Twentieth Century Words

JOHN AYTO

OXFORD
UNIVERSITY PRESS

OXFORD
UNIVERSITY PRESS

Great Clarendon Street, Oxford OX2 6DP

Oxford University Press is a department of the University of Oxford.
It furthers the University's objective of excellence in research, scholarship,
and education by publishing worldwide in

Oxford New York

Athens Auckland Bangkok Bogotá Buenos Aires Calcutta
Cape Town Chennai Dar es Salaam Delhi Florence Hong Kong Istanbul
Karachi Kuala Lumpur Madrid Melbourne Mexico City Mumbai
Nairobi Paris São Paulo Singapore Taipei Tokyo Toronto Warsaw

with associated companies in Berlin Ibadan

Oxford is a registered trade mark of Oxford University Press
in the UK and in certain other countries

Published in the United States
by Oxford University Press Inc., New York

British Library Cataloguing in Publication Data

Data available

Library of Congress Cataloging in Publication Data

Ayto, John
Twentieth Century Words/John Ayto
1. English language—New words—Dictionaries.
2. English language—20th century—Dictionaries.
3. Civilization, Modern—20th century—Dictionaries.
I. Title PE1630/A98 1999 423'.1—dc21

ISBN 0-19-860230-8

10 9 8 7 6 5 4 3 2 1

Typeset in Minion, Officina Sans and Trade Gothic
by Alliance Phototypesetters
Printed in Great Britain by
Biddles Ltd
Guildford and King's Lynn

Introduction

On 1 January 1900 there were approximately 140 million native speakers of English in the world. A century later that figure has almost tripled to nearly 400 million. Add to them about 100 million who speak English as a second language. Consider how English has become the international language of communication, both conventional and digital, in the 20th century. Think, moreover, of the massive increase in literacy since 1900, the legacy of the spread of universal education in the late 19th century. The English language is in an unprecedented number of hands.

In that same period, the world itself has changed almost beyond recognition. In 1900, no powered heavier-than-air craft had left the Earth's surface; Dr Hertz's discovery of radio waves had yet to be put to practical commercial use; it was a mere three years since Joseph Thomson had detected the existence of the electron; and Claude Monet was painting his waterlilies. A hundred years later we look with complacency at pictures of the Earth taken from outer space; various forms of electronic communication have brought all corners of the globe into instantaneous touch with each other; the second half of the century has been lived in the shadow of the nuclear bomb; and avant-garde art proposes the dead sheep as an object of contemplation. The old European colonies have become independent nations. Two savage and prolonged world wars have claimed millions of lives and radically rearranged the planet's political geography. A clash of empires, East and West, has arisen and subsided. Sigmund Freud and his successors have delved into the recesses of the human psyche. The computer has grown, and shrunk, from a set of winking throbbing cabinets big enough to fill a room to a miniaturized component of everyday life, a progenitor of cyberspace, holding the threat and the promise of the future in its microcircuits.

Given that huge increase in the number of English-speakers since 1900, and the myriad new ideas, inventions, discoveries, and schemes that have proliferated in that period, it would be astonishing if the vocabulary of English had not grown substantially. And so it has. We shall never know how many new words were coined during the 20th century. Many were the inspiration of a moment, lost before they could be committed to paper (or recorded by any other means). Others were not common enough to catch the attention of dictionary compilers, or if they were, failed to convince the lexicographers that they deserved the stamp of approval. Those that slipped through the net are without number. But of the remainder we can speak with some confidence. The *Oxford English Dictionary* and its supplementary volumes record about 90,000 new words, and new meanings of old words, that have come into the English language in this century. In other words, every year on average 900 neologisms have come into existence which sooner or later make a sufficient mark to be considered as established in the language, and worthy of record in English's largest dictionary. The figure represents approximately a 25 per cent increase in the total vocabulary of the language as it had evolved in the thousand and more years up to 1900.

It is this newly minted lexicon of the 20th century that forms the basis of this book. It would have been unwieldy and ultimately unenlightening to list all the new words and usages. This is a selection, which attempts to present the most salient new English vocabulary of the past hundred years. The key new terminology of science and technology; the names of important new movements in politics and the arts; the vocabulary of fashion, in clothing, music, dances, hair-styles, food; the latest slang, most of it ephemeral but on everyone's lips at the time.

The words of each decade are given a chapter to themselves. They are listed alphabetically, with a brief introduction bringing together the main strands of lexical development within that period or setting them against their historical background. Each entry word has a date after it. I cannot emphasize too strongly that this represents the earliest date from which a printed or other written record of the word exists in the OED or its files—nothing more and nothing less. It is *not* meant to suggest that the word necessarily 'entered' the language in that year. It is not uncommon for words to escape immediate notice if they slip unobtrusively into the language rather than being announced with a fanfare; and slang and other colloquial items routinely take some time to find their way into the written record. Sometimes English is slow to adopt a term for a phenomenon, movement, etc. which to modern eyes seems the obvious one, and sometimes, no doubt, the record of an earlier adoption has yet to come to light (for example, Max Planck originated his quantum theory in 1900, but the terms *quantum* and *quantum theory* are not recorded in English until the second decade of the century; art nouveau was an important style of art of the last decade of the 19th century, but the term is not recorded as an English word until 1901). So, unless specifically documented details of a word's coinage are given, the date should be regarded simply as an indication of when a particular usage first appeared. The explanation of the word is followed by one or more examples of it in use, which often put further flesh on the bones of the definition. One of them may be the earliest recorded instance of the word in print, but this is not necessarily always the case.

Words are a mirror of their times. By looking at the areas in which the vocabulary of a language is expanding fastest in a given period, we can form a fairly accurate impression of the chief preoccupations of society at that time and the points at which the boundaries of human endeavour are being advanced. Table 1 summarizes the semantic fields which grew most rapidly in the succeeding decades of the 20th century. The new technology of cars, aircraft, radio, and film dominated lexical innovation in the 1900s (*dashboard, aerodrome, wireless, cinema*), along with the vocabulary of psychology and psychoanalysis (*libido, psychoanalysis*). These last two were not so dominant after the 1910s, but the others continued to be major sources of neologisms well into the 1930s. However, in the decade of World War I they were not surprisingly overshadowed by the broad spectrum of military vocabulary (*gas mask, shell shock, tank*), and in the 1920s the lexicon of national post-war relief, the bright young things and the Jazz Age, dominated the scene (*Charleston, Oxford bags*). Then in the 1930s the build-up to and start of a new war (*dive-bomb, Blitzkrieg, black-out*) put such frivolities in their place. In the first half of the 1940s, World War II was again providing the majority of new usages (*doodlebug, gas chamber, kamikaze*), but the return of peace brought other concerns to the fore: reconstruction, national and international (*National Health, Marshall Plan, super-power*), and the nuclear threat (*the bomb*). A small trickle of computer terminology (*electronic brain, hardware*) was to become a flood in the second half of the century. Similar small beginnings for the vocabulary of space exploration (*booster, re-entry*) reached their apogee in the 1960s.

TABLE 1: LEXICAL GROWTH-AREAS BY DECADE

1900s   Cars Aviation Radio Film Psychology
1910s   War Aviation Film Psychology
1920s   Clothes/dance/youth Transport Radio Film
1930s   War/build-up to war Transport Film/entertainment
1940s   War Post-war society/international affairs Nuclear power Computers Space
1950s   Media Nuclear power Space Computers Youth culture
1960s   Computers Space Youth culture/music Media Drugs
1970s   Computers Media Business Environment Political correctness
1980s   Media Computers Finance/money Environment Political correctness Youth culture/music
1990s   Politics Media Internet

The 1950s saw the first significant burgeonings of youth culture (*beatnik, teen*), which in its various manifestations has continued to be a prolific contributor to the English language throughout the rest of the century. It was also the decade in which television combined with other forms of communication and entertainment in a new vocabulary of the media (*hi-fi, transistor radio, videotape*) that would dominate the next fifty years. Both had particular off-shoots in the psychedelic sixties in the language of music (*the twist, Merseybeat*) and the language of drugs (*acid, speed*). In the 1970s, concerns about the destruction of the environment became a long-term source of new vocabulary (*green, global warming*), and the language of political correctness and its proponents began to get into its stride (*chairperson, herstory*). The 1980s were the decade of money, typified both by financial jargon (*dawn raid, white knight*) and by the lifestyle terminology of those who made and enjoyed it (*yuppie, dinky*). The major new player on the 1990s lexical scene was the Internet (*cybernaut, web site*).

Movements and trends in human affairs do not necessarily fit neatly into a particular decade, of course, and the terms we associate with them sometimes anticipate their high-water mark. We tend to think of *appeasement*, for instance, as essentially a phenomenon of the 1930s, and that was indeed the decade in which the negative connotations the word has today began to gather around it; but in fact the concept originated in the second decade of the century. Similarly that quintessentially Cold War expression *iron curtain* can be traced back to the 1920s. It is not at all uncommon for a new term to potter along for decades in obscurity (often as a piece of jargon known only to specialists), and then to find itself suddenly thrust into the spotlight: *greenhouse effect*, for example, was coined in the 1920s, but few non-climatologists had heard of it until the 1980s. Bear in mind, too, that one of the chief characteristics of human language is that it enables us to talk about things which do not exist yet: it can still cause a frisson to read H. G. Wells discussing the *atomic bomb* in 1914.

So although it may at first sight seem odd that some terms that are central to 20th-century life, and particularly to its technological culture (such as *car* and *aircraft*), are not represented in this collection, the answer in most cases is that they are pre-20th-century coinages. Table 2 gives a selection of high-profile or striking examples of this phenomenon, in chronological order.

TABLE 2: PRE-20TH-CENTURY COINAGES

flying machine (1736)	electron (1891)
parachute (1785)	ouija (1891)
aircraft (1850)	homosexual (adj) (1894)
Communist (1850)	spaceship (1894)
acid rain (1859)	automobile (1895)
commuter (1865)	feminism (1895)
aeroplane (1873)	modern art (1895)
biplane (1874)	motor car (1895)
Venusian (1874)	car (1896)
benefit 'financial assistance' (1875)	motion picture (1896)
relativity (1876)	motor (verb) (1896)
phonograph (1877)	moving picture (1896)
old-age pension (1879)	bad 'good' (slang) (1897)
Labour party (1886)	photosynthesis (1898)
department store (1887)	radioactive (1898)
contact lens (1888)	aspirin (1899)
milk shake (1889)	auto 'car' (1899)

But it is not only the areas of activity characterized by high vocabulary growth that give us clues about the direction the human race is going in. Our changing modes of social interaction have a lexical fingerprint too. Take, for example, the 20th century's rehabilitation of the notorious 'four-letter words', formerly so beyond the pale that no dictionary would print them. As their common (and often euphemistic) epithet 'Anglo-Saxon' suggests, they have been around a long time, and no doubt have been used very widely in casual speech, but the taboo imposed on them means that printed examples from the 19th century and earlier are quite rare. In 1896, for instance, J. S. Farmer became involved in a lawsuit when his publishers refused to let him include certain obscene words in his and W. E. Henley's *Slang and its Analogues* (1890–1904), an extensive and distinguished dictionary of slang. It appears to have been the great melting pot of World War I, bringing together people of all classes and backgrounds, that encouraged the spread of such words (see *fuck off* (1929)). You still ran a great risk if you printed them, though: between the wars, the likes of James Joyce and Henry Miller had their work banned when they tried to, and as recently as 1960 in Britain the use of 'Anglo-Saxon words' was one of the main issues in the trial of the Penguin Books edition of D. H. Lawrence's *Lady Chatterley's Lover* for obscenity. When the critic Kenneth Tynan used the word *fuck* on British television in 1965 ('I doubt if there are very many rational people in this world to whom the word *fuck* is particularly diabolical or revolting or totally forbidden') it caused a brief but noticeable national convulsion. But perhaps a more significant straw in the wind was the publication in the same year of the *Penguin English Dictionary*, the first mainstream general English dictionary to include *fuck* and *cunt*. Its imprimatur was confirmed by that of the *Supplement to the OED* in 1972, and by the end of the century these words are included as a matter of course in any unabridged English dictionary.

This is not simply a matter of lexicographers catching up with reality. It represents a genuine change in public usage over the course of the century. In the 1990s, *fuck, fucking*, etc. are common currency in feature films, familiar enough not to raise an eyebrow on post-water-shed television, and waved through on many newspapers (although some —generally speaking those aimed at the 'lower' end of the market—do protect their more unworldly readers with a well-placed asterisk, or the coyly euphemistic *f-word*); in 1992 *fuck* even appeared in a government-sponsored warning against Aids: 'So if you are going to fuck, it makes sense to use one of the stronger variety [of condoms]'. This state of affairs would have been quite unthinkable in the 1950s. It seemed that *cunt* was still holding the line (its taboo maintained, some claimed, not on account of its obscenity but because it was sexist), but in 1998 it was used on national television in Britain for the first time (in a dramatization of the life of Oswald Mosley on Channel 4). The last bastion had fallen.

What does this revolution in usage tell us about changes in English-speaking society? Given that World War I made these words much more widely available, what has happened, especially in the second half of the century, to sanction their more general toleration? It certainly seems to be part of a more widespread tendency to upgrade the status and acceptability of spoken English. Up to at least the 1960s, the notion of 'Standard English' was based exclusively on written English, and the colloquial language was regarded as an irrelevant but occasionally annoying or embarrassing offshoot that needed to be kept in its place. At the end of the century that is no longer so, and colloquial usages (both lexical and syntactic) are widely accepted in situations (including quite formal writing) where they would once have been considered inappropriate. Behind this may be perceived a more general breaking down of social barriers, a valuing of mateyness above reserve, a profound shift away from role models who found *fuck* distasteful or morally undermining. 'Four-letter' status seems destined for the history books. But a passing thought: English would appear to be in danger of depriving itself of some valuable letting-off-steam words for use in extremis, without any obvious replacements in sight. The only 20th-century coinage in this area to have caught on widely is *motherfucker*.

On the other hand, there are a good many usages which once went unremarked, but which we now dare not allow to pass our lips. In the 19th century, for instance, it was socially acceptable, if not positively desirable, to be fat, and there was no stigma attached to the word *fat*. It could even be used approvingly (Princess Alice wrote gleefully in 1864 'My fat baby is a great darling!'). At the end of the 20th century, however, thinness is fashionable, and to call someone fat is a monstrous insult. We have evolved a range of euphemisms, from the colloquial *chunky* to the ponderous *circumferentially challenged*, to avoid the direct accusation.

It sometimes seems as if the 20th century were the century of euphemism. Much of the doublespeak is counterbalanced by areas in which frankness has latterly become the rule (the earlier part of the century boasted a bewildering array of circumlocutions for 'menstruation', for example, whereas 1990s television advertisements for *sanpro* products are studiedly in-your-face), but there is no doubt that there are many areas which English-speakers have become embarrassed to talk about in the last hundred years. The one with the highest profile is probably racial differences. Post-colonial guilt has ensured that the casual, unconsidered racial insult of the first half of the century has become unmentionable in the second (in the 1990s it seems bizarre that Agatha Christie could have entitled one of her mystery novels *Ten Little Niggers* in 1939; it has now become *And Then There Were None*). But the usual lesson of euphemism applies: if underlying tensions remain, a change of name will not stick. The fragmented history of English words for black people down the decades illustrates this. Terms such as *black* and *nigger* fell under a taboo in the middle part of the 20th century. They tended to be replaced by *negro*, but this (even more its feminine form *negress*) went out of favour in the 1960s, perhaps on account of its anthropological overtones. Back stepped *black*, revived by blacks themselves as a term of pride. In the US it was joined by *Afro-American* and later *African-American*, in Britain by *Afro-Caribbean*. The politically correct lobby enthusiastically revived the 18th-century *person of color*, and added its own rather unwieldy *member of the African Diaspora*. Then in the 1980s US blacks subverted the whole process by reclaiming *nigger*, in the assertive new spelling *nigga*.

The term *racism* dates from the 1930s, but the broader concept of *-ism*, in the sense of a censured discrimination on unacceptable grounds, is a creature of the 1960s. *Sexism* led the way (it is first recorded in 1968), but it was followed in the subsequent decades by many disciples. The era of non-discriminatory vocabulary was arriving (often labelled 'politically correct', especially by its detractors). It proved easy to ridicule (*person of restricted growth* for 'someone short' can surely only have been coined by somebody with a sense-of-humour deficit), but it was remarkably tenacious. Numerous examples are recorded in the sections on the 1970s and 80s (see in particular the entries for *challenged* (1985) and *person* (1971), and see also p. 456). Its rise and subsequent chequered career maps neatly on to the idealism of the 60s, the militancy of the 70s, and the cynicism of the 80s.

In 1999, following representations, the American dictionary publisher Merriam-Webster withdrew an on-line thesaurus containing a section of words for homosexuals that included such taboo items as *faggot* and *fruit*. It further indicated that future editions of 'printed material' would be reviewed to remove these offending words. So at the end of the century the high tide of tolerance that admitted *fuck* to English dictionaries is seen to be receding, and the fingers of censorship are beginning once again to pick at the fabric of the lexicon.

By what mechanisms did English expand its vocabulary in the 20th century? There are fundamentally five ways in which neologisms are created: by putting existing words to new uses; by combining existing words or word-parts; by shortening existing words; by borrowing words from other languages; and by coining words out of nothing.

By far the commonest in English is the second—combining existing elements. It accounts for close on three-quarters of the new vocabulary coming into the language. It can be divided into two main categories, both of which are as old as the English language itself: two or more words can be combined in such a way that together, they mean something different from what they would mean separately (*dirty dancing, dreadnought*); or an existing word can have a prefix or a suffix added to it (*unbundle, beatnik*). But there is one particular sort of compound that is highly characteristic of the 20th century: the blend. To create a blend, you do not just put two words side by side; you concertina them together, so that the end of the first merges into the start of the second: for example, *motor + hotel* becomes *motel*. It is a pattern that seems to have had its beginnings in Victorian word-play, and certainly its most celebrated early exponent was the English mathematician and children's author Lewis Carroll. He created several still-famous nonsense-blends (such as *mimsy*, from *miserable* and *flimsy*), and he inspired the blend's alternative name—'portmanteau word' ('Well, "slithy" means "lithe" and "slimy"… You see it's like a portmanteau—there are two meanings packed up into one word', *Through the Looking-glass* (1871)). The pattern was establishing itself at the end of the 19th century (*brunch* is first recorded in 1896), and the 20th century has taken to it with great enthusiasm. Blends often have the air of journalistic jokes (for instance the ever-popular names for hybrid animals, such as *liger* and *shoat*), but many prove to have remarkable stamina (*chunnel, stagflation*), and not a few have become highly respectable members of the lexical community (*pulsar*). The 1980s and 90s in particular have been addicted to the blend's cool snappiness (hence all the cross-genre terms such as *infotainment* and *docusoap*).

The most effort-free way of expanding the vocabulary of a language is to put an existing word to a new use. This generally implies modifying its meaning. It is a phenomenon that is not easy to measure statistically, as there is often an element of subjectivity involved in judging whether the meaning of a word has changed sufficiently to qualify it as a new usage, but estimates of the percentage of such modifications among the total of neologisms are between 10 and 15—a significant proportion. Much rarer, but also much more controversial, is the process known as conversion. This is when the word-class of a word changes, so that, for instance, a noun is used as a verb (e.g. 'to garage a car'). It is a long-standing feature of the language (Shakespeare was fond of playing with word-classes), but in the 20th century it has become a *bête noire* of the linguistic purists, who seem to see in it a threat to the coherence of the language. There is no sign that English-speakers have given up on it, though (for example, the verb *doorstep* and the noun *dry* from the 1980s).

If you want to shorten an existing word, the most straightforward way is to knock off the end (e.g. *hood* for *hoodlum, porn* for *pornography, recce* for *reconnaissance*). But there is a particular subset of these shortened words (nearly all verbs) that are created by deleting a suffix, thereby usually altering the word-class (*destruct* from *destruction, escalate* from *escalator*). They are known as back-formations, and they have proliferated in 20th-century English, particularly in US military and scientific jargon—a fact that perhaps has contributed to making them yet another target of the language police.

An extreme form of shortening a word is to leave only its first letter. This process of abbreviation produces what are often known as initialisms (*GI, LP, BSE*). When the resulting string of letters is pronounced as if it were an ordinary word, it is termed an acronym (*Aids, Cobol, Dora, NATO, PEP*). Acronyms have been the 20th century's great new contribution to English word-formation. They were virtually nonexistent at its start, but by the 1990s they seemed to have seeped into almost every aspect of modern life (see *acronym* (1943)). The main reasons for this are non-linguistic: the proliferation of organizations and other entities with multi-word names (a process which received a considerable boost during World War II), and an increasingly rushed world which prefers not to waste time on saying or writing such long names.

Foreign borrowing, which has so enriched the English language in previous periods, has provided it with approximately 5 per cent of its new words in the 20th century. The majority owe their adoption to some novel cultural influence. The Anglo-Saxon nations' attitude to foreign food, for instance, has undergone a sea change in the past fifty years. Cuisines once superciliously ignored have been enthusiastically assimilated, and they have brought an abundance of new culinary vocabulary with them: *balti, chow mein, ciabatta, courgette, doner kebab, pizza, quiche, tandoori.* Scientific and technological developments in a particular country can lead to a sudden inrush of foreign terminology (the prominence of France in early aircraft technology, for example, lies behind the abundance of French aerospace vocabulary in English—*aerodrome, aileron, fuselage, hangar, nacelle*). And interaction at a political or diplomatic level often contributes (admittedly time-bound) neologisms to English (*anschluss* and *führer, glasnost* and *perestroika*).

Dreaming words up out of thin air accounts for less than one per cent of English neologisms. The great majority of them are proprietary names or commercial names (*nylon, spam* (possibly a blend), *Teflon*), but some technical terms are devised in this way, either directly (*googol*) or by a piece of judicious borrowing from a literary source (*quark*). That leaves a tiny residue of strange coinages which sometimes catch the public imagination through their very outlandishness (*supercalifragilisticexpialidocious*).

Surveyors of the past are often tempted to sign off with a predictive flourish, outlining possible future developments. But not even the foolhardiest student of words would dare to guess at the state of English vocabulary in the year 2100. Words are the servants of events. Who in 1900 could have foreseen the combination of economic and social conditions that led in the 1980s to the craze for inventing *yuppie*-clone lifestyle acronyms (*buppie, guppie, Juppie, dinky, glam, woopie*)? And if by chance anyone had then possessed a working crystal ball, would it also have successfully predicted that it would be *yuppie* and not its original rival *yumpie* that took the decade by storm? All that can with confidence be said is that in the next century people will think new thoughts, have new experiences, make new discoveries, and that they will need new words to communicate them. Somehow, the English language will provide.

I owe a particular debt of gratitude to Michael Proffitt (new words editor of the OED) and to Susanne Charlett and Jonathan Blaney of the OED lexicographic team, for their endless resourcefulness in unearthing from OED files and archives, information without which this book would not have been possible. My thanks go too to members of the publishing and editorial staff of Oxford University Press, notably Susie Dent, Kate Wandless, Vicki Rodger, Elizabeth Knowles, and Kendall Clarke, for their unfailing help and support, and to Jan Palmowski of Christ Church, Oxford, who read the manuscript of the book and made scores of invaluable suggestions. Any errors and omissions that remain are entirely of my own making.

JOHN AYTO

London, 1999

Chronologies

1900s

1900 Relief of Mafeking (South African War); Max Planck originates the quantum theory
1901 Death of Queen Victoria
1902 End of South African War (Boer War)
1903 First powered flight in a heavier-than-air craft, by the Wright brothers
1904 *Entente cordiale* between Britain and France
1905 First Russian Revolution; Einstein's special theory of relativity
1906 Labour Party formed in Britain; Rutherford deduces the existence of the atomic nucleus
1908 Geiger counter invented
1909 Ford Model T car introduced

1910s

1910 Post-impressionist exhibition in London
1911 Amundsen reaches the South Pole
1912 *Titanic* sinks
1913 Stravinsky's *Rite of Spring*
1914 Assassination of Archduke Franz Ferdinand at Sarajevo; World War I begins
1915 Gallipoli campaign; Zeppelin raids on Britain; Einstein's general theory of relativity
1916 Battles of Verdun and the Somme; the tank first used; Easter Rising in Dublin, Ireland
1917 Russian Revolution; US enters World War I
1918 World War I ends; women over 30 get the vote in Britain
1919 Treaty of Versailles; League of Nations established; Alcock and Brown fly the Atlantic

1920s

1920 Prohibition of alcohol comes into effect in the US
1921 Southern Ireland becomes Irish Free State
1923 German putsch organized by Hitler fails
1924 First Labour government in Britain; Surrealist Manifesto published
1926 General strike in Britain; first television
1927 Stalin comes to power in Soviet Union; Lindbergh flies the Atlantic; BBC founded; first talking picture; Walt Disney's Mickey Mouse makes debut
1928 Penicillin discovered
1929 Wall Street Crash; the Depression begins

1930s

1930 Turbojet engine patented by Whittle; Empire State Building opened in New York
1931 Depression worsens; national (coalition) government formed in Britain
1932 Oswald Mosley's British Union of Fascists formed; Cockroft and Walton split the atom
1933 Hitler appointed Chancellor of Germany
1934 Stalin purges begin in Soviet Union
1936 Edward VIII abdicates; Spanish Civil War begins; BBC begins television broadcasts
1938 Munich Agreement; nuclear fission discovered; nylon patented in US
1939 Poland invaded by Germany; World War II begins

1940s

1940 France invaded by Germany; British retreat from Dunkirk; Churchill becomes British prime minister; Battle of Britain
1941 Soviet Union invaded by Germany; Pearl Harbor bombed by Japanese; US enters the war
1942 Allied victories at El Alamein and Midway; Beveridge Report published
1943 Germans surrender at Stalingrad
1944 D-Day invasion of Europe; Paris liberated
1945 US drops atom bombs on Hiroshima and Nagasaki; World War II ends; United Nations formed
1946 Cold War begins
1947 India independent
1948 Berlin airlift; welfare state inaugurated in Britain; apartheid legislation in South Africa; transistor developed in US
1949 NATO formed; People's Republic of China declared

1950s

1950 Korean War begins; first successful kidney transplant
1952 Elizabeth II becomes queen of United Kingdom; US tests hydrogen bomb
1953 Crick and Watson demonstrate structure of DNA; Mount Everest climbed
1954 First commercial television in Britain; Roger Bannister runs first four-minute mile
1955 Bill Haley's 'Rock Around the Clock' popularizes rock 'n' roll
1956 Suez crisis; first commercial nuclear power stations; Elvis Presley's 'Heartbreak Hotel'
1957 EEC formed; first Soviet Sputnik flight
1958 Silicon chip invented in US
1959 Castro takes power in Cuba

1960s

1960 Laser developed in the US; oral contraceptives marketed
1961 Kennedy becomes US president; Berlin Wall built; first manned spaceflight (Gagarin)
1962 Cuban missile crisis; The Beatles' 'Love Me Do'
1963 President Kennedy assassinated

1964 US enters Vietnam War
1965 Introduction of the miniskirt
1966 Beginning of Cultural Revolution in China
1967 Abortion legalized in Britain; first human heart transplant (Barnard)
1968 Soviet forces invade Czechoslovakia; student protest movements throughout Europe and US; violence begins in Northern Ireland
1969 First man on the moon (Armstrong); first Concorde flight

1970s

1971 Decimal currency introduced in Britain
1972 Video cassette recorder marketed
1973 Britain joins EEC; OPEC raises oil prices, triggering economic difficulties in the West
1974 Watergate scandal in the US; President Nixon resigns
1975 Vietnam War ends
1976 Mao Tse-tung dies
1978 First test-tube baby born
1979 Shah of Iran deposed by Khomeini's Islamic revolution; Thatcher becomes British prime minister

1980s

1981 Reagan becomes US president; US space shuttle
1982 Falklands War; compact discs introduced; Aids identified
1983 Cruise missiles installed in Britain and Germany; peace movements active
1984 Miners' strike in Britain
1985 Gorbachev begins liberalization in Soviet Union
1986 Chernobyl nuclear disaster in Soviet Union; 'Big Bang' on British Stock Exchange
1987 Collapse of world stock-market prices
1989 Berlin Wall broken; Communist regimes deposed in Eastern Europe; Tiananmen Square massacre in China

1990s

1990 East and West Germany reunited
1991 Soviet Union breaks up; Warsaw Pact dissolved; Gulf War
1992 Conflict in former Yugoslavia begins
1993 Clinton becomes US president
1994 Mandela becomes South African president; Channel Tunnel opened
1996 British beef banned worldwide
1997 Blair becomes British prime minister; Scottish Parliament and Welsh Assembly approved in referendum; Diana, Princess of Wales killed in car crash
1998 Northern Ireland peace terms agreed
1999 Launch of single European currency; US President Clinton acquitted after impeachment trial

The 1900s

It is 1900. In Britain, Queen Victoria is still on the throne. At the start of the Victorian era, over sixty years before, the railways were a novelty; the only means of taking to the air was the balloon; the voting franchise was still biased towards the landed classes; and the crinoline had not been heard of. Now, the motor car has made its first noisy appearance on the roads; in the US, Orville and Wilbur Wright are planning the first powered flight in an aeroplane; women are agitating for the vote; and the coming thing in female fashion is the *motor veil*. The scientific and technical advances of the late 19th century are about to transform the world, especially in terms of speed of movement. We are shortly to be introduced to *atomic energy* and *hydroelectricity*, *gamma rays* and *hormones*, and the concept of the *world war*. Welcome to the 20th century.

The first decade of the century laid down the basic pattern of transportation that was to be elaborated over the succeeding ninety years, particularly on the roads and in the air. Motor vehicles had become commercially available in the 1890s, but not until the new century did they establish themselves as a serious alternative (and soon successor) to the horse (by the start of World War I, over 130,000 cars were registered in the UK). As automotive technology developed and the infrastructure of motoring began to be put in place, English had to evolve and absorb an enormous amount of new vocabulary. There were all the various bits and pieces of a car, the components and spare parts: *accelerators* and *sumps, big ends* and *dashboards, radiators* and *chassis, speedometers* and *windscreens* (or in the US, *windshields*). There were various sorts and styles of vehicle: *landaulettes, limousines*, and *saloons, tricars* and *bubbles*, not to mention *motor bicycles* and *autocycles*. Roads made for the 19th century's *hippomobiles* needed to be upgraded into *motor roads, motorways*, or *speedways*, with *flyovers* and *underpasses* and *loop roads*. The basic terminology of *automobile, motor car, car, auto*, and the short-lived *horseless carriage* had been established in the 1890s, but the new century joined in with *motor* and the less successful *motor carriage*.

Having put on his *motor coat*, taken his *Rolls Royce* out of its *garage* (or *motor stable*) and *petrolled* it (or given it some *juice*), the *autoist* (or his *chauffeur*) could set off for a *day trip* (or perhaps indulge in some *week-ending*). To ensure that his passengers did not get *carsick* (and that he did not attract the attention of the *traffic police*), he would need to avoid *speeding* (or *overspeeding*). *Road signs* would guide him to his destination. Those unwilling to take to the wheel themselves might prefer to get a *taxi*.

Powered flight was born at Kittyhawk in 1903, when the Wright brothers' biplane took to the air; the *heavier-than-air* aircraft had come to stay. Expansion was rapid, and a new terminology needed to be assembled in a hurry (a lot of it—such as *aileron, fuselage*—was borrowed from French; and much, too, was already in place—*aeroplane, biplane*—thanks to the extended late-19th-century period of development that led to that first momentous take-off). A lot has proved durable (*aerofoil, airliner* (originally applied to airships), *pilot*); other coinages have fallen by the wayside (*aerial liner, aeroplanist, hydroaeroplane*). *Aerodromes* are still around, *flying grounds* are no more. Aircraft are still kept in *hangars* (another French borrowing), but not in *harbours* or *sheds*. From over the horizon in Germany there loomed the *Zeppelin*.

Meanwhile, below ground, *electrification* was making underground railways a practical proposition. In London, the *Tube* was beginning its 20th-century expansion. Amongst the amenities were *escalators* to carry its passengers into the depths. *Straphangers* who suffered from claustrophobia might contemplate the alternative of the *motor bus* or even the *electrobus*.

Scientists were unlocking the secrets of the atom (*splitting the atom* was the colloquial phrase that has stuck), probing the foundations of life, developing new materials. *Electronic* and *half-life* and radioactive *decaying* entered the language, as did *adrenaline* and *antibody, clone* and *genetics*. The transforming material of the 20th century, *plastic*, made its first appearance, initially in the form of *bakelite*. The *stratosphere* was named, and the potentiality of *solar power* and *wind power* examined. But the most momentous theoretical advance of the decade, if not of the century, was marked by the publication in 1905 of Albert Einstein's special theory of relativity. The term *relativity* itself was not a new one—the Scottish physicist James Clerk Maxwell is on record as using it in this same general sense in 1876, and it crops up sporadically in the last quarter of the 19th century—but its elucidation revolutionized our view of the universe and its laws.

In 1901, Guglielmo Marconi succeeded in transmitting a radio signal across the Atlantic Ocean; the era of modern communication media had begun. Both *radio* and *wireless*, which would enjoy a keen terminological rivalry in the ensuing decades, made their first appearance in the language, as did *aerial* and *antenna*. Understandably, a lot of early radio vocabulary—*Marconigram, Marconist*—eponymized its pioneer; you could even *marconi* a message to someone. But the fame was shortlived. The way of the future could already be seen. The *cathode-ray tube* had been invented, and people were discussing the possibility of *television*.

In 1902 the South African War (Boer War) came to an end (it had produced the joky gerund *mafficking*, capturing a mixture of national relief and celebration, but also the ominous *concentration camp*), but before the decade was over Britain was building its *dreadnoughts* in preparation for a forthcoming contest. Several terms that were to become all too familiar in World War I made their debut in the language: *dug-out* and *tin hat, no man's land* and *firing squad, Lee-Enfield* and *surprise attack*. *Gas* was now something for killing people with; and *bomb* was being used as a verb, anticipating the sort of aerial bombardment that was to drag civilian populations into the inferno of 20th-century warfare.

It was the decade in which the concepts *pacifism* and *war crime, non-aggression* and *détente* first found a word, but it was also the decade of *expansionism, propaganda*, and new *pogroms*. The radical unrest of the 19th century was still in the air, and the world first heard of *militants, palace revolutions,* and *revisionism.* In Britain, though, the *Lib-Lab* pact offered hope of political stability.

The upper classes may have been starting to worry about the *servant problem,* but it was also the decade of the *bread-line,* the *hunger march,* and the *poverty line.* The beginnings of a state response to such problems are reflected in such terms as *welfare* and *social security.* That 20th-century Aunt Sally the *social worker* made her (or his) first appearance. The *women's movement* was becoming increasingly impatient in its search for female enfranchisement, and *suffragettes* were chaining themselves to railings. It was a decade in which more 'advanced' views on the relationship between the sexes were taking hold, particularly in Bohemian circles: the era of *mixed bathing* and the *trial marriage.* Relationships between the races were appearing on the agenda, too: the term *racialism* entered the language, along with *colour prejudice, ethnocentric, segregation,* and *white supremacy.*

If one man above all others has dictated the way in which the 20th century has viewed the workings of the human mind, it has been the Austrian psychologist Sigmund Freud (1856–1939). Somewhat under a cloud at the end of the century, in this its first decade he was becoming more widely known in the English-speaking world, through translations of his works, and his terminology was beginning to make its way into the English language, notably *psychoanalysis* and its shortened form *analysis,* and also *libido.* The science of the mind was expanding on all fronts, bringing with it expressions like *anxiety neurosis* and *manic depressive, masochistic* and *repressed, complex* and *depression* and *narcissism,* against which the introspective, anxious 20th century could examine itself. And as if they were not enough, *sexology* took its bow.

For the escapist there was the *cinema.* What better way to forget your anxiety neurosis than going to see a *film*—silent, of course (although someone in the pit might be producing *sound effects*). The first public film performance had taken place in 1895, but it was not until the first decade of the 20th century that the industry became organized on a serious footing. Entrepreneurs built *cinematograph theatres* (or *picture palaces,* or *nickelodeons*); the words *camera-man* and *subtitle* entered the language; and *Kinemacolor* offered an intriguing glimpse of the future. The *bioscope* had come to stay (although that particular term did not stay long, except in South Africa). If music were more your thing, there were the latest products of *Tin Pan Alley,* or the more genteel strains emanating from the *palm court,* or you could do it (almost) yourself with a *Pianola.* To dance to there were the *cake walk* and the *veleta.* The sportingly inclined could choose between *ping-pong* and *table football.*

Models (or *mannequins*) were showing off the latest fashions (but not, as yet, *panties* or other *undies*). *Cloche hats* were in, as were *beehives.* For men, the *lounge suit* put in its first appearance. Tonsorially, waves were the thing: women wanted a *permanent wave,* and the *marcel* was the market leader. If your own hair was not quite up to it, you could always try a *transformation.* Other *beauty culture* services available at the *beauty shop* included *electrolysis.*

In the home, the first of the 20th century's mod cons were making their appearance, including *central heating* and the *vacuum cleaner.* *Home helps* were no doubt enormously grateful for the advent of *floor polish* and *Jeyes fluid,* while upstairs the mistress of the house luxuriated in her *bath-salts*-scented bath. For breakfast there were *cornflakes,* and to spread on your toast (which you would conscientiously *Fletcherize*), *Oxford marmalade* and the improbably named *Nutter.* The canning industry gave the world *pineapple chunks,* and fast food made significant advances with *hot dogs* and the *club sandwich* (probably washed down with *Coke* or its new rival, *Pepsi Cola*). There were *meat-lozenges* for the carnivore, while vegetarians could enjoy *Marmite* and the ineffable *nut cutlet.* Chinese food began its 20th-century infiltration of Western cuisine with the *chow mein.*

In the US, *big business* was gearing itself up for its decades of dominance. In *filing-cabinet*-lined offices, *executives* dictated to *shorthand typists* (or to a *Dictaphone*).

Western science 'discovered' the *okapi*, unearthed the much more mediagenic *tyrannosaurus*, and decided that the *panda* was a panda (not a bear). But undoubtedly the animal of the decade was the *teddy bear.*

accelerator *n* (1900) a device that controls the speed of a motor vehicle. At first *accelerator* was applied to quite a wide range of such devices, but it very soon became established as the term for the pedal depressed to increase speed. The word was not new: it had been used in the past with meanings as diverse as 'a light vehicle to convey letter-carriers to their districts, and accelerate the delivery of letters' and 'a substance used to shorten the duration of development of a photographic negative'

> 1900 W. W. Beaumont: The other governor control is known as the accelerator.

> 1902 A. C. Harmsworth et al.: If the driver wishes to slow down…he does not necessarily change his gear, but operates the accelerator.

action photograph *n* (1904) a photograph representing the subject in action. Early examples of such 'action' shots were carefully posed, but the term has continued in use in modern live photo-journalism

> 1904 G. W. Beldam (*title-page*): *Great Golfers* Illustrated by 268 action-photographs.

addict *n* (1909) someone who is addicted to a drug. A noun use of the verb *addict*

> 1924 *Westminster Gazette*: People who…get into the habit of going to the chemist for drugs to induce sleep, and often end up by becoming opium, morphine, or heroin addicts.

adrenaline *n* (1901) a hormone secreted by the adrenal glands and affecting circulation, muscular action, etc. The discovery of the hormone and the coining of its name are both disputed; they may have been the work of Dr. Jokichi Takamine (see the quote below), or of Dr. Norton L. Wilson

> 1901 *American Journal of Physiology*: The most important contribution to our knowledge of the active principle of the suprarenal gland…is from Dr. Jokichi Takamine who has isolated the blood-pressure-raising principle of the gland in a stable and pure crystalline form… To this body…he has given the name 'Adrenalin'.

aerial *n* (1902) a wire or other device for transmitting or receiving radio waves. A shortening of either *aerial conductor* (coined by Guglielmo Marconi, the inventor of radio, in 1899) or *aerial wire*. See also **antenna (1902)**

> 1906 A. F. Collins *Manual of Wireless Telegraphy*: Aerial, a word much used instead of the longer term *aerial wire*.

> 1908 *Westminster Gazette*: The four aerials connected with the mast cover about an acre and a half.

aerialist *n* (1905) a performer on the high wire or trapeze. A word first recorded in a Barnum and Bailey circus programme

> 1961 *Guardian*: The aerialists are so high and perilous that their bland composure fools no one.

aerial liner *n* (1909) a passenger aircraft. A very short-lived term, which, like **airliner (1908)**, seems mainly to have been applied to airships. Compare **aero-liner (1908)**, **liner (1905)**

> 1909 *Flight*: Baron v. Roenne gives some interesting particulars regarding a proposed aerial liner.

aerial war *n* (1908) (a) war as fought out between aircraft. Wells described the as yet nonexistent phenomenon in his *War in the Air* (1908) (although in fact the anonymous coiner of *aerial warfare* in 1895 was somewhat more prescient, as that term has survived better than *aerial war*)

> 1908 H. G. Wells: The early battles of the aerial war were no doubt determined by attempts to realise the old naval maxim, to ascertain the position of the enemy's fleet and to destroy it.

aerodrome *n* (1909) an area with runways where aircraft can take off and land. The word was originally coined (from Greek *aerodromos* 'traversing the air') in the early 1890s by S. P. Langley. He used it to denote an aeroplane ('An actual working aerodrome model with its motor', *Experimental Aerodynamics* (1891)). This usage did not survive beyond the first decade of the 20th century, losing out to the much longer established *aeroplane* (1873).

An entirely new word *aerodrome* appeared in 1902, meaning 'a hangar for a balloon or other aircraft'. This was borrowed from French *aérodrome*, which had been coined from Greek *dromos* 'course, racecourse' on the model of such words as *hippodrome*. It persisted into the 1920s ('The building…was easily recognisable as a huge aerodrome,' Marie Corelli, *The Secret Power* (1921)), but then faded from the scene.

The application to an airfield developed towards the end of the decade, and at first was not universally well received (see the quote below). It established itself in the 1910s, but as such facilities became bigger it gradually lost out to **airport (1919)**. US English preferred the variant **airdrome (1917)**

> 1909 F. W. Lanchester: I regret to see that the misuse of the word 'aerodrome' is receiving support in your [i.e. *Flight* magazine's] columns… I suppose because a hippodrome is a big open space for horses, you think that an aerodrome should be a big open space for flying machines.

aerodyne *n* (1906) a heavier-than-air aircraft. A back-formation from *aerodynamic*, it seems not to have survived beyond the 1930s

> 1906 W. Turnbull: I use the word 'aërodyne' in preference to 'flying-machines', to denote an aëroplane-supported machine, driven by mechanical power through the air.

aerofoil *n* (1907) any lifting surface of an aircraft, such as a wing, aileron, or tailplane

> 1907 F. W. Lanchester: The author does not employ the term *aeroplane* outside its correct signification, that is to say, to denote other than a true or *plane* aeroplane; the misuse of the word being avoided by the introduction of the word aerofoil, to denote a supporting member, or organ of sustentation of undefined form.

aero-liner *n* (1908) a passenger aircraft. This short-lived term seems to have been used to refer to aeroplanes, in contrast with the fledgling **airliner (1908)**, early recorded examples of which all refer to airships. Compare **aerial liner (1909)**

> 1908 *Daily Mail*: The Aero-Liner. The future liner, the giant aeroplane.

> 1911 H. Gernsbeck: The afternoon transatlantic aeroliner is not due yet.

aeromotor *n* (1902) a motor-powered heavier-than-air aircraft. The term did not survive the decade

> 1902 F. Walker: The construction of dirigible balloons, aërostats, aëroplanes, and aëromotors to be…illustrated by various types already made.

aeroplanist *n* (1906) someone who flies an aeroplane. A usage which staggered into the 1930s before dying out (*aeroplane* itself dates from the 1870s). The struggle for this particular semantic niche was won by **pilot (1907)**

> 1906 *Daily Mail*: The first successful aeroplanist in Great Britain will win…as much money as the Soap Trust has already lost.

> 1934 *Times Educational Supplement*: Model aeroplanists [wend their way] to Hampstead Heath.

age-group *n* (1904) all people of a particular age, considered as a group. Part of the terminology of the relatively new science of demography, which was to measure and record the 20th century

> 1904 *General Report of the Census of England & Wales 1901*: The following Table, which gives the proportions of blind per million living at the earlier age-groups, shows [etc.].

aileron *n* (1909) one of the hinged flaps on the trailing edge of a wing of an aeroplane for maintaining or restoring its balance when flying. Like much early aeronautical terminology, a borrowing from French, where it was a diminutive of *aile* 'wing'

> 1909 *Aero*: The ailerons or small planes between the main surfaces are used instead of wing-flexing for balancing.

airliner *n* (1908) a passenger aircraft. Comparatively rare in early use, it has now largely taken the place of **liner (1905)** in the same sense. In the first recorded example, below, the term refers to an airship, and this was its main early application (German airships were the pioneers of commercial passenger air transport); the first unequivocal record of *airliner* for an aeroplane is in the 1929 edition of the *Concise Oxford Dictionary* (but see **aero-liner (1908)**). See also **aerial liner (1909)**

> 1908 *Daily Mail*: The cost of working the air-liner was represented as small.

> 1955 *Times*: Twenty people died in the airliner, which crashed on…a scheduled flight.

air vehicle *n* (1902) an aircraft. A neologism which failed to catch on

> 1902 *Aeronautical Journal*: Some accomplishment on the part of an air vehicle.

All Black *n* (1905) a member of the New Zealand Rugby Union team. The term (based on the colour of the team's shirt and shorts) was coined as a nickname by British journalists at the beginning of the team's 1905 tour of Britain, and has since become semi-official
> 1905 *Daily Mail*: The record of the 'All Blacks' now stands at 310 points…against seven.

analyse *v* (1909) to psychoanalyse. **Psychoanalyse** itself is not recorded before 1911
> 1921 Rose Macaulay: I think you'd be awfully wise to get analysed.

analysis *n* (1906) psychoanalysis (see **psychoanalysis (1906)**)
> 1907 *Brain*: In hysteria with very little trouble the complex may be revealed by analysis, and with a good prospect of therapeutic advantage.

anorexic *adj, n* (1907) (someone) suffering from anorexia nervosa. English acquired Latin *anorexia* in the 16th century in the anglicized form *anorexy*, meaning broadly 'lack of appetite'. Its specialized medical usage did not develop until the mid 19th century. Its original adjectival derivative was *anorectic*, but this is mainly used in technical contexts; *anorexic* has become the preferred general adjective and (along with *anorexia*) has become much more familiar in the last quarter of the century, as increasing numbers of adolescent girls are being diagnosed with the condition. See also **bulimia (1976)**
> 1907 P. Janet: If food is introduced by force…into the stomach of the most anorexic hysterical…you will recognize that the digestion…comes to be completely effected.

> 1913 S. E. Jelliffe: These patients are what are known as mental anorexics, who…have lost a quarter, a third, and sometimes a half of their weight.

> 1983 *Listener*: Compulsive runners share the same symptoms as anorexics.

antenna *n* (1902) a wire or other device for transmitting or receiving radio waves, an aerial (see **aerial (1902)**)
> 1902 J. A. Fleming: The great improvement introduced by Marconi was the employment of this vertical air-wire, aerial, antenna, or elevated conductor.

antibody *n* (1901) a protein in the blood that is produced in reaction to foreign substances and neutralizes them. A partial translation of German *Antikörper*
> 1901 Hektoen & Riesman: Substances which appear during spontaneous or artificial infection or intoxication are known as antibodies (*Antikörper*) and antitoxins.

anxiety neurosis *n* (1904) a mild mental illness characterized by unjustified or excessive anxiety. An English translation of Sigmund Freud's term *Angstneurose*, which first appeared in print in 1895
> 1904 G. S. Hall: The anxiety neurosis was relatively more common in women than in men.

arbitrage *v* (1900) to trade in two markets in order to profit by the difference in prices. The noun *arbitrage* 'such trading' on which this verb was based was acquired from French in the 1870s. See also **arb (1983)**
> 1923 J. M. Keynes: The surcharge representing the profit of a bank for arbitraging between spot and forward transactions may much exceed the moderate figure indicated above.

art nouveau *n* (1901) a style of art developed in the last decade of the 19th century, characterized by the free use of ornament based on organic or foliate forms and by its flowing (i.e. non-geometrical) lines and curves. It was in and out of fashion throughout the century: reviled between the wars, idolized in the late 1960s. A borrowing from French, literally 'new art'
> 1901 *Times*: It is much to be regretted that the authorities of South Kensington have introduced into the Museum specimens of the work styled, 'L'Art nouveau'.

> 1908 George Bernard Shaw: A model cemetery with Art Nouveau tombstones.

> 1909 J. Thorp: The *art nouveau*, with its meandering tulips and inconsequent squirms and dots.

arty *adj* (1901) pretentiously artistic. The even more damning rhyming elaboration *arty-farty* is first recorded in 1967
> 1901 *Academy*: The *Kensington* is its title; it is broad in the page, handsomely printed, and decidedly *Art-y*.

> 1910 *Daily Chronicle*: The house filled with badly made 'arty', not artistic, furniture.

> 1939 George Orwell: They were arty-looking houses, another of those sham-Tudor colonies.

atomic energy *n* (1906) the energy released by the fission of the atomic nuclei of certain heavy elements such as uranium 235 or plutonium or by the fusion of light nuclei. 1906 was the year in which Ernest Rutherford discovered the atomic nucleus. Also called **atomic power (1914)**. The alternative *nuclear energy* is first recorded in 1930

> 1906 *Nature*: Nevertheless, there is a sense in which it may be said that we are profiting by atomic energy.

> 1914 H. G. Wells: Holsten…was destined to see atomic energy dominating every other source of power.

> 1924 *Scientific American*: Atomic energy is the phrase of the hour.

> 1952 *Literary Guide*: Ours is the age of atomic energy…of psycho-analysis and abstractionism in the arts.

attaboy *interj* (1909) An exclamation of encouragement or admiration. Mainly US. Probably from a casual pronunciation of 'That's the boy!'

> 1909 *American Magazine*: Back of Chance's war cries, 'At-a-boy', or 'Now ye're pitching', may be hidden a whole command to his team.

auto-cycle *n* (1905) An alternative term for *motor-cycle*, which survived into the middle of the century

> 1958 *Oxford Mail*: Auto-cyclist…killed yesterday when the auto-cycle he was riding was involved in a collision with a Land Rover.

autoist *n* (1903) someone who uses or drives an automobile. Very briefly a US rival to *motorist* (1896), but it was really no contest

> 1903 *Scientific American*: Bills giving equal rights to autoists and the drivers of horses.

automat *n* (1903) a cafeteria in which food is obtained from compartments by the insertion of a coin or token. US. The probable inspiration for several other English words ending in -*mat* later in the century (e.g. **Laundromat (1943)**)

> 1921 P. G. Wodehouse: The Automat?… The food's quite good. You go and help yourself out of slot-machines, you know.

automatic *n* (1902) an automatic pistol

> 1902 *Sears Catalogue*: Forehand Perfection Automatic, small frame, rebounding lock.

bakelite *n* (1909) a type of plastic used in a wide variety of manufactured goods in the early part of the century. The invention of the Belgian-born physicist Leo Baekeland (1863–1944), after whom it was named, it was the first plastic that hardens permanently when heated and does not go soft when reheated. The term was coined in German in 1909 as *Bakelit*, and immediately exported to English

> 1920 V. W. Pagé: The distributor head and rotor are made of bakelite.

> 1933 *Practical Wireless*: A heavy flexible metal shielding fits tightly over these bakelite shells, and through the shells ordinary rubber-covered lead-in wire is threaded.

ballyhoo *n* (1901) a flamboyant performance outside a circus or carnival tent, intended to encourage people to enter. First encountered in American English, but its precise origins are unclear. There is an obsolete nautical slang term *ballyhoo* meaning 'an unseaworthy vessel', which apparently comes from Spanish *balahú* 'schooner'; there is a village called *Ballyhooly* in Ireland; and there is an isolated reference in 1880 to a *ballyhoo bird*, a facetious name given to an artificial bird put together from wood and pasteboard to fool a bird-hunter: but none of these is particularly relevant to attracting custom to a show. The wider meaning 'sensational or vulgar (self-)advertising', which is more familiar in present-day English, had developed before the end of the decade

> 1901 *World's Work*: First there is the ballyhoo—any sort of a performance outside the show, from the coon songs of the pickaninnies in front of the Old Plantation, to the tinkling tamborines of the dancers on the stage of 'Around the World'.

> 1908 *Saturday Evening Post*: It is the practice of almost every statesman to prepare the country for his performance by beating the drum and blatting a few lines of ballyhoo.

Barnardo *adj* (1904) Applied to a child brought up in any of the homes for orphans founded in Britain by Dr Thomas John Barnardo (1845–1905). Although the homes date from 1867, the epithet did not become widely used until the 20th century

> 1904 Rudyard Kipling: All the time the beggar was a balmy Barnardo Orphan!

> 1910 E. F. Murphy: Two Barnardo boys look on and enjoy the sport.

bat *n* **like a bat out of hell** (1909) very fast. Slang, originally US

> 1921 John Dos Passos: We went like a bat out of hell along a good state road.

bath salts *n* (1907) soluble salts for softening or perfuming bath-water. Their use faded out in the last quarter of the century

> 1920 Aldous Huxley: A very hot bath with lots of verbena bath-salts.

beat it (1906) to go away, clear out. Slang, originally US

> 1906 Helen Green: I told 'em to beat it.

beauty culture *n* (1909) use of cosmetics, etc., to improve a person's appearance. Originally US. A highfalutin term which initially turns up mainly in book titles (e.g. W. A. Woodbury's opus *Beauty Culture: A Practical Handbook on the Care of the Person* 1911). The derivative *beauty culturist* is first recorded in 1911

> 1911 W. A. Woodbury: The successful beauty culturist must, above all, be modest, tactful, and discreet.

> 1933 *Times Literary Supplement*: A small American town, whose main interests are bridge, poker, 'beauty-culture' and gossip.

beauty shop *n* (1901), **beauty parlour** *n* (1908) an establishment where cosmetic and other treatments are given to improve personal beauty. Originally US. The synonymous **beauty salon** is not recorded until the 1920s

> 1908 *Harper's Weekly*: The 'beauty parlors' of a large department store. There are a number of booths divided off by wooden partitions.

> 1969 Bill Knox: Janey Milton…on her way to have her hair set at a local beauty shop.

beddy-bye *n* (1906) A nursery and facetious term for 'bed' or 'sleep'. The form *beddy-byes* later became the established one

> 1906 Edward Dyson: Booser M'Gunn…went ter beddy-bye.

> 1946 Sarah Russell: Mrs. Chalmers rolled up her knitting and said she supposed it was time for beddy-byes.

beehive *n* (1909) a hat shaped like a domed beehive. See also **beehive (1960)**

> 1909 *Westminster Gazette*: A useful hat…is one of the new shape, which some milliners are calling the 'Beehive'.

> 1937 Noël Coward: Gertie Millar in *Our Miss Gibbs*, wearing a beehive.

big business *n* (1905) large-scale commercial operations, especially when regarded as (excessively) powerful. Originally US

> 1913 Theodore Roosevelt: We demand that big business give the people a square deal; in return we must insist that when any one engaged in big business honestly endeavors to do right he shall himself be given a square deal.

big end *n* (1906) the end of an engine's connecting rod that is attached to the crankshaft. British

> 1909 *Westminster Gazette*: The big-end bearings can be examined and adjusted.

bilge *n* (1908) nonsense, rubbish. Slang; from the earlier sense, 'unpleasant material which gathers in a ship's bilge'

> 1908 Desmond Coke: Let's go… This [excursion] is awful bilge.

> 1954 P. G. Wodehouse: She wrote this novel and it was well received by the intelligentsia, who notoriously enjoy the most frightful bilge.

biometry *n* (1901) the application of mathematics to biology, especially the study of resemblances between living things by statistical methods. The word had previously been used in the 19th century to mean 'the calculation of the average duration and expectation of life', but Galton's usage is apparently a new coinage

> 1901 Francis Galton: The primary object of Biometry is to afford material that shall be exact enough for the discovery of incipient changes in evolution which are too small to be otherwise apparent.

bioscope *n* (1908) The South African word for **cinema**. It had started life as the name of an early sort of film projector (it is first recorded in this sense in 1897); it had spread to South Africa by 1908, but survived and evolved there, while elsewhere in the English-speaking world it withered and died out

> 1908 *Cape Times*: The Electro-Chrono ('King of Bioscopes'). A Machine for exhibiting Living Pictures of exceptional brilliance.

> 1958 *Observer*: I saw the film…on the quivering screen of a Central African bioscope.

biota *n* (1901) A collective term for the animal and plant life of a region, coined from Greek *biotē* 'way of life'

> 1901 L. Stejneger: The author, like many other writers…has felt the need of a comprehensive term to include both fauna and flora which will…designate the total of animal and plant life of a given region or period…also any treatise upon the animals and plants of any geographical area… As such a term I would suggest *Biota*.

bird watching *n* (1901) the hobby of observing birds in the wild. The term is first recorded as the title of a book by E. Selous. He also established *bird watcher* by using it in the title of a book: *The Bird Watcher in the Shetlands* (1905)

> 1930 J. S. Huxley: From the bird-watcher pure and simple it is but a step to the bird-watcher naturalist.

birthday card *n* (1902) a greetings card sent to someone on their birthday

> 1902 *Little Folks*: Miss Shaw seemed to appreciate Moya's birthday card very much.

blood-count *n* (1900) (the finding of) the number of blood cells contained in a given volume of blood

> 1907 *Practitioner*: A blood-count, made two years ago, showed: Red cells, 5,000,000 [etc.].

blue baby *n* (1903) a baby suffering from congenital cyanosis, which causes blue discoloration of the skin. Widespread in the first three quarters of the century, the term has latterly fallen into disuse, perhaps because of too great a suggestion of freakishness

> 1903 R. H. Babcock: The little patient had been a blue baby from birth.

bomb *v* (1909) to attack with bombs. *Bomb* had been used as a verb since the late 17th century, but it referred to the firing of mortar shells (Lord Nelson wrote in 1797 'The intention of bombing us still goes on'). The application (of the noun as well as the verb) to an explosive device placed by hand or dropped from an aircraft is an early 20th-century development (in the early months of World War I *The Times* reported 'A German aeroplane flew over the outskirts of Paris early this morning and threw several bombs,' 9 October 1914; and such tactics had been practised before the war: 'There have been many contests by aviators in "bomb-dropping" ', Richard Ferris, *How it Flies* 1910). The term **air bomb**, distinguishing such devices from other sorts of bomb, is first recorded in 1914; it continued in use for some years: 'And most murderous of all devices Are poison gases and air-bombs Refinements of evil,' D. H. Lawrence, *Last Poems* a1930). The first quote below refers to terrorist activities in British India

> 1909 *Daily Chronicle*: Attempts had been made to blow up Sir Andrew Fraser, to bomb trains known to contain Europeans, and to murder policemen and officials.

> a1917 E. A. Mackintosh: He turned to bomb the big dug-out.

> 1940 *Times*: One of the aircraft which bombed a marshalling yard only a few miles from the heart of Berlin.

borstal *n* (1907) an establishment in Britain in which offenders aged 15 to 21 could be detained for corrective training. A generic use of the name of the first such institution, situated in the village of

Borstal, near Rochester, Kent. Under the terms of the Criminal Justice Act 1982, borstals were replaced by *youth custody centres*

> 1907 *Daily Chronicle*: The 'Borstal prisoner'.

> 1917 *Times*: Four youths have escaped from the Borstal Institution, Rochester.

> 1951 *Lancet*: The only open borstal for girls is at East Sutton… A survey of 300 borstal girls.

bovrilize *v* (1901) to concentrate the essence of; to condense. British colloquial. Bovril, a brand of concentrated beef essence, was introduced in 1889, and in a dozen years had become sufficiently familiar to inspire this fanciful coinage. It was in vogue for only a couple of years, but it was still well enough remembered two decades on for examples of its use to be recorded in the 1920s

> 1901 *Daily News*: Here…is one of these 'bovrilised' announcements…: Wanted, Sit. as Comp. by Eng. lady, 35; good Fr.; good refs.; would trav. R.R., 100.

> 1928 *Musical Times*: The exercises…are short enough not to fatigue the attention, and they bovrilise the difficulties or virtues admirably.

Boy Scout *n* (1908) a member of a boys' organization founded by Robert Baden-Powell in 1908 and intended to develop character and self-reliance. Baden-Powell seems to have got the inspiration for the name from a corps of boys which was formed to help in the defence of Mafeking in the Boer War

> 1908 *Scout*: Although the Boy Scouts have only been set going within the last two months, they are rapidly increasing all over the country.

> 1909 *Daily Mail*: The following message from the King was read at Lieutenant-General Baden-Powell's review of the Boy Scouts at the Crystal Palace on Saturday… 'The King is glad to know that the Boy Scouts are holding their first annual parade. Please assure the boys that [etc.]'.

brassière, brassiere *n* (1909) a women's undergarment worn to support the breasts. A euphemistic borrowing of French *brassière* in its decidedly dated sense 'bodice' (in 20th-century French it has mainly been used, in the plural, to mean 'leading-strings'; the French word for a 'brassière' is *soutien-gorge*). The shortened form *bra* is first recorded in the 1930s (see **bra (1936)**). The general idea dates from the late 19th century (a design for 'health braided wire dress forms' was patented in 1885), but a recognizably modern bra (made with a pair of handkerchiefs) was not patented until 1914, by Mary Phelps Jacob

> 1909 *Vogue*: A brassière for dressy occasions.

> 1911 *Daily Colonist*: (Victoria, British Columbia) (advert): Brassieres of fine cambric, lace and embroidery trimmed.

> 1912 *Queen* (advert): The stylish figure of To-Day requires a Brassiere.

bread-line *n* (1900) a queue of destitute people waiting to receive bread. The term first occurs in, and as the title of, a magazine story by A. B. Paine. The shift in meaning in British English to 'subsistence level' (probably occasioned by a misunderstanding of American English *line* 'queue', and also perhaps by an association with **poverty line (1901)**) seems to have become established by the 1920s

> 1900 *Lippincott's Magazine*: That's the bread line. They get a cup of coffee and a loaf of bread every night at twelve o'clock.

> 1959 *New Statesman*: The average African family in the urban areas lived calamitously below the bread-line.

brogue *n* (1906) a strong shoe for country and sports wear, with characteristic bands of ornamental perforations. A step up for what had once been a much less refined item of footwear, defined by the OED as 'a rude kind of shoe…worn by the inhabitants of the wilder parts of Ireland and the Scotch Highlands'

> 1906 Hasluck, *Boot & Shoe Pattern Cutting*: Brogue Shoes.-The gentleman's brogue is always a strong shoe for shooting, golf, fishing, etc.

bubble *n* a car. US humorous slang—a curtailed version of *automobubble* (1902), which itself was a jokey flight of fancy based on *automobile*. It was already well on its way out by the end of the 1910s—the resemblance to **bubble car (1957)** is purely coincidental

> 1918 P. G. Wodehouse: From the direction of the street, came the roar of a starting automobile…
> 'Gee! He's beat it in my bubble—and it was a hired one!'

buck *n the buck* (1908) the responsibility. Originally, and usually, in the phrase *pass the buck*, but there are other variations (notably *the buck stops here*, attributed to US President Harry Truman (see the second quote below)). The expression seems to come from earlier US slang *buck* denoting an object passed round during a game of poker to indicate the dealer—but the origins of this are unknown

> 1912 W. Irwin: The Big Commissioner will get roasted by the papers and hand it to the Deputy
> Comish, and the Deputy will pass the buck down to me, and I'll have to report how it happened.

> 1952 Harry Truman: When the decision is up before you—and on my desk I have a motto which
> says 'The buck stops here'—the decision has to be made.

bucked *adj* (1907) cheered, encouraged, elated. A British colloquialism, distinctly dated by 1950. Formed from *buck up* 'to cheer up'

> 1907 *Varsity*: We are very 'bucked' that he fitted in a visit this Term.

Buggins's turn *n* (1901) the principle of assigning an appointment to people in rotation rather than according to merit. There was no particular Buggins behind the term—it is merely a randomly selected surname

> 1901 Lord Fisher: Favouritism was the secret of our efficiency in the old days… Going by seniority
> saves so much trouble. 'Buggins's turn' has been our ruin and will be disastrous hereafter!

bulk carrier *n* (1909) a ship that carries cargo in bulk

> 1909 W. S. Tower, *The Story of Oil*: Before long tank steamers were also added to the fleet of bulk
> carriers.

bump off *v* (1907) to remove (someone) by violence; to kill (someone). Slang, originally US

> 1910 W. M. Raine: I've got several good reasons why I don't aim to get bumped off just yet.

bun *n* (1901) a drunken condition. Slang. Usually used in such phrases as *get a bun on* and *have a bun on*, meaning 'to get drunk', it did not survive much beyond the middle of the century. Its origins are obscure

> 1901 Hugh McHugh: You've got another bun on! How dare you trail into my flat with your tide high
> enough to float a battleship?

cake-walk *n* (1902) a strutting dance, popular in the early years of the century, based on a promenade or walk (originally amongst blacks in the southern US) in which the participants who performed the most complicated or outlandish steps won a cake as a prize

> 1902 William Harben: I was doing the cake-walk with that fat Howard girl from Rome.

camera-man *n* (1908) a man who uses or operates a camera professionally. Latterly applied only to film or television cameramen

> 1908 *Westminster Gazette*: After both had posed to the inevitable camera-men.

> 1920 *Quarterly Review*: The camera-man will film you anything.

camp *adj* (1909) outrageously affected or exaggerated in style. Usually used with connotations of male homosexuality. First recorded in a book by J. Redding Ware called *Passing English of the Victorian Era*, its origins remain obscure. It may have come from French *camper* 'to portray, pose', or from English dialect *kemp* 'uncouth'. Its circulation was mainly restricted to theatrical slang in the early years of the century, but it 'came out' in the 1960s

> 1909 J. R. Ware: *Camp* (*Street*), actions and gestures of exaggerated emphasis. Probably from the
> French. Used chiefly by persons of exceptional want of character. 'How very camp he is.'

canned *adj* (1904) Of music, laughter, etc.: mechanically or artificially reproduced. A dismissive epithet coined while recording technology was still in its infancy. See also **tinned (1924)**

> 1904 O. Henry: 'The Latin races…are peculiarly adapted to be victims of the phonograph.' 'Then,'
> says I, 'we'll export canned music to the Latins.'

> 1908 *Westminster Gazette*: The latest invention is the 'canned speech' delivered by a gramophone.

card vote *n* (1902) a method of voting in which each delegate's vote counts for the number of those who delegated him or her. A usage particularly associated with voting at British trade union conferences

> 1902 *35th Annual Report of the Trades Union Congress*: Should a card vote be demanded, it would of course be taken.

carrier bag *n* (1907) a large paper or, latterly, plastic bag for carrying shopping. British

> 1907 *Yesterday's Shopping*: The 'Sensible' carrier bag. With strings…is the only paper Bag with a firm bottom, and capable of carrying wet fruit, pastry &c., without…bursting the bag.

car-sick *adj* (1908) sick from the motion of a car. Modelled on *sea-sick*

> 1908 *Lancet*: Individuals who are car-sick may be good sailors and *vice versâ*… By car-sickness is meant a series of unpleasant symptoms, as giddiness, staggering, nausea, and vomiting due to riding in a vehicle or even in a baby-carriage.

Caterpillar *n* (1908) The proprietary name (registered in the US in 1911 and in Britain in 1915) of a type of tractor which travels on two endless steel bands, one on each side of the machine, to facilitate travel over very rough ground. In modern use it mainly designates these steel bands (*caterpillar tracks*). An invention crucial to the development of the **tank (1916)**

> 1908 *Scientific American*: The 'Caterpillar' Tractor. For some months past the British military authorities have been experimenting with a new type of tractor for the haulage of heavy vehicles over rough and unstable ground… The soldiers at the Aldershot military center, where it is in operation, promptly christened it the 'caterpillar'.

> 1915 Winston Churchill: The caterpillar system would enable trenches to be crossed quite easily.

cathode-ray tube *n* (1905) a vacuum tube in which cathode rays are projected on a fluorescent screen (as used in television sets). The term is first recorded in an article called 'Some Applications of the Braun Cathode-Ray Tube' in the journal *The Electrician*

> 1934 *Discovery*: The advances made in the use of short waves and the introduction of cathode-ray tubes have enabled us to transmit images on screens 3 or 4 feet square.

central heating *n* (1906) (apparatus for) heating a building from a central heat source. Mainly British. The idea dates from Roman times, but the terminology is 20th-century

> 1906 *International Library of Technology*: For use in connection with central heating plants, such as are frequently installed for heating the various buildings of a university or state institution, the vacuum system of heating is well adapted.

> 1921 R. Hichens: There was no central heating on.

cerealist *n* (1905) someone who advocates a cereal diet. As a coinage it had little stamina

> 1905 *Daily Chronicle*: Cerealists preach absolute abstention from pheasant, turbot, and turtle.

chain letter *n* (1906) a letter written with an invitation to the recipient to pass (copies of) it on, the process being repeated in a continuous chain until a certain total is reached

> 1906 *Daily Chronicle*: In 1896 Miss Audrey Griffin, of Hurstville, New South Wales initiated a 'chain letter' with the object of obtaining 1,000,000 used postage stamps.

chassis *n* (1903) the base frame of a motor vehicle, with its mechanism, as distinguished from the body or upper part. From French *châssis* 'frame'

> 1903 *Scientific American*: The motor is placed in the center of the chassis and the boiler is now quite in the rear.

chauffeur *n* (1902) a paid driver of a private motor vehicle. English first borrowed *chauffeur* from French at the very end of the 19th century in the broader sense 'motorist' ('All the members of the Italian Royal Family are enthusiastic *chauffeurs*', *Lady's Realm* (1903)), but this was soon elbowed aside by the current meaning. The French word is derived from *chauffer* 'to heat', and originally denoted a 'stoker'

> 1902 *Westminster Gazette*: As to the driver, 'chauffeur' seems at present to hold the field.

chest *n* get something *off one's chest* (1902) to relieve one's mind by admission or confession. Colloquial

1902 *Daily Chronicle*: The desire is either to deliver a message to the world or to express the individual personality—to 'get it off your chest' is the horrid, vulgar phrase.

chiropractor *n* (1904) a therapist who works by manipulating the backbone and other bodily structures. A derivative of *chiropractic*, which was coined in the 1890s from Greek *kheir* 'hand' and *praktikos* 'effective, practical'

1904 *Backbone*: He is fitted to become an all-round family Chiropractor.

chow mein *n* (1903) a southern Chinese dish consisting of fried noodles served with a thick sauce or stew composed of chopped meat, vegetables, etc. The dish and its name (literally 'fried flour' in Chinese) were acquired via Chinese immigrants on the West Coast of the US

1903 R. L. McCardell: Chaw main is good, too. That's chicken and ginger and mushrooms and bamboo sprouts and other stuff.

cigarette card *n* (1902) a picture card inserted by the makers in a packet or box of cigarettes. They remained a major promotional tool until well after World War II, as people eagerly sought to collect complete sets. In early usage they were often also called *cigarette pictures*. See also **cartophilist (1936)**

1902 *Little Folks*: 2d. a dozen for cigarette cards (Ogden's Guinea Gold)… 90 cigarette pictures (not all different) to dispose of at 90 for 1s.

1967 A. Davis: Cigarette cards…were originally intended as stiffeners (and always known in the trade by this name). The first printed stiffeners were produced in America in 1879.

cigarette heart *n* (1908) a condition of the heart brought about by excessive smoking of cigarettes. Not a term which caught on

1908 *Daily Chronicle*: Witness examined his heart and found no organic disease; it was a 'cigarette heart'.

cinema *n* (1909) A shorter alternative to *cinematograph* (1896). English originally acquired the word at the end of the 19th century from French, as *cinéma*, and it is not clear whether the present-day form is an anglicization of this (itself an abbreviation of *cinématographe*) or an independent English formation. The earliest record of its use in the sense 'a building where films are shown' (short for *cinema hall, cinema theatre*, etc.) is from 1913. See also **kinema (1914)**

1910 *Daily Chronicle*: 'Cinematograph'—which has just been cut down in a glaring advertisement to 'cinema'.

1913 V. Steer: The so-called 'comic' films from France which one sees on the cinema.

cinematograph theatre *n* (1909) a cinema

1909 *Report of the Joint Select Committee on Stage Plays (Censorship)*: The case which is now arising of the performances at what are known as cinematograph theatres.

city centre *n* (1904) the central (often largely non-residential) part of a city. An early occurrence of a term which did not come into common use until after World War II

1904 George Bernard Shaw: In city centres…the [housing] schemes are commercially hopeless.

1957 John Braine: The maze of side-streets off the city centre.

Clapham *n* **man on the Clapham omnibus** (1903) the ordinary or average man; the 'man in the street'. British; an evocation of the extreme ordinariness (and hence representativeness) of a commuter travelling in by bus to work in central London from Clapham (in 1903 a south-western suburb, by the end of the century virtually inner-city). Originally largely a legal figment appealed to by lawyers, but latterly in wider use. The general idea seems to have been around as long ago as the mid 19th century: 'So thoroughly has the tedious traffic of the streets become ground into the true Londoner's nature, that…your dog-collar'd occupant of the knife-board of a Clapham omnibus, will stick on London-bridge for half-an-hour with scarcely a murmur', *Journal of the Society of Arts* (1857)

1903 *Law Report* (King's Bench Division): 'Fair', therefore, in this collocation certainly does not mean that which the ordinary reasonable man, 'the man on the Clapham omnibus', as Lord Bowen phrased it, the juryman common or special, would think a correct appreciation of the work.

1959 *Listener*: It is 'the man in the street', 'the man in the jury box', or (to use the phrase so familiar to English lawyers) 'the man on the Clapham omnibus'.

clip-on *adj* (1909) attached or fitted into position with a clip. An early example of a type of word (an adjective formed from a verb and a particle) which became common later in the century (e.g. **tie-on (1910), roll-on (1941), see-through (1950), wind-up (1979)**)

> 1909 *Chambers's Journal*: A spring clip-on handle is provided, gripping the top and bottom edges of the opened tin, so that it is converted into a mug.

cloche hat *n* (1907) a woman's close-fitting hat of a bell shape, of a type very fashionable in the early part of the century. From French *cloche* 'bell'

> 1907 *Westminster Gazette*: The mondaine's big cloche hat.

> 1923 *Daily Mail*: The narrow-brimmed, high-crowned cloche.

clone *n* (1903) Originally, in botanical terminology, a group of cultivated plants the individuals of which are transplanted parts of one original stock; later used more broadly to denote any group of cells or organisms produced asexually from a single sexually produced ancestor. The form of the word as originally proposed by H. J. Webber in the journal *Science* was *clon*; the amendment to *clone* was put forward by C. L. Pollard in the same journal, on the grounds that it better represents its Greek source *klōn* 'twig, slip'. The verb *clone* did not appear until the 1950s (see **clone (1959)**)

> 1903 H. J. Webber: Clons…are groups of plants that are propagated by the use of any form of vegetative parts.

> 1905 C. L. Pollard: I therefore suggest *clone* (plural *clones*) as the correct form of the word.

closed shop *n* (1904) a shop, factory, trade, etc., in which normally only trade-union members are employed. Originally US

> 1904 *New York Evening Post*: An increase in wages, recognition of the union, and 'closed shops' are demanded.

club sandwich *n* (1903) a thick sandwich containing several ingredients, such as chicken or turkey, lettuce, tomato, mayonnaise, etc. Mainly US

> 1903 R. L. McCardell: All we need is a club sandwich and a bottle of beer.

coin-box *n* (1906) a receptacle for the coins in a coin-operated telephone or the like

> 1906 *Annual Report of the American Telegraph and Telegram Company*: Prepayment coin boxes…have been provided.

coitus interruptus *n* (1900) sexual intercourse in which the penis is withdrawn from the vagina before ejaculation

> 1900 Havelock Ellis: Onan's device was not auto-erotic, but was an early example of withdrawal before emission or coitus interruptus.

coke *n* (1908) the drug cocaine. Slang, originally US

> 1908 R. S. Baker: They buy the 'coke' in the form of powder and snuff it up the nose.

> 1928 Edgar Wallace: It's your 'coke' trade that's stirring up the Yard.

Coke *n* (1909) Coca-Cola. A colloquial abbreviation, registered as a trademark by the Coca-Cola Company. The original name *Coca-Cola* dates from 1887

> 1909 *Coca-Cola Bottler* (Philadelphia): If you…ask to be served with 'Ice Cold Cokes' you will be presented with a very good bottle of carbonated Coca-Cola.

colour prejudice *n* (1905) prejudice on the grounds of racial difference

> 1905 William Baucke: In the case of the Maori, this is deterred by a colour prejudice.

complex *n* (1907) a connected group of repressed ideas which give rise to particular patterns of thought, feeling, and action. The use of the term was established by C. G. Jung in 1907 (*Ueber die Psychologie der Dementia Praecox*), but it originated with Neisser in 1906 (*Individualität und Psychose*). It is commonly used with a qualifying term (e.g. **inferiority complex**, **Oedipus complex**)

> 1907 Petersen & Jung: The complex robs the ego of light and nourishment, just as a cancer robs the body of its vitality.

concentration camp *n* (1901) a camp where non-combatants are incarcerated during a war. The term was originally applied to the camps set up by Lord Kitchener during the South African War

(Boer War) of 1899–1902, the underlying idea being that the inmates were 'concentrated' in one place (see the first quote below), where they could not give help to the fighting forces. It gained even further notoriety when it was applied to camps for the internment, brutalization, extermination, etc. of Jews, gypsies, and political prisoners organized by the Nazi regime in Germany before and during World War II

> 1901 *Hansard*: The policy of placing the women and children confined in the concentration camps in South Africa, whose husbands and fathers are in the field, on reduced rations.

> 1934 *Annual Register 1933*: Germany…For dealing with the masses of prisoners special concentration camps were opened.

> 1940 H. G. Wells: The White Paper of Nazi atrocities in the concentration camps and elsewhere.

conditioned reflex *n* (1906) a reflex or reflex action which through habit or training has been induced to follow a stimulus not naturally associated with it. A term made familiar through the work of the Russian experimental psychologist Ivan Pavlov, who won the Nobel prize for physiology and medicine in 1904

> 1906 *Nature*: The latter actions…are termed by Prof. Pawlow 'conditioned reflexes', to distinguish them from the ordinary or unconditioned reflexes.

conspiracy theory *n* (1909) the theory that an event or phenomenon occurs as a result of a conspiracy between interested parties. Originally a neutral term, but more recent usage (dating from around the mid 1960s) is often somewhat derogatory, implying a paranoid tendency to see the hand of some malign covert agency in any unexplained event. The derivative *conspiracy theorist* is first recorded in the 1960s

> 1975 *New York Times*: Conspiracy theorists contend that two of the men have strong resemblances to E. Howard Hunt Jr. and Frank A. Sturgis, convicted in the Watergate break-in.

conveyor belt *n* (1906) an endless belt of rubber, canvas, etc., running over rollers, on which objects or material can be conveyed. A key element in the mass production which has characterized 20th-century industry

> 1906 *Westminster Gazette*: Electric energy…is used…for the conveyor belts.

> 1948 J. B. Priestley: I don't admire the mass production and conveyor-belt system of education.

cork-tipped *adj* (1907) Of a cigarette: having a filter of a cork-like substance at one end. In later use applied to any filter-tipped cigarette, especially one with a cork-like design covering the filter

> 1928 *Punch*: Really nice girls smoke Player's Cork-Tipped.

cornflakes *n* (1907) a kind of breakfast cereal made from flaked and flavoured maize. Originally US. The archetypal 20th-century manufactured breakfast cereal (the second quote below refers to the World War I period)

> 1908 *Saturday Evening Post*: There are 13 imitations of Kellogg's Toasted Corn Flakes.

> 1960 John Betjeman: And, in the morning, cornflakes, bread and tea, Cook's Farm Eggs and a spoon of marmalade.

crawl *n* (1903) a high-speed swimming stroke in which the swimmer, lying face-downwards, makes alternate overhand arm-strokes assisted by the quick movement of the legs

> 1903 Sinclair & Henry: A young swimmer named R. Cavill, who revolutionised all ideas about speed swimming for short distances by introducing a further modification of this style [i.e. the 'Trudgen'], which was at once termed the 'crawl' stroke.

cryogenic *adj* (1902) relating to the production or use of very low temperatures. A coinage based on Greek *kruos* 'frost, icy cold'. Compare **cryonic (1968)**

> 1902 *Encyclopaedia Britannica*: Within recent years several special cryogenic laboratories have been established.

dashboard *n* (1904) the panel beneath a motor vehicle's windscreen on which electrical instruments and controls are mounted. An adaptation of the earlier meaning, 'a board in front of a vehicle to stop mud being splashed (or *dashed*) up from the horses' hoofs into the vehicle'

> 1904 A. B. F. Young: A cooling apparatus has now been fitted behind the bonnet and in front of the dashboard.

day-trip *n* (1903) an excursion to a place and back in one day. A form of mini-break which apparently found a name around the end of the 19th century (*day-tripper* is first recorded in 1897); daily excursions organized by Thomas Cook date back to the 1840s

> 1903 Arnold Bennett: He had gone to London by a day-trip on the previous Thursday.

decay *v* (1900) Of radioactivity: gradually to diminish in intensity

> 1900 Ernest Rutherford: The intensity of the 'excited' radiation falls to half its value in about eleven hours, or one decays 660 times faster than the other.

deficient *n* (1906) someone unable (e.g. through mental deficiency) to cope fully with the demands of living in society. One of the periodic attempts to establish a euphemism in this area (an earlier one, at the end of the 19th century, had been *defective*); this one seems not to have survived beyond the 1920s

> 1927 Carr-Saunders & Jones: [Authorities] vary notoriously… Some are active, while others close their eyes to the existence of deficients within their areas.

deevy, devey *adj* (1900) delightful, charming. An affected alteration of **divvy (1903)**. It lasted longer than *divvy*, but by the 1920s it too was a distantly remembered piece of Edwardian slang

> 1900 Elinor Glyn: Miss La Touche…said my hat was 'too devey for words'.

> 1905 E. F. Benson: How too deliciously eerie! How deevily mysterious!

depression *n* (1905) a melancholic state often accompanied by feelings of inadequacy and lack of energy. In use since the 17th century as a general word for 'dejection', but in the 20th century adopted as a clinical term

> 1905 *Psychological Review*: If these symptoms of depression—the motor retardation, the difficulty of apprehension and of association—become aggravated, one finds various forms of melancholia.

détente *n* (1908) the easing of strained relations, especially in a political situation. A borrowing from French, where it means literally 'loosening, relaxation'. Quite common in the language of international diplomacy throughout the century, but not generally familiar until the Cold War period, when it referred to a hoped-for relaxation of tension between East and West

> 1908 *Times*: A change in the European situation…had…set in… The characteristic feature of this transformation may be called a *détente*.

> 1976 *National Observer* (US): All that detente brings the United States, Reagan says, is 'the right to sell Pepsi-Cola in Siberia'.

Dictaphone *n* (1907) a machine on which dictated matter is recorded for subsequent audio playback and typing. Registered as a trademark in 1907. Subsequently widely known by the generic term **dictating machine (1907)**. The first such machines were phonographs (it was the first commercial exploitation which Thomas Edison attempted for his invention; only later did he realize that it might be more successful for playing musical recordings); the tape recorder version came much later

> 1907 *Daily Chronicle*: The 'dictaphone', an adaptation of the phonograph.

> 1961 *Evening Standard*: Dictaphone Typist urgently required.

dictating machine *n* (1907) Originally an alternative name for a **Dictograph (1907)**, but this usage soon died out. Its present-day use, as a synonym for **Dictaphone (1907)**, is first recorded in 1957

> 1957 *Economist*: Most people like Stenorette Dictating Machines… A Stenorette takes an average day's dictation on one spool of magnetic tape that can be used over and over again indefinitely.

Dictograph *n* (1907) The proprietary name (registered in 1907) of a device used as an internal telephone without mouthpiece or earpiece, by means of which speech in one room is picked up by a sensitive microphone and reproduced through a loudspeaker elsewhere in the building. Modelled on *phonograph*

> 1907 *Times*: Mr. [K. M.] Turner of New York [one of the inventors]…had the honour of exhibiting the Dictograph before the King and Queen.

divvy *adj* (1903) delightful, charming. British slang. Formed from the first syllable of *divine*

> 1903 *Daily Chronicle*: I heard one of them say that 'the dimpy was divvy', and this, when translated, meant that a certain dinner party was divine.

dolly *n* (1906) an (attractive) young woman. Slang. A usage which probably gave rise to the *dolly birds* of the 1960s (see **dolly (1964)**)

> 1906 Edward Dyson: Now I wouldn' turn it [i.e. beer] down fer ther toffest Dolly on ther block.

door-to-door *adj* (1902) conducted by calling at every dwelling in a neighbourhood

> 1943 *Our Towns* (*Women's Group on Public Welfare*): The door-to-door salesmanship which is one of the pests of town life.

dorothy bag *n* (1907) a woman's handbag gathered at the top by a drawstring and slung by loops from the wrist. The term lingered into the 1960s. The identity of the original Dorothy is unknown

> 1923 *Daily Mail*: An effective Dorothy bag for evenings.

> 1962 *Harper's Bazaar*: The matching dorothy-bag purse has an expanding frame.

do's and don'ts *n* (1902) things one should and shouldn't do. First used in the title of a book, the expression has since spread into the general language

> 1902 'Stancliffe' (title): Golf do's and don'ts.

> 1962 Y. Olsson: There are certain do's and don'ts that he should keep in mind.

double-cross *v* (1903) to deceive by doing what one had promised not to do. Based on the noun *double cross*, which goes back to the early 19th century

> 1903 George Ade: Although he had been double-crossed and put through the Ropes, he still had a Punch left.

dreadnought *n* (1906) any of a class of British battleships having their main armament entirely of big guns of one calibre. These formidable firing-platforms were the keystone of Britain's pre-World War I arms build-up. The name (which originally belonged to a naval ship of Drake's era) was given to the first of the class to be launched (on 18 February 1906), and later generalized to its sister-ships

> 1906 *Outlook*: The Atlantic Fleet will consist of three *Dreadnoughts* and five of the *Canopus* class.

> 1909 *Daily Chronicle*: Our Dreadnought strength and our strength in pre-Dreadnought ships, in comparison with those of Germany.

drop-volley *n* (1907) a softly played volley which drops quickly after crossing the net. Much of the modern vocabulary of lawn tennis was in place before World War I

> 1927 *Daily Express*: She would leap forward and summarily cut short the rally with a deft drop-volley.

duck soup *n* (1902) something easy to do. US slang. The origins of the expression (which was used as the title of a 1933 Marx Brothers film) are obscure

> 1912 A. H. Lewis: 'Them Gophers are as tough a bunch as ever comes down the pike.' 'Tough nothin'!' returned Slimmy: 'they'll be duck soup to Ike.'

dug-out *n* (1904) a roofed shelter used in trench warfare. A specialized use of the earlier sense, 'a rough dwelling formed by excavation'

> 1904 *Westminster Gazette*: The following telegram from General Sakharoff…has been received at St. Petersburg:…Our troops, thanks to their dug-outs, warm clothing, and plentiful food, do not suffer from the cold.

> 1920 M. A. Mügge: The second wave going over the top; it 'mops up', 'cleans up' the enemy's dug-outs.

ectoplasm *n* (1901) a viscous substance which is supposed to emanate from the body of a spiritualistic medium, and to develop into a human form or face. It was not until the 1920s, when people seeking contact with loved ones lost in World War I turned in large numbers to spiritualism, that the term gained wide currency

> 1901 F. W. H. Myers: In describing…imperfectly aggregated ectoplasms we have already touched on the next class, that of quasi-organic detached ectoplasms.

> 1926 Arthur Conan Doyle: The ectoplasm pictures photographed by Madame Bisson and Dr. Schrenck Notzing…may in their first forms be ascribed to the medium's thoughts or memories taking visible shape in ectoplasm.

Edwardian *adj* (1908) of the reign of Edward VII (1901–10). In early usage it was sometimes spelled *Edvardian*

> 1908 *Westminster Gazette*: That the Edwardian age is more placidly disposed towards such a threat [*viz*. 'your beer will cost you more'] than the times of the King's great-grandfather, George III.

> 1911 Max Beerbohm: Miss Dobson now, in the midst of the Edvardian Era, was the toast of two hemispheres.

electrify *v* (1900) to introduce electric power into (a system of railways, a factory, etc.). The derivative *electrification* is first recorded in 1900. Alternative terms that were canvassed contemporaneously were *electralize* [sic] and *electrolization* or *electrilization* ('The electrolisation of the inner circle, with its twenty-six stations', *Westminster Gazette* (1900)), but these completely failed to catch on

> 1900 *Westminster Gazette*: It is not very astonishing that the directors of the District Railway should be in no violent hurry to start upon the electrifying of their line.

> 1904 *Daily Chronicle*: Electrification Perils. Risk Entailed by the Transformation of the 'Underground'.

electrobus *n* (1906) a bus powered by electricity. The name was short-lived, although such buses were successfully used in the first two thirds of the century

> 1906 *Westminster Gazette*: About January…the first of the electrobuses will be placed in regular running.

electrocardiogram *n* (1904) a record of the electric currents produced in the body by the heartbeats of a patient. An adaptation of German *Electrocardiogramm*, coined by W. Einthoven in 1894

> 1904 *Scientific American*: The human electrocardiogram discovered by A. D. Waller.

electrocute *v* (1909) to kill accidentally by means of electricity. A generalized use of a verb which was coined in the late 1880s with the specific meaning 'to execute with electricity', denoting the action of the newly invented electric chair ('Kemmler, the murderer sentenced to be "electrocuted" ', *Voice* (New York) (1889))

> 1909 *Yorkshire Post*: [A boy] who was electrocuted on the Mersey Railway last Saturday.

electrolysis *n* (1909) destruction of hair roots by an electric current. The term had been applied by surgeons since the middle of the 19th century to the use of electricity to destroy unwanted body tissue, such as tumours, and also stones in the kidney, gall bladder, etc., but this rather more trivial usage has now taken the word over

> 1909 *Daily Mirror*: Electrolysis. Superfluous hair permanently removed; ladies only; consultations free.

electronic *adj* (1902) Originally, relating to electrons. The word's main present-day application, to the control of a device by the conduction of electrons in a vacuum, a gas, or a semiconductor, seems to have emerged in the late 1920s, and to have been originally used in the context of musical instruments and the music made by them. Its wider employment followed on the development of computers after World War II. Similarly, *electronics* (first recorded in 1910) initially denoted simply the study of the behaviour of electrons, and was not used in the context of electronically controlled systems until the 1940s

> 1902 J. A. Fleming (*title*): The electronic theory of electricity.

> 1910 *Chemical Abstracts*: Radio activity and electronics.

> 1930 *Electronics*: Electronic Musical Instruments…Examples of such instruments are the electronic organ of M. Coupleaux of Paris.

> 1945 *Times*: The committee's report said…that 'knowledge of electronics promises the ability to detonate atomic bombs at great distances by radio'.

> 1962 Marshall McLuhan: As we experience the new electronic and organic age with ever stronger indications of its main outlines, the preceding mechanical age becomes quite intelligible.

empathy *n* (1904) the power of mentally identifying oneself with (and so fully comprehending) a person or object. Introduced as a technical term in the field of aesthetics as in effect a translation of the parallel German term *Einfühlung*, which had been coined by T. Lipps in 1903. This in turn was based on Greek *empatheia*, literally 'in-feeling'. Around the middle of the century it escaped from the jargon of aestheticians and began to be used almost synonymously with *sympathy*. See also **empathize (1924)**

> 1928 Rebecca West: The active power of empathy which makes the creative artist, or the passive power of empathy which makes the appreciator of art.

engram *n* (1908) a memory-trace; a permanent and inheritable physical change in the nerve tissue of the brain, posited to account for the existence of memory. An adaptation of German *Engramm*, which was coined by R. Semon, the originator of the theory, from Greek *gramma* 'letter', and first used in his book *Die Mneme* (1904)

> 1927 C. E. M. Joad: What I am aware of when I appear to remember something is not the past occurrence which, as I say, I remember, but a present state or modification of my body. This present state or modification is called an engram.

escalator *n* (1900) a moving staircase made on the endless-chain principle, so that the steps ascend or descend continuously, for carrying passengers (especially those using an underground railway) up or down. Originally a US trademark. Familiar enough by the 1920s to have a verb *escalate* back-formed from it ('I dreamt I saw a Proctor "escalating", Rushing up a quickly moving stair', *Granta* (1922)), but its later much vilified metaphorical use was far in the future (see **escalation (1938)**, **escalate (1959)**)

> 1900 *New York Journal*: The escalator…is a movable stairway built by the Otis Elevator Company for the use of passengers of the Manhattan Elevated Railway.

> 1923 *Spectator*: Three escalators will serve the Bakerloo Tube.

ethnocentric *adj* (1900) regarding one's own race or ethnic group as of supreme importance. Originally strictly a technical term amongst ethnologists, but in the second half of the century familiar to a wider audience

> 1900 W. J. McGee: In primitive culture the epocentric and ethnocentric views are ever-present and always-dominant factors of both mentation and action.

exclusive *adj* (1901) Of clothing, furniture, etc.: of a pattern or model exclusively belonging to or claimed by a particular establishment or firm. The first recorded appearance of a usage which was to become a cliché of 20th-century marketing terminology

> 1901 *Tatler*: Some very charming artistic novelties in exclusive and original designs are now ready for inspection.

> 1924 *Queen*: The absurdly low prices of the most exclusive gowns in London… Practical designs for golfing, country and travelling wear. Exclusive but inexpensive.

executive *n* (1902) someone holding an executive position in a business organization; a business person. Originally US

> 1902 G. H. Lorimer: They will never climb over the railing that separates the clerks from the executives.

> 1951 Marshall McLuhan: Do you have a personality? Our executive clinic will get rid of it for you.

> 1960 *Guardian*: There are three types [of private patients]—the snobs…the queue-jumpers…and the business executive.

expansionism *n* (1900) advocacy of, or furtherance of, a policy of expansion, especially territorial expansion. This particular sense of *expansion* dates from the 1880s

> 1900 *Daily News*: By Imperialism British Liberals ought not to understand militarism or even expansionism.

expressionism *n* (1908) a style of painting in which the artist seeks to express emotional experience rather than impressions of the physical world. Initially a descriptive term, it does not seem to have evolved into a (capitalized) name for a specific school of painters until the second decade of the century, in the wake of abstract expressionists such as Kandinsky. (The term *expressionist* in this general sense dates from around 1850)

> 1921 John Galsworthy: Expression! Ah, they were all Expressionists now, he had heard, on the Continent… He wondered where this—this Expressionism—had been hatched. The thing was a regular disease!

fed up *adj* (1900) satiated, bored. Colloquial. Originally British, it had spread to the US by the time of World War I. See also **feed (1933)**

 1900 *Westminster Gazette*: It may be quite true that, to use an expression often heard in South Africa just now, the men are 'fed up' with the war.

 1906 *Daily Chronicle*: I am about 'fed-up' over this motor-car.

 1914 *Evening News*: We have also seen hundreds of German prisoners, mostly looking 'fed up'.

 1971 *Jamaican Weekly Gleaner*: She's...fed up of kass-kass [i.e. quarrelling] with customers.

ferro-concrete *n* (1900) concrete strengthened with steel bars or metal netting. The first recorded reference to what was to become the major building material of the 20th century came in a British patent filed by G. L. Mouchel. More commonly known as **reinforced concrete (1902)**

 1914 *Scotsman*: The tall white ferro-concrete telegraph posts lining many of the main roads.

 1928 *Oxford Poetry*: Fierce ferro-concrete blares, On Woolworth, on!

fibre *n* (1909) dietary material that is resistant to the action of the digestive enzymes, consisting mainly of the cell walls of plants. Compare **roughage (1927)**

 1975 *Washington Post*: The need for fiber or, as grandmother used to call it, roughage.

fibrositis *n* (1904) inflammation of fibrous connective tissue, especially in the muscles of the back

 1904 W. R. Gowers: I think we need a designation for inflammation of the fibrous tissue which has not such results [i.e. the production of suppuration]... We may conveniently follow the analogy of 'cellulitis' and term it 'fibrositis'.

filing cabinet *n* (1907) a cabinet with drawers for holding files, documents, etc. A key information-retrieval system of the 20th-century office, first recorded in a stage direction in George Bernard Shaw's play *John Bull's Other Island*

 1911 H. S. Harrison: West went to a filing cabinet in the corner of the room.

film *n* (1905) a cinematographic representation of a story, drama, episode, event, etc.; a movie. The term has become standard in British English, in preference to *motion picture* (1890s) and **movie (1912)**

 1905 *Westminster Gazette*: A firm who took cinematograph films of his operations... The films once obtained have been sold and even exhibited at country fairs.

 1911 *Times*: The great majority of heroic and patriotic films shown here make United States sailors and roughriders the heroes.

firing squad *n* (1904) a squad of soldiers detailed to fire shots. In early use the term seems quite often to have been synonymous with *firing party* (i.e. 'a squad detailed to fire over the grave of someone buried with military honours'), but during World War I, when such things were much in use, the current sense 'a squad detailed to shoot someone sentenced to death by a court-martial' became firmly established

 1959 T. S. Eliot: The ones who don't get out in time Find themselves in gaol...Or before a firing squad.

flake *n* (1906) A term officially nominated in Britain as the commercial name of the dogfish, whose reputation made it difficult to sell under its own name. It was ousted later in the century by **rock salmon (1931)**

 1906 *Daily Chronicle*: A meeting of the Sea Fisheries Committee...had approved of the change of the name from dogfish to flake, and after the dinner the company unanimously affirmed that flake was a most excellent...form of food.

 1932 *Times Literary Supplement*: There is also long-line fishing for dog-fish (renamed 'flake' for marketing).

Fletcherize *v* (1903) to masticate thoroughly. *Fletcherism* (1906) was all the rage in the mid 1900s. Its central—indeed only— tenet was that in order to be digested properly, food must be relentlessly chewed before swallowing. It was named after its proponent, the American author Horace Fletcher (1849–1919). Its terminology remained in the memory long enough to be used humorously in the 1920s

1903 *Literary Digest*: It is now proposed to speak of the 'Fletcherizing' of food that is thoroughly chewed.

1922 P. G. Wodehouse: The raffish mongrel was apparently endeavouring to fletcherize a complete stranger of the Sealyham family.

flex *n* (1905) flexible insulated electric wire

1905 C. C. Metcalfe: Flexible cord, generally known in the wiring trade as 'Flex', consists of two flexible conductors laid together, each insulated from the other.

floating voter *n* (1905) a voter not committed to one particular political party. The term *floating vote* dates from the mid 19th century

1958 *Economist*: That now well-known and inoffensive favourite of the touchy floating voter, Mr. Aneurin Bevan.

floor polish *n* (1907) a manufactured substance for polishing floors. An early example of the mass production of housework materials

1926 *Daily Colonist* (Victoria, British Columbia): Floor polishes, you may say, are pretty much alike. But try 'Poliflor' just once and you will immediately realize what a vast difference there can be.

floosie, floozie *n* (1902) A contemptuous term for a (young) woman or girlfriend, usually implying promiscuity and/or blowsiness. Originally US. Early spellings are very variable (*flusy, fluzie, floozy*, etc.). Its antecedents are not entirely clear, but it could be a variant of its more-or-less contemporary but now defunct synonym *flossy*, which was probably based on the idea of fluffiness and softness

1927 H. A. Vachell: I'm beginning to think that baby is half vamp and half floosie.

flying-ground *n* (1909) An early but unsuccessful rival to **aerodrome (1909)**

1909 *Westminster Gazette*: Those who, in spite of the half-gale which was blowing, went to the flying-ground.

fly-over *n* (1901) a railway or road bridge over another (e.g. a local over a main) line or road. The application to roads (as opposed to railways) is first recorded in the 1930s

1901 *Daily News*: The junction for the Aldershot branch…is being…rearranged on the 'fly-over' system, that is, the down line…is being brought over the top of the main line by means of a skew bridge… This 'fly-over'…will abolish a fruitful source of delay.

1937 *Daily Express*: Whitehall's idea now is that great motoring highways be driven across the parks from one end to the other. They would meet at fly-overs, where one road would be built over the other.

fool-proof *adj* (1902) so simple and straightforward that even the most foolish or careless person could not fail with it. Originally US

1902 A. C. Harmsworth: The car…is comparatively 'fool-proof'.

for it (1909) in for trouble. Originally, apparently, military slang, denoting an impending appearance on the charge sheet

1909 *Captain*: 'He'll give the whole show away?' 'Then, I suppose, we'll all be for it.'

fuel-tank *n* (1900) a tank for containing the liquid fuel for an engine

1900 A. H. Goldingham: The oil is stored under pressure in the fuel-tank.

funk-hole *n* (1900) a place of safety into which one can retreat. The word really came into its own during World War I, when it was used as a wryly humorous term for a dug-out; thereafter it went into a long-term decline. Based on *funk* 'panic'

1918 W. J. Locke: 'J. M. T. and I have looked Death in the face many a time—and really he's a poor raw-head and bloody-bones sort of Bogey; don't you think so, old chap?' 'It all depends on whether you've got a funk-hole handy.'

fuselage *n* (1909) the main body of an aeroplane, to which the wings and tailplane are attached. Like many early aeronautical terms, a borrowing from French (it is derived ultimately from *fuseau* 'a spindle', a reference to its shape)

1909 *Flight*: The aeroplane itself was considerably damaged, the fuselage which carries the elevating-plane in front…being completely broken.

futurism *n* (1909) an art movement, originating in Italy, characterized by violent departure from traditional forms, the avowed aim being to express movement and growth in objects, not their appearance at some particular moment. Also applied to similar tendencies in literature and music. A term modelled on Italian *futurismo* and French *futurisme*

> 1909 *Daily Chronicle*: 'Futurism' is the declaration of the new school of literature grounded by the International Review 'Poesia'.

> 1915 W. H. Wright: Marinetti, a poet, is the spiritual (and monetary) father of Futurism.

gamma ray *n* (1903) a stream of electromagnetic radiation emitted by atomic nuclei, shorter in wavelength than X-rays. So named because it was originally regarded as the third and most penetrating kind of radiation emitted by radium (gamma (γ) being the third letter of the Greek alphabet), but now known to be identical with very short X-rays

> 1903 Ernest Rutherford: The γ rays, which are non-deviable by a magnetic field, and which are of a very penetrating character.

garage *n* (1902) a building for the storage and shelter of motor vehicles while not in use. To begin with mainly a large commercially owned building accommodating many cars, a usage which by natural evolution soon came to cover an establishment offering repair and refuelling facilities. A borrowing from French, where it was derived from *garer* 'to shelter'. An early but unsuccessful synonym was **motor stable (1907)**

> 1902 *Daily Mail*: The new 'garage' founded by Mr. Harrington Moore, hon. secretary of the Automobile Club… The 'garage', which is situated at the City end of Queen Victoria-street,…has accommodation for eighty cars.

> 1934 P. A. Reynolds: The third type of garage is…the Full Service business, which caters, in addition to the services already mentioned, for repairs of every description.

garden suburb *n* (1905) a suburban area planned so as to combine the advantages of town and country. A development of the concept of the 'garden city', put forward by Ebenezer Howard at the end of the 19th century (the term *garden city* is first recorded in 1898, *garden town* in 1915)

> 1905 S. A. Barnett: My wife has had a very busy week, interviewing people *re* the Garden Suburb.

> 1915 Patrick Geddes: The conditions for labour and its real wages, in the innumerable garden-towns and villages which are springing up.

gas *n* (1900) a poisonous or irritant gas used in warfare

> 1916 *King's Royal Rifle Corps Chronicle 1915*: The Germans opened a burning gas attack upon the front of the trenches we had captured from them ten days before.

genetics *n* (1905) the scientific study of heredity and variation. The word had already been used in the late 19th century, to mean 'the principles or laws of origination' and 'the branch of biology concerned with the study of natural development when not complicated by human interference', but neither of these usages caught on

> 1905 William Bateson: The best title would, I think, be 'The Quick Professorship of the study of Heredity'. No single word in common use quite gives this meaning…, and if it were desirable to coin one, 'Genetics' might do.

Gentleman's Relish *n* (1907) The proprietary name (registered in 1907) of a type of savoury paste

> 1918 H. G. Wells: Perhaps a sandwich, Gentleman's Relish or shrimp paste.

geopolitical *adj* (1902) relating to the influence of geographical factors on international relations. A term adapted from Swedish, where it was coined as *geopolitisk* around 1899

> 1902 E. Reich: History is made by minorities of men, if by majorities of geo-political factors.

geriatrics *n* (1909) the branch of medicine dealing with the health of old people. Coined from Greek *geras* 'old age' and *iatrikos* 'of a physician', on the model of *paediatrics*. The term made a slow start (the derived adjective **geriatric** is not recorded until the mid 1920s), but more than made up for it in the latter part of the century

> 1909 I. L. Nascher: Geriatrics, from geras, old age, and iatrikos, relating to the physician, is a term I would suggest as an addition to our vocabulary, to cover the same field in old age that is covered by the term paediatrics in childhood.

Gibson girl *n* (1901) a fashionable American girl of the late 1890s and early 1900s. The epithet commemorates Charles Dana Gibson (1867–1944), the American artist and illustrator; he typically portrayed girls dressed in a tailored shirtwaister with leg-of-mutton sleeves, and a long skirt. His main model and inspiration was his wife, Irene Langhorne

> 1901 *Cosmopolitan*: It is a saying among artists that nine out of ten models who come…seeking employment say they are the original 'Gibson girl' or the 'Diana of the Garden'.

Girl Guide *n* (1909) a girl who is a member of the Girl Guides Association, an organization of girls, established in 1910, corresponding to the Boy Scouts. The abbreviated *guide* is first recorded in 1912; in 1994 it became the official designation. See also **Brownie (1916)**

> 1909 *Boy Scouts' Headquarters' Gazette*: Where it is desired to start 'Girl Guides' it would be best for ladies interested to form a Committee.

Girl Scout *n* (1909) An early alternative to **Girl Guide**, which became the standard term in US English

> 1909 *Daily Chronicle*: The girl-scout has arrived… This writer saw six of them…on Saturday—neat blue serge skirts, straw hats, haversacks, and poles.

glad rags *n* (1902) one's best party clothes or evening wear. Colloquial, originally US. Originally the term alternated with *glad clothes* ('Only when starvation stares him in the face will he relinquish his "glad clothes", as the cowboys call them,' *Daily Chronicle* (1905)), but this seems to have died out by 1910

> 1902 Dorothy Dix: All the Females Assembled in their Glad Rags and proceeded to go through their particular Stunts for his Benefit.

gongoozler *n* (1904) someone who stares protractedly at nothing. The word was originally applied, reputedly in the dialect of the Lake District, specifically to someone who stares at activity on a canal. Its origins are obscure, but its elements may have some connection with Lincolnshire dialect *gawn* 'to stare vacantly or curiously' and *gooze* 'to gape'

> 1986 *New Yorker*: I stopped off in the Galeana sports park…to watch a game on one of three huge outdoor screens that the city had provided for gongoozlers like me.

googly *n* (1903) (in cricket) an off-break bowled with a leg-break action. The origins of the name are not known, although it is fairly typical of the sort of nonsense vocabulary popular at the time. A contemporary source credits Australian journalists, but it has remained mainly a British term—Australians favour *wrong 'un* or *bosie* (1912)

> 1903 C. B. Fry: You must persuade that Bosanquet of yours to practise…those funny 'googlies' of his.

goo-goo eyes *n* (1900) amorous glances. Slang, which retains some currency in American English at the end of the century

> 1900 Godfrey & Hilbury: She'd make goo-goo eyes at the bandsmen above.

grafter *n* (1900) a (hard) worker. Colloquial; derived from the verb *graft* 'to work', which dates from the mid 19th century

> 1900 Henry Lawson: 'What are we to do now?' enquired Andy, who was the hardest grafter, but altogether helpless, hopeless, and useless in a crisis like this.

guest *n* (1900) a performer who is not a regular member of the company with which he or she is performing. Commoner later in the century in the compounds *guest artist* (1934) and *guest star* (1942)

> 1900 W. A. Ellis: She…appeared four times as 'guest' at the theatre…, playing Preziosa, Maria Stuart, [etc.].

> 1968 *New York Times*: Playing the 'special guest star' in a series of schlocky European films.

hair-tidy *n* (1907) a receptacle for hair-combings. A piece of dressing-table furniture which mercifully had gone out of fashion by the middle of the century

> 1935 *Punch*: The whole affair of the rejection of Miss Rinse's beaded hair-tidy from our Institute Exhibition has been most unfortunate.

half-life *n* (1907) the time in which the quantity of a radioactive substance in a sample decreases by half. In earliest usage it occurs in the expression *half-life period*; it is not recorded on its own until the early 1950s

> 1907 *Journal of the Chemical Society*: Rutherford and others have shown that whilst radium A, B, and C have a life-period of only a few hours, radium D has a half-life-period of forty years.

> 1972 *Nature*: Because 244Pu has an 82 m.y. half life, its presence today, 56 half lives after the formation of the Earth, is a most impressive accomplishment.

hangar *n* (1902) a shed for the accommodation of aircraft. Like many other English aeronautical terms of this period, a borrowing from French (where its ultimate source was probably Medieval Latin *angarium* 'a shed for shoeing horses')

> 1902 *Daily Chronicle*: Mr. Santos Dumont…will construct a hangar in the Bois de Boulogne.

hangover *n* (1904) the unpleasant after-effects of drinking too much alcohol. Originally US; apparently a development of an earlier usage, 'something or someone "left over" from before'

> 1935 Dorothy Sayers: 'How's Miss Cattermole?' 'Bad hang-over. As you might expect.'

harbour *n* (1909) an airship shed or hangar. Appropriately enough, much early airship terminology was nautical in inspiration; this example seems not to have survived World War I

> 1909 *Chambers's Journal*: Work in connection with the other Zeppelin air-ships is so far advanced that as soon as the halls, or harbours, as they are called, are ready it will only be necessary to put the parts together.

heavier-than-air *adj* (1903) Designating an aircraft whose weight is greater than the weight of the air which it displaces, and whose lift is not dependent on light gases; also applied to the use of such aircraft in flight. The basic verbal template had been in place since the 19th century ('To form a "Free Association for Aerial Navigation by means of Machines heavier than Air"', *Marion's Wonderful Balloon Ascents* (1870)), but it was not fully lexicalized until the year in which flight in aeroplanes (as opposed to balloons) became a reality

> 1903 *Westminster Gazette*: The only example of the heavier-than-air machine.

> 1909 *Daily Chronicle*: For a long time, Mr. Cody has practised heavier-than-air flying on Laffan's Plain.

hep *adj* (1908) well-informed, knowledgeable, aware. Slang, originally US. Its antecedents are unknown. The synonymous **hip**, which is presumed to be a variant of *hep*, is roughly contemporary. See also **hep-cat (1938)**

> 1908 *Saturday Evening Post*: What puzzles me is how you can find anybody left in the world who isn't hep.

heterosexuality *n* (1900) the condition of being heterosexual. The term *heterosexual* had been introduced into English in the early 1890s (in C. G. Chaddock's translation of Krafft-Ebing's *Psychopathia Sexualis*), but the derived noun had to wait until the 20th century

> 1900 H. Blanchamp: Psycho-sexual hermaphroditism, in which there are traces of hetero-sexuality, though homo-sexuality predominates.

hip *adj* (1904) well-informed, knowledgeable, aware. Slang, originally US. Probably a variant of **hep**, which is not recorded in print until 1908

> 1904 G. V. Hobart: At this rate it'll take about 629 shows to get us to Jersey City, are you hip?

hippomobile *n* (1904) A word used in the early days of motor vehicles for a horse-drawn vehicle. Based on Greek *hippos* 'horse'. It had died out by the end of the decade

> 1905 *Westminster Gazette*: How much longer, motorists may be tempted to ask, is such a dangerous mode of locomotion as the hippomobile to be tolerated?

home help *n* (1900) someone paid to do another's housework. Latterly in Britain applied specifically to someone provided by the social services to do domestic work for those unable to do it for themselves

> 1939 Margaret Spring Rice: While women…go into hospital…trained home helps can be provided to look after the father and children.

hormone *n* (1905) a chemical substance produced in an endocrine gland which is transported in the blood to a particular organ or tissue and has an effect on its function. From the present participle of Greek *horman* 'to stir up, urge on'

> 1905 E. H. Starling: These chemical messengers, however, or 'hormones'…as we might call them.

> 1930 R. A. Fisher: The investigation of the influence of the sex hormones has shown how genetic modifications…can be made to manifest themselves in one sex only.

hospitalize *v* (1901) to place or accommodate in a hospital. A useful coinage which attracted little adverse comment at first, but latterly has come to be viewed as objectionable by language purists

> 1901 *Daily Chronicle*: The disease was spreading rapidly owing to the people refusing to hospitalise first cases.

> 1918 Alexander Woollcott: My present brief hospitalization is traceable to eye-strain.

hot dog *n* (1900) a hot sausage enclosed as a sandwich in a bread roll. Originally US. What was to become one of the mainstays of 20th-century American fast-food culture may owe its name to an earlier sense of *hot dog*—'someone particularly skilled or excellent'. So the edible hot dog would be a sort of 'super' sausage sandwich

> 1926 *Spectator*: The President of the Brooklyn team asked them to his box and gave them hot dogs.

humdinger *n* (1905) a remarkable or outstanding person or thing. Slang. Originally US, although its antecedents are unknown. In the earliest known record of its use, it is clearly an admiring term for a beautiful woman

> 1926 *British Weekly*: She was a humdinger. She even puts a brand on Brangwyn, and she's no slouch.

hunch *n* (1904) a presentiment. This appears to come from an earlier *hunch* meaning 'a hint or tip', which in turn developed from the sense 'a push or shove'—the underlying notion perhaps being that of giving someone a nudge in the ribs to alert or inform them

> 1904 S. E. White: 'I hope your hunch is a good one,' replied Dick.

hunger march *n* (1908) a march by the unemployed and poor to protest about their condition. A term remembered with particular poignancy by those who lived through the 1920s and 30s

> 1908 *Westminster Gazette*: A statement of the purpose of the 'Hunger March'.

> 1922 *Westminster Gazette*: Unemployed hunger marchers are persisting in their determination to see the Prime Minister.

hydro-aeroplane *n* (1909) an aeroplane with a hull-shaped fuselage enabling it to land on and take off from water. The term (and its near-contemporaries *hydroplane* and *water-plane*, and the American *hydroairplane*) came off second best in competition with *seaplane* and soon died out. *Hydroplane* is probably a contraction of *hydro-aeroplane*, and therefore not quite the same word as *hydroplane* 'horizontal rudder on a submarine' (1901), which was formed from *plane* and is still very much in use

> 1909 *Westminster Gazette*: Before the present year expires the hydro-aeroplane will be an accomplished fact.

> 1913 Winston Churchill: We have decided to call the naval hydroplane a seaplane, and the ordinary aeroplane or school machine, which we use in the Navy, simply a plane.

> 1913 *Times*: Mr. Howard Wright…was attempting to rise from the sea on a waterplane at Cowes yesterday afternoon when the machine capsized.

> 1932 Chatfield & Taylor: The term *seaplane*…is synonymous with *hydroairplane*, a word too clumsy ever to have come into common use.

hydroelectricity *n* (1904) electricity generated by using the motive power of water

> 1904 *Electrical Magazine*: Hydro-electricity in California.

> 1959 *Petroleum Handbook* (Shell International Petroleum Co.): There are…limitations to the future growth of hydro-electricity.

iddy-umpty *n* (1906) A colloquial verbal representation of the dots and dashes of the Morse code. British. First recorded in 1906, but its previous existence is suggested by an earlier record of *umpty* (1905), being used to mean 'an indefinite number' (a usage which led to **umpteen (1918)**)

> 1914 *Daily Express*: To see men practising the 'iddy-umpty', as they call it, with the back of a sheath-knife on the top of an empty tobacco-tin in lieu of a regulation 'dummy-key'.

identity card *n* (1900), **identification card** *n* (1908) a card which gives personal particulars. Both terms survive, *identity card* more vigorously

> 1900 *Westminster Gazette*: When troops are going on service each man has issued to him what is known as a field dressing and an identity card.

> 1969 *New Yorker*: Residents will show identification cards to gain admittance.

image *n* (1908) the impression which people in general have of a particular person or thing. There is no evidence to link this early and apparently short-lived usage with the later 20th-century concept of a public impression deliberately created by advertising or other means (see **image (1958)**

> 1908 G. K. Chesterton: When courtiers sang the praises of a King they attributed to him things that were entirely improbable… Between the King and his public image there was really no relation.

industrial relations *n* (1904) relationships between employers and employees. An isolated early example of a term which did not become established until after World War II

> 1904 S. A. Barnett: Luxury…leads to cruelty in our industrial relations.

> 1958 *Economist*: Both employers and unions are to blame for the dogfight that at present passes for industrial relations at BOAC.

in-group *n* (1907) a small group of people whose common interest tends to exclude others. Originally mainly sociologists' jargon, but it gradually spread to the general language

> 1907 W. G. Sumner: Thus a differentiation arises between ourselves, the we-group, or in-group, and everybody else, or the others-groups, out-groups.

inhalatorium *n* (1906) a building or room used for the treatment of respiratory complaints by vaporized medicaments. Modelled on *sanatorium*, it gradually faded from use as such establishments went out of fashion

> 1906 *Chambers's Journal*: In the medical institute called the Inhalatorium special rooms are set apart for the use of patients, who sit for half-an-hour at a time breathing an atmosphere charged with the vapour suited to their special complaints.

> 1912 *World*: The inhalatoria and gurgling-rooms [Don't ask— ed.].

institutionalize *v* (1905) to put into or house in an institution; to subject to institutional life. The past participle adjective has come to have connotations of dependence and apathy

> 1905 *Daily Chronicle*: He has been 'institutionalised', and I never yet knew the average man survive that pauperising ordeal.

> 1969 *Daily Telegraph*: Because he was hopelessly institutionalised he was unable to look after himself when free.

intelligentsia *n* (1907) the part of a nation, originally in pre-revolutionary Russia, that aspires to intellectual activity; the class of society regarded as possessing culture and political initiative. A borrowing of Russian *intelligéntsiya*, which itself was adapted from Latin *intelligentia* 'intelligence'

> 1907 Maurice Baring: [The revolutionaries] fear that if the question of a Republic is brought forward there will be a general massacre of the educated bourgeoisie, the so-called 'Intelligenzia'.

> 1921 Aldous Huxley: The English colony [at Florence] is a queer collection; a sort of decayed provincial intelligentsia.

it *pron* (1904) sex appeal. First recorded, perhaps somewhat improbably, in the works of Rudyard Kipling, this coy euphemism did not really take off until the 1920s, when the romantic novelist Elinor Glyn used it as the title of a book. The silent-film star Clara Bow (1905–65) became known as the 'It Girl'. See also **sex appeal (1924)**, **oomph (1937)**

> 1904 Rudyard Kipling: 'Tisn't beauty, so to speak, nor good talk necessarily. It's just It. Some women'll stay in a man's memory if they once walk down a street.

> 1927 Elinor Glyn: He had that nameless charm, with a strong magnetism which can only be called 'It'.

> 1971 *Illustrated Weekly of India*: Dev closes the generation gap between Hema and him by the handsome device of welcoming this idli-white 'It Girl' with open arms.

jazz *n* (1909) a type of ragtime dance. This appears to be the original meaning of the word *jazz*. Its first appearance (see the quote below) is in the lyrics of a song called 'Uncle Josh in Society', recorded in the US in 1909. Its use to denote the music to such a dance, and hence (broadly) a type of improvised syncopated music, is not recorded until 1913. Its ultimate origins remain a mystery, despite many ingenious suggestions (e.g. that it comes from the nickname of one Jasbo Brown, an itinerant black musician along the Mississippi (*Jasbo* perhaps being an alteration of *Jasper*), or that it crossed the Atlantic with West African slaves)

> 1909 C. Stewart: One lady asked me if I danced the jazz.

> 1919 *Punch*: 'Whitehall,' says a society organ, 'has succumbed to the Jazz, the Fox-trot and the Bunny-hug.'

Jeyes fluid *n* (1900) The proprietary name in Britain of a disinfectant consisting of a saponified solution of phenols, resins, and other ingredients, manufactured by Jeyes' Sanitary Compounds Company. For the first two thirds of the century the word *Jeyes* conjured up the smell of disinfectant to British speakers

> 1974 Roy Strong: The first three weeks at the V & A were HELL. The dreary Civil Service-ness of it all, the terrible forms, files, signing, the filth, the smell of Jeyes fluid, the dirty loos, all the things I can't stand.

jigsaw, jigsaw puzzle *n* (1909) a puzzle formed by cutting into small irregular pieces (originally with a jig-saw, a type of thin-bladed saw) a picture mounted on a sheet of wood, cardboard, etc. See also **zigsaw (1912)**

> 1909 *Daily Mirror*: These jigsaw geography puzzles should be introduced into all the Council schools in London.

> 1910 *Punch*: What if the jig-saw epidemic spreads?

jojoba *n* (1900) a desert shrub of Mexico and the southern US which produces an oil used in cosmetics. Ultimately from a native American word *hohohwi*; the Spanish form *jojoba* did not become widely known in English until the 1980s, when cosmetics made with it were suddenly fashionable

> 1986 *Look Now*: The Renewer Lotion contains collagens, jojoba oil and a special firming ingredient to smooth and soften the skin.

juice *n* (1909) fuel for an engine. Humorous slang

> 1918 E. M. Roberts: Then I discovered that the tank [i.e. of the aircraft] was nearly empty. That meant that I would have to go in search of 'juice'.

jumper *n* (1908) a pinafore dress. North American. A development of the earlier application of *jumper* (dating from the mid 19th century) to a kind of loose outer jacket or shirt reaching to the hips, made of canvas, serge, coarse linen, etc., and worn by sailors, truckmen, etc.; this in turn probably came from the now obsolete *jump* 'a man's loose jacket', which was probably a variant of *jup*, from obsolete French *juppe* 'jacket'. By the mid 1920s the term was being applied to a woman's knitted blouse in the style of a jacket, and this seems to have been the origin of the present-day British sense 'jersey', which was established by the 1940s

> 1908 *Sears, Roebuck Catalog*: The jumper is made in surplice effect.

> 1928 John Galsworthy: He came on Anne herself, without a hat, sitting on a gate, her hands in the pockets of her jumper.

> 1945 *Wales*: He turned up the cuff of his jumper and showed her the word 'Sue' tattooed with a border of foliage on his forearm.

kewpie doll, kewpie *n* (1909) a chubby doll with a curl or topknot on its head, from a design by Rose O'Neill (1874–1944). Originally and mainly US. The term was coined by O'Neill from *cupid*, and registered by her as a trademark in 1912

> 1909 Rose O'Neill: The reason why these funny, roly-poly creatures are called Kewpies…is because they look like little Cupids.

Kinemacolor *n* (1909) The proprietary name of a method of producing motion pictures in natural colours by means of revolving colour screens. The word **kinema** itself (as a variant of **cinema**) is not recorded before 1914

> 1918 Homer Croy: By the Kinemacolor process colored motion pictures were made of the Coronation.

knock for six (1902) to discompose or defeat (someone) utterly. A colloquialism derived from cricket, where a six (scored by hitting the ball in the air over the boundary) is the maximum punishment the batsman can inflict on the bowler. The rule allotting six runs to such a stroke was not introduced until 1910; before that a hit over the rope officially counted for only four runs

> 1902 J. Milne: 'It knocked me for six', is the statement we have about a bullet in the knee.

labour camp *n* (1900) a penal settlement where the prisoners have to do labouring work

> 1900 *Journal of the Society of Arts*: Prisoners…might serve their time in…quarries, which would be turned into labour camps.

landaulette *n* (1901) a type of car with a leather hood above the rear seats. The word was adapted from *landaulet*, the name of a sort of horse-drawn carriage that was like a small landau, and was originally applied to a particular Peugeot model. It gradually went out general use after 1920

> 1905 *Daily Chronicle*: Now the 'landaulette' is the popular car of the moment.

lebensraum *n* (1905) territory which the Germans believed was needed for their natural development. A borrowing from German, literally 'life's space'. It did not become widely known and used in English until the 1930s, when the Nazis began to put the idea into practice

> 1939 *War Illustrated*: Moravia and Bohemia had been overrun by the Nazi armies and declared German Protectorates-part of the German people's 'lebensraum'.

> 1957 *Encyclopaedia Britannica*: Hitler was convinced that…Germany…needed Russian territory for *Lebensraum*.

Lee-Enfield *n* (1902) a type of rifle used by the British Army in the Boer War and, modified, in World Wars I and II. Named after J. P. Lee (1831–1904), American designer of the bolt action, and Enfield, a town in Greater London, site of the British Royal Small Arms Factory, designers of the rifling form

> 1917 A. G. Empey: *Lee Enfield*, name of the rifle used by the British Army. Its caliber is .303 and the magazine holds ten rounds. When dirty it has a nasty habit of getting Tommy's name on the crime sheet.

libido *n* (1909) psychic drive or energy, especially that associated with the sexual instinct

> 1909 A. A. Brill, translating Freud's *Selected Papers on Hysteria*: The anxiety neurosis goes along with the most distinct diminution of the sexual libido or the psychic desire.

> 1972 *Scientific American*: It has also been observed that removal of the ovaries does not reduce the libido of human females.

Lib-Lab *adj, n* (1903) A contraction of *Liberal-Labour*. Originally it denoted those Labour members of parliament in the first decade of the century who were affiliated to the Liberal Party (as opposed to those who belonged to the Independent Labour Party). It continued in use thereafter, but with less specific application, and in the late 1970s it was used of the arrangement with the Liberals by which the minority Labour government managed to stay in power

> 1903 *Review of Reviews*: The Progress of the Lib-Labs. The Lib-Lab party is carrying all before it.

> 1963 *Annual Register*: Mr Gaitskell stiffly shot down the idea of a formal Lib-Lab alliance.

lie-detector *n* (1909) an instrument intended to indicate when someone is lying by detecting changes in their physiological characteristics. Originally US

║ 1974 Andrew Garve: When a politician talks of frankness most voters reach for their lie-detectors.

lift-off *adj* (1907) removable by lifting. An early example of an adjective formed from a verbal phrase, quite a common phenomenon in 20th-century English

║ 1907 *Yesterday's Shopping*: Art cloth box, with lift off lid.

lighting-up time *n* (1900) the time when lights are switched on, especially the time when lights on vehicles are required by law to be switched on

║ 1900 Jerome K. Jerome: On sunny afternoons you used to ride about with that lamp shining for all ║ it was worth. When lighting-up time came it was naturally tired, and wanted a rest.

limit *n* (1906) **the limit** someone or something very extreme— often, extremely exasperating. Originally US slang; now fairly dated. Often preceded by such words as *absolute, frozen,* and *giddy,* to reinforce the meaning

║ 1949 Agatha Christie: This house is the absolute limit!… I don't see why I should have to be bur-║ dened with such peculiar parents.

limousine *n* (1902) a (luxury) car with a compartment for the passengers and a separate compart-ment for the driver. Originally the driver's seat was outside though covered with a roof. This was thought to resemble a type of cloak worn in Limousin, a former province of France

║ 1902 A. C. Harmsworth: With certain kinds of engines, too, it is difficult to adopt any other form of ║ car than the Tonneau, or for the wet weather the Limousine.

liner *n* (1905) a passenger aircraft. A term originally adopted from the world of maritime transport. The first quote below is from Rudyard Kipling's 'With the Night Mail', a futuristic story about air travel set in the year 2000. Kipling envisaged airships as having conquered the skies, their pilots navigating by means of huge beams of light shone up from the ground, and aeroplanes having only a very minor role. *Liner* in the first quote refers to an airship, and Kipling uses other ship nomenclature in the same way (*war-boat, yacht, mail packet*). It survived to be applied to real air-craft of this type, but has been superseded as the main term by **airliner (1908)**

║ 1905 Rudyard Kipling: A Planet liner, east bound, heaves up in a superb spiral and takes the air of ║ us humming.

║ 1933 *Boys' Magazine*: Mile after mile of seemingly endless country unfurled itself beneath the ║ flying wings of the giant liner.

loan shark *n* (1905) A derogatory term for someone who lends money at very high rates of interest. Originally US, but it had reached British English by the late 1920s

║ 1928 *Daily Telegraph*: It is hoped by this plan virtually to put out of business the 'loan shark', who ║ exacts usurious rates of interest from the person of small means.

lone wolf *n* (1909) someone who likes to live or work alone. Originally US

║ 1909 F. H. Tillotson: Occasionally the police run across Panhandlers known as 'lone wolves'—that ║ is they do not mix with others of their class.

long time no see (1900) Used as a greeting after prolonged separation. Originally a parody of the broken English of American Indians

║ 1900 W. F. Drannan: When we rode up to him [i.e. an American Indian] he said: 'Good mornin. ║ Long time no see you.'

║ 1939 Raymond Chandler: Hi, Tony. Long time no see.

loop-road *n* (1909) a road which leaves and later re-joins a main road, especially to relieve traffic congestion. A precursor of, and largely superseded by, **by-pass (1922)**

║ 1909 *Daily Mail*: To construct loop-roads for fast motor traffic round villages.

lotta, lotter (1906) A colloquial contraction of *lot of*. Compare **lotsa (1927)**

║ 1906 E. Nesbit: I gets a lotter green paint and I paints her stem to stern.

║ 1965 Dell Shannon: A lotta people know my name who I don't know.

lounge suit *n* (1901) a man's ordinary daytime two-piece suit. The original literal meaning was 'a suit for lounging in'

> 1970 *Daily Telegraph*: Mr Bronson cooks and receives diners alternately…wearing a boutonnière in the lapel of his dark lounge suit.

lowbrow *adj, n* (1906) (someone) of low intellect. Colloquial, originally US. Modelled on its antonym *highbrow*, which emerged in the 1880s

> 1913 H. A. Franck: With all its excellences it would be unjust to complain that the Zone 'Y.M.' is a trifle 'low-brow' in its taste.

luxury tax *n* (1904) a tax levied on goods or possessions considered 'luxuries'

> 1904 *Hansard*: The luxury tax at that time was 6d.

maffick *v* (1900) Used, especially in newspapers, to designate the behaviour of the crowds (in London and other towns) that celebrated with uproarious rejoicings the relief of the British garrison besieged in Mafeking (17 May 1900) during the South African War (Boer War). A back-formation from *mafficking*, a humorous alteration (as if it were a present participle) of *Mafeking* (now *Mafikeng*), the name of a South African town. The word enjoyed a brief career thereafter as a general term for indulgence in extravagant demonstrations of exultation on occasions of national rejoicing, but it does not seem to have survived the first decade of the century

> 1900 *Pall Mall Gazette*: We trust Cape Town…will 'maffick' to-day, if we may coin a word, as we at home did on Friday and Saturday.

mandarin *n* (1907) a person of much importance, a great man. Colloquial; often applied specifically to high government officials who exercise wide power with little political control. Based on the power and inscrutability of a Chinese mandarin (= high government official)

> 1907 *National Review*: Our Parliamentary Mandarins are ineffably shocked at the impiety of an independent Radical.

> 1925 Fraser & Gibbons: The Mandarins of the War Office.

manic depressive *adj* (1902) Denoting a psychosis in which periods of manic elation alternate with depression. The related noun *manic depression* is not recorded until the 1950s

> 1902 A. R. Defensdorf: Manic-Depressive Insanity. This term is applied to that mental disorder which recurs…throughout the life of the individual and in which a defective hereditary endowment seems to be the…prominent etiological factor.

> 1958 Michael Argyle: The upper and middle classes have higher rates for manic depression and neurosis.

mannequin *n* (1902) a woman (or occasionally a man) employed in the showrooms of dress-makers, costumiers, etc., to wear and show off garments. A borrowing from French, now largely replaced in everyday usage by **model (1904)**

> 1930 *Daily Express*: Autumn Mannequin Parades will be held on Tuesday and Wednesday this week.

marcel *v* (1906) to wave (hair) in the 'Marcel' fashion. This was a kind of artificial wave (known as a *Marcel wave*) produced by using heated curling-tongs. Fashionable around the turn of the century, it was named after François Marcel Grateau (1852–1936), the French hairdresser who invented it

> 1906 B. von Hutten: A gentleman who *marcelled* heads in an Oxford Street shop.

marconi *v* (1908) to transmit by radio (to). A usage commemorating Guglielmo Marconi (1874–1937), who invented a system of wireless telegraphy. The earliest recorded example is a figurative extension, but the literal meaning remained in use until the 1920s

> 1908 *Isle of Man Weekly Times*: An author sometimes dreams of the ideal actress who shall 'Marconi' across the footlights the puppet he has given birth to.

> 1922 *Glasgow Herald*: These figures represent a code which can be wired, cabled, or marconied anywhere.

Marconigram *n* (1902) a telegram. Named after Guglielmo Marconi (see **marconi (1908)**). The term did not survive the first decade of the century

> 1902 *Daily Chronicle*: When do you expect to start sending Marconigrams at commercial rates across the Atlantic?

Marconist *n* (1900) the operator of a Marconi radiotelegraphy system. Rather surprisingly, in view of the relatively short life of most words based on the name of Marconi, there is evidence that *Marconist* was still being used in the 1930s

> 1933 *Journal of the Royal Aeronautical Society*: On board of the machine, an increase of the crew to probably three pilots, two Marconists and one mechanic.

Marmite *n* (1907) The British proprietary term (registered in 1920) for an extract made from fresh brewer's yeast. A *marmite* was originally a type of cooking pot used for rich stews (a picture of which appears on the label of Marmite jars), so there is a subliminal suggestion of meat extract. Compare **Vegemite (1923)**

> 1928 Rose Macaulay: Doctors…prefer that one should breakfast…on marmite, Ry-Vita biscuits, and an apple.

masochistic *adj* (1904) deriving sexual pleasure from having pain inflicted on one. The term *masochism* had been coined in the early 1890s, commemorating the name of Leopold von Sacher-Masoch (1836–95), an Austrian novelist who (in the words of the OED) 'described the thing'

> 1904 G. S. Hall: Women may acquire a Massochistic [sic] love of violence and pain for the ideal of pleasure.

matinée idol *n* (1902) a handsome actor of a type supposed to be especially attractive to matinée audiences. The implications of the term are usually somewhat ironic

> 1902 Hugh McHugh: Mrs. John…you should be proud of this matinee idol husband of yours.

> 1973 *Times*: In the heyday of the matinee idol he had commanded…a sober, serene and loyal admiration.

mazuma, mazume *n* (1904) money, cash. US slang, acquired from Yiddish. Common in the first half of the century, it has gradually faded out thereafter

> 1913 C. E. Mulford: 'What's this?' he demanded… 'Money,' replied Hopalong. 'It's that shiny stuff you buy things with. Spondulix, cash, mazuma.'

meat-lozenge *n* (1903) a lozenge made from concentrated meat—essential fuel for the Edwardian Polar explorer

> 1903 *Longman's Magazine*: I took only some tins of Brand's essence of beef, chocolate, meat-lozenges [etc.].

Meccano *n* (1907) The proprietary name (registered in 1907 by Frank Hornby) of a set of metal pieces, nuts, bolts, etc., and tools, specially designed for constructing small models of buildings, machines, or other engineering apparatus

> 1928 *Television*: String, cardboard, and pieces of rough wood with Meccano parts;…all combined to make the television machine.

> 1930 J. B. Priestley: It seemed only yesterday when he was…putting the Meccano set by the boy's bedside.

microsecond *n* (1906) a millionth of a second

> 1906 A. E. Kennelly: If we call the one millionth part of a second one microsecond for convenience of description, then one complete wave would pass off in 1/2.5 microsecond.

Middle East *n* (1902) A term designating a variable geopolitical entity roughly approximating to southwestern Asia. The coinage reflects the oil-rich area's growing importance to the Western powers

> 1902 A. T. Mahan: The Middle East, if I may adopt a term which I have not seen, will some day need its Malta, as well as its Gibraltar.

militant *adj, n* (1907) (someone) vigorously seeking political or industrial change by employing or advocating the use of direct action, demonstrations, etc. Originally applied specifically to suffragettes taking direct action, but later an all-purpose term of opprobrium against those actively pursuing radical goals. See also **Militant Tendency (1979)**

> 1907 M. McMillan: Why did the militant Suffragette ever come to the door of the House of Commons?

> 1914 Emmeline Pankhurst, *My Own Story* (heading): The making of a Militant.

> 1968 *Daily Telegraph*: Ultra-left militants in the Electrical Trades Union are planning another demonstration today.

mine-sweeper *n* (1905) a ship used to clear away mines

> 1905 *Westminster Gazette*: Mine-sweepers are to play a great part, it seems certain, in future naval warfare.

misandry *n* (1909) hatred of men as a sex. Adapted from Greek *misandria* (from the stem *andr-* 'man'), on the model of *misogyny*. Never in common usage, but taken up by the feminist movement in the latter part of the century

> 1960 B. Kaye: Such women are common in…Kwangtung Province, where there is a tradition of misandry.

mitochondrion *n, plural* **mitochondria** (1901) a microscopic body inside a cell which is the site of energy production. The term is a borrowing from German, where it was proposed in 1898 by the microbiologist C. Benda; it was formed from Greek *mitos* 'thread' and *khondrion* 'little granule'

> 1901 *Journal of the Royal Microscopical Society*: Meves believes that this term [sc. *Nebenkern*] should lapse, and himself employs for the separate granules Benda's term *mitochondria*, and for the *Nebenkern* which may be formed by their union, the term *mitochondrial corpuscle*.

mixed bathing *n* (1901) simultaneous bathing in the same place by people of both sexes

> 1901 *Graphic*: The case against mixed bathing has passed into the academic or empty stage.

Möbius strip *n* (1904) a surface having only one side and one edge, formed by twisting one end of a rectangular strip through 180 degrees and joining it to the other end. Named after the German mathematician August Ferdinand Möbius (1790–1868), who invented it

> 1970 *New Yorker*: Barbara, taking a pair of scissors…turned the clipping on fragrant Christmas gifts into a Möbius strip.

model *n* (1904) someone, often a woman, who is employed to display clothes by wearing them, or to appear in displays of other goods. An extension of the earlier sense 'someone who poses for an artist'. It competed with and eventually defeated the contemporary **mannequin (1902)**. See also **supermodel (1977)**

> a1911 D. G. Phillips: She was dressed in the sleek tight-fitting trying-on robe of the professional model.

> 1958 *Woman's Own*: The first lesson every model learns is to stand and walk correctly.

modernism *n* (1901) (in the Roman Catholic Church at the beginning of the 20th century) a tendency or movement towards modifying traditional beliefs and doctrines in accordance with the findings of modern criticism and research

> 1901 G. Tyrell: [Kegan Paul] simply rants against Modernism, and glories in what ought to be our shame.

mood *n* (1902) a general feeling among a group of people, a prevailing temper. A usage which did not really come into its own until the last quarter of the century

> 1972 Brian Moore: There were no miracles, there was no hysteria, there was not even a special fervour. The mood was nostalgic.

moon *v* (1901) to indulge in sentimental reverie, or to gaze adoringly. Colloquial

> 1901 M. Franklin: It was daily dinned into my ears that the little things of life were the noblest, and that all the great people I mooned about were the same.

Mother's Day *n* (1908) a day on which mothers are particularly honoured (the placement of the apostrophe varies). In the US, where the idea originated, it is observed on the second Sunday in May; in Britain, where the idea did not really catch on until after World War II, it has often suffered from confusion with the rather more ancient *Mothering Sunday* (mid 19th century). See also **Father's Day (1943)**

> 1908 *Congressional Record*: Resolved, That Sunday, May 10, 1908, be recognized as Mothers' Day.

> 1958 *Listener*: As uniquely and inimitably American as John Foster Dulles or Mothers' Day.

motor *n* (1900) a car. A shortened form of *motor car* (1895) or of the long defunct **motor carriage (1901)**. Common in British usage up to World War II, it has gone into a decline since then, although it has occasional surges in popularity (e.g. in late-20th-century London slang). The verb *motor* 'to travel or convey in a motor vehicle' is first recorded in 1896

> 1900 *Chambers's Journal*: The purchase by the Prince of Wales of a six horse-power Daimler motor should still further…popularise automobilism.

> 1902 A. C. Harmsworth: Many doctors who use motors have joined the Automobile Club.

motor-bicycle, motor-bike *n* (1903) a cycle with a petrol engine. These two terms were preceded by *motor-cycle* (1896) and *motor-cyclette* (1898). See also **auto-cycle (1905)**

> 1903 *Hardwareman*: The side car is…the most sociable attachment for a motor bicycle.

> 1927 H. G. Wells: I remember my wild rush on my motor-bike to London.

motor-bus *n* (1901) a motor-driven bus. *Bus* as a shortened form of *omnibus* dates back to the 1830s—but all previous ones had of course been horse-drawn

> 1901 H. G. Wells: 'You really think such a thing is possible?'… 'As possible,' said Gibberne, and glanced at something that went throbbing by the window, 'as a motor-bus.'

motor carriage *n* (1901) a car. A stately but long vanished usage harking back to the days of the horse-drawn carriage

> 1901 *Scientific American*: Alcohol as fuel for motor carriages… The champions of the alcohol motor scored another triumph in the Paris-Roubaix races.

motor-coat *n* (1909) a coat designed to be worn by motorists. A short-lived usage; its later replacement *car-coat* (1963) denoted a much shorter garment

> 1909 W. J. Locke: Shrugging himself into his motor-coat, which the chauffeur brought him.

motor race *n* (1900) a race between cars. The derived *motor racing* is virtually contemporary

> 1900 *Racing Rules & Regulations* (Motor Car Club): In all Motor Races held under the Rules of the Motor Car Club it must be stated on all Entry Forms…that they are so held.

> 1905 *Official Programme, International Tourist Trophy*: A new departure in the history of motor racing.

motor road *n* (1909) a road suitable for use by motor vehicles

> 1909 *Westminster Gazette*: Of more dramatic interest is the second part of the Bill, with its proposal for the creation of motor-roads.

motor stable *n* (1907) a building for housing motor vehicles. An early but unsuccessful rival to **garage (1902)**

> 1907 Lady Monkswell: The beautiful Surrey landscape looks down into this purgatory of motor stables & everything that motors require.

motor veil *n* (1907) a veil worn by ladies when motoring, to protect the face

> 1926 Walter de la Mare: She was a rare one for the fashions: scarves and motor-veils, and that kind of thing.

motorway *n* (1903) a specially designated class of highway with two or more lanes in each direction, designed and regulated for use by fast motor traffic. As the quotations below suggest, motorways were thought of and named long before they were built, at any rate in the UK (the first stretch of motorway in Britain was the Preston by-pass, opened in 1958)

> 1903 *Car*: The Motor-way is *bound* to come!

> 1955 *Times*: Motorways, 345 miles in total length, for motor traffic only, are to be built by the Government.

muck-raker *n* (1906) someone who looks for and exposes scandal in a sensationalist way. The word was inspired by a reference by US President Theodore Roosevelt in 1906 to 'the Man with a Muck-rake', a character in John Bunyan's *Pilgrim's Progress* who was actually intended as an emblem not of unsavoury scandal-mongering but of absorption in the pursuit of worldly gain: 'The men with the muck-rakes are often indispensable to the well-being of society; but only if they know when to stop raking the muck' (the original literal *muck-rake* was a rake for moving and spreading manure). The derived *muck-raking* is first recorded in 1911

> 1906 S. Ford: That's the style you live in when…you've got to be a top-notch grafter that the muck-rakers ain't jungled yet.

> 1911 *New York Evening Post*: The same articles brought President Roosevelt to the defence of the Senate, and led him to apply the word 'muck-raking' to the literature of higher exposure.

musicology *n* (1909) the academic study of music. An early indication of the 20th century's inclination to put art under the microscope. First recorded as the title of a book by M. S. Logan, the term was probably borrowed from French *musicologie*, but it may be a new English formation

> 1915 W. S. Pratt: 'Musicology', if it is to rank with other comprehensive sciences, must include every conceivable scientific discussion of musical topics.

nancy *n* (1904) an effeminate or homosexual man or boy. A common term of contempt in the first three quarters of the century (often in the form *nancy-boy*), it is a shortened form of the earlier dialectal *Miss Nancy*, with the same meaning

> 1931 Roy Campbell: Sharing out my last desires and fancies With tough old suffragettes and ageing nancies.

narcissism *n* (1905) self-love and admiration that find emotional satisfaction in self-contemplation. Originally a technical term in psychology, although over the century it has found its way into general English (there is actually an isolated instance of the general use recorded from 1822 in one of Samuel Taylor Coleridge's letters ('Of course, I am glad to be able to correct my fears as far as public Balls, Concerts, and Time-murder in Narcissism'), but it does not seem to have caught on). The sexologist Havelock Ellis suggested in 1898 the analogy with the beautiful Greek youth Narcissus who fell in love with his own reflection in a fountain, but the term itself was coined by Näcke in German as *Narcissismus* in 1899

> 1905 Havelock Ellis: I have referred to the developed forms of this kind of self-contemplation…and in this connection have alluded to the fable of Narcissus, whence Näcke has since devised the term Narcissism for this group of phenomena.

naturopathy *n* (1901) a theory of the nature of disease and a system of therapeutic practice founded on the supposition that diseases can be cured by natural agencies

> 1901 *Kneipp Water Cure Monthly*: There is no doubt that you can get cured without operation by Naturopathy.

news flash *n* (1904) a brief item of news, especially as broadcast in other than a regular bulletin. Originally applied to telegraphic news dispatches, the term came into its own with the advent of the broadcast media

> 1904 *Post Express* (Rochester, New York): News Flashes from All Over.

> 1974 Eric Ambler: There was a television news flash. The announcer didn't get your father's name quite right.

nickelodeon *n* (1907) an early type of cinema in which admission usually cost a nickel (five cents). US. The *-odeon* element probably came from *melodeon* 'music hall' (1840). The later use of *nickelodeon* for 'jukebox' is first recorded in the 1930s (see **nickelodeon (1938)**)

> 1921 *Ladies' Home Journal*: It is this class which first patronized the old nickelodeon, and undoubtedly it imposed its tastes and its traditions on the picture makers.

nineteenth hole *n* (1901) A facetious name for the bar-room in a golf club-house, first recorded in the title of a novel by W. G. Sutphen: *The nineteenth hole, being tales of the fair green* (1901). There are eighteen holes on a standard golf course

> 1948 Josephine Tey: A good chap who played a very steady game and occasionally, when it came to the nineteenth, expanded into mild indiscretions.

no man's land *n* (1908) the terrain between the front lines of armies entrenched opposite one another. A term made notorious during World War I, but foreshadowed in earlier conflicts. It originally, in the 14th century, denoted a plot of ground lying outside the north wall of London which was used as a place of execution, and thereafter it was used for any piece of unclaimed ground lying between two others

> 1908 *Blackwood's Magazine*: Here and there in that wilderness of dead bodies—the dreadful 'No-Man's-Land' between the opposing lines—deserted guns showed up singly or in groups.

> 1915 G. Adam: Perilous work it is repairing wire in the No Man's Land between trenches.

non-aggression *n* (1903) avoidance of hostility between nations. Although *non-aggression* came to the fore in the language of international relations during the post-World War I peace conference at Versailles, Morley's quoting of William Gladstone shows that it was around in the latter part of the 19th century

> 1903 John Morley, *Life of Gladstone*: Then he would go on—'…—My name stands in Europe as a symbol of the policy of peace, moderation, and non-aggression.'

> 1925 Arnold Toynbee: Mr. Lloyd George broached to the French delegation his project for a Pact of Non-aggression.

nosey parker *n* (1907) an excessively inquisitive person. British slang; said to have been applied originally as a nickname to a man who spied on courting couples in Hyde Park, London

> 1915 P. G. Wodehouse: 'But Nosey Parker is what I call him,' she said. 'He minds everybody's business as well as his own.'

not *interj* (1900) Used humorously following a statement to indicate that it should not be taken seriously, or sarcastically to negate a statement made immediately before. Mainly US; used sporadically through the century, and repopularized in 1989 by the 'Wayne's World' sketches on the NBC television programme *Saturday Night Live*

> 1900 George Ade: Probably they preferred to go back to the Front Room and hear some more about Woman's Destiny not.

> 1992 *Observer*: Including the fabulous *Head Over Heels*, described as 'a seven-part series about a rebellious rock and roller at a girls' finishing school in the Fifties'. That sounds like copper-bottomed quality entertainment—*not*.

novella *n* (1902) a short novel or long short-story. Originally borrowed from Italian, it has since become a standard element in the terminology of literary criticism

> 1902 W. D. Howells: Few modern fictions of the novel's dimensions…have the beauty of form many a novella embodies.

nut *n* (1904) a fashionable or showy young man. British slang. Despite the isolated example from 1904, the heyday of the *nut* (or **knut (1911)**, as the word was also whimsically spelled) was in the two or three years leading up to World War I

> 1904 *Notes and Queries*: I'm one of the nuts, one of the nibs.

> 1920 Rose Macaulay: He always looked the same, calm, unruffled, tidy, the exquisite nut.

nut cutlet *n* (1908) a cutlet-shaped patty of chopped nuts. First described in F. A. George's *Vegetarian Cookery*, it has become an archetypal vegetarian dish, and a hackneyed means of poking fun at vegetarians

> 1925 D. H. Lawrence: So Sonya will never cook us another goose, only marmite pie and nut-cutlet.

Nutter *n* (1906) The proprietary name of a substitute for butter made from the oil of nuts. Strange though it may sound to late-20th-century ears, *Nutter* survived into the 1970s. But once the slang *nutter* 'insane person' (first recorded in 1958) had established itself, it could scarcely be taken seriously

> 1958 *Catalogue, County Stores* (Taunton): Vegetarian foods…Cooking Fat, Nutter lb. 2/1.

okapi *n* (1900) a rare ungulate mammal, *Okapia johnstoni*, of the giraffe family, about the size of a horse and reddish-brown in colour, with horizontal white stripes on the legs. It lives in forested regions of the Congo, and was one of the last large African mammals to be 'discovered' by Western science. Its finder, in 1900, was Sir Harry Johnston (1858–1927), the English explorer. *Okapi* is its name amongst the local people

> 1900 Harry Johnston: I found the Bambuba natives dwelling alongside the dwarfs called it 'Okapi'.

olive oil *interj* (1906) A joky mispronunciation of *au revoir*, still in use as recently as the 1960s

> 1933 Eric Partridge: For 'good-bye', the boys at Dulwich already in 1906 used...*olive oil* (au revoir).

olympiad *n* (1907) the four-yearly celebration of the modern Olympic Games, revived in 1896. The term had originally denoted the four-year period between the ancient Greek Olympic Games

> 1907 *Westminster Gazette:* When the last Olympiad was held at St. Louis, U.S.A., in 1904, it was decided to hold the next in Rome.

operative *n* (1905) a detective or agent employed by a detective agency; a secret-service agent

> 1905 *New York Press:* The word 'detective' became so offensive...that it was dropped by some successful [detective] agencies. The word chosen by the Pinkertons to take its place was 'operative'.

opinion-former *n* (1906) someone whose views shape the opinions of others. Not widely in use until the 1960s

> 1906 G. W. E. Russell: A Journalist of this type once said to me, with all imaginable gravity, 'I should, I confess, resent any change which interfered with my position as chief opinion-former in the neighbourhood of'—Leeds or Plymouth, or whatever was the name of his town.

> 1967 *Economist:* The opinion-formers have begun their debunking.

organ *n* (1903) the penis. A euphemism which began in full as *male organ* and then (like the parallel *member* (13th century)) shrank to *organ*

> 1967 M. Campbell: He had the largest organ that anyone had ever seen. It was a truncheon.

orthodontist *n* (1903) a practitioner who corrects badly aligned teeth. In Britain, where such work is done mainly by ordinary dentists, the word had to wait until the end of the century before it really began to catch on

> 1903 *Dental Annals:* Orthodontist, a newly-coined word, already considerably used in the United States to signify one who studies and practises orthodontia, or the treatment of irregularity, malposition, or malocclusion of the teeth.

outmoded *adj* (1903) no longer in fashion, out-of-date. Perhaps coined partly on the model of French *démodé*

> 1903 *Academy:* Jesse Berridge is a poet, not a poetess, to use a somewhat outmoded word.

Ovaltine *n* (1906) The proprietary name (registered in Britain in 1906) of a powder composed principally of malt extract, milk, and eggs; also, a hot drink made from this. Presumably based on *oval* (from the eggs), it was registered by the originally Swiss company Albert Wander. The popularity of the drink (the archetypal soothing nightcap) was considerably boosted in the 1930s by the brilliant marketing coup of the 'Ovaltineys', a children's club promoted by radio advertising

> 1937 John Betjeman: He gives his Ovaltine a stir And nibbles at a 'petit beurre'.

overspeed *v* (1906) to drive faster than the legal speed limit. A usage long since superseded by **speeding (1908)** and **speed (1931)**

> 1906 *Westminster Gazette:* The police had been...engaged elsewhere to look out for over-speeding drivers.

Oxford marmalade *n* (1907) a type of thick-cut marmalade originally made in Oxford (registered as a trade-mark by Frank Cooper in 1908 and 1931). An English breakfast tradition not quite stretching back to the 19th century

> 1942 Christopher Morley: There was Cooper's bitter Oxford marmalade-the only Oxonian product to which Uncle Dan would grant supremacy.

Oz *n* (1908) Australia. A colloquial representation of the pronunciation of the first syllable. The earliest spelling was *Oss*, which is more phonetically precise. The established form *Oz* (first recorded in 1944) probably comes from **Ozzie (1918)**

1908 *Bulletin* (Sydney): My home is near Kingston, which is in the S.E. of South Oss.

1970 Barry Humphries: If they guess I'm from Oz the shit will really hit the fan.

pacifism *n* (1902) the policy or doctrine of rejecting war and every form of violent action as means of solving disputes, especially in international affairs. A direct adaptation of French *pacifisme*. The derivative *pacifist* is first recorded in 1906. At first a neutral term, it acquired decidedly contemptuous overtones during World War I

1902 *Proceedings of the 10th Universal Peace Congress*: M. Emile Arnaud… Speaking at length, in French,…said:… The negative programme of Pacifism is anti-War-ism.

1906 *Times*: The French 'Pacifists' will appeal to England's example in order to induce France also to cut down her naval programme.

1919 George Bernard Shaw: There was only one virtue, pugnacity: only one vice, pacifism. That is an essential condition of war.

paediatrician *n* (1903) a specialist in the diseases of children. A derivative of *paediatric*, which was coined around 1880

1903 *Medical Record* (New York): Dr. L. Emmett Holt said he thought all pediatricians would agree that most of the cases which had given trouble in diagnosis were those in which there was a prolonged fever.

paedophilia, pedophilia *n* (1906) an abnormal (sexual) love of young children. The derivative *paedophile* is not recorded until the 1950s (see **paedophile (1951)**)

1906 Havelock Ellis: Paidophilia or the love of children…may be included under this head [i.e. abnormality].

palace revolution *n* (1904) the overthrowing of a sovereign, etc., without civil war, usually by other members of the ruling group. Possibly a translation of German *Palastrevolution*

1907 Jack London: They will be like the guards of the palace in old Rome, and there will be palace revolutions whereby the labour castes will seize the reins of power.

Palestinian *n* (1905) a native or inhabitant of Palestine. *Palestine* (an ancient name from biblical times) was revived as an official political title for the land west of the Jordan mandated to Britain in 1920, but *Palestinian* preceded it as a term for Jews who wished to go and live there. At the other end of the 20th century it denotes Arab peoples who left the area when the state of Israel was established

1905 *Daily Chronicle*: Territorialists…flooded the hall with leaflets declaring that 200 Russian Palestinians were illegally present.

1979 *Time*: The Administration's first goal then, would be to bring Palestinians, perhaps even some P.L.O. officials, into the talks between the Israelis and the Egyptians on the future of the West Bank and Gaza.

palm court *n* (1908) a courtyard or patio, especially in a hotel, containing palm trees. The term is mainly associated with the 'palm-court orchestra', which from the early years of the century played undemanding light music ('palm-court music') in such venues. It survived into the 1960s, but with an increasingly anachronistic air

1910 *Bradshaw's Railway Guide*: Plymouth, Royal Hotel…Magnificent Palm Court. Orchestra plays daily.

1955 *Radio Times*: David Galliver sings with the Palm Court Orchestra in Grand Hotel at 9.0 tonight.

panda *n* (1901) a large, black and white, bear-like mammal of China. 'Discovered' by Western scientists in 1869, it was originally known as the 'parti-coloured bear' (see the first quote below). Its zoological relationship to the red panda was established in 1901, and thereafter it shared its cousin's name (which apparently comes from a Nepali word). The fuller, distinguishing form *giant panda* is first recorded in 1928. Its cuddly appearance has ensured that whenever specimens appear in Western zoos, they become the subject of much media attention

1901 E. R. Lankester: *Æluropus* must be removed from association with the Bears…and is no longer to be spoken of as 'the Parti-coloured Bear', but as 'the Great Panda'.

1928 *Proceedings of the Zoological Society*: The systematic position of the Giant Panda…is a question about which there has been much disagreement amongst zoologists.

1966 Ramona & Desmond Morris: There were panda postcards…, panda toys (almost obliterating the teddy bear for a brief period), panda novelties, panda strip-cartoons, panda brooches, and panda hats.

panties *n* (1908) knickers worn by women and girls. Originally *panties* (a cute diminutive of *pants*) was a somewhat dismissive term for men's trousers or shorts, and it continued to be used in this sense until around 1930 ('Panties for boys and skirts for girls…are being made very short,' *Weekly Dispatch* (1928)). The earliest reference to it as a female garment comes in a book on dolls' clothing, and it does not seem to have been widely used for women's knickers until the 1930s. See also **underpants (1931)**

1908 Mary Morgan: The under-garment is…easily made, for the little waist and panties are cut in one piece.

1932 *New Yorker*: There is a lace brassière top on a circular satin slip, and panties…are built in underneath.

paper handkerchief *n* (1907) a disposable handkerchief made from soft tissue paper

1907 *Yesterday's Shopping*: Handkerchiefs, Paper (Medicated)—These soft, silky papers are specially prepared for invalids, and are invaluable to sufferers from bronchial affections, catarrh, &c.

paratyphoid fever *n* (1902) a fever similar to, but generally milder than, typhoid fever

1902 *American Journal of Medical Science*: Paratyphoid fever closely resembles typhoid in its course, temperature curve, and abdominal symptoms.

parent *v* (1902) to bring up as a parent. An early isolated example of a usage which did not become widespread until the 1970s, in the form of the gerund **parenting (1959)**

1902 *Daily Chronicle*: The best parented children have to suffer exile at times.

pay-as-you- *prefix* (1908) A prefix probably inspired by the expression *pay as you go*, which dates from the early 19th century. Later formations include **pay-as-you-earn (1940s)** and *pay-as-you-view* (1950s)

1908 *Scientific American*: The pay-as-you-enter cars [i.e. carriages] which it is proposed to install on the New York city lines will be equipped with a device for collecting and automatically registering fares.

peak *adj* (1903) relating to a period of greatest use or demand

1924 *Westminster Gazette*: A drop of nearly 40,000,000 in pensions expenditure since the 'peak' year of 1920–21 is mentioned.

1937 *Architectural Review*: Traffic congestion at the 'peak hours' is deplorable.

peanut butter *n* (1903) a spread made with ground roasted peanuts

1903 *Harper's Magazine*: Four sandwiches… Two of wholewheat bread with peanut butter.

pentathlon *n* (1905) a sporting competition consisting of fencing, shooting, swimming, riding, and cross-country running. In ancient Greece the term referred to a contest consisting of jumping, running, throwing the discus, throwing the spear, and wrestling (it means literally 'five contest'). It was revived in English for the modern Olympic Games, and the event was first held in 1912

1948 E. A. Bland: In 1912, when the Swedish Olympic Committee was deliberating upon the programme of events for the Vth Olympiad, they sought a test which would produce the best all-round sportsman in the world… The contest known as the Modern Pentathlon was the result.

Pepsi-Cola *n* (1903) The proprietary name (filed in the US in 1903) of a popular soft drink. Pepsi's great rival *Coca-Cola* dates from the 1880s

1903 *New Bern* (North Carolina) *Journal*: Pepsi-Cola. At Soda Fountains… Aids Digestion.

permanent wave *n* (1909) (a process intended to produce) a long-lasting artificial wave in the hair. The first recorded example of the term refers to the rather alarming use of X-rays to achieve the effect; the more familiar chemical method did not get into its stride as a widely used beauty aid until after World War I (the abbreviation **perm** is first recorded in 1927, the mainly American **permanent** in 1926)

> 1909 *Hairdresser*: Children who have undergone the X-ray treatment for ringworm are growing curly hair… Would it be possible for a lady who desires to secure a permanent wave to undergo the treatment?

> 1922 Upton Sinclair: Would you like to see how we make eet—the permanent wave?

Perrier *n* (1907) The proprietary name (registered in 1907) of an effervescent natural mineral water. It comes from the spring from which the water is obtained, the *Source Perrier*, situated at Vergeze in the South of France.

> 1928 Aldous Huxley: If only Grace could be bottled like Perrier water.

petrol *v* (1902) to supply (a motor vehicle) with petrol. A usage from the early days of motoring which never caught on: no other examples of it have been found

> 1902 *Daily Mail*: The cars can be fed, groomed, and petrolled for a nominal charge.

petrol engine *n* (1902) an engine fuelled by petrol. Despite the dismissive tone of its first recorded use in print, the term has been in continuous mainstream use ever since

> 1902 R. J. Mecredy: 'Petrol Engine' is a slang term for an engine driven by a series of explosions of a mixture of the vapour of a light spirit of petroleum with air.

photographophone *n* (1901) an instrument for recording and reproducing sounds by means of kinematographic photographs of a sensitive flame which are caused to affect a selenium cell, with telephones attached. Dr. Ruhmer of Berlin's invention did not, alas, prove a success

> 1901 *Westminster Gazette*: Dr. Ruhmer, of Berlin, has invented what he calls a 'photo-graphophone', a new scientific marvel, with which he expects to be able to record a series of sounds of the human voice.

physiotherapy *n* (1905) the treatment of disease, injury, or deformity by physical methods, such as massage, exercise, and the application of heat, light, fresh air, and other external influences. The derivative *physiotherapist* is first recorded in 1923, its abbreviation *physio* in 1962

> 1905 *British Medical Journal*: The first congress of physiotherapy will be held at Liège on August 12th.

> 1962 *Times*: They should, like the orthopaedic physiotherapists, also be nurses… I tell my physios: 'Keep your hands off, keep your minds on.'

Pianola *n* (1901) Coined as the proprietary name of a mechanical device which when attached to a piano can be made to play tunes on it; also applied to a piano with such a device fitted. The popularity of the Pianola did not long survive the inexorable rise of the gramophone record, but early rolls preserve many historical performances

> 1901 *Scotsman*: The pianola…is…a mechanical attachment to the piano…a small cabinet…easily adjustable to the keyboard of the piano and, being fed by a perforated roll of paper, and furnished with wind-power by means of bellows, can play the most difficult music without the performer…touching the keyboard.

picture palace, picture theatre *n* (1908) a cinema. *Picture palace* is long disused except in evocations of the past; *picture theatre* survived longer. See also **cinematograph theatre (1909)**

> 1908 *Stage Year Book*: There are now indications that before long these picture 'palaces' will be a feature of London and the larger provincial towns.

> 1952 Nevil Shute: There's a little picture theatre… It's a bit of a bug-house.

pilot *n* (1907) someone who controls an aeroplane in flight. An adaptation of the earlier usage 'someone who controls an airship or balloon', which dates from the mid 19th century, and which in turn goes back ultimately to 'someone who steers a ship' (still current, of course; in early use, it was often necessary to specify *air pilot*). It has become the standard term, despite competition from the somewhat broader *aviator* (coined in the 1880s in deliberate contrast to *aeronaut* 'someone who flies a balloon'), the short-lived **aeroplanist (1906)**, and the later, briefly popular *flyer* (1934). First recorded as a verb in 1911

> 1907 *Navigating the Air* (Aero Club of America): In order to qualify as a pilot one must make ten ascensions, one of which must be made at night, and two of which must be made alone.

> 1911 *Daily News*: The Dutch aviator has decided to pilot a…monoplane…instead of a…biplane.

> 1923 J. W. Simpson: The confident courage that inspires air-pilots.

pineapple chunks *n* (1903) tinned pineapple cut into small cubes. First mentioned in Atkinson and Holroyd's *Practical Cookery*, they have gone on to be a staple of 20th-century convenience desserts

> 1976 Clement & La Frenais: Stealing your tin of naffing pineapple chunks? Not even my favourite fruit.

ping-pong *n* (1900) table tennis. The game seems to have been invented in the 1880s (the term *table tennis* is first recorded in 1887), and this alternative term for it was inspired by the sharp 'ping' emitted by the bat when striking the ball

> 1900 *Daily Chronicle*: Our correspondent seems to hope that the unclean, playing Ping-Pong with the clean, will become unpleasantly conscious of his uncleanness and reform.

ping-pong *v* (1901) to play ping-pong. The literal usage did not survive long, but in the second half of the century *ping-pong* was used figuratively to mean 'to send back and forth' or 'to pass around aimlessly'

> 1901 *Times*: [He] is only required to be agreeable and to ping-pong.

> 1976 *Times*: The report [of a Senate committee] states that 'investigators were repeatedly "ping-ponged" to neurologists, gynaecologists, internists, [etc.]'.

ping-pongist *n* (1901) a ping-pong player. A coinage which did not survive the initial wave of enthusiasm for the game: no further examples are recorded. The later *ping-ponger* proved rather more durable ('It cannot be, and is not, good for anyone to enjoy the high moments or ecstasies of lawn tennis without sharing its physical dangers; yet that is what the ping ponger is trying to do', *Times* (1933))

> 1901 *Daily Chronicle*: The competitors were presumably the pick of 'Ping-Pongists' in London.

pip-pip (1904) Originally used in imitation of a repeated high-pitched sound, especially the sound of a motor-horn, it began to take on a life of its own as a sort of retort, and by the 1920s had become fashionable slang for 'goodbye'

> 1907 George Bernard Shaw: Sarah (touching Lady Britomart's ribs with her finger tips and imitating a bicycle horn) Pip! pip!

> 1920 P. G. Wodehouse: 'Well, it's worth trying,' said Reggie. 'I'll give it a whirl. Toodleoo!' 'Goodbye.' 'Pip-pip!' Reggie withdrew.

plane *n* (1908) A shortening of *aeroplane* (1873). Condemned periodically as excessively colloquial, it has survived more vigorously than *aeroplane*

> 1908 *Times*: Mr. Wright refused to give any details on the propeller employed, but on the general construction of the plane he said it was full of movable diversely articulated parts.

> 1910 *Daily Mail*: To the builders of aeroplanes he cries: 'Construct me planes capable of the maximum speed.'

plastic *n* (1909) any of a range of mouldable materials based on polymerized organic compounds. The original meaning of *plastic* is 'pliable' (it is derived ultimately from Greek *plassein* 'to mould'). It was being applied as a noun to mouldable substances as early as 1905 ('Models sufficiently perfect cannot be made from impressions taken in modelling compound or other of the plastics', E. H. Angle in *American Text-book of Operative Dentistry*), but the first reference in print to the specific type of material now known as *plastic* comes in 1909, from Leo Baekeland, the inventor of bakelite (see **bakelite (1909)**)

> 1909 L. H. Baekeland: As an insulator…[bakelite] is far superior to hard rubber, casein, celluloid, shellac and in fact all plastics…It can be used for similar purposes like knobs, buttons, knife handles, for which plastics are generally used.

> 1911 E. C. Worden: Pyroxylin plastic is extensively used for the bits of pipe stems, and consists of ordinary plastic containing…dyestuffs, picric acid, [etc.].

plastic explosive *n* (1906) an explosive of putty-like consistency that can be shaped by hand and so placed in close contact with its target. One of the main weapons of terrorism in the latter part of the century

1906 C. E. Bichel: Add to the trinitrotoluol liquid resins…in such wise that…the crystalline trinitro-toluol with or without warming is worked in suitable mixing machines into a plastic explosive that detonates well.

plimsoll *n* (1907) a type of rubber-soled canvas shoe. British. So named because of the resemblance of the edge of the sole to a *plimsoll line*, the load line round a ship, named after the English MP Samuel Plimsoll (1824–98), who advocated its introduction. Eventually the **trainer (1978)** took its place

1922 *Times*: When Seabrook appeared in court he was wearing white plimsolls.

plug *n* (1902) an advertisement; an instance of publicity; a method of drawing attention to a product, an entertainment, etc., especially by repeatedly referring to it. Colloquial, originally US. The related verb is first recorded in 1906

1902 George Ade: They were friendly to the prosperous Bachelor and each one determined to put in a few quiet Plugs for Sis.

1906 Helen Green: I ain't got any music, so you kin plug any publisher's stuff an' play what you wanter.

plywood *n* (1907) a structural material made of thin layers of wood glued together. Much used in the manufacture of early aircraft

1919 A. W. Judge: The ply-woods chiefly employed in aeroplane work may vary from ⅛ to ¼ in. in thickness, and are made of ash or birch with an intermediate layer of poplar.

pogrom *n* (1905) Originally, an organized massacre in Russia for the destruction or annihilation of any body or class, especially the Jews. Hence, an organized, officially tolerated, attack on any community or group. Borrowed from Russian, where it means literally 'devastation, destruction'. There had been pogroms in Russia since 1881, but a new wave of them in 1903 propelled the word into English; it remains particularly associated with eastern and central Europe

1905 *Daily News*: The only means of combating the 'pogroms' is armed resistance.

1931 *Times Literary Supplement*: Refugees to England from pogrom-haunted Russia.

pointillism *n* (1901) a method, invented by French impressionist painters in the late 19th century, of producing luminous effects by crowding a surface with small spots of various colours, which are blended by the eye. A borrowing of French *pointillisme* (which was formed from *pointille* 'dot'), soon anglicized to *pointillism*. The derivative *pointillist* had already been acquired in the 1890s

1901 *Saturday Review*: Impressionism in France had…passed through the phases of luminism, vibration, pointillisme, independence and neo-impressionism, all comparatively short-lived extreme phases.

poll *n* (1902) a canvassing of the opinion of a number of people on a particular topic. An adaptation of the earlier sense, 'vote'. The term did not begin to become common (usually in the form (*public*) *opinion poll*) until the late 1930s

1939 George Gallup: The development during the last few years of the public-opinion survey or unofficial poll has raised…a host of new and far-reaching questions.

pomato *n* (1905) A name used by Luther Burbank (1849–1926), an American horticulturist, for the fruit of a hybrid potato, which resembled a tomato. The fruit was a nine-days' wonder, and its name disappeared from view, apparently for good; but it was revived in the 1970s to designate the result of attempts to hybridize the potato and the tomato, by grafting or other methods. One of the earliest of the portmanteau blends naming hybridized species which became popular in the 20th century (see also **liger (1938)**, **tigon (1927)**)

1905 *Century Magazine*: The 'pomato', one of the most wonderful creations, now under way. This may be called a tomato growing upon a potato. It produces in abundance a white, fragrant, succulent, delicious fruit upon potato tops.

1980 *Garden*: Am I the only person who doesn't grow pomatoes?

poodle *n* (1907) someone who does another's bidding subserviently; a lackey. A usage coined by Lloyd George when attacking in parliament the House of Lords' willingness to do anything the Conservative leader, Arthur Balfour, asked of it

> 1907 David Lloyd George: The House of Lords consented. This is the defender of property! This is the leal and trusty mastiff which is to watch over our interests… A mastiff? It is the right hon. Gentleman [A. J. Balfour]'s poodle. It fetches and carries for him. It barks for him. It bites anybody that he sets it on to.

poodle-faker *n* (1902) a man who cultivates female society, especially for the purpose of professional advancement; a ladies' man. Originally services' slang

> 1902 *T.C.D.*: The 'poodle-faker' is just as much a social necessity as tea-cakes.

post-war *adj* (1908) (characteristic) of a period after a war. An adjective whose connotations shift according to one's generation (see **pre-war (1908)**)

> 1908 *Daily Chronicle*: There has been a reduction of some £2,000,000 since 1904–5, the first post-war year.

> 1971 *Scientific American*: The postwar 'baby boom' and rapid growth of the economy in the 1950's pushed the population growth rate up to 18.5 percent.

poverty line *n* (1901) a minimum level of income consistent with a decent standard of living. First used as a socio-economic term by B. S. Rowntree in his 1901 book *Poverty*. See also **bread-line (1900)**

> 1901 Winston Churchill: Families who cannot provide this necessary sum, or who, providing it do not select their food with like discrimination are underfed and come below the 'poverty' line.

power station *n* (1901) an establishment where electricity is generated

> 1901 *Daily Express*: The development of power-stations all over the country.

premium bond *n* (1908) a debenture earning no interest but eligible for lotteries. The term had been in use since the early years of the century (and indeed its origins can be traced back to the late 19th century, when lottery loans had been called 'Premium Loans', so as not to put off people who considered lotteries a form of gambling, and therefore wicked), but it became much more widely known in Britain in the 1950s, when it was applied (in full as *Premium Savings Bond*) to a government bond not bearing interest but with the periodic chance of a cash prize. See also **Ernie (1956)**

> 1908 *Economist*: The practical man in the street who knows anything about premium bonds is quite aware that they are in their nature and intention lotteries.

> 1931 *Star*: Every trick—from premium bonds to guessing the number of beans in a bottle—seems to have been tried.

> 1956 Harold Macmillan: Finally, I have something completely new for the saver in Great Britain—a premium bond.

> 1957 *Observer*: New National Savings reported last week totalled £26,689,000 (including £1,200,000 Premium Bonds and £2,566,000 accrued interest).

pre-war *adj* (1908) (characteristic) of the period before a war. An adjective of shifting connotation, depending on your generation. In the earliest recorded example it refers to the Boer War, but later in the century it would be understood particularly to mean 'pre-World War I' and 'pre-World War II'. **Post-war** is also first recorded in 1908

> 1908 *Daily Chronicle*: The Transvaal Government…are thoroughly honest—a great difference from the pre-war days.

> 1946 *RAF Journal*: All the women were free…to resume their pre-war occupation… Already they have resumed their pre-war studies.

probation officer *n* (1906) someone who supervises an offender on probation. The system of probation, and the name *probation*, originated in the US in the 1870s

> 1906 *Report of the New York Probation Commission*: The duties of the probation officer were to inquire into the previous history of any defendant when so directed by the court.

probe *n* (1903) a penetrating investigation or inquiry. *Probe* has maintained its original reputation as a favourite of newspaper headline writers

> 1903 *Christendom*: Few words are commoner in newspaper headlines than 'probe', which is newspaper English for an investigation of alleged abuses.

1948 Ivor Brown: I have just seen an inquiry into a fatal explosion in a factory described as a Blast Probe.

progeria *n* (1904) a disease characterized by premature senility. The term was suggested by James Rhoades and Professor Arthur Sidgwick, based on Greek *progērōs* 'prematurely old'. Until the latter part of the century it was little known outside medical circles

1969 *Guardian*: A post-mortem examination will be carried out on…a 9-year-old girl who died of a disease that gave her the physical characteristics of a 90-year-old woman. Norma…was the second member of her family to be suffering from progeria.

progressive *adj* (1908) characterized by (the desire to promote) change, innovation, or experiment; avant-garde. A more generalized use of a term which had been in vogue in politics since the 1880s, in the sense 'favouring reform'

1908 H. G. Wells: It was always a very rhetorical and often trying affair, but in these progressive times you have to make a noise to get a living.

1949 Josephine Tey: The great house in the park was a boarding-school for the unmanageable children of parents with progressive ideas and large bank accounts.

prom *n* (1909) a seaside promenade. A term first recorded in the song 'I do like to be beside the Seaside', and redolent of British seaside holidays of the early and middle part of the century

1909 J. A. Glover-Kind: I do like to stroll upon the Prom, Prom, Prom.

Prom *n* (1902) one of the Henry Wood Promenade Concerts, given annually in London since 1895. See also **Promenade (1901)**

1902 *Free Lance*: There is never one of the programmes at the Proms…unworthy of the…most cultured music lover.

Promenade *n* (1901) a Prom. A potential rival colloquialism to **Prom**, in fact it did not survive the decade

1902 *Westminster Gazette*: The Promenades go on from triumph to triumph…, if the audiences might sometimes be larger, they could not possibly be more appreciative.

propagand *v* (1901) to spread propaganda. A back-formation from **propaganda** which survived until after World War II

1923 *Westminster Gazette*: Russia was spending large sums out of her Secret Service in order to propagand in the East against British interests.

propaganda *n* (1908) the systematic dissemination of a particular doctrine by circulating polemical material. The term originally denoted a committee of Roman Catholic cardinals responsible for overseeing the propagation of the faith. It came to be used in English from the late 18th century for any association or movement for the propagation of a particular doctrine or practice ('*a* propaganda'). The shift to the modern connotation of spreading partisan material intended to indoctrinate was a gradual one. The previous entry shows that it had got under way well before the earliest record of it in 1908. That quote still contains echoes of its religious origins, but as the century progressed *propaganda* became a key weapon of oppression and warfare

1908 Lilley & Tyrrell: The Church…soon felt a need of new methods of propaganda and government.

1929 G. Seldes: The term propaganda has not the sinister meaning in Europe which it has acquired in America… In European business offices the word means advertising or boosting generally.

1937 Arthur Koestler: One of the most effective propaganda campaigns launched by the rebels was that relating to the alleged shooting of hostages by the Madrid Government.

protest *v* (1904) to protest against (an action or event). An American usage which has yet to establish itself in British English

1904 *Brooklyn Eagle*: Many of the students are much incensed at the judges and will probably protest the decision.

psychoanalysis *n* (1906) a therapeutic method originated by Sigmund Freud for treating disorders of the personality or behaviour by bringing into a patient's consciousness his or her unconscious conflicts and fantasies. Freud's original term for this was *psychische Analyse* (rendered in English as *psychic analysis* in 1898) or *klinischpsychologische Analyse*, but in a paper in the *Revue Neurologique* in 1896 he used the French word *psychoanalyse*, which formed the basis of the English term. See also **psychoanalyse (1911)** and **psychoanalyst (1911)**

> 1906 *Journal of Abnormal Psychology*: Their importance with relation to treatment (by the method of 'psycho-analysis') is made clear.

psychoanalytic *adj* (1906), **psychoanalytical** *adj* (1908) relating to psychoanalysis

> 1906 *Journal of Abnormal Psychology*: The strict 'cathartic', psycho-analytic method advocated by Freud.

questionnaire *n* (1901) a (printed) set of questions designed to elicit information, as in a survey. A borrowing from French which was at first strongly resisted in some quarters, apparently on the grounds that the anglicized form *questionary* already existed (see the first quote below). Henry Fowler, in his *Dictionary of Modern English Usage* (1940), called it 'too recent an importation to be in the OED'. Other die-hards for a long time insisted on pronouncing it as a French word, with an initial /k/ rather than /kw/. However, it has gone from strength to strength, and *questionary* is now virtually unknown except in medical usage

> 1901 E. B. Titchener: The questionary or 'questionnaire' is a series of questions bearing upon the matter to be investigated, and submitted to a large number of persons for introspective answer.

> 1920 *Glasgow Herald*: Valuable information, never previously collected, is being obtained through a questionnaire by the Federation of British Industries concerning the fuel requirements of the great industrial centres.

racialism *n* (1907) belief in the superiority of a particular race leading to prejudice and antagonism towards people of other races. In early use, often in a South African context. *Racism*, which has come to be used synonymously with *racialism* and to some extent superseded it, dates from the 1930s (see **racist (1932)**)

> 1910 *Westminster Gazette*: What appears to me to be the greatest results of the Botha-Smuts Government is the abolition of Racialism and the construction of roads.

> 1938 *Sun* (Baltimore): The Italian Jews are thus to be added to the victims of Hitler's imbecile 'racialism', now adopted by Mussolini as a sop to superior force.

radiator *n* (1900) a cooling device in an internal-combustion engine in which circulating fluid acts as the coolant. *Radiator* in the sense 'heating device' dates from the late 19th century

> 1900 *Scientific American*: The present water circulating plan…has…the defect of complicating the mechanism by the addition of tanks, radiators and pumps, causing multiplied trouble.

radio *n* (1907) the transmission of speech and other uncoded signals by means of electromagnetic waves, without the use of a wire. *Radio* (ultimately from Latin *radius* 'ray') began life in English as a prefix, in such words as *radiotelegraphy* and *radiotelephony*, in the late 1890s. Its first known use as an independent form was in **radio receiver** (see below), but even here it was only part of a compound noun. The quote from 1907 shows it for the first time in a more free-ranging role, while the first 1917 quote is the first known instance of its not preceding another noun. 1917 is also the first year in which it is recorded in the sense 'radio set'.

At first, *wireless* was much more widespread in general use, and it remained so until World War II (although *radio* was far from uncommon—Edward VIII referred to it, for instance, in his abdication broadcast). From then on, however, perhaps partly from a preference for *radio* in military terminology, their relative frequency has steadily reversed, and at the end of the century few of even the oldest or most conservative English-speakers talk unironically about the *wireless*. See also **radio (1919)**, **radio (1922)**

> 1907 Lee de Forest: This factor, damping, is of far more vital import than any regulation of wavelengths… Radio chaos will certainly be the result until…regulation is enforced.

> 1917 *Electrical Experimenter* (heading): Election returns flashed by radio to 7,000 amateurs.

> 1917 *Electrical Experimenter*: When the German spies…found that it was not very healthy to operate their outfits in attics or in house chimneys…they simply put their radios in touring cars, cleverly concealing the aerial wires inside of the car bodies.

> 1936 King Edward VIII: Science has made it possible for me…to speak to you all over the radio.

> 1968 *New Society*: Non-U *radio*/U *wireless* is no longer true; the U call it a radio too.

radiology *n* (1900) the medical use of X-rays, especially in diagnosis

> 1900 *Popular Science Monthly*: An International Congress of Medical Electrology and Radiology has been connected with the International Congress system of the Paris Exposition, 1900.

radio receiver *n* (1903) an apparatus for receiving radio signals. The shortened form *radio* did not appear with this meaning until the next decade. The quotation below is the earliest known example of *radio* being used as an independent form (as opposed to an element in words such as *radiotelegraphy*—see **radio** above)

> 1903 C. H. Sewall: The first radio-receiver in which cause and effect were observed and recognized was devised by Hertz in 1886.

radiotherapy *n* (1903) the treatment of disease by means of X-rays or other forms of ionizing radiation.

> 1903 *Boston Medical & Surgical Journal*: He had been interested in comparing the effects of phototherapy and radiotherapy.

rain forest *n* (1903) a dense forest in an area of high rainfall with little seasonal variation, especially a tropical forest characterized by a rich variety of plant species. A direct translation of German *Regenwald*, a term proposed by A. F. W. Schimper in his *Pflanzengeographie* (1898), and intoduced into English in W. R. Fisher's version of Schimper's book

> 1903 W. R. Fisher: The Rain-forest is evergreen, hygrophilous in character, at least thirty meters high, but usually much taller, rich in thick-stemmed lianes, and in woody as well as herbaceous epiphytes.

rap *n* (1903) a criminal accusation, charge. Slang, mainly US. Probably a development of the earlier sense 'a rebuke'

> 1903 H. Hapgood: 'What makes you look so glum?'…'Turned out of police court this morning.' 'What was the rap, Mike?' 'I'm looking too respectable. They asked me where I got the clothes.'

ratty *adj* (1909) annoyed, bad-tempered. A colloquialism that has survived vigorously. It is not altogether clear why rats should have been seen as models of ill temper, but since the middle of the 19th century *ratty* had been used as a general term of disapproval for anything of poor quality or disgusting condition, and in Australian English it meant 'mad' or 'eccentric'

> 1976 Tim Heald: I'd simply have asked her what the hell she was so ratty about.

reinforced concrete *n* (1902) An alternative (and to the lay person more familiar) name for **ferroconcrete (1900)**

> 1906 *Daily Chronicle*: There is undoubtedly a great future for reinforced concrete.

remote control *n* (1904) control of an apparatus at a distance. By the 1920s the term was being applied to a device used for remote control. The abbreviated form *remote* is first recorded in this sense in 1966

> 1921 *Wireless World*: The instrument is assembled from a Mk III ebonite top,…the parts of an aeroplane 'remote control', etc.

repress *v* (1909) Of a patient or person who is the object of study: to keep (unacceptable memories or desires) out of the conscious mind, or suppress them into the unconscious. A translation of Sigmund Freud's term *verdrängen*. The derived noun *repression* was introduced into English in the same year

> 1909 A. A. Brill, translating Freud's *Selected Papers on Hysteria*: The patient has not reacted to psychic traumas because the nature of the trauma…concerned things which the patient wished to forget and which he therefore intentionally inhibited and repressed from the conscious memory… If I could now make it probable that the idea became pathogenic in consequence of the exclusion and repression, the chain would seem complete.

rev *n* (1901) A colloquial shortening of *revolution*, in the sense 'rotation', inspired by the newly omnipresent internal-combustion engine. See also **rev (1920)**

> 1901 *Catalogue of the Mechanical Engineering Collection* (Victoria & Albert Museum): The example has 3 in. cylinders, with 4 in. stroke, and is intended to run at 300 revs. per min.

revisionism *n* (1903) a policy first put forward in the 1890s by Edward Bernstein (1850–1932) advocating the introduction of socialism through evolution rather than revolution, in opposition to the orthodox view of Marxists; hence used as a term of abuse within the communist world for an interpretation of Marxism which is felt to threaten the official policy

> 1958 *Times*: It is not only over Yugoslav 'revisionism' that China has lately taken a distinctive and uncompromising attitude.

riot *n* (1909) something spectacularly successful or amusing, especially an uproariously successful performance or show. A piece of theatre slang which survived into the latter part of the century

> 1976 John Snow: His rendering of 'Barnacle Bill the Sailor' was a riot and became his party piece.

road sign *n* (1904) an official sign giving instructions or information to drivers

> 1904 *Car*: Road signs… The conference held…to consider the desirability of uniformity of action with regard to signs and notice boards.

rock *n* (1908) a precious stone, especially a diamond. Slang, originally US

> 1908 Helen Green: 'So that's his new wife, eh?' said Goldie later. 'Did you pipe the rocks she had on?'

Rolls-Royce *n* (1908) a Rolls-Royce car. The trademark, incorporating the names of the car's first designers, C. S. Rolls (1877–1910) and Sir Henry Royce (1863–1933), was registered in 1908, and has since become synonymous with luxury, expensiveness, and purringly smooth travel. The colloquial abbreviation *Rolls* is first recorded in 1928

> 1928 Edgar Wallace: Dick knew the gentleman very well by name; indeed, he had recognised his big yellow Rolls standing outside the hotel.

> 1932 D. H. Lawrence: Do you hear my Rolls Royce purr, as it glides away?

> 1974 *Daily Telegraph*: Vintage port—the Rolls-Royce end of the trade—accounts for only about one per cent. of port production.

röntgenoscopy *n* (1904) examination by means of X-rays. The name of the German physicist Wilhelm Conrad Röntgen (1845–1923), who discovered X-rays in 1895, was widely used in English X-ray terminology in the late 19th and early 20th centuries (e.g. *röntgen ray* (1896), *röntgenology* (1905), *röntgen therapy* (1910)), but it has gradually faded from the scene as the 20th century has progressed. Its (to English eyes) awkward spelling, whether with *oe* or the umlauted *ö*, has no doubt not helped its cause

> 1914 *Journal of the American Medical Association*: Roentgenoscopy has proved that ossification may…occur in the epiglottis.

roquette *n* (1902) a plant with bitter-tasting leaves that are used in salads. A reborrowing of French *roquette*, which was originally acquired in the 16th century and anglicized to *rocket*. Not widely used until the 1980s, when the plant suddenly became popular and sellers wished to give its name some French polish

Rottweiler *n* (1907) a large black-and-tan dog with a short, coarse coat, docked tail, and a broad head. Named after Rottweil, a town in Württemberg, southern Germany. It did not begin to acquire its fearsome reputation as a guard dog and attack dog in Britain until the 1970s. The metaphorical possibilities of this were explored in the 1980s

> 1989 *Sunday Correspondent*: 'It's only working if it's painful' are…the words of a Chancellor with Rottweiler tendencies rather than poodle qualities when it comes to standing up to Mrs Thatcher.

safari *n* (1907) a cross-country expedition, often lasting days or weeks, originally in East Africa and on foot, especially for hunting; later often applied to a trip with motorized vehicles, for tourism, adventure, or scientific investigation. A borrowing from Swahili, where it means literally 'journey, expedition'

> 1907 J. H. Patterson: [He] had left me and gone on safari (a caravan journey) to Uganda… They join another caravan and begin a new safari to the Great Lakes.

1928 *Daily Express*: The royal safari—as a shooting expedition of this nature is described in Africa—is complete to the minutest detail.

saleing *n* (1901) shopping at sales. A British usage which seems to have died out after about 1930

1928 *Daily Express*: 'Saleing' has become a specialised art.

saloon, saloon car *n* (1908) a type of car with a closed body for four or more passengers. The full form *saloon car* is first recorded in 1915

1908 *Motor Manual*: Other forms of bodies fitted to more expensive cars include the brougham, landaulet, saloon, double phaeton, [etc.].

1931 Dorothy Sayers: I observed Mr. Gowan's saloon car standing before the door.

scouting *n* (1908) the activities practised by Boy Scouts. A term introduced by Robert Baden-Powell in his book *Scouting for Boys* (1908), in the year in which he launched the Boy Scout movement (see **Boy Scout (1908)**)

1908 R. S. S. Baden-Powell: Instruction in scouting should be given as far as possible through practises, games, and competitions.

segregation *n* (1903) the enforced separation of different racial groups in a country, community, or institution. A term that through the century has been mainly applied to discriminatory practices against blacks in South Africa and the southern states of the US. Compare **apartheid (1947)**

1903 T. T. Fortune: The Afro-American people have been held together rather by the segregation decreed by law...than by ties of consanguinity.

1957 *Times*: The ruling of the Supreme Court that racial segregation in public schools [in South Africa] was unconstitutional.

send off *v* (1906) to order (a player) to leave the pitch as a punishment

1906 W. Pickford: A referee may send a player off at once and without any previous caution, if he is guilty of violent conduct.

servant problem *n* (1909) the difficulty caused to upper- and middle-class employers by the lack of people willing to enter domestic service. A constant theme of bourgeois complaint as the century progressed and patterns of employment changed. It was particularly exacerbated by World War I, after which people who had seen the alternatives that life offered were reluctant to go back into service

1916 Arnold Bennett: The servant problem had been growing acute.

sexology *n* (1902) the scientific study of sex and sexual relationships. Originally used as the title of a book by W. H. Walling. The derivative *sexologist* is first recorded in 1914

1914 *American Journal of Clinical Medicine*: There may be some homosexuals who are reconciled to or even proud of their abnormality, as some sexologists claim, but I must confess that I have not met such types.

1977 E. J. Trimmer: Reich is...in all the history of sexology, perhaps the most single-minded believer in the centrality of sex to human lives.

shadow cabinet *n* (1906) a group of members of an opposition party nominated as counterparts of the government cabinet. By the 1920s the use of *shadow* had broadened out to designate any opposition counterpart, although it does not seem to have become widespread or to any extent institutionalized until after World War II

1906 A. J. Balfour: If we are to have, as you suggest, a Committee consisting of members selected from the Front Bench in both Houses,...what we should really have would be a shadow Cabinet once a week.

1953 Earl Winterton: I was in Mr. Churchill's 'Shadow Cabinet' from 1945 to 1950.

1958 *Spectator*: The Chancellors and Shadow-Chancellors.

shed *n* (1909) a hangar. Long obsolete as a general term, it is still occasionally pressed into service when speaking specifically of airship hangars (its original application)

1909 *Daily Chronicle*: They have been watching the great shed gradually nearing completion..., and have been eagerly awaiting the advent of the airship.

> 1916 Horatio Barber: The Aeroplane is wheeled out of its shed on to the greensward of the Military Aerodrome.

shoppy, shoppie *n* (1909) a (young female) shop assistant. One of a range of fairly dismissive terms ending in *-y/-ie* that were applied to female workers (e.g. **clippie** 'bus-conductress' (1941), *tweeny* 'type of maid' (1888)); this one seems to have died out in the 1930s

> 1909 P. Webling: Her manner towards him…had none of the affectation of the ordinary 'young lady in business', or the vulgar intimacy of a poorer class of 'shoppie'.

shop-steward *n* (1904) a union member chosen by fellow workers to represent them in dealings with management

> 1904 *Rules of the Amalgamated Society of Engineers*: Committees may also appoint shop-stewards to…keep the committee posted with all events occurring in the various shops.

shorthand-typist *n* (1901) someone who takes down dictation in shorthand and then types out the text

> 1901 *Phonetic Journal*: To a large extent the occupation of the shorthand-typist has hitherto been synonymous with the lady typist.

show-down *n* (1904) a confrontation which brings a disputed issue to a conclusion. An extension of the earlier usage, poker players' slang for 'the act of laying down one's cards with their faces up'. The underlying metaphor is of revelation

> 1904 Francis Lynde: 'You don't mean to say there is any doubt about our ability to do it?' 'Oh, no; I suppose not, if it comes to a show-down.'

smog *n* (1905) fog intensified by smoke. In Britain the term is particularly associated with the very severe smog that afflicted London in the early 1950s, resulting in many deaths (see also **smog mask (1954)**)

> 1905 *Globe*: The other day at a meeting of the Public Health Congress Dr. Des Vœux did a public service in coining a new word for the London fog, which was referred to as 'smog', a compound of 'smoke' and 'fog'.

snakes and ladders *n* (1907) a board-game in which the hazards and advantages are provided by snakes and ladders depicted on the board

> 1907 *Yesterday's Shopping*: Snakes and Ladders. An interesting and most exciting game of chance.

social security *n* (1908) a system of state financial assistance for those citizens whose income is inadequate or non-existent owing to disability, unemployment, old age, etc. The term was coined by Winston Churchill, but did not come into widespread use until the 1930s

> 1908 Winston Churchill: If we were able to underpin the whole existing social security apparatus with a foundation of comparatively low-grade state safeguards, we should in the result obtain something that would combine the greatest merits both of the English & the German systems.

> 1942 *Times*: Social security as envisaged in this report is a plan to secure to each citizen an income adequate to satisfy a national minimum standard… As regards unification, Sir William Beveridge suggests that there should be a Ministry of Social Security.

social worker *n* (1904) someone professionally trained to provide help and advice to the poor, the aged, and those with domestic problems. A derivative of *social work*, which dates from around 1890. By the end of the century its connotations were not altogether positive

> 1904 *Annual Register of the University of Chicago*: A training center for social workers.

> 1958 *Times Literary Supplement*: She writes well, and—somewhat unusually for a social worker— quotes poetry. She seasons her facts with many 'true-life' stories.

> 1977 Barbara Pym: A real bossy social-worker type.

solar heating *n* (1903) utilizing the sun's rays for space or water heating. Exploitation of renewable energy sources is not the preserve of the last quarter of the 20th century

> 1903 C. H. Pope: Another patent for solar-heating devices was obtained…from the British Government.

sound effects *n* (1909) artificially produced sounds imitating natural sounds (e.g. an explosion, horse's hooves), as used in a film, radio programme, etc. The earliest sound effects were produced live as an accompaniment to silent films

> 1909 *Moving Picture World*: Yerkes & Co... Manufacturers of high grade sound effects for moving pictures.

> 1928 *Exhibitor's Herald & Motion Picture World*: The experts of Victor…will…arrange for the synchronized orchestration and sound effects for this picture, in which airplane battles will have an important part.

spastic *adj* (1903) affected with spastic paralysis. The corresponding noun use, meaning 'a person with spastic paralysis', is first recorded in the 1890s. Both have fallen out of favour in the latter part of the 20th century because of the widespread colloquial use of *spastic* to mean 'incompetent, stupid'. The term *spastic paralysis* itself dates from the 1870s

> 1903 Tubby & Jones: Transformation of the pronator radii teres and transplantation of the carpal flexors were effected in spastic children.

speeding *n* (1908) driving a motor vehicle fast, especially at an illegal speed. **Speed** itself is not recorded as a verb until the 1930s (presumably as a back-formation from *speeding*). Both quickly overtook **overspeed (1906)**

> 1908 *Evening Star* (Washington): Baby carriages are required to carry lights at night in Chicago. That rapid city may yet find it necessary to provide special police to keep the baby carriages from speeding.

> 1931 John Galsworthy: 'I'm going to speed,' said Jean, looking back. The speedometer rose rapidly.

speedometer *n* (1904) a speed-indicator, especially one in a motor vehicle

> 1904 *Times*: His 'speedometer'…showed he was going at only ten miles an hour.

speedway *n* (1903) a road on which traffic can drive fast. Originally fairly general in application (it seems to have developed from a late 19th-century US term for a track for fast horse-driving), it later came to be used virtually as a synonym for **motorway**. This was elbowed out by the now current sense, 'dirt-track motor-cycle racing', which evolved in the 1920s

> 1903 *New York Times*: The numerous owners of rapid roadsters are devoting no inconsiderable portion of their Summer leisure to spirited brushes on the new speed-way.

spiflicated *adj* (1906) drunk. Slang, originally US. Presumably from *spiflicate* 'to overcome, destroy', a fanciful formation dating from the late 18th century

> 1906 O. Henry: He uses Nature's Own Remedy. He gets spifflicated.

split the atom (1909) to cause atomic nuclei to undergo fission (see **fission (1939)**). The British physicist Sir Joseph Thomson, referred to in the first quote below, discovered the electron, but it is John Cockroft and Ernest Walton, who in 1932 used a particle accelerator to split an atomic nucleus of lithium, who at the end of the century were more usually thought of as the men 'who split the atom'

> 1909 *Busy Man's Magazine*: [Professor J. J. Thomson] is known both as 'The Man of Ion', and as the man 'who split the atom'.

> 1964 Margaret Gowing: [Cockroft and Walton] bombarded a foil of the metal lithium, disrupting the lithium nuclei which, after combining with incident protons, split into two alpha particles. The experimenters had 'split' atoms by artificial means.

spoonerism *n* (1900) an accidental transposition of the initial sounds, or other parts, of two or more words (as in 'soda and gobbly' for 'sober and godly'). Named after the Reverend William Spooner (1844–1930), Warden of New College, Oxford, who was notorious for making such slips. The word is reported to have been known in colloquial use in Oxford from about 1885, but this is the first written reference to it

> 1900 *Globe*: To one unacquainted with technical terms it sounds as if the speaker were guilty of a spoonerism.

spork *n* (1909) a piece of cutlery combining features of a spoon and a fork. A Lewis Carrollish port-manteau word with a chequered history. It is mentioned in the 1909 supplement to the *Century Dictionary*, but no more is heard of it until the 1970s, when it was registered as a trademark

> 1975 *Equipment for the Disabled: Home Management*: The spork can be adapted by bending and/or lengthened by rivetting on an extension.

stall *v* (1904) to cause (an aircraft, vehicle, engine, etc.) to stall. The intransitive usage of the verb is not recorded before the 1910s, but no doubt it came into existence around the same time as the transitive. In origin it is a metaphorical use of *stall* in the sense 'to become stuck in mud, a snow-drift, etc.'

> 1904 Wilbur Wright: He allowed the machine to turn up a little too much and it stalled it.

stalloy *n* (1906) A blend of *steel* and *alloy* which was used as a trade-name before World War I

> 1906 *Daily Chronicle*: The remarkable new steel alloy called 'stalloy'.

standardize *v* (1900) to make uniform. *Standardize* in its literal sense 'to bring to a standard size, composition, etc.' dates from the 1850s, but this metaphorical use is a 20th-century development

> 1911 F. Harrison: Life and Society have been standardised.

stand up *v* (1902) to fail to keep an appointment with (someone). Originally US

> 1902 O. V. Limerick: I am awfully sorry I had to stand you up last night.

Stepney wheel *n* (1907) a spare wheel for a motor vehicle, comprising a ready-inflated tyre on a spokeless metal rim, which could be clamped temporarily over a punctured wheel. Named after Stepney Street in Llanelli, where it was first made. Long since defunct in British English, the term persists in the English of Malta and of the Indian subcontinent, where it denotes any spare wheel

> 1907 *Westminster Gazette*: The popularity of the Stepney Wheel has never been more clearly demonstrated than at the Olympia Show.

> 1977 *Navbharat Times* (Bombay): Yezdi stepney wheel complete with tyre, tube, hub and bearings.

straphanger *n* (1905) a passenger, especially a commuter, who has to stand and hold on by the strap in a full bus, compartment of a railway carriage, etc. Colloquial. Often used as a sympathetic or contemptuous synonym for *commuter*

> 1905 *Punch*: I am a Straphanger. I am one of a million swaying souls who travel underground to the vast city.

stratosphere *n* (1909) the region of the atmosphere extending from the top of the troposphere up to a height of about 50 km. (the stratopause), in the lower part of which there is little temperature variation with height in temperate latitudes while in the higher part the temperature increases with height. In early use, the term was applied to the lower part of this region only (up to a height of about 20 km.). It is based on *stratum*, from the idea of a 'layer' of the atmosphere

> 1909 *Science Abstracts*: Variation in height of the stratosphere (isothermal layer).

streamline *adj* (1907) having or being a shape such that the flow of a fluid round it is smooth; hence, more widely, shaped so as to reduce air or water resistance. A key design-goal of the 20th century. The synonymous **streamlined** is not recorded before 1913

> 1914 *Automobile Topics*: That beautiful stream-line Car.

student *n* (1900) someone attending a place of primary or secondary education. Originally a US usage, it took a long time to spread to British English, where *student* remained exclusively in the realm of tertiary education until quite late in the century

> 1900 E. E. Brown: In these laboratories [high school] students perform representative experiments in the science they are pursuing.

> 1936 *Evening Citizen* (Glasgow): [In the United States] even schoolboys and schoolgirls are students.

> 1976 *Times*: We have primary school students, presumably working for BAs in Plasticine; the National Union of School Students; and graduation day for high school students… Formerly people were schoolboys or schoolgirls until they became undergraduates.

studio apartment *n* (1903) See **studio flat (1934)**

subatomic *adj* (1903) relating to the constituent parts of an atom

> 1905 *Athenæum*: Experiments have been made with sub-atomic particles from one or other of these sources.

sub-title *n* (1909) a caption which appears on a cinema screen, especially to translate the dialogue or (originally, in silent films) to explain the action

> 1909 *Moving Picture World*: If the audience is not given time to read the sub-titles or if they are indistinct…the spectators lose the thread.

> 1957 Margaret Summerton: The French film was mediocre. I ignored the sub-titles, testing my ear on the dialogue.

suffragette *n* (1906) a female supporter of the cause of women's political enfranchisement, especially one of a violent or militant type. Coined from *suffrage* 'the right to vote', it has the advantage of succinctness over *woman suffragist*, which had been in use since the mid 1880s. In the years when such campaigners were in the news (roughly, until World War I), the word spun off various derivatives, including *suffragettism*, *suffragetty*, and even a verb *suffragette*. See also **women's movement (1902)**

> 1906 *Daily Mail*: Mr. Balfour and the 'Suffragettes'… It was not surprising that Mr. Balfour should receive a deputation of the Suffragettes.

> 1909 H. G. Wells: And her straight hair was out demonstrating and suffragetting upon some independent notions of its own.

> 1912 Clementine Churchill: Amy is kind, but more Suffragetty, Christian Sciency and Yankee Doodle than ever.

> 1913 George Bernard Shaw: That is the sort of thing that you vaguely lump into a cloud of abomination as Suffragettism.

suitcase *n* (1902) a piece of luggage for carrying clothes and other belongings. Originally, as its name suggests, it was designed specifically for carrying a man's suit, but the usage soon broadened out to what it is today

> 1902 *Times*: Captain Clive…sent on his suit-case and other luggage by another train.

> 1981 D. M. Thomas: She realized they were travellers, for they were weighed down by rucksacks and suitcases.

sump *n* (1907) a depression in the bottom of the crankcase of an internal-combustion engine, which serves as a reservoir of lubricating oil

> 1907 *Westminster Gazette*: The oil is forced by a gear-driven pump from a sump in the crankchamber.

Sunday supplement *n* (1905) an illustrated section issued with a Sunday newspaper, sometimes characterized by the portrayal of voguish living

> 1905 Edith Wharton: The photographer whose portraits of her formed the recurring ornament of 'Sunday Supplements'.

> 1971 Alan Bennett: Since then N.W.1 has been used as a catchphrase to indicate Sunday supplement trendiness which people now find rather suspect.

superman *n* (1903) an ideal superior man conceived by the German philosopher Friedrich Nietzsche (1844–1900) as being evolved from the normal human type; hence, more loosely, a man of extraordinary power or ability, a superior being. A translation of German *Übermensch*. Earlier versions had been *overman* (1895) and *beyond-man* (1896), but the success of *superman* was no doubt assured by the title of George Bernard Shaw's play *Man and Superman* (1903) (and later reinforced by the name of the superhuman American comic-strip hero, created in the late 1930s (see **Superman (1938)**)

> 1903 *Speaker*: It is possible by breeding, by education, by social reconstruction, that the Superman may be attained.

supertax *n* (1906) an additional duty of income tax levied on incomes above a certain value: abolished as an official term in the UK in 1929, but still in common use, especially before nouns

1906 *Westminster Gazette*: The powers that would…be necessary to obtain a full disclosure of income…under a system of super-tax.

1978 F. Olbrich: The Taj Mahal Hotel['s]…clientele consisted exclusively of those in the super-tax bracket.

surprise attack *n* (1900) an attack which one's opponent is not expecting. Not a new tactic, but the term is first recorded in the context of the Boer War

1900 *Daily News*: Our surprise attacks only surprised ourselves by the thoroughness of the enemy's preparation for them.

swank *v* (1903) to behave pretentiously, put on airs; hence, to boast. Slang. The verb is first recorded in dialect dictionaries of the early 19th century with the meaning 'to swagger, strut', which suggests that its ultimate origin may have been Middle High German *swanken* 'to sway'. There is an isolated record of its use in the sense 'to boast' in Hotten's *Slang Dictionary* (1874), but it did not come into general slang use until the beginning of the 20th century. See also **swank** the noun **(1913)**

1903 A. McNeill: To see your wife in the Peeresses' Gallery on great occasions, and your sons swanking about town with Hon. before their names.

1914 George Bernard Shaw: I used to boast about what a good boy Bobby was. Now I swank about what a dog he is; and it pleases people just as well.

table football *n* (1907) a game played on a table with moves simulating the action of soccer. It did not achieve great popularity until after World War II, in the form manufactured by Subbuteo. Alas, the alternative name *Wibley Wob* never caught on

1907 *Yesterday's Shopping*: Wibley Wob or Table Football. A game for 2 or 4 players, to be placed upon an ordinary dining table.

tabloid journalism *n* (1901) journalism featuring newspapers in a small format which handle stories in an easily assimilable and often sensational way. *Tabloid* was originally a trademark (registered in 1884) for a small medicinal tablet, but subsequently took off as a metaphor for anything produced in small or concentrated form (during World War I it was used as the nickname of a type of small Sopwith biplane, and as late as the 1930s the term *tabloid cruiser* was coined for a small cruising yacht). The use of **tabloid** as a noun to denote a newspaper of this sort is not recorded before 1918

1901 *Westminster Gazette*: He advocated tabloid journalism.

tail *v* (1907) to follow secretly as a detective or spy. Colloquial, originally US; a usage based on the earlier sense 'to follow or drive cattle'

1907 *Everybody's Magazine*: Detectives were assigned to 'tail' him.

tanker *n* (1900) a sea-going vessel fitted with tanks for carrying oil or other liquids in bulk. The idea of such a ship dates from the late 19th century, but the word appears to be 20th-century. The earliest record of the compound noun *oil tanker* dates from 1920

1900 *Boston Herald*: The wreck was a tanker.

1926 *British Gazette*: Many vessels have been docked and undocked, including oil tankers.

tape record *n* (1905) a recording on tape. With the introduction of steel tape in the 1930s, and later plastic tape, *tape-recording* came to be the preferred term. See **tape recorder (1932)**

1905 *Talking Machine News*: A tape record could be made to be reproduced by either the cylinder or disc type of machine.

Tarmac *n* (1903) The trade-mark (registered in 1903) of a kind of tar macadam consisting of iron slag impregnated with tar and creosote. Now usually used without an initial capital

1905 *Times*: He suggests that the club…should entirely remake some…stretch of road near London with Tarmac.

taxi, taxi-cab *n* (1907) a passenger-conveyance with a fare calculated by a taximeter. Short for *taximeter* (1898), an adaptation of French *taximètre*, which was based on *taxe* 'tax, charge'. In early usage sometimes spelled *taxy*

1907 *Daily Chronicle*: Every journalist…has his idea of what the vehicle should be called. It has been described as the (1) taxi, (2) motor-cab, (3) taxi-cab, (4) taximo,…(7) taximeter-cab.

1907 *Daily Chronicle*: The 'taxicab', as the new taximeter motor-cab is called, is fast becoming a familiar feature in the streets of London.

1908 *Daily News*: Many ladies...now take a 'taxy' regularly for the morning's shopping. There are about 350 horsed 'taxies' on the road.

teddy bear *n* (1906) a stuffed figure of a bear, made of rough plush, used as a toy. It was so called in humorous allusion to Theodore ('Teddy') Roosevelt (President of the US 1901–1909). Roosevelt's bear-hunting expeditions occasioned a celebrated comic poem, accompanied by cartoons, in the *New York Times* of 7 January 1906, concerning the adventures of two bears named 'Teddy B' and 'Teddy G'; these names were transferred to two bears (also known as the 'Roosevelt bears') presented to Bronx Zoo in the same year; finally in 1907 the fame of these bears was turned to advantage by toy dealers, whose toy 'Roosevelt bears', imported from Germany, became an instant fashion in the US

1906 *American Stationer*: Probably no novelty of recent years has been so popular as the Teddy Bears.

1907 *New England Magazine*: The Teddy-bear has come, and one suspects that he has come to stay.

telectrograph *n* (1909) an apparatus for producing at the receiving end a copy of a photograph or print at the transmitting end, by means of electric telegraphy. The technology was late 19th-century, and the term originally applied to it was *telephotograph* (also used for the photograph itself), but this died out in the face of the use of the same word for 'a long-distance photograph' (see **telephotograph (1900)**)

1909 *Daily Mirror*: The pictures were wired from Manchester to London last night in six minutes by the Thorne-Baker telectrograph.

telephone *v* (1901) to establish a system of telephones in (a place). *Telephone* in the now more familiar verbal sense 'to communicate with by telephone' dates from the 1870s. This new usage was distinctly ephemeral

1904 *Daily News*: If the United Kingdom were 'telephoned' in the same proportion there would be nearly 800,000 instruments on its various exchange systems, instead of some 250,000 only.

telephone box *n* (1904) a small enclosure containing a public telephone. The synonymous *call-box* dates from the 1880s

1904 *McClure's Magazine*: Golden could snatch only two opportunities to step into the telephone box that morning.

telephone directory *n* (1907) a book with an alphabetical list of telephone subscribers and their numbers. The synonymous *telephone book* is first recorded in 1915

1913 W. P. Eaton: We fail to find this sort of thing any more thrilling or 'literary' than the telephone directory.

telephotograph *n* (1900) a photograph of a distant object taken with a telephoto lens. A back-formation from *telephotographic* (1890s) which appears not to have survived the decade. The abbreviation *telephoto* is first recorded in 1898

1900 *Army & Navy Journal*: Good telephotographs have been obtained at a distance of over forty miles, and those taken beyond artillery range (ten miles) are on a sufficiently large scale to be of practical use.

teletype *n* (1904) a teleprinter. At first a generic term (coined from *tele-* and *typewriter*), it was registered as a trademark in the 1920s

1904 *Scientific American*: At Brussels it is the telecryptograph of Engineer Malcotti, at Berlin the teletype and the Heljes apparatus.

television *n* (1907) a system for reproducing an image at a distance on a screen by radio transmission. Theoretical discussion of such a system long preceded its implementation. The first name proposed for it appears to have been *televista* ('Dr. Low talks very modestly of the "televista" (the name he has given to his "seeing by wire" invention)', *Daily News* 1904). *Television* proved much more durable, although for many decades it was widely condemned by purists for being a 'hybrid' word—*tele-* being ultimately of Greek origin and -*vision* of Latin origin. See also **vision (1910)**, **televisor (1926), telly (1940),** and **TV (1948)**

> 1907 *Scientific American*: Now that the photo-telegraph invented by Prof. Korn is on the eve of being introduced into general practice, we are informed of some similar inventions in the same field, all of which tend to achieve some step toward the solution of the problem of television.

> 1913 *Wireless World*: The tele-vision,…being based upon the same principle as photo-telegraphy, is possible in itself.

> 1926 *Glasgow Herald*: Mr. John L. Baird, a native of Helensburgh,…recently invented an apparatus which makes television possible.

> 1942 T. S. Eliot: There are words which are ugly because of foreignness or ill-breeding (e.g. *television*): but I do not believe that any word well-established in its own language is either beautiful or ugly.

telewriter *n* (1908) an instrument which electrically reproduces in facsimile a written message; a sort of early fax machine. The term did not survive long, but long enough to have a verb *telewrite* coined from it by back-formation

> 1908 *Times*: An apparatus called a 'telewriter' for electrically reproducing at a distance handwriting, drawings [etc.].

> 1908 *Daily Chronicle*: The Lord Mayor, 'telewriting' to the Lord Mayor of Manchester, tendered his cordial greetings to him and his fellow-citizens from the City of London and himself.

temperamental *adj* (1907) liable to peculiar moods, having an erratic or neurotic temperament. *Temperamental* had been in use since the 17th century, but hitherto only in the neutral sense 'relating to temperament'

> 1907 *American Magazine*: The Celtic race is above all things temperamental.

Thermos flask *n* (1907) a flask capable of being kept hot or cold by the device (invented by Sir James Dewar) of surrounding the interior vessel with a vacuum jacket to prevent the conduction of heat. *Thermos* (from Greek *thermos* 'warm') was registered as a trademark in 1907

> 1909 *Westminster Gazette*: Lieutenant Shackleton testified to the fact that the Thermos flask helped him to perform his wonderful feats in the Antarctic.

thick ear *n* (1909) an ear swollen by a hard punch. Slang

> 1916 'Taffrail': I sed I'd give yer a thick ear if yer went on worryin' me.

third degree *n* (1900) an interrogation of a prisoner by the police involving the infliction of mental or physical suffering in order to bring about a confession or to secure information. Colloquial, originally US; the underlying idea seems to be of the 'third or highest degree' of severity

> 1900 *Everybody's Magazine*: From time to time a prisoner…claims to have had the Third Degree administered to him.

tin hat *n* (1903) a metal helmet, especially one worn for protection against shrapnel. A colloquialism usually associated with World War I and II usage

> 1903 A. M. Binstead: A Tommy in a tin hat as I squared with a couple o'blow.

> 1940 *War Illustrated*: 'Tin Hats' for the Heads of Britain's Defenders.

Tin Pan Alley *n* (1908) the world of the composers and publishers of popular music. Often rationalized as the nickname of a street in which such people congregate, have their offices, etc.: in New York, 28th Street and in London, Denmark Street. *Tin pan* was formerly a slang term for an old decrepit piano

> 1908 *Hampton's Broadway Magazine*: Oh it's a world in itself, is Tin Pan Alley. It has its laughter and its tears.

token *n* (1908) a voucher exchangeable for goods or services

> 1908 Rupert Brooke: Dear Mother, I am so sorry about the Boots token. I quite failed to realize…that it was wanted at once.

toodle-oo, tootle-oo *interj* (1907) goodbye. Its origins are uncertain: it could be an English mangling of French *à tout à l'heure* 'goodbye', but it might also have something to do with *toot* representing the sound of a motor-horn, signalling departure (compare **pip-pip (1904)**—the portmanteau form *tootle-pip* is first recorded in print in 1977, but is probably of the same antiquity as *toodle-oo*)

> 1907 *Punch*: 'Toodle-oo, old sport.' Mr. Punch turned round at the amazing words and gazed at his companion.

torch *n* (1901) a battery-powered portable lamp. A Briticism which often bewilders Americans new to it. In North America, *torch* persists in its original meaning 'flaming brand', and in early British usage the term *electric torch* was commonly used to distinguish the new sense from the old

> 1901 E. W. Hornung: I saw Raffles on my right striking with his torch; a face flew out of the darkness to meet the thick glass bulb with the glowing wire enclosed.

> 1902 *Windsor Magazine*: The 'Ever-Ready' Portable Electric Torch.

towelette *n* (1902) a small towel. Often serving as a genteel variation on the equally euphemistic *sanitary towel* (1896)

> 1902 *Great-Grandmama's Weekly*: Artmann's Hygienic towelettes. Superior to any other Sanitary Towels.

town planning *n* (1906) designing of urban areas so that houses, roads, and public amenities are planned as an integrated whole

> 1906 *Official Report of the Housing Deput. to the Prime Minister* (subject heading): Town Planning and Village Development Commission.

tractor *n* (1903) a rugged powerful motor vehicle for drawing farm machinery, especially one with large rear wheels and an elevated driving seat. The word (in Latin literally 'puller') was originally applied to a traction-engine for supplying power to machinery (it is first recorded in this sense in 1901), but the 'vehicle' sense soon ousted this

> 1903 *Motor Annual*: Rhodesia has appealed to motor manufacturers to supply motor-wagons or tractors for use specially in hilly country.

> 1917 *Isle of Ely & Wisbech Advertiser*: This Tractor will operate on any land… It maintains a firm grip without injuring the lightest surfaces.

traffic police *n* (1906) the branch of the police concerned with road traffic control

> 1906 *Collier's*: The effort to find out how it feels to be 'regulated' by the traffic police of New York.

transformation *n* (1901) an artificial head of hair worn by women. A further euphemism added to the already richly euphemistic nomenclature of the wig, but one which seems not to have survived beyond the first decade of the century

> 1906 *Referee*: When he got to the exit door he discovered to his horror that he had dragged off the lady's 'transformation', and it was hanging to his sleeve-link.

travelogue *n* (1903) an (illustrated) lecture about places and experiences encountered in the course of travel. Later applied to a film or broadcast about travel

> 1903 *Daily Chronicle*: Mr. Burton Holmes, an American entertainer new to London, delivered last evening the first of a series of 'Travelogues'.

> 1921 *Glasgow Herald*: The…Travelogue film, 'With Allenby in Palestine and Lawrence in Arabia'.

trial marriage *n* (1906) a period during which a couple live together to see if they are compatible enough for marriage. **Trial separation** is not recorded until 1968

> 1930 *New Statesman*: The Bishops of Miss Dunbar's Church recently gave an episcopal blessing to birth control, one prominent clergyman approving trial marriage.

tricar *n* (1903) A term applied to both a car with three wheels (also called a *tri-motor-car*) and a motor tricycle with a seat for a person or a carrier for luggage in front. At least in the former case the idea has survived, just (in the shape of the Reliant Robin), but the name has not

> 1904 *Saturday Review*: There is a great future for the useful tri-car.

> 1905 *Westminster Gazette*: Returning home in a tri-motor-car.

trinitrotoluene *n* (1908) a type of yellow crystalline compound used as a high explosive, better known by its abbreviated name **TNT (1915)**

Triscuit *n* (1906) The proprietary name (registered in 1906) of a type of American savoury cracker or biscuit, formed punningly from *biscuit*

> 1980 *Times*: Ketchup in a bottle, salt in a shaker, triscuits (a savory snack biscuit) in the box.

trivia *n* (1902) things of little importance; trivial matters. Originally used as the title of a book by L. P. Smith; from there it spread into the general language

> 1920 *Glasgow Herald*: [Arnold Bennett's] method suggests the amount of human interest and knowledge that may lurk in the trivia of holiday experience.

trouble-shooter *n* (1905) someone who traces and corrects faults in machinery and equipment. The word was originally applied specifically to someone working on a telegraph or telephone line

> 1905 *Strand Magazine*: A good looking young 'trouble-shooter'—as a mender of telephone lines is called—had…asked her to marry him.

trunk murder *n* (1905) a murder after which the body is hidden in a trunk (and often then dispatched by rail to a distant destination). A usage particularly prevalent in the inter-war years, when this method of disposing of the corpse seems to have been unusually popular in Britain

> 1925 P. Selver: At Madame Tussaud's…in the catalogue I found…Arthur Devereux, hanged 1905, known as the 'trunk murderer', because he hid the corpses of his victims in trunks.

> 1936 Graham Greene: Another clue in a trunk murder case.

tube *n* (1900) an underground railway. Usually applied specifically to the London underground railway system. As early as 1847 Queen Victoria was referring in her journal to a 'tube' for trains to run through ('We passed the famous *Swilly Rocks*, and saw the works they are making for the tube for the railroad'), but London's first underground railways (in the 1860s) were built by the 'cut-and-cover' method. The first genuine 'tube' was the electric City to Stockwell line, opened in 1890. The actual term *tube* seems to have originated with the so-called 'Twopenny Tube', the Central London Railway, opened in 1900

> 1902 *Westminster Gazette*: When the phrase 'the twopenny tube' came into existence…a similar electric 'tube' had been in regular running for close upon ten years.

> 1903 *Westminster Gazette*: Thousands of Tube travellers.

> 1905 Rider Haggard: The first part of my journey…was by Tube.

tube, tube it *v* (1902) to travel by underground railway. A British colloquialism which did not survive the first decade of the century

> 1902 *Daily Chronicle*: Yet my cherished hope was this—That under our Metropolis From end to end I'd tube it.

> 1907 *Daily Chronicle*: Shoppers can 'tube' to the West-end.

tube railway *n* (1900) an underground railway. British; a usage which has not survived

> 1900 *Daily News*: One of the most useful of the new tube railways.

tube-train *n* (1901) an underground train. British

> 1901 *Daily News*: Journeying to and from the scenes of their labour in tube-trains.

tyrannosaurus *n* (1906) a large carnivorous dinosaur of the Cretaceous period. The name (literally 'tyrant lizard' in Greek) was coined in 1905 by H. F. Osborn, and first appeared in a 1906 issue of the *Bulletin of the American Museum of Natural History*. The species name *Tyrannosaurus rex* is also first recorded in 1906

> 1927 Haldane & Huxley: The Tyrannosaurus…stood over twenty feet high.

underpass *n* (1904) a (section of) road providing passage beneath another road or a railway; a subway. Originally US

> 1904 Springfield (Massachusetts) *Weekly Republican*: The need of an underpass at the union railroad station in this city.

undies *n* (1906) articles of girls' or women's underwear. Colloquial

> 1906 *Punch*: She'd blouses for Sundays, And marvellous 'undies' Concocted of ribbons and lace.

vacuum cleaner *n* (1903) an electrical appliance for removing dust (from carpets and other floor-ing, soft furnishings, etc.) by suction. The earliest known record of the term is in the name of a commercial company, the 'Vacuum Cleaner Company'. The abbreviated form *vacuum* is first recorded in 1910. A very short-lived alternative designation was *vacuum cleanser* (1903). See also **Hoover (1926)**

> 1903 *Westminster Gazette*: There is a machine at work, called the 'vacuum cleanser', which gives them all, in turn, a thorough 'spring cleaning'.

> 1907 *Yesterday's Shopping* (1969): The 'Witch' Dust Extractor is a vacuum cleaner suitable alike for carpets, upholstery, clothing, &c.

> 1910 *Judge*: A vacuum was the only thing she could be trusted to handle with safety.

veleta *n* (1900) a ballroom round dance for couples in triple time, originating in England in 1900 and popular before World War I. The name comes from Spanish *veleta* 'weather-vane'

> 1978 S. Sherlock: We danced the Veleta, the Gay Gordons, the Dashing White Sergeant.

velodrome *n* (1902) a stadium at which cycle races are held. A borrowing from French, at a time when cycling was a very popular sport and pastime in Britain

> 1902 *Times*: The Alexandra Palace Velodrome.

Veronal *n* (1903) Used as a trade-name for barbitone, a drug used as a sedative or to induce sleep. It was formed from *Verona*, the name of a city in northern Italy

> 1903 *Merck's Annual Report*: Veronal has been thoroughly tested in a large number of noted pub-lic and private hospitals.

vet *v* (1904) to examine carefully and critically for deficiencies or errors. Often applied specifically to investigating the suitability of someone for a post that requires loyalty and trustworthiness. Originally a facetious adaptation of an earlier (and now little used) sense 'to examine (an animal) medically'

> 1904 Rudyard Kipling: These are our crowd… They've been vetted, an' we're putting 'em through their paces.

> 1963 *Times*: He asked whether Vassall had been vetted as necessary for his special post, and was told that he would be revetted before he went.

vote-getter *n* (1906) a person, policy, etc. that attracts votes. The converse *vote-loser* is not recorded before the 1960s

> 1906 Springfield (Massachusetts) *Weekly Republican*: He is also a strong campaigner, and has proved himself a vote-getter.

voyeur *n* (1900) someone who gains sexual satisfaction from observing others' sex organs or sexual activities. A borrowing from French, where it was derived from *voir* 'to see'. See also **voyeurism (1924)**

> 1900 H. Blanchamp: The houses of ill-fame have a *clientèle* of 'voyeurs' of both sexes.

war crime *n* (1906) an act committed during a war which contravenes the conventions of warfare. The term *war criminal* is also first recorded in 1906. See also **war trial (1949)**

> 1906 L. Oppenheim: Violations of rules regarding warfare are war crimes only when committed without an order of the belligerent government concerned. If members of the armed forces commit violations by order of their government, they are not war criminals and may not be punished by the enemy; the latter can, however, resort to reprisals.

> 1945 *Daily Express*: The United Nations War Crimes Commission announced last night: Hermann Goering's name was placed…on the first list of persons charged with war crimes.

water wings *n* (1907) inflatable floats which can be fixed to the upper arms of someone learning to swim, in order to give increased buoyancy

> 1907 *Yesterday's Shopping*: All Water Wings…support a man as easily as a boy…on just the level at which a person can swim or float comfortably.

week-end *v* (1901) to spend a week-end holiday. A fashionable pastime among the leisured classes in the years before World War I, productive also of usages such as *week-ending* and *week-endize*

1901 *Daily Chronicle*: Where shall we week end?

1906 B. Vaughan: You see 'week-endings' have become part of the British Constitution, and nowadays everybody…has to be out of town in the season, say from Saturday to Tuesday.

1910 Robert Bridges: I was glad to get your note saying that you wd week-endize.

welfare *n* (1903) maintenance or improvement of the social and economic conditions of a particular group of people. In early usage the term usually refers to provision made by firms for their employees, but from the 1930s onwards it increasingly connotes help for the poor and other disadvantaged members of society, especially as provided by the government. The word initially appears only in compound forms, such as *welfare work* and *welfare manager*; it is not recorded in isolation until 1918

1904 *Century Magazine*: The welfare manager…who may be either a man or a woman, is a recognized intermediary between the employers and employees of mercantile houses and manufacturing plants.

1918 Arnold Bennett: Canteens, and rest-rooms, and libraries, and sanitation, and all this damned 'welfare'.

wellington *n* (1907) a waterproof boot usually reaching the knee, worn in wet or muddy conditions. The more or less synonymous *gumboot* dates from the middle of the 19th century. The original *wellington* (*boot*) (commemorating the Duke of Wellington, and dating from around 1817) was a type of high leather boot covering the knee in front and cut away behind. See also **welly (1961)**

1907 *Yesterday's Shopping*: Black glazed rubber boots. Ladies' Wellingtons.

white supremacy *n* (1902) the theory that white people are inherently superior to and therefore entitled to rule over black people. The term lay relatively dormant until the late 1950s, when events in southern Africa and the southern states of the US brought it to the surface

1931 Winston Churchill: Upon the rebound from this there must inevitably have been a strong reassertion of local white supremacy.

1967 *Freedomways*: The black student is being educated in this country as if he were being programmed in white supremacy and self-hatred.

wholewheat *n* (1903) wholemeal

1903 *Harper's Magazine*: Four sandwiches… Two of wholewheat bread with peanut butter.

willy, willie *n* (1905) (A children's word for) the penis. British. From the male forename. First recorded as a dialect form from the northwest of England

1977 J. Wilson: A younger male [baboon]…fingered its crimson penis… 'It's playing with its *willie*!' Nicky squealed.

wind of change *n* (1905) change thought of metaphorically as a wind. Institutionalized as a phrase by its use by British prime minister Harold Macmillan in a speech to the South African parliament in Cape Town on 3 February 1960

1905 S. Naidu: The wind of change for ever blows Across the tumult of our way.

1960 Harold Macmillan: The wind of change is blowing through the continent.

1960 *Economist*: This is but one way in which the mining complex of De Beers, Anglo American and Rhodesian Anglo American is adapting itself to the winds of change in Africa.

wind-power *n* (1903) power generated by harnessing the energy of the wind. A concept as old as the windmill, but the term anticipates late-20th-century ecological concerns

1903 *Daily Chronicle*: Wind-power, water-power, and solar-power are running to waste.

windscreen *n* (1905) the front window of a motor vehicle. A specialization of the general sense 'something that screens you from the wind', which dates from the mid 19th century

1905 *Westminster Gazette*: With its hood and wind-screen, [the car] is well fitted for the use of the general practitioner.

windshield *n* (1902) A mainly US alternative to **windscreen (1905)**

> 1911 *New York Times*: Speedwell 1911 four-passenger, semi-racer…extraordinary equipment includes top, windshield, shock absorbers, [etc.].

wireless *n* (1903) the transmission of speech and other uncoded signals by means of radio waves. *Wireless* began life as an adjective in the early 1890s, when it was used in such expressions as *wireless telegraphy* and *wireless telephony* to talk about the new systems being developed by Marconi and others to transmit signals through the air by electromagnetic waves, without the aid of wires. Below is the first known example of its being used as a noun in print. It was first used in the sense 'a radio receiver' in the 1920s. Its replacement by **radio (1907)** was a long but inexorable process which got properly under way around the time of World War II

> 1903 *New York Commercial Advertiser*: First in this great field of making the 'wireless' a handmaid of commerce is the de Forrest system, which has won the approval also of the United States government.

> 1927 T. E. Lawrence: We have no wireless, and I don't look at papers.

wire-tapping *n* (1904) making a (usually secret) connection to a telephone or telegraph circuit in order to intercept messages or eavesdrop. Originally US. A derivative of *wire-tapper*, which dates from the 1890s

> 1904 *Outing*: Despite the habitual exposure in American newspapers of the…'wire-tapping' swindle, the victim continues to be parted from his thousands with painful frequency.

women's movement *n* (1902) the movement promoting women's political and other rights. The term was relatively little used until the 1960s. See also **suffragette (1906), women's liberation (1966)**

> 1902 H. Blackburn: The Married Women's Property Bill occupied the main attention of those engaged in the women's movement.

> 1968 *Ramparts*: The most active of the new radical women's movements is in Berkeley—which should surprise no one.

world war *n* (1909) a war involving all or many of the most powerful nations in the world. Initially a theoretical term (probably translated from German *Weltkrieg*), it was being applied to the 1914–18 war in its first year

> 1909 *Westminster Gazette*: This…is the type of dirigible by which in a world-war…360,000 German troops could be transported from Calais to Dover in half an hour.

> 1914 B. Vaughan: What the South African War failed to teach I really believe this world-war will bring home to us.

wump *n* (1908) a foolish or feeble person. A word of unascertained origins, although it obviously has some semantic and phonological affinity with **wimp (1920)**. The first recorded occurrence of it is in one of Rupert Brooke's letters. It does not seem to have survived the 1930s

> 1908 Rupert Brooke: Abercrombie…is a Metrical Motor Bicyclist, a mumbly Wump, but often splendid.

yellow pages *n* (1908) Originally, in the US, an index printed on yellow paper. The specific application to the classified section (later a separate supplement) of a telephone directory, listing services by category, seems to date from the 1950s. The pages first appeared in British phone books at the end of the 1960s

> 1908 *Sears, Roebuck Catalog*: See the yellow pages in back of this book.

> 1985 *Punch*: I started by ringing a few cowboys through the Yellow Pages, just to check on prices.

Zeppelin *n* (1900) a dirigible airship, originally and specifically one of a type constructed by Count Ferdinand von Zeppelin in Germany in 1900. See also **Zep (1915)**

> 1900 *Whitaker's Almanack*: The Zeppelin Air-ship, now in construction on an island of the Boden See, is a cylindrical frame of aluminium in partitions, each holding a gas-bag.

zip *n* (1900) energy, force. Colloquial. A figurative use of *zip* in the sense 'a brief, sharp, hissing sound'

> 1900 George Lorimer: I need…a little more zest for my food, and a little more zip about my work.

zwitterion *n* (1906) a molecule or ion with separate positively and negatively charged atoms or groups. Borrowed from German, where it had been coined in 1897 by F. W. Küster, from *Zwitter* 'hermaphrodite'

> 1906 G. Mann: Ions which are simultaneously electro-positive and electro-negative (Bredig), and which Küster calls 'Zwitter-ions', i.e. hermaphrodite-ions.

In the second decade of the 20th century the world was convulsed by four years of terrible war. By the time the armistice was signed in November 1918, all the major English-speaking nations of the world had become embroiled in the conflict, and over 8.5 million lives had been lost in action. The massive scale of the slaughter, the appalling conditions on the Western Front, and detailed coverage in the press combined to impress the *Great War* deeply on contemporary minds, and not surprisingly a large proportion of the new vocabulary coming into English during the decade arose from it. There was plenty of demand for neologisms, too: new methods of warfare, new types of weapon, the advent of military aircraft, not to mention the unprecedented levels of civilian involvement, all played their part in expanding the English lexicon.

In the trenches of the *Western Front* the troops were *strafed* by *creeping barrages, trench mortars* (or *toc emmas*, or *Minnies*), *pipsqueaks*, and *whizzbangs*. At the battle of Ypres in 1915 the Germans used *poison gas* for the first time, and *gas attack* became the great fear; *gas masks* were developed to protect against the deadly *mustard gas*. Trench life was a matter of waiting, in a wilderness of mud and *shell holes*, for the moment to go *over the top* into a hail of machine-gun fire—purveyed on the Allied side by the *Lewis gun*. The incidence of *shell shock* was high. Horrendous injuries—not to mention afflictions such as *gas gangrene* and *trench foot*—left the field hospitals and *clearing stations* full of *amputees* and potential *basket cases*. The *walking wounded* could consider themselves lucky if they had an injury serious enough to warrant a return to *Blighty*. In 1916, German troops peering over the parapet with their equivalent of the *trenchoscope* would have seen *tanks* advancing towards them for the first time.

In the skies above the battlefields, the principles of *air warfare* were being laid down by the *air forces* of both sides. The *dogfights* and the air *aces* had the high profile, but *aerial reconnaissance* had an important part to play too. The distinction between *fighters* and *bombers* was established (the latter equipped in due course with *bomb bays*). Although protected by *camouflage*, they had *anti-aircraft* fire (colloquially *Archibald*) and *tracer* to deal with (which might *spike-bozzle* them). Both the *Allies* and the Germans knew that in the new warfare of the 20th century, *air supremacy* was becoming a prerequisite of victory.

At sea, the new shape on the horizon might be a *battle cruiser*, a *carrier*, or even a *Q ship* (or *mystery ship*). To counter the threat of German *U-boats* (and indeed Allied *subs*), *depth charges* were being developed.

On the *home front*, meanwhile, the *war effort* was being pursued by other means. *Munitioneers* and *munitionettes* toiled day and night in the factories, turning out the weapons and ammunition needed at the front, while others in *reserved occupations* kept the home fires burning. *Salvage* recycled valuable materials. There was *rationing* to put up with (although *food parcels* could still be sent to the troops), and the predations of the *profiteers*. *Coupons* ruled people's lives, as they would again during World War II, and in the US people were encouraged to *Hooverize*. For the first time in a war, civilians were subjected to *air-raids*; German *Zeps* were flying over England, and towns had to be *blacked out*. In France, cities were bombarded by the Germans' *Big Berthas*. Anti-German feeling was whipped up to fever pitch—the *Hun* (or *Boche*, or *Fritzes*, or *Jerry*, or *krauts*) had become baby-bayoneting hate figures, and German shepherd dogs had to be renamed *Alsatians*— and the animus was scarcely less against the *conscientious objectors*, or *conchies*, who refused to fight, and received contemptuous nicknames such as *Cuthbert* and *Percy*. Anything that smacked of *defeatism* had to be ruthlessly suppressed. Meanwhile there was a steady demand for new recruits to *join up* (or to be conscripted into *national service*, or in the US *selective service*). When they got to France, they would have encountered several mangled French expressions that had infiltrated the argot of the trenches, a few of which (*napoo, san fairy ann, toot sweet*) found their way home and survived for several decades.

The *ceasefire* came on 11 November 1918, a day commemorated thereafter as *Armistice Day*. Those who had survived for the *duration* (sometimes as *POWs*) would return to a very different world from the one they left. A *New World Order* was proclaimed; plans for a *League of Nations* were put in place; *appeasement* was not yet a dirty word. But in Russia there had been a revolution, bringing such terms as *Bolshevik* and *commissar, Leninist* and *Trotskyite, Comintern* and *soviet* into the English language, not to mention the portentous monosyllable *red* 'communist'. *Spanish flu* killed more than had died during the war. And already the possibility of an *atomic bomb* existed in the minds of scientists.

The exigencies of war had advanced aeronautical technology by leaps and bounds, and aeronautical terminology was keeping pace. Pilots could *land* their aircraft (at an *airport* or *air station*) and *taxi*, and also, alas, *crash* (hopefully wearing a *crash helmet*— but your plane would be a *write-off*). They could do *aerobatics* in their '*bus*'. The commercial possibilities of flying began to be exploited, with terms like *airmail* (or *air-post*), *airbus* (or *aerial bus*), and *airline* coming into the language. We first became acquainted with *cockpits* and *undercarriages*, with *test pilots* and *automatic pilots*.

The commercial development of the private motor car, on the other hand, had to take a back seat during the war years, and the terminology of *motorism* expanded far more slowly than it had in the previous decade. The *convertible* appeared, complete with *hubcaps*, and the sound of the *klaxon* was heard for the first time. Traffic arrangements developed, with *one-way* streets, *traffic signals* (ignored by *jaywalkers*), and *parks* for leaving your vehicle in; on the down side, however, the *traffic jam* appeared.

In the world of science, Albert Einstein followed up his special theory of relativity (see p. 2) with the general theory of relativity, and the concept of *space-time* made its first appearance. The *isotope* and the atomic *nucleus* were named, as were *radon*, the *curie*, and *superconductors*. The biological sciences gained *chromosomes, genes*, and *vitamins*.

The trickle of Freudian terminology which began in the 1900s increased to a flood, including *Freudian* itself; we learned about the *Oedipus complex* and *anal eroticism, fixation, denial, repression*, and the *unconscious*. It was joined by a new set of terms introduced by the Swiss psychologist Carl Gustav Jung, who had been a colleague of Freud but split with him in 1912: *extrovert* and *introvert, collective unconscious, persona,* and *psyche.* It was a productive time for the science of the mind, whose other new lexical contributions included *autism, behaviourism, schizophrenia,* and *sex drive.* On the subject of sex, it was also the decade that saw the first recorded use of *homosexual* as a noun. *Bisexual* and *cross-dressing* made their debut too, but the time for advanced *homo-erotic* views could scarcely be said to have arrived when they were joined by *faggot, poofter,* and the use of *normal* to mean 'heterosexual'. The latest euphemism for 'contraception' was *birth control.*

The development of radio for public entertainment was put on hold for World War I, although new terms like *cat's whisker, crystal receiver,* and *static* would become familiar when it got under way in the next decade. In its absence, you could always do a *crossword puzzle.* But by far the most popular form of public entertainment was the cinema. The *movies* were all *silent,* of course (although there was talk of *talkies*), but none the less eagerly devoured for that. Down at the local *cinema* (or *movie theater,* or *picturedrome*), fans could see the latest *feature film* (or *picture play*)—perhaps a *western*—and swoon over their favourite *film stars* (or *movie stars,* or *cinema stars*). Additionally they would probably be able to watch a *newsreel,* a *topical,* or a *cartoon.* Terms like *director* and *script-writer* became familiar, as did *location, scenario, pan,* and *studio.* The appearance of the terms *Cinephone* and *Technicolor* gave promise of developments to come.

Dance crazes of the time included the *bunny hug,* the *cooch,* the *shimmy,* and the *tango.* The *foxtrot* also made its debut. But in the long run it would be *jazz* and the *blues* that made a permanent mark on 20th-century music.

Cellophane-wrapped *instant* foodstuffs bought in the local *self-service* store (or *cash-and-carry,* or *groceteria*) could be stored in the *kitchenette* of your *double-glazed maisonette*—where you might also have a shiny new *toaster,* some *stainless steel* cutlery (no more need for those old-fashioned knife polishers), a *pressure cooker,* some *Pyrex* dishes, and an *immersion heater* for constant hot water.

Fashion from the *front line* introduced the *trench coat,* but at home it was the era of the *hobble skirt,* the *split skirt,* and the *liberty bodice.* The *scarf* became a head-covering (so necessary for those breezy motor-car journeys—although not, perhaps, if you had had your hair boyishly *bobbed*).

In the visual arts, the defining 20th-century term *abstract* made its bow. The *avant-garde* proclaimed the arrival of *Cubism* and *Fauvism, post-impressionism* and *vorticism.*

abstract *adj* (1915) Of painting, sculpture, etc.: dealing with abstract form; non-representational. A key term in 20th-century fine art, both as a technical label and—perhaps particularly—as a put-down by those out of sympathy with such work

> 1915 *Forum* (New York): This painter no doubt has tried to be significantly abstract... Dore shows an uninteresting abstract canvas.

ace *n* (1917) an outstanding pilot. Applied specifically during World War I to one who had shot down ten enemy aircraft. A translation of French *as*

> 1917 *Times*: Second Lieutenant Lufbery, the 'ace' of the American Lafayette flying Squadron.

> 1975 *Daily Mail*: A gang of 'real stinkers' have raided a top wartime air ace and stolen his most prized souvenir—a 6ft. German propellor.

adviser *n* (1915) a soldier sent to advise or help the government or army of a foreign country. Often a euphemism for a combatant soldier—a usage which became particularly notorious during the Vietnam War

> 1915 *Handbook of the Turkish Army* (Intelligence Dept., Cairo): There is every reason to believe that it was the policy of the Turkish military authorities and their German military advisers to form a certain number [of reserve divisions].

> 1972 *Guardian*: If the Australian Labour Party wins the election and the troops come home—there are only 150 'advisers' left in Vietnam—no one doubts that ANZUK would break up.

aerial bus *n* (1910) a passenger aircraft. This early application of the terminology of land transport to the air (sometimes abbreviated to *bus*) soon died out, but *bus* continued in use as a slang term for an aeroplane (see **bus (1916)**), and *gun-bus* was used as the name of a World War I Vickers aeroplane which carried a machine-gun. See also **airbus (1910)**

> 1910 *Flight*: A Blériot 'Bus' being Built... M. Blériot...has nearly completed a four-seater mono-plane...The day of the aerial 'bus will soon be with us.

aerial mail, aerial post *n* (1911) See **airmail (1913)**

aerial reconnaissance *n* (1914) military reconnaissance conducted from an aircraft. A tactic widely exploited during World War I

> 1914 *R.F.C. Training Manual*: Aerial reconnaissance...may be considered under three heads: strategical, tactical and protective.

aerobatics *n* (1917) feats of expert aviation, especially as performed for display. Coined on the model of *acrobatics*. In the inter-war heydey of aerial displays, the verb *aerobat* was back-formed from it ('Mr. George Murray aerobated in Capt. Broad's special Moth', *Flight* (1930))

> 1917 *'Contact'*: Watching the aerobatics and sham fights of the pool pupils.

> 1958 Nevil Shute: Rather than keep him at the dreary round of circuits and bumps I had been teaching him aerobatics.

aerocar *n* (1910) a flying conveyance; a (passenger) aircraft. A term that failed to survive the 1920s

> 1910 *Flight*: Airmen...are either Aeronauts or Aviators, according as the Aerocar that they control is an Airship or an Aeroplane.

> 1926 *Chambers's Journal*: Aero-cars may take off from here.

aero-engine *n* (1913) an engine used for powering an aircraft

> 1963 *Listener*: Rolls-Royce are to put 16,000 employees in their aero-engine division on short time.

air bomb *n* (1914) See **bomb (1909)**

airbus *n* (1910) a passenger aircraft. A word which initially enjoyed little success (compare **aerial bus (1910)**), but was subsequently revived as a specific term for a wide-bodied jet carrying a large number of passengers over a relatively short distance (see the second quote below)

> 1910 *Times*: Probably when there are air-buses we shall call their drivers airmen.

> 1960 *Aeroplane*: A subsonic short- to medium-stage high passenger-density aircraft, for operation at low fares. This we call the Air-Bus.

air cavalry *n* (1917) a formation of aircraft which flies into action in a way reminiscent of cavalry riding into action. Originally a short-lived coinage, produced during a war in which horses still played an important part, but revived during the Vietnam War for formations of ground-attack helicopters

> 1917 *'Contact'*: We shall see a great extension of ground attacks by air cavalry.

> 1965 *Observer*: The United States is about to reinforce its troops in Vietnam with a new high-powered 'air-cavalry' division.

airdrome *n* (1917) See **aerodrome (1909)**

air force *n* (1917) that branch of a country's armed forces which is concerned wth air warfare. A term apparently originally applied to the newly formed Royal Air Force in Britain, but soon the general term for any such organization

> 1917 *Act of Parliament*: An Act to make provision for the establishment, administration, and discipline of an Air Force, the establishment of an Air Council, and for purposes connected therewith.

airline *n* (1914) (an organization offering) a service of scheduled (passenger) flights. A re-application of the earlier sense of *line*, '(a company operating) a shipping service over particular routes', which dates from the mid 19th century. Despite the early Australian example, the term does not seem to have come into its own before the 1930s

> 1914 *Argus* (Melbourne): The Defence flying school at Point Cook has been inaccessible...except by air line.

airmail *n* (1913) mail conveyed by air; a service for conveying letters, parcels, etc., by air. Not the earliest term for this— *air-post, aerial mail,* and *aerial post* predate it—but easily the longest-lived

> 1913 *Stamp Collecting*: There have been many other German air mail flights.

airport *n* (1919) a place where civil aircraft take off and land, usually with surfaced runways and passenger facilities. The term was fairly well established by the middle of the 1920s

> 1919 *Aerial Age Weekly*: There is being established at Atlantic City the first 'air port' ever established, the purposes of which are...to provide a municipal aviation field,...to supply an air port for trans-Atlantic liners, whether of the seaplane, land aeroplane or dirigible balloon type.

air-post *n* (1911) See **airmail (1913)**

> 1911 *Daily Mail*: First Air-Post... An air post cannot be expected as yet to behave with the same clockwork regularity as an earth post.

air-raid *n* (1914) an attack by hostile aircraft, especially with bombs. One of the key terms of 20th-century warfare. The alternative *aerial raid* is first recorded in 1915, but it does not appear to have survived very long

> 1915 *Lancet*: The dangers of an aerial raid.

> 1916 F. W. Lanchester: Air-raids on Great Britain by Zeppelin do not pay.

airspace *n* (1911) the atmosphere above a country, deemed to be under its jurisdiction. A concept in international law which only assumed importance after the development of aeroplanes

> 1911 R. Wallace: A State should have full dominion in the air space above its territory.

air station *n* (1911) an airfield with facilities for the maintenance of aircraft. A usage which gradually lost currency as the century progressed, except (in Britain) as part of the designation of Royal Naval Air Service bases

> 1911 *Aeronautics*: Starting and Landing Stations... A cumbersome expression... 'Air Stations' have been suggested as alternatives.

air supremacy *n* (1916) dominance of one country's air force over another's

> 1916 *Sphere*: The latest German attempt to challenge British air supremacy.

air terminus *n* (1919) the terminal point of an airline. A term quickly replaced by **air terminal (1921)**

> 1919 *Sphere*: The air terminus for London is Hounslow.

air warfare *n* (1916) warfare involving the use of aircraft, both offensively and defensively. A prospect fully foreseen before the end of the 19th century, and originally lexicalized as *aerial warfare* ('Aerial warfare...likely to ensue when aerial navigation becomes an accomplished fact,' *Knowledge* (1895))

> 1916 *Fortnightly Review*: Air warfare on the scale indicated...opens up possibilities in the way of air raids for landing considerable bodies of men.

alcohol-free *adj* (1913) containing little or no alcohol. A word with a stop-start career: although first recorded in 1913, there is no further evidence of its existence for over 60 years; its modern usage began to blossom in the late 1970s

> 1979 *Washington Post*: Now C. Schmidt & Sons, a Philadelphia brewery, has something the Saudis want—alcohol-free beer.

allergy *n* (1911) hypersensitivity to the action of some particular foreign material, for example certain foods, pollens, micro-organisms, etc. An adaptation of German *Allergie*, which was coined by C. E. von Pirquet in 1906 from Greek *allos* 'other' and *ergon* 'activity', the underlying meaning being 'changed reaction'. English acquired the adjective *allergic* in the same year

> 1911 C. E. von Pirquet: We might rightly use the word 'allergy'...as a clinical conception... The practical method of diagnosis by the allergic reactions will be extended to other diseases.

Allies *n* (1914) the allied forces or states which fought against the Central Powers in World War I, or against the Axis in World War II

> 1914 *Times*: A Note was to have been presented to the Porte on Friday asking for...the withdrawal of the German officers and men from the Turkish ships [etc.]... Failing satisfaction in these respects, diplomatic relations with the Allies would cease.

Alsatian *n* (1917) a large breed of dog of German origin and somewhat wolf-like appearance. Its German name is *deutscher Schäferhund*, and it was introduced into the US with an English version of this, *German shepherd dog*. This would not have gone down very well in Britain during World War I, however, so there it was registered with the Kennel Club as the *Alsatian*. It has no known connection with Alsace

> 1922 Robert Leighton: The dogs lately introduced into Great Britain as the Alsatian Wolfdog and into the United States as the German sheepdog...The Alsatian was known in England before the war.

Alzheimer's disease *n* (1912) a serious disorder of the brain which manifests itself in premature senility. The term, first published in the *Journal of Nervous and Mental Diseases* in 1912, commemorates the German neurologist Alois Alzheimer (1864–1915). It remained largely in the vocabulary of medical specialists until the 1970s, when the higher profile of the disease brought it forcibly to public notice. The abbreviated name *Alzheimer's* is first recorded in 1954

> 1912 S. C. Fuller (title): Alzheimer's Disease (*senium præcox*): the report of a case and review of published cases.

amputee *n* (1910) someone who has lost a limb or other part of the body by amputation. The first recorded instance of the word suggests that it may originally have been a facetious formation, but by the time of World War II there was no question of its seriousness

> 1910 *St. Bartholomew's Hospital Journal*: Please put the patient both to bed, and then, perhaps, we'll see Which is the amputated part and which the amputee.

> 1939 *Lancet*: In place of endless gadgets we now have a few standard 'set ups' round which limbs to suit any particular amputee can be constructed.

anal eroticism, anal erotism *n* (1913) erotic gratification from stimulation in the anal region. An adaptation of German *analerotisch*, coined by Sigmund Freud in 1908. See also **anal (1930)**

> 1913 Ernest Jones (*title*): Hate and Anal Erotism in the Obsessional Neurosis.

anti-aircraft *adj* (1914) used for defence against hostile aircraft. The abbreviation *AA* is first recorded in the same year. See also **Archibald (1915)**

> 1914 *Scotsman*: An anti-aircraft gun of the Third Army Corps.

anti-freeze *adj, n* (1913) (a substance) added to water, especially in an engine, to stop it freezing. The noun is first recorded in 1935

> 1937 D. Aldis: They kept the Ford out in the street in front of the house. It worked all right if they remembered to get it filled with anti-freeze.

Anzac *n* (1915) A word made up from the initials of *Australian and New Zealand Army Corps*, and used colloquially for a member of that corps, or to designate any Australian or New Zealand serviceman.

> 1915 *Sphere*: The term, Anzac, which recent events on the Gallipoli Peninsula have rendered so prominent, is derived as follows [etc.].

> 1920 *Chambers's Journal*: The thing had been started by one of the Anzacs venturing the modest opinion that if Britain had had a million Australian troops, they…would be…in Berlin.

appeasement *n* (1919) pacification of an enemy. The extension of the original general sense 'appeasing' into the geopolitical sphere began after World War I with positive connotations of bringing peace and lessening the likelihood of a renewed outbreak of conflict. It was not until the late 1930s, when British prime minister Neville Chamberlain applied the term to his policy towards Germany, which was reviled in many quarters as conciliation by the offering of excessive concessions, that the word took on the negative aspect which it has retained ever since. The verb *appease* in this sense is first recorded in 1939

> 1919 *General Smuts' Messages to the Empire*: In our policy of European settlement the appease-ment of Germany…becomes one of cardinal importance.

> 1920 Winston Churchill: Here again I counsel prudence and appeasement. Try to secure a really representative Turkish governing authority, and come to terms with it.

> 1936 Anthony Eden: I assure the House that it is the appeasement of Europe as a whole that we have constantly before us.

> 1938 *Times*: The policy of international appeasement must of course be pressed forward… There must be appeasement not only of the strong but of the weak… With the policy of appeasement must go the policy of preparation—preparation not so much for war as against war.

> 1939 *Annual Register*: One of the new Foreign Minister's first steps was to extend to Germany the methods of appeasement—as the Prime Minister was fond of calling them—which were now being tried with Italy… So far were they from trying to 'appease' the Dictators that they might rather be described as 'facing up' to them.

> 1939 *New Statesman*: First, provided that there is a Russian pact, proposals that now smell of appeasement in the most dangerous sense at once become proper and, indeed, the only possible policy.

Archibald, Archie *n* (1915) an anti-aircraft gun. British military slang. Originally applied to those used by the Germans in World War I, but it survived to be around at the beginning of World War II. Also used as a verb, meaning 'to fire at with an anti-aircraft gun'. Allegedly the name came from a British pilot who when he was fired at in the air quoted a popular music-hall refrain of the time—'Archibald, certainly not!'

> 1915 *Sphere*: They laugh at the 'Archibalds' which fling destruction at them whenever they come within range.

> 1917 'Contact': Only somebody who has been Archied from Plusprès can realise what it means to fly right over the stronghold at four thousand feet.

> 1939 *News Review*: On each occasion fighters and heavy 'Archie' barrages drove the Nazis off.

Armistice Day *n* (1919) the day, 11 November 1918, on which the armistice was concluded which brought World War I to an end; hence, any anniversary of that day. See also **Remembrance Day (1921)**

> 1919 *Times*: The Armistice-day service at St. Paul's Cathedral will be the office of Holy Communion… The first anniversary of Armistice Day was celebrated throughout the Empire yester-day.

artificial *adj* (1913) Denoting an apparatus that performs the functions of a particular human organ in place of a diseased or injured organ

1913 *British Medical Journal*: Salicylic acid injected into a vein was excreted in some cases more rapidly by this artificial kidney than by the normal excretory channels.

assembly line *n* (1914) a group of machines and workers concerned with the progressive assembly of some product. Originally US. The key concept of 20th-century mass production made its original impact in the US motor industry

1914 *Engineering*: The study of the finishing and assembling of front-axle components shows how labor-costs may be…reduced…by the use of sliding assembly lines, chain-driven for the final assembling, but having the partial assemblies moved by hand.

atomic bomb *n* (1914) a bomb whose explosive power derives from the fission of heavy atomic nuclei. At the close of the 20th century it can still cause a frisson to recall that although such weapons were not built in reality until the mid 1940s, they were being discussed while World War I was in progress. The alternative **atom bomb** is not recorded before 1945

1914 H. G. Wells: The three atomic bombs, the new bombs that would continue to explode indefinitely.

1917 S. Strunsky: When you can drop just one atomic bomb and wipe out Paris or Berlin, war will have become monstrous and impossible.

atomic power *n* (1914) the power released by the fission of heavy atomic nuclei. Virtually a synonym of the slightly earlier **atomic energy (1906)**. In time applied more specifically to the power of nuclear weapons and to the electricity produced by nuclear power stations

1914 H. G. Wells: The year of crisis that followed the release of atomic power.

audio *adj, n, prefix* (1913) Coined (from Latin *audire* 'to hear', and perhaps partly on the model of *audiometer* (1879)) to denote sound, especially recorded or transmitted sound. At first largely restricted to the combination *audio-frequency*, but in the 1930s its use began to broaden out. Compare **video (1935)**

1913 *Proceedings of the Institute of Radio Engineers*: The audio-frequency produced is equal to the difference in the fundamental oscillation frequencies.

1934 *Wireless World*: The division between radio and audio at 10 kilocycles is quite arbitrary.

Aussie *n, adj* (1917) (an) Australian. A colloquialism whose currency was no doubt spread by Australian soldiers' participation in World War I

1957 S. Hope: Most Aussies, contrary to popular belief, are town-dwellers.

autism *n* (1912) A term coined by E. Bleuler (originally in the Latinized form *autismus*) to denote a mental condition characterized by extreme self-absorption and lack of contact with reality. The specific modern application to a childhood mental illness characterized by the inability to communicate with or relate to other people appears to be a post-World War II development. The word means literally 'self-ism'. The derivatives *autistic* and *autistically* are also first recorded in 1912

1912 E. Bleuler: When we look more closely we find amongst all normal people many and important instances where thought is divorced both from logic and from reality. I have called these forms of thinking *autistic*, corresponding to the idea of schizophrenic autismus… The unconscious can think logically or autistically.

1912 A. Hoch: The chief traits which had existed before the mental breakdown were those which I at that time called the shut-in tendencies—tendencies to which Professor Bleuler has recently applied the term autism.

1962 *Guardian*: London County Council has opened an experimental unit at the health centre in Guildford Street for the treatment and diagnosis of autistic children.

automatic pilot *n* (1916) a device in an aircraft for maintaining a set course and height. Originally applied to a device of this sort manufactured in Britain by Sperry. See also **autopilot (1935)**

1921 *Aeronautics*: The automatic pilot…enables the pilot of an aeroplane to leave the machine entirely to its own devices.

avant-garde *n* (1910) the pioneers or innovators in any art in a particular period. A borrowing from French, where it means literally 'vanguard'

1910 *Daily Telegraph*: The new men of mark in the *avant-garde*.

aviette *n* (1912) an engineless aeroplane or glider. A borrowing from French. It did not survive beyond the 1920s, and although the search for viable human-powered flight continued thereafter, the word was never revived

> 1912 *Daily News*: It is called an aviette competition, an aviette being a flying machine propelled by muscular force alone.

babe *n* (1915) an attractive young woman. Originally US college slang (probably as an extension of the earlier *babe* 'sweetheart', which dates from the late 19th century). It continued in US slang usage throughout the century, but was propelled into a wider arena by its use in the early 1990s in the sketch 'Wayne's World' on the US television show *Saturday Night Live* (see also **babelicious (1991)**). Its transferred application to attractive young men is first recorded in 1973

> 1922 Sinclair Lewis: The bonniest bevy of beauteous bathing babes in burlesque.

> 1991 *Sassy*: He has gray hair, is on the short side and is not what I would refer to as a babe.

> 1992 *Harper's Magazine*: Sean said, 'You look good, Mom. A little modern, but good. David thinks you're a babe'.

back-packing *n* (1916) the sport of hiking, camping, etc. carrying a pack on one's back. Originally US. The term *back-pack* itself is first recorded in 1914, but *back-packing* does not seem to have got up much head of steam until the 1940s (*back-packer* is first recorded in 1946)

> 1916 H. C. Kephart: Back-packing is the cheapest possible way to spend one's vacation in the wilderness.

banner, banner headline *n* (1913) a headline in large type, especially one running across a whole page in a newspaper. Originally US

> 1915 G. M. Hyde: Banner headlines have undergone a strange evolution. They were invented to assist in street sales by advertising the news.

basket case *n* (1919) someone, originally a soldier, who has had all four limbs amputated. US slang; the underlying black joke is 'someone who has to be carried in a basket'

> 1919 *US Official Bulletin*: The Surgeon General of the Army…denies…that there is any foundation for the stories that have been circulated…of the existence of 'basket cases' in our hospitals.

battle cruiser *n* (1911) a warship the size of a battleship but faster and more lightly armoured. One of the new breed of warships being developed as part of the Anglo-German arms race in the years leading up to World War I

> 1911 *Times*: In order to distinguish the armoured cruisers of earlier dates from those of the 'Invincible' and later types the latter vessels are to be…classified as battle cruisers.

bed and breakfast *n* (1910) (in a hotel, boarding house, etc.) the provision of a bed for a night and breakfast the following morning

> 1910 *Bradshaw's Railway Guide*: Residential Hotel… Bed and breakfast from 4/-.

bed-jacket *n* (1914) a short garment for the upper body, worn over a nightdress when sitting up in bed

> 1914 Millicent, Duchess of Sutherland: Our nurses cut out red flannel bed-jackets and tried to take photographs.

behaviourism *n* (1913) a theory and method of psychological investigation based on the study and analysis of behaviour, and regarding unconscious ideas and feelings as unimportant. The approach, founded in the US by J. B. Watson, and later developed by, among others, I. P. Pavlov and B. F. Skinner, stresses the importance of conditioning in determining behaviour

> 1913 J. B. Watson: Psychology as the behaviorist views it is a purely objective experimental branch of natural science. Its theoretical goal is the prediction and control of behavior… I feel that *behaviorism* is the only consistent and logical functionalism.

bellhop *n* (1910) a hotel page-boy; a bellboy. US. A shortening of the earlier but short-lived *bell-hopper* (1900), so called because at the sound of the summoning bell the boy (supposedly) responds with alacrity

> 1910 George Ade: He is not a bell hop—the boys used to dress like that.

Bertha *n* (1914) Allied soldiers' nickname for various very large-calibre German artillery pieces of World War I; in particular, three huge guns used to bombard Paris, christened *Big Bertha*. The nickname was originally the Germans' own: their soldiers coined it in disrespectful reference to Frau Bertha Krupp von Bohlen und Halbach, owner of the Krupp steelworks in Germany, which made a particularly successful 42 cm mortar. *Big Bertha* is a translation of German *dicke Bertha* 'fat Bertha'

> 1918 *Sphere*: Big Bertha spoke for the first time on March 23, and at the sound of her voice Paris was intensely surprised.

bimbo *n* (1919) a (feeble or contemptible) fellow. US slang. From Italian *bimbo* 'baby', and used in the US slang sense of *baby*. See also **bimbo (1920)**

> 1919 *American Magazine*: Nothing but the most heroic measures will save the poor bimbo.

birth control *n* (1914) contraception. Compare **family planning (1931)**. *Contraception* itself dates from the 1880s

> 1914 *The Woman Rebel* (heading): The Birth Control League.

> 1936 D. V. Glass: Condoms are listed as preventatives of disease and not as birth-control appliances, and are thus easily available.

bisexual *adj* (1914) sexually attracted to individuals of both sexes. A term originally coined in the early 19th century, with the meaning 'hermaphroditic'. This new sense remained largely in technical usage until the 1950s. Its use as a noun, meaning 'a bisexual person', is first recorded in 1922. See also **bi (1956)**

> 1914 *American Medicine*: By nature all human beings are psychically bisexual— capable of loving a person of either sex.

> 1986 P. Booth: Jo-Anne tells me there's another problem, Lisa. I didn't know you were bisexual.

black out *v* (1919) to extinguish or conceal all lights in (a place) as an air-raid precaution. The associated noun is first recorded in the 1930s (see **black-out (1935)**)

> 1919 *Illustrated London News*: No longer 'blacked out': London herself again.

> 1939 *Daily Mail*: It took about three visits from courteous wardens before my house was properly blacked out.

black-out *n* (1913) the darkening of a stage during a performance. The original meaning of the noun; further senses emerged in the 1930s (see **black-out (1935)**)

> 1913 George Bernard Shaw: The more I think of that revolving business the less I see how it can be done… There will have to be a black-out.

Blighty *n* (1915) one's home country. Used by British soldiers serving abroad, especially during World War I, to refer to Britain. Originally picked up by British servicemen in India from Hindi *bilāyatī* 'foreign', hence 'British'

> 1916 *Notes & Queries*: One poem I have recently seen begins:—Oh, send me back to Blighty.

blighty *n* (1916) Applied by British soldiers serving abroad during World War I to a wound that secured return to Britain. An extended use of the previous word

> 1916 *Daily Mail*: So-and-so stopped some shrapnel and is back at the base in hospital,…he wasn't lucky enough to get a blighty.

blimp *n* (1916) a small non-rigid airship originally consisting of a gas-bag with the fuselage of an aeroplane slung underneath. During World War II the name was sometimes applied to a barrage balloon. Its precise origins are unclear, but it seems likely that it was based on the airship's original official designation as of the type 'B (limp)' (as opposed to 'A (rigid)'). Its coinage is variously attributed to the aviator Horace Shortt (see the quotation below) and to Lieut. A. D. Cunningham. See also **Blimp (1934)**

> 1918 *Illustrated London News*: Nobody in the R.N.A.S. ever called them anything but 'Blimps', an onomatopœic name invented by that genius for apposite nomenclature, the late Horace Shortt.

blood group *n* (1916) any of the genetically determined types into which human blood can be divided on the basis of its compatibility with the blood of other individuals. At first denoting one of the four original red cell groups

1916 W. V. Brem: Isohemolysins cannot be used, therefore, in determining blood groups.

blues *n* (1912) a style of jazz which developed from black southern American secular songs and is usually characterized by a slow tempo and flattened thirds and sevenths. The name comes from *the blues*'sadness', reflecting the generally melancholic aspect of the music

1912 W. C. Handy (tune-title): Memphis Blues.

1923 *Daily Mail*: Noisy 'jazz' music…is being driven out…by the soft pulsing of muffled melody in new tunes known as 'Blues'.

blurb *n* (1914) a promotional description, as found on the jackets of books. Allegedly coined in 1907 by US humorist and illustrator Gelett Burgess (1866–1951) in a comic book jacket embellished with a drawing of a beautiful young lady whom he facetiously dubbed Miss Blinda Blurb

1914 Gelett Burgess: On the 'jacket' of the 'latest' fiction, we find the blurb; abounding in agile adjectives and adverbs, attesting that this book is the 'sensation of the year'.

bob *v* (1918) to cut (the hair of a woman or girl) short and even all round. From the earlier use of *bob* meaning 'to cut short a horse's tail'. The noun *bob*, denoting such a hairstyle, is not recorded before 1926. See also **bingle (1925)** and **shingle (1924)**

1918 *Punch*: Alarming spread of bobbing.

1918 *Home Chat*: There is quite a craze for 'bobbed' hair, for big and little girls alike.

1926 John Galsworthy: Her hair, again in its more natural 'bob', gleamed lustrously under the light.

Boche *n* (1914) A contemptuous term applied to German soldiers, mainly during World War I but to a certain extent also in World War II. Originally a French word, borrowed by British soldiers from their allies on the Western Front (at first it was often spelt in English *Bosche*, German-style). It is a shortening of *alboche*, which may be compounded of *allemand* 'German' and *caboche* 'pate, hard skull' (source of English *cabbage*). Compare **Fritz (1915)**

1914 *Daily Express*: Monsieur had better come under cover. The 'Bosches' are still firing this way.

1916 Philip Gibbs: It was obvious that the blinking Boche had got the wind up.

1917 G. S. Gordon: Our Archibalds are peppering a Boche aeroplane.

1940 Winston Churchill: All Europe, if [Hitler] has his way, will be reduced to one uniform Boche-land.

Bolshevik *adj, n* (1917) (a member) of that part of the Russian Social-Democratic Party which took Lenin's side in the split that followed the second congress of the party in 1903, seized power in the 'October' Revolution of 1917, and was subsequently renamed the (Russian) Communist Party. The term is derived ultimately from Russian *bolshoi* 'big'; they were in fact in a minority after the split, but they adopted the name on account of a majority they achieved on a particular vote at the 1903 congress. Non-anglicized versions of the word are recorded in English texts before 1917, but this appears to be the year in which it was naturalized, along with the derivatives *Bolshevism* and *Bolshevist*.

1917 *New Europe*: It was from this Conference [of Socialists at Stockholm, 1903] that the cleavage between Bolševiks and Menševiks dates, the former being those who held a 'majority' at the Conference, the latter a 'minority'… The good sense of Russian democracy threw off the yoke of Bolševism.

1917 *19th Century*: The reign of Bolshevists and Terrorists.

bolshy, bolshie *adj* (1918) having supposedly Bolshevistic tendencies, especially being uncooperative or recalcitrant

1918 D. H. Lawrence: The railway people, when one travels, seem rather independent and Bolshy.

1938 Evelyn Waugh: There was a time in the early twenties when the word 'Bolshie' was current. It was used indiscriminately of refractory schoolchildren, employees who asked for a rise in wages, impertinent domestic servants, those who advocated an extension of the rights of property to the poor, and anything or anyone of whom the speaker disapproved.

bomb bay *n* (1918) a compartment in an aircraft for carrying bombs

1918 *Aeronautical Inspection Directorate Data Book*: The bomb bay [of the Handley Page V/1500] is rectangular, and built entirely of spruce.

bomber *n* (1915) someone who throws or places a bomb. This is the first recorded use of the word, preceding 'bombing aircraft' by two years (see next). In this particular example, it means 'one of a bombing party'

> 1915 John Buchan: The bombers...seizing one of these rocket-like bombs from their belts...hurl them high above the parapet.

bomber *n* (1917) a military aircraft designed to carry and drop bombs. Compare **fighter (1917)**

> 1917 *'Contact'*: The fighters guard the bombers until the eggs are dropped.

bouncer *n* (1913) In cricket, a fast short-pitched delivery aimed at the batsman. See also **bodyline (1933)**

> 1913 *Cricket*: Every bowler pitches short sometimes, and when...he does so the result-ant...'bouncer'...is no more than an ordinary risk.

broad *n* (1911) a woman. US slang. Many of the earliest recorded examples of the word suggest 'immoral woman' verging on 'prostitute', and this may well have been the original sense. Its ultim-ate origins are unclear, although some connection has been suggested with obsolete US *broadwife* 'female slave separated from her husband', from *abroad* + *wife*

> 1911 *Hampton's Magazine*: Pretty soon what is technically known as a 'broad'—'broad' being the latest New Yorkese—hove into view.

Brownie *n* (1916) a member of the junior section of the Girl Guides. The name reflects the colour of their uniforms, and appears to have been borrowed from *brownie* 'a benevolent spirit or goblin, of shaggy appearance, supposed to haunt old houses'. A key characteristic of these sprites was that they were supposed to help out with the housework at night—an attribute which it was no doubt hoped would rub off on the fledgling Guides. See also **Rosebud (1914)**

> 1916 *Home Chat*: For the younger girls who are not eleven, and therefore not old enough to become Girl Guides, the Brownie movement has been started.

Brown Owl *n* (1918) The name given to the adult leader of a Brownie pack

> 1918 Robert Baden-Powell: The Brown Owl (that is, the leader of the Pack) takes her place by the toadstool.

bug *n, v* (1919) (to equip with) a security alarm system. US slang; a forerunner of *bug* '(to equip with) a hidden microphone' (1935)

> 1919 M. Acklom: The possibilities of the joint being bugged.

bum's rush *n* (1910) forcible ejection. Slang, originally US

> 1925 L. O'Flaherty: They might give him 'the bum's rush', breaking his neck silently like a rabbit's neck.

bunny hug *n* (1912) a dance in ragtime rhythm, popular in the early part of the 20th century. Originally US

> 1912 *Daily Mirror*: Fashionable society in New York...is fighting upon the great question as to whether...'The Bunny Hug'...shall be...allowed.

bus *n* (1916) an aeroplane. A colloquialism favoured by early aviators. Possibly it arose from the slightly earlier application of *bus* to a multi-seater passenger aircraft (see **aerial bus (1910)**)

> 1916 Horatio Barber: A brand new, rakish, up-to-date machine it is...perfectly 'streamlined' to minimise drift... 'Clean looking 'bus... Ought to have a turn of speed with those lines.'

buzz off *v* (1914) to go away. Slang, usually used in the imperative. There was contemporary com-petition from another *buzz off*, meaning 'to ring off on the telephone' ('Are you the *Bainbridge*? Then buzz off!... You there—have you had a call from the *Bainbridge*?', *Pears' Christmas Annual* (1914)), but this failed to survive

> 1914 E. Pugh: 'Here you!' to the Cub, 'you'd better buzz off—quick!'

camouflage *n, v* (1917) (to conceal from the enemy with) methods or materials such as paint, smoke-screens, shrubbery, etc. A borrowing from French, which in turn got it from Italian *camuf-fare* 'to disguise', but its ultimate origins are unknown

1917 *Daily Mail*: The act of hiding anything from your enemy is termed 'camouflage'… The King paid a visit to what is called a camouflage factory… The King saw all the latest Protean tricks for concealing or, as we all say now, for 'camouflaging' guns, snipers, observers.

cap *n* (1916) a contraceptive device, usually made of rubber, covering the neck of the womb. The full form *Dutch cap* is not recorded until 1922, the synonymous *diaphragm* not until 1933

1918 Marie Stopes: The great advantage of this cap is that once it is in and properly fitted it can be entirely forgotten.

carrier *n* (1917) a ship that carries and serves as a base for aircraft. Originally applied to a ship from which an aircraft could take off only; it had to land on the sea and be winched back on board. The actual combination *aircraft carrier* is not recorded until 1919

1917 W. L. Wade: The big cruising sea-plane, operating either from port or from a seaplane carrier.

1919 L. R. Freeman: Aeroplanes launched from the 'carrier' *Furious*.

1919 *Times*: The aircraft carrier Hermes…is to be towed from the Tyne to Devonport.

cartoon *n* (1915) a cinema film with animated cartoon figures. First recorded in 1915, but such animated cartoons seem to have been introduced around 1912

1915 *Harper's Weekly*: Even cartoons began to come in—'animated' cartoons, as they are called.

cash and carry *n* (1917) a system by which purchasers pay cash for goods and take them away themselves. Originally US. By the middle of the 1920s the word was also being applied to a shop or supermarket operating on this system

1917 *Ladies' Home Journal*: I would recommend to every woman that you follow the 'cash and carry' plan of buying in preference to the 'credit and delivery' plan.

1927 *Magazine of Business*: I located my store in a veritable nest of 'cash and carries'.

cat's whisker *n* (1915) a fine adjustable copper or gold wire in a crystal wireless receiver or in certain types of electronic circuit. The frustratingly finicky manipulation of the wire was a major drawback of early radios. See also **crystal set (1924)**

1915 A. F. Collins: Adjust the wire until the pointed end presses on the crystal and you will have what is called a cat-whisker detector.

cease-fire *n* (1918) a cessation of shooting or fighting; an armistice. From the earlier military command to stop firing guns, which dates from the mid 19th century

1918 *Times*: The 'Cease fire' of yesterday must be final and universal.

Cellophane *n* (1912) The proprietary name of a glossy transparent material made from regenerated cellulose, latterly used mainly for wrapping goods, food, etc., but put to a range of other uses earlier in the century. It is formed from *cellulose* and the suffix *-phane*, meaning literally 'appearing like cellulose'

1912 Cross & Bevan: The 'viscose film' (cellulose) under the powerful auspices of the Société Industrielle de Thaon is at length a fait accompli, and is an article of commerce under the descriptive term 'Cellophane'.

1935 *Times*: A frock in a mixture of cellophane and wool.

chain store *n* (1910) one of a series of stores belonging to one firm and dealing in the same type of goods. Originally US

1910 *Saturday Evening Post*: There were loud declarations of war from the manager of the association that buys goods for retail grocers fighting the chain stores.

cheerio *interj* (1910) goodbye. British. The original form of the word was *cheero*, but the alternative *cheerio* soon came into use (no doubt under the influence of *cheery*), and *cheero* gradually died out

1910 *Punch*: [One loafer to another] Cheero, Charlie.

1914 Rupert Brooke: Cheeryo! (as we say in the Navy).

chemical warfare *n* (1917) warfare using asphyxiating or nerve gases, poisons, defoliants, etc.

1917 Winston Churchill: Chemical warfare must be one of the…leading features of our campaign of 1918.

C.I.D. *n* (1910) An abbreviation of *Criminal Investigation Department* (a 19th-century term), the detective branch of the British police

> 1910 E. H. Richardson: Detective F. H. Carr of the C.I.D.

cigarette girl *n* (1916) a young female cigarette seller, especially in a cinema, night-club, etc.

> 1918 Arnold Bennett: The programme girls, the cigarette girls, the chocolate girls, the cloak-room girls.

cinema *n* (1913) a building where films are shown. English originally acquired the word *cinema* around 1909 in the sense 'cinematograph', and this extended meaning probably represents a shortening of such terms as *cinema hall* and *cinema theatre* (although our record of these is either contemporary with or later than *cinema* on its own)

> 1913 *Punch*: Our Village Cinema.

> 1915 *'Bartimeus'*: The advertisement of a cinema theatre occupied a hoarding near the landing place.

cinema star *n* (1913) See **film star (1914)**

cinematize *v* (1916) to adapt (a play, story) to the cinema; to make a film of. A term which seems to have died out by World War II

> 1928 *Musical Times*: In the cinematizing of a novel only the story is taken.

Cinephone *n* (1913) An early name for an apparatus designed for the production of a film with audible dialogue. It failed to make it into the actual era of talkies

> 1913 *Kelso Chronicle*: The Cinephone, which will enable the actor without any restriction to play his part and to have his voice and action recorded in absolute union.

Citizen's Charter, Citizens' Charter *n* (1913) a document concerning the rights of citizens. A term coined by C. E. Innes and used as the title of a book in which he expounded his 'scheme of national organisation'. It has surfaced periodically since, most recently in Britain in the early 1990s, denoting a plan to guarantee standards in public services

> 1991 John Major: What we now aim to do is to put in place a comprehensive Citizen's Charter. It will work for quality across the whole range of public services.

clearing hospital *n* (1914), **clearing station** *n* (1915) a military hospital for the temporary reception and treatment of sick and wounded

> 1915 Aldous Huxley: Whereabouts unknown—but a wire from the clearing-station brought back by one of Dr. H's assistants in France, prognosticates 3 weeks.

climax *n* an orgasm. Apparently a coinage by the birth-control pioneer Marie Stopes to avoid mystifying her readers with *orgasm*, which in the course of the 19th century had become the technical term for what the OED, with stately definition, calls 'the height of venereal excitement in coition', but which was likely still to be unfamiliar to the layperson. Subsequently also used as a verb

> 1918 Marie Stopes: In many cases the man's climax comes so swiftly that the woman's reactions are not nearly ready.

> 1982 Shirley Conran: After he climaxed, he kissed her gently on the lips.

cockpit *n* (1914) the space in an aircraft (or, later, a spacecraft) occupied by the pilot and crew (and, in small aircraft, a passenger). Probably from the earlier application to the area on a ship from which it is steered

> 1914 *Report and Memorandum* (Advisory Committee on Aeronautics): There are several speed indicators…in which the pressure of the air in the cockpit is allowed to act on one side of the recording diagram.

collective farming *n* (1919) See **collective farm (1925)**

collective unconscious *n* (1917) In the theory of C. G. Jung, that part of the unconscious mind which derives from ancestral experience and is additional to the personal unconscious

> 1917 D. Hecht: The collective unconscious is the sediment of all the experience of the universe of all time, and is also an image of the universe that has been in process of formation for untold ages.

colour-bar *n* (1913) racial discrimination, especially by whites against blacks

> 1913 W. C. Willoughby: The colour of the African is so strikingly different from ours, that it…serves in such phrases as colour-bar to indicate the whole difference.

> 1914 W. G. Lawrence: Relations between English and Hindu professors are bad, and there is a distinct colour bar except in the Mission colleges.

come off it (1912) stop talking nonsense! A British colloquialism

> 1912 A. M. N. Lyons: Mrs. de Courcy Allendale requested me to 'come off it'.

> 1930 Somerset Maugham: 'Come off it, Roy,' I said. 'I'm too old a bird to be caught with chaff.'

Comintern *n* (1919) the Communist International, the international organization of the Communist Party, founded in 1919 and dissolved in 1943. The term was acquired (originally in unanglicized form) from Russian *Komintérn*, which was formed from the Russian equivalents of *communist* and *international*

> 1925 *Glasgow Herald*: The international relations of the S.S.S.R. and the problems of the Komintern in connection with it.

commissar *n* (1918) (during and after the Revolution of 1917 in Russia) a representative appointed by a Soviet, a government, or the Communist party to be responsible for political indoctrination and organization, especially in military units. Borrowed from Russian *komissar*

> 1921 *Chambers's Journal*: The Bolsheviks retreated in a panic, killing their own commissars as they fled.

Commonwealth *n* (1917) an association of states comprising Britain and most of its former colonies and dominions. The expression 'commonwealth of nations' had been used with reference to the British empire by Lord Rosebery in 1884 ('The British Empire is a commonwealth of nations'), but it was the South African statesman Jan Smuts who formulated the modern concept of the Commonwealth and suggested its name. The 'British Commonwealth of Nations' was established by the Statute of Westminster in 1931. After World War II the name was modified to simply 'British Commonwealth', and the 'British' was frequently dropped

> 1917 J. C. Smuts: The British Empire is much more than a State… We are a system…of nations and states…who govern themselves, who have been evolved on the principles of your constitutional system, now almost independent states, and who belong to this group, to this community of nations, which I prefer to call the British Commonwealth of nations.

> 1926 *Report of the Committee on Inter-Imperial Relations*: Status of Great Britain and the Dominions… They are autonomous Communities within the British Empire, equal in status, in no way subordinate one to another in any aspect of their domestic or external affairs, though united by a common allegiance to the Crown, and freely associated as members of the British Commonwealth of Nations.

> 1940 Winston Churchill: So bear ourselves that if the British Commonwealth and Empire lasts for a thousand years men will still say, 'This was their finest hour.'

> 1947 *Times*: It has for some time been clear…that the titles of the Secretary of State for Dominion Affairs and the Dominions Office…should now be changed and steps are accordingly being taken…to alter the titles to Secretary of State for Commonwealth Relations and Commonwealth Relations Office respectively.

> 1958 *Times*: It is proposed to change the name of Empire Day forthwith to Commonwealth Day.

commune *n* (1919) a communal division or settlement in a Communist country. A term no doubt at least partly inspired by the *Commune of Paris*, originally a name assumed by a body which usurped the municipal government of Paris, and in that capacity played a leading part during the Reign of Terror, till suppressed in 1794, and subsequently applied to the government on communalistic principles established in Paris by an insurrection for a short time in the spring of 1871

> 1919 translation of Lenin: For the mercenary and corrupt parliamentarism of capitalist society, the Commune substitutes institutions in which freedom of opinion and discussion does not become a mere delusion.

conchy, conchie *n* (1917) A term of contempt in Britain during World Wars I and II for a **conscientious objector (1916)**

> 1917 *Daily Mail*: The assembly of eleven hundred 'conscientious' objectors at one spot, Princetown, on Dartmoor, where they are known as 'conchies'.

> 1960 *Spectator*: There were more than forty thousand of us—weirdies and beardies, colonels and conchies, Communists and Liberals.

conscientious objector *n* (1916) someone who refuses on grounds of conscience to do military service. The term was actually coined at the end of the 19th century for 'someone who objects on principle to being inoculated', but came into its own during World War I, when people who refused to fight were the subject of widespread public scorn. See also **Cuthbert (1917)**, **Percy (1916)**

> 1916 Aldous Huxley: Conscientious objectors were not so disgustingly hectored as they seem to have been in London.

conurbation *n* (1915) an aggregation of urban areas. A coinage based on Latin *urbs* 'city', probably on the model of French *conurbation*

> 1915 Patrick Geddes: Some name, then, for these city-regions, these town aggregates, is wanted… What of 'Conurbations'?… For our first conurbation the name of Greater London is…dominant.

convertible *n* (1916) a car with a top that can be folded back. Originally US

> 1937 Rex Stout: Gerbert had climbed into a neat little convertible.

cooch *n* (1910) a type of erotic dance. US slang. A shortening of *hootchy-kootchy* (1898) in the same sense, whose origins are obscure. Also used as a verb

> 1927 *Variety*: Where they cooch in New York they 'tease' here.

copacetic *adj* (1919) fine, excellent. US slang. Its origins remain unknown, despite various attempts to derive it from Latin, Yiddish, Italian, Louisiana French, and even various Native American languages. It remained in use at the end of the century, although it has never been successfully exported across the Atlantic

> 1919 I. Bacheller: 'As to looks I'd call him, as ye might say, real copasetic [sic].' Mrs. Lukins expressed this opinion solemnly… Its last word stood for nothing more than an indefinite depth of meaning.

copywriter *n* (1911) someone employed to write advertising copy

> 1911 T. Russell: An advertiser can…employ what are known as copy-writers—professional writers of advertisements.

coupon *n* (1918) any of a series of tickets entitling the holder to a share of rationed food, clothing, etc. (The term also became more ephemerally familiar in Britain at this time as a result of the so-called 'Coupon' Election of 1918, in which Lloyd George distributed slips of paper ('coupons') containing recommendations of particular parliamentary candidates)

> 1918 *Times*: A whole coupon [at the Express Dairy] entitled one to have stewed steak and carrots, two sausages, or cold ham and tongue.

> 1948 Nevil Shute: I ought to get another suit, but there never seem to be any coupons.

cover girl *n* (1915) a glamorous young woman (of the sort) who appears on magazine covers. Originally US; a shortening of earlier *magazine-cover girl*

> 1915 *Harper's Weekly* (caption): Unveiling the statue of Charles Dana Gibson at the annual picnic of the magazine cover girls at Lakewood.

crash *v* (1910) Of an aircraft or its pilot: to fall or come down violently with the machine out of control. The derived noun is first recorded in 1917. The application to motor vehicles comes from this aeronautical usage; it is not recorded until the 1920s

> 1910 R. Loraine: The machine leapt higher,…then—paff!—I came to earth, having stalled and crashed.

> 1917 *Sphere*: This particular victim of a 'crash' had been compelled to lie abed…for several weeks.

crash helmet *n* (1918) a helmet designed to prevent head injury in the event of a crash. Originally applied to such a head-protector for pilots, but, as the quote below indicates, soon diverted to similar helmets for motor cyclists

   1923 *Motor Cycle*: 5,000 New Crash Helmets…ex-R.A.F.

creeping barrage *n* (1916) a curtain of artillery or machine-gun fire moving before and directed from behind advancing troops. A tactic of trench warfare deployed during World War I.

   1916 Harry Yoxall: The creeping barrage which went in front of our assaulting lines was almost geometrically straight, and lifted each time to the second.

crime passionnel *n* (1910) a crime due to passion, specifically a murder resulting from jealousy. A borrowing from French (although English often spells *passionnel* with one *n*)

   1910 *Encyclopedia Britannica*: In cases of what is termed 'crime passionel [sic]', French juries…almost invariably find extenuation.

cripes *interj* (1910) An exclamation of surprise or dismay, representing a euphemistic watering down of *Christ*. By the end of the century it was fast disappearing from use

   1910 A. H. Davis: 'By cripes!' he gasped,…'I've lost th'…th' *cheques!*'

cross-dressing *n* (1911) A translation of German *Transvestismus*, which later appeared in English more lightly adapted as *transvestism* (1928)

   1911 E. Carpenter: Cross-dressing must be taken as a general indication of, and a cognate phenomenon to, homosexuality.

crossword puzzle *n* (1914) a puzzle in which a pattern of chequered squares has to be filled in from numbered clues with words which are written usually horizontally and vertically. The first crossword puzzle appeared in the *New York World* on 21 December 1913, but it was originally called a *word-cross*. By January 1914 this had been transposed to *cross-word*

   1914 *New York World* ('Fun'): Solution to last week's cross-word puzzle.

crystal receiver *n* (1917) An earlier term for a **crystal set (1924)**

   1917 *Wireless World*: The balanced crystal receiver, by keeping signals at a reasonable strength, enables the operator to receive in conditions which would otherwise make work impossible.

Cubism *n* (1911) a movement in painting and sculpture, initiated by Pablo Picasso and Georges Braque, which emphasized the structure of objects by combining geometric shapes to give several simultaneous viewpoints. An anglicization of French *cubisme*, which dates from 1908 and was allegedly coined by a member of the Hanging Committee of the Salon des Indépendants. As a canvas by Braque was being carried by, this person is supposed to have exclaimed 'Encore des Cubes! assez de cubisme!' ('Still more cubes! That's enough cubism!'). The derived *cubist* entered English in the same year

   1911 *Illustrated London News*: Paris is perturbed by the Cubism and the Cubists of the Salon d'Automne.

cuckoo *adj* (1918) crazy, mad. Slang, originally US. From the noun *cuckoo* 'fool, simpleton'

   1923 P. G. Wodehouse: He pottered about the room for a bit, babbling at intervals. The boy seemed cuckoo.

curie *n* (1910) Originally, a quantity of radon in radioactive equilibrium with one gramme of radium; later extended to denote an equivalent quantity of any of the decay products of radium. Later (from the early 1950s), a unit of radioactivity equal to 3.7×10^{10} disintegrations per second. Named after Pierre Curie (1859–1906), the co-discoverer (with his wife Marie (1867–1934)) of radium

   1910 Ernest Rutherford: It was suggested that the name Curie, in honour of the late Prof. Curie, should…be employed for a quantity of radium or of the emanation… The name Curie should be used as a new unit to express the quantity or mass of radium emanation in equilibrium with one gram of radium (element).

cushy *adj* (1915) Of a post, job, etc.: easy, comfortable, 'soft'. Also applied during World War I to a wound, meaning 'not dangerous or serious'. Slang; originally an Anglo-Indian word, from Hindi ḳhūsh 'pleasant'

> 1915 D. O. Barnett: The billets here are very good…and we have rooms to ourselves… It's all very cushey and nice.

Cuthbert *n* (1917) A contemptuous name in Britain during World War I for a man who deliberately avoided military service. Often applied specifically to one who did so by getting a job in a government office or the civil service. The earliest record of it is in a caption to a cartoon by 'Poy' in the *Evening News.* See also **Percy (1916)**

> 1919 *Mr Punch's History of the Great War:* As a set-off to the anti-'Cuthbert' campaign in the Press the War Cabinet has…declared that 'the whole Empire owes the Civil Service a lasting debt of gratitude'.

D-Day *n* (1918) The military code-name for a particular day fixed for the beginning of an operation. It is particularly associated with the day (6 June 1944) of the invasion of the Atlantic coast of German-occupied France by Allied forces (see **D-Day (1942)**, but its origin long predates that. The 'D' simply represents the first letter of *day*

> 1918 *Field Order No. 8, First Army, Allied Expeditionary Force:* The First Army will attack at H-Hour on D-Day with the object of forcing the evacuation of St. Mihiel salient.

> 1928 J. M. Saunders: The word went out that 'D' day was to be Sept. 12.

dealership *n* (1916) an authorization from the manufacturer to sell a particular product. The ambition of every 20th-century auto trader

> 1916 W. P. Werheim: Getting more business, establishing more agencies and dealerships.

death ray *n* (1919) a ray that causes death. A staple of pulp science fiction in the middle years of the century

> 1919 B. Munn: Had the man once used his death rays he was watched carefully enough to have been caught…red-handed.

debag *v* (1914) to remove the trousers from (someone) as a punishment or for a joke. Dated British slang, redolent of (grown-up) schoolboy japes of the pre-World War II period. Coined from slang *bags* 'trousers' (1853)

> 1914 Compton Mackenzie: At Oxford…we should be out of sympathy with him, even up to the point of debagging him… 'We ought to debag him,' he cried. Appleby was thereupon debagged; but as…he continued to walk about trouserless and dispense hospitality without any apparent loss of dignity, the debagging had to be written down a failure.

decathlon *n* (1912) In the modern Olympic games and similar athletics contests, a composite contest consisting of ten specific events. Coined from Greek *deka* 'ten' and *athlon* 'contest'

> 1912 *Times:* The Decathlon was brought to a close to-day, the events to be decided being the pole jump, throwing the javelin…and 1,500 metres flat race.

defeatism *n* (1918) readiness to accept defeat. A borrowing of French *défaitisme*, and originally used in English mainly in the context of Irish politics. The derived *defeatist* is also first recorded in 1918

> 1918 *Observer:* Irish Nationalists will henceforth support Pacifism, and that means defeatism… The political creed of the party,…is to support the Government in winning the war and in defeating the intrigues of Pacifists and Defeatists.

denial *n* (1914) the usually unconscious suppression of painful or embarrassing feelings, reactions, or desires. Introduced into English as a technical term in psychoanalysis by A. A. Brill's translation of Sigmund Freud's *Psychopathology of Everyday Life.* It became known to a wider public in American English in the 1980s, in the phrase *in denial*

> 1992 *Village Voice* (New York): 'You're living in denial. Abortion is killing your baby.' He sounds the prolifers' warning of never-ending guilt, as if morality were mere avoidance of pain.

depth charge *n* (1917) an anti-submarine explosive charge detonated underwater

> 1917 *War Illustrated:* Telegraph to seamen…who prepare to drop Depth Charges to destroy U-boat.

detention camp *n* (1916) a camp in which aliens and others were kept under restraint during World War I

> 1916 John Buchan: The lieutenant discoursed a lot about prisoners and detention-camps.

dialysis *n* (1914) the process of allowing blood to flow past a suitable membrane on the other side of which is another liquid, so that certain dissolved substances in the blood can pass through the membrane and the blood itself be purified or cleansed in cases of renal failure, poisoning, etc. The term is a specialized application of the earlier sense 'separation of substances via a membrane', and comes ultimately from Greek *dialusis* 'separation, dissolution'. The derived verb *dialyse* is also first recorded in 1914, but neither word was common before the procedure came into wider use in the 1940s

> 1914 *Journal of Pharmacology and Experimental Therapeutics*: We have devised a method by which the blood of a living animal may be submitted to dialysis outside the body, and again returned to the natural circulation… An apparatus made of [a] dialysing membrane.

digger *n* (1916) an Australian or New Zealander. In World Wars I and II, applied to an Australian or New Zealand soldier, usually specifically a private. From the earlier sense 'someone who digs for gold', from the high profile of such people in late 19th-century Australia

> 1917 *Chronicles of the New Zealand Expeditionary Force*: He ain't no digger; that's the colonel or the sergeant-major… Two hefty diggers escorted the little lady to her home.

direct action *n* (1912) the use of demonstrations, strikes, sabotage, etc. to exert pressure on governments, employers, etc.

> 1912 J. R. MacDonald: The Programme of Direct Action.

> 1920 Sidney & Beatrice Webb: Trade Unionists object to Direct Action…for objects other than those connected with the economic function of the Direct Actionists.

director *n* (1911) someone who directs a film. This meaning of *direct* is itself not recorded before 1913, but the two words probably emerged hand in hand

> 1913 F. W. Sargent: *Director*, one who produces photoplays, directing the preparation and action.

> 1914 R. Grau: The world-famous director, D. W. Griffith.

Dobermann pinscher *n* (1917) a type of German dog with a smooth coat and docked tail. Named after Ludwig Dobermann, a 19th-century German dog-breeder of Thuringia

> 1917 *Policeman's Monthly*: Nowadays four breeds of dogs are being used for police purposes: the Continental Sheepdog, the Airedale Terrier, the Doberman Pinscher and the Rottweilers.

dogfight *n* (1919) an aerial battle, especially between fighter planes. First recorded in 1919, but current during World War I (of which dogfights formed a small but characteristic feature). A re-application of an earlier, more general sense 'scrap, mêlée'

> 1919 A. E. Illingworth: The battle develops into a 'dog-fight', small groups of machines engaging each other in a fight to the death.

dogs *n* (1913) the feet; often used in the context of tired or aching feet. Originally US; short for rhyming slang *dog's meat*. Frequent in British English in the middle part of the century, it went out of use, but was re-introduced into youth and sports slang of the mid 1990s from the US

> 1939 Monica Dickens: I feel more like goin' to bed and sleeping for a week than prancing round the ballroom on me poor dogs.

dollar diplomacy *n* (1910) the use of US investment in foreign countries to further the commercial interests of the US and enhance its influence

> 1910 *Harper's Weekly*: An attempt is made…to outline…what is meant by the term 'Dollar Diplomacy', as it has come to be commonly applied to certain of the activities of Secretary Knox…in Honduras, in Liberia, [etc.].

donor *n* (1910) someone who gives blood for use in a transfusion. The term *blood-donor* is not recorded before 1921

> 1910 *Johns Hopkins Hospital Bulletin*: The serum of both donor and donee is capable of agglutinating the corpuscles of the other.

> 1921 *Lancet*: In a recent number of the *Guy's Hospital Gazette* the editor protests against the too free use of students as blood-donors.

donor *n* (1918) an animal or person, alive or dead, from whom an organ or tissue is removed for surgical transplantation. The earliest recorded examples denote an animal; the term does not seem to have been applied to human beings until the 1950s

> 1918 *Journal of Medical Research*: In a number of cases the second lobe of thyroid from the third guinea-pig (the second donor) was transplanted into a control guinea-pig.

> 1971 *Daily Telegraph*: Doctors should only be allowed to remove an organ if the donor has given his consent in writing.

Dora *n* (1917) A facetious personification of the British 'Defence of the Realm Act', based on the female name. The Act was first passed in August 1914 and provided the British Government with wide powers during World War I (e.g. for arresting and detaining anyone held to be compromising the war effort)

> 1921 *Punch*: To judge by his description, Dora's daughter [i.e. the Emergency Powers Act of 1920] will be not a whit less drastic in her action than the old lady herself.

double-glazed *adj* (1910) having two panes of glass separated by an air space, for insulation. The noun **double-glazing** is not recorded before the 1940s

> 1910 *Westminster Gazette*: Side windows and skylights, all of which are double-glazed, in order…to guard against changes of temperature.

do well out of *v* (1919) to profit by or from. A phrase made famous in Maynard Keynes's devastating characterization of wartime profiteers. See also **profiteer (1912)**

> 1919 J. M. Keynes: They are a lot of hard-faced men…who look as if they had done very well out of the war.

> 1987 *Daily Telegraph*: Russell is often portrayed as one of the greediest of the Tudor 'New Men' who did well out of the Dissolution of the Monasteries.

duration *n* (1916) the time during which a war lasts. Usually in the phrase *for the duration* 'until the end of the war'; this came from the British term of enlistment for World War I 'for four years or the duration of the war'

> 1916 *Punch*: 'I've got a lot of contracts to finish.' 'How long will they take?' 'Oh, about three years— or the duration of the War.'

economic war *n* (1916) the use of economic measures as a means of bringing pressure to bear on another country. In due course the variant *economic warfare* became the commoner expression

> 1916 G. L. Dickinson (title): Economic war after the war.

> 1939 Winston Churchill: Nazi Germany is all the time under the grip of our economic warfare falling back in oil and other essential war supplies.

edge *n the edge* (1911) someone or something very extreme—often, extremely exasperating. British slang, long since defunct. It was often preceded by such words as *absolute* and *outside*. The inspiration of **the limit (1906)** is evident

> 1911 Ian Hay: Cheating again! My word, Nicky, you are the absolute edge!

egghead *n* (1918) A derisive term for an intellectual. Originally US journalistic slang. Popularized during the 1952 US presidential election campaign, when it was applied to supporters of the Democratic candidate Adlai Stevenson. Versions differ as to whether this was on account of Stevenson's intellect or his baldness, but in the popular imagination baldness has often been interpreted as a sign of intelligence, and the first recorded instance of the word *egghead* (1907) is in the sense 'bald person'

> 1952 *Cleveland* (Ohio) *Plain Dealer*: A good many intelligent people…obviously admired Stevenson. 'Sure,' was the reply, 'all the egg heads love Stevenson.'

> 1955 *Scientific American*: I fear that, while publicly unspoken, anti-intellectualism and suspicion of 'eggheads' may have been a factor.

emote *v* (1917) to display emotion; to act emotionally. Often used with reference to actors, when there can frequently be an implication of over-acting. An early example of a verb created by taking the end off a noun, one of the 20th century's favourite methods of word-formation

> 1927 A. W. L. Fawcett: In these surroundings the players must 'emote' all they know.

> 1931 *Observer*: 'What were your emotions when you looked down…on to the Sea of Galilee?,' I asked Mr [G. B.] Shaw. 'I did not emote,' he replied a trifle reproachfully.

endocrine *adj* (1914) Denoting an organ whose secretions pass directly into the bloodstream. The term was coined from Greek *endon* 'within' and *krinein* 'to separate, secrete'

> 1914 E. A. Schäfer: Organs…passing such material into the blood or lymph are termed internally secreting or endocrine organs.

> 1914 *Lancet*: The organs of internal secretion, or endocrine glands.

eurhythmics *n* (1912) a system of rhythmical bodily movements, especially dancing exercises, with musical accompaniment, often used for educational purposes, and originally taught by Émile Jacques-Delcroze. Professor Delcroze did not so much invent the word, as is claimed in the quote below, as adapt it from Greek *eurhuthmia* 'the quality of being well-proportioned or rhythmical'. At the end of the century, best known for being the name of a pop group, founded in 1980

> 1912 *Standard*: Eurythmics [sic] is…the new craze. Eurythmics is a word which Professor Jacques-Dalcroze has invented to describe his 'rhythmic gymnastics'.

eventide home *n* (1918) a home for old people. An early example of the 20th-century euphemization of old age. The term was originally applied specifically to such an institution run by the Salvation Army

> 1918 Henrietta Barnett: An eventide-home for those…near the end of their pilgrimage.

extrovert *n* (1918) a person whose behaviour is characterized by an interest in interacting with other people and the external world. Originally a technical term in psychology, but subsequently used more generally for 'an outgoing person'. It first appeared in 1915 in the form *extravert*, which actually makes more etymological sense (from Latin *extra* 'outwards'), but the spelling *extrovert*, which was modelled on **introvert (1918)**, has swept the board

> 1918 P. Blanchard: Jung's hypothesis of the two psychological types, the introvert and extrovert,- the thinking type and the feeling type.

facial *n* (1914) a beauty treatment for the face. Originally US

> 1914 G. Atherton: I've got fourteen heads to dress…and most of them want a facial, too.

faggot *n* (1914) a (male) homosexual. Slang, originally and mainly US. Probably the leading American term of abuse for gays in the 20th century. It was adapted from the earlier sense, 'an (unpleasant old) woman'. See also **fag (1921)**

> 1914 Jackson & Hellyer: All the fagots (sissies) will be dressed in drag at the ball tonight.

Fanny Adams *n* (1919) nothing at all. British slang. The original Fanny Adams was the victim of a murder in the late 1860s. British sailors perpetuated her name by using it as a slang term for 'tinned meat', and during World War I the coincidence of her initials with those of *fuck all* led to its use as a euphemistic substitute, usually in the phrase *sweet Fanny Adams*. The expression lasted well into the post-World War II period

> 1949 J. R. Cole: What do they do? Sweet Fanny Adams!

Fany *n* (1918) An unofficial acronym (based on the female name *Fanny*) formed from the initial letters of *First Aid Nursing Yeomanry*, a British corps of military nurses. The term continued in use during World War II, presumably to the consternation or amusement of US troops (*fanny* is US slang for the buttocks)

> 1940 *War Illustrated*: Two volunteers of the First Aid Nursing Yeomanry, known as 'Fanys', are cleaning their ambulance.

farmerette *n* (1918) a woman or girl who farms land. Originally US. Coined at a time when women were taking over many jobs from men away at war, but it survived until such feminine forms began to become politically incorrect

> 1918 *Independent* (New York): The farmerettes are producing food which creates the bodies and minds of mankind.

Fauvist *n* (1915) a member of a movement in painting, chiefly associated with Henri Matisse (1869–1954), which flourished in Paris from 1905, and which is mainly characterized by a vivid use of colour. An adaptation of French *fauviste*, which was derived from *fauve* 'wild animal'. The name was coined by the French art critic Louis Vauxcelles at the Autumn Salon of 1905; coming across a quattrocento-like statue in the midst of works by Matisse and his associates, he remarked 'Donatello au milieu des fauves!' There is no record of the term reaching English until 1915

> 1915 Wyndham Lewis: May the mortality amongst Cubists, Carnivorists, Fauvists and Vorticists at the front be excessive.

feature film *n* (1911) the principal film in a programme at a cinema. First recorded in D. S. Hulfish's *Cyclopedia of Motion-Picture Work*

> 1913 *Moving Picture Annual*: The rapid growth of what has come to be known as the 'feature film'…characterizes the year 1912… Features rather than 'first runs' became the popular cry.

fighter *n* (1917) a high-speed military aircraft designed for aerial combat. Compare **bomber (1917)**

> 1917 'Contact': The fighters guard the bombers until the eggs are dropped.

film star *n* (1914) a popular film actor or actress. The synonymous *cinema star* is first recorded a year before, but soon lost out to *film star*. *Movie star*, the preferred American term, is first recorded in 1919

> 1913 V. Steer: To become a cinema 'star' is not an easy matter.

> 1914 Robert Grau: The greatest film stars in the world.

> 1918 D. H. Lawrence: I dreamed you were a sort of *prima ballerina*—which is the translation of a cinema star, I suppose.

> 1919 H. L. Wilson: [They saw] how much they were paying their president…quoted beside some movie star's salary.

fire-power *n* (1913) the total effectiveness of the fire of guns, missiles, etc., of a military force

> 1913 R. Meinertzhagen: What I should have liked to see is more automatic fire-power in the hands of both the battalion commander and the company commander.

five-star *adj* (1913) Denoting a hotel classified as first-class and designated by five asterisks

> 1913 *Autocar Handbook*: The Association has classified on a 'five star' basis a very large number of British hotels.

fixation *n* (1910) Originally, in Freudian theory, the arrest of a component of the libido at an immature stage, leading a person to abnormal attachments to people or things, etc.; hence, more broadly, an obsession. The back-formed verb *fixate* is first recorded in 1926; it is usually used in the passive

> 1910 A. A. Brill: A phase of very intense but short-lived fixation on the woman (usually on the mother).

> 1926 William McDougall: According to this theory [i.e. the theory of the Oedipus complex] the libido…of every infant normally becomes fixated upon the parent of the opposite sex.

> 1945 George Orwell: It is clear that for many years he remained 'fixated' on his old school.

fixit *n* (1911) someone who mends, puts right, or 'fixes' things. Colloquial, originally North American. The usage seems to have originated with *Little Miss Fixit*, the name of a musical by Hurlbut and Smith, and continues to be usually prefixed with a title, typically *Mr*

> 1972 *Village Voice* (New York): Peter M. Flanigan…became an assistant to the President and acquired a reputation as 'Richard Nixon's "Mr. Fixit" when it comes to powerful business interests'.

flame-thrower *n* (1917) a weapon that projects a steady stream of ignited fuel. A translation of German *Flamenwerfer*. The contemporary synonym *flame machine* did not last long

> 1917 Philip Gibbs: There were eight of these flame-throwers brought against the Sussex lads.

> 1917 *Times*: The Germans have used flame machines for the first time in the Balkans.

flipping *adj, adv* (1911) Used as a euphemistic substitute for *fucking*

> 1911 D. H. Lawrence: 'Ain't it flippin' 'ot?' drawled Creswell.

food parcel *n* (1919) assorted foodstuffs sent in a parcel to supplement low supplies. A familiar feature of 20th-century wartime life was the dispatch of food aid from areas of plenty to beleaguered nations (e.g. from North America to Britain), and from home to those incarcerated in prison camps

> 1919 E. H. Jones: He was comfortable enough himself (thanks to the contents of our food parcels).

footage *n* (1916) the length in feet of cinema or television film used in photographing a scene, etc. In later usage often applied to what is shot on that film

> 1916 B. M. Bower: He visualized a stampede and the probable amount of footage it would require.

> 1967 *Spectator*: NBC decided to puff the footage up into a fifty minute documentary.

fox-trot *n* (1915) a dance of American origin consisting chiefly of alternating measures of long and short steps. Originally a term in equestrianism for a pace with short steps, based on the idea that foxes take short steps

> 1915 *Truth*: A new dance, the 'Fox-trot', a relation of…'Ragtime'.

Freudian *adj* (1910) of Sigmund Freud (1856–1939), the Austrian psychiatrist who developed psychoanalysis. The term quickly picked up connotations of repressed sexuality (see the second quote below), but there is no evidence of its use in the sense 'unwittingly revealing one's true (sexual) feelings' until the 1950s (see **Freudian slip (1959)**)

> 1910 *American Journal of Psychology*: I recently dreamt that I was travelling to Italy on my way to the next Freudian Congress (which is to be held in March).

> 1915 E. B. Holt: The idea has gone abroad that the term 'Freudian' is somehow synonymous with 'sexual'.

Fritz *n* (1915) A contemptuous term applied to a German soldier or soldiers, mainly during World War I but to a certain extent also in World War II. From the German male forename *Fritz*, a nickname for *Friedrich*. Compare **Boche (1914)**

> 1915 D. O. Barnett: By that time, of course, Fritz had made himself scarce.

> 1916 *Daily Mail*: An effective bombardment of the enemy's lines or a successful trench raid [is] described by Tommy as 'strafing the Fritzes'.

front line *n* (1915) the most forward line of a military combat force. Originally used in the context of the trench warfare in France in World War I

> 1915 Ian Hay: That sudden disturbance in the front-line trench.

> 1917 Ford Madox Ford: I hope to get to Mesopotamia as I am not fit for the front line.

furphy *n* (1916) a false report or rumour; an absurd story. Australian slang. From the name of a firm, J. Furphy & Sons Pty. Ltd. of Shepparton, Victoria, manufacturing water and sanitary carts used in World War I: the name 'Furphy' appeared on such carts, whose drivers were sources of gossip

> 1933 *Bulletin* (Sydney): The persistent rumour that they were introduced to check ragwort is a furphy.

gangland *n* (1912) the world of gangsters; the underworld. Originally US

> 1912 A. H. Lewis: The first lesson of Gangland is never to inform nor give evidence.

garden town *n* (1915) See **garden suburb (1905)**

gas attack *n* (1916) an attack using poison gas

> 1916 *King's Royal Rifle Corps Chronicle*: The Germans opened a burning gas attack upon the front of the trenches we had captured from them ten days before.

gas gangrene *n* (1914) a rapidly spreading form of gangrene characterized by the formation of gas bubbles in the surrounding tissue. A common affliction in the trenches of World War I, although it has nothing to do with the use of gas as a weapon

> 1914 *Journal of the Royal Army Medical Corps*: There are some ten different organisms that have been isolated from cases of gas gangrene in man.

gas helmet *n* (1915) An early but short-lived synonym of **gas mask**

> 1915 *Punch*: Will officers please state how many Gas Helmets they possess?

gas mask *n* (1915) a mask used as a protection against poisonous gas

| 1915 *War Illustrated*: French soldiers wearing anti-poison gas masks and respirators.

gasper *n* (1914) a cigarette, especially a cheap or inferior one. Slang. From the respiratory effect on the smoker. The usage was probably at its height in the 1910s and 1920s, but it survived until after World War II

| 1921 S. P. B. Mais: Why should one prefer a Corona cigar to a 'gasper'?

gene *n* (1911) a hereditary unit located on a chromosome which determines a specific characteristic or function in the organism. An adaptation of German *Gen*, coined in 1909 by Johannsen (see the quote below) from the Greek base *gen-* 'be born'

| 1911 W. Johannsen: I have proposed the terms 'gene' and 'genotype'…to be used in the science of genetics. The 'gene' is nothing but a very applicable little word, easily combined with others, and hence it may be useful as an expression for the 'unit-factors', 'elements' or 'allelomorphs' in the gametes, demonstrated by modern Mendelian researches.

go-getter *n* (1910) an enterprising person. Colloquial, originally US. The underlying idea is of someone who goes and gets something, rather than waiting for it to arrive. The related adjective *go-getting* is not recorded before 1921

| 1921 Sewell Ford: Think you're one of these go-getters, do you?

| 1921 J. G. Frederick: The true forward-looking 'go-getting' American business point of view.

golfer *n* (1911) a cardigan. From the characteristic garb of golf players. The usage survived at least into the 1960s

| 1911 *Alfred Weeks' Sales Catalogue*: Our Stock of Golfers will be disposed of at one price only…2/11³/₄.

grand *n* (1915) a thousand dollars. US slang. Later used in British slang for 'a thousand pounds'. Originally the plural was often *grands*, but by the middle of the 1920s *grand* had become the established form. See also **G (1928)**

| 1921 *Collier's*: 'A hundred and fifty grands!' I breathed. 'You're cuckoo.'… '*I lose twenty-five thousand dollars!*… Twenty-five grand!

grass roots *n* (1912) the rank-and-file of the electorate or of a political party. Originally US. A specific political use of a more general metaphor, first recorded in 1901: 'the fundamental level'. By the end of the century it was firmly ensconced as a political cliché

| 1912 *McClure's Magazine*: From the Roosevelt standpoint, especially, it was a campaign from the 'grass roots up'. The voter was the thing.

| 1966 *New Statesman*: The grassroot Tory still prefers to touch his forelock and reverence his 'betters'.

Great War *n* (1914) World War I. The name had previously been used of the Napoleonic wars, and from the 1870s onwards it was commonly applied to the widely anticipated war between Britain and Germany (in the early 1890s, for example, Admiral Sir Philip Colomb and others produced the doomful *The Great War of 1892*). It continued to be the main term (alongside the colloquial *Kaiser's War*) for the conflict of 1914–18 among the generation that had lived through it, but once **World War I (1939)** and **World War II (1939)** had been coined it gradually went out of general use. See also **First World War (1947)**

| 1914 *Maclean's Magazine*: Some wars name themselves… This is the Great War.

| 1915 Grahame-White & Harper (*title*): Aircraft in the Great War.

groceteria *n* (1913) a grocery store in which customers serve themselves and pay the cashier as they leave. A sort of early **supermarket (1933)**. The word was registered as a trademark in 1913, and remained in use in North America until well into the 1960s. It is one of a range of terms modelled on *cafeteria* (e.g. *washeteria* (1959))

| 1916 *Illustrated World* (Chicago): In Pomona, California, a small grocery store has suddenly sprung into prominence…by adopting the 'wait-on-yourself' plan of a cafeteria. A 'Groceteria' if you please.

hate *n* (1915) a (German) artillery bombardment. A jocular usage on the Western Front, based on the German 'Hymn of Hate', which was ridiculed in the magazine *Punch* on 24 February 1915, in the caption of a cartoon, 'Study of a Prussian household having its morning hate'

> 1915 D. O. Barnett: There are some unhealthy spots, 'Suicide Corner', 'Deadman's Alley' and others, where they drop shells regularly, trying to catch our transport at night. We call it the 'Evening Hate'.

> 1926 Ford Madox Ford: There is not going to be a strafe. This is only a little extra Morning Hate.

hobble skirt *n* (1911) a close-fitting skirt usually confined by a wide band below the knees and above the ankles

> 1911 *Smart Set*: A hobble skirt is an awful habit to get into.

> 1954 C. G. Bradley: The hobble skirt of 1914 was worn even on long walking excursions. The slit skirt of the same year brought protests from bishops and ministers.

home front *n* (1919) (matters concerning) the civilian population of a country at war

> 1919 *Mr. Punch's History of the Great War*: The trials…on the home front.

> 1938 *Annual Register*: Sir A. Sinclair complained that the Government was concentrating its energies too much on preparations for attack, to the neglect of …'the home front'.

homo-erotic *adj* (1916) characterized by a tendency for erotic emotions to be centred on a person of the same sex. Originally a technical term in psychology, but often used subsequently as a general synonym for *homosexual*

> 1916 Ernest Jones: The development of a homo-erotic obsessional neurosis.

homosexual *n* (1912) a homosexual person. The earliest recorded instance of the noun in English is in a text translated from German, as is the earliest record of the adjective *homosexual* (1892). See also **homosexualist (1931)**

> 1912 E. Paul: An adult homosexual who as a child once did some needlework for a joke.

> 1932 Stella Gibbons: There were many homosexuals to be seen in Hyde Park.

Hooverize *v* (1917) to be sparing or economical, especially in the use of food. US. A brief commemoration of the name of Herbert C. Hoover (1874–1964), food commissioner 1917–19, and later President of the US 1929–33. The term did not survive long once the frugality was over

> 1917 H. B. Gross: It is now assured that Mr. Hoover is about to become our food regulator…and since he has…exhorted the public to exercise the utmost economy in the use of foodstuffs…I suggest that 'to Hooverize' be universally adopted as expressing the assistance every one of us…can render in that direction.

> 1919 W. T. Grenfell: All hands were forced to 'Hooverize'.

hop it *v* (1914) to go away quickly. British slang

> 1915 *Scotsman*: The Zeppelin kept a few miles in the rear of us, and finally hopped it.

hormone therapy *n* (1914) therapeutic treatment by the administration of hormones. The more specific *hormone replacement therapy* is not recorded until 1967

> 1914 H. R. Harrower: At present the application of hormone therapy in general practice is the exception rather than the rule.

hot flash, hot flush *n* (1910) a sudden unpleasant feeling of heat in the skin, experienced by many women during the menopause. *Hot flash* is the main US term, *hot flush* the British one

> 1910 W. B. Bell: The 'hot flushes'…are produced by rapid changes in the condition of the vasomotor system.

hub cap *n* (1913) a covering for the hub of the wheel of a vehicle

> 1913 *Collier's*: Their wheels, perhaps, have plain hub caps.

Hun *n* (1914) A derogatory name during World War I and afterwards for a German (soldier) or for Germans collectively. The term originally denoted a nomadic Asiatic people who invaded Europe in the Dark Ages, and had actually been applied dismissively to Germans in English since the late 18th century. This rather more specific usage was inspired by a speech delivered by Wilhelm II to the German troops about to sail for China on 27 July 1900, in which he enjoined them to fight like Huns (*The Times* reported (30 July 1900): According to the Bremen *Weser Zeitung* the Emperor said:-'…No quarter will be given, no prisoners will be taken. Let all who fall into your hands be at your mercy. Just as the Huns a thousand years ago, under the leadership of Etzel (Attila) gained a reputation in virtue of which they still live in historical tradition, so may the name of Germany become known in such a manner in China that no Chinaman will ever again even dare to look askance at a German')

1914 Rudyard Kipling: Stand up and meet the war. The Hun is at the gate!

1915 *Daily Mail*: She [*sc.* a Norfolk girl] told me how the eldest [brother 'at the front'] had held up three 'Huns' in a mill… She used the word 'Hun' quite naturally, with no hint of contempt or bitterness.

hush-hush *adj* (1916) A doubled form of the exclamation *hush!* used, often semi-facetiously, to denote any object of manufacture, process, plan, or policy, the details or existence of which are kept secret. Originally applied to secret weapons and other clandestine matters during World War I

1916 Harry Yoxall: The hush-hush Tanks were splendid.

hydroplane *n* (1911) See **hydro-aeroplane (1909)**

illegal operation *n* (1910) A euphemism for *abortion* which remained in common use in British English until the reform of the abortion law in 1968 greatly broadened the conditions under which such operations were legal

1910 G. K. Chesterton: Mr. Granville Barker's play of *Waste*, in which the woman dies from an illegal operation.

1927 *Review of English Studies*: There is a very interesting misuse of words…due…to a yet older human failing: taboo. As instances may serve *lavatory, illegal operation, social evil*.

immersion heater *n* (1914) a usually thermostatically controlled device for heating liquid in which it is immersed. A standard 20th-century method of providing domestic hot water in the days before central heating

1914 M. Lancaster: The water in cylinder A…is heated by the immersion heater B.

immunology *n* (1910) the science which deals with the phenomena and causes of immunity

1910 *Journal of the American Medical Association*: Relations between pharmacology, immunology and experimental therapy.

imperialism *n* (1918) (in Communist usage) the imperial system or policy of the Western powers. A Cold War mantra. The derived *imperialist* is first recorded in 1963

1918 *Manchester Guardian*: The Menshevik and the small bourgeois parties have published a declaration calling on workers all over the world to rally to the support of the Russian Revolution against the Imperialism attacking it.

1959 *Daily Telegraph*: Hence, perhaps, the decision to revert to 'Western imperialism' as target of a fresh hate-campaign in Iraq.

1963 *New Statesman*: The reported Chinese memorandum…[refers to] Krushchev's 'capitulation-ist' attitudes towards the 'imperialists'.

incendiary bomb *n* (1911) a bomb used to start a fire. The noun use of *incendiary* in this sense is first recorded in 1940. The synonymous *fire-bomb* dates from the late 19th century

1911 *Aero*: The following are reckoned…to be the principal offensive uses of the war-aeroplane: (1.) Attacking supply stores and setting them on fire with incendiary bombs.

1917 H. Woodhouse: The Zeppelins also dropped incendiary bombs intended to set places on fire.

1940 *Flight*: The pilot found his objective at once and his incendiaries started four large fires.

info *n* (1913) A colloquial abbreviation of *information*

1925 P. G. Wodehouse: So you've only to pool your info' to bring home the bacon?

instant *adj* (1912) Of a processed food: that can be prepared for use immediately. Originally US. See also **instantize (1962)**

1912 *Ladies' Home Journal* (advert): Instant Postum…is regular Postum [a type of coffee substitute] in concentrated form—made in the cup—no boiling required.

1915 E. B. Holt: I wish I had…drunk less of that hot-wash that my wife calls instant coffee.

intelligence test *n* (1914) a test to measure someone's mental skills

> 1914 *Eugenics Review*: General ability, estimated by intelligence tests, is largely hereditary.

introvert *n* (1918) a person whose behaviour is characterized by a lack of interest in interacting with other people and the external world. Originally a technical term in psychology, but subsequently used more generally for 'a shy self-absorbed person'. Compare **extrovert (1918)**

> 1918 P. Blanchard: Jung's hypothesis of the two psychological types, the introvert and extrovert,—the thinking type and the feeling type.

invasion scare *n* (1915) a widespread fear amongst the public that an invasion is imminent. Used particularly (in Britain) in the contexts of World Wars I and II

> 1915 Mrs. Belloc Lowndes: No, I do not believe in either Zeppelins or an invasion… There is an invasion scare but I don't believe in that.

> 1923 Winston Churchill: An invasion scare took a firm hold of the…authorities.

> 1940 'Gun Buster': Then happened one of our monthly 'flaps' (invasion scares).

invisible *adj* (1911) relating to items other than goods, for which payment is received from abroad, for example services, profits on foreign investment, money spent by visitors from a country with a different currency, etc. See also **invisibles (1958)**

> 1911 C. G. Robertson: Prior to the Industrial Revolution the seaborne and carrying trades, with their invisible exports, are an expanding source of wealth, but are not indispensable.

-ish *suffix* (1916) Added to names of hours of the day to denote: round about, somewhere near (the time of)

> 1916 'Peter': 'What time shall I come?' 'Elevenish,' Sam replied.

> 1925 Ben Travers: I shall be going to Shady Nook at about tenish.

isotope *n* (1913) one of two or more atoms with the same atomic number that have different numbers of neutrons. Coined from Greek *isos* 'equal, same' and *topos* 'place'

> 1913 F. Soddy: The same algebraic sum of the positive and negative charges in the nucleus, when the arithmetical sum is different, gives what I call 'isotopes' or 'isotopic elements', because they occupy the same place in the periodic table.

jamboree *n* (1919) The name given to the 1920 International Rally of Boy Scouts, and subsequently applied to any large scout rally. It was taken from the earlier *jamboree* 'lively celebration', but the ultimate origins of the word are obscure

> 1919 *Times*: The Council of the Boy Scouts Association announce that a 'Jamboree' will be held at Olympia, for about eight days next August.

jankers *n* (1916) punishment for defaulters, or the defaulters themselves. British services' slang, of unknown origin, which continued in use until well after World War II

> 1916 J. N. Hall: The 'jankers' or defaulters' squad was always rather large.

jaywalker *n* (1917) a pedestrian who walks across the road in defiance of traffic signals. Originally US. Based on US slang *jay* 'foolish person'

> 1917 *Harper's Magazine*: The Bostonian…has reduced 'a pedestrian who crosses streets in disregard of traffic signals' to the compact *jaywalker*.

jazz *n* (1913) a type of improvised syncopated popular music, originally as played by black bands in the southern US to accompany a ragtime dance known as 'jazz' (see **jazz (1909)**). It was after World War I that jazz spread from New Orleans and the Deep South to New York, Chicago, and other big US cities, and began to establish itself as one of the main musical art-forms of the 20th century (see **jazz age (1922)**)

> 1913 *Bulletin* (San Francisco): The team which speeded into town this morning comes pretty close to representing the pick of the army. Its members have trained on ragtime and 'jazz'.

> 1916 *Ragtime Review*: The 'Jaz' bands that are so popular at the present time.

> 1917 *Sun* (New York): Jazz is based on the savage musician's wonderful gift for progressive retarding and acceleration guided by his sense of 'swing'.

> 1918 *Era*: John Lester's Frisco Five. The Jollities of 'Jazz'.

> 1922   C. Engel: Jazz is rag-time, plus 'blues', plus orchestral polyphony; it is the combination, in the popular music current, of melody, rhythm, harmony, and counterpoint.

Jerry *n* (1919) a German. During World Wars I and II, applied specifically to a German soldier, or to German forces collectively (there is ample circumstantial evidence of use during World War I, although no written example has been found before 1919). Probably an alteration of *German*, presumably at least partly on the model of the male name *Jerry*. While not exactly affectionate, it does not contain the venom and contempt of **kraut (1918)** and **Hun (1914)**

> 1919   J. B. Morton: There was three Jerries waiting for 'im to get tired and chuck it.

join up *v* (1916) to enlist in the armed forces

> 1916   'Boyd Cable': Just joined up to get a finger in the fighting?

> 1922   D. H. Lawrence: Egbert went and joined up immediately as a private soldier.

kamerad *n* (1914) The German word (borrowed from French) for 'comrade', used as a placatory expression of surrender. Much used in sensational journalism, pulp fiction, etc. to suggest the spinelessness of German soldiers in World Wars I and II

> 1914   *Illustrated London News*: How the enemy surrenders, saying, 'Kamerad...Pardon!'

> 1917   Patrick MacGill: 'Kamerad! Kamerad!' they whined.

kinema *n* (1914) An alteration of **cinema (1913)**, with the *k* re-intoduced from Greek *kinema* 'movement'. As a current usage it does not seem to have survived the 1930s. See also **Kinemacolor (1909)**

> 1914   *Evening News*: It was my first step in the path of the kinema actor.

> 1928   *Western Morning News*: The new kinema on the site of the old Post Office at Totnes.

kitchenette *n* (1910) a small room or alcove in a house, flat, etc., combining kitchen and pantry. Originally US

> 1910   *Variety*: Mr. and Mrs. Nellie are going to have a swell apart. and they call the 'cook house' in a swell apart. a kitchenette.

> 1922   *Glasgow Herald*: The New York business woman...wants her kitchenette and her home cooking, be it ever so simple.

klaxon *n* (1910) an (electric) horn or warning hooter, originally one on a motor vehicle. Originally US. The name comes from that of the company which first made them, and seems to have been based on Greek *klazein* 'to roar'

> 1910   *Saturday Evening Post*: The Klaxon has never taken a life; it has saved thousands.

knut *n* (1911) a fashionable or showy young man of the pre-World War I period. British slang, probably a whimsical variant of **nut** in the same sense (1904), and variously pronounced 'nut' or 'kernut'

> 1913   L. A. Harker: He was...a 'knut' of the nuttiest flavour.

> 1915   A. Wimperis, *Gilbert the Filbert* (song): I'm Gilbert, the Filbert, The Colonel of the Knuts.

kraut *n* (1918) A contemptuous term for a German, and especially a German soldier of World Wars I and II. A tribute to the stereotypical prevalence of sauerkraut in the German diet

> 1918   G. E. Griffin: But he always loved a soldier, be he...'Krout' or 'Mick'.

ladies' *n* (1918) a women's public lavatory. The parallel sense of *gentleman's* is not recorded until the late 1920s

> 1918   Katherine Mansfield: Also, when she goes to the 'Ladies', for some obscure reason she wears a little shawl.

land *v* (1916) to bring (an aircraft) to the ground. First recorded in print in 1916, although no doubt in use well before then: its intransitive counterpart, 'to come to ground from the air', dates from the late 18th century (initially in the context of balloons)

> 1916   Horatio Barber: I'll guarantee to safely land the fastest machine in a five-acre field.

lav *n* (1913) A colloquial shortening of *lavatory*

> 1913   Compton Mackenzie: Tell the army to line up behind the lav. at four o'clock.

League of Nations *n* (1917) an association of self-governing states, dominions, and colonies created by a covenant forming part I of the Peace Treaty of 1919 'in order to promote international co-operation and to achieve international peace and security'. The US did not join it, and the association's failure to deal effectively with the bellicosity of Japan, Italy, and Germany in the 1930s meant that it had become an irrelevance in international affairs by the outbreak of World War II. It was subsequently replaced by the *United Nations* (1942). The third quote below gives something of the history of its name (which was often shortened to simply *League*)

> 1917 H. N. Brailsford (title): A League of Nations… The programme of the British 'League of Nations Society' is as follows.

> 1919 *League of Nations Journal*: The Union…Resulting…from the amalgamation of the League of Nations Society and of the League of Free Nations Association,…includes members of a society which has been working since May, 1915, for the establishment of a League of Nations.

> 1934 H. G. Wells: The term 'League of Nations' is of English origin and it seems to have been first used by a small group of people meeting in the house of Mr. Walter Rea… (E. M. Forster in his life of Lowes Dickinson (1934) gives reasons for ascribing the term to that writer, who may have used it for the two possible 'leagues' he sketched in the first fortnight of the war.) These people founded a League of Nations Society…early in 1915.

> 1950 Theimer & Campbell: The Assembly did not meet again until April 1946, when it decided to dissolve the League, already replaced by the United Nations.

legend in one's lifetime *n* (1918) someone so famous that they are the subject of popularly repeated stories even in their own lifetime

> 1918 Lytton Strachey: [Florence Nightingale] was a legend in her lifetime, and she knew it.

Leninist *adj, n* (1917) (a follower or supporter) of the Russian revolutionary leader V. I. Lenin (1870–1924) or of his doctrine. Coined contemporaneously with *Leninite*, which however barely survived a couple of years. The derivative *Leninism* is first recorded in 1918. Leninists believe in Marxism-Leninism (the term is first recorded in English in 1932), a version of Marxism adopted by Lenin to reflect contemporary developments in Russia and in capitalist societies

> 1917 *Times*: General Korniloff has been placed under the same ban as M. Kerensky, and renewed instructions for the arrest of both have been issued by the Leninist committee…Trotsky, on behalf of the Leninite 'Government', has telegraphed to all the representatives of Russia abroad.

> 1918 *Times* (caption): From Tsardom to Leninism.

Lewis gun *n* (1913) a type of light machine-gun. It was widely used by the Allies in World War I, both on the ground and fitted to aircraft. It was named after its inventor, Col. Isaac Newton Lewis (1858–1931) of the US Army

> 1919 *King's Royal Rifle Corps Chronicle 1916*: Stokes mortars and Lewis gun fire subdued the enemy's resistance.

liberty bodice *n* (1916) a vest-like undergarment for women and children, with buttons down the front. A British trademark. Still in use in the 1970s, but by then old-fashioned enough to raise a titter

> 1916 *Child*: The 'Liberty Bodice' Factory, of Market Harborough, have made a speciality of the 'Liberty Bodice'.

> 1973 *Radio Times*: The wiser you are, the more you appreciate the comfort of a liberty bodice.

limey *n* (1918) a British sailor, and hence more broadly, a British person. US slang. A truncated version of *lime-juicer*, a dismissive US term for a British ship or sailor which dates from the mid 19th century and which refers to the lime-juice drunk as an anti-scorbutic by sailors in the Royal Navy

> 1918 R. D. Paine: Squads of the American navy patrol began to stroll about…displaying no sympathy…for the shipmate who…loudly announced that he could whip any three 'Limies' that ever trod a British deck.

location *n* (1914) an exterior place, away from a film-studio, where a scene is filmed. Often in the phrase *on location* (first recorded in 1918)

1914 *Scribner's Magazine*: It was his duty…to pick out 'locations', as are called the scenes and backgrounds of a moving-picture play.

1918 Homer Croy: Now many actors are…in the studio or on location.

lorribus, lorry-bus *n* (1919) a lorry used as a public passenger vehicle. A word which eventually found a home in West African English

1919 *Daily Mail*: In the welter of London's crowded streets we grasped at the relieving 'lorribus' (the converted Army lorry doing the duty as an emergency omnibus).

1963 *Economist*: Ghana's ubiquitous lorry-buses, or mammywagons.

lounge lizard *n* (1918) a man who spends his time idling in fashionable society, especially in search of a wealthy patroness. Slang, redolent particularly of the inter-war period, but still about at the end of the century. Originally US

1928 'Sapper': 'A lounge lizard. A ball-room snake. What matter that his Black Bottom is the best in London.' 'My Gawd! sir,' gasped the other. 'His 'ow much?'

maisonette *n* (1912) a type of multi-floor flat, often with direct external access. Mainly British. A borrowing from French (where it is spelled *maisonnette*), literally 'little house'. An early contribution to the 20th-century vocabulary of restricted living-spaces

1912 *Chambers's Journal*: Flats or maisonettes, such as Queen Anne's Mansions, Westminster, London.

massage parlour *n* (1913) an establishment offering massage and usually also various sexual services for payment. From the beginning the word's connotation 'brothel' was widely recognized (see the quote below)

1913 *Collier's*: Along with them go the announcements of 'massage parlors' (an all-too-obvious euphemism), free whiskies, and other agencies of public injury.

ministry *n* (1916) The name given to certain departments of the British government. Hitherto they had gone under such designations as *office* and *board*. *Ministry* became the favoured term for any newly founded government department, and remained so until the 1960s, when it began to be overtaken by *department*

1916 *Whitaker's Almanack*: Munitions, Ministry of, Minister, Rt. Hon. D. Lloyd George, M.P.

Minnie *n* (1917) a German trench-mortar, or the bomb discharged by it. Army slang. A shortened version of German *Minenwerfer* 'trench-mortar' (literally 'mine-thrower'), on the model of the female forename *Minnie*. During World War II came the further refinement *Moaning Minnie*, so named because of the noise made by its projectiles

1917 A. G. Empey: A German 'Minnie' (trench mortar) had exploded in the next traverse.

M.O. (1916) An abbreviation of *medical officer*

1916 Ford Madox Ford: The M.O. …has just sounded my poor old lungs again.

mobster *n* (1917) a member of a criminal gang. Slang, originally US. Over the succeeding decade the term came to used in the context of organized crime in the US, and *the Mob* would denote 'the Mafia'

1917 *Lincoln* (Nebraska) *Evening News*: Many mobsters have left the city, it is asserted, and leaders of the mob are going to be hard to find.

moron *n* (1910) an adult with a mental age of between eight and twelve. The term (based ultimately on Greek *mōros* 'stupid') was first adopted and given this meaning by the American Association for the Study of the Feeble-minded in 1910. Already by the 1920s it was being used (as is commonly the fate of new technical terminology attached to the mentally subnormal) as an insult, and it is no longer in technical use

1910 H. H. Goddard: The other (suggestion) is to call [feeble-minded children] by the Greek word 'moron'. It is defined as one who is lacking in intelligence, one who is deficient in judgement or sense.

1919 H. Woodrow: The term *moron*…is a new term… [Its] desirability…arose from the fact that the term feeble-minded, which is used in England to designate only the highest class of mental defectives, had long been used in America to include all three classes.

motion study *n* (1911) See **time and motion study (1932)**

motorcade *n* (1913) a procession of motor vehicles. Originally US. A blend of *motor* and *cavalcade*. Not the first of such formations based on *cavalcade* (*camelcade* dates from the 1880s), but the most durable

> 1913 *Arizona Republican*: This 'motorcade' came from a suggestion thrown out by the sporting editor of the Republican. It was immediately accepted by several local automobile owners, whereupon, the sporting editor [Lyle Abbott] became the busiest man in Phoenix and hammered away at the 'motorcade' a term which he had invented sometime before in order that newspapers might keep pace with the developments of vehicular transportation.

motorism *n* (1913) the use or prevalence of motor vehicles; the world of motoring

> 1913 *Chambers's Journal*: It is but ten or twelve years since the time when the tide of motorism began to flow.

> 1952 *Birmingham* (Alabama) *News*: If you want to be in the forefront of motorism these days, it seems you have to have headlamps outside the fenders.

motorize *v* (1913) to provide with a motor. In the earliest known reference to this verb, in a supplement to *Webster's Dictionary*, it denotes the equipping of a previously horse-drawn organization with motor vehicles, but it has subsequently acquired other meanings, including 'to fit a vehicle with a motor'

> 1922 *Daily Mail*: These machines have gone beyond the stage of motorised pedal cycles and are in all respects real motor-cycles.

> 1972 Gavin Black: Angels mightn't be watching over them, but a good third of the motorized police in the State were.

motor-sledge *n* (1910) a sledge powered by a motor. A term made familiar by Captain Scott's (disastrously unsuccessful) use of such vehicles on his 1910–12 South Pole expedition

> 1910 *Chambers's Journal*: The 'final dash' [to the Pole]…will be made with the help of motor-sledges.

Mountie *n* (1914) a member of the Royal Canadian (formerly North West) Mounted Police

> 1924 A. J. Small: A sentence that is at once the badge and boast of the Mounted—'the Mounties never come in without their man'.

movie *n* (1912) a motion picture, a film. An abbreviation of *moving picture* (1896). Originally (and still mainly) US. Often used in the plural to denote the motion-picture industry, or a film show

> 1912 *Survey* (New York) (*heading*): 'Movies' and the law.

> 1913 *Home Chat*: The comparatively small towns [in America] have installed 'movies'—as they call them over there—in their schools.

movie house *n* (1914), **movie theater** *n* (1915) a cinema. Mainly US

> 1914 *Automobile Topics*: Selected bits of the picture…are being shown in the local 'movie houses'.

> 1915 *Film Flashes*: It's a long lane that has no movie theatre.

movie star *n* (1919) See **film star (1914)**

moving staircase *n* (1910) An alternative for **escalator (1900)**. In the early part of the century this and the variations *moving stair* and *moving stairway* were the preferred terms in British English. The first such staircase in Britain was opened in 1911 at Earls Court underground station

> 1910 *Daily News*: In the course of the hearing counsel referred to a proposed moving staircase as an 'escalator'.

> 1911 *Engineer*: The escalator or moving stairway connecting the 'Piccadilly' and District Railway.

> 1922 *Granta*: I dreamt I saw a Proctor 'escalating', Rushing up a quickly moving stair.

mug's game *n* (1910) a futile activity. Slang. Based on *mug* 'a fool', which dates from the middle of the 19th century. In the earliest recorded example, *mug* is personalized, but by the end of the decade the expression had become established in its now familiar form

1910 Hilaire Belloc: One cannot arrest millionaires with impunity… Even in a wild democracy to arrest them is Mug's game.

1918 *Flying*: Flying's a mug's game, mater, A fact I know full well.

munitioneer *n* (1916) a worker in a munition factory. A term revived in World War II

1916 E. V. Lucas: In the need for copper there is quite a good price for engraved plates, and theirs have been weeded out for the munitioneers.

1940 *New Statesman*: The munitioneer can see no difference in the management or control of his factory.

munitionette *n* (1915) a female worker in a munition factory. British colloquial. A World War I term: it did not reappear during World War II, though the female munition workers did

1917 *Daily News*: A shell-shop filled with blue-clad mob-capped cheering munitionettes.

mushroom *n* (1916) a cloud (of smoke, dust, etc.) that spreads upwards and outwards, in the shape of a mushroom. A metaphor which found its natural home in 1945 when the first atom bomb was detonated (see **mushroom cloud (1958)**)

1916 John Buchan: There was the dull shock of an explosion and a mushroom of red earth.

1945 *New York Times*: A giant column that soon took the shape of a supramundane mushroom.

mustard gas *n* (1917) a colourless, oily liquid which is a powerful poison and blistering agent, and which was first used in warfare by the Germans in 1917, at Ypres

1917 *Nation* (New York): The Germans have just invented a new and particularly powerful weapon in their so-called 'mustard gas'.

mystery ship *n* (1914) an armed and camouflaged merchant ship used in World War I as a decoy or to destroy submarines. Later also known as a **Q boat (1918)** or **Q ship (1919)**

1914 *Daily Mail*: The grey, gaunt outline of the mystery ship took definite shape.

napoo, napooh *interj, adj, v* (1915) Originally an exclamation meaning 'done, finished, no more', but subsequently used adjectivally in the sense 'finished', and also 'dead', and as a verb, 'to finish or kill'. It represents a British soldiers' version of French (*il n'y e*)*n a plus* 'there's no more', picked up during war service in France. It proved to be one of the more durable pieces of World War I slang

1915 Ian Hay: You say 'Na pooh!' when you push your plate away after dinner… 'Poor Bill got na-poohed by a rifle-grenade yesterday.'

1943 J. B. Priestley: You're as good as dead—just waitin' to stiffen. Fini—napoo!

national service *n* (1916) a statutory obligation to serve in the armed forces for a specified period, introduced in Britain in 1916. See also **national serviceman (1949)**

1916 *Hansard*: It is proposed to appoint at once a director of National Service, to be in charge of both the military and civil side of universal national service.

nature reserve *n* (1915) a tract of land managed in order to preserve its fauna, flora, physical features, etc.

1915 R. Lankester: A society has been founded for the formation of 'nature-reserves' in the British Islands.

neon *n* (1911) Used in designating light sources using fluorescent neon-filled tubes, which became a characteristic feature of 20th-century urban nightscapes

1913 *Transactions of the Illuminating Engineers' Society* (US): The neon light is physiologically excellent on account of its dull luminescence.

1940 Louis MacNeice: And the neon-lamps of London Stain the canals of night.

neutral *n* (1912) a position of the driving and driven parts in a gear mechanism in which no power is transmitted

1912 G. Harris: With clutch still disengaged, the transmission lever is moved from neutral to first speed position.

newly-wed *n* (1918) someone newly married

> 1918 *Cosmopolitan*: A Newly-wed can live on Marmalade for about three months.

newshound *n* (1918) an (over-)investigative journalist. Originally US. The synonym *newshawk* is first recorded in 1931

> 1926 *Time*: In a jazzed age no news hound delved through the reference 'morgue' of his paper to turn up the great story.

newsreel *n* (1916) a short cinema film dealing with news and current affairs. The staple form of in-motion news reporting until television news came of age in the late 1950s. See also **news theatre (1933)**

> 1916 *Wells Fargo Messenger*: Some companies issue their news reels twice a week.

> 1928 *Manchester Guardian Weekly*: There are four motion picture newsreel cameramen, and four 'still' photographers.

new town *n* (1918) (in Britain) a planned urban area designed to ease the congestion of a nearby large city, usually one with special provision for housing, employment, and amenities for a de-limited population. First recorded in the title of a pamphlet in 1918, but it did not come into general use until such towns started being built after World War II

> 1948 Josephine Tey: The little house on the outer rim of the 'new' town.

New World Order *n* (1919) a vision of a world ordered differently from the way it is at present. It is a concept that has tended to arise from the ruins of a world shattered by war, and indeed the first recorded occurrences of it are as the title of two books published just after World War I (the 'war to end wars'). More recently it has been applied to a new set of conditions, principles, laws, etc. governing world events, and specifically the global balance of power following the end of the Cold War

> 1919 S. Z. Batten (title): The new world order.

> 1920 F. C. Hicks: From Ladd's time to the present there has been a rapid increase of interest in plans for a new world order for the purpose of maintaining peace.

> 1940 H. G. Wells: There will be no day of days, then, when a new world order comes into being.

> 1977 *US News & World Report*: His basic aim: Build a new world order based on a U.S. commitment to moral values rather than an 'inordinate fear of Communism'.

> 1991 George Bush: And now, we can see a new world coming into view. A world in which there is a very real prospect of a new world order.

Nissen hut *n* (1917) a tunnel-shaped hut made of corrugated iron with a cement floor. Named after its inventor, Lt.-Col. Peter Norman Nissen (1871–1930). It became a familiar part of the dreary landscape of British military establishments of the middle part of the century, housing genera-tions of service personnel. See also **Quonset hut (1942)**

> 1917 E. F. Wood: Recently I met the inventor of the now famous Nissen hut.

normal *adj* (1914) heterosexual

> 1914 E. M. Forster: Against my will I have become normal. I cannot help it.

nuclear *adj* (1914) of atomic nuclei (see **nucleus (1912)**)

> 1914 *Engineering*: A point raised by Professor Rutherford concerning the effective nuclear charge.

> 1945 H. D. Smyth: The pile was first operated…on December 2, 1942… This was the first time that human beings ever initiated a self-maintaining nuclear chain reaction.

> 1963 *Oxford University Gazette*: The University has established a Professorship of Nuclear Structure in the Department of Nuclear Physics.

nucleus *n* (1912) the positively charged central constituent of the atom, comprising nearly all its mass but occupying only a very small part of its volume and now known to be composed of pro-tons and neutrons. Physicists as far back as Michael Faraday in the 1840s had used the term *nucleus* (from Latin, literally a 'kernel') for the hypothetical central point of an atom, so the way was pre-pared for Ernest Rutherford to employ it when the real nature of atomic structure had been eluci-dated. In his original 1911 paper (see the quote below) he referred to it simply as a 'central charge'; *nucleus* followed in 1912

> 1912 Ernest Rutherford: In a previous paper [1911] I have given reasons for believing that the atom consists of a positively charged nucleus of very small dimensions, surrounded by a distribution of electrons in rapid motion, possibly of rings of electrons rotating in one plane.

nutarian *n* (1914) a vegetarian who lives mainly on nuts. Apparently a serious coinage, first recorded in the 1914 supplement to *Chambers's English Dictionary*, but not very long-lived

> 1922 James Joyce: Why do they call that thing they gave me nutsteak? Nutarians, Fruitarians. To give you the idea you are eating rumpsteak.

Oedipus complex *n* (1910) The name given by Sigmund Freud to the complex of emotions aroused in a child by its subconscious sexual desire for the parent of the opposite sex, which, if not resolved naturally, may lead to repression, guilt feelings, and an inability to form normal emotional or sexual relationships. Based on the plot of Sophocles' play *Oedipus Tyrannus*, in which Oedipus unknowingly kills his father and marries his mother

> 1910 Ernest Jones: The Œdipus-complex as an explanation of Hamlet's mystery.

okeh *adj, n, v* (1919) OK. *OK* dates back to the late 1830s (this is not the place to go fully into the much-contested details of its origin, but it was probably short for *orl korrect*, then current slang among the Boston smart set, and since this coincided with the initials of 'Old Kinderhook', the politician Martin van Buren, it was used as a slogan by his supporters in 1840). Hitherto it had been written only as two (capital) letters, but the immediate post-World War I period saw the first moves towards spelling it as it sounds. This initial version (said to have been initiated by US President Woodrow Wilson—see the fourth quote below) seems not to have survived beyond the early 1930s, being ousted by **okay (1929)**

> 1919 H. L. Mencken: Dr. Woodrow Wilson is said…to use *okeh* in endorsing government papers.

> 1925 *Dollar Magazine*: To find new and more vivid forms of expression…in the hope that they will, in time, receive the okeh of the reading public.

> 1930 *American Speech*: Parachute company stock sale okehed.

> 1939 E. B. Wilson: Approval was designated by 'Okeh, W.W.' on the margin of a paper. Someone asked why he did not use the 'O.K.' 'Because it is wrong,' Mr. Wilson said. He suggested that the inquirer look up 'okeh' in a dictionary. This he did, discovering that it is a Choctaw word meaning 'It is so'.

old hat *adj* (1911) old-fashioned, out of date, or unoriginal. Slang

> 1911 Arthur Quiller-Couch: Men have…put it, with like doctrines, silently aside in disgust. So it has happened with Satan and his fork: they have become 'old hat'.

one-step *n* (1911) a ballroom dance in quick time, in which the steps resemble simple walking, popular in the 1910s and 1920s

> 1911 *Home Chat*: Camilla is just mad about the 'One-step'.

> 1914 V. Castle: Simply *walk* as softly and smoothly as possible, taking a step to every count of the music. This is the One Step, and this is all there is to it.

one-way *adj* (1914) Designating traffic systems in which the vehicles are allowed to go in one direction only

> 1914 *World's Work*: Some little has already been done in the small streets off Piccadilly to request drivers to avoid some streets when going north and others when going south, thereby aiming at 'one-way' traffic, but there is no power to enforce the requests… Where streets are too narrow to permit of the rotary system the difficulty can be overcome by one-way streets.

oojah *n* (1917) an unnamed thing; a whatsit. British, originally military slang. An invented word, which had variants with assorted rococo knobs on—notably *oojah-ka-piv* and **oojiboo** (see next). It proved remarkably durable, continuing in use for as long as its original generation of English-speakers were around to use it, and in a variety of roles (e.g. as a euphemism for *lavatory*). See also **oojah-cum-spiff (1930)**

> 1925 Fraser & Gibbons: *Oojah* (also *Ooja-ka-pivi*), a substitute expression for anything the name of which a speaker cannot momentarily think of, *e.g.* 'Pass me that h-m, h-m, oojah-ka-pivi, will you?'

oojiboo *n* (1918) an unnamed thing; a whatsit. British military slang. A refinement on **oojah (1917)**, but not so long-lived—it had largely faded out by the end of the 1920s

> 1918 *Daily Express*: The oojiboo may be a hammer, a saw, a spanner, but Jimmy, or anyone else, knows exactly what is wanted... I dropped the old oojiboo [a kitbag] on the platform and nipped into the refreshment-room. Wasn't gone two minutes, but d-n me if somebody hadn't won the oojiboo [stolen the kitbag].

op *n* (1916) a military operation. Usually used in the plural. See also **op (1925)**

> 1916 Wilfred Owen: We had 'Night Ops.' yesterday till 9.30!

outcry *n* (1911) a vehement public protest. Hitherto *outcry* had simply meant 'loud clamour'. George Bernard Shaw appears to have originated this metaphorical usage

> 1957 Winston Churchill: Andrew Jackson's victory at New Orleans and the success of the peace negotiations produced an outcry against the disloyalty of New England.

Ozzie *n, adj* (1918) (an) Australian. A phonetic spelling of **Aussie (1917)**

> 1919 *New York Times*: There was nothing an Ozzie liked so much as fighting with a Yankee company.

panel *n* (1913) In Britain, the official list of doctors in a district who accepted patients under the National Health Insurance Act of 1913. The system came to an end with the introduction of the National Health Service in 1946, but the term clung on for some decades after that

> 1914 *Times*: Of these [doctors] 1500 are already on the panel for the county.

> 1964 G. L. Cohen: Working people still talk about 'going on the Panel' when they're off sick, and don't see why they should use another term.

panoram *v* (1915) Of a film (or, later, a television) camera: to move so as to follow a moving object. A shortening of *panorama* or *panoramic*, but a less durable one than **pan (1930)**

> 1915 *Wells Fargo Messenger*: We are before the Erie cut, and as the camera 'panorams' around, we get a glimpse of our splendid Eleventh Avenue Stable in Jersey City.

> 1917 C. N. Bennett: Sweeping round the camera...is called panoraming.

parapsychic, parapsychical *adj* (1918) of phenomena such as telepathy, psychokinesis, etc., for which no adequate scientific explanation exists. An earlier attempt to introduce a term that would bring some academic respectability to an area of study popularly associated with spiritualists and séances was *metapsychical*, introduced by Oliver Lodge in 1905 as an adaptation from French *métapsychique*. It did not survive long, but *parapsychic* has done better. Its associated noun *parapsychology* dates from the mid 1920s

> 1918 D. Wright: Unless we choose to coin a special word for the purpose, such as 'parapsychical', as suggested by Dr. Boirac.

park *n* (1916) an open space where cars and other vehicles can be left. Usually preceded by the name of the type of vehicle. The compound **car-park** is not recorded until 1926

> 1916 Arnold Bennett: Audrey's motor-car...was waiting in the automobile park.

parsec *n* (1913) a unit of length equal to the distance at which a star would have a heliocentric parallax of one second of arc (about 3.26 light-years); now a standard unit of astronomical measurement. Coined from *parallax + second*

> 1913 F. W. Dyson: There is need for a name for this unit of distance... Professor Turner suggests *Parsec*, which may be taken as an abbreviated form of 'a distance corresponding to a parallax of one second'.

peace offensive *n* (1918) a sustained campaign or effort to bring about peace; often implying a cynical attempt to further one's own warlike aims by appearing to promote peace

> 1918 Siegfried Sassoon: There are indications that the enemies' peace offensive is creating the danger which is its object.

> 1939 *War Illustrated*: Mr. Chamberlain stated...that nothing in the German 'peace offensive' could modify the attitude which Great Britain had felt it right to take.

pelmanize *v* (1919) to practise **pelmanism (1923)**

> 1919 *Honey Pot*: Lots of our fellows are Pelmanising out here.

Percy *n* (1916) a conscientious objector. A term of contempt used in Britain during World War I, and apparently based on a perception of *Percy* as an effete or feeble name. See also **Cuthbert (1917)**

> 1916 George Bernard Shaw: Mobbed and pilloried and photographed in the 'Daily Sketch' as 'Percy' (all Percies are now—shade of Hotspur!—supposed to be cowards).

persona *n* (1917) the set of attitudes adopted by individuals to fit themselves for the social roles which they see as theirs. Originally a technical term in Jungian psychology, but subsequently used more generally for 'the personality an individual presents to the world'

> 1917 C. E. Long: The persona is always identical with a *typical* attitude, in which *one* psychological function dominates, e.g. feeling, or thought, or intuition.

phonogram *n* (1911) a telegram that the sender dictates over the telephone. The word was originally coined around 1860 by Isaac Pitman for a letter or symbol representing a particular sound in his system of phonetic shorthand. From the late 1870s it was also used for a recording made by or played on a phonograph. This new application, based on *telegram*, has enjoyed particular success in Australian English

> 1911 D. Murray: Economic necessity will…lead to a great increase in telephone-telegrams, or, as the British Post Office already calls them, 'phonograms'.

> 1976 *Sydney Telephone Directory*: Phonograms. To save time, telephone your telegrams.

Photostat *n* (1911) The proprietary name of a kind of photocopying machine, later also applied to a copy made on such a machine, and used as a verb (first recorded in 1914). The term was registered as a trademark in the US in 1911. It means literally 'making light stationary'

> 1912 *Chambers's Journal*: By means of the photostat a new filing method is possible.

> 1914 *American Machinist*: A prism is used to 'turn the corner', making it more convenient than if the book or other object being 'photostated' had to be set up on edge.

> 1928 P. S. Allen: I should be glad to have the photostats (where does the word come from?) quickly.

picturedrome *n* (1914) a cinema. Coined on the model of *hippodrome*. It was still going reasonably strong at the end of World War II

> 1914 *Durham Advertiser*: Arrangements are being made…for the 'Varsity students' 'rag'…to be shown at the Assembly Rooms Picturedrome.

> 1945 *Gen*: A cinema owner can extol the modernity of his 'Picturedrome'.

picture-play *n* (1911) a cinema film drama. The term seems not to have outlived the 1920s

> 1923 George Ade: Two or three weeks ago I picked up a picture magazine and read the outline of the new picture play called 'Fury'.

Piltdown (1912) The name of a village near Lewes in East Sussex, England, where fossil bones of a supposed advanced hominid were found in 1912 by Charles Dawson. It was widely used attributively in connection with the find, and the creature became popularly known as *Piltdown man*. In 1953 the bones were shown to be a hoax

> 1912 *Times*: [A. S. Woodward] inclined…to the theory that…surviving modern man might have arisen directly from the primitive source of which the Piltdown skull provided the first discovered evidence.

> 1955 J. S. Weiner: The end of Piltdown man is the end of the most troubled chapter in human palaeontology.

pinball *n* (1911) See **pin-table (1936)**

pipped *adj* (1914) annoyed, irritated. Fairly short-lived British slang; it goes with *have the pip* 'to be fed-up' and *give someone the pip* 'to annoy someone', which date from the late 19th century and derive from *pip* the name of a type of chicken-disease

> 1914 A. M. N. Lyons: 'How's Leverton?' 'Rather pipped, thank you,' replied Miss Disney. 'Poor old Ma was raw-beefing him when I left.'

pipsqueak *n* (1910) A contemptuous term for a small or insignificant person. From *pip* 'small weak sound', so the underlying idea is of a young weedy creature capable only of making trivial noises.

The expression did not come into widespread use until the 1920s, probably given a boost by **pip-squeak** 'shell' (see next), and by Pip, Squeak, and Wilfred, three animal characters featured in a comic strip in the *Daily Mirror* from 1920 onwards

1930 G. Macmunn: It does not pay in the East to let pip-squeaks beard the mighty.

pipsqueak *n* (1916) a small type of high-velocity shell distinguished by the sound of its flight

1916 E. V. Lucas: Whatever else there is to grumble at over here, wet, and rats, and Pip-Squeaks and Jack Johnsons…we do get two things up to sample.

1917 A. G. Empey: *Pip squeak*, Tommy's term for a small German shell which makes a 'pip' and then a 'squeak', when it comes over.

podiatry *n* (1914) the diagnosis and treatment of disorders of the foot. Coined (together with its derivative *podiatrist*) from the Greek stem *pod-* 'foot' and *iatreia* 'healing', in a conscious attempt to supplant *chiropody* and *chiropodist* (the latter coined in 1785). These were felt to have unfortunate connotations of unskilled corn-cutting (*chiropodist* was defined as 'one who treats corns and bunions' in a late 19th-century medical dictionary). *Podiatry* originated in the US but took a long time to catch on even there (see the second quote below); in general British English it remains uncommon

1914 F. von Oefele: The practice of foot lesions may hereafter be styled 'Helotomy' or, 'Heliatry', or more generally 'Podiatry'… We should prevent the possibility of such a ridiculous misunderstanding by substituting the word 'podiatrist' (physician of the foot) for the unscientific term 'chiropodist'.

1958 *Technology*: The National Association of Chiropodists has announced that it has changed its title to The American Podiatry Association and that its members will henceforth be known by the 'more dignified' style of podiatrists.

poison gas *n* (1915) a lethal gas (e.g. phosgene) used in warfare

1915 H. W. Wilson: After the great chemical experiment with poison gas in April, the Germans had been able to advance to the manor-house.

poison pen *adj* (1914) relating to the writing of malicious and usually anonymous letters

1914 *New York World*: Women…crowded the Union County Court room…hoping to hear some plausible elucidation of the 'poison pen' mystery.

1956 Angus Wilson: To all the other clergymen she was busy addressing poison-pen letters.

pommy, pommie *n, adj* (1912) A derogatory term amongst Australians and New Zealanders for an immigrant from the United Kingdom; hence, more broadly, an Englishman or Englishwoman, a Briton. A shortening of the contemporary but now defunct *pomegranate*, which is said to be an alteration of *immigrant*. The further abbreviated *pom* is also first recorded in 1912

1912 *Truth* (Sydney): The comic British citizen, That leans against a post; They used to say colonials did, But I'm very much afraid, Upon the 'Poms' I'd put my quid.

1916 *Anzac Book*: A Pommy can't go wrong out there if he isn't too lazy to work.

poofter *n* (1910) An insulting term for a male homosexual. Originally Australian, it is a fanciful extension of *poof* (*c*1850). For a later development, see **woofter (1977)**

1910 O'Brien & Stephens: *Pouf or poufter*, a sodomite or effeminate man.

posh *adj* (1918) At first in the meaning 'smart, stylish, first-rate', but the connotations of snobbish exclusivity or refinement which mark its present-day use soon crept in. Colloquial. The origins of the word have been much discussed but remain mysterious. The suggestion that it is derived from the initials of 'port outward, starboard home', referring to the more expensive side for accommodation on ships formerly travelling between Britain and India, is often put forward but lacks foundation. There may be some connection with obsolete 19th-century slang *posh* 'a dandy'

1918 *Punch*: Oh, yes, Mater, we had a posh time of it down there.

1923 P. G. Wodehouse: Practically every posh family in the country has called him in at one time or another.

1929 J. B. Priestley: I'd like to have…a very cosy car, small but frightfully posh.

1957 John Osborne: *Jimmy*: Haven't you read the other posh paper yet? *Cliff*: Which? *Jimmy*: Well, there are only two posh papers on a Sunday.

postcard *v* (1910) to send a postcard (to). A verbification of the noun which seems to have had a certain currency in the first half of the century

> 1910 *Westminster Gazette*: Patterns ready for sending by return post. Postcard us to-day.

> 1947 *Ki-grams* (Washington, D.C. Kiwanis Club): Zeddie Blackistone post-cards about the flowers, the sunshine and golf at Palm Beach.

post-impressionism *n* (1910) a school of painting, exemplified especially by Cézanne, Gaugin, and van Gogh, which rejected the more strictly representational aspects of impressionism and emphasized personal vision. The term (and the derived adjective and noun *post-impressionist*) were introduced to Britain via an exhibition of such paintings organized by Roger Fry in 1910

> 1910 C. Holmes: The tradition of Post-Impressionism,…if any principles so youthful can be called a tradition, is the expression of personal vision.

> 1910 *Poster*: Grafton Gallery. Manet and the Post-Impressionists.

P.O.W. (1919) An abbreviation of *prisoner-of-war* which seems not to have come into widespread use until World War II

> 1941 *War Illustrated*: P.O.W. camps in Germany and Poland are shown in this map.

preadolescent *adj* (1910) having nearly reached the beginning of adolescence

> 1910 A. C. Perry: It is probably true that the preadolescent girl can pursue her school work side by side with the boy without the slightest danger.

premature ejaculation *n* (1910) excessively early ejaculation during sexual intercourse. A first appearance in English for a term which had hitherto hidden in the decent obscurity of Latin *ejaculatio praecox*

> 1910 A. Abrams: Occasionally onanism is followed by various grades of impotency (usually psychic) and premature ejaculation.

prenuptial agreement *n* (1916) a legal contract made between two people prior to marriage, especially one detailing the legal and financial rights and responsibilities, etc. of each in the event of their separation or divorce. A common legal term in the US throughout the century, but familiar in Britain only towards its end. See also **prenup (1990)**

> 1916 *New York Supplement*: We have…a prenuptial agreement that if the plaintiff would marry testator he would make a will by which he should leave her…all of his property.

> 1994 *Observer*: Pre-nuptial agreements are an accepted fact of financial life in the US, but they have yet to catch on here.

pressure cooker *n* (1915) an airtight container in which food can be cooked in steam under pressure, so that a higher temperature is reached and the food is cooked more quickly. A mod con which went out of favour in the last third of the century

> 1915 *Journal of Home Economics*: Why should the modern household reject a tool of value? This question might well be asked concerning pressure cookers.

prestigious *adj* (1913) having high status or glamour; conferring prestige. A usage that has found disfavour in some purist quarters, on the grounds that the etymological (hence, 'true') meaning of the word is 'involving trickery, illusory'. However, the use of *prestige* for 'high status, glamour' goes back to the early 19th century, and it is somewhat bizarre to take exception to the employment of the derived adjective in the same sense. Objections to it seem to have surfaced after World War II: there is no reference to it in early editions of *Fowler's Modern English Usage*, and the awkward *prestigeful*, recommended by some usage writers for those who could not stomach *prestigious*, is not recorded before 1956. The controversy has now largely faded away

> 1913 Joseph Conrad: 'You have had all these immense sums… What have I had out of them?' It was perfectly true. He had had nothing out of them—nothing of the prestigious or the desirable things of the earth.

profiteer *n* (1912) someone who seeks to make excessive gain (e.g. by the extortionate sale of necessary goods). This and the associated noun *profiteering* came into their own during World War I as terms of opprobrium for those who made a profit out of manufacturing or supplying material for the Allied war effort. A law was passed against the practice in Britain in 1919, called the Profiteering Act. See also **do well out of (1919)**

1914 *Englishwoman*: The tricks of the armament profiteers are fresh in the public mind.

1914 *New Age*: England is at war upon profiteering.

project *n* (1916) an exercise in which pupils or students are set to study a topic, either independently or in co-operation, from observation and experiment as well as from books, over a period of time. A key term in 20th-century educational theory and practice

1916 D. Snedden: [We] began using the word 'project' to describe a unit of educative work in which the most prominent feature was some form of positive and concrete achievement.

psyche *n* (1910) the conscious and unconscious mind and emotions, especially as influencing and affecting the whole person. An adoption into psychiatric terminology of a word previously denoting more vaguely the soul or spirit (as distinguished from the body). Ultimately from Greek *psukhē* 'breath, life, soul'

1910 C. G. Jung: Disease is an imperfect adaptation; hence in this case we are dealing with something morbid in the psyche.

psychoanalyse *v* (1911) to subject to or treat by psychoanalysis. A back-formation from **psychoanalysis (1906)**, on the model of *analysis, analyse* (**analyse** itself is first recorded in the sense 'to psychoanalyse' in 1909)

1911 *American Journal of Psychology*: It is…hoped that Freud will…psychoanalyze Goethe.

psychoanalyst *n* (1911) someone who practises or has training in psychoanalysis

1911 *American Journal of Psychology*: The business of the psychoanalyst is to provide a means by which the emotion attached to a repressed complex may find expression.

psychokinesis *n* (1914) a psychic power by which some people are held to be able to move objects by other than physical means. *Telekinesis* (1890) implies movement without physical contact, without necessarily invoking psychic powers

1914 H. Holt: Perhaps we are as nearly ready to consider what I shall call Psychokinesis as people were a generation ago to consider Telekinesis.

public relations *n* (1913) activities to promote a favourable relationship and good image with the public. A prophetic example of the term is recorded over a hundred years before in the writings of American statesman Thomas Jefferson ('Questions calling for the notice of Congress, unless indeed they shall be superseded by a change in our public relations now awaiting the determination of others' (1807)), but it did not establish itself until the 20th century. The abbreviation **PR** is first recorded in 1942

1913 *Electric Railway Journal*: Effective publicity to deal with questions of public relations and to consider the molding of public opinion by the presentation of real facts.

pyjama party *n* (1910) a party at which the party-goers are dressed in pyjamas

1910 *Westminster Gazette*: A pyjama party held a couple of days ago at the residence of Mrs. Edwin Avon, a well-known member of Chicago society.

Pyrex *n* (1915) The proprietary name of a hard heat-resistant glass. The name gives the appearance of having some connection with Greek *pur* 'fire', but according to the original manufacturers it was based on *pie*, one of the first products made from it having been a pie-dish

1915 *American Cookery*: Pyrex is a new-process glass, fire-proofed to withstand the heat of the hottest oven.

quantum *n* (1910) a discrete quantity of electromagnetic energy proportional in magnitude to the frequency of the radiation it represents. From Latin, the neuter of *quantus* 'how great'. The concept was introduced by the German physicist Max Planck in 1900. He called it an *Energieelement* 'energy element', not a *quantum*, but he did use *quantum* in a reference to the electronic charge ('das Elementarquantum der Elektricität'). The first to use it in its current sense was Albert Einstein (1905) in a paper in German discussing the nature of light

1910 *Science Abstracts*: The absorption of the corresponding light-quantum.

1913 *Report of the British Association for the Advancement of Science*: Assuming that an oscillator can only emit definite, discontinuous quantums of energy, Planck showed that their magnitude is proportional to the frequency.

quantum theory *n* (1912) a theory of matter and energy based on the concept of quanta, developed from ideas of Max Planck and Albert Einstein, and forming the basis of **quantum mechanics (1922)**. Originally called *quanta theory*, but the singular form prevailed

> 1912 *Monthly Notices of the Royal Astronomical Society*: The constant of nature in terms of which these spectra can be expressed appears to be that of Planck in his recent quantum theory of energy.

Q boat *n* (1918), **Q ship** *n* (1919) an armed and camouflaged merchant ship used as a decoy or to destroy submarines. Originally known as a **mystery ship (1914)**

> 1919 *Boy's Own Paper*: One of the finest examples of coolness, discipline, and good organisation in the history of Q-ships.

> 1972 J. Broome: The Q-ship's lure-power lay in her half-sunken appearance appealing to the U-boat captain for his coup-de-grâce.

race relations *n* (1911) interaction between people of different races. First recorded in the title of a paper, 'Race relations in the Eastern Piedmont region of Georgia', in the *Political Science Quarterly*, it has been a key socio-political term of the century, particularly in the contexts of the US and South Africa, and also of post-colonial Britain

> 1977 *Whitaker's Almanack*: A Lords amendment to the Race Relations Bill…was reversed in the Commons on Oct. 27.

racialist *n* (1917) an advocate or practitioner of **racialism (1907)**

> 1917 *Debates in the Canadian House of Commons*: We all become nationalists in the true sense of the word, as distinguished from provincialists and racialists.

radio *v* (1919) to transmit or send by radio

> 1919 *Popular Science Monthly*: He radios the information to the ship.

radon *n* (1918) a radioactive gaseous element formed by disintegration of radium. A borrowing from German, where it was coined in 1918 from *Radium*

> 1927 *Observer*: The Radium Institute sends radium, or rather radon, its active principle, to hospitals all over the country.

railophone *n* (1911) a telephone in a train. Also used as a verb. The device and its name were short-lived, and the name was not revived when public telephones on trains were introduced in Britain towards the end of the century

> 1911 *Times*: Any train fitted with the Railophone can be instantly spoken to.

> 1912 *Morning Post*: Last year the first public installation of the railophone…was made on the Stratford-on-Avon and Midland Junction Railway.

ration book *n* (1918) a book entitling its holder to a ration. A familiar household item in the food-starved days of the two world wars and their aftermath

> 1918 *Times*: The Ministry of Food wish to remind the public that persons registered with retailers for tea must renew their registration as soon as possible by depositing with the retailer the 'spare counterfoil 2' on leaf 7 of their new ration books.

rationing *n* (1917) the distribution of food, fuel, etc. in restricted allocations. See also **coupon (1918)**

> 1917 *Times*: The German Government now knows all about rationing, but while it has been learning the German people has eaten up its supplies.

Realpolitik *n* (1914) policy determined by practical and rational, rather than moral or ideological, considerations. A borrowing from German, where it means literally 'realistic politics'. The vernacular *practical politics* dates from the late 18th century

> 1914 George Bernard Shaw: [Friedrich von Bernhardi] prophesies that we, his great masters in Realpolitik, will do precisely what our Junkers have just made us do.

red *adj, n* (1917) (a) Bolshevik or communist. The use of *red* as a (generally negative) synonym for *socialist* or *anarchist*, both adjective and noun, goes back to the middle of the 19th century ('I dreamt that I stood in the Crystal Halls, With Chartists and Reds at my side', *Punch* (1851)). It referred to the colour of a party badge. It was therefore ready and waiting after the revolution of

1917 to be applied to Russian communists, who themselves adopted the symbolism of the colour (e.g. in their flag)

> 1919 *Times*: To create a Red Revolution in England.

> 1922 Sinclair Lewis: Say, juh notice in the paper the way the New York Assembly stood up to the Reds?

refugee *n* (1914) someone driven from their home by war or the fear of attack or persecution; a displaced person. English originally adapted the word from French *refugié* at the end of the 17th century as a term for the French Huguenots who came to England after the revocation of the Edict of Nantes in 1685. For the next 250 years it denoted an asylum-seeker, but this new meaning, with its accent on flight from home rather than seeking refuge, has been made familiar by the wars of the 20th century

> 1914 E. A. Powell: The road from Antwerp to Ghent…was a solid mass of refugees.

regression *n* (1910) a return in one's mind to an earlier period or stage of life as a result of mental illness or through hypnosis or psychoanalysis. A term introduced by Sigmund Freud, and applied by him specifically to the tendency of the libido, under the stress of frustration, to return to a simpler and more satisfying stage of development. The related verb *regress* is first recorded in 1926

> 1910 translation of Sigmund Freud: The flight from the unsatisfying reality into what we call…disease, but which is never without an individual gain in pleasure for the patient, takes place over the path of regression, the return to earlier phases of the sexual life, when satisfaction was not lacking.

> 1926 J. I. Suttie: Now the stage to which these two neurotics regressed seems to be the infantile stage of the first year of life.

relegate *v* (1913) to demote a team to a lower division of a league; specifically, in soccer, to reallocate to a lower division of the Football League an agreed number of teams scoring the fewest points in a division in the course of a season's play. The related noun *relegation* is first recorded in 1924

> 1913 *Times*: Norwich County…will…be relegated to the Second Division next season.

> 1924 *Times*: Fractions in goal averages decided promotion and relegation.

reserved occupation *n* (1915) a high-priority civilian occupation, most of those employed in which are exempted from military service. A term in use particularly in Britain during World Wars I and II

> 1915 *Local Government Board Circular No. R.2 2*: A list has been prepared…of still further occupations (to be known as 'reserved occupations'), to which, in the public interest… it is desirable to extend some measure of protection.

> 1944 Angela Thirkell: Her girls wished to go straight into the Forces…while their parents wanted them to…get a job in a reserved occupation.

rocket *n* (1919) an engine that provides thrust by the ejection of burnt fuel; also, any elongated device or craft (such as a flying bomb, a missile, or a spacecraft) in which such an engine is the means of propulsion. Hitherto, the word's application had been restricted to the firework

> 1919 R. H. Goddard: It is possible to convert the rocket from a very inefficient heat engine into the most efficient heat engine that ever has been devised.

> 1920 *Photo Play*: The theory of a Professor Goddard that a rocket could be sent to the moon.

rodeo *n* (1914) a public entertainment featuring cowboy skills (e.g. bronco-busting, lassooing). Originally US. The word first came into English in the 1830s in the sense 'cattle round-up'; it was borrowed from Spanish

> 1914 B. M. Bower: They have them rodeos on a Sunday, mostly, and they invite everybody to it, like it was a picnic.

role *n* (1913) the behaviour that an individual feels it appropriate to assume in adapting to any form of social interaction. A key term in the jargon of social psychology. See also **role model (1957)** and **role-playing (1943)**

> 1913 G. H. Mead: This response to the social conduct of the self may be in the rôle of another—we present his arguments in imagination and do it with his intonations and gestures… In this way we play the rôles of all our group; indeed, it is only in so far as we do this that they become part of our social environment.

Rosebud *n* (1914) a member of the junior section of the Girl Guides. Mercifully this winsome coinage was soon ditched in favour of **Brownie (1916)**

> 1914 Agnes Baden-Powell: The age at which a Rose Bud may join the Baden-Powell Girl Guides is eight years.

> 1914 Olave Baden-Powell: I am so glad to hear that some of you are taking up the work of training Rosebuds, to follow in your footsteps.

ruddy *adj* (1916) A British euphemism for *bloody*, no doubt in use before 1916, but essentially a word of the first two-thirds of the 20th century. As the need to euphemize *bloody* has waned, so has *ruddy*. It had the advantages of rhyming and of suggesting blood-redness

> 1916 'Taffrail': Go on, Ginger!…Slosh 'im one on the ruddy boko!

sabotage *n* (1910) deliberate destruction of property or disruption of systems in order to obstruct normal functioning. A borrowing from French which was at first treated as a foreignism, but quickly became naturalized. Its use as a verb is first recorded in 1918. The French word itself is a derivative of *sabot* 'wooden shoe', and the underlying connotations are of clattering about noisily in such shoes, and hence of working clumsily and wrecking things

> 1910 *Church Times*: We have lately been busy in deploring the *sabotage* of the French railway strikers.

> 1918 *New Appeal*: Testimony…that the companies are sabotaging the government.

sacred cow *n* (1910) someone or something that must not be criticized. Originally US journalists' slang, based on the veneration of cows as sacred by the Hindus

> 1910 *Atlantic Monthly*: These corporations were jocularly referred to as 'sacred cows'.

salariat *n* (1918) the salaried class; salary-earners collectively. A term borrowed from French, where it was coined from Latin *salarium* on the model of *proletariat*

> 1918 Reckitt & Bechhofer: Hypnotized by the round 'O' in the figure of their pay, the salariat feel that they really are important members of the industry.

salmonella *n* (1913) any of a range of rod-shaped bacteria of the genus *Salmonella*, many of which cause disease, notably food poisoning. Named after the American veterinary surgeon Daniel E. Salmon (1850–1914)

> 1913 H. J. Hutchens: Lignières proposed to designate all those organisms which had the…attributes of the bacillus of hog-cholera…by the name Salmonella after Salmon.

salvage *n* (1918) In wartime, especially World War II: the saving and collection of waste material, especially paper, for recycling; also, the material collected

> 1918 *Times*: A National Salvage Council has been set up with the approval of the War Cabinet to deal with the problems of civil salvage and the recovery of waste products generally.

> 1941 Richmal Crompton (heading): William—the Salvage Collector.

> 1942 *Annual Register 1941*: Such special occasions as a Salvage Drive.

> 1946 Rosamond Lehmann: Found last week in turning out old papers for salvage.

sanctions *n* (1919) action taken by one state or alliance of states against another as a coercive measure, often to enforce a violated law or treaty. A key tool of 20th-century power-diplomacy

> 1919 George Bernard Shaw: Such widely advocated and little thought-out 'sanctions' as the outlawry and economic boycott of a recalcitrant nation.

> 1943 H. A. Wallace: He witnessed the collapse of sanctions under the League of Nations.

sandwich *adj* (1913) Denoting a form of training involving alternate periods of practical and theoretical instruction. An apparently isolated early instance of a usage which did not become widespread until the mid 1950s (*sandwich course* is first recorded in 1955). The underlying metaphor is of practical work being like the filling of a sandwich, between layers of theoretical instruction

> 1913 Fleming & Bailey: A sandwich arrangement comprising short alternating periods of technical and practical training until the full course in each is completed.

> 1955 *Times*: This professional training scheme is organized over four or five years on a 'sandwich' basis… This can be arranged in the 'sandwich' course, which alternates periods of study in college with periods of training in industry.

sandwich counter *n* (1913) a counter at which sandwiches are sold. An establishment which became a familiar feature of the lives of 20th-century office workers. Its first cousin *sandwich bar* is first recorded in 1955

    1913 S. Story: Cafés…have been elbowed away by vulgar bars and automatic sandwich counters.

san fairy ann (1919) it doesn't matter, never mind. One of the many distortions of French which entered English via the soldiers serving on the Western Front during World War I: in this case, of *ça ne fait rien*. It remained on the active list in British English until its original users had faded away

    1973 *Times* (advertisement): San fairy Ann… It doesn't matter to us whether it is fixed wing or helicopter because we sell the best of both.

scarf *n* (1917) a square piece of material worn tied round the head. An adaptation of an existing term to denote a new fashion, originally worn to protect the coiffure of female motorists

    1917 *Harrods General Catalogue*: Chiffon Motor Scarf, wide hem-stitched border…in all the latest shades. 4/6.

scenario *n* (1911) a film script with all the details of scenes, appearances of characters, stage-directions, etc., necessary for shooting the film. An adaptation of the earlier application to the outline of the plot of a play, opera, etc.

    1911 *Chambers's Journal*: Many of the leading dramatists now devote their energies seriously to the elaboration of scenarios for picture-plays.

schizophrenia *n* (1912) a psychotic disorder involving withdrawal from reality, hallucinations, delusions, etc. Originally coined in German by E. Bleuler in 1910 as *Schizophrenie*, from Greek *skhizein* 'to split' and *phrēn* 'mind'

    1912 *Lancet*: This little volume is a translation of a series of articles by Professor Bleuler…, in which he advances a theory of the negativism so frequently met with in…schizophrenia.

scientifiction *n* (1916) A blend of *scientific* and *fiction*, it denoted what later came to be known as **science fiction (1929)**. It remained in use until the second half of the century, but its battle with *science fiction* was lost

    1916 H. Gernsback: I am supposed to report Münchhaussen's doings; am supposed to be writing fiction, *scientifiction*, to be correct.

    1940 George Orwell: H. G. Wells…is the father of 'Scientifiction'.

scooter *n* (1916) a child's foot-powered vehicle consisting of a footboard with a wheel at each end and an upright steering handle; also (in full *motor-scooter*), a motor-powered vehicle based on this. As the quotes below show, the toy scooter was in use before World War I, but written records of it are lacking. The first motor-powered scooter, made in New York in 1915, was called the 'Auto-Ped'. The first commercially successful one was the Vespa (see **Vespa (1950)**). See also **scooter (1957)**

    1917 *Autocar*: For some months past it has been known in this country that the 'scooter' in America has developed into something rather beyond the child's plaything so popular in the British Isles. Until quite recently, however, the American motor-driven 'scooter' has not been seen in London.

    1919 *Times*: The 'scooter' we knew before the war was a new terror to the pavement.

    1919 *Isis*: The Proctor…on a motor-scooter, accompanied by a couple of attendant 'bullers' on a push-bike.

script-writer *n* (1915) someone who writes the dialogue for a film

    1915 C. J. Caine: A script writer should make it a point to see that wherever a leader is broken into a scene it is not only absolutely necessary, but also somewhat of a help to the artistic value of the scenario.

scrummy *adj* (1915) excellent, smashing; enjoyable, delicious. A British colloquialism (based on *scrumptious*) which has survived the century well, perhaps helped by its frequent use in the 'William' books of Richmal Crompton

    1915 Mrs. Humphry Ward: You've got to change and rest…before dinner!… You've got to put on a scrummy frock too!

    1923 Richmal Crompton: The cakes had been scrummy.

selective service *n* (1917) a US system of military service from 1917 to 1973 under which draftees were selected from those required to enrol. Compare **national service (1916)**

> 1917 *New Republic*: The New Republic advocated the principle of selective service for this emergency.

self-determination *n* (1911) freedom to decide one's own form of government. Originally a translation of German *Selbstbestimmung*, a coinage of the philosopher Johann Gottlieb Fichte, but given currency in English initially by US President Woodrow Wilson's frequent use of it in the aftermath of World War I, and latterly by the worldwide decolonizations of the second half of the century

> 1911 *Encyclopedia Britannica*: The more enlightened of the emperors…made a genuine endeavour to give a due share in the work of government to the various subject races. But nothing could compensate for the lack of self-determination.

self-service *adj, n* (1919) (operating) a system by which customers in a shop, restaurant, etc., serve themselves instead of being attended to or waited on by the staff. A later synonym was **serve-your-self (1937)**

> 1919 *Ladies' Home Journal*: The Duffy-Powers Company, operating a full-fledged department store in Rochester, New York, inaugurated self-service—that is, the customers, not the store, provide the service—in its grocery department… After several months…, not only are all the self-service departments reported on a self-supporting basis, but with sales increasing.

semi *n* (1912) a semidetached house. A British colloquial abbreviation that was to become synonymous with suburban banality

> 1912 Rose Macaulay: To settle down in the new semi and 'do for' her Ben,…what had heaven to offer more than that?

> 1958 Julian Symons: These were the moments when the watchers in their suburban semis wriggled most deliciously in their overstuffed armchairs.

serial *n* (1914) a film shown in a number of episodes; hence, a radio or, later, a television play broadcast in usually weekly episodes. An adaptation of the earlier application to a novel published in serial form, which dates from the mid 19th century

> 1914 Robert Grau: The latter arranged with…Thomas W. Hanshew…to prepare a serial.

> 1939 *BBC Handbook*: An interesting aspect of the year's radio-dramatic work was the development of serial plays. The serial feature, which is the backbone of American radio, had made comparatively few appearances here before 1938… Publishers…found that the 'Monte Cristo' serial caused a great demand for the novel.

sex discrimination *n* (1916) unfavourable treatment motivated by prejudice against members of a particular sex. Originally US. Not in widespread use until the 1960s (when it was joined by *sexual discrimination*)

> 1916 *Campaign Text-Book*: Enfranchised women in the United States regard the removal of sex discrimination from our national constitution as a political need of primary importance.

sex drive *n* (1918) the impulse which motivates satisfaction of sexual needs. Also termed *sex urge* (1920)

> 1918 R. S. Woodworth: The association is not entirely a spreading of the sex drive into the esthetic sphere.

> 1920 M. Sanger: This man is not concerned with his wife's sex urge, save as it responds to his own at times of his choosing.

sex object *n* (1911) a person towards whom or thing towards which the sexual impulse is directed. Originally a technical term in psychology, but latterly, under the influence of feminist writing, applied to a person regarded only as the object of sexual desire

> 1911 *American Journal of Psychology*: [Leonardo da Vinci] directed [the 'sex impulse'] towards the physical Jesus in toto. It was simply the substitution of one sex object for another.

> 1980 Graham Greene: Deane is not an actor: he is a sex object. Teenage girls worship him.

sexologist *n* (1914) See **sexology (1902)**

sex symbol *n* (1911) a person who is the epitome of sexual attraction and glamour

> 1911 D. G. Phillips: Men…might regard her as nothing but sex symbol.

> 1976 Botham & Donnelly: The olive skin of the man [i.e. Rudolf Valentino] who would…become the world's first and most enduring sex symbol.

shell-hole *n* (1916) a hole caused by the explosion of a shell on a battlefield

> 1916 'Boyd Cable': The stretcher-bearers who lifted him from the shell-hole.

shell shock *n* (1915) a severe neurosis originating in trauma suffered under fire. A term particularly associated with World War I, in which soldiers on the Western Front were subjected to a seemingly incessant barage of shell-fire. Compare **bomb-happy (1943)**

> 1915 *British Medical Journal*: The necessity of investigating cases of 'shell shock'…in order to differentiate those that are functional from those that are due to organic lesions.

> 1918 E. A. Mackintosh: The Corporal…collapsed suddenly with twitching hands and staring, frightened eyes, proclaiming the shell-shock he had held off while the work was to be done.

shimmy *n, v* (1918) (to dance) a lively modern dance resembling a foxtrot accompanied by simulated quivering or shaking of the body. It became one of the key dances of the Roaring Twenties. Its name early on usually appeared in *shake the shimmy*, suggesting that this *shimmy* may be the same word as *shimmy* 'chemise', a dialectal form familiar in the US, where the dance originated. There is also on record from 1917 *shimme-sha-wabble*, which may be an anticipation of *shimmy* ('The opening number was programed as a combination of "Strutter's Ball", "Shimme-Sha-Wabble" and "Walking the Dog" ', *Variety*). See also **shimmy (1923)**

> 1918 *Dancing Times*: It is still very, very crude-and it is called 'Shaking the Shimmy'… It's a nigger dance, of course, and it appears to be a slow walk with a frequent twitching of the shoulders.

> 1919 *New York World* (heading): Shimmy dance is banned in greater New York.

> 1919 A. J. Piron (song-title): I wish I could shemmi like my sister Kate.

shish kebab *n* (1914) a dish consisting of pieces of meat, usually lamb, grilled on skewers. A borrowing of Turkish *şişkebap*, which was formed from *şiş* 'skewer' and *kebap* 'roast meat'. See also **doner kebab (1958)**

> 1914 Sinclair Lewis: I'm sure you'll like shish kebab.

shopping list *n* (1913) a list of purchases to be made

> 1913 *Vanity Fair*: You can easily clip half a dozen and attach them to your own shopping list.

silent *adj* (1914) Of a cinema film: unaccompanied by sound recording. A term which came into use only after the possibility of talking pictures had been contemplated (see **talkie (1913)**)

> 1914 *Writer's Bulletin*: Even in filmdom…there are a dozen who hold the art of the silent drama in reverence.

> 1918 *New York Times* (heading): Two opera stars in silent films.

slit skirt *n* (1913) a tight skirt slit upward from the hem

> 1913 *Punch*: Four young women who last week promenaded Fifth Avenue, New York, in slit skirts…were surrounded by an enraged mob.

small advertisement, small ad *n* (1919) a brief newspaper advertisement in small type

> 1922 James Joyce: Best paper by long chalks for a small ad.

> 1937 Margery Allingham: Uncle William put down *The Times*. He had been looking at the small advertisements.

snapper *n* (1910) a taker of snapshots; a photographer. A colloquialism of some stamina, latterly often used with reference to press photographers or paparazzi

> 1910 *Chambers's Journal*: There is no relief in a protest, for the rampant 'snapper' knows that the law is on his side.

> 1977 *Ripped and Torn*: And thanks a lot to all you budding photographers for the offers of photos, just send 'em in you snappers.

snout *n* (1910) a police informer. Slang. Probably from the idea of the mouth, the organ of speech, being situated in the 'snout' or 'muzzle'

> 1910 C. E. B. Russell: He was in reality a 'snout' or 'nark',…and from time to time had 'given away' many of his comrades.

somewhere *adv* (1915) Used, in the phrase *somewhere in* …, to refer to some locality in the theatre of war without identifying it (because of the restrictions of censorship); hence, in extended use, somewhere unspecified for reasons of security

> 1915 *Illustrated London News* (caption): The War Area as seen by the Airman: 'somewhere in Flanders' photographed from a reconnoitring Aeroplane.

> 1939 *War Illustrated*: From his bed in an R.A.F. medical receiving station hidden away in the woods 'somewhere in France'.

sorry *interj* (1914) Used for expressing apology or regret. So common at the end of the 20th century that it is hard to believe it has not always been around, plain *sorry* is first recorded in print in 1914 (although no doubt it was widespread in spoken English before that). It is a cut-down version of such phrases as *I'm sorry*, which themselves seem to date back no further than the mid 19th century

> 1914 George Bernard Shaw: Sorry. Never heard of him.

S.O.S. *n* (1910) The international radio code-signal of extreme distress, used especially at sea. The letters were chosen because they are easy to transmit in Morse, but they are conventionally interpreted as 'Save Our Souls'. Their most famous early use was in the fruitless distress signals put out by the sinking *Titanic* in 1912. Their use was discontinued in 1998

> 1910 J. A. Fleming: This signal, S,O,S, has superseded the Marconi Company's original high sea cry for help, which was C,Q,D.

soviet *n* (1917) any of a range of elected legislative and executive councils operating at all levels of government in the USSR. A borrowing of Russian *sovet* 'council', which was also applied to various revolutionary councils set up prior to the establishment of socialist rule in 1917. See also **Soviet (1920)**

> 1917 *Times*: A meeting of the Central Committee of the Soviet was held…at which the situation on the front was considered.

space-flyer *n* (1911) An early but unsuccessful rival to *spaceship* (1894) and the eventual 'serious' term **spacecraft (1930)**. It was revived in the 30s with the meaning 'astronaut'

> 1911 *Modern Electrics*: He knew now that Fernand 600 10 had carried off his sweetheart in a space-flyer and that the machine by this time was probably far out from the earth's boundary.

space-time *n* (1915) time and three-dimensional space regarded as fused in a four-dimensional continuum containing all events. A translation of German *Raumzeit*

> 1915 E. Cunningham: Newtonian Relativity consists in the fact that either (x, y, z, t) or (x', y', z', t') are equally valid as space-time coordinates.

Spanish influenza, Spanish flu *n* (1918) influenza caused by an influenza virus of type A. Applied originally to the pandemic which began in 1918, and killed 20 million people worldwide (more than twice as many as had died in action in World War I). Perhaps so called after a similar great epidemic of 1557, which seems to have started in Spain

> 1918 Wilfred Owen: About 30 officers are smitten with the Spanish Flu.

speedboat *n* (1911) a high-speed motor-boat

> 1911 *New Fry's Magazine*: The number of speed-boats, pure and simple, has grown greatly.

speed king *n* (1913) Journalists' hyperbole for 'a motor-racing champion'. Originally US; mainly a pre-World War II term

> 1913 *Illustrated Technical World* (caption): Ralph De Palma. The 'speed king' of 1912.

> 1938 C. Graves: German princes, English speed-kings…are usually to be found here.

spike-bozzle *v* (1915) to destroy (an enemy plane, etc.) or render it unserviceable. British military slang. It outlasted World War I, but was fairly moribund by the end of World War II. *Spike* probably comes from the expression *spike someone's guns* 'to thwart someone's plans' (originally 'to make a gun unserviceable by driving a spike into the touch-hole'); the second element may be from *bamboozle*

> 1915 H. Rosher: Last night 'old man Zepp' came over here… Two machines went up to spike-bozzle him, but…never even saw him.

spill the beans (1919) to reveal a secret. Slang, originally US

> 1919 T. K. Holmes: 'Mother certainly has spilled the beans!' thought Stafford.

split personality *n* (1919) a condition in which a person manifests two or more distinct personalities. Often used loosely to mean 'schizophrenia'

> 1919 M. K. Bradby: The split personalities of hysterics and mediums…have a subjective meaning.

spooking *n* (1919) the calling up of spirits at a séance. A colloquialism of the first third of the century, when spiritualism was a popular hobby among those with little better to do

> 1919 E. H. Jones: 'What's the suggestion?' Alec asked. 'Spooking,' said I. 'Cripes!' said Alec… Matthews brought in the…table… Little wrote a letter of the alphabet on [squares] and arranged them in a circle… I polished the tumbler… We had constructed our first 'Ouija'.

spring chicken *n* (1910) a young person, especially a woman. Usually used in negative contexts, to indicate euphemistically that someone is quite old. Originally US

> 1910 *National Police Gazette* (US): She wasn't a Spring chicken, by any means, yet she wasn't old.

squadrilla *n* (1914) a unit of military aircraft. Apparently a blend of *squadron* and *flotilla*, it was used sporadically during World War I, but then disappeared

> 1914 *Daily Mail*: A squadrilla of five German aeroplanes caused a hundred casualties in the suburbs of Warsaw.

stainless steel *n* (1917) a chromium-steel alloy that does not rust or tarnish

> 1917 *Scientific American*: A steel that does not stain or tarnish is one of the latest new materials… It is called 'stainless steel'.

static *n* (1913) random hissing or crackling noise from a radio receiver. A term common in the early days of radio

> 1913 *Wireless World*: Communication will also be had with New Orleans, which the static formerly prevented.

> 1938 Dorothea Canfield: That woman who talks about cooking is coming on splendidly. Not a speck of static. Wouldn't you like to bring your sewing over and listen?

steel helmet *n* (1916) a helmet made of steel (or other metal), worn as a form of protection in wartime

> 1916 R. Asquith: One fearful addition to the honours of War since I have been away is the steel helmet which we all have to wear now, when in the shell area.

storm troops *n* (1917) Originally a general term (translated from German *Sturmtruppen*) for 'shock troops'—high-calibre soldiers specially trained to lead an attack. From the 1920s it was also applied specifically to the troops of the Nazi Sturmabteilung. The derivative *storm-trooper* is first recorded in 1933

> 1917 *Punch*: Special 'storm troops'—men picked for their youth, vigour and daring, to carry out counter-attacks—are now a feature of the German Armies.

> 1923 *Times*: Bands of 'storm troops' paraded the streets, singing the Fascist war songs.

> 1933 *Palestine Post*: The Nazi storm-troopers at noon on Friday, cleared the Berlin law courts of Jewish judges.

strafe *v* (1915) A word picked up by British soldiers in the early days of World War I from German *strafen* 'to punish', and in particular from the phrase *Gott strafe England* 'God punish England', a common salutation in Germany in 1914 and the following years. It was used in a variety of senses, including 'to punish', 'to do damage to', and 'to attack fiercely'. The specific application to attacking ground positions in a low-flying aircraft is a World War II development (see **strafe (1942)**)

> 1916 Letter from a soldier on the Western Front: There is not much Hun artillery fire, but as our guns strafe them well every day, I expect they will wake up and return the compliment.

1916 *Daily Mail*: Not only is an effective bombardment of the enemy's lines or a successful trench raid described by Tommy as 'strafing the Fritzes,' but there are occasions when certain 'brass hats'…are strafed by imprecation. And quite recently [I] heard a working-class woman…shout to one of her offspring 'Wait till I git 'old of yer, I'll strarfe yer, I will!'

streamlined *adj* (1913) having a streamline form (see **streamline (1907)**). After World War I, the sort of flowing lines and slender elongated rounded forms demanded by streamlining became a distinguishing feature of contemporary design in general

1913 *Aeroplane*: [The aeroplane's] small span and carefully streamlined body.

1934 Herbert Read: 'Streamlined' is popularly, if inaccurately, used as a term of approval for the design of any object in daily use.

1934 *Punch*: This 'streamlining' bunkum is spreading from the sordid realms of mere mechanics to those of everyday life, even to human physiognomy.

studio *n* (1911) a room in which films are shot. A usage which evolved from the earlier sense, 'a room in which a photographer works' (1881)

1911 C. N. Bennett: Covered-in studios provided with expansive glass roofs for daylight work…are hardly among the first flights of commercial Kinematographic enterprise.

sub *n* (1917) A colloquial abbreviation of *submarine* (1899)

1917 J. M. Grider: We were supposed to look out for gulls which they say usually follow in the wake of a sub.

summer time *n* (1916) a standard time (in advance of ordinary time) adopted during the summer months. The English term arose from the introduction of such a standard in the British Isles in 1916, and was enshrined in the Summer Time Act. The period was from 21 May to 30 September. It was also known as *British Summer Time* (first recorded in 1930)

1916 *Times*: Of the changes which have already proved themselves to be changes for the better, that which immediately affects the greatest number of people is the introduction of 'summer time'.

1937 Dorothy Sayers: October 2nd—sun would be setting about half-past five. No, it was Summer Time. Say half-past six.

sun-lounge *n* (1910) a room built largely of glass to admit the maximum amount of sunlight

1910 *Bradshaw's Railway Guide*: Linden Hall Hydro… Splendid winter garden and sun-lounge.

superconductor *n* (1913) a substance which has virtually no electrical resistance at temperatures close to absolute zero. A translation of Dutch *suprageleider*, coined by H. K. Onness

1913 H. K. Onness: A pushing forward of the electrons in the galvanic current through a super-conductor without performance of work.

superstate *n* (1918) a dominant political community, especially one formed from an alliance or union of several nations. In later use a synonym of **superpower (1944)**

1918 O. Gregory: The Super-State must borrow from the Socialists the conception of an all-embracing power and activity.

1935 J. E. C. Welldon: I have felt that the Darwinian theory of the survival of the fittest…was responsible for the German doctrine of the super-state, which, as the Germans conceived it, could only be Germany.

1974 M. B. Brown: The nation states, apart from the super-states—USA, EEC, Japan and the USSR—are forced into a client relationship with the giant companies.

surf *v* (1917) to ride on a surfboard

1917 *Chambers's Journal*: The depth of the lagoon is trifling…, and this it is which makes surfing there so safe and enjoyable.

Svengali *n* (1914) The name of a musician and hypnotist, a character in the novel *Trilby* (1894) by George Du Maurier, used allusively to designate one who exercises a controlling or mesmeric influence on another, often for some sinister purpose

1914 Rudyard Kipling: I'm glad Zvengali's [sic] back where he belongs [referring to a dog with a mesmeric stare].

> 1919 Compton Mackenzie: The juggler…passed into the category of the Svengalis, and became one of a long line of romantic impossibilities.

swank *n* (1913) someone who swanks (see **swank (1903)**). British slang

> 1923 Richmal Crompton: He was a pariah, outside the pale, one of the 'swanks' who lived in big houses and talked soft.

swizzle *n* (1913), **swizz, swiz** *n* (1915) a disappointment or 'swindle'. British slang of the schoolboy variety. Often 'What a swizz(le)!'. Probably an alteration of *swindle*

> 1915 Wilfred Owen: What a swizz about Harold!

> 1950 Anthony Buckeridge: It was a rotten swizzle, sir, because we flew through low cloud and we couldn't see a thing.

tabloid *n* (1918) a popular newspaper which presents its news and features in a concentrated, easily assimilable, and often sensational form, especially one with smaller pages than those of a regular newspaper. A noun use of a word which had first appeared with journalistic connotations in the expression **tabloid journalism (1901)**. As the quotes below make clear, the credit for the tabloid goes to Lord Northcliffe (Alfred Harmsworth), founder of the *Daily Mail* and of the modern concept of popular journalism

> 1918 W. E. Carson: Since 1908 Alfred Harmsworth, like his famous 'tabloid', has disappeared from view.

> 1926 *Encyclopedia Britannica*: The introduction of tabloids may be explained…by the passing remark of Lord Northcliffe, 'If some American does not start one I shall have to come over to do it.'

talkie *n* (1913) a picture with audible dialogue (as opposed to a silent film). Formed from *talking picture*, on the model of **movie (1912)**, and most often used in the phrase *the talkies*. The term preceded the commercial introduction of such films by about fifteen years, and went out of active use towards the end of the 1930s, once the novelty of such things had worn off. Nowadays it is applied only to early sound films. See also **smellie (1929)**

> 1913 *Writer's Bulletin*: The silent 'Movies', so popular to-day, will become tame in comparison with the 'Talkies'.

> 1921 *Daily Colonist* (Victoria, British Columbia): All have seen the movies, now people are to have the opportunity of seeing and hearing the 'Talkies'… The author…of the remarkable speaking photoplay, 'Shell Shocked' is in the city.

tango *n* (1913) a Latin American dance in duple time, with long gliding steps and sudden dramatic poses. One of the most popular dances of the inter-war period, its exaggerated movements facilitated by women's new freedom from whalebone and stays. The word comes from American Spanish, and originally denoted an Afro-American drum dance; its ultimate source may be one of the Niger-Congo languages of West Africa.

> 1913 *Daily Graphic*: 'A Peeress' talks about the Tango. This is a most graceful dance.

> 1913 *Punch*: 'Do you tango?' she asked me as soon as we were comfortably seated.

tank *n* (1916) an armoured military vehicle moving on a tracked carriage and mounted with a gun, designed for use in rough terrain. The word was originally officially adopted in December 1915 as a secret code name for use during development work. It was supposedly chosen because the vehicle was thought to look like a benzene tank. Tanks were first put into commission on the Western Front on 15 September 1916

> 1916 *Times*: 'Tanks' is what these new machines are generally called, and the name has the evident official advantage of being quite undescriptive.

> 1916 E. Montagu: Cannot the idea of the Tank be so extended as to use a Tank-like machine to protect our Infantry.

tanker *n* (1919) a member of a tank crew

> 1919 *W.R.A.F. on the Rhine*: What jolly boys those Tankers were!

> 1940 *Sun* (Baltimore): There are tankers who long ago served in the same regiment when it was fully horsed.

tankodrome, tankdrome *n* (1918) an area where military tanks are kept. Inspired by **aerodrome (1909)**, but it never caught on; *tank park* became the accepted term

> 1918 *Illustrated London News*: A 'tankdrome' on the Western Front.

taramasalata *n* (1910) a Greek fish pâté made from the roe of the grey mullet or the cod. In Greek literally 'roe salad'. The term remained exotic in English until the 1960s

> 1910 Z. D. Ferriman: Red caviar…is pounded with garlic and lemon juice into what is called *tarama salata*.

taxi *v* (1911) Of an aircraft or its pilot: to travel slowly along the ground under the machine's own power. Apparently from *taxi* 'a hired passenger vehicle'—the noun was also used as a slang term for an aircraft at this period ('An airplane was…usually [called] a boat, ship, bus, or taxi,' *New York Times Magazine* (1919))

> 1911 *Aeroplane*: The only way to get—'s 'bus into the air is to 'taxi' to the sewage farm *remou* [a localized eddy of air] and get pulled off the ground by it!

tear gas *n* (1917) a tear-causing gas used in warfare and crowd-control

> 1917 Wilfred Owen: It was only tear-gas from a shell, and I got safely back (to the party) in my helmet.

> 1927 *New Republic*: The troopers on the outskirts…hurled tear-gas bombs and charged.

Technicolor *n* (1917) A proprietary name (originally registered in the US in 1917) for various processes of colour cinematography, especially ones employing dye transfer and separation negatives. The *Techni-* element of the term is supposedly a tribute to the Massachusetts Institute of Technology, the alma mater of Technicolor pioneer Herbert T. Kalmus. Often spelled *Technicolour* in British English, despite its trademark status

> 1930 *Punch*: *Show of Shows*… the latest and greatest of technicolour talkie reviews.

> 1932 *Discovery*: The subtractive process…has been familiar to picture-goers in the many Technicolor films shown in this country.

technocracy *n* (1919) the control of society or industry by technical experts. The word received a particular boost from the founding in New York in 1932–3 by Howard Scott of Technocracy, Inc., a group advocating the technical control of society. It is from this period that the derivative *technocrat* dates

> 1919 W. H. Smyth: For this unique experiment in rationalized Industrial Democracy I have coined the term 'technocracy'.

> 1932 *New York Herald-Tribune*: Technocracy…the name for a new system and philosophy of government, in which the nation's industrial resources should be organized and managed by technically competent persons for the good of everyone.

temporary gentleman *n* (1916) A snobbish and condescending British term for an officer commissioned only for the duration of a war (originally World War I). Originally recorded in its abbreviated form, *TG*

> 1916 Naomi Mitchison: Last night about half a dozen [officers] came into the salon and started a conversation… They were awful TGs mostly.

> 1918 James Barrie: Socially he had fallen…; even…in his uniform the hasty might say something clever about 'temporary gentlemen'.

test pilot *n* (1917) a pilot who test-flies an aircraft. First recorded as a verb in the late 1940s, when test pilots in Britain such as Geoffrey de Havilland, Neville Duke, John Derry, and Peter Twiss were becoming national heroes in their efforts to break the sound barrier

> 1917 W. L. Wade: Now with Parnell and Sons, of Bristol, as chief test pilot.

> 1947 *Saturday Evening Post*: They reminded him of the fiery trail left by the high-altitude jet plane he had test-piloted in the last week of the war.

theatre *n* (1914) a particular region in which a war is being fought. A specific application of an earlier more general sense of *theatre*, 'the scene of a particular activity', which was often used in the context of warfare

1914 Winston Churchill: The hand of war will I expect be heavy upon us in the Western Theatre during the next four weeks.

1961 G. F. Kennan: Real fighting took place between Allied and Bolshevik forces only in one theater, in the Russian north.

thousand island dressing *n* (1916) a pink mayonnaise-based salad dressing with tomatoes, chilli, green peppers, etc. Apparently named after the Thousand Islands, a group of over 1800 small islands in the St. Lawrence river, between the USA and Canada

1916 *Daily Colonist* (Victoria, British Columbia): Mrs. Porter's Thousand Island Salad Dressing, bottle 35¢.

tie-on *adj* (1910) that can be fixed on by tying. Compare **clip-on (1909)**

1910 *Times*: Tie-on labels should not be used.

time study *n* (1911) See **time and motion study (1932)**

TNT *n* (1915) An abbreviation of **trinitrotoluene (1908)**, a powerful explosive used in bombs and shells and also for blasting

1915 D. O. Barnett: The yellow muck doesn't choke you, though, like the black greasy smoke (T.N.T.) which they generally have in the 6 and 8-inch shells.

1962 Edgar Snow: A responsible Western physicist's estimate that the world then possessed a nuclear weapons stockpile roughly the equivalent of forty tons of TNT for each person alive.

toaster *n* (1913) an electric appliance for toasting bread

1913 *Maclean's Magazine*: Electric cooking appliances—the shining nickel-plated or aluminum utensils, including coffee percolators, toasters, chafing dishes…

1913 *Technical World Magazine* (advert): The economy electric toaster.

toc emma, tock emma *n* (1916) a trench mortar. British military slang. From the two military code words then in use for *t* and *m*

1916 *B.E.F. Times*: Completely oblivious of the dangers I encountered from our own artillery and Tock Emmas!

toot sweet *adv* (1917) straight away; promptly, quickly. One of the many manglings of French vocabulary that found their way into British military slang during World War I, and thence into the general language. This one was based on *tout de suite* 'immediately', and lasted as long as those who were young when it was coined

1917 *Punch*: Tommy (to inquisitive French children): 'Nah, then, alley toot sweet, an' the tooter the sweeter.'

1967 *Guardian*: Your two brace of crocodiles[' eggs] have arrived—Yes. I'll get 'em incubated toot sweet.

top *n over the top* (1916) over the parapet of a trench at the start of an attack

1916 *War Illustrated*: Some fellows asked our captain when we were going over the top.

1917 'Contact': When, at a scheduled time, the infantry emerge over the top behind a curtain of shells, the contact patrol buses follow their doings.

topical *n* (1912) a brief film dealing with topical events; a British usage which seems to have died out by about 1920

1917 C. N. Bennett: Fourpence or fivepence a foot will be the most a country showman will pay for a local topical.

tracer *n* (1910) Originally, a trail produced in flight by bullets or shells, so that their course can be seen or 'traced'. The term soon came to be applied to the bullets or shells themselves, and this is its present-day use

1910 *Blackwood's Magazine*: The projectiles of airship guns may possibly give out a jet of flame and a smoke 'tracer' on discharge.

1937 *Times*: This was a most spectacular demonstration, the machine-guns using tracer and the new smoke observation projectiles.

traffic jam *n* (1917) (a stoppage caused by) a condition in which road traffic cannot proceed freely and comes to a standstill. Originally US. (A previous near-synonym was *traffic block* (1896), which survived well into the 20th century: 'Soon they were embedded in a traffic block in the Strand,' Evelyn Waugh, *Vile Bodies* (1930))

> 1926 *Sunset*: Traffic jams: how Western cities are trying to reduce congestion on down-town streets.

traffic signal *n* (1917) a signal (e.g. a traffic light) for controlling traffic. Originally US. A near-contemporary US synonym was *automobile signals*—see the quote at **road safety (1920)**. See also **traffic light (1929)**

> 1917 *Harper's Magazine*: The Bostonian…has reduced 'a pedestrian who crosses streets in disregard of traffic signals' to the compact *jaywalker*.

> 1934 *Architectural Review*: Traffic signals did not come to Hyde Park Corner until 1932.

trench-coat *n* (1916) a waterproof overcoat worn by officers in the trenches during World War I. Later applied to a long, belted raincoat

> 1916 Wilfred Owen: My poor troops were wet to the bone. (But I had my Trench Coat.)

trench-foot *n* (1915) a painful condition of the feet caused by prolonged immersion in cold water or mud, marked by swelling, blistering, and in severe cases death of tissue. A further misery to afflict soldiers in the trenches of World War I

> 1915 *Lancet*: The term trench-foot appears to us to be the most suitable for a condition…met with in those who have had to remain for long periods in the trenches.

> a1918 Wilfred Owen: But never…fever, trench-foot, shock, Untrapped the wretch. And death seemed still withheld.

trench-mortar *n* (1915) a small mortar designed to propel bombs from a front trench into enemy trenches. See also **toc emma (1916)**

> 1915 D. O. Barnett: In the afternoon we had a trench-mortar duel with the Allymans.

trenchoscope *n* (1915) a kind of tube-and-mirror apparatus used in trench warfare. A conflation of *trench periscope*, which was also in use at the time. Another variation was *trenchscope*, first recorded in 1918

> 1915 *Morning Post*: The Adams trenchoscope is the latest periscope for use in the trenches.

triped *n* (1916) a three-legged animal. Sporadically recorded subsequently during the century, but there is no evidence of continuous use. Probably it was newly coined each time (often facetiously), from the Latin stem *triped-* 'three-footed'

> 1916 *Daily Colonist* (Victoria, British Columbia): A three-legged chicken is the pride of a brood of a dozen hatched last week… The triped is quite lively and is putting lots of joy into the life of the Simpson barnyard.

trip-wire *n* (1916) a wire stretched near the ground to trip up enemies, trespassers, etc.

> 1916 A. Knebworth: He walks forward, he has found his landmark. He thinks he knows where the Huns are. He is coming to the Hun trip wire. He has cut the German trip wire.

Trotskyite *adj* (1919) of or supporting Leon Trotsky (1879–1940), Russian revolutionary and politician. *Trotskyism* and *Trotskyist* are not recorded until the 1920s. (The quote below reflects Trotsky's belligerent stance towards Germany, in contrast to Lenin, who wanted to sue for peace)

> 1919 *Mr. Punch's History of the Great War*: Which am I…Pro-German or Pro-Trotskyite?

trunk call *n* (1910) a call from one telephone exchange to another. An everyday term before the introduction of direct dialling

> 1910 *Times*: The telephone is still open, but…a message into the country usually involves a trunk call.

typewriter *n* (1915) a machine-gun or sub-machine-gun. Military slang. A piece of trenches gallows-humour, inspired by the quick rat-tat sound of machine-guns

> 1915 A. D. Gillespie: The only typewriter here is the machine-gun—the men's nickname for it.

U-boat *n* (1913) a German submarine. An adaptation of German *U-boot*, which is a contraction of *Unterseeboot*, literally 'undersea-boat'. Described by the OED in 1913 as being 'in recent use', but no actual examples of the word are recorded before 1916

    1916 *Times*: The U boat is stated to be unarmed.

umpteen *adj, n* (1918) an indefinite (large) number; lots. A humorous coinage based on *umpty*, a fanciful rendering in military slang of the Morse code dash, which was itself used to denote 'an indefinite number' (see **iddy-umpty (1906)**)

    1918 *Blackwood's Magazine*: Men from five continents and umpteen colonies.

    1918 E. A. Mackintosh: That's the umpteenth Bosche that I've killed today.

unconscious *n* (1912) that part of the psyche not subject to direct conscious observation but inferrable from its effects on conscious behaviour. In his psychoanalytic theory, Freud applied the term specifically to processes activated by desires, fears, or memories which are unacceptable to the conscious mind and so repressed

    1912 Sigmund Freud: The term *unconscious*…now comes to imply something more. It designates not only latent ideas in general, but especially ideas with a certain dynamic character, ideas keeping apart from consciousness in spite of their intensity and activity.

undercarriage *n* (1911) the landing-gear of an aircraft. In modern usage the term generally denotes the aircraft's wheels and their struts, but originally it covered any of a range of skids, floats, etc. It is an aeronautical adaptation of a word which originally referred to the framework that supports the body of a carriage, wagon, etc.

    1911 Harper & Ferguson: The under-carriage was formed of wheels alone.

underclass *n* (1918) a subordinate social class. An early and apparently isolated coinage of a word which did not start its fully-fledged career as a technical term in sociology until the 1960s, when it was introduced as a translation of Swedish *underklass*, meaning 'the lowest social stratum in a country or community, consisting of the poor and the unemployed'

    1918 J. Maclean: The whole history of Society has proved that Society moves forward as a consequence of an under-class overcoming the resistance of a class on top of them.

    1963 Gunnar Myrdal: Less often observed…is the tendency of the changes under way to trap an 'underclass' of unemployed and, gradually, unemployable persons and families at the bottom of a society.

undergraduette *n* (1919) a female undergraduate. Coined from *undergraduate* and the feminine suffix *-ette*. It seems to have gone out of general use before it could be the target of late-20th-century political correctness

    1919 *Observer*: The audience was chiefly composed of under-graduates and under-graduettes.

    1980 *Listener*: In the Oxford of 1939…I remember a red-headed 'undergraduette' (as we then rather quaintly would have called her).

up *adj* (1911) Of a woman's hair: worn tied or pinned on top of or at the back of the head, not hanging down. At this period among the middle and upper classes this was an indication of entry into adult society

    1911 Max Beerbohm: Her hair, tied back at the nape of her neck, would very soon be 'up'.

    a1976 Agatha Christie: I was now ready to 'come out'. My hair was 'up'.

vamp *n* (1911) an alluring woman who uses her sex appeal to entrap and exploit men. Often applied to a stock character in plays and films. Both noun (from *vampire*) and verb (see the second quote below) belong essentially to the era of melodrama and silent movies, and neither survived in common usage much beyond the 1930s

    1911 G. K. Chesterton: Thackeray took it for granted that Mary Stuart was a vamp.

    1918 *New York Times*: Enid Bennett In a New 'Vamp' Story… 'The Vamp'…is a pleasing light comedy…in which Enid Bennett…appears as Nancy; an ingenuous wardroom girl at a musical comedy theatre where she hears sophisticated chorus girls tell how the female of the species may make the male buy her dinners and diamond bracelets by 'vamping' him.

vanishing cream *n* (1916) a cosmetic cream that is readily absorbed by the skin, used as a powder base or skin cleanser. A staple of women's make-up until well past the middle of the century, especially in the version manufactured by Pond's

> 1932 *Woman's Pictorial*: Use a pure vanishing cream…for the powder base.

vision *n* (1910) (the transmission or reproduction of) television images; in broadcasting terms, the visual partner of *sound*

> 1910 H. N. Casson: Some future Carty…may transmit vision as well as speech.

visual aid *n* (1911) a picture, model, film, etc., used as an aid to learning. Originally US

> 1911 P. Monroe: The last century of schoolroom practice has been marked by a great increase in the use of natural objects, models, pictures, maps, charts, and other visual aids.

vitamin *n* (1912) any of a range of naturally occurring substances essential for the control of the body's metabolic processes. The original form of the word was *vitamine*. It was coined by C. Funk from Latin *vita* 'life' and *amine* (because he thought vitamins contained amino acids). The main modern spelling *vitamin* was introduced to avoid any erroneous connection with amines (see the 1920 quote below)

> 1912 C. Funk: It is now known that all these diseases, with the exception of pellagra, can be prevented and cured by the addition of certain preventive substances; the deficient substances, which are of the nature of organic bases, we will call 'vitamines'; and we will speak of a beri-beri or scurvy vitamine, which means a substance preventing the special disease.

> 1920 J. C. Drummond: The criticism usually raised against Funk's word Vitamine is that the termination '-ine' is one strictly employed in chemical nomenclature to denote substances of a basic character, whereas there is no evidence which supports his original idea that these indispensable dietary constituents are amines… The suggestion is now advanced that the final '-e' be dropped, so that the resulting word Vitamin is acceptable under the standard scheme of nomenclature…which permits a neutral substance of undefined composition to bear a name ending in '-in'. If this suggestion is adopted, it is recommended that the somewhat cumbrous nomenclature introduced by McCollum (Fat-soluble A, Water-soluble B), be dropped, and that the substances be spoken of as Vitamin A, B, C, etc.

vorticism *n* (1914) a British art-movement of the early 20th century, characterized by abstractionism and machine-like forms. Also applied to similar tendencies in literature. Coined by the poet Ezra Pound from the Latin stem *vortic-* 'vortex'. The derivative *vorticist* is also first recorded in 1914

> 1914 Ezra Pound: The image is not an idea. It is a radiant node or cluster; it is what I can… call a *Vortex*, from which…ideas are constantly rushing… And from this necessity came the name 'vorticism'.

> 1914 *Daily News*: My Scot one morning preached me a fiery sermon on the poetry of lawn tennis, and…I became a Vorticist.

Waldorf salad *n* (1911) a salad made from apples, walnuts, lettuce and/or celery, dressed with mayonnaise. Named after the Waldorf-Astoria Hotel in New York, where it was first served. The term (and the recipe) are first recorded in Leiter & Van Bergh's *Flower City Cook Book*

> 1930 Edna Ferber: She was the first to electrify the ladies of the Twentieth Century Culture Club by serving them Waldorf salad—that abominable mixture of apple cubes, chopped nuts, whipped cream, and mayonnaise.

walking wounded *n* (1917) Originally, in World War I, casualties able to make their way on foot to treatment stations, not in need of a stretcher

> 1917 Philip Gibbs: The long trails of the walking wounded, marvellously brave, wonderfully full of spirits.

walrus moustache *n* (1918) a large moustache which overhangs the lips (thus resembling the whiskers of a walrus). A not uncommon male facial adornment of the late 19th and early 20th centuries, and one often featuring in pictures of the stereotypical 'old soldier' of this period (e.g. 'Old Bill', a cartoon character created during World War I by the British cartoonist Bruce Bairnsfather)

> 1918 Wilfred Owen: An old soldier with a walrus moustache.

war bride *n* (1918) a woman who marries a serviceman during wartime

    1918 Arnold Bennett: She was becoming hysterical: the special liability of the war-bride.

war cabinet *n* (1916) a cabinet with responsibility for the political decisions of a country during a war

    1916 *Times*: It is an immense gain to have the Prime Minister definitely…committed to the creation of a small War Cabinet, constantly…devoted to the prosecution of the war.

    1940 John Reith: I asked if the job carried War Cabinet rank and he said no.

war effort *n* (1919) the effort of a nation to win a war, or of an individual or group to contribute to that end

    1919 *Maclean's Magazine*: Britain's wonderful war effort.

    1954 Noël Coward: A job which…would be of real value to the war effort.

water-plane *n* (1912) See **hydro-aeroplane (1909)**

western *n* (1912) a film portraying life in the American West in the 19th century, usually through idealized stock situations and characters, especially cowboys and gun-fights. The adjective *western* in this sense is first recorded a couple of years earlier ('It is almost impossible to criticize these Wild Western films, because cowboys are likely to do almost anything', *Moving Picture World* (1910))

    1912 *Moving Picture World* (advert): 'The Fight at The Mill'… A powerful Western, distinctly unusual among typical 'Westerns' containing a beautiful story and a dashing Indian battle that will interest and instruct.

Western Front *n* (1914) the front in Belgium and northern France in World Wars I and II

    1914 Lloyd George: These objects cannot be accomplished by attacks on the Western Front.

    1915 *Times*: Lord Kitchener…explained that the operations on the Western front have for some time resolved themselves into a state of siege warfare.

    1939 *War Weekly*: The incalculable factor on the Western Front is the mind of Hitler.

white collar *adj, n* (1919) (wearing) the white collar regarded as characteristic of someone who does non-manual work. Originally US. Compare **blue-collar (1950)**

    1919 Upton Sinclair: It is a fact with which every union workingman is familiar, that his most bitter despisers are the petty underlings of the business world, the poor office-clerks…who, because they are allowed to wear a white collar…, regard themselves as members of the capitalist class.

    1921 *Ladies' Home Journal*: Urban chain restaurants have accustomed white-collar boys and girls to tasty viands, albeit in limited amounts.

white hope *n* (1911) Originally, a white boxer who might beat Jack Johnson, the first black to be world heavyweight champion (1908–15), but soon generalized to refer to any person who, or a thing which, it is hoped will achieve much

    1911 *Daily Colonist* (Victoria, British Columbia): A New York promoter has succeeded in arranging for a match between Albert Palzer, New York's most prominent white hope, and Carl Morris, the giant locomotive engineer.

    1941 Lord Berners: He was a composer: the white hope (thus a critic had described him) of English music.

whizz-bang *n* (1915) the shell of a small-calibre high-velocity German gun. British military slang. So called from the noise it made (*whizz-bang* had been used for a whizzing sound ending with an explosion since at least the early 19th century)

    1915 Ian Hay: A whizz-bang is a particularly offensive form of shell which bursts two or three times over, like a Chinese cracker.

wiggle waggle, wiggle woggle *n* (1910) a fairground amusement consisting of a promenade moved by machinery on which people walk to the accompaniment of music. The form with *woggle* seems to have been more durable than *waggle*

    1910 *Penny Guide to the Japan-British Exhibition*: Fun on the Wiggle Waggle.

    1938 George Orwell: A dreadful thing called the Wiggle-Woggle at the White City Exhibition.

wind *n* **get** or **put the wind up** (1916) to become or make apprehensive. Slang. Wars are rich sources of jokey euphemisms for fear. This one probably comes from the idea of the fart-inducing quality of terror. See also **windy (1916)**

> 1916   Philip Gibbs: It was obvious that the blinking Boche had got the wind up.

wind tunnel *n* (1911) a tunnel-like apparatus for producing an air-stream of known velocity past models of aircraft, buildings, etc., in order to investigate flow or the effect of wind on the full-size object

> 1911   *Aeronautical Journal*: The planes were tested in a 'wind tunnel'.

windy *adj* (1916) apprehensive, frightened. Slang. From the expression *get the wind up*, which is first recorded in the same year

> 1916   D. Hankey: The anticipation of danger makes many men 'windy'.

Wolf Cub *n* (1916) a member of the junior section of the Boy Scouts

> 1916   Robert Baden-Powell: Hullo, Wolf Cubs! What swells you are to have a newspaper all to yourselves!

woman's magazine *n* (1912) a magazine devoted to women's interests. The alternative form *women's magazine* is first recorded in 1920, and has gradually become the preferred variant

> 1912   *Magazine Maker* (title): Making a woman's magazine.

> 1920   P. G. Wodehouse: Heaven knows what a women's magazine wants with my sort of stuff, but they are giving me fifteen thousand of the best for it.

> 1981   J. B. Hilton: There were shopping notes, memos…a pile of women's magazines.

woofits *n* (1918) a vague unwell feeling. World War I military slang, of unknown origin, which had largely died out by the middle of the century

> 1918   J. M. Grider: Curtis says he is suffering from the Woofits, that dread disease that comes from overeating and underdrinking… I drank too much coffee before getting up and I'm as nervous as a kitten now. Must be getting the Woofits.

write-off *n* (1918) an aircraft, motor vehicle, etc., so badly damaged as to be not worth repair; a wreck. Originally Air Force slang

> 1918   J. M. Grider: He wasn't hurt but the Spad [an aircraft] was a write-off.

X chromosome, Y chromosome *n* (1911) the two types of sex chromosome, one of which (X) is associated with femaleness and the other (Y) with maleness. The symbol *X* had first been applied to this chromosome (in German) by H. Henking in 1891, in the *Zeitschrift für wissenschaftliche Zoologie*. The earliest example of its use in English is in a paper by T. H. Montgomery in the *Transactions of the American Philosophical Society* in 1902: 'One of these three [chromosomes], that designated *x* in Figs. 119–123, imposes by its relatively very large volume… We shall call this the "chromosome *x*"'. The parallel use of *Y* is first recorded in a paper by E. B. Wilson in *Science* in 1909: 'The X-element…appears as a "large idiochromosome" which has a synaptic mate… The latter chromosome…I shall designate as the "Y-element"'. But the actual formulations *X chromosome* and *Y chromosome* are not found before 1911

> 1911   *Biological Bulletin*: We have associated the X and Y chromosomes of the male with sex-determination, but possibly they have some other meaning.

yes-man *n* (1912) a man who agrees from self-interest or fear with everything put to him by a superior; an obsequious subordinate. Originally US

> 1912   *Century Magazine*: We're both yes-men, Edward. We've got to take orders now.

you *adj* (1918) expressive of or suited to your taste, personality, etc. Colloquial

> 1918   Roger Fry: I've read your *Lucretius*… I feel sure it's both immensely him and also very much you.

> 1936   U. Orange: 'I think it's lovely,' said Jane unkindly, 'So *you*, somehow.'

zabernize *v* (1914) to adopt bullying or aggressive tactics, especially in a military context. The term was based on an incident at Saverne (a town in Alsace whose German name is Zabern) in 1913. This probably involved German soldiers insulting the local population, although a more sensational account has it that a young German officer killed a lame cobbler for smiling at him. The noun *zabernism* soon followed, but neither lasted long into the 1920s

> 1914 *Daily News & Leader*: A quaint illustration of an attempt to 'zabernise' in business life…is published…to-night.

> 1920 *Glasgow Herald*: The advance of the Government troops into the Ruhr district, coupled with a marked exhibition of 'Zabernism', has stiffened the Spartacist resistance.

Zep, Zepp *n, v* (1915) A colloquial abbreviation of **Zeppelin (1900)**, the name of a German airship used in air attacks during World War I. The verb denoted 'to bomb from a Zeppelin'

> 1915 J. Pope: The night those Zeps bombarded town.

> 1920 W. J. Locke: 'So you've been Zepped, I hear,' she said.

Ziegfeld (1913) The name of the American theatre manager and producer Florenz Ziegfeld (1869–1932), used to designate the extravagant revues that he staged annually from 1907 to 1931

> 1913 *Green Book*: Never before was so much beauty shown so much as in this latest of the Ziegfeld nonsensicalities.

> 1915 *New Republic*: Ziegfeld Follies 1915, a musical comedy produced by F. Ziegfeld Jr.

zigsaw, zigzaw *n* (1912) Alternative forms of **jigsaw (1909)** which enjoyed a brief popularity in the 1910s. The durability of the puzzle was greater than that of the word, despite the quote

> 1912 H. Maxwell: One of those zigzaw puzzles which had a fleeting vogue two or three years ago.

The twenties, if the old cliché is to be believed, roared (the expression *roaring twenties* is not actually recorded until 1930: 'The giants of the roaring 'twenties ought to be able to achieve glory of some sort in half as many years', *Saturday Review*). After the horrors and traumas of the Great War, the world was hungry for gaiety. A generation of youth had been 'lost', and those who stepped into its shoes were determined to enjoy themselves. So for the leisured and the moneyed this was the decade of the *flapper* and the *bright young thing* and the *hearty*, and also of the *good time girl* and the *gold-digger*. They danced their flippant dances—the *black bottom*, the *Charleston*, the *camel walk*, the *heebie-jeebie*, the *shimmy* (1918)—with fierce determination. They visited the *flicks*, and went to *cocktail bars*, where they drank *delish gimlets* and *sidecars*. All too too *sick-making* (1930) if you didn't have the *lettuce*.

The trivialities of personal appearance could once more be paid serious attention: the 20s saw the first *beauticians* and *beauty salons*, and also the first *beauty queens* and *bathing beauties*; and *face-lifting* was now possible. The hair could be *shingled* or *bingled*, or disciplined into a severe *Eton crop*; and (fittingly) more permanently, the *perm* put in its first appearance. *Oxford bags* and *plus-fours* proved to be a passing fad, but *Levi's* have survived the century, as have the *sweatshirt* and the *T-shirt*. Women for the first time wore *scanties* and *teddies*, and *girdles* and suchlike *foundation garments* presaged the demise of 19th-century whalebone and laces. But perhaps the greatest sartorial advance of the 1920s was the *zipper* (or, as the British called it, the *zip*), which so neatly encapsulates the 20th century: instead of wasting five or six precious seconds of your life laboriously buttoning or unbuttoning your fly, you can do it in one with the zip (whose very name promises efficient speed).

On the subject of unbuttoning, in the 1920s people were beginning to find it easier to talk about sex. *Sex* itself as a term for sexual intercourse dates from then, as do *sexy*, *sex appeal*, *sexpert*, and *sexationalism*. The words *heterosexual* and *lesbian* are first recorded as nouns in the 20s (but homophobia was still the orthodoxy: *fag*, *pansy*, and *queer* are 20s words too). In the cinemas, girls could swoon over the *sheik* (played by Rudolph Valentino, the first truly mass-appeal idol), while round the corner in the burlesque theatre, men were getting their first eyeful of *stripping*.

All this in the world of the haves. But what of the have-nots? As the world turned to peaceful pursuits after the conflagration of 1914–18 (*demob* and *deration* are both words of the 20s), survivors came home with hopes for a better society and jobs for all. But *recession, redundant,* and *deflation* are 20s words too. For the many, there was not harmony and plenty, but want. It was the era, too, that saw the beginning of *organized crime,* and of *racketeering.*

On the international scene, the consequences of the war started to fester. In the 20s, the world first heard of *Fascism, National Socialism, black shirts, goose-steppers, putsches,* and the *Duce.* The terms *totalitarian* and *liquidate* came ominously on the scene, as did *bacteriological warfare* and *chemical weapon.* Against all this, new concepts such as *peaceful co-existence* (a Soviet invention), *non-violence,* and *security* can have inspired little confidence in the future.

Science and technology still offered a way forward, however, and the 1920s saw additions to the lexicon such as *proton* and *photon, insulin, oestrogen,* and *penicillin, Geiger counter* and *cosmic ray.* The last perhaps smacks more of *science fiction* than of science fact, and the 20s was a fruitful period for the crystal-ball school of word-creation, particularly in the area of space-travel. Among its contributions to the future were *astronaut, colour television, rocket ship,* and *spacesuit.* But perhaps the most famous coinage of this sort was *robot,* originally a Czech word, which has come to be seen as the vehicle by which 20th-century humanity will realize its aspiration to leave behind the mundane physical tasks of everyday life and devote itself to leisure and contemplation.

For in many ways the 20s were the first decade of the modern age (the term *modernism,* in its application to the arts, dates from then). Many aspects of the 19th century survived into the first fifteen years of the new century, but World War I blew a lot of them away. Many of the key features of later 20th-century life, along with their terminology, began to be put in place during the 20s. Take transport. On the roads, the products of the automakers' tireless assembly lines were becoming widely available, and a whole new vocabulary of mass car culture was called into being: *A road* and *by-pass, hit-and-run* and *hitchhike, ringroad* and *roundabout, road sense* and *road safety, speed cop, traffic lights,* and *white lines, car parks,* and *petrol stations* (or, in the US, *parking lots, filling stations,* and *gas stations* (1932)). If you could not afford a car of your own, you could take a *trolleybus* or a *chara. Airgirls* like Amy Johnson and Amelia Earheart were pioneering new airline routes, and *air terminals* were being constructed for the comfort of passengers.

The technology of radio transmission had developed to a stage at which, early in the decade, public broadcasting could begin. A whole new lexicon had to evolve in a very short period to accommodate it, and *listeners-in* soon became familiar with terms like *crystal set* and *valve set, news bulletin* and *news reader, outside broadcast* and *on the air, commentary* and *commentate,* and even such basic items as *broadcast* and *programme.* Although the word *television* dates from the first decade of the century, the 20s saw the first practical demonstration of television, and the words *televise* and *look in* were born (as also, less successfully, were *televisor* and *watch in*). In the cinema, the films began to talk in earnest. The development had already been anticipated in the term *talkie* (1913), but again the actuality entailed a mushroom growth of new vocabulary (*soundtrack, phonofilm, Movietone, Vitaphone*).

Nearly every decade has its fads and crazes that give it a certain quirky individuality. In the 1920s, people suddenly went mad for the *pogo stick. Pelmanism* was all the rage; and in genteel drawing rooms where previously bridge had been the rule, they could not get enough of *mah-jongg.* Could these be the same people who now embraced the German passion for going around with no clothes on? Certainly English found room for two words for this (*naturist* and *nudism*) in the 20s.

This postwar decade saw the coming of age of the blend—a type of word which is formed by merging two existing words together. Some still familiar ones had emerged before 1900 (*brunch*, for instance; see p. x), but it was the 1920s that really started taking a liking to them. Perhaps the best-known of all dates from then—*motel*. *Chunnel* was coined long before the Channel tunnel itself was constructed (after which its rate of usage seems to have nosedived), and *mirthquake* and *sexationalism* have belied their apparent ephemerality. Such items are meat and drink to journalists and headline writers, and if you can combine them with (more or less) cuddly animals, you have neologisms to die for—hence the extensive press coverage given to *swooses, tigons,* and (later) *ligers* (1938).

abominable snowman *n* (1921) a creature alleged to exist in the Himalayas, but sighted more regularly in the pages of the English-speaking press during the rest of the century. A literal translation of the Tibetan term (see the quote below). See also **yeti (1937)**

> 1921 *Times*: The men were never seen…but footprints were found which were suspected of being those made by these men, who are apparently known to the Tibetans as Meetoh Kangmi, or 'Abominable Snowmen', and small colonies of these people are believed to exist on the slopes of Everest, Chumalhari, and Karola.

absenteeism *n* (1922) the persistent absence of employees from their place of work or of pupils from school. The word originated in the early 19th century, denoting landlords who lived far away from their estates. See also **presenteeism (1989)**

> 1941 *Punch*: Committee on National Production…we shall do our best to decrease absenteeism during the coming winter.

Adam and Eve *v* (1925) to believe. A piece of Cockney rhyming slang which has survived in genuine use to the end of the century

> 1956 E. A. Thorne: A *baby*! Would you Adam-and-Eve it!

adjustment *n* (1922) psychological adaptation. The associated verb and adjective *adjust* and *adjusted* are contemporaneous

> 1922 R. S. Woodworth: Much used…are 'adjustment' and 'mental set', the idea here being to liken the individual to an adjustable machine which can be set for one or another set of work.

> 1924 J. J. B. Morgan: It is the function of the parent and teacher to encourage the successfully adjusted children… It may be that the child will not adjust and will later develop a more serious form of dissociation.

aerosol *n* (1923) a system of colloidal particles dispersed in the air or in a gas. Coined from *aero-* + *solution*. The meaning '(the substance in) a dispenser packed under pressure', more familiar to lay people, is not recorded before the 1940s

> 1923 R. Whytlaw-Gray: Aerosol is a convenient term to denote a system of particles of ultra-microscopic size dispersed in a gas, suggested to us by Prof. Donnan.

> 1957 *Times*: Special foam shaving cream in aerosol container, price 12s. 6d.

air *n* (1927) the air considered as a medium for the transmission of radio waves. Used mainly in the expressions *on the air* and *off the air* (later *on air* and *off air*) 'being/not being broadcast' and *over the air*

> 1927 *Observer*: The only New York church which is 'on the air'.

air ambulance *n* (1921) an aircraft for transporting the sick or injured. The alternative *ambulance plane* is also first recorded in 1921. See also **blood wagon (1922)**

> 1921 *Aeronautics*: The first air ambulance…is painted aluminium with a large Red Cross painted on the fuselage and beneath the wings.

> 1921 *Flight*: American ambulance 'plane comes to grief.

airgirl *n* (1928) a female aviator. A coinage from the days of flying pioneers, among whom women figured significantly (e.g. Amy Johnson, Amelia Earheart, Jean Batten)

> 1928 *Daily Express*: All first impressions vanished… The boyish airgirl [Amelia Earheart] became a feminine woman.

air terminal *n* (1921) an establishment with facilities for the reception of air passengers

> 1921 *Aircraft Year Book*: The principal communities which are situated along this air route should create thoroughly modern air terminals.

> 1935 C. G. Grey: Though Hounslow Heath was actually the first London Air Terminal, it was given up because it was on the wrong side of London.

all-electric *adj* (1920) using only electric power. Electricity still had novelty value in 1920

> 1920 *Electrical Review*: On Friday, last week…a Press visit to the 'All-Electric House' exhibited…at the Ideal Home Exhibition, took place.

ambisexuality *n* (1924) sexual attraction to people of either sex. The term never fully caught on: there is no contemporary record of the adjective *ambisexual* (it did not surface with this meaning until after World War II), and it was never able to capture the ground established by *bisexuality* (1892). It has, however, retained a toehold in the language

> 1924 Havelock Ellis: Ferenczi, again…accepts 'the psychic capacity of the child to direct his originally objectless eroticism to one or both sexes', and terms this disposition ambisexuality.

ambulance plane *n* (1921) See **air ambulance (1921)**

anorak *n* (1924) a waterproof hooded jacket. Originally applied to such garments worn by Greenland Eskimos (from whose language the word comes); it does not seem to have been used for Western imitations of these until the 1930s

> 1924 *Chambers's Journal*: He was habited…in anorak and skin breeches and mukluks.

anschluss *n* (1924) the union of Austria with Germany (either the actual union in 1938 or as proposed before that date). When it finally happened, it was seen as one of the key events on the road to World War II, signalling Hitler's willingness to ignore world opinion and march into other countries. In German the word means literally 'joining' or 'union', and it was used by Hitler to gloss over the fact that Austria had, in fact, been annexed. Around the World War II period it was briefly used as a verb

> 1924 *Annual Register 1923*: This…could be explained by the decline of interest in the Anschluss idea, due to the calamitous condition of Germany.

> 1939 J. N. L. Baker: The Anschluss with Austria, proposed periodically since 1917 and forbidden by the treaty, was accomplished by force in March 1938.

> 1945 *American Speech*: Hitler's next big coup was to anschluss Austria.

A road *n* (1921) In Britain, a road officially designated first-class. The term *B road* for second-class roads was introduced at the same time

> 1921 *Autocar*: It is not…intended to deal with the numbering of the B roads until that of the A roads has been completed.

artificial sunlight *n* (1927) light radiated from an ultra-violet lamp. A feel-good term popular particularly in the inter-war period, when great stress was placed on the importance for public health of getting people out of dark and verminous slums into the sunlit open air. The nearly contemporary **sun-ray (1928)** has proved longer-lasting

> 1927 *Lancet*: London clinic for artificial sunlight treatment.

> 1927 *Punch*: It is interesting to observe that in spite of artificial sunlight, television, winter sports and the heebie-jeebie there are still some stalwarts who stand by the old traditional amusements of the English people.

astronaut *n* (1929) a traveller in space. Coined when the concept was mere ambition, it survived to become the accepted term when such people actually existed. The adjective *astronautical* is first recorded in the same year. Compare **cosmonaut (1959), spaceman (1942)**

> 1929 *Journal of the British Astronomical Association*: That first obstacle encountered by the would-be 'Astronaut', viz., terrestrial gravitation… Prof. Oberth…has just been awarded the £80 prize offered for the most successful solution of the 'astronautical' question.

> 1957 Patrick Moore: The astronauts taking off for the planet Hesikos remain standing upright.

> 1961 *Times*: President Kennedy spoke to Commander Alan Shepard by radiotelephone a few minutes after the astronaut was delivered by helicopter to the deck of the aircraft carrier Lake Champlain.

athlete's foot *n* (1928) ringworm of the foot. A new name for an old affliction, coined in the US

> 1928 *Literary Digest*: Athlete's foot…from which more than ten million persons in the United States are now suffering.

atonal *adj* (1922) Applied to a style of musical composition in which there is no conscious reference to any scale or tonic. An important feature of 20th-century avant-garde serious music. The noun *atonality* is also first recorded in 1922. See also **twelve-tone (1926), serial (1947)**

> 1922 A. E. Hull: I have been working for two years at a system of non-tonal harmony, which I had long been unable to christen. Now, after visiting no less than seven foreign countries I not only find that the thing is widely known as Atonality, but [etc.]… Keyboard chord-writing as well as linear, tonal as well as Atonal.

autogiro *n* (1923) a type of aircraft with a conventional engine-powered propeller but deriving its lift mainly from a system of freely rotating horizontal vanes, and capable of landing in a very small space. It was developed to some degree of sophistication in the 1920s and 1930s, but fell out of use when the helicopter came in in the 1940s. The word was based on Spanish *giro* 'a turning round, a revolution or whirl'

> 1923 *Flight*: Some tests have recently been carried out at Getafe, near Madrid, with an extremely interesting and original type of machine, the invention of a young Spanish engineer, Don Juan de la Cierva. This machine is known as the 'Autogiro', and is what might be described as being midway between the aeroplane and the helicopter.

bacteriological warfare *n* (1924) the use, as a means of war, of bacteria to spread disease in the enemy. An earlier and more specific term than **biological warfare (1946)**. Also more colloquially known as **germ warfare (1938)**

> 1924 *League of Nations Official Journal*: The present report deals successively with the *known* effects of chemical warfare and the *possible* effects of bacteriological warfare.

Balkanize *v* (1920) to divide (a region) into a number of smaller and often mutually hostile units, as was done in the Balkan Peninsula in the late 19th and early 20th centuries. The noun *Balkanization* is first recorded in the same year

> 1920 *19th Century*: Great Britain has been accused by French observers of pursuing a policy aimed at the Balkanisation of the Baltic provinces.

baloney *n* (1922) nonsense, rubbish. Slang, originally US; often used as an exclamation. The usage appears to be an extension (perhaps influenced by *blarney*) of a slightly earlier sense 'idiot', which is generally accepted as coming from (a colloquial pronunciation of) *bologna* (the sausage)

> 1928 *Saturday Evening Post*: Gee, that's a long shot. Boloney! That's not the ball—it's the divot.

Band-Aid *n* (1924) A proprietary name for a type of sticking-plaster with a gauze pad; registered in the US by Johnson & Johnson in 1924, with a claim of use since 1920. See also **Elastoplast (1928)**

> 1926 *Army & Navy Stores Catalogue*: Band Aid…'a protective dressing for cuts and wounds'…tin 1/-.

bandoneon, bandoleon *n* (1925) a kind of button accordion typical of the Argentine tango orchestras popular in the 1920s. It was invented (around 1840) by and named after Heinrich Band. The original form is *bandoneon*, but *bandoleon* (perhaps a subconscious blend of *bandolier* and words like *Aeolian, Napoleon,* and *simoleon* 'dollar'—and possibly also *banjolele*) was quite common

> 1925 *Daily News*: The Tango band consists of piano, harmonium, guitar, symphonic mandoline, concertina and bandoleons.

banjolele, banjulele *n* (1925) a stringed musical instrument of a type between a banjo and a ukulele, which enjoyed a certain popularity in the interwar years. The name, like the instrument, is a blend, and the spelling depends on which of the elements is emphasized

> 1925 *Glasgow Herald*: A native band playing on banjoleles, a sort of zither, from which the tones are provided by gourds filled with varying amounts of water.

barrage balloon *n* (1923) a captive balloon forming part of a set of such balloons designed to form a hindrance to low-flying enemy aircraft. They became a familiar sight around British cities during World War II

> 1923 *Aviation*: The employment of barrage balloons…permits the realization of economy in the distribution of 'active means' of anti-aircraft defense.

bathing beauty *n* (1920) an attractive young woman in a bathing suit, especially one taking part in a beauty contest. An alternative term was *bathing belle*. By the 1960s both were sounding distinctly passé

1920 Ben Levy: It would be hard to throw a stone…upon the American Vaudeville stage without hitting what the eight-sheets describe as 'California Bathing Beauties'.

1924 Philip Macdonald: Minister murdered by Bathing Belle.

1955 *Times*: Tell the miners what Yarmouth has to offer—Tommy Trinder, Charlie Chester, Ronnie Ronalde, 'hot-dogs', bathing beauties, and all.

Bauhaus *n* (1923) The name (literally 'building-house' in German) of a school of design founded in Weimar, Germany, in 1919 by Walter Gropius (1883–1969). Later used to denote the principles or traditions characteristic of the Bauhaus

1923 H. G. Scheffauer: The Staatliche Bauhaus of Weimar represents one of the most interesting and significant enterprises in the vivifying of modern arts and crafts.

beautician *n* (1924) someone who runs a beauty salon; a beauty specialist. Originally US

1926 *Glasgow Herald*: The immense growth of 'beauty parlors' in the United States has added to the American language the word 'beautician'.

beauty queen *n* (1922) the winner of a beauty contest. Originally US (*beauty contest*, incidentally, is first recorded in 1899). See also **Miss (1922)**

1922 *New York Times*: The winning beauty will be heralded as America's 'Beauty Queen'.

beauty salon *n* (1922) an establishment where cosmetic and other treatments are given to improve personal beauty. Originally US. A slightly more up-market name for a **beauty shop (1901)**

1922 *American Hairdresser*: A. Simonson on September 5 opened new beauty salons at 54 West 57th street.

bee's knees *n* (1923) the very best; the height of excellence. Slang, originally US; one of a range of bizarre 1920s 'excellence' terms based on various parts of animals' anatomy (see **cat's whiskers (1923)**). A more risqué contemporary alternative was *the bee's nuts*. *Bee's knee* as a metaphor for something tiny or insignificant dates back to the late 18th century

1923 H. C. Witwer: You're the bee's knees, for a fact!

1958 *Times*: Lord Montgomery…holds that to label anything the 'cat's whiskers' is to confer on it the highest honour, and the 'bee's knees' is not far behind it as a compliment.

Bible Belt *n* (1926) the South and the Middle West of the US, where Protestant fundamentalism is a powerful force. Reputedly coined by the American journalist H. L. Mencken

1926 Sinclair Lewis: I'm collecting parsons, Gilbert… That's why I've been living in Kansas City. It's the centre of the Bible belt.

big band *n* (1926) a large band of musicians playing dance-music, swing, jazz, etc.

1926 *Melody Maker*: [It] gives the lie to those who say that a 'big band' is unwieldy.

1955 *Jazzbook 1955*: [Duke Ellington] is the only man who has consistently created big band jazz of more than ephemeral value.

bimbo *n* (1920) a young woman, especially one who is promiscuous or unintelligent. Slang, originally US; by extension from the male *bimbo* (1919). The notion of empty-headedness (already present in the 1920s) may have been reinforced by the subliminal influence of *dumbo* 'fool' (1932). The term enjoyed a surge of usage around 1987–88, when it was widely applied to young women who were prepared to 'kiss and tell', ending their affairs with the rich and famous by selling their stories to the popular press. See also **bimbette (1982), himbo (1988)**

1937 *Detective Fiction Weekly*: We found Durken and Frenchy LaSeur, seated at a table…with a pair of blonde bimboes beside them.

1988 *Guardian*: So J. Danforth Quayle has 'bimbo-problems'… Paula Parkinson kissed and told.

bingle *n*, *v* (1925) (to cut in) a short hairstyle for women, between a bob and a shingle. A portmanteau term much shorter-lived than its two elements, **bob (1918)** and **shingle (1924)**

1925 *Punch*: This lady complains that you have—ah—completely bungled her bingle.

1925 *Westminster Gazette*: The shingled or bingled head is firmly established in popularity.

biotechnics *n* (1925) the practical application of discoveries in the biological sciences. An early stab at a term which the world seems not to have felt a need for until the 1970s (when **biotechnology** was preferred)

> 1925 Geddes & Thomson (heading): The Applications of Biology (Biotechnics).

bitchy *adj* (1925) malicious, spiteful. Colloquial, originally US

> 1947 John Steinbeck: There wasn't anything mean or bitchy about her.

Black and Tans *n* (1921) A colloquial name for an armed force specially recruited to combat the Sinn Fein rebellion in Ireland in 1920, so named from the mixture of police (black) and military (khaki) uniforms worn by them. Officially auxiliary members of the Royal Irish Constabulary, most were British ex-servicemen; their often brutal methods have ensured that their name lives on in memorious Ireland

> 1921 Lord Braye: I rise to ask His Majesty's Government…whether they will…recall the Black and Tans.

black bottom *n* (1926) a dance, popular in the mid to late 1920s, that involved a sinuous gyrating of the hips. Originally US. The name probably reflects the hip movements, but it may also have been subconsciously prompted by the already existent *black bottom* 'low-lying area inhabited by blacks'. Also recorded as a verb

> 1926 *New York Times*: It occurred to the producer that if you could dance before the beat you would have a new rhythm… The result is the Black Bottom.

> 1927 *Daily Express*: Miss Bradhurst had black bottomed nineteen miles…before she collapsed.

blackshirt *n* (1922) a member of the Fasci di Combattimento, paramilitary units founded by Mussolini in 1919 and forming the backbone of the Fascist party of Italy. Named after the black shirts (in Italian *camicia nera*) they wore. In the 1930s the term was also applied to British Fascists. See also **brown-shirt (1932)**

> 1922 *Youth's Companion*: The 'black shirts' have beaten down Communism by force of arms.

> 1934 H. G. Wells: It was a gathering of Mosley's black-shirts.

> 1934 *Daily Mail* (headline): Hurrah for the Blackshirts.

blind date *n* (1925) a date between two people not known to each other. Originally US. First recorded in 1925, but instances of the synonymous use of *blind* as a US slang noun since 1921 suggest that it was in circulation well before that

> 1925 *Literary Digest*: No, got a blind date on to-night.

blood-donor *n* (1921) See **donor (1910)**

blood wagon *n* (1922) an ambulance. British slang. Originally applied to an air ambulance, but later in wider usage

> 1922 *Flight*: 'The old blood wagon', as the air ambulance…was generally called.

> 1957 Stirling Moss: Out came the 'blood wagon' and back to the ambulance station in the paddock I went.

blue-eyed boy *n* (1924) a particularly favoured person, especially a young man. Mainly British

> 1924 P. G. Wodehouse: If ever there was a blue-eyed boy, you will be it.

bogy, bogey *n* (1924) a detective; a police officer. British slang. Probably from the earlier use of *bogy* as a name for the Devil, or more broadly for any object of dread

> 1936 James Curtis: One of the bogies from Vine Street reckernizes me.

bomb load *n* (1921) the weight of bombs that an aircraft can carry

> 1921 *Aeronautical Journal*: The bomb load of the standard…four-engined machines amounted to 3,000 kilograms.

Bonzo *n* (1927) the figure of a comically-shaped puppy which came into vogue in Britain through a series of drawings by G. E. Studdy (the first of which appeared in *The Sketch* 8 November 1922), used in various forms, as toys, etc. The word was an arbitrary formation dreamed up by Capt. Bruce Ingram, the editor of *The Sketch*. Although its origins were widely forgotten well before the end of the century, it remains in existence in British English as a stereotypical (if seldom used) dog-name (perhaps reinforced by the 'Bonzo Dog Doodah Band', an eccentric musical combo formed in 1965)

> 1927 *Bulletin*: The craze for vanity bags in the form of Teddy Bears, Bonzos, and other zoological specimens.

boobs *n* (1929) the female breasts. Slang, originally US; probably a shortening of the much older *boobies*. Popular as a semi-daring euphemism amongst women in the latter part of the century

> 1949 Henry Miller: I felt her sloshy boobs joggling me but I was too intent on pursuing the ramifications of Coleridge's amazing mind to let her vegetable appendages disturb me.

> 1968 *Daily Mirror*: If people insist on talking about her boobs, she would rather they called them boobs, which is a way-out word,…rather than breasts.

boogie-woogie *n* (1928) a style of playing blues, usually on the piano, marked by a persistent bass rhythm. Originally US, Black English. A fanciful reduplication of *boogie*, which is first recorded in 1917 in the sense '(rent) party', as part of the title of a jazz number ('Boogie rag'). See also **boogie (1941)**

> 1928 (*title*): Pinetop's Boogie Woogie.

> 1935 *Swing Music*: This side [of the record] might be an instruction disc in Swedish Drill…only it's a lesson in Boogie Woogie.

bridge roll *n* (1926) a soft oval bread roll—staple genteel party fare of the middle years of the century. The origin of the name is not entirely clear, but it probably comes from the rolls being served at gatherings at which bridge was played

> 1926 D. D. C. Taylor: Social Tea…Bridge Rolls and Cress, White and Brown Bread and Butter.

bright young people *n* (1927), **bright young thing** *n* (1928) (a member of) the younger generation in fashionable society, especially in the 1920s and 1930s, noted for exuberant and outrageous behaviour

> 1927 *Punch's Almanack*: Since a section of the 'Bright Young People' literally 'set the Thames on fire', things have been a little quiet.

> 1929 G. K. Chesterton: If the bright young thing cannot be asked to tolerate her grandmother…why should the grandmother…have tolerated the bright young thing?

broadbrow *n* (1927) someone with broad artistic or intellectual tastes, between those of highbrows and lowbrows. The word enjoyed a brief vogue in the late 1920s, but soon lost out to the nearly synonymous **middlebrow (1925)**

> 1927 A. P. Herbert: Ballads for Broad-brows.

> 1927 *Observer*: It is no longer highbrow versus lowbrow. We are all broadbrows, and what we want to listen to depends on our mood.

broadcast *v* (1921) to transmit by radio or television. The verb originally denoted scattering seed by hand, so the underlying idea is of disseminating widely. The corresponding noun, and the derivative *broadcaster*, are first recorded in 1922. All were in place for the imminent start of public broadcasting

> 1921 *Discovery*: The [wireless] station at Poldhu is used partly for broadcasting Press and other messages to ships, that is, sending out messages without receiving replies.

> 1922 *Daily Mail*: The largest and most powerful wireless station that can broadcast to the world… Government arrangements for broadcasting…[headline] World Broadcast.

> 1922 *Daily Mail*: The Prince of Wales…made a great hit as a 'broadcaster'…when he delivered a message by wireless to the Boy Scouts.

bungaloid *adj* (1927) like a bungalow; having many bungalows. British. A term of contempt coined (on the model of *fungoid*) to condemn the rash of cheap post-World War I suburban housing (often in the form of flimsy one-storey shacks) and ribbon development. The first bungalows in Britain (modelled on Indian originals) had been built in the mid Victorian period

> 1927 *Daily Express*: Hideous allotments and bungaloid growths make the approaches to any city repulsive.

> 1928 *Sunday Dispatch*: Mr. Shaw designates our modern urban communities 'bungaloid promiscuities', and refuses them the more dignified term of civilisations.

bung-ho, bungo *interj* (1925) An exclamation used at parting or as a drinking toast. Current mainly in the 1920s and early 1930s

> 1928 Dorothy Sayers: 'Dry Martini,' said Wimsey… 'Bung-ho!'

business lunch *n* (1926) a midday meal at which business deals are discussed or done. Originally US. A key feature of 20th-century commercial life (although proverbially they consist more of lunch than of business)

> 1926 Sinclair Lewis: I don't really know a soul…except for meeting them at business lunches.

buy *v* (1926) to believe, accept as true. Slang

> 1926 Edgar Wallace: 'It's rather early in the day for fairy-tales,' he said, 'but I'll buy this one.'

buzz-box *n* (1920), **buzz-wagon** *n* (1923) a car. Slang, which did not long survive the 1920s

> 1923 Ian Hay: Let's go to the stable and start up your little friend's buzz-wagon.

> 1934 *Passing Show*: Ring up Mason's yard…and ask 'em to send round the old buzz-box.

by-line *n* (1926) a line giving the name of the writer of an article in a newspaper or magazine. Originally US

> 1926 Ernest Hemingway: I sorted out the carbons, stamped on a by-line.

> 1938 Irene Kuhn: The thing I wanted most was a by-line—that magic inch of print above a story I had written which would identify me as the author of the gem.

by-pass *n* (1922) a road built around a town, congested area, etc. so as to relieve traffic. See also **ring road (1928)**

> 1922 *Daily Mail*: New roads and by-passes, which should remove some of these danger spots.

> 1923 *Times*: The Kingston by-pass will begin at the Robin Hood gate.

Caesarian *n* (1923) a Caesarian section. Originally US. The term *Caesarian section* dates from the early 17th century, and alludes to the legend that Julius Caesar (or an ancestor of his) was born in this way. The article quoted below, incidentally, is by the surgeon who performed the operations, not by a woman who underwent them. The abbreviation *Caesar* is first recorded in 1952

> 1923 S. P. Warren (*heading*): What I have learned from my one hundred and six cesareans.

camel-walk *n* (1921), **camel-trot** *n* (1923) a popular dance of the early 1920s, involving supposedly camelish movements

> 1921 *Frontier*: The morbid minded may read them as openly as they danced the shimmy and the camel-walk a year ago.

> 1923 *Weekly Dispatch*: They call the modern dances camel-trots.

candid camera *n* (1929) a camera for photographing or filming people without their knowledge. The term achieved notoriety in the 1950s as the name of a television programme featuring surreptitiously taken films of people in amusing or embarrassing situations, originally shown in the US and subsequently in Britain

> 1929 *Graphic*: At the foreground table, unaware of the proximity of the candid camera, will be seen Dean Inge enjoying his cigar.

car-park *n* (1926) an open space, a building, etc. for the parking of motor vehicles. Compare **parking lot (1924)**

> 1926 *Daily Mail*: Glastonbury Car Park. Indignation has been aroused…by a proposal…to purchase part of the land…as an extra parking space for motor cars.

cat *n* (1920) a fellow, guy; also, in later use, a person of either sex. Slang, originally US, especially Black English. Later strongly reinforced by *cat* 'jazz enthusiast' (1931). Often in the phrase *cool cat*

> 1959 A. Anderson: 'At-dam, man, youre the selfishest kat I seen yet.

> 1963 Raven McDavid: A cool cat...is...much of the time stoned on wine, pot..., heroin or an over-dose of Zen Buddhism.

cat's whiskers *n* (1923) the very best; the height of excellence. Slang, originally US. One of the best-known and longest-lasting of a whole range of bizarre 'excellence' words based on various parts of animals' anatomy and other attributes, which enjoyed a fashion in the 1920s. Others based on *cat* included *cat's meow, cat's pajamas,* and the more risqué *cat's nuts,* but other animals got in on the act too: *canary's tusks, flea's eyebrows,* for instance (although such formations were highly ephemeral). See also **bee's knees (1923)**. A later formation on the same model was *dog's bollocks* (1989)

> 1924 P. G. Wodehouse: 'Well, if this ain't the cat's whiskers!' said Miss Peavey.

centrist *n* (1923) someone taking a position in the political centre; a moderate. A borrowing from French, originally (in the 1870s) as a term for a member of the Centre Party in France

> 1923 E. A. Ross: The 'Berliner Tageblatt' and the 'Vossische Zeitung' demand an understanding with Russia by all means. The Centrists favor an agreement.

Chaplinesque *adj* (1921) characteristic of Charlie Chaplin (1889–1977), the English-born film actor and producer, whose comical-pathetic figure 'the Tramp' was probably the most famous creation of the silent-film era

> 1921 George Bernard Shaw: The Chaplinesque invention of Simon of Nantua and the *papegai.*

chara *n* (1928) See **charry (1926)**

Charleston *n* (1923) a dance characterized by side kicks from the knee. Probably the most popular and characteristic dance of the decade. Originally US, and first recorded as the title of a song by C. Mack and J. Johnson. The name comes from Charleston, the capital city of Charleston county, South Carolina. It is first recorded as a verb in 1927

> 1926 *Glasgow Herald*: In these days of fox trots and Charlestons it is refreshing to watch such clean dancing.

> 1928 D. H. Lawrence: 'Do you Charleston?' she said.

charry *n* (1926), **chara** *n* (1928) Short-lived colloquialisms for *char-à-banc.* This (literally 'benched carriage' in French) had been in use in English since the early 19th century, applied to a horse-drawn vehicle, but it really came into its own in Britain in the 1920s, when motorized versions carried day-trippers in their thousands enjoying their new-found mobility and holidays with pay. However, by the middle of the century it was well on its way out, replaced by *coach*

> 1926 *British Weekly*: The motor-omnibus...is another formidable competitor to the 'charry'.

> 1928 F. E. Baily: I don't approve of them charas on the Kingswear Road.

chemical weapon *n* (1920) a weapon that depends for its effect on the release of a toxic or noxious substance

> 1920 E. S. Farrow: The following types of chemical weapons have been approved for use by infantry: Incendiary grenades, gas grenades, smoke grenades. [etc.]

chewy *adj* (1925) having a texture that requires chewing. A positive term in the hands of 20th-century advertising copywriters

> 1925 *Golden Book Magazine* (advert): It was made for those who prefer firm and 'chew-y' chocolates.

Chinese gooseberry *n* (1925) the fruit of the vine *Actinia chinesis*, later better known as the **kiwi fruit (1966)**. China was its original home

> 1925 *Weekly News* (Auckland): The Chinese gooseberry...has been introduced into Auckland.

chorine *n* (1922) a chorus girl. Originally US. Essentially a word of the inter-war period, although it outlived that in US English

> 1922 *Moving Picture Stories*: Pearls continue to be popular, especially with soubrettes and even chorines.

Chunnel *n* (1928) a tunnel under the English Channel, connecting Britain and France. An isolated instance of this blend of *channel* and *tunnel* is recorded in 1928 (in a glossary rather than in a spontaneous text), but there is no evidence that it was in widespread use around that time. It did not take off (and then mainly in newspaper-ese) until the late 1950s, when another of the periodic surges of interest in building such a tunnel took place. When the tunnel was actually built, in the 1980s, the word *Chunnel* was comparatively little in evidence outside the occasional newspaper headline. See also **fixed link (1974)**

> 1957 *New York Times Magazine*: A channel tunnel?... My newspaper christened the project 'The Chunnel'.

chute *n* (1920) A colloquial abbreviation of *parachute*

> 1920 *Ace*: Jumping backwards from the wing...Heenan dropped over 1,000 feet before the chute opened.

cine camera *n* (1920) a film camera

> 1920 V. Steer: Crowds of ebullient amateurs all so eager to 'strut their little hour' in front of the cine camera.

clerkess *n* (1923) a female clerk. A Scotticism, still an entry in the Scottish *Chambers 21st-Century Dictionary* in 1996

> 1965 J. Caird: She was clerkess in an office.

cocktail bar *n* (1929) a bar at which cocktails are served. They come in many shapes and sizes, domestic as well as commercial, but the concept is the key: the Art Deco-ish sophistication of interwar café society (see also **cocktail party (1928)**, **cocktail cabinet (1933)**). You can get spirits at a cocktail bar, and probably also champagne, but decidedly not beer

> 1934 Aldous Huxley: The last word in cocktail bars and peach-pink sanitary fittings.

cocktail party *n* (1928) a drinks party, usually in the early evening. Concoctions called 'cocktails' had been drunk in the US since at least the early 19th century, but it was not until the mid 1920s that the modern cocktail, with its whole associated culture of parties and bars and its veneer of sharp modern sophistication, impinged significantly on the rest of the Western world. See also **Gibson (1930)**, **gimlet (1928)**, **sidecar (1928)**

> 1928 D. H. Lawrence: She almost wished she had...made her life one long cocktail party and jazz evening.

cold turkey *n* (1921) a method of treating drug addicts by sudden and complete withdrawal of the drug, instead of by a gradual process. Slang, originally North American. Presumably from the earlier adverbial usage, 'suddenly, without preparation or warning' ('I'd lost five thousand dollars..."cold turkey"', Robert Service (1910)), but the origins of that are unknown. See also **withdrawal symptoms (1924)**

> 1921 *Daily Colonist* (Victoria, British Columbia): Perhaps the most pitiful figures who have appeared before Dr. Carleton Simon...are those who voluntarily surrender themselves. When they go before him, [drug addicts] are given what is called the 'cold turkey' treatment.

collective farm *n* (1925) a farm, especially in the USSR, consisting of the holdings of several farmers, run by a group of people in co-operation, usually under state control. The term was slightly preceded into English by *collective farming*, in a translation of a text by Lenin: 'The local and central Soviet authority aims... to foster collective farming' (1919)

> 1958 *New Statesman*: From a visit to two collective farms...he concludes that Israeli Left-wingers are doctrinaire and spartan.

colour television *n* (1929) television in which the pictures are transmitted and displayed in colour rather than black and white. John Logie Baird gave a demonstration of colour television in London in 1928 (referred to in the first quote below), but it was not until 1953 that the first successful system was adopted for broadcasting, in the US

> 1929 Sheldon & Grisewood: Baird was partially successful in color television in 1928.

> 1955 *Oxford Junior Encyclopedia*: The colour-television receiver has three separate cathode ray tubes, one for each of the signals from the three cameras.

columnist *n* (1920) someone who writes a newspaper column. Originally US. This particular application of *column* to a regular newspaper article by a particular writer (in which sense it was, to begin with, often facetiously spelled *colyum*) seems to have emerged in the US around the turn of the century: 'The most important development on America's editorial pages during the past quarter of a century has been the evolution of the "colyum"', H. W. Davis (1926)

> 1920 *Blackwood's Magazine*: The 'colyumist' [sic] of a New York paper.

> 1926 *Spectator*: One of the best known 'columnists' of the American press.

combine harvester, combine *n* (1926) a harvesting machine that cuts, threshes, and cleans grain. Originally US. Probably the biggest single technological development in arable farming in the 20th century, which transformed much of the British landscape from a pattern of small medieval fields into a mini-prairie. *Combined* had been used in the designations of multi-purpose agricultural machines since the middle of the 19th century ('In the afternoon the combined mower and the Illinois mower were put upon trial, in a beautiful field of timothy', *Illinois State Register* (1857)), and the variant *combined harvester* is also on record

> 1926 *Kansas City Star*: Hundreds of combines will be in the fields in southern, central, and western Kansas by Wednesday.

> 1929 *Institute of Agricultural Engineering Bulletin*: Throughout this report the Combine Harvester or Harvester-Thresher is referred to as the 'combine'.

comic strip *n* (1920) a series of drawings telling a story, typically appearing in a newspaper, comic, etc. The 1920s and '30s were perhaps the Golden Age of the comic strip, beginning with the likes of Little Orphan Annie and going on with such characters as Li'l Abner, Popeye, Rupert the Bear, and Jane. British English has the alternative term **strip cartoon (1936)**

> 1928 *Daily Sketch*: I keenly appreciate the qualities that make Pop the greatest comic strip in the world. No comic strip artist…has the same facile and generic lines the creator of Pop possesses.

commentary *n* (1927) a description of some public event broadcast or televised as it happens. Originally always in the expression *running commentary*, to distinguish it from comment on previous happenings

> 1927 *B.B.C. Hand-book 1928*: Running commentaries fall easily under two different -headings— Sporting and purely Descriptive.

> 1930 *B.B.C. Year-book 1931*: The above events were dealt with either by commentaries broadcast while the event was taking place, or by accounts by eye-witnesses broadcast after the event.

commentator *n* (1928) someone who gives a broadcast commentary on a live event (see **commentary (1927)**).

> 1935 *Punch*: If Perry puts a forehand drive into the far corner, right or left, the commentator has to say so in so many words.

compact *n* (1921) a small case for compressed face-powder, rouge, etc.

> 1921 *Daily Colonist* (Victoria, British Columbia): Luxor Compacts in three shades.

conservation *n* (1922) the preservation of the environment, and especially of natural resources. To begin with, an ecologists' term; it did not start to become a buzzword until the late 1950s. *Conservationist* is first recorded in the same year

> 1922 *Encyclopedia Britannica*: A very important by-product of the conservation-movement was the development at Washington of a mania for the establishment of reservations in Alaska… The most ardent of the conservationists failed to recognize the urgent importance of conserving the salmon and halibut fisheries.

> 1958 *New Biology*: Conservation as a world problem.

corgi *n* (1926) a small, short-legged dog of Welsh origin, introduced as a pet breed in the 1920s and still popular with the British royal family towards the end of the century. In Welsh, its name means literally 'dwarf dog'

> 1926 *Glasgow Herald*: A certain amount of talk in praise of a tiny Welsh dog, the Corgy.

> 1970 *Times*: The Queen, with a firm hand on the leash for a reluctant corgi, arriving at Euston station.

cosmetic *adj* (1926) Of surgery: improving or modifying the appearance. The term *plastic surgery* is first recorded in 1839

> 1926 *Encyclopedia Britannica*: Cosmetic and plastic surgery, especially of the face, has undergone considerable improvement following our large experience in the war.

cosmic rays *n* (1925) high-energy radiations from outer space with great penetrative power which reach the surface of the earth. Discovered by the American physicist R. A. Millikan

> 1925 R. A. Millikan: Our experiments brought to light…a cosmic radiation of…extraordinary penetrating power… We obtained good evidence that these cosmic rays shoot through space in all directions.

cossie, cozzie *n* (1926) a bathing-costume. Formed from a shortening of *costume*. An early example of a colloquialism formed with the familiar suffix *-ie* that has been a characteristic of Australian English in the 20th century (others include **barbie (1976)**, *carby* 'carburettor' (1957), and **tinny (1974)**)

> 1931 *Surf*: Where's y'r cossy? Didn't y' come here to swim?

cotton on *v* (1922) to begin to understand; to catch on. Colloquial

> 1922 D. H. Lawrence: Oh…I didn't want to… Didn't want to—didn't cotton on, like.

council house *n* (1923) a house erected by a local council and provided at a subsidized rent. British

> 1929 *Times*: The Reigate Rural District Council are now insisting on building a street of council houses along one of the most beautiful lanes in Surrey.

cover charge *n* (1921) a charge for service added to the basic charge in a restaurant. The original reference had nothing to do with 'covering' the cost: it comes from the noun *cover* in the sense 'place-setting at a table'

> 1921 *Nation* (New York): As levied here, the cover charge is a compulsory blanket assessment for nothing in particular; it commonly includes bread and butter.

crackers *adj* (1928) crazy, mad. Slang, originally and mainly British. A combination of the idea of having a 'broken' head (as in *cracked* and *crack-brained*) with the suffix *-ers* (see **preggers (1942)**)

> 1928 *Daily Express*: I shall go 'crackers' (meaning mad) if anything happens to Ted.

craftsperson *n* (1920) a craftsman or craftswoman. See **salesperson (1920)**

> 1920 William de Morgan: The winding of these wools was out of all proportion to the craftsperson's output.

crazy paving *n* (1925) pavement of irregular pieces of flat stone or tile. A usage apparently inspired by *crazy quilt*, a late-19th-century US term for a patchwork quilt made of pieces of cloth of all kinds in irregular patterns

> 1925 A. S. M. Hutchinson: Under the blue tile…of the crazy-paving just by the rain-water butt.

crisp *n* (1929) a thin sliver of potato fried until crisp and eaten cold. As a commercial product they achieved great popularity in the 1930s, particularly, in Britain, the Smith's brand, sold in paper packets with a little blue-paper twist of salt inside. Initially they were usually called in full *potato crisps*, but by the second half of the century the abbreviated form was the norm. Neither term is very familiar in the US, where these delicacies are usually called *potato chips*

> 1929 *Star*: Potato Crisp Factory.

> 1935 Harold Nicolson: We went to Harry's Bar…and there was a Pekinese being fed with crisps.

> 1950 T. S. Eliot: Potato crisps? No I can't endure them.

crime wave *n* (1920) a prolonged period with a high incidence of crime

> 1920 *Times* (headline): Crime Wave. Murder, robbery and theft.

cruise *v* (1927) to go around in search of homosexual partners. A development of an earlier application to prostitutes walking the streets in search of customers, which has been traced back to the lowlife slang of the mid 17th century

> 1927 A. J. Rosanoff: In the most respectable class [of homosexuals] are those who do no 'cruising'.

crystal set *n* (1924) a radio using a semiconducting crystal in contact with a fine metal wire (see **cat's whisker (1915)**) as a detector. An earlier recorded synonym is **crystal receiver (1917)**. Compare **valve set (1929)**

> 1943 C. L. Boltz: Some years ago thousands of people regularly used crystal sets for listening to broadcast programmes.

cultivar *n* (1923) a variety of plant that has arisen in cultivation

> 1923 L. H. Bailey: I now propose another name, cultivar, for a botanical variety, or for a race subordinate to species, that has originated and persisted under cultivation.

cuppa *n* (1925) A representation of a colloquial pronunciation of *cup of*. An early example of a type of written form that proliferated modestly as the century progressed (see also **lotsa (1927)**, **pinta (1958)**, and **loadsa (1987)**). In British usage it has become synonymous with 'a cup of tea'

> 1925 P. G. Wodehouse: Come and have a cuppa coffee.

> 1968 Mordecai Richler: 'Good morning,' Joyce said. 'Coffee?' 'If it's no trouble I'd prefer a cuppa.'

current affairs *n* (1920) events of public interest in progress. Originally a fairly general term (for which the synonym *current events* is first recorded in the middle of the 19th century); the more specific application to 'political or international events of public importance' does not seem to have become firmly established until the time of World War II, and the even more specific implication of television coverage of these followed in the 1960s

> 1920 Max Beerbohm: Swinburne did, from time to time, take public notice of current affairs.

> 1979 *Journal of the Royal Society of Arts*: What is reported on the news, and current affairs, something very different indeed from…election round-up programmes.

customs *n* (1921) the area at a seaport, airport, etc., where goods, luggage, and other items are examined and customs duties levied. Hitherto, *customs* had simply been applied to the duties themselves

> 1921 C. Crow: Travelers should note that…if goods other than personal effects are taken out of the country it is necessary to pass them through the customs before they can be accepted by the shipping companies.

dab *n* (1926) a fingerprint. British slang

> 1926 Norman Lucas: The finger-print system is without doubt the crooks' greatest enemy… The verifying of their 'dabs' soon brings their dossier to court.

Dada *n* (1920) an international movement in art and literature, characterized by a repudiation of traditional conventions and reason, and intended to outrage and scandalize. The name comes from that of a review which appeared at Zürich first in 1916, founded by Tristan Tzara (a Rumanian poet), Jean Arp (a French artist), and Richard Hülsenbeck (a German poet). This in turn was an arbitrary use of French *dada*, baby-talk for 'hobbyhorse'

> 1920 *Athenæum*: The movement 'Dada'…has its headquarters in Paris, and its principal promoters are Francis Picabia and Tristan Tzara, neither of whom is of French nationality.

date *n* (1925) a (potential) sexual partner with whom one has a date. Originally and mainly US. *Date* meaning 'courtship assignation' seems to have surfaced at the end of the 19th century, although early examples are not always easy to distinguish from the more general (and roughly contemporary) 'appointment'. See also **blind date (1925)**

> 1925 *American Speech*: My date was late last evening.

deadline *n* (1920) a time by which material has to be ready for inclusion in a particular issue of a publication. Originally US. It appears to have come from the earlier printers' sense 'a guide-line marked on the bed of a printing-press', which in turn was based on the US military sense 'a line drawn round a military prison, beyond which a prisoner is liable to be shot down', which dates from the mid 19th century

> 1920 *Chicago Herald & Examiner*: Corinne Griffith…is working on 'Deadline at Eleven', the newspaper play.

debunk *v* (1923) to expose or ridicule the falseness or exaggerated claims of. Originally US. The derivation of the word is explained in the first quote below

> 1923 W. E. Woodward: De-bunking means simply taking the bunk out of things... To keep the United States thoroughly de-bunked would require the continual services of...half a million persons.

> 1927 *British Weekly*: The somewhat ruthless process which in America is called 'debunking'—that is, pricking pretentious bubbles [etc.].

decibel *n* (1928) a unit used in comparing the intensities of two sounds. A coinage (based on *bel*, which in turn commemorates the US inventor Alexander Graham Bell) originally restricted to technical contexts, but by the 1940s it had become more familiar in general use

> 1928 *Electrical Communication*: If common logarithms are used, the reproduction is obtained in Decibels.

> 1948 *Punch Miscellany*: No one misses a single decibel of your conversation.

deflation *n* (1920) an increase in the value of money and a reduction of general price levels. The reverse of *inflation*, which dates from the 1830s

> 1920 *Glasgow Herald*: The process of deflation likely to result from the new rights of the Federal Reserve system to discount on a graded scale.

dehydrate *v* (1922) to remove the water from (food), so as to preserve it and reduce its bulk. One of the earliest steps in the 20th-century industrialization of food-production

> 1921 C. V. Ekroth: One of the most important features of the food conservation movement since the outbreak of the war has been the practice of dehydrating fruits and vegetables.

delish *adj* (1920) A colloquial abbreviation of *delicious*

> 1920 *Punch*: Their music, I gather, is wholly delish.

> 1953 Nicholas Blake: Have a glass of port, won't you? It's rather delish.

demob *v* (1920) A colloquial abbreviation of *demobilize* (1882)— i.e., 'to release from military service'. Like **deration (1920)**, an 'end-of-the-war' word. The parallel noun, short for *demobilization*, seems not to have come on the scene until the conclusion of World War II (see **demob (1934)**)

> 1920 *Glasgow Herald*: Some young soldiers...who had been recently demobbed.

denationalize *v* (1921) to transfer (an industry, etc.) from national to private ownership. See also **privatization (1959)**

> 1921 *Times*: The object of the...agitation is not to improve the [telephone] service, but to get it denationalized, 'to get it handed over to private capitalists'.

dendrochronology *n* (1928) the science of arranging events in the order of time by the comparative study of the annual growth rings in (ancient) timber. A coinage based on Greek *dendron* 'tree'. The rather charming Germanic alternative *tree-time* mentioned in the quote below never caught on, but *dendrochronology* has gone on to have wide currency

> 1928 A. E. Douglass: We are measuring the lapse of time by means of a slow-geared clock within the trees. For this study the name 'dendro-chronology' has been suggested, or 'tree-time'. This expression covers all the dating and historic problems...as well as the study of cyclic variations and the distribution of climatic conditions.

deplane *v* (1923) to leave an aircraft. The first quote below actually refers to jumping out with a parachute, but in later usage more conventional disembarkation at one's destination is usually implied

> 1923 *Blackwood's Magazine*: Dudley left me, saying...that he was to 'deplane' now.

> 1967 Leigh James: After clearing immigration control, he...watched the crowd of deplaning passengers.

deration *v* (1920) to free (a rationed commodity) from rationing

> 1920 *Glasgow Herald*: The Food Controller was able to announce...last night that sugar will be de-rationed as from Monday.

dilatation and curettage *n* (1920) an operation involving the opening of the cervix and removal of the lining of the uterus, carried out for diagnostic purposes, to terminate a pregnancy, or to stop irregular menstrual bleeding. The alternative formulation *dilatation and curetting* is recorded as long before as 1906, but *dilatation and curettage* has become the standard term. See also **scrape (1968)**

> 1920 H. S. Crossen: The safe method of securing the necessary fixation of the cervix, for Dilatation and Curettage.

discussion group *n* (1921) a meeting of several people to discuss an issue (possibly the embryo which grew up into the **think tank (1959)**)

> 1921 H. J. Laski: A discussion group to thresh out the problems of governmental re-organisation.

dissociation of sensibility *n* (1921) T. S. Eliot's term for a separation of thought from feeling, which he considered to be first manifested in poetry of the later 17th century

> 1921 T. S. Eliot: The poets of the seventeenth century…possessed a mechanism of sensibility which could devour any kind of experience… In the seventeenth century a dissociation of sensibility set in, from which we have never recovered.

Dodgem *n* (1921) a fairground amusement consisting of a number of small electrically powered cars (*dodgem cars*) steered about in an enclosure.

> 1947 Nevil Shute: Among the hurly-burly of his swings and roundabouts and flip-flops and dodgem cars.

dogs *n the dogs* (1927) a greyhound race meeting. British colloquial. Large-scale organized greyhound racing got underway in Britain in 1926, and for several decades was the best-attended spectator sport in the country. See also **gracing (1928)**

> 1928 A. P. Herbert: Going to the Dogs. Well Trix darling at last I've been to these *contagious* greyhounds.

doolally *adj* (1925) mad, crazy. British services' slang; first recorded in print in 1925, but noted then as 'old Army'. It is a shortened form of *doolally tap*: *doolally* is soldiers' mangling of *Deolali*, the name of a town in Marashtra, India, where there was a British army camp; obsolete *tap* 'malaria' comes ultimately from Persian *tap* 'fever, heat'. It was often used in the phrase *doolally-tap in the boodle* 'mad in the head'. At the end of the century it was still remembered and, occasionally, used

> 1936 James Curtis: What's the matter with that bloke? Doolally?

Duce *n* (1923) The title assumed in 1922 by Benito Mussolini (1883–1945), the creator and leader of the Fascist state in Italy. From Italian, literally 'Leader'

> 1923 B. Quaranta di San Severino: Three…important elements account for the success of the 'National Fascista Party'…above all, the personality of Mussolini himself, the 'Duce', as he is called.

Dutch elm disease *n* (1927) a disease of elm trees, first discovered in Holland, caused by the fungus *Ceratocystis ulmi*. By the early 1930s it had spread across Britain and continental Europe and crossed to North America. The new epidemic of the 1970s was caused by a more virulent strain of the fungus

> 1927 *Gardeners' Chronicle*: The Dutch Elm Disease… The disease was first observed in Holland in September, 1919.

> 1976 *Daily Telegraph*: Three thousand Zelkova trees imported from Germany are being planted in Peterborough to replace elms killed by Dutch Elm disease.

Elastoplast *n* (1928) A proprietary name for a type of sticking-plaster, originally made of stretchable fabric and subsequently also of other materials. Widely used as a generic term in British English in the middle years of the century. See also **Band-Aid (1924)**

> 1948 Graham Greene: Now iodine… Now the elastoplast.

empathize *v* (1924) to treat with empathy. Originally transitive, but in modern usage (presumably on the model of *sympathize*) more usually intransitive, followed by *with*, and meaning 'to feel empathy' (see **empathy (1904)**)

> 1931 T. H. Pear: One may…'empathise' with the speaker.

equalize *v* (1925) to bring the scores level, especially in a football match. Mainly British

> 1925 S. J. Southerton: Soon after half-time Millington should have equalised from a penalty kick.

equal opportunity *n* (1925) equal chance and right to seek success in one's chosen sphere regardless of social factors such as class, wealth, race, religion, and sex. As a general phrase, or slogan, this has probably always taken second place to the synonymous *equality of opportunity*, first recorded in 1891 ('It will possibly, however, be contended that here the ideal is equality of Opportunity', *Economic Review*), but it has acquired a niche for itself in adjectival use since the 1960s in the specific context of anti-discriminatory legislation, especially in the area of employment

> 1925 D. H. Lawrence: They talk about 'equal opportunity': but it is bunk, ridiculous bunk. It is the old fable of the fox asking the stork to dinner.

> 1963 *New York Times*: Mr. Screvane proposed to the Board of Estimate that $3,400,000,000 in city pension funds be invested only in securities of equal-opportunity employers.

Eskimo pie *n* (1928) a bar of ice-cream coated with chocolate. A proprietary name in the US, apparently coined in 1921 (see the quote below) and recorded in the shortened form *Eskimo* in 1922 ('Chocolate eggs filled with ice-cream and known as "Eskimos" ', *Glasgow Herald*). Compare **choc-ice (1951)**

> 1928 Turnbow & Raffetto: Chocolate-coated ice cream bars were introduced in 1921 as 'Eskimo Pies'.

establishment *n* (1923) a social group exercising power generally, or within a given field or institution, by virtue of its traditional superiority, and by the use especially of tacit understandings and often a common mode of speech, and having as a general interest the maintenance of the status quo. Henry Fairlie, in the *Spectator* article quoted below, is generally credited with bringing the term into wide currency, although, as the other quotations show, it had been around for some time before 1955

> 1923 Rose Macaulay: The moderns of one day become the safe establishments of the next.

> 1945 D. Goldring: It was a head-on collision between two acknowledged leaders of the literary avant-garde and the powerful forces of what Ford Madox Ford used to call the Establishment.

> 1955 Henry Fairlie: By the 'Establishment' I do not mean only the centres of official power—though they are certainly part of it—but rather the whole matrix of official and social relations within which power is exercised.

estrogen *n* (1927) See **oestrogen (1927)**

Eton crop *n* (1926) a style of cutting women's hair close to the head all over, popular in the 1920s and resulting in a boyish appearance, like the pupils of Eton College

> 1926 Edgar Wallace: The masculinity of the powerful face was emphasized by the grey hair cut close in an Eton crop.

extra-marital *adj* (1929) taking place outside marriage. In practice always applied to sexual intercourse, in the context of its social prohibition to those not married to each other. A marker of the post-World War I world's ability to refer to such matters with at least a degree of objectivity, without resorting to coy euphemisms of the *free love* type (an early 19th-century coinage)

> 1929 Bertrand Russell: We, however, wish to appeal to reason, and we must therefore employ dull neutral phrases, such as 'extra-marital sexual relations'.

face-lifting *n* (1922) cosmetic plastic surgery to improve the appearance of facial skin. Early terminology was in a state of flux, as the quote below shows; the long-term winner, **face-lift**, is not recorded until 1934. See also **lift (1922)**

> 1922 Florence Courtenay: The 'face-raising' or 'face-lifting' process which does away with wrinkles, mouth and eyelines and sagging cheeks by literally 'lifting' off part of the old face and replacing it.

> 1934 Rose Macaulay: What I needed…was a face-lift… I should have a new, young, tight face.

fag *n* (1921) a male homosexual. US slang; a shortening of **faggot (1914)**

> 1923 Nels Anderson: Fairies or Fags are men or boys who exploit sex for profit.

family allowance *n* (1924) an allowance paid by the state to parents who have a specified number of children, or by an employer to employees with families. In Britain, the term in its former sense was officially replaced in 1975 by **child benefit**

> 1924 E. F. Rathbone: Family allowances in an extremely rudimentary form were started in France in 1890 by the Railway Companies.

fan mail *n* (1924) letters sent to a celebrity by his or her fans. This use of *fan* (short for *fanatic*) dates from the late 19th century

   1937 Auden & MacNeice: A poet's fan-mail will be nothing new.

fantasize *v* (1926) to indulge in fantasies

   1926 *Spectator*: Certainly one may fantasize to one's own taste.

fascism *n* (1922) the principles and organization of a body of Italian nationalists, which was orga- nized in 1919 to oppose communism in Italy, and, as the *partito nazionale fascista*, under the lead- ership of Benito Mussolini (1883–1945), controlled that country from 1922 to 1943. The term first appeared in English texts in 1920 in the original Italian form *fascismo*, but the anglicized version dates from 1922, as does *fascist*, which itself had been used in English in the Italian plural form *fascisti* in 1921. The word is based on Italian *fascio* 'bundle, group' (the Fascists used the ancient Roman 'fasces', a magistrates' emblem of authority consisting of a bundle of rods bound round an axe, as their symbol). The term was being applied to a similar right-wing movement in Germany as early as 1923

   1922 *Quarterly Review*: A section of the Press…now veered completely round to the cause of Fascism. The Fascist terror increased in intensity.

   1922 *Daily Mail*: Signor Mussolini, the Fascist leader, to-day made his first speech in the Chamber.

   1923 *Contemporary Review*: Fascism in Germany will never be more than one of several factors.

fascistization *n* (1925) the action or process of making something fascist

   1925 *Glasgow Herald*: The complete 'fascistisation' of Italy.

fast one *n* (1923) a sly and deceiving trick done to gain an advantage. Colloquial; usually in the phrase *pull a fast one*, although this is not recorded before 1932

   1923 H. C. Witwer: He's trying to put over a fast one!

   1932 J. Sayre: Brick pulled a fast one in the St. Mary's game.

fast worker *n* (1921) someone who makes rapid progress. Originally (and often subsequently) applied colloquially to someone who loses no time in chatting up a prospective sexual partner

   1921 Sewell Ford: The dark stranger is getting a bit free. He is patting Inez on the arm… 'One of these fast workers, I take it,' says I.

fat cat *n* (1928) an inordinately wealthy person. In original US slang use the term was applied specifically to a rich backer of a political party, but since then it has broadened out into a general term of opprobrium for people who have more money than others think they should have and have acquired it without hard work

   1928 F. R. Kent: These capitalists have what the organization needs—money to finance the cam- paign. Such men are known in political circles as 'Fat Cats'.

   1998 *Private Eye*: It's hard to see how his campaign to charge British Library readers fees, while giv- ing fat cat bosses handouts, fits with Demos' concern for 'information have-nots'.

filling station *n* (1921) an establishment where drivers can buy fuel. Originally US. See also **gas station (1932)** and **petrol station (1926)**

   1921 *Outing* (US): He should not attempt the trip without a small reserve can of gasoline…enough to carry him to a filling station in case of leakage.

fixate *v* (1926) See **fixation (1910)**

flapper *n* (1921) a pleasure-seeking young woman who flouted the conventions of the time, and was looked upon by those who disapproved of such things as flighty and indecorous. The antecedents of the word are not easy to disentangle. In the foregoing sense it is one of the defining words of the 'Roaring Twenties', but this may well be a compound of two separate sources. From the 1880s onward a *flapper* was both a 'prostitute' (there may be some connection with Northumberland and Durham dialect *flap* 'flighty young woman') and a 'teenage girl' (apparently so called because her hair had not yet been 'put up', and so it still 'flapped' around—either unrestrained or in a pig- tail). There are strong traces of these uses (particularly the latter) in *flapper* (and derivatives like *flapperish* and *flapperdom*) during the 1920s, and it is not always clear whether the previous or the newer meaning is intended. The introduction of full female suffrage in Britain in 1928 gave rise to the so-called 'flapper vote' (previously only women of 30 and above could vote)

> 1921 S. Thompson: The…attention bestowed…by her 'flapper' cousins on these ordinary, pleasant-faced young men.

> 1957 *Observer*: Mrs. Rosenthal, who launched the 'Maiden-form' brassiere thirty-three years ago at the height of the flapper era…, sent me over from New York the original sketch of this most modest, flattened bust-line.

flatlet *n* (1925) a small flat, usually of one or two rooms. British

> 1925 *Glasgow Herald*: There is a large scheme evolving by which big well-built houses…are adapted to provide one–two-roomed flatlets at a very moderate rental.

flaunt *v* (1923) to flout. A solecism of long standing which does not begin to appear in books on 'correct' usage (such as Fowlers' *English Usage*) until after World War II

> 1923 C. Garstin: He achieved strong local popularity, a priceless asset to a man who lives by flaunting the law.

flick *n* (1926) a film; also used in the plural to denote 'the cinema'. Colloquial. Probably a back-formation from *flicker* (although that is not recorded until the following year), the underlying idea being the flickering effect of early movies on the screen. Relatively common in the middle years of the century, it has faded from use latterly

> 1926 Edgar Wallace: We'll occupy the afternoon with a 'flick'. I love the movies—especially the romantic ones.

> 1927 W. E. Collinson: We all know the word movies, but still use pictures or cinema [si'nima] in preference to the American term… Mr. Titley adds the slang flicks or flickers, unknown to me.

floodlight *n* (1924) a light providing a beam of intense illumination. The term *floodlighting* is recorded in the previous decade ('A Resumé of Flood-lighting', *Electrical News* (1917)), so conceivably *floodlight* is a back-formation

> 1924 J. F. Hobart: Another means of illumination is by floodlights which are mounted at a distance from the space to be lighted.

flow chart *n* (1920) a diagram showing the movement of goods, materials, or personnel in any complex system of activities and the sequence of operations they perform or processes they undergo. An essential tool of 20th-century production control

> 1920 C. E. Knoeppel: What should be considered in making up these flow charts are [etc.].

flying doctor *n* (1926) a doctor who habitually uses an aircraft for visiting patients in areas remote from his or her headquarters

> 1932 *Lancet*: In May 1928 Dr. K. St. Vincent Welch, the first 'flying doctor', set up practice at Cloncurry in Queensland.

football pool *n* (1929) a gambling pool in which people pay to bet on the results of soccer matches. British. Usually used in the plural, and very often in the abbreviated form *pools*. From their inception after World War I until the advent of the National Lottery in the 1990s, the pools were the largest form of mass gambling in Britain. The term *football coupon* for the form filled in to do the pools is first recorded in 1918

> 1936 *Economist*: We may…put… the total 'rake off' of football pool promoters…at not less than 30 per cent. of the amounts staked.

> 1938 *Mass-Observation: First Year's Work, 1937–38*: The Pools provide an outlet for personal frustration, ambition and faith.

foreplay *n* (1929) sexual stimulation that precedes intercourse. A key term in the clinical vocabulary of 20th-century sexology

> 1929 J. B. Eggen: The difference between perversion and fore-play.

> 1953 Alfred Kinsey: Many persons…feel that the intensity of the ultimate orgasm is heightened by extended foreplay.

formula *n* (1927) the class or specification of a racing car, usually expressed in terms of engine capacity. In modern usage best known in such expressions as *Formula One* and *Formula Ford*

> 1927 *Autocar*: Half an hour later we knew for certain that we had won the race on formula.

> 1965 *Listener*: This was the weekend of the Monaco Grand Prix, when the faded Edwardian pensions seemed stunned and shaken by the noise of Formula One racing engines.

foundation garment *n* (1927) an item of (women's) underwear, such as a bra or corset, intended to support and shape the figure. Undoubtedly there was an element of euphemism in the coinage, but it is also a useful collective term

> 1927 *Daily Express*: These are best described as cami-bockers, plus a skirt, and are quite the most sensible foundation garment.

> 1957 *Times*: It is wise first of all to give thought to the question of the right foundation garments. Unconditioned muscles tire less with the support of a well-fitted brassière and pantie-belt.

fridge, frig *n* (1926) A colloquial abbreviation of *refrigerator*, probably at least partly modelled on the trade-name *Frigidaire*. The earlier spelling was *frig* (or *'frig*), and this survived well into the second half of the century

> 1926 E. F. Spanner: Best part of our stuff here is chilled, and with no 'frig plant working, the mercury will climb like a rocket.

> 1935 C. Brooks: Do you mean that you keep a dead body in a fridge waiting for the right moment to bring her out?

> 1939 Monica Dickens: Your frig is out of order and the trifle hasn't got cold.

friendly *adj* (1925) belonging to or allied with one's own armed forces. Originally a World War I expression, applied for example to shells fired by one's own artillery as they whizzed over the trenches on their way to the enemy's lines. Later associated particularly with the phrase *friendly fire*, used in the Vietnam War and the Gulf War as a euphemism for bombardments which hit one's own troops or installations

> 1941 *Civil Engineering* (US): The range of friendly bombing aircraft permits assembly of tactical operating units.

> 1991 *Independent*: Since the war began, more American troops are thought to have been killed by 'friendly fire' than by the Iraqis, most by air-launched missiles.

Frigidaire *n* (1926) The proprietary name of a brand of refrigerator which has enjoyed some currency as a generic term, mainly in the US, its country of origin. It is pseudo-French in form, based on Latin *frigidaria* 'cold larder'. It probably contributed to the spelling of *frig* (see **fridge (1926)**)

> 1926 *Publishers' Weekly*: Vacuum cleaners, frigidaires, radios.

> 1932 Evelyn Waugh: The Legges' Frigidaire is broken and they can't get it mended until after the war.

front *n* (1921) the interface between air masses of different temperatures

> 1921 Bjerknes & Solberg: In the first case, the boundary line at the ground will be the front of advancing cold air, or, to introduce a shorter expression, a 'cold front'. In the latter case, the boundary line will be the front of advancing warm air, or simply a 'warm front'.

fry *v* (1928) to be executed in the electric chair. US slang

> 1929 *Flynn's*: I'll fry for it, I suppose—that's the law, Doc.

fuck off *v* (1929) to go away. *Fuck* in its literal sense has been around since at least the 13th century, but written references to its various extended uses are extremely thin on the ground before the end of the 19th century. No doubt *fuck* as an expletive, *fucking* as an intensifier, *fuck off*, and so on had been in widespread use for a long time, but they existed under a taboo which denied them access to print. Post-World War I writers such as James Joyce, Henry Miller, and (as in the quote below) Frederic Manning broke the taboo, but only at the cost, initially, of having their work banned. It was not until 1965 that *fuck* and its companion 'four-letter word' *cunt* found their way into a mainstream English dictionary—the *Penguin English Dictionary*. See also **four-letter word (1934)**

> 1929 Frederic Manning [the time-frame is World War I]: As soon as a bit o' shrapnel comes their way, [they] fuck off 'ome jildy, toot sweet.

fundamentalism *n* (1923) a religious movement, which originally became active among various Protestant bodies in the US after World War I, based on strict adherence to certain tenets (e.g. the literal truth of Scripture) held to be fundamental to the Christian faith. The corresponding noun *fundamentalist* is first recorded in 1922. The application of the term to other religions (e.g. Islam) is first recorded in the 1950s

> 1923 *Daily Mail*: Mr. William Jennings Bryan…has been exerting the full force of his great eloquence in a campaign on behalf of what is termed 'Fundamentalism'.

> 1981 *Observer*: The new, or rather very old, Islam, the dangerous fundamentalism revived by the ayatollahs and their admirers.

fuzz *n* (1929) the police. Originally US underworld slang, but its ultimate antecedents are unknown: perhaps some equation of fluff or dust with contemptible people, or an obscure Black English reference to the head and body hair of white people. It became widely known and used in British slang in the 1960s

> 1929 E. Booth: Don't run, and rank yourself—the fuzz don't know what's doin' yet.

G *n* (1928) a thousand dollars. Originally US gambling slang, short for **grand (1915)**

> 1928 J. O'Connor: They had me in the bag for nearly ten G's before I pulled the string and let the joint go blooey.

G, g *n* (1928) a unit of force equal to the force exerted by gravity on a body at rest. Used particularly in expressing the gravitational forces acting on pilots and astronauts. *G* as an abbreviation of *gravity* dates from the late 18th century

> 1928 N. Macmillan: Sustained high manœuvre loadings…are referred to for brevity as 1G, 2G, or 6G. The question of G affects the pilot as well as the aeroplane.

gang shag *n* (1927) an occasion on which many people have sex successively with one person. Slang, originally US. A precursor of **gangbang (1945)**

> 1927 F. M. Thrasher: The gang shag includes boys from sixteen to twenty-two years of age. It is a party carried on with one woman by from fifteen to thirty boys from one gang or club. A mattress in the alley usually suffices for this purpose.

gate-crasher *n* (1921) someone who gains unauthorized admission, originally to a sports stadium but subsequently to any limited-access function, such as a private party. Originally US. The companion *gate-crashing* soon appeared

> 1927 *Daily News*: 'One-eyed Connolly', the champion American 'gate crasher' (one who gains admittance to big sporting events without payment)… The Committee of the White Rose Ball…dealt severely with a few cases of 'gate crashing'.

> 1929 *Daily Mail*: Helly Cozzonis…was the gate-crasher at the Mansion House reception.

gazump *v* (1928) to swindle, especially by reselling something at an increased price. Its ultimate origins are unclear, but it had fairly wide currency in British underworld slang from the late 1920s onwards. It was in the early 1970s that it emerged into the public domain with the specific application to raising the price of a house after accepting an offer for it; its spelling, which had varied considerably (see the first quote below), settled at *gazump*

> 1928 *Daily Express*: 'Gazoomphing the sarker' is a method of parting a rich man from his money. An article is auctioned over and over again, and the money bid each time is added to it… I 'gazoomphed' a friend of mine with complete success last night.

> 1971 *Guardian*: 'Gazumping'—a system of profiteering by double selling and pushing prices up—is creeping into the property market… The word is car trade slang for selling to one buyer and then, as values rise, to a second buyer.

Geiger counter *n* (1924) an instrument for detecting and counting ionizing radiation, used especially for measuring radioactivity. Named after the German physicist Hans Geiger (1882–1945); he invented it in 1908, but the term is not recorded in English until the 1920s

> 1924 *Science Abstracts* (title): The Geiger counter as a sensitive detector of X-radiation.

geriatric *adj* (1926) See **geriatrics (1909)**

ghost *v* (1922), **ghost-write** *v* (1927) to write for someone else who takes the credit for authorship. The noun *ghost*, referring to someone who does this, dates from the 1880s, but it does not seem to have engendered this nest of new usages until the 1920s (*ghost-writer* is first recorded in 1927 too)

▎ 1922 *Glasgow Herald*: 'A certain general' for whom he did some 'ghosting'.

▎ 1927 *Literary Digest*: A ghost-writer may do all the work.

▎ 1932 *New Republic*: The autobiographical boloney ghost-written by Samuel Crowther for Ford.

gig *n* (1926) an engagement for a musician or musicians playing jazz, dance-music, etc., especially a one-night stand. Origin unknown

▎ 1927 *Melody Maker*: This seven-piece combination does many 'gigs' in S.E. London, but is hoping to secure a resident engagement at Leamington in the near future.

gimlet *n* (1928) a cocktail made with gin or vodka and lime-juice. Presumably so named for its penetrating effect on the drinker. Originally US, an early product of the surge in fashionability of the cocktail from the mid 1920s

▎ 1928 D. B. Wesson: The 'Gimlet' we were introduced to…at the Golf Club: and it proved to be the well and flavorably known ricky, but described as 'gin, a spot of lime, and soda'.

girdle *n* (1925) a foundation garment that holds in the stomach, hips, and buttocks. Originally US. At least partly a euphemism for *corset*, but also applied specifically to an elasticated flexible corset that does not go above the waist. As women abandoned such undergarments in the last quarter of the century, it began to fade from the memory

▎ 1925 *Eaton's News Weekly*: Brassiere of rayon jersey silk and girdle of mercerized cotton and silk brocade with panels of elastic.

gob-stopper *n* (1928) a large, hard, usually spherical sweet for sucking, so named because, before it has been sucked, it fills the mouth and makes speech difficult. British

▎ 1928 Walter de la Mare: *Gob-stoppers* and *toffee*—are these not 'good' names for goodies?

go-getting *adj* (1921) See **go-getter (1910)**

gold-digger *n* (1920) a woman who attaches herself to a man merely for gain. Slang, originally US. The back-formed verb *gold-dig* is first recorded in 1926

▎ 1926 Sinclair Lewis: I gold-dig you for all the money I can get.

▎ 1928 *Sunday Dispatch*: The professional gold-digger is generally a girl of good family who finds she can supplement her allowance by going out with, say, half-a-dozen men.

gong *n* (1925) a medal or other decoration. British services' slang; first recorded in print in 1925, but noted then as being 'an old Army term'. The reference is to the circular shape

▎ 1942 B. J. Ellan: Wilf, G— and F/Sgt. S— had all been awarded 'Gongs' (medals to you!) after Dunkirk.

good-time girl *n* (1928) a young woman who lives only for pleasure. Originally US, and often a euphemistic cover-up for sexual promiscuity

▎ 1928 *Publishers' Weekly*: Gerry Harris was 'a good time girl', who sought men only as playmates.

goofus *n* (1928) a musical instrument similar to a saxophone but with 25 finger-holes, each with its own reed, and therefore capable of producing chords. It failed to achieve long-term success, perhaps held back by its unfortunate name

▎ 1928 *Melody Maker*: With the coming of Rollini to the Savoy Hotel, the Goofus has leapt into popularity. It is an original instrument with two chromatic octaves, and plays both melody and accompaniment at the same time.

goon *n* (1921) a stolid person. US slang. A term introduced to a wider world by Frederick Lewis Allen, who is reported as saying that it had been in use in his family for some time, but that he did not know whether a family member had invented it. After this sighting *goon* disappears from view, and when it reappears in the 1930s with the meaning 'stupid person', it is not at all clear that it is the same word (see **goon (1938)**)

▎ 1921 F. L. Allen: A goon is a person with a heavy touch as distinguished from a jigger, who has a light touch. While jiggers look on life with a genial eye, goons take a more stolid and literal view.

goose-stepper *n* (1923) someone who does the goose-step. Often used with the implication of a zombie-like soldier serving a tyrannical dictatorship. The term *goose-step*, denoting a ceremonial march performed without bending the knees, dates from the early 19th century, but in the 20th century it became particularly associated with militaristic German regimes ('Doing the Prussianist goose-step by way of *pas de triomphe*', C. E. Montague (1922))

> 1923 H. L. Mencken: The first made them almost incapable of soldierly thought and conduct; the second converted them into cringing goose-steppers.

gracing, greycing *n* (1928) A contracted form of *greyhound racing*, which enjoyed some currency in British English while the sport was in the first flush of its popularity in the 1920s and '30s (see **dogs (1927)**)

> 1928 *Star*: Gracing at Wimbledon.

> 1928 *Daily Express*: Greycing… Programmes…for tonight's greyhound racing meetings.

greenhouse effect *n* (1929) the phenomenon whereby the surface and the lower atmosphere of a planet are maintained at a relatively high temperature owing to the greater transparency of the atmosphere to visible radiation from the sun than to infra-red radiation from the planet. Although the term was coined in the 1920s, the phenomenon did not begin to give public concern until the 1980s, when the resultant warming of the atmosphere was seen as posing a long-term threat to the environment

> 1929 W. J. Humphreys: Their joint effect on earth radiation is far greater, so much so, indeed, that they produce a very marked greenhouse effect.

> 1989 *Which?*: The destruction of the tropical rain-forest is also contributing to the greenhouse effect, since forests help to regulate the amount of carbon dioxide in the atmosphere.

guinea-pig *n* (1920) a person or thing used like a guinea-pig as the subject of an experiment

> 1923 H. G. Wells: And may I ask…the nature of this treatment of yours, these experiments of which we are to be the-guinea pigs, so to speak? Is it to be anything in the nature of a vaccination?

gunboat diplomacy *n* (1927) diplomacy supported by the use, or threatened use, of military force. Usually applied to attempts by Western or colonial powers to coerce those who oppose their interests

> 1927 *US Naval Institute Proceedings*: It has been said that the days of 'gunboat diplomacy' in China are over.

> 1961 *Daily Telegraph*: The Iraqi delegate called the British action in Kuwait 'gunboat diplomacy at its worst'.

hand-held *adj* (1923) compact or light enough to be held and operated in one's hand. Applied originally to cameras, and subsequently to a wide range of other devices, including microcomputers

> 1969 *Daily Telegraph*: The photograph was taken by astronaut Anders with hand-held Hasselblad.

happy-dust *n* (1922) cocaine. Slang. From its immediate effect on the user

> 1922 E. F. Murphy: The boxes were found to contain cocaine, or 'happy-dust'.

health farm *n* (1927) a residential centre to which people go to improve their health or fitness (e.g. by exercise or dieting). Originally US. Early evidence of the Western middle classes' increasing obsession with their bodies as the century progressed

> 1927 Ernest Hemingway: Jack started training at Danny Hogan's health farm over in Jersey.

hearing aid *n* (1922) a small electronic device worn in the ear to amplify sound. The colloquial alternative *deaf-aid* is first recorded in 1934

> 1922 *Lancet*: These electrical instruments should go far towards destroying the too general prejudice against the use of hearing aids.

hearty *n* (1925) a keen sportsman, especially at a university. British; often used disparagingly, to imply a distaste or inaptitude for intellectual pursuits

> 1925 *Weekly Dispatch*: The leaders in the sport ['debagging'] are a band of 'hearties' who hail mostly from Magdalen and 'The House'.

heebie-jeebies *n* (1923) a feeling of discomfort, apprehension, or depression; the jitters. Slang, originally US. A fanciful coinage, which in the middle of the decade was transferred to a short-lived dance craze

> 1923 W. De Beck: You dumb ox—why don't you get that stupid look offa your pan—you gimme the heeby jeebys!

> 1926 *Bulletin*: The latest dance, the 'Heebie-Jeebies' is said to represent the incantations made by Red Indian witch doctors before a human sacrifice.

heffalump *n* (1926) A child's word for an elephant. Introduced to the world by A. A. Milne in *Winnie-the-Pooh*, it continues in facetious or playful adult use, especially in the expression *heffalump trap*, which also appeared in Milne's *House at Pooh Corner* (1928)

> 1926 A. A. Milne: He would go up very quietly to the Six Pine Trees now, peep very cautiously into the Trap, and see if there *was* a Heffalump there.

> 1958 *Spectator*: The Conservatives are not going to leap into the heffalump-trap in which their opponents…reside.

helicopterist *n* (1923) a helicopter pilot. The word *helicopter* had been in use in English since the late 19th century on a purely theoretical basis, and it was applied to many experimental vertical-takeoff aircraft in the early decades of the century. The first genuinely successful helicopter, to a design by Igor Sikorsky, flew in 1939, and the word *helicopterist* does not seem to have been around to see it

> 1923 *Daily Mail*: M. Raoul de Pescara, the helicopterist.

herpes virus *n* (1925) any of a range of viruses that cause inflammation of the skin and mucous membrane (e.g. cold sores). In later usage often spelled as one word

> 1968 A. Rook: The particles of herpesvirus are first found in the nucleus and later appear in the cytoplasm from which the virus is gradually released with destruction of the cell.

heterosexual *n* (1920) a heterosexual person. A noun use of the adjective *heterosexual*, which dates from the early 1890s. This early example is in a translation of a text of Sigmund Freud's, and it did not come into widespread use until the 1960s

> 1920 Joan Riviere: To convert a fully developed homosexual into a heterosexual.

hijack *v* (1923) Originally a Prohibition-era slang term, denoting the theft of contraband in transit, or robbing a bootlegger of his illicit goods. The main modern connotation, of comandeering a vehicle, and especially an aircraft, in transit, did not develop until the 1960s. The word is perhaps a back-formation from *hijacker* (also first recorded in 1923), which may have been coined from *highway* + *jacker* 'one who holds up'. See also **skyjack (1961)**

> 1923 *Literary Digest*: 'I would have had $50,000,' said Jimmy, 'if I hadn't been hijacked.'

> 1925 *Times*: A shooting affray between bootleggers and 'hijackers' (men who prey on bootleggers) took place…in a lodging~house on the west side of New York.

> 1927 James Barbican: So we landed the cargo as quickly as we could, and took the chance of the cargo being seized or hijacked on shore.

hincty, hinkty *adj* (1924) conceited, snobbish, stuck-up. US slang. Its origins are unknown, although it has been suggested that it may be a much eroded form of *handkerchief-head* (= 'an Uncle Tom Negro')

> 1936 *Esquire*: 'She couldn't be mixed up in no murder trial. She's too respectable.' 'A hinkty hussy!' said Sling.

hit-and-run *adj* (1924) Denoting the action of the driver of a motor vehicle who fails to stop after an accident for which he or she is responsible. The early alternative *hit-run* survived until at least the 1960s

> 1924 *Scientific American*: With the bumper in circuit with the ignition, there would be no more 'hit-and-run' driving.

hitch-hike *v* (1923) to travel by means of lifts in vehicles. Originally US. By 1927 it had been joined by the nouns *hitch-hike* and *hitch-hiker*

> 1923 *Nation*: Hitch-hiking is always done by twos and threes.

> 1927 *Glasgow Herald*: There are apparently hitchhikers in the United States who boast they can travel 500 miles free of charge without walking more than 10.

holism *n* (1926) A term coined from Greek *holos* 'whole' by the South African soldier and statesman Jan Smuts (1870–1950) to designate the tendency in nature to produce wholes (i.e. bodies or organisms) from the ordered grouping of unit structures. With it came the adjective *holistic*, which became something of a buzz-word in the latter part of the century (see **holistic medicine (1960)**)

> 1926 J. C. Smuts: The whole-making, holistic tendency, or Holism, operating in and through particular wholes, is seen at all stages of existence.

Hollywood *n* (1926) the world of American film-making, as typified by Hollywood, an area near Los Angeles in California, the chief production centre of the US cinema industry. The 1920s also saw the first of a range of *Hollywood* derivatives, such as *Hollywoodesque* and *Hollywoodish*

> 1926 Aldous Huxley: What is this famous civilisation of the white man which Hollywood reveals?

> 1927 *Daily Express*: The cottage is so picturesque and Hollywoodesque that…it is more like a 'set' than a real house.

> 1928 *Daily Express*: Mr. Douglas Fairbanks…is meditating…a slap-up, original Hollywoodish sequel of his own devising.

hooey *n* (1924) nonsense, rubbish. Slang, originally US; often used as an exclamation. Origin unknown

> 1924 Percy Marks: My prof's full of hooey. He doesn't know a C theme from an A one… 'Bunk!' he exclaimed. 'Hooey!'

Hoover *n, v* (1926) (to clean with) a vacuum cleaner, originally one of a type with the proprietary name 'Hoover' (registered in 1927). The US Hoover company, named after its founder W. H. Hoover (1849–1932), began manufacturing vacuum cleaners in the first decade of the 20th century. As a generic term, *Hoover* is almost exclusively British

> 1926 *Army & Navy Stores Catalogue*: A Hoovered room…is…free from dust.

> 1934 *Punch*: Her bodywork's smart and strikes the eye Clean-swept as though with a Hoover.

hot *adj* (1925) (recently) stolen, and therefore actively sought by the police and hazardous to possess. Slang, originally US

> 1925 *Collier's*: Stolen bonds are 'hot paper'; stolen diamonds 'hot ice'.

hot diggety *interj* (1924) an exclamation of joy or surprise. US slang. It probably originated as a fanciful variation on the synonymous *hot dog* (first recorded in 1906), and often appears in the full form *hot diggety dog*

> 1927 *Sun* (Baltimore): When it comes to 'hot dog', there's no more to be said, unless it is, perhaps, to add a frill and make it 'hot diggety dog'.

> 1939 Ryerson & Clements: I'll…get cleaned up and into my…tux!…Hot diggity!

housing estate *n* (1920) an area of houses planned and built as a group. A manifestation of 20th-century **town planning (1906)**

> 1920 *Times*: It will afford… much-needed means of access to the L.C.C. Housing Estate at Dagenham.

humpty *n* (1924) a low padded cushion seat. British. Perhaps a shortening of *humpty-dumpty*, although the dialectal adjective *humpty*, meaning 'humped' or 'hump-backed', is recorded in the 19th century. Humpties do not appear to have survived the 1920s

> 1926 *British Weekly*: The ladies of the village are busy making 'humpties', soft cushion seats to pull up on the rug before the peat fire.

hunger-striker *n* (1922) someone who is on a hunger-strike. The term *hunger-strike* actually goes back at least to the 1880s, but there is no record of *hunger-striker* before 1922

> 1922 *Blackwood's Magazine*: He gave his orders for the release of the hunger-strikers.

ice cube *n* (1929) a small artificially made piece of ice, used especially for cooling drinks. Originally US. One of the cornerstones of 20th-century American/Western civilization

> 1929 Max Lief: She dashed into the kitchen and came back with a bowl of ice-cubes and some more bottles.

id *n* (1924) the part of the psyche associated with instinctive impulses and demands for immediate satisfaction. A use of Latin *id* 'it', as a rendering of German *es* 'it', which was adopted by Sigmund Freud (*Das Ich und das Es* 'The I and the It' (1923)) following its use in a similar sense by G. Groddeck (*Das Buch vom Es* 'The Book of the It' (1923)). In the quote below, Freud's first English translator explains how the appropriate English equivalent was decided on

> 1924 Joan Riviere: The essay…describes the various allegiances the ego owes, its mediate position between the outer world and the id, and its struggles to serve all its masters at one and the same time. [*Translator's note*.] To translate the German '*es*', which means 'it' and thus implies the impersonality of the mind apart from its ego, the Latin '*id*' has been selected… Keep in mind this dissection of the mental apparatus that I have proposed, namely, into ego, super-ego and id.

inferiority complex *n* (1922) a neurotic condition resulting from a persistent unrealistic sense of inadequacy, often compensated for by aggressive behaviour

> 1922 A. G. Tansley: Thus the 'inferiority complex' may account for a whole series of well-known human traits.

infrastructure *n* (1927) all the elements that together make up the basic supporting structure of an undertaking. A borrowing from French, where it is first recorded in 1875. As the second quote below shows, by the middle of the century it had already acquired its bad reputation as a jargon word

> 1927 *Chambers's Journal*: The tunnels, bridges, culverts, and 'infrastructure' work generally of the Ax to Bourg-Madame line have been completed.

> 1950 Winston Churchill: In this Debate we have had the usual jargon about 'the infrastructure of a supra-national authority'.

insulin *n* (1922) a hormone produced in the islets of Langerhans (in the pancreas) which controls blood glucose levels. The word originated in French. Based on Latin *insula* 'island' (from its place of secretion), it was coined in 1909 by J. de Meyer as *insuline*. This was introduced into English by E. A. Schäfer in 1916 (see the 1926 quote below), but it did not make much impact. It was not until the team of Canadian scientists, led by Banting, Best, and Macleod, who discovered the use of the hormone for treating diabetes, reintroduced it in the anglicized form *insulin* in 1922 that it became widely known

> 1922 F. G. Banting, C. H. Best, etc.: Purified alcoholic extracts of pancreas, for which we suggest the name insulin, when injected subcutaneously into normal rabbits cause the percentage of sugar in the blood to fall within a few hours.

> 1926 E. A. Schäfer: To this autacoid the name insulin is applied. [Note] The term was introduced by de Meyer (Arch. di fisiol., vii., 1909). In ignorance of this it was employed as a convenient term to denote the autacoid of the islet tissue in the first edition of this work, published in 1916. It was independently adopted by the Toronto workers [i.e. Banting and Best] in 1922.

intelligence quotient *n* (1921) a number arrived at by means of intelligence tests and intended to express the degree of intelligence of an individual in relation to the average for the age-group, which is fixed at 100. A translation of German *Intelligenz-quotient*, which was coined in 1912 by W. L. Stern. The abbreviated form *I.Q.*, first recorded in 1922, has become much better known than the full version.

> 1921 C. L. Burt: If a child's mental age be divided by his chronological age, the quotient will state what fraction of ability the child actually possesses… This fraction may be termed…the child's 'intelligence quotient'.

> 1922 R. S. Woodworth: Brightness or dullness can also be measured by the intelligence quotient, which is employed so frequently that it is customarily abbreviated to 'I.Q.'

interior design *n* (1927) the design of the interior of a building, including wallpaper, furniture, fittings, etc., according to artistic and architectural criteria. The derivative *interior designer* is first recorded in 1938. (The more homely *interior decoration*, incidentally, dates from the early 19th century)

> 1938 *Decorative Art*: The favourable attention of all leading Interior Designers can be secured…through a single publication, 'Interior Design and Decoration'.

ionosphere *n* (1926) a region of the outer atmosphere, beginning at a height of 50–80 km. (30–50 miles), which contains many ions and free electrons and is capable of reflecting radio waves

> 1926 Robert Watson-Watt: We have in quite recent years seen the universal adoption of the term 'stratosphere'…and…the companion term 'troposphere'… The term 'ionosphere', for the region in which the main characteristic is large scale ionisation with considerable mean free paths, appears appropriate as an addition to this series.

I.Q. *n* (1922) See **intelligence quotient (1921)**

I.R.A. *n* (1921) the Irish Republican Army

> 1921 George Bernard Shaw: The I.R.A. is flushed with success.

iron curtain *n* (1920) the hypothetical barrier between the Soviet bloc and the West, especially during the Cold War. It was Winston Churchill who, in his speech at Westminster College, Fulton, Missouri, on 5 March 1946, effectively established the term *iron curtain* in the English language, where it was to outlast the bloc which it circumscribed. But he did not invent it. The first person on record as using it was Ethel Snowden (the wife of Philip Snowden, the British Labour politician), in a book called *Through Bolshevik Russia*, although it is unclear whether she actually coined it herself. It caught on to some extent, but more as a general term for an inviolable barrier (as the 1924 quote demonstrates) than as one for a specific East-West divider. The impetus for this, towards the end of World War II, appears to have come from Germany: Josef Goebbels, the German propaganda minister, wrote of 'ein eiserner Vorhang', which means 'an iron curtain', but was translated in *The Times* on 23 February 1945 as 'an iron screen', and on 3 May of the same year *The Times* reported the German foreign minister Schwerin von Krosigk as speaking of 'the iron curtain'. It was soon taken up in the English-speaking world: in an article in the *Sunday Empire News* entitled 'A Curtain Across Europe', Sir St. Vincent Troubridge wrote of 'an iron curtain of silence' separating East from West. See also **bamboo curtain (1949)**

> 1920 Mrs. P. Snowden: We were behind the 'iron curtain' at last!

> 1924 Lord D'Abernon: Stresemann considered that it was essential for the Rhineland to be frankly part of Germany, also for Danzig to be reincorporated. Without this there could be no permanent peace. I put forward my view of the reciprocal iron curtain or strip of inviolable territory as a protection.

> 1945 *Times* (23 February): If the German people lay down their arms, the whole of eastern and south-eastern Europe, together with the Reich, would come under Russian occupation. Behind an iron screen mass butcheries of peoples would begin.

> 1945 *Times* (3 May): In the East the iron curtain behind which, unseen by the eyes of the world, the work of destruction goes on is moving steadily forward.

> 1945 Sir St. V. Troubridge: Yet at present an iron curtain of silence has descended, cutting off the Russian zone from the Western Allies.

> 1946 Winston Churchill: From Stettin, in the Baltic, to Trieste, in the Adriatic, an iron curtain has descended across the Continent.

> 1953 *Encounter*: If they live behind the Iron Curtain they can do none of these things—for, while the Communists agree that knowledge is power, they are persuaded that they are already in essential possession of both.

isolationism *n* (1922) a national policy of not engaging in economic or political relations with other countries. Often applied specifically to the policy of the US in the first part of the century. The related *isolationist* is first recorded in 1899

> 1930 *Headway*: Add to this the fact that half the people…who have emigrated to America in the last generation or so are Europeans who have left Europe because they wanted to get away from Europe, and the secret of America's 'isolationism' is very largely explained.

jalopy *n* (1929) a battered old motor vehicle. Colloquial, originally US. The word's origins are obscure and, as the examples below demonstrate, its spelling was at first highly variable

> 1929 Hostetter & Beesley: *Jaloppi*, a cheap make of automobile; an automobile fit only for junking.

> 1936 John Steinbeck: Mac and Jim circled the buildings and went to the ancient Ford touring car. 'Get in, Jim. You drive the gillopy.'

jazz age *n* (1922) the era of jazz (see **jazz (1913)**). Used by F. Scott Fitzgerald as part of the title of a collection of short stories, *Tales of the Jazz Age* (1922), but in retrospect usually applied specifically to the period between 1919 and 1929

> 1959 Thomas Griffith: In the years between the Armistice and the stock-market crash, came the period we used to call…the Jazz Age.

jeepers *interj* (1929) An exclamation of great surprise or consternation. Originally and mainly US. It is a euphemistic phonetic disguise for *Jesus*, and the extended form *jeepers creepers*, first recorded in 1937, conceals *Jesus Christ* (as the halfway form in the first quote below suggests). *Jeepers creepers* became more widely known thanks to a 1938 song by Mercer and Warren: 'Jeepers, creepers, where'd ya get those peepers; jeepers, creepers, where'd ya get those eyes?'

> 1929 W. D. Edmonds: Jeepers! A cat wouldn't stand no show at all… Spinning swore. 'I'll bet that's right. Jeepers Cripus! How can they expect us to help a marshal if he don't let us know who he is?'

> 1937 *Saturday Evening Post*: Jeepers Creepers! Where are you going to find a couple of goats and a red wagon on Christmas Eve in three hours?

jive *n* (1928) talk or conversation, especially talk that is misleading, untrue, empty, or pretentious. Also first recorded as a verb in the same year, meaning 'to assail or mislead with such talk'. Originally US slang, but its antecedents are obscure

> 1928 Louis Armstrong: Don't jive me.

> 1932 Muse & Arlen: Thus the enamoured customer completed his meal, without ever having taken his eyes off that tantalizing brown, with her suave Birmingham jive.

> 1935 *Swing Music*: Maybe you think that that is all jive. You are wrong if you do. It is the way I felt about these new records.

Jixi, Jixie *n* (1926) Very short-lived British slang for a type of two-seater taxi licensed in 1926 while Sir William Joynson-Hicks (1865–1932) was British Home Secretary. His nickname was 'Jix', so, *Jix* + *taxi* …

> 1926 *Westminster Gazette*: Jixi is the name given by the Westminster Gazette, and now used by everyone, to 2-seater taxicabs.

> 1927 *Observer*: The first 'Jixie' or two-seater taxicab will probably be seen on the streets of London at the end of the present week.

jobless *adj* (1923) out of work, unemployed. A common 20th-century synonym for *unemployed*, which dates from the late 17th century. The noun *joblessness* is also first recorded in 1923

> 1923 *Glasgow Herald*: The demand that would ensue for land users would mean jobs for jobless men.

kayo *v* (1923) to knock out. Colloquial, originally US. Later used also as a noun, denoting 'a knock-out', but it was as a verb that it initially made headway, perhaps because of some perceived difficulty in using *KO* (of whose pronunciation it was a representation) verbally (see **KO (1922)**)

> 1923 H. C. Witwer: You never been knocked cold in your life—why go out of your way to get kayoed?

kitsch *n* (1926) art (in the broadest sense) which is vulgar, sentimental, or pretentious. A borrowing from German, of uncertain ultimate origin. The adjective *kitschy* is first recorded in 1967

> 1926 Brian Howard: A healthy week…riding, chasing dogs and listening to 'Kitsch' on his wireless.

> 1969 Rhona Petrie: Her family owned a furniture factory. 'We make…mostly kitschy bits fit to furnish Grimm's fairy tales.'

Kleenex *n* (1925) The proprietary name of an absorbent disposable cleansing paper tissue. Originally US. (The generic **paper handkerchief** is first recorded in 1907)

> 1925 *Picture-Play Magazine* (advert): This secret of famous stage beauties…is simply the use of Kleenex in removing cold cream and cosmetics… This soft velvety absorbent is made of Cellucotton… Use it once, throw it away.

KO *n, v* (1922) An abbreviation of *knock(-)out*, as both a noun and a verb. Initially the verb at least seems often to have been treated strictly as a written abbreviation, with no inflected endings shown

> 1922 T. Burke: As a youth the ring attracted him... A few k.o.'s put an end to that.

> 1928 *Daily Express*: Young Stanley...was then k.o. by a right swing to the jaw.

landscape *v* (1927) to lay out (a garden or other piece of ground) in the form of an aesthetically pleasing landscape

> 1927 *British Weekly*: Even factories...frequently have lovely landscaped grounds.

learning curve *n* (1922) a graph showing progress in learning. For most of the century a technical term in psychology; only latterly has it come to mean 'a process of acquiring skill or experience'

> 1922 R. S. Woodworth: Learning curve for the rat in the maze.

leotard *n* (1920) a close-fitting one-piece garment worn by acrobats and dancers. Named after the French trapeze artist Jules Léotard (1830–70)

> 1920 J. W. Mansfield: Leotards...are used by acrobats and aerial performers.

lesbian *n* (1925) a female homosexual. The adjective *lesbian*, commemorating the alleged homosexuality of the Greek female poet Sappho who lived on the island of Lesbos, was in use at the end of the 19th century, but this is the first known instance on record of the noun. (The similarly inspired *Sapphism* 'female homosexuality' also dates from the late 19th century, but has not survived so well)

> 1925 Aldous Huxley: After a third-rate provincial town, colonized by English sodomites and middle-aged Lesbians, which is, after all, what Florence is, a genuine metropolis will be lively.

lettuce *n* (1929) money. US slang; from the crisp green-and-whiteness of US dollar bills

> 1967 P. G. Wodehouse: How are you fixed for lettuce, Hank?... Dough. Cash. Glue... Money.

Levi's, Levis *n* (1926) a type of (originally blue) denim jeans or bibless overalls, with rivets to reinforce stress-points, patented and produced as working clothes in the 1860s, and adopted as a fashion garment in the 20th century. The form *Levi's* is a proprietary term in the US. The name comes from the original American manufacturer, Levi Strauss

> 1926 R. Santee: My Levis was brand-new.

> 1957 Jack Kerouac: Dean was wearing washed-out tight levis and a T-shirt.

liaise *v* (1928) to contact and communicate; maintain liaison. Originally services' jargon, and the sort of back-formation unpopular with those who see such usages as undermining the language, it has nevertheless prospered and widened its range of use. It is first recorded in print in 1928, but as the first quote below suggests, it was probably around during World War I

> 1928 C. F. S. Gamble: [Lord Fisher said in 1916] 'I want a soldier...to keep in touch with the Navy and so "liaise" or exchange inventions which may be suitable.'

> 1941 *American Notes & Queries*: The kind of grammatical economy found in a recent (British) Home Guard instruction sheet—in the event of certain circumstances, it stated, two groups were ordered to 'liase' with two others.

> 1942 *New Statesman*:'To liaise'...was at first frowned on by the pundits: its usefulness...soon came to outweigh its objectionableness.

lift *v* (1922) to perform plastic surgery on (especially the face) so as to remove wrinkles or sag. See also **face-lifting (1922)**

> 1931 *Daily Express*: A woman can now have her face lifted one day and appear among her friends the next.

lipid *n* (1925) any of a range of fats and fatlike substances that together with carbohydrates and proteins constitute the principal structural material of living cells. The term was originally coined in French as *lipide* by G. Bertrand, and first published in the *Bulletin de la Société de Chimie biologique* in 1923. He based it on Greek *lipos* 'fat'. As the quote below records, alternative but related terms were at first in competition—*lipoid* (1906) and *lipin* (1910)—but it is the anglicized form of *lipide* that has become the established name

> 1925 W. R. Bloor: Three terms have been suggested for the group, namely, 'Lipins' by Gies and Rosenbloom, 'Lipides' by the International Congress of Applied Chemistry, and the old term 'Lipoids' by the author. The term lipins has been used in a different sense by Leathes, and was later adopted by McLean in his monograph as a name for a subgroup containing the cerebrosides and the phosphatides. The term lipoids is understood by many to exclude the fats, although used in the wider sense by many workers on the Continent. For these reasons, and for the sake of uniformity, the author recommends the use of the term Lipides as the general group name.

liquidate *v* (1924) to put an end to, abolish; to wipe out; to kill. An adaptation of Russian *likvidírovat* 'to liquidate, wind up' which has become a key element in the 20th-century euphemization of oppression

> 1939 V. A. Demant: The Trotskyists…are 'liquidated' as being insufficiently dialectical to see that the policy of the Russian State at any moment has absolute finality.

liquorice all-sorts *n* (1928) sweets of various colours and shapes made from liquorice and sugar icing

> 1931 Winifred Holtby: Pink sugared hazel nuts, and Liquorice All Sorts.

listener-in *n* (1922), **listener** *n* (1923) someone listening to the radio. The verb *listen in* had its beginnings in the wireless telegraphy of the first decade of the century, and it embraced domestic listeners when public broadcasting came on the scene in the early 1920s ('Radio today is a continuous performance. You…listen in…to the music of today…the news of the minute, stock quotations, and so on', *Scientific American* (1922)). It was also turned into a noun ('A listen-in. The Queen…listened to a recitation sent out from Marconi House', *Daily Mail* (1922)) and an adjective ('*Husband* (to listening-in Wife). 'What's the matter, dear? Is it bad news or Stravinsky?' *Punch* (1926)). *Listener-in* was born at the same time, but all began to go out of use around the middle of the century: *listen in* completely, as watching television replaced listening to the radio as the chief source of domestic entertainment (see **look in (1927)**), and *listener-in* replaced by the more-or-less contemporary *listener*

> 1922 *Daily Mail*: The limited service has already established itself in high favour with 'listeners-in'.

> 1923 *Radio Times*: It seems to me that the B.B.C. are mainly catering for the 'listeners' who own expensive sets.

litter lout *n* (1927) someone who carelessly or deliberately drops litter in public places. Mainly British. The US equivalent **litterbug** is not recorded before 1947

> 1927 *Children's Newspaper*: It is time the Litter Lout was taken seriously in hand.

loaf *n* (1925) the head. British slang, a shortened version of rhyming slang *loaf of bread*. Originally in fairly general use, but by the end of the century mainly in the phrase *use your loaf* 'act sensibly or cleverly'

> 1971 B. W. Aldiss: You want to use your bloody loaf, Stubbs, or we'll never win this war the way you're carrying on.

long-playing *adj* (1929) Designating a gramophone record that plays for longer than the standard time, specifically a microgroove record designed to be played at 33⅓ revolutions per minute. The specific application dates from the late 1940s, when the new type of microgroove record was introduced; the abbreviation **LP (1948)** came on the scene then too. The synonymous *long-play*, first recorded in 1954, enjoyed some currency

> 1929 *Wireless Magazine*: Long-playing dance records.

> 1948 *Electronic Engineer*: A new library of recorded music has been announced…which consists of a series of long-playing 10 and 12 in. records run at 33⅓ r.p.m.

> 1954 F. Ramsey (title): A guide to longplay jazz records.

look in *v* (1927) to watch television. A usage based on *listen in* (see **listener-in (1922)**), which gradually faded out in the 1950s, '60s, and '70s. Contemporary and directly inspired by **listener-in** was *looker-in* 'someone watching television', which, when actual television services began in the 1930s, was elbowed aside by **viewer (1935)**. See also **watch in (1928)**

> 1927 *Pictorial Weekly*: We shall then 'look-in' by wireless and see events and scenes at a distance…A speech which the 'looker-in' can actually see being delivered.

1928 *Daily Telegraph*: This afternoon 'lookers-in' will be given a chance of seeing the first still pictures to be publicly broadcast in this country.

loss leader *n* (1922) an article put on sale at a non-profit-making price in order to attract potential buyers of other articles

1922 Hayward & White: Many chains have a fixed policy of featuring each week a so-called 'loss leader'. That is, some well known article, the price of which is usually standard and known to the majority of purchasers, is put on sale at actual cost to the chain or even at a slight loss...on the theory...that people will be attracted to this bargain and buy other goods as well. Loss leaders are often termed 'weekly specials'.

lost generation *n* (1926) Often applied specifically to the generation of the World War I period, a high proportion of whose men were killed in the trenches of France; also used more generally of any generation judged to have 'lost' its values, etc.

1926 Ernest Hemingway (title-page): 'You are all a lost generation.'—Gertrude Stein in conversation.

lotsa (1927) Representing a casual pronunciation of *lots of*. Compare **lotta (1906)** and **loadsa (1987)**

1927 *Flynn's Weekly*: I never shot nobody... Lotsa times I don't carry a gun. That's one thing I try to dodge—the hot chair.

loud-speaker *n* (1920) a device that converts electric signals to (amplified) audible sound. Hitherto, the term used to characterize such devices had generally been *loud-speaking* (as in 'loud-speaking telephone'), which dates from the 1870s. There is a record of *loud-speaker* from the 1880s, but it seems to have been a one-off coinage which did not survive. The shortened form **speaker** is first recorded as early as 1926

1920 *Telegraph & Telephone Journal*: It was quite remarkable how far and how distinctly it was possible to hear the talk from the loud-speakers.

luncheonette *n* (1924) a small restaurant or snack bar serving light lunches. Originally US. See also **dinette (1930)**

1924 *Public Opinion*: Luncheonettes supply icecream soda and a ham sandwich.

lysozyme *n* (1922) a type of enzyme that can act as a mild antiseptic

1922 Alexander Fleming: In this communication I wish to draw attention to a substance present in the tissues and secretions of the body, which is capable of rapidly dissolving certain bacteria. As this substance has properties akin to those of ferments I have called it a 'Lysozyme', and shall refer to it by this name throughout the communication.

macho *adj* (1928) male, and especially manly or virile. The earliest example may be an isolated one; the word does not seem to have come into common use (originally in the US), with all its connotations of overweening masculinity, until the 1950s. It was borrowed from Mexican-Spanish. See also **machismo (1940)**

1928 *Nation*: Here was I in their midst, a Macho Yankee Gringo, yet treated with consideration.

1959 Norman Mailer: Every American writer who takes himself to be both major and *macho* must sooner or later give a *faena* which borrows from the self-love of a Hemingway style.

mah jong *n* (1922) a Chinese game resembling certain card games but played with small tiles. It was introduced into the West in the early 1920s and enjoyed a considerable vogue. The word comes from a Chinese dialect term meaning literally 'sparrows', apparently from the figure of a sparrow on a leading piece of one of the suits. It is first recorded in English in the title of a book about the game by R. E. Lindsell (1922)

1923 *Daily Mail*: There will be...demonstrations of Mah Jongg, the wonderful Chinese game which threatens to oust Bridge.

malarkey *n* (1929) exaggerated or meaningless talk; nonsense. Originally US slang, it soon spread to Britain, and was in quite common use in the middle years of the century. Where it came from, though, remains a mystery

> 1934 *Esquire*: Daughter of Mrs. Sally Alden, father unknown! What malarkey! All hooey, even protected by the official records of a friendly republic.

manor *n* (1924) a police district; the area in which a particular police officer works. British slang

> 1928 Edgar Wallace: I wouldn't advise you to break in on Gennett's 'manor'—he's rather touchy, and he's got charge of the case.

marbles *n* (1927) mental faculties; brains; common sense. Slang, originally North American. Usually in such phrases as *lose one's marbles* and *have all one's marbles*. The antecedents of the metaphor are lost

> 1957 Margaret Millar: She's a fattish little *hausfrau* with some of her marbles missing.

> 1958 P. G. Wodehouse: Do men who have got all their marbles go swimming in lakes with their clothes on?

market *v* (1922) to place or establish (a product) on the market, especially by means of promotion strategies. A back-formation from *marketing*, first recorded in this sense in the 1880s

> 1922 A. P. Mills: The ground grappiers [lumps of unburnt lime] are also separately marketed as a special cement known as grappier cement.

market research *n* (1926) the systematic investigation of the demand for particular goods

> 1926 *Market Research Agencies Guide*: With large sums of money being spent for market research…the necessity of having an inventory of accomplishments becomes obvious.

mass media *n* (1923) the media of communication (such as radio, television, newspapers, etc.) that reach a large number of people

> 1923 S. M. Fechheimer (title): Class appeal in mass media.

> 1946 Julian Huxley: The media of mass communication—the somewhat cumbrous title (commonly abbreviated to 'Mass Media') proposed for agencies, such as the radio, the cinema and the popular press, which are capable of the mass dissemination of word or image.

May-day *n* (1927) an international radio-telephone signal of distress, based on the pronunciation of French *m'aider* 'help me!'. Compare **S.O.S. (1910)**

> 1929 *Times*: The pilot, after wirelessing the S.O.S. of the Air Service 'May Day'…endeavoured to return to Lympne aerodrome with the power still at his disposal.

mean *adj* (1920) remarkably clever, adroit, etc.; formidable. Colloquial, originally US

> 1920 H. C. Witwer: Everything was jake until K. O. Krouse shook a mean dice and win $28 from Battlin' Lewis on the way to Toledo… You never heard tell of Kane Halliday?… The big… football star, the weights thrower…what they call a round-about athalete? You know, one of them bimbos which flings a wicked spear and hurls a mean hammer and that there stuff, get me?… Your wonder child may pack a mean wallop.

media *n* (1923) newspapers, radio, television, etc., collectively, as vehicles of mass communication. Originally a shorthand form for **mass media** (in which collocation it is first recorded). It did not become widespread outside advertising-industry jargon until the 1950s, when its increasingly frequent use as a mass noun, with a singular verb, began to enrage purists wedded to its status as a Latin plural. The heavily ironic respelling *meeja*, intended partly to poke fun at the media's perceived self-importance, is first recorded in 1983

> 1923 S. M. Fechheimer (title): Class appeal in mass media.

> 1929 E. O. Hughes: The advertising media to which reference will be made…are newspapers, journals, magazines and such-like printed publications.

> 1958 *Times Literary Supplement*: The media which appeal to our visually conscious age call for organizing ability as well as individual talent.

> 1966 Kingsley Amis: The treatment of media as a singular noun…is spreading into the upper cultural strata.

> 1971 *Radio Times*: The media have an ambiguous relationship with the radical left.

> 1972 *Times*: Miss Allen seems to be under the impression that the media is confined to newspapers.

> 1983 *Guardian Weekly*: Part of the reason Mailer is such fun is his self-appointed mission to smash the consensual tea party held by the cultural bureaucrats and 'meeja' liberals.

mercy *adj* (1927) intended to alleviate suffering. A usage probably based ultimately on French *coup de grâce*, which had been translated into English as long ago as 1702 as *mercystroke*. Over the decades it has become most firmly established in the euphemistic *mercy killing*

> 1927 *Daily Express*: The 'mercy bullet'…contains a chemical which is released on striking the animal. The fluid in the blood will cause temporary unconsciousness.

> 1930 *Commonweal* (New York): Mercy murders once more: euthanasia.

> 1935 *American Speech*: On the trail of the…mercy killer…the public follows day by day.

> 1957 *Observer*: This [melodrama], with its brilliant young scientist strangling his wife and volunteering for deep freeze and being mercy-killed by his boss.

method *n* (1923) a theory and practice of acting associated with the Russian actor and director Konstantin Stanislavsky (1863–1938), in which actors seek the complete illusion of reality by identifying themselves as closely as possible with the part they play. References to Stanislavsky's 'method' date from the early 1920s, but its institutionalization as a term (as shown by, for example, its capitalization and its use before other nouns, as in *method actor*) does not seem to have come about until the 1950s

> 1923 O. M. Sayler: 'My method, though imperfect,' [Stanislavsky] says, 'I consider psychologically natural.'

> 1956 Kenneth Tynan: This is Stanislavsky without Freud, physiological acting without the psychiatric glosses beloved of American 'method' actors.

> 1957 *Observer*: Eli Wallach, the American disciple of the Method…, was admirably solid, but not noticeably more absorbed in his role than some of our own best actors look to be in theirs.

metricalization *n* (1924) An unsuccessful forerunner of **metrication (1965)**

> 1924 *Glasgow Herald*: The question of the metricalisation of our coinage.

Metroland *n* (1926) the area surrounding a metropolis; usually applied specifically to the district around London served by the (Metropolitan) underground railway, viewed as a semi-rural dormitory. Evelyn Waugh publicized the name in the character of Margot Metroland in *Decline and Fall* (1928), but it was John Betjeman's eulogies of pre-lapsarian suburban rusticity that really established its place in the language

> 1926 Rose Macaulay: That house at Great Missenden…will suit them exactly. In metro-land, and such nice people all about… They must have a car, though; relying entirely on the Met. is too awkward, with so many strikes and so few late trains… After all, it's not London; metro-land can't be London.

> 1938 John Betjeman: The houses of Metroland and beechy Bucks dot the landscape.

Mickey Finn *n* (1928) an alcoholic drink that is surreptitiously drugged. In the first recorded example (see below) the reference is simply to a very stiff drink, although the intention is clearly to incapacitate. The modern implication of spiking with a drug became established in the 1930s. Who the original Mickey Finn was is not known

> 1928 M. C. Sharpe: I got a bottle of brandy… He was lit up…but I shot a few more Mickey Finns (double drinks) into him.

> 1931 *American Mercury*: But he never slipped an obstreperous customer the croton oil Mickey Finn of the modern night club.

microclimate *n* (1925) the climate of a very small or restricted area, or of the immediate surroundings of any individual or object of interest, especially as it differs from the climate generally. A term coined by L. F. Roussakov

> 1925 *Review of Applied Mycology*: Temperature, absolute and relative humidity, aeration, insolation, &c., which prevail at various levels…are comprised by him under the term 'microclimate'.

middlebrow *adj, n* (1925), **mid-brow** *adj, n* (1928) Dismissive terms for (someone with) tastes considered artistically or intellectually limited or conventional by highbrows. Modelled, of course, on *highbrow* (1884) and **lowbrow (1906)**. A contemporary synonymous coinage was *mezzo-brow*, based on Italian *mezzo* 'middle' ('I am not a "high-brow", but what I believe is now called in America a "mezzo-brow", an Uncompromising Mezzo-brow! And if you imagine that to be a "mezzo-brow" means that one has no positive opinions…I give you the lie,' Nigel Playfair (1925)), but it has not stood the test of time. Equally unsuccessful was the nearly synonymous **broadbrow (1927)**. The basic pattern continued to be exploited throughout the century ('A sort of upper-middle-brow equivalent of the horror-comic', Robert Conquest (1956))

> 1925 *Punch*: The B.B.C. claim to have discovered a new type, the 'middlebrow'. It consists of people who are hoping that some day they will get used to the stuff they ought to like.

> 1928 *Observer*: The standard of 'middle-brow' music and plays is always rather low.

> 1928 *Sunday Express*: Delighting the low-brow, the mid-brow, and the high-brow with equal facility.

milliardaire *n* (1924) someone who owns a milliard (a thousand million) units of a particular currency. A term which enjoyed a certain vogue in the 1920s, but is not recorded thereafter; the synonymous *billionaire* (1861) already existed in US English, and increasingly came to have that meaning in British English too

> 1927 *Spectator*: Including…a respectable proportion of the Royal Families and aristocracy of most European countries, besides a sufficiency of 'milliardaires' from both Americas.

mirthquake *n* (1928) a film, book, etc. that provokes uncontrollable laughter. A 'humorous' blend of *mirth* and *earthquake* which enjoyed a slight vogue, mainly in newspaper language, in the late 1920s and the 1930s

> 1928 *Daily Express*: I found Prince George…among the first to see Harold Lloyd's new 'mirthquake'.

Miss *n* (1922) Used as the title of young woman (e.g. *Miss Universe, Miss America, Miss Wolverhampton*) chosen for beauty, personality, etc., to represent a country, region, etc. (The earliest record of *Mr* being used in a parallel way is in 1962)

> 1922 *New York Times*: Miss Margaret Gorman of Washington, winner of the 1921 contest, will be known as 'Miss America'.

> 1953 S. Spewack: Attention, everybody. We now bring you the results of the beauty contest…to pick Miss Human Ant of nineteen fifty-three.

> 1968 *Radio Times*: The first Miss World in 1951 measured 37–23–36.

modernist *n, adj* (1927) (an artist) deliberately departing from classical and traditional methods of expression. Originally used in the field of visual arts, but subsequently also applied to music, literature, architecture, etc. The related noun *modernism* is first recorded in 1929

> 1927 F. J. Mather: Modernist pictures are becoming discreet, almost cautiously monotonous in colour… In comparison the Modernists have attained nothing of the coherence or authority of a school.

> 1934 R. Blomfield: I have already called attention to the disastrous effect of Modernism on architecture, painting, and sculpture… I find the same insidious and repulsive influence at work in a good deal of contemporary music… The Modernist seems to glory in his own obscurity.

monkey gland *n* (1924) a gland or testicle from a monkey, grafted on to a man as a possible means of rejuvenation. Enthusiastically touted by quacks and charlatans in the 1920s (notably Professor Serge Voronoff), they remained objects of ridicule for some decades afterwards

> 1924 George Bernard Shaw: Fortified…against old age by…weekly doses of monkey gland.

> 1971 Robert Dentry: Stop talking like Noel Coward after a shot of monkey glands!

monkey trial *n* (1925) the trial in 1925 of a Tennessee school-teacher, J. T. Scopes, for teaching evolutionary theories. The nickname is an allusion to anti-evolutionists' accusations that Darwinians claimed that human beings were descended from monkeys. It remained in the folk memory for many decades

> 1925 *Evening Sun* (Baltimore): Washington is getting the reflex of increasing European interest in the so-called monkey trial.

> 1969 D. F. Horrobin: It is associated more with the summer heat of the monkey-trial country of Tennessee rather than with the coolness of the dreaming spires of Oxford.

motel *n* (1925) a hotel catering primarily for motorists, especially one comprising self-contained accommodation with adjacent parking space. Originally US. An early and classic example of the 20th century's passion for blends

> 1925 *Hotel Monthly*: The Milestone Interstate Corporation…proposes to build and operate a chain of motor hotels between San Diego and Seattle, the hotels to have the name 'Motel'.

Movietone *n* (1927) The proprietary name of a system used in the making of sound films, in which the picture and sound are recorded on the same film. In later use it came to be mainly associated with the style of presentation of newsreels formerly produced by the Movietone Company

> 1927 *Glasgow Herald*: The movietone…is a vast improvement on previous talking films.

> 1969 *Listener*: A reading from the Old Testament about the death of Moses delivered in a hushed movietone voice.

multiracial *adj* (1923) of or comprising several races, peoples, or ethnic groups, especially as living in the same community on amicable and equal terms

> 1923 *Overseas*: The interests of modern civilisation and, I think, Christian ethics, are better expressed in large, bi-racial or multi-racial States,…where racialism is accounted a public curse rather than a civic virtue.

myxomatosis *n* (1927) a highly infectious virus disease of rabbits, originally detected in Brazil, characterized by fever, swelling of the mucous membranes, and the presence of benign tumours called 'myxomata'. The term, based ultimately on Greek *muxa* 'mucus, slime', was an adaptation of German *Myxomkrankheit*, coined around 1898 by G. Sanarelli. It did not become familiar to lay people until the 1950s, when the disease was deliberately introduced in Britain and Australia to control rabbit populations

> 1953 *Times*: The Ministry of Agriculture and Fisheries announced yesterday that in the past week myxomatosis, a virus disease of rabbits, was discovered near Edenbridge, Kent.

nappy *n* (1927) a piece of material worn by a baby to absorb excreta. Mainly British. As the first quotation shows, it was originally merely a nursery version of *napkin* (which dates in this meaning from the first half of the 19th century), but by the end of the century it had become the standard British term, and *napkin* was all but forgotten

> 1927 W. E. Collinson: Mothers and nurses use pseudo-infantile forms like pinny (pinafore), nappy (napkin).

> 1938 Stephen Spender: The babe's scream till the nurse brings its nappy.

narcotic *n* (1926) an illegal drug. Originally and mainly US. A re-application of a term that, in the strict pharmacological sense, means 'a drug that dulls the senses or induces sleep'

> 1926 *Proceedings of the First World Conference on Narcotic Education*: How the police catch the crook or the narcotic dealer;…it is only when someone tells the police who the narcotic addict or peddler is that the police get them.

National Socialist *adj, n* (1923) (a member) of the German National Socialist Workers' Party led by Adolf Hitler after 1920. The pronunciation of the first two syllables of the original German, *Nationalsozialist*, is the source of **Nazi (1930)**. See also **National Socialism (1931)**

> 1923 *Times*: At the conclusion of a National Socialist meeting last night Herr Hitler's storm troops…attempted to march through Munich.

naturist *n, adj* (1929) (an advocate or practitioner) of naturism. The term is first recorded a few years before *naturism* (see **naturism (1933)**), and seems from the beginning to have had rather wider currency. Its attractions as a euphemism are obvious (see the 1963 quote below), but it is also intended to convey attention to environmental concerns, healthy living, etc. and a return to 'nature', as the quote from Parmelee's *Nudity in Modern Life* suggests. See also **nudism (1929)**

> 1929 M. Parmelee: We have all heard of so-called 'naturists', who insist that man…should discard everything artificial such as…clothing, books, cooked food, etc.

> 1963 *Daily Telegraph*: The description 'a nudist camp', according to the naturist terminology, is defunct… Instead club members are asked to use the expression 'sun club' or 'naturist club'.

needle *n* (1923) competitive spirit, antagonism provoked by rivalry. Colloquial, used mainly in sporting contexts

1923 *Daily Mail*: It may be, of course, that there was too much 'needle' (to employ a boxing term which means bad spirit) about this contest.

neurosis *n* (1923) a mental illness or disorder characterized by anxiety, fear, depression, etc. The word *neurosis* had been used in English since the 18th century to mean simply 'a nervous disease', and the contrast with *psychosis* was established in the late 19th century, but this specific usage reflects Sigmund Freud's terminology. Before the end of the 1920s it was being used colloquially for any sort of anxiety or malaise

1967 J. R. Ackerley: One more neurosis, shared with my mother: I was worried about bad teeth.

neutron *n* (1921) an electrically uncharged sub-atomic particle whose mass is very slightly greater than that of the proton. Before its discovery in 1932 it was conceived as a close association of a proton and an electron. Rutherford (who communicated Glasson's 1921 paper to the Royal Society) discusses this concept in a paper of 1920 cited by Glasson, but without using the word *neutron*. Harkins (of Chicago) seems to have coined the term independently.

1921 W. D. Harkins: Any complex atom has a mass and weight 0.76 per cent. less than the hydrogen atoms (neutrons) from which it may be assumed to be built... The term neutron represents one proton plus one electron.

1921 J. L. Glasson: In the ordinary atom of hydrogen we have a single electron separated from the nucleus by a distance of the order of 10^{-8} cm. It is here contemplated that a more intimate union of the two is possible... Such a particle, to which the name neutron has been given by Prof. Rutherford, would have novel and important properties. It would, for instance, greatly simplify our ideas as to how the nuclei of the heavy elements are built up.

1930 Ernest Rutherford et al.: The existence of a neutron, i.e. a close combination of a proton and electron, has been suggested.

never-never *n* (1926) a system of paying for purchases by periodic instalments over an extended period. British colloquial; the more sober *hire-purchase* dates from the 1890s

1926 Edgar Wallace: Her uncle...drove a taxi which he...had purchased on the 'never never' system. You pay £80 down and more than you can afford for the rest of your life.

news bulletin *n* (1923) a brief television or radio programme in which the news is announced. The abbreviated *bulletin* is first recorded in this sense in 1925

1923 *Radio Times*: 10.0.—Time signal, general news bulletin. Broadcast to all stations, followed by London News and Weather Report.

1925 *Times*: The news given out as a bulletin on a very recent Sunday from the London Station must have made many listeners pause.

news reader *n* (1925) someone who reads a news bulletin on the radio (or, later, televison) (see also **newscaster (1930)**)

1925 *Daily Herald*: Instead of receiving a shock at a national calamity, the news reader breaks it to you in a calm and quiet voice.

nippy *n* (1925) a waitress in one of the restaurants of J. Lyons & Co. Ltd., London; hence, any waitress. A live term only up until about the middle of the century, but lingering much later in the memories of former Lyons patrons. The name is a tribute to the waitresses' speedy service

1925 *Punch*: I can't mike up me mind wevyer to be a lidy's 'elp or a 'nippy'.

1948 G. V. Galwey: His hands stuck out in front of him like a Nippy carrying a tray.

nitwit *n* (1922) a stupid person, a person of little intelligence. Britsh colloquial. Originally dialectal, it had become firmly established in the general language by the end of the decade. The underlying meaning is probably 'someone with the brains of a head-louse' (i.e. a nit). The shortened version *nit* is first recorded in 1941. See also **twit (1934)**

1930 *Musical Times*: Music...of the type that the nitwits who write...to the Radio Times call dry and highbrow.

non-violence *n* (1920) the principle or practice of abstaining from the use of violence. A key element in the philosophy of Gandhi, which he stressed throughout his campaign to gain the independence of India

1920 M. K. Gandhi: I believe that non-violence is infinitely superior to violence, forgiveness is more manly than punishment.

non-white *adj* (1921) not of the white race. Originally US, but taken up in South Africa in the more specific and legal sense 'not of European descent'

1921 *Scientific American*: The States that have the greatest proportion of non-white residents.

1952 B. Davidson: No serious South African will argue any longer (at least in private) that *apartheid*, the complete and geographical segregation of the white from the non-white at all levels, can work.

nudism *n* (1929) the doctrine or practice of living in the nude. The cult began in Germany after World War I, and has since spread to other parts of the Western world, to the bemusement of those who do not follow it. The name is apt to provoke sniggers, and from the beginning *naturism* has often been preferred by practitioners (see **naturist (1929)**). The noun and adjective *nudist* is also first recorded in 1929

1929 *Time*: Made in Germany, imported to France, is the cult of Nudism, a mulligan stew of vegetarianism, physical culture and pagan worship… Much publicity has been given the Nudist colony on an island in the Seine near Paris… A U.S. parallel would be if elegant Editor Frank Crowninshield of Vanity Fair should suddenly appear as a vegetable-eating, hairy-chested Nudist.

1935 *Punch*: 'A real tent… Think of the saving. Hotel bills, nothing. Meals, practically nothing. Clothes, nothing whatever.' 'Pamela,' I said imploringly, 'not Nudism.'

oestrogen *n* (1927) a hormone produced mainly by the ovary and responsible for the development and maintenance of female secondary sex characteristics. First recorded in the US form **estrogen**, which was registered as a proprietary name in 1927 (see the quote below). It was coined from *oestrus/estrus* 'period of ovulation'

1936 *Journal of the American Medical Association*: 'Estrogen' is a registered trade mark belonging to Parke, Davis and Company… This firm has commendably agreed to relinquish its proprietary rights in the name on its adoption by the Council as a generic term.

ofay *n* (1925) A derogatory term for a white person. US, mainly Black English. Probably ultimately from a West African language, although the precise source has never been identified. Another suggestion, that it is a Pig Latin reversal of *foe*, lacks plausibility

1925 *Inter-State Tattler*: We hear that 'Booker Red' has three ofays on his staff.

okay, okey *adj, n, v* (1929) OK. By the early 1930s this had virtually replaced **okeh (1919)**, an earlier stab at a spelled-out version of *OK*. There was some vacillation at first between *okay* and *okey*, but the former eventually established itself as overwhelmingly the main form

1929 J. P. McEvoy: *Jimmy (dashing out door)*: I'll kill the son of a—*Girl (going back to kitchenette)*: Okay, big boy.

1945 Evelyn Waugh: 'Don't let on to anyone that we've made a nonsense of the morning.' 'Okey, Ryder.'

1968 *Listener*: Okayed by Western governments, the Prague festival enjoyed a substantial dollar bonus in the form of the Illinois State University Jazz Band.

1970 Germaine Greer: His secretary had…moved out of Haight Ashbury when it ceased to be okay to live there.

1973 *Freedomways*: Nothing goes down without his okay.

olde worlde *adj* (1927) spuriously old-fashioned or quaint. An (equally spurious) antiquated spelling of *old world*, with the *es* decidedly pronounced (as the spelling in the first quote below shows). See also **shoppe (1933)**

1927 Cyril Connolly: There remain consolations, such as finding places that aren't spoilt and not being surprised by their destruction into the…oldie worldie type.

1934 Constant Lambert: We…pour our bootleg gin into cracked leather bottles with olde-worlde labels.

op *n* (1925) a surgical operation. Colloquial, mainly British. See also **op (1916)**

1932 Agatha Christie: Just before my op… Operation. For appendicitis.

organized crime *n* (1929) widespread criminal activities planned and controlled in the manner of a business operation. The phenomenon may not have been new (see the quote below), but the term arose out of the co-ordinated criminal activities in the US during the Prohibition era. See also **racketeering (1928)**

> 1929 J. Landesco: Organized crime is not, as many think, a recent phenomenon in Chicago.

outside broadcast *n* (1927) a radio or television broadcast coming from outside a studio. The insiders' abbreviation *O.B.* is also first recorded in 1927

> 1927 *B.B.C. Handbook*: *Outside broadcast*, a broadcast item taking place at some point other than the studio… Every O.B. of the simplest…nature necessitates the provision of two complete telephone line circuits…between the site of the performance and the Station Control Room.

Oxford bags *n* (1927) a style of trousers very wide at the ankles, fashionable in the 1920s. The precursor *Oxford trousers* is recorded in 1925 ('Perils of the Dance. The terror of the Oxford trousers', *Punch*)

> 1938 John Betjeman: The pale-faced mechanics in Oxford bags and tweed coats, walk down the Cornmarket.

package *v* (1928) to wrap up, make into a package. A verbal use of the noun *package* which was originally condemned as 'commercial cant' (M. H. Weseen, *Crowell's Dictionary of English Grammar* (1928)), but has since established itself seamlessly in the language

> 1947 Mary McCarthy: An image of happiness as packaged by the manufacturer.

pansy *n* (1929) an effeminate man; a male homosexual. One of the main insult-words applied to male homosexuals in the middle years of the century, the underlying image being that of the delicate flower. First recorded in adjectival use in the same year

> 1929 Jean Devanny: 'Thanks. Don't bother.' The voice was warm… A rich telephone voice. To an artist a pansy voice; a purple pansy.

> 1937 Margery Allingham: You don't want to feel that every other user of the road privately feels that your club is nothing but a pack of pansies on bicycles.

paranormal *adj* (1920) going beyond the bounds of ordinary experience or scientifically explainable phenomena. First recorded in the 1920 addendum to Webster's *New International Dictionary*, but it did not really get its feet under the table of the language until the 1950s, as a noun—*the paranormal*

> 1958 J. Blish: He has no belief in the supernatural—or, as we're calling it in our barbarous jargon these days, the 'paranormal'.

paraphilia *n* (1925) abnormal sexual behaviour; a sexual deviation. A term coined (from Greek *para-* 'beside' and *philia* 'love') by the Viennese-born psychotherapist Wilhelm Stekel (1868–1940), and introduced into English in translations of his work. It and its derivatives (*paraphiliac* and so on) did not come into widespread use until the 1950s

> 1958 *Times Literary Supplement*: Stekel…says that pluralistic orgies are tribal in derivation, and that frequently the paraphiliac who engages in them seeks a family combination.

parking lot *n* (1924) an area of ground used for the parking of vehicles. Originally and mainly US. Compare **car-park (1926)**

> 1924 Homer Croy: Some of the people still lingered under the arc light, with its summer collection of bugs still in it, waiting for the two to come from the parking lot.

Parkinsonism *n* (1923) (the symptoms seen in) Parkinson's disease. The term *Parkinson's disease* (which was originally coined in French as *maladie de Parkinson*) dates from the 1870s; it commemorates the English surgeon James Parkinson (1755–1824), who described such a disorder in 1817

> 1923 *Brain*: Post-encephalitic Parkinsonism is usually due to degeneration of the substantia nigra.

paso doble *n* (1927) a Latin American ballroom dance in duple time. From Spanish, literally 'double step'

> 1927 Victor Silvester: The Paso Doble is danced very little in this country, but it is popular in certain parts of the Continent. It is often referred to as the Spanish one-step. The walk is short and springy, not unlike a very modified Quickstep.

Paul Jones *n* (1920) a ballroom dance during which the dancers change partners after circling in concentric rings of men and women. Named after John Paul Jones (1747–92), a Scottish-born naval officer noted for his victories for the Americans during the War of Independence

> 1920 *Atlantic Monthly*: The whole sprightly, smiling, hand-clapping population seems engaged in one vast 'Paul Jones'…with no one…refusing to join the dance.

peaceful coexistence *n* (1920) In the foreign policy of the Soviet Union, peaceful relations with other countries. The early quotation from Lenin has never been thoroughly verified, and certainly the term did not come into widespread use in English until the time of the Cold War, when it had the additional connotation of avoidance of nuclear confrontation

> 1920 *New York Evening Journal* [Interview with Lenin]: Our plans in Asia? The same as in Europe: peaceful coexistence with the peoples, with the workers and peasants of all nations.

> 1961 *Times*: Mr. Khrushchev,…at a New Year banquet… in the Kremlin,…raised his glass and bade the whole company drink to peaceful coexistence.

peachy *adj* (1926) attractive, outstanding, marvellous, etc. Slang

> 1926 Elinor Glyn: He…whispered to the man behind him— 'Peachy bit in the eighth row—Look at the pearls.'

pecking order *n* (1928) a pattern of behaviour first observed in hens and later recognized in other groups of social animals, in which those of high rank within the group are able to attack those of lower rank without provoking an attack in return. A translation of a term coined in German as *Hackliste* by T. J. Schjelderup-Ebbe in the early 1920s. The now familiar metaphorical usage, applied to human beings, is not recorded before the 1950s, but the potential for it is evident in the first quote below

> 1928 Aldous Huxley: Observing the habitual and almost sacred 'pecking order' which prevails among the hens in his poultry yard…the politician will meditate on the Catholic hierarchy and Fascism.

> 1955 Harold Nicolson: In a perfect classless society…similar pecking orders must exist.

pelmanism *n* (1923) a system of memory training taught by the Pelman Institute for the Scientific Development of Mind, Memory and Personality, founded in London in 1899 by Christopher Louis Pelman. His name had been lexicalized in various ways by the early 1920s (*pelmanist, pelmanize*, etc.), many of the coinages originating in the Institute's own publicity, but it was *pelmanism* that really stood the test of time—at least until around the 1950s. It also became attached to a type of card game embodying the principles of the memory system—indeed that is what its earliest known quote refers to

> 1919 *Honey Pot*: Lots of our fellows are Pelmanising out here.

> 1920 *Pelman Pie*: A very large proportion of its readers are 'Pelmanists'.

> 1923 *Hoyle's Games Modernized*: Pelmanism is…a splendid exercise for the memory, besides a source of amusement to the players—of whom there may be any number.

> 1934 E. M. Delafield: Short exercise in Pelmanism enables me to connect wave in her hair with first name, which is Marcella.

penicillin *n* (1929) an antibiotic obtained from penicillium moulds. The original agent named by Alexander Fleming was obtained from a culture of *Penicillium notatum*, but in its fully realized form, as isolated and purified by Howard Florey and E. B. Chain at Oxford, it can be produced from a variety of species. It revolutionized the treatment of infection, and saved many lives on the battlefield in World War II

> 1929 Alexander Fleming: In the rest of this article allusion will constantly be made to experiments with filtrates of a broth culture of this mould, so for convenience and to avoid the repetition of the rather cumbersome phrase 'Mould broth filtrate', the name 'penicillin' will be used. This will denote the filtrate of a broth culture of the particular penicillium with which we are concerned.

> 1941 H. W. Florey, etc.: Enough evidence has now been assembled to show that penicillin is a new and effective type of chemotherapeutic agent, and possesses some properties unknown in any antibacterial substance hitherto described.

penthouse *n* (1921) a separate flat, apartment, etc., situated on the roof of a tall building. Previously *penthouse* had denoted a subsidiary structure attached to the wall of a main building

    1921 *Country Life*: Two of the elevators were designed to run to the roof, where a pent-house…was being built.

perm *n, v* (1927) Short for *permanent*, as in **permanent wave (1909)**. A term which survived far longer than other early 20th-century terms for hair-waving techniques (compare, for example, **marcel (1906)** and **water waving (1925)**)

    1927 *Home Chat*: How long does a 'perm' last?

    1928 *Daily Express*: These girls took their chairs at 7.30 p.m… Three hours later they rose 'permed', as one says in the profession.

    1949 *Women's Own*: Give yourself a Toni Home Perm today!

permanent *n* (1926) A shortened form (mainly US) of **permanent wave (1909)**

    1932 *New Yorker*: A deep-wave marcel permanent styled for you alone in the modern manner.

petite *adj* (1929) Of a garment: suitable for a woman of small stature. Part of the 20th-century fashion industry's armoury of euphemisms for mitigating the despair of customers who are not of a standard size

    1929 *Radio Times*: This Stylish Coat…From Petite to Matrons' Sizes.

    1960 *Harper's Bazaar*: Afternoon dress…in 'petite' sizes for the 5'2" and under.

petrol station *n* (1926) A British synonym for **filling station (1921)**

    1926 *Times*: Wanted, hard, ambitious, and independent worker with £750, to erect and operate new petrol station under exceptionally favourable supply contract.

petting *n* (1920) erotic fondling, carressing, kissing, etc. Originally US. A word with which the 1920s liked to mildly shock itself. Derivatives (*petter* and the back-formation *pet*) soon followed

    1920 F. Scott Fitzgerald: That great current American phenomenon, the 'petting party'.

    1922 Sinclair Lewis: Babbitt had heard stories of what the Athletic Club called 'goings-on' at young parties; of girls 'parking' their corsets in the dressing-room, of 'cuddling' and 'petting', and a presumable increase in what was known as Immorality.

    1924 Percy Marks: I'm a bad egg. I drink and gamble and pet. I haven't gone the limit yet…—but I will.

    1925 *College Humor*: Have a nice evening? Jean's some high-type petter, isn't she?

phonofilm *n* (1921) a cinema film with a soundtrack. Originally a proprietary name in the US, registered in 1921, but virtually disused by the mid 1930s. The inventor of the process was Dr Lee de Forest

    1928 *Manchester Guardian Weekly*: The Prime Minister for a quarter of an hour delivered to an audience of half a dozen people and two phonofilm cameras a farewell address.

photocopy *n, v* (1924) (to make) a photographic reproduction of something. The history of the term is not entirely clear. In the first quote below, the combination could well be *photo + copying machine*, not *photo copying + machine*. The first uniquivocal reference to *photocopy* comes in the second edition of Webster's *New International Dictionary of the English Language* (1934), but its use does not appear to have become widespread until the 1940s, with the advent of modern methods of xerography. See **xerography (1948), Xerox (1952)**

    1924 C. W. Hackleman: Photo copying machines. In Fig. 2015 is shown a machine for making copies of records, drawings,…flat merchandise, etc., by a simplified method of photography, the copies being made in enlarged, reduced or natural size directly upon sensitized paper.

    1948 *Library Association Record*: There are private photocopying firms in most cities.

    1959 *Economist*: For more than 20 to 25 copies it will prove cheaper to use some kind of duplicator than even the cheapest type of photocopier.

photogenic *adj* (1928) making a good subject for photography; that shows to good advantage in a photograph or film. Originally US. Possibly a borrowing from French *photogénique* (which was occasionally adopted unchanged in early use), but the word *photogenic* had been in the language since the early 19th century in various technical senses (including as a synonym for *photographic*). See also **radiogenic (1928)**, **microgenic (1931)**, and **telegenic (1939)**

> 1931 Sam Goldwyn: An actor may be 'photogenic' and have personality and appearance, but that is not enough.

photon *n* (1926) a quantum of light or other electro-magnetic radiation, regarded as a type of elementary particle. The word, based on Greek *phōt-* 'light', was actually coined around 1916 by the US psychologist and physicist L. T. Troland (1889–1932) to denote a unit of retinal illumination, but this later usage caught on and caused a good deal of confusion, and in the mid 1940s Troland's own name was adopted as the term for the optical unit, leaving the field clear for the quantum of light

> 1926 G. N. Lewis: I therefore take the liberty of proposing for this hypothetical new atom, which is not light but plays an essential part in every process of radiation, the name *photon*.

planetarium *n* (1929) a device for projecting an image of the night sky at various times and places on to the interior of a dome for public viewing. The name is a reassignment of a term coined in modern Latin in the 18th century for 'a machine illustrating by the movement of its parts the motions of the planets'. In late 20th-century lay usage it is most commonly applied to a building housing the device

> 1929 *Encyclopedia Britannica*: Planetarium is the name given to an arrangement made by Zeiss of Jena, for producing an artificial sky. By optical methods images of the sun, moon, planets and stars are projected on a large hemispherical dome and by mechanical and electrical means the apparatus can be revolved so as to show the principal motions.

> 1973 Carl Sagan: Several million people visit planetariums in North America and Britain each year.

plus fours *n* (1920) men's baggy knickerbockers gathered below the knees. Stereotypical 20s garments, so named from the four inches that had to be added to ordinary knickerbockers to make them overhang the knees

> 1920 *Isis*: The desuetude of the traditional grey flannel 'bags' of the undergraduate... 'Plus fours' have succeeded them.

pogo stick *n* (1921) a stilt-like pole on which one jumps about. When they first came into vogue, they were often called simply 'pogos', but the coiner of the term has not left his or her name to history. There was another brief pogo craze in the late 1950s

> 1921 *Glasgow Herald*: What is a Pogo? It is a four-foot pole, hollowed at the foot for the insertion of a strong spring, with a rubber cushion at the end of it. About half a foot above the spring are two steps. To Pogo you place one foot on each step, clutch the top of the pole firmly in both hands, and hop.

> 1921 *Oxford Times*: On Thursday afternoon two undergraduates were seen racing along Cornmarket Street on Pogo sticks.

> 1958 *Daily Mail*: On stilts and pogo sticks (their latest craze).

Politburo *n* (1927) the highest policy-making committee of the U.S.S.R., or of some other Communist country or party. Adapted from Russian *politbyuró*, a conflation of *politícheskoe byuró* 'political bureau'

> 1927 *Daily Express*: Stalin has packed the Politburo, which...is practically the Cabinet, with his friends.

polyester *n* (1929) a polymer in which the units are joined by the ester linkage -COO-. A word which stayed largely in the laboratory until the 1950s. Polyester resins are widely used in plastics, paints, etc. but it was the discovery of polyester fibre in the early 1940s (see the second quote below) that paved the way for its widespread use as a clothing fabric in the second half of the century

> 1929 *Journal of the American Chemical Society*: Polyintermolecular condensation requires as starting materials compounds in which at least two functional groups are present in the same molecule (e.g., hydroxy acids...might lead to poly-esters,...amino-acids, to poly-amides...).

1958 *Manchester Guardian*: Polyester fibre was discovered in 1941 by Mr. J. R. Whinfield and Dr. J. T. Dickson in the laboratories of the Calico Printers' Association.

1977 *R.A.F. News* (advert): 'Tootal' Polyester/Cotton Wedgwood Blue Shirts.

polystyrene *n* (1927) a polymer of styrene, used as a hard plastic for moulding or, in a light expanded form, for packing and insulation. One of the most familiar plastics in everyday use in the latter part of the century

1970 N. Saunders: Sack chairs…consist of a chair-shaped bag three-quarters full of expanded polystyrene granules.

pooch *n* (1924) a dog, especially a mongrel. Originally US slang, but its origins are obscure; a connection has been suggested with the German term of endearment *putzi*

1924 Ben Hecht: All you do is sink your teeth in my shoulder and make noises like a basket full of hungry pooches.

pop *adj, n* (1926) Denoting music of wide popular appeal, especially to young people. As a noun, *pop* originally denoted an individual popular song or other piece of music, a usage which gradually died out except in certain fixed phrases, such as *top of the pops*. The current application to popular music in general is first recorded in 1954. At first the term designated merely popularity, and covered a wide range of styles (e.g. varieties of jazz). The sense of a specific genre (featuring, for example, strong rhythms and electronic amplification) did not begin to emerge until the 1950s

1926 *American Mercury*: She coos a pop song.

1935 *Hot News*: Turn the record over and you have another winner—'Add a Little Wiggle'—a masterpiece made out of a song-and-dance 'pop'.

1945 S. Hughes: Cole Porter's 'Begin the Beguine'…has twice the regulation number of bars that a good 'pop' should have.

1947 A. J. McCarthy: Jelly would play one of his new 'pop' songs, watching…for its effect.

1954 *Unicorn Book 1953*: A magazine…each December publishes a list of the year's top pop music and musicians.

1970 *Observer*: In the world of pop, the death of Jimi Hendrix on Friday from a suspected overdose of drugs will seem as if Tchaikovsky or Mozart had also been struck down at only 24.

Poppy Day *n* (1921) a day on which those killed in World War I (and later World War II) are commemorated in Britain by the wearing of an artificial poppy. From the choice of the Flanders poppy as the emblem of those who died on the Western Front (and elsewhere) in World War I. Alternatively called **Remembrance Day (1921)**

1921 *Daily Mail*: To-day [11 November]…is Poppy Day. Twenty million red Flanders poppy emblems will be on sale in the streets.

popsicle *n* (1923) an ice lolly. US. Registered as a trademark in the US in 1923 by Frank Epperson of Oakland, California, who dreamed up the idea of a frozen lollipop. British **ice lolly** is not recorded before 1949

1941 S. V. Benét: The usual crowd…Kidding the local cop and eating popsicles.

potty *adj* (1923) thoroughly infatuated; madly in love. British colloquial

1923 E. V. Lucas: I'm potty about her.

pre-packed *adj* (1928) packaged or wrapped on the site of production or before retail

1928 *Daily Express*: The public…would abandon bread altogether in favour of pre-packed foods, all of them comparatively expensive.

presidium, praesidium *n* (1924) the presiding body or standing committee in a Communist organization, especially in the Supreme Soviet. A borrowing of Russian *prezidium*, which itself was taken from Latin *praesidium* 'garrison'

1924 *Observer*: In a second decree the Presidium of the Union C.E.C. decided to replace the sentence of ten years strict isolation passed on the Catholic Archbishop Ciepliak by the All-Russian C.E.C. by expulsion from the territories of the Union of Socialist and Soviet Republics.

pressure group *n* (1928) a group or association of people representing some special interest, who bring concerted pressure to bear on public policy
> 1928 P. H. Odegard: The character of pressure groups as of individuals can frequently be understood from the manner in which they spend their money.

primal scene *n* (1925) the first time that a child is emotionally aware of his or her parents copulating. A term of Sigmund Freud's, introduced into English in Strachey's translation of his work
> 1925 James Strachey: We will proceed with the study of the relations between this 'primal scene' and the patient's dream.

prison-camp *n* (1925) a camp in which prisoners, especially political prisoners or prisoners-of-war, are confined
> 1925 *Scribner's Magazine*: The scene is a Turkish prison-camp during the recent war.

problem child *n* (1920) a child that is difficult to deal with, especially because of some personality disorder. Used as the title of a book by the educationist A. S. Neill in 1926
> 1920 J. Taft: The placing and replacing of a problematic child…is also costly… The problem child is such a costly, nagging, persistent proposition that… we are forced to bring intelligence to bear upon his case.

programme *n* (1923) a radio (or, later, television) show
> 1923 *Radio Times*: From November 14th last year…we have…transmitted roughly 1,700 distinct evening programmes.

Prohibition *n* (1922) (the period (1920–33) of) the banning of the manufacture, sale, and transportation of alcoholic drink in the US. The term *prohibition* had been used in the US for the banning of alcohol since the 19th century ('The State of Vermont has struggled arduously to arrive at the summit level of entire prohibition', *Annual Report of the Executive Committee of the American Temperance Union* (1851)), and it is not always possible to distinguish this usage from early references to the period during which the ban was in force. See also **Volstead (1920)**. (Incidentally, the term *bootlegger* 'a smuggler of illicit alcohol', which came into prominence during Prohibition, dates from the late 1880s; it probably originally referred to someone who concealed contraband in his boot)
> 1922 *Daily News*: So far as the movement against Prohibition is concerned, the victory of Mr. Edwards, Governor of New Jersey, is only a gesture. As Governor he promised to make the State as wet as the Atlantic.

project *v* (1923) to attribute (an emotion, state of mind, etc.) to an external object or person, especially unconsciously
> 1923 Julian Huxley: Certain neurotic types project their depression so as to colour everything that comes into their cognizance a gloomy black.

promotion *n* (1925) the furtherance of the sale of something by advertisement or other modes of publicity. Originally US. A specialized 20th-century application of the more general sense 'furtherance, advancement', which dates from the 15th century. The related usage of the verb is not recorded before 1930
> 1928 *Publishers' Weekly*: Promotion cannot be done without waste… But the idea back of the new mergers is the idea of outlets, of promotion, of selling more goods.
> 1930 *Publishers' Weekly*: The books all to be individualized in appearance and fully promoted.

proton *n* (1920) a positively charged elementary particle that is a constituent of all atomic nuclei. The term *proton* (coined from Greek *prōton* 'first') had already been used by embryologists in the 1890s for a 'primordial body part', but it never really caught on. Its application to the atomic particle appears to have been at least partly inspired by the name of the English chemist and physician William Prout (1785–1850), who suggested that hydrogen was a constituent of all the elements (see the first quote below)
> 1920 *Engineering*: Sir Ernest [Rutherford], replying, said that…a clear nomenclature was certainly wanted; the term 'prouton' or 'proton' might be suitable for the H nucleus.
> 1922 J. Mills: The hydrogen atom is composed of only one proton and one electron.

psychiatrize *v* (1929) to treat psychiatrically. A coinage that has enjoyed limited success: a few examples of it are recorded from the second half of the century
> 1929 *Sunday Dispatch*: Parents may also be psychiatrised to study their traits and home-life.

psycho *n* (1921) A colloquial abbreviation of **psychoanalysis**. It does not seem to have survived beyond the middle of the century, perhaps elbowed aside by **analysis (1906)**
> 1921 Rose Macaulay: 'Psycho-analysis, I mean.' 'Oh, psycho… Not that insomnia is always a case for psycho, you know.'

P.T.A. (1925) An abbreviation of *parent-teacher association* (a term first recorded in 1915)
> 1925 *Kansas City* (Missouri) *Star*: P.-T.-A. plans celebration.

public *n* (1921) an author's, entertainer's, etc. readers, followers, or supporters
> 1921 Hart Crane: I am 'sold out' and will have to rush rhymes and rhythms together to supply my enthusiastic 'public' as fast as I can.

publicity stunt *n* (1926) something done only for the purpose of gaining publicity
> 1926 'Sapper': It was just an advertisement—an elaborate publicity stunt.

publicize *v* (1928) to bring to the notice of the public; to give publicity to; to advertise
> 1928 *Weekly Dispatch*: Nowadays the potential star has to be managed and publicised.

putsch *n* (1920) an attempted revolution. A borrowing from Swiss German, where it means literally a 'knock' or 'blow'—also the literal meaning of French *coup*. It had already made a back-door entry into English at the end of the 19th century in the term *putschism*, denoting the advocacy of putsches
> 1922 *Quarterly Review*: King Charles has made his second attempt to ascend the Hungarian Throne. In the circumstances out-lined above it was doomed to failure. So was Louis Napoleon's second *coup d'état—Putsch* is the modern word—at Boulogne.

Put-u-up *n* (1924) A proprietary name for a sofa or settee which can be converted into a bed. British. Later in the century the spelling *put-you-up* began to replace the trademark form
> 1978 *Morecambe Guardian*: Besides traditional beds, there are the convertible put-you-up types which are essential when space is short.

pylon *n* (1923) a lattice-work metal tower for overhead electricity lines. One of the most obvious marks of the 20th century on the countryside. Hitherto, a *pylon* had been 'an ancient Egyptian monumental gateway' (its original meaning) and 'a tower for guiding pilots'
> 1923 E. Shanks: Half a mile up the mountain, a cable, a thin black line, traversed the crystal air, borne up on pylons.

> 1930 W. H. Auden: Pylons fallen or subsiding, trailing dead high-tension wires.

quantum mechanics *n* (1922) a theory of matter, incorporating **quantum theory (1912)**, based on the concept that elementary particles possess wave properties. The first known instance of the term comes from 1922, but it is not there being used in the full sense that had become established by the middle of the decade
> 1922 *Report of the British Association for the Advancement of Science*: The spectrum theory is far the most important branch of the quantum theory, as it has led and is still leading to extensions of quantum mechanics.

> 1925 *Proceedings of the Royal Society* (heading): The fundamental equations of quantum mechanics.

queen *n* (1924) a male homosexual, especially the effeminate partner in a homosexual relationship. Slang. Probably the same word as *queen* 'female ruler', although later spellings associate it with *quean* 'woman'
> 1930 Evelyn Waugh: 'Now what may you want, my Italian queen?' said Lottie as the waiter came in with a tray.

> 1935 D. Lamson: We did hear startling tales…of 'family' life, of marriage ceremonies, of fights with knives for the favor of some 'quean', as the perverts are called in prison.

queer *adj* (1922) homosexual. Originally US. The usage does not seem to have become widespread until the 1930s, when it is first recorded as a noun, meaning 'a homosexual person'. One of the main insult-words for homosexuals in the middle part of the century, changing social attitudes from the 1960s onwards gradually placed it under a taboo

> 1922 *The Practical Value of the Scientific Study of Juvenile Delinquents* (Children's Bureau, US Department of Labor): A young man, easily ascertainable to be unusually fine in other characteristics, is probably 'queer' in sex tendency.

> 1936 Lee Duncan: There was even a little room…where the 'fairies', 'pansies', and 'queers' conducted their lewd practices.

qwerty (1929) Part of the series of letters that label the first row of letter keys on typewriters and similar keyboards in English-speaking countries, used adjectivally to designate a keyboard or machine that incorporates this type of non-alphabetical lay-out. The lay-out was devised in the 1870s in order to slow typists down—typewriters of that era tended to jam if adjacent keys were pressed in too quick succession, and the qwerty keyboard separates the commonest letters widely

> 1929 *Times Literary Supplement*: The 'qwerty' keyboard appears first on the Yost in 1887.

racketeering *n* (1928) a system of organized crime directed chiefly to extorting money from business firms by intimidation, violence, or other illegal methods. Originally US. *Racketeer*, as both a noun and a verb, is first recorded in the same year. See also **organized crime (1929)**

> 1928 *New York Times*: Two gang murders within the last week prompted Judge Edwin O. Lewis…to order the August Grand Jury to delve to the bottom of 'racketeering' in Philadelphia.

> 1928 *Time*: In the old days it was a mark of distinction to be seen at gangster funerals, but during the Loesch prosecutions, probably not even U.S. Senator Deneen of Illinois would care to be seen near the bier of a 'racketeer'… In 36 years in Chicago I have never been held up, robbed, or racketeered.

radiation sickness *n* (1924) disease caused by exposure of the body to ionizing radiation

> 1924 *Lancet*: Dodds and Webster have recently summarised the literature of radiation sickness in *The Lancet*

radical feminism *n* (1923) advocacy of radical left-wing views designed to counter the traditional dominance of men over women. A term which did not come into widespread use until the 1970s

> 1923 A. R. Wadia: These would also have to be studied so as to enable us to judge how far they afford a stable basis for the advocates of radical feminism.

radio *n* (1922) sound broadcasting. See also **radio (1907)**

> 1922 *Scientific American*: Radio today is a continuous performance. You purchase your ticket in the form of a receiving set…and then listen in…to the music of today…the news of the minute, stock quotations, and so on.

radiogenic *adj* (1928) well suited for broadcasting by radio; providing an attractive subject for a radio broadcast. An adjective (probably based on **photogenic (1928)**) particularly of pre-television days, but it survived into the last quarter of the century. See also **telegenic (1939)**

> 1928 *Radio Times*: Their object is to discover…a form (or forms) of drama which shall be truly 'radiogenic'.

radioize *v* (1922) to equip with radio. Not a long-lived coinage (although another sighting of it, probably as a re-coinage, is on record from 1950)

> 1922 *Science & Invention* (advert): Radioize your phonograph with a guaranteed adapter.

> 1950 *Sun* (Baltimore): Russia is in the middle of an all-out campaign to 'radioize' the entire population of its sprawling Soviet Socialist Republics.

radish *n* (1920) an anti-communist who professes to be an enthusiastic communist. The quote below explains the metaphor, and also suggests its origin. The underlying idea prefigures words applied later in the century to blacks who adopt white cultural characteristics (e.g. **Oreo (1968)** and *coconut* (1988))

> 1920 *Times*: A 'radish' is a man who fervently professes devotion to the Communist cause while harbouring a secret longing for its overthrow. Red outside, but white…inside. The epithet was invented by Trotsky.

railodok, railodoc *n* (1924) an observation car, running on rails and conveying visitors round the British Empire Exhibition at Wembley in 1924. Pretty much a forgotten word by the end of the decade

> 1924 *Glasgow Herald*: Her Majesty…toured the Exhibition in a railodok car.

raspberry *n* (1920) (a sign of disapproval, accompanied by) rejection or dismissal. Slang. From the earlier sense 'a derisive sound', which itself was probably short for rhyming slang *raspberry tart* 'fart'

> 1920 P. G. Wodehouse: Convict son totters up the steps of the old home and punches the bell! What awaits him beyond? Forgiveness? Or the raspberry?

rationalize *v* (1922) to give plausible reasons for (one's behaviour) that ignore, conceal, or gloss its real motive. Used both transitively and intransitively

> 1922 H. Somerville: It is clear that patient is rationalising, and that as a matter of fact he is eaten up with jealousy.

> 1925 Joan Riviere: The patient's consciousness naturally misunderstands them and puts forward a set of secondary motives to account for them—rationalizes them, in short.

rationalize *v* (1926) to organize (economic production or the like) according to rational or scientific principles so as to achieve a desired or predictable result. Often subsequently used as a euphemistic camouflage for reducing the size of an operation, firing employees, etc.

> 1926 E. Grossmann: International cartels will be able to rationalise production in a way impossible in the present state of affairs.

> 1962 *Listener*: Their numbers go down: they are 'rationalized'. In 1920 there were nine evening newspapers in London; now there are two.

rave *n* (1926) a highly enthusiastic or laudatory review or notice of a book, play, film, etc. Originally US. Latterly often used as an adjective, meaning 'full of praise'. Despite the comment in the first quote below, no earlier definite example of the usage has been traced in *Variety*

> 1926 *American Mercury*: One of the paper's [i.e. *Variety*'s] coinages should be officially embraced by the dictionary and bred into the language. It refers to a flattering, enthusiastic review by a sycophantic critic as a *rave*.

> 1951 P. G. Wodehouse: Of course he can open the safe. He's an expert. You should have read what the papers said of him at the time of the trial. He got rave notices.

rayon *n* (1924) (a fabric made from) fibres and filaments composed of or made from regenerated cellulose. Originally US: the quote below explains how the word (perhaps a borrowing of French *rayon* 'ray of light') was selected as a commercial name in place of the cumbersome *artificial silk* (1884). Another alternative was *art silk*, first recorded in 1922

> 1924 *Drapers' Record*: 'Glos' having been killed by ridicule, the National Retail Dry Goods Association of America has made another effort to produce a suitable name for artificial silk. This time their choice has fallen on 'rayon'.

readership *n* (1923) the total number of (regular) readers of a periodical publication, such as a newspaper or magazine. Originally US

> 1923 O. G. Villard: The appeal of the *News* to the masses has been so successful that it now has a readership of some forty thousand.

recession *n* (1929) a temporary decline or setback in economic activity or prosperity. There was more than a hint of euphemism in the coining of this term, traces of which remain even at the end of the century

> 1929 *Economist*: The material prosperity of the United States is too firmly based, in our opinion, for a revival in industrial activity—even if we have to face an immediate recession of some magnitude—to be long delayed.

> 1938 Eric Ambler: 'Trade recession' they called it… As far as I could see there wasn't a great deal of difference between a trade recession and a good old-fashioned slump.

recycle *v* (1926) to reuse (a material) in an industrial process. Originally a technical term used mainly in the oil-refining industry and, later, in the nuclear industry. The more widespread application to the processing of waste to make it usable is not recorded until 1960

> 1960 *Aeroplane*: It has systems which reduce all organic waste to a small amount of ash and re-cycle urine and waste water into drinkable water.

red menace *n* (1925) the political or military threat regarded as emanating from the Soviet Union. A roughly contemporary but short-lived synonym was *red peril*, inspired by *yellow peril* 'the alleged threat that Chinese or other Far Eastern people will invade or destroy Europe or the West' (1898)

> 1925 B. Coan: It is time, right now, to get down to cases about this thing we hear called the 'red menace'.

> 1927 *Observer*: We have to guard against the Red Peril on our borders.

red shift *n* (1923) displacement of spectral lines towards the red end of the spectrum; increase in the wavelength of electromagnetic radiation, caused by the Doppler effect or by gravitation

> 1923 Arthur Eddington: The red shift in the spiral nebulae.

redundant *adj* (1928) no longer needed at work; unemployed because of reorganization, mecha-nization, change in demand, etc. A term with euphemistic origins which has become a key part of 20th-century British industrial-relations vocabulary

> 1934 J. B. Priestley: You may do a good stroke of work by declaring the Stockton shipyards 'redun-dant', but you cannot pretend that all the men who used to work in those yards are merely 'redun-dant' too.

Remembrance Day *n* (1921) 11 November (or, latterly in Britain, the Sunday closest to 11 November, also called *Remembrance Sunday* (1942)), kept in remembrance of those killed in World War I, and subsequently in World War II. See also **Armistice Day (1919)**, **Poppy Day (1921)**

> 1929 *Radio Times*: Remembrance Day, Nov. 11. Wear a Flanders Poppy.

> 1942 C. Milburn: Remembrance Sunday, and great news today! American troops have landed in North Africa.

rent-a- *prefix* (1921) Used before a noun to designate the rental of the thing specified, originally and mainly a motor vehicle. Originally US. The broadening out of the usage to apply to things other than means of transport dates from the 1960s (see **rent-a- (1961)**)

> 1921 *Chicago Central Business & Office Building Directory*: Rent-a-Ford (Inc.) 1450 S. Michigan av.

> 1935 *Archives of Dermatology & Syphilology*: A man…who owned a 'rent-a-car' business.

rent party *n* (1926) Originally, a party aimed at raising money to pay the rent of a house; later, any jam session in a house or apartment. US. Apparently a shortening of *house-rent party*, first recorded the previous year ('I am a tamer of wild women and bitterly against house-rent parties', *Inter-State Tattler*)

> 1926 Carl Van Vechten: There were…the modest rent-parties.

reparations *n* (1921) compensation for war damage owed by the aggressor. *Reparation* has been used for 'compensation' in English since at least the early 15th century, but this specific 20th-century use of the plural seems to have come from the presence of *réparations* in the French text of the 1919 peace treaty, detailing payments to be made by Germany (the English text in the same place says *reparation*)

> 1921 *Glasgow Herald*: The mere purchase of foreign securities to meet reparations…simply means the transference of worthless papers from one body of financiers to another.

request *n* (1928) a letter, etc., asking for a particular record, song, etc., to be played on a radio pro-gramme; hence, a record played or a song, etc., sung in response to such a request

> 1928 *Radio Times*: The B.B.C. can never promise to comply with requests, for…suitable oppor-tunities may not arise for weeks or even months… Children's Hour request week… The Fourth Request Week will begin on January 7, 1929.

> 1949 *Radio Times*: Listeners' requests played by Sandy Macpherson at the BBC theatre organ.

rest home *n* (1925) a residential establishment for rest and recuperation. Over the decades the term evolved into a euphemism for *old people's home*

1925 *Daily Herald*: The organization of rest homes, where workers may spend their vacation, is a unique development.

rev *v* (1920) to (cause to) operate at an increased rate of revolutions. Based on the noun **rev (1901)**

1920 *Blackwood's Magazine*: British Fighter whose pilot was revving up his 250-horse-power Rolls Royce Falcon.

ribbon development *n* (1927) the building of houses in a single line along a main road, usually one leading out of a town or village. A post-World War I phenomenon widely condemned at the time and legislated against. *Ribbon building* was a contemporary synonym

1927 *Garden Cities and Town Planning*: The writers are well aware of the disadvantages of 'ribbon' development.

1928 *Daily Express*: Ribbon-building should be abolished.

1929 *Times*: Your condemnation of ribbon development building along arterial roads is especially applicable to the new arterial Reigate to Dorking road.

ring road *n* (1928) a by-pass road encircling a town or other urban area. See also **by-pass (1922)**

1928 *Daily Express*: London has no form, no symmetry. I suggest that we could give her this by cutting a broad ring-road through the old nineteenth century suburbs.

Ritz *n put on the Ritz* (1926) to assume an air of superiority. US colloquial, based on the luxurious connotations of the Ritz hotels in New York, London, Paris, and elsewhere, which themselves commemorate the Swiss hotelier César Ritz (1850–1918)

1926 Ring Lardner: If you mention some really worth while novel like, say, 'Black Oxen', they think you're trying to put on the Ritz.

roadability *n* (1925) suitability for being driven on the road; roadworthiness; road-holding ability. A coinage apparently of the advertising industry, which seems not to have survived in widespread usage after the 1920s (although a further isolated example is recorded in 1973). There is also the adjective *roadable* (1929), probably a back-formation from *roadability*

1928 *Sunday Dispatch* (advert): Wider track, lower centre of gravity, improved roadability.

1929 *Bookman* (New York): Motor car advertising of the past decade has brought forth the remarkable word 'roadability'... A car that has 'roadability' is, presumably, 'roadable'; that is, it can be roaded—whatever that might mean.

1935 A. P. Herbert: What sort of a car, I wonder, is a car which is not 'roadable'?

road safety *n* (1920) elimination of the danger of traffic accidents

1920 *Scientific American*: Automobile Signals for Danger Spots... New illustrations of old ideas for street comfort and road safety.

road sense *n* (1923) the ability to use roads and negotiate traffic safely

1923 *Daily Mail*: The good driver uses care instinctively because he has the imagination or 'road-sense' which tells him instantly what he can and what he cannot do.

robot *n* (1923) Originally denoting one of the mechanical men and women in Karel Čapek's play *R.U.R.* ('Rossum's Universal Robots') (1920), and subsequently applied to a machine (sometimes resembling a human being in appearance) designed to function in place of a living agent, especially one which carries out a variety of tasks automatically. Čapek (1890–1938) coined the word from Czech *robota* 'forced labour', which is related to German *Arbeit* 'work'. Its first recorded occurrence in English is in Selver's translation of Čapek's play

1923 P. Selver: You see...the Robots have no interest in life. They have no enjoyments.

1923 *Times*: If Almighty God had populated the world with Robots, legislation of this sort might have been reasonable.

1998 *Sunday Times*: Scientists in Albuquerque have already made robots the size of sugar cubes.

rocket plane, rocket airplane *n* (1928), **rocket aeroplane** *n* (1932) a rocket-powered aeroplane. Only a theoretical possibility in the late 1920s, but such an aircraft (the Messerschmitt Me 163) was produced and put into service by the Germans during World War II

1928 *Popular Mechanics*: Valier has calculated that a rocket plane could be shot from Berlin to New York in ninety-three minutes.

1929 *Amazing Stories*: The series of experiments were given their first impetus by the German rocket airplanes, successfully designed for the Berlin-to-New York air service.

rocket-ship *n* (1927) a rocket-powered spacecraft. See also **spacecraft (1930)**

1927 *Literary Digest*: [Max Valier] is even now building a rocket-ship.

1936 *Forum & Century*: But the question of whether rocket ships will ever reach the planets can be even approximately answered only when intensive research has been carried on over many years.

Rorschach test *n* (1927) a type of personality test first devised by the Swiss psychiatrist Hermann Rorschach (1885–1922), in which a standard set of ink blots of different shapes and colours is presented one at a time to a subject with the request that he or she should describe what they suggest or resemble

1927 Moir & Gundlach: Each subject was given the Rorschach test.

Rosie Lee, Rosy Lee *n* (1925) British rhyming slang for 'tea'. Also used in the shortened form *Rosie*. Originally probably services' slang of the World War I period, it has survived and spread more widely through the language since then, and remains reasonably familiar at the end of the century. There was probably no particular Rosie Lee behind the coinage, although it was no doubt reinforced by the name of the American striptease artiste Gypsy Rose Lee

1929 J. B. Priestley: 'Ow about a drop o' Rosie Lee?

1968 J. Boland: Want a drop of rosie, do yer, Dad?

roughage *n* (1927) the indigestible fibrous matter or cellulose in vegetable foodstuffs. A favourite term of the digestion-obsessed, particularly in the middle part of the century; later supplanted by **fibre** (see **F Plan Diet (1982)**)

1948 *Good Housekeeping Cookery Book*: Much constipation is due to insufficient quantities of roughage in the diet.

roundabout *n* (1927) a junction at which traffic moves one way round a central island. The British term for what in the US is called a *rotary* (1940) or *traffic circle* (1942). It gradually replaced the French *rond-point* (1903), which had been used hitherto

1927 *Glasgow Herald*: There is only one draw-back to the roundabout, and that is the inconvenience caused to pedestrians.

1927 *Report of the Commissioner of Police of the Metropolis 1926*: During the past year roundabout systems of traffic have been put into operation at Parliament Square [etc.].

1947 *Daily Mail*: Removal of the Mansion House to make room for a big round-about.

royal *n* (1920) A name projected, but never adopted, for a decimal unit of currency. In the 16th and 17th centuries there had been an English gold coin called a 'royal', and the word was also used into the 18th century as the English name for the Spanish *real* coin, so there was a good precedent for the suggestion, but it was never officially accepted, either in Britain or in Australia

1920 *Report of the Royal Commission on Decimal Coinage*: The second scheme (Lord Leverhulme's) proposes the creation of a new unit of 100 halfpennies to be called a Royal.

1963 *Guardian*: The Cabinet decided today that Australia's main currency units will be the Royal and the Crown… The royal, equal to 10 of the present Australian shillings, will be subdivided into 100 cents.

rumba *n* (1922) a complex syncopated Afro-Cuban dance. By the end of the decade the term was being applied to a ballroom adaptation of this dance. The word comes from American Spanish, where it was derived from *rumbo* 'carousel'

1922 Joseph Hergesheimer: Her life…was incredibly, wildly, debauched. Among other things, she danced, as the mulata, the rumba, an indescribable affair.

runway *n* (1923) a specially prepared surface on an airfield for the taking off and landing of aircraft. Originally US

1923 *Aviation*: A wonderful landmark—Boston Airport with its T type runways.

Ryvita *n* (1925) The proprietary name of a type of crispbread, registered in Britain in 1925. It was coined from *rye* and Latin *vita* 'life'. The generic term *crispbread* is first recorded in 1926

> 1930 Arnold Bennett: Oldham softly entered with the tea-tray... 'I've brought you some hot ryvita in case you should fancy it, sir.'

S.A. *n* (1926) An abbreviation of **sex appeal (1924)**

> 1926 *American Mercury*: The girl is a looker with an armful of S.A. (sex appeal).

> 1932 Philip MacDonald: A Gallic young woman with apparently some looks and, let us say, 98 per cent. vigorous S.A.

salesperson *n* (1920) a salesman or saleswoman. This and **craftsperson (1920)** appear to be the earliest examples in English of job-names coined with the element -*person*, with the deliberate intention of making no distinction between female and male. However, they do not seem to have started a trend: it was not until the early 1970s that the usage sudenly proliferated (see **-person (1971)**)

> 1920 *Harper's Magazine*: We have long been familiar with *salesman* and *saleswoman*—even, alas! with *saleslady*; and the latest member of the family to whom we have been introduced to, *salesperson*, a name intended to apply to employee of either sex.

sales resistance *n* (1925) reluctance to buy something offered for sale. Originally US

> 1925 *New Yorker*: 'Beggar on Horseback' presents no sales resistance problem... The buying public flocks.

samey *adj* (1929) identical; lacking in variety, monotonous. Colloquial

> 1929 Ernest Raymond: The days that followed, becoming 'samey'..., sank out of memory's sight.

sardines *n* (1924) a party game of hide-and-seek, in which each seeker joins the hider upon discovery until one seeker remains. In US English it is generally called *sardines-in-the-box*. The underlying idea is of tightly packed sardines in their tin

> 1924 Mendel & Meynell: *Sardines* is gaudier still. Only one player hides, all the others seek; the first to find him hides with him, the next...squashes in alongside,...till everybody's hiding in the same spot but one Seeker.

> 1925 F. Scott Fitzgerald: 'Hide-and-go-seek' or 'sardines-in-the-box' with all the house thrown open to the game.

scanties *n* (1928) underwear, especially women's knickers. A winsome euphemism (first recorded in the singular form *scanty*) which has not enjoyed the long-term success in British English that it has in its original US

> 1928 J. P. McEvoy: The hottest little wench that ever shook a scanty at a tired business man.

> 1951 Monica Dickens: No don't go, dear. You've seen me in my scanties, anyway.

schizoid *adj, n* (1925) like or tending towards schizophrenia, but with milder or less developed symptoms (e.g. an absence of delusions); also, a schizoid person. A term coined in German by the psychologist E. Kretschmer and introduced in his book *Körperbau und Charakter* (1921). It first appeared in English in Sprott's translation of this. In lay language it has come often to be used merely as a synonym for *schizophrenic*

> 1925 W. J. H. Sprott: One may for convenience call the transitional stages between illness and health, and the pathological abortive forms, 'schizoid' and 'cycloid'...We sometimes find schizoids, who look just as if they had already been through a schizophrenic psychosis before they were born.

science fiction *n* (1929) imaginative fiction based on postulated scientific discoveries or spectacular environmental changes, often set in the future or on other planets and involving space or time travel. The term is actually first recorded in 1851 in the work of one W. Wilson, but it did not have quite the same connotations as the modern word, and there is no evidence of any continuity of usage between then and the late 1920s. The abbreviation *S.F.* is also first recorded in 1929; **sci-fi** not until 1955

> 1929 *Science Wonder Stories*: The editor of this publication [H. Gernsback] addressed a number of letters to science fiction lovers. The editor promised to pay $50.00 for the best letter each month on the subject of 'What Science Fiction Means to Me.'... The S.F. Magazine. (Science-Fiction).

scofflaw *n* (1924) somene who treats the law with contempt, especially one who avoids various kinds of not easily enforceable laws. US. An instructive example of a manufactured word which has made a lasting place for itself in the language, albeit in a rather wider sense than was originally intended during the Prohibition period

> 1924 *Boston Herald*: Delcevare King of Quincy last night announced that 'scofflaw' is the winning word in the contest for the $200 he offered for a word, to characterize the 'lawless drinker' of illegally made or illegally obtained liquor. 'Scofflaw' was chosen from more than 25,000 words, submitted from all the states and from several foreign countries. The word was sent by two contestants, so the prize will be equally divided between Henry Irving Dale…and Miss Kate L. Butler.

> 1977 *Saturday Review* (US): The illegal phone-dialing devices called 'blue boxes' are about to be put out of business… By…pressing its rewired dial-tone buttons, a scofflaw could bypass phone company billing systems.

scoptophilia *n* (1924) voyeurism. The word should have been *scopophilia*, but Joan Riviere, translating a text of Sigmund Freud's, mistakenly gave it as *scoptophilia*, and this stuck for a while; the 'correct' form is not recorded in English until 1937

> 1924 Joan Riviere: The obscure psychical processes implicit in the repression of scoptophilia and in the outbreak of psychogenic visual disturbance.

scram *v* (1928) to leave quickly. Slang, originally US. It is generally taken to be a shortened form of *scramble*, but German *schramm*, the imperative singular of *schrammen* 'to depart', may also have had a hand in it (the specific origin reported in the first quote below is unconfirmed). The Pig Latin version *amscray* is first recorded in 1934

> 1928 Walter Winchell: [Jack Conway's] popular slang creations include…'scram', meaning 'git out!'

> 1933 *Punch*: Son, beat ut, d'ya get me?—Gwawn—S-C-R-R-A-M!

security *n* (1925) the maintenance of peaceful relationships between the nations of the world. See also **collective security (1934)** and **Security Council (1944)**

> 1925 *Times*: The jurists…are discussing the technical details of the proposed Security Pact at the Foreign Office.

> 1955 *Bulletin of Atomic Science*: 'Security', as it relates to the continuing struggle between the free world and the Soviet bloc, is an abundantly common yet widely misunderstood word.

serious *adj* (1929) considerable in amount or extent; worth taking seriously. Used in US business jargon (especially in the phrase *serious money*) down the decades, but not more widely current until the money-loving 1980s took it up. See also **seriously (1981)**

> 1929 *American Speech*: If you wish to boast of having a great deal of money, you may speak of having *gobs, oodles, piles, scads,* or *wads* of it… Recently we have begun to hear…of *important* or *serious* money or of *heavy sugar*.

> 1975 *Forbes*: Very few of the thousands upon thousands of hard-working money managers, brokers and security analysts who are highly educated and full of facts ever make serious money.

> 1989 Alice Walter: She wore these three-inch heels…I'm talking serious stiletto.

service charge *n* (1929) a charge (usually a percentage of the total bill) made for services rendered. A method of extracting more money from customers, especially in restaurants, with which the 20th century has become increasingly familiar

> 1955 Raymond Chandler: I paid a service charge on the bill… This service charge is supposed to take the place of tipping.

sex *n* (1929) sexual intercourse. Commonly in the phrase *have sex* (*with*)

> 1929 D. H. Lawrence: If you want to have sex, you've got to trust At the core of your heart, the other creature.

> 1962 *Listener*: Why wasn't Bond 'more tender' in his love-making? Why did he just 'have sex' and disappear?

> 1962 *Woman's Own*: Those trends in our society that make sex before marriage so easy.

sex appeal *n* (1924) attractiveness that arouses sexual desire. The daring new term was initially also used as a verb, but once the bloom had worn off this disappeared. See also **it (1904)** and **S.A. (1926)**

> 1924 *American Mercury*: An actress with sex appeal is four times out of five a more effective actress.

> 1924 G. R. Chester: She'd sex appeal me all right!

sexationalism *n* (1927) sexual sensationalism. This and the related *sexational* (1928) have become firm tabloid favourites

> 1927 *Time*: Newspaper sensationalism has developed into sex-ationalism.

> 1937 *Time*: Sexational, robustious Cinemactress Mae West appeared on a commercial broadcast for the first time in four years.

> 1976 *West Lancs. Evening Gazette*: 1st Blackpool showing of the Sexsational *Highway through the Bedroom* (X).

sexpert *n* (1924) an expert on sexual matters. There is no record of the term between the two examples quoted below, and it may well be that recent usage represents a re-coinage

> 1924 W. Fabian: The sexperts, which is a combination of sex and expert: I glued it together myself. Not so dim; yes?

> 1979 *Radio Times*: Every other interviewed sexpert seemed to come from California where…you can graduate in any old spurious subject.

sex urge *n* (1920) See **sex drive (1918)**

sexy *adj* (1925) concerned with sexual activity; sexually attractive. Colloquial. The first known record of the word is actually in a French text, in the sense 'about or full of sex' ('Depuis que Joyce a publié un livre qu'ils croient "sexy"—cet état d'esprit n'a pas d'équivalent français—on s'en empare…que sa méthode sert de modèle à des gens qui…se disent surréalistes', *La Nouvelle Revue Française* (1925)), but this is backed up by an instance of the derived noun *sexiness* from the same year

> 1925 *Glasgow Herald*: The stallion seems to vanish altogether near the end of the story, and the Welsh groom is put into prominence, with mere 'sexiness' thus supplanting magnificent vitality.

> 1928 *Sunday Dispatch*: Australian audiences…like sex plays, but they mustn't be too sexy.

S.F. *abbreviation* (1929) See **science fiction (1929)**

sheik *n* (1925) a strong, romantic lover; a lady-killer. A usage inspired by *The Sheik*, a bodice-ripping novel in an Arabian setting by E. M. Hull (1919), and more particularly by its film adaptation *The Sheikh* (1921), starring Rudolph Valentino, who made young womanhood of the 1920s swoon (despite being a closet gay)

> 1925 *Literary Digest*: We hear almost nothing more of the matinée idol any more… The 'sheik' has taken his place.

> 1932 Stella Gibbons: The mask smiled…from a great silver screen: 'Seth Starkadder in "Small-Town Sheik".'

shelf life *n* (1927) the length of time that a commodity can be kept for sale or stored without becoming unfit for use or consumption

> 1927 *Manufacturing Confectioner*: What is the shelf life of your hard candy?

shih-tzu *n* (1921) a small long-coated dog of Chinese origin. From Chinese, literally 'lion-son'

> 1921 V. W. F. Collier: These books [i.e. the imperial dog-books]…portray dogs closely resembling the 'Pekingese' type, as also the 'Shih-tzu' dog and the 'Pug'.

shimmy *v* (1923) to come or go unobtrusively or effortlessly; to glide. A coinage probably based on **shimmy (1918)** the dance, but also influenced by *shimmer*, which Wodehouse used in the same way ('Jeeves shimmered off, and Cyril blew in, full of good cheer and blitheringness' (1923))

> 1923 P. G. Wodehouse: I bounded into the sitting-room, but it was empty. Jeeves shimmied in.

shingle *v, n* (1924) (to cut a woman's hair in) a close-cropped layered style in which the hair is full at the back of the head and tapers in to the nape of the neck. The use of *shingle* in US English as a verb to denote the close cropping and laying of the hair (so as to resemble the 'shingles' or tiles on a roof) dates back to the mid 19th century, but as a name for this specific style it is characteristic of the 1920s. See also **bob (1918)** and **bingle (1925)**

  1924 *Hairdressing* (caption): Based on the 'shingle'.

  1924 *Punch*: It moves me not if Araminta shingles Her locks, or Evelina has them bobbed.

shotgun wedding *n* (1927), **shotgun marriage** *n* (1929) a forced marriage, especially due to pregnancy. Originally US. The underlying scenario is that the scandalized father or relatives force the groom to marry at gunpoint

  1927 Sinclair Lewis: There were, in those parts and those days, not infrequent ceremonies known as 'shotgun weddings'.

sidecar *n* (1928) a cocktail made of brandy and lemon juice with a dash of an orange liqueur. Presumably named after the vehicle attached to a motorcycle, but the reason behind the metaphor is not known

  1928 Sinclair Lewis: Mame took a Bronx, and Delmerine took a side-car.

skiffle *n* (1926) Formerly, in the US, a style of jazz music popular at rent parties, deriving from blues, ragtime, and folk music, and played on standard and improvised instruments. In the 1950s the term came to have slightly different connotations, especially in Britain (see **skiffle (1957)**). The ultimate origins of the word are unknown

  1926 (jazz-music title): Chicago skiffle.

  1930 *Paramount Dealers' List*: Home Town Skiffle—Part I. Descriptive Novelty—All Star.

skint *adj* (1925) having no money; broke. British slang. Originally a variant of the now obsolete *skinned* in the same sense, metaphorically 'stripped of money', which dates back at least to the early 19th century

  1935 George Ingram: Edina offered him a shilling. 'That's all right… I ain't "skint" yet.'

sky-writing *n* (1923) tracing of legible signs in the sky, especially for advertising purposes, by means of smoke trails made by aircraft. See also **sky-shouting (1932)**

  1926 H. Barr: Invented in 1910 by John Clifford Savage, it was not until twelve years later that sky-writing became an accomplished fact.

  1935 H. G. Wells: Sky writing by the new planes.

slalom *n* (1921) a race in which skiers go down a zigzag course between artificial obstacles, usually flags. A borrowing of Norwegian *slalåm*, which means literally 'sloping track'

  1927 Arnold Lunn: However, the Slalom was worth a trial, and in 1922 the Alpine Ski Challenge Cup became a Slalom race.

sleeping dictionary *n* (1928) a (temporary) sexual partner from whom one learns (the rudiments of) a foreign language. Euphemistic or humorous slang

  1928 J. B. Wharton: We picked up two beauties… Oo-la-la-I've learned French—out uv a sleepin' dictionary—dat's what dey're called.

slenderize *v* (1923) to cause to be or appear slender. Also used intransitively to mean 'to lose weight, so as to be thinner', but this usage seems not to have survived beyond the 1930s—perhaps driven out by **slim (1930)**

  1923 *Weekly Dispatch*: A slight figure will be more essential than ever. 'You must slenderise,' said one, coining a useful word.

  1923 *Daily Mail* (advert): Corsets for slenderising full figures.

slinky *adj* (1921) Of a woman: slim and felinely sinuous in movement; also applied to close-fitting female clothing that contributes to this effect. Colloquial

  1921 *Ladies' Home Journal*: Even now I seem to see in memory a slinky, slant-eyed person with long, slender finger nails, who wears green.

1923 *Glasgow Herald*: Jessica was swathed in a slinky gown of flat crepe in a deep blue shade.

smacker *n* (1920) a dollar or pound. Slang, originally US. The underlying idea is probably of slapping money down on to a counter or into an open palm

1920 *Chicago Herald & Examiner*: Along comes Earl Gray and knocks off the U.S. treasury for 13,000,000 smackers.

smash and grab *n, adj* (1927) a form of robbery in which the thief smashes a shop window and takes some of the objects on display. Popular with criminals in the 1920s and 1930s, before the technology of glass-toughening thwarted them. Their eventual riposte was the **ram-raid (1987)**

1927 J. C. Goodwin: 'Smash and Grab' raids seem to be the order of the day.

smash hit *n* (1923) a film, song, etc., which enjoys enormous popular success. Subsequently often also in the abbreviated form *smash*

1923 *Variety*: 'Rosie O'Reilly' and 'The Fool', Loop's Two Smash Hits.

1931 *Daily Express*: The magnates who had contracted to buy the picture indulged in fits of doubt concerning its prospects as a box-office 'smash'.

smellie *n* (1929) a (hypothetical) cinema or television film in which smell is synchronized with the picture. A mainly fanciful or facetious coinage based on **talkie (1913)**

1929 A. P. Herbert: These early smellies made a great sensation, particularly Fish, a strong story written 'around the life of a San Francisco fishwife of homicidal tendencies'.

1977 *Time*: Another treat in the works: smellies—a futuristic device attached to the [television] set will emit aromas into the living room.

so-and-so *adj* (1929) A euphemistic substitute for an abusive or obscene epithet. The parallel noun usage (as in 'You little so-and-so!') is first recorded in 1897

1929 Edgar Wallace: 'That's what we pay rates and taxes for, and no so-and-so policemen in sight!' He did not say 'so-and-so', but Mr. Reeder thought his profanity was excusable.

1959 *Listener*: Some [clients] are good, some are indifferent, some are a so-and-so nuisance.

social climbing *n* (1924) the attempt to advance oneself socially, especially by gaining acceptance in fashionable society. *Social climber* is more or less contemporaneous, and equally a put-down

1924 Winifred Holtby: The careful tact of years of social climbing.

1926 Sinclair Lewis: You sniveling little social climber!

Social Credit *n* (1920) a political theory put forward by the British engineer C. H. Douglas, according to which the supposed chronic deficiency in the purchasing power of consumers was to be remedied through a reduction of prices by means of subsidies to producers or through the giving of additional money to consumers. Subsequently used as the name of a Canadian political party which advocated the theory

1920 A. R. Orage: The effect is inherent in the separation of Real Credit from Financial Credit— Social Credit, that is to say, from Financial Credit privately controlled.

socialite *n* (1928) someone prominent in fashionable society

1928 *Time*: Splendorous as hostess & socialite was Princess Clara in both Germany and England.

social mobility *n* (1925) the possibility of movement between different social levels that exists in a society, or to different fields of employment or interest, or to new areas, within the same social level. A term coined by the sociologist P. A. Sorokin, and used by him as the title of a book in 1927. More academically respectable than the contemporaneous **social climbing**

1925 P. A. Sorokin: We used to think that in the United States 'social mobility' was greatest.

sonny boy *n* (1928) A term of address to a boy or young man. Originally made famous in a song of the same name by Al Jolson and others, but subsequently more widely used, often threateningly

1928 Al Jolson: Climb upon my knee, Sonny Boy; You are only three, Sonny Boy.

1955 William Gaddis: Lie back and don't try to remember everything now, sonny boy.

son of (1929) A common formula in the middle years of the century for the title of a sequel to a book or film, and hence used facetiously to designate a programme, product, institution, etc., that is a derivative of its predecessor

  1929 Edgar Rice Burroughs (title): Son of Tarzan.

  1934 *Picturegoer*: *Son of Kong*… By no means a second King Kong this picture, nevertheless, has some clever technical qualities.

  1966 Osmington Mills: I produced a scintillating piece of non-fiction called…*Elizabethan Domestic Drama*… I got a sequel—Son-of-Elizabethan-Domestic-Drama…—into print as well.

sophisticate *n* (1923) a sophisticated person. Originally US

  1923 Gertrude Atherton: All the Sophisticates (as Clavering had named them, abandoning 'Intellectuals' and 'Intelligentsia' to the Parlor Socialists) were present.

Soroptimist *n* (1921) a member of an international service club for professional and business women, founded in California in 1921. The word was coined from Latin *soror* 'sister', probably on the model of the *Optimist* Club, founded in 1911. The organization is roughly the women's equivalent of the Rotarians

  1921 *Charter* (Soroptimist Club, Oakland, California): Whereas, the persons who [sic] names appear at the foot hereof…having enrolled themselves as Charter Members of the Soroptimist Club (Oakland), [etc.].

soundtrack *n* (1929) the narrow strip at one side of a cine film that carries the sound recording. A term which soon became familiar to devotees of the new talking pictures

  1957 P. G. Wodehouse: This is not always the laughter of a real studio audience. Frequently, it is tinned or bottled. They preserve it on sound tracks, often dating back for years.

Soviet *n, adj* (1920) (a citizen) of the Soviet Union. See also **soviet (1917)**

  1920 *Commercial & Financial Chronicle*: [Clemenceau] insisted upon writing the final paragraph, 'affirming that the Allies had not changed their attitude towards the Soviets'.

  1920 *Russian Economist*: This is the secret of 'bourgeois' diplomacy, and this riddle is being solved by Soviet diplomacy and with it by all the Russian-speaking people.

spacesuit *n* (1929) a protective pressurized garment worn by someone going into space. Yet another instance of science fiction anticipating real life

  1929 *Science Wonder Stories*: Normal communication by speech would be impossible. Of course, this is not true of enclosed, air-filled rooms… But it is true when one is out 'in the open' (in the space suit).

  1962 John Glenn: G-suits are not to be confused with pressure suits (or, now, spacesuits) which the Astronaut wears during space flight to maintain atmospheric pressure at high altitudes.

speaker *n* (1926) Short for **loud-speaker (1920)**

  1926 *Journal of the Franklin Institute*: This speaker employs a six-inch cone driven by an electro-magnetic power unit.

speakie *n* (1921) a stage play in contrast to a (silent) film. A term apparently coined by the comedy film actor Charlie Chaplin, presumably based on **movie (1912)** and **talkie (1913)**. It did not survive very long, and by the end of its brief career it was being confused (understandably) with **talkie**

  1921 J. M. Barrie: The ordinary stage drama he [sc. Charlie Chaplin] called the 'Speakies'.

  1927 *Observer*: She prophesied the downfall of the 'speakies' and the triumphant survival of the 'movies'.

  1928 *Sunday Dispatch*: 'Talkies' or 'speakies' as they are calling them in Hollywood, have very definitely arrived.

speed cop *n* (1924) a police officer detailed to enforce traffic laws, especially a motorcycle patrolman. Colloquial

  1933 *American Speech*: His Grace, on being stopped, demanded 'Are you a speed-cop?' The patriotic magistrates fined him £10. 10s. and suspended his license for three months.

spermaticide *n* (1923), **spermicide** *n* (1929) a substance which kills spermatozoa, especially one used as a contraceptive. The earlier form was used, if not coined, by the birth-control pioneer Marie Stopes, but was eventually ousted by *spermicide* on, if the second quote below is to be believed, aesthetic grounds

> 1923 Marie Stopes: Of all the chemical substances used as spermaticides, undoubtedly quinine is in the most general use.

> 1931 *Journal of Hygiene*: The words 'spermicide' and 'spermicidal' are preferred, on grounds of euphony, to 'spermaticide' and 'spermaticidal'.

spin-dry *v* (1927) to remove excess water from (washing) by spinning it rapidly in a rotating perforated drum. The term *spin-drier* is not recorded before 1939

> 1927 *Saturday Evening Post*: It takes the Savage [Washer & Dryer] just one-tenth the time to spin-dry the entire load in its own tub.

> 1939 *Architectural Review*: The laundry is all electric, and is equipped with a Rotary Washer and Spin Dryer, and Rotary Ironer, in which all the laundry of the house can be done without resort to clothes lines.

squandermania *n* (1920) an insane desire or obsession to spend money recklessly. What could have been a short-lived journalistic coinage has proved to be a durable addition to the language

> 1920 *Public Opinion*: The public are deeply roused upon the Squandermania issue.

> 1976 *Times*: Sheer 'squander-mania'…has currently invaded our society.

Stalinism *n* (1927) the policies pursued by Josef Stalin (1879–1953), leader of the Soviet Communist Party and head of state of the Soviet Union, based on but later deviating from Leninism, especially the formation of a centralized, totalitarian, objectivist government. The derivative *Stalinite* is also first recorded in 1927, the longer-lived *Stalinist* in 1928

> 1927 *Daily Telegraph*: A violent denunciation of 'Stalinism' and its 'terrorising of the party'… The struggle between the Trotskists and the Stalinites.

> 1928 *Observer*: Open calculations measured in advance by the Stalinists.

starkers *adj* (1923) completely naked. British slang, based on *stark* (*naked*). It is first recorded in Joseph Manchon's 1923 French dictionary of English slang, *Le Slang*. See **preggers (1942)**

> 1952 Margery Allingham: We was all starkers and painted black.

starlet *n* (1920) a young promising performer, usually an actress, in the world of entertainment

> 1920 J. Ferguson: Some 'starlet' sings, Into the footlights' glare.

station wagon *n* (1929) a car with a rear door or doors, capable of carrying goods as well as passengers. Originally and mainly US. An adaptation to the motorized age of a term originally applied to a sort of horse-drawn vehicle used for conveying passengers to and from a railway station

> 1929 *New York Times*: The Ford Motor Company is having its own exhibition… The three new models added to the line are on display there. These are the town sedan, the convertible cabriolet, and the station wagon.

steamed up *adj* (1923) excited or roused, especially to anger. Colloquial

> 1923 H. C. Witwer: I was a bit steamed up about her making my popular sex ridiculous by going boy-crazy at fifty.

stereophonic *adj* (1927) giving the impression of a spatial distribution in reproduced sound; especially, employing two or more channels of transmission and reproduction so that the sound may seem to reach the listener from any of a range of directions. See also **stereo (1954)**

> 1927 *Wireless World*: A marked improvement in quality of reproduction will be noticed, due to the phase-difference introduced by the distance between loud-speaker and phones. This phase-difference also varies with the frequency of the sounds reproduced, and thus a constantly varying difference in phase produces the stereophonic effect so superior to ordinary reproduction.

strip *n* (1928) strip-tease. Originally US. See **strip-teaser (1930)**

> 1928 *Variety*: Why do women principals try to do strip numbers against the competition of experienced runway specialists?… Columbia, by the way, seems to be leery of the limit in strip at this telling.

strip *v* (1929) to perform a strip-tease. Originally US. See also **stripper (1930)**

> 1929 *Variety*: She has the unadornment stuff to herself, since the other gals never strip beyond regulation soub garb.

> 1939 James Joyce: She stripped teasily for binocular man.

struggle-buggy *n* (1925) a car, especially an old or battered one. US slang

> 1925 *College Humor*: I'll say you can park in my struggle buggy.

strut one's stuff (1926) to display one's ability. Slang, originally US

> 1926 Carl Van Vechten: Some one cried, Strut your stuff, Lasca!

sub-machine-gun *n* (1920) a light portable machine-gun firing ammunition of the same type and calibre as a pistol

> 1920 *Army & Navy Journal*: Colonel Thompson is now connected with the Auto-Ordnance Corporation of New York City, which has put the Thompson sub-machine gun on the market.

sugar-daddy *n* (1926) an elderly man who lavishes gifts on a young woman in return for (or hopes of) sexual favours. Slang, originally US

> 1935 P. G. Wodehouse: The morning papers had come aboard, reassuring citizens…that sugar daddies were still being surprised in love-nests.

sun-bather *n* (1929) someone who sits or lies in the sun (e.g. to get a tan). *Sun-bathing* is first recorded as long ago as 1600, and the now almost disused *sun bath* was quite common in the 19th century, but it was the 1920s that saw the beginnings of the 20th century's love affair with the sun ('If preparing for a sun-bath, a swim, or both, slip into the Jantzen Sun-suit!', advert, *Punch* (1929)). The verb *sun-bathe* (probably a back-formation) is first recorded in 1941

> 1929 *Daily Express*: The groups of Lido sun-bathers.

> 1941 Agatha Christie: I oiled myself and sunbathed.

sun-ray *adj* (1928) Denoting the therapeutic use of ultraviolet rays (see **artificial sunlight (1927)**)

> 1928 *Daily Express*: The speedy development of sun-ray clinics all over the country.

> 1930 M. Kennedy: I wonder if sunray treatment would do her good… Sir Ivor knew nothing of sun-ray, and he had no faith in doctors.

supercharger *n* (1921) a compressor that increases the pressure of the fuel-air mixture supplied to the cylinders of an internal-combustion engine. Derived from the verb *supercharge*, which is first recorded in 1919

> 1921 A. W. Judge: The power required to drive the supercharger is about 6 per cent.

super-ego *n* (1924) According to the theories of Sigmund Freud, that part of the psyche which acts as a conscience for the ego

> 1924 Joan Riviere [translating Freud]: Keep in mind this dissection of the mental apparatus that I have proposed, namely, into ego, super-ego and id.

super-giant *n* (1927) a very large star that is even brighter than a giant, in many cases despite being relatively cool

> 1927 H. N. Russell: Certain very bright stars, much more brilliant than the ordinary giants, are sometimes called super-giants.

superhighway *n* (1925) a multi-lane road for high-speed traffic. Originally US, and largely restricted to that variety until the last two decades of the century, when metaphorical use took it worldwide: see **information superhighway (1985)**

> 1925 *American City Magazine*: The Super-Highway is unique… It will furnish an express motor traffic highway.

supertanker *n* (1921) an oil-tanker of very large capacity (in late-20th-century terms, 275,000 tons or more)

> 1921 *Mex Fuel Oil* (Anglo-Mexican Petroleum Co.): These losses are being made good by the building of several supertankers, commencing with the San Florentino…18,000 tons.

surrealist *adj, n* (1925) (a practitioner) of a movement in art and literature evolving from Dada (see **Dada (1920)**) and seeking to express the subconscious mind by any of a number of different techniques, including the irrational juxtaposition of realistic images and the creation of mysterious symbols. The French term *surréalisme*, coined by Guillaume Apollinaire around 1917, was taken over by the poet André Breton as the name of the movement, which he launched with his *Manifeste du Surréalisme* in 1924. At first it and its derivative *surréaliste* were taken over in their French form into English, and it was not really until the 1930s that the anglicized versions we are familiar with today became established (*surrealism* is first recorded in 1931)

> 1925 Roger Fry: That beastly young Surrealist Masson.

> 1931 *French Review*: Since the opening of the twentieth century, only three schools have counted [in French literature], unanimism, between 1908 and 1911, surrealism, about 1924, and populism in 1929.

sweatshirt *n* (1929) a sort of long-sleeved cotton jumper. Originally US, but by the end of the century an almost universal item of casual wear

> 1929 *Sears, Roebuck Catalog*: Every Man and Boy Wants A Sweat Shirt.

sweetie-pie *n* (1928) A term of endearment which has survived to the end of the century

> 1928 P. G. Wodehouse: 'Hello, sweetie-pie,' said Miss Molloy.

swoose *n* (1920) a bird that is the offspring of a swan and a goose. Hybrid animals have been given hybrid names since ancient times (as witness *camelopard* for the giraffe, which struck early witnesses as being a cross between a camel and a leopard), but 20th-century skill in genetic manipulation has boosted the phenomenon (see also **tigon (1927)**, **liger (1938)**, **shoat (1969)**, and **geep (1971)**). Sightings of *swoose* crop up fairly regularly during the century (latterly mainly in Australia), but it is not clear whether they represent a continuous usage or successive reclonings

> 1920 *Daily Mail*: A bird prodigy of evil and hybrid character is the despair of a Norfolk farmer. It rejoices in the name of the 'swoose', a portmanteau word indicating its origin, for its father was a swan and its mother a goose. This ill-assorted pair had three children—three 'sweese'.

> 1976 *Sydney Sun*: Like the 'swoose' (a cross between a swan and a goose) the 'churkey' is a mythical bird.

tap dancer *n* (1927) an exponent of a form of exhibition dancing characterized by rhythmical tapping of the toes and heels, which became popular in the late 1920s. *Tap dancing* is first recorded in 1928

> 1927 *New Republic*: That fair singer, good tap-dancer, born-to-the-purple, bred-in-the-bone, works-while-she-sleeps comedian, the plump May Barnes.

> 1928 *Daily Express*: The inventor of tap dancing.

> 1929 Damon Runyon: Miss Billy Perry is worth a few peeks, especially when she is out on the floor of Miss Missouri Martin's Sixteen Hundred Club doing her tap dance.

Tarzan *n* (1921) a person, especially a man, of great strength, muscularity, or agility but limited intellect. Based on the name of a character in a series of novels (beginning with *Tarzan of the Apes* (1914)) by the American author Edgar Rice Burroughs (1875–1950), and in subsequent films and television series, who is orphaned in West Africa in his infancy and reared in the jungle by a mother-ape. The main connotation in the earliest recorded example (see the first quote below) seems to be the ability to swing agilely from branch to branch, but subsequently (probably because of the cinematic treatment of Tarzan) the word has come to imply more 'virility' and 'muscular development'

> 1921 *Glasgow Herald*: At fruit picking time there is a regular colony of Tarzans disporting themselves in the branches.

> 1938 Margery Allingham: Ramillies was ruddy pleased... Saw 'imself a Tarzan.

> 1981 Robert Barnard: Gordon began his morning liturgy of exercises... 'Bloody Tarzan,' said Brian.

tease *v* (1927) to do the strip-tease (see **strip-tease (1936)**). Also recorded in this year in the expression *tease number* 'strip-tease dance'. See also **cooch (1910)**

> 1927 *Variety*: Where they cooch in New York they 'tease' here... The four feminine principals alternated in 'tease' numbers with the help of the chorus.

> 1930 *Variety*: With a fair voice, a nice figure and lots of personality, Miss Almond clicked easily in her tease numbers.

teddy *n* (1924) a woman's undergarment combining chemise and panties. Originally and mainly North American. The origins of the term are unclear; it has been suggested that there might be some underlying reference to the shape (or lack of it) of a **teddy bear (1906)**

> 1924 H. C. Witwer: She added...she'd personally get enough enjoyment out of standing before her mirror garbed in a sheer silk teddy to warrant any sacrifice.

teenage *adj* (1921) Denoting someone in their teens. Originally North American. See also **teenager (1941)**

> 1921 *Daily Colonist* (Victoria, British Columbia): All 'teen age' girls of the city are cordially invited to attend the mass meeting to be held this evening.

teeth *n* (1925) power, especially the power of enforceablity by the exaction of penalties

> 1931 *Week-End Review*: It is even more urgent to take steps which will lead to the success of the Disarmament Conference next February than to 'give teeth' to the Paris Peace Pact.

teleplasm *n* (1927) An alternative name for **ectoplasm (1901)** which never enjoyed wide currency

> 1927 *Daily Express*: Teleplasm...was shown issuing from the face of the tranced woman.

teleprinter *n* (1929) a telegraph instrument for transmitting telegraph messages as they are typed on a keyboard and printing incoming ones

> 1929 *Telegraph & Telephone Journal*: The first Teleprinters to be tried in this country were produced by the Morkrum Corporation under the proprietary name of 'The Teletype'.

televise *v* (1927) to transmit or broadcast by television. A back-formation from *television*, based on other verbs ending in -*ise*, such as *revise*

> 1928 *Television*: The subject who is being 'televised' had to face a powerful battery of blinding lights.

televisor *n* (1926) a television. The name was applied to the form of television designed and patented by John Logie Baird (1888–1946), but when this failed to be adopted its name virtually died with it

> 1926 *Glasgow Herald*: The Televisor... The scene in front of the transmitting televisor is turned into electrical impulses.

> 1984 *Financial Times*: A rare John Logie Baird televisor of around 1930 sold for £1,760.

threads *n* (1926) clothes. Slang, originally and mainly US

> 1959 R. Bloch: Mitch got into some decent threads—he had this one blue suit and he wore a white shirt and a tie too.

throw-away *adj* (1928) designed to be thrown away after use. A convenient if glib metaphor for 20th-century civilization. See also **disposable (1943)**

> 1928 *Weekly Dispatch*: You can...clean your face at intervals with those throwaway hankies you buy from any chemist.

tigon *n* (1927) the offspring of a tiger and a lioness. A blend of *tiger* and *lion* which delighted the press when it first appeared, and far from being a lexical flash in the pan, is still in occasional use at the end of the century, along with its alternative formulations *tigron* and *tiglon*. See also **liger (1938)**

> 1927 G. Jennison: It should be noted particularly that the markings of the Tigon are not stripes, but rhomboids, almost like the markings on the Clouded Leopard.

> 1938 *Times*: The name liger is given to the offspring of a male lion and tigress, the opposite cross being called a tigron.

> 1947 *Partisan Review*: Mr. Gielgud's gravity, his sensitive, melancholy profile, here becomes exquisitely comic—he looks like a tiglon with a heart.

tinned *adj* (1924) Of music, laughter, etc.: mechanically or artificially reproduced. Historically the British equivalent of *canned* in all senses, but it never really took firm hold in this metaphorical application (see **canned (1904)**)

> 1924 John Reith: The sound is metallic and unsatisfying, and...we do not like our music tinned.

toffee-nosed *adj* (1925) snobbish, supercilious. Originally British services' slang (the quote below, and other sources, suggest R.A.F., but it is first recorded in Fraser and Gibbons's *Soldier and Sailor Words and Phrases*). Its origins are not entirely clear, but probably there is some pun on *toffy* 'grand, like a toff' involved

> 1928 T. E. Lawrence: A premature 'life' will do more to disgust the select and superior people (the R.A.F. call them the 'toffee-nosed') than anything.

toiletries *n* (1927) preparations for use in washing or grooming. Note the pseudo-French form in the first quote below

> 1927 *Glasgow Herald*: One really up-to-date shop coins a new and compact name for these indispensable odds and ends and calls them 'toiletteries'.

> 1927 *Hollis Street Theatre Programme* (US): Her keen individuality finds in the inimitable Djer-Kiss odeur a refreshing complement; she fastidiously insists upon it in all her toiletries!

tommy gun *n* (1929) a Thompson or other sub-machine-gun. Colloquial, originally US; associated initially with the extravagant fire-power of American organized crime in the interwar years. The designation *Thompson* (dating from 1919) commemorates the name of US General John T. Thompson (1860–1940), who conceived the gun and whose company financed it

> 1934 Ernest Hemingway: The nigger shot him in the belly with the Tommy gun.

totalitarian *adj* (1926) Denoting a regime or system of government which imposes a monolithic unity by authoritarian methods. An adaptation of Italian *totalitario* 'complete, absolute; totalitarian'. The noun *totalitarianism*, also presaging the era of European dictators, is first recorded in this year too

> 1926 B. B. Carter: Anti-Fascism…has, however, a positive sense if it is taken to represent an element antagonistic to the 'totalitarian' and absolute position of Fascism… This would mark the end of Fascist 'totalitarianism' and the renewal of political dualism.

traffic light *n* (1929) one of a set of changing coloured lights for the regulation of traffic; usually used in the plural. The term *traffic light* seems actually to have been coined by Rudyard Kipling. He used it in a futuristic story called 'As Easy as A.B.C.' (1912), and applied it to a light used for the guidence of aircraft ('They began turning out traffic-lights and locking up landing-towers'). This never caught on in real life, however. When the sort of traffic lights we are familiar with today were introduced after World War I, they were initially known as *traffic regulation lights* (1920), but the shorter form soon became established in general usage. See also **traffic signal (1917)**

> 1929 *Saturday Evening Post*: T is for Traffic Light, bane of all motorists.

trailer *n* (1928) an excerpt of a film, broadcast, etc., used as advance publicity

> 1930 *Dancing Times*: In a 'trailer' advertising the film, it is announced that the producers have aimed more at entertainment than historical accuracy.

transvestite *n* (1922) a person with an abnormal desire to wear the clothes of the opposite sex. An adaptation of German *Transvestit*, which was coined from Latin *trans*- 'across' and *vestire* 'to dress'. First recorded as an adjective in 1925. The related noun *transvestism* is first recorded in 1928 (the alternative *Eonism*, which was suggested by the sexologist Havelock Ellis—see the quote below— but never really caught on, was based on the name of the Chevalier Charles d'Éon (1728–1810), a French adventurer who wore women's clothes)

> 1922 J. van Teslaar: Among the transvestites (personifiers) we find the most pronounced examples of marked homosexuality and stressed bi-sexuality.

> 1925 A. L. Kroeber: The transvestite sexual perverts recognized by all North American tribes.

> 1928 Havelock Ellis: It was clearly a typical case of what Hirschfeld later termed 'transvestism' and what I would call 'sexo-aesthetic inversion', or more simply, 'Eonism'.

treen *n* (1927) wooden dishes and utensils. A pseudo-archaism dreamed up in the inter-war period, as the debased legacy of the Arts and Crafts movement filled bourgeois British homes with lumpy *objets d'art* in brass, copper, and dark wood. *Treen* as an adjective, meaning 'wooden', dates back to the Old English period; it is a derivative of *treow*, which meant 'wood' as well as 'tree'

1927 H. V. Morton: 'Before people used pewter for plates and tankards,' he explained, 'wooden trenchers, drinking cups and bowls—called "treen"—were used by everyone.'

tripe-hound *n* (1923) a contemptible person. A widely used term of abuse in the middle years of the century

1937 Ngaio Marsh: You damned little tripe-hound.

trolley-bus *n* (1921) a trackless passenger vehicle that gets its power from an overhead cable by means of a pole and a grooved pulley (known as a 'trolley'). A successor to trams on many urban streets in the middle of the century, and a familiar element of the London traffic scene

1921 *Daily Colonist* (Victoria, British Columbia): The trolley-buses...are of the single-deck type, with seats for twenty-four passengers.

T-shirt *n* (1920) a simple short-sleeved collarless garment for the upper body. Originally US. The first T-shirts were men's undershirts of this design, and they were so called because they formed the shape of a letter T when laid out flat

1920 F. Scott Fitzgerald: Amory, provided with 'six suits summer underwear...one sweater or T shirt...' set out for New England, the land of schools.

twelve-tone *adj* (1926), **twelve-note** *adj* (1928) Denoting music based on the atonal arrangement of the traditional twelve chromatic notes devised by Arnold Schoenberg; *twelve-tone* is the more usual US form, *twelve-note* the main British one. Schoenberg originally referred to his system in a letter dated December 1923: 'Mir handelt es sich ausgesprochen dabei um gar keine anderen Theorien, als um die Methoden der "Komposition mit 12 Tönen", wie ich das—nach vielen Irrtümern und Abschweifungen—heute (hoffentlich endgültig) nenne' ['..."composition with 12 notes", as I...today (I hope finally) call it']. See also **atonal (1922)**, **serial (1947)**

1926 *Modern Music*: [Schoenberg], too, is convinced that no tone of the twelve tone system should dominate and that the new structural elements should be sought in sequence of twelve tones.

two-time *v* (1924) to deceive (especially a person to whom one owes loyalty); to be unfaithful to (a spouse or lover). Slang, originally US. The ground had been prepared for the verb by the adjective *two-time* 'happening twice, double', which dates from the late 19th century

1924 J. Edwards: She'll two-time you like she double-crossed me.

ultrasonic *adj* (1923) faster than sound; also, using or operated by sound waves with a frequency above the range of human hearing. Both meanings are still in use, although **supersonic (1934)** is now more usual for the first

1923 *Proceedings of the Royal Society of Canada*: The wave-lengths of ultra-sonic waves are very convenient for experiment.

1923 *Proceedings of the Royal Society of Canada*: Two ultra-sonic generators...were placed facing one another, 60 cms. apart, in a large tank of water.

1985 *Sunday Times*: An ultrasonic beam passed through liquid generates bubbles which act as a cleansing agent.

unilateral disarmament *n* (1929) disarmament by one state, irrespective of whether others take similar action. Since the 1950s the term has come to imply specifically 'nuclear disarmament' (it is from around that time that the derivative *unilateral disarmer* begins to appear in the record)

1929 *Times*: Lord Salisbury agreed that unilateral disarmament had probably reached its limits.

1935 Clement Attlee: I want to recall to the House what our position is as a party on the question of defence... We do not stand for unilateral disarmament.

1960 *Guardian*: One can be a pacifist and a unilateral disarmer, prepared to accept the consequences for oneself and one's country.

1984 Sue Townsend: Went back to Pandora's and watched the Labour Party Conference vote for unilateral disarmament... If elected the Labour Party would chuck all their nuclear weapons away.

uplift *n* (1929) the support or lift gained from a garment that raises part of the body. Latterly associated particularly with advertisers' claims for the effect of bra on bust, but that was not the original connotation in the flat-chested 1920s

1929 *Radio Times*: A supporting stocking… Its gentle uplift massaging action has a beneficial effect upon the varicose veins.

1959 *Housewife*: The bra that gives a natural uplift.

usherette *n* (1925) a female usher in a cinema or theatre. Originally US

1926 *Bulletin*: Thirty beautiful girls…will receive visitors to…the Plaza, at its opening on Tuesday. They will be called 'usherettes'.

valve set *n* (1929) a radio in which amplification is effected by means of valves. Compare **crystal set (1924)**

1929 *Radio Times*: Her nursery…is wired for broadcasting and…her movements or cries are now heard loud in the sitting-room…where our valve set is placed.

vampish *adj* (1922) characteristic of a **vamp (1911)**

1922 Sewell Ford: I have got something more over the footlights than just my ankles and a few vampish hip motions.

V.D. (1920) An abbreviation of *venereal disease*. This term had its origins in the 17th century, but then and for some time afterwards it denoted specifically 'syphilis'. Its institutionalization as a general word for all sexually transmitted diseases may be signalled by the appearance of this euphemistic abbreviation

1920 *Annual Report of the Chief Medical Officer, Ministry of Health*: V.D. clinic. Suggested plan of arrangement of a…hut.

1920 F. Fox: I do not know where the idea sprang from that v.d. was very common in the Army.

Vegemite *n* (1923) A proprietary name (registered in Australia in 1923) for a type of spread made from a concentrated yeast extract. A prototypical Australian foodstuff, on which all Ockers are weaned. The word was coined from *vegetable* and the final syllable of **Marmite (1907)**

1990 *Times*: Australia: I acclimatized on the plane by spreading the Vegemite thick.

virgin *n* (1923) a cigarette made of Virginia tobacco. Short-lived British slang

1940 Graves & Hodge: In the early Twenties…in offering a cigarette-case one would say, 'I hope you don't mind: it's only a Virgin.'

Vitaphone *n* (1926) A name (based on Latin *vita* 'life') given to a process of sound film recording in which the sound track was recorded on discs and played in synchronization with the projection of the film. It was used for what is generally acknowledged to be the first 'talkie', *The Jazz Singer* (1927) starring Al Jolsen, but it was not a long-term success, other systems involving a soundtrack proving more effective (see **Movietone (1927)**, **phonofilm (1921)**, **soundtrack (1929)**)

1926 *Westminster Gazette*: A method of talking-motion pictures has been developed in America. The invention is called the vitaphone… It is claimed that the synchronisation of picture and voice…is perfect.

vo-do-deo-do *n* (1927) A meaningless jazz refrain (with many variations) that often puts in an appearance in popular songs of the late 1920s and 30s. It is first recorded in the 1927 song *Crazy Words, Crazy Tune* by J. Yellen: 'Sings the same words to ev'ry song. Vo-do-de-o. Vo-do-do-de-o-do'. Often used adjectivally to designate a style of singing or a song characterized by speed, energy, and the repetition of such a refrain or insistent rhythm

1934 Constant Lambert: The most irritating quality about the Vo-dodeo-vo, poop-poop-a-doop school of jazz song is its hysterical emphasis on the fact that the singer is a jazz baby going crazy about jazz rhythms.

1937 Noël Coward: Slick American 'Vo do deo do' musical farces, in which the speed was fast, the action complicated, and the sentimental value negligible.

voguish *adj* (1927), **voguey** *adj* (1928) that is in vogue or temporarily fashionable. *Voguish* has stood the test of time rather better than *voguey*

1927 *Daily Express*: Hundreds of the voguish Jumper Suits await your selection.

1928 *Observer*: An achievement…which steers a happy course between the 'arty' and the 'voguey'.

Volstead (1920) The name of Andrew J. Volstead (1860–1947), American legislator, originator of the legislation to enforce prohibition which was passed in 1919 by the US Congress, used to designate this legislation or the period during which prohibition was in force. The noun *Volsteadism*, denoting 'prohibition', is also first recorded in 1920. See also **Prohibition (1922)**

> 1920 *Current Opinion*: The Wet leaders…will wage a campaign for the election…of Congressmen favorable to changes in the Volstead Act.

> 1920 *Harvey's Weekly*: The Republicans would have to stand for Volsteadism or incur defeat.

voyeurism *n* (1924) gratification gained from observing the sex organs or sexual activities of others. A derivative of **voyeur (1900)**. See also **scoptophilia (1924)** and **scopophilia (1937)**

> 1924 J. S. van Teslaar: *Voyeurism*, erotic gratification experienced at looking at another's sexual organs; morbid desire to peep into secrets.

wah-wah, wha-wha *n* (1925) a musical effect gained by applying a mute to a brass instrument and then rapidly withdrawing it. Originally a jazz musician's term, imitative of the sound itself, and first recorded in a musical direction in the score of Gershwin's *Rhapsody in Blue*

> 1925 George Gershwin: Wha Wha effect.

> 1926 H. O. Osgood: Then there is the clown of mutes. Leading philologists of the jazz world are at odds over the correct spelling of the name; some favour wow wow, others prefer wha wha, but there is authority for the simplification wa-wa.

Wall Street crash *n* (1929) the collapse of the American stock-market which took place in October 1929

> 1929 *New York Times*: Commenting on the Wall Street crash of yesterday, the German press unanimously agrees that Germany has no reason to mourn.

war to end war(s) *n* (1921) a war which is intended to make (or assumed to have made) subsequent wars impossible. A term usually applied, with a naive optimism, to World War I, probably on the model of H. G. Wells's *The War that Will End War* (1914)

> 1921 George Bernard Shaw: There was a war called the War to End War. In the war which followed it about ten years later, none of the soldiers were killed; but seven of the capital cities of Europe were wiped out of existence.

> 1949 Ernest Benn: If…war debts between nations had been wiped off the slate, and reparations in money never attempted, the 'war to end war' might have achieved its high purpose.

> 1967 Walter Lippman: Each of the wars to end wars has set the stage for the next war.

watch in *v* (1928) to watch television. An extremely short-lived alternative to **look in (1927)**

> 1928 *Daily News*: Pictures by Wireless. Where to 'watch-in' this week…Watchers-in will be able to judge for themselves the value of picture transmissions during this week.

water waving *n* (1925) a method of waving hair with water. The early part of the century delighted in exploring new techniques for mitigating nature's cruelty in giving a woman straight hair in an age of waves (see also **marcel (1906)** and **perm (1927)**)

> 1925 *Daily Telegraph*: Wanted, smart man… Must be thoroughly competent in perm. waving, Marcel and water waving.

wavicle *n* (1928) an entity (e.g. an electron or a photon) having characteristic properties of both waves and particles.

> 1928 Arthur Eddington: We can scarcely describe such an entity as a wave or as a particle; perhaps as a compromise we had better call it a 'wavicle.'

weepie *n* (1928) a sentimental film, story, play, etc.; a tear-jerker. Colloquial, presumably modelled on **talkie (1913)** and the like

> 1928 *Sunday Dispatch*: There are undoubtedly times when a film calculated to raise buckets of tears has its appeal. Someone recently christened this type of picture…a 'weepie'.

well- *combining form* (1921) Used in designating health-care facilities dedicated in particular to preventive medicine. Originally North American. The initial combination was *well-baby*; *well-woman* did not come on the scene until the 1970s

1921 *Daily Colonist* (Victoria, British Columbia): A well-baby clinic will be held at the Saanich Health Centre…An invitation is extended to all mothers to bring their infants.

1977 *PEN Broadsheet*: A range of leaflets on contraceptive methods, well-women care, sex-related diseases.

white dwarf *n* (1924) a faint highly dense star towards the end of its life

1924 *Monthly Notices of the Royal Astronomical Society*: The white dwarfs Sirius (*comes*) and O$_2$ Eridani.

1925 *Nature*: Invoked to decide the truth of a suspicion of transcendently high density in the 'white dwarf' stars, [Einstein's theory of gravitation] has decided that in the companion of Sirius matter is compressed to the almost incredible density of a ton to the cubic inch.

white line *n* (1924) a narrow white strip painted on the road surface to guide or direct motorists, especially one that separates adjacent traffic lanes

1924 *Oxford Times*: The experiment of the white line, which has proved so successful in encouraging the careful driving of motors round corners in Worcestershire, might with advantage be tried in this district.

whoopee *n* (1929) a lively or rowdy party. Short-lived slang of the Bright Young Things. An adaptation of the exclamation *whoopee!*, which is now most familiar in the expression *make whoopee* 'to have a boisterous good time'. This first appears in G. Kahn's 1928 song *Makin' Whoopee* ('Another bride, another June, Another sunny honeymoon, Another season, another reason for making whoopee!'), but there it means 'to make love'; it is not recorded in its modern sense until the early 1930s

1929 *Punch*: A London hostess, writing to a gossip page, said—'I am giving a Whoopee. Do come to it.'

1930 Evelyn Waugh: Noel and Audrey are having a little whoopee on Saturday evening.

wimp *n* (1920) a feeble, spineless, or ineffectual person. Colloquial, originally US. The origins and development of the word remain something of a mystery. There is one isolated example of it from 1920 (see below), but then it disappears from view in print until the 1960s. This fleeting early appearance is, however, supported by a sighting of the derived adjective *wimpish* in 1925. It would seem that *wimp* lay relatively dormant for about forty years, before undergoing a sudden surge of popularity in the early to mid 1960s, which has sustained it in widespread use until the end of the century. It infiltrated British English in the 1970s. Its source has never been definitely established, but the likeliest explanation is that it is a back-formation from *whimper*; there appears to be no connection with **wimp (1923)**, which is exclusively British. See also **wimpy (1967)**

1920 George Ade: Next day he sought out the dejected Wimp.

1925 Sinclair Lewis: They looked like lunching grocers: brisk featureless young men;…wimpish little men with spectacles, men whose collars did not meet.

1984 *Sunday Telegraph*: In daily life Ronnie Lee is a wimp. Put him in a balaclava and he thinks he's a he-man.

wimp *n* (1923) a woman. British slang. The only record of it is in dictionaries or books of slang (none later than 1950), and its origins are murky: conceivably it was just an alteration of *woman*. What was presumably the same word is reported by Morris Marples in his *University Slang* (1950) as having been 'used as a verb at Oxford *c*. 1917, e.g. *to go wimping*' (i.e. 'to go chasing women')

withdrawal symptoms *n* (1924) unpleasant physiological reactions resulting from the process of ceasing to take an addictive drug. See also **cold turkey (1921)**

1924 *British Journal of Inebriety*: The withdrawal symptoms of addiction disease.

work to rule (1927) to work strictly according to all the rules of one's job, however trivial, as a form of industrial action. Mainly British. The noun *work-to-rule* is first recorded in 1940

1927 W. E. Collinson: The inconveniences of lightning-strikes, ca' canny policy (deliberate restriction of output) and working-to-rule.

wow *n* (1920) a sensational success. Slang, originally US. From the exclamation *wow*

1920 *Collier's*: In Round Five they stalled some more… The sixth innin' was a wow!

Wurlitzer *n* (1925) The proprietary name of various musical instruments made by the Rudolf Wurlitzer Company of Cincinnati, Ohio. The name was registered in 1926, but with a claim of use since 1857. It was originally associated most closely with player-pianos, but as the century progressed it came to connote chiefly a type of large electric organ, known as the 'Mighty Wurlitzer'

> 1925 Theodore Dreiser: A Victrola and Wurlitzer player-piano furnished the necessary music.

> 1980 *Times*: The daily organ recital on what must be the world's best known Mighty Wurlitzer.

yippee *interj* (1920) An exclamation of delight or excitement. Originally US

> 1920 Sinclair Lewis: She galloped down a block, and as she jumped from a curb across a welter of slush, she gave a student 'Yippee!'

yobbo, yobo *n* (1922) a lout, a hooligan. Slang. An extended form of *yob*. This originated as a back-slang version of *boy* in the middle of the 19th century, and its modern negative connotations do not seem to have become established until the 1920s

> 1922 *Contemporary Review*: To him the boys are always the 'yobos'.

> 1960 *News Chronicle*: The local Teddies and yobbos swing their dubious weight behind the strike.

zap (1929) Used to represent the sound of a ray gun, laser, bullet, etc. A key representative of the iconic onomatopoeic language of US comic book fiction which has entered partially into the mainstream of 20th-century English

> 1929 P. F. Nowlan: Ahead of me was one of those golden dragon Mongols, with a deadly disintegrator ray… Br-r-rr-r-z-zzz-zap.

Zinoviev letter *n* (1924) a letter published in the British press in 1924 as having been sent by Zinoviev (the assumed name of Y. A. Radomyslsky (1883–1936)), a Russian statesman, to British Communists and urging them to commit subversive acts; it was later discovered to be a forgery

> 1924 *Times*: If the Zinovieff letter is a forgery, it shows the amount of scoundrelliness with which we are surrounded.

zip fastener, zip fastening *n* (1927), **zip** *n* (1928) a zipper. The more usual British versions of the word

> 1927 *Daily Express*: Many of the new sports suits have zip-fasteners.

> 1927 *Daily Express*: The airwoman's costume of tango suède, complete from the zip fastening to the little hat…is attracting many admirers.

> 1928 E. M. Forster: He felt the shirt…and he gave the zip at the throat a downward pull.

zipper *n* (1925) a form of fastener for clothes, luggage, etc., consisting of two flexible strips with interlocking projections closed or opened by a sliding clip pulled along them. Originally US. *Zipper* was registered in the US as a trade mark in April 1925 (with use of the term claimed since June 1923), but in the sense 'boots made of rubber and fabric'. It is no longer a proprietary term in any of its uses

> 1925 *Harper's Bazaar* (advert): A 'zipper' closing bag sometimes used to carry champagne.

> 1925 *Scribner's Magazine* (October, advert): No fastening is so quick, secure, or popular as the 'zipper'.

The 1930s The 1930s
The 1930s The 1930s The
1930s The 1930s The
1930s The The 1930s
The 1930s The The

The
1930s

After the febrile gaiety of the 1920s, the gloom—the hangover, almost—of the 1930s. It was a decade constantly in waiting, it seemed, for the fate which seemed certain to befall it: a renewed conflagration in Europe, which would perhaps consume the whole world. From the *Depression* at its beginning to *World War II* at its end it was a dark and fearful time, and this is reflected in the vocabulary of the era.

1930 found the world in the depths of an economic slump. Jolted by the spasm of the 1929 Wall Street crash, which stifled economic activity in the US, the world's industry and trade slowed down to danger levels, and millions were thrown out of work. It was the era of *skid row* and of *Hoovervilles*, and also of the remembered danger of *hyperinflation*. Steps were taken—there was *reflation*, and in the US Roosevelt's *New Deal*—but far-reaching damage had been done: in Germany, the Depression contributed to the rise of Hitler's Nazi movement.

English-speakers became familiar in the 1930s with a large amount of new terminology emanating from Germany, which by the end of the decade would send a chill down their spines. They read of *brownshirts* and *swastikas*, of the *gestapo* and the *Third Reich*. They were introduced to the concept of the *Aryan*, and the cult of the *Führer* and his *Hitlerite* followers. Above all they learned the word *Nazi*, which came to stand as the symbol of the evil which overtook Europe and the rest of the world.

In the other side of the scales were *appeasement* (a term first used at the end of World War I) and diplomacy. Internationalism was refining itself and producing ambitious new terminology: this was the age of *co-existence*, of *collective security*, of *defence*, of *power politics*—of a *brave new world*, even. But it all came to nothing at *Munich*. As the world prepared for war in 1939, it could look back on a shoddy decade of *fellow travellers* and *fifth columnists*, of *show trials* and *stateless persons*.

By the time hostilities actually started, the 1930s had a mere four months left to run. But so well anticipated was the event that a good deal of later familiar wartime vocabulary was already in place. Various aspects of *civil defence* had been dinned into people. They knew all about *air-raid precautions* (for instance, the *black-out*). They were prepared to be chivvied into their *Anderson shelters* by *air-raid wardens* if the threat of German *dive-bombing* became reality. They realized they might be *evacuated*, or have *evacuees billeted* on them. Perhaps they had heard the new term *Blitzkrieg* too, although they could scarcely have realized what significance it would hold for many of them by the end of 1940.

Some of the hardware of war had introduced itself, too—*Bren guns* and *Asdic, ack-ack* and *flak*, the new *interceptor* fighters, and the mysterious and ominous *secret weapon* (product of the 1930s *arms race*). Chillingly, *germ warfare* announced its presence as well. The concepts of the *partisan* and of *resistance* were in place by 1939, as was *scorched earth*.

Against this background of menace and fear, what did people do to cheer themselves up? New forms of mass entertainment were coming of age in the 1930s. There were talking pictures and the wireless, and by the end of the decade public television broadcasting had begun. For the first time in Britain, filmgoers were visiting *Odeons* to see all the *Oscar*-winners from Hollywood (or perhaps a more modest locally produced *quota quickie*). They also had the chance to drop in casually to a *news theatre* to catch the latest newsreel or cartoon, or even a *documentary*. On the wireless, *soap operas* were in the US starting their extraordinary march towards the centre of people's lives, and *newscasters* and *sportscasters* were bringing the most up-to-date world developments into their homes. The *crooners'* latest offerings could be heard, as could *commercials*, with their catchy *jingles*. If you wanted to make your own musical selection, you could use the new *record players* and *radiograms*, *juke boxes* and *nickelodeons*, and the *tape recorder* was making its debut. Those fortunate enough to have television sets could *view* the novel *telecasts*, and rejoice in being the first *televiewers*.

If live entertainment was what you wanted, you could go and see a *musical*, or a *revusical*. And for more active involvement still, there was no shortage of new dances in the 1930s, from the *jitterbug* and the *jive*, the *Lindy hop* and the *Susie Q*, to the more homely *conga*, *palais glide, Lambeth Walk*, and *Knees up, Mother Brown*. For those whose inclination was more voyeuristic than participative, there were the new *fan dancers* and the even more daring *striptease* dancers. Or you could simply stay at home and play *Monopoly*—or manipulate your *yo-yo*.

Key elements of later 20th-century underwear terminology fell into place in the 1930s: *bras, briefs*, and *underpants* all put in their first appearance, not to mention the *negligee*. The concept of *casual* clothes was born, and that powerful icon the *twin set* came on the scene. The *trouser suit* and *platform soles* were heard of briefly, before disappearing until the 1970s—a resurrection not to be achieved by the *co-respondent shoe*. Cosmetic innovations included *eye shadow* and *lip gloss*. But undoubtedly the major newcomer in the fashion field was *nylon*, first of the man-made fibres which were to transform the clothes we wear in the second half of the 20th century.

Fashions in food were not ripe for change yet. A trickle of adventurous new items was maintained—*courgettes, pasta, pizzas*—but the *burger* is probably the most influential gastronomic contribution of the 1930s. *Scampi* were exotic novelties, and *muesli* was still on the wilder shores of vegetarianism. There were *fruit gums* and *Mars bars* for the kiddies, *Gibsons* and *gin-and-its* for the grown-ups; *Rice Krispies* for breakfast and *rock salmon* for supper. *Lounge bars, milk bars*, and *snack bars* catered for every taste. And before the decade was over, the first of the wartime make-do foodstuffs had appeared—*macon* and *Spam*. But the most telling pointers to humanity's eating habits in the second half of the 20th century were *quick frozen* food and *supermarkets*.

The internal-combustion engine was tightening its stranglehold on Western society. To placate it, we built *dual carriageways* and *clover leaves, lay-bys* and *traffic islands, car ports* and *drive-ins. Parking meters* made their debut, in the US, while in Britain *Belisha beacons* sprouted on city streets. The concept of the *learner* (*driver*) emerged, and the *drunkometer* was tried out as a solution to *drunk driving*.

Science uncovered *mesons, neutrinos,* and *positrons,* and put a name to *deoxyribonucleic acid.* In the field of *nuclear physics, fission, heavy water,* and *deuterium* anticipated the exploding of the first atomic bomb, while the *Turing machine* gave a theoretical foretaste of the computer. The terms *electron microscope, polythene, satellite, semiconductor,* and *test-tube baby* all made their first appearances, and a new planet was named—*Pluto.*

The 1930s were the decade of the masses, of unified populaces. In a highly regimented society, large numbers of people could be affected at a stroke: *mass observation, mass hysteria, mass murder.* There were *social services* for the *underprivileged, marriage guidance* for unhappy couples, and lessons in *parentcraft* for anxious mothers- and fathers-to-be. The appearance of *dailies* and *baby-sitters* reflected the post-World War I servant problem, and hinted at further *embourgeoisement* to come. Whether you lived in an *open-plan* house, a *studio flat,* or a *Tudorbethan* villa, mod cons such as *washing-up machines, sink units,* and *electric blankets* made up for the absence of domestic help.

The 1930s were also the decade that produced perhaps the most notorious of the century's euphemisms, *senior citizen.* It signalled the growing difficulty the 20th century experienced in referring to old age, just as *underprivileged, slow learner,* and *defence* indicated that we were becoming squeamish about poverty, lack of intelligence, and the use of military power. Other circumlocutions, though, like *smallest room,* looked back to Victorian embarrassments.

The slang of the 1930s looked in two directions too. The likes of *feeding, oojah-cum-spiff,* and *shy-making* conjure up a passing British era, but in the jazz clubs of the US, Black English was brewing up *cool, groovy, hep cat,* and *send,* which in the 1940s and 50s would be on the lips of the young all round the English-speaking world.

Abyssinia *interj* (1934) goodbye. Slang, originally US; a facetious pun on *I'll be seeing you*, possibly given a boost by the Italian conquest of Abyssinia (Ethiopia) in 1935. As a live usage it barely survived the decade. See also **see you later, alligator (1957)**

> 1939 M. Harrison: 'Coming, young Figg?'... 'Well, I'll be back.' 'Abyssinia!' said Mr. Flowerdew.

ack-ack *n* (1939) anti-aircraft gunfire, or an anti-aircraft gun. Originally an abbreviation of *anti-aircraft*, using the then current military signalling code *ack* for the letter *a*

> 1939 *Collier's*: One unscheduled move and the machine would have been blown from the air by those long, lean guns the British call Aak Aaks, signalers' code for anti-aircraft.

> 1940 R. Walker: Engine failure due to ack-ack fire.

ackamarackus *n* (1933) pretentious nonsense, bullshit. Slang, originally US; usually in the phrase *the old ackamarackus*. Apparently a fanciful pseudo-Latin coinage, possibly by the US author Damon Runyon, who is responsible for the earliest recorded examples of it

> 1934 Damon Runyon: This is strictly the old ackamarackus, as the Lemon Drop Kid cannot even spell arthritis.

affirmative action *n* (1935) positive action by employers to ensure that minority groups are not discriminated against during recruitment or employment. US; not in widespread use until the 1960s

> 1935 *New York Times*: If...the Board shall be of the opinion that any person...has engaged or is engaging in any such unfair labor practice, then the Board shall...issue...an order requiring such person...to take such affirmative action, including reinstatement of employees with or without back pay, as will effect the policies of this Act.

> 1961 *New York Times*: The contractor will take affirmative action to ensure that applicants are employed, and that employees are treated, during employment, without regard to their race, creed, color or national origin.

Aga *n* (1931) A proprietary name, registered in 1931, for a type of large cooking stove or range burning solid fuel and (later) gas or oil. An acronym formed from the initial letters of Swedish *Svenska Aktienbolaget Gasackumulator* 'Swedish Gas Accumulator Company', the original manufacturers. See also **Aga saga (1992)**

> 1938 Louis MacNeice: Four Siamese cats, very large, sat on the Aga cooker.

air-conditioning *n* (1930) the process of cleaning air and controlling its temperature and humidity before it enters a room, building, etc. The term had been in use since the first decade of the century with reference to various industrial processes, but it was not until the 1930s that it (and derivatives such as *air-conditioned* and *air-conditioner*) became familiar in the context of controlling (and particularly cooling) indoor human environments

> 1930 *Engineering*: Air-conditioning is dealt with fully, with the methods for washing, cleaning, humidifying, cooling and drying the air.

> 1935 *Burge Complete Book of Aviation*: Air conditioners have been designed to supply fresh air, and to maintain a comfortable cabin temperature while a machine is on the ground.

> 1937 *Times*: The trustees of the National Gallery will discuss a scheme to air-condition the gallery.

air hostess *n* (1934) a female flight attendant on a passenger aircraft. It gradually superseded the earlier **stewardess (1931)**. The abbreviated **hostess** is first recorded in 1936, the sexless **flight attendant** not until 1947

> 1934 *Baltimore Sun*: The air hostess was the overnight guest of Captain and Mrs. W. O. Schrum.

> 1939 *Flight*: The K.L.M. has found it wiser to employ stewards rather than Air Hostesses on the London line.

air-raid precautions *n* (1935) measures (especially legally enforceable ones) taken to minimize casualties and damage in the event of an air-raid (e.g. extinguishing lights—see **black-out (1935)**). More generally known in Britain during World War II by the abbreviation *A.R.P.*

> 1935 *Lancet*: Mr. Mander asked the Home Secretary the precise nature of the work to be carried out by the Home Office Air-raids Precautions Department at 5, Princes-street, Westminster.

1937 *Lancet*: A.R.P. These sinister initials are being made more and more familiar by a spate of books on air-raid precautions.

air-raid warden *n* (1936) a person responsible for the enforcement of air-raid precautions, and for providing help in the event of an air-raid

1936 *Lancet*: Each subdivision being required to make its own plans for police and fire brigade services, rescue, [etc.]…and air-raid wardens.

algorithm *n* (1938) a process, or set of rules, usually one expressed in algebraic notation. Contemporary usage in the fields of computing, machine translation, and linguistics dates from around 1960. In origin the term is a variant of *algorism*, a word of Arabic ancestry denoting the Arabic system of numbers

1938 Hardy & Wright: The system of equations…is known as Euclid's algorithm.

1960 E. Delavenay: *Algorithm* or *algorism*…, used by computer programmers to designate the numerical or algebraic notations which express a given sequence of computer operations, define a programme or routine conceived to solve a given type of problem.

American dream *n* (1931) the ideal of a democratic and prosperous society which is the traditional aim of the American people; a catch-phrase used to symbolize US social or material values in general

1931 J. T. Adams: If the American dream is to come true and to abide with us, it will, at bottom, depend on the people themselves.

anal *adj* (1930) of the second stage of Freud's suggested process of libidinal development (lasting from about the age of eighteen months to three years), dominated by toilet training; hence, displaying character traits thought to result from fixation at this age, such as obsessive orderliness, parsimony, or obstinacy. See also **anal eroticism (1913), anal retentive (1958)**

1930 W. Healy: The 'anal character' was the first to be discovered and investigated.

1990 *Premiere*: As long as we're being anal about it, the guest that Monday was not Sammy Davis, Jr., but Flip Wilson.

Anderson shelter *n* (1939) a small prefabricated air-raid shelter devised by Mr. (later Sir) William Paterson, a Scottish engineer, and adopted in Britain while Sir John Anderson was Home Secretary (1939–40)

1939 *New Statesman*: Goats sheltered from high explosive in Anderson shelters were claimed to be quite unhurt.

1940 *New Statesman*: Where's my rabbits?…Kept 'em in the Anderson.

appease *v* (1939) See **appeasement (1919)**

arms race *n* (1936) competition between unfriendly nations or other groups in the accumulation and development of weapons. A phenomenon which, in its modern form, probably dates from the years preceding World War I, but was first conceptualized, or at least lexicalized as *arms race*, in the 1930s, when the world was again arming itself for coming conflict. It persisted into the Cold War, in the context of nuclear weapons

1936 *Hansard Commons*: This House cannot agree to a policy which in fact seeks security in national armaments alone and intensifies the ruinous arms race between the nations, inevitably leading to war.

1964 *Annual Register 1963*: In a speech of 10 June…Mr. Kennedy called for a halt to the arms race.

Aryan, Arian *adj, n* (1932) In Nazi ideology, (a member) of a Caucasian Gentile race, especially of a Nordic type. The term originally denoted the precursor of the languages spoken in most of modern Europe and parts of southwest Asia and India, which would now be called *Proto-Indo-European*. It came to be applied to the speakers of this language, and in the 19th century it was taken up by various nationalistic historical and romantic writers. It was given especial currency by M. A. de Gobineau, who linked it with the theory of the essential inferiority of certain races. The Nazis revived and distorted it in the 1920s

1932 Louis Golding: What you and many of your followers imagine is the Arian manner.

> 1933 W. Norman Brown (title): The Swastika, a Study of the Nazi Claims of its Aryan Origin.

> 1933 *Times* (translation of Hitler's *Mein Kampf*): The exact opposite of the Aryan is the Jew.

Asdic *n* (1939) an echo-sounding device for the detection of submarines. An acronym formed from the initial letters of the somewhat inelegant *Allied submarine detection investigation committee*

> 1939 *War Illustrated*: Asdic…mentioned by Mr. Churchill in one of his speeches…[is] a type of secret apparatus now used by the Navy.

Asian *adj* (1930) of Asia. Not strictly speaking a new usage—it has been around since at least the 16th century—but it had always been relatively unusual. The standard term had been *Asiatic*. However, this was coming to be seen as offensive or discriminatory by some Asians (see the second quote below), and gradually, over the middle decades of the century, it went out of use, to be replaced by *Asian*. At the end of the century it had a distinctly dated feel

> 1930 *Kenya Legislative Council Debates*: The first thing I notice about the motion is the word 'Asian'. I have tried to look it up, but I can find no dictionary which gives it—it is usually 'Asiatic'.

> 1953 *Times Literary Supplement*: Asian Review… After 68 years of existence the widely circulated quarterly hitherto known as the *Asiatic Review* makes a slight but important change of designation. The reason is to be found in the sensitiveness of the cultured classes of Asia about nomenclature… The term 'Asiatic' has come to be regarded with disfavour by those to whom it applied, and they feel entitled to be brought into line with usage in regard to Europeans, Americans and Australians.

audio-visual *adj* (1937) Denoting material such as gramophone records, tape recordings and various visual aids used as an adjunct to teaching

> 1937 Townsend & Stewart (title): Audio-visual aids for teachers.

autopilot *n* (1935) A concertinaed version of **automatic pilot (1916)**

> 1935 *Flight*: No information is available concerning the degree of accuracy which the 'Autopilot' will give in bumpy weather.

Axis *n* (1936) the political association of 1936 (becoming in 1939 a military alliance) formed between Italy and Germany; later extended to that between Germany, Italy, and Japan

> 1936 *Times*: The 'Rome-Berlin axis' is a conceit which has its momentary attractions.

> 1942 *Times Weekly*: The 26 anti-Axis nations are united…in the broad conduct of the war.

baby-sitter *n* (1937) someone who looks after a child while its parents are out, especially in the evening. Originally US. The derived verb *baby-sit* is first recorded in 1947. By the 1960s *sit* was being used on its own with the same meaning, and later in the century it began to attach itself to other objects of guardianship (mainly in *house-sit*)

> 1937 C. R. Walker: There are two high-school girls in the neighborhood who hire out for twenty-five cents an evening as 'baby sitters' when the family wants to go to the movies.

> 1947 in *American Speech* (1949): Offer to 'baby sit' with her little boy.

> 1966 John Gloag: He wondered if Willy would be able to get Mrs Hillman in to sit. Friday was a bad night.

bale out, bail out *v* (1930) to parachute from an aircraft, especially in an emergency. Originally US. The original spelling, and one still widely used in US English, was *bail*, as if it were based on the idea of ladling out, as in a waterlogged boat; the *bale* spelling relies on the idea of letting a 'bale' or bundle through a trapdoor

> 1930 C. J. V. Murphy: Some say the pilot 'bailed out' the moment he went into the spin.

> 1939 F. D. Tredrey: If you bale out and land in water…a smart rap will release the whole lot and you can swim free.

balls-up *n* (1934) a confusion, a muddle, a mess. Slang; perhaps from *ball up* 'to entangle, muddle up, confuse, spoil' (which dates from the 19th century), but with a strong hand played by *balls* 'testicles, nonsense'

> 1945 *Penguin New Writing*: 'What d'you make of this case, corporal?' 'Bleeding balls-up, between you and me.'

banana republic *n* (1935) a small state, especially in Central America, whose economy is almost entirely dependent on its fruit-exporting trade. Colloquial; the term's usual connotations are of capricious and unstable government, with frequent revolutionary punctuations

> 1935 *Esquire*: We strung along with Major Brown on the inhuman aspects of war in the banana republics.

barbecue *n* (1931) a grill or similar apparatus for cooking food over an open fire of wood or charcoal, usually out of doors. The word goes way back, to late-17th-century America, when it was applied to a sort of makeshift wooden frame for sleeping on ('[We] lay there all night, upon our Borbecu's', William Dampier (1697)). It came ultimately from an indigenous Caribbean language. Its use as a frame for grilling or roasting is first recorded in the 18th century, but the object which modern mankind would recognize as a barbecue is a 20th-century phenomenon. See also **barbie (1976)**

> 1931 *Sunset* (heading): How to build a barbecue.

> 1986 *Practical Householder*: The delicious aroma drifting across a neighbour's fence of food cooking over charcoal is enough to make anyone yearn for a barbecue of their own.

bathysphere *n* (1930) a spherical diving apparatus for deep-sea observation. The 'Greek prefix' mentioned in the quote below comes from *bathus* 'deep'. See also **bathyscaphe (1947)**

> 1930 W. Beebe: When I was writing the name of a deep-sea fish—*Bathytroctes*—the appropriateness of the Greek prefix occurred to me: I coined the word *Bathysphere*, and the name has stuck.

battery *n* (1931) a series of hutches, cages, or nesting-boxes in which laying hens are confined for intensive laying or poultry reared and fattened. In the second half of the century the term absorbed all the negative connotations of modern industrialized agriculture (see **factory farming (1964)**)

> 1931 G. W. Wrentmore: The system is best carried out with birds that have been in Batteries from the start.

> 1953 A. Watkyn: It ain't right to ask 'uman beings to live like Battery Hens.

Belisha beacon *n* (1934) a post about seven feet high surmounted by a flashing amber-coloured globe and erected on the pavement in Britain at officially recognized pedestrian crossings of the highway. Named after Leslie Hore-Belisha, Minister of Transport 1931–7

> 1934 *Punch*: One of the clever people who have been going about stealing and even shooting the Belisha Beacon globes—(1) 'as a protest against their futility'; (2) 'because they slow down the traffic'.

benzedrine *n* (1933) a type of amphetamine drug. Registered in 1935 as a proprietary name, based on *benzoic* and *-edrine* (as in *ephedrine*)

> 1933 *Lancet*: A new drug has recently been introduced into rhinology under the name of benzedrine. It is a synthetically prepared compound, the carbonate of benzyl-methyl-carbinamine, which is described as a racemic mixture of bases having the formula $C_6H_5CH_2.CH.NH_2.CH_3$.

berk *n* (1936), **burk, burke** *n* (1938) a fool. British slang; short for *Berkeley* (or *Berkshire*) *hunt*, rhyming slang for *cunt*. No doubt current well before the 1930s, but publishers were shy of committing such words to print. The spelling *burk(e)* was presumably influenced by the surname *Burk(e)*

> 1936 James Curtis: 'The berk.' Jealousy and savage contempt blended in the Gilt Kid's tone.

> 1938 Walter Greenwood: 'Stick the burke in a taxi,' he said.

billet *v* (1936) to assign quarters to (civilian evacuees). Often used with *on*. Used especially with reference to children evacuated from British cities during World War II

> 1936 in R. M. Titmuss (1950): The evacuation of London needs to be thought out in terms, not of transport only but of reception, housing (by compulsory billeting if necessary) and feeding.

> 1939 *Punch*: It was when you first heard that little Sidney and the others were to be billeted on you.

billetee *n* (1939) a person who is billeted. British

> 1939 *Times*: Mrs. Miniver...will cope in a wonderful manner with refractory billetees.

> 1958 D. Wallace: A lot of our dear billettees weren't even house-trained.

bingo *n* (1936) a game (often played in public halls, etc. for prizes) in which numbers are called out at random and the winner is the first person to cross off all the corresponding pre-numbered squares on his or her card. The name, which presumably came from *bingo* the exclamation of pleasurable surprise, originated in the US; it was not until the 1950s that it began seriously to spread to British English, where hitherto the game had usually been called **housey-housey (1936)**. The game itself is a slightly modified version of what had previously been known as *lotto* or *tombola*

> 1936 *Time*: In many a U.S. Catholic diocese during the past few years the simple gambling game of bingo…has served as a prime money-raiser.

> 1949 Noel Streatfeild: Such heavenly things were happening on deck… There was a game called Bingo.

> 1953 *Oxford Mail*: For some time now Bingo drives have been gaining in popularity at Oxford social gatherings. Bingo…is very closely akin to what used to be known as 'Housey Housey'.

biomass *n* (1934) the total weight of the organic substance (e.g. plankton) or organisms in a particular area

> 1934 B. G. Bogorov: Weighing is the main method of obtaining the biomass. The conception 'biomass' may be applicable also to the quantity of substance, characteristic for a given species at its different stages of development.

black market *n* (1931) unauthorized dealing in commodities that are rationed or of which the supply is otherwise restricted. After a slow start in the 1930s, mainly in the area of currency dealing, the term really took off in the disrupted economic circumstances of World War II and its aftermath, when items notionally rationed or unobtainable could often be bought if you knew the right person and had the right money. It was at this point that a range of derivative terms appeared, such as *black marketer, black marketeer*, and *black marketeering*, as well as the concertinaed form **blacketeer (1942)**. See also **spiv (1934)**

> 1931 *Economist*: The growth of an unofficial or 'black' market in sterling exchange.

> 1941 *New Statesman*: There is evidence of a 'black market' where food can be bought without restriction if the price is high enough.

> 1942 *New Republic*: The most skilled black marketer…is the sort of man who used to be a confidence man or other City hanger-on.

> 1942 *New Statesman*: If Jewish black-marketeers flourish in England, it is an indication of the inefficiency of the Government in checking this pursuit.

> 1942 *Times Literary Supplement*: The profits of black marketeering.

> 1943 E. M. Almedingen: People black-marketed in currency, in timber…in leather and in steel.

black-out *n* (1935) the extinguishing, covering, or obscuring of lights as a precaution against air-raids, etc.; also applied to the resulting darkness. A derivative of the verb **black out (1919)** in the same sense; it came into its own during World War II, when British civilians became used to dark streets and windows heavily muffled against the escape of even a chink of light

> 1935 *Lancet*: Mr. Harcourt Johnstone asked the Prime Minister whether instructions for compulsory 'black-outs' in districts where experiments were being carried out against air attacks were issued by authority of any Government department.

> 1940 *Annual Register 1939*: Of the inconveniences the most serious continued to be the 'black-out'.

blasé *adj* (1930) bored or unimpressed through over-familiarity. A borrowing suited to the world-weariness and cynicism of post-war society. In French it originally meant 'exhausted by enjoyment, sated'

> 1930 Noël Coward: Don't laugh at me, you mustn't be blasé about honeymoons just because this is your second.

Blattnerphone *n* (1931) an early type of tape recorder, which recorded on magnetic steel tape (see **tape recorder (1932)**). Named after its inventor, L. Blattner (1881–1935)

> 1931 *Wireless World*: A few days ago I was privileged to see and hear the Blattnerphone in operation.

Blimp *n* (1934) a character (in full *Colonel Blimp*) invented by the cartoonist and caricaturist David Low (1891–1963), pictured as a rotund pompous ex-officer voicing a rooted hatred of new ideas. A reactionary militaristic figure who struck a chord in 1930s Britain, to the extent of inspiring adjectives such as *blimpish* and *blimpian* and nouns like *blimpery* and *blimpism*. The ultimate inspiration for the term was the tubby airship of the same name (see **blimp (1916)**)

> 1934 *Evening Standard*: Prime Minister Blimp: 'Gad, sir, the Air League is right. We must oppose all proposals for the abolition of military aviation.'

> 1937 George Orwell: Easy to laugh at…the Old School Tie and Colonel Blimp.

> 1938 *New Statesman*: The modern clothes Hamlet at the Old Vic has excited a lot of Blimpish indignation.

> 1943 Cecil Beaton: Blimpism, plus the Cairene climate, are two of Hitler's strongest weapons.

Blitzkrieg *n* (1939) an attack or offensive launched suddenly with great violence with the object of reducing the defences immediately—a tactic (supported by dive-bombing and rapid armoured advances) successfully deployed by Germany in invading its neighbours in the early years of World War II. In German the word means literally 'lightning war'. See also **blitz (1940)**

> 1939 *War Illustrated*: In the opening stage of the war all eyes were turned on Poland, where the German military machine was engaged in *Blitz-Krieg*—lightning war—with a view to ending as soon as possible… Everything was ready for the opening of the 'Blitzkrieg' on the West.

B.O. *n* (1933) See **body odour (1933)**

bobby pin *n* (1936) a kind of sprung hair-pin or small clip, originally for use with bobbed hair. US. See also **bobby socks (1943)**

> 1936 J. Lawrence: She wondered whether she had lost all the bobby-pins from her marcelled hair.

bodyline *adj, n* (1933) Denoting intimidatory short-pitched fast bowling directed at the batsman's head or upper body. The term had its genesis in the threat posed by Donald Bradman, the most prolific batsman of all time. Desperate for a way to get the Australian out cheaply, Douglas Jardine, appointed captain of the M.C.C. team to tour Australia in 1932–33, fixed on this idea of fast leg-theory, with several fielders close in on the leg side to catch the ball as the batsman fended it off. It was to be carried out by Harold Larwood, one of the fastest bowlers ever, and Bill Voce. Predictably, several Australian batsmen were hit (although not Bradman), and the Australian board of control protested strongly (see the quote below), using the new and graphic term *bodyline*

> 1933 *Times*: The Australian Cricket Board of Control has sent the following telegram to the M.C.C.: 'Body-line bowling has assumed such proportions as to menace the best interests of the game, making the protection of his body by a batsman his main consideration [etc.].'

body odour *n* (1933) the smell of the human body, especially the unpleasant odour of stale sweat. A 20th-century advertisers' euphemism, used in the promotion of soap, deodorants, etc. (the earliest recorded example (see the quote below) is from *Murder Must Advertise* by Dorothy Sayers, who had herself been an advertising copy-writer). Best known in the abbreviated form *B.O.*, first recorded in the same year

> 1933 Dorothy Sayers: Do you ever ask yourself about Body-Odour?

> 1933 *Saturday Evening Post*: Those 'B.O.' ads. I laughed at—is the joke on *me*?

bourgeoisification *n* (1937) See **embourgeoisement (1937)**

boxer *n* (1934) a smooth-coated, square-built, fawn or brindle breed of dog of the bulldog type, originating in Germany. English acquired the word from German, which in turn had borrowed it from English, from *boxer* 'fighter'—an allusion to the dog's pugnaciousness

> 1934 *Hutchinson's Dog Encyclopaedia*: Boxer. This dog, which appears to derive from the 'Dogues' that had been made use of, during past centuries, for animal-baiting, is very little known in Britain.

bra *n* (1936) a brassière (see **brassière (1909)**). Originally a colloquial abbreviation, but quickly established as the standard term. At first, *bra* vied with *bras* (pronounced /bræz/), as in the first quote below, but it was not a prolonged contest

> 1936 W. B. M. Ferguson: She wore nothing but a 'bras', the briefest of French knickers, and the sheerest of white silk hose.

> 1936 *New Yorker* (advert): Bras...50 c.

> 1937 *Night & Day* (advert): The Bra is one of the famous 'Alphabet' Bra's.

brave new world *n* (1933) a society in which 'progress' has produced a nightmarish 'utopia'. Ultimately the expression comes from Shakespeare's *Tempest* 5:1 ('How beauteous mankind is! O brave new world, that hath such people in't'), but it was Aldous Huxley's use of it as the title of a novel (1932), a fable about a future scientifically trouble-free but stultifying and alienating society, that propelled it into the language

> 1933 *Annual Register 1932*: The driving force that sweeps Mr. Huxley on to presenting every nook and cranny of his Brave New World to the fiercest light of inquiry is the heart-corroding disgust he feels for human society as it will become according to his vision.

> 1935 H. G. Wells: I will *go* for this Brave New World of theirs—tooth and claw.

bread *n* (1935) money. Originally US criminals' slang. Suggested by the synonymous *dough*, which dates from the mid 19th century

> 1952 *Down Beat*: If I had bread (Dizzy's basic synonym for loot) I'd certainly start a big band again.

Bren gun *n* (1937) a type of light quick-firing machine-gun. The name was coined from Brno, the town in Czechoslovakia where the gun was first produced, plus the first syllable of Enfield, the north London borough (then in Middlesex) housing the British Royal Small Arms Factory

> 1939 *War Illustrated*: A long train of Bren gun carriers is passing towards the front.

briefs *n* (1934) very short knickers. See also **panties (1908)**, **underpants (1931)**

> 1934 *Books of To-Day*: I'm bored to tears with 'scanties', I'm sick to death of 'briefs'.

> 1959 Margot Neville: Cathy, in minute briefs and bra, struggling into her dress.

brown-shirt *n* (1932) a member of the Sturmabteilung, a Nazi German militia founded in 1921, reorganized by Ernst Röhm in 1930, and notorious for its violent methods; so called from the brown shirt worn as part of the uniform. See also **blackshirt (1922)**

> 1932 *Observer*: The concession made to Herr Hitler's brown shirts.

> 1939 R. C. K. Ensor: The heavy jack-booted hero afterwards idolized by the Brown-shirts.

bubble dancer *n* (1936) See **fan dancer (1936)**

bubble-gum *n* (1937) chewing-gum which can be blown into large bubbles. Originally US. (The term *chewing-gum*, incidentally, is first recorded in 1850)

> 1937 *Night & Day*: Bubble Gum...is particularly intriguing.

bug *n*, *v* (1935) (to equip with) a hidden microphone or other listening device. Originally US; a development of the slightly earlier sense '(to equip with) a burglar alarm'

> 1946 W. L. Gresham: That would have been a beautiful place to plant a bug if you wanted to work the waiting room gab angle.

> 1949 *Times* (Los Angeles): Cohen seemed well aware that his house was 'bugged' and that his conversations were tapped.

bulldozer *n* (1930) a heavy caterpillar tractor fitted with a broad steel blade in front, used for removing obstacles, levelling uneven surfaces, etc. Originally US. A transferred use of a 19th-century US slang term which meant 'a strong-arm man who coerces people with threats of violence'. The element -*dozer* was subsequently used in the names of other similar heavy vehicles, such as *angledozer* (1940), and also colloquially as a synonym for *bulldozer* itself

> 1930 *Water Works & Sewerage* (US): The bulldozer is built for heavy duty.

> 1942 *Infantry Journal* (US): The blade of the dozer is not much good.

bumf, bumph *n* (1930) excessively bureaucratic and boring documents, memos, forms, etc. British colloquial; an ironic diversion of the earlier meaning, 'toilet paper' (first recorded in 1889), which gives a clue to the word's origin: short for *bum fodder*

> 1938 Evelyn Waugh: I shall get a daily pile of bumf from the Ministry of Mines.

bum-freezer *n* (1932) a short jacket, particularly of the kind worn by schoolboys at Eton. Jocular British slang

> 1955 Howard Spring: A nice little Eton suit—what Greg inevitably called my bum-freezer.

burger *n* (1939) a hamburger. The term *hamburger* (or in full *hamburger steak*) is first recorded in 1889. By the 1930s its last two syllables were being used as a suffix in the names of various similar products with different ingredients (e.g. *nutburger* (1934), *chickenburger* (1936) ('The barbecues which began to dot the country with the rise of the automobile soon offered chickenburgers as well as hamburgers', H. L. Mencken (1936)), *cheeseburger* (1938), *porkburger* (1939)), and by the end of the decade it had become a word in its own right. The syllable *ham-* no doubt encouraged this proliferation, although of course there is no ham in a hamburger; its name comes from the German city of Hamburg. See also **beefburger (1940), Vegeburger (1972)**

> 1946 *American Speech*: Burger, hamburger sandwich. 'Burger steak' is hamburger steak.

> 1966 Truman Capote: 'Perry, baby,' Dick said, 'you don't want that burger. I'll take it.' Perry shoved the plate across the table.

burk, burke *n* (1938) See **berk (1936)**

café society *n* (1937) a group of people who frequent fashionable restaurants, night-clubs, and resorts. Originally US

> 1937 *Fortune*: A blending of old socialites and new celebrities called Café Society.

car-port *n* (1939) a car shelter, open at the side or front, adjoining or built into a house. Originally US

> 1939 *Life*: At the left is the 'carport' which opens on main entrance of building.

cartophilist *n* (1936) someone who collects, arranges, and studies cigarette-cards and similar items as a hobby. The word was based on French *carte* or Italian *carta* 'card'. Cigarette-cards (small picture cards inserted in cigarette packets to encourage sales) had been around for some time (the term is first recorded in 1902), but their heyday was probably the 1930s and '40s. This was when the mania for collecting them (*cartophily*, also dating from 1936) was at its height

> 1936 C. L. Bagnall in *Cigarette Card News*: 30,000 people in the British Isles…collect cigarette cards… I have coined a new word for my clients and call them cartophilists.

> 1936 *Morning Post*: There is a magazine entirely devoted to 'cartophily'… For every one serious 'cartophilist' in 1930 there are 25 now.

casual *adj* (1939) Of clothes: suitable for informal wear

> 1939 M. B. Picken: Casual, designed for easy, informal wear; of sports or semi-sports type; as, a casual coat.

> 1952 *Evening News* (advert): 560 Prs. casual shoes.

cat *n* (1931) a jazz enthusiast or performer. Originally US jazz slang, and presumably a specialization of the earlier *cat* 'fellow, guy' (1920). It subsequently spread into general youth slang, with musical connotations wider than just jazz, and in the 1950s became familiar in British English. See also **hep-cat (1938)**

> 1932 *Melody Maker* [quoting Louis Armstrong]: All the cats were there.

> 1935 *Down Beat*: The slanguage of swing-terms that 'cats' use.

> 1955 Shapiro & Hentoff: Minton's was just a place for cats to jam… When you went in you'd see cats half-stewed who weren't paying much mind to what was happening on stage.

> 1958 *Woman's Own*: 'It's got beat and a lot of excitement,' said one teenage 'cat' I talked to.

> 1958 *Observer*: On one side was the frenetic…bumptiousness of the rock-'n'-rollers, on the other the calculated indifference of the cool cats.

cheeseburger *n* (1938) See **burger (1939)**

cheesecake *n* (1934) photographs of sexually attractive young women scantily clothed. Slang, originally US

> 1934 *Time*: Tabloid and Heartsmen go after 'cheesecake'—leg-pictures of sporty females.

chicken *adj, n* (1933) (someone) cowardly. Slang, originally US. *Chicken* was used as a slang term for 'coward' in the 17th and early 18th centuries ('*Gib*. You assure me that Scrub is a Coward. *Bou*. A Chicken, as the saying is', George Farquhar, *The Beaux' Stratagem* (1706)), but this seems to have died out (although it has left us *chicken-hearted* (1681)). The 20th-century usage is apparently a completely independent development. See also **chicken out (1941)**

> 1933 Boehm & Gelsey: Ain't turnin' chicken, are ya?

> 1938 Wilbur & Sherman: You guys have turned out to be a fine bunch of chickens.

> 1952 Stanley Ellin: You'd just holler for the cops? Why, man, you're chicken.

civil defence *n* (1939) the organization and training of civilians for the preservation of lives and property during and after air raids or other enemy action

> 1940 *Annual Register 1939*: Some 20,000 men and women, representing every branch of Civil Defence.

clip-joint *n* (1932) a club, bar, etc., charging exorbitant prices. Slang, originally US. The underlying idea is probably that customers have their money 'clipped' off them, as if with a pair of scissors

> 1933 S. Walker: The worst creature, of all the army of parasites who carried on their trade along Broadway during the speakeasy period, was the proprietor of the 'clip joint'… The clip joint preys on the New Yorker and the out of town sport alike.

clover-leaf *n* (1933) a system of intersecting roads from different levels, in form resembling a four-leafed clover. Originally US. The idea behind it is to avoid interrupting traffic flow at busy junctions by means of curving access and exit roads. The pattern, strikingly photogenic from the air, quickly became a signature of the new road systems being built in the US and Germany

> 1937 *Times*: For straight cross-roads where traffic is heavy and the amount of turning traffic considerable, the 'clover-leaf' type of bridge system used both in America and Germany would…justify the expense.

cocktail cabinet *n* (1933) a cupboard, often of vulgar design, in which alcoholic drinks are kept. A term which hijacks the 1920s sophistication of *cocktail* (see **cocktail party (1928)**) for an article of furniture which may contain anything from a decanter of whisky to a half-empty bottle of faded sherry

> 1958 *Times*: He can afford to buy, on hire purchase, telly, cocktail cabinet, and washing machine.

> 1968 *Listener*: A friend likened it [i.e. a vacuum cleaner] to a property speculator's cocktail cabinet.

coelacanthid *adj, n* (1939) (a fish) of the family *Cœlacanthidæ*, characterized by a hollow spine. Long thought extinct, a coelacanth was discovered off the coast of South Africa in 1938. The word *coelacanth* itself (from the Greek for 'hollow spine') is first recorded in 1857

> 1939 *Nature* (caption): Coelacanthid fish from East London, South Africa.

co-exist *v* (1931) Of opposing political or economic systems: to exist side by side peaceably, with neither trying to obliterate the other. The term is particularly applied to the simultaneous existence of capitalist and communist systems, and was foreshadowed by Lenin in 1920: 'You ask me about our plans in Asia. They are the same as in Europe: peaceful, neighbourly life with all peoples; with the workers and peasants of all nations.' It, and especially its derivative *co-existence*, really came into prominence during the Cold War, notably in the phrase *peaceful co-existence*

> 1931 *Economist*: The question may then well arise whether the plan-economy of Russia and the capitalist economy of Western Europe can co-exist in amity.

> 1955 Harry Hodgkinson: Co-existence or 'peaceful co-existence'… The phrase…does not mean 'living peaceably together'. It is compatible with propaganda against, isolation from and peripheral risings against the non-Communist world.

1957 *Listener*: We have not yet achieved a way of coexisting in real peace with the Soviet Union.

collective security *n* (1934) a system by which international peace and security are maintained by an association of nations

1934 Winston Churchill: The great principle of collective security…is the only principle that will induce hon. Gentlemen opposite to make any preparation for the defence of this island.

colour *n* (1938) picturesque, evocative, and authentic but extraneous detail

1938 Evelyn Waugh: We're paid to supply news… Of course there's colour. Colour is just a lot of bull's-eyes about nothing… They gave Jakes the Nobel Peace Prize for his harrowing descriptions of the carnage—but that was colour stuff.

coloured *n* (1938) a dark-skinned person, especially a black. In South Africa applied specifically to a person of mixed race, constituting a distinct grouping under the apartheid laws

1938 N. Devitt: The bulk of the menial labour is done by coloureds who are not highly paid for their services.

1965 *Listener*: In his own country [he] will put on his 'to let' signs 'no coloureds please'.

colour supplement *n* (1939) a supplement in a newspaper, etc., containing coloured illustrations. By the 1960s the term had acquired the connotation 'sophisticated lifestyle'

1939 D. A. Spencer: For editorial illustrations in the colour supplements of newspapers, this lack of subtlety is of little account.

1965 *New Statesman*: Brainwashed into cultural coolness by Sunday papers and colour-supplements.

1966 *Listener*: The young Poles long for western luxuries like cars and clothes and the other bonuses of colour-supplement living.

commercial *n* (1935) an advertisement broadcast on radio or television. Originally US

1935 *Fortune*: We used no media other than radio to feature this soup…using one-third of our commercials on Campbell's Chicken Soup.

1942 *Quarterly Journal of Speech*: The mixture of ghastly, forced gayety and jolly-doggism in this commercial makes it a comic example.

conga *n* (1935) a Latin-American dance of African origin, usually performed by several people in single file and consisting of three steps forward followed by a kick. Often resorted to, especially in the middle decades of the century, when a party reached a particular level of conviviality. The word comes from American Spanish *danza Conga*, the dance from the Congo. Also used as a verb

1935 *Dancing Times*: The 'Conga' is not a ball-room dance, at any rate in Cuba.

1941 J. Cavanaugh: I came, I saw, I conga'd; It's plain to see you conquered me.

1958 *Times*: Nor was he above leading a 'Conga' through the halls and corridors of Buckingham Palace.

cool *adj* (1933) Used as a term of approval. The history of *cool* in the 20th century is somewhat complex. It first emerged recognizably with the meaning 'excellent, wonderful' in US Black English in the interwar years, but it is not entirely clear where this came from. Perhaps it was a development of an earlier US slang sense 'shrewd, clever', which itself probably evolved from general English 'impudent'. It reached a wider audience via jazz musicians after World War II, by which time it was being overlaid with connotations of 'laid-backness' (this was probably a jazz contribution) and of 'fashionableness' or 'stylishness' (harking back to an earlier sense 'suave, sophisticated', which itself grew out of 'shrewd, clever'). It was a core item of youth slang in the 1940s and 50s (e.g. in expressions like *cool cat*). As is usually the case with such items, the next generation found it laughably passé, but it made a comeback towards the end of the century. See also **supercool (1970)** and **cool Britannia (1993)**

1933 *American Negro Stories*: Sho wisht [his wealth] wuz mine. And whut make it so cool, he got money 'cumulated. And womens give it all to 'im.

1948 *New Yorker*: The bebop people have a language of their own… Their expressions of approval include 'cool'!

1953 *Time*: The latest Tin Pan Alley argot, where 'cool' means good, 'crazy' means wonderful.

> 1958 *Observer*: On one side was the frenetic…bumptiousness of the rock-'n'-rollers, on the other the calculated indifference of the cool cats.

> 1959 *Observer*: They got long, sloppy haircuts and wide knot ties and no-press suits with fat lapels. Very cool.

> 1999 Eddie Izzard: Be cool you kids!

> 1999 *Observer*: 'They [i.e. interactive Teletubby dolls] are extremely cool,' says Strommen, a designer at Actimates. 'I consider them to be the best toy we've done'.

cope *v* (1934) to deal competently with a particular problem, or with the problems of life in general. Essentially a back-formation from *cope with*, which dates from the 17th century

> 1934 Elizabeth Bowen: Angela rang the bell wildly for someone to come and cope.

> 1958 Ivor Brown: 'She suffers from copelessness.' I have heard this said of an unsatisfactory employee. The use of cope as a verb by itself to describe dealing with all kinds of situations is a recent usage. In my youth we tried, or were told to try, to cope with this or that problem. We were not required to cope in general.

core curriculum *n* (1935) that part of a school curriculum which is essential or compulsory as opposed to that which is optional. Originally US. Long restricted to the technical jargon of educationists, the term entered the public domain in British English towards the end of the century, in the wake of education reforms carried out by the Thatcher and Major governments

> 1935 *Californian Journal of Secondary Education*: 'Shall there be a core curriculum in secondary schools?': a symposium.

co-respondent shoes *n* (1934) A jocular name for men's two-toned shoes of a type fashionable in certain quarters in the interwar years. From the idea of them being worn by the type of man who gets cited in divorce cases. From an end-of-century perspective they are more comical or preposterous than louche

> 1934 A. G. Macdonell: A pair of those singularly repulsive shoes of black and white which are called 'Co-respondents' (quite wrongly called, incidentally, for co-respondents at least get and give some fun, and these shoes do neither).

courgette *n* (1931) a variety of small vegetable marrow. Still a novelty to the Anglophone world in the early part of the century, and liable to be italicized as a foreignism (it comes from French, a diminutive of *courge* 'gourd'). The more usual American and Australian term for the vegetable, *zucchini*, is first recorded in 1929

> 1931 E. Lucas: *Courgettes* may be…treated in the same way as vegetable marrows.

> 1951 Elizabeth David: You can bring back…baby *courgettes* or marrows.

> 1958 *Sunday Times*: A luncheon…starting with courgettes stuffed with shrimp.

crooner *n* (1930) a male vocalist who sings popular sentimental songs in a low, smooth voice, especially into a closely held microphone

> 1933 *Punch*: Bing Crosby the crooner…croons to his feminine class and is crooned to in reply.

> 1954 *Granta*: Dickie Valentine turns out, from his old cuttings, to be a crooner, as I had suspected.

crumpet *n* (1936) women regarded as (potential) sexual partners. British slang; the origin is unclear, but it probably comes from a male equation of sexually available women with toothsome delicacies (as with *tart*). Towards the end of the century it came to be applied even-handedly to men

> 1936 James Curtis: Fancy staying up as late as this and not having no crumpet.

> 1987 *Observer*: His performance as a trendy and hung-up LA painter in 'Heartbreakers' made him the thinking woman's West Coast crumpet.

cull *v* (1934) to select and kill (wild animals or birds), usually in order to improve the stock or reduce the population. A usage which arose out of *cull* 'to pick out livestock according to quality', employed in Australian and New Zealand animal husbandry circles since the late 19th century. It did not become widely known until the 1960s, when its euphemistic overtones made it a hate-word among animal-rights campaigners

1934 *Evening Post* (Wellington, New Zealand): With the object of determining the best method of culling deer in the Tararuas…the sum of £10 was granted by the Wellington Acclimatisation Society last night.

1978 *Orcanian*: Lord Cranbrook…said that 10,000-plus [seal] pups had been culled in the last ten years.

curvaceous *adj* (1936) having a voluptuous figure; shapely. Colloquial, originally US

1936 *Screen Book Magazine*: The curvaceous lady [i.e. Mae West] receives from Paramount just as many dollars per week for her scenario work as she receives for her acting.

cyclotron *n* (1935) an apparatus for accelerating charged atomic particles by subjecting them repeatedly to an electric field as they revolve in orbits of increasing diameter in a constant magnetic field. Despite the author of the quote's confident assumption, the origin of the term may be in need of some explanation: *cyclo-* refers to the orbit of the particles, and *-tron* is from the Greek suffix *-tron*, denoting an implement or device (it was subsequently used in the name of other types of particle accelerator and similar apparatuses, such as *betatron* (1941) and *levitron* (1960))

1935 E. O. Lawrence: An apparatus of the type developed by Lawrence and Livingston was used to produce a beam of high speed deuterons… Since we shall have many occasions in the future to refer to this apparatus, we feel that it should have a name. The term 'magnetic resonance accelerator' is suggested… The word 'cyclotron', of obvious derivation, has come to be used as a sort of laboratory slang for the magnetic device.

cystic fibrosis *n* (1938) a congenital metabolic disorder, usually causing early death, in which exocrine glands (such as the pancreas) secrete very viscid mucus, which accumulates and blocks the passageways of the body

1938 *American Journal of the Diseases of Children* (heading): Cystic fibrosis of the pancreas and its relation to celiac disease.

daily *n* (1933) a domestic cleaner or servant who does not live on the premises. British; a manifestation of the 'servant problem' which hit the middle classes after World War I: live-in servants could no longer be afforded, and recourse had to be had to cleaners who came in on a daily basis

1933 D. C. Peel: In my youth there were charwomen but the 'daily' is a new invention.

decolonization *n* (1938) the withdrawal from its former colonies of a colonial power; the acquisition of political or economic independence by such colonies. A major geopolitical feature of the mid 20th century

1938 M. J. Bonn: A decolonization movement is sweeping over the continents. An age of empire-breaking is following an age of empire-making.

1957 *Economist*: Nor did the postwar return of the colonial powers reverse or halt the process of 'decolonisation'.

decrypt *v* (1936) to decipher (an encrypted message), originally without the use of a key, but latterly used more broadly

1936 *Cryptogram*: Those who succeeded in decrypting Message No. 1 of the last issue.

defence *n* (1935) the military resources of a country. Mainly applied to equipment, personnel, etc. which is just as likely to be used for attack as for defence, but at the end of the century the usage has so successfully insinuated itself into the language that its euphemistic origins are no longer immediately obvious

1935 Clement Attlee: We talk about the co-ordination of defence; the co-ordination of the peace forces of the world is quite as important…as the co-ordination of the different services of this country… I am glad to hear that the Government are thinking of the question of having a Defence Minister.

1937 *Annual Register 1936*: The official title of the new Minister would be 'Minister for the Co-ordination of Defence'.

demo *n* (1936) A colloquial abbreviation of *demonstration*, originally in the sense 'a public display of group opinion'

1936 James Curtis: The anti-war demo last week.

1949 Angus Wilson: Norman's out at the demo. At Trafalgar Square.

demob *n* (1934) A colloquial abbreviation of *demobilization* 'release from military service at the end of hostilities'. A term on many lips in 1945 and '46, often preceding another noun (as in *demob suit*, a suit issued to a soldier on demobilization). The verb *demob* 'to demobilize' is first recorded in 1920

> 1945 *Daily Mirror*: It's 'total' demob. now—Many home by year's end.

> 1949 G. Cotterell: The mockery of the black Homburgs and umbrellas, the demob suits, whose patterns one often recognised [etc.].

deoxyribonucleic acid *n* (1931) any of the nucleic acids which yield deoxyribose on hydrolysis, which are generally found in and confined to the chromosomes of higher organisms, and which store genetic information. The original form of the term, as first recorded in Levene and Bass's book *Nucleic Acids*, was *desoxyribonucleic acid*, but *deoxyribonucleic*, which also dates from the 1930s, has largely replaced it. The more manageable and familiar abbreviation **DNA** is first recorded in 1944

> 1938 *Journal of the Chemical Society*: Secondly there are deoxyribonucleic acids, in which the sugar component is d-2-deoxyribose and of which 'thymus nucleic acid' is the classical example.

> 1944 *Journal of Biological Chemistry*: The key rôle of the desoxyribose type of these substances in the reproduction of inheritable characteristics has been emphasized by the identification of desoxyribose nucleic acid (DNA) as a major component of chromosomal nucleoprotein.

depression *n* (1934) the financial and industrial slump of 1929 and subsequent years. A specific application of a term which had been in general use, in expressions like *depression in commerce* and *depression of trade*, since the late 18th century

> 1934 Aldous Huxley: Since the depression, books on Mexico have been almost as numerous…as books on Russia.

> 1935 J. Guthrie: 'I thought you had a baby.' 'No, darling,' said Carol. 'None of us are having them now. It's the depression.'

deuterium *n* (1933) an isotope of hydrogen which has a neutron as well as a proton in the nucleus. Combined with oxygen it makes **heavy water (1933)**. It was discovered by H. C. Urey in 1932. He based the name on Greek *deuteros* 'second', since it is the second in the series of possible hydrogen isotopes

> 1933 H. C. Urey et al.: We wish to propose that the names for the H^1 and H^2 isotopes be protium and deuterium.

dig *v* (1934) to understand. Slang, mainly US Black English; originally jazz slang. The origins of the usage, which certainly was not widespread before the mid 1930s, are obscure. It has been claimed that it was introduced into the vocabulary of jazz by Louis Armstrong in the mid 1920s, but this has never been substantiated. Nor have suggestions that it came from an African language (such as Wolof *deg* or *dega* 'to understand') or from Romany *dik* 'to look, see'. Probably it is just an unexplained metaphorical extension of *dig* 'to excavate'. See also **dig (1939)**

> 1941 *Life*: Dig me?

> 1958 *Punch*: The lines of communication get tangled. In other words the people don't quite 'dig' you.

dig *v* (1939) to appreciate, like, admire. Slang, mainly US Black English; originally jazz slang. From **dig** 'to understand' (see above)

> 1943 Max Shulman: Awful fine slush pump, I mean awful fine. You ought to dig that.

> 1949 Leonard Feather: Dizzy didn't dig the band's kind of music and the band didn't dig Dizzy.

dinette *n* (1930) a small room or part of a room set aside for meals. Originally US. Compare **luncheonette (1924)**

> 1930 *Ladies' Home Journal*: Two clumsy, heavy French doors between the living room and the dinette.

dive-bomb *v* (1935) to attack with bombs at a low level after diving. A technique pioneered and perfected by the German Luftwaffe, particularly using the Junkers Ju 87 'Stuka'. Its principal object was to terrorize civilians. The noun *dive-bomber* (probably a direct adaptation of German *Sturzkampfflugzeug*, of which *Stuka* is an abbreviation) is first recorded in 1937

> 1935 *Evening News*: In dive-bombing, which is the most accurate form of aerial attack on surface targets yet devised, the aircraft is aimed bodily at the target in the course of an almost vertical dive, which is maintained for several thousands of feet.

> 1939 *Times*: The North Sea Attack. Failure of German Dive-Bombers.

> 1940 *Times*: Patrolling off the South Coast, three Hurricane pilots spotted 16 Me. 110s flying line astern to dive-bomb a convoy.

documentary *n* (1932) a film based on real events or circumstances, and intended primarily for instruction or record purposes. The noun usage arose out of a slightly earlier adjectival one: 'The Documentary or Interest Film, including the Scientific, Cultural and Sociological Film', P. Rotha (1930). The genre was pioneered in Britain by John Grierson, who is often credited with introducing the term into English

> 1932 *Cinema Quarterly*: Documentary is a clumsy description, but let it stand. The French who first used the term only meant travelogue.

> 1936 *Times Literary Supplement*: The documentary film—or, *tout court*, 'documentary'.

doodle *n* (1937) an aimless scrawl made by a person while his or her mind is more or less otherwise applied. The related verb is also first recorded in 1937

> 1937 *Literary Digest*: 'But everbody doodles.' So Gary Cooper, as Longfellow Deeds, in 'Mr. Deeds Goes to Town', defended himself. He wasn't crazy because he drew squares and circles on scraps of paper—he was just 'doodling'.

> 1942 *Punch*: Mr. Clement Attlee, the Premier's deputy, industriously drew doodles of intricate pattern.

drive-in *adj* (1930) Denoting a restaurant, cinema, bank, etc., into or up to which customers can drive their cars and, without leaving them, have a meal, see a film, conduct a business transaction, etc. Originally US. First recorded as a noun, 'such a restaurant, cinema, etc.', in 1937

> 1930 Cecil Beaton: The diehards hang on…working at 'drive-in' quick-lunch counters.

> 1937 *American Speech*: At roadside *drive-ins*, where one may secure curb service while sitting in his car.

drop-out *n* (1930) someone who withdraws from participation, especially in a course of study or in society in general. Colloquial, originally US. First recorded in 1930, but the 1960s and 70s were the word's heyday

> 1930 *Saturday Evening Post*: The drop-outs are usually those with inferior mental capacity.

> 1960 *Times*: The bored students—mostly boys—and the 'drop outs'.

> 1967 *New Statesman*: An international gathering of misfits and drop-outs, smoking pot and meditating in the Buddhist temples.

drum-majorette *n* (1938) a girl who leads or takes part in a parade or the like, twirling a baton, etc. Originally US. Also in the abbreviated form *majorette*

> 1938 *Life*: Drum majorettes are latest in ballyhoo.

> 1941 *San Francisco Examiner*: During the past few years the drum major…has given way to the so-called majorette.

drunk driving *n* (1937) driving while drunk. The alternative formulation **drink driving** is not recorded before 1964

> 1937 *Literary Digest*: In view of the rise in accidents from this cause, we will concentrate on just one thing—drunk driving.

drunkometer *n* (1934) a device for measuring the alcoholic content of a person's breath. Originally US. A forerunner of the **breathalyser (1960)**, and to begin with the name was also applied to the breathalyser itself

> 1934 *Journal of the American Medical Association*: Exhibit of automatic demonstration of the use of the 'drunkometer', a device for detecting drunkenness by testing the subject's breath.

> 1960 *New Statesman*: Since the drunkometer has been used in New York, convictions for drunken driving have increased from 30 to 85 percent.

dual carriageway *n* (1933) a road with separate carriageways, divided by a central strip, for up and down vehicular traffic. A feature of British inter-city and suburban road-building in the 1930s, as traffic densities began to build up; a key staging-post between traditional single-carriageway roads and multi-lane motorways

> 1933 *Proceedings of the Institute of Municipal & County Engineers*: The intention of such roads was to so design them as to enable them to carry very fast traffic safely. The only method of doing that was by providing dual carriageways with central strips which could be so treated as to make them a delightful amenity.

dumb down *v* (1933) to simplify or reduce the intellectual content of (especially published or broadcast material) so as to make it appealing or intelligible to a large number of people. Originally US; for the later intransitive version see **dumb down (1991)**

> 1980 James Michener: Education has taken very backward steps in the last 20 years—for example, the so-called dumbing down of the textbooks.

Durex *n* (1932) The British proprietary name of a type of contraceptive sheath, often used generically for a condom. Said to have been coined in 1929 by the chairman of the London Rubber Company, A. R. Reid, when he was travelling home by train one evening

> 1932 *Trade Marks Journal*: Durex…Instruments, apparatus, and contrivances, not medicated, for surgical or curative purposes, or in relation to the health of men or animals, but not including surgical adhesive tape… The London Rubber Company, London.

> 1971 B. Thornberry: Boys use sheaths, sometimes called durex, skins, or French letters.

dustbowl *n* (1936) a region subject to drought where, as a result of the loss or absence of plant cover, the wind has eroded the soil and made the land unproductive. Applied particularly to western Kansas and parts ('panhandles') of Oklahoma and Texas lying just to the south of it, where the native grasslands had been uprooted to make way for wheat, and during the drought years of 1934–37 hundreds of tons of loose topsoil were blown into the Gulf of Mexico. The sufferings of the farmers were graphically portrayed by John Steinbeck in his novel *The Grapes of Wrath* (1939)

> 1936 *Durant* (Oklahoma) *Daily Democrat*: The panhandle 'dustbowl' was outside the path of the wind.

> 1936 *Dallas Morning News*: They say he nearly defeated himself by urging Landon's election among the dust bowl farmers.

dyke, dike *n* (1931) a lesbian, especially one of markedly masculine appearance or manner. Slang, originally US; it probably started out as a cut-down version of *morphadike*, a US dialectal variant of *hermaphrodite*. First recorded in this form in 1931, but the synonymous compound *bulldyker* is on record from 1925, and the verb *bulldyke*, meaning 'to engage in lesbian activities', is known from even earlier (1921)

> 1931 Peter Tamony: Benches in the more obscure parts are used continually by couples, pansies and dykes.

> 1964 Eric Ambler: You know about that dike partner of hers?

economical with the truth *adj* (1932) concealing part of the truth. Usually used as a euphemism for lying, or at best misrepresenting the facts. A phrase mainly associated in the minds of British speakers at the end of the century with Sir Robert Armstrong, former head of the British Civil Service, who used it when giving evidence in an Australian court in 1986 on behalf of the British government about a book by the former spy Peter Wright (see the second quote below), but it is of much longer ancestry than that. It can be traced back ultimately to the expression *economy of truth*, in which *economy* was originally used in its etymological sense 'judicious handling', hence 'suitable presentation' (i.e. an early form of 'spin'), and already by the 18th century was being interpreted as 'being sparing'. The phrase *economical of the truth* evolved from this ('On the other hand, he was, by temperament, economical of the truth', Rudyard Kipling (1904))

> 1932 H. C. Bailey: 'I've put the old scamp of a solicitor through it and made him admit he had heard talk of turning the firm into a trust.' 'Oh, yes, I thought he was being economical with the truth.'

> 1986 Robert Armstrong: It contains a misleading impression, not a lie. It was being economical with the truth.

> 1995 *Sunday Times*: You just have to be economical with the truth… You have to say things. You should never lie, but it's very difficult.

ecosystem *n* (1935) a community of organisms and its environment which function as an ecological unit. A word which has become common currency at the end of the century, with the spread of eco-awareness, but it took some time to establish itself even as a technical term after its coinage by A. G. Tansley in the 1930s

> 1935 A. G. Tansley: There is constant interchange…within each system, not only between the organisms but between the organic and the inorganic. These *ecosystems*, as we may call them, are of the most various kinds and sizes. They form one category of the multitudinous physical systems of the universe.

electric blanket *n* (1930) an electrically warmed blanket. The early 20th century's love affair with the wonders of electricity extended into the 1930s, throwing up ever more ingenious subjects for electrification

> 1930 *Punch*: Had a rotten night. My electric blanket fused and I had to get up to mend it.

electron microscope *n* (1932) a microscope in which the resolution and magnification of minute objects is obtained by passing a stream of electrons through a system of electron lenses. An adaptation of the German term *Elektronenmikroskop*, coined in 1932 by E. Brüche

> 1941 *Annual Register 1940*: An important advance during the year was the construction of an electron microscope with about twenty times the resolving power of the best light microscope with oil immersion.

eleven plus *n* (1937) the age (between 11 and 12) at which pupils in Britain leave primary schools. The term became better known in the 1950s as the name of an exam taken at this age before entering one of the various types of secondary school

> 1937 E. Garnett: The age known in state educational circles as 'eleven-plus' (that year of destiny for all elementary school children with any ambition).

> 1958 *Economist*: Labour…turns to the Rent Act, the block grant, the 'iniquitous eleven-plus'.

embourgeoisement *n* (1937) adoption, especially by the proletariat, of middle-class attitudes or life-style. A key term in socialist theory and, some would argue, a key element in the evolution of socialism as the century wore on, culminating in the embracing of the free market by parties nominally of the left. The word was borrowed from French, but was immediately also turned into English as *bourgeoisification*. Later on the hybrid form *embourgeoisification* appeared

> 1937 F. Borkenau: It could not have succeeded had the Spanish proletariat ever undergone that process of 'embourgeoisement' which is characteristic of the industrial proletariat all over the world.

> 1937 J. M. Murry: 'The bourgeoisification of the English proletariat', which [Marx] deplored.

> 1970 *Daily Telegraph*: Hence [the Labour party's] reluctance to welcome the *embourgeoisement* of the wage-earners into a house-owning, two-car, fashion-conscious, home-entertaining, overseas-holidaying middle class.

> 1973 *Listener*: They were frightened…that they would not be able to afford the 'fair rents' which would be charged after conversion, and saw the Trust as yet another agent of creeping, expensive embourgeoisification.

end *n the end* (1938) the limit of what can be endured; the worst imaginable. British colloquial

> 1938 Ngaio Marsh: The sort of people who go there are just simply The End…the most unspeakable curiosities.

> 1959 Gillian Freeman: Donald, you really are the absolute end.

-eroo *suffix* (1931) See **flopperoo (1931)**, **switcheroo (1933)**

escalation *n* (1938) incremental succession. Originally applied to the arms race, then to increases in prices and wages, and, during the Cold War, to the development of 'conventional' warfare into nuclear warfare, or the use of successively more powerful types of weapons in war. Originally US. The usage has attracted the hostility of those who appear to think that a higher authority has decreed that *escalat-* words (see also **escalate (1959)**) should only refer to moving staircases (see **escalator (1900)**)

> 1938 *Kansas City Star*: *Escalation* means the building of bigger battleships when other nations do so.

> 1949 *New York Times*: Sales contracts permit upward adjustment through 'escalation' as a result of wage increases granted by the vendors.

> 1960 *Guardian*: The 'escalation' of a minor conventional war into a major nuclear one.

escapist *n, adj* (1930) (someone) seeking escape from reality or routine. The related noun *escapism* is first recorded in 1933

> 1930 J. C. Ransom: It is much more likely that they betoken a defeated and escapist people.

> 1933 C. S. Lewis: 'And you have never heard Mr. Halfways either.' 'Never. And I never will. Do you take me for an escapist?'

> 1933 *Encyclopedia of Social Sciences*: The bibulous, aphrodisiac lyrics strummed out by Anacreon of Teos at the banquets of Polycrates, tyrant of Samos, are an example of escapism, comparable to the songs of Alcaeus and Sappho in strife ridden Mytilene.

evacuate *v* (1938) to remove (inhabitants of an area liable to aerial bombing or other hazards) to safer surroundings

> 1938 *Times*: Authorities of our large towns will wonder whether or not to evacuate more than children.

evacuee *n* (1934) an evacuated person. First recorded in 1934 in the second edition of Webster's *New International Dictionary* as a French borrowing in the form *évacué*, with *évacuée* for females, but actual usage shows it quickly assimilated to English in a decade of insecure domicile (see **evacuate** above). See also **vacky (1940)**

> 1939 *Times Weekly*: The embarcation of these, mostly unwilling, evacuees is illustrated.

existential *adj* (*a*1937) concerned with human existence as seen from the point of view of existentialism. *Existential philosophy* was a slightly earlier term for what is more usually termed **existentialism (1941)**

> *a*1937 M. Geiger: 'Existential Philosophy' is a collective term for many problems, many methods of thinking, many points of view… The distinguishing feature of all existential philosophy is the fact that its basic category is existential significance.

> 1956 Colin Wilson: Kierkegaard's attitude is so Existential that his Christianity is a religion that regards God as the intermediary between himself and his fellow human beings, and cannot even accept their existence without first accepting the existence of God.

extra-sensory perception *n* (1934) perception by other means than those of the known sense-organs (e.g. by telepathy, clairvoyance, etc.). Commonly abbreviated to *ESP*

> 1934 J. B. Rhine: Let us merely say…'perception by means that are outside of the recognized senses', and indicate this meaning by 'Extra-Sensory Perception' or E.S.P.

> 1946 Aldous Huxley: When tests for ESP can be repeated under standardized conditions, the subject…achieves…a measure of scientific respectability.

eye shadow *n* (1930) cosmetic colouring applied to the eyelids or around the eyes

> 1930 Helena Rubinstein: The most successful way of lending depth and mystery to the eyes is with the eye shadow.

face-lift *n* (1934) See **face-lifting (1922)**

family planning *n* (1931) the planning and controlling of the number of children in a family and the intervals between them. Often used as a euphemistic cover for *contraception*. See also **birth control (1914)**

> 1945 *Lancet*: Growing numbers of women attending 'family planning' centres.

fan dancer *n* (1936) a female cabaret dancer, usually naked or scantily clothed, who manipulates large fans to conceal her body as she moves about. The term *fan dance* dates from at least the 1870s, but this particular titillatory version, comparatively hot stuff in the days before striptease had come into its own, could produce pleasurably scandalized shock in the middle decades of the century. Out of the same stable came the *bubble dancer* (1936), who used balloons rather than fans ('*Pre-honeymoon* is concerned with the love of a U.S. Senator for a bubble dancer,' *Time* (1936))

▌ 1936 R. E. Sherwood: Shirley is the principal, a frank, knowing fan dancer.

fantastic *adj* (1938) wonderful, marvellous. Colloquial. The usage rapidly took over from earlier senses of the word, such as 'bizarre' and 'illusory', much to the alarm of some purists ('This abuse of a once-useful word is beyond cure. All that you can do is to keep to a minimum the childish informal use of *fantastic*', *The Right Word at the Right Time* (1985)), and at the end of the century was its main meaning

▌ 1938 Margery Allingham: Oh, Val, isn't it *fantastic*?…It's amazing, isn't it?

fave *adj, n* (1938) (a) favourite. Slang, originally US; it did not make much headway in British English until the expression *fave rave* caught on in the mid 1960s, denoting an especially popular song, musician, etc. There is an isolated record of *fav* from 1921, but it is not clear whether it represents the same usage

▌ 1938 *Variety*: Lester Harding, heavy fave here, clicks with pop songs.

▌ 1967 *Melody Maker*: Smith's quartet version with Stan Getz was one of the fave rave records of the period.

feed *v* (1933) to bore or tire; to make fed-up. British slang; a fairly short-lived back-formation from **fed-up (1900)**, used either as a finite verb or in the adjectival form *feeding*

▌ 1933 Georgette Heyer: Anyone can have the super motor boat as far as I'm concerned. Joan, too. She bars it completely, which feeds Brother Basil stiff.

▌ 1940 Morris Marples: 'It's *feeding*, isn't it?' (i.e. calculated to make one *fed-up*).

feel up *v* (1930) to fondle the sexual organs of, especially through the clothing; grope. Slang, originally US

▌ 1930 John Dos Passos: She's awful hot. Jez I thought she was going to feel me up.

fellow-traveller *n* (1936) someone who sympathizes with the Communist movement without actually being a party member. A direct translation of Russian *poputchik*, which was used of noncommunist writers sympathizing with the Revolution

▌ 1936 *Nation* (New York): The new phenomenon is the fellow-traveler. The term has a Russian background and means someone who does not accept all your aims but has enough in common with you to accompany you in a comradely fashion part of the way. In this campaign both Mr. Landon and Mr. Roosevelt have acquired fellow-travelers.

▌ 1942 Evelyn Waugh: 'I was never a party member.' 'Party?' 'Communist party. I was what they call in their horrible jargon, a fellow traveller.'

fibreglass *n* (1937) a composite material consisting of glass fibres in resin. Registered as a proprietary name in the US in 1937 (spelled *Fiberglas*)

▌ 1941 *Flight*: A fabric made of 'fibre glass' for wing covering.

fifth column *n* (1936) Originally the column of supporters which General Mola declared himself to have in Madrid, when he was besieging it in the Spanish Civil War, in addition to the four columns of his army outside the city (in Spanish, *quinta columna*); hence, applied during World War II to a body of one's supporters in an attacked or occupied foreign country, or to the enemy's supporters in one's own country. The derived *fifth columnist* is first recorded in 1940

▌ 1939 *War Illustrated*: This looks to me like the Nazis' 'fifth column' in Belgium ready for the invasion.

▌ 1940 Winston Churchill: Parliament has given us the powers to put down Fifth Column activities with a strong hand.

▌ 1940 George Bernard Shaw: If you call Stalin a bloodstained monster you must be shot as the most dangerous of Fifth Columnists.

Filofax *n* (1931) A proprietary name, registered in 1931 and based on a colloquial pronunciation of *file of facts*, for a portable filing system for personal or office use, consisting of a loose-leaf notebook with separate sections for appointments, notes, addresses, etc., usually in a wallet with spaces for pens, credit cards, and other personal items. A notable sleeper of a word: it subsisted in obscurity for many decades before leaping to sudden fame, even notoriety, in the 1980s as the quintessential yuppie accessory. See also **personal organizer (1985)**

> 1985 *Company*: Paul Smith was first to spot and stock the now ubiquitous Filofax, which the media crowd took so completely to their hearts and pockets.

filter-tip *n* (1932) (a cigarette with) a filter at one end to remove some of the harmful substances from the smoke. Such cigarettes began to dominate the market in the 1950s, when the health-risks of smoking became more evident, although they had existed before then

> 1932 *Daily Mail* (advert): The Filter Tip that holds throat irritants in check.

> 1957 *New Yorker*: When I ran out of American filter-tips, I chose the nearest equivalent I could find—a Bulgarian make.

fission *n* (1939) the splitting, either spontaneously or under the impact of another particle, of a heavy nucleus into two approximately equal parts, with resulting release of large amounts of energy. The technical term was long preceded by the demotic **split the atom (1909)**. See also **fission bomb (1941)**

> 1939 Meitner & Frisch: By bombarding thorium with neutrons, activities are obtained which have been ascribed to radium and actinium isotopes. Some of these periods are approximately equal to periods of barium and lanthanum isotopes resulting from the bombardment of uranium. We should…like to suggest that these periods are due to a 'fission' of thorium.

> 1948 *Physics Abstracts*: Nuclear fission reactors.

flak *n* (1938) anti-aircraft fire. A borrowing from German, where it was formed from the initial elements of the compound *Fliegerabwehrkanone*, literally 'pilot-defence-gun'; this denoted an anti-aircraft gun, which is what the first quote below refers to. The metaphorical sense 'adverse criticism' is first recorded in 1968

> 1938 *Jane's Fighting Ships*: [On a German vessel] A.A. guns. 4.1 inch, 3.5 inch on H.A. mounts ('Flak').

> 1941 *Times*: Blenheim and Beaufort aircraft of Coastal Command flew through intense flak.

> 1972 *New Yorker*: Getting much flak from Women's Lib?

flopperoo *n* (1931) a flop, failure. US colloquial. The first recorded coinage based on the fanciful suffix **-eroo**. This was probably an arbitrary alteration (based on words like *buckaroo* and *kangaroo*) of the equally meaningless *-erino*, which had been popular in the first decade of the century. Its use was popularized by the influential US newspaper columnist Walter Winchell, and it survived to the end of the century (joined in the 1960s by the even more elaborate *-eroonie*)

> 1931 *American Speech*: Walter Winchell loves to…[see] *terpsichorines*…in *revusicals* which might even turn out *floperoos*.

> 1936 *American Speech* (1937): John Oliver in the Richmond *News-Leader* for Dec. 26, 1936, terms Georgia Tech the '*greatest flopperoo*' in football of the sports season.

four-letter word *n* (1934) a word considered obscene, especially any of several monosyllabic English words referring to the sexual or excretory functions or organs of the human body. It has been argued that the emergence of this euphemism reflects a proliferation in the use of such words during World War I (see **fuck off (1929)**)

> 1934 *American Speech*: For most people, the bare word forms of these four-letter words have become sexual fetishes.

> 1960 *Times*: Having regard to the state of current writing, it seems that the prosecution against *Lady Chatterley* can only have been launched on the ground that the book contained so-called four-letter words.

fruit gum *n* (1938) a fruit-flavoured gum; specifically, in Britain, one of a type manufactured by Rowntree's. In the early days of television advertising they were marketed under the slogan 'Don't forget the Fruit Gums, Mum!'

> 1938 Graham Greene: The packets of fruit gums came dropping out.

fruit machine *n* (1933) a coin- or token-operated gambling machine which pays out according to the combination of symbols (often representations of fruit) appearing on the edges of wheels spun by the operation of a lever. Originally something of a colloquialism, but long since the standard term. The blackly humorous synonym **one-arm(ed) bandit** is first recorded in 1938

> 1933 *Times*: Committed to trial…on a charge of receiving 20 automatic 'fruit' machines…knowing them to be stolen.

führer, fuehrer *n* (1934) Part of the title (*Führer und Reichskanzler* 'Leader and Imperial Chancellor') assumed by Adolf Hitler in 1934 as head of the German Reich, on the model of *Duce* (see **Duce (1923)**). Originally in English denoting Hitler himself, but later also applied ironically to any authoritarian leader

> 1934 *Notes & Queries*: Since the Führer refuses permission for this, it is thought probable the German stamps will show the swastika.

> 1959 *Sunday Times*: The cold and pointless ferocity of the gang fights came out vividly in interviews…with two or three young fuehrers.

gaff *n* (1932) a house, shop, or other building. Slang. Apparently an extension of a much earlier underworld slang usage, 'a fair or other place of entertainment', but its ultimate origins are obscure

> 1932 G. S. Moncrieff: He went back to his gaff and broke into the gas meter.

gas station *n* (1932) A US synonym for **filling station (1921)**

> 1932 Edmund Wilson: The city…cannot afford to have the gas stations go broke.

gay *adj* (1933) homosexual. Originally US. The adjective had been used to mean 'sexually dissolute' since the 17th century, and by the early 19th century it was being applied to people earning a living by prostitution. It is possible that male prostitutes catering to homosexual men provided the conduit through which it passed from 'living by prostitution' to 'homosexual'. Another element in the equation may be *gaycat*, US hobos' slang for a tramp's companion, usually a young boy, and often his catamite; this is first recorded about the turn of the 20th century, but its origins are unknown. An earlier clue still is a reported 1868 song called 'The Gay Young Clerk in the Dry Goods Store' by the US female impersonator Will S. Hays, but the precise semantic status of *gay* here remains speculative. Whatever its antecedents, the earliest reliable printed record of it comes from 1933; it was largely restricted to the private argot of homosexuals until the mid 1960s, but from then on it started to 'come out', and by the 1980s had become a standard English term. It is first recorded as a noun, meaning 'homosexual person', in 1953

> 1933 Ford & Tyler: Gayest thing on two feet.

> 1951 E. Lambert: In a way it was an odd threesome. It occurred to me that Esther rather hung round our two gay boys.

> 1974 Kate Millett: I talked at DOB in August, candid, one gay to another.

germ warfare *n* (1938) the deliberate dissemination of disease-germs among an enemy as a weapon of war; a layperson's alternative to **bacteriological warfare (1924)**

> 1938 *Harper's Monthly*: Lurid descriptions of death rays, rocket planes, germ warfare.

> 1953 *Encounter*: The stories of germ warfare in Korea.

Gestapo *n* (1934) the secret police of the Nazi regime in Germany, notorious for their brutal methods. A German acronym based on the early letters of *Geheime Staats-Polizei* 'Secret State-Police', the name of an organization set up by Hermann Göring in Prussia, 1933, and extended to the whole of Germany in January 1934. The term has often been used subsequently in English as a metaphor for any investigative body thought of as resembling the Gestapo

> 1937 *New York Times*: The spokesmen of the regime,…are taking every opportunity…to ridicule the idea that every German servant girl abroad is a disguised Gestapo agent or a spy.

> 1944 George Bernard Shaw: The municipal statesman sends his sanitary Gestapo into an unhealthy private house and prosecutes the tenant.

G.I. *n* (1939) an enlisted man in the US Army. The term appears to have originated as an abbreviation of *galvanized iron*. It was in use as early as 1907 in the US Army in semiofficial designations such as *G.I. can*. This came to be misinterpreted as *government-issue*, and was applied to words such as *shoe* and *soap*. It also went with *soldier*, and in due course this combination was shortened to simply *G.I.* The term became familiar in Britain in the latter years of World War II, when thousands of US troops were stationed there. See also **G.I. bride (1945)**

1944 *Spectator*: Relations between British other ranks and their equivalents, the American G.I., notoriously vary.

Gibson *n* (1930) a cocktail consisting of gin and vermouth garnished with a cocktail onion. A variation on the *martini* (1894). The identity of the original Gibson has not been preserved, although it may be a tribute to Charles Dana Gibson (see **Gibson girl (1901)**). See **cocktail party (1928)**

1951 Helen McCloy: Two double Gibsons, very dry…icy, oyster-white liquid that was almost pure gin with only a dash of vermouth.

gift-wrap *v* (1936) to wrap (an article intended as a gift) attractively. Originally US

1936 *American Speech*: During the holiday season many department stores advertised, 'We Gift-Wrap Here.'

gin-and-it *n* (1932) a drink of gin and Italian vermouth, fashionable in Britain in the middle third of the century

1932 B. Worsley-Gough: As I was sipping my gin-and-it before lunch.

1960 Kingsley Amis: Her lighter and chocolates and gin-and-its with two cherries on sticks.

glamour boy *n* (1939) a young man who possesses glamour; in World War II British slang often applied specifically (and, by other services, with a tinge of envy) to members of the R.A.F., particularly fighter pilots, whose exploits in the Battle of Britain and well cultivated reputation for swashbuckling had made them contemporary heroes

1939 M. Brinig: People do him a great injustice by calling him a glamour boy.

1941 *New Statesman*: Glamour boys, R.A.F., especially flying crews.

G-man *n* (1930) an F.B.I. agent. US slang; an abbreviation of *government man*, and first used with reference to political detectives in Ireland around 1917 ('The bloody old lunatic is gone round to Green street to look for a G. man', James Joyce, *Ulysses* (1922))

1930 F. D. Pasley: He offered a G man (Government agent) ten gran' to forget it.

1958 *Spectator*: Mr. Hoover has built up…an immense personal reputation…by creating a legend of the G-man that has largely transferred the romantic interest from the robbers to the cops.

gnome *n* (1938) a statue or ornamental figure of a gnome, especially one placed in a garden. Often occurring in the expression *garden gnome*, first recorded in 1946 (when the objects were evidently already in bad odour—see the second quote below). Such figurines are widely taken as touchstones of British bad taste. They were first produced in the 19th century, and were very popular with the Victorians; their belated appearance in the written record probably reflects the mass inter-war sales that precipitated their loss of esteem

1938 Dennis Kincaid: An imitation pergola and a coloured plaster gnome or two.

1946 *Woman & Beauty*: Garden gnomes—*some* people like them.

1966 M. Kelly: The owners of plastic flowers and garden gnomes, and plaster teal taking wing across the wall of the lounge-diner.

goon *n* (1938) a stupid person; a fool; also, someone hired, especially by racketeers, to terrorize workers; a thug. Slang, originally US. The immediate inspiration seems to have been 'Alice the Goon', a slow-witted, muscular character in the comic strip 'Thimble Theater, featuring Popeye' by E. C. Segar, which first appeared in 1933. It remains unclear whether Segar knew, and was prompted by, the earlier **goon** 'stolid person' (1921)

1938 Raymond Chandler: Some goon here plays chess. You?

1959 S. Clark: There, you goon. You'll bump into them if you don't watch out.

1971 *Blitz* (Bombay): Attempts on his life by goons allegedly employed by the Calcutta police authorities.

go-slow *n* (1930) a form of industrial protest in which employees work at a deliberately slow pace

1937 *Daily Herald*: Drivers on the Morden-Edgware tube and the Bakerloo line had been adopting a 'go-slow' policy, because it is alleged, they resented being reprimanded by inspectors for speeding on bends.

> 1955 *Times*: The men's representatives undertook that there would be no further 'go slows' or stoppages and that every man would work his full shift.

gotcha, gotcher (1932) A representation of the colloquial pronunciation of (*I have*) *got you*, usually in the sense either 'I have caught or destroyed you' or 'I have understood you'. It was the former usage (in the form *gotcha*) which achieved notoriety when the *Sun* newspaper used it (4 May 1982, first edition only) as a triumphalistic banner headline celebrating the sinking of the Argentinian battleship *General Belgrano* during the Falklands War

> 1932 Edgar Wallace: The 'plane was nearing the centre of Cavendish Square, when it suddenly heeled over. Its tail went down and it fell with a crash in the centre of the garden which occupied the middle of the square. 'Gotcher!' It was Jiggs' triumphant voice.

> 1983 Robert Harris (title): Gotcha! The Media, the Government and the Falklands Crisis.

> 1994 George Bain (title): Gotcha! How the Media Distorts the News.

grass *n* (1932) a police informer. British criminals' slang. Probably short for *grasshopper*, rhyming slang for *copper* 'policeman' (also said to be rhyming slang for *shopper* 'one who "shops" or betrays', which would be slightly more appropriate but lacks supporting evidence). The verb, meaning 'to betray (someone) to the police', soon followed

> 1936 James Curtis: Tell you the details and then you'll do the gaff on your jack…or else turn grass… Anyhow it was a dirty trick grassing his pals.

> 1938 Graham Greene: I wouldn't grass, Spicer said, unless I had to.

grass *n* (1938) marijuana. Slang, originally US

> 1943 *Time*: Marijuana may be called…grass.

green belt *n* (1932) an officially designated belt of open countryside in which all development is severely restricted, usually enclosing a built-up area and designed to check its further growth

> 1935 *Planning*: Mr. Herbert Morrison's offer of a sum of £2 millions to neighbouring local authorities in order to create a green belt round London represents a belated assumption by the L.C.C. of the wider responsibilities already recognised last century by the City Corporation.

groove *n in the groove* (1932) performing exceptionally fluently or well; hence more generally, doing well. Originally US jazz slang

> 1932 *Melody Maker*: Having such a wonderful time which puts me in a groove.

> 1933 *Fortune*: The jazz musicians gave no grandstand performances; they simply got a great burn from playing in the groove.

groovy *adj* (1937) in the groove; hence, used as a term of general commendation: wonderful, excellent. Originally US jazz slang

> 1941 *Pittsburgh Courier*: Love is Groovie.

gruntled *adj* (1938) pleased, satisfied, contented. A jocular back-formation from *disgruntled*

> 1938 P. G. Wodehouse: He spoke with a certain what-is-it in his voice, and I could see that, if not actually disgruntled, he was far from being gruntled.

G-string, gee-string *n* (1936) a tiny garment worn by striptease dancers, consisting of a strip of cloth passing between the legs and supported by a waistband. The term had previously been applied to a sort of skimpy loincloth worn by North American Indians, but this old usage was understandably driven out by the new one

> 1936 John Dos Passos: One of the girls…wiggled her geestring at him.

> 1939 Aldous Huxley: It had happened, but quite unwillingly…at Congo Club with nothing on but a G-string and some talcum powder.

guesstimate *n* (1936) an estimate which is based on both guesswork and reasoning. Originally US; a blend of *guess* and *estimate*

> 1936 *New York Times*: 'Guesstimates' is the word frequently used by the statisticians and population experts.

guinea-pig *n* (1939) an evacuee or billetee in World War II. British slang; so called because the billeting allowance was a guinea (£1.05)

1939 *Daily Dispatch*: We are known here [West of England] as the *guinea-pigs*…and we are being treated locally like those tailless rodents.

heavy water *n* (1933) a type of water, especially deuterium oxide, consisting (almost) exclusively of molecules containing hydrogen with a mass number of 2, used in some types of nuclear reactor. The term was held in some awe by the non-scientist in the early days of nuclear energy, and there was much head-shaking during World War II over reported attempts by Germany to get its hands on supplies of the substance for its own nefarious purposes

1936 *Punch*: 'Heavy-water', the newly-discovered fluid, costs £120 a teaspoonful.

1941 in Margaret Gowing (1964): We know that Germany has taken a great deal of trouble to secure supplies of the substance known as heavy water.

hep-cat *n* (1938) a devotee of jazz, swing music, etc.; someone who is up-to-date or stylish. Slang, originally US; see **hep (1908)**

1938 *American Speech*: Hep cat,…guy who knows what [swing music is] all about.

1940 F. Scott Fitzgerald: Suddenly they were at work again—taking up this new theme in turn like hepcats in a swing band and going to town with it.

1955 *Science News Letter*: This is not cool chatter between some young hep-cats in a smoke-filled jazz joint.

high *adj* (1932) under the influence of a drug. Slang, originally US; an extension of the earlier meaning 'drunk', which goes back to the 17th century

1951 *San Diego Evening Tribune*: He'd been 'getting high' on heroin week-end after week-end.

Hitler *n* (1934) a bumptiously or psychotically dictatorial person, reminiscent of Adolf Hitler (see **Hitlerite (1930)**). Often in the phrase *little Hitler*

1934 J. Spenser: Sparkes wanted to be the Hitler of that kitchen.

1957 Joyce Cary: Preedy has been taken to pieces by experts. They say, 'The typical schizoid—a little Hitler. You find him everywhere—the village boy who goes from Mass to do murder is the basic type.'

Hitlerite *adj, n* (1930) (a follower) of Adolf Hitler (1889–1945), chancellor of the German Reich (1933–45) and leader of the National Socialist (Nazi) Party in Germany. From the beginning, the tone or context of the word was largely negative or hostile, as were those of later parallel formations, notably *Hitlerist* (1931), *Hitlerian* (1934), and *Hitlerish* (1935)

1930 *Times*: These Hitlerite outbursts may disturb German Liberals and Socialists.

1930 *New Statesman*: One may magnify or minimise the role of the Hitlerites, but [etc.].

1934 Aldous Huxley: Dislike and fear of Hitlerian Germany.

Hitler moustache *n* (1934) a narrow moustache in the middle of the upper lip, like that worn by Adolf Hitler (see **Hitlerite (1930)**)

1934 Evelyn Waugh: He was comic; huge feet and hands, huge mouth, and an absurd little Hitler moustache.

hobbit *n* (1937) In the stories of J. R. R. Tolkien (1892–1973), any of a race of diminutive people, resembling human beings but with furry feet. Tolkien, who originated the word, claimed in a piece of post-hoc etymologizing that its underlying meaning was 'hole-builder'. When the Tolkien cult began to grow in the 1960s, a number of *hobbit*-derivatives sprang up, such as *hobbitomane* and *hobbitry*

1937 J. R. R. Tolkien: In a hole in the ground there lived a hobbit.

home movie *n* (1939) a home-made movie; a film made of the activities of one's own circle

1939 *Army & Navy Stores Catalogue*: Home movie camera.

homosexualist *n* (1931) a homosexual. The word enjoyed some currency in the middle years of the century as an alternative to **homosexual (1912)**, but by the end any residual usage was mainly facetious

1933 Henry Williamson: His book…proving…that Hamlet should be played as a homosexualist in vain love with Horatio had just been published.

honky-tonk *n* (1933) rag-time music or jazz of a type played in the sort of insalubrious drinking-saloons or dance-halls known as 'honky-tonks', especially on the piano. Originally US. That 'drinking-saloon' usage dates from the late 19th century, but it is not known where it came from

> 1936 *Swing Music*: Superficially, 'Honky Tonk' is the musical interpretation of a train journey; fundamentally it is a twelve-bar blues.

hood *n* (1930) a thug or violent criminal. Slang, mainly US; associated particularly with the gang warfare in American organized crime from the 1920s onwards. An abbreviated form of *hoodlum*

> 1930 *American Mercury*: None of those St. Louie hoods are going to cut in here, see?

Hooverville *n* (1933) a temporary shanty town. US. The name commemorates Herbert Hoover (1874–1964), President of the US 1929–33, years of economic depression

> 1933 *New Republic*: Hoovervilles are in a separate nation, with separate codes.

> 1939 John Steinbeck: There was a Hooverville on the edge of every town.

hopefully *adv* (1932) it is to be hoped (that). Originally US, and possibly modelled on German *hoffentlich* in the same sense. A usage which latterly has excited a good deal of hostility, for no very good reason. It was little used in British English before the 1970s, and its arrival set off a spate of ill-informed anti-Americanism (in fact US purists tend to get just as steamed up about it as British ones do). See also **thankfully (1966)**

> 1932 *New York Times Book Review*: He would create an expert commission…to consist of ex-Presidents and a selected list of ex-Governors, hopefully not including Pa and Ma Ferguson.

> 1971 *Guardian*: Prototype wooden rocking horses… Hopefully they will be available in the autumn at prices from £120.

hostess *n* (1936) See **air hostess (1934)**

hotcha *adj* (1937) Of jazz: producing strong excitement through driving rhythm, high speed, loud volume, etc.; hot. Slang. The word seems to have originated as a fanciful extension added on to the end of the traditional interjection *hey nonny nonny* ('Good morning, Phipps. What ho, what ho, with a hey nonny nonny and a hot cha-cha', P. G. Wodehouse (1937))

> 1937 Stephen King-Hall: I seemed to notice a tendency, towards the end of 1936, for what one of my daughters calls 'Hotcha' music to be replaced by 'Swing' music.

house arrest *n* (1936) detention in one's own home. A popular way of dealing with political dissidents in the 20th century, particularly as the term (as in the quote below) can give a euphemistic gloss to the proceedings

> 1936 F. L. Schuman: He was subjected to 'house arrest' for his protection.

housey-housey *n* (1936) The British term in the middle decades of the century for the game latterly known mainly as **bingo (1936)**. It is an elaboration of the earlier name *house*, which apparently originated in the army and presumably refers to the winner getting a full 'house' of numbers on his or her card

> 1938 in H. L. Mencken's *American Language* (1945): The game so popular in army circles in Hong Kong under the name of tombola is now sweeping South London as a craze called housey-housey. It is played for the most part by housewives who are attracted to open-door booths by a glittering display of cutlery and chromium-plated clocks.

hydroponics *n* (1937) the process of growing plants without soil, in beds of sand, gravel, or similar supporting material flooded with nutrient solutions. A coinage based on Greek *hudor* 'water' and *ponos* 'work'

> 1937 W. F. Gericke: 'Hydroponics', which was suggested by Dr. W. A. Setchell, of the University of California, appears to convey the desired meaning better than any of a number of words considered.

hyperinflation *n* (1930) an acute form of economic inflation, as in Germany after World War I. Often applied specifically to inflation over 20 per cent

> 1930 F. D. Graham (title): Exchange, prices and production in hyper-inflation.

include someone **out** *v* (1937) to exclude someone. One of the first and best-known 'Goldwynisms'—surreally paradoxical twistings of the English language supposedly perpetrated by the American film producer Sam Goldwyn (1882–1974), but in fact mainly dreamed up by his studio's press office. Others include 'In two words— impossible' and 'Verbal contracts aren't worth the paper they're written on'. See also **microgenic (1931)**

> 1937 A. Johnston: An ordinary man, on deciding to quit the Hays organization, might have turned to his fellow producers and said, 'Gentlemen, I prefer to stand aloof,' or, 'Gentlemen, I have decided to go my own way.' Sam [Goldwyn] said, 'Gentlemen, include me out.'

> 1938 *Hansard Commons*: It may be that the First Commissioner of Works…will now label the 'Aye' Lobby the 'Sez you' Lobby, and the other the 'Include me out' Lobby.

infanticipate *v* (1934) to be expecting a child. US; a blend of *infant* and *anticipate*. Witty, but it never strayed far from newspaper English, and slowly petered out after the 1930s. Possibly it was too much like *infanticide*

> 1934 Walter Winchell: The J. Clark Baldwin, 3ds,…are infanticipating… The Alan Mowbray infanticipation is due in late October.

> 1941 in *American Speech*: 'Storkettes' for 'infanticipating' friends of yours.

infiltration *n* (1930) the gradual or surreptitious penetration of enemy lines by small numbers of troops. The back-formed verb *infiltrate* is first recorded in 1934, the derivative *infiltrator* in 1944

> 1930 *Economist*: They thus succeeded…in reaching the outlying quarters of Peshawar, albeit in small numbers, by a process of nocturnal 'infiltration'.

> 1944 *Times*: Skilfully infiltrating through the chain of Japanese outposts and garrisons, the force penetrated hostile territory as far as the Shan States.

> 1944 *Infantry Journal* (US): Our men had orders not to leave the lines in case of any infiltration, because our rear elements would take care of the infiltrators.

insecure *adj* (1935) lacking in self-confidence; chronically apprehensive. Used with very general application since at least the 17th century, but its adoption as a term in psychology— originally mainly child psychology—dates from the 1930s

> 1935 F. B. Holmes: Karl is very insecure and clings to adults… The fearful children were more frequently described as being dependent upon adults for help…and as appearing generally insecure.

> 1941 Pritchard & Ojemann: The term 'insecurity' and its correlative 'desire for security' appear extensively in child development literature… We need methods by which we can discriminate between the relatively secure and the relatively insecure children.

> 1960 R. D. Laing: The ontologically insecure person is preoccupied with preserving rather than gratifying himself.

interceptor *n* (1930) a fast aircraft which is designed specifically to intercept and shoot down hostile aircraft. A change in the concept of the fighter aircraft from one which fought 'dogfights' with other similar aircraft (as in World War I) to one whose main role was to shoot down enemy bombers

> 1930 *Flight*: For a normal fighter, tanks to carry fuel for a flight of…$2\frac{1}{2}$ hours are sufficient. The new class of 'interceptor fighters' require even less endurance than that.

> 1934 *Times*: The modern interceptor was evoked by the fast day bomber.

interdisciplinary *adj* (1937) relating two or more disciplines or branches of learning; contributing to or benefiting from two or more disciplines. An educational buzzword of the latter part of the 20th century

> 1972 *Language*: Child language acquisition has proved to be one of the more important interdisciplinary areas of the past decade.

interwar *adj* (1939) of the period 1919 to 1939 between the two world wars

> 1939 Osbert Lancaster: The inter-war period through which we have just passed.

> 1944 William Temple: There must be no slipping back into the self-seeking and self-indulgence of the interwar years.

iron lung *n* (1932) a kind of respirator for giving prolonged artificial respiration mechanically, consisting of a metal case that fits over the patient's chest or trunk with an air-tight aperture for the neck, so that air can be forced into and out of the lungs by producing rhythmic variations in the air pressure in the case. Originally US. A grim apparatus which became familiar as a polio counter-measure in the middle decades of the century

> 1938 *Times*: Eric Baker, aged 11, died at Braintree…from infantile paralysis. He was taken ill on Monday and was placed in an iron lung.

Jacobethan *adj* (1933) See **Tudorbethan (1933)**

Jehovah's Witness *n* (1933) a member of a fundamentalist millenary sect, the Watchtower Bible and Tract Society, founded around 1879 (under the name 'International Bible Students') by Charles Taze Russell (1852–1916), which rejects institutional religion and refuses to acknowledge the claims of the State when these are in conflict with the principles of the sect

> 1933 M. S. Czatt (title): The International Bible Students, Jehovah's Witnesses.

> 1944 George Bernard Shaw: May he choose…a tribal idol as the sect called Jehovah's Witnesses now do?

jingle *n* (1930) a short verse or song in a radio or television commercial or in general advertising. A word which in its very sound seems to encapsulate the perceived annoyingness and triviality of 20th-century advertising. It is a specific usage of the more general sense 'a simple, repetitive, catchy rhyme or tune', which dates back to the 17th century

> 1930 A. Flexner: Let the psychologists study advertising…in order to understand what takes place when a jingle like 'not a cough in a carload' persuades a nation to buy a new brand of cigarettes.

> 1972 Diana Ramsay: The jingle, a singing commercial for a detergent, was being recorded.

jitterbug *n* (1934) a jittery or nervous person. Colloquial. First recorded as the title of a song by Cab Calloway and others, but later in the decade used as a political taunt against those apprehensive of war

> 1934 Cab Calloway: They're four little jitter bugs. He has the jitters ev'ry morn, That's why jitter sauce was born.

> 1939 *Times*: [The Government] is the only body capable of giving the information which would largely dispel the apprehensions of the 'Jitter-bugs', who, though perhaps few in number, are vocal and often influential.

jitterbug *n, v* (1938) (to dance) a dance, popular especially in the early 1940s, performed chiefly to boogie-woogie and swing music, and consisting of a few standardized steps augmented by much improvisation. Originally US. From **jitterbug** 'nervous person' (see above) by way of the intermediate sense 'jazz player or enthusiast'

> 1939 Raymond Chandler: This jitterbug music gives me the backdrop of a beer flat. I like something with roses in it.

> 1939 *American Magazine*: Susy Shag…begins thinking seriously of marrying the guy she's been jitterbugging with.

> 1943 *Dancing Times*: The wildest Jitterbug yet is danced by Dorothy Lamour.

jive *v* (1939) to dance to fast lively music, originally a form of jazz and later rock-and-roll. Also used as a noun, to denote this sort of dancing. Originally US. The original meaning of the word, dating from the 1920s, is 'misleading or empty talk', but it is not known where it came from

> 1939 *San Francisco News Letter*: If you should dance to the rhythms of either gentleman you will be jiving.

> 1957 *Observer*: Young people from the East End and the West End came there [the Humphrey Lyttelton Club] to jive or listen.

juke, jook, jouk *v* (1933) to dance, especially at a juke-joint or to the music of a juke-box. Slang, mainly US. Presumably derived from the noun **juke**, although that is not recorded until slightly later

> 1933 W. Roland (title of disc): Jookit Jookit.

> 1937 C. R. Cooper: In the 'jukin' joints' there is, of course, the prime requisite of liquor.

> 1941 *American Speech*: 'Let's jouk' is an invitation to dance, but 'let's go joukin' is a request for a date.

juke, jook, jouk, juke-house, juke-joint *n* (1935) a roadhouse or brothel, especially a cheap roadside establishment providing food and drinks, and music for dancing. US Black English slang; probably from *juke* or *joog*, a word meaning 'wicked' or 'disorderly' in the Gullah language, a creolized English of South Carolina, Georgia, and northern Florida

> 1935 Z. N. Hurston: They talked and told strong stories of Ella, Wall, East Coast Mary,…and lesser jook lights around whom the glory of Polk County surged.

> 1937 *Florida Review*: Back yonder a 'juke' was a place, usually a shack somewhere off the road, where a field negro could go for a snort of moonshine… There were negro juke-joints as far back as I can remember.

juke-box *n* (1939) a machine that automatically plays selected gramophone records when a coin is inserted. An earlier synonym was *juke organ* (1937), but it did not survive long

> 1939 *Time*: Glenn Miller attributes his crescendo to the 'juke-box', which retails recorded music at 5¢ shot in bars, restaurants and small roadside dance joints.

keep-fit *adj* (1938) Denoting exercises, classes, etc. to keep people fit and healthy

> 1938 M. Carter: Gardening comes into their day's programme and 'keep fit' exercises.

> 1939 Nicholas Blake: A healthy, bouncing, Keep-Fit sort of girl.

kibbutz *n* (1931) a collective settlement in Israel (or, in early use, Palestine), owned communally by its members, and organized on co-operative principles. From modern Hebrew *ḳibbūṣ* 'gathering'

> 1931 *Annual Report of the Central Tenuvah Federation* (Palestine) *1930*: 'Tenuvah' is a co-operative marketing association… Its members are the kvutzoth (collective farms), moshavim (smallholders' settlements), and kibbutzim (large farm training groups).

killer *n* (1937), **killer-diller** *n* (1938) an impressive, formidable, or excellent person or thing. Originally US jazz slang

> 1937 *Metronome*: That Zutie drummer-man is really a killer!

> 1938 *Life*: The hot musician…shudders when he hears Benny Goodman announce his next radio number as a 'killer-diller'.

knees up, Mother Brown *n* (1939) a dance in which the knees are vigorously raised to the accompaniment of the song 'Knees up, Mother Brown!' The song, by Weston and Lee, appeared in 1939, and both it and the dance were immemsely popular in wartime Britain. The use of the abbreviated *knees-up* for any boisterous party is first recorded in 1963

> 1939 Weston & Lee: Ooh! Knees up Mother Brown! Well! Knees up Mother Brown!…knees up, knees up! Don't get the breeze up Knees up Mother Brown.

> 1945 *Daily Mirror*: We are dancing the Conga and the jig and 'Knees up, Mother Brown'.

> 1963 Peter Willmott: We went to another house on the banjo for a 'knees-up'.

L (1936) Abbreviation of *learner*. Initially it was used mainly in *L-plate*, denoting a sign with a capital *L* on it which in Britain must be displayed on a car driven by a learner, but its application soon spread out to other aspects of learning to drive

> 1936 *Motor Manual*: 'L' plates must be carried at the front and rear of the car.

> 1936 *Punch*: Ermyntrude, inspired by blind jealousy (and aided by some rather L driving by Rachel), emerged from the garage.

Lambeth Walk *n* (1937) a Cockney song and dance first performed by Lupino Lane in the revue *Me and my Gal* in 1937, and popular in Britain at the end of the 1930s and during World War II. The song was written by Furber and Gay. It takes its name from a street in Lambeth

> 1942 J. W. Drawbell: She can hardly pull herself away from that cheerful, excited London throng— from the people who have fought fires while the bombs fell and can still sing and dance the Lambeth Walk.

language laboratory *n* (1931) a classroom, equipped with tape recorders, computers, etc., where foreign languages are learnt by means of repeated oral practice. The arts embraced 'science', or at least technology, in the days before the **two cultures (1956)** had been heard of

> 1931 R. H. Waltz (title): Language laboratory administration.

1946 *French Review*: A large Language Laboratory was installed… Phonographs and records were available at all times of the day.

lay *n* (1932) (a person—originally usually a woman—readily available for) an act of sexual intercourse. Slang, originally US. Recorded marginally earlier than the corresponding verb (see next), but the two evidently came as a package

1932 J. T. Farrell: A foursome passed homeward; two of the group were girls whom Jack and George agreed were swell lays.

1936 John Dos Passos: There never been a girl got a spoken word by givin' that fourflusher a lay.

lay *v* (1934) to have sex with. Slang, originally US. One of the staples of 20th-century throwaway sex terminology, but its affinity with the Biblical *lie with* ('Shechem the son of Hamor…tooke her, and lay with her, and defiled her', Genesis 34:2) reveals the euphemistic impulse that underpins it

1934 John O'Hara: I'm going to take Teddy out and get him laid tonight… 'You're wrong about one thing,' said Julian… 'I didn't lay that girl.'

lay-by *n* (1939) an area adjoining a road where vehicles can park without interfering with the traffic. Mainly British. The word originally (in the early 19th century) denoted 'a slack part of a river in which barges are laid by out of use'

1939 *Nature*: 'Lay-byes' and 'drawn-ins' should be made on every few miles of highway.

1972 *Daily Telegraph*: Caravanners who park in lay-bys causing litter and hygiene problems will face prosecution.

learner driver, learner *n* (1930) someone who is learning to drive but has not yet passed the driving test. See also **L (1936)**

1930 Anthony Armstrong: Conversational freedom between…taximen and private 'learner drivers'.

1934 R. F. Broad: A provisional licence will be issued to enable learners to receive instruction qualifying them for the official test.

liger *n* (1938) the offspring of a lion and a tigress. Compare **tigon (1927)**

1938 *Times*: Two young Whipsnade-bred tigresses have been sent to London with the intention that they shall be paired with lions to produce the so-called ligers.

Lindy Hop *n* (1931) a type of jitterbug dance which originated among blacks in Harlem, New York City. The Lindy element probably comes from the nickname of Charles Lindbergh (1902–74), the American pilot who in 1927 was the first to make a solo non-stop transatlantic flight and became a sort of US folk hero

1931 *Zit's Theatrical Newspaper*: The winners of the all-Harlem Lindy Hop contest…drew rounds of applause nightly.

lip gloss *n* (1939) a glossy cosmetic applied to the lips; a more glamorous alternative to *lipstick* (first recorded in 1880)

1939 *Army & Navy Stores Catalogue*: Max Factor… Lip gloss–2/6.

live *adj* (1934) (of a performance) heard or watched at the time of its occurrence, as distinguished from one recorded on film, tape, etc. Modern recording technology has broken the bond between time and events, posing an existential challenge to the concept 'alive': dead performers can speak on the radio and move on the screen, and need to be distinguished from those who are actually breathing at the moment of transmission. *Live* does the job (later in the century the waters were muddied with such usages as 'recorded live')

1934 *B.B.C. Year-Book*: Listeners have…complained of the fact that recorded material was too liberally used…but…transmitting hours to the Canadian and Australasian zones are inconvenient for broadcasting 'live' material.

1947 *Penguin Music Magazine*: The standard of playing…has suffered…because…there was an unprecedented demand for live performances.

lobotomy *n* (1936) incision into the frontal lobe of the brain, especially in the treatment of mental illness

1936 Freeman & Watts (heading): Prefrontal lobotomy in agitated depression.

Loch Ness monster *n* (1933) a large unidentified aquatic creature alleged to live in Loch Ness, a long deep lake in northern Scotland. Periodic claimed sightings of it from the 1930s onwards have provided much-needed relief to news editors on slow days. The pet-name *Nessie* is first recorded in 1945

> 1933 *Inverness Courier*: The Loch Ness 'monster' was seen near the west end of the Loch.

> 1971 *Stornoway Gazette*: Preparations are now complete and they set off in a few days' time to try and capture that elusive denizen of the deep—the Loch Ness Monster.

logical positivism *n* (1931) the theories and doctrines of philosophers active in Vienna in the early 1930s (the Vienna Circle), which were aimed at evolving in the language of philosophy formal methods for the verification of empirical questions similar to those of the mathematical sciences, and which therefore eliminated metaphysical and other more speculative questions as being logically ill-founded. The noun *logical positivist* is first recorded in the same year

> 1931 Blumberg & Feigl: To facilitate criticism and forestall even more unfortunate attempts at labelling this aspect of contemporary European philosophy, we shall employ the term 'logical positivism'…The principle of causality is for the logical positivist not a categorical necessity of thought.

> 1968 Max Black: Logical Positivism has seen its best days.

logo *n* (1937) the identifying symbol of an organization, publication, or product. An abbreviation of *logotype*, which was originally a printers' term for a piece of type with two or more separate elements

> 1937 *Advertising & Selling*: He wrote the first ad ever written for that new-fangled mechanical pencil called 'Eversharp'. Designed a logo for it, too.

lounge bar *n* (1937) a bar in a pub which is furnished with the amenities of a lounge. A salubrious facility introduced by pub owners in an effort to attract the sort of clientele scared off by the spit-and-sawdust image of public bars. The effect aimed at was bourgeois comfort rather than the fashionable sophistication of the cocktail bar (see the quote below)

> 1937 *Hotel & Catering Management*: Smoke-room or lounge bars are obviously larger than cocktail bars, and provision has to be made for the serving of draught beers.

luxury *adj* (1930) of high quality, and usually expensive; also, providing sumptuous comfort. A key adjective in 20th-century advertisers' hyperbole

> 1930 T. E. Lawrence: We must do our best to get the whole of the luxury edition placed before the date of publication.

> 1934 George Bernard Shaw: The rich tourists in the palace hotels and luxury liners.

macon *n* (1939) mutton salted and smoked like bacon. Among the first of the bizarre foodstuffs forced on the long-suffering British public by wartime privations (not so bizarre in sheep-producing areas, where such fare is traditional)

> 1939 *Daily Express*: *Macon* has now been adapted by other newspapers as a name for mutton bacon. This is only the latest of many words and phrases originally coined in this office which have later been used generally.

> 1939 *Times*: Macon was introduced…at the Savoy Hotel yesterday… Mr. Cecil Rodd, introducing macon…said he did not pretend to know how the word macon came into being; it just happened.

> 1968 *Punch*: The Ministry of Food then stood in for Mrs. Beeton, instructing them how to…work wonders with such unlikely raw materials as macon (bacon made from mutton, children)…and…coelacanth.

magazine *n* (1936) a periodical broadcast programme comprised of varied items of entertainment linked together as a single series. The fuller form *magazine programme* is first recorded in 1941

> 1936 *Radio Times*: 'Picture Page'. A Magazine of Topical and General Interest.

> 1970 *Times*: B.B.C. Newcastle…will have its own budget which will be sufficient to allow the production of another 30-minute weekly magazine programme.

> 1975 *ITV Evidence to Annan Committee*: A thirty-minute news magazine is taking shape for 6 pm transmission.

magic eye *n* (1938) a photo-electric cell or similar electrical device used for identification, detection, or measurement. The term was originally a proprietary name (registered in the US in 1936) for a sort of tuning indicator on a radio

> 1938 *Sun* (Baltimore): Eleven pairs of 'magic eyes'…have counted approximately 7,000,000 motor vehicles during the last year.

Magnum *n* (1935) The proprietary name of a type of very powerful handgun, registered in the US by Smith and Wesson in 1935

mainline *v* (1934) to inject (a drug) intravenously. Slang, originally US. First recorded in the derivative form *mainliner*, but the verb is probably contemporary. It comes from *main line*, slang for 'a large vein into which a drug can be injected' (first recorded in 1933)

> 1934 *Detective Fiction Weekly*: The addict who shoots stuff into the veins is said to be a gutter, or mainliner.

> 1959 Ed McBain: Snorting?… Skin pops?… Larry, Larry, are you mainlining?

-making (1930) See **shy-making (1930)**

marriage guidance *n* (1935) the giving of advice on problems connected with marriage, usually as a form of social service

> 1935 *Time*: Old Stone Church is one of an increasing number whose pastors run 'marriage guidance bureaus'.

> 1970 Germaine Greer: Women are not happy even when they do follow the blue-print set out by…marriage guidance counsellors and the system that they represent.

Mars, Mars bar *n* (1932) The proprietary name (registered in Britain in 1932) of a chocolate-covered bar with a toffee-like filling

> 1943 *Penguin New Writing*: Mars are made from the finest available materials—including chocolate…, glucose…, separated milk.

martial art *n* (1933) any of various fighting sports or skills mainly of Japanese origin, such as judo, karate, and kendo. The term, a translation of Japanese *bujutsu*, is first recorded in 1933, but did not become familiar until the 1960s, when a range of such sports began to be better known and more widely practised in the West. See also **karate (1955), kung-fu (1966)**

> 1933 *Official Guide to Japan* (Japanese Government Railways): Contests [of kendo] take place nowadays at the annual meetings of the Butoku-kai, or Association for Preserving the Martial Arts, in Kyoto.

> 1974 *Isle of Wight County Press*: Mr. Singleton, who holds a Kendo black belt, a brown belt in Karate, and has just taken up Ju-Jitsu, said he had no intention of 'cashing in' on the current martial arts boom.

mass hysteria *n* (1934) the irrational behaviour of a large mass of people. The 20th century's way of naming and explaining the way people are capable of doing deplorable or foolish things in a crowd which they would never dream of on their own

> 1934 Aldous Huxley: The mindless mass hysteria of howling mobs.

> 1973 *Times*: There is an argument for introducing rationing in London where some form of mass hysteria seems to have occurred.

mass murder *n* (1931) the murder of very large numbers of people, either serially or (more usually) simultaneously. A term for which the century found ample use as it ground on. See also **genocide (1944)**

> 1931 S. Nearing (title): War: organized destruction and mass murder by civilized nations.

> 1967 Hannah Arendt: The bulk of the armed SS served at the Eastern front where they were used for 'special assignments'—usually mass murder.

mass observation *n* (1933) the study and recording of the social habits of people *en masse*. A very '30s name (with its accent on the social laboratory, and on the populace as a unified concept and potential specimen) for what was in many ways the forerunner of later 20th-century public-opinion surveying. In 1937 it was taken as the designation of an organization set up in Britain for this purpose by Charles Madge and Tom Harrisson. This helped to establish the term and also gave rise to a range of derivatives, such as *mass observer* and *mass observationist*

> 1937 Madge & Harrisson: If after reading the pamphlet you should wish to co-operate by becoming a Mass-Observer, send a card… A group of people started Mass-Observation, which aims to be a scientific study of human social behaviour, beginning at home.

> 1948 John Betjeman: The Mass-Observer with the Hillman Minx.

means test *n* (1930) an official investigation into someone's financial circumstances to determine whether they are eligible for a welfare payment. A notable 20th-century political football, reviled by the left as demeaning and intrusive, supported by the right as discouraging scroungers. First recorded as a verb in 1963

> 1930 *Economist*: We should not cavil greatly at the principle of granting, on the basis of a means test, maintenance allowances for children compelled to attend school.

> 1963 *Economist*: All university awards are means-tested now.

mentholated *adj* (1933) treated or impregnated with menthol. Applied mainly to cigarettes. The process, and the term, enabled tobacco manufacturers to add a new layer of sophistication to their product, and in the middle decades of the century mentholated cigarettes outsold other types in the US

> 1933 *Tobacco World*: And now say 'hello' to KOOL, B & W's mild mentholated new cigarette.

mercy killer, mercy killing *n* (1935) See **mercy (1927)**

Mickey Mouse *adj* (1936) Denoting something small, insignificant, or worthless. Often applied specifically to inferior dance-band music, similar to that played as a background to a cartoon film. From the name of a mouse-like character in a series of animated cartoons designed by the American cartoonist Walt Disney (1901–66)

> 1936 George Orwell: You have moved too much away from the ordinary world into a sort of Mickey Mouse universe where things and people don't have to obey the rules of space and time.

> 1938 *Down Beat*: A strictly 'mickey mouse' band is still box office.

> 1951 *San Francisco Examiner*: 40th Division. Troops Lack Equipment. Woes of 'Mickey Mouse Army'.

microfilm *n* (1935) (a length of) photographic film containing microphotographs of the pages of a book, periodical, etc.

> 1939 *Nature*: The so-called micro-film…offers one means for the photographic reproduction of bulky reports.

microgenic *adj* (1931) Of a voice: that sounds well when transmitted by microphone; well suited to broadcasting. Coined by the ineffable Sam Goldwyn (see **include out (1937)**), with scant regard for the confusion it would be likely to cause. Against all the odds, and in the face of some ridicule, it seems to have survived for a while

> 1931 Sam Goldwyn: An actor may be 'photogenic'…but that is not enough. He must also be 'microgenic', that is to say, he must have a voice that is suitable to the microphone.

> 1944 *Evening Standard*: It seems strange that words like flak…should escape censure by the austere…while such bitter eloquence is directed against…microgenic (good for broadcasting).

microwave *n* (1931) electromagnetic radiation with a wavelength between infrared and short-wave, roughly one millimetre to one metre. The familiar modern application to cooking dates from the 1960s (see **microwave oven (1965)**)

> 1931 *Telegraph & Telephone Journal*: When…trials…with wavelengths as low as 18 cm. were made known, there was undisguised surprise…that the problem of the micro-wave had been solved so soon.

milk bar *n* (1935) a place where drinks made from milk (and often also other refreshments) are sold. Popular and wholesome places of youthful resort in the middle decades of the century, but long since consigned to the museum of mass catering. Top of the menu were milk shakes (the term *milk shake* is first recorded in 1889, but in its fully evolved form it is really a drink of the 1930s)

> 1935 *Forres Gazette*: The milk bar, or place where milk drinks are sold, is a popular institution all over Australia, and plans are on foot for installing…them in Britain.

> 1937 *Daily Herald* (caption): Mrs.—…sampling a milk shake after she had opened a milk bar in Tottenham Court-road yesterday.

mini- *prefix* (1934) very small of its kind. A suffix formed from the first two syllables of *miniature* (probably also with some input from *minimum*). Its origins in the 1930s were largely as an element in proprietary names, such as *minipiano* and *minicamera* (the latter was subsequently abbreviated to *minicam*: 'Their photographs, largely contributed by "minicam" amateurs', Graves & Hodge (1940)). It was the 1960s that saw the real explosion in the use of *mini-*, possibly initiated by the popularity of the *Mini-Minor* (1959), a small car manufactured originally by the British Motor Corporation, and reinforced by the fashionability of high hemlines, which encouraged coinages like **miniskirt (1965)** and **minidress (1965)**

> 1934 *Trade Marks Journal*: Minipiano… Pianos. Brasted Bros. Ltd.,…London,…piano manufacturers; and C.A.V. Lundholm Aktiebolag (a Joint Stock Company organised under the laws of Sweden),…Sweden; merchants.

> 1936 *Miniature Camera Magazine*: It is perhaps to be expected that all sorts and conditions of industries and businesses should have sprung up around the successful Minicamera.

> 1949 *Railway Gazette*: The equipment exhibited by Westinghouse Garrard Ticket Machines Limited at…Olympia, includes… The Westinghouse mini-printer,…with four or six printing units.

> 1954 *Life*: The new 'mini-pig'…is ideal for medical research, which is what he was bred for.

> 1962 *Punch*: A cycle firm is bringing out a mini-bike.

> 1966 *Times Review of Industry*: With the 'mini-budget' having withdrawn another 500m. from internal demand.

> 1970 *New Scientist*: The minipill was developed for one reason alone: because it was believed to provide safe contraception.

mitigate against *v* (1932) to militate against. A malapropism increasingly commonly recorded in the last quarter of the century, and one which seldom fails to evoke the expected Pavlovian response from the language police

> 1932 William Faulkner: It's as though there were some intangible and invisible social force that mitigates against him.

> 1977 *New Zealand Listener*: However, money is not big enough to attract other top world players and the grass-court scene here, plus travel distances, are the other two factors mitigating against the bigger names coming to Auckland.

mod con *n* (1934) Short for *modern convenience* 'an amenity, device, fitting, etc., of the sort that is usual in a modern house', a piece of estate agents' jargon first recorded in 1926. The abbreviation itself started out amongst the house agents, but has since established itself (often tongue in cheek) in the general language. Usually used in the plural

> 1934 *Punch*: An advertisement…describing just such a house as we wanted. Just the right number of rooms, 'five minutes from the station, h. & c. in all bedrooms, all mod. cons.'

> 1966 Hugh MacDiarmid: We had no 'mod cons', and were getting too old to put up with really primitive conditions.

modoc, modock *n* (1936) a man who becomes a pilot for the sake of the glamorous image it conveys. US slang. A term redolent of the frontier days of flying (goggles, flying boots, white silk scarf, etc.), up to and including World War II, when to be a pilot guaranteed instant charisma and sex appeal. Similar impulses in Britain led to R.A.F. aircrew being dubbed **glamour boys** or *Brylcreem boys*. The origins of *modoc* are entirely mysterious

> 1936 Allen & Lyman: A *modoc*, the derivation of which is obscure, is a flashy chap who goes around wearing helmet and goggles, and more than likely, leather boots and riding breeches, too, and talking about the big things he is going to do for aviation.

Monopoly *n* (1935) The proprietary name of a game (invented by Charles Darrow) in which the players use imitation money to engage in simulated financial dealings

1935 *New York Times*: Heading all other 'board games'...is the season's craze, 'Monopoly', the game of real estate.

1939 Graham Greene: There were 'Monopoly' parties.

Moral Rearmament *n* (1938) (the beliefs or principles of) a religious group advocating spiritual revival, founded by the American evangelist Frank Buchman (1878–1961), who was previously the moving spirit behind the Oxford Group in the 1920s. Its underlying agenda is anti-Communist

1938 *Times*: Moral rearmament, which is the true basis of national fitness, is an individual responsibility.

1940 Earl of Athlone: Moral Re-Armament stands for a change of heart, for that new spirit which must animate all human relationships.

1940 Nancy Mitford: If the British people had gone all out for moral rearmament and real appeasement, things need never have reached this pass.

muesli *n* (1939) a dish, originating in Switzerland, consisting of a cereal (usually oats) and fruit to which milk is added, often eaten as a breakfast dish. It had first been introduced into Britain in the 1920s under the name *Birchermuesli*, after its proponent Dr Bircher-Benner, who served it to patients in his 'natural health' clinic in Zürich. Originally restricted largely to the health-food fringe, it leapt to fame in the high-fibre boom of the 1970s, becoming the trendy breakfast dish

1939 Bircher-Benner & Bircher: The fact that it is cold is never harmful as long as the müesli is well chewed and thus sufficiently warmed in the mouth.

Munich (1938) The English name of München, the capital of Bavaria, used allusively with reference to a meeting of representatives of Germany, Britain, France, and Italy on 29 September 1938, when (by the 'Munich Agreement') the Sudetenland of northern and western Czechoslovakia was ceded to Germany. Its connotations were usually of naive and dishonourable appeasement, particularly on the part of the British prime minister who concluded the agreement, Neville Chamberlain. In the succeeding years a small range of opprobrious derivatives were formed from it, including *Municheer*, *Munichism*, and *Munichite*

1938 Harold Nicolson: Go up to Leicester. Bertie Jarvis says that I have put the women's vote against me by abusing Munich.

1939 Aldous Huxley: These last months, since the Anschluss and Munich, one had found that political discussion was one of the unpleasant things it was wise to avoid.

1942 *Sun* (Baltimore): Writer finds people hostile to war officialdom, Commons and Municheers.

1962 Michael Foot: At Bridgwater, Vernon Bartlett,...won a spectacular victory in the teeth of all the 'peace' propaganda of the Munichites.

musical *n* (1938) a film or a theatrical piece (not opera or operetta) of which music is an essential element. The earlier *musical comedy*, which it has largely supplanted, goes back to the 18th century

1940 *Illustrated London News*: Some of these 'musicals' have proved extremely popular.

Muzak *n* (1938) The proprietary name (registered in Britain in 1938) of a system of piped music for factories, restaurants, supermarkets, etc.; also used loosely, and generally disparagingly, to designate recorded light background music generally. Reputedly it was coined as a blend of *music* and *Kodak*

1959 *Observer*: Several firms have already arranged to receive Muzak in the factories.

1968 *Times*: If muzak be the food of love, no wonder it is commonly to be found...among the frozen mint-flavoured peas and the crinkle-cut chips.

national government *n* (1931) a coalition government. A term which now has weaselly connotations: it is suspected on the one hand of trying to cover up *coalition*, which smacks a little too much of compromise and indecision, and on the other of making inflated claims about subordinating party differences to the national interest in a time of crisis. It was fatally holed on its first outing, when Ramsay MacDonald, hitherto prime minister of a Labour government (the first such) formed a coalition government with the Conservatives in Britain in 1931 following the economic crisis, and called it the 'National Government'. He was reviled ever after in the Labour party as a turncoat

1931 John Reith: A wire…informed me that the Labour government had resigned, that MacDonald was prime minister of a National government.

1931 *Economist*: Sir John Simon…stated that…'if the broad base National Government finds it [i.e. a particular tariff] necessary, I am not going on that ground to refuse to support the National Government.'

national grid *n* (1930) an interconnecting system that joins together all of a country's major power stations and electricity distribution centres

1930 *Times*: There will be no great rush of new business consequent on the completion of the national 'Grid' system, as was contemplated in some quarters.

National Socialism *n* (1931) the ideology and practice of the Nazis, including particularly racist nationalism and state control of the economy. See also **National Socialist (1923)**

1933 J. J. Bronowski: National Socialism pictures itself as persecuted, not only by the political world but by art, science and philosophy.

naturism *n* (1933) a movement for, or the practice of, communal nudity in private grounds (see **naturist (1929)**)

1933 *Gymnos*: This book…is the first serious attempt to link Nudism with…Naturism, and Feminism.

1961 *Daily Telegraph*: Delegates…at the annual conference of the British Sun Bathing Association…agreed…to substitute 'naturism' for 'nudism'.

Nazi *adj, n* (1930) (a member) of the National Socialist (Workers') Party in Germany, led by Adolf Hitler from 1920 and in power from 1933 to 1945. The form of the word is a German representation of the pronunciation of the first two syllables of German *Nationalsozialist*. Before the end of the 1930s *Nazi* was being applied to similar fascist parties and organizations elsewhere, and in due course it became a general term of condemnation for any sort of right-wing oppression. See also **National Socialist (1923)**

1930 *Times*: Herr Hitler, the leader of the victorious National-Socialists (Nazis), has very carefully refrained from saying anything… Herr Hitler, the leader of the National Socialists, speaking at the last big Nazi election meeting.

1938 *Sun* (Baltimore): The center of Santiago was kept in turmoil after Chilean Nazis…seized the National University.

1942 Winston Churchill: The horde of divisions provided by Finland, Rumania, Hungary, and others of the Nazi-ridden or Fascist-ridden states.

1973 *Guardian*: 'Nazi' has become an indiscriminate political cliché applied to insensitive bureaucrats, Americans in Vietnam, IRA Provos, British paras in Ulster, Black September, Zionists, *et al*.

Nazify *v* (1933) to cause or force to adopt Nazism

1933 *Times*: Dr. Dollfuss…is resisting…the combined efforts of the German and Austrian Nazis to nazify Austria.

1934 *Sun* (Baltimore): Such events do not augur well for the future of the 'unified', i.e., Nazified, Evangelical Church of Germany.

negligee *n* (1930) a woman's dressing-gown, usually made of flimsy, semi-transparent fabric trimmed with ruffles, lace, etc. A semi-anglicization of French *négligé* which had been used previously in the 18th century for a sort of loose gown worn by women, and also for an informal garment worn by men

1930 M. Story: The negligée, this garment for intimate occasions may be…silky, lacy, colorful, and dainty.

neutrino *n* (1934) any of a range of electrically neutral particles, thought to be massless. A borrowing from Italian, literally 'little neutral one', coined in 1933 by the physicist Enrico Fermi

1934 *Science Abstracts*: A quantitative theory of the emission of beta-rays is explained. This admits the existence of the 'neutrino', a new particle proposed by Pauli having no electric charge and mass of the order of magnitude of that of the electron or less.

New Deal *n* (1932) the programme of social and economic reform in the US planned by the Roosevelt administration of 1932 onwards. The term spawned derivatives such as *New Dealer, New Dealish,* and *New Dealism*

> 1932 F. D. Roosevelt: I pledge you—I pledge myself—to a new deal for the American people.

> 1934 *American Mercury*: Fifty New Dealers who are helping the President make the country laugh.

> 1940 H. G. Wells: The New Deal is plainly an attempt to achieve a working socialism and avert a social collapse in America.

newscaster *n* (1930) someone who reads the news on radio or television. Originally US; it did not spread significantly to British English until the mid 1950s, when it was consciously introduced by the newly formed Independent Television (see the second quote below). Based, of course, on *broadcaster*, similar later US formations include *sportscaster* and *racecaster*, both first recorded in 1938

> 1930 *Observer*: Graham MacNamee, the news-caster of our American newspaper newsreel, takes the part of an unseen dramatist.

> 1956 *Annual Register 1955*: I.T.A. news was planned, intentionally, as something different from the traditional, wholly dignified, and impartial B.B.C. news, and was given instead from a personal angle, from less orthodox sources, by a skilful team of 'newscasters'.

> 1981 Ed McBain: The sportscaster read off the baseball scores.

news theatre *n* (1933), **news cinema** *n* (1935) a cinema showing a succession of short films, cartoons, newsreels, etc. A familiar sight on inner-city streets, at railway stations, etc. in the middle decades of the century. As people turned more and more to televison for the sort of diet they provided, they gradually faded out

> 1933 J. B. Priestley: He paid his shilling and entered one of the little News Theatres.

> 1935 *Punch*: Trousers go wrong the moment you move in them. The news-cinemas and photographs in the papers tell you that.

> 1961 S. Chaplin: We nipped into the News Theatre one night and saw one of these Barbecue affairs, in colour.

nice nellyism, nice nellieism *n* (1936) excessive prudishness of speech or behaviour. North American slang; based on *nice Nelly*, a conventional name for an excessively respectable woman

> 1936 *New Republic*: Perhaps it is true as charged that the British press is displaying a brand of Nice Nellyism in refusing to mention the subject [i.e. the divorce of Mrs Simpson, later Duchess of Windsor].

nickelodeon *n* (1938) a machine that automatically plays selected gramophone records on the insertion of a coin; a jukebox. Originally and mainly US. The term initially denoted a theatre or motion-picture show for which the admission fee was a nickel (see **nickelodeon (1907)**), and then a place containing automatic machines to provide amusement, which could be used for a nickel. These two senses were current in the 1920s. It was probably based ultimately on *melodeon*, in the sense 'music-hall'

> 1949 *Saturday Evening Post*: A nickelodeon at the end of the street emits a tinny piano tinkle.

night starvation *n* (1936) Originally an advertising copywriter's metaphor for night-time hunger, used in promoting the drink Horlicks as a nourishing nightcap, but it also enjoyed some currency in the middle decades of the century as a mysterious euphemism for deprivation of sexual intercourse

> 1936 George Orwell: What they asked for was a really telling slogan; something in the class of 'Night-starvation'…that would rankle in the public consciousness.

> 1971 Dan Lees: It wasn't as if I was suffering from night starvation. Val was easily one of the best screws in the business.

nobody's business *n* (1931) something extraordinary or unheard of. A rather curious colloquialism of the middle decades of the century, often used in the phrase *like nobody's business* 'to an extraordinary extent, like mad'

> 1931 Eric Linklater: 'How I love you is just nobody's business,' she said.

> 1938 P. G. Wodehouse: The fount of memory spouting like nobody's business.

nuclear physics *n* (1933) the scientific study of the forces, reactions, and internal structures of atomic nuclei

> 1933 *Discovery*: Lord Rutherford of Nelson, to whom so much of what is best in modern nuclear physics is due.

nylon *n* (1938) a type of high-strength synthetic material. One of the earliest and best-known of the man-made fibres which had such a transforming effect on 20th-century life. Amongst the first products was the nylon stocking, which almost attained the status of an unofficial currency when brought to war-deprived Europe by US service personnel (*nylons* in this sense is first recorded in 1940).

The origin of the name *nylon* has excited speculation, particularly in the light of its resemblance to the initial elements of *New York* and *London*. The matter was clarified in the following letter to *Women's Wear Daily* by John W. Eckelberry of the du Pont Co. in 1940: 'The word is a generic word coined by the du Pont Co. It is not a registered name or trademark... We wish to emphasize the following additional points: First, that the letters n-y-l-o-n have absolutely no significance, etymologically or otherwise... Because the names of two textile fibers in common use—namely "cotton" and "rayon", end with letters "on"...it was felt that a word ending in "on" might be desirable. A number of words...were rejected because it was found they were not sufficiently distinct from words found in the dictionary, or in lists of classified trademarks. After much deliberation, the term "nylon" was finally adopted'

> 1938 *New York Times*: 'Nylon' is a generic name, coined by the du Pont chemists, to designate all materials defined scientifically as 'synthetic fiber-forming polymeric amides having a protein-like chemical structure; derivable from coal, air and water, or other substances, and characterized by extreme toughness and strength and the peculiar ability to be formed into fibers and into various shapes, such as bristles and sheets'.

> 1940 *Journal of the Royal Aeronautical Society*: Possible use of synthetic textile Nylon as a parachute material.

> 1940 *Woman* (US): Dunk your nylons in rich suds of neutral soap.

> 1951 Marshall McLuhan: Food and nylons...are consumed and promoted with moral fervor.

oblige *v* (1933) to work as a charwoman. A bizarre British euphemism of the middle decades of the century

> 1933 D. C. Peel: The mother took in washing and went out to 'oblige' and earned roughly 22s. a week and some of her food.

> 1958 Joanna Cannan: I'm not in service. I oblige by the hour.

Odeon *n* (1933) any of numerous cinemas in a chain built in Britain by Oscar Deutsch or his company in the 1930s. The word is an adaptation of Greek *odeion*, which denoted a building for musical performance. It became almost synonymous with *cinema* in British English in the middle decades of the century, and continues to convey many of the connotations of the lavish architectural style in which the originals were built

> 1977 *Times*: M. Barrier designed his own restaurant under the influence of fin-de-siècle, early Odeon, and fifties tubular.

on *prep* (1936) addicted to or regularly taking (a drug or drugs). Colloquial, originally US

> 1955 Shapiro & Hentoff: I don't think all musicians are on junk by any means.

one-arm bandit, one-armed bandit *n* (1938) An alternative name (originally US) for the **fruit machine (1933)**; so called from the single handle at the side, and the fact that most of its customers end up poorer

> 1938 *Sun* (Baltimore): The Court of Appeals at Annapolis yesterday declared...that the so-called 'one-arm bandit' type of slot machine is illegal.

one-stop *adj* (1934) Denoting a shop or the like that can supply all a customer's needs within a particular range of goods or services. Originally US

> 1934 *American Speech*: Plenty of one-stop service stations for washing, minor repairs, lubrication, etc.

oojah-cum-spiff *adj* (1930) all right, O.K. Ephemeral British slang, a fanciful extension of the already surreal **oojah** 'unnamed thing' (1917)

> 1930 P. G. Wodehouse: 'All you have to do,' I said, 'is to carry on here for a few weeks more, and everything will be oojah-cum-spiff.'

oomph *n* (1937) sex appeal, glamour, attractiveness; vitality, enthusiasm. Slang, originally US. In many ways a follow-up to the earlier **it (1904)**

> 1937 *Saturday Evening Post*: With actors, the 'it' quality has to do with their visual personality—sex appeal, magnetism, or whatever you care to call it. Back of the camera, we refer to the ingredient as 'umphh'.

> 1939 *Life*: Three cheers for the Oomph Girl—yours, *Look's* and *Collier's*—all in one week!... This Ann Sheridan certainly must have oomph to win the attention of three such important magazines in issues which hit the newsstands at the same time.

open plan *n* (1938) an architectural style allowing for no (or few) internal walls or partitions within a building, especially an office or a school. Often used adjectivally

> 1938 *Architectural Review*: The open plan is almost universal but perhaps less easy to work than it looks.

> 1954 *Architectural Review*: A few are more experimental, influenced either by the pre-war work of Arne Jacobsen and Mogens Lassen or, more recently, by the open-plan American house.

Oscar *n* (1936) one of the statuettes awarded by the Academy of Motion Picture Arts and Sciences, Hollywood, U.S.A., for excellence in film acting, directing, etc. These awards have been made annually since 1928. Margaret Herrick, a former secretary of the Academy of Motion Picture Arts and Sciences, is said to have remarked in 1931 that the Art Deco-style statuette reminded her of her 'Uncle Oscar', namely Oscar Pierce, an American wheat and fruit grower; the name stuck

> 1936 *Time*: Neither Director Ford nor Screenwriter Nichols appeared to claim their prizes—small gold statuettes which Hollywood calls 'Oscars'.

overspill *n* (1930) the movement of surplus population from a city to a less heavily populated area of the same country; also applied to the surplus population itself. A favourite word of 20th-century town-planners, although it had its origins in the late 19th century as a term for surplus population leaving a country

> 1930 *Times*: On the south lie the famous South Downs, within range of the overspill from the seaside towns.

> 1945 *Annual Register 1944*: The Bill for the purchase of so-called 'overspill' areas where those who were crowded out could be accommodated.

> 1946 *Nature*: Public interest has been stimulated equally by the controversies over the proposals for dealing with Manchester's overspill in a new town at Mobberley, or the even larger overspill problem of Liverpool.

owner-occupier *n* (1935) someone who owns their dwelling (as opposed to, for example, renting it). A term which did not come into its own until after World War II, when this form of occupancy became much commoner (although its previous existence is suggested by an isolated record of the derivative *owner-occupiership* from 1924)

> 1935 *Planning*: There are for example the approaches of State ownership at the one extreme, and of sub-division among many thousands of small owner-occupiers at the other extreme.

> 1958 *New Statesman*: Here and there an enterprising tenant, owner-occupier or determined landlord has repaired and repainted and the contrast is startling.

package *n* (1931) a combination or collection of interdependent or related abstract things. Compare **package (1947)**

> 1931 *Social Science Abstracts*: Insurance in a 'package'... The exact size of the 'package' offered to any employee depends upon age, sex, and length of service.

> 1958 *Economist*: The [US] Administration is thinking of proposing a simplified 'package' [for summit talks].

palais glide *n* (1938) a type of ballroom dance in which large groups dance together. The 'palais' in its name comes from *palais de danse*, a high-falutin word for a dance hall which was in vogue between the wars (first recorded in 1919)

> 1938 A. Moore: The Palais Glide can hardly be termed a dance; it is reminiscent of the Gallop which has been a feature of Hunt Balls for many years… It can be danced to any Foxtrot tune…and it is played at a tempo of about 30 bars a minute.

pan *v* (1930) to move (a film or television camera) so as to follow moving action. A shortening of *panorama*. *Pan* had actually been used in a similar way in the early days of silent movies, with the person or thing filmed as its object ('We'll "pan" you right down the middle of the picture to the raft', *Saturday Evening Post* (1913)), but this usage seems never to have caught on widely. The intransitive use, now the commonest, is first recorded in 1931. See also **panoram (1915)**

> 1930 *Electronics*: With the advent of sound, the operation of 'panning' the camera to afford a changing point of view became a more complicated process.

> 1932 A. Buchanan: The camera 'pans' around the room, bringing to view the shabby furniture.

parentcraft *n* (1930) knowledge of, and skill in, the rearing of children. Part of the 20th century's avid codification of activities and functions which in more innocent times had just involved doing what came naturally. Later the fashionable term was **parenting (1959)**

> 1930 *Lancet*: The teaching of parentcraft.

> 1945 *Times*: The Ministry were discussing various schemes regarding children under two, and they had lately set up a committee to go into the question of parentcraft.

parking meter *n* (1936) a coin-operated meter which registers the time a vehicle has been parked. Originally US; often abbreviated to simply *meter*. The devices were not intoduced in Britain until the end of the 1950s

> 1936 *American City*: In July…there came to the attention of the officials in Dallas a device known as the parking meter.

> 1960 *Daily Telegraph*: What promises to be the most important experiment in traffic control starts next Monday, when car parking over the whole of Mayfair becomes subject to meters.

partisan *n* (1939) During World War II, a guerrilla, especially one working in enemy-occupied territory in Eastern Europe and the Balkans

> 1939 C. Gubbins (title): Partisan leader's handbook.

> 1942 *Daily Telegraph*: Behind the fighting front the Russian 'partisan front' in the German rear forms a skeleton army.

> 1944 *Hutchinson's Pictorial History of the War*: In the autumn of 1941 Marshal Tito's partisans began a wild and furious war for existence against the Germans… The partisan movement soon out-stripped in numbers the forces of General Mikhailovitch.

patrol car *n* (1931) a police car used for patrolling the streets. Originally US

> 1931 *Chicago Police Problems*: Each district normally has two small patrol cars.

> 1951 A. Martienssen: In the Aberdeen system, the patrol cars and the beat constables have been formed into teams.

Pavlovian *adj* (1931) Denoting the theories, experiments, or methods of the Russian physiologist Ivan Petrovich Pavlov (1849–1936), especially those aspects of his work connected with conditioning the salivary reflexes of a dog to the mental stimulus of the sound of a bell. In later usage often applied more broadly to any automatic, 'knee-jerk' response

> 1931 Aldous Huxley: The effects of such sociological reforms as Pavlovian conditioning of all children.

> 1974 *Daily Telegraph*: The report does not hesitate to name names, a procedure that will inevitably touch off a Pavlovian response from Leftist circles to deride it as a 'Reds under the Beds' scare.

payola *n* (1938) a secret or indirect payment or bribe to someone to use their position, influence, etc., to promote a commercial product, service, etc., especially such a payment to a disc-jockey for plugging a record or song. Colloquial, originally US. Coined from *pay* plus the ending -*ola*, perhaps as in *Victrola*, the proprietary name of a type of record player

1938 *Variety*: Plug payolas perplexed… The payola element had made their deals with bandleaders on the expectation that they continue to get 19c, thereby making it profitable to do business with the plug at a rate of around 10c a point.

peanuts *n* (1934) something inadequately small, especially a derisory payment. Slang, originally US. Possibly from the idea of peanuts being something one feeds thoughtlessly to animals

1941 Budd Schulberg: They got you working for peanuts.

1959 John Osborne: There's a thousand pounds a week from record sales…it ain't peanuts.

pen-friend *n* (1933), **pen-pal** *n* (1938) a friend with whom contact is maintained (almost) exclusively by correspondence

1933 *Boy's Magazine*: Any reader at home or abroad who would like to correspond with a 'pen-friend' in another land is invited to send his name, address, and age to the Editor.

Pentothal *n* (1935) A proprietary name (registered in 1936) for thiopentone sodium, a barbiturate drug used especially as an intravenous anaesthetic. It is an arbitrary reworking of the generic name *thiopental*

1940 *Notes & Queries*: I observe in the press mention of two drugs to induce sleep with new names, Evipan and Pentothal.

personal space *n* (1937) the area immediately surrounding each individual which is felt to be his or her own, and into which others cannot usually intrude without giving rise to feelings of anxiety, unease, etc. Originally a technical term in psychology (it is a translation of German *personaler Raum*); it did not spread into everyday use until the last quarter of the century

1977 Desmond Morris: No one can ever become completely immune to invasions of Personal Space.

1988 *Independent*: Half of her sample were smokers… It was…a way of creating a tiny oasis of the personal space they were denied.

Perspex *n* (1935) A British proprietary name (registered in 1935) for polymerized methyl methacrylate, a tough transparent thermoplastic that is much lighter than glass and does not splinter. It was based on Latin *perspect-*, the past participle stem of *perspicere* 'to look through'. In the US Perspex is sold under the names *Plexiglas* and *Lucite*

1943 Leonard Cheshire: I asked Percy to dim his light; it reflected on the perspex in front and I couldn't see out.

pesto *n* (1937) a pasta sauce of crushed basil, garlic, and olive oil. An early outrider of the Italian culinary terms that cascaded into English in the second half of the century

1954 Elizabeth David: When the *pesto* is a thick purée start adding the olive oil.

photo-finish *n* (1936) the finish of a race in which competitors are so close that the result has to be determined by reference to a photograph of the situation

1936 *New York Times*: New…tests will be made tomorrow at Pimlico on the photo finish device… At Belmont Park thirty pictures were called for. Of this number the photo finish awarded the decision to sixteen horses racing on the outside, with fourteen on the inside.

picture window *n* (1938) a large window consisting of a single pane of glass

1938 *American Home*: If you have a large picture window, we suggest sill-length casement drawn curtains.

pinko *n, adj* (1936) (a person whose politics are) left of centre, but closer to the centre than those of a 'red'; (a) liberal socialist. Colloquial, and usually decidedly derogatory; originally US. An elaboration of *pink* in the same sense, a metaphor whose origins can be traced to the early 19th century

1936 J. G. Cozzens: She's a good girl… Now only a healthy pinko. I've snatched her like a brand from the Young Communist League burning.

1972 Dan Lees: He made Ronald Reagan look like a pinko liberal.

pin-table *n* (1936) a table for playing pinball, a bagatelle-like game in which small balls are propelled across a sloping surface towards targets which indicate the score when hit. The term *pinball* is first recorded in 1911, but only as applied to a simple domestic version of the game. It was not until the mid 1930s that automated slot-machine-style pinball took off as an arcade game ('One of the bills would allow the State…to license claw machine and pinball games', *Sun* (Baltimore) (1935))

> 1936 *Architectural Review*: Under one of these, however, peeps out a gay little shop in bright green paint, full of pin-tables, where one can lose one's money in proper Strand fashion.

pirate *n* (1933) someone who transmits radio programmes without a licence. A rather strange volte-face in usage, because in the 1910s and 20s *pirate* had been used of someone who *received* radio broadcasts without a licence ('The thousands who are listening-in without a licence of any description—popularly termed "pirates" ', *Wireless Weekly* (1923)). The term really came into its own in the 1960s, often as an adjective

> 1933 *Practical Wireless*: Wanted, One Radio Pirate! The small Brussels (Schaerbeek) broadcasting station, having complained to the authorities that an illicit transmitter has marred the reception of its broadcasts, a reward of one thousand Belgian francs has been offered to trace the identity of the culprit.

> 1964 *Daily Telegraph*: The activities of the 'pirate' radio ships Caroline and Atlanta have presented the Government with a problem which cannot be solved simply. It is expected that the Cabinet will discuss this week the possibility of legislation to prevent broadcasting from such 'pirate' vessels.

pix *n* (1932) pictures. Slang, originally US journalists', used to save space in headlines. In early use mainly denoting 'motion pictures, films', but latterly usually used in the sense 'photographs'

> 1932 *Variety*: 'Million', Par's all-star pix… Open sesame for Brit. pix in Dominion.

> 1973 Edward Hyams: Barnet said, 'I want the Victoria Lowell pix.'… [He] began looking through the thirty-seven photographs of Victoria Lowell.

pizza *n* (1935) an Italian foodstuff consisting of a breadlike base with various savoury toppings. In Italian the word means literally just 'tart' or 'pie', but its ultimate origins are unknown. Earliest references to it in English are as an exotic foreign dish; not until the 1950s did its career as a fast-food star begin. See also **pizzeria (1943)**

> 1935 Marcelle Morphy: Pizza alla Napoletana… In the south of Italy…all kinds of flat tarts are called 'pizze'.

> 1957 *Sunday Times*: The Pizza Napoletana has travelled the world. In Paris restaurants, in Shaftesbury Avenue milk bars, in South Kensington coffee shops the pizza has become acclimatised.

> 1959 *Times*: The pizza palaces and highway honky-tonks with which we have littered the land.

pizzazz *n* (1937) zest, vim, vitality, liveliness. Colloquial, originally US. It is a made-up word, probably seeking in some way to encapsulate the sound and feeling of zestfulness. Its spelling has never completely settled down—variants on record include *bizzazz* and *pezzazz*

> 1937 *Harper's Bazaar*: Pizazz, to quote the editor of the Harvard *Lampoon*, is an indefinable dynamic quality, the *je ne sais quoi* of function; as for instance, adding Scotch puts pizazz into a drink. Certain clothes have it, too… There's pizazz in this rust evening coat.

platform sole *n* (1939) a thick raised sole. Fashionable in the late 1930s and early 40s and again in the 1970s. Often shortened to plain *platform* (first recorded in 1945)

> 1946 *Sun* (Baltimore): Picture-Pretty Platforms… Two flattering styles to choose from…both mounted on black faille platforms.

> 1973 *Woman's Own*: Today's fashions, with their high-heeled, platform-soled shoes and long, straight trousers can easily make you look taller.

platinum blonde *adj*, *n* (1931) (a woman) with hair of a silvery-blonde colour

> 1931 *Daily Express*: Miss Binnie Barnes, who appears as a platinum blonde in 'Cavalcade', is seen here as a brunette. Nature gave her auburn-red hair.

platter *n* (1931) a gramophone record. Cool enough slang until the 1960s, but then it faded from vogue. Originally US

> 1935 *Vanity Fair* (New York): There ought to be a hot coupling on every platter.

> 1960 *Master Detective*: Rock and Roll, that's what I'm good at. I got a terrific collection of platters.

Pluto *n* (1930) a small planet of the solar system lying beyond the orbit of Neptune, discovered in 1930 by C. W. Tombaugh. By the end of the century its status as a true planet was seriously in doubt. For accounts of the naming (commemorating the Roman god of the Underworld) see the quotes below

> 1930 *New York Times*: 'Pluto' is the provisional name that Italian astronomers have given to the new trans-Neptune planet discovered March 13 at Lowell Observatory in Flagstaff, Ariz… Hugh Rice…yesterday opposed naming the newly discovered planet 'Minerva', as has already been suggested, because an asteroid already bears that name.

> 1930 V. M. Slipher: Many names have been suggested and among them Minerva and Pluto have been very popular… Pluto seems very appropriate and we are proposing to the American Astronomical Society and to the Royal Astronomical Society, that this name be given to it. As far as we know Pluto was first suggested by Miss Venetia Burney, aged 11, of Oxford, England. [Note] Kindly cabled by Prof. H. H. Turner.

> 1930 H. H. Turner: A post-card from the President of the Royal Astronomical Society offered this morning 'congratulations to the suggester of the name Pluto, now adopted'. The reference is to a telegram which I had the honour of sending to the Lowell Observatory on March 15…conveying the suggestion of Miss Venetia Burney, of Oxford, made at breakfast on that day to her grandfather, who sent it on to me… It was a brother of that same grandfather who suggested the names Deimos and Phobos for the satellites of Mars.

Polaroid *n* (1936) A proprietary name (registered in the US in 1936) for a material which in the form of thin sheets produces a high degree of plane polarization in light passing through it. It was further registered for sunglasses in 1942. Its application to a kind of camera which develops the negative and produces a positive print within a short time of the exposure's being made dates from the 1960s (see **Polaroid (1961)**)

> 1936 *Nature*: Another [firm] manufactures ophthalmic instruments employing Polaroid.

> 1959 Colin MacInnes: The water sparkling so that I had on my Polaroids.

polio *n* (1931) poliomyelitis, especially the paralytic form. The term *poliomyelitis*, of which this is an abbreviated form, is first recorded in 1878; it gradually replaced the previous *infantile paralysis*. The abbreviation followed mid-century epidemics, which were brought to an end by the administration of an effective vaccine in the 1950s. See also **iron lung (1932), Salk vaccine (1954)**

> 1931 *Survey* (heading): Panic and polio.

> 1940 *Time* (heading): Polio scare.

polythene *n* (1939) a tough, light, translucent thermoplastic made by polymerizing ethylene and used especially for moulded and extruded articles, as film for packaging, and as a coating. The word is a contraction of *polyethylene*, also first recorded in this sense in 1939, and the preferred form in US English

> 1939 *Plastics*: Polythene, the new polymerized ethylenic resin.

polyunsaturated *adj* (1932) containing long chains of carbon atoms with numbers of double carbon-carbon linkages. For long an obscure item of biochemists' jargon, it gained a higher profile in the early 1960s, thanks to its application to certain types of fat used in margarines and cooking oils, which promote low cholesterol levels

> 1961 *Sunday Times*: American housewives,…concerned about their husbands' health, are shopping for 'poly-unsaturated fats'. The rush is on because medical research has established a connection between arterial diseases and the level of cholesterol in the blood—and cholesterol seems to be formed chiefly from the intake of the 'saturated fats', particularly animal and dairy fats.

polyvinyl chloride *n* (1933) a thermoplastic resin used in a variety of manufactured products (e.g. plastic raincoats). Much better known in the second half of the century under its abbreviated name **PVC (1941)**, and in the US under the proprietary name *Saran*

> 1933 *Industrial & Engineering Chemistry*: Co-polymerization of vinyl chloride and vinyl acetate gives a better resin than the mere admixture of polyvinyl chloride and polyvinyl acetate.

pool *n* the pools (1938) See **football pool (1929)**

positron *n* (1933) the anti-particle of the ordinary (negative) electron, having the same mass and a numerically equal but positive charge

> 1933 C. D. Anderson: Experiments have been carried out which gave conclusive evidence that positrons are ejected from lead by the gamma-radiation of ThC". [*Note*] The contraction positron is here used to denote the free positive electron.

power politics *n* (1937) political action based on or backed by threats to use force. A direct translation of German *Machtpolitik*

> 1942 L. B. Namier: For centuries Vienna and Paris had been the centres of European power-politics.

prefab *adj, n* (1937) (a house or other building) that is prefabricated; in Britain applied specifically to a light, often single-storey house of the kind built in large numbers during and after World War II when it was necessary to rehouse many people in a short time

> 1937 *New Yorker*: Darling, the Prefab Homes man was just here.

> 1942 *Time*: This year 20% of all new houses may be prefabs.

> 1947 Nevil Shute: Any young couple might live in a prefab when they start off first.

prefabricate *v* (1932) to manufacture sections of (a building or similar structure) in a factory or yard prior to their assembly on a site, especially when they are larger or more complex than those considered traditional

> 1932 W. H. Ham: We can prefabricate 90 per cent of a house in the factory, assemble it, and make it a permanent, attractive, useful home.

> 1933 *Architectural Review*: There are a number of houses, one among them being actually of the new 'prefabricated' type.

prezzie, pressie *n* (1937) a present. Colloquial. An elaboration of the earlier and never very common *pres* ('Accept my little pres', James Joyce, *Ulysses* (1922)). At first it seems to have had a fairly limited, 'private-language' style circulation, with no established spelling, but it gained wider currency in Australian English in the early 1960s, and spread back from there to British English

> 1937 E. D. Metcalfe: The rest of the time will be spent shopping (buying presees for Wallis [Simpson, Duchess of Windsor]).

> 1975 *Australian*: From…endeavours yesterday to discover what presents the Whitlams were taking overseas with them, we can inform you of the following piece of government policy: From this day forth no public announcements will be made about the nature of prime ministerial pressies.

production line *n* (1935) (a method of mass-producing goods using) an assembly line (see **assembly line (1914)**). In later usage often with connotations of sterile uniformity

> 1935 T. H. Burnham: Many nice problems arise as to when it is economic to break up a group system and lay down a special production line.

> 1958 *Listener*: I suggest one of those 'production-line' chickens, which is big enough for four.

protagonist *n* (1935) a proponent, advocate, or supporter (of a cause, idea, etc.). Etymologically, a *protagonist* is the leading character in a Greek drama, and those who take a Canute-like view of semantic change have railed against this 20th-century usage (see the first quote below)

> 1935 A. P. Herbert: I heard with horror…that the word 'protagonist' is being used as if it were protagonist—one who is *for* something, and opposed to ant-agonist, one who is against it.

> 1975 *Times Literary Supplement*: Kokan was…an unabashed protagonist of the technical superiority of Western civilization.

pull-in *n* (1938) a café or refreshment stand in a lay-by—the modest forerunner of the motorway services

> 1938 Graham Greene: He didn't speak to her in the bus… The country unwound the other way: Mazawattee tea, antique dealers, pull-ins.

pulp *adj* (1936) producing or being ephemeral literature, typically containing sensational or pornographic subject matter. Originally US. First recorded in 1936, but predated by the noun use of *pulp* to denote a magazine of this sort ('Even should he fail to publish in the big magazines, and never graduate from the "pulps", he can rise to as much as ten cents a word,' *Frontier* (Missoula, Montana) (1931)). The name comes from the rough, unfinished paper on which such publications are often printed

> 1936 *New Yorker*: We found ourselves…talking with an ace pulp writer.

> 1955 L. A. Fiedler: Wordless narrative: digests, pulp fiction, movies, picture magazines.

pusher *n* (1935) a seller of illegal drugs. Slang, originally US

> 1956 Ed McBain: Junkies are easy to trace. Talk to a few pushers, zing, you're in.

pushy *adj* (1936) unpleasantly forward or self-assertive; aggressive. Originally US

> 1936 Margaret Mitchell: [Atlanta] had nothing whatever to recommend it—only its railroads and a bunch of mighty pushy people… Restless, energetic people from the older sections of Georgia.

quick-frozen *adj* (1930) frozen rapidly to facilitate long storage at a low temperature. Preservative freezing (and the adjective *frozen*) had been applied to foodstuffs since the middle of the 19th century, but it was the technique of subjecting them to a sudden low-temperature blast, eliminating the formation of ice crystals, that paved the way for the late 20th century's freezer food-culture. *Quick-frozen* remained the vogue term in the middle years of the century, but it gradually gave way to the simpler *frozen*. See also **fish stick (1953)**, **fish finger (1955)**

> 1930 *Popular Science*: Clarence B. Birdseye…succeeded in placing quick-frozen fish on the market.

quin *n* (1935) any of five children born at one birth. An abbreviation of *quintuplet* popularized when the Dionne quintuplets (born in Ontario, Canada, in 1934) were given saturation media coverage in the mid 1930s. The word *quintuplet* itself dates from the late 19th century

> 1935 *Dionne Quintuplets growing Up* (caption): My, what big girls the 'Quins' are getting to be.

quota quickie *n* (1936) a cheap rapidly made cinema film produced to fulfil a quota. In Britain, the 1927 Cinematograph Film Act required cinemas to show a certain number of home-grown films per year, in order to protect the British film industry from Hollywood overkill. By 1937–38, the annual production had reached a remarkable 228 titles. The use of *quickie* to denote a quickly made film is first recorded in 1926

> 1936 *Economist*: The primary objective of the Board of Trade…was the complete extirpation of the 'quota quickie'.

race gang *n* (1931) a group of petty criminals who frequent race-meetings. Their nefarious activities at British race-tracks, in somewhat pale imitation of US gangsters (notably rearranging their rivals' faces with razors and knuckledusters), were staple fare in tabloid newspapers of the 1930s, and are vividly evoked by Graham Greene in *Brighton Rock* (1938)

> 1931 Margery Allingham: Gipsies and race gangs always hate each other.

> 1937 Eric Rickman: The term 'race gang' is still a very favoured one by newspaper sub-editors.

racist *n, adj* (1932) (an advocate) of belief in the superiority of a particular race, leading to prejudice and antagonism towards people of other races. The associated noun *racism* is first recorded in 1935. In the 1930s, the words were usually used with reference to the Nazis' theories of racial superiority, but in the latter part of the century their context is usually prejudiced treatment of blacks and Asians. They were late-comers in a field already occupied by **racialism (1907)** and **racialist (1917)**, but over the decades they have gradually become the main forms

> 1934 H. G. Wells: So much for the Hitlerite stage of my development, when I was a sentimentalist, a moralist, a patriot, a racist.

> 1936 L. Dennis: If…it be assumed that one of our values should be a type of racism which excludes certain races from citizenship, then the plan of execution should provide for the annihilation, deportation, or sterilization of the excluded races.

> 1977 Martin Walker: A strike of the Asian workers against racism in the factory.

radiogram *n* (1932) a radio and record-player combined in a single cabinet. A shortened version of the short-lived *radio-gramophone* (1927). As televisions replaced radios and tapes replaced records between the 1950s and the 1970s, the word gradually faded from use. Compare **music centre (1974)**

> 1932 G. Wilson: If you have no electricity in your house you should avoid the radio-gram.

> 1933 *Sunday Referee*: In the living-room…is a ply-wood built-in book-case, at one end of which is…a built-in electric radiogram and loud-speaker.

railbus *n* (1933) a vehicle resembling a bus but running on a railway track

> 1933 *Morning Post*: The London and North-Eastern Railway Company will put the new…stream-lined Diesel-electric 'railbus' into regular service on the suburban and outlying railway systems round Newcastle, within the next two weeks.

> 1968 *Drive*: British Rail could save many of their rural routes by introducing rail buses—a sort of single-decker diesel tramcar, operated by a driver-conductor not as a train but as if the vehicle were on the open road.

rally *n* (1932) a competitive event for motor vehicles, usually over a long distance on public roads. The term was borrowed from French, and in the early years the French spelling *rallye* was often used in English

> 1932 *Radio Times*: Some of the big motoring events of the year—the Ulster Motor Rally, [etc.].

> 1949 C. A. N. May: There can be no guarantee of a 1949 Rallye actually taking place.

rat-race *n* (1939) a fiercely competitive struggle or contest. Originally US. The word's main modern connotation, 'a competitive struggle to maintain one's position in work or life', does not seem to have crystallized until the 1950s. It is not clear whether there is any connection with the slightly earlier slang use of *rat-race* as the name of a type of dance

> 1939 Christopher Morley: Their own private life gets to be a rat-race.

> 1958 *Spectator*: Modern economic life is more like a rat-race than a rational way of life.

> 1959 *Observer*: I don't like this rat-race for promotion.

raygun *n* (1931) a weapon that can emit harmful or lethal rays. A term redolent of earlier and (as they seemed at the end of the century) simpler and less sophisticated days of science fiction

> 1931 *Amazing Stories*: The rayguns of the battlecraft, being of superior range, melted down the mortars of the fort at the magazine.

> 1958 *Spectator*: But as a space-veteran who once triggered a ray-gun with Flash Gordon, let me advise you to read on.

record *n* **off the record** (1933) unofficial(ly), confidential(ly). Originally US

> 1933 H. L. Ickes: He met and answered every question, although in some instances his answers were off the record.

> 1935 *Time*: Only a very few Canadian tycoons took a calmer off-the-record view.

recordist *n* (1931) someone who makes (sound) recordings. A term apparently coined deliberately to create a distinction from *recorder*, applied to a machine used for such recordings

> 1938 *Nature*: That highly skilled, imaginative, ingenious, agile and patient collaborator in film-making who bears the regrettable though comprehensible title of 'recordist'.

> 1978 *Daily Telegraph*: All BBC television programme production is threatened from today by an unofficial overtime ban by cameramen and sound recordists.

record player *n* (1934) an electrical device for playing gramophone records. From the 1950s onwards it gradually took the place of the earlier *gramophone* and *phonograph*

> 1934 *Wireless World*: The Collaro record player incorporated in a radio-gramophone cabinet.

> 1939 *New Regal-Zono Records* (advert): The thousands already sold of the Columbia electric record-player prove conclusively how many fully appreciate the facility of playing their records through their radio sets.

redevelop *v* (1935) to rebuild (e.g. a part of a town) according to new plans. Part of town planners' jargon, and not without a tinge of hyperbole and euphemism: it sounds both progressive and impressive, and plays down the considerable destruction often involved. Its associations with high-rise ghettoes have tarnished it. First recorded in the derived noun *redevelopment*

> 1935 *Act of Parliament*: It shall be the duty of the local authority to cause the area to be defined on a map, and to pass a resolution declaring the area so defined to be a proposed re-development area.

> 1936 E. E. Finch & C. G. Eve: It therefore appears that nearly a quarter of the building site area has been redeveloped in the last 30 years.

reflation *n* (1932) a deliberate increase in the supply of money, so as to revive economic activity. A term (modelled on *inflation* and *deflation*) that arose out of efforts to bring to an end the economic depression of the early 1930s. The derivative *reflationary* is contemporary

> 1932 *Economist*: Its purpose has been aptly described as 'reflation', to prevent further deflation…and to undo some of the present extreme deflation.

> 1932 *Hansard Commons*: I propose a different thing altogether [from inflation]. I would describe it as reflation, which I would define as controlled expansion of the note issue to keep pace with increased production.

> 1932 *Times Literary Supplement*: The 'reflationary' policy of the American Government will in the end, he thinks, set prices rising again.

reject *v* (1931) to refuse affection to (someone), specifically to spurn (a child) by denying it the normal emotional relationship between parent and offspring. Originally US. Classic sociologists' jargon of the 20th century

> 1931 *Smith College Studies in Social Work*: Case histories are presented showing the attitude toward their parents…, husbands, and children of twelve mothers who rejected their children.

> 1973 A. Janov: But to feel really rejected means to…feel utterly alone and unwanted as that child.

repossess *v* (1933) to regain possession of or seize (goods being bought by hire-purchase) when a purchaser defaults on his or her payments. Its original mode, apparently, was as a past participle, used in US English as a commercial euphemism for *second-hand*

> 1933 *Sun* (Baltimore) (advert): Repossessed Car Corp., 31 W. North Ave.

> 1969 *Rolling Stone*: The starting point was having their car repossessed in Nashville ten years ago.

resistance *n* (1939) organized covert opposition to an occupying or ruling power, especially (usually with a capital *R*), in World War II, the underground movement formed in France in 1940 (see **Resistance (1944)**)

> 1939 *War Illustrated*: Underground resistance to Hitler has been organized amongst the workers in all the big industrial centres of Germany.

> 1940 *Times*: General de Gaulle…broadcast from London a message to the French nation last night. The text of his speech…is as follows:…Whatever happens the flame of French resistance must not and shall not be extinguished.

revusical *n* (1931) a theatrical entertainment that combines elements of the revue and musical. A portmanteau word (originally US) which belongs essentially to the middle three decades of the century, although there are records of it (apparently as a recoinage) in the late 1960s

> 1936 *Daily Mirror* (New York): Harriet Hoctor's class in 'The Ziegfeld Follies', the revusical.

Rice Krispies *n* (1936) The proprietary name (registered in 1936, under the description 'a food made of rice, for human consumption') of a type of breakfast cereal made from rice. Often spelled *rice crispies*

> 1956 C. Blackstock: The fourteen-year-old at the breakfast table…can devour the Black Mass with her rice crispies.

ripple *n* (1939) an ice cream manufactured with an admixture of coloured syrup that gives it a rippled appearance. Registered as a proprietary name in the US in 1942

> 1976 *Milton Keynes Express*: Ice Cream… Raspberry Ripple, 4 litre £1.10.

robot *n* (1939) See **traffic robot (1931)**

Rockefeller *n* (1938) The name of John D. Rockefeller (1839–1937), American financier and philanthropist, used as the type of an immensely rich man

1938 Isaac Goldberg: Anciently, men looked up to Crœsus…as a man of immense wealth… Thousands of years later men still say, 'He is a Rockefeller'.

rock salmon *n* (1931) A commercial euphemism applied by British fishmongers and fish-and-chip shops to any fish which, if its real identity were known, would put the customers off. The commonest recipients of the name have been the dogfish and the wolffish. It gradually ousted the earlier **flake (1906)**

1931 J. R. Norman: It has been found convenient to market this perfectly wholesome fish [i.e. catfish] under a more pleasing name, and…it is sold as 'Rock Salmon'.

running dog *n* (1937) In Communist terminology, one who is subservient to counter-revolutionary interests; a lackey. A literal translation of Chinese *zougou*, but during the Cold War it became a familiar taunt in all parts of the Communist world

1937 Edgar Snow: Vanguards of young Moslems were…urging the overthrow of the 'Kuomintang running-dog'.

1961 *Mao Tsetung's Selected Works*: Without a revolutionary party,…it is impossible to lead the working class and the broad masses of the people in defeating imperialism and its running dogs.

sad *adj* (1938) Of a person: contemptible, socially inadequate, pathetic. Colloquial; a usage which bumped along the bottom of the graph until the late 1980s, when it suddenly enjoyed a burst of popularity. See also **saddo (1992)**

1938 I. Edman: 'Philosophy's rather highbrow at college. If you go in for that kind of thing, they think you're rather sad.' 'Rather what?' I said. 'Oh, *sad* is…the opposite of tops.' 'Oh, I see; and if you're interested in ideas you're *sad*.'

1989 G. Naylor: Do you really think I'm the sort of pathetic, sad, weasly kind of person who could get erotically aroused by looking at paintings of matronly breasts?

1994 *Guardian*: They find that they are communicating with the kind of sad anorak-wearers they would never have encountered in real life.

Sadie Hawkins day *n* (1939) a day early in November on which, according to a 'tradition' started by the US cartoon series *Li'l Abner*, women can propose marriage to men, demand dates with them, etc. Sadie Hawkins is a character in the series

1952 *Sun* (Baltimore): The dean… was the only man to get away in the Sadie Hawkins Day race this afternoon.

sado-masochism *n* (1935) the co-existence of sadism and masochism in one person, so that they get sexual pleasure from both inflicting and suffering pain. A coinage apparently of the Austrian psychologist Wilhelm Stekel (originator also of **paraphilia (1925)**), and first recorded in English in a translation of his work. (The term *sadism* is first recorded in 1888, *masochism* in 1893)

1935 L. Brink: I do not claim that I have solved the perplexing problem of sadomasochism…The literature concerning sadomasochistic disorders is extraordinarily abundant… All sadomasochists are affect-hungry individuals.

safety island *n* (1933) See **traffic island (1931)**

satellite *n* (1936) a man-made object placed in orbit round an astronomical body, typically the Earth. An English translation of Jules Verne's *Begum's Fortune* in 1880 spoke of a space projectile 'endowing the Earth with a second satellite', but the terminology did not really meet the concept in its modern sense until the 1930s. The science-fiction writer Arthur C. Clarke is often credited as being the first to set out the real possibilities for such an object, in the 1945 article in *Wireless World* quoted below. Theory became practice in 1957 (see **sputnik (1957)**)

1936 *Discovery*: The scheme for building a metal outpost satellite and propelling it in a fixed orbit 600 miles above the earth's surface.

1945 Arthur C. Clarke: This 'orbital' velocity is 8 km per sec. (5 miles per sec), and a rocket which attained it would become an artificial satellite, circling the world for ever with no expenditure of power.

1957 *Times*: The Russian satellite soaring over the United States seven times a day has made an enormous impression on American minds.

scampi *n* (1930) a dish of Dublin Bay prawn tails, typically fried in batter. A borrowing from Italian, the singular form of which, referring to the animal itself, is recorded in English in 1928 ('It is extremely plentiful in the Adriatic and is sold in the Italian ports under the name of "Scampo" ', Russell & Yonge). This never caught on, but the plural *scampi* certainly did: at first somewhat recherché, by the 1960s it was on the menu at most middle-market eating places

> 1930 Evelyn Waugh: I ate *scampi* at Cavaletto and felt no ill effects.

> 1978 *Times*: Bartolomeo Calderoni…introduced scampi to Britain… As for the scampi, he imported them from Venice's Grand Hotel…when he was head chef at Quaglino's in the 1930s.

scopophilia *n* (1937) voyeurism. Due to a mistake by one of Sigmund Freud's translators, the word originally appeared in English as **scoptophilia (1924)**. This form embedded itself quite success-fully in the language, and for some time after the 'correct' version (based on Greek *-skopia* 'obser-vation') was introduced, the two rubbed along side by side. See also **voyeurism (1924)**

> 1937 M. Hirschfeld: One of the principal criteria of pathological scopophilia is the *dominant* char-acter of the urge.

scorched earth *n* (1937) Denoting a policy of destroying all means of sustenance or supply in a country that might be of use to an invading enemy. The English term is apparently a translation of Chinese *jiaotu* (*zhèngcè*) 'scorched earth (policy)'

> 1937 C. McDonald: The populace…are still disturbed, in spite of official denials, by wild rumours of a 'scorched earth policy' of burning the city before the Japanese enter.

screwball *n* (1933) an eccentric or irrational person. Slang, mainly US; a development of the earlier baseball sense, 'a pitch thrown with reverse swing, so that it goes against the natural curve'

> 1933 Paul Gallico: McKabe was already heading for the door. He heard Billers say: 'Who is that screwball?'

seat belt *n* (1932) a safety belt for a person in a moving conveyance. Originally applied to one worn in an aircraft, especially at take-off or landing, and later used for one worn in a motor vehicle as a protection in an accident or in an emergency stop

> 1933 *Aeroplane*: 'Please fix seat-belts.' (Note! not safety belts.)

> 1959 *B.S.I. News*: Arising from the interest now being displayed in seat belts for motorists, a new technical committee of the B.S.I. recently held its first meeting, at which it was decided that a British Standard for these articles would serve a useful purpose.

secret weapon *n* (1936) a weapon (often of potentially decisive force) classified as secret. A some-what paranoid term which arose out of the long build-up to war in the 1930s, when potential en-emies were suspected of developing nameless horrors in their weapons research establishments

> 1936 Eric Ambler: He once told me that in these days there was no such thing as a secret weapon.

> 1939 Winston Churchill: The magnetic mine…may perhaps be Herr Hitler's much vaunted secret weapon.

> 1974 *Listener*: The Führer…said he had a secret weapon. Immediately Neville Chamberlain…asked the Intelligence Services what the secret weapon was.

semiconductor *n* (1931) any of a range of solid crystalline substances, such as germanium or sil-icon, that have electrical conductivity greater than insulators but less than good conductors. The word actually goes back to the early 19th century as a fairly general term for something intermedi-ate between a good and a bad conductor, but the specific application to the sort of substance from which transistors are made is a 20th-century phenomenon

> 1931 *Proceedings of the Royal Society*: It is not possible to maintain that the difference between good and bad conductors is one of degree only… There is an essential difference between a semi-conductor, such as germanium, and a good conductor, such as silver, which must be accounted for by any theory which attempts to deal with semi-conductors.

> 1979 *Journal of the Royal Society of Arts*: Sometimes a significant advance in technology may itself create a new market, as did the advent of the semiconductors to the small 'transistor radio' market.

send *v* (1932) to transport with delight; carry away. Slang; originally applied specifically to jazz, and later often to various sorts of popular music and performers

> 1932 *Melody Maker*: I enclose the following wire which Louis (Musicmouth) Armstrong sent to Big John… 'My boy Earl was marvellous as ever yessir he sent me.'

> 1956 Billie Holiday: Meade Lux Lewis knocked them out; Ammons and Johnson flipped them…Newton's band sent them.

> 1958 *Spectator*: The girls wore thick eye-makeup and 'sent' expressions.

senior citizen *n* (1938) an old person, especially one who is past the age of retirement. Originally US. One of the 20th century's classic euphemisms, and an early sign of its uneasiness with the concept of old age

> 1938 *Time*: Mr. Downey had an inspiration to do something on behalf of what he calls, for campaign purposes, 'our senior citizens'.

serve-yourself *adj* (1937) Denoting a shop, restaurant, etc., where the customers serve themselves. Originally US. A variation on the earlier **self-service (1919)**

> 1937 Marjorie Hillis: Those serve-yourself emporiums…often have simple ones [i.e. evening wraps]…which…won't look very different from the costly one on your neighbor.

services *n* (1936) the section of the economy that supplies needs of the consumer but produces no tangible goods

> 1941 *Economist*: The British public spent almost 900 millions in 1937 on services, excluding entertainments, rent, rates and taxes. The largest constituents of the total were travel, domestic service, public utilities, hotels and restaurants…The very considerable increase in the standard of living…explains the growth of the 'service', as distinct from the 'productive' industries since the last war.

shocking pink *n* (1938) a vivid, garish shade of pink, introduced by the Italian-born fashion designer Elsa Schiaparelli (see the second quote below)

> 1938 *Encyclopedia Britannica Book of the Year*: Only one new colour arrived; it is 'Shocking Pink', introduced by Schiaparelli in Feb. 1937, then taken up by other designers, with the result that the vanguard of fashionable women everywhere are now seen wearing this crude, cruel shade of rose.

> 1954 Elsa Schiaparelli: My friends and executives…began to say that I was crazy and that nobody would want it because it was really 'nigger pink'… The colour 'shocking' established itself for ever as a classic. Even Dali dyed an enormous stuffed bear in shocking pink.

shoppe *n* (1933) An archaic spelling of *shop*. The difference in its usage on either side of the Atlantic is marked: in British English, it deliberately evokes a faux-antique quaintness that sets the teeth on edge (the standard inter-war British Tudorbethan package of chintz, oak beams, horse-brasses, etc.); in the US, however, it is used, largely without irony, for any small, boutique-like retail outlet, particularly a gift shop

> 1933 John Betjeman: Arts and Crafts. Gentle folk weaving and spinning; Modern Church Furnishing; Old Tea Shoppes.

> 1948 Joanna Cannan: Expensive and financially unstable gifte shoppes.

show trial *n* (1937) a judicial trial attended by great publicity. Usually used with specific reference to a prejudged trial of political dissidents by a totalitarian government

> 1981 *Annual Register 1980*: Jiang Qing constantly harangued witnesses and shouted defiance at the court—to such effect that she was forcibly removed on two occasions. Thus the trial was not equivalent to the Stalinist show trials of the 1950s.

shy-making *adj* (1930) embarrassing. This sort of compound adjective based on -*making* was lifted by Evelyn Waugh from the slang of the wealthy Guinness set in the late 1920s and used to characterize the louche young things in his novel *Vile Bodies*. It touched a chord and became popular for a time. Other examples include *hot-making* 'embarrassing' ('This, to use the current phrase, hot-making play', *Sunday Times* (1931)), *sad-making* ('"My dear, isn't that rather sad-making for you?" "I'm desperate about it."' Evelyn Waugh (1930)) and **sick-making (1930)**. A more recent exploitation of the formula is **cringe-making (1983)**

> 1930 Evelyn Waugh: I shall just ring up every Cabinet Minister and all the newspapers and give them all the most shy-making details.

> 1940 Margery Allingham: Great heroism, like great cowardice, is shy-making, and they were all…embarrassed.

sick-making *adj* (1930) making one sick—usually in the sense 'upset', but in the first quote below there is a double entendre with 'nauseous'. See **shy-making (1930)**

> 1930 Evelyn Waugh: Sometimes the ship pitched and sometimes she rolled… 'Too, too sick-making,' said Miss Runcible, with one of her rare flashes of accuracy.

> 1949 Nancy Mitford: I'm in a terrible do about my [stolen] bracelet of lucky charms—no value to anybody else—really—too too sick-making.

signature tune *n* (1932) a piece of music that always precedes or follows a particular programme or a performance by a particular entertainer or band

> 1932 *Daily Mail*: B.B.C. Band's 'Signature'. 'Just the Time for Dancing' and 'Till Next Time' are the titles of the 'signature' tunes selected by Mr. Henry Hall for his new B.B.C. Dance Band, to be used every time the band begins or concludes a broadcast.

simonize *v* (1934) to polish by the application of Simoniz. US. *Simoniz* is the proprietary name of a type of wax polish used on cars

> 1949 Arthur Miller: Remember those days? The way Biff used to simonize that car?

sink unit *n* (1939) a kitchen unit comprising a sink and draining-board, usually with cupboards below. See **unit (1937)**

> 1939 Martin & Speight: Wringer unit which can be fixed permanently to an 'Easiwork' sink unit in an ideal position between the sink and copper.

> 1958 *House & Garden*: You can start with an EZEE Sink Unit and gradually build your dream kitchen around it

siren suit *n* (1939) overalls or a boiler-suit, originally designed for wear by women in air-raid shelters; later, worn by either sex (most famously by Winston Churchill), and as a fashion garment

> 1939 *English Autumn*: Ladies' dress-shops ambiguously advertise 'siren suits' for the Air Raid Shelter.

> 1959 Richard Collier: In a minute [Winston Churchill] came—black silk dressing-gown embroidered with gold pheasants over the baby-blue siren suit he called 'my rompers'.

sit-in *n* (1937) a strike, demonstration, etc. in which people occupy a work place, public building, etc., especially in protest against alleged activities there. Originally US

> 1937 *New York Times*: Fifty members of the Workers Alliance who tried to stage a sit-in at City Hall yesterday were removed…by a dozen policemen.

skid row *n* (1931) a run-down area of a town where the unemployed, vagrants, alcoholics, etc., tend to congregate. Slang, originally US. An alteration of the earlier *skid road* in the same sense. This originally denoted literally 'a track formed by skids along which logs are rolled'; it then came to be applied to any part of town inhabited by loggers, and from there moved inexorably downhill. There was no shortage of such places to apply it to in the depression-haunted 1930s

> 1942 *Crisis*: Here, a short walk up from 'Skid Row',…is haven for men of all races.

sky-shouting *n* (1932) the sending of advertisements or messages from an aircraft to the ground by means of a loudspeaker. See also **sky-writing (1923)**

> 1932 *Children's Newspaper*: The inventor…can now quote terms for Sky Shouting or Sky Advertising. Concerning the sky-shouters a really alarming invention has been successfully tried.

slim *v* (1930) to attempt to become thinner by dieting. The word had been preceded by the equally euphemistic **slenderize (1923)**, but it has been *slim* that has come out on top

> 1930 *Punch*: The hostess ate hardly any. She is slimming.

slow learner *n* (1938) A further way-point on the 20th century's agonized and never-ending search for an inoffensive term to denote pupils of below-average intelligence

> 1938 *High Points*: The problem of the slow learner continues to grow…as increased numbers flow into high school.

smallest room *n* (1930) A euphemism for *lavatory*

> 1930 A. Lyall: It is all very baffling for the uninitiated foreigner…who when his host offers to 'show him the geography of the house' finds that his tour begins and ends with the smallest…room.

smear v (1936) to attempt to destroy the reputation of (someone) with malicious unsubstantiated charges. Also used as a noun, denoting such a charge. Originally US

> 1936 W. Irwin: When the Republicans began calling this line of attack the 'smear Hoover' campaign, Michelson…faced the microphone with a masterpiece of ingenious invective.

> 1938 *Sun* (Baltimore): He called the Lobby Committee 'a snooping committee' which was engaged in 'a smear campaign', a campaign of 'terror and intimidation' against newspapers and magazines which dare to criticize activities of the New Deal.

> 1943 *Sun* (Baltimore): 'This is an outright smear,' Stromberg asserted.

snack bar n (1930) a bar or counter at which snacks are served to customers. One of the 1930s' contributions to 20th-century fast-food culture. By the middle of the decade it had been joined by *snackery*, a US coinage

> 1930 *Punch*: A vegetarian snack-bar.

> 1936 *American Speech*: Steve's Snackerie is the sign over a small café in Lincoln, Nebraska.

snazzy adj (1932) smart, stylish, flashy. Colloquial, originally US. Its origins are unclear; it may be a blend of *snappy* and *jazzy*

> 1935 Noel Ersine: That's a snazzy dressup you've got.

snort v (1935) to inhale (a narcotic drug in powder form, especially cocaine or heroin). Slang, originally US

> 1958 H. Braddy: Since ma was a viper And daddy would snort, There wasn't much more I had to be taught.

snowmobile n (1931) a motor vehicle designed for travelling over snow, especially a small, light passenger vehicle supported on runners at the front and a traction chain at the rear

> 1931 *Times Literary Supplement*: The American expedition to the South Pole under…Admiral Byrd was… carried out in the grand manner… It had a 'snowmobile'; but this did not travel very far before meeting disaster on the rough surface.

soap opera n (1939) a radio or television serial dealing especially with domestic situations and often characterized by melodrama and sentimentality. The 'soap' part of the name comes from the fact that some of the early sponsors of the programmes were soap manufacturers. It is foreshadowed in 'These fifteen-minute tragedies…I call the "soap tragedies"…because it is by the grace of soap I am allowed to shed tears for these characters who suffer so much from life', *Christian Century* (1938). The 'opera' element is an echo of the earlier *horse opera* 'a Western' (1927). The abbreviated form *soap* is first recorded in 1943

> 1939 *Newsweek*: Transcontinental Network bubbled up out of the 'soap operas'.

> 1943 *New York Times*: Within these specifications, there is a deal of shrewd craftsmanship in the preparation of the 'soaps'.

social services n (1933) services supplied for the benefit of the community, especially any of those provided by the central or local government, such as education, medical treatment, social welfare, etc.

> 1933 John Buchan: He is not prepared to go back on our social services… All parties go on sluicing out…new benefits from the public funds.

sociopath n (1930) someone with a personality disorder manifesting itself chiefly in anti-social attitudes and behaviour. A term coined (along with its derivatives *sociopathic* and *sociopathy*) by the psychologist G. E. Partridge, on the model of *psychopath*

> 1930 G. E. Partridge: A conspicuous number who…may justly be termed 'sociopathic'… We may use the term 'sociopathy' to mean anything deviated or pathological in social relations… We may exclude from the class of essential sociopaths those whose inadequacy is primarily related to physical weakness, fear, hypersensitiveness, shyness and self-blame.

sound barrier n (1939) the obstacle to supersonic flight posed by such factors as increased drag and reduced controllability, which occur when aircraft not specially designed for such flight approach the speed of sound. It was overcome for the first time by the US Bell X1 rocket aircraft in 1947. Also called the *sonic barrier* (1946)

> 1939 *Journal of the Royal Aeronautical Society*: It is noteworthy that the curve, which at first is flat, rises gradually for a while, without the enormous increases which other experimenters have found between M.n. 0.6 and 0.8, and which have made them speak of a concrete 'sound barrier'.

> 1952 *Times*: Their moment of triumph after breaking once more through the sound barrier.

spacecraft *n* (1930) a vehicle designed to travel in space. The word was destined (along with **space vehicle (1946)**) to become the 'serious' term for such vehicles when they were actually built, with the earlier *spaceship* (1894) being relegated to the sci-fi annexe. See also **rocket-ship (1927)**

> 1930 *Scientific American*: Valier was the principal proponent of working toward the space craft from the known forms of surface or air craft.

> 1932 D. Lasser: Our experience with cosmic speeds and distances is not equal to the task of guiding a space-craft on its perilous journey.

Spam *n* (1937) The proprietary name (registered in the US in 1937) of a type of tinned cooked meat consisting chiefly of pork; also (with lower-case initial) applied loosely to other types of tinned luncheon meat. Probably a conflation of *spiced ham*, although the first quote below tells a different story. In Britain Spam became synonymous with the dull and meagre diet of World War II, and eventually turned into something of a laughing-stock

> 1937 *Squeal*: In the last month Geo. A. Hormel & Co…launched the product Spam… The 'think-up' of the name [is] credited to Kenneth Daigneau, New York actor… Seems as if he had considered the word a good memorable trade-name for some time, had only waited for a product to attach it to.

> 1981 George MacBeth: A plate of Molly's best Spam sandwiches.

speed *v* (1931) See **speeding (1908)**

speedway *n* (1930) a sport in which motorcyclists race several laps round a short oval dirt track. It quickly developed into one of the most popular of spectator sports in Britain in the middle decades of the century

> 1930 S. Elder: Now that Speedway Racing has taken its place as one of our national pastimes.

spin-drier *n* (1939) See **spin-dry (1927)**

spiv *n* (1934) a man who lives by his wits and has no regular employment, especially one engaging in petty blackmarket dealings and often characterized by flashy dress. British slang, probably dating back to the underworld argot of the 19th century but first recorded in 1934. It is very likely related to obsolete slang *spiff* 'a well-dressed man', but the origins of that are obscure. The spiv reached his apotheosis during World War II and the succeeding years, when the disrupted economic conditions allowed ample scope for unofficial trading (a pair of nylons here, a few packets of cigarettes there) and other petty crime. He became a stock figure in the English social comedy, represented on screen by such stereotypes as 'Flash Harry' (played by George Cole) in the St. Trinian's films and Pte. Walker in *Dad's Army*. See also **wide boy (1937)**

> 1934 A. Bracey: *Spiv*, petty crook who will turn his hand to anything so long as it does not involve honest work.

> 1952 Joan Henry: In appearance, he resembled the typical spiv; with coat-hanger shoulders, and pointed shoes, and a smile that would have been an asset to any confidence man.

spliff *n* (1936) a marijuana cigarette. A word of West Indian origin, but its ultimate antecedents are unknown

> 1936 *Daily Gleaner* (Kingston, Jamaica): Here is the hot-bed of ganja smoking…and even the children may be seen at times taking what is better known as their 'spliff'.

sponsor *n* (1931) a firm or individual that pays, or contributes towards, the expenses of a radio or television programme, a performance or other event or work, usually in return for advertising space or rights. Originally US. The corresponding verb *sponsor* is also first recorded in 1931

> 1931 P. Dixon: The sponsor wants a dramatic type of program and is willing to spend one thousand dollars a week for the program… When an advertiser decides that the program's worth sponsoring.

> 1931 F. A. Arnold: The travelogue type of program, sponsored by a tourist agency or a steamship company.

sportscaster *n* (1938) See **newscaster (1930)**

stacking chair *n* (1939) a chair so designed that several can be stacked one on top of another

> 1939 Martin & Speight: Stacking chair, by Alvar Aalto in natural birch or lacquered…20s 0d.

> 1951 *Catalogue of Exhibits, South Bank Exhibition, Festival of Britain*: Cantilevered all-purpose stacking chairs.

Stakhanovite *n* (1935) In the USSR during the 1930s and 1940s, a worker whose productivity exceeded the norms and who thus earned special privileges and rewards. The word is based on the name of the Soviet coal-miner Aleksei Grigorevich Stakhanov (1906–77); the Soviet authorities publicized the prodigious output he achieved in 1935 as part of a campaign to increase industrial output. It came to be used more generally for any zealous and highly productive worker, often with connotations of excessive compliance with management and lack of solidarity with fellow workers

> 1935 *Time*: In the coal mine at Stalino two assistant foremen, a checkweighter and an electrician were arrested for the murder of a fast-working Stakhanovite.

stateless *adj* (1930) not being a citizen of any state; having no nationality. The *stateless person* became a leitmotiv of mid-20th-century Europe, its populations uprooted and scattered by two world wars. See also **displaced person (1944)**

> 1930 E. F. W. Gey van Pittius: A person of dual nationality can at least enter more than one country and seek protection from both while abroad. Not so the stateless person.

> 1957 C. Day Lewis: He travels on, not only blind But a stateless person.

steroid *n* (1936) any of a range of organic chemical compounds that have a 17-carbon-atom ring as a basis (some examples are given in the quote below). The term was coined from *sterol*

> 1936 Callow & Young: The term 'steroids' is proposed as generic name for the group of compounds comprising the sterols, bile acids, heart poisons, saponins and sex hormones.

stewardess *n* (1931) a female attendant on a passenger aircraft who attends to the needs and comfort of the passengers. In due course largely superseded by **air hostess (1934)**. The fuller form *air stewardess* is first recorded in 1936

> 1931 *United Airlines News*: Uniformed stewardesses employed on the Chicago-San Diego divisions of United. The picture shows the original group of stewardesses employed.

> 1936 *Punch*: To Chloe, an 'Air Stewardess'. My Chloe rides the heavens in a roaring silver hull, She serves up morning coffee over Basle and Istanbul.

Stockbrokers' Tudor *n* (1939) A facetiously dismissive term coined by the British writer and cartoonist Osbert Lancaster for a style of mock-Tudor British architecture supposed to be favoured by stockbrokers. See also **Tudorbethan (1933)**

> 1940 Graves & Hodge: In 'Stockbroker's Tudor' houses…ingenuity was displayed in olde-worlde disguise.

storm-trooper *n* (1933) See **storm troops (1917)**

stream of consciousness *n* (1931) a method of narration which depicts events through a flow of thoughts and impressions in the mind of a character. The term originally belonged to psychology, where it denotes 'an individual's thoughts and conscious reaction to external events experienced subjectively as a continuous flow'. Its use in the jargon of literary criticism is foreshadowed in 1918 in a comment on one of Dorothy Richardson's characters (Richardson was one of the earliest exponents of the technique): 'In identifying herself with this life which is Miriam's stream of consciousness Miss Richardson produces her effect of…getting closer to reality than any of our novelists', M. Sinclair

> 1931 *Notes & Queries*: This is in part a development from the 'stream of consciousness' method.

> 1955 L. P. Hartley: Do you think the stream-of-consciousness method has come to stay, or have Joyce and Virginia Woolf exhausted it?

strip cartoon *n* (1936) A British term for a **comic strip (1920)**

> 1936 *Discovery*: Shop-keeper's bill of the early 18th century. Note the smokers conversing about their tobacco, quite in the modern 'strip-cartoon' style.

stripped pine *n* (1934) pine-wood that has had the accretions of paint or varnish removed, so as to reveal the natural grain and colour. First recorded in the 1930s, but it was the 1960s and '70s that were the true age of stripped pine in Britain, when it accounted for the great majority of trendy furniture and domestic woodwork

> 1934 Margery Allingham: The high narrow room with its top lights and stripped pine panelling.

> 1976 *Listener*: He likes corner cabinets and stripped pine.

stripper *n* (1930) a strip-tease dancer; a strip-teaser. Joined towards the end of the decade by *strippeuse*, a US coinage probably based on *danseuse* 'female dancer'. See also **strip (1929)**

> 1930 *Variety*: Detroit censor pinches four stock strippers.

> 1939 *Life*: Last year blonde Della Carroll was première strippeuse at New York's Paradise restaurant.

strip-tease *n* (1936) a kind of entertainment in which a female (or sometimes a male) performer undresses gradually in a tantalizingly erotic way in front of an audience, usually to music. Originally US. Apparently a back-formation from **strip-teaser (1930)**, but the elements of the compound had been in use since the late 1920s (see **strip (1928)**, **strip (1929)**, and **tease (1927)**), and appear to have been assembled in the proto-form *strip and tease* in 1930 ('Girls have the strip and tease down to a science', *Variety*)

> 1936 *Variety*: An undersea ballet, veil waving number and a mild strip tease by the entire chorus, which required little feeling, were nicely executed.

> 1937 *Daily Telegraph*: Can anything be said in defence of the present public interest in 'strip-tease' and nudist or semi-nudist displays on stage?

strip-teaser *n* (1930) a strip-tease dancer

> 1930 *Variety*: The main b[ox] o[ffice] lure is the girls, those known as 'strip teasers'.

> 1935 e. e. cummings: I recommend the Irving Place Burlesk (stripteasers in excelsis).

studio flat *n* (1934) A term that has become a victim of estate agents' hyperbole. To begin with it denoted a flat containing a spacious room with large windows, which was or resembled an artist's studio, but latterly its referent has shrunk to a small one-roomed flat. (The US equivalent, *studio apartment*, is first recorded in 1903)

> 1934 Aldous Huxley: We are in London for the winter—having found a studio flat, miraculously large.

> 1970 Kenneth Giles: He had what they call a studio flat—bed, gas fire and tiny kitchenette.

subsonic *adj* (1937) involving, capable of, or designating speeds less than the speed of sound

> 1958 *Times*: It is…to carry 95–100 passengers, cruising at high subsonic speeds of around 600 m.p.h.

summerize *v* (1935) to prepare (something) for summer use. A US colloquialism which, probably owing to Britian's temperate climate, has never crossed the Atlantic. The corresponding *winterize* is first recorded in 1938 ('A radio announcer…urged his listeners to have their cars winterized', *American Speech*)

> 1935 *Evening Sun* (Baltimore): Let Hutzler's summerize your home.

> 1949 *Sun* (Baltimore): Come to K. Katz and 'summerize'!

superette *n* (1938) a small supermarket. Originally and mainly US

> 1938 *Saturday Evening Post*: It also developed a store called the 'Super-ette', which is a compact, limited-stock, self-service store.

> 1976 *Daily Times* (Lagos): A spacious van for traders, commercial houses,…supermarkets and superettes.

Superman *n* (1938) The name of an invincible hero with superhuman powers, including that of flight, introduced in an American comic strip (1938). He quickly became a cult figure, and his name has often been attached metaphorically to performers of prodigious deeds (although instances of the latter can be difficult to distinguish from the earlier **superman (1903)**)

> 1938 *Action Comics*: So was created…Superman! champion of the oppressed, the physical marvel who had sworn to devote his existence to helping those in need!

> 1976 *Survey*: The…New York Times…in the past presented Henry Kissinger as a species of diplomatic superman.

supermarket *n* (1933) a large self-service shop, selling a wide range of groceries and household goods, and often one of a chain of stores. Originally US. The idea of such a shop was not new (the earliest example had been the chain named 'Piggly-Wiggly', founded in 1916 by Clarence Saunders in Memphis, Tennessee, which had many of the familiar features, such as customers picking their choice of goods from open shelves and paying for them as they left), but the term *supermarket* was. See also **groceteria (1913)**

> 1933 *New York Times*: In a move interpreted by the trade as an effort to help both corporate chains and independent wholesale grocers fight the competition of 'super-markets' which have sprung up in the last two years, the Associated Grocery Manufacturers of America, Inc., yesterday drew up a proposed model law for States which may seek to prevent the sale of standard grocery products at or below purchase price… For three months now a large supermarket in New Jersey has been doing a business reputed to average $100,000 a week.

> 1933 *Chain Store Age*: The 'One-stop-drive-in super market' provides free parking, and every kind of food under one roof.

supernova *n* (1934) a star that undergoes a sudden and temporary increase in brightness like a nova but to a very much greater degree, as a result of an explosion that disperses most of the stellar material

> 1934 Baade & Zwicky: Supernovae flare up in every stellar system (nebula) once in several centuries.

supersonic *adj* (1934) involving, pertaining to, capable of, or designating speeds greater than the speed of sound. *Supersonic* originally denoted sound waves or vibrations with frequencies greater than those audible to the human ear (it is first recorded in that sense in 1919), but that meaning has now been largely taken over by **ultrasonic (1923)**

> 1936 *Aircraft Engineering*: The wing shows what the Germans call a 'supersonic profile', because the aeroplane is supposed to fly the greater part of its route at supersonic speeds.

surreal *adj* (1937) having the qualities of surrealist art; bizarre, dreamlike. A back-formation from **surrealist (1925)**

> 1937 *Burlington Magazine*: Some 'surreal' influence haunts the regions of the Black Forest.

> 1976 Samuel Hynes: As the 'thirties moved on toward the end, there was only the surreal… Even the agents of order were surreal and terrifying.

sus *n* (1936) An abbreviation of *suspicion*, used in British criminals' slang for 'suspicion of having committed a crime' or 'suspicious behaviour, especially loitering'. Used especially in the expression *on sus*, and also in *sus law*, the law by which a person could be arrested on suspicion of committing a crime, or even of looking as if he were going to commit a crime, effective from the passing of the Vagrancy Act in 1824 until 1981

> 1936 James Curtis: What you nick me for? Sus?

> 1970 G. F. Newman: Chance nickings in the street, from anything on sus, to indecent exposure.

> 1981 *Times*: The controversial 'sus' law, under which people can be arrested on suspicion that an offence is likely to be committed, is no more. The Criminal Attempts Act, which comes into force today, abolishes section 4 of the Vagrancy Act 1824… The delight at the passing of 'sus' is, however, mitigated by a degree of apprehension about its replacement, the newly created offence of 'interference with vehicles'.

Suzi(e)-Q, Susie-Q *n* (1936) a type of modern dance popular in the 1930s. It is said to have originated in Harlem, New York, but the reason for the curious name is not known

> 1936 Davis & Coots: A new dance hit the town, It's really gettin' 'round, It's lots of fun, I found, Doin' the Suzi-Q.

swastika *n* (1932) a cross with a right-angled projection at the end of each arm, used as the symbol of Nazism. The word, which comes from Sanskrit *svastika*, a derivative of *svastí* 'well-being, luck', originally denoted an ancient cosmic or religious symbol of this form. English adopted it as the equivalent of German *Hakenkreuz*, literally 'hook-cross'

> 1932 'Nordicus': Thousands flocked to his standard—the 'Hakenkreuz'—(swastika), the ancient anti-semitic cross in a color scheme of red-white-black in memory of the colors of the old army.

swing *n* (1933) a variety of big dance-band music played with a flowing but strongly compelling rhythm. Despite Louis Armstrong's claim below, the true age of swing was from the mid 30s to the mid 40s

> 1933 *Fortune*: The best white ensembles usually compromise by playing both *sweet* and *hot* music. This is true of Ben Pollack's excellent *swing* band of Chicago (with Trombonist Teagarden and other crack soloists).

> 1937 Louis Armstrong: Even now, thirty years after Swing was born, this book is the first history of swing music, and of the men who made it, to be published in the English language.

> 1938 *Saturday Evening Post*: If any one musician brought about the Swing Age, it is Benny Goodman.

switcheroo *n* (1933) a change of position or an exchange, especially one intended to surprise or deceive; a reversal or turn-about. US colloquial. One of the earliest and longest-lived of the coinages based on the facetious suffix -*eroo* (see **flopperoo (1931)**)

> 1933 *Forum*: We'll pull a switcheroo. We'll use olives instead [of cherries].

> 1941 Budd Schulberg: All you gotta do to that story is to give it the switcheroo. Instead of the minister you got a young dame missionary, see.

talkathon *n* (1934) an interminable session of talk or discussion; often applied specifically to a prolonged debate in a legislature or similar body. Originally and mainly US. Modelled on **walkathon (1932)**, and helping to establish the pattern of coinages based ultimately on *marathon* which proliferated in the latter part of the century

> 1934 *American Speech*: Apropos of the walkathons,…a contributor suggests that talkathons will be longer lived, especially in legislative halls.

> 1948 *Times-Dispatch* (Richmond, Virginia): Filibustering Dixie Senators won a major round today in their effort to talk the anti-poll tax bill to death. The presiding officer…decided that an effort to curb the debate was in conflict with Senate rules, and so the talkathon continued.

Tampax *n* (1932) The proprietary name (based on *tampon* and registered in the US in 1932) of a sanitary tampon for women; also applied loosely to any variety of tampon

> 1955 William Gaddis: When we launched the customs almost arrested me, they thought my Tampax was incendiary bombs.

tape recorder *n* (1932) an apparatus for recording sounds, etc. on magnetic tape and afterwards reproducing them. The original machines, also called *wire recorders*, used steel tape, which did not make for easy portability (see also **Blattnerphone (1931)**). The present-day type, using plastic tape covered with iron oxide, came in after World War II. See also **tape record (1905)**

> 1932 *B.B.C. Glossary*: Steel Tape Recorder

> 1949 *Consumer Reports*: The three tape models all proved…substantially more convenient than earlier tape recorders and better than…the wire recorders tested.

telecast *n*, *v* (1937) (to) broadcast on television. Originally US

> 1937 *Atlantic Monthly*: He can be assured that any receiver he buys will give him the telecasts sent out by all the major systems of transmission.

> 1940 *Topeka* (Kansas) *Daily Capital*: Easter Services…were telecast today.

telegenic *adj* (1939) that shows to advantage on television; providing an interesting or attractive subject for a television broadcast. Modelled on *photogenic*

1939 *Sun* (Baltimore): Judith Barrett, pretty and blonde actress, is the first Telegenic Girl to go on record. In other words she is the perfect type of beauty for television… She is slated for the first television motion picture.

teleportation *n* (1931) the conveyance of people or things by psychic power. Originally a spiritualists' term, it was later taken over by the science fiction fraternity and applied to the instantaneous transportation of people across space by advanced but usually unspecified technological means

1931 C. Fort: Sometimes, in what I call 'teleportations', there seems to be 'agency' and sometimes not… Some other time I may be able more clearly to think out an expression upon flows of pigeons to their homes, and flows of migratory birds, as teleportative, or quasi-teleportative.

1951 John Wyndham: Suppose the Russians…could project things or people here by teleportation.

televiewer *n* (1935) a person who watches or is watching television. An early alternative to **viewer** which has persisted at a fairly low level of usage

1935 *Discovery*: An excellent answer to the questions of the…would-be 'televiewer'.

1982 *Daily Telegraph*: Millions of televiewers around the world saw the moving spectacle of Prince Rainier's grief.

telex *n* (1932) a system of telegraphy in which printed messages are transmitted and received by teleprinters using public telecommunication lines. A compound made up of the initial elements of *teleprinter* and *exchange*

1932 *Telegraph & Telephone Journal*: In August 1932, came the opening in London of 'Telex' service, otherwise 'teleprinter exchange service'.

temp *n* (1932) a worker holding a temporary post. In the original US usage, represented in the first quote below, the term denotes specifically a part-time non-civil service employee of the US Post Office. It is not clear whether the British usage of the 1960s onwards, which applies particularly to a temporary secretary, is a continuation of this or a new coinage. By the 1970s it had become a verb, meaning 'to work as a temp' (see **temp (1973)**)

1932 *American Speech*: A temp, a part-timer.

1967 *Economist*: Overstaffing is not solely the result of the unwillingness to use temps.

1970 Reginald Hill: One of his women, a temp, only comes in at weekends [at a pub].

tenderometer *n* (1938) an instrument for testing the tenderness of raw peas for picking, processing, etc.

1981 *Southern Horticulture* (New Zealand): As soon as the tenderometer reading is at its optimum the whole paddock must be cleared within hours.

terrific *adj* (1930) wonderful, marvellous, excellent. Every generation has its own colloquialisms for expressing enthusiastic admiration, and *terrific*, from the middle years of the century, has survived better than most (latterly sometimes colloquialized still further to *triffic*, or even abbreviated to *triff* (1984)). It developed from the earlier sense 'very great or severe' (as in 'a terrific nuisance'), which dates back at least to the early 19th century. See also **fantastic (1938)**

1930 D. G. Mackail: 'Thanks awfully,' said Rex. 'That'll be ripping.' 'Fine!' said Derek Yardley. 'Great! Terrific!'

1981 *Daily Mail*: 'I feel great, really terrific,' said the former Wings guitarist.

testosterone *n* (1935) a male sex hormone which is produced in the testicles and controls secondary sexual characteristics. The word was coined in German in 1935 as *Testosteron*, based on Latin *testis* 'testicle'

1939 Aldous Huxley: With a course of thiamin chloride and some testosterone I could have made him as happy as a sand-boy.

test-tube baby *n* (1935) Applied originally to a baby conceived by artificial insemination, and latterly to a baby that has developed from an ovum fertilized outside the mother's body

1935 Emil Novak: There has been…a good deal of unfortunate newspaper discussion on the subject of artificial insemination and 'test-tube babies'.

1978 *Times*: The world's first test-tube baby, a girl, was born by caesarian section just before midnight at Oldham and District General Hospital, Greater Manchester… The embryo was implanted in Mrs Brown's womb after being fertilized in Mr Steptoe's laboratories.

Third Reich *n* (1930) the German state under the rule of Adolf Hitler and the Nazi party, 1933–45; the regime of Hitler. A partial Anglicization of German *Dritte Reich* 'Third Empire', which is first recorded as the title of a 1923 book by A. Moeller van den Bruck. (The 'First' Empire in this context was the Holy Roman Empire (up to 1806) and the 'Second', the Imperial German state 1871–1918)

> 1930 *Times*: Asked to give some idea of the 'Third Reich', Herr Hitler said the old Germany was a State of great honour and of glorious events, but the conception of 'the people' was not the central pillar of its structure. The second State had placed democracy and pacificism in the centre. They hoped for the Third Reich, which would have as its keystone the conception of the people and the national idea.

> 1933 L. Stowe: On October 18th, four days after he had led the Third Reich out of the League of Nations…Adolf Hitler made the following peace declaration before eight hundred of his party leaders in Berlin.

thumber *n* (1935) someone who 'thumbs' a lift; a hitch-hiker. North American, colloquial

> 1935 *Evening Sun* (Baltimore): Chief of Police…has turned 'thumbs down' on the 'thumbers'.

ticket *n* (1930) an official documentary notification of an offence, especially speeding or illegal parking. Originally US

> 1930 *Outlook*: He wrote the young professor a ticket for speeding.

> 1971 S. Smith: Horsham Police were surprised to receive payment of the £2 parking fine on the Cortina… It came in a plain manilla envelope,…and inside were two pound notes and the parking ticket.

tickety-boo *adj* (1939) in order, correct, satisfactory. A fairly short-lived British colloquialism. Its ancestry is obscure: one possible candidate is Hindi *ṭhīk hai* 'all right' (see the second quote below)

> 1939 Noel Streatfeild: Things ought to have shaped right… Couldn't have looked more tickety-boo.

> 1947 *American Notes & Queries*: Lord Mountbatten, now Governor General of India, is credited in the *New York Times Magazine* (June 22, 1947, p. 45) with 'giving currency' to the phrase 'tickety-boo' (or 'tiggerty-boo'). This Royal Navy term for 'okay' is derived from the Hindustani.

time and motion study *n* (1932) the measurement of the efficiency of an industrial or other operation. A combination of terms which had been around for some time: both *motion study* and *time study* are first recorded in 1911

> 1932 C. Reynolds (heading): Time and motion studies.

> 1959 *Listener*: That sinister figure, the man with the stop-watch, the time-and-motion expert, disliked by union men the world over.

titfer *n* (1930) a hat. British colloquial. A shortened form of rhyming slang *tit-for-tat*, which is not recorded before 1925 but was no doubt in use in the World War I period. It remains in use among older speakers at the end of the century

> 1960 *Observer*: Last week I told you about the time I popped my titfa.

togetherness *n* (1930) the fact of getting on well together or being well suited to one another; a sense of belonging together. *Togetherness* in the more neutral and always rather rare sense 'the condition of being together or united' dates back to the 17th century

> 1930 D. H. Lawrence: Class-hate and class-consciousness are only a sign that the old togetherness, the old blood-warmth has collapsed.

toots *n* (1936) Used as a colloquial term of address, typically to a woman, but also sometimes to men. Originally and mainly US. No doubt a shortened version of the earlier *toots(e)y* in the same sense, which dates from the late 19th century, but where that came from is not clear—perhaps it is the same word as *toots(e)y* 'foot'

> 1936 *American Speech*: Toots used to be used in families here and there as a nickname, or a term of endearment, the vowel sounded as in 'boots'… Is this term the ancestor of the present mode of address in 'O.K., toots!', 'Hello, toots!' etc., the vowel shortened into that of 'full'?

> 1941 H. A. Smith: I…raised my hand in a clumsy wave and cried out: 'Hiya, toots!'… I had called J. P. Morgan 'toots' to his face.

trafficator *n* (1933) a signal arm of a type formerly attached to either side of a motor vehicle, which could be raised and illuminated to indicate the direction in which the vehicle was about to turn. As it came to be replaced in the 1950s by an indicator incorporated in the rear of the car, the term gradually died out

> 1935 *Times*: The least expensive Morris Eight is the two-seater which sells at £118, or £120 10s. with bumpers and trafficators.

traffic island *n* (1931), **safety island** *n* (1933) a raised or marked area in a road to direct traffic and provide refuge for pedestrians crossing the road

> 1931 e. e. cummings: I've just returned from the place de la Concorde…where waited on a traffic-island for 2½hours.

> 1933 *Sun* (Baltimore): A few years ago safety islands were placed in the middle of some of Cambridge's principal thoroughfares to safeguard the lives of pedestrians.

traffic robot, robot *n* (1931) traffic lights. The term made no headway elsewhere, but became standard in South African English

> 1931 *Evening Standard* (headline): Traffic 'Robots' in the City.

> 1939 *Forum* (Johannesburg): The Daily Dispatch, East London, is critical of a proposal to fix robots in the town's streets.

> 1974 *Eastern Province Herald*: Vandals removed the lamps from seven traffic robots and the flashing head from a warning pole.

train set *n* (1939) a set of trains, tracks, etc., required for a model railway

> 1939 *Army & Navy Stores Catalogue*: This excellent train set…comprises a No. 1 Special Locomotive…two No. 1 Pullman Coaches…and rails.

trautonium *n* (1931) an electronic musical instrument, capable of producing notes of any pitch. The name, modelled on *euphonium*, commemorates the inventor of the instrument, the German scientist Friedrich Trautwein (1888–1956). It failed to excite, and little was heard of it after the 1930s

> 1931 *Electronics*: The 'Trautonium' is a recent development at the Radio Research section of the Berlin Academy of Music… Paul Hindemith…is himself an excellent Trautonium player and has written music specially for it.

trouser suit *n* (1939) a woman's suit consisting of matching jacket and trousers. After a period in limbo, it came back into fashion in the 1970s

> 1939 *Vogue*: Digby Morton, famous tailleur, created this trouser suit in a bright tartan 'Viyella'.

> 1975 David Lodge: She was waiting for him…in a cream-coloured trouser-suit.

truck *n* (1935) a popular dance in the US in the mid 1930s, reportedly introduced at the Cotton Club in 1933. Also used as a verb

> 1935 *Sun* (Baltimore): The truck, or truckin', that jerky yet rhythmic dance which combines a bend of the body, a tightening of the hand muscles and a slight strut with the legs, hit the theaters, sidewalks, gin taverns and dance floors of Harlem last summer.

> 1937 *American Speech*: Only negroes can really truck.

Tudorbethan *adj, n* (1933) mock Tudor; imitative of Tudor and Elizabethan styles. A dismissive epithet provoked by the rash of half-timbered suburban villas which broke out in Britain between the wars ('It is almost impossible now to take any real delight in Elizabethan half-timber—logical and honourable as it is—because we are so sickened with the miles of shoddy imitation with which we are surrounded,' Evelyn Waugh (1938)). Contemporary and nearly synonymous is *Jacobethan*, a blend of *Jacobean* and *Elizabethan*. See also **Stockbrokers' Tudor (1939)**

> 1933 Leavis & Thompson: The outbreak of 'Tudorbethan' villas.

> 1933 John Betjeman: The style in which Gothic predominates may be called, inaccurately enough, Elizabethan, and the style in which the classical predominates over the Gothic, equally inaccurately, may be called Jacobean. To save the time of those who do not wish to distinguish between these periods of architectural uncertainty, I will henceforward use the term 'Jacobethan'.

> 1945 *Architectural Review*: Westcombe Park Road…shows an early tendency towards those ornamental features which long afterwards gave the names of 'sham Tudor' and 'Jacobethan' to a rather pathetic phase in domestic design.

> 1975 *Times*: [Liberty's] store was rebuilt in 1924 to the Tudorbethan designs of E. T. and E. S. Hall.

Turing machine *n* (1937) a notional computing machine for performing simple reading, writing, and shifting operations in accordance with a prescribed set of rules, invoked in theories of computability and automata; in effect, the theoretical forerunner of the computer (see **computer (1945)**). It was named after the English mathematician Alan Turing (1912–54), who described such a machine in 1936

> 1937 Alonzo Church: Certain further restrictions are imposed on the character of the machine, but these are of such a nature as obviously to cause no loss of generality—in particular, a human calculator, provided with pencil and paper and explicit instructions, can be regarded as a kind of Turing machine.

twin set *n* (1937) a woman's matching jumper and cardigan; a garment which, paired with pearls, became a cliché of bourgeois female attire in the middle years of the century

> 1944 Marghanita Laski: I've got a Worth frock…I swopped…for my cashmere twin-set.

twit *n* (1934) a fool; a stupid or ineffectual person. Slang, originally British. A word which came into widespread use in the 1950s and 1960s, although it had been around since before World War II; in the 1970s it gained some currency in US English, largely through British television sitcoms. It may be connected with the ancient verb *twit* 'to reproach', but there is probably also some influence of **nitwit (1922)**

> 1934 Eric Linklater: He was…a false hero who flaunted himself in fine colours when he was drunk and dwindled to a shabby twit when sober.

> 1970 N. Fleming: No one but a prize twit or Captain Oates would have ventured out in this weather.

Ugli *n* (1934) The proprietary name of a hybrid citrus fruit, first produced in Jamaica by crossing the Seville orange *Citrus aurantium*, the grapefruit *C. paradisi*, and the tangerine, *C. reticulata*. The name, registered as a trademark in 1938, reflects the fruit's unprepossessing appearance—like a large, mournful, discoloured, semi-deflated grapefruit

> 1934 *Daily Gleaner* (Kingston, Jamaica): Should the name of 'ugli' fruit be changed to a more beautiful name?

> 1975 *Australian Post*: Prince Charles loves an ugli, so said the Queen when she opened London's new Covent Garden market recently.

un- *prefix* (1936) Used in telegrams in place of *not*, to avoid the expense of an extra word. The practice (along with other current telegraphic enormities) was satirized by Evelyn Waugh in his travel book *Waugh in Abyssinia*

> 1936 Evelyn Waugh: Cables were soon arriving from London and New York: '*Require earliest name life story photograph American nurse upblown* [i.e. bombed] *Adowa.*' We replied '*Nurse unupblown,*' and after a few days she disappeared from the news.

> 1967 *Observer*: Regret expelled by Syrians after twenty-four hours unreason given.

underpants *n* (1931) an undergarment covering the lower part of the body (and part of the legs). Typically applied to a man's garment. So firmly established is the whole family of *pants* words for 'underwear' in British English at the end of the 20th century that it seems hard to imagine a pre-*pants* era, but hitherto such items had largely (and the word is used advisedly) been known as *drawers* or, in the case of women, *knickers*. **Panties** is first recorded in 1908, but in reference to dolls' clothing, and it does not seem to have come into general use until the late 1920s; early references to *pants* in this sense can be difficult to disentangle from those meaning 'trousers', but again the usage was current by the late 1920s. **Briefs (1934)** soon joined the party

> 1931 Roy Campbell: The living image of a country lover, In woolly underpants, a sort of Faun.

underprivileged *n* (1935) people without the advantages and opportunities enjoyed by most members of the community. The word is actually recorded as an adjective towards the end of the 19th century, but it did not begin to take off as a key 20th-century euphemism for 'poor people' until the 1930s

> 1935 A. P. Herbert: She had spent a long time persuading one of the 'underprivileged' to go to hospital to have an operation.

unit *n* (1937) a piece of furniture which is fitted in place and typically combines storage space with other elements. A concept which arose out of the mid-century fashion for doing away with large individual pieces of furniture and having the superstructure of a room blended into a seamless whole. See also **sink unit (1939)**

> 1937 *New York Times*: The demand for electrical kitchen units is greatest in the Midwest.

> 1981 M. E. Atkins: I'm going to…start with the kitchen. I'll have units all round, a new sink and cooker.

unit trust *n* (1936) an investment group investing combined contributions from many people in various securities and paying them dividends in proportion to their holdings

> 1936 *Economist*: Three new trusts with different degrees of flexibility have recently appeared, which extend the activities of the unit trust movement into new fields.

> 1980 *Times*: Most of the unit trusts managed not to lose too much money for unit holders last year.

unquote (1935) Used in speaking (usually paired with *quote*) to indicate the end of a quotation. Originally US. It began as a device used in giving dictation, but soon spread into ordinary speech, and thence into writing imitating speech

> 1935 e. e. cummings: But he said that if I'd hold up publication of No Thanks for 15 days he'd kill unquote a page of Aiken… The Isful ubiquitous wasless&-shallbeless quote scrotumtightening unquote omnivorously eternal thalassa pelagas or Ocean.

unwind *v* (1938) to obtain relief from tension or anxiety; to relax. Colloquial

> 1958 *Radio Times* (advert): After interviews Edana finds she can 'unwind' with 'Aspro' and a cup of tea.

up-do *n* (1938) a style of dressing women's hair by sweeping it up and securing it away from the face and neck. Originally and mainly US

> 1938 *Sun* (Baltimore): The 'up-do' hair style does not click with De Paul University men students… The 'up-do' probably will go back down after movie stars get tired of it.

up-tight *adj* (1934) in a state of nervous tension or anxiety; worried, on edge. Slang, originally US. There is a large gap in the record between the first recorded example and the mid 1960s, when this usage really took off, but it seems likely that it was simmering in the spoken language in the interim

> 1934 J. M. Cain: I'm getting up tight now, and I've been thinking about Cora. Do you think she knows I didn't do it?

> 1969 C. Young: He looked worried. Really worried. As the kids say, he was up-tight.

value added tax *n* (1935) a tax levied on the value added to an article or the raw material forming it at each stage during its production or distribution. The term (probably an adaptation of German *Mehrwertsteuer*) did not become familiar outside the jargon of economists and accountants until such a tax was introduced in Britain in the early 1970s (see **VAT (1966)**)

> 1940 *Journal of Political Economy*: A rather imperfect form of a value-added tax was incorporated by Mr. Arthur L. Johnson in his revised old age pension bill in 1939.

video *adj, n, prefix* (1935) Coined (from Latin *videre* 'to see') as a visual equivalent of **audio (1913)**, and applied specifically to that which is displayed on a television screen or other cathode-ray tube. In later US noun use also denoting television as a broadcasting medium. As a prefix it took part in a relatively modest number of formations through the 40s, 50s, and 60s, but the trickle became a flood in the 70s and 80s

> 1935 *Discovery*: They are providing ever better products and service to enable the listening public to get more enjoyment from the 'audio' programmes…and will be ready to cater for those who wish…to see such 'video' items as may become available.

> 1937 *Electronics*: A video amplifier is one that is responsive to picture signals, and therefore, is an extremely good audio as well as a very wide band radio frequency amplifier.

> 1937 *Printers' Ink Monthly*: *Video*, the sight channel in television, as opposed to audio, the sound channel.

> 1946 *Time*: NBC published a 55-page booklet, listing words & phrases commonly used in video.

view *v* (1935) to watch (television). Competition for the already established **look in (1927)**. It eventually took over as the preferred term, but had itself gradually gone out of use towards the end of the century, except in the agent noun **viewer** and certain special combinations such as *viewing figures*

> 1935 *Discovery*: The comfort and interest with which the [television] pictures may be viewed in a semi-darkened room.

> 1936 *Times*: I should be unwilling to lay heavy odds against a resident in Hindhead viewing the Coronation procession.

> 1958 *Listener*: They view on average for thirteen hours a week.

viewer *n* (1935) someone who watches or is watching television. A term which, when public television broadcasting became actual rather than potential, gradually took over from the earlier *looker-in* (1927). See also **televiewer (1935)**

> 1936 *Times*: At Alexandra Palace yesterday, when the new television service of the B.B.C. was officially opened, the Postmaster-General and others had to address themselves not only to listeners, but to 'viewers'. Within a radius of some 25 miles, 'viewers' saw and heard a ceremony which the speakers rightly described as historic... There was a speech by Mr. R. C. Norman, chairman of the B.B.C. who was the first to use the word 'viewers' in its new meaning.

> 1985 *Broadcast*: Failure to cover such events, it is felt, would reflect badly on broadcasters in the minds of viewers.

vinyl *n* (1939) Shorthand for *polyvinyl*, a type of plastic or resin formed by polymerizing the organic radical or group vinyl. The word did not come into widespread lay use until the late 1950s, when the substance started turning up in household articles, records, covering materials, etc.

> 1939 *Nature*: Resins more recently developed, such as vinyl and polystyrene, are slowly making headway.

> 1959 *House & Garden*: Dining-chairs upholstered in washable vinyl.

> 1962 *B.B.C. Handbook*: L.P. vinyl records giving basic pronunciation rules.

V.I.P. *n* (1933) Abbreviation of *very important person* (or, in the earliest recorded instance, *personage*). A usage which proliferated during and after World War II. Occasionally treated as an acronym, and pronounced /vip/

> 1933 Compton Mackenzie: 'At the moment he has a V.I.P. with him'... Miss Glidden seemed to divine his perplexity, for...she turned round and whispered through a pursed up mouth, 'Very Important Personage'.

> 1945 *Fortune*: Very important persons, or 'Vips', usually travel in plush C–54's.

> 1946 Evelyn Waugh: I found I had been categorized VIP—Very Important Person. It seemed odd to be asked 'Are you a VIP?'

walkathon *n* (1932) a long-distance walk; originally a competitive one, now usually one undertaken to raise money for charity. The first in a longish line of 20th-century coinages formed with the ending -*athon*, based on (or 'barbarously extracted from', as the OED disapprovingly puts it) *marathon* (see also **talkathon (1934)**, **telethon (1949)**))

> 1932 *Kansas City Times*: Sure a hick town is a place where they have enough superhicks to put on a walkathon.

> 1979 *Honolulu Advertiser*: Manned booths for various charitable walk-a-thons or walked themselves.

walkie-talkie *n* (1939) a small radio transmitter and receiver that can be carried on the person to provide two-way communication as one walks. Originally US

> 1939 *Sun* (Baltimore): 'Walkie-talkie' is the Army Signal Corps' way of speaking of unit S.C.R.
> 195—a recently developed radio sending and receiving set so small it is carried on the back and one talks while one walks.

washing-up machine *n* (1930) an electrical apparatus for washing dishes. It has never quite ousted *dishwasher*, which was coined in the US in the 1860s for a hand-operated machine and was applied to the new electrical appliances in the 1920s ('Lessen the labors of your wife. Electric wash-ing machines, electric dish washers, [etc.]', *Daily Colonist* (Victoria, British Columbia) (1921))

> 1930 *Daily Telegraph*: Electric washing-up machines…will be sold by auction.

water ski *n* (1931) one of a pair of skis enabling the wearer to skim the surface of water when towed by a motor-boat. As the first quote below suggests, the term came into being in the late 1920s, but there are no written examples on record (along with its derivatives *water-skier* and *water-skiing*) until 1931

> 1931 *New York Times*: In 1928 a young Viennese student and amateur skier named Joseph Krupka, observing a long-legged waterfly racing over the surface of a rain-barrel, conceived the idea of skiing over water as he had done over snow. That night he worked out on paper the construction of a water ski… The 1929 water ski champion, Herr Pribitzer of the water-ski rescue section…has attained speeds of more than twelve miles an hour… The water skier can carry about sixty pounds additional weight… Water skiing is beginning to eclipse canoeing.

> 1931 *Times Educational Supplement*: A schoolmaster…crossed the Channel…on a pair of water skis.

whizz-boy *n* (1931) a pickpocket. British slang

> 1931 Margery Allingham: How many murders do we get in this class… It's navvies, whizz-boys, car thieves…who run off the rails and commit murder.

whodunit *n* (1930) a story about the solving of a mystery, especially a murder; a detective or mur-der story. Colloquial, originally US. A semi-facetious lexicalization of the non-standard *who done it?* (i.e. 'who did it?')

> 1930 D. Gordon: *Half-Mast Murder*, by Milward Kennedy—A satisfactory *whodunit*.

wide boy *n* (1937) someone who lives by his wits, often dishonestly; someone who engages in petty-criminal activities, a spiv. British slang; based on the use of *wide* to mean 'shrewd, sharp-witted' which dates back to the mid 19th century

> 1937 R. Westerby: Jim was turning, or had already turned, into a Smart Aleck, a Wide Boy, a despiser of the Mugs who worked.

wide screen *n* (1931) a cinema screen which presents a wide field of vision in proportion to its height. As the quotes below describe, experiments with such a screen, wider than the standard 4:3 proportions, were carried out in the 1930s, but its commercial exploitation had to wait until the 1950s

> 1931 *Annual Register 1930*: The Wide Screen is still only a matter for experiment, as stand-ardisation has not yet been achieved.

> 1932 *Annual Register 1931*: The 'Wide Screen' invention, though perfected, was not offered to the public by the big producing concerns, seeing that it would involve the studios in huge expenditure.

> 1953 *Manchester Guardian*: Hollywood…had decided to coast for the present on a compromise between 3-D and Cinemascope—namely on the less spectacular development known as Wide Screen.

widget *n* (1931) A generally facetious name for a gadget or mechanical contrivance, especially a small manufactured item. Originally US, and largely restricted to that variety until it became bet-ter known in Britain in the 1990s as the result of an advertising campaign for beer: *widget* was the term chosen for a device that makes beer foam when its can is opened. It probably originated as an alteration of *gadget*

> 1937 E. Lyons: Every time the percentage of widgets turned out by her factory rose her features shone.

> 1997 *Daily Mail*: He has since made a tidy packet from the John Smith 'widget' beer commercials.

witch-hunt *n* (1938) a single-minded and uncompromising campaign against a group of people with unacceptable views or behaviour (in early use, mainly communists), especially one regarded as unfair or malicious persecution

> 1938 George Orwell: Rank-and-file Communists everywhere are led away on a senseless witch-hunt after 'Trotskyists'.

> 1958 *Times Literary Supplement*: The story of a security officer in America in the days when McCarthy witch-hunts were frequent and when communists lurked…under every bed.

> 1977 *Gay News*: During the operation—labelled a 'witch-hunt' by the local gay community—28 men were arrested.

workshop *n* (1937) a meeting for discussion, study, experiment, etc. Originally US. A favourite educational device of the latter part of the century

> 1984 *Times*: Priority bookings for their tastings, wine workshops and special dinners.

World War I *n* (1939) the war of 1914–18. Previously generally referred to as the **Great War (1914)** (a name adhered to by members of its generation), the advent of **World War II** made it hard to resist calling it *World War I* (the alternative formulation **First World War** is first recorded in 1947)

> 1939 *Time*: Exports of arms, munitions and related materials in World War I amounted…to only 25% of total exports to the Allies.

> 1947 *Time & Tide*: The despair and cynicism that followed what it has now become fashionable to call World War One.

World War II *n* (1939) the war of 1939–45. Speculation about such a conflagration, as a follow-up to the war of 1914–18, had produced similar terminology before ('World War No 2', *Manchester Guardian* (heading) (1919)), but there is no evidence of its being fully lexicalized before actual hostilities began. The alternative formulation **Second World War** is first recorded in 1942

> 1939 *Time*: Some of the diplomatic juggling which last week ended in World War II was old-fashioned international jockeying for power.

yeti *n* (1937) The name among the Sherpas of the Himalayas for the creature known familiarly in English as the **abominable snowman (1921)**. It is an adaptation of Tibetan *yeh-teh*, literally 'little manlike animal'

> 1937 *Times*: The Sherpas had no hesitation in pronouncing [the tracks] to be those of a Snowman or 'Yeti'.

yo-yo *n* (1932) a toy in the form of two joined discs with a deep groove between them in which a string is attached and wound, its free end being held so that the toy can be made to fall under its own weight and rise again by its momentum. The word is first recorded in 1915 as the name of a Filipino toy of this type. It was registered as a trademark in 1932 (in Canada), which was the year when a sudden craze for the toy spread through the western world. The word then came to be used also for the pastime of playing with the yo-yo, and also as a verb. There was a re-run of the craze in the 1950s, and again in 1998. (As a toy the yo-yo is far from a 20th-century novelty. In the 19th century a similar plaything was known as a *bandalore*, described already in 1824 as a 'gone-by toy')

> 1932 *Evening Standard*: He asked me to hold his hand until he became proficient, and I experienced a queer thrill as I brought his hand slowly up and down to make the Yo-Yo respond to the twitch of the string.

> 1932 *Daily Express*: Some boys playing yo-yo attracted the Queen's attention… Do you yo-yo?

The 1940s were the pivotal decade of the century. World War II, which began in the last months of 1939, occupied the energies of most nations on the planet for the best part of six years. The two atom bomb explosions at Hiroshima and Nagasaki in 1945, which marked its effective end, were also the hinge of the century. The second half of the 1940s saw the putting in place of the elements that would shape the world's events for the following 40 years: the ideological contest between East and West, decolonization, international cooperation, the development of nuclear weapons, and of the computer.

From the *phoney war* (or *sitzkrieg*) at its beginning to the *war trials* at its end, from the acronyms of its military bureaucrats to the slang of its ordinary soldiers, World War II contributed an enormous amount of new vocabulary to the English language—much of it necessarily ephemeral (few now remember *Coventrate*), but much, too, that still resonates at the end of the century (*final solution, collaboration*).

It was the war, above all, that first stretched out its tentacles towards civilian populations. In Britain, this took the form, in 1940, of the *blitz: bombed out* families surveyed the smoking ruins of their homes; the *bomb-sites* began to appear that would disfigure British cities for decades to come; Coventry was *Coventrated*, and later there came the *Baedeker raids*. Towards the end of the war it would be the *V-1s* (or *buzz bombs*, or *doodlebugs*, or *flying bombs*) and the *V-2s*. To meet the threat of invasion, Britons joined the *Home Guard*; to produce precious fuel, some became *Bevin boys* down the mines; *clippies* 'manned' the buses. It was a time of *cannibalizing* and *make do and mend*. For eating out there were *British restaurants*, while at home there were (if you had the *points*) such delicacies as *luncheon meat* (notably *Spam* (1937)), *national* milk, butter, etc., *Woolton pie*, and, later, *snoek*. To supplement this meagre fare, there were always the *blacketeers*. The Americans (providers of *lend-lease*) arrived, bringing their *Kilroy* to join the British Mr Chad, with his graffiti'd *wot no?* slogan. When they left, they took many *GI brides* with them.

Others, answering the *call-up*, carried the war to the enemy, with *bazookas* and *Sten guns* and *napalm* and *saturation* bombing. They fought in *jeeps, dukws*, and *landing craft*; as *commandos, paratroops*, and *pathfinders*, as *Desert Rats* and as *Chindits*; against *E-boats* and *panzers*. They used *psychological warfare* (but not *biological warfare*). In the Far East they encountered *banzai* and *kamikaze*. Then came *D-Day*, and there were *mulberry harbours* and *Bailey bridges* to be built as the *second front* advanced. Then the enormities of Nazi *genocide*, the *final solution*, the *Holocaust* (1957), came to be revealed: the *concentration camps* (1901), the *extermination camps*, the *gas chambers*. Meanwhile, in occupied countries, the *Resistance* had been active (in France, the *Maquis*); but there was also *collaboration*, and the *Quisling*.

The unprecedented levels of organization and bureaucratization stemming from the mobilization of most of the adult population, the governmental control of most aspects of economic (and other) activity, and multi-level cooperation between the Allied powers led to a mushroom growth of official bodies, committees, military groups, plans and projects. Most of them seemed to have lengthy, multi-word titles which the urgency of war demanded should be abbreviated. Hence the rash of acronyms and other initialisms produced in the 1940s (e.g. *BABS* 'blind approach beacon system', *BAOR* 'British Army of the Rhine', *PLUTO* 'pipeline under the ocean', *SHAEF* 'Supreme Headquarters, Allied Expeditionary Force'; see *acronym* (1943)), which has set a seemingly irresistible pattern followed by the rest of the century.

At the other end of the lexical spectrum, the stress and comradeship of war produced a wealth of slang, much of it of the 'whistling in the face of adversity' type (a dangerous military operation, for instance, became a *party*). To take one small part of the whole as an example, the Royal Air Force (whose aircrew suffered the highest death rates of all British service personnel) was a rich source: *angels* and *bandits*, *stooging*, *getting weaving*, and *going for a burton*, *gremlins* and *shaky dos*, *prangs* and *tail-end Charlies*, all became familiar to a public following the pilots' exploits.

In 1945–46, *demob* (1934), and the problems of peace. On the continent of Europe there were still *displaced persons* in *transit camps*, while in Germany there was still *denazification* work to be done (and *fraternization* to be discouraged). At home there was *austerity*, and simple pleasures (*holiday camps*, and the *baby boom*), but also a promise of a fresh start and a brighter future in the *welfare state* (in Britain exemplified by the *National Health* and *National Assistance*, and also the prospect of *comprehensive* education). In Europe, the *Marshall Plan* and other forms of *aid* set war-ravaged economies on their feet. Pessimists feared *Big Brother*, but the *teenagers* had other things to worry about.

At the end of the war, the Western powers and the Soviet Union were somewhat uneasy allies, but it soon turned sour. The *Cold War* got under way, which was to separate the world into capitalist and Communist power blocks (*West* and *East* (1951), dominated respectively by the two *superpowers*, the US and the USSR) for the next four decades. The *iron curtain* (1920) and the *bamboo curtain* descended. The *terrorist* appeared on the international scene (in Palestine), and English obtained the word *apartheid*. The *card-carrying crypto-communist*, that bogey figure of the 1950s, popped up for the first time.

To set against these depressing developments, international cooperation was producing institutions such as the *United Nations* and the *Security Council*, while in Europe, *Benelux* gave a foretaste of future integration.

The fear which fuelled the Cold War was, of course, largely caused by the *atom bomb* (*A bomb* for short, *fusion bomb* for the technically minded, *superbomb* or simply *the bomb* for the apocalyptically minded, but all anticipated by many decades by *atomic bomb* (1914)), which the US possessed and the Soviet Union acquired in 1949. The world was having to get used quickly to the possibility of being *atomized* by *nuclear* weapons. And as if this were not enough, there was now talk of a *hydrogen bomb*, exploded by nuclear *fusion* and perhaps delivered by a *guided missile*. *Ground zero* was not the place to be. But peaceful uses of nuclear energy were being discussed too, and *fuel rod* and *pile* entered the language.

Another newcomer of far-reaching import was *computer* (*electronic brain* was a contemporary synonym, but it failed to last the course). The development of such machines was only in its embryonic phase, but already many now-familiar elements of computational terminology were falling into place: *analogue* and *digital; bit, data,* and *memory; language* and *program; hardware, punchcard,* and *input.* This was not the only area in which the *boffins* and *backroom boys* had been working during and after the war, though. Other new developments and discoveries of the decade included *radar* and *sonar, radio telescopes* and *transistors, holograms* and *biotechnology, bosons* and *plutonium, antibiotics* and *DDT.* And then there was the *jet engine,* or *turbojet,* which was to revolutionize aviation in the second half of the century; the *delta wing* was the new shape in the sky.

The *space age* was, if not completely in the realms of science fiction, still in the planning stage; *space vehicles, boosters,* and *re-entry* were being discussed, but *spaceman* turned out not to have long-term credibility—its fate lay with *flying saucers* and *aliens.*

As postwar consumerism began to get into its stride, new goodies appeared on the market (many available on *HP*). You could have *double glazing* for your house, a *blender* for the kitchen, *Formica* work surfaces, and write the cheque with a *biro* or *ball-point pen.* You could take a *bubble bath,* and wrap up your sandwiches in *foil.* If you had despaired of dowdy *utility* clothes, the shops now had the *New Look.* The young in the 1940s were wearing *pedal pushers, bobby sox,* and *zoot suits,* and sported *crew cuts* and *peek-a-boo* hairstyles. Women could cultivate their shape with the new lightweight *pantie-girdles* and *roll-ons,* or show it off to sensational effect with the *bikini.*

You could go out and dance to *boogie* and *bop,* or listen to the offerings of *disc jockeys* on the radio. And if you preferred not to, you were probably *square.*

A-bomb *n* (1945) An abbreviation, current during the 1940s and 50s, of **atom bomb (1945)**

> 1945 *Daily Mirror*: Jap Radio says Evacuate—'Ware A-Bombs.

abort *v* (1946) to bring (a mission or other procedure) to a premature end. Originally US; a piece of technical jargon which became more widely familiar during the US space programme of the 1960s

> 1962 John Glenn: A bright red light at the very top of this panel is labelled 'Abort'… You could be aborted automatically…or by a command from the ground.

> 1963 *American Speech*: We lost an engine, so we aborted the mission.

acronym *n* (1943) a word formed from the initial letters of other words. Originally US; coined from the prefix *acr-* 'outer end, tip' (from Greek *akros*) plus -*onym*, as in *homonym*. The precise application of the term varies, but strictly speaking it denotes a combination pronounced as a word (e.g. *NATO* from *North Atlantic Treaty Organization, SHAEF* from *Supreme Headquarters Allied Expeditionary Force*) rather than as just a sequence of letters. It is often taken too to include words formed from initial syllables (e.g. **sitrep** from *situation report*), and hybrids of letters and syllables (e.g. **radar** from *radio detection and ranging*).

It is a quintessentially 20th-century way of creating new words—there is little or no evidence of it before 1900. No doubt the proliferation of polynomial governmental agencies, international organizations, and military units as the century has progressed (the last particularly during World War II) has contributed significantly to its growth. Most remain as simple initialisms ('alphabet soup agencies' they were called in the US during F. D. Roosevelt's presidency), but as soon as the letter-sequence takes on (by accident or design) the lineaments of a pronounceable English word, it seems we cannot resist the temptation to turn it into an acronym.

> 1943 *American Notes & Queries*: Words made up of the initial letters or syllables of other words…I have seen…called by the name *acronym*.

aid *n* (1940) material help given by one country to another, especially economic assistance or material help given by a rich to a poor or underdeveloped country

> 1940 *Economist*: The United States' aid to Britain would be rendered ineffective.

> 1958 *Spectator*: Congress would like to buy missiles with foreign-aid money.

air freshener *n* (1949) a substance or device for introducing 'pleasant' smells into the air of a room, to mask foul odours. Originally US

> 1949 *Good Housekeeping* (New York): Have you ever used an air freshener—a special product that camouflages unpleasant odors with clean countrylike scents?

air-lift *n* (1945) transportation of supplies or troops by air, especially during a state of emergency. A term mainly familiarized by the 'Berlin air-lift' of 1948, when Allied aircraft flew thousands of tons of essential supplies into the city over a period of nearly a year after it had been blockaded by the Russians

> 1945 *Life*: General Ho Ying-chin used the American air lift to pass four crack American-equipped…armies over the heads of the Communists into Shanghai.

> 1948 *News Chronicle*: This is the first British plane to crash on the air lift, which began in June.

air support *n* (1941) the provision by aircraft of cover and other assistance to ground or naval forces in action

> 1941 *Aeronautics*: Fortunately the Royal Navy has never completely neglected the importance of air support to naval forces.

alien *adj, n* (1944) (a being) from another planet, especially one visiting the Earth. A usage largely restricted to science fiction; its negative connotations (hostility, creepiness, etc.) would make it impolitic to use in the presence of a real alien. Popularized in particular by the Ridley Scott film *Alien* (1979). The noun is first recorded in 1953. See also **extraterrestrial (1963)**

> 1944 *Astounding Science Fiction*: An alien ship, all right… He looked at the thing. It was alien…, horribly different from anything on Earth.

> 1953 W. Tenn: The first of the aliens stepped out in the complex tripodal gait that all humans were shortly to know…so well.

analogue *adj* (1946) Denoting a computer which operates with numbers represented by some physically measurable quantity, such as weight, length, voltage, etc. Compare **digital (1945)**

> 1946 D. R. Hartree: The American usage is 'analogue' and 'digital' machines.

> 1947 *Electronic Engineering*: Electrical analogue computing.

angel *n* (1947) an unexplained mark on a radar screen

> 1947 W. B. Gould: Radar equipment…has given fairly consistent unexplainable echoes at altitudes between approximately 300 and 3000 yards. For want of a better term, these echoes have been dubbed 'Angels' by Signal Corps personnel.

angels *n* (1943) height above ground; usually applied specifically to a height of 1,000 feet. R.A.F. slang. Its origins are unclear, but the usual assumption is that it has something to do with the sky as the haunt of angels. *Angel* is recorded slightly earlier as a verb, meaning 'to gain height, climb' ('The boys of Britain's R.A.F. have developed a language all their own. A fighter pilot is told to "scramble", instead of take off; then he "angels upward" ', *Reader's Digest* (1941)), but it seems likely that the noun came first

> 1943 P. Brennan: 'Gain your angels quickly…' We continued to climb… We climbed into sun, Woody advising us to get as much angels as possible.

> 1943 Hunt & Pringle: '20 M.E.s at Angels one owe' means '20 Messerschmitts at 10,000 ft.'

angst *n* (1944) a strong but ill-defined feeling of anxiety. English writers had been using German *Angst* for some time (it appears in a letter written by George Eliot in 1849, and early 20th-century translators of German psychological and philosophical works—e.g. by Freud and Heidegger—often referred to it), but it was always very obviously 'non-naturalized', and often followed by a translation; 'Palinurus' (the pen-name of Cyril Connolly) is the first on record to use it as an English word. The native equivalent has often been deployed in the same context (e.g. in 'The Age of Anxiety', the title of a long poem (1947) by W. H. Auden dealing with man's isolation)

> 1944 'Palinurus': Angst may take the form of remorse about the past, guilt about the present, anxiety about the future… There need be nothing angst-forming about the sexual act.

> 1956 C. P. Snow: Discussing other people whose lives were riven by angst—it domesticated her wretchedness a little to have that label to pin on.

Anthony Eden *n* (1940) a black Homburg hat of the type often worn by the British politician Sir Anthony Eden (1897–1977)

> 1956 Daniel Davin: Dark suit and Anthony Eden hat during the week, tweed jacket and flannels at the week-end.

antibiotic *n* (1944) any of a class of substances produced by living organisms and capable of destroying or inhibiting the growth of micro-organisms, especially one of these substances used for therapeutic purposes. The term *antibiotique* (literally 'injurious to life') was coined in French around 1889. English had adapted it as *antibiotic* before the end of the 19th century, but it was not until the 1940s, with the development of bactericides like penicillin, that it really took off (including conversion into a noun)

> 1944 *Lancet* (title): The Mould Antibiotics.

> 1949 H. W. Florey et al.: The antibiotics comprise substances with diverse chemical structures and biological activities. They range in their action from those which inhibit the growth of certain strains of bacteria in a highly selective manner to those which are relatively toxic to all living cells.

apartheid *n* (1947) The name given in South Africa to the segregation of the inhabitants of European descent from the non-European (Coloured or mixed, Bantu, Indian, etc.), a policy introduced in 1948. It comes from Afrikaans *apartheid*, literally 'separateness', which is first recorded in 1929. See also **separate development (1955)**

> 1947 *Cape Times*: Mr. Hofmeyr said apartheid could not be reconciled with a policy of progress and prosperity for South Africa.

> 1948 *Cape Times*: Mr. P. O. Sauer…will explain the application of the apartheid policy on the railways.

apparatchik *n* (1941) Originally used in the writings of Arthur Koestler to refer to a Communist agent or spy, but later in its more central Russian sense, 'a member of an *apparat*, the organizational and administrative apparatus of the Communist party'. Later still extended to any bureaucratic functionary

> 1941 Arthur Koestler: The dark silhouette of the Tchekist, the 'Aparat-chik', or G.P.U. agent had replaced the once bright and lively symbols of the struggle for a happier world.

> 1973 *Daily Colonist* (Victoria, British Columbia): The United States was indeed being pushed in the direction of a police state. The pushers were not mere apparatchiks such as John Dean, but President Nixon and his closest associates.

atom bomb *n* (1945) a bomb whose explosive power derives from the fission of heavy atomic nuclei. The alternative **atomic bomb** was in use as long before as 1914, but *atom bomb* had to wait until theory became reality with the dropping of two such bombs by the US on the Japanese cities of Hiroshima and Nagasaki in August 1945. Also first recorded as a verb in 1945, meaning 'to drop an atom bomb on'. Often abbreviated to **A bomb (1945)** in the 1940s and 50s

> 1945 *Times*: An impenetrable cloud of dust and smoke had covered the target area after the atom bomb had been dropped at Hiroshima.

> 1945 *Evening News*: Ultimatum to Japs: Accept by 6 p.m.—or be atom-bombed.

atomize *v* (1945) to damage or destroy with an atomic weapon. Colloquial

> 1945 *Daily Mirror*: Nagasaki, the second…Japanese city to be 'atomised'.

austerity *n* (1942) the reduction of non-essentials to a minimum as a war-time measure of economy. Widely used adjectivally during and immediately after World War II before nouns relating to food, clothing, etc., denoting a spartan lack of elaboration or embellishment. Compare **utility (1942)**

> 1942 *Times Weekly*: A General Limitation Order—…which suggests that the United States have got quite a way on the road to austerity.

> 1944 *Times*: Mr. Dalton…said that austerity clothing was not unsaleable. On the contrary, many men evidently thought that at 20 coupons austerity suits were a good bargain.

automatic transmission *n* (1946) an automatic gear-changing system in a motor vehicle. Originally US

> 1946 W. H. Crouse: The Hydra-Matic drive, supplied on Cadillac and Oldsmobile cars as special equipment, combines the fluid drive with an automatic transmission that has four forward and one reverse speed.

automation *n* (1948) automatic control of the manufacture of a product through a number of successive stages. Hence applied more broadly to the application of automatic control to any branch of industry or science, and by extension, to the use of electronic or mechanical devices to replace human labour. The coinage of the word is usually attributed to Delmar S. Harder of the US. The back-formation **automate** is first recorded (in the form *automated*) in 1952

> 1948 *McGraw-Hill Encyclopedia of Science and Technology*: *Automation*, the art of applying mechanical devices to manipulate work pieces into and out of equipment, turn parts between operations, remove scrap, and to perform these tasks in timed sequence with the production equipment so that the line can be put wholly or partially under pushbutton control at strategic stations.

> 1952 *Cleveland* (Ohio) *Plain Dealer*: Another 'automated' line, less spectacular than the block line, machines the cylinder head.

> 1953 *Manchester Guardian Weekly*: Many factories are spending large sums on 'automation', that is, the adoption of automatic machines working together with little labour.

baby boom *n* (1941) a temporary marked increase in the birth-rate. Colloquial, originally US; often applied specifically to one that occurred in the years following World War II. People born then came to be known later as **baby-boomers (1974)**

> 1941 *Life*: Whatever the reasons, the U.S. baby boom is bad news for Hitler.

> 1971 *Scientific American*: The postwar 'baby boom' and rapid growth of the economy in the 1950's pushed the population growth rate up to 18.5 percent.

baby-sit *v* (1947) See **baby-sitter (1937)**

backroom boy *n* (1941) someone engaged in essential but unpublicized work, especially (secret) research. The germ of the term appears in the first quote below, from Lord Beaverbrook, then Minister of Aircraft Production, although it is not recorded in its finished form until 1943

> 1941 Lord Beaverbrook: Now who is responsible for this work of development on which so much depends? To whom must the praise be given? To the boys in the back rooms. They do not sit in the limelight. But they are the men who do the work. Many of them are Civil Servants.

> 1943 *Punch*: He's one of those obscure back-room boys who have lately been so much in the lime-light.

> 1944 *Times*: The man most responsible for the development of the rocket projectile...is Group Captain John D'Arcy Bakercarr,...whose 'backroom boys' at the Ministry of Aircraft Production have worked unremittingly with him.

Baedeker raid *n* (1942) any of a series of raids by the German Luftwaffe in April and May of 1942 on places of cultural and historical importance in Britain. *Baedeker* is the name given to the series of guide-books issued by Karl Baedeker (1801–59) at Coblenz, or by his successors (ironically, it had become synonymous in English with cultured European travel by the 1890s); the reason for its application to the air-raids is given in the second quote below

> 1942 *Daily Mail*: The 'Baedeker' raids have put the Luftwaffe in a grave dilemma.

> 1942 *War Illustrated*: York's Guildhall as it appeared on the night of April 28 after it had been struck by incendiaries in one of Hitler's 'Baedeker raids' on Britain's cultural heritage. After the legitimate R.A.F. raids on Rostock, where the Heinkel factory and other munition works were destroyed, German officials frankly stated that the Luftwaffe would go out for every building in Britain which is marked with three stars in Baedeker's guide-books.

Bailey bridge *n* (1944) a bridge of lattice steel designed for rapid assembly from prefabricated standard parts, used especially in military operations. Named after its inventor, the English engineer Donald Bailey (1901–85)

> 1944 *Times*: A Bailey bridge more than 1,000 ft. long has been built over the Chindwin near Kalewa.

ball pen *n* (1946), **ball-point pen** *n* (1947) a pen in which the writing point is a minute ball which is inked from an inner reservoir. Originally US. The shortened *ball-point* is first recorded in 1959, although no doubt it was in use before then. See also **Biro (1947)**

> 1946 *Esquire* (Chicago): Biro who introduced the first ball-pen presents...a sensational new invention.

> 1958 *Times Review of Industry*: The ball-point pen has a universally inimical effect upon...hand-writing.

bamboo curtain *n* (1949) a political and economic barrier between territories under the control of the Communist régime in China and non-Communist countries. Modelled on **iron curtain (1920)**

> 1949 *Time*: The Communist bosses of Peiping dropped a bamboo curtain, cutting off Peiping from the world.

bandit *n* (1942) a hostile aircraft. R.A.F. slang

> 1942 I. Gleed: One bandit shot down in sea about ten miles out.

banzai *adj* (1945) Applied to a reckless attack by Japanese soldiers, pilots, etc. An adjectival use of the Japanese cry *banzai* (literally 'ten thousand years'), used for greeting the emperor or as a battle-cry. Compare **kamikaze (1945)**

> 1945 *Coast to Coast 1944*: Out in the glaring sky a Zero started its Banzai run.

> 1945 *San Francisco News*: Smashed desperate 'banzai' charges by doomed enemy survivors.

barn *n* (1947) In nuclear physics, 10^{-24} square centimetres, a unit of area used in the measurement of the cross-section of a nucleus. One of those little jokes which scientists permit themselves from time to time: it comes from the association of barns with largeness (as in 'as big as a barn', 'couldn't hit a barn-door', etc.)

> 1947 R. D. Evans: This area has been dubbed the 'barn', 1 barn = 10^{-24} cm2 /nucleus.

bathyscaphe *n* (1947) The name given by the Swiss scientist Professor Auguste Piccard to his deep-sea diving vessel, and subsequently also applied to other similar vessels. He coined it (originally in French) from two Greek words meaning literally 'deep ship'. See also **bathysphere (1930)**

> 1953 Jacques Cousteau: The elderly scientific extremist [Auguste Piccard] had designed the Bathyscaphe ('Depth-craft') a decade before and, after the delay of a world war, it had been built by a brilliant Belgian physicist, Dr. Max Cosyns... The *Bathyscaphe* was to navigate twenty-five times as deep as conventional submarines.

bazooka *n* (1943) a tubular anti-tank rocket-launcher. Originally US. The name was borrowed from a curious home-made jazz instrument, not unlike a trombone, which enjoyed a brief celebrity in the 1930s; it was presumably coined by the instrument's inventor, a Mr Burns, perhaps partly on the model of *kazoo*, an instrument that makes a buzzing sound

> 1943 *Fortune*: A strange gun called the bazooka that fires a rocket projectile.

> 1943 *War Illustrated*: American anti-tank rocket thrower..., known as the 'bazooka'.

beat up *v* (1940) to dive low over (a person or place) in an aircraft as a stunt. Slang

> 1942 Terence Rattigan: I put the old Wimpey into a dive and beat him up—you know, pulled out only a few feet above his head and stooged round him.

bebop *n* (1945) a development of jazz, begun in the US around the end of World War II, characterized by complex harmony, dissonant chords, and highly syncopated rhythm. The word, along with the contemporary, synonymous, but shorter-lived *rebop*, seems to have originated as a nonsense word in jazz lyrics: instances have been traced in recordings as far back as 1928: 'Bop-do-de-de-do-do...Bebop one, bebop two, bebop three', McKinney's Cotton Pickers, *Four or Five Times* (1928). **Bop (1948)** is a reduced form

> 1945 *Down Beat* (title of gramophone record): Dizzy Gillespie. Salted Peanuts/Be-Bop.

> 1946 *Melody Maker*: The re-bop (or, if you prefer it, be-bop: they're using both names for it in America) is clearly evident.

> 1948 *Life*: Boppers go gaga over such bebop classics as OO Bop Sha Bam.

> 1955 Leonard Feather: As musicians gathered outside the clubs along Fifty-Second Street to discuss the music of Charlie Parker...or of Dizzy Gillespie..., they would use an onomatopoetic expression to describe a typical phrase played by these musicians: 'rebop' or 'bebop' they would say.

beefburger *n* (1940) a hamburger. Originally US. Once the element -*burger* had become semi-detached from *hamburger* and begun entering promiscuously into a range of other combinations (see **burger (1939)**), a need was evidently felt to make the hamburger's main ingredient explicit—hence *beefburger*. A later, more upmarket variation was *steakburger* (first recorded in 1960)

> 1940 *American Speech*: Hamburgers are out, beefburgers are in!

Benelux *n* (1947) the customs union of Belgium, the Netherlands, and Luxembourg formed in October 1947. The seed which grew into the European Union, with a fashionable acronym for a name

> 1947 *Foreign Affairs*: The Secretariat prepared a common tariff for the 'Benelux Union'.

> 1947 *Spectator*: Success would make 'Benelux'...the third trading power in the world.

Bevin boy *n* (1944) In Britain during World War II, a young man of age for military service, but selected by lot to work in a coal-mine. Named after Ernest Bevin (1881–1951), Minister of Labour and National Service 1940–5

> 1944 *Manpower*: The 'Bevin boys' selected by ballot undergo preliminary training.

Big Brother *n* (1949) the head of state in George Orwell's novel *1984*; hence, an apparently benevolent, but ruthlessly omnipotent, state authority

> 1949 George Orwell: On each landing...the poster with the enormous face gazed from the wall... *Big Brother is watching you*, the caption beneath it ran.

> 1953 *Economist*: The distrust of the *concierge* who is also a police spy, of the admirable focusing device which the big block provides for the watchful eye of Big Brother.

bikini *n* (1948) a brief two-piece swimsuit for women. The term was coined in French in 1947 ('Bikini, ce mot cinglant comme l'explosion même...correspondait au niveau du vêtement de plage à un anéantissement de la surface vêtue; à une minimisation extrême de la pudeur', *Le Monde Illustré* (1947)), apparently drawing a parallel between the explosive effect of the swimsuit on French males and the US atom bomb test on Bikini Atoll in the Marshall Islands in July 1946

> 1948 *Newsweek*: This...French beauty...shows the 1948 countertrend against the skimpy 'Bikini' style...which swept French beaches and beauty contests last year.

> 1950 *News of the World*: —made an unsuccessful attempt yesterday to swim in a Hampstead Heath pond in her home-made 'Bikini' costume.

> 1957 *Times*: 'What is a bikini?'...'A small pair of pants and a brassière.'

bind *v* (1943) to complain. British services' slang

> 1943 *Penguin New Writing*: 'Stop binding,' said Ginger mechanically... 'When I get back to civvy street I'll never moan about my job again.'

biological warfare *n* (1946) warfare involving the use of toxins, germs, etc., harmful to plants, animals, or human beings. A more comprehensive term than **bacteriological warfare (1924)** and **germ warfare (1938)**

> 1946 *Life*: Biological warfare, using scourges of disease and famine as weapons, is as dreadful as the atomic bomb and far more difficult to control.

biotechnology *n* (1947) the branch of technology concerned with the development and exploitation of machines in relation to the various needs of human beings. A usage which has largely given way to the later 'use of living organisms in production processes' (see **biotechnology (1972)**). **Ergonomics (1950)** is now the more usual term, particularly in British English

> 1947 *Science*: Hours of work, on-the-job feeding, rest periods, etc. are also phases of the physiology of work which form an important part of a comprehensive biotechnology.

bird *n* **for the birds** (1944) trivial, worthless; appealing only to gullible people. Colloquial, originally and mainly US; usually in the phrase *strictly for the birds*. Reputedly an allusion to birds eating droppings from horses and cattle

> 1951 J. D. Salinger: 'Since 1888 we have been moulding boys into splendid, clear-thinking young men.' Strictly for the birds.

> 1953 *Time*: Kinsey's book is strictly for the birds.

Biro *n* (1947) The proprietary name (registered in Britain in 1947) of a particular make of ball-point pen. Subsequently used as a generic term for any ball-point pen. It commemorates the pen's Hungarian inventor Laszlo Bíró (1900–85). See **ball pen (1946)**

> 1948 George Orwell: Thanks ever so for sending the pen... It'll do just as well as a Biro.

> 1967 Margaret Drabble: Even the sight of a broken biro on his windowsill was of interest to her.

bit *n* (1948) a unit of information derived from a choice between two equally probable alternatives or 'events'. The word, a blend of *binary digit*, is usually applied to such a unit stored electronically in a computer. See also **byte (1964)**

> 1948 C. E. Shannon: If the base 2 is used the resulting units may be called binary digits, or more briefly *bits*, a word suggested by J. W. Tukey.

> 1952 *Scientific American*: It is almost certain that 'bit' will become common parlance in the field of information, as 'horsepower' is in the motor field.

> 1957 *New Scientist*: Existing electronic computers can store, in their normal memories, up to about one million bits.

blacketeer *n* (1942) A concertinaed version of *black marketeer* (1942) (see **black market (1931)**). The original term for an operator on the black market was *black marketer* (1941). The change to *blacketeer* probably signals the increasing unpopularity of this figure, seen as unpatriotically exploiting wartime shortages for his own financial gain

> 1942 *Time*: The British people...favor outright imprisonment of guilty 'blacketeers'.

> 1944 *Daily Express*: Alleged blacketeering by Paris 'Gestapo'.

blender *n* (1948) an electrical appliance for puréeing or finely chopping food. One of the first of the new toys in the postwar consumer-boom kitchen. British English tended to prefer the term **liquidizer (1950)**

> 1948 *American Home*: Relax with a blender at your elbow… Start out with the recipes in your blender book.

blitz *n* (1940) an air-raid or a series of air-raids conducted with great intensity and ferocity, specifically the series of air-raids made on London and other British cities by the German Luftwaffe in 1940–41. A shortening of **Blitzkrieg (1939)**. Also used as a verb, meaning 'to bomb intensively' or 'to destroy, drive out, etc. by aerial bombing'

> 1940 *Daily Express*: Blitz bombing of London goes on all night… In his three-day blitz on London Goering has now lost 140 planes.

> 1940 *Daily Sketch*: Neighbourhood Theatre braved the blitz and yesterday presented a new play.

> 1940 *Daily Express*: A south coast town felt the heaviest weight of last night's Nazi blitzing.

> 1941 *New Statesman*: The Home Guard of young architects who spent the night of the City 'blitz' battering out Hitler's incendiaries.

> 1942 *Annual Register 1941*: 70,000 meals had to be provided by the Emergency kitchens for people 'blitzed' out of their homes.

bobby socks, bobby sox *n* (1943) socks reaching just above the ankle, typically white, especially those worn by girls in their teens. Originally and mainly US. The origins of *bobby* are not clear, but it may have something to do with *bob* 'to shorten'. The derivative *bobby-soxer*, denoting an adolescent girl who follows all the current fads in music, fashion, etc., is first recorded in 1944

> 1943 *Time*: Hundreds of…girls in bobby socks sat transfixed.

> 1944 *Birmingham* (US) *News-Age-Herald*: About 6,000 bobby soxers attended the concert.

boffin *n* (1945) someone engaged in 'back-room' scientific or technical research. British colloquial. The term's origins have never been satisfactorily explained. It seems to have been first applied by members of the Royal Air Force to scientists working on radar. They may have got it from Royal Navy slang *boffin* 'elderly officer' (1941), but as it is not known where that came from, it fails to advance the investigation much further

> 1945 *Times*: A band of scientific men who performed their wartime wonders at Malvern and apparently called themselves 'the boffins'.

> 1948 Lord Tedder: I was fortunate in having considerable dealings in 1938–40 with the 'Boffins' (as the Royal Air Force affectionately dubbed the scientists).

bogey, bogy, bogie *n* (1946) a score of one stroke over par for a hole at golf. Originally US. *Bogey* in British golfing terminology used to mean 'the number of strokes a good player ought to need for the course or for a hole'—in other words, what would now be called *par*. The following circumstantial but not altogether plausible story is told of its origins: In 1890 Dr. Thomas Browne, R.N., the hon. secretary of the Great Yarmouth Club, was playing against a Major Wellman, the match being against the 'ground score', which was the name given to the scratch value of each hole. The system of playing against the 'ground score' was new to Major Wellman, and he exclaimed, thinking of 'The Bogey Man', a song popular at that time, that his mysterious and well-nigh invincible opponent was a regular 'bogey-man'. The name 'caught on' at Great Yarmouth, and supposedly spread from there throughout the British game. There is no record of its use after 1910 (although it did spread to other games, such as bridge, as a term for a standard score), and it seems likely that this new usage is a completely independent coinage, based on *bogey* 'something to be feared'

> 1951 *Golf World*: Hall had seven birdies, two eagles and one bogie.

bomb *n* **the bomb** (1945) the atomic or hydrogen bomb, as (threatened to be) used by any country as a weapon of war, and regarded as unique because of its utterly destructive effects. See also **ban the bomb (1960)**

> 1945 *Times* (headline): Victory and the Bomb.

1959 *Sunday Times*: Twenty years ago, I mean: before the war, the Bomb, the satellites, the space-travellers and the nudist paradises.

bombed out *adj* (1940) driven out of one's home or other premises because it has been destroyed by bombing

1940 *New Statesman*: What…is happening to the host of shopkeepers…driven from their shops…or bombed out of them?… Our ruined or bombed-out shopkeeper will pay out of his income.

bomb-happy *adj* (1943) mentally affected by exposure to a bomb or shell explosion at close quarters; shell-shocked. Colloquial. One of a range of compounds based on *-happy* that were popular during World War II to denote the effects of a particular type of stress encountered on active service. Others included *sand-happy*, suffered by those in the North African campaign ('I served with the British Eighth Army in the desert…, but I never heard *sand happy*', *American Speech* (1946)) and *flak-happy*, brought on by exposure to anti-aircraft fire. Compare **shell shock (1915)**

1943 *San Francisco Chronicle*: A barrage so incessant…that many troops of the crack 65th Nazy Division were rendered 'bomb happy' and fell easy prisoners.

bomb-site *n* (1945) an area of ground on which buildings, etc., have been destroyed by aerial bombing. The term was a familiar one in Britain through the 1940s and 50s right into the 60s, when many such desolate holes still disfigured London and other major cities

1959 *Times*: Many of the bomb-site parks in central London are seldom full.

boogie *n* (1941) a style of blues music popular at rent parties. Originally a synonym of **boogie-woogie (1928)**, of which it is a shortened form, the term was adopted by rock groups in the late 1960s for music whose rhythm derived from repeated sequences of blues chords played on guitars. Also used as a verb, meaning 'to dance to this music'

1941 *Brunswick Records Catalog* (title): Scrub me, Mama with a Boogie Beat.

1978 *Daily Mirror*: Night after night she flirts and boogies the hours away.

boom and bust, boom or bust *n* (1943) a period of great prosperity followed by a severe depression. Originally US.

1943 H. S. Canby: The building trade, as usual, suffered from boom-and-bust.

1962 *Times Literary Supplement*: Cataclysmic alternatives—destruction or utopia, boom or bust.

boondocks *n* (1944) rough country; jungle; an isolated or wild region. Originally and mainly US; it was adopted by US personnel serving in the Philippines from *bundok*, the word for 'mountain' in the local language Tagalog. Nowadays it is mainly used in the sense 'somewhere far from centres of civilization'

1944 C. Wynn: The sand and boondocks of Paris Island.

1965 *Spectator*: Those who have been feeling the public pulse out in the boondocks report a good deal of unrest.

booster *n* (1944) an auxiliary engine or rocket, especially one used to give initial speed to a rocket or missile which is afterwards left to continue under its own power

1944 A. L. Murphy: Some being catapulted by booster rockets, while other craft will take off as rockets.

1961 *Spectator*: The huge boosters that launched Major Gagarin's capsule.

bop *n* (1948) An alternative name for **bebop (1945)**. In due course it came to denote more loosely any sort of dancing to pop music

1950 J. Vedey: The BBC has not been lacking in fostering its development, even to the point of broadcasting Bop—most advanced of all jazz forms.

boson *n* (1947) an elementary particle, such as a photon or pion, which has zero or integral spin and obeys Bose-Einstein statistics. Named after the Indian physicist Satyenda Nath Bose (1894–1974), a pioneer of quantum physics

1947 P. A. M. Dirac: The new statistics was first studied by Bose, so we shall call particles for which only symmetrical states occur in nature bosons.

bright-eyed and bushy-tailed *adj* (1942) alert and enthusiastic; lively or active. Originally US; the underlying reference is to conventional descriptions of the squirrel. Popularized by the song 'Bright Eyed and Bushy Tailed' by B. Merrill

> 1953 B. Merrill: If the fox in the bush and the squirr'l in the tree be, Why in the world can't you and me be Bright eyed and bushy tailed and sparkelly as we can be.

> 1968 Harry Harrison: You look very bright-eyed and bushy-tailed this morning.

British restaurant *n* (1941) a government-subsidized restaurant opened in Britain during World War II

> 1941 Winston Churchill: I hope the term 'Communal Feeding Centres' is not going to be adopted... I suggest you call them 'British Restaurants'.

bubble bath *n* (1949) a bath in which the water has been made to foam by a perfumed toilet preparation

> 1949 Leslie Charteris: 'I was having a bubble bath,' said Pauline Stone.

burton *n* **gone for a burton** (1941) killed. Originally R.A.F. slang, applied to pilots killed in action, but later broadened out and trivialized to cover anything missing, destroyed, or spoiled. Various ingenious theories have been advanced to account for its origins, but all remain unproved. The most persistent is that it refers to 'Burton ale' (beer brewed in Burton-on-Trent), and that 'slipping out for a drink' is a typically British stiff-upper-lip euphemistic cover for being killed

> 1947 Nevil Shute: He went for a Burton over France last year.

> 1957 John Braine: We noncoms used to say *got the chopper*. Going for a Burton was journalist's talk.

buzz-bomb *n* (1944) An alternative name for the German flying bomb of World War II (see **V-1 (1944)**). So called either because of the characteristic buzzing noise of its pulse-jet engine, or because it came in at a low altitude, like an aircraft 'buzzing' the ground

> 1944 *News Review*: The Germans sent over 11 pilotless planes or 'Buzz-bombs'.

cake-hole *n* (1943) a person's mouth. Slang, originally and mainly British. It appears to have started out in the services, but during the 1950s and 60s it was widespread, especially in the expression *shut your cake-hole!* 'shut up!'

> 1959 I. & P. Opie: Shut your cake-hole.

call-up *n* (1940) compulsory enlistment for military service; conscription. A nominalization of the verb *call up*, which has been used in this sense since the mid 19th century

> 1945 *News Chronicle*: We still propose to go on calling up young men under 30 as they reach the call-up age.

canasta *n* (1948) a card game of Uruguayan origin, in which two packs are used with four jokers, combining features of rummy and pinochle. Popular particularly in the first two post-war decades. The word in Spanish means literally 'basket'

> 1949 *Bookseller*: A new card game—*Canasta*—is said to be sweeping the world.

cannibalize *v* (1943) to take parts from one unit for incorporation in, and completion of, another (of a similar kind). A word born of the shortages and improvisations of wartime

> 1943 Redding & Leyshon: One by one the other aeroplanes have gone, some destroyed by enemy action, others cannibalized for parts and still others retired because of age.

> 1947 *Hansard Commons*: It would be necessary to dismantle or, as they say, cannibalise half a dozen to provide one good Nissen hut.

cappuccino *n* (1948) white coffee served with white froth on top. Like **espresso (1945)**, another borrowing from Italian, it did not become fully established in English until the 1950s. Its name refers to the habit of the Friars Minor Capuchins, which has a white hood

> 1959 Colin MacInnes: She blew a little brown nest in the white froth of her cappuccino.

card-carrying *adj* (1948) having a membership card of a specified organization, especially the Communist Party. The implication is of complete and avowed commitment. A term which originated in the early Cold War anti-Communist paranoia and hysteria in the US

1948 B. Andrews: The most dangerous Communists in the nation today are not the open, avowed, card-carrying party members.

carry-cot *n* (1943) a portable cot for a baby. An omen of the late-20th-century new man—for the carry-cot, one parent per handle, implied equality in child-care. At one point *carry-cot* was turned into a proprietary name, with the marketer's obligatory orthographic twist: *Karri-Kot*

1943 Honoria Croome: He slept all day long in his carry-cot.

1951 Alexander Baron: Young couples…carrying two-handled carry-cots between them from which…babies bellow.

cat's-eye *n* (1940) any of a succession of light-reflecting studs used to demarcate traffic lanes on roads at night. Invented in 1934 by Percy Shaw (1890–1976)

1940 *New Statesman*: Few motorists…in Oxfordshire will deny that the 'cats-eyes', with which the County Council has studded its main roads, are an improvement for night driving on the old white line.

character assassination *n* (1949) deliberate destruction of someone's reputation. The back-formed *character assassin* is first recorded in 1951

1951 H. MacInnes: Character assassination, they call it… If they can't find out anything against a man, they invent it.

1951 *American Speech*: A period of 'the big lie', of the furtive informer, of the character assassin.

Charley, Charlie *n* (1946) a fool. Colloquial; usually in **proper Charley** or **right Charley**

1957 *Listener*: The plebeian engineer was a proper Charlie to let himself be roped in for it.

1961 Simpson & Galton: I felt a right Charlie coming through the customs in this lot.

cheesed (off) *adj* (1941) bored, disgruntled, exasperated. British slang, of uncertain origin

1941 J. Sommerfield: 'I'm browned off,' announces Taff. 'I'm cheesed.'

1942 Gerald Kersh: Two people, both cheesed off, are better than one.

chicken out *v* (1941) to back down or withdraw out of cowardice. Slang, originally US (see **chicken (1933)**)

1950 *Cornell Daily Sun*: The Harvard Student Council…just plain chickened out… [They] considered the proposal…and sent the resolution back to committee on a technicality.

Chindit *n* (1943) a member of an Allied force fighting during World War II behind the Japanese lines in Burma, led by Orde Wingate (1903–44). The name comes from *chinthé*, a Burmese word for a type of mythical lion; its adoption was probably influenced by *Chindwin*, the name of a river in northern Burma

1943 *Hutchinson's Pictorial History of the War*: Some of Brigadier Wingate's doughty Chindits on their way back from the dangers of the jungle.

chocker *adj* (1942) fed-up. British slang, originally naval; a curtailed version of *chock-a-block* 'full'

1942 *Gen*: When Jenny the Wren is fed up with the world she is 'chokker'.

1945 'Tackline': Says she's chocka with being blonde, and she'll be brown again by the time I see her.

citizens(') band *n* (1948) a short-wave band made available for private radio communication. Originally US. A term which (with its abbreviation **CB (1959)**) did not achieve wide currency until the 1970s, when the inventive slang of CB users (e.g. **Smokey Bear (1974)**) gained it some celebrity

1948 *Radio & TV News*: It has been possible to obtain greater output at higher efficiencies with less heating power in cathode types than in filamentary types at the Citizens Band frequency.

classified *adj* (1944) classified as secret for reasons of national security and forbidden to be disclosed except to specified persons. Originally US

1949 *New York Herald Tribune*: The B-47 will combine characteristics which are still classified, with range equivalent to the B-29 range.

cleavage *n* (1946) the cleft between a woman's breasts as revealed by a low-cut décolletage

1947 *Landfall*: [The film] just goes all out to exploit sex and violence as blatantly as it can, with the result that 'cleavage' has once again become a problem to haunt the dreams of censors.

clippie, clippy *n* (1941) a bus-conductress. British colloquial; so named from the clipping of tickets. Their numbers shot up during World War II

1946 *News Chronicle*: London's 26,000 busmen and clippies are seriously perturbed at the bad name they are getting with the travelling public.

cock-up *n* (1948) something bungled; a mess. British slang. The corresponding verb is also first recorded in 1948. Both were probably inspired by the earlier, anatomically contiguous **balls(-)up**

1959 Ian Jefferies: 'I was thinking of going out to Tikvah today, sir,' I said, and did I make a cock-up of that job.

1967 W. Pine: I've cocked up a little job… An almighty cock-up.

cohort *n* (1944) a group of people having a common statistical characteristic, especially that of being born in the same year. A technical usage in demography, based on the earlier, more general sense 'group of people'

1962 *Lancet*: The number of possible long-stay patients produced by the 1954 cohort of admissions was estimated as 7453.

cold war *n* (1945) hostilities short of armed conflict, consisting of threats, violent propaganda, subversive political activities, etc. First recorded as a general term, but the specific application to the state of affairs existing between the U.S.S.R. and the western powers after World War II was soon in place. It lasted, with periodic changes in temperature, until the Communist regimes in eastern Europe collapsed in the late 1980s. The West declared itself the winner

1945 George Orwell: A State which was…in a permanent state of 'cold war' with its neighbours.

1946 *Observer*: After the Moscow Conference last December,…Russia began to make a 'cold war' on Britain and the British Empire.

1947 Walter Lippmann (title): The cold war. A study in U.S. foreign policy.

1948 *Hansard Commons*: The British Government…should recognize that the 'cold war', as the Americans call it, is on in earnest, that the third world war has, in fact, begun.

collaboration *n* (1940) traitorous cooperation with the enemy. Initially used with reference to local cooperation with the Germans in France and other occupied countries (and as such probably borrowed directly from French). The related verb *collaborate* is first recorded in 1941, its derivative *collaborator* in 1943. See also **quisling (1940)**

1940 *Economist*: Pétain may be outvoted on the question of mitigating the peace terms by some sort of shameful collaboration.

1941 *Annual Register 1940*: The futility of attempts to 'collaborate' with their German conquerors.

1943 *Times*: Not all have a record as black as Laval's… There were some who collaborated with a sick heart.

1946 George Orwell: At this moment, with France newly liberated and the witch-hunt for collaborators in full swing.

commando *n* (1940) a member of a body of picked men trained originally (in 1940) as shock troops for repelling the threatened German invasion of England, later for carrying out raids on the Continent and elsewhere. Subsequently applied to similar troops of other countries. The word was originally used in South Africa for a 'raiding party of Boers' (it is first recorded in this sense in 1809), and became more widely known in English during the South African War (Boer War)

1940 Winston Churchill: Plans should be studied to land secretly by night on the islands and kill or capture the invaders. This is exactly one of the exploits for which the Commandos would be suited.

1942 George Orwell: The rightwing papers…suggest that we can tie down a million troops along the coast of Europe by continuous commando raids.

commitment *n* (1948) the state of being involved in political or social questions, or in furthering a particular doctrine or cause, especially in one's literary or artistic expression; moral seriousness or social responsibility in artistic productions. A translation of French *engagement*, a key term in existential politico-aesthetics, introduced by Jean-Paul Sartre. The adjective *committed* emerged around the same time, and the corresponding reflexive verb *commit oneself* is first recorded in 1950. Alongside this little nest of *commit* words, English also freely used more literal translations of the French originals (see **engaged (1947)**), or even the originals themselves (see **engagé (1955)**)

> 1948 P. Mairet: [An] important Sartrean concept—*engagement*—is here translated as 'commitment'... At the very heart...of existentialism, is the absolute character of the free commitment, by which every man realises himself...What counts is the total commitment, and it is not by a particular case or particular action that you are committed altogether.

> 1956 Colin Wilson: Sartre, whose theory of commitment or 'engagement'...led him to embrace a modified communism.

> 1959 *Books of the Month*: Christopher Logue...has become 'engaged', or 'committed', which means that he is striving to write poetry touching the everyday life of ordinary people.

comprehensive *adj* (1947) Designating a secondary school or a system of education which provides for children of all levels of intellectual and other ability. These levels were characterized, under the reforms introduced in Britain under the 1944 Education Act, as 'grammar', 'modern', and 'technical'. The companion terms *bilateral* (denoting schools offering two such levels) and *multilateral* (two or more levels; see the first quote below) soon faded away, but *comprehensive* (all levels) remained as a touchstone of equal-opportunity education, or a threat to the excellence of traditional grammar schools, depending on your point of view, into and beyond the 1960s, when (almost) universal comprehensive education was introduced in Britain (see **comprehensivize (1958)**). First recorded as a noun, denoting a school of this kind, in 1958

> 1947 *Ministry of Education Circular*: Combinations of two or more types of secondary education are often referred to as bilateral, multilateral or comprehensive... A comprehensive school means one which is intended to cater for all the secondary education of all the children in a given area without an organisation in three sites.

> 1955 *Annual Register 1954*: The L.C.C. had adopted the educational policy of the so-called comprehensive school, where all, whatever their standards, were to be educated together up to the age of 15.

> 1958 *Observer*: Pupils shunted off to the posh new comprehensives.

computer *n* (1945) an automatic electronic device for performing high-speed mathematical or logical operations. The term *computer* had been in use for 'a calculating machine' since the late 19th century; and forerunners of the computer as we would recognize it at the end of the 20th century had been in (theoretical) development for some time too (see **Turing machine (1937)**): so it is not particularly easy to tell when the concept and the term met. Several recorded examples of the word come fairly close, but the consummation of the marriage cannot be dated to before 1945, when the name 'electronic numerical integrator and computer' (usually abbreviated to *ENIAC*) was given to such a device being developed in the US (the first quote below shows that the alternative term *computing machine* was then current). See also **electronic brain (1946)**

> 1945 J. Eckert et al. (title): Description of the ENIAC and comments on electronic digital computing machines.

> 1946 *Electronics*: The servomechanism is part of the computer, and...computers of this type have become known as electronic computers.

> 1947 *Mathematical Tables and Other Aids to Computation*: We are engaged at the RCA Laboratories in the development of a storage tube for the inner memory of electronic digital computers.

consumerism *n* (1944) protection of the consumer's interests. Originally US. Compare **consumerism (1960)** for a radically different take on the meaning of the word

> 1944 *New Republic*: Some of the oldest and most successful consumer enterprises grew independently of the rural impulse that in recent years has been most active in spreading the idea of consumerism.

contrail *n* (1945) Another name for a **vapour trail (1941)**. The word is a conflation of *condensation trail*

1945 *Saturday Evening Post*: With no wind and intense cold, taxiing planes leave ice-crystal contrails behind them, just as Fortresses do at 30,000 feet over Germany.

cortisone *n* (1949) a steroid hormone found in the adrenal cortex and prepared synthetically for use as an anti-inflammatory agent in rheumatoid arthritis, etc. The first quote below explains how its name was arrived at

1949 *New York Times*: The hormone…was named yesterday by its discoverer, Dr. Edward C. Kendall…as 'cortisone', an abbreviation of its long chemical name, 17-hydroxy-11 dehydrocorticosterone.

1950 *Lancet*: Hench's dramatic report on 'Cortisone' in rheumatoid arthritis has opened an entirely new field of work.

counselling *n* (1940) the giving of professional advice or help on social or psychological problems; a notable growth industry of the latter half of the 20th century. At first probably mainly familiar to lay people in the context of marriage guidance (see **marriage guidance (1935)**), by the 1960s it had extended its influence to many areas that had previously been the province of the amateur shoulder to cry on (or, in British culture, of the stoical stiff upper lip). *Counsellor* with the same connotations is also first recorded in 1940

1940 C. R. Rogers: The finest touches of artistry will not make counselling contacts helpful if they are basically unsound in principle… There must be a warmth of relationship between counsellor and counselee.

1945 S. E. Goldstein: When marriage counseling becomes well-established and generally accepted as a profession, it…will be used as, for example, that of the lawyers.

1959 *Listener*: There is no doubt that some students need counselling or even psychological treatment in these testing years.

1987 *Money*: If you are earning $20,000 a year or less, debt counselors say your net income may leave only enough for essentials.

1988 *Daily Telegraph*: Schools and parents…received an offer yesterday of free stress counselling for teachers and children plucked from the wreck.

counter-intelligence *n* (1940) the activity of preventing the enemy from obtaining secret information (the synonymous *counter-espionage* is first recorded in 1899)

1940 S. Thomas: These are but the elementals of counter-intelligence.

1949 J. F. Embree: Members of various divisions…concerned with such matters as counter-intelligence.

Coventrate *v* (1940) to bomb intensively; to devastate sections of (a city) by concentrated bombing, such as that inflicted by German aircraft on Coventry, Warwickshire, in November 1940. *Coventrate* is actually an anglicization of a German verb, *coventrieren*, coined somewhat gloatingly to characterize the massive destruction inflicted on that city (including, famously, its medieval cathedral). It enjoyed an understandably brief vogue

1940 *Hutchinson's Pictorial History of the War*: German bombers made prolonged mass attacks…on Coventry… And…they invented the verb 'to coventrate' to describe the indiscriminate mass murder of civilians.

1942 L. E. O. Charlton: Possibility of another 'coventration' of a manufacturing centre.

crew-cut *n* (1940) a closely cropped style of hair-cut for men (apparently first adopted by boat crews at Harvard and Yale Universities). In the 1940s and 50s it became almost a symbol of stereotypical virile American youth. The term is foreshadowed by *crew-cropped*, which never caught on to the same extent ('Wilson noted his crew-cropped hair', Ernest Hemingway (1938)). First recorded in the form *crew haircut*; *crew-cut* itself is not known to have put in an appearance before 1942

1940 *Time*: Doe-eyed Lucille Ball…gets the affections of Richard Carlson, whose crew haircut makes him the first genuine-looking Princeton undergraduate in cinema history.

1942 R. King: A steward…with a sparkling crew cut of chestnut hair.

crispy *adj* (1940) crisp. *Crispy* had existed as a synonym of *crisp* in the sense 'brittle, crunchy' since at least the 17th century (in 1611 Randle Cotgrave wrote of 'the crispie mammocks [= 'pieces, shreds'] that remaine of tried hogs grese'), but it is not until the second half of the 20th century that it became the advertising copywriter's stand-by term for appetizing crunchiness. Part of its boost no doubt came from **Rice Krispies (1936)**, but originally it was used in the context of Chinese foods (at first noodles, then others) fried to crispness. Once the perception was established that *crispy* things are even crisper (and therefore more delicious) than *crisp* things, it began to be applied to a whole range of foodstuffs: in the world of late-20th-century catering, bacon was never 'crisp', always 'crispy'

> 1940 André Simon: 'Crispy Noodles'… Roll this dough out very thinly and cut into strips as thin as spaghetti… Throw into boiling oil or frying fat, frying a delicate brown.

> 1973 *Harrod's Christmas Catalogue*: 1 metre box of crispy mints—a special chocolate blended in our own factory. £5.25.

crypto-communist *n* (1946) someone who conceals their communist allegiance, typically beneath a disguise of democratic socialism. A common right-wing scare-word of the early years of the Cold War, when communism was painted in the West as the ultimate evil and its supporters as devious and destructive. Often used in conjunction with **fellow traveller (1936)**, as the quote below demonstrates

> 1947 *News Chronicle*: He is an extreme Left-Wing Socialist… In the Commons he is, of course, dubbed a 'fellow-traveller' and a 'crypto-communist'.

cut back *v* (1943) to reduce or decrease (expenditure, etc.). Originally US. The related noun *cut-back* is first recorded in the same year

> 1943 *Saturday Evening Post*: If the Army cuts back a program, it will not need the steel for some other program.

> 1943 *Iron Age*: More than 90 per cent of prime contractors holding Army ordnance contracts are now operating…below capacity because of recent cut-backs in ordnance contracts.

cybernetics *n* (1948) the theory or study of communication and control in living organisms or machines. Its implications of automated decision-making made it a hot concept in the 1940s and 50s. The term was coined by the US mathematician Norbert Wiener (1894–1964) from Greek *kubernētēs* 'steersman' (which also lies behind English *govern*). A similar coinage had actually been made in French (*cybernétique*) over a century before by A.-M. Ampère, with the meaning 'the art of governing'

> 1948 Norbert Wiener: We have decided to call the entire field of control and communication theory, whether in the machine or in the animal, by the name Cybernetics.

> 1958 *Listener*: The claim of cybernetics is that we can treat organisms as if they were machines, in the sense that the same methods of synthesis and analysis can be applied to both.

daddy-o *n* (1948) fellow, man. Used as a term of address by those absorbed in the jazz culture of the late 1940s and the early 50s, until it became something of a cliché

> 1952 R. Ellison: A group of zoot-suiters greeted me in passing. 'Hey, now, daddy-o,' they called.

data *n* (1946) the quantities, characters, or symbols on which operations are performed by computers and other automatic equipment, and which can be stored or transmitted in the form of electrical signals, records on magnetic tape or punched cards, etc. See also **data processing (1954)**

> 1946 *Mathematical Tables & Other Aids to Computation*: The [IBM card] reader scans standard punched cards…and causes data from them to be stored in relays located in the constant transmitter.

D-Day *n* (1942) the day (6 June 1944) of the invasion of the Atlantic coast of German-occupied France by Allied forces. A specialized (and now by far the most familiar) application of an earlier, more general term, designating the day on which an operation is scheduled to begin (see **D-Day (1918)**)

> 1942 *Newsweek*: A major Russian offensive long in preparation abiding the eventful D-day.

> 1944 *Hutchinson's Pictorial History of the War*: By the end of D-Day plus two they had cleared their respective areas of dead and wounded.

D.D.T. *n* (1943) An abbreviation of *dichlorodiphenyltrichloroethane*, a white crystalline chlorinated hydrocarbon used as an insecticide. It had a massive effect both on food production (as an agricultural insecticide) and on disease control. However, problems with the development of resistant strains of insects and its persistence in the environment led to its withdrawal in the early 1970s

> 1943 *Soap & Sanitary Chemicals*: An insecticide material of similar type is now being made in the United States by Geigy & Co., New York, under the name 'DDT'.

> 1944 Winston Churchill: The demand for the new insecticide, D.D.T., is urgent and increasing.

debark *v* (1943) to perform an operation on (a dog) to prevent it from barking. Not, as might have been suspected, a facetious tabloid neologism, but a genuine scientific coinage. It joined two other verbs *debark* already in the language: 'to disembark' (17th century) and 'to remove a tree's bark' (18th century)

> 1943 *Biological Abstracts*: Dogs debarked by removal of the true vocal cords soon learned to bark again.

defibrillation *n* (1940) treatment to stop the heart fibrillating (i.e. beating in an abnormally rapid quivering way). *Defibrillator*, denoting an apparatus used for this treatment, is first recorded in 1956

> 1940 C. J. Wiggers: Defibrillation can be accomplished in the dog by the…application of several comparatively weak shocks.

Delhi belly *n* (1944) an upset stomach accompanied by diarrhœa such as may be suffered by visitors to India (Delhi being the capital of India). A coinage of US troops newly introduced to the Russian roulette of Indian cuisine during World War II (compare **gippy tummy (1943)**)

> 1944 *Newsweek*: Joe was off again—this time to be the first to hit the heat and filth of India and the desolation of China. He got 'Delhi belly' (a form of dysentery) and greeted Tommy Harmon when the flyer walked out of Jap-controlled China.

delta wing *n* (1946) a type of triangular swept-back aircraft wing. The futuristic shape soon became a familiar sight on fast military jets (e.g. in Britain, the Vulcan bomber), and eventually turned up on the Concorde supersonic airliner

> 1946 *Journal of the British Interplanetary Society*: The first effect…can…be reduced but not eliminated by the use of a very low aspect-ratio triangular wing platform (the so-called 'Delta' wing).

> 1951 *Engineering*: Type of…swept-back 'delta'-wing experimental aircraft.

denazify *v* (1944) to free (a person, institution, etc.) from Nazi allegiance, influence, or ideology. A programme of *denazification* (1944) was set up by the Allies in occupied Germany after World War II, to make sure that all Nazi supporters were rooted out of positions of influence

> 1944 *Spectator*: Whenever the problem of…de-Nazifying the young Nazis, is being seriously approached, some encounter or incident turns up to make the…hopelessness of the situation inescapable.

> 1944 *Saturday Review of Literature*: His hope for a de-Nazification of Germany's killers.

Desert Rat *n* (1944) a soldier of the 7th (British) armoured division, whose divisional sign was the figure of a jerboa, and which took part in the desert campaign in North Africa (1941–2)

> 1944 quoted in *Shorter Oxford English Dictionary* (1956): As we stewed our tea—desert-rat style.

> 1945 Winston Churchill: Dear Desert Rats, may your glory ever shine.

digital *adj* (1945) Denoting a computer which operates on data in the form of digits or similar discrete elements. Compare **analogue (1946)**

> 1946 D. R. Hartree: [Computers] of the other class handle numbers directly in digital form… The American usage is 'analogue' and 'digital' machines.

disc jockey *n* (1941) someone who introduces and plays recordings of popular music, especially on radio. Originally US. A term marginally preceded by *record jockey* ('The name bands are come on for the record jockeys who ride herd over not only Decca records but all the others', *Variety* (1940)), but that never really caught on. The abbreviation **DJ** is first recorded in 1961, its orthographic realization **dee-jay** in 1955. See also **veejay (1982)**

> 1941 *Variety*: Gilbert is a disc-jockey who sings with his records.

> 1942 *Time*: Some stations merely hired 'disk-jockeys' to ride herd on swing records, in the tradi-
> tional milk-man's matinee style.

displaced person *n* (1944) someone removed from his or her home country by military or political pressure, especially a non-German compelled to work in Germany during World War II, and
thereafter homeless. Often abbreviated to *DP*. Compare **stateless (1930)**

> 1944 *Saturday Evening Post*: The Refugees…or, as they term these people here…the Displaced
> Persons.

> 1945 *Broadcaster* (US): The real difficulty was and is the care of the slave laborers, men, women
> and children the Germans had imported from all over Europe to do their work for them. These we
> call Displaced Persons and for brevity refer to them as DP's.

disposable *adj* (1943) designed to be thrown away after one use. Originally US. Early usage mostly
relates to nappies, but the word soon spread to other (mainly paper-based) products, perhaps
lending the concept more gravity than the earlier **throw-away (1928)**. First recorded as a noun in
1965

> 1943 L. E. Holt: The disposable paper diapers are a great convenience and involve relatively little
> expense.

> 1965 *Nursing Times*: Wall cupboards for the storage of disposables had also been installed.

> 1965 *Sunday Times* (*Colour Supplement*): A lot of ward equipment is disposable now—things like
> catheters or blood drips… Bed pans and bottles are made of papier maché, to be disposable.

dissident *n* (1940) someone who openly opposes the policies of the government or ruling party,
especially in a totalitarian system.

> 1940 Edmund Wilson: He took the position that the voters…had the right to confer power on whom
> they chose; that for a dissident like himself to refuse to submit to their choice would constitute an
> act of insurrection.

ditch *v* (1941) to bring (an aircraft) down into the sea in an emergency. Colloquial

> 1941 *Times Weekly*: The pilot…must 'ditch' his aircraft in the sea, near enough to a ship for him to
> be picked up.

Dixiecrat *n* (1948) a member of a group of southern US Democrats who seceded from the
Democratic Party in 1948 because they opposed its policy of extending civil rights. US colloquial.
Based on *Dixie*, a word of obscure origin denoting the southern states of the US (for an account of
the coining, see the second quote below)

> 1948 *Birmingham* (Alabama) *News*: Truman finds some Dixiecrats supporting him on A-veto
> stand.

> 1948 *New York Times*: The States Rights Democrats have Bill Weisner, telegraph editor of the
> Charlotte News, to thank for putting Dixiecrat into the American vocabulary. Mr. Weisner was
> writing a headline on a story about the States Rights Democrats which would not fit. Dixiecrats
> would.

DNA *n* (1944) See **deoxyribonucleic acid (1931)**

doodlebug *n* (1944) A nickname applied to the German flying bomb of World War II (see
V-1 (1944)). It is apparently an adaptation of the much earlier US *doodlebug* meaning 'a tiger-
beetle, or the larva of this or other insects'. The term falls into a familiar pattern of belittling objects
of terror by giving them silly names, as a way of setting their reality aside

> 1944 *Times*: The first fighter pilot to shoot down what the R.A.F. men call a 'doodlebug' was Flight
> Sergeant Maurice Rose, of Glasgow.

double glazing *n* (1943) (providing windows with) two layers of glass to reduce the transmission
of heat, sound, etc. A true 20th-century domestic totem. Preceded by **double-glazed (1910)**

> 1957 *Housewife*: The north and south walls consist almost entirely of Plyglass double-glazing.

doublethink *n* (1949) the mental capacity to accept as equally valid two entirely contrary opinions
or beliefs. Coined by George Orwell in his novel *Nineteen Eighty-Four*

1949 George Orwell: His mind slid away into the labyrinthine world of doublethink. To know and not to know, to be conscious of complete truthfulness while telling carefully constructed lies, to hold simultaneously two opinions which cancelled out, knowing them to be contradictory and believing in both of them, to use logic against logic, to repudiate morality while laying claim to it, to believe that democracy was impossible and that the Party was the guardian of democracy.

1959 *Daily Telegraph*: They ask for increases in wages which are plainly impossible; or they pretend they want a shorter working week when they really want more overtime. Their followers know double-think when they see it, as well as the employers.

downpoint *v* (1946) to lower the value in points of (something rationed). A live usage in British English as long as wartime rationing remained in force

1946 *News Chronicle*: The trade would welcome the downpointing of women's coats and costumes.

dreamboat *n* (1947) an extremely attractive member of the opposite sex. Colloquial, originally US. Popular mainly in the 1940s and 50s, but still some residual use at the end of the century

1949 in Wentworth & Flexner: [Ava Gardner] will star opposite James Mason, who she says is a 'dreamboat'.

1951 Terence Rattigan: I thought you'd be quite old and staid and ordinary and, my God, look at you, a positive dream boat.

duck, dukw *n* (1943) an amphibious military vehicle, used e.g. for ferrying troops across rivers. The name originated in a combination of factory serial letters (see the second quote below)

1944 *Hansard Commons*: The marvellous American invention, the 'Duck', spelt D.U.K.W., is a heavy lorry which goes at between 40 and 50 miles per hour along the road, and can plunge into the water and swim out for miles to sea in quite choppy weather.

1945 *Manchester Guardian*: Officially known as 'Dukws'—a combination of the factory serial letters D for boat, U for lorry body, and KW for lorry chassis—they quickly became known in the Army and Navy as 'Ducks'.

dysfunctional *adj* (1949) not functioning properly. The noun *dysfunction* (first recorded in 1916) originated as a medical term, but its derived adjective has become a treasured piece of 20th-century socio-speak

1978 *Times Literary Supplement*: The eighty-six men assigned to the 'dysfunctional' group also lacked any quasi-marital partnership and often expressed regret about their homosexuality, but they were sexually more active and promiscuous.

E-boat *n* (1940) a German World War II torpedo-boat. It is not clear what the *E* stands for: it has been suggested that it is short for German *Eile* 'speed', but there is no evidence that it was ever used thus in German (the usual German word for a speedboat is *Schnellboot*)

1940 *Hutchinson's Pictorial History of the War*: One of our motor torpedo-boats, thinking that the enemy ahead was an E-boat, and being too close to take action, rammed the enemy.

ecdysiast *n* (1940) a strip-tease dancer. A facetious coinage (based on Greek *ekdusis* 'stripping') by the US journalist H. L. Mencken, and later used mainly in the same spirit

1940 H. L. Mencken: It might be a good idea to relate strip-teasing in some way…to the associated zoölogical phenomenon of molting… A resort to the scientific name for molting, which is *ecdysis*, produces both *ecdysist* and *ecdysiast*.

1958 *Time*: Is it possible for a nightclub to lose money with famed Ecdysiast Sherry Britton stripping to bugle beads and pearls?

ejection seat, ejector seat *n* (1945) a seat which ejects the pilot from an aircraft in an emergency

1945 *Aeroplane*: It was the first German aeroplane to employ a pilot-ejection seat… The single-seat cockpit is positioned well forward and the pilot ejection seat is of the explosive cartridge type.

1948 *Flight*: There are no known reports of a pilot getting out of the Vampire. To fit an ejector seat now would be a major operation.

electronic brain *n* (1946) An early and fairly colloquial term for a computer. It started out as a rather general word for any electronic apparatus able to perform calculations or other vaguely cerebral functions ('An "electronic brain", which helps pilots test-fly new airplanes, has been invented by flight research engineers of Consolidated Vultee Aircraft Corporation. Technically, the device is known as a "flight recorder" ', *Aero Products* (1945)), but soon attached itself fairly firmly to the electronic computer

> 1946 *Lancet*: Another war secret now disclosed is an electrical calculating machine which has been built in the United States and has been called an 'electronic brain', or more accurately an Electronic Numerical Integrator and Computer—ENIAC.

engaged *adj* (1947) Of an artist: completely involved in political, moral, or social questions. A translation of the term *engagé* used by French existential philosophers and later imported into English *au naturel* (see **engagé (1955)**). The more usual English equivalent is *committed* (see **commitment (1948)**)

> 1947 John Hayward: This is not to say that literature must become 'engaged', as one school of continental writers now insists; that it must…'take sides' in the social revolution.

espresso *n* (1945) strong coffee made made by forcing steam or hot water at high pressure through powdered coffee beans. An adaptation of Italian *caffè espresso*, which means literally 'pressed-out coffee'. At first treated as an exotic foreignism, it did not get its feet under the English table until the rise of the coffee-bar culture in the 1950s (see **coffee bar (1956)**), by which time it was often being further anglicized to *expresso*

> 1945 A. Boucher: I was drinking a caffé espresso, a strong, bitter, steamed coffee.

> 1955 *New York Times*: Also new are the numerous small Coffee Expresso Snack Restaurants off Dublin's Grafton Street.

> 1957 Angus Wilson: The even more degrading swamps of espresso bar rebellion.

ethnic *n* (1945) a member of an ethnic group or minority (see **ethnic minority (1945)**). Originally US. The adjective *ethnic* had been used as a technical term in anthropology since the middle of the 19th century, denoting social grouping based on a range of physical and cultural characteristics, but it was not until the 1930s, with the increasing compromising of the term *race* (see **racist (1932)**), that it came to be widely used with specific connotations of racial difference (usually in the context of a minority grouping within a larger whole: 'Like other ethnic units, the Jews have their own standard racial character', C. S. Coon (1939)). The noun usage evolved from this, and came to serve a euphemistic function, as also did the adjective ('Its hopelessly reactionary nature is best exemplified not…even by the ethnic comedians', *New Yorker* (1969)). See also **ethnicity (1953)**

> 1945 Warner & Srole: The Irish…had their origins largely in the peasant stratum… The Jews were of the burgher class… These differences in the ethnics' social-class backgrounds will be seen later to have important bearing on their adaptation… The ethnics have conspicuously succeeded in 'getting ahead' in the Yankee City social hierarchy.

> 1963 T. & P. Morris: It is the general view of the prison staff that the majority of 'coloureds' and 'ethnics' are West Indians.

ethnic minority *n* (1945) a group of people differentiated from the rest of the community by racial origins or cultural background, and usually claiming or enjoying official recognition of their group identity

> 1945 *American Sociology Review* (heading): Status and housing of ethnic minorities.

> 1964 Gould & Kolb: R. E. Park and his students have done outstanding research work into the patterns of adjustment, accommodation, and assimilation of ethnic minorities.

existentialism *n* (1941) a doctrine that concentrates on the existence of individuals, who, being free and responsible, are held to be what they make themselves by the self-development of their essence through acts of the will (which, in the Christian form of the theory, leads to God).

The existentialist movement was mainly originated by the Danish writer Søren Kierkegaard (1813–55), who frequently used the term *Existens-forhold* 'condition of existence, existential relation'. It was developed in the 20th century chiefly in continental Europe by Jaspers, Sartre, and others. Its emphasis on the individual alone in an indifferent or hostile universe caught the mood of the middle decades of the century, and it was the fashionable philosophy of the 1940s and 50s. The English word *existentialism* was adapted from German *Existentialismus*, which is first recorded in 1919. The derivative *existentialist* is first recorded in English in 1945, and the related **existential** before 1937

> 1941 J. Kraft: Kierkegaard, Nietzsche, and pragmatism are examples of real or possible starting points of existentialism, capable of being multiplied by further examples.

> 1945 A. J. Ayer: Philosophically, [Sartre] is usually described as an Existentialist.

> 1957 *Observer*: We asked Miss Greco what Existentialism implied. Apparently its essence is summed up by 'whatever you do, you become'.

extermination camp *n* (1945) a concentration camp for the mass murder of human beings, especially one of the camps set up by Nazi Germany during World War II

> 1945 *Atlantic Monthly*: Among the workers a threat of being sent to an extermination camp has its uses.

> 1957 Henriette Roosenburg: The Jews…were sent to the extermination camps.

fail-safe *adj* (1948) capable of returning, in the event of failure or breakdown, to a condition involving no danger

> 1948 *Journal of the Royal Aeronautical Society*: Automatic power plant control including automatic 'fail safe' provision against mechanical trouble or power failure.

falsies *n* (1943) a padded brassière; breast-pads. Colloquial, originally US

> 1943 *New York Post*: 'Falsies'…the term for the pads that convert [nightclub chorus girls] from 32s to 34s.

fanzine *n* (1949) a magazine for fans, especially those of science fiction. Originally US

> 1949 *New Republic*: *Fantasy Commentator*, perhaps the best of the fanzines, once ran a history of fan magazines.

fast-forward *adj, n* (1948) (Designating) accelerated forward motion of a tape, etc., especially to reach a particular place in a recording

> 1955 *Wireless World*: Main control knob with seven positions:—(1) 'off', (2) amplifier only, (3) fast forward, (4) fast rewind.

Father's Day *n* (1943) 'A day for recognition of the respect and gratitude felt by children toward their fathers, commonly observed on the third Sunday in June. Father's Day was originated by Mrs. John Bruce Dodd of Spokane [presumably so that fathers should not feel left out by **Mother's Day (1908)**] and proclaimed by the governor of Washington in 1910 but was not widely observed until twenty-five years later' (Webster 1950), and the term was not recorded in print before 1943. Not until after World War II, when the greeting-card companies had got their act together, did its observation get seriously under way in Britain

> 1943 *Greeley* (Colorado) *Daily Tribune*: Governor Vivian proclaimed Sunday, June 30, as Father's Day.

fax *n, v* (1948) (a copy of a document obtained by) facsimile telegraphy, in which the document is scanned and the resulting signal is transmitted by wire or radio. Originally US; a respelling of the *facs-* of *facsimile*. The technology had been around for a long while, but the word did not start to become really well known until the 1970s (which is when the verb is first recorded)

> 1948 *Time*: The big news about 'fax' was that, technically, the bugs were pretty well worked out of it.

> 1979 *Datamation*: Who will fax the mail?

final solution *n* (1947) A literal translation of German *Endlösung*, the name given to the Nazi policy, from 1941, of exterminating Jewish people in Europe

> 1947 *Trial of German Major War Criminals* (H.M.S.O.): Final solution of the Jewish question.

> 1949 D. Macardle: As the 'final solution', camps fitted with gas-chambers, electrocution plants and huge crematoria were erected in Poland.

fire-watching *n* (1941) keeping on the alert, especially at night, to watch for and report the occurrence or spread of fires, especially those caused by aerial bombardment; a crucial civil-defence precaution in Britain at the time of the Blitz. *Fire-watcher* (in this sense) is first recorded in 1941 too, and also the back-formed verb *fire-watch*

1941 *Manchester Guardian Weekly*: Everyone now realises the great importance of fire-watching and fire prevention.

1941 *Annual Register 1940*: All factories employing not less than thirty persons must have fire watchers.

1941 R. Greenwood: I've got to fire-watch.

First World War *n* (1947) An alternative name for **World War I (1939)**

1947 *Partisan Review*: The mystique of the working class has faded somewhat since the First World War.

fission bomb *n* (1941) a bomb in which the explosion is produced by nuclear fission (see **fission (1939)**). An occasional synonym for **atomic bomb (1914)**

1941 H. D. Smyth: A fission bomb of superlatively destructive power will result from bringing quickly together a sufficient mass of element U-235.

flavour-of-the-month *n* (1946) an ice-cream flavour featured during a particular month. Originally a marketing gimmick in the US ice-cream industry, but now widely used metaphorically in World English to mean 'something that is currently fashionable'

1946 *Ice Cream Review*: Illinois Association of Ice Cream Manufacturers has set up a committee which will give serious study to a suggested flavor and flavor-of-the-month program for 1947.

1984 *Australian Financial Review*: This ranks Australia second only to Hawaii as the most popular holiday spot… 'Australia is the flavour of the month,' as Mr Brian Walsh put it.

flight attendant *n* (1947) A first outing for a non-sex-specific word for someone who looks after passengers on an airliner (compare **stewardess (1931)** and **air hostess (1934)**)

1947 W. L. Grossman: By picking up…the flight coupons, with the passengers' names on them, after the passengers are seated, a flight attendant knows where, say, Mrs. Johnson is located and can address her by name.

flip side *n* (1949) the reverse, or less important, side of a record; the side you 'flip' over to when you have heard the main side. The synonymous *B side* is not recorded before 1962

1949 *Down Beat*: The flip side (*South*) will be a shade slower but with the same general routine.

fluoridate *v* (1949) to add traces of a fluoride or other source of fluoride ions to (water, tooth-paste, food, etc.). The purpose of the process was, and is, to reduce tooth decay, but proposals to treat public water supplies aroused much controversy in the 1950s and 60s on both sides of the Atlantic. The derivative *fluoridation* is also first recorded in 1949

1949 *Bulletin of the American Association of Public Health Dentists*: Many cities throughout the nation…have taken or are taking steps to fluoridate their water supplies.

1949 *Journal of the American Water Works Association*: The present demands for the fluoridation of water supplies are coming from the public and the press.

flying bomb *n* (1944) a pilotless jet-propelled aeroplane with an explosive warhead, originally and specifically one of a type first used by the Germans against England in June 1944 (see **V-1 (1944)**)

1944 *Times*: Strong measures to counter the flying bombs have been continued throughout the week-end.

1946 *Journal of the Institute of Electrical Engineers*: Automatic-following radar…was of the essence of the A.A. gunnery successes against flying bombs.

flying saucer *n* (1947) a disc- or saucer-shaped object reported as appearing in the sky and alleged to come from outer space. The immediate post-World War II period appears to have been chosen by aliens as the right time to pay the Earth (or more usually the US) a visit, a circumstance linked by amateur psychologists with American fears of nuclear attack by the Soviet Union and by conspiracy theorists with secret US weapons tests. However, the comparison of unidentified objects seen in the sky to 'saucers' can be traced back to the 19th century ('When directly over him it [i.e. a flying object] was about the size of a large saucer and was evidently at a great height', *Denison* (Texas) *Daily News* (1878)). Compare **unidentified flying object (1950)**

1947 *Times*: During the past fortnight reports that dish-like objects, nicknamed 'flying saucers', have been seen travelling through the air at great speed…have come from the United States and Canada.

> 1947 *Daily Progress* (Charlottesville, Virginia): Describing what they saw as flat, translucent plates 12 to 15 inches in diameter, several Port Huron, Mich., residents reported seeing the 'saucers'.

> 1948 *Journal of the British Interplanetary Society*: I haven't examined the details carefully, but the 'flying saucers' bear all the hall-marks of mass-suggestion.

> 1965 *New Society*: When Kenneth Arnold saw something from his airplane near Mount Rainier in June 1947, he gave them the happy name of flying saucers.

foil *n* (1946) a very thin sheet of metal, typically aluminium, used for the protective wrapping of foodstuffs. A technological advance taken for granted at the end of the century, when previous generations' waxed paper, grease-proof paper, etc. had been forgotten about

> 1946 *Steelways*: Aluminum foil is the star in frozen foods packaging.

> 1969 *Daily Telegraph*: Cut and trim the toast bread and set it in table position (tightly foil-wrapped to keep it perfectly moist) with the butter.

fork-lift truck *n* (1946) a vehicle fitted with a pronged device in front for lifting and carrying heavy goods

> 1946 *Engineering Index 1945*: Use of carrier fork lift trucks capable of handling filled cable reels.

> 1955 *Radio Times*: Modern package-handling machines—fork-lifts they are called.

Formica *n* (1946) The proprietary name of a hard, durable plastic laminate used especially as a decorative surfacing material. It comes from the name of its original manufacturer, the Formica Insulation Company of Cincinnati, Ohio. They originally registered it in 1922 as the name of a type of electric insulating compound. The now familiar name for the laminate was not registered until 1946. The substance reached into most western homes in the 1950s in the form of table tops, work surfaces, etc.

> 1957 *Oxford Mail*: Red upholstered chairs with chromium legs and tables in formica.

> 1958 *House & Garden*: Furniture surfaced for ever with Formica decorative laminates.

fraternization *n* (1944) contacts between occupying troops and local inhabitants that contravene military discipline. Applied specifically to sexual relations between Allied troops and German women after World War II. A specialization of the general sense 'friendly relations between occupiers and occupied', which dates from the mid 19th century

> 1944 *New Statesman*: The administration of occupied Germany…must necessarily be 'tough'… To judge by his Proclamation No. 1 to the German people, and by his orders forbidding fraternisation, General Eisenhower is going to present his subordinate commanders and staffs with some knotty problems.

> 1945 *New Statesman*: At present it is not clear whether rape [by occupying troops] is a crime to be punished by death, or whether it should be classified as fraternisation, for which the penalty is a fine, or non-fraternisation, which is a laudable act.

freedom-fighter *n* (1942) someone who takes part in a resistance movement against the established political system of a country. A frequent actor in the post-colonial struggles of the second half of the century. The word is notoriously paired and contrasted with **terrorist (1947)**

> 1942 John Lehmann: Their freedom-fighters staining red the snow.

> 1964 *Annual Register 1963*: Mr. Obote had played a prominent part in the Addis Ababa conference…offering training grounds for 'freedom fighters' against South Africa.

free expression *n* (1943) the uninhibited expression of one's thoughts, feelings, creative capacities, etc. A fashionable concept in education in the middle decades of the century

> 1967 Margaret Drabble: The efforts of the American teacher at their nursery group to make the children paint with free expression.

freeze-drying *n* (1944) a method of drying foodstuffs, blood plasma, pharmaceuticals, etc. while retaining their physical structure, the material being frozen and then warmed in a high vacuum so that the ice vaporizes without liquefying. Best known to lay people in the form of the derivative *freeze-dried*, familiarized when food products treated in this way began to come on to the market in the late 1950s

> 1944 *Nature*: Many biological materials can be most conveniently preserved…if they are dried from the frozen state. The success of the 'freeze-drying' procedure appears to be chiefly related to the fact that the resulting 'solid state' prevents the concentration and aggregation of the molecules of protein.

> 1967 *New Scientist*: More recently, freeze-dried coffee extracts have appeared on the market.

French roll *n* (1941) a woman's hairstyle in which the hair is tucked into a vertical roll down the back of the head. Also known as the *French pleat*

> 1941 F. E. Wall: French Roll. This coiffure is particularly becoming to the small woman who wishes to appear taller, but it is equally suitable to a taller woman with a thin face.

fuel rod *n* (1947) an assemblage of nuclear fuel with other materials to form a unit for use in a reactor

> 1947 Clark Goodman: Solid fuel rods, clad with a non-corrosive metallic coating.

fusion *n* (1947) the formation of a heavier, more complex nucleus by the coming together of two or more lighter ones, usually accompanied by the release of relatively large amounts of energy. The reaction is the basis on which the hydrogen bomb is designed (as opposed to the atomic bomb, which works by **fission (1939)**). The aim of harnessing it to produce cheap energy remains one of the holy grails of science at the end of the century

> 1947 *Science News Letter* (heading): Atom fusion gives energy.

> 1952 *Economist*: This may have been a hybrid bomb, part atom, part hydrogen, but enough to prove that the scientists have solved the problem of releasing energy by nuclear fusion.

futurology *n* (1946) the forecasting of the future on a systematic basis, especially by the study of present-day trends in human affairs. A term which had to wait until the 1960s before it gained much momentum (including the coining of the derivative *futurologist*)

> 1946 Aldous Huxley: Thank you for…the interesting enclosure on 'Teaching the Future'. I think that 'futurology' might be a very good thing.

> 1967 *Listener*: Futurology, the systematic study of trends which enable us to forecast the shape of things to come… Here we are with the automation process which, according to well-known futurologists, will lead to enforced leisure for a large part of the population.

Gallup poll *n* (1940) a public-opinion poll conducted along the lines established by the US journalist and statistician George Horace Gallup (1901–84). In 1935 he set up the American Institute of Public Opinion, and in 1936 successfully predicted the result of the presidential election

> 1940 *Illustrated London News*: According to the latest U.S. Gallup poll as we go to press, President Roosevelt is assured of a total of 410 electoral votes.

gamesmanship *n* (1947) skill in winning games, especially by means that barely qualify as legitimate. Coined by the British humorist Stephen Potter, on the model of (and in deliberate contrast to) *sportsmanship*, and used by him in the title of a book on the subject (see the first quote below). He exploited the suffix -*manship* liberally himself to make other creations, and it became a minor word-formation craze for a while (see **-manship (1947)**)

> 1947 Stephen Potter (title): The theory & practice of gamesmanship or the art of winning games without actually cheating.

> 1952 Edward Grierson: This was so like Laura, with whom a hand she could not play was a hand wasted, but Mr. Clarke, a practitioner of 'gamesmanship' himself, would not be rushed.

gangbang *n* (1945) multiple sexual intercourse with a succession of men, usually against the woman's will. Slang, originally US. The lexical concept was not new in 1945: the synonymous **gangshag** is recorded from as early as 1927

> 1968 Bill Turner: What's the next arrangement to be? A gang-bang for the whole Vice Squad?

garden gnome *n* (1946) See **gnome (1938)**

gas chamber *n* (1945) a sealed enclosure in which people are killed by means of poison gas, specifically one of those used by the Germans for their extermination programme during World War II. A grisly new use for a term which had started life innocuously enough in the late 19th century, denoting an apparatus used in microscopy for studying the action of different gases on structures or organisms. A contemporary synonym was *gas oven*, but this gradually went out of use, perhaps because it was seen as robbing the victims of their dignity

> 1945 *Daily Mirror*: The Germans knew what to do with women with white hair, or too exhausted to work. For them was the gas-chamber.

> 1945 George Orwell: Was it true about the German gas ovens in Poland?

> 1953 *Encounter*: In the gas chambers of Auschwitz, Belsen, and other extermination camps, around six million human beings were put to death during the closing phase of the Second World War.

gasser *n* (1944) something or someone that is very pleasing, exciting, impressive, admirable, etc. Originally US jazz slang, derived from the verb *gas* 'to thrill', which is first recorded in 1941. The noun **gas** in the same sense is not recorded until 1953

> 1944 Cab Calloway: When it comes to dancing, she's a gasser.

gen *n* (1940) information; facts. British slang, originally R.A.F. It is not clear where it came from (it may be an abbreviation of *general* in the official phrase 'for the general information of all ranks', or possibly from part of the words *genuine* or *intelligence*), but it was widely used among the World War II generation. *Genned up*, meaning 'well informed', is first recorded in 1945

> 1940 Michie & Graebner: Operations room, where I got my 'Gen' (R.A.F. slang for information, or instructions).

> 1975 *Evening Standard*: Landladies…are far more genned up on local history and things to do (plus some riveting gossip) than the managers of more impressive emporia.

genocide *n* (1944) the deliberate and systematic extermination of an ethnic or national group. A term coined specifically in response to the Nazis' slaughter of six million Jews (about two-thirds of European Jewry) in concentration camps during World War II. See also **Holocaust (1957)**

> 1944 R. Lemkin: By 'genocide' we mean the destruction of a nation or of an ethnic group.

> 1945 *Sunday Times*: The United Nations' indictment of the 24 Nazi leaders has brought a new word into the language—genocide. It occurs in Count 3, where it is stated that all the defendants 'conducted deliberate and systematic genocide—namely, the extermination of racial and national groups…'

G.I. bride *n* (1945) a foreign woman married by a US serviceman while he is on duty abroad

> 1945 *Evening Standard* (headline): Ships soon to take G.I. brides.

ginormous *adj* (1948) exceptionally huge. British, and reportedly originally services' slang; a blend of *gigantic* and *enormous*

> 1977 *Economist*: The state company Egam, declared bust last spring,…is going to cost considerably more than the £500 billion…earmarked by the government last June, probably a ginormous £1,700 billion.

gin-rummy *n* (1941) a version of the card-game rummy for two or more players in which you win by matching all your cards or may end the game by melding when your unmatched cards add up to ten points or less. Originally US. The *gin* part is a rather feeble pun on *rummy* (as if it were based on *rum* the drink)

> 1941 Somerset Maugham: After a good dinner…she suggests a game of gin-rummy.

gippy tummy, gyppy tummy *n* (1943) diarrhœa suffered by visitors to hot countries. Originally British services' slang, used feelingly by troops in North Africa during World War II. *Gippy* had been used by British soldiers as a condescending word for an Egyptian since the late 19th century. World War II seemed to start a trend for naming diarrhœa after the place where it was contracted: another contemporary example is **Delhi belly (1944)**

> 1943 Alan Moorehead: Few set foot in Egypt without contracting 'Gyppy Tummy' which is a mild stomach disorder lasting usually a couple of days. It recurs at irregular intervals and it makes you feel terrible.

git *n* (1946) a worthless person. British slang. It came into general use via World War II services' slang, where it was picked up as a southern variant of northern and Scottish *get* 'illegitimate child, brat'. Ultimately it is derived from the verb *get* in its archaic sense 'to beget'.

1946 *Penguin New Writing*: Chalky! You idle git!

1967 *Listener*: That bald-headed, moon-faced, four-eyed git Garnett gristling on about Harold Wilson.

gizmo, gismo *n* (1942) a gadget, thingumajig. Slang, originally in the US Navy and Marine Corps, but beyond that its origins are a mystery

1949 Robert Heinlein: Now what is this gismo? When you brought it aboard I thought it was a volley ball.

gobbledygook *n* (1944) official, professional, or pretentious verbiage or jargon. Originally US. The term was introduced by Maury Maverick, chairman of the US Smaller War Plants Corporation. He did not invent it out of thin air, though: it is a variation on the earlier US slang *gobbledygoo*, which originally denoted a prostitute specializing in fellatio; this in turn was a lexicalization of the phrase *gobble the goo* 'to perform fellatio'. Presumably it was the sound of the word (suggestive of a fatuous turkey) that drew Maverick to it, rather than its meaning

1944 *American Notes & Queries*: Gobbledygook talk: Maury Maverick's name for the long high-sounding words of Washington's red-tape language.

1945 *Tuscaloosa* (Alabama) *News*: The explanations sound like gobbledegook to me.

googol *n* (1940) A fanciful name (not in formal use) for ten raised to the hundredth power. An often-quoted example of the (fairly rare) phenomenon of a word being coined out of thin air, without recourse to existing words or word-parts (the story of its invention by Milton Sirotta, the young nephew of US mathematician Edward Kasner, is summarized in the first quote below)

1940 Kasner & Newman: The name 'googol' was invented by a child (Dr. Kasner's nine-year-old nephew) who was asked to think up a name for a very big number, namely, 1 with a hundred zeros after it… At the same time that he suggested 'googol' he gave a name for a still larger number: 'Googolplex'.

1966 Ogilvy & Anderson: The googol…can easily be written out in full in about two lines of print.

goon *n* (1945) A nickname given by Allied prisoners of war to their German guards in World War II. Presumably a specialized use of **goon** 'fool, thug' (1938)

1945 G. Morgan: I think it was an Australian who first called the Germans 'Goons'.

1962 *Times*: 'Goon-baiting', which was the favourite occupation of the prisoners.

gremlin *n* (1941) a mischievous sprite imagined as the cause of mishaps to aircraft. Originally R.A.F. slang. Despite numerous conjectures (see, for example, the second quote below), its precise origins are unclear, but presumably its ultimate model was *goblin*. Later usage has broadened out to cover a general embodiment of mischance

1941 Charles Graves: As he flew round, he wished that his instructor had never told him about the Little People—a mythological bunch of good and bad fairies originally invented by the Royal Naval Air Service in the Great War… Those awful little people, the Gremlins, who run up and down the wing with scissors going 'snip, snap, snip' made him sweat.

1942 *Observer*: Behaviour of…machines couldn't always be explained by…laws of aerodynamics. And so, lacking a Devil, the young fliers…invented a whole hierarchy of devils. They called them Gremlins, 'on account of they were the goblins which came out of Fremlin beer bottles'. They were the genii loci of the R.A.F. messes in India and the Middle East, where Fremlin's beer bottles were plentiful.

1944 *Times*: The King said that on his way back from Italy they thought they heard a gremlin in the royal aeroplane.

1959 *New Statesman*: Unfortunately the misprint gremlin has raised its ugly head in my letter to you on 18 April.

ground zero *n* (1946) that part of the ground situated immediately under an exploding bomb, especially a nuclear one (for maximum effect, nuclear bombs are detonated before they actually hit the ground). An alternative term is *hypocentre*

1946 *New York Times*: The intense heat of the blast started fires as far as 3,500 feet from 'ground zero'.

group therapy *n* (1943) psychotherapy involving more than one patient at a time, in which the changing interaction between the patients is part of the therapeutic process. Originally US. A technique pioneered in the early part of the century (see the second quote below), but the term is not recorded before 1943

> 1943 S. R. Slavson (title): An introduction to group therapy.

> 1948 *Science News*: The first recorded use of group therapy was the experiment of Dr. J. H. Pratt in Boston [in 1905].

G-suit *n* (1945) a garment designed to enable a person to withstand high accelerations. See **G (1928)**

> 1945 *Aeroplane*: Many experiments…have been conducted…and success has now been accomplished with the United States Berger G-suit, used by operational fighter pilots.

guided missile *n* (1945) a missile operating by remote control or as directed by equipment carried in the weapon. One of the key 'fear' words of the 1950s, when such weapons, armed with nuclear warheads, were at the cutting edge of Cold War deterrence

> 1945 *Newsweek*: The 'guided missile'—a rocket projectile that can be aimed accurately over great distances.

hardware *n* (1947) the physical components of a system or device (originally and mainly a computer) as opposed to the procedures required for its operation. Compare **software (1960)**

> 1947 D. R. Hartree: The ENIAC [an early type of computer]… I shall give a brief account of it, since it will make the later discussion more realistic if you have an idea of some 'hardware' and how it is used, and this is the equipment with which I am best acquainted.

> 1960 *Times*: Both punched card and computer 'hardware' will continue to develop very rapidly.

Harry *adv* (1941) Used as a sort of intensifier before adjectives ending in -ers. Dated British slang, originally services'. This bizarre usage perhaps arose out of the earlier British nautical slang *Harry Freeman's* (1925) for 'a free gift', although where that came from remains a mystery

> 1941 Charles Graves: Fortunately, the sea has dropped and it is Harry Flatters. Harry Flatters means flat calm, and Harry is used as a predicate for almost any expression.

> 1946 *Lancet*: Get in there, and strip off Harry Nuders.

have had it so good (1946) to possess so many advantages. Colloquial, originally US; mainly used in negative contexts. 'You never had it so good' (referring to favourable economic conditions) was used as a slogan by the Democratic Party in the US presidential election campaign of 1952. It became familiar to British people when the prime minister Harold Macmillan adapted it in a speech in 1957

> 1946 *American Speech*: *You never had it so good*. This is a sardonic response to complaints about the Army; it is probably supposed to represent the attitude of a peculiarly offensive type of officer.

> 1957 *Times* (reporting Harold Macmillan's speech at Bedford on 20 July): Let us be frank about it: most of our people have never had it so good.

> 1958 *Times*: How long can women's magazines have it so good?

heliport *n* (1948) a landing-place for helicopters. Originally US. Alternative names followed ('Helidrome, rotorport, helistop and helihalt are among recent verbal coinage[s] to signify a helicopter station', *Daily Telegraph* (1951)), but *heliport* has largely held the field

> 1948 *American Aviation*: The helicopter is a marvelous vehicle. It just plops down anywhere. All but three of the 12 stops were made right inside towns on small fenced-off portions of vacant lots which have been designated by the super-name of 'heliports'.

highlight *n* (1941) a bleached or light dyed streak in the hair

> 1941 *Hairdressers' Weekly Journal*: One can bring out high-lights on every shade of hair by the appropriate use of toning rinses.

> 1942 Dawn Powell: 'You've had your hair dyed.'… 'Not dyed. High-lighted is the new word,' said Vickey.

hipster *n* (1941) someone who is 'hip' or in touch with fashionable tastes. Slang, originally US. See also **hippie (1953)**

> 1948 *Partisan Review*: Carrying his language and his new philosophy like concealed weapons, the hipster set out to conquer the world.

holiday camp *n* (1940) a complex of chalets, places of entertainment, etc., designed for family holidays. The term was not new—it had been applied before World War II to camps for children (not unlike the US *summer camp*) on the continent of Europe. The institution in the modern sense began before the war too (Billy Butlin opened his first holiday centre at Skegness, Lincolnshire, in 1936), but had its heyday in the 1940s and 50s, catering to those whom the war had deprived of holidays but accustomed to regimentation. See also **redcoat (1950)**

> 1940 *Manchester Guardian Weekly*: Then there were the Holiday Camps, cheap, social, with every modern convenience and all the modern pleasures. Their official hosts and hostesses mapped out the day with a colossal time-table of delights.

> 1958 *Times*: A steel cabinet in the security block at Butlin's holiday camp at Ayr was forced at the weekend.

hologram *n* (1949) a pattern produced when light reflected, diffracted, or transmitted by an object placed in a coherent beam is allowed to interfere with an undiffracted background or reference beam related in phase to the first. When suitably illuminated a photographic hologram causes a two- or three-dimensional image of the original (two- or three-dimensional) object to form in space. The name was coined (based on Greek *holos* 'whole') by the Hungarian-born British scientist Dennis Gabor, who won the 1971 Nobel prize for physics for his work on holography

> 1949 Dennis Gabor: The name 'hologram' is not unjustified, as the photograph contains the total information required for reconstructing the object, which can be two-dimensional or three-dimensional.

Home Guard *n* (1940) the military force organized in 1940 for the defence of Great Britain and Northern Ireland against possible invasion. It was originally called the *Local Defence Volunteers*, but Winston Churchill insisted on the change of name. It was stood down in 1944 and disbanded 31 July 1957. The name was not a new coinage: it dates back to mid-19th-century America, where it was used for a member of a local volunteer force, and in Britain in the early years of the 20th century it was applied to the Territorial Army

> 1940 Winston Churchill: Behind the regular Army we have more than a million of the Local Defence Volunteers, or, as they are much better called, the 'Home Guard'.

> 1942 *Annual Register 1941*: On May 14 the Home Guard celebrated its first anniversary.

hot rod *n* (1945) a motor vehicle specially modified to give high power and speed. Originally US

> 1945 *Life*: A 'hot rod'…is an automobile stripped for speed and pepped up for power until it can travel 90 to 125 mph. Most hot rods are roadsters.

H.P. *n* (1945) An abbreviation of *hire purchase* (1895). The concept (as that date suggests) was well established, but (bypassing the slightly bizarre first quote below) it was the consumer boom of the 1950s that produced the heyday of hire purchase, and encouraged the abbreviation

> 1945 *Daily Mirror*: 'Stop H.P. babies'… Mothers…have to pay for their babies on the hire-purchase system because of the high charges of maternity homes.

> 1959 *New Statesman*: The artisan class lives in new houses and pays off the telly and the car on HP.

hydrogen bomb *n* (1947) an immensely powerful bomb in which the energy released is derived from the fusion of hydrogen nuclei in an uncontrolled self-sustaining reaction initiated by a fission bomb. A successor to the atom bomb which when it was actually made (by the US in 1952, later by the Soviet Union and others) sent the temperature of the Cold War plunging still further. The abbreviation **H-bomb** is first recorded in 1950

> 1947 *New York Times*: Hydrogen bomb. New and improved atomic bombs were discussed at the recently held forum of the Northern California Association of Scientists.

> 1954 Winston Churchill: The development of the hydrogen bomb raises strategic and political issues.

ice lolly *n* (1949) a water ice on a stick. British. Americans had long had the **popsicle (1923)**

> 1949 *Ice Cream Topics*: Ice lollies or iced lollies…sell at 1d. or 2d. and capture the kiddy trade, being cheaper than cones and wafers filled with ice cream.

incendiary *n* (1940) See **incendiary bomb (1911)**

indie *n* (1945) an independent record company. Originally US; a colloquial shortening of *independent*, which had originally been used in the 1920s of independent (non-studio) film producers and film production companies. In the 1980s *indie* came to designate the type of pop music recorded by such independent companies, typically unsophisticated and enthusiastically alternative in style

> 1945 *Billboard*: Several publishers report that they've had difficulty getting dough on a couple of tunes that one indie made.

> 1982 *Face*: Why didn't he get it out for £4.00 like the indies manage to.

> 1990 *Independent*: Hosted by Dave Booth, a mix of indie (Happy Mondays, Stone Roses) and jazz.

input *v* (1946) to feed (data, a program, etc.) into a computer or similar device. The past form is often *inputted* rather than *input*

> 1946 *Nature*: These switches are connected up so that for any two-figure argument x from 00 to 99, input to the function table, the value of the function for that argument is output in the form of pulse groups on the appropriate digit lines.

> 1953 A. D. & K. H. V. Booth: It is possible to input up to 300 decimal digits per second.

integration *n* (1940) the bringing into equal membership of a common society those groups or persons previously discriminated against on racial or cultural grounds. A usage which appears to have begun (ironically) in South Africa. The back-formed verb *integrate* is first recorded in 1948

> 1940 T. J. Haarhoff: For the great task that awaits us in South Africa is a task of integration, of making the Union into a unity.

> 1948 *Richmond* (Virginia) *Times-Dispatch*: Democrats 'integrate' Negroes for campaign.

intercept *n* (1942) (a written transcription of) a conversation, message, code, etc., that is picked up or discovered by the use of a concealed microphone, by listening to a radio communication, etc.

> 1945 *Sun* (Baltimore): In the War Department…the intercepts were shown only to Secretary Henry L. Stimson, [etc.].

intercom *n* (1940) a system of intercommunication by radio or telephone between or within aircraft, offices, vehicles, etc.

> 1940 C. Olsson: The others behind me were gossiping as usual on their 'intercoms'.

> 1941 *War Illustrated*: The rear gunner, I remember, called up on the inter-com., and said, 'I hope you chaps see the next one before I do.'

interfere with *v* (1948) to assault sexually. A decorous euphemism much resorted to in the days before the more clinical but equally euphemistic **abuse (1969)** came on the scene. See also **molest (1950)**

> 1948 David Ballantyne: The former Mayor…who was kicked out of his church for interfering with a youngster in a Sunday School class.

jeep *n* (1941) a small, sturdy, four-wheel-drive US army vehicle, used chiefly for reconnaissance. The name is a spelling of the initials *GP* 'general purpose', probably influenced by the name 'Eugene the Jeep', a creature of amazing resource and power, first introduced into the cartoon strip 'Popeye' on 16 March 1936 by his creator E. C. Segar. It is recorded as being previously applied in 1937 to a type of commercial motor vehicle

> 1941 J. Daniels: Beer wagons moved on the road with the brown jeeps of soldiers and marines.

> 1942 *R.A.F. Journal*: The Canadians…put their dollars on a Jeep. There were a few of these contraptions beetling about the countryside.

jeepable *adj* (1944) negotiable by jeep

> 1946 G. Hanley: The infantry battalions took off their jackets and started to lay thousands of logs across the mud in an endeavour to make the road even 'Jeepable'.

jelly baby *n* (1945) a soft gelatinous sweet in the shape of a baby. The US near-relation *jelly bean* is first recorded in 1905

> 1950 Richmal Crompton: 'Jelly babyth are nithe, too,' said the small shrill voice behind them.

jerrican *n* (1943) a five-gallon usually metal container for petrol, water, etc., of a type first used in Germany and later adopted by Allied forces in World War II. The name comes from **Jerry** 'German' (1919); the second quote below explains the application

> 1943 *Hutchinson's Pictorial History of the War*: Mules carrying 'jerricans' to British troops… Jerricans are a special type of petrol container for transporting water.

> 1944 *Times*: The Germans had a very efficient five-gallon petrol can. The Eighth Army captured some of the cans. They were sent back to England, and the British started manufacturing them. They were called jerricans.

jet *n* (1944) an aircraft powered by a jet engine. The first such aircraft to enter military service was the Messerschmitt Me 262, a two-engined fighter which was deployed by the German Luftwaffe in 1944

> 1944 *Collier's*: The jet…is capable of faster flight at low altitudes than any airplane with conventional engines and propeller.

jet engine *n* (1943) an engine utilizing jet propulsion to provide forward thrust, especially an aircraft engine that takes in air and ejects hot compressed air and exhaust gases. The term *jet propulsion* is first recorded in 1867, and the concept of powering aircraft and spacecraft with a high-speed jet of gas had long been toyed with ('The earth around the huge metal cylinder had been melted by the blasts of its atomic propulsion-jets', Balmer & Wylie, *After Worlds Collide* (1935)), but the first practicable jet engine was not developed until the 1930s, by Frank Whittle (who had patented the idea in 1930). It was a type of gas turbine, and that is how it was generally referred to by those concerned with it ('This invention relates to an aeroplane propelled by a constant pressure gas turbine, the exhaust gases of which are exhausted towards the rear at so high a velocity that their recoiling effect sustains or wholly replaces the propeller', *Journal of the Royal Aeronautical Society* (1935)). The first flight by an aircraft powered by Whittle's engine took place in 1941. *Jet engine* was soon shortened to **jet**, both in isolation and in combination with other nouns (*jet plane, jet fighter*, etc.). See also **turbojet (1945)**

> 1943 *Journal of the Royal Aeronautical Society*: In general, the jet engine performance is given not in h.p. but in kg. of thrust.

> 1944 *Flight*: Now about the jet aircraft. Instead of the jets coming out of the tail, shape the aircraft like an orange pip and have several jets coming out of the shoulders, pressing air against and all round the fuselage.

> 1944 *War Illustrated*: The first enemy jet-plane to fall in Allied lines was shot down over Nijmegen on October 5 by six R.A.F. Spitfires; it was a Me 262.

> 1948 Nevil Shute: The Mark I model…had radial engines, though now they all have jets.

jog *v* (1948) to run at a gentle pace as a form of physical exercise. A specialization of the earlier sense 'to move at an easy pace but slightly joltingly', which dates from the mid 16th century. At first it was mainly used by athletes, with reference to training running at a slower speed than racing. It did not come into general use until the late 1960s, when, as part of a general 'healthy living' obsession, the craze for fitness running swept the western world

> 1948 K. S. Duncan: The runner should start any piece of jogging with the slow jog style.

> 1968 *Chicago Tribune*: Joggers have become an almost familiar sight thruout America in the last year.

> 1976 *New Yorker*: You will always be in good taste with a pair of Adidas jogging shoes.

jolly d *adj* (1949) jolly decent. British middle-class slang of the middle years of the century

> 1949 Nancy Spain: Jolly d. of you to ask us.

> 1960 N. Fairbrother: I *say*. Jolly *d*. It's exactly what I want.

Kafkaesque *adj* (1947) like or suggestive of the nightmarish world conjured up in the writings of the Czech novelist Franz Kafka (1883–1924), in which sinister impersonal forces control human affairs. Even before the adjective was coined, Kafka's name was being invoked in such contexts ('This is the perfect Kafka situation', Malcolm Lowry (1936))

> 1947 *New Yorker*: Warned, he said, by a Kafka-esque nightmare of blind alleys.

> 1954 Arthur Koestler: Long before the Moscow purges revealed that weird, Kafka-esque pattern to the incredulous world.

> 1958 *Spectator*: An authentic Kafkaesque atmosphere of despair and horror.

kamikaze *n* (1945) any of the Japanese pilots who in World War II made deliberate suicidal crashes into enemy targets, usually ships. Also applied to an aircraft, usually loaded with explosives, employed in such an attack, and frequently used adjectivally. The word in Japanese means literally 'divine wind', and was originally used in Japanese lore with reference to the supposed divine wind which blew on a night in August 1281, destroying the navy of the invading Mongols

> 1945 *Newsweek*: As a British task force was hoisting victory pennants a Kamikaze darted out of the clouds toward the ship.

> 1946 *Chemical & Engineering News*: The Army and Navy…provided protective [smoke] screens against the Kamikaze attack of the Japanese.

Kilroy *n* (1945) The name of a mythical person, popularized by American service personnel during World War II, who left such inscriptions as 'Kilroy was here' on walls, etc., all over the world. The explanation in the second quote below is one of numerous unverifiable accounts of the origin of the name

> 1945 *Saturday Evening Post*: On the crib hung a hand-lettered sign which asserted: 'Kilroy slept Here'… Wherever he was, Kilroy had been there and left his mark behind: 'Kilroy Was Here', or 'Kilroy Passed Through' or 'You're in the Footsteps of Kilroy'.

> 1946 *New York Times*: As far as the American Transit Association is concerned, the identity of the elusive Kilroy of 'Kilroy Was Here' fame has been established, and in token of this recognition a street car was shipped today to James J. Kilroy of Halifax, Mass… In brief, Mr. Kilroy's claim is based on the following: During the war he was employed at the Bethlehem Steel Company's Quincy shipyard, inspecting tanks, double bottoms and other parts of warships under construction. To satisfy superiors that he was performing his duties, Mr. Kilroy scribbled in yellow crayon 'Kilroy was here' on inspected work. Soon the phrase began to appear in various unrelated places, and Mr. Kilroy believes the 14,000 shipyard workers who entered the armed services were responsible for its subsequent world-wide use.

knockers *n* (1941) a woman's breasts. Slang, originally US, and mainly used with reference to large breasts. The origins of the word are not clear: probably it just refers to the tendency of pendulous breasts to collide, or conceivably to some feveredly fancied resemblance to a door-knocker, but it has also been suggested that there is some connection with *norks* (1962), Australian slang for breasts—the chronology, however, does not favour this

> 1948 Norman Mailer: Look at the knockers on her, Murray says.

kriegie *n* (1944) an Allied prisoner of war in Germany during World War II. Slang; an abbreviation of German *Kriegsgefangener* 'prisoner of war'

> 1946 Brickhill & Norton: The worn track…which kriegies 'pounded' or 'bashed' (walked) for hours at a time.

lacquer *n* (1941) a fixative for a hairstyle, now usually applied as an aerosol spray

> 1941 F. E. Wall: Many of the coiffures…can be made more lasting through the use of lacquer as a fixative.

> 1943 *Modern Beauty Shop*: A national publicity campaign is informing women everywhere that hair lacquer is best applied with an ordinary toothbrush.

landing-craft *n* (1940) a naval vessel with a shallow draught designed for landing troops, tanks, etc., in an amphibious assault

> 1940 Winston Churchill: Great efforts should be made to produce the landing-craft as soon as possible.

Land-Rover *n* (1948) The proprietary name (registered by the Rover Company in 1948) of a sturdy, four-wheel-drive motor vehicle designed especially for work in rough or agricultural country

> 1948 *Motor*: Also exhibited is the Land Rover, as a closed estate car with seven-seat capacity, a go-anywhere, four-wheel-drive model powered by the '60' engine.

language *n* (1949) any of a wide range of systems of precisely defined symbols and rules for using them (e.g. ASCII, COBOL) that have been devised for writing computer programs or representing instructions and data.

> 1949 E. C. Berkeley: We must translate into machine language, in this case punched holes in the program tape.

launderette *n* (1949) an establishment providing automatic washing machines for the use of customers

> 1949 *Vogue*: A new and interesting development in housekeeping—the advent of the self-service launderette.

Laundromat *n* (1943) Originally the proprietary name (registered in the US in 1943) of a brand of automatic washing machine, but later also, and mainly, used as the equivalent of **launderette (1949)**

> 1951 *American Speech*: The Westinghouse Company has a 'Laundramat', and there are also 'Laundromats'—often called 'Laundermats' and 'Laundrymats'—open for public patronage.

> 1957 Jack Kerouac: I…found nothing but laundromats, cleaners, soda fountains.

lend-lease *n* (1941) Applied originally to an arrangement by which sites in British overseas possessions were leased to the United States as bases in exchange for the loan of US destroyers, devised largely to enable the US to help Britain in its war with Germany without becoming actively involved (which would have enraged the powerful US isolationist lobby). Later extended to various similar arrangements to help strategic countries threatened by Germany and Italy. At first the formulation *lease-lend* was equally common, but this gradually faded out

> 1941 *Economist*: Future disposition of the armaments now being produced is before Congress in the 'Lend-Lease' Bill…The great reduction in American payments under the 'Lease and Lend' Bill.

> 1972 *National Observer* (US): Talks in the State Department are aimed at ending a U.S.–Soviet dispute over lend-lease that goes back to World War II. From 1942 to 1945, the United States supplied Russia with some $10.8 billion in military and civilian equipment under the lend-lease program.

letter bomb *n* (1948) an explosive device sent through the post as a weapon of terror. See also **parcel bomb (1950)**

> 1949 Arthur Koestler: His brother was killed by a letter-bomb sent by the Stern Group.

liberate *v* (1944) to free (an occupied territory) of the enemy. Often used ironically to imply subjection to a new tyranny; also, by a facetious extension of the irony, applied to filching small objects

> 1944 George Bernard Shaw: All your Italian friends must be starving now that we have 'liberated' them.

> 1944 *Daily Express* (caption): Excuse me, Canon, but I rather think you've liberated my matches.

> 1955 *Annual Register 1954*: Chu Teh…expressed China's intention of 'liberating' Formosa.

litterbug *n* (1947) someone who litters public areas with discarded rubbish. Originally US. The mainly British equivalent **litter lout** is first recorded in 1927

> 1947 *New York Herald-Tribune*: 47,000 subway 'litterbugs' pay $107,000 in fines in 1946 drive.

lolly *n* (1943) money. British slang. A rather involved derivation is sometimes suggested from Romany *loli* 'red', used by gypsies to refer to copper coins, and hence to money in general, but a straightforward equation with sweet things seems more plausible. It has stayed in continuous use, and enjoyed a modest revival in the money-obsessed 1980s

> 1943 Michael Harrison: This 'ere bloke touches the Guv'ment fer a nice drop er lolly.

loner *n* (1947) someone who avoids company and prefers to be alone. Originally US

> 1961 *Guardian*: The American ex-patriates along the Seine…are what James Jones calls 'loners'.

loo *n* (1940) the lavatory. British. A word of much discussed but still undetermined etymology. Amongst the most widely touted conjectures are some (usually unspecified) connection with *Waterloo* (in the early 20th century *Waterloo* was a British trade name for iron cisterns, which may be more than a coincidence) and *gardyloo*, a cod-French warning ('Watch out for the water!') shouted to unwary passers-by by 18th-century Edinburgh householders about to empty the contents of a chamber-pot from an upstairs window (untenable chronologically). Perhaps the likeliest explanation is that it comes from French *lieu*, literally 'place', short for *lieux d'aisance* 'places of easement', a euphemism for 'lavatory', brought back from France by British soldiers who served there in World War I. As for when it appeared, there is a probable earlier reference to it in another book by Nancy Mitford, champion of 'U' and 'non-U' (see **U (1954)**): 'The absence in his speech of such expressions as "O.K. loo"…"we'll call it a day" ' (1932). It has rearranged the landscape in that British social minefield, the vocabulary of places of excretion: it initally invaded mainly the territory of *lavatory*, but during the 1970s it started to become more and more frequent among *toilet*-users

> 1940 Nancy Mitford: In the night when you want to go to the loo.

> 1943 Cecil Beaton: They had dressed, teeth brushed, breakfasted, had visited the loo, and were on their precarious journey all in a question of fifteen minutes.

> 1971 *Petticoat*: You can wait until he goes to the loo or, if he appears to have a bladder like an ox, send him to the kitchen for more coffee.

> 1974 *Observer*: The loo rolls unfurling across the pitch.

LP *n* (1948) An abbreviation of *long-playing* (*record*) 'a microgroove gramophone record designed to be played at 33⅓ revolutions per minute'. **Long-playing (1929)** had been used in relation to records since the second decade of the century, but this specific application is first recorded in 1948 ('A new library of recorded music has been announced…which consists of a series of long-playing 10 and 12 in. records run at 33⅓ r.p.m.', *Electronic Engineering*). See also **EP (1954)**

> 1948 *Musical American*: The new disc, called LP (long playing) Microgroove, requires a new pickup.

> 1958 *Times*: Stereo records will give almost as much playing time as present LPs.

luncheon meat *n* (1945) meat, usually pork, processed and pressed into a small loaf shape and usually tinned. A pompous name given to a decidedly mundane foodstuff which loomed large in the immediate postwar years of food shortages, when fillet steak was but a distant memory. The best-known brand was **Spam (1937)**

> 1945 Richmal Crompton: Although it meant opening her last remaining tin of Luncheon Meat.

Lurex *n* (1945) The proprietary name (registered in the US in 1945) of a type of yarn which incorporates a metallic thread. Also applied to a fabric made from this yarn. Over the years the term (not helped by the association with *lurid*) has acquired the subtext 'vulgar'

> 1973 *Guardian*: Plain snakeskin Lurex blousons.

machine translation *n* (1949) translation by computer

> 1949 W. Weaver: Mr. Max Zeldner, in a letter to the *Herald Tribune* on June 13, 1949, stating that the most you could expect of a machine translation of fifty-five Hebrew words which form the 23d Psalm would start out Lord my shepherd no I will lack [etc.].

> 1956 *Nature*: Dr. Booth is optimistic that even the problems of machine-translation of literary work may prove less complex than they at present appear.

machismo *n* (1940) the quality of being macho; male virility, masculine pride. Originally US. Like its parent adjective **macho (1928)**, this acquisition from Mexican Spanish does not seem to have made much headway in English at first, but in the 1960s it found a niche as a put-down

> 1948 B. Griffith: Machismo makes a boy swear big round oaths as a youngster.

Mae West *n* (1940) an inflatable life-jacket, originally as issued to R.A.F. aircrew during World War II. Named after the US film actress Mae West (1892–1980), whose impressive breasts evidently reminded someone of the two prominent front-pieces of the life-jacket

> 1941 *New York Times*: One can understand…why an airman's life-belt should be a 'Mae-West'. It…gives the wearer a somewhat feminine figure.

make do and mend (1947) to repair for continued use something which one might otherwise have thrown away. A philosophy heavily encouraged by Government propaganda in Britain during

World War II, and inculcating habits of minute economy into the wartime generation that stayed with them for many decades afterwards

> 1947 Ivor Brown: This age of bits and pieces, queues, rationing, and make-do-and-mend.

male menopause *n* (1949) a supposed counterpart in middle-aged men to the female menopause, marked by feelings of anxiety, self-doubt, lost opportunity, etc.

> 1949 Ernst & Loth: Another reason which has sometimes been given is that many men reach in middle age a climacteric which is dubbed a male menopause.

-manship *suffix* (1947) the art of coping with the stated thing, and particularly exploiting it to one's own advantage (often by disconcerting or distracting rivals). A long-established suffix in its original, neutral sense 'skill in a particular activity', and from time to time used facetiously ('Parisiennes continue to witch the world with noble bikemanship in their graceful kilted knickerbockers', *Pall Mall Gazette* (1894)), it got a significant boost in Stephen Potter's coining of **gamesmanship (1947)**, which started a fashion for similar creations. See also **brinkmanship (1956), one-upmanship (1952)**

> 1947 Stephen Potter: Psychological tendency, if not temporal necessity, will cause him to drive faster, and—behold! now the gamesman can widen his field and bring in carmanship.

> 1950 *Sunday Times*: Many gamesmen find a specious field for the exercise of their knowledge in the allied craft of queuemanship.

> 1959 *Evening Standard*: His hobbies…include farming, motoring…and general do-it-yourself-manship.

> 1973 *Nature*: He has some useful and pointed things to say on 'grantsmanship'.

Maquis *n* (1944) a secret army of patriots in France during the German occupation in World War II, consisting of members of the Resistance who were known to the Germans and therefore had to go into hiding in the *maquis*, areas of dense scrub-land. See also **Resistance (1944)**

> 1945 Winston Churchill: The tributes which are paid to the heroic French or Belgian Maquis.

marriage bureau *n* (1942) an agency which arranges introductions with a view to marriage. A term which in the latter decades of the century gave way to alternatives such as *dating agency*, as such a frank admission of seeking a spouse became less socially acceptable

> 1942 Oliver & Benedetta: How much better it would be if there were an organization that could arrange the actual match-making and see that suitable people met each other. And this way my idea for the Marriage Bureau.

Marshall plan *n* (1947) a plan initiated in 1947 by George C. Marshall (1880–1959), US Secretary of State from 1947 to 1949, to supply financial assistance to certain Western European countries to further their recovery after World War II. His name was used in a range of other associated compound nouns, particularly *Marshall aid*

> 1947 *New York Times*: If at the end of the first year of the Marshall plan, Europe is not showing dividends, you will see what a collapse there will be.

mass radiography *n* (1943) radiography of the chests of large numbers of people by a quick routine method, especially as carried out in Britain in the decades following World War II, to screen the population for tuberculosis and other lung diseases. More generally known to the population at large as *mass X-ray*

> 1954 Elizabeth Jenkins: These mobile X-ray units for mass radiography.

mastermind *v* (1941) to plan and direct (something); to be the mastermind behind (an enterprise, a crime, etc.). Originally US

> 1941 *True Detective*: Often suspected but never convicted of masterminding some of the plots hatched in his grog shop.

master-race *n* (1942) a race of people considered to be pre-eminent in greatness or power. Originally used very much in terms of the Nazis' concept of the Germans or 'Aryans' as a superior people (it is a translation of German *Herrenvolk*); later broadened out in application, but usually retaining its connotations of megalomania

1942 Julian Huxley: The [German] nation is formidably united behind its own ideal of an 'Aryan' Master-Race.

1974 *Times*: To suggest that I [i.e. Sir Keith Joseph] was arguing for a 'master race'…is…very wrong.

megabuck *n* (1946) a million dollars. Colloquial. Originally US, but the later plural usage, denoting broadly 'a huge amount of money', has spread throughout World English

1946 *Picture Post*: Atomic research is so expensive that American scientists have ceased to use the dollar as their unit. They have laughingly coined the term 'megabuck'—one megabuck equals a million dollars.

1992 *Making Music*: He's out of date, out of touch and he'll rake in megabucks by flogging these turkeys to his ridiculously acquiescent fan base.

melamine *n* (1940) a type of plastic made from a crystalline compound called melamine. This name was coined in German (as *Melamin*) by the chemist Justus Liebig in 1834, based on *Melam*, an apparently arbitrary name he invented for a substance obtained by the distillation of sulpho-cyanide of ammonium (from which he made melamine). It became perhaps over-familiar as a household material in the 1960s and 70s

1972 *Daily Telegraph*: Young couples usually eat in the kitchen, and kitchen/dining tables with white melamine tops are attractive.

memory *n* (1946) that part of a computer in which data or program instructions are stored and from which they can be retrieved when required

1946 *New York Times*: Numerical values covering a wide range of scientific 'constants' are inter-jected as and when they are needed. There are four kinds of 'memory' in the Eniac [an early sort of computer] to accomplish this.

1946 *Nature*: The units in which addition is carried out provide a 'memory' with a capacity of about twenty numbers.

methadone *n* (1947) a powerful synthetic pain-killer which is similar to morphine in its effects but less sedative and is used as a substitute drug in the treatment of addiction to morphine or heroin. The term was coined from elements of the substance's systematic chemical name (see the quote below), and at first was widely used in the form *methadon*

1947 *Journal of the American Medical Association*: The Council voted to recognise the word Methadon as the generic designation for 6-dimethylamino-4,4-diphenyl-3-heptanone.

miniaturize *v* (1946) to produce in a smaller version; to make very small. An early outing for a verb which came into its own in the last three decades of the century, particularly in the area of elec-tronics

1951 *Electronic Engineer*: Miniaturized components generally are becoming more and more read-ily available.

mobile home *n* (1940) a large caravan used as a residence. US. Also called a **trailer home** or *trailer house*

1940 H. G. Wells: In such large open countries as the United States there has been a considerable development of the mobile home in recent years. People haul a trailer-home behind their cars and become seasonal nomads.

Molotov cocktail *n* (1940) a makeshift incendiary hand-grenade, consisting of a breakable con-tainer filled with inflammable liquid, and a means of ignition. Named after Vyacheslav Mikhailovich Molotov (1890–1986), Soviet Minister for Foreign Affairs from 1939 to 1949

1940 *Hutchinson's Pictorial History of the War*: Used with success in the Finnish war, the so-called 'Molotov cocktails' are considered an effective weapon against armoured divisions and have been adopted by the Home Guard.

moussaka *n* (1941) a Balkan and eastern Mediterranean dish of minced beef or lamb, aubergines or potatoes, and onions. Excitingly exotic in the 1940s, after decades of Mediterranean holidays it has become thoroughly domesticated. The word came into English via Turkish from, ultimately, Egyptian Arabic *musakk'a*

1941 H. D. Harrison: Moussaka is another dish which savours of the east.

1972 Joan Aiken: Moussaka…is a sort of super-shepherds-pie with a cheese omelette on top.

Mrs Mopp *n* (1948) a charwoman. British colloquial; a generic use of the name of a character (who first appeared in 1941) in the BBC radio comedy series *ITMA*. The underlying allusion is obvious enough for the term still to be in occasional use at the end of the century among those without the faintest idea where it originated. See also **TTFN (1948)**

> 1950 Agatha Christie: Our Mrs Mopp says he came from one of the big hotels.

> 1972 *Listener*: Today's generation monotonously describe char-women as Mrs Mops [sic].

mug *v* (1948) to attack and rob (someone), especially in the street or other public place. A development of a much earlier boxing slang sense, 'to hit in the face (i.e. the "mug"), to beat up', which dates from the early 19th century. Originally US; the new usage did not become familiar in Britain until the 1970s. The related *mugger* is first recorded in 1942

> 1948 *New York Times*: The police said the victims were mugged in the hallways of their homes.

> 1960 I. Wallach: She's going into Central Park for her constitutional. I hope she gets mugged.

> 1970 *Daily Mail*: Clarendon Road in London's Notting Hill area…is the haunt of the Muggers—men who clobber you and steal whatever you have of value.

mulberry harbour *n* (1945) The code name of the prefabricated floating harbour used in the invasion of the Continent by Allied forces in 1944

> 1945 *Notes & Queries*: The word 'Mulberry' was selected as the secret name for the artificial harbour…from its being that which happened to come next in rotation on the Admiralty's List of Ships' Names then available for use.

> 1958 *Listener*: Further north—in the island of Schouwen-Duiveland—I saw where it had been necessary to float great mulberry harbour caissons in and sink them in the gaps.

name-dropper *n* (1947) someone who, in order to impress others, mentions a famous person in such a way as to suggest personal acquaintance. Originally US. The related *name-dropping* is first recorded in 1950, the back-formed verb *name-drop* in 1955

> 1947 *San Francisco Examiner*: Our newest menace. The name dropper.

> 1955 J. D. Salinger: There's an unwritten law that people in a certain social or financial bracket can name-drop as much as they like just as long as they say something terribly disparaging about the person as soon as they've dropped his name.

napalm *n* (1942) a jelly made from petrol and a type of aluminium soap, used in flame-throwers and incendiary bombs. The name is a conflation of *naphthenic* and *palmitic acid*. Its use as a verb, meaning 'to attack or destroy with napalm', dates from the time of the Korean War

> 1950 *New York Times*: Troops were napalmed when they were found hiding in caves at the dead end of a canyon.

> 1952 René Cutforth: He was no longer covered with a skin, but with a crust like crackling which broke easily. 'That's napalm,' said the doctor.

national *adj* (1940) Used in Britain during World War II to designate foodstuffs made to official specifications for nation-wide distribution

> 1940 *Hansard Commons*: All butter sold by the Ministry of Food is…described as 'National Butter'.

> 1941 *New Statesman*: The bakers are equally reluctant to change their habits. They shake their heads with a mournful smile at mention of the national loaf.

> 1943 *Daily Telegraph*: National Milk-Cocoa—the new food drink evolved by the Ministry's scientific advisers—is already available to all factories and industrial undertakings in limited quantities.

National Assistance *n* (1948) a form of UK welfare payment combining Unemployment Assistance (payment to those out of work) and Public Assistance (payment to the poor), begun in 1948, administered by the National Assistance Board, and replaced in 1966 by Supplementary Benefits

> 1959 John Braine: There isn't any dole for him. It's bankruptcy first and then National Assistance.

National Health *n* (1946) the comprehensive health service provided in Britain, initiated in 1946 and financed by taxation. The term *national health*, denoting the health of the whole nation, was not a new one: in 1908 there had been a 'Women's National Health Association of Great Britain', and the National Insurance scheme introduced just before World War I had been devoted to the cause of 'national health' ('A few weeks ago I had the honour of introducing in the House of Commons a measure dealing with proposals for securing the national health', Lloyd George (1911)). The abbreviation *N.H.S.* for *National Health Service* is first recorded in 1948

> 1946 *Act of Parliament*: National Health Service Act.

> 1948 *Lancet*: Other doctors do not discriminate between private and N.H.S. patients.

> 1952 Agatha Christie: Nowadays even if you've got a chilblain you run to the doctor with it so as to get your money's worth out of the National Health.

national serviceman *n* (1949) a conscript in the British armed forces. The term **National Service** is first recorded in 1916, when compulsory military recruitment was introduced in Britain ('It is proposed to appoint at once a director of National Service, to be in charge of both the military and civil side of universal national service', *Hansard Commons* (1916)), and it was used again when conscription was reintroduced in 1939, but it was not until 1947, when the National Service Act provided for peacetime conscription, that the term found a secure place in the language. Under the system, up to 150,000 civilians were called up for military service every year; it was abolished in 1962

> 1949 *Times*: The Secretary of State for War gave an assurance that no national service man would be posted to the Far East with less than 18 weeks' service.

New Look *n* (1947) a style of women's clothes introduced in Paris by Christian Dior in 1947, characterized especially by skirts longer and fuller than those previously worn. The term itself was popularized and apparently coined by the American press. Subsequently it was also applied to more recent new fashion styles

> 1948 *Economist*: Clothing in styles which the New Look has superseded.

> 1957 *Daily Mail*: When Christian Dior launched the New Look in 1947 it met with an enthusiasm which amounted to hysteria.

news blackout *n* (1944) an official cutting off of the supply of information to the media. A term reflecting the press's increasing assumption of unfettered access to its raw material as the century wore on

> 1944 *Sun* (Baltimore): The whole sector east of the Falaise bottleneck was under an Allied news blackout.

Newspeak *n* (1949) The name of the artificial language used for official communications in George Orwell's novel *Nineteen Eighty-Four*, often applied to any corrupt form of English, especially the propagandist and ambiguous language of some politicians, broadcasters, etc. It became the inspiration for a range of neologisms ending in *-speak* (see **-speak (1957)**)

> 1949 George Orwell: Syme was a philologist, a specialist in Newspeak. Indeed, he was one of the enormous team of experts now engaged in compiling the Eleventh Edition of the Newspeak Dictionary... Do you know the Newspeak word *goodthinkful?*... Newspeak was the official language of Oceania and had been devised to meet the ideological needs of Ingsoc, or English Socialism. In the year 1984 there was not as yet anyone who used Newspeak as his sole means of communication, either in speech or writing.

> 1966 *Punch*: Accusing the Prime Minister of 'the same old excuses', [the *Daily Telegraph*] labelled 'redeployment' as 'new-speak', which would be 'victimisation of the workers' in any but a Labour Government.

N.H.S. *n* (1948) See **National Health (1946)**

-nik *suffix* (1945) A Russian suffix, acquired originally via Yiddish, added to nouns and adjectives to denote a person or thing involved in or associated with the thing or quality specified. Originally and mainly US; often with humorous or pejorative connotations. The original trickle of English words based on it became a flood in the late 1950s following the launch of the first **sputnik (1957)**. See also **beatnik (1958)**, **neatnik (1959)**, **peacenik (1965)**

> 1945 A. Kober: That stuck-upnick fomm the lodge, Sister Leshinsky...she's a regella Yenkee.

1959 *Observer*: It happened that Mr. Werth arrived in Columbus, Ohio, just as the Russian Sputnik soared into the cosmos; before he left the American flopnik had burnt out on its launching pad.

1965 *Times*: Those guitar-plunking protestniks whose St. Joan is Baez.

Nip *adj, n* (1942) (a) Japanese. An abbreviation of *Nipponese* 'Japanese', originally called into being as a term of contempt for Japanese service personnel during World War II

1942 *Time*: I visited a command post in one sector where they had just rounded up a bunch of Nips.

1942 *R.A.F. Journal*: The Nip pilots.

nit *n* (1941) a fool. Slang. Partly short for **nitwit (1922)**, but probably partly also from *nit* 'headlouse egg', which was being used as a term of amused contempt as far back as Shakespeare's time: 'And his Page,...Ah heauens, it is [a] most patheticall nit', *Love's Labour's Lost* (1588). In vogue mainly in the 1950s and early 60s

1962 *Melody Maker*: I could see he wasn't very impressed with this nit sitting across the table.

no *adj* (1944) Used on signs forbidding the stated activity. Possibly a symptom of World War II dirigisme

1944 J. Gunther: I wanted to smoke, but fell asleep before the No Smoking sign was switched off.

1946 *Report of the Departmental Committee on Traffic Signs* (Ministry of Transport): We do not consider it desirable that the words 'Halt' or 'No Parking' should be marked on the carriageway.

no-no *n* (1942) something that must not be done, used, etc.; something that is forbidden, impossible, or not acceptable. Colloquial, originally US

1968 *Washington Post*: What she was doing was a no-no, the protectors of our health announced... She must stop baking things for sale.

nuclear *adj* (1945) using nuclear energy as a source of explosive power, or as a source of electricity. See also **nuclear (1954)**

1945 *Engineering Journal*: In view of the source of the energy, the current terms 'atomic bomb' and 'atomic power' might well be replaced by the more exact terms 'nuclear bomb' and 'nuclear power'... A large stationary power installation might be used for heat and motive power in the Arctic or Antarctic regions...where the difficulty of transporting other fuels...outweigh[s] the disadvantages and difficulties of operating and maintaining a nuclear power plant.

1948 *Nuclear Science Abstracts*: Fourth, nuclear weapons have not reached their maximum size in the present type bomb.

1955 *Tribune*: Nuclear power stations are designed to be safe.

1957 *Observer*: To keep the British nuclear deterrent up to date on its present scale in relation to the Soviet defence will cost more and more each year.

nuclear family *n* (1949) A sociologists' term for the basic family unit or group, consisting typically of father, mother, and offspring

1971 *Guardian*: If they get rid of the nuclear family there won't be grannies any more than there will be widows.

nylons *n* (1940) See **nylon (1938)**

oceanarium *n* (1944) an establishment with a pool in which large marine animals can be kept and observed, especially for public entertainment. Coined from *aquarium*; a trend continued with *seaquarium* (1955) and *dolphinarium* (1969)

1944 E. B. Marks: The aquarium of other days is now slated to be the oceanarium.

office block *n* (1942) a large multi-unit building containing offices; a major feature of the post-war urban landscape. The use of *block* in this sense dates from the mid 19th century, although at first it seems to have been applied largely to residential rather than commercial buildings

1942 *London Replanned*: The large octagonal building prominent in the drawing...is a suggested office block with garden court or car park.

oral *adj* (1948) involving or being sexual activity in which the genitals of one partner are stimulated by the mouth of the other

> 1948 A. C. Kinsey et al.: Most prostitutes are from the lower social levels, and consequently…few of them engage freely in oral activities.

organic adj (1942) Of farming or gardening: growing plants without the use of chemical fertilizers, pesticides, etc., adding only organic (i.e. chemical-free) fertilizers to the soil. This application of *organic* to fertilizers is first recorded in the 1860s, but it remained rare until the 1940s. In the 1970s the usage was extended to foods grown by such methods

> 1942 J. I. Rodale: What is claimed roughly for these organic methods of farming is that they increase the fertility of the soil, produce much better tasting crops,…reduce weeds, do away with the necessity of using poisonous sprays, improve the mechanical structure of the soil.

> 1972 *Daily Telegraph*: The organic food market is booming.

orienteering n (1948) the competitive sport of finding one's way on foot across rough country with the aid of map and compass. It originated in Sweden around 1918, and the word is an anglicization of Swedish *orientering*

> 1948 *American Ski Annual 1949*: Senior Scouts representing 15 Boy Scout Councils from New York and New Jersey met at Snow Ridge Ski Center last winter to compete in the first official Ski Orienteering race to be held in America.

outsider n (1946) In literary criticism: the archetypal artist or intellectual seen as a person isolated from the rest of society. A specific use of the earlier 'someone who does not "fit in" ' (first recorded in 1907), instigated by its adoption as the English title of Albert Camus's novel *L'Étranger*, and later cemented by Colin Wilson's *The Outsider*, a study of alienated heroes in modern fiction

> 1956 Colin Wilson: Many great artists have none of the characteristics of the Outsider. Shakespeare, Dante, Keats were all apparently normal and socially well-adjusted.

> 1957 *Times Literary Supplement*: [Colin Wilson's] original contribution was simply the Outsider gimmick.

Overlord n (1943) The code-name for the allied invasion of German-occupied Normandy in June 1944.

> 1943 John Reith: Meeting…about a ridiculous Churchill demand for a twenty-five per cent increase in Overlord (invasion of Europe) force.

package n (1947) any related group of objects that is viewed or organized as a unit. Compare **package (1931)**

> 1947 Crowther & Whiddington: A late model; it is a 'package', with magnetron and magnet complete with rectangular wave guide out of which power pours.

> 1958 *Observer*: The objectives of this lavish experiment were…to test the interaction of the three stages…and…to achieve a trajectory that could be controlled enough to put the final package within some 50,000 miles of the moon.

pantie-girdle n (1941) a woman's undergarment combining the functions of panties and girdle. A staging-post on the journey from the heavily boned and laced corsetry of earlier generations to the abandonment of such garments later in the century. See also **roll-on (1941)**

> 1941 Hermer & May: We recommend panty-girdles of mesh elastic and net or lace bras.

> 1946 George Orwell: Someone has just sent me a copy of an American fashion magazine… Here are a few sample sentences…'Gentle discipline for curves in lacy lastex pantie-girdle'.

panzer n (1940) Denoting a German armoured unit. In German, *Panzer* means literally '(coat of) mail'

> 1941 *Hutchinson's Pictorial History of the War*: An Imperial division concentrated round Bengazi was left in the air when the German Panzer inrush swept aside the British armoured brigade.

paper towel n (1943) a small disposable towel made of absorbent paper, usually one of a number wound in a roll

> 1943 Dorothy Baker: She jerked a paper towel off the roller and did a careful job of drying.

parapants n (1944) women's knickers made from parachute silk. A product of wartime making-do, when the armed forces had the first call on silk (and most other things)

1944 *Time*: Parapants. In Manhattan, Mrs. Virginia Bell Jack received from her Thunderbolt-pilot husband in England a pair of real silk (German parachute) panties.

parashot *n* (1940), **parashooter** *n* (1940) a member of the British Home Guard in World War II whose task was to shoot down enemy parachutists. A tabloid coinage which caught on for a while

1940 *Star*: Clubs' part in fight against parachute troops… The appeal for parashooters has brought rifle shooting into the news. Clubs are offering free instruction to applicants.

1940 *New Yorker*: A movement to provide parashots with hand grenades.

paratroops *n* (1940) a body of soldiers (to be) dropped by parachute from aircraft flying over enemy territory. The singular *paratrooper* is first recorded in 1941

1940 *Daily Express*: Parashots—the new Local Defence Volunteers now being enrolled to deal with paratroops dropped from planes—will have uniforms of overall material.

1940 *Notes & Queries*: Parachutists dropped as troops, or to establish themselves in the enemy's country…have now been shortened to 'paratroops'.

1941 *Time*: The paratroopers…had never been in an airplane when it was landed.

parking ticket *n* (1947) a ticket attached by an official to a vehicle which has violated parking regulations. Originally US

1947 *Denver Post*: Parking tickets no longer could be fixed.

party *n* (1942) an attack, combat, or fight; an (action-packed) operation. Services' slang, insouciantly making light of potentially fatal encounters

1942 B. J. Ellan: I just fired when something came into my sights and then turned like hell as something fired at me! What a party!

1942 *R.A.F. Journal*: Confirmation came through that the big party was on. And that the target was Cologne.

passion killers *n* (1943) knickers with no frills and a reputation for impenetrability. British slang; originally a services' witticism, applied to standard-issue drawers in the women's forces

1946 J. J. C. Irving: An elastic-bound bifurcated undergarment said to be worn in the women's Services and known…as 'passion-killers'.

1974 *Times*: Stout fleecy lined drawers…which would have been called by this generation 'passion-killers'.

pathfinder *n* (1943) an aircraft or its pilot sent ahead of bombing aircraft to locate and mark out the target for attack

1943 *Times*: Red tracer bullets were continually fired from the ground at the pathfinders' flares.

1946 *R.A.F. Journal*: For the crews of Bomber Command's Pathfinder Force it was all a question of time.

pay-as-you-earn *n* (1943) a system of collecting income tax in which the tax payable is deducted by employers from current earnings. The slightly less cumbrous abbreviation *PAYE* was soon in use. The ultimate model is the maxim 'Pay as you go', denoting the immediate discharge of any financial obligation, which dates from at least the 1840s. The earliest recorded appropriation of the 'pay as you' formula to other purposes is *pay-as-you-enter* (see **pay-as-you- (1908)**)

1943 *Daily Telegraph*: As to deduction of income-tax from wages he warned the House of the experiences of other countries which had attempted the 'pay-as-you-earn' idea.

1944 *Times* (headline): PAYE begins.

Peace *n* (1944) a hybrid tea rose bearing large yellow flowers shaded with pink, belonging to a variety developed by Francis Meilland, French nurseryman, in 1939, introduced into cultivation in France in 1942 (under the name 'Mme A. Meilland'), and named 'Peace' in English (originally in the US) in anticipation of the end of World War II. It was one of the best-selling varieties of rose over the next few decades

1944 R. Pyle: We are persuaded that this greatest new rose of our time should be named for the world's greatest desire: Peace.

pedal-pushers *n* (1944) a type of girls' or women's trousers, reaching only just below the knee, suitable for wearing when cycling, fashionable in the late 1940s and early 50s. Originally US; an adaptation of the earlier *pedal-pusher* 'cyclist'

> 1944 *Life*: When college girls took to riding bicycles in slacks, they first rolled up one trouser leg, then rolled up both. This…has now produced a trim variety of long shorts, called 'pedal pushers'.

peek-a-boo *adj* (1948) Denoting a woman's hairstyle in which the hair, worn long, is allowed to fall over one eye. It was popularized in the early 1940s by the Hollywood filmstar Veronica Lake

> 1948 M. M. Miller: Her 'peek-a-boo' style secured major parts for her, under new name Veronica Lake.

peer *n* (1943) someone of equal standing, especially in age. A term used mainly by sociologists and anthropologists, particularly in compounds such as *peer group* (1943), *peer culture* (1944), and *peer pressure* (1970)

> 1943 Breckenridge & Vincent: Although the adolescent declares his independence of adult standards and controls, he is actually very dependent upon conformity with his peer group.

> 1944 C. M. Tryon: Although in meeting some adult standards girls must undergo less change than boys, in their relation to their own peer culture they must often be more adaptive in relation to changing requirements.

people's republic *n* (1949) A title assumed by a number of left-wing or Communist states (e.g. *People's Republic of China*)

> 1949 *Times*: Mr. Rákosi…said…that 'the Hungarian Republic must be developed into a People's Republic'.

> 1975 *Bangladesh Times*: The Magura Journalists Association in a meeting held recently at Magura hailed the Government of the People's Republic of Bangladesh for creating the new district of Magura.

> 1978 Lord Hailsham: Probably our own monarch would not survive the institution in Britain of…a people's republic.

permafrost *n* (1943) subsoil or other underground material that is at a temperature of less than 0°C throughout the year, as in Arctic regions; permanently frozen ground

> 1943 S. W. Muller: The expression 'permanently frozen ground'…is too long and cumbersome and for this reason a shorter term '*permafrost*' is proposed as an alternative.

personnel department *n* (1943) the department within an organization concerned with the recruitment and well-being of its personnel. Later shortened to *personnel* (first recorded in 1960)

> 1943 J. B. Priestley: Mr. Cheviot…was very keen on the personnel department and welfare generally.

> 1960 Muriel Spark: I'm just mentioning a factor that Personnel keep stressing.

phoney war *n* (1940) the period of comparative inaction at the beginning of World War II, lasting from September 1939 to May 1940. See also **sitzkrieg (1940)**

> 1940 *Times*: When the Allies seemed slow at getting off the mark,…it was whispered to the American public that this was a 'phoney' war.

> 1940 *Manchester Guardian Weekly*: During the eight months of the 'phoney' war everything seemed to be running smoothly between Great Britain and France.

pile *n* (1942) a nuclear reactor

> 1945 *War Illustrated*: The natural uranium (U238) is in the shape of rods embedded in a graphite block and contained in an atomic 'pile'.

pile in *v* (1944) to crash an aircraft. R.A.F. slang

> 1944 G. Netherwood: So low did Pilot Officer Weeks fly as he did the Victory Roll, that those watching him made certain that he would 'pile in'.

pink lady *n* (1944) a cocktail comprising gin, egg white, grenadine, and other ingredients. US

> 1944 Saul Bellow: She had been drinking Pink Ladies, and she was running over.

pin-point *adj* (1944) performed with great positional accuracy. Originally applied to the bombing of targets

> 1944 *Manchester Guardian*: Fighter Command's activities included thirty missions against V2 targets in Holland, where pin-point power-dive attacks resulted in direct hits on erection and launching installations.

pin-up *adj, n* (1941) Denoting a favourite or sexually attractive young person, the typical subject of a photograph fixed to a wall, etc. Originally US

> 1941 *Life*: Dorothy Lamour is No. 1 pin-up girl of the U.S. Army.

> 1943 *Sun*: (Baltimore): Bob Hope, radio and film comedian, today emerged victorious as the official pin-up boy of the WAC contingent here.

pissed off *adj* (1946) angry, irritated; fed-up, depressed. Slang, originally US

> 1948 Norman Mailer: I bet you even look pissed-off when you're with your wife.

pit-bull terrier *n* (1945) a small, stocky, short-coated dog belonging to the American breed so called, usually fawn or brindled in colour, with white markings. It was originally bred for dog-fighting. Its name (often shortened to *pit-bull*) was not well known in Britain before large numbers were imported in the early 1990s. Instances of attacks on children caused a furore and led to the Dangerous Dogs Act (see **dangerous dog (1991)**)

> 1945 *Sun* (Baltimore): Mrs. Dorella Zinke…died within 90 minutes after a mass attack by nine pit bull terriers.

> 1974 Ross Thomas: He held a leash that was attached to an aged English pit bull that waddled…and wheezed.

pixie hood *n* (1940) a pointed hood

> 1950 Barbara Pym: They stood in the doorway,…wearing mackintoshes, and that wet-weather headgear so unbecoming to middle-aged ladies and so incongruously known as a 'pixie hood'.

pizzeria *n* (1943) a place where pizzas are made, sold, or eaten. Originally US. The word and the concept came from Italy but have long since been swamped by international fast-food culture (see also **pizza (1935)**)

> 1977 *New Zealand Listener*: Between performances he telephoned his wife in London, pottered around on the golf course, downed Newcastle ale and frequented 'The Pinocchio', a Sunderland pizzeria.

plasticize *v* (1940) to treat or make with plastic

> 1940 *New Statesman*: An enterprising silk manufacturer…'plasticised' gold lace so that it became a permanent table-cloth when used as a table-surface.

play group *n* (1942) a group, often one organized informally by parents of pre-school children, formed with the object of providing supervised companionship for children

> 1942 C. Landreth: For this group probably the best immediate solution under 1942 conditions is parents' cooperative backyard play groups.

> 1962 *Guardian*: A pre-school play group which a group of mothers are organising.

plutonium *n* (1942) a transuranic metallic element which is formed indirectly from uranium in nuclear reactors and occurs naturally in trace amounts, is chemically similar to uranium, and is very reactive; the longest-lived isotope (plutonium 244) is produced for use in nuclear weapons and as fuel. The name was given to it because it is the next element after neptunium in the periodic table, as Pluto is the planet next beyond Neptune. It was previously applied to barium in the early 19th century, but this usage did not survive long

> 1942 Seaborg & Wahl: Since such formulae are confusing when the symbols '93' and '94' are used, we have decided to use symbols of the conventional chemical type to designate these elements. Following McMillan, who has suggested the name neptunium…for element 93, we are using plutonium…for element 94. The corresponding chemical symbols would be Np and Pu.

point *n* (1940) a unit of value and exchange in rationing

> 1940 *Economist*: Textiles are sharply rationed [in Holland]... On August 12th, the German system of a clothing card of 100 points was introduced.

> 1944 Marghanita Laski: You always seem to forget that breakfast cereals cost points.

> 1944 *Times*: From April 2 imported tinned marmalade will be available on points, and will not be, as hitherto, part of the preserve ration.

polo neck *n* (1944) a high close-fitting roll collar. From the round neckline of the shirts worn by polo players

> 1944 Nevil Shute: A grey jumper with a polo neck.

> 1973 Martin Amis: He was wearing a fashionable black polo-neck jersey (fashionable, that is, among the weasly middle-aged).

polyurethane *n* (1944) a type of synthetic material commonly used in foams and fibres and in flexible forms. The original name was *polyurethan*, but the form with the final -*e* has proved more durable

> 1944 *Chemical Abstracts* (heading): Polyurethans and polyureas.

> 1945 *Modern Plastics*: Polyurethane resin was used on a small scale as an adhesive in aircraft construction.

pool *n* (1940) the unbranded petrol which was the only grade available in Britain during and just after World War II

> 1940 M. Nicholson: In war [petrol] all goes round in grey tankers and is all called 'Pool'.

postindustrial *adj* (1947) Denoting a society no longer based on heavy industry. A buzzword particularly of the final quarter of the century, as traditional 'metal-bashing' took up progressively less and less of the productive capacity of the First World

> 1947 *Partisan Review*: Industrial organization and the postindustrial state are here to stay.

> 1977 *Times*: We are already laying the foundation for the post-industrial future.

postmodern *adj* (1949) subsequent to, or later than, what is 'modern'. Early uses of the term are all fairly general in application, but in the 1960s it began to be employed specifically in the arts to denote a movement in reaction against that designated 'modern' (the derivatives *postmodernism* and *postmodernist* date from this period). It became best known in the late 1970s in its application to a school of architecture that reverted to more traditional, formal, even classical styles

> 1949 J. Hudnut (heading): Post-modern house... He shall be a modern owner, a post-modern owner, if such a thing is conceivable. Free from all sentimentality or fantasy or caprice.

> 1966 Frank Kermode: Pop fiction demonstrates 'a growing sense of the irrelevance of the past' and Top [sic] writers ('post-Modernists') are catching on.

> 1979 *Time*: The nearest man Post-Modernism has to a senior partner is, in fact, the leading American architect of his generation: Philip Cortelyou Johnson.

PR *n* (1942) An abbreviation of **public relations** '(the maintenance of) a good relationship between an organization, firm, etc., and the general public, by means of advertising, positive communication, etc.' This latter term is first recorded as long ago as 1807, in the writings of Thomas Jefferson ('Questions calling for the notice of Congress, unless indeed they shall be superseded by a change in our public relations now awaiting the determination of others'), but it did not become institutionalized in its full modern meaning until the second decade of the 20th century ('Effective publicity to deal with questions of public relations and to consider the molding of public opinion by the presentation of real facts', *Electric Railway Journal* (1913)), since when it has inserted its soft focus into most aspects of our lives

> 1944 A. Jacob: The remains of the P.R. unit set off down the desert road.

> 1963 H. Kubly: Your students are giving you an excellent PR.

> 1977 *Time*: The p.r. man behind this is the star.

prang *v* (1941) to crash or crash-land (an aircraft). Originally R.A.F. slang, but its origins are unknown; later extended in British English to crashing cars, etc. Also used as a noun

> 1941 *Tee Emm* (Air Ministry): Do they give a grateful sigh and shut up shop when the last serviceable aircraft has been pranged against a hangar because its pilot would land towards obstacles?

> 1943 Hunt & Pringle: 'P/O Prune' is the title bestowed upon a pilot who has several 'prangs' on his record.

> 1944 Nevil Shute: After so many operations it was an acute personal grief to him that he had pranged his Wimpey.

precinct *n* (1942) a part of a town or community designated for a specific purpose. Originally a fairly generalized concept in town planning, but by the 1950s the term was being used specifically in the context of areas from which motor vehicles are excluded, especially to allow pedestrians to shop in safety (see **pedestrian precinct (1953)**)

> 1942 H. A. Tripp: A great number of pockets will have been created, each of which will consist of a little local system of minor roads, devoted to industrial, business, shopping or residential purposes... Each pocket represents in its way a separate little community... The best term...seems to be 'precinct'.

> 1958 *Listener*: The exclusion of wheeled traffic from the main shopping precinct.

precooked *adj* (1946) cooked and then preserved in some way (e.g. by freezing) for future consumption. Originally US. A foretaste of dinners to come in the second half of the 20th century; the insensitivity of the coinage (all food that is cooked is by definition 'pre-'cooked) somehow mirrors the underlying attitude to food

> 1946 *Fortune*: A high-priced Restaurant carrying a sideline of precooked quick-frozen meals on plastic plates.

> 1957 *Daily Mail*: Pre-cooked hamburgers...in their little frozen transparent plastic bags.

prefab *n* (1942) See **prefab (1937)**

preggers *adj* (1942) pregnant. British slang. Probably based mainly on other similar adjectives such as **crackers (1928)** and **starkers (1923)**, but also evidence of the continuing vitality of the British upper-middle-class all-purpose suffix -*ers*. It and its singular form -*er* were in widespread use in the last two decades of the 19th century and the first two of the 20th, tacked on to a range of nouns (at one point, for instance, the Prince of Wales was dubbed the 'Pragger-Wagger': 'The P-Wagger came to see us yesterday. I met him coming off parade, and threw a hairy salute', D. O. Barnett (1914)). This was the first flush of its fashionability, initially among Oxford undergraduates. However, as the century has advanced, it has refused to die completely; a sort of nostalgia keeps it going, and in the 1990s it is still used facetiously in nicknames ('Bad miss, Godders', Godfrey Smith (1998)). See also **Harry (1941)**

> 1942 Monica Dickens: Let anyone mention in her hearing that they felt sick, and it would be all over the hospital that they were 'preggers'.

press-up *n* (1947) an exercise in which the body is raised from a prone position by straightening the arms while keeping the hands and feet on the ground and the legs straight

> 1947 James Bertram: Press-ups are a fairly strenuous exercise at the best of times.

probable *n* (1940) an aircraft recorded as probably shot down

> 1940 *Winged Words*: They were the new Heinkel 113s... We got...three or four of what we call 'probables'.

> 1944 *Saturday Evening Post*: I chalked him up with only a probable, because I did not see it crash.

program *n, v* (1945) a set of instructions that are fed into a computer to enable it to perform operations on data. The verb senses 'to supply (a computer) with a program' and 'to organize or convert (data) into a program' are first recorded in the same year. A usage of American origin, so it was eventually the US spelling *program* which became the World English form (although at first *programme* was preferred in British English)

> 1945 J. P. Eckert et al. *Description of ENIAC* (University of Pennsylvania): The problem of programming the ENIAC... In this fashion, problems involving numbers of multiplications far in excess of 24 can be programmed.

> 1946 *Nature*: Control of the programme of the operation of the machine [i.e. ENIAC, an early form of computer] is also through electrical circuits.

psychological warfare *n* (1940) the use of hostile or subversive propaganda to undermine morale and cause confusion and uncertainty. See also **war of nerves (1940)**

> 1940 *Current History*: Psychological warfare and how to wage it… Psychological warfare is the fight conducted by the state with psychological weapons to strengthen its own prestige…and to weaken that of the enemy.

> 1949 *Sun* (Baltimore): Miss Gillars…is accused…of betraying her country by aiding Hitler's psychological warfare program over a period of more than four years.

punch-card *n* (1945) a card in which holes are punched to represent data to be processed by a computer or other machine. The underlying principle was established at the beginning of the 19th century in the Jacquard loom, which used such cards to facilitate the weaving of patterned fabrics, and the term *punched card* is recorded before the end of the century. The adoption of *punch-card* is roughly contemporary with the use of the cards for feeding information to the new-fangled computers

> 1945 J. von Neumann: These instructions must be given in some form which the device can sense: Punched into a system of punchcards [etc.].

purchase tax *n* (1940) a tax levied in Britain between 1940 and 1973 on goods bought at a rate that was higher on luxuries than on more essential goods

> 1940 *Manchester Guardian Weekly*: The purchase tax came into operation on Monday [20 October], amid some confusion and protest… The tax imposes $33\frac{1}{3}$ per cent on the wholesale value of luxury goods and $16\frac{2}{3}$ per cent on other more essential commodities.

> 1972 *Times*: Ribena…was held not to be a drug or medicine and therefore not exempt from purchase tax.

PVC *n* (1941) The abbreviation by which **polyvinyl chloride (1933)** is more commonly known

> 1970 *Oxford Mail*: Courreges' best inspiration for ready-to-wear were his flare-legged cat suits in P.V.C. or cotton.

quiche *n* (1949) an open flan or tart with a savoury filling, a speciality of the Lorraine region of France. Originally in Britain largely confined to cookbooks and cookery columns as an alien strangeness, the quiche was suddenly fashionable and then omnipresent in the 1970s. The predictable reaction set in, and it soon became a sad derided thing in some quarters, with a reputation for vegetarian wimpishness. The word itself comes ultimately, via French, from German *Kuchen* 'cake'

> 1949 André Simon: *Quiche*, a savoury custard in an open tart, a Lorraine spécialité.

> 1979 Posy Simmonds: Quiches are marvellous! They're all out of my freezer. Now, the vegetarian ones are at the front.

Quisling *n* (1940) a traitor to one's country; someone who collaborates with occupying forces, especially during World War II. A generic use of the name of Major Vidkun Quisling (1887–1945), Norwegian officer and diplomat (real name Abraham Lauritz Jonsson), who collaborated with the Germans during their occupation of Norway from 1940 to 1945. The term was taken up with some enthusiasm during World War II (perhaps partly because it has a sound suggestive of mean-spiritedness and untrustworthiness), and was even transformed into a verb, *quisle* 'to betray one's country'

> 1940 *Times*: Comment in the Press urges that there should be unremitting vigilance also against possible 'Quislings' inside the country [i.e. Sweden]… There seem to have been no Quislings, partly because it was unnecessary to 'quisle' in a country which, as the Nazis have always said 'could be taken by telephone'.

> 1941 *Sun* (Baltimore): No report of the size of the attacking fleet…was given, but small craft actually allowed British and Norwegian troops to take 215 Germans and ten 'Quislings' as prisoners.

quiz *n* (1941) a form of competitive entertainment, especially on radio and television, in which questions are put to individuals or to a team. Originally US; a specialization of the earlier sense 'a set of questions to be answered as an entertainment'

1941 *Scribner's Commentator* (heading): Quiz by the Quiz kids.

1946 F. Wakeman: Vic had heard a story of how he went to a sponsor all primed to sell a quiz show.

1956 *B.B.C. Handbook 1957*: Archaeology triumphantly holds its special place with its somewhat unexpected quiz presentation of 'Animal, Vegetable, Mineral?'

Quonset hut *n* (1942) The proprietary name in the US for a kind of prefabricated building consisting of a semi-cylindrical corrugated metal roof on a bolted steel foundation. Effectively the US equivalent of the **Nissen hut (1917)**. The name comes from Quonset Point, Rhode Island, where the hut was first manufactured

1943 *Popular Mechanics*: 'Quonset Huts', those portable barracks, begin replacing the tent city.

radar *n* (1941) a system for detecting the presence of objects at a distance, or ascertaining their position or motion, by transmitting short radio waves and detecting or measuring their return after being reflected. Originally US; an acronym formed from the initial letters of *radio detection and ranging*, which eventually supplanted the synonymous **radiolocation (1941)** in British English. See also **sonar (1946)**

1941 *New York Times*: The Navy undertook a special enlistment campaign today to recruit men for training in maintenance of the radio device known as 'Radar', which is used to locate ships and aircraft that are hidden by fog or darkness.

1943 *News Chronicle*: He described Radar as 'probably the most dramatic new weapon to come out of this war'.

radioastronomy *n* (1948) the branch of astronomy concerned with the study and interpretation of radio waves reaching the earth from space, and with the astronomical use of radio-echo techniques. See also **radio telescope (1948)**

1948 *Science News Letter*: Radioastronomy is a new branch of astronomy only recently announced, Dr. Shapley stated. By use of high-frequency radio waves meteors are tracked in their flight.

radiolocation *n* (1941) The term originally used in Britain for **radar** (1941); the determination of the position and course of ships, aircraft, etc., by means of radar. It had gone out of active use by the end of the 1940s

1941 *Flight*: In the Battle of Britain the advantages of radiolocation were even more apparent.

1942 *R.A.F. Journal*: By what, then, is the R.A.F. kept in the air?… Its radio-location girls,…its operations staff?

radio telescope *n* (1948) an apparatus or installation for detecting and recording radio waves from the sky with great sensitivity and a high degree of resolution, consisting essentially of a large sensitive directional aerial together with a receiver and recording equipment. An invention which has enabled humankind in the latter part of the 20th century to peer into the remotest corners of the universe and pass backwards towards the moment of its creation. The term is actually first recorded long before the device itself existed, but not in this instance as a case of uncannily accurate prediction—it was merely used to denote a fictitious apparatus in which some sort of radio device was attached to an optical telescope ('Well, what do you think of it?… How do you like my radio-telescope?' *Amazing Stories* (1929)). See also **radioastronomy (1948)**

1948 *Newsweek*: The newer radio telescope…is designed to gather radio static in the microwave region.

1953 *New York Times*: The foundations of Britain's million-dollar radio telescope…are now being built at Jodrell Bank, Cheshire.

ramjet *n* (1942) a simple form of jet engine in which the air used for combustion is compressed solely by the forward motion of the engine. The German V-1 flying bomb was powered by a type of ramjet

1942 *29th Annual Report of the US National Advisory Committee on Aeronautics*: An experimental investigation of an idealized ram-jet propulsion system was conducted in the…wind tunnel at the Langley Memorial Aeronautical Laboratory in March 1941.

ratings *n* (1947) an estimate, based on statistical sampling, of the size of the audience of any particular radio or television programme. Originally US. The system was set up by Archibald M. Crossley, who in 1930 began the regular reports of the Cooperative Analysis of Broadcasting. These were at first known, in his honour, as *Crossley ratings*, or just *Crossleys* for short ('You've heard some radio comedian crack, after getting off a poor gag, "There goes my Crossley". He is referring to his popularity rating with one of the services that measure…the size of radio listening audiences', *Business Week* (1939)). The unadorned *ratings* is not recorded in print until 1947

> 1947 *Billboard*: The majority of new shows on the air—so far at least—are failing to show evidence of any particular rating strength. This is especially true when ratings are related to talent budgets.

> 1971 *Daily Telegraph*: Though the two BBC channels between them still share the ratings with ITV on a 50–50 basis, the trend is sufficiently strong to alarm the major companies.

> 1980 *Times*: The ratings war—the battle to win as many viewers as possible for a programme.

recce *n, v* (1941) (to make) a reconnaissance. Military slang. In World War I the abbreviation was *recco* (1917), but World War II *recce* has largely superseded it

> 1942 Evelyn Waugh: The C.O. has just gone forward with his recce group to make his recce.

> 1943 J. H. Fullarton: We're even reccying alternative positions twenty miles back to withdraw to.

redbrick *adj* (1943) Used, often condescendingly, to denote a British university founded in the late nineteenth or early twentieth century in a large industrial city, with buildings of red-brick, as distinct from the older universities (especially Oxford, Cambridge, the ancient universities of Scotland, and some of the London colleges) built predominantly in stone, and also as distinct from the new universities founded after World War II. First recorded in a book called *Redbrick University* by 'Bruce Truscot' (the pseudonym of E. Allison Peers, Gilmour Professor of Spanish at Liverpool University 1922–52)

> 1943 Bruce Truscot: The range of interests represented in a Redbrick staff common-room… It may be natural enough for him to go on to Red-brick, but to…enter Oxbridge is something infinitely more exciting.

> 1944 H. Ashton: Marriner took his professorship at that frightful red-brick university.

re-entry *n* (1948) the return of a spacecraft into the earth's atmosphere. Coined when such an event was no more than a theoretical possibility, but surviving into actuality. See also **re-enter (1961)**

> 1948 *Journal of the British Interplanetary Society*: The technique of atmospheric re-entry will be developed from progressively daring excursions into space.

> 1961 *Guardian*: The vapour trail caused by the re-entry of the capsule.

reffo *n* (1941) a European refugee, especially a refugee who left Germany or German-occupied Europe before World War II. Australian slang, formed with the all-purpose 20th-century Australian colloquial suffix *-o* (other examples include *cemo* for *cemetary*, *euco* for *eucalyptus*, and *garbo* for *garbage (man)*)

> 1951 Cusack & James: 'The woman's a Viennese.' 'Oh, a reffo?'

> 1955 Jon Cleary: She talked even now in her letters of the Dagoes and Balts and reffos, the New Australians, who were taking over the country.

Remembrance Sunday *n* (1942) See **Remembrance Day (1921)**

Resistance *n* (1944) the underground movement formed in France in June 1940 with the object of resisting the authority of the German occupying forces and the Vichy government. A concrete application of the abstract *resistance* (1939). Subsequently applied to similar movements in other countries. See also **Maquis (1944)**

> 1944 *Daily Telegraph*: Mr. Wareing reveals…the existence of a Resistance plan to seize power.

> 1946 Aldous Huxley: I was sent a number of French books recently… Novels about the Resistance—half heroism, half unutterable moral squalor.

rhesus *n* (1941) Used (mainly in compounds such as *rhesus-positive*, *rhesus-negative*, and *rhesus factor*) with reference to a major blood group consisting of three principal antigens to which naturally occurring antibodies are rare, and which are important because hæmolytic disease of the newborn is usually the result of antibodies produced in the blood of a rhesus-negative mother in response to the rhesus-positive blood of the fetus. So called from being first discovered in the rhesus monkey. Commonly abbreviated to *Rh*

> 1941 *American Journal of Obstetrics & Gynecology*: In the great majority of the cases the blood factor involved has been shown to be either identical with or related to the Rh (Rhesus) agglutinogen first described by Landsteiner and Wiener with the aid of rabbit sera prepared by injection of Rhesus blood.

> 1943 *British Medical Journal*: Treat these infants by transfusion with rhesus-negative blood, free of agglutinins and thus test out the recommendation that rhesus-negative blood would produce better results than rhesus-positive blood.

rhubarb *n* (1943) a low-level flight for opportunistic strafing. World War II airforce slang

> 1943 *Time*: When a fighter pilot flies low over France, strafing whatever he finds—trains, troops, airdromes—he is 'on a rhubarb'.

> 1956 Johnny Johnson: Usually our *Rhubarb* efforts yielded little more than a staff car... I loathed those *Rhubarbs* with a deep, dark hatred.

robomb *n* (1944) A blend based on **robot bomb (1944)**. Despite its obvious attractions for newspaper headline writers, it did not survive long

> 1944 *Saturday Night* (Toronto): Germany's robombs another case of 'too little and too late'.

robot bomb *n* (1944) An early but short-lived alternative to **flying bomb (1944)**. Also sometimes shortened to simply *robot*

> 1944 *New York Times*: Germans' robot bomb is a potential menace.

> 1944 *Daily Telegraph*: Many of the robots launched against England on Sunday night finished up in the sea.

robotics *n* (1941) the art or science of the design, construction, operation, and application of robots and the like. Originally coined as a science-fiction term, but now more generally used of automatic processes in industry. The coiner was the Russian-born writer and biochemist Isaac Asimov (1920–92), and it was he too who in 1942 formulated the so-called 'laws of robotics', a set of rules for governing the actions of robots (see the second quote below)

> 1941 Isaac Asimov: There's irony in three of the greatest experts in robotics in the world falling into the same elementary trap, isn't there?

> 1968 Isaac Asimov: Eventually, I formulated these safeguards in the shape of 'The Three Laws of Robotics'. 1. A robot may not injure a human being or, through inaction, allow a human being to come to harm. 2. A robot must obey the orders given it by human beings, except where such orders would conflict with the First Law. 3. A robot must protect its own existence, except where such protection would conflict with the First or Second Law.

> 1979 *Topic* (Imperial College, London): Support is planned for...new computer applications (e.g. industrial robotics).

rock *n* (1946) an ice-cube or crushed ice for use in a drink. Usually used in the plural, in the phrase *on the rocks*, denoting a spirit served with ice. Colloquial, originally US

> 1948 F. Brown: A slug or two of rock and rye won't hurt you.

> 1949 *Life*: Ordering a Scotch on the rocks at the bar.

rock *v* (1948) to perform, or dance vigorously and in an improvised way to, popular music with a strong beat. In early use, the term often had sexual connotations. In the early 1950s it gradually shaded into the more specific 'to play or dance to rock and roll music' (see **rock and roll (1954)**)

> 1948 Moore & Reig (song-title): We're gonna rock.

> 1953 Freedman & De Knight (song-title): We're gonna rock around the clock.

> 1956 *Look*: Elvis Presley. The hottest thing rockin', sings throbbing lyrics that sound almost unintelligible.

rodent officer *n* (1944), **rodent operative** *n* (1944), **rodent operator** *n* (1946) someone who rids houses of rats or other vermin. A respectable-sounding job-title for the lowly rat-catcher. A later refinement was *rodent controller* (1970)

> 1944 *Liverpool Echo*: Westminster City Council's rat-catcher is in future to be called Rodent Officer.

> 1944 *Sunday Times*: When it comes to official jargon, can you beat turning our old friend the rat-catcher into a 'Rodent Operative'?

> 1979 John Gardner: 'Are you a rat-catcher, Mr. Kruger?'…'They are called rodent operatives nowadays.'

role-playing *n* (1943) the deliberate acting of a particular role, often used as a technique in training or psychotherapy. Apparently formed from *role-player* (also first recorded in 1943), which itself was a translation of German *Rollenspieler*

> 1943 J. L. Moreno: It may be useful to differentiate between *role-taking*…—*role-playing*—which permits the individual some degree of freedom—and *role-creating*.

roll-on *n* (1941) a type of elasticated corset designed to be stepped into and rolled up on to the body. Originally US

> 1945 *Richmond* (Virginia) *Times-Dispatch*: A start could be made by changing the corsets—reminiscent of cumbersome bone and lacing styles—and attracting young women with the idea of…roll-ons.

Roxy *n* (1940) The nickname of Samuel Lionel Rothafel (1882–1936), US radio and film entrepreneur, used to denote people and things connected with the chain of cinemas built by him

> 1940 F. Scott Fitzgerald: It's very modern to be taking dramatic criticism although it reminds me vaguely of the school for Roxy ushers.

RSJ *n* (1940) An abbreviation of *rolled steel joist*

> 1978 *Private Eye*: We had…three RSJs put across the ceiling to stop the upstairs coming downstairs.

rumpus room *n* (1940) a room set aside for recreation, which does not need to be kept tidy. Originally North American

> 1940 *Chatelaine*: Off through a double-doored hallway can be seen the 'rumpus room', that dennish haunt of Priscilla and Rosemary.

saturation *adj* (1942) Denoting intensive bombing of an area, with the aim of destroying the target by sheer quantity of bombs

> 1943 *Time*: According to U.S. testimony, the precision bombing of the American forces is more effective, ton for ton, than the saturation bombing of the R.A.F.

scramble *v* (1940) to make a rapid take-off; to become airborne quickly. Originally R.A.F. usage (see the second quote below), applied to Battle of Britain fighter squadrons' swift response when German raiders were spotted. Also used as a transitive verb, meaning 'to order a squadron to scramble', and as a noun

> 1940 G. Barclay: The squadron scrambled and intercepted some Do215s and Me110s… The squadron was off the ground which was the main thing, but they were scrambled too late to intercept… I came on the stage after this scrap and we had three scrambles.

> 1962 R. W. Clark: Another great time-saver was the use of a code for passing instructions to the fighters, and such R.A.F. terms as 'scramble' (for take-off)…were invented during these experiments [on radar interception, 1936].

screw *v* (1949) Used in curses and other impassioned exclamations, as an equivalent to *fuck*. Slang, originally US; based on the use of *screw* for 'to copulate', which dates back at least to the early 18th century

> 1949 Arthur Miller: 'In the business world some of them think you're crazy.'… 'Screw the business world!'

> 1960 Roald Dahl: 'Don't shout. There might be keepers.' 'Screw the keepers!' he cried.

second front *n* (1941) In World War II, a front in Nazi-occupied Europe in addition to the Russian sector of fighting. A concept much discussed in the middle years of the war, and a reality much desired by the Soviet Union, to relieve it of what it saw as its unfair share of the land-war against Germany. Despite various plans hatched by Winston Churchill and others, it did not begin to happen until D-Day in 1944

> 1941 Winston Churchill: There is no chance…of a second front being formed in the Balkans without the help of Turkey.

> 1942 *New Statesman*: The key to victory is to open…that 'second front in continental Europe' for which Stalin has publicly called.

Second World War *n* (1942) An alternative name for **World War II (1939)**. H. G. Wells had anticipated the term in 1930, in a heading in his book *The Autocracy of Mr. Parham*: 'Book the Fourth: The Second World War'

> 1942 *Political Science Quarterly*: The economic developments associated with the second World War have restored to American railroads a volume of traffic comparable to that which they handled before the great depression.

Security Council *n* (1944) a principal council of the United Nations consisting of a core of permanent members (originally the chief victors of World War II: China, France, UK, USA, USSR) and temporarily of ten others, charged with the settlement of disputes. Its peace-keeping role is reflected in its name (see **security (1925)**)

> 1944 *Times*: Tentative proposals have been made for the establishment of a general international organization under the title of The United Nations. The proposals…deal with…its principal organs, including a General Assembly, a Security Council, and an International Court of Justice.

Sellotape *n* (1949) The proprietary name (registered in 1949) of a plastic self-adhesive tape. The element *Sell-* is based on the first syllable of *cellulose*, reflecting the material from which it was originally made. First recorded as a verb, 'to stick with Sellotape', in 1960

> 1957 *Landfall* (New Zealand): Does she want to come a cropper, dashed earthward by wings casually fastened with sellotape?

> 1964 Angus Wilson: He continued to sellotape Beth's caricatures to the walls.

serial *adj* (1947) Applied to a type of musical composition which takes as its starting-point an arrangement of the twelve tones of the chromatic scale (compare **atonal (1922)** and **twelve-tone (1926)**)

> 1947 Humphrey Searle: Fartein Valen, whose *Sonetto di Michelangelo*…uses a serial technique derived from Berg.

service industry *n* (1941) See **services (1936)**

sexploitation *n* (1942) the exploitation of sex, especially in films. Originally US. The blend may have been new in the 1940s, but *sex exploitation* is first recorded as long before as 1914. The lexical template later produced **blaxploitation (1972)**

> 1948 G. V. Desani: Damme, make the eternal triangle pay out a dividend! First that Portuguese feller victimised, then self! Damme, sexploitation!

shaky do *n* (1942) a difficult or risky situation, a close shave. Dated British slang, originally R.A.F.

> 1942 Terence Rattigan: They had rather a shaky do last night.

> 1944 T. H. Wisdom: No. 18 Squadron, which had been involved in many similar 'Shaky do's', was asked to lay on the raid.

shazam *interj* (1940) A magic word used like 'abracadabra' to introduce an extraordinary deed or story. An invented word, reputedly coined from the initial letters of 'Solomon's wisdom, Hercules' strength, Atlas' stamina, Zeus' power, Achilles' courage, and Mercury's speed'

> 1940 *Whiz Comics*: 'Speak my name!' 'Shazam!'…As Billy speaks the magic word he becomes Captain Marvel.

shelterer *n* (1940) someone taking shelter from an air-raid

> 1940 Rose Macaulay: The Central London tube was so crammed with thousands of shelterers that I couldn't get near the platform.

shorty, shortie *adj* (1949) Designating garments which are shorter than the norm. In due course largely superseded by **mini- (1934)** and **mini (1963)**

> 1949 *Sun* (Baltimore): Short and sugary…cool and comfy…these delicious Rayon Jersey Shortie Pajamas in pastel shades.

> 1960 *News Chronicle*: They were sacked…after a party in which they staged their own version of Florence Nightingale in the nurses' home, dancing about in 'shortie' nighties waving lighted candles.

showcase *v* (1945) to display as if in a showcase; to exhibit in a favourable context. Originally US

> 1949 *Journal* (Baltimore): They showcase new acts, who want to be on TV.

shufti *n* (1943) a look. Originally British services' slang; usually used in the expression *have* or *take a shufti*. It appears to have come into English as a verb ('The orderly room sergeant to a Waaf clerk as he sights a squadron of Liberators through the headquarters' window, "Shufty!" ', C. H. Ward-Jackson, 1943), but it did not survive very long in this mode; the noun, however, proved more robust. It was picked up by British service personnel in North Africa from Arabic *šufti* 'have you seen?'

> 1943 *Gen*: Take a shufti at that. That's Stephanie.

> 1947 D. M. Davin: She took another good shufty at us.

simulated *adj* (1942) manufactured in imitation of other, usually more expensive materials or goods. Originally US; part of the small change of 20th-century commercial euphemism

> 1960 *Harper's Bazaar*: Eyelash curlers in simulated gold.

> 1973 *Country Life*: A set of 8 Regency Period Simulated Rosewood Dining Chairs.

simulcast *v, n* (1948) to broadcast (a programme) simultaneously on radio and television. Also, a programme broadcast in this way. Originally US

> 1948 *New York Herald-Tribune*: A press agent at WCAU-TV in Philadelphia has rather timorously launched the verb 'simulcast' into the uneasy seas of the English language.

> 1951 *Time*: Allen alone of the top announcers 'simulcasts'—broadcasts games simultaneously for both radio and TV.

single *n* (1949) a record with only one item (typically, of pop music) on each side

> 1949 *Billboard* (headline): Best-selling pop singles.

> 1965 George Melly: His version of 'Rock Island Line', originally part of a Chris Barber in Concert LP, was requested so often on the radio that it was put out as a single and rose to be top of the Hit Parade.

sitrep *n* (1943) a situation report—services' jargon for a report keeping interested parties informed of the progress of events. World War II saw a huge efflorescence of all sorts of abbreviated forms—initialisms, acronyms, conjunctions of miscellaneous syllables—most of which, like *sitrep*, emanated from the military, where time spent on lengthy locutions was time wasted (see **acronym (1943)**)

> 1943 J. H. Fullarton: The daily Sit. Rep. had now identified seven Italian and at least three German divisions in the line.

> 1955 Evelyn Waugh: The B.G.S. said: 'We got a sitrep from the Halberdiers three hours ago.'

sitzkrieg *n* (1940) a war, or part of a war, marked by a (relative) absence of active hostilities; specifically that phase of World War II lasting from September 1939 to May 1940 (a period also known as the **phoney war (1940)**). Formed on the analogy of **Blitzkrieg (1939)**, as if from German *sitzen* 'to sit' + *Krieg* 'war'

> 1940 *New York Times*: The R.A.F. referred to the war as a 'Sitzkrieg', which it translated as 'sit-down war'.

> 1943 *Sun* (Baltimore) (headline): Temporary 'sitzkrieg' on Garigliano sector.

sixty-four dollar question *n* (1942) Originally, the question posed at the climax of a US radio quiz called *Take It or Leave It* (1941–48) for a prize of sixty-four dollars, used metaphorically to denote a difficult or crucial question. When the show transferred to US television in 1955, its top prize inflated spectacularly to sixty-four thousand dollars, and this too has entered the language

1942 J. R. Tunis: Here's the sixty-four dollar question. Will the team go to Miami?

1957 *Observer*: Mr. Macmillan said…there was only one answer to the 64,000-dollar question—to increase production.

skyway *n* (1940) an overhead motorway. US

1940 *Sun* (Baltimore): It has been suggested that a skyway be built along Pratt street from Monroe to the Fallsway, the western end to connect with the route to Washington.

slimline *adj* (1949) slim, narrow, gracefully thin in style or appearance. Modelled on **streamline**

1961 *Economist*: Stereophonic equipment, slim-line television, the second wireless set.

slingback *n, adj* (1949) (a woman's shoe) which has an open back and is held on by a strap across the heel. The adjective *sling-backed* is first recorded in 1948

1949 *10 Eventful Years* (*Encyclopedia Britannica*): They were soft suede slippers, little leather sling-backs, ankle-high boots, and ballet slippers of all colours and materials.

snafu *n* (1941) An acronym formed from the initial letters of *situation normal, all fucked up* (sometimes euphemistically explained as *all fouled up*), used in the US military as an expression conveying the common soldier's laconic acceptance of the disorder of war and the ineptitude of his superiors. It soon became a noun, originally denoting 'confusion, muddle', later 'a mix-up or mishap'

1943 *Yank*: They worked hard and steadily, with a minimum of snafu.

1963 Mrs. L. B. Johnson: Pretty soon the German plane rolled in, overshooting the red carpet by a few feet, so there was a slight snafu and they had to hop around to get onto it.

snoek *n* (1947) a large marine food fish found in large shoals in colder parts of Southern Hemisphere oceans. The claim in the quote below is actually far from the literal truth—the word (a borrowing from Dutch) was first used in English in the late 18th century—but it is true that it made a sudden unprecedented (and short-lived) impact in the late 1940s, for the reason stated

1963 S. Cooper: In October 1947…the hungry British first heard the word 'snoek'. Ten million tins of it from South Africa were to replace Portuguese sardines.

snog *v* (1945) to kiss and cuddle. British colloquial. Also used as a noun. Its origins (despite the claim put forward for India in the first quote below) are obscure, although it may have something to do with dialectal *snug* 'to lie close together, cuddle'. It has maintained a remarkable consistency of usage among adolescents over the decades, and in the 1990s enjoyed a new lease of life as a transitive verb

1945 C. H. Ward-Jackson: *Snogging*, courting, running around with the opposite sex. Comes from India. Thus, 'On my leave I'm going up to the hills for a bit of snogging.' Also used as a verb.

1959 W. Camp: Let's pretend we're teenagers and stop for a nice snog.

1995 *Private Eye*: A line of 'nutters' queueing for a turn to snog the Princess of Wales.

snowdrop *n* (1944) a US military policeman. The reason for the nickname is given in the quote below. It persisted for several decades after its coinage

1944 *New York Times*: 'Snowdrops'—the London nickname for white-helmeted American military police—were patroling the sidewalks.

sonar *n* (1946) a system using transmitted and reflected sound waves to detect and locate submerged objects. An acronym based (on the model of **radar (1941)**) on *sound navigation ranging*

1946 *US Navy Press Release*: The word 'sonar' was coined from abbreviations for sound, navigation and ranging, and includes various types of underwater sound devices used in detecting submarines and other submerged objects and in obtaining water depths.

sonic barrier *n* (1946) See **sound barrier (1939)**

sophisticated *adj* (1945) Of equipment, techniques, theories, etc.: employing advanced or refined methods or concepts; highly developed or complicated. A usage which at first attracted the hostility of the linguistic diehards, particularly when, in the 1950s, it began to be widely applied to machinery, weapons, etc. Their objection, that *sophisticated* 'really' means 'refined, cultured', or even (its now moribund original sense) 'adulterated', has cut little ice in the long run. The corresponding use of *sophistication* is first recorded in 1959

> 1945 C. S. Lewis: The man was so very allusive and used gesture so extensively that Mark's less sophisticated modes of communication were almost useless.

> 1956 *New York Times*: Navy scientists are virtually exploring multidimensional space in a time machine in the search for what they call 'sophisticated' high-yield weapons.

> 1959 *Time*: In the past the usual comment was that Russian space vehicles are big and brawny because of more powerful launching rockets, but that U.S. space vehicles, small and elegant, made up for the Russians' gross size by their sophistication.

soul *n* (1946) the emotional or spiritual quality of Black American life and culture, manifested especially in music. See also **soul music (1961)**

> 1954 *Grove's Dictionary of Music*: Louis Armstrong declared that 'Anything played with beat and soul is jazz.'

space age *n* (1946) the period of human exploration and exploitation of space. Often used adjectivally to designate products supposed to be characteristic of this age

> 1946 H. Harper: We have had an age of steam-power, an age of electricity and of the petrol engine, and an age of the air, and now with the coming of atomic power the world should, in due course, find itself in the space age.

> 1980 *Times Literary Supplement*: Our space-age Palace of History—the new computerized Public Record Office at Kew.

spaceman *n* (1942) someone who travels in space. The sense 'someone who comes from another planet' is a later development. When space travel became a reality, **astronaut (1929)** was the largely preferred term, *spaceman* being somewhat tainted by its science-fiction origins

> 1942 *Thrilling Wonder Stories*: Maybe Lambert was a spaceman. Maybe he wasn't, but if he knew anything at all about spaceman's lingo he'd have to give now.

> 1962 Alison Lurie: Amateur experts…Visitors from another world… They think they're space men.

space vehicle *n* (1946) a spacecraft, especially a large one (see **spacecraft (1930)**)

> 1946 *New York Times*: They are to serve as pioneers for the long-range guided missiles and 'space' vehicles.

> 1959 *Times*: In putting a space vehicle on to the moon the Russians have provided the most complete…proof of the length of the lead that they now hold.

sprog *n* (1941) a new recruit; a trainee. British, originally services' slang. It was used in this way particularly in the R.A.F. The Navy, on the other hand, applied it to children, and it was mainly this meaning that later seeped out into the general language. It is not clear where it came from, although it might be related to the obsolete *sprag* 'lively young fellow'

> 1943 J. Hillier: Never mind, Wendy, you sprogs of 'B' flight will learn to fly yet—if you live long enough!

> 1949 Eric Partridge: Nobby Clark's gone on leave, his wife's just had a sprog.

> 1973 Martin Amis: Here I attempted a few minutes' work, not easy because the fifty bawling sprogs had classes there in the afternoon.

squander-bug *n* (1943) A symbol of reckless extravagance and waste, used in Britain in publicity campaigns promoted by the National Savings Committee from 1943 onwards to promote wartime economy and represented as a devilish insect

> 1943 *Times* (advert): Beware the treacherous Squander Bug! He's the prince of fifth-columnists—doesn't believe in a nest-egg for the future—doesn't believe in making money fight for Britain… Join a Savings Group to defeat the Squander Bug!

square *adj, n* (1944) (a person) holding conventional or old-fashioned views. Originally US jazz slang, the opposite of **hep** or **hip**; later, especially in the 1950s, used as general term of teenage condemnation for anyone obviously over 21. The adjective is first recorded in 1946. See also **cube (1957)**

1944 *Sun* (Baltimore): *Square*, in musician's jargon, anyone who is not cognizant of the beauties of true jazz.

1944 Dan Burley: Are you going to be a square all you days?

1950 J. Vedey: Consummate performer that Ellington is, he put these numbers over to the delight of all types of audience, young and old, sophisticated and 'square'.

1956 Ed McBain: This guy is from Squaresville, fellas, I'm telling you. He wouldn't know a .45 from a cement mixer.

1961 *John o' London's*: Where Squareness is the ultimate low, anything can get by if it proclaims itself Hip loudly enough.

square-bashing *n* (1943) military drill. British services' slang

1975 Gavin Black: Attached to a Malay regiment, supervising weapon training and square bashing.

squillion *n* (1943) a very large but indefinite number. Colloquial, originally US; based, like the equally facetious and rather more successful **zillion (1944)**, on *million.*

1943 Z. N. Hurston: The deep blue sea…was a pearly blue, like ten squillion big pearl jewels dissolved in running gold.

Stateside, stateside *adj, adv* (1944) of, in, or towards the United States of America. Originally US

1945 *Sun* (Baltimore): 'Stateside' is a mighty popular word out here [i.e. in Guam] because a service man going 'stateside' is going home.

1963 Len Deighton: Fernie fixed the consignment to a ship heading stateside. I notified my contacts in New York.

steady state *n* (1948) a cosmological theory which embraces the principle that on a large scale the universe is essentially unchanging in time and space. Usually applied specifically to the theory propounded by Bondi, Gold, and Hoyle of a universe expanding at a constant rate, with matter being continuously created so that mean density of the universe remains constant. Compare **big bang (1950)**

1948 Bondi & Gold (heading): The steady-state theory of the expanding universe.

1969 *Times*: The steady state theory…says that the universe looks roughly the same from any position and at any time in the past, present or future.

steel band *n* (1949) a band composed of musicians who play calypso-style music on drums made out of oil drums with one end beaten down and divided into grooved sections to give different notes

1949 *Caribbean Quarterly*: The audience was introduced to…Trinidad's own steel band.

Sten gun *n* (1942) a type of light rapid-fire sub-machine-gun. Its name comes (on the model of **Bren**) from the first letters of the names of its designers, R. V. Shepherd and H. J. Turpin (but see the first quote below), plus the *En-* of Enfield, the north London borough (then in Middlesex) housing the British Royal Small Arms Factory

1942 *Times*: [The gun] was known as the Schmeisser gun, and the Sten was merely a slight modification of it… The Ministry of Supply was not justified in taking to itself high praise for the speed of production of the Sten, and in giving the country the false impression that 'Colonel S' and 'Major T' invented and designed the gun.

1942 George Orwell: Last night for the first time took a Sten gun to pieces.

step out *v* (1942) to parachute out of a (disabled) aircraft. R.A.F. slang

1942 B. J. Ellan: If you are unlucky enough to get shot down yourself, you…step out.

stick *n* (1940) a number (usually five or six) of bombs dropped in quick succession from an aircraft

1940 *Illustrated London News*: A 'stick' of five bombs has just burst across her bows.

stonk *n, v* (1944) (to bombard with) concentrated artillery fire. Military slang; probably from the earlier *stonk* denoting a type of marble, or a game of marbles, which itself may represent the sound of marbles making forceful contact

1944 *Daily Telegraph*: Here was one more message before we left—that British troops on a captured ridge were being 'stonked' heavily.

> 1981 Lord Harewood: You could never tell…if your arrival would bring down an artillery 'stonk' on your head.

stooge *v* (1941) Of an aircraft or pilot: to fly with no particular aim in view; to cruise. R.A.F. slang

> 1941 *Illustrated London News*: We just stooged about watching the bombers drop their loads.

> 1942 Terence Rattigan: We were stooging along over the Dutch coast.

strafe *v* (1942) to attack (a ground target) in a low-flying aircraft. A World War II specialization of a word which entered English with a much wider application during World War I (see **strafe (1915)**)

> 1944 *Sun* (Baltimore): Most of the fighter escort of the 1,600 bombers…dropped to telephone-pole level to strafe trucks and trains heading from Frankfurt to the Saarbrucken battle zone.

straight *adj* (1941) conforming to the conventions of society; especially, heterosexual. Originally US slang. From the idea of not deviating. See also **straight (1967)**

> 1965 *San Francisco Examiner*: A lot of us have 'straight' friends.

sun-bathe *v* (1941) See **sun-bather (1929)**

superbomb *n* (1940) Used as an awestruck name for a projected new bomb of unprecedented destructive power—originally an atomic bomb (the term **atomic bomb** is first recorded in 1914), later a hydrogen bomb

> 1940 O. R. Frisch: Since the energy release in this reaction would be about 105 times larger than in ordinary chemical reactions…it has been feared that it might form the basis for the construction of a super-bomb exceeding the action of ordinary bombs by a factor of 106 or more.

> 1951 W. L. Laurence: 'Is it true about the superbomb?' I asked him. 'Will it really be as much as fifty times as powerful as the uranium or plutonium bomb?'

supercalifragilisticexpialidocious *adj* (1949) wonderful, fantastic. The word (34 letters long in the established spelling) first appeared, recognizably but in slightly different guise, as the title of a song by Parker and Young. It was made popular by the Walt Disney film *Mary Poppins* in 1964. Life Music Co. and the two song-writers brought a copyright-infringement suit in 1965 against the makers of the film. In view of earlier oral uses of the word sworn to in affidavits and dissimilarity between the songs the judge ruled against the plaintiffs. At the end of the century it was still familiar enough to be adapted punningly in a national advertising campaign in Britain ('As far as we know, Sainsbury's offer more kinds of alliaceous vegetables (onions, shallots, garlic, leeks and chives) than any other supermarket. Which must make Sainsbury's the most supercalifragilistic-expialliaceous supermarket in the country' (1997))

> 1949 Parker & Young (unpublished song-title): Supercalafajalistickespialadojus.

> 1964 R. M. & R. B. Sherman (song-title): Supercalifragilisticexpialidocious!

> 1967 *Decisions of the US Courts involving Copyright 1965–66*: The complaint alleges copyright infringement of plaintiff's song 'Supercalafajalistickespeealadojus' by defendants' song 'Supercalifragilisticexpialidocious'. (All variants of this tongue twister will hereinafter be referred to collectively as 'the word'.)

> 1971 *Daily Telegraph*: If you can stand more than a day of Supercalifragilisticexpialidocious entertainment you can settle in at the concrete Contemporary Resort Hotel.

super-duper, super-dooper *adj* (1940) exceptionally good or wonderful. Colloquial, originally US; a reduplicated extension of *super*

> 1942 *Sun* (Baltimore): A week ago officers knew before the curtain rose that something super-duper was about to be staged.

superpower *n* (1944) a nation or state which has a dominant position in world politics, or has the power to act decisively in pursuit of interests which embrace the whole world; usually applied specifically in the post-World War II period to the United States of America and the Union of Soviet Socialist Republics

> 1944 W. T. R. Fox: There will be 'world powers' and 'regional powers'. These world powers we shall call 'super-powers', in order to distinguish them from the other powers…whose interests are great in only a single theater of power conflict.

> 1978 John Updike: Capital investments cleverly pried from the rivalry between the two super-powers (and that shadowy third, China, that has the size but not as it were the mass, the substance, to be called super).

supersonic *adj* (1947) exceptionally good or wonderful. Colloquial; used (especially by boys, small and large) in the days when breaking the sound barrier was still a great adventure (see **supersonic (1934)**)

> 1955 G. Dorman: Ginge's eyes gleamed and he said eagerly,…'Gee, Wing! This is supersonic! Can I be in it too?'

supremo *n* (1944) someone holding the highest (military) authority. A word acquired from Spanish (*generalissimo*)*supremo* 'supreme general', and used sporadically in English in the late 1930s in Spanish contexts. It attached itself as a nickname to Earl Mountbatten of Burma during his period as Supreme Allied Commander, South-East Asia (see the first quote below), and hence came to be applied to anyone holding the highest military command. By the 1960s it was being used colloquially for someone in overall charge in any sphere (see **supremo (1963)**)

> 1944 *Daily Express*: Why the Supremo?… A handsome, romantic figure [i.e. Mountbatten]. Hence the Latin-sounding nickname.

> 1958 *Daily Express*: Now their advice and complaints can reach the Cabinet or the Prime Minister only through their 'supremo'—the chairman of the staff chiefs.

swan *v* (1942) to move about freely or in an (apparently) aimless way. Originally British military slang, and used particularly with reference to armoured vehicles, and to pilots in aircraft. The metaphor derives from the laid-back gracefulness of gliding swans. Also used as a noun

> 1942 *Daily Telegraph*: Breaking up his armour into comparatively small groups of…tanks, he began 'swanning about', feeling north, north-west and east for [British tanks].

> 1946 Lord Montgomery: A recurrence of what was then becoming known in the Eighth Army as the 'annual swan' between Egypt and El Agheila.

> 1980 Dirk Bogarde: She swanned about at the party like the Queen Mother.

sweater girl *n* (1940) a girl, especially a model or actress, who wears tight-fitting sweaters; originally a name applied to the American actress Lana Turner (1920–95) who wore such a sweater in the film *They Won't Forget* (1937), and in subsequent publicity photographs

> 1940 *Movie Mirror*: Sweet and sophisticated sixteen: Lana Turner, at the time her face hit a thousand papers as the 'Sweater Girl'.

> 1941 *Life*: Mr. Breen's letter left movie-makers wondering…what to do with their up-and-coming sweater girls.

tail-end Charlie *n* (1941) a crew member who mans the gun at the rear of a bomber aircraft; a rear-gunner. R.A.F. slang

> 1941 *Illustrated London News*: The 'tail-end Charlie' of a 'Halifax' gives the 'thumbs up' sign just before his machine takes off.

take-over *n* (1946) the assumption of control or ownership of a business concern by another company, especially by the acquisition of the majority of its shares, either by agreement or after a bid. Initial usage seems to have been mainly attributive

> 1946 *Sun* (Baltimore): I am giving this 'take-over' plan the pitiless publicity it deserves.

> 1953 *Times*: A certain type of financial operation described in general terms by Lord Hacking—the recent epidemic of 'take-over bids'.

> 1959 *Punch*: A surge of sentiment for Harrods has set in since the Fraser take-over.

teenager *n* (1941) someone in their teens. Originally US; formed from **teenage (1921)**, and confirming the status of the pre-twenties as a force to be reckoned with (and often patronized) in the second half of the 20th century. See also **teen (1951)**

> 1941 *Popular Science Monthly*: I never knew teen-agers could be so serious.

> 1952 Marguerite Steen: Do we have to behave like a couple of hysterical 'teen-agers?

Teflon *n* (1945) A proprietary name (registered in the US in 1945 by du Pont) for polytetrafluoroethylene, a type of thermoplastic resin with a very low coefficient of friction. The name did not become widely known until the substance began to be used for nonstick pans in the 1960s. Its metaphorical potential began to be exploited in the 1980s (see **Teflon (1983)**)

  1965 *Family Circle*: Won't scratch, scar or mar Teflon coated cookware.

telethon *n* (1949) an especially prolonged television programme used to raise money for a charity or cause. Originally US. The pattern of naming protracted events after the marathon had been set by **walkathon (1932)** and **talkathon (1934)**, but *telethon* was probably the first successful coinage of this sort to adopt the shortened suffix *-thon* (others on record include *moviethon* and *pianothon*)

  1952 *Sun* (Baltimore): Bing Crosby and Bob Hope, in a 14½-hour coast-to-coast telethon today raised more than $1,000,000 in contributions and pledges for the United States Olympic fund.

telly, tellie *n* (1940) A colloquial shortening of **television (1907)**. Original examples are US, but it was later confined largely to Britain, where there is little evidence of its widespread use before the mid 1950s. At first it was quite commonly spelt *tele*, decorously preserving its status as an abbreviation rather than a colloquialism

  1955 Margery Allingham: He…walked back to the village and the telly.

  1956 Angus Wilson: I see him on the Tele.

  1957 *Observer*: For all practical purposes, if it hasn't been on telly, it doesn't exist.

terrorist *n* (1947) a member of a clandestine or expatriate organization aiming to coerce an established government by acts of violence against it or its subjects. A term, as is well known, used by those who do not share the organization's aims; if you think they are laudable, the members are **freedom-fighters (1942)**. The term actually has a long prehistory: it was originally applied (as an anglicization of French *terroriste*) to the Jacobins and their agents and partisans in the French Revolution, especially to those connected with the Revolutionary tribunals during the 'Reign of Terror'; and in the mid 19th century it was used to denote members of any of the extreme revolutionary societies in Russia

  1947 *Annual Register 1946*: The latest and worst of the outrages committed by the Jewish terrorists in Palestine—the blowing up of the King David Hotel in Jerusalem.

  1956 Harold Nicolson: When people rise against foreign oppression, they are hailed as patriots and heroes; but the Greeks whom we are shooting and hanging in Cyprus are dismissed as terrorists. What cant!

Terylene *n* (1946) A proprietary name (registered in Britain in 1947 and in the US in 1949) for polyethylene terephthalate used as a textile fibre. Coined from the first element of *terephthalate* and the last element of *polyethylene*

  1946 *Nature*: A new fibre-forming polymer…to which the name 'Terylene' has been provisionally assigned.

  1958 *New Statesman*: The men who had nylon shirts and terylene suits before those fabrics got into Marks and Spencer's where the rest of us buy our clothes.

Third World War *n* (1947) a hypothetical war, subsequent to World War II, involving most of the world's nations. The concept was in people's minds before World War II ended ('You will have to postpone your visit until the brief interlude between this war & world-war no 3', Duke of Bedford (1945)), and remained there throughout the Cold War. Also termed **World War III (1959)**

  1947 *Civil & Military Gazette*: Sir John Boyd Orr…said in an interview…that a Third World War would be in the making unless some sort of world food plan was established.

thought police *n* (1945) In a totalitarian state, a police force established to suppress freedom of thought. Originally applied specifically in pre-war Japan to the Special Higher Police (*Tokubetsu Koto Keisatsu* or *Tokko*); its use by George Orwell in *1984* popularized it (so to speak) more widely

  1945 *Sun* (Baltimore): It is an order imposing freedom of speech, thought, religion and assembly on the Japanese people, and requiring the immediate liberation of those imprisoned for political offenses by the so-called 'thought police'.

  1949 George Orwell: He had denounced his uncle to the Thought Police after overhearing a conversation which appeared to him to have criminal tendencies.

thrift shop *n* (1947) a shop at which second-hand goods, especially clothes, are sold, usually in aid of charity. Originally and mainly US; the usual British (partial) equivalent is *charity shop*

> 1947 S. J. Perelman: A mound of shawls, brocades, bracelets, necklaces, purses, fans, and bric-a-brac resembling the contents of a thrift shop.

throw *v* (1941) to disconcert or confuse. Colloquial, originally US

> 1941 Budd Schulberg: Don't let Julian's worries throw you.

toecover *n* (1948) an inexpensive and useless present. Colloquial; an interesting example of what apparently began as a piece of private language within a family and spread outwards

> 1948 Betty MacDonald: Toecover is a family name for a useless gift. A crocheted napkin ring is a toecover.

> 1983 *Listener*: Gifts are given, not only the completely useless trivia or 'toe-covers' which litter the surgery, but more substantial gifts, such as briefcases.

tog *n* (1945) a unit of thermal resistance used to express the insulating properties of clothes and duvets. The term is taken from the colloquial *togs*'clothing', on the model of the earlier US term *clo*

> 1945 Peirce & Rees: So that practical clothing may be described conveniently by a range of small integers, the unit of thermal resistance, to be called the 'tog', is the resistance that will maintain a temperature difference of 0.1°C. with a flux of 1 watt per square metre, or in more practical terms, 10°C. with a flux of 1 watt per square decimetre. This is the resistance of a light summer suit, and 10 togs represents about the thickest clothing…practicable to wear.

Tony *n* (1947) any of the medallions that have been awarded annually since 1947 by the American Theatre Wing (New York) for excellence in some aspect of the theatre. The name is taken from the nickname of the US actress, manager, and producer Antoinette Perry (1888–1946)

> 1948 *New York Times*: John Garfield represented the Experimental Theatre in accepting a 'Tony' for 'experiment in theatre'.

trailer home *n* (1940) An alternative term for **mobile home (1940)**. US

> 1940 H. G. Wells: In such large open countries as the United States there has been a considerable development of the mobile home in recent years. People haul a trailer-home behind their cars and become seasonal nomads.

transistor *n* (1948) a semiconductor device in which the load current can be made proportional to a small input current, so that it acts like a valve but is much smaller and more robust, operates at lower voltages, and consumes less power and produces less heat. Invented at Bell Labs in the eastern US in 1947. The word is a blend of *transfer* and *resistor* (a referrence to the transfer of electrical signals across a resistor). Despite the lukewarm prediction in the second quote below, the transistor made possible the development of the computer and all the other electronic devices that have so shaped the second half of the 20th century (including the **transistor radio (1958)**). See also **transistorize (1953)**

> 1948 *New York Times*: A device called a transistor, which has several applications in radio where a vacuum tube ordinarily is employed, was demonstrated for the first time yesterday.

> 1952 *Electronic Engineer*: Although it is unlikely that the transistor will ultimately displace the electronic valve, there is no doubt that for many electronic applications the transistor…will be preferred because of its robust and compact form.

transit camp *n* (1943) a camp for the temporary accommodation of service personnel awaiting posting, refugees, prisoners-of-war, etc. A classic term of the rootless 1940s, when it seemed sometimes that half the population of Europe was en route to somewhere else, propelled by the ill winds of war

> 1946 Eric Linklater: [He] made his escape…from a transit camp for prisoners of war near Bari.

traymobile *n* (1948) a small wheeled table or stand on which food, etc., can be transported. Australian and New Zealand

> 1948 Vance Palmer: Her attention was on the traymobile the girl had wheeled in beside her. She began to pour out the tea.

trickle-down *adj* (1944) of or based on the theory that economic benefits to particular groups will inevitably be passed on to those less well off. Also used as a noun, meaning 'a filtering down (of money or ideas)'. Originally US; the term did not gain a footfold in British English until the 1980s, when right-wing economic theorists used it to justify the Thatcher government's policy of easing the tax burden on the rich

> 1944 *Antioch Review*: In agriculture, as in business, they are devotees of the trickle-down philosophy.

> 1984 *New Yorker*: To Fink this often sounded suspiciously like Republican trickle-down economics.

trick or treat (1947) a formula used at Hallowe'en by children who call on houses threatening to play a trick unless given a treat or present. Originally a US practice, but in the last two decades of the century it spread to Britain. *Trick-or-treating* was an early derivative

> 1947 *American Home*: The household larder needs to be well stocked on October 31, because, from dusk on, the doorbell rings, bright eyes peer through crazy-looking masks, and childish voices in ghostlike tones squeal, croak, or whisper, 'Trick or Treat!'

> 1950 *Sun* (Baltimore): So let the kids go out tonight and have a grand time with their masquerading and trick-or-treating.

trigger-happy *adj* (1943) over-ready to shoot at anything at any time or on slight provocation. The noun *trigger-happiness* is first recorded in 1942

> 1943 F. J. Bell: Yes, they missed us, and the G hereby absolves whoever it was along that section of coast that got a little trigger-happy early one December morning.

TTFN *interj* (1948) goodbye. British colloquial; an initialism conjured from *ta-ta for now* by the character Mrs Mopp (see **Mrs Mopp (1948)**) in the BBC radio comedy series *ITMA* (see the first quote below). It caught on with the public and survived a considerable time in the vocabulary of those initially exposed to it

> 1948 F. Worsley: The beloved Cockney Charlady, Mrs. Mopp (played by Dorothy Summers)…did not make her first appearance…until 10th October, 1941… Another of her famous sayings were the letters 'T.T.F.N.'—a contraction of 'Ta-ta for now' with which she made her exit.

> 1976 *Observer*: JY [i.e. Jimmy Young] said TTFN to Mr Healey.

Tube Alloys *n* (1942) the code name of a section of the British Department of Scientific and Industrial Research formed in 1940 and concerned with research into the production of an atomic bomb

> 1945 Winston Churchill: Imperial Chemicals Industries Limited agreed to release Mr. W. A. Akers to take charge of this directorate, which we called, for purposes of secrecy, the Directorate of 'Tube Alloys'.

turbojet *n* (1945) a jet engine in which the jet gases also power a turbine-driven compressor for compressing the air drawn into the engine. The standard type of jet engine used in aircraft

> 1945 *Aeronautics*: The turbo-jet shows definite advantages in comparatively light aircraft designed to operate at high speeds.

> 1950 *Annual Register 1949*: Propelled by…turbo-jet engines,…the Comet flew at an altitude of 35,000 feet.

TV *n* (1948) An abbreviation of **television (1907)**. Originally US. Sometimes also rendered orthographically as *teevee*, especially in the US

> 1948 *Fortune*: It is not where TV has gone,…but the pace at which it is going that causes all the excitement… The average capital investment for a TV station is about $375,000.

> 1949 *New York Mirror*: Warners, unworried about teevee, showed a 1948 profit of 3 million.

unarmed combat *n* (1947) fighting using no weapons except one's hands. Conceptualized and named as part of commando training during World War II

> 1947 Nevil Shute: 'You went on to a course in unarmed combat. What did they teach you to do there?' 'We was taught how to attack an armed man just with our hands and feet.'

under-arm *adj* (1947) relating to the armpit and various problems of personal hygeine associated with it. *Underarm* is recorded as a noun, synonymous with *armpit*, in the 1930s ('An extensive scar remained upon her right breast, underarm and back', *Southwestern Reporter* (1933)), but it was the advertising industry (evidently terrified of the word *armpit*) that was responsible for its postwar boom as an adjective. The noun in due course received the same euphemistic gloss (see the second quote below)

1947 H. M. McLuhan: The means of defeating under-arm odour.

1966 in G. N. Leech: Veet 'O' leaves skin satin-soft, makes underarms immaculate, arms and legs fuzz-free.

underbelly *n* (1942) a vulnerable part. A usage popularized by the British World War II prime minister Winston Churchill, who favoured it particularly when referring to the southern coast of Europe as an access point for striking at the Nazi homeland (a project dear to his heart). It is mainly used in the phrase *soft underbelly*

1942 Winston Churchill: We make this wide encircling movement in the Mediterranean…having for its object the exposure of the under-belly of the Axis, especially Italy, to heavy attack.

1949 *Life*: An all-out attack on the 'soft under-belly' of socialism.

underdeveloped *adj* (1949) Designating a country or other region in which economic and social conditions fail to reach their potential level or an accepted standard. Originally a kid-glove term, replacing the abrasively frank *backward*, but when in due course (as usually happens) it too began to sound patronizing, it was replaced by **developing (1964)**

1949 Harry Truman: Fourth, we must embark on a bold new program for making the benefits of our scientific advances and industrial progress available for the improvement and growth of underdeveloped areas.

1956 Thomas Balogh: The typical under-developed country even in the more recent past has only attracted capital for the exploitation of primary products.

United Nations *n* (1942) Originally, the Allied nations who united against the Axis powers in World War II; hence, used as the title (in full *United Nations Organization*) of an international peace-seeking organization of these and many other states, founded by charter in 1945. Commonly abbreviated to *U.N.* (1946) or the acronym *U.N.O.* (1945). The name had originally been coined in 1918 by Raleigh C. Minor for a federal league of nations proposed by him

1942 *Daily Telegraph*: But at any rate it will be long enough for Japan to inflict…losses upon all of the United Nations who have…possessions in the Far East.

1945 *Tuscaloosa* (Alabama) *News*: The ideas range like this…let the United Nations Organization (UNO) handle it [etc.].

1946 *New York Times*: If the U.N. remained at Hunter or went to Lake Success, it would have to erect an auditorium.

1974 Paul Gore-Booth: Mrs Eleanor Roosevelt came to propose that the organization be called 'The United Nations'… I put forward a motion to the effect that we accept Mrs Roosevelt's proposal subject to a committee of jurists being satisfied that the term 'United Nations' presented no legal difficulty.

unputdownable *adj* (1947) Of a book: too interesting, exciting, etc. to put down unfinished. This pattern of adjectives formed by adding *un-* and *-able* to verb-adverb or verb-preposition combinations goes back at least to the 17th century (*uncomeatable* (1694)), and was very popular in the 19th century (*undowithoutable* (1844), *ungetonable-with* (1873), *untalkaboutable* (1862)), but the vast majority of the coinages were one-off affairs (an exception which has lasted is *ungetatable* (1862)). In the 20th century, a few have been longer-lived—including (apart from *unputdownable*) *unswitchoffable* (1974) and *unwearoutable* (1968)

1947 Raymond Chandler: I found it absolutely…unputdownable.

upward mobility *n* (1949) movement from a lower to a higher social level. Mainly restricted to sociologists' jargon until the 1960s (when the related **upwardly mobile** is first recorded)

1949 *American Journal of Sociology*: These children were learning attitudes and habits leading to upward social mobility.

1964 *Sunday Times*: The barriers within that structure…can be crossed by upwardly-mobile Jews.

utility *adj* (1942) In Britain during and after World War II, designating clothes and household goods made in a standardized form in accordance with an official allowance of materials. Compare **austerity (1942)**

1942 *Daily Express*: Frankly, Meadows, can you see me in a utility suit?

1943 *Architectural Review*: An exhibition has recently been held of utility furniture and utility pottery.

1952 Marghanita Laski: Mrs. Wilson made the tea and then they both sat down on their camp-beds and sipped it out of thick white Utility cups.

V (1941) An abbreviation of *victory*, used in a range of contexts to symbolize the aims and ambitions of the Allies in World War II: for example, the first four notes of Beethoven's Fifth Symphony, which correspond to the code for *v* in Morse, were used to introduce radio broadcasts to occupied Europe. See also **V sign (1941)**

1941 Clara Milburn: The V campaign (…) was launched by Mr Churchill today. V for victory, the opening notes of Beethoven's V (fifth) symphony.

1973 David Westheimer: She raised her hand in a peace sign… He realized it was not the peace sign at all. To those of the old woman's generation it was V for Victory.

V-1 *n* (1944) a pilotless jet-propelled aeroplane with an explosive warhead used by the Germans against Britain between June 1944 and March 1945, killing over 5500 civilians. The *V* in its name was short for German *Vergeltungswaffe* 'reprisal weapon'. It was powered by a pulse jet which made a characteristic and ominous buzzing noise (hence one of its nicknames, **buzz-bomb**). People on the ground quickly came to dread the silence after the engine cut out, which meant that the bomb was on its way down. Other current names for it, of varying degress of officialness, were **flying bomb, doodlebug, robot bomb,** and **robomb**

1944 *Times*: For two weeks London has now been subjected to ceaseless bombardment by the German weapon V1.

V-2 *n* (1944) a long-range liquid-fuelled rocket with an explosive warhead used by the Germans against Britain and the Low Countries in 1944 and 1945. It became the basis for both US and Soviet postwar rocket design. For the significance of its name, see **V-1 (1944)**

1952 Margery Allingham: Night. V2 time… Remember V2's?… Suddenly, no warning, no whistle, wallop!

vacky, vakky *n* (1940) an evacuee, especially a child evacuated from the city to the country at the beginning of World War II. British colloquial

1949 E. E. Coxhead: I was a vakky. My home's in Clapham really, but our school was sent to Bedfordshire.

vapour trail *n* (1941) a visible trail of condensed water vapour in the sky, in the wake of an aircraft. Their patterns became a familiar sight in the skies of southern England during the Battle of Britain. A later synonym was **contrail (1945)**

1941 *Picture Post*: The vapour trails are left by the R.A.F. fighters weaving in and out of the German formation.

VE Day *n* (1944) a day (8 May 1945) officially designated as the day of victory for Allied forces in Europe during World War II. See also **VJ Day (1944)**

1944 *Washington Post*: James F. Byrne, director of War Mobilization, found a new designation for the two victory days… Last night he referred to the date of Germany's impending surrender as V-E (victory in Europe) Day, and the day of Japan's defeat as V-J (Victory over Japan) Day.

1945 *Daily Mirror*: Today is VE-Day—the day for which the British people have fought and endured five years, eight months and four days of war.

vegan *n* (1944) a person who on principle abstains from all food of animal origin. Coined to distinguish strict *vegetarians* (1839) from backsliders who eat cheese, eggs, etc. The pronunciation note in the second quote below applies to British English, but in the US the *veg-* is usually pronounced the same as the first syllable of *vegetarian*

1944 D. Watson: 'Vegetarian' and 'Fruitarian' are already associated with societies that allow the 'fruits' of cows and fowls, therefore…we must make a new and appropriate word… I have used the title 'The Vegan News'. Should we adopt this, our diet will soon become known as the vegan diet, and we should aspire to the rank of vegans.

1945 D. Watson: Two members have asked how 'Vegan' is pronounced. Veegan, not Veejan.

venture capital *n* (1943) money that is put up for speculative business investment. The synonymous *risk capital* is first recorded in 1948

> 1943 M. A. Shattuck: Industry during the last decade has not only lacked venture capital for new enterprises; it has also lacked venture capital for established concerns.

victory roll *n* (1942) a rotational manœuvre about a longitudinal axis performed by an aircraft as a sign of triumph

> 1942 *Tee Emm*: On returning to his aerodrome he began a victory roll, got into a spin and failed to recover.

VJ Day *n* (1944) a day officially designated as marking the defeat of Japan in World War II, either (in Britain) 15 August 1945, when Japan ceased fighting, or (in the US) 2 September 1945, the day of Japan's official surrender. See **VE Day (1944)**

> 1956 *B.B.C. Handbook 1957*: VJ-day was recalled by the Overseas Services in a series of talks.

voice-over *n* (1947) narration spoken by an unseen narrator on a film or television broadcast. A word which remained largely locked away in the professional jargon of film and television until the 1960s

> 1968 *Listener*: In slow motion she loped muzzily through sylvan glades, and it was a matter of judgment whether the voice-over announcer would come on to plug the sexual properties of petrol, hand lotion or tooth-paste.

V sign *n* (1941) Originally applied to the letter V used as a written symbol of victory during World War II, or to the Morse Code representation of this (see **V (1941)**), and subsequently to a two-fingered gesture representing V for victory, made palm outwards, which was made famous by the British prime minister Winston Churchill. The same name was later given to a gesture similar in form but made palm inwards, and with obscene intention

> 1941 Winston Churchill: The V sign is the symbol of the unconquerable will of the occupied territories, and a portent of the fate awaiting the Nazi tyranny.

> 1942 Harold Nicolson: Winston…gives the V-sign to an audience which does not greet him with any tumultuous applause.

> 1973 *Daily Telegraph*: Two 'louts'…taunted him outside his home by shouting obscenities and making V-signs.

wakey, wakey *interj* (1941) A British services' elaboration on the theme 'Wake up!', formerly used as a command to soldiers at reveille (often in combination with *rise and shine*). It continued in jocular use among the World War II generation for several decades, and was familiar for a while as the catchphrase of the bandleader Billy Cotton. Also used as a noun, meaning 'reveille'

> 1945 *Gen*: The sarnt came round yelling wakey-wakey.

> 1973 Tim Heald: 'Wakey Wakey, rise and shine,' said Brother Barnabas in an unconvincing demonstration of joviality.

waldo *n* (1942) a device for handling or manipulating objects by remote control. US. From the name of Waldo F. Jones, the inventor of such gadgets in a science-fiction story in *Astounding Science Fiction* by Robert Heinlein (writing under the pen-name 'A. MacDonald')

> 1942 A. MacDonald: Even the…humanoid gadgets known universally as 'waldoes'…passed through several generations of development…in Waldo's machine shop before he redesigned them for mass production. The first of them…had been designed to enable Waldo to operate a metal lathe.

> 1978 D. A. Stanwood: The bathyscaphs are both equipped with remote manipulators—the experts call them 'Waldos'—for working under the extreme pressure.

war of nerves *n* (1940) a period of psychological warfare (see **psychological warfare (1940)**)

> 1940 *Annual Register 1939*: The British public…did not allow the 'war of nerves' organised by the Nazi Government to interfere in the least with its August holiday.

war trial *n* (1949) the trial of a person for a war crime or crimes. Used originally with reference to the series of trials of former Nazi leaders for alleged war crimes and crimes against humanity presided over by an International Military Tribunal formed from the victorious Allied Powers and held in Nuremberg in 1945–6. See also **war crime (1906)**

> 1949 Raymond Chandler: There is an element of hypocrisy in these war trials.

weave *v get weaving* (1942) to begin promptly or briskly. British colloquial, originally R.A.F.

 1942 Terence Rattigan: We'd better get weaving, or we'll find this chemist feller has gone to lunch.

welfare state *n* (1941) (a country with) a social system in which the welfare of members of the community is underwritten by means of state-run social services. The term is sometimes said to have been coined by Sir Alfred Zimmern in the 1930s, but it has not been traced in his published writings; the earliest known reference to it is in *Citizen and Churchman* by William Temple, Archbishop of Canterbury (see the first quote below). The theory was put into practice in Britain by the Labour government elected in 1945 (although many elements of a recognizable welfare state— such as state-funded old-age pensions—were in place long before the term was first thought of)

 1941 William Temple: We have…seen that in place of the conception of the Power-State we are led to that of the Welfare-State.

 1950 *Times*: This is one of the achievements for which the 'welfare State', with its vast apparatus of taxation, subsidies, family allowances, school meals, and other services, can claim credit.

West *n* (1946) the non-Communist states of the world in opposition to the Soviet bloc during the Cold War. More of a political than a geographical concept, so although most of its constituent states are to the west of the Soviet Union and its satellites— in Western Europe and North America—countries decidedly to the east, such as Australia, are admitted too. Compare **East (1951)**

 1946 Harold Nicolson: He is convinced that the Russians wish to dominate the world… The only way in which the West can counter this is to pool their philosophy of liberalism, put up a united front.

whammy *n* (1940) an evil influence or 'hex'. Slang, originally and mainly US. From the 1950s, often with reference to the comic strip *Li'l Abner* (see the second quote below), mainly in the phrase *a double whammy* (even, later on, *a triple whammy*). Latterly used more broadly for 'something effective, upsetting, problematic, etc.' It enjoyed a vogue in British English in the early 1990s after it was used as a campaigning slogan by the Conservatives in the 1992 General Election

 1940 J. R. Tunis: Interest round the field now centered in the Kid's chances for a no-hit game… On the bench everyone realized it too, but everyone kept discreetly quiet on account of the Whammy. Mustn't put the Whammy on him!

 1951 *Al Capp's Li'l Abner*: *Evil-Eye Fleegle* is th' name, an' th' '*whammy*' is my game. Mudder Nature endowed me wit' eyes which can putrefy citizens t' th' spot!… There is th' '*single whammy!*' *That*, friend, is th' full, *pure power* o' *one* o' my evil eyes! It's *dynamite*, friend, an' I do not t'row it around lightly!… And, lastly—th' '*double whammy*'—namely, th' *full power o' both eyes*—which I hopes I never *hafta* use.

 1992 Ian Lang: Scotland has rejected separatism. Britain has rejected Socialism. It's a double whammy!

 1995 *Modern Woman*: Choose orange to feel stimulated, blue to feel relaxed, green to feel healthy—or try all three bath-oil bead colours for a triple whammy!

whistle-stop *adj* (1949) Denoting a journey with a lot of brief halts, especially one by a campaigning politician that takes in many undistinguished places in this way. Originally US. The usage comes from *whistle-stop* 'a small station or town at which trains do not stop unless requested by a signal given on a whistle'; its application to political campaigning developed during the run-up to the 1948 US presidential election ('President Truman told a railroad station crowd here tonight that "before this campaign is over I expect to visit every whistle stop in the United States" ', *New York Times* (1948))

 1949 *Time*: Louis Johnson…raised enough money…to pay for Harry Truman's whistle-stop campaign.

 1952 *Manchester Guardian Weekly*: On the whistle-stop tour down California's Central Valley.

whizzo *adj* (1948) excellent, wonderful. An adjectivization of the earlier exclamation *whizzo!*, signifying delight. It seems to have begun as R.A.F. slang, and spread to middle-class small boys

> 1948 *R.A.F. Review*: It's whizzo when you get a fried egg sunny-side-up for tea.

> 1948 Ivor Brown: A father who told his son that he had…arranged for the boy to visit Norway received the following answer: 'Absolutely wizard, flash, whizz-o, grand, lovely to beetle up to Norway.'

wilco *interj* (1946) An abbreviation of *will comply*, used to express acceptance of instructions, especially those received by radio or telephone

> 1960 Hillary Waugh: 'Roger, wilco, and out,' the staticky voice sang.

-wise *suffix* (1942) from the point of view of, as regards. A usage which has its origins back in the Old English period, in expressions like *in cross wise* 'in the manner of a cross'. By the 14th century, the free noun *wise* had come to function as a suffix—thus, *crosswise*. This state of affairs continued undisturbed until the 20th century, when US English (perhaps under German influence) began using *-wise* to mean 'in respect of'. It attracted a good deal of hostility from purists, but at the end of the century it was fairly well ensconced

> 1942 E. R. Allen: It should be noted that there are two types of hydrogen atoms position-wise.

> 1948 *Saturday Review*: Plotwise, it offers little more or little less of what-happens-next interest than may be found [etc.].

> 1958 *Spectator*: John Robert Russell, 13th Duke of Bedford…in twelve TV performances, was the greatest, successwise, among the aristocrats.

Woolton pie *n* (1941) a vegetable pie publicized by the British government to help people eke out their meagre wartime meat ration. It took its name from F. J. Marquis (1883–1964), 1st Earl of Woolton, who was at that time Minister of Food

> 1941 *Food Facts for the Kitchen Front*: Lord Woolton Pie. The ingredients of this pie can be varied according to the vegetables in season. Potato, swede, cauliflower and carrot make a good mixture.

> 1955 Evelyn Waugh: The London crowd shuffled past, surfeited with tea and Woolton pies.

wot no …? (1945) In Britain during World War II, a catchphrase protesting against shortages (e.g. 'Wot, no beer?'), written as the caption accompanying a Chad, a figure of a human head appearing above a wall, etc. The origins of Chad's name are a mystery never penetrated

> 1945 Sunday Express: Chad is the Watcher… He peers over walls and asks, 'Wot, no—?'

> 1950 M. Kennedy: She drew a picture of Mr. Chad on the terrace wall saying: 'Wot? No black amber?'

xerography *n* (1948) a dry copying process in which an electrically charged surface retains both the charge and a pigmented powder on areas not illuminated by light from bright parts of the document, so that a permanent copy can be immediately obtained by placing paper on the surface and applying heat to fuse the powder to it. Photocopying had been around for some time (see **photocopy (1924)**), but it was this simple inkless process that turned it into the leading method of in-office text reproduction, consigning older procedures such as cyclostyling to the print museum. The word *xerography* itself (based on Greek *xeros* 'dry') never caught on to any extent, but its offspring was the ubiquitous proprietary name **Xerox (1952)**

> 1948 *New York Times*: A revolutionary process of inkless printing…was announced yesterday… Invented by Chester F. Carlson, a New York lawyer, and known as 'Xerography', this basic addition to the graphic arts reproduces pictures and text at a speed of 1,200 a minute… Even an unskilled person can make good Xerographic prints easily.

> 1962 *Daily Telegraph*: Xerography is capturing a growing share of a market in office copying.

youth club *n* (1940) a social club provided for the spare-time activities of young people

> 1940 *Times*: Youth clubs may be found in all districts of the city.

> 1957 John Osborne: I was teaching Art to a bunch of Youth Club kids.

zillion *n* (1944) a very large but indefinite number. Colloquial, originally US; based, like the equally facetious **squillion (1943)**, on *million*. *Zillionaire*, meaning 'someone worth zillions of dollars', is first recorded in 1946, also in the writings of Damon Runyon

> 1944 Damon Runyon: I love him a zillion dollars' worth.

> 1947 *Esquire*: Faithful to their zillions of fans.

zone *v* (1942) to restrict the distribution of (a foodstuff) to a designated area, as was done in Britain in the latter part of World War II

> 1942 *Hansard Lords*: We have arranged that the deliveries of bread shall be zoned.

> 1943 *Daily Express*: Compelling some grocers to buy their zoned cake through the co-ops.

zoot suit *n* (1942) a type of man's suit of exaggerated style popular in the 1940s (originally worn by US blacks), characterized by a long, draped jacket with padded shoulders, and high-waisted tapering trousers. The *zoot* part is just a fanciful alteration of *suit*

> 1942 Gilbert & O'Brien: I want a Zoot Suit with a reat pleat, with a drape shape.

> 1949 Raymond Chandler: Taking knives away from grease-balls in zoot suits.

In the 1950s, prosperity danced with anxiety. As the decade opened, the last of the postwar austerities were being shuffled off as, fuelled by the powerhouse of the US economy, Western nations began to feel affluent again. The 50s saw the start of the long consumer boom that reached a peak in the 60s, and did not receive a real check until the oil crisis of the 70s. Underpinning this economic *growth* were continuing scientific advances on all fronts, from medicine to computers—and towards the end of the decade came the greatest coup of all, as the holy grail of flight into space was grasped. But there was a worm in the bud. Science was not all peace and progress; it had also produced the nuclear bomb. The threat of human annihilation loomed over the 50s, like the very *mushroom cloud* of the bomb itself. The title of W. H. Auden's 1947 poem 'The Age of Anxiety' was appropriate to the coming decade.

To the 1940s, nuclear weapons were a novel terror. In the 50s they became part of the landscape, a background to daily lives. They even acquired a pet name: *nukes*. They progressed in destructive power (the *H-bomb*) and in the sophistication of their means of delivery (from the *V bomber* to the *ICBM*). The banal vocabulary of *thermonuclear* warfare had a shocking familiarity: *fall-out, overkill, megadeath*. Everyone had heard of *kilotons* and *megatons*, of *strategic* and *tactical* nuclear weapons, and of comfortable old *conventional* weapons. There were many, though, who did not accept the official *deterrent* line. Towards the end of the decade the anti-nuclear protest movement began to grow. Groups such as *CND* were formed, and the term *unilateralist* was added to the nuclear lexicon.

This was the background against which the Cold War ideological conflict between the *free world* and the *East* solidified. *NATO* and the *Warsaw Pact* forces peered suspiciously at each other over the Iron Curtain, while *Kremlinologists* tried to fathom Soviet intentions. *Summit* conferences were convened, at which differences between the two sides would hopefully be resolved, but all too often the outcome was a Russian *niet*. Meanwhile, in 1949, another Communist regime had established itself, in China, and the West had *Maoism* for a new enemy, berating it with a fresh set of insults (*paper tiger*). There were fears that the *domino* theory was about to be proved. Back home in the US, anti-Communist paranoia manifested itself in *McCarthyism*. For nations that had decolonized and were unwilling to replace one dependency with another, *non-alignment* seemed the sanest alternative. As far as Europeans were concerned, the answer to war was unity; the 50s were the decade when the terms *common market* and *EEC* entered our vocabulary.

Among the most unsettling set-backs of the period for the West was the launch of the Soviet *sputnik* in 1957. Up till now, the US had assumed it was comfortably ahead in the *space race*, but suddenly there was a real prospect that the winners would be *cosmonauts* rather than astronauts. The result was an all-out US effort for a spectacular *moon-shot* in the next decade, culminating, hopefully, in a *soft landing*. Towards the end of the 50s the US public, and television viewers worldwide, watching the *count-down* to *blast-off*, started to become familiar with the *aerospace* jargon that would dominate the next two decades, as the *space programme* evolved. Meanwhile, on the lunatic fringe, the flying saucer had been respectablized as the *UFO*.

Computers were starting to move out of university laboratories into commercial estab-lishments, albeit still as very large whirring boxes with flashing lights. *Artificial intelligence, information technology*, and *data processing* had their beginnings, and terms like *bootstrap* and *modem, on-line* and *real time, print-out* and *RAM, Algol* and *FORTRAN* entered the language.

The *double helix* was discovered, and the *big bang* postulated. Surgeons operated on the *open heart*, performed *by-passes* and *transplants*, and fitted *pacemakers*. The *Salk vaccine* banished the mid-century scourge of polio, but, ominously, before the decade was out, *thalidomide* had appeared on the scene. Meanwhile, the world was going down with *Asian flu*.

Following the convulsions of wartime, Western society was establishing itself in new patterns that rejected the stratified deference of previous decades and the dirigisme of the 1940s. The 50s were the period of the *beat generation*, the *angry young man*, and the *crazy mixed-up* kid, of the *kitchen sink* and the *coffee bar*. It was the *teen* age: the decade in which young people thrust their way into the spotlight, whether they were *Teddy boys* (or their Australasian equivalent, *bodgies*), or *Hell's Angels*, or *beatniks*, or early *hippies*. It was the decade of *protest*, and sometimes of violence (the *flick knife* the weapon of choice), and to be old was to be a *cube*. The slang of the period was US teenspeak, much of it inherited from the argot of jazz: *far out* and *way out, with it* and *swinging, a gas* and *the most, split* the *scene, see you later alligator*, anything ending in *-ville*. Not that the old order was entirely mori-bund, at least in Britain, where people still got very steamed up over the difference between *U* and *non-U*.

Music was a key element in the new youth culture— notably, of course, *rock and roll*, but there were other favourites, such as *country and western* and *skiffle*. The concept of the *group* was born, although it was not to achieve its apotheosis until the 1960s. *Deejays* played their records in *discotheques*, where the teenagers danced in their *jeans* and *ponytails*. But in the affluent 50s, the kids could also afford their own record players, and their money pro-pelled songs into the *hit parade*, the *top ten, top of the pops*.

Other record buyers were playing their *albums* on the new *hi-fi* and *stereo* systems. But the biggest developments in electronic entertainment were going on in television, which in the course of the 1950s grew exponentially to become the world's leading medium of com-munication. From being an esoteric toy of the well-off at the start of the decade, it had by the end made the transition to being a taken-for-granted part of everyday life. In Britain, the turning point was the Coronation of Elizabeth II in 1953. New *Elizabethans* in their thousands bought televisions to watch the event, and millions of their neighbours huddled round their tiny screens to share the experience. The bug was caught, and the *goggle-box*— or simply *the box*—was there in the corner to stay, even though the audience had to make do with *panel games* rather than coronations. Meanwhile, in the US *pay television* and *breakfast-time television* were taking their first steps. In the cinema, directors experimented with *Cinerama, CinemaScope*, and even *Smell-o-Vision*, but a more significant long-term development was the appearance of *videotape*. The *transistor radio* also made its bow.

Our surroundings began to take on a spartan modernism. *High-rise* blocks (long familiar in the US but new to Britain) and *pedestrian precincts* dominated the new urban landscape, and architects embraced the *new brutalism*. In the visual arts it was the decade of *abstract expressionism* and *action painting*, and of the beginnings of *pop art*.

In the world of fashion, the *A-line* graced the middle of the decade, but by the time of the *sack dress* inspiration had run dry. We first wore *Bermuda shorts, Y-fronts*, and *stiletto heels* (though not as an ensemble), and *tracksuits* made their first appearance (initially confined to athletics tracks—very useful if you had just run a *four-minute mile*). Technology made its contribution with *Lycra* and the *drip-dry* shirt. The *bouffant* hairstyle came in, reliant on *hair spray* and *back-combing*, while for men, if the *DA* was not for you, you could go for a *Tony Curtis*.

Technology was beginning to dominate our diet, too. We could buy *sliced bread*; the first *fish finger* announced the arrival of frozen prepared dishes; and *fast food* appeared on the high street. But there were also signs of a growing penetration of foreign cuisines into the staid Anglo-Saxon gastronomic repertoire, exemplified by the likes of *doner kebabs, garlic bread, tandoori*, and *woks*.

On the roads, small and nippy were the watchwords. If you did not want a *bubble car*, or one of the new Minis, you could *scooter* around on a *moped* or a *Vespa*—but watch out for the *traffic wardens* and *meter maids*. In the air, the helicopter came of age as a means of transport, and went into battle in the Korean War—hence *chopper* and *whirlybird*. And a completely new type of vehicle came on the scene: the *hovercraft*.

The *permissive* sixties were coming, ushered in by *the pill*. There were *sex kittens* on the screen and *kinky* sex in the Sunday papers. But the time was not yet ripe for *consenting adults* to come out of the *closet*. Meanwhile the teenagers of the next decade were still at home, playing with their *hula hoops*.

abstract expressionism *n* (1952) a school of painting characterized by the active and free application of the paint on to the canvas (see **action painting (1952)**) and its nonrepresentational design

> 1952 *American Artist*: From abstract expressionism to new objectivity.

> 1957 B. S. Myers: The New York school of Abstract Expressionism led by such artists as Jackson Pollock (1912–1956) and Willem de Kooning (b. 1904).

> 1958 L. Alloway: The term Abstract Impressionism seems to have been coined by Elaine De Kooning in 1951 at the Arts Club, 8th Street, New York.

action painting *n* (1952) a form of abstract art in which the paint is placed in strokes or splashes on the canvas by the spontaneous or random action of the artist. Its chief exponent was the US painter Jackson Pollock

> 1952 H. Rosenberg: The American action painters… Action painting is painting in the medium of difficulties.

admass *n* (1955) A term coined by the English writer J. B. Priestley (1894–1984) for that section of the community which is easily influenced by mass methods of publicity and entertainment; also applied to the advertising, etc., processes or agents themselves. Priestley based it on *advertisement* and *mass*. It did not remain in active use much beyond the 1950s

> 1955 J. B. Priestley & Jacquetta Hawkes: *Admass*. This is my name for the whole system of an increasing productivity, plus inflation, plus a rising standard of material living, plus high-pressure advertising and salesmanship, plus mass communications, plus cultural democracy and the creation of the mass mind, the mass man.

> 1957 *Listener*: Ordinary, intelligent people…who do not wish to be caught up in the Admass culture, yet whose education has not provided them with a complete means to resist it.

adult *adj* (1958) pornographic. A euphemism based ostensibly on the notion of access restricted to adults, but suggesting the subtext 'likely to appeal to adults'—a rather seedy reflection on adulthood

> 1958 *New Musical Express*: Unusual adult photo sets. S.a.e. Free exciting offer.

> 1984 *Tampa* (Florida) *Tribune*: Rentals for adult videos outstrip purchases by 12 to 1.

adventure playground *n* (1953) a playground where children are provided with miscellaneous equipment, often waste material, from which they can contrive their own amusement

> 1953 Lady Allen: How does an Adventure Playground differ from the usual playground? There is no asphalt, no see-saws, swings or slides, except those created by the children themselves out of waste material freely available on the site.

aero-space *n* (1958) the earth's atmosphere and outer space. Widely used, often adjectivally, to refer to the technology of flight in the atmosphere and in space, and to the industrial aspects of such flight

> 1963 *Guardian*: The change from an aircraft industry to an aerospace industry is one which has not yet been made in Britain.

> 1963 *Wall Street Journal*: Aerospace workers at McDonnell Aircraft Corp.'s plants.

Afro-Caribbean *adj, n* (1958) of both Africa and the Caribbean. Applied especially to West Indians of African descent. A further item in the late-20th-century litany of would-be politically correct terms for black people

> 1958 *Oxford Mail*: Lessons in Afro-Caribbean dancing…for…members of the Oxford University Ballet Club.

> 1959 *Encounter*: In the bad old days, when…the Afro-Caribbeans had little but humiliation.

agonizing reappraisal *n* (1953) a reassessment of a policy, position, etc., painfully forced on one by a radical change of circumstances, or by a realization of what the existing circumstances really are. A catch-phrase which rapidly became a cliché

> 1953 John Foster Dulles: If…the European Defence Community should not be effective; if France and Germany remain apart… That would compel an agonizing reappraisal of basic United States policy.

> 1958 *Star*: As if in response to new directions from an agonising reappraisal in MCC's room at lunch, the scoring spurted as Cowdrey twice swung Benaud to the leg fence.

agribusiness *n* (1955) the group of industries concerned with the processing and distribution of agricultural produce or with farm machinery and services. Originally US. Subsequently also applied to agriculture conducted as a modern business, especially making use of advanced technology

> 1955 *Harvard Business School Bulletin*: 'Agri-business'—a term coined to define the many diverse enterprises which produce, process, and distribute farm products or which provide supporting services.

> 1968 Mervyn Pyke: Science will inevitably bring agriculture, as it has so far been understood, to an end, and cause 'agribusiness' to take its place.

air-time *n* (1955) broadcasting time allocated for a particular purpose. From the notion of being 'on the air'—i.e. broadcasting

> 1955 T. H. Pear: The listening public's approval or disapproval of the 'air-time' given to each.

a.k.a. *abbreviation* (1955) also known as. Originally US; used in giving someone's alias, pseudonym, or other alternative name

> 1970 *New Yorker*: Cassius Clay, a.k.a. Muhammud Ali.

album *n* (1957) an LP containing several different pieces of music, especially pop music, light music, jazz, etc.

> 1963 *Oxford Mail*: Many jazz album covers have little connection with the contents.

Algol *n* (1959) an international algebraic language for use in programming computers. Coined from *algorithmic* and the *l* of *language*. See **FORTRAN (1956)**

> 1961 *Times*: Algol…is used widely as a communication language.

A-line *n* (1955) the shape of a garment, especially a dress or skirt, which is flared from the shoulder or waist to the hem like a letter A. The brain child of the French fashion designer Christian Dior (1905–57) (see also **New Look (1947)**)

> 1955 *Punch*: Christian Dior's A-line—the most significant cipher since the S-curve of the Edwardian Gibson Girl.

> 1969 *Sears Catalog*: A-line skirt. Jute belt; contour top.

alligator *n* (1957) See **see you later, alligator (1957)**

amniocentesis *n* (1958) a prenatal diagnostic technique in which a sample of amniotic fluid is withdrawn from the uterus through a hollow needle and examined for information about the fetus. Coined from Greek *amnion* 'caul' and *kentesis* 'pricking'

> 1958 H. M. Parrish: The term 'transabdominal amniocentesis' is introduced as being descriptive of the procedure and is suggested in lieu of previous terminology including: amniotomy, abdominal paracentesis…and paracentesis uteri.

anal retentive *adj, n* (1958) (someone) displaying excessive orderliness and parsimony, interpreted by psychoanalysts as the result of fixation at the anal phase of development (see **anal (1930)**). By the end of the century it had become an all-purpose term of abuse for a tidy, mean, or up-tight person

> 1984 Sue Townsend: My mother said, 'You're an anal retentive, aren't you?' and my father said, 'You're tight-fisted, and you've always got your perfectly groomed head in a book.'

angry young man *n* (1957) a young man who is dissatisfied with and outspoken against the prevailing state of affairs, current beliefs, etc. The expression had been in use since at least the late 1930s, and in 1951 the Irish writer Leslie Paul used it as the title of a book, but it first became commonly used, especially by journalists, after the production of John Osborne's play *Look Back in Anger* (first performed 1956). The phrase did not occur in the play but was applied to Osborne by G. Fearon, a reporter (see the first quotation below), thence used particularly of young writers, usually of provincial and lower middle-class or working-class origin, who denounced or satirized the 'Establishment' and the abuses of the time; later applied by extension to any person, group, etc., in Britain and elsewhere who considered the times to be out of joint

1957 G. Fearon, *Daily Telegraph*: I had read John Osborne's play. When I met the author I ventured to prophesy that his generation would praise his play while mine would, in general, dislike it… 'If this happens,' I told him, 'you would become known as the Angry Young Man.' In fact, we decided then and there that henceforth he was to be known as that.

1958 *Times*: The angry young man who feels that life is short, and that he must make his mark early by carping at established ideas and institutions.

anti-matter *n* (1953) a hypothetical form of matter consisting of anti-particles. The existence of anti-particles, elementary particles of the same mass as a given particle but having an opposite electrical charge, was predicted in 1930 by the British physicist Paul Dirac ('We may call such a particle an anti-electron', Paul Dirac (1931))

1953 *Science News Letter*: The existence or creation of anti-matter, or the negative analogue of the proton…is theoretically possible.

anti-missile missile *n* (1956) a missile designed to intercept and destroy attacking missiles

1956 *Newsweek*: The 'Nike B' is designed as an antimissile missile as well as an improved version of the anti-aircraft 'Nike' weapons.

après-ski *n, adj* (1954) (worn, taking place, etc.) at the time when skiing is over for the day. Borrowed from French (literally 'after-ski') at a time when at least the better-heeled British were resuming winter-sports holidays in the Alps. The translated version *after-ski*, first recorded in 1962, has never made so much of an impression

1954 R. Martin: The 'après-ski' outfit…is based on the outdoor version… There is always a queue of Britons to read it [i.e. an English newspaper], during the hours of 'après-ski'.

1961 *Sunday Express*: The ski-suit above…[is] for the indoor après-ski party.

aqualung *n* (1950) a portable diving apparatus consisting of containers of compressed air strapped on the back which feed air automatically through a valve and mouthpiece to the diver

1953 Cousteau & Dumas: In June 1943…a new and promising device…an automatic compressed-air diving lung conceived by Émile Gagnan and myself… No children ever opened a Christmas present with more excitement than we did when we unpacked the first 'aqualung'.

ArmaLite *n* (1958) A proprietary name (registered in the US in 1958) for a type of small-bore weapon. Mainly associated with a rifle (the *ArmaLite rifle*) that has come latterly to be synonymous with terrorist violence

1985 *Economist*: In 1982 Sinn Fein…decided to fight through the ballot box as well as with its Armalite rifles.

artificial intelligence *n* (1956) (the study of) the capacity of machines to simulate intelligent human behaviour. Commonly abbreviated to *AI* (first recorded in 1971—the 1970s was the decade when work in this field got seriously under way)

1956 M. L. Minsky: In the random decisions desired in the domain of artificial intelligence, I am confident that the 'precision' required of pseudo-random sequences will be very much less than for mathematical or numerical purposes.

1971 *New Scientist*: The first major effort of the AI scientists was directed towards writing computer programs to translate automatically between languages.

A.S.A.P. *abbr* (1955) as soon as possible. Apparently originally a US Army usage

1985 *Washington Post*: It is selfish and inconsiderate for a guest [at a party] to conclude that he/she will not be entertained adequately and must therefore bail out ASAP.

Asian flu *n* (1957) The popular name of a kind of influenza caused by a virus first identified in Hong Kong in 1957, which spread round the world in the late 1950s

1958 *Punch*: Three days later…all of us, including the cat, were struck down with Asian flu.

attrit *v* (1956) to erode (the resources or morale of an enemy) by means of an unrelenting military offensive; to grind down. Originally US airforce jargon, familiarized to the general public by the Vietnam War; a back-formation from *attrition* (as in 'war of attrition')

1969 *Atlantic Monthly*: Wear him down. Wear the Cong down, and he'll quit. Put him through the meat grinder. Attrit him. He is hurting.

> 1991 *Newsweek*: His defense was designed to attrit us… Every American you kill, it's another family protesting the war.

autocue *n* (1958) a script device, placed out of range of the camera, which prints the words to be spoken by a speaker on television as a memory aid. British. See also **teleprompter (1951)**

> 1958 Ivor Brown: The autocue is…one of the gadgets introduced by television. The speaker or recorder of news has in front of him a screen over which his text passes. Thus he can read without looking down or fidgeting with papers.

automate *v* (1952) to convert to largely automatic operation; to introduce automatic control to (the manufacture of a product, etc.). Originally US; a back-formation from **automation (1948)**. The contemporary *automatize* ('The estimated cost of complete instrumentation of a new modern plant to automatize it as fully as possible', *Scientific American* (1952)) never caught on to the same extent

> 1952 *Cleveland* (Ohio) *Plain Dealer*: Another 'automated' line, less spectacular than the block line, machines the cylinder head.

> 1955 *Controller*: PanAm Automates.

ayatollah *n* (1950) (An honorific title for) an Iranian Shiite religious leader. It comes ultimately from Arabic, where it means literally 'miraculous sign of God'. It made little impression on English until the late 1970s, when the Ayatollah Khomeini became religious leader of Iran following the overthrow of the Shah. His reputation for dogmatism and intransigence provoked an outburst of metaphor

> 1950 D. N. Wilber: A very few of the most important Iranian religious leaders, resident either in Iran or at the Shi'a shrines in Iraq, bear the honorary title of Ayatollah.

> 1979 *Observer*: Mr Frank Chapple…said 'self-styled ayatollahs' were leading a 'conspiracy of academics and professional people to keep ordinary people and their views out of the party'.

back-comb *v* (1955) to comb the under layers of the hair towards the roots, creating a bouffant effect. Fashionable among (mainly) women in the late 1950s and 60s

> 1955 C. Brown: She had back-combed her hair so that it stood out.

> 1960 *Sunday Express*: Backcombing madly…my favourite hairdresser…built up some splendid, puffed out effects.

backlash *n* (1957) a sudden and adverse reaction, especially to a political or social development. A metaphorical extension of the earlier 'recoil produced by interacting parts of a mechanism', which dates from the early 19th century. It apparently originated in the context of racial tensions in the US in the 1950s

> 1957 *Saturday Evening Post*: You're going to get a backlash—segregation's going to spread.

> 1964 *Listener*: The notorious white backlash (the voters, especially of immigrant origins, who fear the Negroes will move into their jobs and depress the value of their little houses).

bank *n laugh/cry all the way to the bank* (1956) to relish/deplore the fact that one is making money, especially undeservedly or at the expense of others. The original form of the phrase is *cry all the way to the bank*, which started life as an ironic observation by the flamboyant pianist Liberace, weighing the size of his takings against the low opinion of the critics (see the first quote below). The more straightforward, non-ironic version *laugh all the way to the bank* has proved more durable for everyday use

> 1956 *Daily Mirror*: On the occasion in New York at a concert in Madison Square Garden when he had the greatest reception of his life and the critics slayed him mercilessly, Liberace said: 'The take was terrific but the critics killed me. My brother George cried all the way to the bank.'

> 1985 *National Trust*: The taxpayer may be called in to 'save' it [i.e. a great house] for the nation. Then the owner laughs all the way to the bank, and the devil can take his conscience.

baryon *n* (1953) a subatomic particle that participates in strong interactions, has a half-integral spin, and is more massive than a meson. Coined from Greek *barus* 'heavy'

> 1953 *Progress in Theoretical Physics*: It seems practical to have a collective name for these particles and others which possibly may still be discovered… It is proposed to use the fitting name 'baryon' for this purpose.

beat generation *n* (1952) An expression applied at first to a group of young people, predominantly writers, artists, and their adherents, in San Francisco, later to similar groups elsewhere, adopting unconventional dress, manners, habits, etc., as a means of self-expression and social protest. The etymology of the term is uncertain: it is generally associated with *beat* 'rhythm (of jazz)' or with *beat* 'worn out, exhausted', but its originator, the US writer Jack Kerouac (1922–69), connected it with *beatitude* ('Beat means beatitude, not beat up')

> 1952 J. C. Holmes: It was the face of a Beat Generation… It was John Kerouac…who…several years ago…said 'You know, this is really a beat generation'. The origins of the word beat are obscure, but the meaning is only too clear to most Americans. More than the feeling of weariness, it implies the feeling of having been used, of being raw. It involves a sort of nakedness of mind.

> 1955 Jack Kerouac: Jazz of the Beat Generation… Here we were dealing with the pit and prune juice of poor beat life itself and the pathos of people in the Godawful streets.

beatnik *n* (1958) a member of the beat generation. A term coined early in 1958 by the San Francisco columnist Herb Caen, no doubt under the influence of the contemporary buzzword **sputnik (1957)**. In due course the older generation took it up, often with obvious distaste, as a general word for a long-haired bohemian

> 1958 *Daily Express*: [San Francisco] is the home and the haunt of America's Beat generation and these are the Beatniks—or new barbarians.

> 1959 *Guardian*: He calls a flat a 'pad' (Beatnik language).

> 1966 *English Studies*: In the mid-twentieth century the typical Bohemian has become the beatnik poet or pseudo-philosopher.

Bermuda shorts *n* (1953) knee-length shorts, characteristic of US holiday-makers on the Atlantic island of Bermuda

> 1953 Raymond Chandler: Loafing around one of the swimming pools in Bermuda shorts.

bi *adj* (1956) A colloquial abbreviation of **bisexual**

> 1966 Maureen Duffy: My luck she should turn out to be bi. Don't expect it in a butch.

bible-black *adj* (1953) deep black, like the cover of a bible. A coinage of the Welsh poet Dylan Thomas, made famous in his popular radio play *Under Milk Wood* (1954)

> 1953 Dylan Thomas: It is spring, moonless night in the small town, starless and bible-black.

big bang *n* (1950) the explosion of a single compact mass, in which (according to one cosmological theory) the universe originated. For a decade or two the **steady state (1948)** theory competed hotly with the explosion theory, but by the end of the century it was generally agreed that the big-bangers had it

> 1950 Fred Hoyle: One [idea] was that the Universe started its life a finite time ago in a single huge explosion… This big bang idea seemed to me to be unsatisfactory.

> 1969 *Observer*: A unique and inscrutable primeval atom, out of which all matter was born in some mysterious First Explosion—the famous 'Big Bang'.

biological clock *n* (1955) an innate mechanism that regulates various cyclic and rhythmic activities of an organism

> 1955 *Proceedings of the National Academy of Sciences*: Such a biological clock would seem theoretically to be a necessary component in the mechanism of the normally precise rhythms of solar and lunar frequency.

biopic *n* (1951) a biographical film; a film biography. Colloquial, originally US. A coinage of the 1950s, but it did not make much headway until the 1970s

> 1951 *Memphis* (Tennessee) *Commercial Appeal*: 'Variety' coins another word for show biz— 'biopic', meaning a biographical film.

> 1976 *Time Out*: Old fashioned Hollywood biopic.

blast off *v* (1951) Of a rocket or spacecraft: to take off, be launched into space. The related noun *blast-off* is also first recorded in 1951

> 1951 Ray Bradbury: You could still smell the hard, scorched smell where the last rocket blasted off when it went back to Earth.

> 1952 Arthur C. Clarke: We were supposed to keep out of the pilot's way at blast-off.

> 1969 *Times*: It only remains for three veteran space travellers…to blast off on Sunday.

blinder *n* (1950) something dazzlingly good or difficult, especially a brilliantly played football game. British slang

> 1950 Walter Hammond: Striking out at an innocent-looking ball, I've sent a blinder—dead into the fieldsman's hands.

> 1960 David Storey: You played a blinder… It was the best game I ever saw.

blokeish *adj* (1957) characteristic of a bloke. Colloquial British. Its original connotations were 'straightforward, unaffected, down-to-earth, one of the lads', but towards the end of the century more negative tones of brash and insensitive machismo were often added to the blend. Compare **laddish (1991)**

> 1993 *Sunday Times*: The Mayles then popped up in a restaurant in Provence, Lindsay Duncan all cutesy and John Thaw all blokeish ('When you're ready, maestro!').

Bloody Mary *n* (1956) a drink containing vodka and tomato juice. The name, a reference to the drink's colour, comes from the nickname of Mary Tudor, Queen of England 1553–58, earned by her enthusiastic execution of Protestants

> 1956 *Punch*: Those two…are eating raw steaks and drinking Bloody Marys.

blue-collar *adj* (1950) Designating a manual or industrial worker, as distinct from a 'white-collar' worker. Originally US; from the stereotypical blue overalls of the artisan. Compare **white collar (1919)**

> 1950 *Tuscaloosa News*: 'Blue collar' workers also include helpers, laborers, and supervisors.

> 1958 *Listener*: The blue-collar people, the machine operators.

bodgie, bodgy *n* (1950) a teenage boy who wears long hair and jackets and behaves anarchically; the Australasian counterpart of a **Teddy boy (1954)**. Australian and New Zealand. Probably coined from Australian slang *bodger* 'something fake or worthless'; reputedly the term was originally applied in the mid 1940s to inferior cloth passed off as American, and was transferred to teenage boys who affected an American accent. See also **widgie (1950)**

> 1950 *Sunday Telegraph* (Sydney): The bizarre uniform of the 'bodgey'—belted velvet cord jacket, bright blue sports shirt without a tie, brown trousers narrowed at the ankle, shaggy Cornel Wilde haircut.

body bag *n* (1954) a strong bag in which a corpse is placed and transported (e.g. from the scene of an accident). Originally US; the sight of body bags on television was said to have been a major factor in the US public's turning against the Vietnam War

> 1976 Newton Thornburg: Maybe I just scooped up too many guys and dumped them in body bags.

bonkers *adj* (1957) mad, crazy. British slang; perhaps from the earlier naval slang *bonkers* 'slightly drunk', which itself may have been based on the idea of a *bonk* or 'blow' on the head. Compare **crackers (1928)**

> 1961 Simpson & Galton: By half-past three he'll be raving bonkers.

bootstrap *n* (1953) the computing procedure of using a fixed sequence of instructions to initiate the loading of further instructions and ultimately of a complete program (especially the operating system); also, the initial fixed sequence of instructions used for this. Subsequently used as a verb, meaning 'to prepare (a computer) for operation by causing an operating system to be loaded into its memory from a disc or tape', usually abbreviated to **boot (1980)**. The underlying idea is that the first-loaded instructions pull the subsequent ones up 'by their bootstraps'

> 1953 *Proceedings of the Institute of Radio Engineers*: A technique sometimes called the 'bootstrap technique'…Pushing the load button…causes one full word to be loaded into a memory address previously set up…on the operator's panel, after which the program control is directed to that memory address and the computer starts automatically.

> 1978 *Practical Computing*: The system is boot-strapped as soon as the power is turned on.

bottle *n* (1958) courage, spirit, guts. British slang; especially common in the phrase *lose one's bottle* 'to lose one's nerve'. The usage probably derives from the phrase *no bottle* 'no good, useless'. It is however often popularly associated with the rhyming slang term *bottle and glass* 'arse' and other similar expressions. It did not come into general use until the 1970s, when it was introduced to a wider audience mainly via television crime dramas. See also **bottle out (1979)**

> 1958 Frank Norman: We all began to ask each other…why he hadn't made a dash for it. 'What's the matter Frank, your bottle fallen out?'

> 1969 *It*: You've gotta have a helluva lot of bottle to do something like that, and I believe that Morrison did it out of sheer contempt.

> 1985 *TV Times*: I don't think I handled the intrusion so well. I tend to lose my 'bottle'.

bouffant *adj, n* (1955) (a hair-style that is) puffed out, arranged in a swelling or fluffy style; fashionable in the late 1950s and early 60s. A borrowing of French *bouffant* 'swelling'

> 1955 *Vanity Fair Guide for the Bride*: René…designed a simple hairstyle… Watch that smooth but bouffant silhouette.

> 1959 *Sunday Times*: The bouffant, hair-styler's joy and milliner's grief.

boutique *n* (1953) a small fashion-shop or department that sells ready-to-wear clothes designed by a couturier; a small shop selling trendy clothes or other articles, especially for young or fashionable people. Often used adjectivally, to denote the sort of articles bought in such a shop. A re-importation of a French word which had been used sporadically in English since the mid 18th century in the more prosaic sense 'small shop'. It enjoyed particular success in the 1960s, when, applied to a self-contained shop rather than an in-store department, it became almost synonymous with 'Swinging London', Carnaby Street, etc.

> 1953 *New York Times*: The usual boutique sports clothes were not so evident as swirls of summer cocktail and evening dresses went by.

> 1957 *Observer*: The idea of 'Boutiques', those small shops set inside couture establishments to sell ready-to-wear.

> 1966 *Vanity Fair*: I…love the look of boutique clothes.

> 1966 Mary Quant: It was agreed that if we could find the right premises for a boutique…we would open a shop. It was to be a bouillabaisse of clothes and accessories…sweaters, scarves, shifts, hats, jewellery, and peculiar odds and ends.

box *n the box* (1958) television. British colloquial; see also **goggle-box (1959)**

> 1963 E. Humphreys: I saw one of your plays, Dicky. On the old box.

brain-washing *n* (1950) the systematic and often forcible elimination from a person's mind of all established ideas, especially political ones, so that another set of ideas can take their place; this process regarded as the kind of coercive conversion practised by certain totalitarian states on political dissidents. The term is a literal translation of Chinese *xi nao*, and English acquired it via the Korean War. *Brain-washer* and the back-formed verb *brain-wash* soon followed

> 1950 E. Hunter: 'Brain-reform' is the objective, popularly referred to as 'brain-washing'.

> 1952 *Times*: Ai Tze-chi was Red China's chief indoctrinator or, as he was generally called, Brainwasher No 1.

> 1953 *Saturday Evening Post*: The anticommunist soldiers…may be blackmailed or brain-washed or third-degreed.

breakfast-time TV *n* (1952) television broadcasting in the morning, especially at or around breakfast time. Originally US. The variant *breakfast television*, which proved more popular when such broadcasting began in Britain in the early 1980s, is not recorded until 1971

> 1952 *New York Times*: Breakfast-time TV has been a commercial success in some cities outside of New York.

> 1971 *Life*: I felt I had performed reasonably well on midnight radio and breakfast television from Boston to San Francisco.

> 1980 *Economist*: Channel Four…is meant to start then [i.e. in 1982] (so too is Breakfast TV, but its revenue is likely to be less than 1% of total TV advertising)… What the IBA wants from contenders is profitability. The only major innovation it is encouraging is national breakfast-time television.

brinkmanship *n* (1956) the art of advancing to the very brink of war but not engaging in it. Coined by the US politician Adlai Stevenson (1900–65) in response to a remark by John Foster Dulles, the US Secretary of State: 'Says Dulles "…Of course we were brought to the verge of war… If you try to run away from it, if you are scared to go to the brink, you are lost… We walked to the brink and we looked it in the face" ', *Time* (1956). His model was Stephen Potter's **gamesmanship** and similar formations (see **-manship (1947)**)

> 1956 *New York Times*: [Adlai Stevenson] derided the Secretary [i.e. J. F. Dulles] for 'boasting of his brinkmanship—the art of bringing us to the edge of the nuclear abyss'.

> 1958 *Annual Register 1957*: Anglo-French 'brinkmanship' over Suez had failed to stop at the brink.

bubble car *n* (1957) a miniature car with a transparent domed top, fashionable in Britain in the late 1950s, until the Mini stole its thunder

> 1957 *Observer*: The B.M.C…are not interested in bubble cars as now known, but only in properly engineered vehicles.

> 1958 *Spectator*: The tiniest bubble-car I ever set eyes on.

bucket bag *n* (1956) a woman's bag, resembling a bucket in shape. In mid- and late-1950s Britain such bags were seemingly omnipresent; then, just as suddenly, they had gone

> 1956 Josephine Bell: Mrs. Weaver produced a fat envelope from her bucket bag.

budget *adj* (1958) designed or suitable for someone of limited means. A marketing department euphemism, designed to win over customers who would be offended by *cheap*

> 1958 *Woman*: This is just the drink to give party guests a glow—at a budget price.

> 1969 *Woman's Own*: Budget meals for the family.

by-pass *n* (1957) (an operation to create) a permanent alternative pathway within the circulatory system (especially in or near the heart or brain), alimentary canal, etc., incorporating a transplanted or synthetic vessel or chamber

> 1961 *Lancet*: The patient was on bypass for eighty-one minutes… The first open repair on the heart, using a cardiopulmonary bypass, was carried out by Cooley et al. (1958).

> 1964 H. Laufman: The saphenous vein…is not always available in sufficient length for by-pass surgery.

candy floss *n* (1951) a sweet confection, usually pink, of fluffy spun sugar, typically sold at fairgrounds, at the seaside, etc. First recorded in an American publication, although the more usual US term is *cotton candy*

> 1951 *Springfield Sunday Republican* (advert): Salt water taffy…pop corn—candy floss.

> 1961 *Observer*: Something called 'cotton candy' (*anglice* 'candy floss') is sold at seashore resorts; it is made by expanding under pressure a tiny amount of sugar into a huge tasteless blob.

catalytic converter *n* (1955) a device fitted to the exhaust system of some internal-combustion engines which catalyses the oxidation of some of the exhaust gases, making them less harmful as pollutants. A term scarcely familiar to lay audiences until the 1980s, when such pollution had reached alarming levels

> 1989 J. Button: In the USA the compulsory fitting of catalytic converters has cut carbon monoxide emission by 90 per cent.

CB *n* (1959) An abbreviation of **citizen's band (1948)**

> 1959 *Popular Electronics*: Manufacturers eager to get their CB equipment on the market.

> 1964 *Electronics World*: CB was intended to serve the needs of small business.

cha-cha, cha-cha-cha *n, v* (1954) (to dance) a type of ballroom dance to Latin-American rhythm, with small steps and swaying hip movements, fashionable in the mid to late 1950s. A borrowing of American Spanish *cha-cha-cha*

> 1954 *Melody Maker*: What Touzet means by 'cha-cha', as far as I can make out, is simply a mambo with a pronounced güiro rhythm.

> 1955 *Melody Maker*: 'Cha-cha-cha' is danced very much more delicately over here than in England.

> 1959 *Cambridge Review*: We called on an old boy, to find him cha-cha-cha-ing with a young lady.

chambré *adj* (1956) Of a red wine: brought to the temperature of the room in which it is served. A borrowing from French, the past participle of Swiss-French *chambrer* 'to bring to room temperature'. The Anglo-Saxons were beginning to find out more about wine, but as with others of these French gastronomic past participles (*flambé, sauté*), they were frequently puzzled as to whether they should leave them as they were or put an English -*ed* on the end

> 1956 Constance Spry: As a general rule red wines should be served at room temperature or, as the French term it, *chambré*.

> 1970 J. Burke: Unless you order well in advance, you can hardly expect a bottle to be *chambré*'d.

charisma *n* (1959) marked personal charm or magnetism which gives one the power to influence others. The word was originally brought into English around 1930 as a term used by the German social scientist Max Weber (1864–1920), denoting a gift or power of leadership or authority. The later 20th century made it at once more metaphysical and more mundane. Its ultimate source is Greek *kharisma* 'favour, divine gift'

> 1967 *Spectator*: Like many of his generation, he succumbs to the Kennedy charisma, identifies himself with his hero.

charm school *n* (1950) an establishment where people are taught the social graces. Often used metaphorically, in criticizing someone's politeness

> 1962 L. Grex: Steve Blaine might be top of his class in Charm School, but [etc.].

choc-ice *n* (1951) a small bar of ice-cream covered with chocolate. In the US they had long gone under the name **Eskimo pie (1928)**

> 1968 Mordecai Richler: The children skipped off to the dining-hall, where choc-ices, a conjurer, and a Popeye cartoon awaited them.

chopper *n* (1951) a helicopter. Slang, originally US. See also **whirlybird (1951)**

> 1951 *New York Herald Tribune*: The Korean War has added some new words to the American soldier's vocabulary…Chopper: Helicopter.

> 1952 *New York Times Magazine*: Oil and gas producers use the 'chopper' to patrol long and rugged gas and oil pipelines.

chunder, chunda *v* (1950) to vomit. Australian slang; familiarized to British readers from the late 1960s through the exploits of Barry Mackenzie (as chronicled by Barry Humphries). It probably comes from the earlier *Chunder Loo*, rhyming slang for 'spew'. This was inspired by *Chunder Loo of Akim Foo*, a cartoon character originally drawn by Norman Lindsay and appearing in advertisements for Cobra boot-polish in the Sydney *Bulletin* between 1909 and 1920

> 1950 Nevil Shute: The way these bloody Nips go on. Makes you chunda.

> 1970 *Private Eye*: Many's the time we've chundered in the same bucket.

CinemaScope *n* (1953) The proprietary name of a form of cinema film using a very wide screen

> 1953 *Economist*: One of the major film companies has released the first film made in CinemaScope, 'The Robe'.

Cinerama *n* (1951) The proprietary name of a form of cinema film projected on a wide curved screen by three cameras. A blend of **cinema** and *panorama*

> 1952 *Daily Telegraph*: Cinerama, a new 'three-dimensional' system for projecting films, was given an enthusiastic welcome when it was displayed for the first time last night at the Broadway Theatre, New York… It uses a curved screen about six times as large as a normal cinema screen. The image on the screen is not one picture but three, converging into each other to create an impression of depth.

circadian *adj* (1959) Designating physiological activity which occurs approximately every twenty-four hours, or the rhythm of such activity. Coined from Latin *circa* 'around' and *dies* 'day'

> 1963 J. Leith: Circadian rhythms in animals, unlike plants, are almost always acquired.

clone *v* (1959) to propagate or cause to reproduce so as to form a clone (see **clone (1903)**)

> 1959 *Nature* (heading): A New Technique for Isolating and Cloning Cells of Higher Plants.

> 1968 *Observer Colour Supplement*: One of the most extraordinary of the possibilities now being explored…is referred to as 'cloning people'—the creation of genetically identical individuals from body cells.

closet *adj* (1952) secret, unacknowledged. Originally US; from the idea of being hidden in a 'closet' or cupboard. The earliest recorded example relates to a secret drinker of alcohol, but it was with reference to homosexuality that the usage took off in the late 1950s, especially in *closet queen* (first recorded in 1959). The phrase *come out of the closet* 'to acknowledge publicly one's previously concealed homosexuality', first recorded in 1971, appears to derive from the adjectival usage rather than vice versa. See also **out (1990)**

> 1961 *Social Problems* (US): 'Secret'…homosexuals…in the…'gay world'…are known as 'closet fags'.

> 1972 *Saturday Review* (US): Today's homosexual can be open ('come out') or covert ('closet').

> 1984 *Mail on Sunday*: His colleagues' retort is that Jimmy is a closet queen because he doesn't live with a woman.

> 1985 *Sunday Telegraph*: His defection [to Rome] is a blow because he was not a closet Papist intoxicated by bells and fancy vestments.

CND *n* (1958) An abbreviation of *Campaign for Nuclear Disarmament*, an organization formed in 1958 to campaign for Britain's nuclear disarmament. See also **ban the bomb (1960)**

> 1958 C. Judd: There are major points in the policy of the CND which UNA cannot support.

coca-colonization *n* (1950) the spread of US commercial culture throughout the world (as epitomised by the omnipresent American soft drink Coca-Cola)

> 1950 Edward Hyams: The coco-colanization [sic] of the viticultural regions.

> 1960 Arthur Koestler: One might call it the coca-colonization of Western Europe.

> 1990 *BBC Wildlife*: Let's not forget the 'coca-colonisation' of Africa, as Kenyan historian Ali Mazuri has so aptly termed it.

co-existence *n* (1954) See **co-exist (1931)**

coffee bar *n* (1956) an establishment where coffee and other non-alcoholic drinks are sold. The term is actually first recorded in 1905, but it was not until the 1950s that the concept (fuelled by newly fashionable Italian coffees—see **espresso (1945)**, **cappuccino (1948)**) took off: coffee bars became the centres of a now innocent-seeming youth culture, stimulated by nothing more intoxicating than rock 'n' roll and talk

> 1956 Louis McIntosh: This is Oxford's latest coffee-bar… The others are getting so tatty.

> 1957 *Times Literary Supplement*: The seedy group of coffee-bar philosophers…spouting their sad rehash of dated Fascist clichés.

common market *n* (1954) a group of countries imposing few or no duties on trade with one another and a common tariff on trade with outside countries. The term (with capital initials) later became the name of the trade association of France, the German Federal Republic, Italy, Belgium, the Netherlands, and Luxembourg instituted in 1958, and joined in 1973 by Britain, Denmark, and Ireland. It gradually gave way to **EEC (1958)**

> 1954 *Annual Register 1953*: The provisions…for the gradual establishment of a European common market.

> 1957 *Economist*: The Common Market: a treaty to set up a European Economic Community signed at Rome in March by six countries.

comprehensivize *v* (1958) to make (a school or system of education) comprehensive (see **comprehensive (1947)**). Widespread comprehensivization in Britain was initiated by the Labour government in 1965

> 1958 *Economist*: Attempts by local authorities to 'comprehensivise' schools… Newport has revised its drastic comprehensivisation plans down to a single comprehensive school.

> 1966 Daniel Jenkins: The compulsory 'Comprehensivisation' of schools.

cone *n* (1953) a cone-shaped warning sign placed on the roadway, etc., and used in (temporary) road traffic control. Originally US. Often in the phrase *traffic cone*. The verb **cone off** 'to close off (a section of road) with traffic cones' is first recorded in 1996 ('Before very long I can see the pavements being coned off for the different grades of pedestrians', *Market Trader & Shopkeeper*)

> 1953 *Construction & Maintainance Bulletin* (Texas Highway Dept.): Safety through use of traffic cones… By proper placement of these cones, a work area can be isolated… The cones should be set to channelize traffic in the proper lane to bypass the work area.

> 1976 A. Price: Stacks of *police—no parking* cones were dotted in readiness round the village.

consenting adult *n* (1957) an adult who takes part voluntarily in a sexual act, especially a homosexual act. Hence sometimes used as a facetious euphemism for 'homosexual'. A usage publicized in Britain by the Wolfenden Report on homosexuality in 1957 (see the first quote below)

> 1957 *Report of the Committee on Homosexual Offences & Prostitution*: We accordingly recommend that homosexual behaviour between consenting adults in private should no longer be a criminal offence.

> 1968 Osmington Mills: No, I'm not a consenting adult. But I'm not sex-starved, either.

containerize *v* (1958) to pack into, or transport by means of, large box-like receptacles of standardized design, known as 'containers', for the transportation of freight by road, rail, or sea

> 1958 *Times*: Express containerized cargo.

> 1959 *Times*: New developments which may affect our business, such as the bulk carrier, containerisation of cargo, [etc.].

continuous assessment *n* (1959) the evaluation of a pupil's progress throughout the course of study, based on course-work as well as, or instead of, examinations

> 1959 *15 to 18: Report of the Central Advisory Council for Education* (*England*) (Ministry of Education): Some Institutes of Education are using analogous methods of continuous assessment instead of examinations.

conventional *adj* (1955) Of bombs, weapons, warfare, etc.: not nuclear. The usage can be seen in embryo in 'We must decide whether the new fire package [i.e. the hydrogen bomb] will permit a reduction of our more conventional military weapons', *New York Herald Tribune* (1952)

> 1955 Max Beloff: The knowledge that all-out war would almost certainly mean the annihilation of organized society of the country initiating it…must enter into the calculations of modern statesmen as a deterrent to war in a way in which the limited horrors of 'conventional war' could not.

> 1955 *Hansard*: This unique difference…between the hydrogen and the atomic weapon on the one hand and conventional weapons on the other.

cool *v cool it* (1953) to relax, calm down, take it easy. Slang, originally US

> 1959 *Encounter*: The Wizard took my arm, and said, 'Cool it, kiddo.'

cosmetic *adj* (1955) that affects appearance only, superficial; intended merely to improve appearances

> 1955 T. H. Pear: Phrases and 'cosmetic' modifications of vowels are invented, adopted and discarded.

cosmonaut *n* (1959) an astronaut, especially a Russian one. An Anglicization of Russian *kosmonavt*, on the model of **astronaut**. (The adjective *cosmonautic(al*) had previously been coined in English, apparently as a completely independent creation, with no particular reference to Russian space-travel. It is first recorded in 1947: '[Von Pirquet]…called it the 'cosmonautic paradox', Willy Ley)

> 1959 A. Shternfeld's *Soviet Space Science* (translation): Naturally, cosmonauts could leave an artificial satellite and move in outside space.

> 1964 *Annual Register 1963*: The visit of three Russian cosmonauts…was followed by the official goodwill visit…of President Ayub Khan of Pakistan.

couch *n* (1952) a couch on which a patient lies when undergoing psychoanalysis or psychiatric treatment

> 1963 A. Heron: It seems reasonable to accept in general the psychoanalytic approach…but to predict that its most useful application may well prove to be preventive rather than therapeutic; in the home and school rather than on the couch.

count-down *n* (1953) the action of counting in reverse, from a given number to zero, usually in seconds, to mark the lapse of time before an explosion, the launching of a missile, etc. Originally US

> 1953 *News* (Birmingham, Alabama): Observers on the mountain were able to hear the count-down on the drop from the control tower.

> 1958 *Observer*: The count-down began. At the count of 11 the very top of the rocket started spinning. Two…one…and then the firing command.

counter-productive *adj* (1959) having the opposite of the desired effect, tending to act against the attainment of an objective. Originally US

> 1959 Dwight D. Eisenhower: The holding of a summit meeting…would be…absolutely impractical and as the State Department says, counterproductive.

country-and-western *adj, n* (1959) a type of music originating in the southern and western US, consisting mainly of rural or cowboy songs accompanied by a stringed instrument such as the guitar or fiddle

> 1970 *Listener*: Musically, Liverpool has always preferred Country and Western music to virtually any of the current national trends.

cowabunga *interj* (1954) An exclamation of exhilaration or satisfaction. Originally US. It was created (in the form *kowa-bunga*) by Eddie Kean as an exclamation of anger for the cartoon character Chief Thunderthud in *The Howdy Doody Show*. In the 1960s it became incorporated in surfers' slang (by now as a shout of triumph), but it did not achieve worldwide fame until 1990, when it was taken up as the rallying cry of the Teenage Mutant Ninja Turtles, a group of four comic-book fantasy characters for children which enjoyed a brief but intense vogue

> 1954 *Howdy Doody*: 'Princess will give me her magic necklace!' 'But I can't do that!' … 'Kowabunga! Then me fix you good! You be sorry!'

> 1963 *Time*: Shouting…'cowabunga!' they climb a 12-ft. wall of water and 'take the drop' off its shoulder.

> 1990 *Teenage Mutant Hero Turtles*: 'Hey, Mike, I didn't know that you could drive!' 'Me neither…cowabunga!'

crazy mixed-up *adj* (1955) Applied to someone whose mind is driven distracted by conflicting and unresolved emotions. Colloquial

> 1955 *Melody Maker*: Full of the most peculiar phrases…something else is a 'crazy, mixed-up creep'.

> 1957 John Braine: As they say in the films, I'm just a crazy mixed-up kid.

credit card *n* (1952) a card issued by an organization authorizing a named person to draw on its account or to make purchases on credit. Originally US; a reuse of a term which in the late 19th century had been used for a 'traveller's cheque'. Compare **debit card (1975)**

> 1952 *New York Times*: Anyone who can sign his name and pay his bills can charge his way through some of the better hotels, restaurants and night clubs of the country under a new credit card system known as the Diners Club.

> 1958 *Business Week*: American Express will present its new credit card to society Oct. 1.

credit squeeze *n* (1955) the restriction of financial credit facilities through banks etc. *Squeeze* in the sense 'a financial restriction' dates back at least to the 1870s

> 1955 *Times*: As early as last February I applied a little of the curb—what is sometimes called the credit squeeze.

> 1956 *Annual Register 1955*: Influential bankers and industrialists complained that the 'credit squeeze' had been overdone and warned against the danger of deflation.

cruise missile *n* (1959) a weapon in the form of a guided pilotless jet aircraft carrying a warhead and able to fly at low altitudes. Originally US

> 1959 *Aviation Week*: Severest test to date for Bomarc A was a simulated operational launch against North American X–10 test vehicle from the Navaho cruise missile program.

> 1983 *Daily Telegraph*: The threat to peace was not from the Cruise missile.

cube *n* (1957) an extremely conventional or conservative person. Youth slang, originally US; modelled punningly on **square (1944)**

> 1957 J. D. MacDonald: Work was for the cubes—the quintessence of a square.

> 1959 John Osborne: He's strictly from Cubesville.

D.A. *n* (1951) a style of haircut in which the hair at the back of the head is shaped like a duck's tail, favoured by Teddy-boys. Short for *duck's arse* (or, with facetious coyness, *duck's anatomy*). Alternative, toned-down versions with no need to hide behind euphemistic initials were *duck's behind* and *duck's tail* or *ducktail* (Teddy-boys were known in South Africa as *ducktails*)

> 1951 *Sunday Pictorial*: The D.A. [haircut], so called because of its remarkable resemblance to a duck's rear… The D.A. therefore stands for Duck's Anatomy—or some such word.

> 1955 D. Keene: The blond youth was in this up to his ducktail haircut.

> 1961 J. I. M. Stewart: His girl had…made him quit that Duck's Behind for a straight sleeking back with oil.

> 1969 Nik Cohn: He looked like another sub-Elvis, smooth flesh and duck-ass hair.

data processing *n* (1954) the performance by automatic means of any operations on empirical data, such as classifying or analysing them or carrying out calculations on them. Usually applied specifically to such an operation carried out on a computer

> 1954 *Instruments & Automation*: New 'Model CRC 102-A Electronic Computer' and its auxiliary…are designed for…data processing.

> 1985 *Times*: Electronic point of sale (EPOS) systems…link cash registers to larger computers for data processing.

Day-Glo *n* (1951) A proprietary name (registered in Britain in 1951) for a make of fluorescent paint or other colouring matter. Commonly applied loosely (and with an implication of tastelessness) to the eyeball-shrivellingly vivid colours characteristic of Day-Glo paints

> 1963 *Punch*: Sailing ladies can wear…day-glo vermilion jackets.

> 1968 *Sunday Times*: The George Mitchell Choir, greasepaint and day-glo and soft-shoe, was hamming it up on the jetty.

dee-jay *n* (1955) a disc jockey (see **disc jockey (1941)**). Originally US; an orthographic representation of the abbreviation **DJ** (which itself is not recorded before 1961). See also **veejay (1982)**

> 1956 *Life* (US): Some 1,200 radio disk jockeys…journeyed…to Nashville…to attend…'Dee Jay' (for disk jockey) convention.

destruct *v* (1958) to destroy. Originally US; a back-formation from *destruction*. A usage which originated within the aero-space community, and seems to have had a wider appeal only in the form **self-destruct (1966)**—perhaps from its use in the title-sequence of the popular US television drama series *Mission Impossible* (first broadcast in 1966)

> 1958 *Times*: The rocket…turned back…towards the shore; at this point it was destroyed (or 'destructed' as the official explanation puts it) by remote control.

> 1963 *New Scientist*: A brief stop at the 'arming tower', where the 'destruct' equipment is installed.

> 1969 *Daily Colonist* (Victoria, British Columbia): This message will self-destruct in 10 seconds but the printed message is the one that lives on.

deterrent *n* (1954) the nuclear weapons of any one country or alliance, viewed as likely to deter potential aggressors. The principle on which the long-running stand-off of the Cold War was founded: attack by atomic weapons is so appalling in its effect that no one in their right mind would provoke it

> 1954 *Statement on Defence* (*Parliamentary Papers 1953–54*): The primary deterrent, however, remains the atomic bomb and the ability of the highly organised and trained United States strategic air power to use it.

> 1959 *Observer*: Britain should also be prepared to give up her independent deterrent and stop the manufacture of nuclear weapons.

diabolical *adj* (1958) outrageous, disgraceful; disgracefully bad. British slang; often used in the clichéd phrase *diabolical liberty*

> 1958 Brendan Behan: Why ain't I given a chance to follow my trade in 'ere, eh?…It's a diabolical liberty. Geezers get no chance to follow their trade.

> 1986 *Observer*: From my point of view that pitch was dangerous. In fact, it was diabolical.

dialogue *n* (1953) discussion or diplomatic contact between the representatives of two nations, groups, or the like. Latterly extended to any supposedly valuable or constructive discussion or communication

> 1953 *Times*: M. Mayer went on to speak of the 'dialogue' which was tending to establish itself between east and west.

> 1970 *Guardian*: The new society, based on dialogue between all sections of society.

dianetics *n* (1950) a system, developed by the American writer L. Ron Hubbard (1911–86), that has as its aim the relief of psychosomatic illnesses by a process of cleansing the mind of harmful mental images. The word was coined by Hubbard from a variant of *dianoetic* 'relating to the thought processes'. See also **Scientology (1951)**

> 1950 *Time*: A new cult is smouldering through the U.S. underbrush. Its name: dianetics. Last week its bible, *Dianetics: The Modern Science of Mental Health*, was steadily climbing the U.S. bestseller lists.

> 1950 Aldous Huxley: We have been looking into dianetics.

diminished responsibility *n* (1957) a state of mental disturbance or abnormality, not classifiable as insanity, but recognized in law as a ground for exempting a person from full liability for criminal behaviour

> 1957 *Act of Parliament*: Persons suffering from diminished responsibility. Where a person kills…he shall not be convicted of murder if he was suffering from such abnormality of mind…as substantially impaired his mental responsibility.

> 1958 *Spectator*: Suppose that at his trial Taper should plead diminished responsibility, alleging that Sir Reginald's speeches had driven him…barmy.

Dinky *adj, n* (1950) A proprietary name (registered in Britain in 1950 by Meccano Ltd.) for a make of toy model motor vehicles, etc.; based on *dinky* 'small'

> 1957 *Economist*: As [children] often seem to bring back the same toy from each party—most usually, a surplus dinky car.

> 1977 *Private Eye* (advert): Collector wishes to purchase Dinky toys.

discotheque *n* (1954) a club, etc., where recorded music is played for dancing. A borrowing from French, and in the 1950s mainly used still in the French form *discothèque*, referring to such establishments in France. It was not until dancing clubs playing pop records became fashionable in the early 1960s that it was fully naturalized (and abbreviated to **disco (1964)**, which soon became the usual form)

> 1954 *New Yorker*: The St.-Germain-des-Prés *discothèque* night clubs…where phonograph *disques* are played for dancing.

> 1964 *TV Guide* (US): A discotheque is a small, intimate night club that plays recorded music for dancing—and discotheque dresses make dancing the frug, the monkey, and the Watusi a delight because they move with the beat.

disinformation *n* (1955) (the dissemination of) deliberately false information, especially when supplied by a government or its agent to a foreign power or to the media, with the intention of influencing the policies or opinions of those who receive it. Possibly an Anglicization of Russian *dezinformatsiya*. This in turn may have been adapted from French *désinformation*, although the known chronology is not in favour of this sequence (the Russian word is first recorded in 1949, the French in 1954)

> 1955 *Times*: The elimination of every form of propaganda and disinformation, as well as of other forms of conduct which create distrust or in any other way impede the establishment of an atmosphere conducive to constructive international cooperation and to the peaceful coexistence of nations.

dock *v* (1951) to join (a space vehicle) to another in space; also used intransitively. A vigorous survivor from speculation to actuality

> 1951 *Journal of the British Interplanetary Society*: The idea of 'docking' a spaceship inside…a space-station is suicidal lunacy.

> 1969 *Guardian*: Astronauts Neil Armstrong and Edwin Aldrin soared up and away from the moon's surface to dock with the command module.

do-it-yourself *n* (1952) doing one's own household repairs and maintenance, usually as opposed to employing someone else to do it. A term arising in large part from the great increase in home ownership in the second half of the century. In earlier times, when accommodation was much likelier to be rented, there was little incentive to save one's landlord money by doing repairs oneself. The phrase has been around in proverbial expressions for centuries ('If a man will haue his businesse well done, he must doe it himselfe', Thomas Drax (1616)), and Richard Barham endorsed its message of self-reliance in the *Ingoldsby Legends* ('If it's business of consequence, *Do it yourself*' (a1845)). The derived *do-it-yourselfer* is first recorded in 1954, and the abbreviation *DIY* in 1955

> 1952 *Time*: Do-it-yourself has brought similar gains, and market shifts, to other industries.

> 1954 *New York Times*: To the do-it-yourselfer, plywood is as essential as paint, tools, plastics and ordinary lumber.

> 1955 *Pract. Householder* Dec. 203/1 A central pool such as a 'D.I.Y. Club' from which…tools can be hired is the obvious advantage.

domino *n* (1954) Applied metaphorically to a theory that a political event or development in one country, etc., will lead to its occurrence in others. First recorded as being used by US President Eisenhower, but the expressions *domino theory* and *domino effect*, in which it is now most often encountered, did not emerge until the 1960s. It was commonly advanced by US strategists as a justification for the Vietnam War, the reasoning being that once one Southeast Asian country had been allowed to fall to Communism, the rest would follow (and then Australia, and so on), like one toppling domino knocking over the next in a row

> 1954 Dwight D. Eisenhower: You had broader considerations that might follow what you might call the 'falling domino' principle. You had a row of dominoes set up, and you knocked over the first one, and what would happen to the last one was the certainty that it would go over very quickly.

> 1965 *New Statesman*: There was as much domino talk ('With the collapse of South Vietnam, Laos…would speedily be swallowed…') then as now… Even if…the domino theory works out in practice.

doner kebab *n* (1958) a Turkish dish which consists of slices of lamb or mutton, layered with herbs and spices on a vertical spit and roasted as it revolves against a tall narrow grill. As the surface is cooked the meat is sliced thinly downwards and served, often with pita bread. A borrowing of Turkish *döner kebap*, literally 'rotating kebab'. The earliest references to it in English are as an exotic item, in books of Eastern Mediterranean cookery and the like, but then a wave of Turkish immigration brought the dish to Britain. In the mid 1970s, doner kebab houses became well-patronized inner-city fast-food joints, and *kebab*, *tout court*, came to denote not a shish kebab but a doner kebab

> 1974 *Times*: The Open Space in Tottenham Court Road…is within easy reach of…the kebab houses around Charlotte Street.

> 1986 J. Milne: A take-away doner kebab…The nice thing about doner is…enough raw onion and chili sauce on it.

Dormobile *n* (1952) A proprietary name (registered in 1952) for a type of motor-van with a rear compartment convertible for use as a caravan. A blend of *dormitory* and *automobile*

> 1966 Peter Willmott: We're going in a big Dormobile and we'll have four chalets and a caravan.

dosh *n* (1953) money. British slang; origin unknown. It appears to have been in use in the US in the second half of the 19th century (there are records of it from 1854 and 1871); no more is known of it until 1953, but it would be highly coincidental if there were no connection between the two usages. It enjoyed a revival of popularity in the money-conscious 1980s

> 1953 Hugh Clevely: He hadn't enough dosh on him.

> 1989 *Looks*: Chances come your way to make extra dosh so try your luck.

double helix *n* (1954) the structure of a DNA molecule, consisting of two spiral chains of polynucleotides coiled round the same axis. The term was introduced in a paper in the *Proceedings of the Royal Society* by Francis Crick and James Watson who, with the help of Maurice Wilkins and Rosalind Franklin, worked out the structure in the early 1950s. Watson used it as the title of a book in 1968

> 1954 Crick & Watson (heading): Detailed configuration of the double helix.

> 1968 *New Scientist*: The symbol of the molecular biological age is without doubt the 'double helix' of DNA.

downtime *n* (1952) time, or an occasion, when a machine or vehicle is out of action or unavailable for use. Originally US

> 1952 *Bell Telephone System Monograph*: The amount of 'down time' due to faulty machine operation is very low.

> 1954 *Journal of the Association of Computing Machinery* (table): Number of unscheduled down times.

drag (race) *n* (1954) a race between specially modified cars (*dragsters* (1954)) to see which can accelerate the fastest. Originally US. Compare **hot rod (1945)**

> 1954 *American Speech*: There are different types of drag racing: (1) drags from a dead stop; (2) drags from a rolling start… Dragster is one of the classifications in official acceleration competition.

> 1962 *American Speech*: An establishment where youthful drivers congregate to plan illegal activities such as highway drag-races.

drainpipe trousers, drainpipes *n* (1950) narrow tightfitting trousers, of a type typically worn by Teddy boys

> 1950 *Strand Magazine*: 'Drain-pipes haven't caught on,' says Eddie. 'The money won't run to them. We can't wear them for work.'

> 1955 M. Berger-Hamerschlag: But even Jeff entered the class in a new outfit of that macabre character, with drainpipe trousers, both sides braided with black silk.

drip-dry *v, adj* (1953) Of certain synthetic or chemically treated fabrics: to dry when hung up to drip, without subsequently requiring wringing or ironing; also used transitively. Hence as an adjective, meaning 'that will drip-dry'

> 1953 *Woman*: With this permanently pleated nylon nightie…you just…rinse out, drip dry, and you don't even think of ironing.

> 1954 *Science News Letter*: It will not shrink, fade or wrinkle and it drip-dries without pressing.

> 1957 *Woman*: Cottons and rayons with a special finish—that is ones that have been made crease-resistant, drip-dry or non-iron.

duck's arse *n* (1951), **ducktail** *n* (1955) See **D.A. (1951)**

early retirement *n* (1957) retirement from one's occupation before the normal retirement age, especially on advantageous financial terms. An early sign of the shortage of work to go round in the post-industrial world

> 1957 *Life*: If it works, early retirement can produce the blissful by-product shown on the next page.

East *n* (1951) the states of eastern Europe during the Cold War; the Communist powers; the Soviet bloc. Almost always used in conjunction with *West* 'the non-Communist states' (see **West (1946)**)

> 1951 *Annual Register 1950*: There were more 'espionage' convictions…and the closing of the Czech Consulate-General in New York. These incidents, significant of the growing estrangement of East and West, were also…evidence that neither party wished to push its claims to the limit.

> 1959 *News Chronicle*: The harsh reality of the cold war, of East-West tension.

economy size *n, adj* (1950) Applied, especially in advertising, to objects which are sold in a size that is said to be economically advantageous to the customer— typically, but not always, the largest packet, etc., in a series. Originally US

> 1950 R. P. Bissell: The only trouble with the economy size tube of shaving cream is that it takes up more room in the valise than a pair of rubber boots.

EEC *n* (1958) An abbreviation of *European Economic Community*, the name of an association of (originally six) Western European states for the purpose of economic cooperation, formed by treaty in 1958. See also **common market (1954)**, **EC (1973)**, **European Union (1991)**

> 1958 *Times Review of Industry*: Exchanges with the other members of E.E.C. accounted for 27 per cent. of imports.

> 1958 *Spectator*: The Common Market Treaty, laying down the conditions under which the European Economic Community…is to be established, came into force on 1st January 1958.

eiderdown *n* (1950) a quilt filled with eider-duck feathers or any similar soft material.

> 1950 *Times*: I ask you…to lend your pen to scotching the unwarrantable…term 'eiderdown' when applied to the ordinary goose-down quilt.

electro-convulsive therapy *n* (1952) the treatment of mental disease by the application of an electric shock to the central nervous system. Used especially in cases of severe depression. Usually shortened to *ECT*, which is first recorded in 1953

> 1953 Hinsie & Shatzky: Electric convulsive therapy, or E.C.T., is indicated in mania, depressions, and certain cases of schizophrenia.

Elizabethan *adj, n* (1953) (a person) of the reign of Elizabeth II, Queen of the United Kingdom 1952–. For a while the new reign was characterized as 'New Elizabethan', and Her Majesty's new subjects as 'New Elizabethans', as if some of the confidence and bravado of the earlier Elizabethan age would rub off

> 1953 F. E. Halliday: It still remains…one of the best accounts that we possess of life in Elizabethan England, a quality that should appeal to Elizabethans of the new age.

> 1957 D. J. Enright: The 'New Elizabethan' theme, cooking in the minds of statesmen, leads to nothing more glorious than the devastation of an Arab quarter.

engagé *adj* (1955) The up-market, original-French version of **engaged (1947)**

> 1955 Graham Greene: I don't know what I'm talking politics for. They don't interest me and I'm a reporter. I'm not *engagé*.

environment *n* (1956) the combination of external conditions that impinge on organisms living on the Earth. A specialized application of the more general 'the objects or the region surrounding something', which goes back to the early 19th century

> 1956 P. S. Sears: The situation is clouded by a widespread confidence that this impact of man upon environment can continue indefinitely.

> 1967 K. Mellanby: Perhaps the most obvious way in which man has contaminated his environment is by polluting the air with smoke.

EOKA *n* (1955) An abbreviation of modern Greek *Ethniki Organosis Kupriakou Agonos* 'National Organization of Cypriot Struggle (for the furthering of the Greek cause in Cyprus)', the name of a Greek-Cypriot liberation movement led by Archbishop Makarios and General Grivas which became familiar in Britain in the late 1950s. Many on both sides were killed in the struggle to drive out the island's British colonial rulers

> 1955 *Times*: These were the first terrorist outrages for a week, and may have been caused by a 'lone wolf' terrorist, as Eoka, the underground movement, has refrained from all activity.

EP *n* (1954) An abbreviation of *extended play*, denoting a record seven inches in diameter, each side playing for about six minutes at 45 revolutions per minute. Compare **LP (1948)** and **single (1949)**

> 1954 *Gramophone*: The second batch of EPs to appear… The other side of the new EP.

ergonomics *n* (1950) the scientific study of the efficiency of human beings in their working environment. A coinage based on Greek *ergon* 'work'

> 1950 *Lancet*: In July, 1949, a group of people decided to form a new society for which the name the 'Ergonomics Research Society' has now been adopted.

> 1952 *Oxford Mail*: [K. F. H. Murrell] found it necessary to invent the word 'ergonomics' to cover the kind of work he and other people are doing in studying work in relation to environment.

Ernie *n* (1956) An acronym formed from the initial letters of *electronic random number indicator equipment*, the name given to the device used in Britain for drawing the prize-winning numbers of premium bonds (see **premium bond (1908)**). This was one of the first such anthropomorphic acronyms (made up from a heavily manipulated name) to which the British public had been exposed with the full backing of a press campaign, and it made a considerable initial impression

> 1957 *Times*: Ernie here is a pleasant enough fellow and…will be a lot more efficient at picking winning premium bonds.

escalate *v* (1959) to increase or develop by successive stages. Often used, especially originally, with specific reference to development from conventional warfare into nuclear warfare. A word that got picked out in the lottery of linguistic condemnation: purists continue to wince at it at the end of the century, although objectively it is little better or worse than scores of similar formations that pass unremarked. See also **escalation (1938), escalator (1900)**

> 1959 *Guardian*: The possibility of local wars 'escalating into all-out atomic wars'.

> 1961 *Economist*: Using tactical nuclear weapons which would be likely to escalate hostilities into a global nuclear war.

ethnicity *n* (1953) the fact of belonging to a particular ethnic or racial group. Over the second half of the 20th century, an increasingly used term in the field of race relations. See also **ethnic (1945)**

> 1953 D. Riesman: The groups who, by reason of rural or small-town location, ethnicity, or other parochialism, feel threatened by the better educated upper-middle-class people.

Europe *n* (1957) Used allusively with reference to (British) membership of the European (Economic) Community (formerly the Common Market; see **common market (1954)**)

> 1957 *Times*: The defeat shortly after this success of the plan for a European Defence Community was a setback for 'Europe'.

> 1962 *Listener*: The decision to go into Europe.

Eurovision *n* (1951) the television network of the European Broadcasting Union, through which programmes are exchanged or relayed

> 1954 *New York Times*: Europe's leading television engineers will twirl dials with crossed fingers tomorrow when they tune in the first eight-nation 'Eurovision' hook-up through Lille.

fab *adj* (1957) wonderful, marvellous. Slang. A shortening of **fabulous** (which is not recorded in print in this sense until 1959). The usage really took off around 1963, when it became attached to the Beatles (sometimes called the 'Fab Four') and other Merseyside pop groups. After lying dormant for a while, it enjoyed a revival in the 1980s (see **fabbo (1984)**)

> 1963 *Times*: She stretched her stockinged toes towards the blazing logs. 'Daddy, this fire's simply fab.'

> 1963 *Meet the Beatles*: Most of the Merseyside groups produce sounds which are pretty fab.

> 1988 *National Lampoon*: And I just think it's fab!

fabulous *adj* (1959) wonderful, marvellous. Colloquial

> 1959 *Cambridge Review*: Miss Mitchell, looking, one must admit, fabulous, played down her frenzy.

> 1962 *Radio Times*: I think [Salford]'s a fabulous place.

> 1963 Alan Ross: Trueman puffed at a cigarette and said he felt fabulous.

fall-out *n* (1950) radioactive refuse of a nuclear bomb explosion; also, the process of deposition of such refuse. A substance about whose invisible perils its potential victims were much exercised during the Cold War

> 1952 *New York Times*: Nevertheless, a good deal of radioactive stuff is picked up and carried by the wind and deposited all over the country… So far there have been no dangerous concentrations of radioactive 'fall-out', as it is called, that is outside of the proving grounds in Nevada.

> 1961 *John o' London's*: The make-it-yourself fallout shelter.

far-out *adj* (1954) Of jazz: of the latest or most progressive kind. Hence used more generally, to mean 'avant-garde' or 'far-fetched', or as a broad term of approval: 'excellent, splendid'. Slang, originally US

> 1954 *Time*: Jazz lingo becomes obsolescent almost as fast as it reaches the public ear… A daring performance was 'hot', then 'cool', and now is 'far out'.

> 1963 Kingsley Amis: She was…several times more attractive than her with-it off-beat far-out co-religionist deserved.

> 1970 *Science Journal*: Talking with computers, so much a far-out idea when this journal discussed IBM's work on it four years ago, now seems quite straightforward.

fast food *n* (1951) convenience food of a type which can be served quickly at a catering outlet or prepared quickly at home; mainly used adjectivally with reference to eating places where foods are kept hot and ready to serve, or partially prepared so that they can be served quickly. Originally US. See also **convenience (1961)**

> 1951 *Fountain & Fast Food Service*: The partners have become old hands at spotting the type of conventioneer that will patronize their fast food service.

> 1977 *Times*: 'Fast food' requires no preparation by the customer. Traditional 'fast food outlets' like fish-and-chip shops are being superseded by Chinese, Indian, Kebab and fried chicken houses.

felt-tip pen *n* (1957) a pen with a writing point made from compressed fibres. Variations first recorded slightly later are *felt-tipped pen* (1964) and *felt pen* (1965)

> 1966 *Guardian*: The secret bards [i.e. graffiti-writers] have taken to felt-tipped pens.

> 1966 Dick Francis: Mike…was already writing names on disposable cups with a red felt pen.

> 1978 *Times Literary Supplement*: Others are hastily scrawled in blunt pencil,…or a child's mauve felt tip.

fibre optics *n* (1957) the study and application of the transmission of images by means of total internal reflection through fibres of glass or other transparent solids (see **optical fibre (1970)**)

> 1956 *Times*: If one beam of light can be transmitted along a glass tube, why not transmit detailed images along the same path?… Dr. Narinder Singh Kapany, 30, has succeeded by applying a technique he refers to as 'fiber optics'.

fish stick *n* (1953), **fish finger** *n* (1955) a small finger-shaped or rectangular section of fish coated in batter or breadcrumbs; *stick* is the preferred alternative in America, while the British go for *finger*. Introduced by Birds Eye in the early 1950s, this was the first significant contributor to the frozen-food revolution which swept over Western eating habits in the second half of the 20th century

> 1953 *Time*: Birds Eye brought out fish sticks (fresh fish coated with a special batter, breaded, fried, packed and then frozen).

> 1962 *Listener*: Cornflakes and frozen fish-fingers, oven-ready chickens, and wrapped, sliced bread.

flaky, flakey *adj* (1959) eccentric, crazy, unbalanced. Slang, originally and mainly US; it did not become familiar to British speakers until 1986, when US President Ronald Reagan used it to describe Libyan head of state Moamar al Gaddafi. Its ultimate source may be US drug users' slang *flake* 'cocaine, especially in flaked form', which dates from the 1920s. Eric Partridge included a suggestive quote in his *Dictionary of the Underworld*: 'We couldn't help enjoying the name Flaky Lou. She was named after cocaine, which was flaky in appearance' (1945)

> 1983 John Le Carré: We hear she's currently allied with a very flakey anarchist guy, some kind of crazy.

> 1986 *New Yorker*: People can choose their own words to describe Qaddafi's mental state— President Reagan called him 'flaky', and later denied that he considered Qaddafi mentally unbalanced.

flick knife *n* (1957) a knife with the blade held in the handle by a catch which can be released with a flick of the finger. A weapon favoured by gang-fighting youths, which caused a tremor of concern among the authorities when it appeared on the scene in the mid 1950s

> 1957 *Times*: Mr. Justice Streatfeild said at York Assizes yesterday: 'What an invention of the Devil is the "flick" knife, which unhappily so often features in crimes of violence in this country, often committed by young people.'

flying bedstead *n* (1955) an experimental aircraft, shaped like a bedstead, for testing methods of vertical take-off. See **VTOL (1955)**

> 1955 *Science News Letter*: Rolls-Royce, in Britain, has designed a model dubbed the 'flying bedstead'. It is thrust into the air vertically by two jet nozzles pointed downward in the front and rear.

FORTRAN *n* (1956) a high-level programming language used chiefly for scientific and mathematical calculations. Originally US; the quote below explains how the word (the earliest of the major computer-programming-language coinages) was put together. See also **Algol (1959)**, **Cobol (1960)**, **BASIC (1964)**

> 1956 *Computers & Automation*: More recently, John Backus' group at IBM has prepared FORTRAN (FORmula TRANslation) for the IBM–704 computer. FORTRAN will translate into computer language a program written very close [*sic*] the language of the mathematician or scientist.

four-minute mile *n* (1955) a mile run by an athlete in four minutes or less (first achieved by Roger Bannister at Oxford in 1954). The holy grail of middle-distance runners at a time when breaking arbitrary barriers was all the rage (compare **sound barrier (1939)**)

> 1955 Thomas Sterling: These people would believe I was going to die if they saw me running the four minute mile.

Freefone *n* (1959) The proprietary name, initially in Britain and subsequently (from 1984) in the US, for a telephone service by which the charge for calls made to an organization, typically for information or to make use of a service, is borne by the organization itself rather than the caller. Often spelt *Freephone*. Compare **toll-free (1970)**

> 1990 *She*: For further information on the Peugeot range, call Freefone 0800–678 800.

free world *n* (1955) the non-Communist countries of the world. A partisan usage, favoured by non- or especially anti-Communists

> 1955 *Bulletin of Atomic Science*: The Soviet World and the Free World are running neck and neck in the training of scientists.

> 1963 *Guardian*: The free-world countries involved were Britain and Greece.

Freudian slip *n* (1959) an unintentional mistake that seems to reveal a subconscious intention. Named after the Austrian psychiatrist Sigmund Freud and (not surprisingly, given the nature of his preoccupations) often applied (facetiously) to a slip of the tongue which reveals thoughts of a sexual nature

> 1963 Nicholas Blake: It was an odd little slip of the tongue… They call them Freudian slips nowadays.

Frisbee *n* (1957) The proprietary name (registered in the US in 1959) of a concave plastic disc which spins when thrown into the air and is used in a catching game. The disc was invented by Fred Morrison, who is said to have got the idea (and the name) from the aerodynamic pie tins of the Frisbie bakery in Bridgeport, Connecticut

> 1957 *Newsweek*: The object of the game is simply for one player to toss the Frisbee, or disk, into the air and try to keep it from his opponent's grasp.

funky *adj* (1954) Of jazz or similar music: down-to-earth and uncomplicated; emotional; having the qualities of the blues. Slang, originally US Black English. Probably ultimately from *funky* 'musty, foul-smelling'

> 1957 *New Yorker*: One of the leaders of an increasingly fashionable school of modern jazz called…'hard bop' or 'funky' is Horace Silver.

> 1971 *Frendz*: Brown Sugar and Bitch are Jagger at his foxy, dirty, funky best.

garlic bread *n* (1951) bread flavoured with garlic, moistened with oil or butter, and re-heated. An early sign of British people's reconciliation with garlic, after more than a century's Dracula-like aversion. A mixture of wartime service abroad, the evocative cookery-writing of Elizabeth David and others, and (especially later in the decade) foreign holidays were reawakening them to the pleasures of other cuisines

1960 I. T. Ross: She brought a basketful of garlic bread from the oven.

gas *n* (1953) something or someone that is very pleasing, exciting, impressive, admirable, etc. Originally US jazz slang; often in *a gas*. Probably derived from the synonymous **gasser (1944)**

1957 James Baldwin: Brand-new pianos certainly were a gas.

1971 *Frendz*: The Stones…were a screaming, speeding, sexy gas.

gay *n* (1953) See **gay (1933)**

glitterati *n* (1956) the celebrities or 'glittering' stars of fashionable society, or of the literary and show-business world. Originally US; a punning coinage based on *literati*, not in widespread use until the late 1970s. Thereafter, *-ati* became a buzz-suffix, producing much ephemera (e.g. *slopperati* (1986), *jazzerati* (1987), *numerati* (1988), *blazerati* (1998))

1956 *Time*: Bobbing and weaving about the premises are a passel of New York glitterati. There is a highbrow editor of a popular magazine who is keen on starting a new literary journal [etc.].

1978 *New York Times Magazine*: So say the formerly beautiful people, once the jet set, now called the glitterati, which appears to be a combination of literati, or illuminati, with a glittering generality.

gnome *n* (1956) an international financier or banker, specifically one who is Swiss. Used mainly in the hostile phrase *the gnomes of Zurich*, which was apparently originated by the British Labour politician and future prime minister Harold Wilson (1916–95)

1956 *Hansard Commons*: All these financiers, all the little gnomes in Zurich and the other financial centres about whom we keep on hearing.

1964 *New Statesman*: The gnomes of Zurich and their related goblins in the more politically involved capitals.

goggle-box *n* (1959) a television set; the television. British slang, part humorous, part patronizing. See also **box (1958)**

1959 *Guardian*: Switch the goggle-box on at 10 a.m.

1967 *Times*: Mr. Wilson was…so good at television appearances, that he had convinced himself that he, single-handed, could win elections 'with the help of the goggle box'.

go-kart *n* (1959) a light, low-framed vehicle with small wheels and engine, used for recreational racing. A commercial respelling of *go-cart*, a word which dates back to the late 17th century. At first it denoted a wheeled walking-frame for toddlers, then, in the 18th century, a hand-cart, and in the 19th century a sort of light open carriage. *Go-kart* is often shortened to *kart*, and the sport of driving these mini racing cars is called *karting* (both also first recorded in 1959)

1959 *Times*: The R.A.C. are prepared in principle to accept the control in Britain of go-kart racing— the new miniature car racing popular in the United States.

1959 *Motor*: The whole affair may well seem reprehensible to those who feel that an injustice has been wrought on the children or that karting is too juvenile for adults, but after trying a kart, although one must admit that they are a joke, there is no doubt that they are one of the very best jokes to come out of the U.S.A. since Thurber's dogs. After 10 minutes' karting the cynic is invariably asking where he can get one.

goon *n* (1951) any of the members of the cast of a popular British radio comedy series, *The Goon Show* (originally called *Crazy People*), noted for its crazy and absurd brand of humour. The history of the word *goon* is remarkably complicated. In the 1930s it meant both 'a thug' and 'a fool' (see **goon (1938)**). The former (with perhaps a sprinkling of the latter) probably led to 'a prisoner-of-war guard' (see **goon (1945)**), but Spike Milligan, creator of the Goons, denies that he got the name from that source (see the fourth quote below). He claims that it came from a cartoon character, presumably the same 'Alice the Goon' who inspired the original 1938 *goon*. No doubt the intervening years of use in the sense 'fool' had played a part too. Subsequent uses of *goon* to mean 'someone who behaves crazily' are not easy to distinguish from the earlier 'fool', but derivatives such as *goonery* and *goonish* were no doubt inspired by the radio Goons

1951 *Radio Times*: Crazy people… Radio's Own Crazy Gang 'The Goons'… Spike Milligan…has compiled the 'Goon Show' material.

> 1951 *Picture Post*: Four young comics—Michael Bentine, Harry Secombe, Spike Milligan and Peter Sellers—have at last got together in a radio programme. In 'Crazy People' they put across their favoured kind of humour. This they call 'goonery'.

> 1959 *Sunday Times*: Photographs by Inge Morath that have that air of solemnity suppressing a giggle that has become known, in this country at least, as 'goonish'.

> 1971 Spike Milligan: Prisoners of war called their German guards goons but I got it from Popeye. There was a creature called the Goon which had nothing in the face at all except hair... I liked the word and we called it *The Goons*.

gross *adj* (1959) disgusting, repulsive. US, originally students' slang; an extension of its earlier use as an intensifying adjective, applied to unpleasant things (as in 'gross discourtesy')

> 1978 J. Hyams: 'She really thinks he's gross, huh?'... 'The pits,' said Freda.

group *n* (1958) an ensemble of pop musicians, typically numbering between three and six. First recorded in the compound *skiffle group*, but the term did not really take off until the early 1960s, with the rise of groups such as the Beatles and the Rolling Stones. Often in the compounds *pop group* and *rock group*. By the late 1960s *group* was becoming uncool, and was widely substituted by *band*

> 1964 *Gramophone Popular Record Catalogue* (Artist Section): *Barron-Knights, The...* Call up the groups. Medley.

> 1967 *Listener*: Two of the Rolling Stones 'pop group' are sent for trial on drugs charges.

> 1967 *Melody Maker*: Groups who are going to give us action.

> 1967 *Listener*: As a rock group, then, the Kinks don't rate musically.

growth *n* (1952) an increase in economic activity or profitability; economic expansion. The underlying *raison d'être* of 20th-century Western capitalism

> 1952 W. W. Rostow: Growth is defined as a relation between the rates of increase in capital and the working force,...and in population,...such that per capita output (not necessarily consumption) is rising.

> 1965 Harold Wilson: I am now fighting a losing battle on another word I dislike—growth—which had a certain medical and agricultural connotation. 'Economic growth involves more purposeful work than leaving it to nature.'

growth industry *n* (1957) an industry which has been, or is in process of, developing at a faster rate than other industries. Widely applied metaphorically to any activity which is on the increase

> 1957 *Economist*: The pattern of growth in Britain's biggest growth industry...is not a balanced one.

> 1964 *Spectator*: In time private enterprise snoopery could become a growth industry and major job-supplier for our unemployed.

hair spray *n* (1959) a fixative solution sprayed on to the hair to keep a hairstyle in place. Necessitated by the contemporary female fashion for large hair (see **bouffant (1955)**, **beehive (1960)**). (**(Hair) lacquer**, latterly a synonym, is first recorded in the 1940s, when it was used for a substance that had to be applied with a brush)

> 1969 *Honey Book of Beauty*: Outdoor girls who swear by hair spray must be careful in their choice.

hallucinogenic *n* (1952) Of a drug: causing hallucinations. The related noun *hallucinogen*, denoting such a drug, is first recorded in 1954. At first familiar only to chemists and aficionados, in the LSD-taking 1960s both became common currency

> 1952 *Journal of Mental Science*: There are many other hallucinogenic drugs, but none has either such striking properties or such a simple chemical constitution as mescaline.

> 1954 Aldous Huxley: Lysergic acid, an extremely potent hallucinogen derived from ergot.

happening *n* (1959) an improvised or spontaneous theatrical or pseudo-theatrical entertainment. Originally US

> 1959 *Nation* (New York): The first exhibition is not of painting but is an 'event' consisting of eighteen 'happenings' by Allan Kaprow.

1963 *Observer*: The last day…gave us our notorious nude, who was towed across the musicians' gallery as part of a rehearsed 'Happening'.

1974 Roy Strong: I want provocative exhibitions…happenings in the quadrangle…huge catalogues to appear, publications to take off.

hard *adj* (1955) Of a drug: dangerous and habit-forming, addictive (e.g. heroin and cocaine). Compare **soft (1959)**

1967 *Listener*: Nothing on earth would persuade me to try LSD or the hard drugs.

hard shoulder *n* (1955) a reinforced verge at the side of a motorway on which vehicles may drive and stop only in an emergency. British; part of the new terminology of motorways to which English-speakers had to become used in the late 1950s (see **motorway (1903)**)

1955 *Times*: The motorways are to be constructed to modern standards, with hard shoulders of 9 ft.

H-bomb *n* (1950) The abbreviated name of the **hydrogen bomb (1947)**

1950 *Hansard, Commons*: I am not one who criticised the right hon. Gentleman…for drawing attention to the H-bomb.

1952 *Manchester Guardian Weekly*: The first test model of the H-bomb will be followed shortly by even more violent versions.

Hell's Angel *n* (1957) A name given in the 1950s in the US (later to similar people elsewhere) to a member of a group of lawless, usually leather-jacketed, motor-cyclists notorious for their disturbances of civil order in California (featured, but there called 'Black Rebels', in a 1954 film entitled *The Wild One*). The origin of the term may be a 1930 film called *Hell's Angels*, about air-battles in World War I. It is also on record as an aircraft name in World War II ('The ten-man crew which manned the flying fortress, "Hell's Angel", on her thirty-three raids across the English channel', *Examiner* (San Francisco) (1943))

1957 *Chronicle* (San Francisco): It also attracted several hundred cyclists who are not American Motorcycle Association members, but who belong to such clubs as the Vampires, Scavengers and Hell's Angels group that rides in the Bay Area.

1971 *New Scientist*: The Hell's Angels created rather than prevented disorder when Mick and the Stones were dispensing their magic.

hi-fi *n, adj* (1950) that part of acoustics and electronics that deals with the design, construction, and use of equipment for the recording and reproduction of sound to a fairly high standard. In this original usage, *hi-fi* is simply an abbreviation of the noun *high fidelity* (first recorded in 1934), but it was soon being used adjectivally (see the second quote below), and in due course this became its main role. A new noun sense, 'a hi-fi record-player or other system', is first recorded in 1959

1950 *Audio Engineer* (title): Hi-fi at seven-and-a-half.

1952 *Time*: Until last week, most 'hi-fi' sets, which reproduce music in the home with the clarity and realism of the concert hall, were custom-made from standard parts by small radio and phonograph shops at a cost of from $150 to $2,000.

1953 *House & Garden*: What do they mean when they talk about hi-fi?

1959 Colin MacInnes: I put a disc on to his hi-fi.

high-rise *adj* (1954) Of a building: tall, multi-storey. A term that ushered in the period—roughly from the mid 1950s to the mid 70s—when very tall blocks of flats were considered to be the best way of housing large numbers of the less well-off. The antonym *low-rise* is first recorded in 1957

1954 *Architectural Review*: In general form—podium and high-rise accommodation—this scheme follows the general pattern of current thought.

1957 *Fortune*: What kind of people…prefer 'high-rise' apartment buildings, what kind of people prefer two-to-five-storey 'low-rise' houses?

hippie, hippy *n* (1953) Originally a low-profile synonym of **hipster (1941)**—i.e. someone who is 'hip' or in touch with fashionable tastes—*hippie* suddenly made it into the big time in the mid 1960s as the name for a member of a culture, originally mainly on the West Coast of the US but eventually spreading throughout the youth of the Western (and indeed parts of the Eastern) world, characterized by an emphasis on nonviolence and universal love and a general rejection of the mores of conventional society, especially regarding dress, personal appearance, and way of life. Numerous derivatives, such as *hippiedom* and *hippieness*, soon followed. Long after the original hippies themselves have wandered off into the sunset, the word remains current as a patronizing term for casualness or unconventionality of appearance or behaviour, especially in the young. See also **flower people (1967)**

> 1953 D. Wallop: Man, I really get a bellyful of these would be hippies.

> 1967 *Daily Telegraph*: These people, 'writers, musicians, psychedelic popsters and hippies…' see London as a 'focal city for permissive experiments' in art and life.

> 1967 *Sunday Truth* (Brisbane): A hippie is the LSD Age's equivalent of a beatnik, and they turn on with marihuana, LSD, benzedrine or merely with the idea of turning-on.

> 1967 *New York Times*: There are two philosophical trends in hippiedom.

> 1968 *Blues Unlimited*: I guess California, and psychedelia, and hippieness have had the influence.

> 1998 *Food Illustrated*: The French seem impervious to the politics of food—while an organic movement exists, it is generally disdained as hippy.

hit parade *n* (1958) a list of the best-selling recorded songs over a given period. See also **top ten (1958)**, **charts (1963)**

> 1958 *Times*: The numbers listed in the hit parade all have a structure of professionalism.

> 1965 George Melly: His version of 'Rock Island Line'…was put out as a single and rose to be top of the Hit Parade.

Holocaust *n* (1957) the mass murder of the Jews by the Nazis in World War II. The specific application was introduced by historians during the 1950s, probably as an equivalent to Hebrew *hurban* and *shoah* 'catastrophe' (used in the same sense); but it had been foreshadowed by contemporary references to the Nazi atrocities as a *holocaust* (in the sense 'great slaughter', which dates from the early 19th century): 'The Nazis go on killing… If this rule could be relaxed, some hundreds, and possibly a few thousands, might be enabled to escape from this holocaust', *Hansard, Lords* (1943). At first the term was in common use mainly among Jews, but it gradually spread to a more general domain. See also **genocide (1944)**

> 1957 *Yad Washem Bulletin*: Research on the Holocaust Period.

> 1962 Brian Glanville: The holocaust…was the inevitable end, the logical conclusion of the pogroms, the Mosley marches, the hatred.

Hooray Henry *n* (1959) a type of loud, rich, rather ineffectual or foolish young society man. Often applied in British English since the mid 1970s specifically to a fashionable, extroverted, loud-voiced, but conventional upper- or upper-middle-class young man—a sort of male equivalent to the female **Sloane Ranger (1975)**. Commonly shortened to the equally derogatory *hooray*. Apparently an alteration of an earlier *Hurrah Henry*, recorded in use by Damon Runyon in 1936

> 1959 Colin MacInnes: That garden-party's for the ooblies and the Hooray Henries, anyway.

> 1979 *New Statesman*: A gang of Hooray Henrys from Sotheby's travel round the country crying 'Bring out your junk'.

> 1986 *Expression!*: A blanket or rug is also a good idea (tartans for hoorays; kilims for aesthetes).

hooter *n* (1958) the nose. British slang. Popular in the late 1950s and the 60s, not least through its use by Tony Hancock in his radio and television comedy programmes of the time

> 1958 Frank Norman: He held [the handkerchief] up to his face as though he was going to blow his hooter.

hot line *n* (1955) a direct, exclusive communication channel between two points. The term first made the headlines in the early 1960s, when it was applied to the direct telephone link between the US and Soviet governments, intended as an aid to mutual understanding in times of international crisis

> 1955 *New York Times Magazine*: To hold this breakthrough to a minimum is 'ConAd's' job. It has twelve air divisions, tied in by 'hot line' communications with one another and with the Army, Navy and Civil Defense Administration.

1963 *Daily Telegraph*: Hot line. At Geneva yesterday the United States and Russia signed an agreement to set up a direct link between the Kremlin, the Pentagon and, presumably, the White House.

househusband *n* (1955) a husband who carries out the household duties traditionally associated with the role of housewife. Originally US

1955 *Scientific American*: To a chemist 'kitchen-sink fluoridation' is only a minor nuisance, well worth the little trouble and infinitesimal cost, but the average housewife and househusband may find it less easy.

1986 *Sunday Express*: John Lennon tried being the house husband for some years, but I'd prefer not to give up my work.

hovercraft *n* (1959) a vehicle or craft that can be supported by a cushion of air ejected downwards against a surface close below it, and can in principle travel over any relatively smooth surface (e.g. a body of water, marshland, gently sloping land) while having no significant contact with it. Invented by the British engineer Sir Christopher Cockerell; the concept was patented in 1955. For some years from 1961 *Hovercraft* was registered as a proprietary term, but it is now in the public domain. Alternative names include *air-cushion vehicle* ('Air cushion vehicles—or hovercraft, if you prefer the term', *Guardian* (1965)) and the short-lived *cushion-rider* ('This year's Farnborough flying display will feature…a "cushion-rider" ', *Times* (1959))

1959 *Daily Mail*: The sea-saucer has been officially christened the Hovercraft.

1961 Christopher Cockerell: My wife and I tried to find a name and settled for the not altogether appropriate word 'Hovercraft'.

hula hoop *n* (1958) a tubular plastic hoop used for spinning round the body with movements like those of the hula, a Hawaiian dance. There was a major but very short-lived craze for the hula hoop in Britain in the late 1950s. It put in a brief but ignominious reappearance in the 1980s, presumably at the hands of a speculator who had bought up a warehouse-ful of unused hoops

1958 *Times Literary Supplement*: Hoops, also of ancient origin, had virtually disappeared from shops and streets, until the sudden recent craze for 'hula' hoops brought them out in a new form.

1970 *Which?*: Remember hula-hoops and dislocated hips?

hydrofoil *n* (1959) a vessel fitted with vanes for raising it clear of the water when in motion

1962 *Daily Telegraph*: The United States Maritime Administration…believes there is a big future for hydrofoils as passenger vessels.

hyperdrive *n* (1955) a hypothetical device by which a spaceship is enabled to travel from one point to another in a shorter time than light would take (usually by passing out of ordinary space into 'hyperspace' for the journey). A concept beloved of science-fiction writers. The term is probably a mixture of *hyperspace* and *overdrive*

1955 B. Davenport: A 'hyperdrive'…may be defined simply as something that does enable ships to travel faster than the speed of light, no matter what Einstein says.

1968 M. S. Livingston: No responsible scientist would attempt to justify support for research in this field with prediction of an 'anti-matter engine'…or a 'hyper-drive' for spaceships.

ICBM *n* (1955) An abbreviation of *intercontinental ballistic missile* (also first recorded in 1955), a missile capable of being fired from one continent and landing on another, typically carrying a nuclear warhead. One of the sinister fruits of Wernher von Braun's rocketry work, which carried atomic warfare into the space age

1955 *Newsweek*: The Air Force is now calling the Intercontinental Ballistic Missile the ICBM.

identity crisis *n* (1954) a period of disorientation and anxiety that results from difficulties experienced in resolving personal conflicts, adjusting to social demands and pressures, etc. Widely used more loosely to denote a lack of confidence in oneself and in one's place (and relevance) in society—common features of late-20th-century zeit-angst

1954 *Journal of the American Psychoanalytical Society*: George Bernard Shaw arranged for himself a psycho-social moratorium at the age of twenty when his identity crisis led him to leave…his family, friends and familiar work.

1974 *Times Literary Supplement*: A middle-aged cuckold with piles and an identity crisis.

image *n* (1958) a concept or impression, especially a favourable impression, created in the minds of the public, of a particular person, institution, product, etc. A usage which came into the general domain from the advertising industry, and has become for cynics a key word of the 20th century, with its emphasis on appearance at the expense of substance. A closely related use is recorded in the first decade of the century (see **image (1908)**, but there is a lack of intermediate evidence linking the two. See also **image-maker (1960)**

> 1958 J. K. Galbraith: The first task of the public relations man, on taking over a business client, is to 're-engineer' his image to include something besides the production of goods.

> 1958 M. Mayer: David Ogilvy, of Ogilvy, Benson & Mather, apostle of the 'brand image'.

> 1961 *Listener:* [Lord Reith] created what in modern jargon would be called a public image of the B.B.C. Programmes moved with smooth efficiency…behind a screen of anonymity.

> 1962 *Listener:* Mr Gaitskell has improved his image by his determination at Scarborough and after.

immune system *n* (1955) the part of the body's make-up and functioning responsible for producing an immune response and maintaining immunity. A specialist term which did not enter the public domain until the Aids crisis of the 1980s

> 1955 *International Archive of Allergy & Applied Immunology:* With the protein immune systems, the weight of antigen injected intravenously corresponded…to one-half the amount of antibody.

> 1986 *Daily Telegraph:* These young women have a 10 to 30 per cent chance of developing [Aids], which kills by destroying the immune system thus exposing sufferers to a variety of lethal infections.

information technology *n* (1958) the branch of technology concerned with the dissemination, processing, and storage of information, especially by means of computers. Originally US; the abbreviation *IT* is not recorded before 1982

> 1958 Leavitt & Whisler: The new technology does not yet have a single established name. We shall call it information technology.

> 1984 *National Westminster Bank Quarterly Review:* The development of cable television was made possible by the convergence of telecommunications and computing technology (…generally known in Britain as information technology).

in-house *adj, adv* (1956) (done) internally within a business or other institution, without outside assistance

> 1966 *Electronics:* Under the new arrangement it's expected that more of the work will be done in-house at the Marshall Space Flight Center.

> 1973 R. W. Burchfield: Making full use…of in-house photocopying apparatus.

innit (1959) A representation of a casual British pronunciation of *isn't it*, used initially as a tag question after statements containing *is*, with the person in the question referring back to the subject of the verb in the statement, but latterly, especially in London slang, these restrictions have been abandoned, and *innit* has become an all-purpose tag, rather like French *n'est-ce pas*

> 1959 Michael Gilbert: That's right, innit?

> 1989 Martin Amis: 'Would you burp her for me? Just for a second.' 'Can't. Watching TV innit.'

integrated circuit *n* (1959) a small unit or package which is made as a single indivisible structure (such as a chip) and is electrically equivalent to a conventional circuit of many separate components

> 1962 *Electronics, Reliability & Microminiaturization:* In integrated circuits the [circuit] element may be a region in a block of the material rather than a separate device.

interferon *n* (1957) a protein released by an animal cell, usually in response to the entry of a virus, which has the property of inhibiting further development of viruses of any kind in the animal (or in others of the same species)

> 1957 Isaacs & Lindenmann: To distinguish it from the heated influenza virus we have called the newly released interfering agent 'interferon'.

Interpol *n* (1952) the International Criminal Police Commission (founded in 1923), with headquarters in Paris. Originally a telegraphic address (see the first quote below), coined by conflating *International police*

> 1952 Söderman & O'Connell: All national bureaus of the ICPC have adopted the telegraphic address of 'Interpol'.

> 1958 *Daily Mail*: British police last night sent a call to Interpol, the international police organisation, for help in solving the riddle of a British airman whose father believes he is still alive 15 years after he was shot down over Germany.

intoximeter *n* (1950) a device for measuring the alcohol content of a person's breath, especially in cases of suspected drunken driving. Originally a proprietary name in the US (registered in 1950, with claim of use since 1946). Compare **breathalyser (1960)**

> 1984 *Daily Telegraph*: One of four intoximeters tested by the Government before the device was introduced for detecting drink-drivers was faulty.

investigative *n* (1951) Denoting journalism or a journalist actively investigating and seeking to expose malpractice, miscarriage of justice, etc. Originally US. A mode of journalism which the late 20th century likes to think of as peculiarly its own (although William Howard Russell (for instance), who exposed in the *Times* the mismanagement of the Crimean War, might not have agreed)

> 1951 *Editor & Publisher*: 'Newspapers must turn more and more to great reporters,' declared Mr. Walters. 'They will be known as investigative reporters.'... Investigative reporting has as its goal the stimulation of sufficient indignation to force a new code of ethics on the public officeholder.

invisibles *n* (1958) imports and exports of services, such as tourism, banking, and insurance, as opposed to goods. A noun use of the adjective **invisible**, first recorded in this sense in 1911

> 1958 *Economist*: Net earnings from commercial services ranked as invisibles also rose.

jeans *n* (1956) close-fitting trousers made of denim, typically blue (*blue jeans*). The word had been used since the mid 19th century to denote a garment made of jean, a type of twilled cotton cloth, and blue trousers of this general sort had been manufactured in the US by Levi Strauss since the 1860s, but it was the mid 1950s that saw their adoption as a worldwide teenage uniform

> 1956 Jean Potts: She...swung her blue-jeaned legs.

> 1957 *Times*: For miles and miles of suburban area you will rarely see a young woman out of blue jeans, shorts or slim-jim pants during the day.

> 1958 *Economist*: Girls in tight jeans and dazzle socks.

jet set *n* (1951) a smart set of wealthy people who conduct business by jet travel, or who make frequent journeys, e.g. to holiday resorts, by jet aircraft; also used more broadly to denote rich, sophisticated, fashionable people. Originally US. Regular commercial jet travel actually began in 1952, when the De Havilland Comet entered service with B.O.A.C.

> 1951 *San Francisco Examiner*: You're strictly jet set...if you stake your claim in the dunes...never descend to ocean level except for a quick dunk.

> 1964 *Saturday Review*: The Jet Set...has rediscovered St. Tropez.

job satisfaction *n* (1955) the extent to which someone's expectations and hopes about the job they are employed in are fulfilled. A term of social psychologists and management consultants which gradually filtered into the public domain

> 1972 M. Argyle: Many studies have shown that job satisfaction is affected by relationships in the work group.

junk mail *n* (1954) unsolicited circulars, advertisements, etc., sent by post to a large number of addresses. Originally US

> 1954 *Reader's Digest*: The argument for junk mail is that sorting requires little time—the postman simply delivers one throwaway to each home.

karate *n* (1955) a Japanese system of unarmed combat in which hands and feet are used as weapons. Probably the first of the 'new' wave of Eastern martial arts to become popular in the West (judo had been well known since the late 19th century). Schoolboys everywhere regretted trying to karate-chop bricks. The word in Japanese means literally 'empty hand'

> 1955 E. J. Harrison: Karate resembles both jujutsu and judo... A single karate technique...is capable of inflicting fatal injury upon its victim.

kiloton *n* (1950) a unit of explosive power, equal to that of one thousand tons of T.N.T. Used in describing the potency of nuclear weapons. See also **megaton (1952)**

> 1952 *Birmingham* (Alabama) *News*: According to informed forecasts, the new bomb will have an explosive power of between 200 and 300 kilotons.

kinky *adj* (1959) suggestive of or having unusual or exotic sexual tastes. Colloquial; at one extreme a humorous, throw-away word, at the other a homophobic one. See also **kink (1965)**, **kinky boot (1964)**

> 1959 Colin MacInnes: Suze…meets lots of kinky characters…and acts as agent for me getting orders from them for my pornographic photos.

> 1964 *Times Literary Supplement*: Zoo men receive a constant stream of kinky letters.

kitchen sink *adj, n* (1954) Used initially to designate, dismissively, (the work of) a group of English realistic painters of the 1950s, and soon afterwards a group of English realistic playwrights and other authors of the same period. It is the latter usage, applied to the likes of Shelagh Delaney, John Osborne, and Arnold Wesker, that has become the most familiar. Their form of drama, portraying the lives of working-class or lower-middle-class people, invaded the fragrant drawing rooms portrayed by Noël Coward and Terence Rattigan and condemned them to several decades of oblivion. *Kitchen sink* has since come to be used more broadly as a metaphor for domestic squalor

> 1954 David Sylvester (title): The kitchen sink… The post-war generation takes us back from the studio to the kitchen… The kitchen sink too… It is evident that neither objectivity nor abstraction is the aim of the young painters of the kitchen-sink school.

> 1960 *Times*: Mr. Ronald Duncan is reported as saying that the English Stage Company…presents only left wing 'kitchen sink' drama.

> 1963 *Times*: If the British new wave were interested only in easy money they would stick to the slag-heap and the kitchen sink.

Kite mark *n* (1952) a quality mark, similar in shape to a kite, granted for use on goods approved by the British Standards Institution

> 1956 *Observer*: It is hoped that eventually the B.S. Kite-Mark will certify the quality of many…consumer goods.

kooky *adj* (1959) cranky, crazy, eccentric. Slang; probably formed from **kook** 'crazy person', although this is not recorded before 1960. The ultimate source is no doubt *cuckoo*

> 1959 *Motion Pictures*: Get set for some far-out talk on teen-age romance by the kookiest cat in town—Edd Byrnes.

> 1960 *Daily Mail*: A kook, Daddy-O, is a screwball who is 'gone' farther than most.

Kremlinology *n* (1958) the study and analysis of the Soviet government and its policies. From the *Kremlin*, the central citadel of Moscow, containing government headquarters, used metonymically since the 1930s for the Soviet government

> 1958 *Oxford Magazine*: For all his interest in Kremlinology…the author is not really very good at it.

> 1960 *Daily Telegraph*: Kremlinologists, versed in the mysteries of Marx and Lenin, Mao Tse-tung and Mr Khruschev, tell us that the signs are that Mr Khruschev has won yet another battle, at least on points.

leak *n* (1950) an improper or deliberate disclosure of information (e.g. for political purposes). The verb usage from which this derives dates back at least to the 1860s

> 1950 H. D. Lasswell: Americans are accustomed to 'government by leak'.

> 1957 *Economist*: The allegation of a 'leak' about last Thursday's increase in Bank rate has brought forth understandable indignation from those City dealers whose fingers were burned, and an equally understandable demand by the Labour Party for a full inquiry.

Lego *n* (1957) The proprietary name (registered in Britain in 1957) of a constructional toy consisting principally of small interlocking plastic blocks. It was borrowed from Danish, where it is a respelling of the phrase *leg godt* 'play well'

> 1971 *Habitat Catalogue*: No self-respecting toy-box…should be without Lego.

> 1991 Dorris & Erdrich: He constructed labyrinthine Lego cities, but refused to tie his own shoes.

life-support system *n* (1959) a system designed to make possible the continued normal functioning of the body in hostile or dangerous environments, or when it is otherwise incapable of sustaining its own life. Originally a space-technology term, but latterly widely used medically, in the context of keeping people alive 'artificially'

    1962 F. I. Ordway: A life support system for a manned base on the Moon…will be exceedingly complex.

like *adv* (1950) Used as a preposed emphatic filler. Slang, originally US. The usage is presumably a development of the postposed filler *like*, which is frequently condemned as characteristic of debased late-20th-century (youth) speech but in fact goes back at least to the late 18th century, and is widely evidenced in representations of 19th-century dialectal speech ('Might I be so bold as just to ax, by way of talk like, if [etc.]', Edward Peacock (1870)). Preposed, it can precede either a single word (often adjective or interjection) or a whole clause

    1950 *Neurotica*: Like how much can you lay on [i.e. give] me?

    1959 *She*: Like wow…wonderful.

    1971 *Black Scholar*: Man like the dude really flashed his hole card.

liquidizer *n* (1950) an electric food processor, used to blend, purée, etc. ingredients. An alternative (generally preferred in British English) to the earlier **blender (1948)**

    1972 Beale & Johnston: The liquidizer reduces dried peas, beans, lentils, rice, etc., into powder speedily.

low-rise *adj* (1957) See **high-rise (1954)**

LSD *n* (1950) the drug lysergic acid diethylamide, used in experimental medicine and taken illegally as a hallucinogenic, especially in the 1960s. Probably a borrowing from German, where it is first recorded in 1947 as an abbreviation of *Lysergsäure-diäthylamid*

    1950 *Diseases of the Nervous System*: We believe that L.S.D. 25 is a drug which induces a controllable toxic state within the nervous system, that re-activates anxiety and fear with apparently just enough euphoria to permit recall of the provoking experiences.

    1964 *Daily Telegraph*: The tablets are believed to be a solid form of LSD, lysergic acid diethylamide. They can be obtained in certain clubs and public houses in London and other big cities.

luncheon voucher *n* (1955) a money voucher given to employees which is exchangeable for meals at certain restaurants. A form of payment in kind widely used in Britain in the third quarter of the 20th century, mainly for office workers. Note the genteel *luncheon*. Often abbreviated to *LV*

    1955 *Evening Standard*: Doorman/timekeeper for staff and goods entrance… Pension scheme, welfare fund, luncheon vouchers, etc… Copy typist with some experience of statement work, required by City firm. Commencing salary…according to age & ability plus L.V's.

    1973 *Times*: The notes in our wallets, stamps for letters…luncheon vouchers…are a few of the little pieces of paper so essential to modern life.

lurgy *n* (1954) an unspecified but virulent illness. British colloquial; usually in the phrase *the dreaded lurgy*. The word was popularized by the BBC radio comedy series *The Goon Show* (see **goon (1951)**), and in the 1950s and 60s aficionados would bring *the dreaded lurgy* into the conversation at suitable points. It was probably invented, either by the main writer Spike Milligan, or by one of the other contributors to the show

    1954 *Radio Times*: The Goon Show… Poor Arnold Fringe is suddenly stricken with the Dreaded Lurgi… Within a few days Lurgi has claimed nine thousand victims.

    1974 Hamish MacInnes: I was beginning to feel weak and knew that I had caught the dreaded swamp lurgy.

Lycra *n* (1958) The proprietary name (registered in the US in 1958) of an elastic polyurethane fibre and fabric used especially for underwear and swimming costumes

    1968 *Vogue*: This…pantie-corselette…of softest lycra power net.

McCarthyism *n* (1950) the policy of hunting out (suspected) Communists and removing them from government departments or other positions. Originally and mainly applied to the campaign instigated in the US in the early 1950s by Senator Joseph R. McCarthy (1908–57). Decidedly a negative term, suggestive of paranoia and persecution; the McCarthyites certainly did not apply it to themselves

> 1950 *New York Post*: To call McCarthyism a fascist atmosphere would be descriptive enough.

> 1952 *New York Times*: McCarthyism breeds fear, suspicion and unrest. It turns neighbor against neighbor and makes every American a suspected traitor until and unless he can prove his innocence by McCarthyite standards.

Maoism *n* (1951) the Marxist-Leninist theories of Mao Tse-Tung developed and practised in China, emphasizing the peasantry's role in a revolution. From the name of Mao Tse-Tung (1893–1976), Chairman of the Central Committee of the Chinese Communist Party. See also **Mao (1967)**

> 1951 B. I. Schwartz: The essential features of Maoism… Another peculiar feature of the Maoist strategy…is the preference for 'border area' bases.

marginal *adj, n* (1951) (of or being) a constituency, etc., in which an election or issue is likely to be closely contested and the majority very small. British. The noun usage is first recorded in 1966

> 1951 *Times* (heading): Marginal seats… A significant feature of today's General Election polling is the substantial number of constituencies which may be described as marginal, and where the result of the voting is problematical.

> 1966 *New Statesman*: For Labour MPs in 'marginals'…it means that their perilous positions could be secured.

maser *n* (1955) a laser, especially one that emits microwaves. The first masers emitted microwaves. Later ones emitted in other parts of the spectrum, and these were also called masers for a time until **laser (1960)** came to be adopted as the general name for all such devices. The word is an acronym coined from the initial letters of *microwave amplification by stimulated emission of radiation*

> 1955 *Science News Letter*: Scientists can, for the first time, generate microwaves of extremely high frequency by tapping directly the energy of molecules, Dr. Charles H. Townes of Columbia University's physics department reported in New York. His device for doing so is known as the 'maser'… Work on the maser began three years ago.

Mau Mau *n* (1950) an African secret society originating among the Kikuyu, having as its aim the expulsion of European settlers and the ending of British rule in Kenya. It instigated an armed revolt which lasted from 1952 to 1957. The origins of the name are unclear

> 1950 *East African Standard*: We have arrived at a state of dissatisfaction and insecurity, bitterness and delusion which has given rise to the formation of such societies as the 'Dini ya Mswambwa' and the 'Mau Mau Association'.

> 1952 *New York Times*: Large groups of natives fled today to lofty mountain hideouts to escape the Government drive…against Mau Mau terrorists, who have sworn death to the white man.

megadeath *n* (1953) the death of a million people, as a unit in estimating the possible effects of nuclear warfare. A still more grisly coinage was *megacorpse* (first recorded in 1958), denoting a million dead bodies resulting from a nuclear war. See also **overkill (1958)**

> 1953 *Birmingham* (Alabama) *News*: He does not deal in numbers of atomic bombs or precise methods of delivery, in kilotons or megadeaths.

megaton *n* (1952) a unit of explosive power equal to that of one million tons of T.N.T. A coinage called into being by the unparalleled power of the hydrogen bomb (throughout the whole of World War II only six megatons were used). Compare **kiloton (1950)**

> 1952 *New York Herald-Tribune*: The first true super-bomb to be detonated is expected to have a power of two megatons.

meritocracy *n* (1958) government by people selected on the basis of merit in a competitive educational system; also, a society so governed, or a ruling or influential class of educated people. A term introduced by Michael Young in his book *The Rise of the Meritocracy* (1958); derivatives such as *meritocrat* and *meritocratic* soon followed

> 1958 Michael Young: Before the meritocracy was fully established, age-stratification as a substitute for the hereditary order may have been necessary for the sake of social stability.

> 1958 *Economist*: Mr Young's meritocratic Britain, though described with ostensible enthusiasm, is an odious place.

> 1961 Daniel Jenkins: One of Young's most unlikely prognostications is that the best public schools will be taken over by the meritocrats.

meter maid *n* (1957) a female traffic warden. Colloquial, originally US. See **parking meter (1936)**

> 1957 *American Speech*: Surveys conducted in cities using 'meter maids' have found that their meter revenue increased.

microcircuit *n* (1959) an integrated circuit or other minute electrical circuit (see **integrated circuit (1959)**)

> 1959 *Electronics*: New circuit fabrication techniques such as are used in microcircuits.

microfiche *n* (1950) a flat piece of film, usually the size of a standard catalogue card, containing microphotographs of the pages of a book, periodical, etc. A formation based on French *fiche* 'slip of paper, index-card'

> 1953 *Library Science Abstracts*: The translucent microfiche is considered by some people to be better than the opaque microcard.

middle management *n* (1957) middle-ranking company executives responsible for the day-to-day running of a department. Originally US. *Middle manager* is first recorded in 1966 ('The middle managers have, understandably, resisted any change', *New York Times* (1966))

> 1966 S. Phipps: The opposite swing of the same pendulum may be seen in the groups of middle-management-type bungalows that are appearing round the fringes of English villages.

modem *n* (1958) a combined modulator and demodulator (such as is used in connecting a computer to a telephone line) for converting outgoing signals from one form to another and converting incoming signals back again. Coined from the initial elements of *modulator* and *demodulator*

> 1975 *Daily Colonist* (Victoria, British Columbia): They communicated over regular telephone lines, using teletypewriters connected to the lines by electronic devices known as modems.

Mogadon *n* (1956) A proprietary name (registered in Britain in 1956) for nitrazepam, a type of sleeping tablet

> 1973 *Guardian*: Police found a total of 156 drug tablets including a bottle of Mogadon.

molest *v* (1950) to assault (a child) sexually. The origins of this euphemistic usage go back to the much earlier, non-sexual sense 'to meddle with (someone) injuriously or hostilely', which dates from the 15th century. We find *molest* being used by Thomas Hardy to denote a sexual attack on a woman ('No average man—no man short of a sensual savage—will molest a woman by day or night, at home or abroad, unless she invites him', *Jude the Obscure* (1895)), and in the 1920s there is this hint at what is to come: 'Every person who annoys or molests any school child…is a vagrant', *Statutes of California* (1929). Towards the end of the century *molest* gradually gave way to **abuse (1969)**. See also **interfere with (1948)**

> 1950 *Collier's*: When child molesters got to the courts, like as not they were let off with $100 fines… How many cases of child molestation were never reported to the police?

> 1992 *Globe & Mail* (Toronto): An Ontario woman awarded $284,000 in damages against the father who molested her from the time she was 5.

moonlight *v* (1957) to do paid work, usually at night, in addition to one's regular employment. Colloquial, originally US

> 1957 *Reporter* (New York): He takes two or three hours off and then…departs for a second job… The practice is known as 'moonlighting'.

moon-shot *n* (1958) the launching of a spacecraft to or towards the moon. Colloquial, originally US

> 1958 *Washington Post*: Yesterday's moon shot blew up 50,000 feet and 77 seconds after the launching at Cape Canaveral.

moped *n* (1956) a light motorcycle, not over 50cc. British; a borrowing from Swedish, where it was coined (around 1952) by taking the elements *mo-* and *ped-* from *tramp-cykel med motor och pedaller* 'pedal cycle with engine and pedals' and joining them together. As this suggests, the original version had auxiliary pedals

> 1956 I. Dunlop: You must have a license to drive an autocycle ('moped').

> 1957 *Times*: The accompanying recommendation that the minimum age limit for riding mopeds should be reduced from sixteen to fifteen will be less readily accepted.

most *n the most* (1953) the best, (something that is) extremely good, most exciting; also used adverbially, in the sense 'to the greatest degree'. Slang, originally US

> 1954 *Time*: Last week the general and even the Pentagon conceded that the bop campaign was the most, to say the least.

> 1958 *Sunday News* (New York): Of her husband, she said, 'Adam and I dig each other the most. We have a perfect understanding. It couldn't be better.'

> 1968 *Listener*: I would infinitely prefer to listen to the Kenny Everett programme—'the show that's the most with your tea and toast', as that masterly DJ himself puts it.

mother-fucker *n* (1956) a despicable person; someone or something very unpleasant. Slang, originally US. The still taboo suggestion of incest provided a much needed new obscenity in a sociolinguistic environment in which traditional 'four-letter words' were beginning to lose their power to shock—even *fuck* (see **fuck off (1929)**). The related *mother-fucking* is first recorded in 1959

> 1956 *American Speech*: This linguistic vacuum is being filled by a new obscenity symbol, *mother-fucker*.

> 1959 Norman Mailer: They could smash some mother-f—ing Reds.

> 1960 James Baldwin: You've got to fight with the elevator boy because the mother f*****'s *white!*

Ms (1952) A title prefixed to the surname of a woman, regardless of her marital status. Originally US; an orthographic and phonetic compromise between *Miss* and *Mrs*. Although proposed in the early 1950s, it did not begin to make real headway until the 1970s, when it was vigorously championed by the burgeoning feminist movement. Despite a strong rearguard action by diehard opponents (whose arguments have included its alleged unpronounceability and its confusability with the abbreviation for *manuscript*), by the end of the century it had firmly established its place in the language. Sometimes written as *miz*, especially when used other than as a title

> 1952 *The Simplified Letter* (US): Use abbreviation Ms. for *all women* addressees. This modern style solves an age-old problem.

> 1952 *The Simplified Letter* (revised edition): Use abbreviation Ms. if not sure whether to use Mrs. or Miss.

> 1971 *Publishers' Weekly*: A crowded New York press conference heard this morning that a new magazine, called *Ms.* (pronounced 'Miz'), will begin publication in January.

> 1972 *Village Voice* (New York): Cavett addressed her as Mrs. Morgan and asked her if she would rather be called a miz and she said she didn't care.

> 1974 *Daily Telegraph*: The Passport Office yesterday conceded the right to women to call themselves Ms (pronounced Miz) on their passports instead of Mrs or Miss. This followed a month's campaign by Women's Lib.

MS *n* (1955) An abbreviation of *multiple sclerosis*, a degenerative disease of the central nervous system. The term *multiple sclerosis* is first recorded as long ago as 1885, but it was not widely enough used to call for abbreviation until after World War II

> 1955 *Science News Letter*: The search for twins with MS, or multiple sclerosis, has yielded 33 identical sets so far, but the National Multiple Sclerosis Society would like to locate about 350 more, fraternal as well as identical.

Murphy's law *n* (1958) A name humorously given to various aphoristic expressions of the apparent perverseness and unreasonableness of things. Originally US; British English has tended to prefer the alternative formulation *sod's law* (first recorded in 1970). The account of the name's origin in the second quote below may be apocryphal

> 1958 *Nation* (New York): There is an old military maxim known as Murphy's Law which asserts that where-ever there is a bolt to be turned, someday there will be someone to turn it the wrong way.

> 1962 John Glenn: We blamed human errors like this on what aviation engineers call 'Murphy's Law'. 'Murphy' was a fictitious character who appeared in a series of educational cartoons put out by the U.S. Navy... Murphy was a careless, all-thumbs mechanic who was prone to make such mistakes as installing a propeller backwards.

mushroom cloud *n* (1958) the cloud of smoke that forms above the site of a nuclear explosion, with the characteristic shape of a tall pillar with a broad, flattish top. The resemblance had already been noticed by early observers of atom-bomb explosions ('At first it was a giant column that soon took the shape of a supramundane mushroom', *New York Times* (1945))

> 1964 M. M. Gowing: Dr Penney was one of the scientific observers who saw the mushroom cloud rise from the ruins of Nagasaki.

naff off *v* (1959) to go away. British slang; a euphemistic substitute for *fuck off*, usually used in the imperative. The origins of *naff* are uncertain; it may come from *eff* (a phonetic spelling of *f*, a euphemistic reduction of *fuck*), with the addition of the final -*n* of a preceding word (as in the noun phrase *an eff*), or alternatively there may be some connection with obsolete backslang *naf* = *fan* 'female genitals'

> 1959 Keith Waterhouse: Naff off, Stamp, for Christ sake!

> 1975 Clement & La Frenais: 'It's all been arranged, it's all set up, right? So naff off', I said.

> 1982 *Sunday Times*: Princess Anne...lost her temper with persistent photographers and told them to 'naff off'.

name *v* (1950) to specify officially (someone) by name to whom certain political (usually Communist) affiliations are imputed, especially in South Africa under the Suppression of Communism Act, 1950, and in the US during the period of McCarthyism. See also **name and shame (1991)**

> 1950 *Times*: Senator McCarthy has been ordered by Senator Tydings...to name to-morrow the high State Department official who he has alleged in the Senate intervened to protect an employee who was regarded as a bad security risk.

Native American *adj, n* (1956) (a member) of the indigenous peoples of North America. A term not in wide use until the 1970s, when the political incorrectness of referring to such people as 'Indians' began to be more keenly felt. Before very long it too succumbed, the offending component being 'native'

> 1956 Aldous Huxley: Thank you for your most interesting letter about the Native American churchmen.

> 1973 *Black Panther*: Appearing at the awards in Brando's behalf was the beautiful, gracious, and now famous Native American woman, Sacheen Littlefeather, who, dressed in the traditional garments of her people, read a prepared statement.

N.A.T.O. *n* (1950) An acronym formed from the initials of *North Atlantic Treaty Organization*, a North American/Western European military alliance set up in 1949

> 1950 *Newsweek*: Nato is the newest synthetic word in the international gobbledygook and stands for the North Atlantic treaty organization.

neatnik *n* (1959) someone who is neat in their personal habits (as opposed to the archetypally dirty and scruffy beatnik). Slang, originally and mainly US; inspired, of course, by **beatnik (1958)**, and not always entirely complimentary

> 1959 *New York Times*: The beatniks and the neatniks had at each other this week.

> 1960 *New York Times*: Seeing how you're a Neatnik, you'll be buying things like soap and ties and stuff from now on.

need-to-know *adj* (1954) Used to denote a principle or practice, especially in counter-espionage, whereby people are kept ignorant of things which they do not need to know

> 1969 Alfred Marin: You will notice that there are some gaps in the Clay material. Part of the information is...strictly on a 'need to know' basis.

nerd *n* (1951) an ineffectual, unstylish, or socially inept person, usually male, especially one who is excessively or annoyingly studious. Slang, originally US; the usage did not get up a head of steam until the late 1960s, on college campuses and among surfers and hot-rodders, and it spread from there to the general language. Its origins are unclear: a link has been suggested with *turd*, but it may simply come from the name of the character invented by the US children's author 'Dr. Seuss' (Theodore Geisel) ('And then, just to show them, I'll sail to Ka-Troo And Bring Back an It-Kutch, a Preep and a Proo, a Nerkle, a Nerd, and a Seersucker, too!', 'Dr. Seuss', *If I Ran the Zoo* (1950)). The derived adjective *nerdy* is first recorded in 1978

   1971 *Observer*: Nerds are people who don't live meaningful lives.

   1978 *New York Times*: The nerdiest nerds on TV are really smart cookies.

   1986 M. Howard: He feels…like a total nerd in his gentleman's coat with the velvet collar.

new brutalism *n* (1953) a style of art or architecture characterized by deliberate crudity of design

   1954 *Architectural Review*: The attitude taken by certain younger English architects and artists, and known, half satirically, as the New Brutalism.

   1959 *Manchester Guardian*: Churchill College at Cambridge will be built by a modern architect— perhaps even by a 'new brutalist'.

niet *n* (1957) a blunt refusal, especially on the part of a Soviet politician. As part of the Cold War shadow-play, the Soviet Union became notorious for its unwillingness to agree to anything suggested by the West, and its frequent pithy expression of this in the one Russian word *nyet* 'no' made for good newspaper headlines

   1957 *Time*: The *Nyet* Man… Gromyko's televised image became a symbol of the Cold War… As Russia's first U.N. representative, his *nyet*, uttered in the course of 26 Soviet vetoes, was a byword.

   1959 *Daily Mail*: Sir David has become Moscow's Mr. Niet. He has said 'No' to insistent demands for bigger credits for Russia.

nig-nog *n* (1959) A contemptuous British term for a black. One of a small but potent range of anti-black epithets which arose in the developing racist climate in Britain in the 1950s and 60s, in the wake of large-scale Commonwealth immigration (the first race riot took place in London in 1958). This one was based on *nigger*, perhaps with an element of rhyme on *wog*, and conceivably also with a memory of the earlier colloquial *nig-nog* 'fool'. Political correctness consigned it to the taboo bin in the last quarter of a century

   1959 Marshall Pugh: First lot, and look lively. Lot of nig-nogs off the trees.

nit-picker *n* (1951) a pedantic critic; someone who searches for and over-emphasizes trivial errors. Originally US; *nit-picking* soon followed. The underlying idea is of poring over someone's scalp, looking for the egg-cases of headlice

   1956 *Time*: The members of the Cabinet commented on the draft of the message, then commented upon one another's comments. 'No nit-picking,' Vice President Nixon adjured his colleagues, but the Cabinet eventually sent out to the President a file of verbatim reaction that piled $1\frac{1}{2}$ inches high.

no comment (1950) A conventional statement of refusal to comment on a situation, especially when answering a journalist, interviewer, etc.

   1950 *Time*: Questioned on a press report that 'a close adviser to President Truman' was predicting Johnson's resignation, White House Press Secretary Charles Ross issued a perfunctory 'no comment'.

non-alignment *n* (1955) absence of political or ideological affiliations with other nations, especially with the most powerful nations. A geopolitical concept which emerged in response to the polarization of the two Cold War power blocks. The related adjective **non-aligned** is first recorded in 1960

   1955 *Times*: He extolled 'non-alignment' and co-existence.

   1960 *New Left Review*: The non-aligned powers have grown in strength.

non-stick *adj* (1958) Of a cooking utensil: to which food does not adhere

   1958 *Listener*: Silicones are used…for…coating cooking pans to make them 'non-stick'.

   1968 *Guardian*: The cost of the non-stick oven lining adds £6 10s to the price of a cooker.

non-U *adj* (1954) See **U (1954)**

notelet *n* (1955) a folded card or sheet of paper on which a note can be written, having a picture or design on the face of the first leaf. A coinage of toe-curling genteelness

> 1955 *Stationery Trade Reference Book*: Macniven & Cameron Ltd…manufacturers of social and gift stationery. 189/1 Notelets Products. Macniven & Cameron Ltd.

> 1971 *Countryman*: S.A.E. brings our list of Christmas gifts, cards, notelets, calendars for country lovers.

nuclear *adj* (1954) of, possessing, or employing nuclear weapons. See also **nuclear (1945)**; compare **conventional (1955)**

> 1954 *Commonweal* (heading): Nuclear war: a false dilemma.

> 1956 *Foreign Policy Bulletin* (heading): Nuclear tests: psychological defeat for West.

> 1958 *Annual Register 1957*: The resolution urged that the United Nations and the 'nuclear' Powers should immediately suspend all such tests.

> 1958 *New Statesman*: The response to last Monday's inaugural meetings of the Campaign for Nuclear Disarmament suggests that it is becoming a focus for a real movement of opinion on this issue.

nuke *n* (1959) a nuclear bomb, missile, etc. Originally US military slang; a cosily familiar term for a weapon of mass destruction. It was soon in use as a verb too (see **nuke (1962)**)

> 1959 *New York Times Magazine*: Soon there may be 5-inch nuclear shells and portable Davy Crockett 'nukes' for the infantryman.

> 1964 *Daily Mirror*: The generals should be allowed to decide whether to use tactical nuclear weapons, or as the current ugly phrase has it: 'Where and when to put in the nooks.'

numerate *adj* (1959) acquainted with the basic principles of mathematics and science. Coined from Latin *numerus* 'number', on the model of *literate*. The related noun *numeracy* is first recorded in the same year

> 1959 *15 to 18: Report of the Central Advisory Council for Education* (*England*) (Ministry of Education): Little is done to make science specialists more 'literate' than they were when they left the Fifth Form and nothing to make arts specialists more 'numerate', if we may coin a word to represent the mirror image of literacy… It is perhaps possible to distinguish two different aspects of numeracy that should concern the Sixth Former.

nut-case *n* (1959) a crazy person. Colloquial

> 1959 *Punch*: I couldn't get anyone to talk about it openly. The way they clammed up you'd have thought I was a spy or a nut-case.

> 1965 Allan Prior: He knew the nut-cases, the convicted sexual offenders.

nymphet *n* (1955) a sexually attractive young girl. A term introduced by Vladimir Nabokov (1899–1977) in his novel *Lolita*, whose academic antihero Humbert Humbert lusts after pre-adolescent girls

> 1955 Vladimir Nabokov: Between the age limits of nine and fourteen there occur maidens who, to certain bewitched travellers, twice or many times older than they, reveal their true nature which is not human, but nymphic (that is, demoniac); and these chosen creatures I propose to designate as 'nymphets'.

> 1971 *Southerly*: She is…at her first appearance a shameless nymphet of thirteen already indifferent to the number of boys who have enjoyed her favours.

ombudsman *n* (1959) an official appointed to investigate complaints by individuals against maladministration by public authorities. A word borrowed from Swedish, where it means literally 'commission-man'. It is applied in Sweden to the deputy of a group, particularly a trade union or a business concern, appointed to handle the legal affairs of the group and protect its interests generally. There is a specific office held in Sweden by the *justitieombudsmannen*, whose remit is to guard against the abuse of state power. It was this office which was established in New Zealand in 1962, and for which English adopted Swedish *ombudsman*. When it was introduced in Britain in 1967 it was officially termed *Parliamentary Commissioner for Administration*, but most people referred to it as *ombudsman*. In the early 1970s other more specialized ombudsmen were appointed in Britain (e.g. local government ombudsmen in 1974)

> 1959 *Listener*: Sweden has been running the Ombudsman system for 150 years, and Denmark has a very active Ombudsman.

> 1966 *New Zealand News*: Britain's Ombudsman, Sir Edmund Compton, is now in New Zealand consulting New Zealand's Ombudsman, Sir Guy Powles, about the workings of his office and the way in which he deals with complaints.

> 1978 *Times*: The appointment of local ombudsmen has had a considerable impact on local authority procedures, in the view of the authors of the first critical appraisal of their work.

one-upmanship *n* (1952) the art or practice of getting a psychological advantage over another person. Coined by Stephen Potter (see **-manship (1947)**) on the basis of colloquial *one up* 'holding an advantage over someone', which is first recorded in 1919

> 1952 Stephen Potter (title): One-upmanship.

> 1957 *Economist*: This piece of applied relativity…may go down in the annals of international one-upmanship as the sputnik ploy.

on-line *adj* (1950) directly connected, so that a computer receives an input from or sends an output to a peripheral device, process, etc., as soon as it is produced; carried out while so connected or under direct computer control.

> 1950 W. W. Stifler: For some applications, of which the most prominent are those in which the reduced data are used to control the process being measured, the input must be developed for on-line operation. In on-line operation the input is communicated directly…to the data-reduction device.

> 1965 *Mathematics in Biology and Medicine*: Without time-sharing, the 'on-line' use of a fast modern machine would be unthinkably costly.

open heart *n* (1950) a practically bloodless heart that has been temporarily by-passed and cut open for examination or surgery. Now mainly used adjectivally

> 1950 *Surgery*: Recent rapid strides in the field of vascular surgery are leading inevitably to the point where a direct surgical attack on the open heart is possible.

> 1977 *Private Eye*: As he recovers from open-heart surgery (new valves) Sir Christopher Soames is confident of an early return to Parliament.

overkill *n* (1958) the capacity, especially of nuclear weapons, to kill and effect destruction in excess of strategic requirements

> 1958 *Time*: A word coming more and more into Pentagon usage is 'overkill'—a blunt but descriptive term implying a power to destroy a military target not once but many times more than necessary.

> 1971 *Guardian*: The nuclear club reached the point of H-bomb overkill.

pace-maker *n* (1951) an artificial device which supplies electrical signals to the heart, stimulating it to beat at an appropriate rate. A transferred use of a term originally applied to the heart's sino-atrial node, which controls heartbeat

> 1963 *Daily Telegraph*: A transistorised pacemaker little bigger than a match box and weighing only a few ounces has been devised for implanting in the abdominal wall.

paedophile, pedophile *n* (1951) someone who is sexually attracted to young children. A derivative of **paedophilia (1906)**. At first largely restricted to specialist psychology texts, it began to emerge into the public domain in the 1970s, and by the end of the century was everyday tabloid fare

> 1951 *Group Psychotherapy* (heading): Psycho-dramatic treatment of a pedophile.

> 1976 *Publishers Weekly*: Hilary is nine… She's at the mercy of the old man she calls the Devil, actually a pathetic pedophile.

panel game *n* (1953) a quiz or similar game played before an audience by a small group of people (known as **panellists (1952)**), typically on radio or television. A popular TV staple of the 1950s and 60s. Sometimes alternatively termed a *panel show* (1954)

> 1953 *Evening News*: The first edition of the new TV panel game 'Down You Go' was not an unqualified success.

> 1954 Groucho Marx: The gibbering idiots on panel shows, quiz shows, and other half hours of tripe.

panellist *n* (1952) someone on the panel in a **panel game (1953)**

> 1958 Kingsley Amis: Bowen…had something of the air of a television panellist.

paper tiger *n* (1952) a person, country, etc., that appears outwardly powerful or important but is actually weak or ineffective. A translation of a Chinese expression originally applied by Mao Tse-tung to the US, and mainly used in the context of Communist Chinese anti-Western rhetoric

> 1952 Han Suyin: America is only a paper tiger… That's what the Peking government says.

> 1958 *Peking Review*: In August 1946 Comrade Mao Tse Tung gave an interview to the American journalist Anna Louise Strong and expressed his famous view point that all reactionaries are paper tigers.

paramedic *n* (1951) a person trained to be dropped by parachute to give medical aid. A usage swiftly driven out when *paramedic* 'paramedical worker' (1970) came on the scene

> 1951 *Sunday Mirror* (New York): Para-medics from air-sea rescue squadrons…were in the search planes.

parcel bomb *n* (1950) a bomb wrapped up so as to resemble a parcel, sent through the post as a weapon of terror. See also **letter bomb (1948)**

> 1950 *Times*: Injured by parcel bomb. A small parcel addressed to Mr. Thomas Rose…blew up when he opened it on Sunday night.

parenting *n* (1959) the care and upbringing of a child. Not in wide use until the right-on 1970s; an earlier term had been **parentcraft (1930)**. See also **parent (1902)**

> 1970 L. B. Ames: New parents have a great deal to learn from those already experienced in what Dr. Fitzhugh Dodson calls the art of parenting.

Parkinson's law *n* (1955) a principle enunciated by the British historian and journalist Cyril Northcote Parkinson (1909–93): work expands to fill the time available for its completion. He used the term as the title of a book, first published in 1957

> 1955 *Economist*: Before the discovery of a new scientific law—herewith presented to the public for the first time, and to be called Parkinson's Law—there has…been insufficient recognition of the implications of this fact in the field of public administration.

> 1958 C. N. Parkinson: Parkinson's Law or the Rising Pyramid. Work expands so as to fill the time available for its completion.

pay television, pay TV *n* (1956) a system of supplying an extra television channel to viewers paying either by subscription or by inserting coins into a box attached to the television receiver. It was introduced in the US in the mid 1950s, and has gone under a range of alternative names, including *pay-as-you-see television* ('Sir Alexander Korda intends to seek permission of the United Kingdom authorities to operate "pay as you see" television', *Times* (1955)), *pay-as-you-view television* ('The vital issue of whether a Pay-As-You-View television service is allowed to operate in this country', *Spectator* (1958)), *slot television* ('If slot television gets a real hold on the public, commercial cinema…is doomed', *Kinematograph Weekly* (1958)), *subscription television* ('An unmanned roving vehicle on Mars could probably be supported by subscription television', Carl Sagan (1973)), and *toll television* (US) ('The principle of toll television is that the viewer should pay only for films…he wants to see', *Spectator* (1960)). The latest variant is *pay-per-view television* (see **pay-per-view (1978)**, but *pay television* remains the most popular

> 1956 *Britannica Book of the Year*: Also introduced from the United States—though not yet fully accepted into British English—were such expressions as Pay TV, [etc.].

> 1957 *Economist*: The Federal Communications Commission has tentatively opened the airwaves to 'pay television'.

pedestrian precinct *n* (1953) an area reserved for pedestrians only, usually in a town centre or shopping centre. A term associated particularly with the brave new towns built in the early 1950s. See also **pedestrianize (1963), precinct (1942)**

1953 Frederick Gibberd: A system of pedestrian precincts as short cuts between shopping streets can be developed in a large centre.

1977 *Belfast Telegraph*: The police officers chased the gunmen through a pedestrian precinct into Water Street.

peepie-creepie *n* (1952) a portable television camera used for close shots on location. Originally US; a facetious alternative to *walkie-lookie*, first recorded in 1946. The ultimate model for both was **walkie-talkie (1939)**. Neither survived very long

1952 *Time*: Most startling TV innovation was a portable camera known as the walkie-lookie, or peepie-creepie, with which the enterprising TV reporter could sneak up to Mr. Delegate and catch him yelling his head off or scratching his nose.

permissive *adj* (1956) tolerant, liberal, allowing freedom. From the mid 1960s mainly used with the implication of freedom in sexual matters (see also **permissive society (1968)**)

1956 C. A. Tonsor: I realize that in the face of the permissive tendencies of the age, there is not much respect for rules.

1971 *Daily Telegraph*: Perhaps it is time...for Parliament to have another look at the whole subject of abortion, family planning and perhaps permissiveness in general.

pheromone *n* (1959) a substance that is secreted and released by an animal, usually in minute amounts, and causes a specific response when detected by another animal of the same (or a closely related) species. A coinage based on **hormone**, and taking its first element from Greek *pherein* 'to convey'

1959 Karlson & Lüscher: We propose...the designation 'pheromone' for this group of active substances.

pill *n the pill* (1957) the contraceptive pill. Not a practical reality until the early 1960s

1957 C. H. Rolph: He gives a modestly exciting account of the quest now going on...for what laymen like myself insist on calling 'the Pill'; and by this phrase...I mean the simple and completely reliable contraceptive taken by the mouth.

1960 *Economist*: For about thirty years a campaign has been carried on for the reform of Britain's abortion law... It...looks as if the search for the 'Pill'—a simple, safe contraceptive—may be rewarded first.

1969 *New Scientist*: As contraceptives, IUDs are not as effective as the pill.

pinta *n* (1958) A representation of an informal pronunciation of *pint of*. Introduced in Britain in 1958 in a National Dairy Council advertising slogan for milk (see the first quote below), and widely used thereafter for 'pint of milk'

1959 *Times*: Referring in his opening speech to the 'Drinka pinta milka-day' campaign, Mr. Amory said:...'I drink a pint and a half a day.'

1960 *Harper's Bazaar*: Your daily pinta is the best glamour food there is.

pits *n the pits* (1953) the worst or most despicable example of something; often applied to a person or place considered particularly obnoxious or contemptible. Slang, originally and mainly US; said to be a shortening of *armpits*

1953 *Newsweek*: A bad exam experience would be 'I'm wasted' at Howard,...'It was the pits' at Vassar.

1981 *Observer*: I've never been fined for saying something obscene. It's always been for saying 'You're the pits,' or something.—John McEnroe.

place-mat *n* (1951) a table-mat for an individual place-setting. *Table-mat* is recorded as far back as the 1830s, but hitherto generally as something to place hot serving-dishes on; the *place-mat* foreshadowed the widespread postwar demise of the table-cloth

1951 Thomas Sterling: The waitress took the mangled place-mat...and brushed the shreds of paper from the table.

polo sweater *n* (1950), **polo-necked sweater** *n* (1955) a sweater with a **polo neck (1944)**. The quotes below suggest some of its 50s connotations

1950 **Arthur Koestler**: A member of the intelligentsia could never become a real proletarian, but his duty was to become as nearly one as he could. Some tried to achieve this by forsaking neckties, by wearing polo sweaters and black fingernails.

1955 **N. Fitzgerald**: I always wear…flannel bags, a polo sweater.

1955 **Macdonald Hastings**: She had changed into a pair of black ski trousers and a polo-necked sweater.

ponytail *n* (1952) a hair-style in which the hair is gathered back through a band or other fastening to resemble the shape of the tail of a horse or pony

1952 *Sun* (Baltimore): The panel of high-school boys and girls discusses the latest teen-age fashions, including…the pony tail.

pop art *n* (1957) art that uses themes drawn from popular culture. The term is applied specifically to an art form which flourished in the US and Britain in the 1960s, characterized by the depiction of commonplace subjects using strong colour and imagery, sharp features, and a photographic technique of representation. Leading exponents included Andy Warhol, Roy Lichtenstein, Claes Oldenburg, Richard Hamilton, and Peter Blake. Often shortened to simply *pop*

1957 *Listener*: A sophisticated apologia for subtopia is to call it 'pop art' which the middle-aged are perverse to frustrate.

1967 **Lawrence Alloway**: The term 'Pop Art' is credited to me, but I don't know precisely when it was first used. (One writer has stated that 'Lawrence Alloway first coined the phrase "Pop Art" in 1954'; this is too early.) Furthermore, what I meant by it then is not what it means now. I used the term, and also 'Pop Culture', to refer to the products of the mass media, not to works of art that draw upon popular culture. In any case, sometime between the winter of 1954–55 and 1957 the phrase acquired currency in conversation, in connection with the shared work and discussion among members of the Independent group.

1972 **Edward Lucie-Smith**: The first example of Pop is now generally conceded to have been a small collage made by the English painter Richard Hamilton…in 1956.

population explosion *n* (1953) a rapid or sudden marked increase in the size of a population. Originally US

1953 *Time*: Latin America is in the midst of a 'population explosion'. Its people are multiplying 2½ times as fast as the populations in the rest of the world.

porno *adj* (1952) A colloquial abbreviation of *pornographic*. The alternative **porn**, which eventually became the preferred form, is first recorded in 1962

1952 **Norman Mailer**: It is dirty, downright porno dirty, it is a lewd slop-brush slapped through the middle of domestic exasperations and breakfast eggs.

1963 **Desmond Cory**: Judging from the script…it might be just the *tiniest* bit porno.

print-out *n* (1953) (a sheet or strip of) printed matter produced by a printer connected to a computer. The verb *print out* is also first recorded in this sense in 1953

1969 *New Scientist*: Everyone should be entitled to a print-out of the information in the data bank in regard to him.

privatization *n* (1959) reversion from public to private ownership; denationalization. The related verb *privatize* is not recorded until 1970, and neither the noun nor the verb achieved a particularly high public profile in Britain until the Thatcher government of the 1980s started putting the idea into practice

1959 *News Chronicle*: Erhard selected the rich Preussag mining concern for his first experiment in privatisation.

1960 *News Chronicle*: Complete privatisation was opposed by the Socialists…because they feared…the little man selling out his shares to the big capitalists.

1970 *New Society*: Is the Office of Health Economics trying to hint that the best place to start totally privatising the National Health Service is at eye level?

probe *n* (1953) a small, usually unmanned, exploratory spacecraft (other than an earth satellite) for transmitting information about its environment

> 1953 *Journal of the British Interplanetary Society*: The probe will arrive at Mars nine months after opposition.

> 1977 *Whitaker's Almanack 1978*: A Russian space probe has revealed that the lower layers [of Venus] are extremely dense.

protest *adj* (1953) composed, performed, or performing as a protest, especially against the prevailing establishment

> 1953 J. Greenway: Protest songs are unpleasant and disturbing.

> 1968 *Guardian*: Brave new causes for brave new protest singers.

> 1969 *Listener*: Can [Bob Dylan] have forgotten entirely the horrors that gave such a fine edge to his protest music?

psephology *n* (1952) the study of public elections, and statistical analysis of trends in voting; also used more broadly to denote the prediction of electoral results. The basis of the coinage is outlined in the first quote below by Professor David Butler, the British political scientist whose writing and broadcasting on general and other elections did much to spread awareness of the term

> 1952 D. E. Butler: It…seems appropriate to preface this book with a discussion of why elections merit study and an examination of how much has been…learnt from psephology… I am indebted to Mr. R. B. McCallum for the invention of this word to describe the field of research in which he is so eminent a pioneer. It is derived from *psephos*—the pebble which the Athenians dropped into an urn to vote.

> 1952 *New York Herald-Tribune*: He [i.e. R. B. McCallum] suggested I [i.e. D. E. Butler] call myself a psephologist.

> 1952 *Daily Express*: Psephologically speaking: you may vote for a good-looking party.

psychedelic *adj, n* (1956) (a drug) producing an expansion of consciousness through greater awareness of the senses and emotional feelings and the revealing of unconscious motivations, often symbolically. The word, coined from Greek *psukhe* 'mind' and *deloun* 'to make manifest, reveal', was originally suggested by H. Osmond in a letter to Aldous Huxley early in 1956. He put it into the public domain in a scientific paper in 1957. It came into its own in the LSD-culture of the mid to late 1960s, when its application broadened out to denote the effect or sensation produced by a psychedelic drug, especially vivid colours, often in bold abstract designs or in motion. See also **psychedelia (1967)**

> 1956 H. Osmond: To fathom Hell or soar angelic, Just take a pinch of psychedelic (Delos to manifest).

> 1957 H. Osmond: I have tried to find an appropriate name for the agents under discussion: a name that will include the concepts of enriching the mind and enlarging the vision… My choice, because it is clear, euphonious, and uncontaminated by other associations, is psychedelic, mind-manifesting.

> 1967 *Wall Street Journal*: Psychedelic fabrics are becoming the rage.

> 1968 *Globe & Mail* (Toronto): 'Topless' dancers gyrating in the glow of psychedelic slides and lights.

> 1969 *Observer*: The very latest psychedelic colours, electric purples and greens.

rabbit *v* (1950) to talk volubly. Slang. From rhyming slang *rabbit and pork* for 'talk'

> 1959 *Encounter*: The next thing I knew, I was rabbiting away to a geezer.

RAM *n* (1957) An acronym formed from the initial letters of *random-access memory* 'a computer memory or file all parts of which are directly accessible, so that it need not be read sequentially'

> 1957 R. K. Richards: 'Random access storage' (or RAM, for 'random access memory').

> 1977 *Design Engineering*: The MM5799…contains 1,536 8-bit instructions in its ROM, and its RAM can store 96 BCD digits of 4 bits each.

Rastafarian *adj, n* (1955), **Rasta** *adj, n* (1955) (a member) of the Ras Tafari sect, a Jamaican sect which believes that blacks are the chosen people, that the late Emperor Haile Selassie of Ethiopia (1892–1975) is God Incarnate, and that he will secure their repatriation to their homeland in Africa. Members typically have dreadlocks (see **dreadlocks (1960)**) and wear beret-like hats called toms.

Ras Tafari is the name by which Haile Selassie was known from 1916 until his accession in 1930 (*ras* is Amharic for 'chief')

> 1955 G. E. Simpson: Emphasis…is placed on love and kindliness to fellow Ras Tafarians… The 'Rasta' people consider Marcus Garvey…as the forerunner of their movement.

> 1960 *Guardian*: The bearded Marijuana-smoking Rastafarian sect… The Rastafarians run a campaign to get Jamaican negroes to return to Africa.

real time *n* (1953) the actual time during which a process or event occurs, especially one analysed by a computer, in contrast to time subsequent to it when computer processing can be done, a recording replayed, or the like

> 1953 *Mathematical Tables & Other Aids to Computation*: With the advent of large-scale high-speed digital computers, there arises the question of their possible use in the solution of problems in 'real time', i.e., in conjunction with instruments receiving and responding to stimuli from the external environment. The criteria for satisfactory operation in such real-time service are different from those generally encountered.

> 1964 *Listener*: A higher speed in computers means that their complexity can increase very rapidly, too, and that they can more easily engage in activites in what we call 'real time'. That is to say, they can calculate at the actual speed of the events taking place.

redcoat *n* (1950) a steward at a Butlin's holiday camp. They were required to wear red jackets

> 1950 *Butlin Holiday Book 1949–50*: The snow eventually disappeared and the 'Redcoats' prepared to return to the Holiday Villages.

rock *n* (1957) Originally an abbreviation of **rock and roll**, but latterly often used to encompass most modern pop music with a driving beat

> 1957 *Beat*: 'It's the answer to Rock,' said one and all… But a new sound package of diluted Rock, Hill-Billy tunes and ersatz Blues assails our ears.

> 1959 *Punch*: Richard, like most rock singers, dances from the knees in a style borrowed from African warriors.

> 1967 *Listener*: Is there an analogy between films and rock music?

> 1978 Gore Vidal: A rock band deafened us… Deafening was what H.V.W. would call the din from the rock stars' dressing rooms where electric guitars whined.

rock and roll, rock 'n' roll *n* (1954) a type of popular dance-music characterized by a heavy beat and simple melodies, combining elements of rhythm and blues with country and western music. Originally US. The expression, which in Black English is a euphemism for sexual intercourse, had been used in connection with popular dancing since at least the 1930s (there is a 1934 song by S. Clare called 'Rock and roll'), but this specific conjunction of music and name had to wait until the early 1950s. Amongst the music's earliest and now legendary exponents were Bill Haley and Elvis Presley. The spelling *rock 'n' roll* is first recorded in 1955, the derivative *rock 'n' roller* in 1956. Sometimes abbreviated to *r 'n' r* (perhaps on the model of *r and b* 'rhythm and blues', first recorded in 1949). See also **rock (1957)**

> 1954 *Billboard*: Alan Freed…will sponsor his first 'Rock and Roll Jubilee Ball' at the St. Nicolas Arena here on January 14 and 15.

> 1955 *Life*: But parents and police were startled by other rock 'n roll records' words which were frequently suggestive and occasionally lewd… On a list of 10 top juke box best-selling records last week, six were r'n r.

> 1956 *Time*: *My Boy Elvis*…is a real rock 'n' roller.

> 1969 Nik Cohn: In 1951, a DJ called Alan Freed launched a series of rhythm reviews at the Cleveland Arena… These shows featured coloured acts but were aimed at predominantly white audiences and, to avoid what he called 'the racial stigma of the old classification', Freed dropped the term R&B and invented the phrase Rock'n'Roll instead.

role model *n* (1957) someone on whom others model their behaviour or actions

> 1957 W. Thielens: By the time students enter law or medical school, those whose decisions were made earliest are most likely to have a role model.

> 1977 *New York Times Magazine*: If the teacher was a 'role model', parents were obviously unaware of it.

rotisserie *n* (1953) a cooking appliance which has a rotating spit for roasting and barbecuing meat. The Anglo-Saxon cook rediscovers the spit, made more desirable by a sophisticated French name. It came into its own with the fashionability of the kebab in the 1960s, but in the long run lost out to the barbecue (see **barbecue (1931)**, **barbie (1976)**)

> 1953 *Home Beautiful*: Cooking on a rotating spit or rotisserie is high gourmet cooking.

> 1960 *Guardian*: All the glittering machines, the washers, the electric rotisseries.

sack dress *n* (1957) a short unwaisted dress, usually narrowing at the hem, fashionable during the second half of the 1950s. Often shortened to simply *sack*

> 1957 *Punch*: After all, the belted sack-dress, in some form or another, is a perennial we have known all down the years, flowering chiefly in the suburbs and the provinces.

> 1957 *Daily Mail*: The sack has swept London like a prairie fire.

> 1959 *Listener*: The sack is out. Now, it's the Empire line.

Salk vaccine *n* (1954) the first vaccine developed against poliomyelitis, made from viruses of the three immunological types inactivated with formalin. Named after Jonas Edward Salk (1914–95), US virologist, who developed the vaccine in 1954

> 1954 *Journal of the American Medical Association*: There is no chance that injections of Salk vaccine will cause human Rh-negative subjects to produce Rh antibodies.

> 1958 *Oxford Mail*: Chicago has been completely free from polio this year for the first time, states the Health Department, which credited this to the extensive use of Salk vaccine.

sandwich course *n* (1955) See **sandwich (1913)**

scene *n* (1951) a place where people of common interests meet or where a particular activity is carried on. Hence, more loosely, an activity or pursuit (especially a fashionable or superior one, or one which one favours); a situation, event, or experience; a way of life. Originally US jazz slang; it was taken up by the beatniks of the later 1950s, and retained a place in the 'cool' slang of succeeding decades

> 1951 Elliot Paul: 'Nobody comes on this scene wearin' any green,' said another taller Negro.

> 1958 G. Lea: Something on the scene you don't dig… It was a bad scene. It scared me, man.

> 1967 *Punch*: They come here to work because it's exciting and new and because it's the scene.

> 1975 David Lodge: Washing up was more his scene than body language.

Scientology *n* (1951) a system of beliefs based on the study of knowledge and claiming to develop the highest potentialities of its members, founded in 1951 by L. Ron Hubbard (1911–86). *Scientology* was registered in the US as a proprietary term in 1970. It was coined by Hubbard, perhaps on the basis of the earlier German *Scientologie* (first recorded in 1937). See also **dianetics (1950)**

> 1951 L. Ron Hubbard (title): Handbook for Preclears: Scientology.

> 1952 L. Ron Hubbard: Scientology means knowing about knowing, or science of knowledge… The E-Meter is available from The Hubbard Association of Scientologists.

sci-fi *n* (1955) A colloquial abbreviation of **science fiction (1929)**

> 1955 *Britannica Book of the Year*: The popularity of science fiction was reflected in the contracted form Scifi.

> 1957 *MD Medical Newsmagazine*: Modern sci-fi writers follow an honorable tradition.

scooter *v* (1957) to travel by motor-scooter. The motor-scooter was a fashionable mode of transport among the young in the late 1950s and early 60s ('The rising popularity of new types of machines—the scooter and the moped', *Times* (1957)); see also **Vespa (1950)**

> 1957 Christine Brooke-Rose: He climbed on to his Lambretta and scootered off towards Oxford Street.

Scrabble *n* (1950) The proprietary name (registered in the US in 1950, with claim of use since 1948) of a game in which players use tiles displaying individual letters to form words on a special board

> 1954 *Newsweek*: To help Scrabble fans, crossword-puzzle addicts, and other persons troubled for a word ending in 'x', 'y', or 'z', a 'reverse' dictionary has been compiled at the University of Massachusetts.

scrambler *n* (1950) an electronic device used, especially in telephony and radio, to make speech signals unintelligible, usually by dividing the signal into distinct frequency ranges which are separately inverted and displaced in frequency

> 1950 Gilbert Hackforth-Jones: This line, which linked me directly with the Rear-Admiral, was fitted with a device known as a 'scrambler' which was completely secure against listening in and it was therefore possible to speak freely and at length at all times.

> 1981 A. Melville-Ross: You can get me…the Minister's Private Secretary…on the scrambler.

scuba *n* (1952) an apparatus designed to enable a swimmer to breathe while under the water. An acronym formed from the initial letters of *self-contained underwater breathing apparatus*. Now mainly used in *scuba diving* and *scuba diver*

> 1952 Hahn & Lambertsen: Within the last 3–5 years we have witnessed…a rapid increase in the numbers of self contained underwater breathing apparatus (SCUBA) in use… SCUBA are now in relatively large scale use by spearfishermen and sports swimmers.

> 1962 (title): The new science of skin and scuba diving.

see-through *adj* (1950) Of a fabric or a garment, typically a woman's: that can be seen through; transparent

> 1950 *Life*: See-through fabrics bring undercovering to the surface.

> 1951 *Sunday Pictorial*: 'See-through' nighties…may be heavenly for women, but they have many disadvantages.

see you later, alligator (1957) A catch-phrase used on parting. It comes from a song of the same name by R. C. Guidry (see the first quote below), which is often quoted (or rather, slightly misquoted) more fully in a dialogue as *see you later alligator—in a while, crocodile*. The reason for *alligator* is that from the 1930s to the 50s it was US jazz slang for 'a devotee of swing music' ('You are there as an alligator, so don't applaud', *Delineator* (1936))

> 1957 R. C. Guidry: See you lat-er, al-li-ga-tor, Aft-er 'while, croc-o-dile,—Can't you see you're in my way, now, Don't you know you cramp my style?

> 1959 I. & P. Opie: Rhyme seems to appeal to a child as something funny and remarkable in itself, there being neither wit nor reason to support it… Hence the way lines of current dance songs become catch phrases…'See you later, alligator'—'In a while, crocodile', repeated ad nauseam.

sensitive *adj* (1953) involved with or likely to affect (national) security

> 1953 *Manchester Guardian Weekly*: People in 'sensitive' jobs or departments—that is in positions having access to top secret or policy information.

separate development *n* (1955) the systematic development or regulation of a group or race by itself independently of other groups or races in a society. Originally used in South Africa as an English synonym of **apartheid (1947)**

> 1955 *Summary, Report of the Committee on the Socio-Economic Development of Bantu Areas of South Africa* (heading): Objections to the policy of separate development.

sex-kitten *n* (1958) a young woman who exploits her sex appeal. Colloquial; largely a journalistic usage

> 1958 *Daily Sketch*: Clever film men have moulded her sex-kitten type.

> 1966 *Guardian*: Brigitte Bardot…the original sex kitten with the French charm.

sexpot *n* (1957) a sexually exciting person, especially a woman. Colloquial

> 1957 F. Morton: How pitiful the American who cannot command the smile of a sexpot.

> 1975 *New Yorker*: Graham Chapman, John Cleese…with Connie Booth and Carol Cleveland as their sexpot aides.

short sharp shock *n* (1959) a brief but harsh custodial sentence imposed on an offender, especially a young one, in an attempt to discourage further offending. A term which crops up periodically, as the remembrance of the futility of the practice fades

> 1959 *Penal Practice in a Changing Society*: It has been found possible to adapt the original conception of the 'short sharp shock' to include that of a limited but positive form of training.

> 1993 *Independent*: The detention centre is meant to be a short sharp shock.

silent majority *n* (1955) the mass of people whose views remain unexpressed, especially in political contexts; those who are usually overlooked because of their moderation. As a metaphor for 'those who have died (and gone to heaven)' the expression dates back to the 19th century, but its political status was established by Westley and Egstein's 1969 book *The Silent Majority*. See also **Moral Majority (1979)**

> 1955 C. V. Wedgwood: The King in his natural optimism still believed that a silent majority in Scotland were in his favour.

> 1970 *Time*: Who precisely are the Middle Americans?… They make up the core of the group that Richard Nixon now invokes as the 'forgotten Americans' or 'the Great Silent Majority'.

sin bin *n* (1950) an enclosure to which an ice-hockey player must go for a fixed period after he or she has been sent off for foul play. Originally North American

> 1958 *Herald Tribune* (Grand Prairie, Alberta): [The] game saw 37 minutes spent in the sin-bin.

skiffle *n* (1957) a mainly British form of pop music in which the vocal part is supported by a rhythmic accompaniment of guitars or banjos and other more or less conventional instruments (e.g. a washboard). The name was borrowed from a much earlier US usage (first recorded in 1926), applied to a type of jazz played on improvised instruments. The word's ultimate origins are unknown

> 1957 *Times*: Earnest young women will not consent to hear even skiffle, unless they are sure of the reverberation factor of the sitting room.

> 1957 Christine Brooke-Rose: A skiffle group—consisting of two guitarists, a thimble-fingered drummer with a wooden washboard, and a man sweeping a carpet-brush rhythmically over three metal strings drawn taut across a saucepan.

skijamas *n* (1958) a pair of pyjamas in the style of a ski suit. North American; a word with a relatively limited life-span

> 1958 Lorna Whishaw: I…then, dressed in my skijamas, ate my dinner in peace.

Skylon *n* (1950) a spindle-shaped filigree spire, illuminated at night, forming a prominent feature of the South Bank exhibition at the Festival of Britain in London in 1951. The name was presumably a blend of *sky* and *pylon* (see the quote below for an account of its origin). The Skylon itself was demolished after the exhibition, but its name was occasionally revived for similar structures. Compare **Millennium Dome (1997)**

> 1950 *Times*: Mrs. A. G. S. Fidler, the wife of the chief architect to the Crawley Development Corporation, was informed yesterday that her suggestion of the name of 'Skylon' for the vertical feature of the Festival of Britain exhibition had been accepted.

sleeper *n* (1955) a spy, saboteur, etc. who remains inactive for a long period before engaging in spying or sabotage or otherwise acting to achieve his ends. Reportedly the term used in the trade, in preference to the more headline-friendly **mole (1974)**

> 1955 H. Roth: Hollister… was a sleeper—a member of the Communist Party whose whole life was dedicated to the one big moment.

> 1976 *Times*: There almost certainly exists within our political establishment, what is known as a 'sleeper'—a high level political figure who is in fact a Soviet agent, infiltrated into the system many years ago.

sliced bread *n* (1958) bread sold already sliced (and wrapped). Such a boon was this article to late-20th-century men and women with no time to cut bread that it gave rise to the expression *the greatest thing since sliced bread* (first recorded in 1969) to denote anything or anyone particularly splendid, worthy to compare with the most stunning technological advances. Foodies, on the other hand, generally regard sliced bread with great distaste

> 1958 J. Mortimer: The trouble with living here, the butter gets as hard as the rock of Gibraltar. It blasts great holes in your sliced bread.

> 1972 P. G. Wodehouse: Bodkin regards you as the best thing that's happened since sliced bread.

slipped disc *n* (1953) an intervertebral disc that is ruptured or injured, causing pain in the back or (if nerve roots are compressed) in other parts of the body. An anatomical misnomer that has established itself firmly in the home doctor's vocabulary

> 1953 Edith Simon: The slipped disk everybody nowadays is suffering from.

> 1972 J. Minifie: God help the farmer who 'pulled his back', as they used to say before 'slipped disc' became the fashionable term.

slumlord *n* (1953) someone who lets slum property to tenants, especially one who allows the property to fall into disrepair. Originally US; a conflation of *slum landlord*, which is first recorded in 1893. Compare **Rachmanism (1963)**

> 1953 *Chicago Daily News*: Reporters…found that slumlords frequently twist Illinois' trust laws into blinds for escaping detection.

smaze *n* (1953) a mixture of smoke and haze. Originally US; a rival to **smog (1905)** which survived into the 1960s

> 1960 *Daily Telegraph*: A Weather Bureau official described the condition as a kind of smog-like haze. 'Call it smaze,' he said.

Smell-o-Vision *n* (1958) a style or technique of film presentation in which pictures on the screen are accompanied not only by sound but also by appropriate smells released into the auditorium. The idea was not new (see **smellie (1929)**), but this latest break-through in smell technology found few takers. The term was revived in the US in 1986 as the proprietary name for a special-effects technique involving 'scent-emitting stickers' with televised film

> 1987 *Guardian*: Whatever happened to Smellovision?

SMERSH, Smersh *n* (1953) The colloquial name of the Russian counter-espionage organization, originating during World War II, which was responsible for maintaining security within the Soviet armed and intelligence services. In Russian, a shortened form of *smert shpionam*, literally 'death to spies'. It was popularized in the West in the 1950s via espionage films and novels

> 1953 Ian Fleming: He would take on SMERSH and hunt it down. Without SMERSH, without this cold weapon of death and revenge, the M.W.D. would be just another bunch of civil servant spies.

smog mask *n* (1954) a mask to prevent the breathing in of smog (see **smog (1905)**)—a necessary precaution in London in the early 1950s, when smog caused many deaths, but largely redundant in Britain since the 1956 Clean Air Act came into force

> 1954 *Annual Register 1953*: The year 1953 might well be remembered as the one in which 'smog' masks first appeared.

snorkel, schnorkel *n* (1953) a short breathing-tube used by underwater swimmers. An adaptation of German *Schnorchel*, which was earlier applied to a sort of airshaft which allowed diesel-powered submarines to operate submerged for an extended period

> 1953 Jacques Cousteau: They claimed we drove away fish, damaged nets, looted their seines, and caused mistrals with our schnorkels.

> 1958 *Oxford Mail*: The American film television series, *Sea Hunt*, claims to be boosting the sport of skin-diving. If that is true there is soon going to be a big demand for snorkels and spear-guns in the Midlands.

soft *adj* (1959) Of a drug: comparatively non-addictive and safe to use (e.g. cannabis, LSD, amphetamines). Compare **hard (1955)**

> 1959 *Oxford Mail*: Dr. D. C. M. Yardley of Oxford found that of about 50 university users of soft drugs (mostly marihuana) about 20 were regular takers, and that although the latter were convinced they could give it up at any time, in fact they hardly ever did so without professional help.

soft landing *n* (1958) a landing of a spacecraft that is slow enough for no serious damage to be incurred

> 1958 *Proceedings of the Lunar & Planetary Exploration Colloquium*: With a soft landing on the moon one might put down a payload of 225 to 800 pounds, but…only about 10 to 25 percent of this would be usable for instruments.

solid-state *adj* (1959) utilizing the electronic properties of solids (as in transistors and other semi-conductor devices, in contrast to the partial vacuum of valves)

> 1959 *Economist*: The transistor, best known of the 'solid-state' devices that employ these materials [i.e. semiconductors], can do most of the jobs of a valve while taking far less space.

son et lumière *n* (1957) a form of entertainment using recorded sound and lighting effects, usually presented at night at a historic building and giving a dramatic narrative of its history. A borrowing from French, literally 'sound and light'

> 1957 *Times*: A dinner party…on the occasion of the preview of the *Son et Lumière* spectacle… In the five years since M. Paul Robert-Houdin first introduced the technique at…Chambord, *son et lumière* has been adopted at…buildings of historic interest in France.

> 1959 *Times*: Son et lumière performances are being given this week, starting to-night at Greys Court, Henley-on-Thames.

sonic boom *n* (1952), **sonic bang** *n* (1953) the sudden loud noise heard when the shock wave from an aircraft travelling faster than sound reaches the ears. A familiar sound in the skies in the early 1950s, when aircraft developers were obsessed with breaking the **sound barrier (1939)**. By the time the supersonic airliner *Concorde* entered service in the mid 1970s the novelty had worn off; its sonic boom had it banned from many overland air-routes

> 1952 *Times*: Aircraft travelling at about the speed of sound cause a loud bang, which has become known as the 'sonic boom'.

> 1953 *Science News*: Subsequently two sonic bangs were heard of the same intensity with a small time interval apparently the same as that between the vapour puffs.

space programme *n* (1958) a programme of exploration of space and development of space technology

> 1958 *New Statesman*: It was Congress, rather than the President, that took the initiative in pushing a space programme.

space race *n* (1959) the competition between nations (usually specifically the US and the Soviet Union) to be first to achieve various objectives in the exploration of space

> 1959 *Listener*: The possible nature of Britain's contribution to the space race.

space station *n* (1952) a large manned satellite designed for permanent orbit around Earth and used for scientific research or military reconnaissance, or as an assembly point for long-range spacecraft. A term which survived the transition from theory to practice

> 1952 W. Ley: The space station…is always spinning, and obviously it cannot be stopped just to enable a space taxi to enter one of the turrets.

> 1970 Neil Armstrong: An orbiting space station and the 'space taxi'…to take astronauts there and back.

-speak *suffix* (1957) a particular variety of (spoken) language; a characteristic mode of discourse. An element extracted from *Newspeak*, the name of the artificial language used for official communications in George Orwell's novel *Nineteen Eighty-Four* (see **Newspeak (1949)**). Since a leading characteristic of this is that it was put to corrupt purposes, not surprisingly most -*speak* formations tend to be negative in connotation

> 1957 M. Buttle: In the literary weeklies, the languages of criticism and theology have become one and book reviews all sound like sermons written in the most holy 'Double-Speak'.

> 1981 *Times* (headline): Haigspeak rewrites the grammar.

> 1981 *Guardian*: 'I am very sorry that I cannot be with you today… I am most grateful and touched that you have decided to name a locomotive after me,' [the telegram] said in classic royalspeak.

split *v* (1954) to leave, depart. Slang, originally US. Also used transitively, mainly in the phrase *split the scene*

> 1956 O. Duke: But that's why the cat split… Naw, man—I split that scene.

1956 Billie Holiday: I grabbed him and told him to do something because I had to split for the bathroom again.

sputnik *n* (1957) an unmanned artificial earth satellite, especially a Russian one. The term is applied specifically (usually with capital initial) to any of a series of such satellites launched by the Soviet Union between 1957 and 1961. The first Sputnik, launched on 4 October 1957, was the first artificial satellite. This Soviet space coup, which left the hitherto complacent Americans stunned, made *sputnik* one of the in-words of the late 1950s, and did much to promote the popularity of the ending -*nik* in English (see **beatnik (1958)**). *Sputnik* in Russian means literally 'travelling companion'; it is formed from *s* 'with' and *put* 'way, journey', plus the agent suffix -*nik*

1957 *Times*: Pride in the launching of the sputnik ('fellow-traveller'), as the satellite is called, as well as the guided missile, were reflected in a speech by Mr. Krushchev…last night… Mr. Khrushchev replied: 'To peace and to the sputnik as a symbol of peace!'… The régime which sends a second Sputnik girdling the earth has just emerged from another of its secretly contrived shifts of political power.

1957 *Times Literary Supplement*: America's defeat in the sputnik race.

sputnikitis *n* (1957) hysterical enthusiasm for sputniks. A short-lived term for a short-lived phenomenon

1957 *Observer*: We rang up Hamley's to see how Sputnikitis was hitting them… 'No, I'd not say our space toys were on the up… It's always in competition with cowboys and Red Indians, you see.'

status symbol *n* (1955) a possession or asset sought or acquired as a symbol of social prestige

1957 *Wall Street Journal*: The most common sources of interoffice rivalry over status symbols involve such obvious executive trappings as the size of the desk, the quality of drapes and carpets in private offices, [etc.].

steam radio *n* (1957) sound radio, considered as being outmoded by television. Colloquial; a measure both of the rapid advance of television in the 1950s, and of the obsolescence of steam as a power source (steam locomotion in Britain was on its last legs)

1957 Val Gielgud: The flight from 'steam-radio' to television has become an admitted rout.

1961 *Radio Times*: I am the proud possessor of 'square eyeballs', but still feel that the good old 'steam' radio has a winner in the *Scrapbook* series.

stereo *adj, n* (1954) Originally an abbreviation of the adjective **stereophonic (1927)**, it is first recorded as a noun in the sense 'stereophonic sound' in 1956, and in the sense 'a stereophonic apparatus' in 1964. In this latter usage it has virtually come to denote any system for playing recordings (stereophony being the norm)

1954 *Wireless World*: The first full-length stereophonic film to be released was Walt Disney's 'Fantasia',…with stereo sound photographically recorded on four tracks on a separate sound film.

1956 *Radio & Television News*: What should stereo do?

1958 *Times*: What stereo discs have achieved is to combine these two channels in one groove traced by one stylus.

1964 *House & Garden*: The wall unit houses the stereo.

stiletto heel *n* (1953) (a woman's shoe with) a very narrow, high heel, fashionable especially in the 1950s. Often curtailed to simply *stiletto*

1953 *Daily Telegraph*: One of the models…in the…winter collection…has the new stiletto heel, $3\frac{1}{2}$ in high and just large enough at the base to cover a sixpence.

1959 *New Statesman*: She came…smooching forward, her walk made lopsided by the absence of one heel of the stilettos.

strange *adj* (1956) Applied to those sub-atomic particles that have a non-zero value of the strangeness quantum number, a number denoting the property of being conserved in strong but not in weak interactions (this use of *strangeness* is also first recorded in 1956). So called originally because the particles had lifetimes much longer than was expected from their being produced by the strong interaction

1956 Murray Gell-Mann: We shall refer to the nucleon…, the antinucleon…, and the pion…as 'ordinary particles' to distinguish them from the 'strange particles', K-particles and hyperons… Since we have S = 0 for ordinary particles and S / 0 for 'strange' ones we refer to S as 'strangeness'.

strategic *adj* (1957) of, delivering, or being nuclear weapons intended to destroy an enemy's capacity to make war. The contrast is usually with **tactical**, denoting nuclear weapons intended for short-range use, which is also first recorded in 1957

> 1957 *Listener*: Nobody has managed…to draw an effective distinction between 'strategic' and 'tactical' atomic weapons.

> 1969 *Times*: The discussions which will open between the United States and Russia in Helsinki next month are…the long awaited Salt discussions—the strategic arms limitation talks.

structuralism *n* (1951) Originally, any theory or method in which a discipline or field of study is envisaged as comprising elements interrelated in systems and structures at various levels, the structures and the interrelations of their elements being regarded as more significant than the elements considered in isolation. Later, the term came to be applied to theories, particularly in anthropology, sociology, and literature, concerned with analysing the surface structures of a system in terms of its underlying structure. The leading figure in this sort of structuralism (which was heavily influenced by contemporary work in linguistics) was the French social anthropologist Claude Lévi-Strauss

> 1951 *Mind*: Braithwaite evidently believes that the whole philosophy of structuralism breaks down over the question of a combining relation.

> 1955 Raymond Firth: All British social anthropologists are structuralists in their use of the analytical principles developed by this method. But the rigidity and limitations of a simple structuralism alone have come to be more widely perceived.

> 1980 *London Review of Books*: Structuralism is the philosophy of those in the universities and thereabouts who are not philosophers.

stuff *v* (1952) Used in various expressions of dismissive contempt based on the notion of inserting an object into a bodily orifice (notably *get stuffed* and *stuff it*), and linked with *stuff* 'to copulate with' (first recorded in 1960).

> 1952 Miles Tripp: 'Get stuffed,' he said savagely.

> 1955 Philip Larkin: Ah, were I courageous enough To shout *stuff your pension*!

> 1958 Frank Norman: The geezer just got up and told him to stuff his job.

subtext *n* (1950) an underlying theme in a piece of writing (especially in a novel, play, or screenplay). Originally a term in the theory of acting developed by Konstantin Stanislavsky (see **method (1923)**)

> 1950 E. R. Hapgood: What do we mean by subtext? What is it that lies behind and beneath the actual words of a part?… It is the manifest, the inwardly felt expression of a human being in a part, which flows uninterruptedly beneath the words of the text, giving them life and a basis for existing.

> 1973 *Times*: Also admirable was the manner in which Prince underlined the subtext of naturalism that lies beneath the very obvious symbolic superstructure.

subtopia *n* (1955) a suburban area that has been developed in an unattractive or unsightly way. British; an ironic blend of *suburban* and *utopia*, with no doubt a side-glance at *suburbia*. Its coiner, Ian Nairn, had his wish that it would 'stick' (see the first quote below)

> 1955 *Architectural Review*: There will be no real distinction between town and country. Both will consist of a limbo of shacks, bogus rusticities, wire and aerodromes, set in some fir-poled fields… Upon this new Britain the *Review* bestows a name in the hope that it will stick—Subtopia… The other is the panic reflex to the spread of Subtopia, which attempts improvements using standards which are themselves Subtopian.

> 1971 *Country Life*: Will there still be English villages as we know them, or will they have merged into an unending subtopia in which town and country have become indistinguishable?

sudsable *adj* (1951) Of a garment: washable in soapy water. North American. Largely an advertising copywriter's creation, but it is based on a genuine verbal use of *suds* ('to wash in soap-suds') which dates back at least to the 1830s ('Colors perk up—brighten up—when you suds your washables in Ivory Flakes', in Marshall McLuhan (1951))

> 1951 *Sun* (Baltimore) (advert): She never has too many blouses…so lovable…so wearable…so sudsable.

summit *n* (1950) the level of heads of state or heads of government, especially of the superpowers. Churchill's metaphor (see the first quote below) probably engendered the usage, but it did not really get under way until the middle of the decade, when characteristic compounds such as *summit conference* and *summit meeting* are first recorded. In due course *summit* came to be used elliptically for *summit conference*

> 1950 Winston Churchill: It is not easy to see how things could be worsened by a parley at the summit, if such a thing were possible.

> 1955 *Times*: The senator's resolution demanding that the United States should refuse to attend the 'summit' conference.

> 1955 *New York Times*: I say at this moment I see no reason for that summit meeting.

> 1967 *Spectator*: The most certain result of the Glassboro summit, in fact, is no more than that Mr. Johnson's standing at home is now rather higher.

summitry *n* (1958) the practice of convening or holding summit meetings, or of using them as a diplomatic device

> 1958 *Economist*: The Western dislike of time-wasting summitry is due…to a feeling that even an inconclusive get-together would fill the democracies with a false sense of security.

> 1967 *Spectator*: Mr. Macmillan likened the preliminaries to the summitry so dear to his heart to a stately minuet.

supportive *adj* (195) providing moral or emotional support. The adjective has been in use since the 16th century in the general sense 'providing support'; this specific application emerged from the jargon of US psychotherapists

> 1954 H. C. Shands: It is necessary that the anxious individual have available a supportive pattern of relationship to depend upon through the learning period.

> 1968 A. J. Tannenbaum: They have worked with the children…in order to win their confidence and provide supportiveness.

> 1980 *Daily Telegraph*: Most American psychotherapists now advertise themselves as 'supportive'.

surfer *n* (1955) someone who rides a surfboard. The somewhat less common *surfboarder* is first recorded in 1953. 1955 is also the first known year for *surfing*

> 1955 Alan Ross: The essential art of surfing is timing… The heads of the surfers bob over several ignored undulations.

surgery *n* (1951) a session at which a Member of Parliament, local councillor, etc., is available to be consulted locally by his or her constituents, usually on regular occasions. British. A usage directly inspired by the general practitioner's regular consultations

> 1951 *Hansard, Commons*: It is a practice of mine…to call personally upon as many of my constituents as I can, and I find that by doing this a different set of problems is presented to me from those which my post-bag or even my weekly 'surgery' bring.

surplus *n* (1951) goods that are sold off as being surplus to requirements. A usage which thrived in the post-World War II years, when huge amounts of ex-military clothing and equipment came on to the market

> 1951 Roger Senhouse: Jean de Touzac—is in the surplus store racket. What a set!

> 1952 Hammond Innes: They wore war surplus clothing relieved by bright scarves.

> 1952 E. C. R. Lorac: Grey blankets, (good 'government surplus').

swinging *adj* (1958) uninhibited, ignoring conventions; lively and up to date: applied to people and places (notably, in the 1960s, *swinging London*) and to the decade of the 60s itself (the *swinging Sixties*). Also used as a general term of approval: wonderful, marvellous, great. Colloquial. As the first quotation suggests, the usage arose out of US jazz parlance. See also **swinger (1964)** and **swinger (1965)**

> 1958 *Publications of the American Dialect Society*: Swingin', the highest term of approval. May be applied to anything a jazzman likes, or any person.

> 1959 *Guardian*: [She] informed him that she wants a large place 'in a swinging part of town'…so he is looking around in Chelsea and Knightsbridge.

1964 **Norman Vaughan**: When people ask me how I feel about the months ahead, I tell them: 'Sometimes it's a bit dodgy, but most of the time it's swinging!'

1965 *Weekend Telegraph*: Diana Vreeland…editor of Vogue…has said simply 'London is the most swinging city in the world at the moment'.

1966 *Time*: I know this world, this swinging London… But I wouldn't describe myself as a swinger.

1967 *Listener*: He does not fit into the Zeitgeist of the swinging 'sixties.

1971 **Harold Wilson**: The press publicized what they called the new swinging style of the Downing Street receptions.

tactical *adj* (1957) of, delivering, or being nuclear weapons intended for short-range use. The contrast is usually with **strategic**, denoting nuclear weapons intended to destroy the enemy's capacity to wage war, which is also first recorded in 1957. The usage arose out of the earlier application of *tactical* to bombing in support of one's ground forces, which evolved during World War I

1976 **Lord Home**: The balance of argument through the years moved towards a substantial conventional force, but it was gradually rendered somewhat academic by the introduction of the tactical nuclear weapon.

tandoori *adj, n* (1958) (a dish) cooked (as if) in a tandour, a type of clay oven used in northern India and Pakistan. A borrowing from Urdu or Punjabi. One of the new wave of Indian culinary terms that came into English after World War II, thanks to the restaurants set up by immigrants to Britain from India and Pakistan; they joined those (such as *curry* and *chutney*) which had previously made the transition through the Raj connection

1958 **Robin Howe**: Tanduri chicken is always eaten with the fingers.

1969 *Guardian*: The restaurant specialises in exclusive Indian cuisine: Tandoories—meat and chicken grilled in clay ovens over a charcoal fire.

tat, tatt *n* (1951) rubbish, junk, worthless goods. Colloquial, mainly British. Probably a back-formation from *tatty*, but there may also be a memory of the earlier, now seldom encountered *tat* 'a shabby or slovenly person' ('You should have seen the company: a couple of old tats got up as Elizabethan pages', Noël Coward (1936))

1951 **William Sansom**: He was talking of his business in Georgian and early Victorian objets d'oeil. He called it tat.

1958 **Angus Wilson**: It was filled…with a jumble of pleasing, valuable antique furniture and hideous, worthless bric-a-brac… 'I like tatt,' he had said.

tax-deductible *adj* (1954) allowable as an expense that can be deducted from gross income in calculating taxable income

1954 **Ira Levin**: We are…beginning the construction of a new gymnasium… Perhaps your father would be interested in making a contribution… Such contributions are tax-deductible.

Teddy boy *n* (1954) a youth affecting a style of dress and appearance held to be characteristic of Edward VII's reign, typically a long velvet-collared jacket, 'drainpipe' trousers, and sideburns. The style began in the late 1940s among a group of Guards officers calling themselves the 'Edwardians', who dressed in mock-Edwardian manner. It was taken up by the homosexual community and then, in the early 1950s, with an admixture of the 'spiv' look, by working-class youths. The Teddy boys' reputation for gang fighting soon led to the term being used more broadly for any youthful street rowdy. The abbreviated *Teddy* is first recorded in 1956, as is the still shorter *Ted*. The underlying allusion is, of course, to the familiar form of the name *Edward*

1954 **A. Heckstall-Smith**: Craig was just such a fellow. Ronald Coleman, the leader of the 'Edwardians' or the 'Teddy Boys', the gang of young hooligans who ran amok on Clapham Common, was another.

1955 *Times*: Young soldiers are now forbidden to 'walk out' when off duty in plain clothes of unorthodox pattern, particularly the so-called Edwardian or 'Teddy boy' style… The forbidden style is not specifically defined in the order but is understood to be that of the long, draped-fronted jacket with velvet collar, and tight trousers shortened to show white socks at the ankles.

1956 *Time*: The Ted's notion of sartorial splendor ranges from a caricature of Edwardian elegance to the zoot padding of a Harlem hepcat.

Teddy girl *n* (1955) a girl who associates with or behaves like Teddy boys.

> 1957 *Sunday Times*: The girls who are an integral part of the gangs—the so-called Teddy-girls—are probably the worst influence of all.

teen *n* (1951) a teenager. A usage anticipated in the early 19th century ((*title*) 'Advice to the Teens; or, Practical Helps to the Formation of Character', I. Taylor (1818)), but in modern times mainly US. See also **teenager (1941)**

> 1951 *Deseret News* (Salt Lake City): Doing something fun like redecorating your room…is really interesting biz for a teen who loves being busy.

teleconference *n* (1953) a conference held by people who, though separated physically, are linked by telecommunication devices (e.g. telephones, television screens, etc.). Not a practical proposition until the late 1970s, when the derivative *teleconferencing* was coined

> 1953 *Language*: A general at a teleconference writes out a message for transmission.

> 1975 *Financial Times*: The psychological and travel-replacement aspects of teleconferencing were underlined in a paper by Quebec University.

teleprompter *n* (1951) an electronic device used by a speaker or actor on television, which, unseen to the audience, slowly unrolls the script, assisting or replacing memory. Formerly a proprietary name in the US (the equivalent British name is **autocue (1958)**)

> 1951 *Life*: Set at the eye level of performers, the Teleprompter unrolls a script whose inch-high letters, printed by special typewriter, can be read 25 feet away.

telerecording *n* (1953) a recording of a television programme made while it is being transmitted. The back-formed verb *telerecord* is first recorded in 1955

> 1953 *Radio Times*: A telerecording of the Abbey Ceremonies and a special Coronation edition of Television Newsreel.

> 1955 *Radio Times*: Monday's telerecorded programme *The Secret Arts*.

tenure *n* (1957) guaranteed tenure of office, as a right granted to the holder of a position (usually in a university or school) after a probationary period and protecting them against dismissal under most circumstances. Originally US. The related *tenured* 'having or carrying such a tenure' is first recorded in 1969 ('Left-wing professors, whose only protection is tenured appointment', *Guardian* (1969))

> 1957 Vladimir Nabokov: who had no life tenure at Waindell, would be forced to leave—unless some other literature-and-language Department agreed to adopt him… 'Naturally, I am expecting that I will get tenure at last,' said Pnin rather slyly. 'I am now Assistant Professor nine years.'

thalidomide *n* (1958) a non-barbiturate sedative and hypnotic which was found to induce abnormalities when taken early in pregnancy, sometimes causing malformation or absence of limbs in the fetus. Babies born deformed to women who had taken the drug to relieve certain side-effects of pregnancy were dubbed in the press *thalidomide babies*. Over 500 such babies were born in Britain between 1959 and 1962. The drug was withdrawn in 1961. The name was extracted from its full name, *phthalimidoglutarimide*, which in turn was based ultimately on an abbreviated form of *naphthalene*

> 1961 *Lancet*: We have just received reports from two overseas sources possibly associating thalidomide ('Distaval') with harmful effects on the fœtus in early pregnancy.

> 1962 *Guardian*: There is still no information about the number of 'thalidomide babies' in the country.

them and us (1957) people who are privileged or in authority and ordinary people. The implication is that the latter (the mass of the people) are exploited or oppressed by the former (a controlling élite). This use of *them* predates its joining up with *us* ('The magic circle of "Them", the great ones. "They" were the élite, the prefects and the games captains', Winifred Holtby (1924))

> 1957 Richard Hoggart: To the very poor, especially, they compose a shadowy but numerous and powerful group affecting their lives at almost every point: the world is divided into 'Them' and 'Us'.

> 1966 *Guardian*: The 'ordinary people' who looked on, who made…the Them and Us division [between the physically handicapped and other people].

thermonuclear *adj* (1953) Denoting (the use of) weapons that utilize a nuclear reaction that occurs only at very high temperatures, namely fusion of hydrogen or other light nuclei— in other words, the hydrogen bomb. A military-political use of a word that had been a technical term in nuclear physics (designating such a reaction) since the 1930s

> 1953 *Time*: Secretary of Defense Wilson, at his press conference, cast doubt on a suggestion that the Russians had a thermonuclear bomb 'in droppable form'.

> 1955 *Annual Register 1954*: Mr. Adlai Stevenson…inquired whether the 'New Look' meant leaving the country with 'the choice of inaction or a thermo-nuclear holocaust'.

think-tank *n* (1959) a research institute or other organization providing advice and ideas on national or commercial problems; an interdisciplinary group of specialist consultants. The term was originally a facetious US colloquialism for 'the brain' (first recorded in 1905)

> 1959 *Times Literary Supplement*: Even the Institute of Advanced Studies at Princeton does not quite meet the bill, nor does the 'think tank', the Center for Behavioral Sciences at Palo Alto.

> 1968 *Sunday Times*: The private research corporations, or 'think tanks' (in the current American terminology) which are paid, mostly by departments of Government, to think about problems.

three-D, 3-D *adj, n* (1952) An abbreviation of *three-dimensional* (which dates from the 1870s), used especially to denote a stereoptic method of filming, giving the effect of depth and perspective to the image on the screen for those willing to don the special red- and green-lensed spectacles necessary to see it

> 1953 *Sun* (Baltimore): We receive with mixed reaction the news that three-dimensional motion pictures, coyly called '3-D', will shortly come into general distribution.

> 1953 Alistair Cooke: One big studio has done a Technicolor 3-D movie of 'Kiss Me, Kate' which…has the effect of whisking the audience into the most privileged seat in a live theatre.

time warp *n* (1954) a distortion of space-time that is conceived as causing or enabling a person to remain stationary in time or to travel backwards or forwards in time. Originally a science-fiction-writer's term, but non-specialists soon found they had a use for it

> 1954 W. M. Miller: They showed me a dozen pictures of moppets with LTR-guns, moppets in time-warp suits, moppets wearing Captain Chronos costumes, [etc.].

> 1971 *Guardian*: The time warp effect was…intensified by having David Frost—essentially an early sixties figure.

titchy *adj* (1950) insignificantly small, diminutive, tiny. British colloquial; mainly a child's word. Based on *ti(t)ch* 'small person' (1934), which itself came from 'Little Tich', the stage-name of the diminutive English music-hall comedian Harry Relph (1868–1928), who was given the nickname as a child because of a resemblance to the so-called 'Tichborne claimant' (Arthur Orton (1834–98), who claimed to be the long-lost Roger Tichborne, heir to an English baronetcy)

> 1950 Anthony Buckeridge: Well, anyway,…there'll be a titchy hunk all round, so no one'll have any reason to grumble.

ton *n* (1954) a speed of one hundred miles per hour. British colloquial; used especially with reference to motor-cycle riders. Often in the phrase *do the* (or *a*) *ton*. From the earlier sense 'a score of one hundred', which apparently originated in darts in the 1930s. See also **ton-up (1961)**

> 1959 *News Chronicle*: The dangerous noddles who boast about doing the ton on the public roads.

> 1973 *Hansard Lords*: In that case, you must have been doing a 'ton', if very few cars passed you.

Tony Curtis *n* (1956) The professional name of the US film actor Bernard Schwarz (b. 1925), used to designate a style of haircut in which the hair at the sides of the head is combed back and that on the forehead is combed forwards

> 1956 *People*: The blokes with crew cuts or Tony Curtises.

top of the pops *n* (1958) the most popular or the best-selling record over a given period. Also widely used figuratively, meaning 'highly successful or popular' (indeed, that is how it is first recorded, and it soon became a sign of fuddy-duddiness to refer to a literal record in this way)

> 1958 *Punch*: 'Wagon Train' stays top of the pops in ITV features on every channel.

1978 Graham Greene: The top of the pops for any given year came as readily to Davis's memory as a Derby winner.

top ten *n* (1958) the first ten tunes or records, CDs, etc. in the popularity charts (see **charts (1963)**) at a particular time. *Top twenty* is first recorded in 1959. See also **hit parade (1958)**

1958 J. Asman: Traditional jazz records vie with the accepted 'pop' Top Ten in selling power.

1959 Francis Newton: Jazz has until recently simply not been big business in Britain, in the terms in which those who prepare records for the 'hit parade' of the 'top ten' or 'top twenty' think of it.

tracksuit *n* (1955) a loose two-piece garment, elasticated at the wrists and ankles; originally as worn by athletes while training and before and after contests, but later adapted as fashion-wear

1955 Roger Bannister: Not having had the importance of warming up explained to me I did not wear a track suit.

1980 *Times Literary Supplement*: His…wife…memorably fetching in her pink towelling track suit.

trad *adj, n* (1956) A colloquial abbreviation of *traditional* (*jazz*)—a style of jazz originating in New Orleans, characterized by collective improvisation by a front line of trumpet, trombone, and clarinet accompanied by a rhythm section. The term *trad* was also applied to its adherents

1956 *Melody Maker*: The great trad battle… The 'trads' belong to a strange sort of exclusive society.

1957 *Observer*: Lyttelton, who found 'trad' (traditional jazz) became play-acting and a dead-end, has travelled far from the revival days.

1958 *Spectator*: A raucous trad-jazz group struck up 'Basin Street Blues'.

traffic warden *n* (1959) a person employed to enforce regulations about the parking of motor vehicles and the use of parking meters. British. See also **meter maid (1957)**

1959 *Punch*: Any supposed similarity of function between the police and the newly-proposed traffic wardens vanished with the official statement that the wardens 'would help motorists to find parking space'.

1980 J. McNeil: It was a Ford, parked by the opposite kerb on…double yellow lines. A traffic warden was…preparing to write a ticket.

tranquillizer *n* (1956) any of a large class of drugs in widespread use since the 1950s for the reduction of tension or anxiety and the treatment of psychotic states. The alternative term *ataractic* (or *ataraxic*), proposed in 1955, never really caught on

1956 Aldous Huxley: Our impressions of the cutting short of the mescalin experience by this new tranquillizer.

1957 *Times*: The rapidly increasing use of drugs described as 'tranquillizers' and 'ataraxics'…has become a cause of concern in many countries.

transformational *adj* (1955) of or being a linguistic model or method of analysis based on the generation of surface structures from underlying structures by 'transformations', operations by which one syntactic structure is converted into another by the application of specific rules (the term *transformation* in this sense is also first recorded in 1955). *Transformational* first appears in 'Transformational Analysis', the title of the 1955 PhD dissertation of Noam Chomsky (b. 1928), the US language theorist who devised the method. It revolutionized the study of linguistics

1957 Noam Chomsky: Correspnding to the level of phrase structure, a grammar has a sequence of rules of the form $X \rightarrow Y$, and corresponding to lower levels it has a sequence of morphophonemic rules of the same basic form. Linking these two sequences, it has a sequence of transformational rules.

1965 *New York Times*: Transformational grammar grew in part from M.I.T. computer experiments to produce mechanical translations of foreign languages.

transistorize *v* (1953) to design or make with **transistors (1948)** (rather than valves)

1953 *Science News Letter*: Because of their ruggedness, 'transistorized' amplifiers should eliminate many an electronic headache under the restless sea.

1976 A. Hope: When the craze for transistorising everything got under way, in the 1960s, very few true hi-fi enthusiasts would touch a transistor amplifier with a barge pole.

transistor radio *n* (1958) a small portable radio with transistors and other solid-state devices in place of valves. Often abbreviated to simply *transistor*. A liberating boon or mobile noise-pollution, depending on your point of view. See also **tranny (1969)**

> 1958 *Spectator*: The new miniature transistor radios.

> 1966 John Betjeman: The endless anonymous croak of a cheap transistor Intensifies the loneliness I feel.

transplant *n* (1951) an operation in which an organ, tissue, etc., is transplanted from one person or animal to another. The verb *transplant* is first recorded in this sense in the late 18th century, but the organ concerned (as in the first record of the noun, quoted below) was a tooth. The earliest reference to internal organs comes at the start of the 20th century ('A…case in which a child…suffering from cretinism, had a portion of its mother's thyroid gland transplanted into its spleen', *Daily Chronicle* (1906)). The term did not become widely familiar until Christiaan Barnard performed the world's first successful heart transplant operation at the Groote Schuur Hospital in Cape Town in 1967

> 1951 *Sun* (Baltimore): He decided to try a transplant [of a tooth].

> 1963 *Guardian*: Surgeons at St Bartholomew's Hospital, London, this week carried out the hospital's first kidney transplant operation.

> 1971 *Daily Telegraph*: Prof. Christian Barnard…is standing by to carry out his first transplant for two years.

transsexualism *n* (1953) the condition of being transsexual, manifested in an overwhelming desire to belong to the opposite sex. The original related adjective and noun was *transsexualist* (1954); the now standard *transsexual* is not recorded before 1957

> 1953 H. Benjamin: Transvestitism…is the desire of a certain group of men to dress as women, or of women to dress as men. It can be…overwhelming, even to the point of wanting to belong to the other sex and correct nature's anatomical 'error'. For such cases the term Transsexualism seems appropriate.

> 1957 *American Journal of Psychotherapy*: Other kinds of secondary experiences might give rise to transsexual tendencies… Marriage, motherhood, and a husband are a woman's life and he wants that as a fulfillment of his femininity. These persons form the group aptly termed 'transsexuals'.

Travolator *n* (1955) A proprietary name (registered in the US in 1959) for a moving pavement designed for use at railway stations, airports, shopping centres, etc. A combination of *travel* and *elevator*

> 1955 *Science News Letter*: A moving sidewalk with cleated escalator treads had been developed by the Otis Elevator Company… Designers foresee use of the moving platform, called 'Trav-o-lator', for such congested areas as airports, subway stations, [etc.].

> 1957 *Economist*: Two 300 foot 'travelators'—stepless escalators that carry pedestrians along slight gradients—are expected to be in operation at the Bank underground station in London towards the end of next year.

treble chance *n* (1951) a form of football pool in which various points are awarded for a draw, an away win, and a home win

> 1951 Michael Innes: 'Heard what was last week's treble chance?' he asked. 'Ninety-eight thousand.'

triffid *n* (1951) In the science-fiction novel *The Day of the Triffids*, by John Wyndham (1903–69), one of a race of menacing plants, possessing a poisonous sting and able to move about, which threaten to overrun the world. Hence used allusively of vigorous plants, or of anything invasive or rapid in development. Perhaps based on *trifid* 'split into three parts'; the plant was supported on 'three bluntly-tapered projections extending from the lower part' of the body

> 1951 John Wyndham: A catchy little name originating in some newspaper office as a handy label for an oddity—but destined one day to be associated with pain, fear and misery—*triffid*.

> 1978 R. H. Lewis: Books 'taking over' in Triffid style is a common experience.

trip *n* (1959) a hallucinatory experience induced by a drug, especially LSD. Slang. The related verb, 'to experience drug-induced hallucinations', is first recorded in 1966

> 1959 Norman Mailer: I took some mescaline… At the end of a long and private trip which no quick remark should try to describe, the book of *The Deer Park* floated into mind.

> 1966 *Time*: Such dangers do not deter the acid heads or 'psychedelics'—even though some users are willing to admit that they found no great 'show', or had a 'freak trip' (a bad one) or 'tripped out' (the worst kind).

tumbler-drier *n* (1956), **tumble-drier** *n* (1962) a machine for drying washing in a heated drum that turns about a horizontal axis

> 1956 *Good Housekeeping Home Encyclopedia*: Electric Tumbler Dryers dry by means of a revolving drum in a heated cabinet.

> 1972 James McClure: The lady next door has a tumble drier so you put your clothes outside and I'll take them round.

Tupperware *n* (1956) The proprietary name (registered in the US in 1956, with claim of use since 1951) of a range of plastic vessels, containers, etc., sold exclusively at 'parties' in private homes to which potential purchasers are invited. Named after Earl S. Tupper, President of the Tupper Corporation

> 1965 *Which?*: Are more expensive brands [of food container], in particular Tupperware, better than cheaper brands at storing foods?

> 1966 Thomas Pynchon: Mrs Oedipa Maas came home from a Tupperware party whose hostess had perhaps put too much kirsch in the fondue.

twin town *n* (1955) one of a pair of towns, usually in different countries, that have established official links. An earnest of the postwar mood of international amity and cooperation. *Twinned* is first recorded in this context in 1957

> 1957 *Harrogate Advertiser*: Harrogate was the first town in the country to be twinned with a French town—Luchon…

> 1976 *Southern Evening Echo* (Southampton): Wickham entertained 11 French visitors from their proposed twin town of Villers-Sur-Mer at the Kings Head.

two cultures *n* (1956) the arts and the sciences, regarded as being hermetically separated from each other in modern culture, with exponents of each being ignorant of the other. The concept and the phrase were introduced by the British novelist and scientist C. P. Snow (1905–80) in an article in the *New Statesman*, and the phrase was later used by him in the title of a book, *The Two Cultures and the Scientific Revolution* (1959)

> 1956 C. P. Snow: The separation between the two cultures has been getting deeper under our eyes; there is now precious little communication between them… The traditional culture…is, of course, mainly literary…the scientific culture is expansive, not restrictive.

> 1961 *Listener*: The lack of communication between scientists and non-scientists, which has been so much discussed recently in terms of 'the two cultures'.

U *adj* (1954) An abbreviation of *upper class*, used particularly in the context of vocabulary and other aspects of linguistic usage. Contrasted specifically with *non-U* (1954), denoting that which is not (and by implication is not up to the standard of, less admirable or pleasing than) upper class. The two terms were introduced by Professor Alan Ross in a paper entitled 'U and non-U' in the journal *Neuphilologische Mitteilungen*, but it was not until 1956, when Nancy Mitford publicized them in a book called *Noblesse Oblige*, that they were taken up by non-linguists. For a time assigning synonyms to one camp or another became a popular dinner-party game, and sheep were divided from goats by whether they said *note paper* or *writing paper*

> 1954 A. S. C. Ross (title): U and non-U… In this article I use the terms upper class (abbreviated: U, correct, proper),…to designate usages of the upper class; their antonyms (non-U, incorrect, not proper,…) to designate usages which are not upper class… As a boy I heard *not quite a gent*…used by non-U speakers.

> 1957 Ogden Nash: The Wicked Queen said 'Mirror, mirror on the wall' instead of 'Looking glass, looking glass on the wall'… So the Wicked Queen exposed herself as not only wicked but definitely non-U.

> 1958 *Oxford Magazine*: He…dropped the final 'g's' of his present participles in a manner then 'U'.

> 1962 Alison Lurie: 'I don't think he's really U, though, do you?' 'Oh no. Shabby genteel, maybe.'

UFO *n* (1953) An abbreviation of **unidentified flying object (1950)**, usually treated as an acronym and pronounced /ˈjuːfəʊ/

> 1953 D. E. Keyhoe: The UFO was estimated to be between 12,000 and 20,000 feet above the jets.

> 1956 E. J. Ruppelt: UFO is the official term that I created to replace the words 'flying saucers'.

under-achievement *n* (1951) consistent failure to reach a level predicted by intelligence tests or other measures of ability. Like most technical terms related to low intelligence, this, and in particular the derived *under-achiever* (1953), has been exploited by euphemizers and drained of meaning by widespread extended use

> 1951 *School Review*: Factors related to over-achievement and under-achievement in school.

> 1953 *Journal of Abnormal Psychology*: If his grades fell a full rank below prediction he was labelled an 'underachiever'.

> 1973 E.-J. Bahr: I identify with the underachievers of this world.

underground *adj, n* (1953) Denoting a subculture which seeks to provide radical alternatives to the socially accepted or established mode, especially as manifested in its literature, music, press, etc. Compare **alternative (1970)**

> 1953 *Observer*: Its detached picture of barren tragic love…in a furtive fantastic 'underground' sector of London.

> 1969 *Oz*: He talked solidly for nearly forty-five minutes—he'd said it all before… to all the underground papers in the States.

underwhelm *v* (1956) to leave unimpressed, to arouse little or no interest in. Colloquial, usually in the form of the participial adjectives *underwhelmed* and *underwhelming*. Originally a facetious play on *overwhelm*, which has established its own niche in the language

> 1956 T. K. Quinn: He wrote…commending the action of one of the giant corporations for a…price reduction at a time when prices were rising. I was underwhelmed, and investigated.

> 1984 *Observer*: He was…fluent in speech and crashingly dull. If there was an opportunity to be underwhelming, he unfailingly seized it.

unflappable *adj* (1958) not subject to nervous excitement or anxiety; imperturbable. Colloquial. A usage apparently popularized by its application to, if not actually coined to describe, Harold Macmillan, British prime minister 1957–63

> 1958 *Observer*: Six months ago even the unflappable Mr. Macmillan had his doubts and sometimes asked in bewilderment what he was doing wrong.

> 1959 *Economist*: The Prime Minister…has no doubt been reflecting on the virtues of the legend of unflappability.

unidentified flying object *n* (1950) A term introduced to lend an air of scientific respectability to what had hitherto been known mainly as **flying saucers (1947)**. Usually abbreviated to **UFO (1953)**

> 1950 *Chambers's Journal*: Project Saucer revealed that it had analysed 375 incidents of 'unidentified flying objects'.

unilateralism *n* (1959) advocacy of nuclear disarmament on the part of one's own country, irrespective of the policy or actions of other nations. The derivative *unilateralist* is first recorded in the same year

> 1959 *Guardian*: He said that unilateralism would take Britain out of N.A.T.O… Defeats among unilateralists were matched by defeats among believers in the 'great deterrent'.

urban renewal *n* (1955) the clearance and redevelopment of slum areas, waste land, ghettos, etc., within a city or town. Originally US

> 1955 *Statutes at Large U.S.A.*: The heading of title I of the Housing Act of 1949…is hereby amended to read Title I—Slum Clearance and Urban Renewal… A fund…known as the 'Urban Renewal Fund', shall be available for advances, loans and capital grants to local agencies for urban renewal projects.

use *v* (1953) to take drugs. Slang, originally US; probably a back-formation from *user*, which is first recorded in the sense 'drug-addict' in 1935

1953 William Burroughs: The reason it is practically impossible to stop using and cure yourself is that the sickness lasts five to eight days. Twelve hours of it would be easy, twenty-four possible, but five to eight days is too long.

vacuum-pack *v* (1951) to pack (something) in an air-tight container from which the air has been withdrawn

1951 *Good Housekeeping Home Encyclopedia*: Coffee that is both freshly ground and freshly roasted (or vacuum-packed).

V-bomber *n* (1955) any of three types of long-range jet bomber (the Avro Vulcan, Handley Page Victor, and Vickers Valiant) which from the mid 1950s formed the main delivery system of Britain's nuclear weapons. They were gradually superseded from the late 1960s by submarine-based missiles. The only time they saw active service was when some rather ageing Vulcans bombed Argentinian positions during the Falklands War

1955 *Britannica Book of the Year*: Concentration on air-power was reflected in terms like *V-bomber* (the initial referring to the types, Victor, Vulcan and Valiant).

Vespa *n* (1950) A proprietary name for an Italian make of motor scooter, first produced by Piaggio in 1946 and much favoured by the young and sufficiently affluent in the 1950s and early 1960s. It means literally 'wasp' in Italian. The make's main rival brand was the *Lambretta* (see the quote at **scooter (1957)**). See also **scooter (1916)**

1965 Daphne du Maurier: The young were everywhere, pouring out of lecture rooms, laughing, talking, getting on to vespas.

video *n* (1958) a video recorder, recording, or player

1958 *Observer*: The Video is like a combined tape-recorder and cinema camera. It records your television appearance complete with sound track and can be played back at the touch of a switch.

1968 *Observer*: The days of the disc, in the pop world at least, are numbered. For soon will come the video. We will have the top 20 videos which you plug into your home video-machine.

1981 *Church Times*: They…went down to BBC television… Later he popped round to the school and showed them a video of themselves.

1984 Sue Townsend: We are the only family in our street who haven't got a video.

videophone *n* (1955) a telephone incorporating a television screen on which the person at the other end of the line can be seen speaking. The earliest examples of the word are science-fiction crystal-ball-gazing, but by the last quarter of the century the videophone had become reality. See also **Picturephone (1964)**

1955 C. L. Moore: He…called Maltzer's apartment by videophone.

1976 *TV Guide* (US): To reach other videophone outlets, the user merely dials the telephone.

videotape *n* (1953) magnetic tape on which moving visual images, such as television programmes, can be recorded

1953 *Wall Street Journal*: With further development of video tape techniques, numerous possibilities will open up. Small portable television cameras are already in wide use in industry, in stores, banks and schools.

1958 *Times*: The BBC's VERA which tape-records complete television shows, picture and sound combined, and the AMPEX and R.C.A. videotape machines which do the same job for the independent television contractors, will greatly facilitate the provision of such Press shows.

Viet Cong *n* (1957) the Communist guerilla force active in Vietnam between 1954 and 1976. The name in Vietnamese means literally 'Vietnamese Communist'

1957 *Annual Register 1956*: Though small groups of dissidents remained in the jungles they ceased to be a danger, and the Communist dissidents known as the Viet Cong were equally ineffective.

-ville *suffix* (1956) Used to designate a particular quality suggested by the word to which it is added. Since the late 19th century the place-name suffix -*ville* had been used colloquially in the US in phrases of the type *an x from Xville* (e.g. *a slugger from Sluggersville* and *a bonehead from Boneheadville*), but it was hepcats of the 1950s who propelled it front of stage in formations describing degrees of (or usually lack of) hipness. These eventually often turned virtually into adjectives. The English *city* was sometimes substituted for the slightly French *-ville* ('All my life I'm taught by my family *to keep it going*, don't get boring at the dinner table. When I learned I could do that by just being honest, whole vistas of trouble opened up. I get on a talk show, I get talking and *whoa*! Trouble city!', *Rolling Stone* (1979)). See also **dullsville (1960)**

> 1956 Ed McBain: This guy is from Squaresville, fellas, I'm telling you. He wouldn't know a ·45 from a cement mixer.

> 1961 *Woman*: No need to feel cubesville (that's worse than being a square) if you don't follow Kookie patter; even many Americans reckon it odd!

> 1967 J. Aitkin: University? Man, that's just dragsville.

vital statistics *n* (1952) the measurements of a woman's bust, waist, and hips. A colloquial appropriation of the earlier, serious sense, 'statistics relating to birth, marriage, death, etc.'

> 1957 *Times*: Those feminine measurements which have become known, in the entertainment world, as vital statistics.

VTOL *abbr* (1955) vertical take-off and landing: a term applied to aircaft whose take-off is effected by jet thrust or conventional propellers rather than (as with helicopters) a rotor. Much experimentation was done in this field in the 1950s (see **flying bedstead (1955)**), but the British Harrier jet was the only successful outcome in terms of operational military aircraft (see **jump jet (1964)**). The abbreviation is usually pronounced as a semi-acronym, /veetol/

> 1955 *Wall Street Journal*: Bell Aircraft Corp. announced it has built and flown the first jet-propelled vertical rising airplane which takes off and lands without needing a runway. The test VTOL (vertical take-off and landing) airplane weighs about 2,000 pounds, is 21 feet long, has a wing span of 26 feet, and carries only the pilot.

> 1979 N. Slater: The basic [aircraft] design owed much to the VTOL Harrier.

wall-to-wall *adj* (1953) Of carpeting: covering the whole floor of a room; fitted. The metaphorical and usually disparaging sense 'omnipresent, constant' is first recorded in 1967

> 1953 Arthur Upfield: I detest wall-to-wall carpets.

> 1973 *Listener*: A respite from wall-to-wall Mozart on Radios 3 and 4.

> 1984 *New Statesman*: Their sponsors include the IBA…and the BBC (in whose Reithian corridors the epithet 'wall-to-wall *Dallas*' was reputedly coined).

Walter Mitty *n* (1950) a person who indulges in day-dreams; someone who imagines a more adventurous or enjoyable life for himself than he actually leads. From the name of the hero of James Thurber's short story *The Secret Life of Walter Mitty*, which appeared in the *New Yorker* in 1939. Often used adjectivally

> 1950 Budd Schulberg: I've had daydreams of how I'd come back. Walter Mitty stuff about arriving in style.

> 1960 *Sunday Express*: Women…live in a dream world of their own imagining—a Walter Mitty-ish 'Other Life'.

warfarin *n* (1950) a chemical compound used as a rat poison and medicinally as an anticoagulant, to treat thrombosis. The name was originally registered as a trademark by the Wisconsin Alumni Research Foundation, where the compound was developed, and it was coined by adding the initials of their name to *coumarin*, the name of a similar substance

> 1968 *Times*: Rats which are immune to warfarin, the most widely used rat poison in the world, are spreading.

Warsaw Pact *n* (1955) a military alliance of the Soviet Union with Bulgaria, Czechoslovakia, East Germany, Hungary, Poland, Romania, and Albania, formed by the Treaty of Warsaw, signed on 14 May 1955. Principally established as a Communist counterpart to N.A.T.O. It was dissolved in 1991, when the Soviet empire collapsed

> 1955 *New York Times*: It would be a mistake to discount the Warsaw pact.

way out *adj* (1959) unconventional, extreme, progressive. Slang; soon after came **way in (1960)**

> 1959 *Encounter*: The ego-ideal of the Beatnik is the 'cool hipster'—…the man who is 'way out'.

> 1964 J. Dunbar: One thing I like about Cambridge, people don't try to be too way out. At places like Oxford, or Reading, I've seen blokes going around barefoot and wearing ear-rings.

weirdo *n* (1955) a strange or eccentric person. Slang. At first mainly applied to people of unconventional appearance, which in the 1960s and 70s generally meant a hippyish untidiness and long-hairedness. (In this usage it was shadowed by *weirdie*, first recorded in this context in 1949.) Latterly it has tended to be used about people suspected of having strange sexual preferences

> 1958 *Observer*: He is worried by Press reports which represent him as 'a weirdo—there is another word for it'.

> 1972 James McClure: A shock-haired, bearded weirdo in a tartan dressing-gown and wellington boots.

> 1984 *Melody Maker*: This record is for the real weirdos.

wham-bam, wham-bang *interj* (1956) Used with reference to sexual intercourse conducted quickly and without tenderness, especially in the phrase *wham, bam, thank you ma'am*. Slang, originally US

> 1956 Billie Holiday: With my regular white customers, it was a cinch. They had wives and kids to go home to. When they came to see me it was wham, bang, they gave me the money and were gone.

> 1971 S. Firestone: Men are interested in nothing but a screw (wham, bam, thank you M'am!).

whirlybird *n* (1951) a helicopter. Slang, originally US. Helicopters saw action for the first time in the Korean War, and their pilots and others lost no time in dreaming up colloquial names for them; see also **chopper (1951)**

> 1951 *Air Facts*: The biggest untold story out of Korea is of a few score unarmed American helicopters and a handful of pilots who have flown themselves and their 'whirlybirds' into military history.

white-wall tyre *n* (1953) a tyre with white side surfaces, considered to be characteristic of large flashy American automobiles of the post-World War II period. Originally US. The fuller form *white-sidewall tyre* is first recorded in 1949

> 1953 L. Z. Hobson: A Buick Roadmaster... Fully equipped, radio, heater, white wall tyres.

widgie, weegie *n* (1950) an Australasian Teddy girl, the female counterpart of a **bodgie (1950)**. Australian and New Zealand; origin unknown

> 1950 *Sun* (Australia): There'll be...prizes for the most colorfully dressed 'bodgy' and 'weegie'.

> 1956 Stanton Hope: A popular district with bodgies and widgies is 'the Cross'.

wife-swapping *n* (1959) the interchange of marital partners for sexual purposes within a social group. Necessary to prove your credentials as a swinger in the 1960s and 70s

> 1959 Marshall Pugh: He began to discuss the wife-swapping parties held locally... 'But how do they get away with it here?... The town's so small. I would have thought that after six months...they'd have to convene a mass divorce trial.'

Windsor knot *n* (1953) a large loose knot in a tie, as favoured by the Duke of Windsor (formerly Edward VIII) (1894–1972) and consequently fashionable for a while

> 1953 *Man about Town*: How to tie the 'Windsor' knot.

wine snob *n* (1951) a social menace (defined in the first quote below) particularly active in the 'little-knowledge' period between the postwar re-awakening of interest in wine in Britain and its supermarket-led demystification towards the end of the century

> 1951 Raymond Postgate: A Wine Snob is a man...who uses a knowledge of wine, often imperfect, to impress others with a sense of his superiority.

> 1966 H. W. Yoxall: There's been much talk recently about wine snobbery, most of it rather stupid.

with it *adj* (1959) up-to-date, trendy. Slang; a quickly worked-out seam among its original youthful users, but, as often happens with such items, the older generation then took it up and succeeded only in sounding past it

> 1959 Richard Condon: They are with it, Raymond. Believe me, they are even away ahead of me.

> 1960 *Guardian*: The new *Time and Tide*, to borrow the language of the teen-ager, is 'with it'.

> 1962 *Listener*: Curtain designs for the really with-it 'contemporary home'.

> 1977 J. I. M. Stewart: The silly woman just thought it a with-it thing to say to a celebrated dramatist.

wok *n* (1952) a bowl-shaped frying pan used in Chinese cookery. A borrowing from Cantonese which in early use was often transcribed as *wock*. Not until the 1970s, when the utensil began to appear widely in Western domestic kitchens, did the spelling *wok* establish itself

> 1952 D. Y. H. Feng: A well-stocked Chinese kitchen usually has…several convex-bottomed circular pans hammered out of thin iron or copper called *wock*.

> 1977 *Sunday Times* (Colour Supplement): Wok cooking is about to sweep the Western world.

> 1983 *Listener*: By 1972 I needed a small pantechnicon to convey all my books on macrobiotic cookery, my plants, wall-hangings and floor cushions, my astrological tables, women's-lib posters and my wok.

wolf-whistle *n* (1952) a distinctive whistle expressing sexual admiration

> 1952 *Time*: No one took exception to U.S.N. wolf-whistles at the señoritas.

> 1953 Nigel Balchin: Some vulgar female person let out a low wolf-whistle as she passed him.

wonk *n* (1954) someone obsessed with an activity, and especially its minutiae; a nerd or anorak. Originally US, but popularized more widely in the 1980s in the field of politics and administration, in the phrase *policy wonk* 'someone with an obsessive interest in minor details of policy'. Its ultimate origins are unknown

> 1970 Erich Segal: Who could Jenny be talking to that was worth appropriating moments set aside for a date with me? Some musical wonk?

> 1993 *Washingtonian*: The president's furrow-browed band of policy wonks.

worktop *n* (1953) a flat surface suitable for working on, especially in a kitchen. A product of the space-saving kitchens of the second half of the century, where areas for food preparation must be conjured out of the tops of cupboards. *Working top* is an occasional alternative

> 1953 *Architectural Review*: Though not as highly resistant to abrasion as Formica it is considerably cheaper, and suitable for anything but worktops where there is much cutting and sliding.

World War III *n* (1959) An alternative name for the **Third World War (1947)**
> 1968 Kenneth Bird: Rattling their rifles as if they were fighting World War Three.

X (1950) Used to denote films classified as suitable for adults only, or to which only those older than a certain age are to be admitted. In Britain replaced by *15* and *18* in 1983

> 1950 *Report of the Departmental Committee on Children & the Cinema*: We recommend that a new category of films be established (which might be called 'X') from which children under 16 should be entirely excluded.

> 1950 *Times*: The X certificates…will cover films other than those of a 'horrific' character, which are 'wholly adult in conception and treatment'.

Xerox *n* (1952) A proprietary name (registered in 1952) for a make of photocopiers, based on **xerography (1948)**. It did not begin to make headway in the general language until the 1960s, when it became virtually a generic term, used both for 'a photocopy' and as a verb, meaning 'to photocopy'. See also **reprography (1961)**

> 1966 *Economist*: In most American offices executives instruct subordinates to 'make me a Xerox of this report' rather than 'make me a copy of it'.

> 1972 Marcia Williams: The Rank Organization in Brighton installed a xerox copying machine in the office [at 10 Downing Street] and we also had an electric duplicating machine.

Y-fronts *n* (1953) men's close-fitting briefs with Y-shaped seaming at the front. British; from *Y-front*, a proprietary name for men's underwear registered in 1953
> 1978 M. Page: He stripped to his Y-fronts and plunged into the pool.

zebra crossing *n* (1950) a pedestrian crossing marked by broad black and white stripes on the road and Belisha beacons on the kerb. The zebra was the first of a mini-menagerie of black-and-white creatures enlisted to lend their names to various road-crossing configurations (see also **panda crossing (1962)** and **pelican crossing (1966)**)

| 1950 *Surveyor*: The initial values of the percentage of drivers giving way are higher on the 'zebra' crossings than on the plain.

Zimmer *n* (1951) A proprietary name (registered in Britain in 1951) for a range of orthopædic appliances. It became best known in *Zimmer frame*, the name of a lightweight metal frame used as a support when walking, which in the last two decades of the century became a frequent metaphor for the infirmity of the elderly

| 1982 E. Dewhurst: Incapable of walking without a Zimmer frame.

The 1960s

If ever a decade confidently announced that it had broken with the past and was setting off down heady new paths it was the 1960s. The children of the 1940s baby boom were making their presence felt, armed with ample spending power; the exploration of space was providing a spectacular swan-song to the era of confidence in scientific progress (and doing it on small screens in the world's living rooms); the computer was beginning to send its invisible threads through all our lives. There were not just new inventions and new discoveries to talk about—in plenty. We sought new ways of looking at the world, and new modes of vocabulary to describe our experience of it.

The 1960s were the decade when the blend and the acronym entrenched themselves still further in the language, and prefixes and suffixes raised their profiles. Acronyms—words formed from the initial letters of other words—were essentially the children of World War II (see p. 254), but it was in the 1960s that they really established themselves in a big way outside the military field. Terms like *Cobol, laser, SALT*, and *zip code, Lem, AWACS*, and *GIGO* slipped into the language, some so unobtrusively that their acronymic origins went largely unnoticed. Blending—the formation of compounds by partially merging two words—gained further ground, with the likes of *advertorial, docudrama, faction, identikit, medevac*, and *stagflation* entering the language; it was even responsible for the name of a new country: *Tanzania* (formed from *Tanganyika* and *Zanzibar*). The trend towards creating verbs out of nouns continued, with *access, action, format, keyboard*, and *nuke* joining the lexicon.

The encroachment of prefixes on to the territory of adjectives has been a feature of 20th-century English, and in no decade has it been more salient than the 1960s. *Mini-* led the way (see *mini-* (1934)), and its enthusiastic reception in the fashion industry (*minidress, miniskirt*) opened the door to length variations in *midi-* and *maxi-*. *Eco-* and *Euro-* began highly successful careers in the 1960s, as, on a less exalted level, did *renta-*. This was also the key decade for the suffix *-in* (as in *love-in, laugh-in*, and *teach-in*, as well as *sit-in*—its origins were in the 1950s).

Our closer acquaintance with the wider universe was reflected in our vocabulary—not only as observed from the surface of the planet (*black hole, pulsar, quasar, singularity*), but experienced at first hand. From the moment Yuri Gagarin's rocket blasted off in April 1961, space travel stepped from the wilder shores of science fiction to everyday reality, and the subsequent years of the decade familiarized us with such concepts as *re-entry, splash-down, launch windows*, and *moon walks*. We learnt to handle the jargon for all the hardware:

lander, module, moon buggy (1971), *shuttle*. When astronauts reassured mission control that the situation was *nominal*, we nodded sagely.

But undoubtedly the area of technology that made the greatest lexical advances in the 1960s was computer science. As yet it was largely confined to specialists, but as *computeracy* spread and one by one various aspects of our lives became *computerized*, we would learn the significance of *bytes, chips, cursors, databases, mice, peripherals*, and *software*. We could *format* and *access* to our heart's content, fluent in *ASCII, BASIC*, and *Cobol*. We had the key to the computer's limitations—*GIGO* ('garbage in, garbage out'). And for our leisure moments there were *computer games*—and *computer dating*.

Out on the street in the 1960s, in the clubs and campuses, it was youth that was setting the agenda, and it is their vocabulary that in many ways carries the most telling resonances of the decade—60s' *vibes*. Their terms of commendation (*in, with it* (1959), *switched on, gear, fab* (1957), *knock-out, together*) and condemnation (*grotty, naff*) expressed the crucial judgments of the day. Their clans (*mods, rockers*) made the headlines, often with threats of *aggro* or *bovver*. But above all, it was the music. Picking up the impetus of 1950s rock 'n' roll, the pop music scene exploded in the 1960s, and its sheer diversity contributed sackfuls of new vocabulary to the language. Each new music style or dance had a name more out-landish than the last (*the twist, bossa nova, frug, hully gully, Watusi, ska, acid rock*). In Britain, the *Merseybeat* reversed many years of American domination of the *charts*, and the *Beatlemania* that sent *popsters, groupies*, and *teeny-boppers* into a frenzy soon spread to the US. For those with ears not attuned to all this, the 1960s was also the decade in which the concept of *easy listening* first adorned our musical life.

In acknowledgment of the new commercial realities, the world of fashion shifted its beady eyes from haute couture to the lucrative youth market. Teenagers set the trends, and the hemlines—*minis, midis, maxis, kinky boots* and *Chelsea boots, flares* and *hipsters, thongs* and *caftans*. *Tights* (or *pantyhose*) saw off stockings and suspenders. As male hair lengthened, the *unisex* look came in.

As part of the same package came recreational drugs—comparatively innocent-sounding in retrospect, shocking though they were to authority's sensibilities at the time: *poppers* and *tabs, speed* and *acid, purple hearts* and *angel dust*. They opened the door in the latter part of the decade to the *alternative* (1970) world of the *flower children*, the *alternative society, psychedelia, be-ins* and *love-ins, Hare Krishna*, and the *Age of Aquarius*.

But hippies were not the only ones taking drugs in the 1960s. In an age of growing emphasis on the individual and their psyche, *uppers* and *downers* and *tranks* found a wide market, and there was no lack of customers for *Librium* and *Valium, Mandrax* and *diazepam*. A self-absorbed concern with health found lexical expression in items as diverse as *cellulite* and *holistic medicine, biorhythms* and *shiatsu*.

The 1960s were also the decade of the *permissive society*, when traditional four-letter words first appeared in respectable dictionaries. But in spite of the *swingers* hoping to *score* with *bunny girls* in *topless* bars, you still had a hard time if you deviated from the norm: *homophobia* was rife, and *kinks* kept a low *profile*.

The communications revolution was getting well under way, with *comsats, bleepers, pagers*, and, ominously, *news management* and *image makers*. We could watch (or listen to on our *trannies*) *chat-shows, sitcoms, docudramas, phone-ins*, and *radiothons*. And, if we wanted to be independent of the network offerings, we had *cassettes* and *videos*. A less welcome sign of things to come was the first appearance of the *paparazzi*.

Other straws in the wind for future decades were civil rights legislation and moves towards racial desegregation in the US (where *bussing* provided a long-running controversy) and the beginnings of environmentalism (photos of the Earth taken from the Moon were a forceful argument for the *global village*: *biodegradable* and *unleaded* entered our vocabulary, species became *endangered* or *threatened*, and *eco-* was a strong contender for prefix of the decade) and of political correctness (the terms *sexism, ageism,* and *tokensim* were all coined in the 1960s).

In a world still frozen deeply in the Cold War, *doves* talked of *non-proliferation* and *SALT* while the minds of the *hawks* were more on *flexible response* and *surgical* strikes. Despite the *peaceniks,* it was the hawks who largely got their way over the Vietnam war—providing the US with a long-lasting scar on its national psyche, and ensuring that the English language now embraces such unlovely or ominous terms as *body count, dink, frag* (1970), and *Agent Orange* (1970).

abuse *n, v* (1969) Applied to sexual or physical assault on a regular basis. Originally US; a euphemism which in the last quarter of the century has largely replaced **interfere with (1948)** and **molest (1950)**

> 1969 *New York Times*: The committee…made the charge in connection with the publication of 'A Series of Recommendations for the Protection of Abused Children Within New York City'.

> 1972 *Newsweek*: Other themes scheduled for prime-time dramatic treatment include impotency, castration,…and child abuse.

access *v* (1962) to gain access to (data, etc., held in a computer or computer-based system, or the system itself). A conversion of noun into verb which began as a piece of computer jargon but in the 1970s spread into the general language

> 1962 A. M. Angel: Through a system of binary-coded addresses notched into each card, a particular card may be accessed for read and write operations.

> 1978 *Verbatim*: The University of California at Berkeley…announces the hours during which its business office 'may be accessed'.

acid *n* (1966) the hallucinogenic drug LSD (lysergic acid diethylamide), the favourite pschedelia-inducer of the 1960s. Slang, originally US; an extract of the drug's full scientific name. Devotees were widely known as *acidheads* (also first recorded in 1966)

> 1968 Adam Diment: Acid heads are such nice people they want to be friends with the whole world.

> 1970 John Lennon: I was influenced by acid and got psychedelic, like the whole generation, but really, I like rock and roll and I express myself best in rock.

acid rock *n* (1966) a type of electronically amplified rock music with a pronounced beat. The allusion is to its supposed inspiration by LSD-induced states of consciousness ('Acid rock is considered to be the musical equivalent of an LSD-induced state', E. E. Landy (1977))

> 1966 *Life*: True 'acid rock' goes deeper psychedelically than just lyrics.

action *v* (1962) to take action on (a request, etc.), to process; to put into effect. Used especially in business jargon

> 1962 Len Deighton: The E.M.P…promised to action it for me if I let his A.D.C. have details in writing.

adult *adj* (1968) Of accommodation: designed for the use of elderly people. Also used more generally to mean 'of or relating to the elderly'. A North American euphemism which has never caught on elsewhere, perhaps because of the existence of the other euphemistic usage, 'pornographic'

> 1968 *Globe & Mail* (Toronto): Forest Hill, 1 bedroom, small adult building.

> 1984 *Tampa* (Florida) *Tribune*: According to our recently released study of adult home buying habits in Hillsborough County, The Tampa Tribune has strong readership among all types of home buyers.

advertorial *n* (1961) an advertisement written in the form of an editorial, which purportedly provides objective information about a commercial or industrial subject. Compare **infomercial (1981)**

> 1968 *Heidelburg News*: There has been talk lately about 'advertorials', wrapping up an advertisement to look like an editorial.

aerobics *n* (1968) (a method of) physical exercise for producing beneficial changes in the respiratory and circulatory systems by activities which require only a modest increase in oxygen intake and so can be maintained. Both the method and the term originated in the US, and caught on in Britain in the early 1980s

> 1968 *Chicago Tribune*: Under the aerobics program, a person is awarded a number of points according to the amount of exercise he does each week.

> 1982 *Observer*: Aerobics have become the latest fitness craze.

African-American *adj, n* (1969) Designating American citizens of African descent; (a) black American. Although an isolated instance of the term is on record from as long ago as 1863, it did not begin to establish itself in a big way until the 1970s. By the second half of the 80s it had become the preferred term for US blacks

> 1969 *New York Times*: Albert Vann, president of the African-American Teachers Association…said that the editorial had evoked little response.

> 1987 *Washington Post*: What made him the target of four years of government infiltration, investigation, persecution and eventual prosecution was his championing the cause of racial independence for African-Americans.

> 1991 *New York Times Magazine*: Justice Marshall has long avoided using the term *black*, preferring *Negro* or, more recently, *Afro-American*. Jesse Jackson has been pressing the appellation *African-American*.

Afro *adj, n* (1966) Denoting a hairstyle in which the hair is shaped into a wide frizzy bush, popular especially among blacks. Originally US. A reassertion of black identity in the face of decades, even centuries, of Europeanized hairstyles

> 1966 Thomas Pynchon: The same goes for boys who like to wear…Afro haircuts.

> 1971 Bernard Malamud: A black man with a thick full beard, wearing a spiky Afro like a dangerous plant on his head.

ageism, agism *n* (1969) prejudice or discrimination against people on the grounds of age, especially old age. Originally US; one of the earliest of the spate of late-20th-century '-isms' inspired by **racism (1936)** and *sexism* (1968). The derivative *ageist* is first recorded in 1970

> 1969 *Washington Post*: Dr. Robert Butler…believes many of his Chevy Chase neighbors suffer from 'age-ism'.

> 1970 *Daily Telegraph*: The jack-booted agists of West Sussex must be stopped before they subject the elderly to the whole terror-apparatus of the Police State.

> 1974 *Newsweek*: She called him 'a sexist, age-ist pig'.

agenda *n* (1961) the things which a person, organization, etc. has it in mind to do; a notional list of intentions. In the last two decades of the century, often in the expression **hidden agenda (1968)**, denoting a concealed motivation

> 1963 *Times Review of Industry*: Union agendas are increasingly devoted to industrial and economic issues.

> 1986 *Cambridge* (Massachusetts) *Chronicle*: There's family politics, sure, but our jobs are not being threatened… So when we get into disagreements there's no hidden agenda.

Age of Aquarius *n* (1967) an astrological age characterized by world freedom and brotherhood, which is said to have begun during the 1960s. Thanks largely to the success of the song in which it figured (see the quote below), it came to symbolize the freedom and permissiveness of the late 60s. See also **New Age (1971)**

> 1967 Ragni & Rado (song): This is the dawning of the age of Aquarius.

aggro, agro *n* (1969) aggravation, aggression; deliberate trouble-making or harassment (especially formerly by skinhead gangs), violence, trouble; annoyance, inconvenience. British slang. An abbreviation of *aggravation* or *aggression* + *-o*

> 1972 Daniel & McGuire: This didn't stop the gang from searching out provocative situations, looking for 'aggro'.

-aholic, -oholic, -holic *suffix* (1965) someone who is addicted to, obsessed by, or inordinately fond of (something). Taken from *alcoholic* 'someone who suffers from alcoholism'. The first widely used formation was **workaholic (1968)**, and this was the inspiration for a wide range of other (usually one-off, facetious) forms. See also **chocoholic (1976)**

> 1965 P. Wyden: I was a sugarholic…Mom kept saying, 'You eat your spinach and I'll give you a piece of candy.'

> 1971 *Southern Living*: Donald Goldstein…probably knows more manufacturers personally than Porter and other club manufacturers. Goldstein, you see, is a 'golfaholic'.

alternative society *n* (1969) the aggregate of (predominantly young) people whose social organ-ization (or lack of it) and cultural values purport to represent a preferable and cogent alternative to those of the established social order. See also **alternative (1970)** and **counter-culture (1970)**

> 1969 *It*: Brother Simon Tugwell is planning a 3-day talk-in on the alternative society.

anabolic steroid *n* (1961) a synthetic hormone used to increase muscle and bone growth. Its il-legitimate use as a performance-enhancer by sportsmen and sportswomen remained contro-versial to the end of the century

> 1974 M. C. Gerald: Anabolic steroids…have been used by football players, weight lifters, and athletes.

anchor *v* (1961) to present (a radio or television news programme). Also used as a noun, 'a compère of a radio or television programme, especially the host presenter of a news programme'. In both cases a back-formation from *anchorman*, which is first recorded in 1958

> 1961 *Sunday Times*: They employed Mr. John Freeman to anchor an hour of absorbing re-capitulation.

> 1965 *Guardian*: 'Panorama' will continue… Richard Dimbleby remains the anchor.

angel dust *n* (1969) the drug phencyclidine, used as a hallucinogen. Slang, originally US. See also **angel dust (1990)**

> 1969 *Rolling Stone*: Parsley can give a more powerful high on marijuana. The garden herb, says Olas Hendrickson, is the basic ingredient in a new psychedelic substance called 'Angels' Dust'.

> 1985 *Sunday Times*: PCP or 'angel dust', a strong anaesthetic which came after LSD in 1960s drug fashions…has recently emerged anew. Now they call it 'rocket fuel' in Chicago and mix it with peanut butter.

answering machine *n* (1961) a machine which answers incoming telephone calls by repeating a pre-recorded message to the caller (and by recording a message left by the caller for subsequent audio playback). The alternative **answerphone (1963)** is now the generally preferred term, but *answering machine* continues in use

> 1961 *Daily Mail*: The quarterly rent for a coin box is to go up from 11s 3d to £1, but for an answering machine it will go down from £10 to £8.

answerphone *n* (1963) a telephone answering machine. Originally a US proprietary name, spelt *Ansafone*; the generic spelling *answerphone* is not recorded before 1976

> 1984 *Daily Telegraph*: Clients on the third line will hear an answerphone message asking them to try again five minutes later.

A-OK, A-okay *adv, adj* (1961) in perfect order or condition. Originally US; an abbreviation of *all (systems) OK*. Reputedly originated and used by astronauts and their mission-controllers, but see the second quote below

> 1963 K. Peters: Always make a short test run before starting a dubbing session. This ensures that all systems are functioning A-O.K.

> 1970 Neil Armstrong: 'A-OK', an expression coined by a public affairs announcer, and one which the astronauts…never did use.

art deco *adj, n* (1966) The name applied subsequently to a style of interior design (furniture, tex-tiles, ceramics, etc.) popular in the 1920s and 30s, characterized by geometrical shapes and harsh colours. It comes from an abbreviation of French *art décoratif*, literally 'decorative art' (from the name of the exhibition *L'Exposition Internationale des Arts Décoratifs et Industriels Modernes* held in Paris in 1925)

> 1966 *Times*: Earlier this year the Musée des Arts Decoratifs in Paris staged a fascinating exhibi-tion…which highlighted the style now known by connoisseurs as Art Deco.

ASCII *n* (1963) An acronym formed from the initial letters of *American Standard Code for Information Interchange*, a standard seven-bit character code by which information is stored and transmitted in a computer or a data transmission system

> 1967 D. H. Hamsher: Through the use of the shift and control keys in conjunction with the other keys, all 128 code combinations of ASCII can be generated.

atrium *n* (1967) a usually skylit central court in a public building rising through several storeys and surrounded by galleries at each level with rooms (shops, offices, etc.) opening off them. A favourite of late-20th-century architects with a hankering for impressive spaces. Originally US. A development of the earlier application, ' a central hall or glassed-in court in a house that may be used as a sitting-room'

> 1967 *Interiors*: The unsuspecting visitor enters the…hotel…through a dark-brown tunnel-like entrance. He then walks smack into…a 24-story atrium full of breathtaking fantasy.

attitude *n* (1962) aggressive or uncooperative behaviour; a resentful or antagonistic manner. Slang, originally US. In the 1970s the usage started to take on a positive aspect, with implications of an independent or self-possessed outlook, and even of style or swagger. By the time it reached Britain in the 1990s it was even being applied to things, in the sense 'strong stylishness'

> 1985 *Sunday Times*: I can't believe this restaurant. I ask the waiter for a clean fork and all I get is attitude.

> 1994 *Toronto Star*: In the early '70s, crepes were the foodstuff that ushered in the eating revolution—the pancake with attitude that took us from meat and potatoes into the modern world of gastrohype.

au pair, au pair girl *n* (1960) a foreign girl who does housework in exchange for board and lodging. From French *au pair* 'on an equal footing'. The term has been in use in English since the late 19th century to denote the arrangement under which au pairs work. It is first recorded as a noun, applied to the girl herself, in 1960, although the usage was certainly quite common by the late 1950s

> 1960 *Oxford Times*: Au pair to help with young children.

auteur *n* (1962) a film director whose personal influence over films is so great that he or she may be regarded as their author. From French, literally 'author'; the term was introduced in the 1950s by critics (including François Truffaut and Jean-Luc Godard) writing in the influential journal *Cahiers du cinéma*

> 1998 *Guardian*: What if, in truth, the Great Hollywood Auteur never really existed in the first place?

AWACS *n* (1966) an airborne long-range radar system for detecting other aircraft, including low-flying ones, and controlling weapons directed against them. Originally US. An acronym from the initial letters of *Airborne Warning and Control Systems*

> 1977 *RAF News*: A British contribution to a Nato AWACS force…will be very costly.

awesome *adj* (1961) staggering, remarkable. Originally and mainly US. A weakening of the earlier sense, 'awe-inspiring'. In due course it weakened still further, to 'marvellous' (see **awesome (1980)**)

> 1975 *Economist*: A garrulous old African with an awesome memory.

> 1986 *New Yorker*: To begin with, there is her awesome record… Over the last thirteen years, she has won at least one major title each year—a feat no other tennis player…has accomplished.

bag *n* (1964) a person's particular area of interest or expertise. Slang, originally US Black English. From the slightly earlier jazz slang sense, 'a category' (from the notion of a bag being something you put things in). Still in use in the 1980s, although by then it sounded decidedly dated

> 1970 *Harper's*: Black Studies is not my bag.

ball game *n* (1968) a state of affairs. Used in such expressions as *a different* (*whole new*, etc.) *ball game*, denoting one in which new factors come into play. Colloquial, originally US; the ultimate reference is to a baseball game, but intermediately the term had been used in US slang for 'a challenging or competitive situation' since at least the 1930s

> 1968 *Globe & Mail* (Toronto): 'Then it will look like a different ball game,' he said. 'We might see these recent attacks as a kind of last gasp.'

> 1971 *New Yorker*: If an invasion took place the Chinese might enter the war. If this were to happen, some official…would no doubt announce that we were in a 'whole new ballgame'.

ballpark *n* (1960) a broad area of approximation, similarity, etc.; a range within which comparison is possible. Originally US. A *ballpark* is literally 'a baseball stadium', and the metaphor was originally applied specifically to the area within which a spacecraft is expected to return to earth. The phrase *in the* (*right*) *ballpark*, meaning 'plausibly accurate, within reasonable bounds', is first recorded in 1968

> 1960 *San Francisco Examiner*: The Discoverer XIV capsule…came down 200 miles from the center of its predicted impact area, but still within the designated 'ballpark' area.

> 1967 *Wall Street Journal*: I gave them a guess of somewhere around £1.5 billion… I thought it was a ball-park figure.

> 1968 *San Francisco Examiner*: The figures I have indicate this pay-out is 'in the ball park'.

ban the bomb (1960) The slogan of those advocating nuclear disarmament, used (with hyphens) as an adjective. See **bomb (1945)**; see also **CND (1958)**

> 1960 *News Chronicle*: The ban-the-bomb campaigners are well advanced with their arrangements to make a new challenge.

Barbie doll *n* (1966) a type of slim, large-breasted teenage fashion doll. The name *Barbie* (a diminutive of *Barbara*) was registered in the US as the proprietary term for such a doll in 1959. It has since become widely used allusively to refer to a pretty but passive or characterless woman

> 1966 J. D. MacDonald: She was all erotic innocence… She made me think of a Barbie Doll.

> 1984 A. F. Loewenstein: He thinks I'm cute, she thought, a cute little professional doll with a brief-case. A Barbie doll.

bar code *n* (1963) a machine-readable code consisting of a series of alternating lines and spaces of varying width, used especially for stock control. It did not begin to come into general commercial use until the early 1970s

> 1963 W. J. Bijleveld: Addressograph-Multigraph suggests the use of digits with an external bar code… The digits with their bar-code to match are shown in fig. 67.

> 1970 O. Dopping: Certain cash registers can record a machine-readable bar code on the internal control tape with ink.

BASIC *n* (1964) Acronym of *Beginners' All-purpose Symbolic Instruction Code*, a high-level computer programming language originally developed as a general-purpose language similar to English and easy to learn, and now widely used with personal computers. Invented by J. G. Kemeny and T. E. Kurtz.

> 1964 *BASIC Instruction Manual*: An instruction in BASIC consists of three parts, an instruction number, an operation, and an operand.

battered *adj* (1962) systematically assaulted and injured by a parent, guardian, or partner. The original usage (usually in the phrase *battered baby*) referred to young children; the application to adults (usually in *battered wife* and *battered woman*) developed in the 1970s

> 1963 *British Medical Journal*: Multiple epiphysial injuries in babies ('battered baby' syndrome)… The x-ray changes in the 'battered baby' are…like those often described in infantile scurvy.

> 1973 *Nursing Times*: Erin Pizzey is always hot under the collar about the lack of help a battered wife can get.

Beatlemania *n* (1963) addiction to the British pop group 'the Beatles' and their characteristics; the frenzied behaviour of their admirers. The pattern was later followed to encapsulate the adulation of other pop groups (e.g. *Rollermania*, caused by the Bay City Rollers in the mid 1970s)

> 1963 *Times*: The social phenomenon of Beatlemania, which finds expression in handbags, balloons and other articles bearing the likeness of the loved ones, or in the hysterical screaming of young girls whenever the Beatle Quartet performs in public.

> 1964 *Daily Telegraph*: Outside, hundreds of squealing Beatlemaniacs carried such signs as 'We love you—never leave us'.

beautiful people *n* (1964) wealthy, fashionable people; the 'smart set'. Originally US. Later in the decade the term was also applied to hippies

> 1964 *Vogue*: What the beautiful people are doing to keep fit.

> 1966 Mrs. L. B. Johnson: 'The Beautiful People' are all heading for Acapulco and in the list of the beautiful people was Lynda Bird's name.

beehive *n* (1960) a high beehive-shaped hair-style, of a sort fashionable at the end of the 1950s and still widely worn when démodé in the 1960s. The term had previously been applied to a hat (see **beehive (1909)**)

> 1960 *Guardian*: Three East Berlin peroxide girls whose beehives tower over provocative curves.

be-in *n* (1967) a public gathering of hippies. Modelled on **teach-in (1965)** and the like (see **-in (1960)**). The ultimate 1960s existential experience

> 1967 *Daily Telegraph*: Thousands of people with painted faces and chests and love on their minds pranced through New York's Central Park yesterday to celebrate Easter Sunday with a 'be-in'.

Biafran *adj, n* (1967) (a native or inhabitant) of Biafra, a region in West Africa that seceded from federal Nigeria in 1967 and was reunited with it, after a savage civil war, in 1970

> 1967 *Guardian*: The Biafrans naively thought them dead, ambled up, and were themselves killed.

> 1967 *Times*: Enugu radio claimed today that the Biafran air force…had killed about 1,000 federal troops.

bike *n on your bike* (1967) go away, push off. British slang. Since the early 1980s also used with the implication that the hearer should get up and start doing something useful. This implication was popularized by a speech given by Employment Secretary Norman Tebbit at the Conservative Party Conference in October 1981, in which he pointed out that his father had not rioted in the 1930s when unemployed, but had 'got on his bike and looked for work'

> 1981 *Times*: 'On your bike, Khomeini', the crowd shouted outside the Iranian Embassy during the siege.

> 1983 *Economist*: He 'got on his bike' and looked for work. 'On yer bike, Tebbit!' became the slogan of right-to-work marchers, to the delight of Mr Tebbit's supporters.

biodegradable *adj* (1961) susceptible to the decomposing action of living organisms, especially of bacteria. A key approval-term of the late-20th-century ecological movement, applied to things that can be thrown away or otherwise released into the environment without permanently damaging it

> 1969 *Nature*: Biodegradable detergents are now a reality.

bionics *n* (1960) the science of the application of biological systems to engineering problems. Coined from *bio-* + *electronics*. The derived adjective **bionic** is first recorded in 1963; its extended meaning 'having ordinary human capabilities increased (as if) by the aid of such devices' was promoted by the US television series *The Six Billion Dollar Man* in the mid 1970s (see **bionic (1976)**)

> 1960 J. E. Keto: The title of this session is Bionics. This is a new term referring to a relatively new but rapidly expanding area of activity—the study of systems which function after the manner of or in a manner characteristic of or resembling living systems.

> 1978 *Guardian*: The 'bionic' hands look and work like real ones, responding to tiny electronic impulses from the body.

biorhythm *n* (1960) a cyclic variation in some aspect of an organism's bodily functioning, such as the daily cycle of sleeping and waking, or the annual cycle of dormancy and activity in some animals. Originally a technical term in biology, but applied in the later 1960s to each of three alleged cycles of different periods involving a person's physical, emotional, and intellectual activity, as used to explain or predict behaviour

> 1960 *New Scientist*: Hibernation is not simple sleep, nor is it continuous sleep. It proceeds in a biorhythm of the same sort as causes Man to sleep and waken at regular intervals.

> 1986 *New Health*: An exclusively prepared biorhythm chart will help you at a glance to overcome those 'off' days and capitalize your energies during periods of peak performance.

black box *n* (1964) A colloquial term for a *flight recorder* (which is first recorded in 1948). It originated in World War II RAF slang, when it was applied to a navigational instrument in an aeroplane; it was later extended to denote any automatic apparatus performing intricate functions

> 1964 *Daily Telegraph*: The flight recorder is an indestructible 'black box' which automatically records the key functions in the aircraft… The 'black box' can…tell what went wrong in a crash.

black hole *n* (1968) a region within which the gravitational field is so strong that no form of matter or radiation can escape from it except by quantum-mechanical tunnelling, and thought to result from the collapse of a massive star. The name was no doubt partially inspired by the *Black Hole of Calcutta*, an incident in 1756 in which 146 people were incarcerated for a whole night in the punishment cell of the barracks in Fort William, Calcutta. By the 1980s its metaphorical possibilities (bottomlessness, threateningness, etc.) were being widely exploited

> 1968 *American Scientist*: Light and particles incident from outside emerge and go down the black hole only to add to its mass and increase its gravitational attraction.

> 1980 *Time*: To the 1.7 million people added to the jobless rolls in April and May, the U.S. economy may well seem to have…been sucked into a black hole.

Black Panther *n* (1965) a member of a militant organization of blacks in the US seeking to establish black supremacy by force. The first quote below explains the origin of the name

> 1965 *San Francisco Examiner*: SNCC [Student Nonviolent Co-ordinating Committee] has chosen a black panther to adorn its party emblem—a requirement of parties in Alabama…SNCC's 'black panther' movement is viewed by some as a form of black nationalism at the local level.

> 1966 *Economist*: Good sense (or fear of white retaliation) led Negroes in Lowndes County, Alabama, to reject the 'Black Panthers', who stand for 'black power'.

black power *n* (1966) power for black people; used as a slogan of varying implication by, or in support of, black civil-rights workers and organizations. Originally US

> 1966 *Times*: Young Negroes…, supporters of the 'black power' group led by Mr Stokely Carmichael.

bleeper *n* (1964) a miniature radio receiver that emits a bleeping sound when activated, usually by telephone, used to contact the person carrying it. A semi-colloquialism later partly replaced by **pager (1968)**. The verb *bleep* 'to summon or alert with a bleeper' is first recorded in 1976 ('The Federal Government is to spend more than $60,000 so that Members of Parliament can be "bleeped" to notify them of telephone calls when they are out of their offices', *Telegraph* (Brisbane))

> 1964 J. R. L. Anderson: After I had finally got off early in the morning, my bleeper…woke me up.

blow *v blow someone's mind* (1965) Originally, to induce hallucinatory experiences in a person by means of drugs, especially LSD, but also, and more widely, used metaphorically, meaning 'to produce in a person a powerfully pleasurable (or shocking) sensation'. Slang, originally US. See also **mind-blowing (1967)**

> 1967 *San Francisco Examiner*: On a hip acid (LSD) trip you can blow your mind sky-high.

> 1970 *Rolling Stone*: Blue blazer, grey flannel pants, shirt and a beautiful scarf with a chunky Mexican turquoise/silver bracelet and ring which blew the white-shirted jury's minds.

blow-dry *v* (1966) to style and dry (hair) with a brush or comb and hand-held hair-dryer

> 1966 J. S. Cox: Blow waving, the setting of waves in the hair by means of a comb and a hair dryer with a flattened nozzle by which the wave is shaped and blow-dried into position.

blusher *n* (1965) a cosmetic used to give an artificial colour to the face

> 1965 *Vogue*: 'Ultima II' blushing creme… You can do no wrong with this 'transparesscent' blusher—it is so blendable, so edgeless, so atmospheric in texture.

body count *n* (1968) in the Vietnam war, the count of enemy soldiers killed by US and allied troops in combat

> 1968 *Economist*: The Americans have largely abandoned the 'body count' system, according to which a Vietcong was supposed to be reported dead only if his body was actually seen and counted.

body language *n* (1966) the gestures and movements by which a person unconsciously or indirectly conveys meaning. Apparently a translation of French *langage corporel*

> 1983 *Chemical Engineer*: Various types of 'body language'—such as shuffling feet, yawns, glances at watches…and so on—may signal that it's time to call for a break.

body stocking *n* (1965) a tight one-piece woman's undergarment for the torso, sometimes also with sleeves and legs. Often worn to give the impression of nudity under a transparent dress

> 1965 *Vogue*: New body stocking…body-coloured, body-shaped Lycra, just about invisible.

born-again *adj* (1961) characterized by (an experience of) new birth in Christ or spiritual renewal; of a Christian: placing special emphasis on this experience as a basis for all one's actions; evangelical. Originally US, and associated particularly with the activities of the religious right in the last quarter of the century. Based on John 3: 3 'Jesus answered and said unto him, Verily, verily, I say unto thee, Except a man be born again, he cannot see the kingdom of God.' Later widely used metaphorically (see **born-again (1977)**)

> 1961 *Church & People*: Each was a born-again Christian.

> 1977 *Time*: Encouraged by the presence of a born-again Southern Baptist in the White House,…the far-flung residents of the new Bible Belt are loosely lumped together under the name Evangelicals.

BOSS *n* (1969) the state security service of the Republic of South Africa, established in 1969 and renamed *National Intelligence Service* in 1978. An acronym formed from *Bureau of* (properly *for*) *State Security*

> 1971 *Guardian Weekly*: The group is convinced that there have been between eight and 20 BOSS agents working in Britain.

bossa nova *n* (1962) a style of Brazilian music related to the samba; also, a dance performed to this music, briefly in vogue in the early 1960s. From Portuguese, literally 'new tendency'

> 1962 *Daily Mail*: In a hesitant way the bossa nova is already starting. At Edmundo's club…his band plays bossa nova while the customers perform their own version, a kind of lazy samba.

bottom line *n* (1967) the final analysis or determining factor; the point, the crux of the argument. Originally US; a metaphorical extension of the earlier accountants' usage, ' the last line of a profit-and-loss account, showing the final profit (or loss)'

> 1967 *San Francisco Examiner*: George Murphy and Ronald Reagan certainly qualified because they have gotten elected. I think that's the bottom line.

bovver *n* (1969) trouble, disturbance, or fighting, especially caused by skinhead gangs. British slang. Representing a Cockney pronunciation of *bother*

> 1969 *New Society*: 'We show 'em because they're useful if there's a bit of bovver.' Bother is the crophead word for fight; indeed, a lot of them call their footwear 'bovver boots'.

> 1972 Daniel & McGuire: Around the Collinwood there was about twenty on average but with bovver there was sometimes more than that.

bovver boot *n* (1969) a heavy boot with toe-cap and laces, of a kind characteristically worn by skinheads. British slang

> 1980 *Daily Telegraph*: Yesterday at Brighton…police…confiscated hundreds of pairs of laces from 'bovver boots' so that the youngsters wearing them could not kick anyone.

brain death *n* (1964) irreversible loss of function in the cerebrum and brain-stem of such a degree that respiration and circulation continue only if artificially maintained. A concept introduced to define death more narrowly, in the face of medical advances in keeping injured people alive artificially. See also **brain-dead (1976)**

> 1964 *Journal of the American Medical Association*: Medicolegal texts do not mention the consideration of brain death by EEG.

> 1979 *Removal of Cadaveric Organs for Transplantation*: In diagnosing brain death the criteria laid down by the Colleges should be followed.

brain drain *n* (1963) the loss of highly trained or qualified people by emigration, particularly to the US. A journalistic coinage which achieved some success in the early 1960s, and continues to emerge from time to time when the phenomenon asserts itself

> 1963 Peter Fairley: Nearly one quarter of Britain's best young scientists and technologists are being magnetised to jobs in North America. About 10 per cent are settling there. This is the shock finding of experts who have spent months investigating the 'brain drain' across the Atlantic.

breathalyser *n* (1960) a device for measuring the alcohol content of a breath sample, and used in particular to identify drunk drivers. Coined from *breath* + *analyser*. The verb *breathalyse*, a back-formation, is first recorded in 1967. Earlier terms for similar devices include **drunkometer (1934)** and **intoximeter (1950)**

1960 *Times*: The Breathalyser, an American instrument for measuring the percentage of alcohol in the blood from a breath sample, was put on view…yesterday.

1967 *Times*: 'Would it not be sensible to amend the Bill so that the police power to stop and 'breathalyse' people should be limited?

bull bar *n* (1967) a metal bar or framework fitted to the front of a vehicle to provide protection in the event of a collision with a bull or (in its original home, Australia) a kangaroo. In the 1990s bull bars became a *cause célèbre* when they were added as a fashion accessory to heavy off-road-type vehicles and the like, undoing decades of safety work on vehicle front-ends

1995 *Independent on Sunday*: As well as the physical results of accidents involving bull bars, there is also growing evidence of psychological effect on drivers, turning them into macho maniacs.

bunny girl, bunny *n* (1960) a night-club hostess dressed in a costume which partly resembles a rabbit. The inspiration of Hugh Heffner, who introduced them in his Playboy clubs. Their allure relied more on their heavily cantilevered cleavages (they had to bob rather than lean over when serving, so as not to over-excite customers) and their heavily accentuated bottoms than on their rabbit's ears and tail

1963 *Daily Mail*: These bunnies are the newest import to London night-club life from America.

bus *v* (1961) to transport (people) by bus from one place to another, especially in order to encourage or achieve racial integration. US; the practice of *bussing* was the cause of considerable controversy in the US in the 1960s (and later). *Bus* was originally turned into a verb in the 19th century, in the phrase *bus it* 'to go by bus'

1965 *Economist*: Local authorities should adopt the policy known in the United States as 'bussing'—that is to say, spreading immigrants' children around over a wide area.

1969 *New Yorker*: Nine thousand children are now bused—about half as many as would have to be bused in the final stage of integration.

byte *n* (1964) a group of eight consecutive bits operated on as a unit in a computer. An arbitrary formation, probably influenced by **bit (1948)** and *bite*

1964 *IBM Journal of Research & Development*: When a byte of data appears from an I/O device, the CPU is seized, dumped, used and restored.

cable television *n* (1965) a system of television rediffusion whereby signals from a distant station are picked up by an antenna and transmitted by cable to subscribers' sets. Originally mainly a method of overcoming the intereference which in certain areas hampered reception by aerial, but in the 1980s, as the possibilities grew for including telecommunications facilities in the system, it was vastly expanded. Often abbreviated to *cable TV*, or just *cable*. See also **cable (1979)**, and compare **satellite television (1966)**

1965 *Variety*: The state of Indiana has been asked to exercise its regulatory charges for the use of telephone facilities in the transmission of cable television.

1982 L. Block: I'm watching a movie on cable.

caftan, kaftan *n* (1965) a wide-sleeved, loose-fitting shirt or dress worn in Western countries, resembling the original garment worn in the Near East. It became a fashion item in the mid 1960s, largely on the back of a vogue for the East and its religions and cultures

1966 *Daily Telegraph*: Caftans, the season's fashion talking point, won murmurs of delight in light-weight silk, hand-painted, in versions both short and long from artist Noel Dyrenforth.

1967 *Daily Mail*: I'd like to see men in this country wearing kaftans—those long cotton robes—to relax at home.

caravanette *n* (1961) a motor vehicle designed with a caravan-like rear compartment for eating, sleeping, etc., especially while on holiday; a motorized caravan or camper

1974 *Oxford Times*: A sleeping man was flung to his death when an articulated lorry crashed into his parked caravanette.

caring *adj* (1966) that cares; compassionate, concerned. From the mid 1970s often used specifically with reference to professional social work, care of the sick or elderly, etc., in such phrases as *caring profession, society*. See also **carer (1978)**

1966 *Punch*: This was good, caring, committed television, of the kind I am always begging for in these columns.

1976 *Economist*: The shift from relative scarcity to relative abundance in the supply of social service manpower has meant that it is now much more difficult to enter the 'caring professions'.

1980 Margaret Drabble: The welfare state itself, and all the caring professions, seemed to be plunging into a dark swamp of uncertainty.

cash dispenser *n* (1967) an automatic machine from which bank, building society, etc. customers may withdraw cash, especially from a current account. The synonymous **automated teller machine** is 1970s

1967 *Bankers' Magazine*: Following 'Barclaycash'…and the Westminster's 'cash dispenser service'…the National Provincial has started up its 'cash cards' dispenser—like the others good for £10 when inserted into a machine located outside a branch.

cassette *n* (1960) a closed container of magnetic tape with both supply and take-up spools, so designed that it needs merely to be inserted into a suitable tape recorder, computer, or video recorder to be ready for use. The invention which transformed the cumbersome reel-to-reel tape recorder into something handily portable that could be listened to on the move

1960 *Tape Recording and Hi-Fi Yearbook 1959–60*: One of the new decks…is the first British product designed to operate with cassettes.

catch 22 *n* (1961) a supposed law or regulation containing provisions which are mutually frustrating; a set of circumstances in which one requirement, etc., is dependent upon another, which is in turn dependent upon the first. Often used before a noun, especially in *catch 22 situation*. From a paradoxical rule postulated in the novel *Catch-22* (1961, released as a film in 1970), by Joseph Heller (b. 1923), US author. There is no evidence of the widespread use of the term generically until the early 1970s, after the release of the film

1961 Joseph Heller, *Catch-22*: There was only one catch, and that was Catch-22… If he flew them [more missions] he was crazy and didn't have to; but if he didn't want to he was sane and had to.

1974 *Sumter* (S. Carolina) *Daily Item*: His Public Interest Group now finds itself in a Catch 22 situation. It cannot prove the device works without EPA funds, but EPA won't grant the funds unless they prove the device works.

cellulite *n* (1968) a special lumpy form of fat supposed to occur in some women, especially on the hips and thighs, sometimes producing a yellowish puckering of the skin. From French *cellulite*. The marketing of patent methods of eliminating it continues to be profitable

1968 *Vogue*: In Europe treatments for cellulite vary from acupuncture…to sea baths.

1982 Shirley Conran: Joujou lay back on the bed, having her cellulite massaged away.

centrefold *n* (1966) the centre spread of a newspaper or magazine, especially one depicting a nude model; also applied to someone whose picture appears on a centrefold. Originally US

1966 *McCall's Magazine*: The reader is treated to an illustrated biography of the young…maiden, replete with details of her wholesome family life…before stumbling on her stretched over the center fold in full bloom and triple exposure.

Charlie, Charley *n* (1965) the North Vietnamese and Vietcong; also, a North Vietnamese or Vietcong soldier. US services' slang. Suggested by *Victor Charlie*, military communications code for *VC* (= **Vietcong**), perhaps also with some memory of World War II US services' slang *Charlie* 'a Japanese soldier, the Japanese forces', which in turn probably came from 1930s US derogatory slang *Charlie* 'an Asian man', suggested by the fictional Chinese detective *Charlie Chan*

1965 *Newsweek*: A Ranger captain…shouted: 'Don't you tell me Charlie [GI slang for Vietcong] isn't hiding here!'…The rubber planter…answered 'Charlie? Who is Charlie?' The plantation manager, of course, knew perfectly well who Charlie was.

charm *n* (1964) one of the quantum properties or flavours that distinguish the different quarks, being possessed only by the *c* quark

1964 Bjørken & Glashow: A new quantum number 'charm' is violated only by the weak interaction, and the model predicts the existence of many 'charmed' particles.

charts *n* (1963) a list of the records or songs that are most popular or selling best at a particular time. See also **top of the pops (1958)**, **top ten (1958)**

> 1963 *The Beatles*: More chart-topping discs on the way; more packed audiences to drown the frantic beat with cheering.

> 1967 *Scottish Daily Mail*: Engelbert Humperdinck's six-week-long reign at the top of the charts with *The Last Waltz* has finally been broken by the Bee Gees with *Massachusetts*.

chat show *n* (1969) a television programme in which guests are interviewed by the host. First recorded later than the synonymous *talk show* (1965), but it has weathered somewhat better

> 1969 *TV Times*: Like a lot of women—and men I guess—in New York I thought I'd reached chat-show saturation point, but Frost made me think again.

> 1972 *Times*: The apotheosis of the chat show arrives tonight when Muggeridge guests for Parkinson.

Chelsea boots *n* (1962) elastic-sided boots. Named after the district of west London. In the early 1960s their Edwardian retro-chic earned them a brief vogue

> 1963 *Honey*: The Beats wear…polo-sweaters and Chelsea boots.

chicken kiev *n* (1964) chicken breast fried or baked with a stuffing of garlic butter. One of the first signs of the great British eating public becoming modestly adventurous in their approach to 'Continental'-style food (albeit in a debased, mass-produced form); this was one of the earliest successful supermarket ready-made dishes. Named after Kiev in the Ukraine

> 1964 Len Deighton: I…had…lasagne and followed it with chicken Kiev.

chip *n* (1962) a tiny square of thin semi-conducting material which by suitable etching, doping, etc., is designed to function as a large number of circuit components and which can be incorporated with other similar squares to form an integrated circuit. The miniature foundation stone of the late-20th-century information revolution; it was invented in the US in 1958

> 1962 B. G. Bender: A device must have a semiconductor element in any event, but economical techniques have been developed for producing chips for the Microseal component effort which have advanced the state of the art.

> 1965 *Scientific American*: Engineers…saw the possibility of producing complete circuits within a silicon chip by forming all the circuit elements by diffusion.

chisel *adj* (1961) Designating a type of shoe with a squared toe, in vogue for a while in the 1960s

> 1961 *New Statesman*: Where I live, the latest is an Italian-styled navy blue double-breasted suit, and chisel shoes.

cinéma vérité *n* (1963) a film or films which avoid artificiality and have the appearance of real life; the making of such a film; documentary films collectively. From French. The compressed form *ciné-vérité* is first recorded in 1964

> 1963 *Observer*: The trouble with *cinéma-vérité* is that it all depends how interesting your *vérité* is.

clubbing *n* (1966) visiting night clubs, especially in order to dance. A term particularly associated with the club scene of the 1980s and 90s

> 1966 *Guardian*: Clubbing…has all the sanction of social fashion in Manchester.

> 1992 *Daily Telegraph*: We are not a glitzy duo who go out clubbing every night.

cluster bomb *n* (1967) an anti-personnel bomb containing numerous metal pellets which spray out over a wide range on impact. A new refinement first tried out against the Vietnamese. Also used as a verb

> 1968 *New York Review of Books*: The deadliest weapon of all, at least against personnel, were CBUs—cluster bomb units… It should prove interesting to hear…the defense of cluster-bombing a row of houses in the hope of finding a suspect.

Cobol, COBOL *n* (1960) An acronym formed from *Computer Business Oriented Language*, a computer language designed for use in business operations

> 1961 *Times*: Ideally if a Cobol translator were written for every computer, a programme once written in Cobol could be translated and then used on any machine.

community care *n* (1966) long-term care for the mentally ill, the elderly, and people with disabilities, within the resources offered by the community rather than in hospitals or institutions. A term whose profile was raised in Britain in 1990 when the government launched a programme to get long-stay patients out of old crumbling institutions, especially mental hospitals, and integrate them into the community. Often alternatively formulated as *care in the community*

> 1976 *National Observer* (US): Mental patients have the right to receive community care as an alternative to institutional 'warehousing' or release without care, according to a ruling by a Federal court in Washington, D.C.

> 1995 *Economist*: The government's failure to make community care work is discrediting a progressive policy.

commute *n* (1960) a journey made in commuting, especially to or from one's place of work; the distance travelled. Originally US. From the verb *commute* 'to travel in this way', which is first recorded (in the US) in 1889. This in turn was based on the notion of buying a *commutation ticket*, US English for *season ticket*. *Commuter*, archetypal 20th-century suburban animal, is first recorded in 1865

> 1960 *Time*: He frequently test-drives a competitor's car on his commute to Ann Arbor.

compassion fatigue *n* (1968) a state or feeling of weariness and indifference among the general public resulting from excessive appeals to donate to charitable causes

> 1968 A. W. Farmer: You have been hearing and perhaps using, as I have, the phrase 'Compassion Fatigue'. We are just tired out with all the repeated appeals to do good.

> 1987 *Listener*: What the refugee workers call 'compassion fatigue' has set in. Back in the 1970s, when the boat people were on the front pages, the world was eager to help. But now the boat people are old news.

composite *n, v* (1962) (to form into) a composite resolution put before a Trades Union Congress, which has been compiled from several related resolutions proposed by trade unions or constituency Labour parties. A term familiar in the high days of trade-union influence in Britain, in the 1960s and 70s. On its pronunciation, see the second quote below

> 1962 *Economist*: The Liberal executive keeps a watch over this agenda by compositing into multi-point motions the ideas.

> 1971 *Daily Telegraph*: From the agendas…resolutions are plucked…to be amended…and finally extruded in a series of 'composites' (pronounced for obscure reasons to rhyme with 'kites').

computeracy *n* (1969) knowledge of or experience in computing. Formed from *computer* on the model of *literacy*. The word was apparently coined in 1969, but it did not come into general use until the early 1980s, when its derivative **computerate** is first recorded

> 1969 *Times*: 'Let M.I.T. have their computers… What has it to do with industry, or management?'… It has everything to do with the level of computeracy.

> 1985 *Guardian*: Computeracy will not solve all your problems.

computer dating *n* (1966) the use of a computer to match potential partners, according to pre-specified criteria of compatibility, desirability, etc.

> 1966 *Look*: With all the joys and ploys of computer dating, social life at sexually segregated schools in the Ivy League remains plenty anxiety-laden.

computer game *n* (1965) a game played on a computer, especially one (e.g. Space Invaders) involving graphics and operating in real time. A novelty in the 1960s, a fixture in most kids' bedrooms in the 90s

> 1965 *Times Educational Supplement*: We have found that it is very instructive to use what we call the *computer game* in this respect.

> 1993 *Wired*: Zero's life revolves around computer games. He only ventures out of his six-mat in Kawagoe to acquire new gameboards.

computerize *v* (1960) to operate by means of a computer; to install a computer or computers in (an office, etc.)

> 1960 *Times*: The initial paperwork for each computerized job is therefore often formidable.

1964 *Bookseller*: To computerize our invoicing and accounts departments in the hope of maintaining a faster flow of invoices.

comsat *n* (1962) A contraction of *communications satellite*, an artificial satellite used to relay radio, television, and telephone signals around the earth's surface (e.g. Telstar, launched in 1962)

1962 *Flight International*: A martyr to the comsat cause.

condominium *n* (1962) (an apartment in) an apartment house in which the units are owned individually, not by a company or co-operative. Originally and mainly North American. A re-application of the legal term *condominium* 'joint ownership or sovereignty'. The colloquial abbreviation *condo* is first recorded in 1964

1964 *Financial Times*: The condominium—or the 'condo' as Chicagoans have come to know it—is essentially a development from the co-operative concept.

confrontation *n* (1963) the coming of countries, parties, etc., face to face: used of a state of political tension with or without actual conflict. Previously, *confrontation* had denoted a more general notion of bringing people face to face with each other, without necessarily any suggestion of hostility

1963 *Daily Telegraph*: There is reason and good sense in the Malaysian Prime Minister's attitude that there can be no talks with Indonesia while 'confrontation' is going on. For those who seek a clearer definition of President Soekarno's vocabulary, this word means intimidation, guerrilla warfare, arson, loot and confiscation.

conglomerate *n* (1967) a large business group or industrial corporation resulting from the merging of originally separate and diverse commercial enterprises—very much the commercial fashion in the 1960s and 70s. Previously *conglomerate* was largely a geological term, referring to a type of composite rock

1967 *Economist*: Textron Inc., a leading 'conglomerate'—its 28 divisions sell everything from chickens to rocket engines.

consciousness-raising *n* (1968) the increasing of social, political, etc. sensitivity or awareness, so that people realize, for example, how they have been exploited all these years. Originally US; a key element in the right-on vocabulary of the 1970s

1968 *Notes from the First Year*: If there is anything we can learn from the black liberation movement, it is that the primary job is consciousness-raising.

1976 *Spare Rib*: We're raising consciousness, affecting some concrete issues like age discrimination, putting lousy pay on the agenda too.

consensus *adj* (1966) involving or advocating mutual agreement (with the implication of a degree of compromise). In adjectival use, one of the political buzzwords of the last third of the century. As a noun, meaning 'the general or shared opinion', it dates from the mid 19th century

1966 *New Statesman*: The essence of consensus politics is directly related to consensus communications.

consumerism *n* (1960) a doctrine advocating a continual increase in the consumption of goods as a basis for a sound economy. An altogether more red-in-tooth-and-claw usage than the previous **consumerism** 'protection of consumers' interests' (1944), but the latter made a comeback in the 1960s and 70s (see **consumerist (1965)**), and at the end of the century was the more widely used

1960 Vance Packard: A leading apostle of 'consumerism'…pointed out that every recent United States recession had been caused by…a failure to see that consumption kept pace with production.

1962 Eve Godfrey: Consumerism has become the guiding force of our economy.

consumerist *n* (1965) an advocate of **consumerism** 'protection of consumers' interests' (1944)

1965 *Printers' Ink*: Why consumerists think advertising is a waste.

1972 *Times*: Ralph Nader and his consumerists appear to have scored a minor victory.

convenience *adj* (1961) designed for convenience; easy and quick to prepare or use. A quality much prized in the middle of the century, when considerable ingenuity and research went into technological methods of reducing the domestic drudgery of earlier years. As the decades passed, however, *convenience* (mainly applied to food) came to connote lack of spontaneity and originality. Originally US. See also **fast food (1951)**

> 1961 *Economist*: Even the Thanksgiving turkey has now become a 'convenience' food.

> 1965 *Daily Express*: The 'convenience store' is always open in America.

> 1967 *Boston Sunday Herald*: Send us your favorite recipe using convenience foods (frozen or refrigerated prepared foods, canned soups, sauce mixes, cake mixes etc.) and you may win a $10 prize.

cost-effective *adj* (1967) effective in terms of cost. Dated to 1967, although the noun *cost-effectiveness* is actually first recorded in 1964

> 1967 *Guardian*: Does Mr McNamara's cost-effective thinking pass the Soviet leaders by?

coulis *n* (1960) a thin light sauce of puréed fruit or vegetables. A French culinary term which did not raise its English profile until the 1980s, when the sauce became a fashionable element in the 'pictures-on-a-plate' school of nouvelle cuisine

> 1960 Elizabeth David: The straightforward sauces, of which tomato sauce is typical,… are really purées, or *coulis*, needing no sort of extra thickening.

> 1984 *Times*: Starters such as…vegetable terrine with tomato coulis.

courtesy *adj* (1968) supplied, especially for use, free of charge. A perfumed commercialism which goes overboard in its obsequiousness. Mainly in the terms *courtesy car, courtesy coach*, and *courtesy phone*. Originally North American

> 1968 *Globe & Mail* (Toronto): Courtesy car supplied only at Eglinton Caledonia Volkswagen.

> 1975 David Lodge: He tries to read a courtesy copy of Time, but can't concentrate.

> 1984 *Times*: In-bound passengers…can wait comfortably in a 'buffer lounge' (with pay phones and courtesy phones for car-hire and hotel bookings).

crash *v* (1965) to sleep, especially for a single night or in an emergency. Slang. *Crash* in the simple sense 'sleep' is first recorded in 1943, but this particular usage arose in the hippie culture of the mid 1960s. Latterly often followed by *out*

> 1969 *Win*: The two people who had come for help agreed to take these guys home with them, turn them on, feed them, give them a place to crash, love them a lot and keep them close to them all the next day.

> 1975 *Sing Out!*: Probably where the engineers crash out while waiting for the trains.

credibility gap *n* (1966) a disinclination to believe a person, a statement, etc. (used especially of the non-acceptance at face-value of official statements); a disparity between facts and what is said or written about them

> 1966 *Guardian*: Official American statements are no longer taken on trust… The phenomenon…is called the 'credibility gap'.

crudités *n* (1960) an hors-d'œuvre of mixed raw vegetables. A borrowing from French, where it means literally 'raw things'. Terribly chic and sophisticated when they first appeared, within a couple of decades both word and dish had become a shade naff

> 1960 Elizabeth David: With a *plat de crudités* is usually served…a slice or two of *pâté de campagne*.

cryonic *adj* (1968) involving the technique of deep-freezing the bodies of people who have died, usually of an incurable disease, with the aim of reviving them once a cure has been found. Based ultimately on Greek *kruos* 'frost, icy cold' (compare **cryogenic (1902)**). A fashionably (pseudo-) scientific way for the rich to try and cheat death in the latter part of the century

> 1968 *Courier-Mail* (Brisbane): Steven Jay Mendell…who died last Sunday will have a so-called cryonic interment.

CS *n* (1960) a substance that causes irritation of the skin, crying, coughing, etc., and is used in the form of a finely divided solid as a quick-acting irritant for riot control and other purposes. Its name commemorates B. B. Corson and R. W. Stoughton, American chemists who discovered its properties in 1928. In the final third of the century it was in the armoury of every regime with something to fear from its population. Usually in the expression *CS gas*

1970 *Daily Telegraph*: CS gas has been used by British troops during peace-keeping operations in Ulster, and by American forces in Vietnam.

cultural revolution *n* (1966) a cultural and social movement in Communist China, begun in 1965, which sought to combat 'revisionism' and restore the original purity of Maoist doctrine. See also **Red Guard (1966)**

1966 *Economist*: Lin Piao…has loyally used the army as a guinea-pig for the 'cultural revolution' dose of salts with which Mao is now purging the whole country.

cursor *n* (1967) a distinctive symbol on a VDU display (e.g. a flashing underline or rectangle) that indicates the position at which the next character will appear or the next action will take effect. From the earlier application, 'a part of a mathematical, astronomical, or surveying instrument which slides backwards and forwards'

1967 Stotz & Cheek: The cursor on the screen 'follows' the motion of the 'mouse'.

cyborg *n* (1960) a person whose physical tolerances or capabilities are extended beyond normal human limitations by a machine or other external agency that modifies the body's functioning; an integrated man-machine system. A blend of **cybernetic** and *organism*

1970 Alvin Toffler: Advanced fusions of man and machine—called 'Cyborgs'—are closer than most people suspect.

Dalek *n* (1963) a type of evil robot appearing in 'Dr. Who', a BBC Television science-fiction programme. Its mobile-dustbin appearance and tinny voice intoning 'Exterminate! Exterminate!' made it a cult figure in the 1960s and 70s. It made its debut in the second Dr. Who adventure, written by Terry Nation, who got the inspiration for the name from an encyclopedia volume labelled DA—LEK

1963 *Radio Times*: Dalek voices: Peter Hawkins, David Graham.

1969 C. Hodder-Williams: Under what interesting new law do you propose to enforce this regime? Or have you hired the Daleks?

damage limitation *n* (1965) the action or process of restricting damage caused by an accident, error, etc., or of attempting to do this. Originally a piece of military jargon, it is in the area of political news management that the term has become widely known

1965 Herman Kahn: 'Damage limitation' is current jargon for capabilities and tactics that attempt to limit damage if deterrence fails and war breaks out… The United States can buy a very important increment in damage-limiting capability.

1987 *Economist*: The damage limitation after the Reykjavik summit, brilliantly managed by the White House staff, went down the plug hole in the flood of post-Iran doubts.

dancercise *n* (1967) dancing performed as an exercise; organized physical exercise which incorporates the rhythms of (modern) dance. Formerly (from 1971) a proprietary term in the US. One of the earliest examples of a mini-trend for creating blends based on *exercise* (later ones include *aquacise* (1969), *jazzercise* (1977), and **boxercise (1985)**)

1967 Debbie Drake: Dancercize not only remolds your body, but gives you grace, poise and beauty.

1983 *Sunday Telegraph*: While 'Dancercise' was a London-based phenomenon in its youth, classes are spreading all over England.

database *n* (1962) a structured collection of data held in computer storage, especially one that incorporates software to make it accessible in a variety of ways. Hence, any large collection of information

1962 *Technical Memo* (System Development Corporation, California): A 'data base' is a collection of entries containing item information that can vary in its storage media and in the characteristics of its entries and items.

1985 *Sunday Times*: CIR went through its data-base looking for companies interested in investing in new ideas in electronics.

1985 *Ashmolean*: A museum and its records are one vast database.

D-day *n* (1963) Short for *decimalization day*, denoting the day on which a decimal currency is introduced (in the United Kingdom, 15 February 1971). Modelled on **D-day** designating the day of the Allied invasion of Europe (1940s)

1963 *Report of the Committee of Inquiry on Decimal Currency*: We hope…that as many organisations as possible will change on 'D-day' [in South Africa].

1971 *Oxford Mail*: D-day dawned with a minimum of fuss, and shoppers were taking the new coinage in their stride.

decriminalization *n* (1968) the legalization of (the possession and use of) certain narcotic drugs. A specialization of a term that is first recorded in the more general sense 'reclassification as legal' in 1945. The related sense of the verb *decriminalize* is not recorded until 1972. The arguments pro and con have continued to reverberate from the upsurge of the drug culture in the 1960s until the end of the century

1968 *New York Times*: Dr. Fort…called present drug laws 'extreme, barbaric and inefficient', and said that 'immediate de-criminalization of the whole thing' was needed.

1972 *New York Times Magazine*: Glasser would decriminalize heroin and make it available in pharmacies for addicts.

dedicated *adj* (1969) Of equipment, a facility, etc.: designed, manufactured, or installed so as to be available only for a particular purpose or a particular category of user

1969 *Times*: The bulk of M.I.T.'s computers are the so-called 'dedicated' computers, like the stolen one. They are dedicated, that is, to a particular function—usually some on-line process control function.

defoliation *n* (1964) the deliberate destruction of foliage (for military purposes). A tactic employed by US forces during the Vietnam war, in order to deny the Vietcong hiding places in the jungle ('The most powerful technological nation in the world has deployed its invention in massive weight; from 70,000-ton attack carriers, through flying headquarters equipped with computers, to defoliants for stripping the jungle of concealing vegetation', *Punch* (1967))

1965 *Times*: Mr. Goldwater was demanding the nuclear defoliation of the Vietnamese jungles.

demystify *v* (1963) to remove the mystery from; make less complex, ambiguous, or obscure

1963 *Times Literary Supplement*: And so he has devoted himself to 'demystifying politics'.

Denver boot, Denver shoe *n* (1967) a kind of wheel clamp used to immobilize an illegally parked vehicle, apparently first used in Denver, Colorado. The British equivalent **wheel clamp** dates from the 1980s

1974 *Ottawa Citizen*: The notice…said a large locking device had been attached to one of my wheels… This locking contraption is called a Denver Boot.

deregulation *n* (1963) the removal of regulations and restrictions, especially those fixing prices. The verb *deregulate*, coined by back-formation from *deregulation*, is first recorded in 1964

1963 *Petroleum and Chemical Transporter*: We cannot bear to think of the awful consequences of deregulation.

1964 *Economist*: The only rates to be de-regulated were…on agricultural and fishery products transported in bulk.

deselect *v* (1968) to choose not to select; to remove from selection. Often applied euphemistically to the dismissal of an employee. Originally US. The sense 'to remove as a parliamentary candidate' is a later development (see **deselect (1979)**)

1968 *New York Times*: The road from applicant to trainee to overseas volunteer is a hard one. Many individuals do not follow through. Many are 'de-selected'.

designer *adj* (1966) Denoting goods bearing the name or label of a famous designer, with the implication that they are expensive or prestigious. Originally US; later broadened out, especially in the 1980s, to designate anything fashionable among the smart set (e.g. *designer food*, prepared in minimalist quantities by fashionable chefs). See also **designer drug (1983)** and **designer stubble (1987)**

1966 *New York Times*: Designer scarves join name-dropping game.

1984 *Times*: Small wonder Perrier is called Designer Water. My local wine bar has the cheek to charge 70p a glass.

1985 S. Lowry: He loves seafood…and detests designer dishes.

desktop *adj, n* (1968) Designating a computer system, especially for word-processing, that is small enough to use at a desk. A revolutionary concept at a time when previously computers had been huge boxes whirring away in a room of their own. The template *desktop* later inspired **lap-top (1984)** and **palm-top (1987)**

> 1968 *Daily Telegraph*: Desk-top computers for use in homes…may be made possible by an invention described today.

> 1985 *Personal Computer World*: If you use an hp-150 pc, ibm pc, xt or an ibm compatible you will be glad to know that the desktop and the Portable can talk to each other.

developing *adj* (1964) Of a poor country: in the process of developing higher economic, industrial, and social conditions. The latest in the litany of 20th-century euphemisms which English has come up with to avoid sounding patronizing to poor countries: in this case the previous offender which needed replacing was **underdeveloped (1949)**

> 1964 H. Myint (title): The economics of the developing countries.

> 1969 R. Blackburn: Bourgeois economists once talked about the economically 'backward' countries; then 'underdeveloped' was felt to be a kinder adjective. They now prefer to refer to poor capitalist countries as 'developing nations'.

diazepam *n* (1961) a minor tranquillizer of the benzodiazepine group with sedative, anticonvulsant, and amnesic properties. Coined from *benzodiazepine* + the invented suffix *-am*

> 1977 *Scientific American*: Alcohol, barbiturates and antianxiety drugs, such as chlordiazepoxide (Librium) or diazepam (Valium) seem to share brain mechanisms for tolerance and dependence.

digital *adj* (1960) Designating (a) recording or broadcasting in which the original waveform is digitally coded and the information in it represented by the presence or absence of pulses of equal strength, making it less subject to degradation than a conventional analogue signal. The method was originally used for making high-quality audio recordings, but at the end of the century it was being phased in as a broadcasting medium

> 1960 *Institute of Radio Engineers, Transactions on Electronic Computers*: The nature and features of digital recording.

> 1978 *Gramophone*: It would be a great pity if this opportunity for a 'quantum leap' in audio standards were spoilt by the emergence of several conflicting, incompatible digital discs.

> 1999 *Radio Times*: ITV is only on digital terrestrial.

dink *n* (1967) A derogatory or contemptuous term for a Vietnamese person. US military slang. Origin uncertain: apparently earlier an Australian term of contempt for an East Asian person, but probably influenced by *dinky* 'small', *Chink* 'Chinese person', and earlier US slang *dink* 'twerp'

> 1969 *Eugene* (Oregon) *Register-Guard*: He also criticized U.S. military training, which he said permits references to the Vietnamese as 'gooks, dinks, or slopes'.

dirty tricks *n* (1963) Originally applied to covert intelligence operations, especially those carried out by the Central Intelligence Agency (the plans division of which was nicknamed the 'department of dirty tricks'); subsequently also used to designate any underhand political activity designed to discredit an opponent

> 1963 J. Joesten: In the 'Department of Dirty Tricks',…our Intelligencers behave like babes in the wood.

> 1976 *Economist*: As for Watergate, Mr Weicker's record—and his strong stand against dirty tricks—should help him with many voters.

disco *n* (1964) An abbreviation of **discothèque (1954)** which rapidly superseded the full form in general use. Originally US. In the 1970s the word came to denote also a style of pop music frequently played in discos, characterized by a heavy bass beat. First recorded as a verb, 'to dance at a disco', in 1979

> 1964 *Playboy*: Los Angeles has emerged with the biggest and brassiest of the discos.

> 1975 *Time*: Though New York City's blacks and Puerto Ricans have been doing the Hustle for years, its current vogue among people of all colors and ages has coincided with the explosion of 'disco' sound—rhythm and blues with a strong Latin beat.

1979 *New York Post*: It was a hot night the following spring and she was at Studio 54 and she was discoing with a kid who looked like Bruce Jenner.

DJ *n* (1961) An abbreviation of **disc jockey (1941)**. First recorded in print in 1961, but previous references to it in the spelling **dee-jay (1955)** show that it been around well before that

1965 *Daily Telegraph*: The BBC is plainly fascinated by the phenomenon of the disc jockey, now abbreviated to DJ.

DNA fingerprint *n* (1969) a **genetic fingerprint (1969)** obtained by examination of DNA

1988 *Mouse News Letter*: Inbred strains of mice have less complex DNA fingerprints than wild mice.

docudrama *n* (1961) a dramatized film (usually for television) which is based on a semi-fictional interpretation of real events; a documentary drama. Originally North American. In many eyes a suspect genre, which blurs the distinction between reality and fiction. Compare **faction (1967)**, and see also **docusoap (1998)**

1975 *Toronto Star*: CBC producer Ralph Thomas and director Peter Pearson were completing under wraps the most controversial of the network's five new hour-long 'docu-dramas' series.

1981 *Listener*: In the excellent docudrama film, *This is Elvis*, there is a painful sequence…when Elvis…attempts to sing 'Are You Lonesome Tonight?'.

dolly *adj* (1964) Of a young woman: attractive, fashionable. Usually in such phrases as *dolly bird* and *dolly girl*, denoting the sort of wide-eyed miniskirted adolescent sex objects that characterized the mid 1960s. British colloquial. *Dolly* had been used on its own for 'an attractive young girl' since the first decade of the century (see **dolly (1906)**)

1964 *Telegraph* (Brisbane): Take note, girls… Our London men report that you haven't really been given top-of-the-pops praise by your boyfriend unless he has called you a Dolly Bird.

1967 *Punch*: It studies tradition, 'dolly girls', protest, pop, film stars, pop art and the American influence.

domestic *n* (1963) a (violent) quarrel between members of the same household, especially husband and wife. Mainly police slang; originally recorded in Australian English, but familiarized in Britain in the 1980s via television police dramas

1986 *Sunday Sport*: Answering a 999 to what the cops call a 'domestic'.

dork *n* (1967) a stupid person. Originally US students' slang. An adaptation of earlier *dork* 'penis', which may have originated as a humorous alteration of *dick*

1974 P. Gzowski: Meeting some of the famous people of the country (some of whom, confidentially, are dorks).

dove *n* (1962) someone who advocates negotiations as a means of terminating or preventing a military conflict, as opposed to one who advocates a hard-line or warlike policy. Originally US. From the stereotype of the dove as a bird of peace. Usually contrasted explicitly with **hawk (1962)**

1962 *Saturday Evening Post*: The hawks favored an air strike to eliminate the Cuban missile bases… The doves opposed the air strikes and favored a blockade.

1966 *Listener*: The term 'hawks and doves'…was put into circulation by Charles Bartlett, President Kennedy's great journalistic confidant, in the course of an apparently inspired account of what took place in the President's own National Security Council at the time of the Cuban missile crisis.

downer *n* (1966) a drug, especially a barbiturate, that has a depressant or tranquillizing effect. Slang

1966 *Observer*: You know what the young take now? They take 'downers'. They want to feel depressed!

Down's syndrome *n* (1961) mongolism. Named after J. L. H. Down (1828–96), an English physician. Introduced to avoid the perceived racialist overtones of *mongol*, which by the end of the century had virtually disappeared

1961 *Lancet*: Our contributors prefer Down's syndrome to mongolism because they believe that the term 'mongolism' has misleading racial connotations and is hurtful to many parents.

dreadlocks *n* (1960) a Rastafarian hairstyle in which the hair is allowed to grow without combing, and forms into matted 'locks' which hang down from all over the head. The abbreviated *dreads* is first recorded in 1977.

> 1966 *Guardian*: An extremist fringe of members distinguished by their long twisted hair or 'dread-locks', which were modelled after pictures of Ethiopian warriors.

> 1977 *New York Times*: The men therefore let their hair grow into long ropelike strands…referred to as the dreadlocks…or 'dreads'.

dream ticket *n* (1960) a pair of candidates for political office ideally matched to attract widespread support for a party in an election. Originally US, and applied specifically to the proposed candidature of Richard Nixon and Nelson Rockefeller for President and Vice-President of the US. British spin doctors and political journalists picked it up in the 1980s. (US *ticket* 'list of candidates' dates from the early 18th century)

> 1960 *Nation's Business*: The G.O.P. professionals in Washington began calling it the 'dream ticket'.

> 1983 *Sunday Telegraph*: Mr Kinnock, a leading left-winger, and Mr Hattersley, an outspoken figure on Labour's Centre-Right, have been described as the dream ticket because they would form a team uniting both wings of the Labour party.

drink-driving *n* (1964) driving or attempting to drive a motor vehicle with an excessive proportion of alcohol in one's blood, especially with an amount that exceeds a legally fixed limit

> 1964 *Daily Telegraph*: 282 arrests for drink driving.

droog *n* (1962) Adapted by Anthony Burgess from Russian *drug* 'friend' as a word for a member of a gang; hence applied generally to a young ruffian or an accomplice or henchman of a gang-leader

> 1962 Anthony Burgess, *A Clockwork Orange*: There was me, that is Alex, and my three droogs, that is Pete, Georgie, and Dim.

> 1967 *Sunday Mail* (Brisbane): 'Get in,' he said, motioning towards the car. 'I'm no droog.'

druggy, druggie *n* (1968) someone who takes or experiments with illegal drugs, a drug-addict. Slang, originally US

> 1968 *Harper's Magazine*: In the case of the new druggies, their rage for 'experience' passes over into a form of hedonism.

dullsville *n* (1960) an imaginary town that is extremely dull or boring; hence, an environment or condition of extreme dullness. US slang. Also used as an adjective. See **-ville (1956)**

> 1960 *New York Times*: *-ville*, suffix connoting a superlative notion and tacked on to words at will to intensify them…as in…'He's from Dullsville'.

> 1966 *Time*: Johnson is square, folksy and dullsville, sounding…like dozens of boring politicians from the past.

dweeb *n* (1968) a contemptible person, especially one who is ridiculed as puny, unfashionable, or excessively studious; a nerd. US, originally college slang. Probably formed by tacking *dw-* (perhaps from *dwarf*) on to US slang *feeb* 'feeble person'

> 1990 *Chicago Tribune*: Any community that can knowingly elect a dweeb like Edwin Eisenrath…as alderman obviously has a precious sense of fun.

easy listening *n* (1965) Designating a category of (recorded) music which is popular without being loud, abrasive, or otherwise demanding

> 1965 *Billboard*: Billboard this week introduces the 'Top 40 Easy Listening' chart.

eco- *prefix* (1969) An abbreviation of *ecological* or *ecology*. *Eco-* had occasionally been used before in the formation of technical terminology (e.g. *ecospecies*, *ecotype* (1920s), **ecosystem (1930s)**, *ecosphere* (1950s)), but its wide-ranging career in non-specialist vocabulary began in the late 1960s, as the environmentalist movement got into its stride. Among the earliest recorded formations of this new phase were *eco-activist*, *ecocatastrophe*, and *ecocide*

> 1969 *Time*: Last week eco-activists staged a 'Damn DDT Day' in San Francisco's Union Square.

> 1970 *Guardian Weekly*: Beyond that lie the use of ecocidal weapons—herbicides in Vietnam—and 'humane incapacitants'.

> 1970 *Natural History*: I've been an ecofreak for 30 years.

ego-trip *n* (1969) an activity, period of time, etc., devoted entirely to indulging in one's own interests or in self-expression. First recorded as a verb in 1970

1969 *It*: They're using the music as a vehicle for character and personality building. I don't think they're half as much a musical ego-trip as people imagine.

1970 *New York*: Father ego-tripping on his children's academic and other achievements.

Elint, ELINT *n* (1961) electronic intelligence-gathering methods. Originally US. A contraction of *electronic* (or *electromagnetic*) *intelligence*. See also **Sigint (1969)**

1977 Breyer & Polmar: A surprising feature of these new ELINT ships is that the electronic gear is scarcely visible.

empty nester *n* (1962) either member of a couple whose children have grown up and left home. A category identified by marketeers as having a sudden access of disposable income

1962 *Economist*: Couples in the 45–65 age bracket—the so-called 'empty nesters', whose children have grown up and who have become bored with their large houses.

encounter group *n* (1967) In group therapy, a group which meets in order to improve the emotional adjustments of its members through body contact, emotional expression, and confrontation. Originally US

1967 C. R. Rogers: Since then I have been involved in more than forty ventures of what I would like to term—using the label most congenial to me—basic encounter groups.

endangered *adj* (1964) Of an animal or plant: in danger of extinction. Used especially in the phrase *endangered species*

1964 *Congress Record*: A partial list of extinct and endangered species of the United States and Puerto Rico is attached.

enjoy *interj* (1960) take pleasure in the thing (typically food or drink) being presented. Originally and mainly US, modelled on Yiddish

1994 *Minnesota Monthly*: Because it is easy and rewarding, Tumis Bunchis is frequently one of the first things children in Indonesia learn how to cook. Enjoy!

entryism, entrism *n* (1963) the policy or practice of joining an organization with the intention of subverting its aims and activities; organized infiltration. Modelled on French *entrisme*, which is thought to have arisen from advice given by Leon Trotsky to his followers in *La Vérité*, September 1934: 'En disant ce qui est, il faut entrer dans le parti Socialiste.' Its use did not become common in English until the mid 1970s, when it was applied to the infiltration of the Labour Party by Marxists and Trotskyists. The derived *entryist* or *entrist*, first recorded in 1964, also took off in the 70s

1963 I. Deutscher: 'Entrism' is the term by which the Trotskyists described and discussed this move even thirty years later [than 1934–5].

1976 *Guardian Weekly*: There was also much huffing and puffing in Labour's parliamentary ranks about the infiltration—or, euphemistically, entryism—into the party by Trotskyists and Marxists.

1977 *Listener*: The 'entrists' who are persuading constituency parties that their MP is a representative and not a delegate.

Euro- *prefix* (1962) conforming to or resulting from European Union (formerly EEC) standards, regulations, etc. Often used jokingly, sarcastically, or dismissively. The organization was founded (under the Treaty of Rome) in 1957, but Britain did not begin to take serious notice of it until the 1960s (Britain first tried to join in 1963)

1965 *Daily Telegraph*: Studies are being made aimed at agreeing on common electrical standards throughout Europe… A common electric plug has been devised… It is called the 'Europlug'.

1967 *Economist*: Germany's second biggest [brewery]…will spend about £600,000 to £700,000 on changing over from the conventional flip top bottle to the 'euro bottle', a Brussels invention.

1985 *Times*: Marking animals with a Eurocode so that their owners can identify them.

Eurocrat *n* (1961) A usually derogatory term for a bureaucrat employed by the European Union

1961 *Economist*: These new 'Eurocrats' are worth watching.

extraterrestrial *n* (1963) a being that comes from outer space. A noun use of an adjective which dates back at least to the 1860s; popularized particularly by the 1982 Steven Spielberg film *E.T.* (short for *extraterrestrial*). See also **alien (1944)**

> 1966 *New Statesman*: Contact with extra-terrestrials will…come suddenly.

extravehicular activity *n* (1965) The rather ponderous jargon used by US space scientists for activity outside a space-vehicle while it is in flight. Often abbreviated to *EVA*. See also **spacewalk (1965)**

> 1965 *Newsweek*: White climbed into a new 'extravehicular activity' (EVA) suit.

> 1966 *New Scientist*: Cernan…had to take repeated rests during his extravehicular activities.

facilitator *n* (1961) a person or organization whose job or role is to facilitate communication or understanding within a group of people, or negotiations between various parties; a mediator. The sort of constipated polysyllable that has given academic jargon, particularly in the social sciences, a bad name in the last third of the century

> 1991 *New Yorker*: I didn't want to leave my parents when they weren't communicating and might need me as a facilitator

faction *n* (1967) a literary genre in which fictional narrative is developed from a basis of real events or characters; documentary fiction. A blend of *fact* and *fiction*. Compare **docudrama (1961)**

> 1967 Publisher's note in *Games* by H. Atkinson: This is the great work of faction of 1967—fiction based on fact, the novel form of our time.

> 1980 *Times*: He is an exponent of the dramatized documentary, sometimes known as 'faction', a method of film-making which has been severely criticized for blurring the dividing line between truth and fiction.

factory farming *n* (1964) agriculture organized on industrial lines. Largely a polemical term, implying cruelly cramped conditions and deprivation of freedom and fresh air. The related *factory farm* dates from the 1890s

> 1964 *New Statesman*: Boycott factory farm food?… Boycott factory farmers?… The essential thing is to amend the Protection of Animals Act (1911) to cover factory-farming techinques.

family values *n* (1966) values supposedly learnt or reinforced within a traditional, close, family unit, especially high moral standards and discipline (viewed as being in decline). A phrase used as a slogan by the political right in the 1990s. Originally US

> 1996 *Times*: A highly disciplined election-year drive to present himself as the champion of conservative 'family values'… He has urged a return to school uniforms to encourage discipline and announced moves denying welfare benefits to teenage mothers who leave school or refuse to live at home.

fine-tune *v* (1969) to adjust (an instrument, measurement, etc.) very precisely. Hence, metaphorically, to make delicate adjustments to (the economy, a situation) so as to bring about a desired improvement. A back-formation from *fine tuning*, which had been used with reference to the tuning of radio receivers since the mid 1920s

> 1969 *Washington Post*: To say that we can 'fine-tune' the economy so that the addition of another $1 billion or so in surplus makes a difference—we're not that smart.

flares *n* (1964) flared trousers. Intermittently fashionable during the last four decades of the century, and at other times the object of derision. Originally US

> 1964 *New York Post*: Belted coats, skimmers, flares, demi-fits, the 'in' silhouettes for dress and casual wear!

> 1985 S. Lowry: The rest of the male world sported peach cord flares.

flash *v* (1968) Of a man: to exhibit or expose the genitals briefly and indecently, especially in a public place. Used transitively since at least the mid 19th century in various picturesque phrases (*flash one's meat, flash one's root, flash it*), but the modern intransitive usage would appear to be no older than the 1960s. The agent noun *flasher* is first recorded in 1974

> 1968 Joan Lock: City parks also have their share of 'flashing'.

1974 *Kingston* (Ontario) *News*: A middle aged man indecently exposed himself to a female student… There were several reports of a so-called 'phantom flasher' in the University…area.

1978 Gore Vidal: Men stared at me. Some leered. None, thank God, flashed.

flexible response (1963) a military strategy based on appropriate responses to a variety of threats. A piece of Pentagon-speak which entered the general consciousness. The underlying idea is 'Don't start a nuclear war over a trivial military incident'

1963 *Time*: Pentagon planning now puts relatively more emphasis than it did a few years ago on 'graduated' or 'flexible' responses.

float *v* (1965) Of a currency: to fluctuate as regards its international exchange rate. The transitive usage, 'to arrange for (a currency) to fluctuate in this way', is first recorded in 1970

1965 *Guardian*: The decision to let the mark float was forced on the German authorities by a sudden inflow of funds.

1970 *Daily Telegraph*: Foreign exchange markets went into a flurry of activity as a result of the decision to float the Canadian dollar.

flower people, flower children *n* (1967) members of a sub-group of hippies in the late 1960s and early 70s who wore or carried flowers as symbols of peace and love. Widely ridiculed for their unworldliness and condemned because of their reputation for drug-taking, sexual promiscuity, etc.

1967 *Guardian*: Beat-reared, Greenwich-nurtured teenagers are running away…to be flower people.

1969 *Listener*: The political innocence of the Hornsey flower children.

flower power *n* (1967) the beliefs and conventions of the flower people

1969 Nik Cohn: As fads go, Flower Power was less than impressive… London was content mostly to ape California. Everyone wore kaftans and beads and bells. Everyone spoke in hushed tones of San Francisco and Monterey, of acid and Love and the Maharishi.

fly-by-wire *n* (1962) a semi-automatic, often computer-regulated system for controlling the flight of an aircraft, spacecraft, etc.

1962 John Glenn: I used the fly-by-wire mode which…utilizes a combination of the manual control stick and the hydrogen peroxide nozzles of the automatic system.

1986 *Aircraft Illustrated*: A 'fly-by-wire' airliner with electrical signalling of all control surfaces.

format *v* (1964) to arrange or put into a format. Used mainly in connection with computers

1965 *Advanced Computers*: These systems have come to be known as formatted file systems, since the input data are arranged into various formats for ease of storage and retrieval.

freak *n* (1967) someone who freaks out; a drug addict. Slang, originally US

1967 *Atavar* (Boston): The life expectancy of the average speed-freak…is less than five years.

freak out, freak *v* (1965) to undergo an intense emotional experience, to become stimulated, especially under the influence of hallucinatory drugs. Slang, originally US. See also **freak out (1970)**

1965 *Village Voice*: Grand Opening!!! Freak with the Fugs!!! The East Side's Most Infinite Hallucination in Person.

1966 *Life*: When my husband and I want to take a trip together…I just put a little acid in the kids' orange juice…and let them spend the day freaking out in the woods.

freaky *adj* (1966) characteristic of someone who freaks out. Slang, originally US

1967 A. K. Baer: Everybody in the car was positive he was on an acid trip. He was freaky.

freedom ride *n* (1961) an organized ride (in buses, etc.) by people demonstrating against racial segregation. An early tactic by civil-rights campaigners in the US. *Freedom rider* is first recorded in the same year

1961 *New York Times*: Freedom Rides…are expected to continue until bus-terminal segregation ends.

1961 *Guardian*: Anti-segregation 'freedom riders' arrived here by bus from Montgomery, Alabama.

frug *n, v* (1964) a type of modern dance which enjoyed a brief vogue in the mid 1960s. The corresponding verb is first recorded in 1965. The origins of the word are a mystery

1965 *Daily Express*: Other guests…were wearing themselves out with the latest dance craze, the Frug.

1965 *Punch*: They were frugging around to a new Who waxing.

1967 *Spectator*: Mr. George Brown went to New York to dance the frug and tell the United Nations about Vietnam.

galleria *n* (1960) a covered shopping mall resembling or inspired by an Italian shopping arcade. From Italian

1964 *Guardian*: A proposal to turn the Covent Garden…central market…into a 'galleria' of small shops…backing on to halls for music and dancing.

game show *n* (1961) a television light-entertainment programme in which celebrities or members of the public compete in a game or quiz, often for prizes. Originally US

1961 *Saturday Evening Post*: The set announced, 'It's Time to Say When!' and after a commercial, the first of the day's 'game shows' began.

1984 *Broadcast*: The year has seen the successful development of a new game show for Channel Four.

garage sale *n* (1966) a sale of unwanted used goods and possessions, usually held in (the garage of) a private house. The US equivalent of the **car boot sale (1985)**

1966 *Daily Union* (Sacramento) *Family Weekly Magazine*: A couple…held a garage sale on three consecutive weekends and…sold out…countless items.

garbologist, garbiologist *n* (1965) a dustman. A delightful piece of (self-)aggrandisement, not to be confused with the very serious term **garbology (1976)**

1966 *New Scientist*: One dustman in court last week called himself a garbologist.

garden centre *n* (1965) a place where plants, seeds, gardening equipment, garden furniture, and similar items are sold. Supermarket methods come to the formerly sedate world of nurserymen and seedsmen

1965 C. Kelway: Look out for [dwarf trees] at the now-popular garden centres where many may be seen growing in containers ready for taking home.

gear *adj* (1963) wonderful, great. Also used as an exclamation of delighted approval. British slang. It appears to have originated in the early years of the century in expressions such as *that's the gear*, meaning 'that's just what's wanted, that's great'. There is a record of its use meaning 'smart, fashionable' from the early 1950s, but its (brief) career as an all-purpose approval-word is closely linked with British youth culture of the mid 1960s, and particularly with the Merseybeat scene

1963 *Today*: They're gear! The Beatles leave for London after their triumphant tour of Sweden.

1964 J. Burke: 'Gear!' John jumped up from his seat. 'Come on, girls, let's have a bit of a dance.'… Once we even all sat down and wrote those letters saying how gear she was and all that rubbish.

gender *n* (1963) the sex of a human being, from the point of view of the social and cultural, as opposed to the biological, distinctions between the sexes. Often used before a noun

1963 Alex Comfort: The gender role learned by the age of two years is for most individuals almost irreversible, even if it runs counter to the physical sex of the subject.

1986 *Financial Times*: It was most important…that schools could intervene in and modify the education of a child regardless of race, gender or class background.

generation gap *n* (1967) an (undesirable) difference in outlook and understanding between older and younger people. No doubt the difference had existed before, but it took the youth-oriented 1960s to take sufficient notice of it to coin the term *generation gap*. It went on to inspire **gender gap (1977)**

1967 *Boston Globe*: He acknowledged that the 'generation gap' is difficult both for the younger and the older generations.

genetic engineering *n* (1969) alteration of the DNA of a cell for the purpose of research, as a means of manufacturing animal proteins, correcting genetic defects, or making artificial improvements to plants and animals. The term, with its built-in contrast between life-processes and metal-bashing, remained an uneasy one at the end of the century, largely because of the seed of doubt sown by that word 'improvements'

> 1969 *New Scientist*: The day may be approaching when genetic engineering may make it possible to make a plant to order.

> 1971 *Guardian*: Human genetic engineering aimed at the elimination of genetic diseases.

genetic fingerprint *n* (1969) a set of genetic characteristics derived from an individual's tissues or secretions, especially when used for identification purposes like a conventional fingerprint

> 1969 E. M. Berkman: The genetic fingerprint of human blood types.

geostationary *adj* (1961) of or being an artificial satellite that revolves round the earth in one day and hence remains above a fixed point on the earth's surface

> 1961 *Aeroplane*: Raising a communication satellite from a low-circular orbit into a geostationary orbit at 22,300 miles.

> 1968 *New Statesman*: The existence of geo-stationary satellites and the enormous investment in world-wide communications will increase the flow of information and disseminate it on a scale that almost defies the imagination.

GIGO *n* (1964) An acronym formed from *garbage in, garbage out*, a principle in computing: if the input or program is incorrect, the output will inevitably be incorrect too

> 1964 T. W. McRae: If the original data supplied to us are inaccurate we have built what the Americans ironically describe as a *gigo* model, that is 'garbage in—garbage out'.

gite *n* (1964) a furnished or self-catering holiday home in France, usually in a rural district, popular with the British middle classes from the late 1960s. From French *gite*, which was originally borrowed into English at the end of the 18th century in the sense 'a stopping-place or lodging', but died out in the mid 19th century

> 1984 *Listener*: Holidays are taken in the Dordogne, on remote Greek islands, in rural gites and in distant Kashmir.

glitch *n* (1962) a malfunction in a system, specifically a surge of current in an electrical circuit; hence more generally, a hitch or snag. Slang, originally US. Probably from German *glitschen* 'to slip, make an error'

> 1962 John Glenn: Another term we adopted to describe some of our problems was 'glitch'. Literally, a glitch is a spike or change in voltage in an electrical circuit which takes place when the circuit suddenly has a new load put on it… A glitch…is such a minute change in voltage that no fuse could protect against it.

> 1988 *New York*: The Quayle announcement was only the most noticeable of a host of glitches affecting the Republicans.

glitzy *adj* (1966) characterized by glitter or extravagant show; ostentatious, glamorous. Often a negative term, implying tawdriness. Probably from German *glitzern* 'to glitter' (perhaps via Yiddish); compare German *glitzerig* 'glittering'. See also **glitz (1977)**

> 1966 *New York Times*: Advertising will stress that Devil Shake is 'glitzy'. This claim will be hard to deny, at least until someone defines the word.

> 1985 *Listener*: The Oscars are the high point of the Western film industry's year—a glitzy, vulgar affirmation that they're getting things right.

global village *n* (1960) A term popularized by Marshall McLuhan (1911–80) for the world in the age of high technology and international communications, through which events throughout the world may be experienced simultaneously by everyone, so apparently 'shrinking' world societies to the level of a single village or tribe

> 1960 Carpenter & McLuhan: Postliterate man's electronic media contract the world to a village or tribe where everything happens to everyone at the same time: everyone knows about, and therefore participates in, everything that is happening the minute it happens. Television gives this quality of simultaneity to events in the global village.

glue-sniffing *n* (1963) inhaling the fumes of plastic cement for their narcotic effects. The agent noun *glue-sniffer* is first recorded in the same year. See also **solvent abuse (1977)**

> 1963 *New Society*: A new threat to teen-age stability…is glue-sniffing, the deliberate inhaling of the fumes from plastic cement… The glue sniffers…frequently fall asleep in class.

> 1971 E. E. Landy: Eventually most glue sniffers outgrow glue and go to more adult-type drugs such as marijuana, [etc.].

gofer *n* (1967) someone who runs errands, especially someone employed for such duties on a film set or in an office; a general dogsbody. Originally and mainly US. Formed from *go for* (see the quote), on the model of *gopher* 'small burrowing mammal'

> 1967 J. O'Hara: 'Teddy's used to being my gofer.' 'Your what?' said Ellis Watson. 'You never worked in radio. A gofer goes for coffee.'

go-go *adj* (1964) fashionable, with it. Slang. A reduplication, probably based on *the go* 'the fashion, the rage'

> 1964 *Punch*: It's fab…and withitly gogo.

go-go *adj* (1965) Applied to a young female erotic-dance performer in a club, disco, etc.

> 1967 *Boston Herald*: Brash, young Gypsy Joe Harris, squirming and twisting like a go-go dancer.

golden-ager *n* (1961) an old person. US, euphemistic. From *golden age* '(past) period of prosperity or excellence'

> 1970 Harry Waugh: Frank bought himself a drink in the bar…while watching the golden agers gossip in the lounge area.

golden handshake *n* (1960) a gratuity given as compensation for dismissal or compulsory retirement. Later semi-facetious coinages which it inspired include **golden handcuffs (1976)** and **golden parachute (1981)**

> 1960 *Economist*: There is little public sympathy for the tycoon who retires with a golden handshake to the hobby farm.

Gonk *n* (1964) The proprietary name (registered in Britain in 1964) of an egg-shaped doll which enjoyed a brief vogue in the mid 1960s. A made-up word

> 1964 *Spectator*: Those neckless dolls called—I think—gonks, which witless adults are said to give to other adults.

> 1964 *Daily Mail*: Gonks…are those nasty, expensive, fat balls of felt and rag that are squatting all over our houses and toy shops.

granny glasses *n* (1968) metal-framed spectacles with round lenses, of a sort stereotypically worn by little old ladies, and fashionable among the flower-children generation of the late 1960s and early 70s

> 1968 J. Hudson: She had a flower painted on her cheek, and large, blue-tinted granny glasses.

grody *adj* (1969) unpleasant, dirty, nasty, ugly, etc.: a general term of disapproval. US slang, which in due course became incorporated in the teenage dialect known as **Valspeak (1982)**. An alteration of earlier *groaty* (1965), which was derived from *grotesque*

> 1982 *Los Angeles Times*: Grody is used to describe a disgusting object. Moon Zappa calls her toenails '*Grody* to the *max*', which means disgusting beyond belief.

grotty *adj* (1964) unpleasant, dirty, nasty, ugly, etc.: a general colloquial term of disapproval which by the end of the decade had spread itself widely amongst British English speakers. Derived from *grotesque*

> 1964 *Sunday Times*: A charming touchline companion called the [hockey] match 'grotty' which seemingly means disappointing.

> 1967 *House & Garden*: The house was a ruin—dirty, really grotty, but with obvious potential.

groupie *n* (1967) a usually young female fan of a rock or pop group who follows the group around on tour, in many cases allegedly with the aim of having sex with them

> 1969 *Private Eye*: Read the sensational story, in her own words, of Katie a nineteen-year-old Groupie, as she 'pulls' from pop group to pop group.

grunge *n* (1965) dirt, filth; filthy or disgusting material. US slang. Origin uncertain: perhaps a blend of *grime* and **gunge**. The earliest record of *grunge* is actually as a term of abuse applied to a person, implying slovenliness, but this usage seems not to have survived the 1960s. The first recorded instance of the meaning 'filth' comes from 1968, but it is implied in 1965 (albeit metaphorically) in the derived adjective *grungy*. See also **grunge (1991)**

> 1965 *New York Times*: Liquor flows freely, jokes are the 'grungiest', fun and games abound.

> 1968 *Current Slang* (University of South Dakota): Did you see the *grunge* we had for lunch?

grunt *n* (1962) an infantry soldier. US slang, familiarized by the Vietnam war. Compare the earlier US slang sense, 'a mechanic's or electrician's mate' (first recorded in the 1920s), whose connotations of 'subordinateness' may underlie the military usage

> 1969 Ian Kemp: The sound of…engines, among the most welcome of all music to the average infantryman—or 'grunt', as we were impolitely called—in Vietnam.

gunge *n* (1969) a sticky mass; any messy or clogging substance, especially one considered otherwise unidentifiable. Also, general rubbish, clutter, filth. Slang. Of uncertain origin; perhaps associated with *goo*, **grunge**, *gunk*, etc. Reported in Partridge's *Dictionary of Slang and Unconventional English* (1970) as being engineers' slang for 'grease' or 'oily dirt' around 1940. The adjective *gungy* is first recorded in 1962, but in a rather generalized derogatory sense; there are no clear examples of it in the sense 'stickily messy' before 1971

> 1969 *Sunday Times*: Recently the Birkenheads received an export order for a rather special type of…er, well, gunge. This was for lissage, which is also known as English Ground Flake, mixed with linseed oil.

gunship *n* (1968) a heavily armed helicopter. The concept and the term were familiarized by the Vietnam war

> 1968 *Times*: Helicopter 'gunships' armed with machine-guns accounted for most of the toll.

gut *adj* (1964) Of an issue, question, etc.: basic, fundamental; also, of a reaction: instinctive and emotional rather than rational. From the idea of feeling something in one's guts

> 1964 *Economist*: For Harold Wilson it was a carefully planned campaign:…the neo-Kennedyism combined with a concentration on gut issues.

> 1968 *Guardian*: The three nights of rioting that followed his murder were an immediate gut reaction.

hands-on *adj* (1969) involving direct participation in an activity (especially the use of computers or a computer keyboard), in order to gain practical experience of it; of experience, training, etc.: practical, rather than theoretical or second-hand. In the 1970s, the scope of the adjective was extended to people, denoting 'prepared to become practically involved in a task'

> 1971 *Computers & Humanities*: At least eighteen seem, from their course descriptions, to offer 'hands-on' experience with computers.

> 1978 *Detroit Free Press*: Must be a hands on person with some mechanical ability.

hard-wired *adj* (1969) using or containing permanently connected circuits designed to perform a specific, unchangeable, function. The metaphorical application to neural cells in the brain and the like is first recorded in 1971

> 1969 *Mechanised Accounting*: Central to the entire System 21 structure is the microprocessor and its various hard-wired microprograms.

> 1971 *New Scientist*: These cells are hard-wired and ready for action as soon as the kitten opens its eyes.

Hare Krishna (1968) The title of a chant or mantra based on a name of the Hindu deity Vishnu, used especially as an incantation by members of a pop religious cult that flourished among the young in the US and elsewhere in the late 1960s and early 70s. From Hindi *hare* 'O God!' + *Kṛishṇa* name of an incarnation of the god Vishnu

> 1968 *New Yorker*: Newspaper pictures of the poet [i.e. Allen Ginsberg] chanting 'Hare Krishna' at one of Leary's sellout psychedelic celebrations.

hawk *n* (1962) someone who advocates a hard-line or warlike policy. Originally US. From the idea of the hawk as an aggressive bird. Usually contrasted explicitly with **dove (1962)**

1965 *Economist*: President Ayub's difficulties in curbing the 'hawks' in his country.

1967 D. Boulton: The committee seems to have become immersed immediately in a struggle between doves and hawks.

hidden agenda *n* (1968) a secret motivation behind the ostensible purpose of an action, statement, etc.; an aim ulterior to that which is openly stated. See **agenda (1961)**

1987 Margaret Atwood: Sex was the hidden agenda at these discussions.

1990 *New York Magazine*: Whenever someone says to me that something can't be done, I figure that the person is either weak, just doesn't want to do it, or has a hidden agenda.

hipsters *n* (1962) trousers that extend from the hips rather than the waist

1962 *Sunday Express*: Top girls are buying camel-hair hipsters with long matching braces.

holistic medicine *n* (1960) a form of medical treatment that attempts to deal with the whole person and not merely with his or her physical condition

1960 F. H. Hoffman: Throughout the United States, concern with teaching about the whole man— 'holistic' or comprehensive medicine—is a growing phenomenon in the medical school curriculum.

homophobia *n* (1969) fear or hatred of homosexuals and homosexuality. Coined from **homosexual** + -*phobia*. An identically spelt word had been coined (from Latin *homo* 'a man') in the 1920s, meaning 'fear of men or of mankind', but there is no record of its use since 1960. The related *homophobic* and *homophobe* are first recorded in 1971. Compare **heterosexism (1979)**

1969 *Time*: Such homophobia is based on understandable instincts among straight people, but it also involves innumerable misconceptions and oversimplifications.

1971 *Gay* (New York): The homophobes tended to disagree significantly more than the others.

1981 *Observer*: Rat-packs of homophobic punks, white or Latino, prowled gay neighbourhoods.

honky, honkie *n* (1967) a white person; white people collectively. US Black English, derogatory slang. The origins of the word are obscure; it may be a variant of US slang *hunky* 'immigrant to the US from east-central Europe', which itself came ultimately from *Hungarian*

1967 *Newsweek*: 'Go for the honkies'… The chemistry in tranquil Nashville, Tenn., spelled riot… Stokely Carmichael…exhorted: 'You have to go for the honkies…who are keeping you in the ghettos… Victims should never, ever apologize for their use of violence.'

hully gully *n* (1964) a dance that is a modification of the frug. Origin unknown

1969 Nik Cohn: Dance-crazes bossed pop right up until the Beatles broke. There was the Hully Gully, the Madison, [etc.].

human resources *n* (1961) people, especially personnel or workers, considered as a significant asset of a business or other organization, as opposed to material resources, etc. An item of US management-speak which in due course crossed the Atlantic, elbowing aside *personnel* and the gender-compromised *manpower*

1961 *Act for International Development: Summary Presentation* (U.S. President's Task Force): The decade can bring significant progress in launching the slow process of developing their human resources and their basic services.

1978 *Times*: James F. Scull…has had a meteoric rise through the corporation over the last 14 years, latterly as vice-president for human resources (personnel, I suppose we would call it).

1990 *Times*: We are seeking a committed personnel professional who will be able to establish and manage the human resources function at the plant.

hype *n, v* (1967) (to publicize with) deceptively inflated advertising or promotion. Originally US. Often taken to be short for *hyperbole*, but it can probably be traced back to an earlier US slang usage, 'to short-change', whose origins are unknown

1967 Norman Mailer: The hype had made fifty million musical-comedy minds; now the hype could do anything.

1969 Nik Cohn: Hype is a crucial word. In theory it is short for hyperbole. In practice, though, it means to promote by hustle, pressure, even honest effort if necessary, and the idea is that you leave nothing to chance. Simply, you do everything possible. Hype has become such an integral part of pop that one hardly notices it any more.

hypertext *n* (1965) machine-readable text that forms an interconnected structure in such a way that related items of information are linked. Although introduced in the 1960s, the term gained little popular currency until the late 80s, when the growth in the power of personal computers, and the rise of media such as CD-ROMs which could contain large amounts of material in multiple formats, meant that some such organization of the information was essential

> 1965 T. H. Nelson: Let me introduce the word 'hypertext' to mean a body of written or pictorial material interconnected in such a complex way that it could not conveniently be presented or represented on paper.

> 1991 *Whole Earth Review*: Links connect nodes in the hypertext software by computer-supported relationships that permit rapid, easy movement across the network of nodes.

identikit *n* (1961) a composite picture of a person whom the police wish to interview assembled from features described by witnesses. It transformed the business of alerting the public to suspected criminals: in place of a vague verbal description or a dubious drawing, Frankensteinish montages began to appear in newspapers and on television. A blend of *identity* and *kit*. See also **photofit (1970)**

> 1961 *Observer*: About forty police forces in this country are now testing an American device called an 'Identi-Kit', which is used to translate witnesses' descriptions of a person into visual terms.

image-maker *n* (1960) someone who creates a favourable **image (1958)** of someone or something in the mind of the public

> 1960 *Guardian*: [Owing] to the failure of the image-makers…neither candidate seems to have put across a strong or provocative personality.

in *adj* (1960) fashionable, sophisticated. Colloquial

> 1960 *Spectator*: A personable young strip-peuse at Vegas (as we 'in' people call Las Vegas).

> 1965 *Melody Maker*: Record companies release more discs in the belief that folk is the new 'in thing'.

> 1970 *Times*: The in-crowd calls [Casablanca] 'Casa', and I offer the information here for anyone who can use it to advantage.

-in *suffix* (1960) Used originally to designate a communal act of protest by blacks in the US against racial segregation (in this case the ultimate model was **sit-in (1937)**); subsequently indicating any group protest or large gathering for some common purpose, especially as held by students. See also **be-in (1967), laugh-in (1968), love-in (1967), teach-in (1965)**

> 1960 *Newsweek*: Into the already-roiled waters of the South, Negroes will wade this summer in a campaign to break down segregation at public beaches—a wade-in counterpart to the widespread lunch-counter sit-ins of recent weeks.

> 1963 *Time*: The 'pray-in' at churches.

> 1965 *New York Times*: There have been sit-ins, lie-ins, stand-ins, eat-ins, shop-ins, sleep-ins, swim-ins, and sing-ins.

> 1966 *Daily Telegraph*: William Bryden-Smith, aged 10, who wrote to us, wants to take part in the cook-in.

> 1971 *Guardian*: A student sleep-in began last night.

incomes policy *n* (1965) Applied originally to a policy introduced in Britain by the Labour Government of 1964–70 for the control of inflation by attempting to restrict increases in wages, salaries, dividends, etc., and subsequently to various similar programmes

> 1965 *New Statesman*: When he first goes into battle over a wage claim or a price increase—when an incomes policy is first translated into action.

> 1972 *Listener*: The publicly and privately expressed views of the Bank of England that a formal incomes policy of some kind was needed.

indexation *n* (1960) an adjustment in rates of payment in money (e.g. wage-rates, bond prices, etc.) to reflect changes in the value of money by means of an index of such changes

> 1960 *Spectator*: The system of 'indexation' by which wages and prices rose in an officially sponsored spiral.

industry *n* (1965) the profitable exploitation of a particular personage, activity, etc.

> 1966 *Listener*: The Shakespeare industry…is a very old one; I have an eighteenth-century snuffbox made from Shakespeare's mulberry tree.

> 1969 *Daily Telegraph*: The way to tackle 'Ulysses' is to plunge into it headfirst,…which is what we all had to do before the Joyce industry began.

inner city *n* (1968) the central area of a city, especially regarded as having particular problems of overcrowding, poverty, etc. Originally US

> 1968 *Saturday Review* (US): The twin concepts of decentralization and community control of the schools developed in response to the failure of schools in the inner city.

> 1971 *Guardian*: Camden's housing problems have often been in the spotlight for revealing inner-city trends.

instantize *v* (1962) to make (foodstuffs) available in **instant (1912)** form

> 1962 R. J. Clarke: 'Instantized' milks, with lowered bulk density are making their appearance.

in-store *adj* (1961) situated or taking place within a store or large shop

> 1961 *Progressive Grocer*: The in-store advancement training program is given much credit for the success of Safeway Stores in his division.

> 1972 *Police Review*: Investigation of all in-store security.

intelligent *adj* (1969) Of a device or machine: able to vary its behaviour in response to varying situations and requirements and past experience; specifically (especially of a computer terminal), having its own data-processing capability; incorporating a microprocessor

> 1969 C. Machover: Because economical general purpose computers are now available, the 'intelligent' terminal almost always uses such a computer for both a refresh memory and the other functions.

> 1986 *Keyboard Player*: An intelligent masterkeyboard…allows control, via MIDI, of up to eight synthesizers in all registrations.

intensive-care unit (1963) a hospital unit in which a patient is kept under concentrated and special observation

> 1963 *Lancet*: Our medical staff found the medical intensive-care unit so valuable that they requested…a separate surgical intensive-care unit.

interactive *adj* (1967) of or being a computer or other electronic device that allows a two-way flow of information between it and a user, responding immediately to the latter's input.

> 1967 *Institute of Electrical & Electronics Engineers Transactions on Human Factors in Electronics*: Multiple-access, on-line interactive man-computer systems.

> 1981 *Event*: Interactive video, TV screens equipped with computer-linked press-buttons for instant Q&A verdicts on the show—asked in the studio and answered in your own home.

interface *n* (1962) a means or place of interaction between two systems, organizations, etc.; a meeting-point or common ground between two parties, systems, or disciplines. From the earlier (19th-century) scientific sense, 'a surface forming the boundary between two portions of matter or space'. The noun and its associated verb, 'to come into interaction' (first recorded in 1967) have become particular targets for attack by those on the look-out for pretentious jargon

> 1962 Marshall McLuhan: The interface of the Renaissance was the meeting of medieval pluralism and modern homogeneity and mechanism.

> 1968 *Lebende Sprachen*: Before turning to a discussion of how this management system…interfaces with functional organization let us try to define what we mean by project management.

into *prep* (1969) interested or involved in; knowledgeable about. Colloquial; the 'in' preposition of the late 1960s and early 70s, much resorted to by those wanting to sound 'cool'

> 1969 *Rolling Stone*: I tend to like the stuff the rock groups are doing because they're creative and original, and that's something I'm very much into.

> 1969 *Down Beat*: She is a Libra, for those of you who are into that.

> 1971 *New Yorker*: First I was into Zen, then I was into peace, then I was into love, then I was into freedom, then I was into religion. Now I'm into money.

-ism, -ist *suffixes* (1965) Denoting unfair or bigoted discrimination on the stated grounds. The prototype is **racist (1932)**, but it was not until the 1960s that the suffixes began to take on a life of their own. First in the new field was **sexist (1965)**, but soon every anti-bias grouping was jumping on the bandwagon (see also **ageism (1969)**). Another burst of new coinages (often frivolous or debunking) was prompted by the political correctness of the 1980s (see also **speciesism (1975)**, **lookism (1978)**, **ableism (1981)**, **sizeist (1981)**)

> 1992 *Out*: Why must we look like what society dictates is fetching? Because we live in a looks-ist world.

> 1994 *Guardian*: I have the right to challenge sizeism and bodyism alongside racism, sexism and ageism.

> 1998 *Observer*: He also…smashed the 'hatist' bigots who look on men who wear headgear as second-class citizens.

Jacuzzi *n* (1966) The proprietary name of a kind of bath incorporating underwater jets of warm water, and used for both therapeutic and leisure purposes. Originally US; the name is that of the firm which manufactures the bath. The generic *whirlpool bath* dates from the 1950s. See also **spa (1974)**

> 1966 *New Yorker*: Now I will go take my Jacuzzi bath!… You know what it is, a Jacuzzi?… The brochure that comes with it describes it as a hydromassage.

> 1984 *Sunday Telegraph*: You'll still hear 'anyone for tennis?', but you're as likely to hear 'anyone for a jacuzzi?'

jet lag *n* (1969) the delayed effects, especially temporal disorientation, suffered by a person after a long flight on a (jet) aircraft

> 1969 Alexander Cade: The long journey, jet-lag and the heat had given him a headache.

job *n* (1963) an operation involving cosmetic surgery to the specified body part. Originally US

> 1963 Thomas Pynchon: Chapter four. In which Esther gets a nose job.

jock *n* (1963) an athlete. Often applied specifically, originally in US college slang, to a male athlete at university. Short for *jock-strap*; from the wearing of jock-straps by athletes

> 1972 *Time*: Rocks for jocks, elementary geology course popular among athletes at Pennsylvania.

jogger *n* (1968) See **jog (1948)**

journo *n* (1967) a journalist, especially a newspaper journalist. Colloquial, originally Australian

> 1973 *Nation Review* (Melbourne): He will be reinstated at the level of an A grade journo, and *not* as executive producer of *TDT*.

juggernaut *n* (1969) a heavy lorry, especially one regarded as being a hazard to other road users, destructive to the environment, and generally dangerous and undesirable. British. The word was originally the name of a huge wagon on which a statue of the Hindu god Krishna is drawn in procession (it comes from a Hindi word meaning literally 'lord of the world'). It has been applied metaphorically in English to a large or heavy vehicle since at least the mid 19th century. The element of destructiveness in this new usage probably comes from apocryphal stories of devotees of Krishna throwing themselves under the wheels of the original Juggernaut

> 1969 *Evening Star* (Ipswich): Experienced colleagues of mine are concerned about container lorries—the 30-ton juggernauts—which are completely disregarding speed limits.

> 1972 *Oxford Mail*: A plan to banish the juggernaut lorry from many Oxfordshire village roads is being prepared.

jumbo jet *n* (1964) a large jet airliner with a seating capacity of several hundred passengers. The abbreviated *jumbo* is first recorded in 1966. See also **wide-bodied (1970)**

> 1964 *Economist*: Some…airlines do not expect…an American supersonic airliner ever to go into production. Jumbo-jets, with 500 seats and two decks,…look much cheaper to fly.

> 1966 *New Statesman*: The competitors…need only a small handful of jumbos…on the popular long-distance routes.

jump jet *n* (1964) A colloquial term for a vertical take-off jet aircraft, and particularly for the Hawker Harrier, developed in Britain in the late 1950s and early 60s. See also **VTOL (1955)**

> 1970 *New Scientist*: The trials that the RAF and RN are now conducting on the employment at sea of the Harrier 'jump-jet'.

jump-suit *n* (1965) a one-piece woman's outfit with legs, reaching from neck to ankles, and usually made of a close-fitting, stretch fabric. It was modelled on a parachutist's costume, for which the name *jump-suit* was coined in 1948

> 1965 H. Kane: Nora was slender and graceful in a crisp white narrow-legged jump suit.

K (1966) Used to represent 1000. Originally used in technical contexts in computer science (from the prefix *kilo-* 'thousand'), but from around 1970 applied more generally—at first, apparently, in quantifying salaries in job advertisements for computer staff

> 1967 Cox & Grose: It seemed desirable…wherever possible to ignore the limitations of the computer available to us (a KDF 9 with a store size of 16 K 48-bit words).

> 1986 *Daily Telegraph*: Financial administrator, Thames Valley, from £12k.

keyboard *v* (1961) to operate a computer or other keyboard, or to input by this means

> 1969 *Scientific American*: After the encyclopedia…has been keyboarded into the computer.

kink *n* (1965) a sexually deviant person. Also, subsequently, applied more loosely to an eccentric person, someone who wears peculiar clothes, behaves oddly, etc. Colloquial. In this usage probably a back-formation from **kinky (1959)**

> 1965 *Harper's Bazaar*: His phone is ex-directory because of all the kinks who used to phone at 2 a.m.

kinky boot *n* (1964) A half mocking, half joky term for a knee-length boot for women, fashionable in the early 1960s (see **kinky (1959)**)

> 1964 *Annual Register 1963*: It [i.e. 1963] was the year…that women adopted the fashionable long 'kinky' boot.

kir *n* (1966) a drink made from dry white wine and crème de cassis. It enjoyed the spotlight in the 1980s, when fashionable restaurants started serving it as an aperitif, but by the 90s it had become yesterday's drink. The term comes from the name of Canon Felix Kir (1876–1968), mayor of Dijon, who is said to have invented the recipe

> 1966 *Times Literary Supplement*: M. Follain's work should be read with a kir, a benedictine or a calvados.

kiss of life *n* (1961) artificial respiration by means of breathing directly into the victim's mouth. A sensational name which gave a significant boost to this new method (supplanting the old arm-pumping technique). After a decade or two, the more sober *mouth-to-mouth resuscitation* had become the more usual terminology

> 1961 *Daily Mail*: Mrs. Alice Lowe…used the 'kiss-of-life' to save her 19-month-old nephew Geoffrey Ahmed at Oldham yesterday.

> 1969 *Private Eye*: Finding her six years old goldfish 'Bubbles' on the carpet beside its tank, a Nottinghamshire woman gave it the kiss of life.

kiwi fruit *n* (1966) the oval edible fruit of a type of climbing plant, which has fuzzy brown skin and pale green flesh with little black seeds. The imprimatur of nouvelle cuisine chefs, who loved it mainly for its colour, made it one of the most fashionable fruits of the 1970s and 80s. Its original name was **Chinese gooseberry**, but when New Zealand growers tried to export it to the US in the 1960s this was found not to be acceptable for political reasons, so a new name, appropriate to one of New Zealand's most high-profile products, was chosen

> 1970 *New Zealand News*: A storage technique first developed for bananas has been tested on Chinese gooseberries, now renamed 'Kiwi fruit'.

knock-out *adj* (1966) wonderful, excellent. Colloquial

> 1966 *Crescendo*: Chasing a real knockout sound? You'll find the most rewarding instrument…is the Hammond organ.

1968 *Listener*: The wit and repartee of the DJ... 'Hi there— it's great to be with you and welcome to another knock-out show.'

knotted *adj* (1963) Used in the phrase *get knotted* as roughly the equivalent of 'go to hell!'. British slang; a popular dismissive phrase of the 1960s

1964 B. W. Aldiss: Get knotted, Duffield, you ruddy trouble-maker.

kook *n* (1960) See **kooky (1959)**

Kruger rand *n* (1967) a South African gold coin bearing a portrait of President Kruger, issued for investment purposes, to enable purchasers to escape restrictions on the private ownership of gold. Widely bought in the UK in the early 1970s. See also **rand (1961)**

1967 *South African Digest*: The Krugerrand is to be minted in limited numbers and is intended for overseas issue.

1974 *Harpers & Queen*: Keep some Kruger rands under your mattress.

kung-fu *n* (1966) a Chinese martial art resembling karate (which may have developed from it). Its popularity in the West was exploited and furthered by a series of films starring Bruce Lee (1940–73). From Chinese, literally 'merit master'

1966 *Punch*: Kung-fu is here.

1974 *Listener*: The plot...hinges on Lee wiping out an ex-monk, Kung-fu (martial arts) vice chief.

lander *n* (1961) a spacecraft, or a part of one, which is designed to land on the surface of a planet or of the moon

1961 *Astronautica Acta*: The rotary drill...is designed to penetrate 1.5 ft or more into the lunar surface and bring samples into the lander for chemical analysis.

laser *n* (1960) a device that is capable of emitting a very intense, narrow, parallel beam of light. Formed from the initial letters of *light amplification by the stimulated emission of radiation*, on the model of the earlier **maser (1955)**. Originally treated as the name of a particular kind of maser (*optical maser*) emitting visible light, *laser* in due course became the general term for all devices of this kind, whatever the wavelength of the emitted radiation.

1960 *New York Times*: The Hughes device is an optical maser, or 'laser', (the 'l' standing for 'light').

1963 *Monsanto Magazine*: A laser beam can generate intense heat–10,000°F. or higher—in a small area.

lateral thinking *n* (1966) a way of thinking which seeks the solution to intractable problems through unorthodox methods, or elements which would normally be ignored by logical thinking

1966 *London Life*: [Dr. Edward De Bono] divides thinking into two methods. One he calls 'vertical thinking'—that is, using the processes of logic, the traditional-historical method... The other type he calls 'lateral thinking', which involves disrupting an apparent sequence and arriving at the solution from another angle.

laugh-in *n* (1968) a demonstration, event, or situation marked by laughter, often staged for this purpose. Originally US, as the name of a television show

1968 *Listener*: There's a kind of cathartic quality about Danny la Rue that is a tremendous relief after weeks of trying to admire the Rowan and Martin Laugh-In.

LEM, Lem *n* (1962) An acronym formed from the initial letters of *lunar excursion module* (1962), a module designed to take an astronaut from an orbiting spacecraft to the moon's surface and back (see **module (1961)**)

1962 *Listener*: We had a discussion of Project Apollo, the American scheme for getting a man on the Moon. The secondary space-craft for this formidable task has been dubbed a 'lunar excursion module', or Lem for short.

1969 *Guardian*: Armstrong: Going to step off the LEM now... That's one small step for man, one giant leap for mankind.

lib *n* (1969) A colloquial shortening of *liberation* in the sense 'emancipation', a usage which developed in the early 1960s, largely in the context of the struggle of US blacks for civil rights. It was taken up by other groups pressing for new freedoms, and it was these to which the abbreviation *lib* attached itself—first *women's lib*, then others. The somewhat trivializing effect of the short form was a strong factor in the later search for alternative terminology (see **women's liberation (1966)**). See also **libber (1971)**

> 1969 *Time*: 'My twelve-year-old son has been hearing a lot about Women's Lib lately,' says Ruth.

> 1970 *Los Angeles Free Press*: Gay Lib Front meets... The Pope hopes that all Gay organizations— Old line, Gay lib, motorcycle, and social—will join in the demonstration.

> 1970 *New Yorker*: The members of Men's Lib say they are tired of 'having to prove our masculinity twenty-four hours a day'

Librium *n* (1960) The proprietary name (registered in the US in 1960) of a white crystalline compound used as a tranquillizer. Along with **Valium (1961)**, a sedative of the jangled nerves of the 1960s

> 1968 *New Scientist*: Hostile tendencies can often be remarkably controlled by drugs, like Librium and diazepam, which are *not* sedatives, and which do not depress the general level of cerebral activity.

life-style *n* (1961) a way or style of living. Originally a specialized term used by the Austrian psychologist Alfred Adler to denote a person's basic character as established early in childhood which governs their reactions and behaviour, and first recorded in this sense in 1929. The much broader modern sense (particularly as used in the jargon of marketing) betrays, in the eyes of cynics, the late 20th century's obsession with style at the expense of substance

> 1961 *Guardian*: The mass-media...continually tell their audience what life-styles are 'modern' and 'smart'.

> 1973 *Times*: Council of churches want freedom for students to create their own life-styles.

> 1990 *M & M*: Al Fares is the only serious upmarket lifestyle magazine in the Middle East.

> 1995 *Independent*: The latest lifestyle choice for the vibrant elderly is the 'retirement village', an American invention pitched somewhere between Club Med and Brookside.

light show *n* (1966) a display of changing coloured lights or varied film strips, often accompanying pop music. Light shows, with various psychedelic effects, enjoyed a vogue at discos and dances in the late 1960s and early 70s

> 1966 *Berkeley Barb*: Led by Tony Martin's light show, which fills the huge wall behind the bands and their 30 foot row of amplifiers and electronics with red shapes shifting in time to the music, the hall is filled with swaying, writhing people.

lite *adj* (1962) Designating a manufactured product that is lighter, especially in calorie content, than the ordinary variety. Originally US. Often used after the noun in product names. A phonetic respelling of *light*

> 1967 *New York Times*: The leotards match the packaging and labeling of Meister Brau Lite, a no-carbohydrate beer to be introduced this week.

liveware *n* (1966) people, personnel, as distinct from the inanimate or abstract things they work with; specifically, computer personnel. Modelled on **hardware (1940s)** and **software (1960s)**

> 1966 *Times*: The three elements which comprise a working computer system are hardware, the equipment itself; software, the vital programming aids; and the 'liveware', or personnel.

living will *n* (1969) a written request that, if the signatory suffers severe disablement or terminal illness, he or she should not be kept alive by artificial means (e.g. a life-support system). Originally US. Increasingly common as the century progressed, but still controversial at its end

> 1969 *Indiana Law Journal*: The document indicating...consent may be referred to as 'a living will'.

> 1995 *Independent*: The BMA is opposed to legalising living wills, although the Law Commission wants the position tidied up.

loon *v* (1966) Of young people: to spend one's leisure time in a pleasurable way, e.g. by dancing to popular music; to lie about or wander about. Origin unknown. See also **loon pants (1971)**

> 1969 *It*: It's sort of music essentially to loon about to.

lotus position *n* (1962) a bodily position in Yogic exercises which is said to resemble a lotus blossom (which is symbolic in Hindu and Buddhist thought). A translation of Hindi *padmasana*, which had been turned into English as *lotus posture* as long ago as the 1880s. *Lotus position* was the version that caught on during the revival of Western interest in Eastern mystic religions in the 1960s

> 1964 Ian Fleming: Since Bond had arrived in Japan he had assiduously practised sitting in the lotus position.

> 1968 *Guardian*: Sitting in the lotus position…concentrating upon one's navel and repeating the mystic syllable, 'Om, Om'.

love beads *n* (1968) a necklace of coloured beads worn by the hippie generation of the late 1960s and early 70s as a symbol of universal love

> 1973 Berkeley Mather: Weirdo fringed shirts, headbands, love beads…as unsavoury a bunch of love children as I have ever seen.

love-in *n* (1967) a gathering for the purpose of establishing and enjoying love relationships, originally as attended by the flower children of California. See also **-in (1960)**

> 1967 *Times*: The 'love-in' in Elysian Park, Los Angeles, was equally odd but caused no more than a traffic jam.

Mace *n* (1966) The proprietary name (in full *Chemical Mace*) of a chemical preparation used as a disabling weapon by being sprayed at a person's face. Favoured as a riot-control substance in the protest-prone late 1960s. First recorded as a verb, meaning 'to use Mace on', in 1968

> 1967 *New York Times*: The gas is called Mace and it comes in a small black aerosol container like a hair spray can.

> 1973 *Black Panther*: They feel that because they are in power they can call ten or 20 pigs for just one man, mace him, beat him up and call him profane names.

mall *n* (1963) a shopping precinct. Originally US. The word was at first applied to an urban shopping precinct consisting of a central pedestrian area surrounded by shops; in this sense it is a development of the earlier *mall* 'a sheltered walkway serving as a promenade'. The application to a suburban shopping centre followed in the late 1960s

> 1963 *Observer*: The central paved avenue, or 'mall' [in a shopping-centre], wider than any street, with booths in the middle.

Mandrax *n* (1963) A proprietary name for tablets containing methaqualone and diphenhydramine hydrochloride, used as a sedative. See also **mandy (1970)**

> 1972 *Police Review*: He admits taking Mandrax tablets obtained on prescription.

Mao *adj* (1967) Denoting a simple style of clothing based on dress in Communist China (e.g. *Mao cap, collar, jacket, trousers*, etc.), adopted by right-on fashion victims in the West. From the name of Mao Tse-tung (see **Maoism (1951)**)

> 1968 *Punch*: Out, apparently, are Mao caps, Guevara beards, Maharishi gowns and Zapata moustaches.

marketeer *n* (1962) an advocate of the UK's entry into the Common Market. The fuller form *Common Marketeer* is also first recorded in 1962. For much of its later career (before it was succeeded by **Euro-sceptic (1986)**, *Euro-enthusiast*, and the like), *marketeer* was mainly used with either of the prefixes *anti-* or *pro-*

> 1962 *Listener*: The Marketeers within the Labour Party.

> 1969 *Guardian*: The TUC General Council is trying to avoid an embarrassing public debate on the Common Market… Pro- and anti-Marketeers united in angry condemnation of Mr. Jenkins's attempts to force the issue on to the agenda.

maxi- *prefix* (1961) denoting things, especially articles of clothing, which are very long or large of their kind. From *maximum*. The *maxiskirt* appeared in the mid 1960s in reaction to the **miniskirt (1965)**, and was followed by the *maxidress* and *maxicoat*, intensely fashionable in the late 60s and early 70s

> 1966 *Times Educational Supplement*: There will be Lady X in Rutland realizing with a gasp of horror that she is wearing the same maxi-skirt as Lady Y.

> 1970 Robert Lowell: The girl's maxi-coat, Tsar officer's, dragged the snow.

medevac, medivac *n* (1966) a military helicopter for transporting wounded soldiers to hospital. US. A blend of *medical* and *evac(uation)*, familiarized by the Vietnam war. First recorded as a verb in 1968

> 1967 *Harper's Magazine*: The two wounded Aid Men continued to crawl about and administer care. There would be no medevac; there was no landing zone for it.

> 1969 *Time*: At My Lai, Ridenhour reported, one soldier shot himself in the foot so that he would be Medevacked out of the area.

Medicare *n* (1962) The name given in the US and Canada to a scheme of health insurance for the elderly. Such a scheme had been under discussion in the US since 1947, when it was first proposed by President Truman, but it was not set up there until 1965

> 1971 *Optometry Today*: At present, optometrists…cannot provide optometric services to American senior citizens under the Medicare program.

meltdown *n* (1965) the melting of a nuclear reactor's fuel rods as a result of a defect in the cooling system, with the possible escape of radiation into the environment. Also used metaphorically since the early 1980s for any disastrous collapse, especially a sudden rapid drop in the value of a particular currency or of assets, shares, etc.

> 1965 *New Scientist*: Overheated fuel may result in 'meltdown' and general contamination of the reactor system.

> 1992 *Financial Times*: Talk of a meltdown in Japan plunging Wall Street into crisis and the US economy back into recession.

menu *n* (1967) a computer-generated list of options, usually displayed on a screen, any of which can be conveniently selected and entered into the computer

> 1982 *Which Computer?*: The operator can re-configure the operating parameters. This is done by a yes/no key located on the enclosure and a menu printed out on paper.

Mersey beat *n* (1963) the kind of pop music associated with the British group 'the Beatles', and with other Liverpool-based groups (e.g. Gerry and the Pacemakers). From the *Mersey*, the river that flows through Liverpool, where the Beatles came from. The similarly inspired *Mersey sound* is first recorded in 1965

> 1963 *Meet the Beatles*: The Beatles, undoubted monarchs of the Mersey Beat scene.

> 1965 S. Jepson: The Mersey sound banged and twanged into the night.

metric *n* (1969) metric measurement; metric weights and measures collectively. A fairly ephemeral British usage called into being by **metrication (1965)**

> 1969 *Times*: Metric is so much easier to teach and to learn.

metrication, metrification *n* (1965) the process of converting to the metric system of weights and measures; the adoption of the metric system. *Metrication* was a new coinage, *metrification* a re-use of an existing technical term in prosody, denoting the construction of a metrical composition. The associated verb, *metricate*, is also first recorded in 1965. The alternative *metricize*, which dates back to the 1880s, seems not to have found much favour in the 1960s

> 1965 *Times*: The N.P.L. [National Physical Laboratory] and the Ministry of Technology chose 'metrication' on the grounds of brevity and euphony.

> 1965 *Observer*: If of old measures we're forsakers…How describe it? There are cries For Metrification, Metricize.

micro *n* (1968) An abbreviation of *microskirt* (1966)

> 1968 *New York Times*: Hemlines go to all lengths. In extremes, there are micros, which barely cover the buttocks; minis, maxis and the nineteen-thirties length.

microelectronic *adj* (1960) of, using, or containing **microcircuits (1959)**

> 1960 *Proceedings of the Western Joint Computer Conference*: Microelectronic data processing systems are analyzed.

microwave oven *n* (1965) an oven in which food is cooked by passing microwaves through it, the resulting generation of heat inside the food making rapid and uniform cooking possible. Not widely used until the 1970s, when the vocabulary expanded (e.g. *microwave oven* was shortened to simply **microwave**, which was also used as a verb, 'to cook with microwaves'). The synonymous *micro-oven* is recorded earlier ('A cooked meal that is quick-frozen and then re-heated in a matter of seconds in a micro-oven', *Punch* (1962)), but it never really caught on

> 1965 *Economist*: Microwave ovens. A meal a minute.

> 1968 *New Scientist*: The microwave oven…is now coming into quite wide use in homes in the United States.

> 1976 *Bon Appétit*: If you have a family that eats in relays, you'll find the microwave ideal.

> 1976 *National Observer* (US): I…microwaved them two at a time for one minute.

midi *n* (1969) a skirt, dress, etc. of mid-calf length. An abbreviation of terms such as *midi-skirt* and *midi-coat*, which are first recorded in 1967

> 1969 *International Herald Tribune*: Almost every designer is nervously groping for the right length; it's touch and go whether the average woman will go for the maxis and midis.

midlife crisis *n* (1965) an emotional crisis occurring in midlife, characterized by the feeling that one is growing old or that life is 'passing one by'

> 1965 E. Jaques: Less familiar perhaps, though nonetheless real, are the crises which occur around the age of 35—which I shall term the mid-life crisis—and at full maturity around the age of 65.

mind-blowing *adj* (1967) breath-takingly astonishing or astounding. Colloquial, originally US; an adjectivization of the expression *blow someone's mind* (see **blow (1965)**)

> 1967 *Jazz Monthly*: While the music lasted little of this was evident; the spectacular mind-blowing ferocity of it all simply carried the group through.

> 1974 Helen McCloy: A mind-blowing mustard yellow for the woodwork and on the walls a psyche-delic splash of magenta and orchid and lime.

mind-expanding *adj* (1963) Of a drug: causing a sensation of heightened consciousness; psyche-delic

> 1963 *News-Call Bulletin* (San Francisco): Professors Richard Alpert and Timothy Leary…started several years ago to experiment with 'psychedelic' or 'mind-expanding' drugs.

> 1967 *Times*: The term flower children has been given to devotees of mind-expanding drugs in California.

mini *n* (1961) An abbreviation of *minicar*, a term used in the 1940s as a name of a type of three-wheeled car made by the British firm Bond. *Mini* itself was first used in 1959 as part of the proprietary name, *Mini-Minor*, of a small car manufactured originally by the British Motor Corporation. By 1961 this had been shortened to *Mini*

> 1961 *Engineering*: The Mini's astonishing success is due purely and simply to good engineering.

mini *adj* (1963) very small, tiny. Colloquial. Either an abbreviation of *miniature* or an adjectival use of the prefix **mini- (1934)**, and probably inspired by the noun **mini**

> 1963 *Daily Telegraph*: A 'mini' census covering one householder in ten will be taken by the Government in 1966.

> 1966 *Daily Telegraph*: M. Redlus insists: 'My minis will be the most mini in Europe but they'll be decent.'

> 1966 *Punch*: Leg make-up…gives sitting-down confidence to the wearer of the miniest skirt.

> 1967 *New Scientist*: The current preoccupation with 'mini-ness' has now extended into the realm of…microbiology.

mini *n* (1966) An abbreviation of **miniskirt (1965)**

> 1966 *Guardian*: The new thing about the Scherrer mini is that it flares.

mini-budget *n* (1966) a budget of limited scope coming between the main annual budgets

> 1966 *Times Review of Industry*: With the 'mini-budget' having withdrawn another £500m. from internal demand.

minicab *n* (1960) a car like a taxi but available only if ordered in advance

> 1960 *Economist*: Current regulations regarding London taxis would not allow the introduction of what Mr. Dennis Vosper, speaking for the Home Office, called 'minicabs'.

minidress *n* (1965) a dress with a miniskirt

> 1965 *Christian Science Monitor*: The fashion pages of British papers sport mini-dresses.

minimal *adj* (1965) A term used in the arts to denote an approach characterized by the elimination of elaboration: applied specifically, in the 1960s, to abstract painting and sculpture eschewing expressiveness and using simple geometric shapes, and in the 1970s to music based on simple elements, often repeated several times with minute variations. The related *minimalism* and *minimalist* are first recorded in the late 1960s

> 1965 R. Wollheim: Such a gesture…would provide us with an extreme instance of what I call minimal art.

> 1969 *Manchester Guardian Weekly*: Tony Smith, usually taken as the original minimalist sculptor…is well represented by large sculptures.

> 1974 Michael Nyman: As in the American minimal music so all the workings of the process are easy to follow audibly.

> 1985 *Radio Times*: In the 1960s [Steve Reich] began exploring the musical effects of repeated musical patterns that incorporate gradual changes over an extended period. The style came to be called minimalism.

miniskirt *n* (1965) a very short skirt. The archetypal 1960s garment, symbolizing at once the exuberance of the baby-boom teenagers and the sexual permissiveness with which the decade has become associated. The French fashion designer André Courrèges is credited with its invention

> 1965 *Economist*: The Fashion House Group of London dumbfounded the…audience of American buyers quite as much by the sight of the British aggressively selling as by their mini-skirts and kooky outfits.

> 1972 Francis Warner: Pretty, miniskirted, and attractive young lady.

Minuteman *n* (1961) a type of US intercontinental ballistic missile. Named after the *minutemen*, militiamen at the time of the American revolution who were supposedly ready for service at a minute's notice

> 1961 *Daily Telegraph*: The American Air Force achieved a spectacular advance today when it launched the first Minuteman missile.

miss *n* (1965) an unsuccessful gramophone record. A usage popularized by the BBC TV programme *Jukebox Jury*, in which a panel adjudicated on the commercial prospects of new pop records

> 1965 *Listener*: Persons invited to give their verdict…are not being asked to say whether the songs are good or bad but merely whether they will be 'hits' or 'misses'.

missionary position *n* (1969) a position for sexual intercourse in which the woman lies underneath the man and facing him. So called because allegedly Christian missionaries forced it on 'primitive' peoples who hitherto had been getting on perfectly well with a range of other positions

> 1969 *Daily Telegraph*: In six States [in the US] a woman may still be awarded a divorce if her husband makes love to her in any other than the missionary position.

mobile phone *n* (1965) a telephone that can operate without being physically linked to a telephone line. In early usage the term was applied to radio-telephones installed in cars. It was not until the late 1970s, when it started to be used for the new cellular telephones (see **cellular (1977)**), that it really began to take off. In the 1980s the *mobile* (the shortened form is first recorded in 1990) became a symbol of success, a yuppie accessory. By the 1990s it was ubiquitous, and a severe source of irritation in trains, restaurants, and other public places subjected to its warble and the one-sided conversation of its user. At the end of the century there were over 10 million mobile phones in Britain alone

> 1965 *Newsweek*: There is a pocket of mobile phone owners in New York…but the fad hasn't yet caught on in other cities, where car phones are generally for professional purposes.

> 1992 Iain Banks: Rather than phone from the airport, Lewis had hired a mobile along with the car but then when they'd tried to use it, it hadn't worked.

mod *n* (1960) a member of a group of young people noted for their sophistication, clothes-consciousness, and tidiness and for their antipathy to **rockers (1963)**. An abbreviation of *modern* or *modernist*. The early 1960s in Britain saw numerous violent clashes between mods and rockers, particularly at seaside towns on bank holidays

> 1960 *New Left Review*: Teds and Mods, Beatniks and Ravers.

> 1963 *Guardian*: Fights between the 'mods' and the 'rockers'.

> 1964 *Observer*: Mods and Rockers have co-existed comparatively well for a year or so—the Mods, neatly dressed and on scooters, the Rockers in studded leather jackets and on motor-bikes.

model *n* (1963) a prostitute. Euphemistic

> 1963 *Observer*: 'Company director' and 'model' are useful euphemisms for those who appear in dubious court cases.

> 1968 Joan Lock: There had been an increase of newsagents' notice-board ads for 'Models'.

model *v* (1965) to devise a mathematical model of (a phenomenon, system, etc.)

> 1965 C. H. Springer: We 'modeled' a business process with the aid of a ready-made algebraic model.

module *n* (1961) a separable section of a spacecraft that can operate as an independent unit. From the earlier, more general sense, 'a separable part of a whole'. See also **LEM (1962)**

> 1961 *New Scientist*: To deal with its dual function the Apollo craft will have three separate sections, or modules: first, a command centre module…; secondly, a propulsion module…; and finally, a so-called 'mission' module.

module *n* (1966) a unit or period of training or education. The related adjective *modular* is first recorded in 1968

> 1966 *Economist*: Eventually the sort of retraining envisaged could fit in with the notion…of periodic training 'modules', whereby skilled men would take repeated periods off productive work to renew their perhaps rusty skills and learn new ones.

> 1972 *Timber Trades Journal*: The courses would be modular, so that a company could send people in to be trained in any particular aspect.

Mohican *adj* (1960) Of a hairstyle: resembling that worn by the Mohican peoples of North America, in which the head is shaved except for a strip of hair from the middle of the forehead to the back of the neck. In the 1970s applied more specifically to a punk style in which the strip is worn stiffly erect and often brightly coloured

> 1960 *Guardian*: A Lowestoft boy…had a 'Mohican' haircut on Saturday and then went back to the barber to have the remaining strip of hair cut.

monetarist *n* (1963) someone who advocates tighter control of the money supply as an important remedy for inflation. The word was originally coined as an adjective around 1914, with the general sense 'having a monetary basis'. The noun *monetarism*, denoting the theory or policies of monetarists, is first recorded in 1969. The theory became fashionable in the 1970s and conventional wisdom in the 80s (when it was implemented by a number of Western governments). One of its main proponents was the US economist Milton Friedman

> 1963 *Economist*: To control inflation by curtailment, as prescribed by the 'monetarists'.

> 1969 *Newsweek*: The combination of Stansian horse-and-buggy finance with Friedmanian go-go monetarism.

monokini *n* (1964) a one-piece beach garment, usually one equivalent to the lower half of a bikini and worn by women. Based on **bikini**, as if the *bi-* meant 'two'

> 1964 *Daily Mirror* (Brisbane): Monokinis are selling in Paris like iceboxes in Alaska.

Montezuma's revenge *n* (1962) diarrhœa suffered by visitors to Mexico. Humorous. From the name of Montezuma II (1466–1520), Aztec ruler at the time of the Spanish conquest of Mexico

> 1970 *Times*: England's World Cup football squad suffered their first casualty in Mexico on Wednesday, when 20-year-old Brian Kidd was struck down by what is known as 'Montezuma's Revenge'.

Moog synthesizer *n* (1969) an electronic musical instrument that produces a wide variety of sounds. Named after R. A. Moog, an American engineer who invented it

> 1969 *Punch*: A moog synthesiser…is an electronic musical instrument capable of generating all kinds of weird sounds.

moon *v* (1968) to expose one's buttocks in public, in order to shock anyone who happens to be looking. Originally US students' slang. Probably from the idea of pale circularity

> 1974 *News & Reporter* (Chester, S. Carolina): The convention…was to last through Saturday afternoon, and we imagine that it did although we did hear a wild rumor that a cut-up named Fannie might pull her own version of 'the streak' during the Sunday breakfast…just to get the Sunday session off to a good start if the session started getting dull. But, Fannie has assured us that she didn't 'moon' anybody.

moon walk *n* (1966) a walk on the surface of the moon. See also **moonwalking (1980)**

> 1969 *Observer*: Hints that the 'moonwalk' will also be brought forward were strengthened when the astronauts' physician, Dr Charles Berry, said that he did not now expect the two men to go to sleep on the moon.

mountain *n* (1969) a stockpile, a surplus. Applied particularly to an undesirably large surplus of a particular agricultural product within the European Union, the blame for which is standardly placed on the Common Agricultural Policy. Compare **lake (1974)**

> 1969 *Times*: In Germany…they are beginning to resent [the price for protection], as the sardonic remarks in the supermarkets about the 'Butter Mountain' reveal.

> 1974 *Times*: Measures designed to disperse the Community's growing beef surpluses. The beef mountain now stands at more than 70,000 tons.

mouse *n* (1965) a small hand-held device which is moved over a flat surface to produce a corresponding movement of a cursor or arrow on a computer's VDU, and which usually has fingertip controls for selecting a function or entering a command. From its shape, and particularly its lead, which resembles a mouse's tail

> 1965 English & Engelhardt: Within comfortable reach of the user's right hand is a device called the 'mouse' which we developed for evaluation…as a means for selecting those displayed text entities upon which the commands are to operate.

multi-media *adj, n* (1962) of or being a form of artistic, educational, or commercial communication in which more than one medium is used. By the 1970s being used as a noun, denoting such combined use. See also **multi-media (1981)**

> 1962 *Times*: The first prong is a multi-media publicity campaign to encourage school children…to obtain adequate educational qualifications.

> 1971 *Black Scholar*: As originator of the practice of reading poetry to jazz, he not only stitched backwards and forward in his lineage and idiom, but wrought a new force in the now obscenely exaggerated concept of multi-media.

naff *adj* (1969) unfashionable, outmoded, or vulgar; unselfconsciously lacking style, socially inept; worthless, rubbishy. Slang, mainly British. Origin unknown; compare northern English dialect *naffhead, naffin, naffy* 'an idiot'; *niffy-naffy* 'stupid'; Scottish *nyaff* 'an unpleasant person'

> 1969 *It*: A lot of these bands are pretty naff anyway.

> 1983 *Sunday Times*: It is naff to call your house The Gables, Mon Repos, or Dunroamin'.

naked ape *n* (1967) a human being, especially as viewed from a zoological point of view, as a creature with physical and mental characteristics that can be compared with those of other animals. The term comes from the title of a 1967 book by Desmond Morris

> 1967 *Spectator*: Even before man has destroyed all other animals to make more room for himself, the naked ape may well destroy himself also.

Nam, 'Nam *n* (1969) A colloquial abbreviation of *Vietnam*, widely familiar once the Vietnam war had been under way for a few years

> 1969 *Time*: 'Nam' or 'The Nam' is widely used by U.S. troops to refer to Vietnam.

name of the game *n* (1966) the object or essence of an action, etc. Colloquial

> 1966 *Legionary* (Ottawa): Where the knight's concerned, quality is the name of the game.

nana *n* (1965) a fool. Slang, originally Australian but popular with British speakers in the 1960s. Perhaps from *banana*

> 1967 Charles Drummond: It seems if you have a bit of cash it snowballs unless you are a proper 'nana.

nanny state *n* (1965) government institutions and practices of the Welfare State collectively, perceived as being overprotective, interfering, or excessively authoritarian, and as stifling initiative. A term first recorded in a *Spectator* article by the Conservative politician Iain Macleod, it came into its own in the 1980s, when one of the Thatcher government's main obsessions was rolling back the nanny state

> 1965 Iain Macleod: The London County Council is dying, but the spirit of the Nanny State fights on.

> 1983 *Washington Post*: The British, we are incessantly told, have now rejected the 'nanny state' and regard the social worker as a boring pest.

National Front *n* (1967) a political group in Britain with extreme right-wing or fascistic views. In the early 1980s its place in the political spectrum was taken over by the British National Party

> 1967 *Spearhead*: On October 7th there took place…an event which may well prove to have historic significance in British politics. This was the first Annual General Meeting of Britain's new party, The National Front.

> c1970 *Facts: National Front*: When the National Front comes to power it will know well how to deal with the murderer and the thug.

Neddy *n* (1962) A colloquial name for the National Economic Development Council, a body formed in the UK for government-management-union consultation on economic development

> 1962 *Engineering*: Since poor Neddy was formed everyone seems to be jumping on to his band wagon.

neo-colonialism *n* (1961) the acquisition or retention of influence over other countries, especially one's former colonies, often by economic or political measures. A favourite accusation-word with which to beat the rich countries of the West in the 1960s and 70s

> 1972 *Scientific American*: Strong elements of neocolonialism persist in the economic relations of the rich and poor countries.

neutron bomb *n* (1960) a bomb that would produce large numbers of neutrons but little blast, and would consequently be harmful to life but not destructive of property. A particularly obnoxious form of nuclear weapon, the prospect of which appealed to many strategists on both sides of the Cold War in the late 1950s and early 60s

> 1960 *Congressional Record*: Although there have been a few fragmentary references to the neutron bomb in the press, I was told…that the matter was classified.

new penny *n* (1966) a penny in the new decimal currency introduced in Britain in 1971, worth one hundredth of a pound. So called initially to distinguish it from the penny in the previous system, of which there were 240 to the pound. By the end of the 1970s the newness had worn off, and people had reverted to simply *penny* (or *pee*—see **pee (1971)**)

> 1966 *New Statesman*: The government has opted for a pound divided into 100 'new pennies'.

> 1971 James Fraser: Game bird soup at twenty new pence a helping.

news management *n* (1969) manipulation of the news media, especially by public relations or press office. A black art further elaborated by politicians and their minions later in the century (**see spin (1978)**)

> 1969 *New Yorker*: Mollentroff specialized in exposés of wrongdoing…he carried on a one-man crusade against government interference with the press, and pursued it with such zeal that, while he may not have coined the phrase 'news management', his name is associated with it in the minds of most people here.

> 1993 *Daily Telegraph*: It is less clear whether the Princess chose or was persuaded by friends and advisers to move from passive acquiescence in sympathetic media coverage to a strategy bordering on active news management of coverage of her marital collapse.

new technology *n* (1964) (a) technology that radically alters the way something is produced or performed, often involving computers

> 1964 Marshall McLuhan: The ability of the artist to sidestep the bully blow of new technology…is age-old.

> 1966 J. G. Burke: This interaction between basic science—that is, pure research—and applied science…is what I have termed the new technology.

new wave *n* (1960) a new movement or trend, especially in the arts. A translation of French *nouvelle vague* (1950s). See also **New Wave (1976)**

> 1960 *News Chronicle*: A 'new wave' is emerging here [in Spain], too, with an up-to-date philosophy.

nitty-gritty *n* (1963) the realities or basic facts or details of a problem, situation, subject, etc.; the heart of the matter. Slang, originally US; probably a rhyming form based on *grit* in various senses

> 1963 *Wall Street Journal*: Says W. C. Patton, field secretary for…the National Association for the Advancement of Colored People. 'Now we're down to the nitty-gritty, the hard core who've never been interested in politics.'

no-cal *adj* (1969) Of a food substance or diet: free from, or very low in, calories. An abbreviation of *no-calory*, which is first recorded in 1961

> 1969 *Guardian*: Young mothers…whose entire diet consists of cottage cheese, yogurt, and gallons of 'no-cal' pop.

nominal *adj* (1966) within prescribed limits; normal. The usage originated in and is mainly confined to the aerospace field

> 1972 *Daily Colonist* (Victoria, British Columbia): As one engineer said, 'She is phenomenally nominal'—nominal being space jargon for operating-as-planned.

non-aligned *adj* (1960) Of a country, government, etc.: pursuing a policy of **non-alignment (1955)**. See also **unaligned (1961)**

> 1960 *New Left Review*: The non-aligned powers have grown in strength.

> 1973 *Caribbean Contact*: The need…for the Non-Aligned world to probe beyond the detente between the big powers.

non-event *n* (1962) an unimportant or unexciting event, especially one which was expected or intended to be important

> 1963 Ian Gilmour: Drugged by their normal diet of non-news stories and non-events, the newspapers tend to lose their heads when…faced with…a news story.

non-proliferation *n* (1965) the prevention of an increase in the number of countries possessing nuclear weapons. Often used before another noun

> 1965 *Newsweek*: The price for a Russian agreement on a non-proliferation pact.

no problem (1963) Used as a polite disclaimer to an (explicit or implicit) suggestion that one has been troubled. Originally US

> 1973 Martin Amis: Finally, every time I emptied my glass, he took it, put more whisky in it, and gave it back to me, saying 'No problem' again through his nose.

notice *v* (1961) to be noticeable. A usage in which the passive sense of the transitive verb is presented intransitively, partially on the model of *show*. It persisted to the end of the century without ever threatening to be accepted into Standard English, but also without becoming a purists' *cause célèbre*

> 1961 Y. Olsson: I have mended the hole now. I don't think it notices.

no way *adv* (1968) it is impossible, it can't be done; no. Colloquial, originally US college slang

> 1970 J. G. Vermandel: 'No way I can do it any faster than that'… But Peter Angel was shaking his head. 'No way, sorry.'

> 1975 *New Yorker*: He said he wouldn't start up a gang today—no way.

no-win *adj* (1962) Of a contest or struggle: that cannot be won. Later in the century US English created the antonym *win-win*

1973 *Daily Colonist* (Victoria, British Columbia): So the trail of broken fixes has put Nixon in a no-win position.

nuke *v* (1962) to attack or destroy with nuclear weapons. Originally US military slang. From the noun **nuke** 'a nuclear weapon' (1959)

1967 *Look*: I remember in Saigon how disturbed General Westmoreland was after talking to a group of American editors…who told him they favored 'nuking' (A-bombing) China.

number-cruncher (1966) a machine with the capacity for performing arithmetical operations of great complexity or length. Colloquial. The derivative *number-crunching* is first recorded in 1971

1966 *New Scientist*: The Flowers report recommended the setting up of some 'regional centres' each with a large 'number-cruncher' to take the bulk-computing load off more local machines.

1971 *Scientific American*: Here's a calculator that speaks your language. You can customize its keyboard, memory size, display, programs and peripherals to suit your number-crunching tasks.

OD *n, v* (1960) A slang abbreviation of *overdose* (of a narcotic drug). The noun is first recorded in 1960, the verb in 1969

1970 S. O'Callaghan: Diana has O.D.'d and she's dead.

1971 *Black World*: A truly brilliant Black filmmaker goes into his grave at 24…an O.D. takes him, he loses a battle of several years—the 'stuff' wins.

offshore fund *n* (1969) an investment fund operating as a unit trust which is registered overseas

1983 *Financial Times*: A government consultative document on proposals to clamp down on international tax avoidance failed to mention offshore roll-up funds.

oil sheikh *n* (1960) the ruler of a Middle Eastern oil-exporting country. A generally resentful usage which achieved its highest profile during the fuel crisis of the mid 1970s, when Arab states placed severe restrictions on oil exports

1974 *Times*: The oil shaikhs put paid to that as club after club buckled before the fuel crisis.

one-parent family *n* (1969) An alternative formulation to *single-parent family* (see **single (1969)**)

1969 *Times*: A committee to consider the problems of one-parent families in society.

on stream *adv, adj* (1965) in or into active use. From the earlier technical sense, 'in or into production', which had been in use since the 1930s (originally in the oil industry)

1972 *Times*: London had become enormously attractive to young people all over the world…because 'le mini', Carnaby Street and the swinging set had come on stream all at more or less the same time.

op art *n* (1964) a form of abstract art and visual decoration in which optical effects are used to provide illusions of movement in the patterns produced. Originally US. A shortening of *optical art*, a term first recorded in the same year which soon became secondary to its abbreviated form

1964 *Time*: No less a break from abstract expressionism than pop art, op art is made tantalizing, eye-teasing, even eye-smarting by visual researchers using all the ingredients of an optometrist's nightmare.

orchestrate *v* (1969) to arrange or organize so as to achieve a desired effect. A favourite late-20th-century metaphor (based on the literal 'to arrange (music) for orchestral performance'), teetering on the edge of being a cliché

1969 *Daily Telegraph*: Russia and America yesterday ratified the treaty banning the spread of nuclear weapons. They chose the same day by a diplomatic agreement typical of the way the two super-Powers are 'orchestrating' their moves in this front.

1977 *Time*: Owen helped to orchestrate the European Community's fishing agreement with the Soviet Union.

Oreo *n* (1968) A derogatory term for an American black who is seen, especially by other blacks, as part of the white establishment. US slang. From the proprietary name of a type of biscuit made of two chocolate wafers with a white filling between

1969 *Harper's Magazine*: Trouble is Negroes been programmed by white folks to believe their products are inferior. We've developed into a generation of Oreos—black on the outside, white on the inside.

Ostpolitik *n* (1961) German policy towards Eastern Europe, associated mainly with the Federal Republic of Germany's cultivation of good relations with the German Democratic Republic and the rest of the Communist bloc during the 1960s, but applied also, by extension, to the policies of other western countries regarding the East as a whole. From German, formed from *Ost* 'east' and *Politik* 'policy'

> 1967 *Economist*: Herr Kiesinger…promised that the government would not pursue its Ostpolitik 'behind the backs of the expellees'.

oven-ready *adj* (1960) Of poultry: having been plucked and had its neck, legs, and entrails removed before sale. A term born largely of the new mass market in poultry brought about by factory farming (see **factory farming (1964)**)

> 1960 *Farmer & Stockbreeder*: A new firm…has been formed with the aim of becoming one of the largest producers of oven-ready turkeys and ducklings in the country.

over-exposure *n* (1969) an excessive number of public appearances by an entertainer, actor, or the like. The related adjective *over-exposed* in this sense is first recorded in 1971

> 1971 *Guardian*: Future plans? A repeat of the 'Basil Brush Show' on the BBC, but careful avoidance of overexposure.

> 1971 *Radio Times*: They hope that by not being over-exposed they'll be able to last longer, keep their standard higher.

pager *n* (1968) a radio device that emits a sound when activated by a telephone call, used to contact a person carrying it. From *page* 'to have a person called by a page', which is first recorded in 1904

> 1968 *Guardian*: There are already…in this country devices called radio pagers. You carry in your pocket the pager, which is linked by radio connection to your telephone. When the telephone rings, the pager blips, and you can answer the call by speaking into the pager. As things stand the pager is illegal.

Paki *n* (1964) a Pakistani, specifically an immigrant from Pakistan. Usually taken to be offensive. It did not take long after the first significant immigration from Pakistan started in the 1950s for the term to take a hold in British English. The expression *Paki-bashing*, denoting assault on Pakistani immigrants, is first recorded in 1970

> 1964 *Guardian*: Some big Paki over the water's got her set up for right trouble.

> 1970 *Observer*: The name of the game is Pakky Bashing… Any Asian careless enough to be walking the streets at night is a fool.

panda car, panda *n* (1966) a British police patrol car, so named from the resemblance of a broad white stripe on the car to the markings of the giant panda. British colloquial

> 1970 *Times*: Five children, who…helped catch two thieves, are to be given a ride in a police panda car.

panda crossing *n* (1962) a pedestrian road crossing in the UK with chevron-shaped road markings, operated by traffic lights. From the resemblance to the panda's black-and-white markings

> 1962 *Times*: Panda crossings, introduced yesterday, held up Croydon's evening traffic.

pantyhose *n* (1963) a women's undergarment combining panties with stockings; tights. Originally US. The death-knell of the stocking (see **tights (1965)**)

> 1963 *New York Times*: Our exclusive panti-hose… She'll enjoy the comfort and freedom of…panty tops and micromesh stockings, all in one. No garters, no seams.

paparazzo *n* (1968) a free-lance photographer who pursues celebrities to take their pictures. From Italian *paparazzo*, which probably came from French *paperassier* 'scribbler'. Mainly used in the plural form *paparazzi*

> 1977 *Maclean's Magazine*: If Margaret was troubled by the publicity or the paparazzi that followed her during her New York stay, she certainly didn't show it.

pass book *n* (1961) In South Africa and Rhodesia, a document issued to non-white residents, authorizing and regulating their movement and residence in particular areas. Also known as a *reference book*. Pass laws were repealed in South Africa in 1986

> 1961 T. Matshikiza: The sergeant…thumbed querulously through each ninety-six paged pass book.

peace dividend *n* (1968) a (financial) benefit from reduced defence spending; a sum of public money which may become available for other purposes when spending on defence is reduced. Originally US. The first supposed provider of such largesse was the ending of the Vietnam War. In practice such hopes proved illusory, and the term vanished from the scene until the late 1980s. The ending of the Cold War saw its revival—a temporary one, since once again governments seemed to find ways of spending just as much on weapons as before

> 1968 *Fortune*: In Washington, the magic phrase is 'the Peace Dividend'... The fact is that peace dividends will neither materialize so quickly nor amount to so much money as many people think.

> 1995 *Economist*: When the Soviet Union began to collapse in 1990, many people predicted a huge and long-awaited 'peace-dividend'.

peacenik *n* (1965) a member of a pacifist movement, especially when regarded as a 'hippy'. Often applied specifically to an opponent of the military intervention of the US in Vietnam

> 1965 *San Francisco Examiner*: Dean Plapowski...described himself as a 'peacenik'. This, he explained, 'is probably a beatnik who's got himself hung up in pacifist and non-violent activity'.

pedestrianize *v* (1963) to make accessible only to pedestrians; to make into a **pedestrian precinct (1953)**

> 1963 *Observer*: [Professor Buchanan] even suggested that some of these central streets...should be closed to traffic and, in the jargon, pedestrianised.

pelican crossing *n* (1966) a British pedestrian-crossing controlled by push-buttons. *Pelican* was coined from 'pedestrian light controlled'

> 1976 *Flintshire Leader*: Residents of Oakenholt are ready to block the main road through the village in their campaign for a pelican crossing.

penetrate *v* (1962) to infiltrate (an organization, especially an enemy espionage network) as a spy

> 1962 Len Deighton: He organized a train-wrecking group until it was penetrated and the survivors fled.

peripheral *n* (1966) a piece of equipment that is used in conjunction with a computer without being an integral or necessary part of it. Usually used in the plural

> 1966 *Economist*: It just has not got the sort of money needed to develop and market a complete line of data processing equipment and the associated 'peripherals'.

permanentize *v* (1961) to make permanent

> 1961 *Guardian*: The latest word to be added to Pentagonese...is 'permanentise'.

permissive society *n* (1968) a society in which sexual freedom is tolerated. A hostile label attached to Western society of the 1960s and 70s, particularly by those who found that there was altogether too much sex going on. See **permissive (1956)**

> 1968 *Listener*: This dreadful dilemma of the puritan in a permissive society.

> 1970 Germaine Greer: The permissive society has done much to neutralize sexual drives by containing them.

phone-in *n* (1968) a live radio or television programme during which listeners telephone the studios to ask questions or express their views. Originally US. First used in 1967 in the sense 'a protest in the form of mass telephone calls of complaint', but this usage did not survive long

> 1968 *Time*: He proposed reducing transit fares for San Franciscans over 65 to 5¢, on a subsequent TV 'phone-in', said he would try to get buses closer to the curb at pickup.

> 1971 *Listener*: One of the most exciting potentials this year has been the phone-in.

Picturephone *n* (1964) A US proprietary name (registered in 1966) for a **videophone (1955)**

> 1964 *New York Times*: The Picturephone was demonstrated yesterday with a see-as-you-talk call between the World's Fair and Anaheim, Calif.

pinger *n* (1968) a timer that makes a ringing or pinging sound after a pre-set number of minutes. Often applied specifically to such a timer attached to an oven, and latterly a microwave oven. From the earlier technical sense, 'a device which transmits regular short bursts of sound' (1950s)

> 1968 J. Bingham: I heard the old vibrant tinkling, like those kitchen ping-ers which tell you when the cabbage is ready cooked.

Pinteresque *adj* (1960) (characteristic) of the British playwright Harold Pinter (b. 1930) or his works, which are famous particularly for their elusive, pause-filled dialogue and an atmosphere of menace

> 1960 *Times*: Mr Adrian writes with a cruel mastery of our slipshod, contemporary idioms, and the long drunken coda to his play is a comic achievement none the less impressive for its Pinteresque overtones.

> 1974 *Listener*: Suddenly everyone…talked like overheard conversations on buses. They invented a word for it—Pinteresque.

pixel *n* (1969) any of the minute areas of uniform illumination of which a television image is composed. From **pix** (plural of *pic* 'picture') + *element*

> 1969 *Science*: An analog tape recorder was used to store the analog video signal from each pixel.

plonker *n* (1966) a fool. British slang. Probably from an earlier sense 'penis', but the origins of this are not recorded. Popularized by its frequent use in the BBC television series *Only Fools and Horses* (first broadcast in 1981)

> 1966 J. Gaskell: If she'd been my daughter in fact I'd never have let her go out with an obvious plonker like myself.

> 1988 *Smash Hits*: I look at a dress and think because it's fashionable it'll look good and then I go out with it on and realise what a plonker I look.

Polaroid *n* (1961) A proprietary name for a kind of camera which develops the negative and produces a positive print within a short time of the exposure's being made. Also applied to a photograph taken with such a camera. From the earlier sense, 'type of plastic which polarizes light' (1936)

> 1961 A. Gordon: How about a nice picture, sir?… I use a Polaroid… I'll have a print for you in a minute.

> 1977 *Rolling Stone*: Grace snapped a couple of Polaroids for the wedding album.

popper *n* (1967) a capsule of amyl or (iso)butyl nitrate, taken by drug-users for its stimulant effect. The capsule is typically crushed or 'popped', and the drug taken by inhalation

> 1967 Joan Didion: Las Vegas…a place the tone of which is set by mobsters and call girls and ladies' room attendants with amyl nitrate poppers in their uniform pockets.

popster *n* (1963) a pop musician or artist; an enthusiast for pop music, pop art, or pop culture in general

> 1963 *Meet the Beatles*: 12.45 p.m. Popsters posing in the park.

Pop-Tart *n* (1964) A proprietary name for a jam-filled pastry case designed to be heated up in a toaster. A delicacy introduced by Kellogg's

> 1976 *Springfield* (Massachusetts) *Daily News*: I glanced over to look at her order: jumbo bottle of soft drink, a box of strawberry poptarts, and a variety of other 'goodies'.

populist *n* (1961) one who seeks to represent the views of the mass of ordinary people. The term had been used since the 1890s with reference to various specific collectivist or socialist parties

> 1977 *Time*: Brogan questions whether Carter is a bona fide populist at all.

porn *n* (1962) A colloquial abbreviation of *pornography*. A usage which hit the streets with the large-scale expansion in the pornographic book and magazine trade in the 1960s. The alternative **porno** is first recorded (as a noun) in 1968, but it never caught on to the same extent. See also the adjective **porno (1952)**

> 1962 *John o' London's*: The central character and narrator, the Captain, is a seedy but not at all unsympathetic individual who makes a precarious living by writing 'porn'.

> 1964 *New Society*: 'There's nothing odd about our customers,' the porn shop assistant said.

Portakabin *n* (1963) The proprietary name (registered in Britain in 1963) of a make of portable building which by the 1970s had become familiar on building sites

> 1975 *Times*: The Portakabin which served as his drawing office.

positive discrimination *n* (1967) the making of distinctions in favour of groups considered disadvantaged or underprivileged, especially in the allocation of resources and opportunities. Compare **affirmative action (1935)**

> 1967 *Children & their Primary Schools* (Central Advisory Council for Education): We ask for 'positive discrimination' in favour of such schools [in deprived areas] and the children in them, going well beyond an attempt to equalise resources.

postcode *n* (1967) a series of letters or numbers, or both, allocated to postal areas to facilitate the automatic sorting and speedy delivery of mail. The alternative formulation *postal code* is first recorded in 1968

> 1968 *Times*: On the back of it is stamped the instruction 'Remember to use the postcode'.

> 1973 *Times*: The Post Office has published a booklet with the postal codes in it.

post-nuclear *adj* (1963) subsequent to the development or use of nuclear weapons

> 1963 *Economist*: China was dreaming of a post-nuclear heaven.

post-structuralist *adj* (1967) of or being a literary-critical philosophy which emphasizes the instability and plurality of meaning and uses the technique of deconstruction (see **deconstruct (1973)**). The noun *post-structuralism* is first recorded in 1977

> 1988 *Nation* (New York): He goes beyond the useful post-structuralist point that facts about the past are structured like texts.

Powellism *n* (1965) the political and economic policies advocated by the British Conservative politician Enoch Powell (1912–98), specifically one of restricting or terminating the immigration of coloured people into the UK. The adjective *Powellite* is also first recorded in 1965

> 1965 *Economist*: In the past few months a new word has found its way into British politics: Powellism.

> 1977 Martin Walker: The NF was deeply concerned that it had missed the Powellite boat, and that it was not expanding as it should… Stories in the press about a split in the movement between Powellites and the rest.

pre-owned *adj* (1964) secondhand. An originally US euphemism pioneered by secondhand-car salesmen, to avoid the stigma of *used*. It has continued to have some currency, despite its transparency

> 1964 *Listener*: Used cars are now referred to as pre-owned [in the US].

pre-teen *adj* (1960) Denoting the years of a child's life (usually immediately) before the age of thirteen. Originally US

> 1960 Vance Packard: Even pre-teen boys' shoes were slated for obsoleting. They were being designed away from their 'sexless' look to a real 'nervous' look of flashy casualness.

prime time *n* (1964) the time of day when a radio or television audience is expected to be at its largest; a peak listening- or viewing-period. Often used before a noun. Originally US. The concept predates the 1960s: 'John Fischer, the editor of Harpers,…asks for an autonomous authority empowered to produce programmes of exceptional merit, financed by a levy on the income of the broadcasters, who will also be under an obligation to transmit these programmes in the cherished prime-viewing hours', *Times Literary Supplement* (1959)

> 1964 *Variety*: For the first time in years, WNBC-TV has copped the number one rating position in prime time, in the highly competitive N.Y. market.

> 1976 *Billings* (Montana) *Gazette*: Jaclyn Smith is one of the gals who's huckstered in TV commercials a committee studied along with prime-time programs to determine the image given women on the small screen.

profile *n* (1961) a (characteristic) way of presenting oneself to the world. Typically used in the phrase *low profile*, first recorded in 1970

> 1970 *Guardian*: The United States…has repeatedly committed itself to keeping its profile low.

> 1972 *Guardian*: The British profile during the present crisis in Vietnam has been as low as could be conceived.

promo *n* (1963) publicity, advertising; often applied specifically to a promotional trailer for a television programme. Originally US. An abbreviation of *promotion*(*al*)

> 1966 *Saturday Review*: 'Will Robin escape?... Will Batman arrive in time to save him? The worst is yet to come!' And sure enough, minutes later on came the second of this trilogy—*The Blue Light*. What a promo!

> 1976 *New Musical Express*: Despite promo pics that make them look like 12-year-olds, their 'charisma' is more David Cassidy style.

pseud *adj, n* (1962) (someone) pretentious. A shortening of *pseudo* 'pretentious' (first recorded in 1945) or of the prefix *pseudo-*. Often used in the expression *Pseuds' Corner*, in allusion to the column in the British satirical magazine *Private Eye* devoted to exposing excruciatingly pretentious writing

> 1962 *Spectator*: Present-day trend-setters, pseud as they come.

> 1964 *Spectator*: The pseuds and intellectual craze-mongers seem to have dropped cinéma-vérité almost as quickly as they took it up.

> 1971 *Guardian*: Woodstock, the drug scene, the race war, Vietnam… The genre is familiar, and the path through it can verge dangerously close to Pseud's Corner.

psychedelia *n* (1967) psychedelic articles or phenomena collectively; the subculture associated with psychedelic drugs (see **psychedelic (1956)**)

> 1967 *Melody Maker*: Apparently today's hippie must be expanded and experienced in the whys and wherefores of psychedelia but it cannot be said that the products of this society are all 'junkie'.

psych out *v* (1961) to analyse in psychological terms; to work out. Slang

> 1974 Kate Millett: Mother's X-ray eyes met Celia once, had it all psyched out in three minutes.

pull *v* (1965) to pick up (a partner for sexual purposes). Slang

> 1965 *Sunday Express*: As a young man I could never pull (pick up) any birds of my own class.

pull-tab *n* (1965) a device, usually comprising a ring and short tongue of metal, by means of which a tin can be opened. Originally US. The simple **tab** is recorded slightly earlier ('The beer drinker opens the can by pulling off the tab', *Wall Street Journal* (1963)). In the prehistoric days before pull-tabs, tins had to be opened with tin-openers—in the case of drinks cans, a piece of metal with a V-shaped tooth. A later term is **ring-pull (1970)**

> 1965 *Economist*: The successful development of pull-tab tops for beer tins, so that they can be opened by hand rather than with an opener.

pulsar *n* (1968) a cosmic source of radio signals that pulsates with great regularity at intervals of the order of a second or less, and is believed to be a rapidly rotating neutron star. Formed from *pulsating star*, on the model of **quasar (1964)**

> 1968 *Daily Telegraph*: An entirely novel kind of star…came to light on Aug. 6 last year and,…was referred to by astronomers as LGM (Little Green Men). Now…it is thought to be a novel type between a white dwarf and a neutron [sic]. The name Pulsar (Pulsating Star) is likely to be given to it… Dr. A. Hewish…told me yesterday: '…I am sure that today every radio telescope is looking at the Pulsars.'

punter *n* (1965) a customer or client; a member of an audience or spectator. British. Often used patronizingly, with the suggestion 'gullible customer'; often also applied specifically to the customer of a prostitute. From the earlier sense, 'a gambler'

> 1977 *Record Mirror*: The punters were well pleased. Some people even…said they preferred my sound, as far as I was concerned I played crap that night.

> 1977 *Drive*: The more confused you are, the more likely you are to accept his offer. Because you are the punter.

purple heart *n* (1961) a tablet of the stimulant Drinamyl. Originally US. So named because of its shape and colour, largely inspired by the previous application of the term to a US military decoration awarded to personnel injured in battle

> 1973 Henry Miller: Drugs. Purple Hearts, amphetamines. The bloke was passing the stuff to kids.

quadraphonic, quadro-, quadri- *adj* (1969) produced by or being a system of sound recording and reproduction that uses four signal sources, two or more channels, and four loudspeakers, these being placed so that the original front-to-back sound distribution can be reproduced as well as the side-to-side one of stereophony. Much trumpeted at the outset as the ultimate in audio experience, it failed to make a long-term impact

> 1969 *High Fidelity*: The four channels might be used for double ping-pong effects—perhaps a quadriphonic version of 'Switched on Bach'.

quark *n* (1964) any of a group of sub-atomic particles (originally three in number) conceived of as having a fractional electric charge and making up in different combinations the hadrons, but not detected in the free state. Coined as a nonsense word by James Joyce ('Three quarks for Muster Mark!', *Finnegan's Wake* 1939), and applied to the fundamental particle by its discoverer, the US physicist Murray Gell-Mann

> 1965 *New Scientist*: Just as atoms are composed of particles (protons, neutrons and electrons) so may the heavy particles themselves be made up of combinations of simpler entities, called 'quarks'.

quasar *n* (1964) any of a class of celestial objects that give a star-like (i.e. unresolved) image on a photograph and have a spectrum showing a large red shift, usually taken to indicate great remoteness and immense power. A contraction of *quasi-stellar* (*object*), coined by H-Y Chiu and first used in a paper in *Physics Today*

> 1964 *Observer*: For the past twelve months, astronomers have been obsessed with these 'quasars' or 'quasi-stars' as they are now called.

quasi-nongovernmental organization *n* (1967) See **quango (1973)**

quasi-stellar *adj* (1963) giving a star-like (i.e. unresolved) image on a photograph but believed not to be a star; mainly in *quasi-stellar object* (1964) and *quasi-stellar* (*radio*) *source* (1963)

> 1963 *Scientific American*: In recognition of their small size, and for lack of a better name, they are called quasi-stellar radio sources.

> 1964 *New Scientist*: The highly enigmatic 'quasi-stellar objects' whose discovery over the past year or so has been of considerable excitement to astronomers.

Rachmanism *n* (1963) exploitation of slum tenants by unscrupulous landlords. From the name of Peter Rachman (1919–62), a Polish-born London landlord who bought up cheaply rented houses controlled under the 1957 Rent Act, used blackmail and physical violence to evict the tenants, and sold off the then decontrolled property for a large profit or let it at exorbitant rates

> 1963 Harold Wilson: The disease of Rachmanism is to buy controlled properties at low prices, and to use every means…to bring about evictions which…have the effect of decontrolling the property.

radiothon *n* (1964) a prolonged radio broadcast by a person or group, usually as a fund-raising event. US

> 1964 *Richmond* (Virginia) *Times-Dispatch*: With only an hour to run, the radiothon had netted the March of Dimes here more than $1,200.

rand *n* (1961) a unit of decimal currency, originally equivalent to ten shillings sterling, and containing 100 cents, adopted by the Republic of South Africa in 1961. Named after the Rand, short for *Witwatersrand*, a gold-mining area of Transvaal. See also **Kruger rand (1967)**

> 1961 *Guardian*: A two-rand (formerly one pound) postal order bought in a Capetown post office.

rap *v, n* (1965) (originally and especially among American blacks) (to engage in) a special type of improvised repartee, or more generally, impromptu dialogue or discussion. Mainly US. A single instance of the verb *rap* in the sense 'to converse' is recorded in 1929, but there is no evidence of continuity of usage between then and the 1960s. The notion of improvised speech led on later to **rap** 'music with improvised words' (1979)

> 1965 Eldridge Cleaver: In point of fact he is funny and very glib, and I dig rapping (talking) with him.

> 1967 J. Horton: Sometimes used synonymously with street conversation, 'rap' is really a special way of talking—repartee… For example, one needs to throw a lively rap when he is 'putting the make on a broad'.

raunchy *adj* (1967) earthy, coarse, vulgar; also, smutty. Compare the earlier sense, 'dirty' (1930s)

> 1967 Ellery Queen: I fell in love with him. In a raunchy sort of way he's beautiful.

> 1973 *Daily Colonist* (Victoria, British Columbia): A drunk at the next table was singing some raunchy songs. The songs kept getting dirtier and dirtier.

rave *n* (1960) a lively party; a rowdy gathering. The usage became further specialized in the late 1980s to mean 'a large gathering with dancing to fast loud electronic pop music' (see **rave (1989)**)

> 1960 *News Chronicle*: I wandered around to a rave I knew was going on in Covent Garden.

> 1968 *Listener*: Have you heard, the Touch-Paceys are economising this year by combining their children's bonfire party with their annual fancy dress rave?

rave-up, rave-in *n* (1967) a rave. *Rave-in* (with the 1960s' favourite **-in** suffix) appears never to have seriously caught on, but *rave-up* went from strength to strength

> 1967 *Melody Maker*: Pop enthusiasts have been treated to rave-ups featuring such world-class stars as the Four Tops.

> 1967 *New Statesman*: Last week police arrested scores of teenagers at a rave-in, and left-wing Catholics staged a pray-in.

read-only *adj* (1961) Applied in computing to a memory whose contents cannot be changed by program instructions but which can usually be read at high speed

> 1977 *Engineering Materials & Design*: The function program for the device is held in a 16 kilobit read only memory.

Reaganism *n* (1966) the policies and principles advocated by Ronald Reagan (b. 1911), American Republican politician, Governor of California 1967–75, and President of the United States 1981–9. The term embraces particularly his free-market, low-tax economic policies (see **Reaganomics (1980)**) and his hard-line anti-Communist foreign policy. It did not come into widespread use before the mid 1970s. The derivative *Reaganite* is first recorded in 1976

> 1966 *Punch*: Reaganism is really rampant now.

> 1975 *Financial Times*: Wits have suggested that 'Reaganism is extremism in defence of Fordism'.

> 1976 *Times*: The Reaganites…have moved on… If organization was the key to success, Mr Ford would never stand a chance.

red-eye *adj* (1968) Denoting an aeroplane flight on which the traveller is unable to get adequate sleep because of the hour of arrival or because of differences in time zones. Informal, originally US. From the passengers' bloodshot eyes

> 1968 Mrs. L. B. Johnson: Lynda was coming in on 'the red-eye special' from California, about 7 a.m., having kissed Chuck good-by at Camp Pendleton last night as he departed for Vietnam.

Red Guard *n* (1966) (a member of) a youth movement during the Cultural Revolution in the People's Republic of China, 1966–76, whose main role was denouncing and harassing 'counter-revolutionary' elements. The name had previously been applied to armed units of village people in the Second Revolutionary Civil War in China, 1927–37

> 1966 *Economist*: The rioters were clearly identified as a new youth group of secondary school and university student activists called the Red Guard. The Red Guard made its first appearance at the monster rally on August 18th, when the students were publicly congratulated for their revolutionary zeal by Mao Tse-tung.

re-enter *v* (1961) Applied to a spacecraft coming back into the Earth's atmosphere. A specific use of a verb in general use since the 15th century. The astronautical use of the noun *re-entry* is earlier (see **re-entry (1948)**)

> 1961 *Times*: Seven minutes after take-off the report came through that the capsule was beginning to reenter the earth's atmosphere.

refute *v* (1964) to deny, repudiate. Historically, the 'correct' meaning of *refute* is 'disprove'. This shift to 'deny' (understandable—the difference between 'assert to be false' and 'prove to be false' is a small if crucial one) probably got under way in the 1950s (Fowler and other prewar writers on acceptable usage make no mention of it). It continues to make headway, and at the end of the century is commoner than 'disprove'. Its typical verbal companion is *allegations*

> 1964 Charles Barber: For people who still use the word in its older sense it is rather shocking to hear on the B.B.C., which has a reputation for political impartiality, a news-report that Politician A has *refuted* the arguments of Politician B.

> 1978 *Observer*: Mr O'Brien, who was first elected general secretary three years ago, refutes the allegations.

reggae *n* (1968) a kind of pop music, of Jamaican origin, characterized by a strongly accentuated off-beat and often a prominent bass. Origin unknown; perhaps connected with Jamaican English *rege-rege* 'a quarrel, row'. The *-gg-* is 'hard'

> 1969 *Observer*: The visiting American executives…dancing the Reggae, Jamaica's successor to the Ska.

> 1977 McKnight & Tobler: So we come to reggae, which the British initially found difficulty in pronouncing, let alone understanding.

renta- *prefix* (1961) Used to denote the easy acquisition or instant availability (usually for some transitory purpose) of the thing specified. An extension of the use of *renta-* in the names of hire companies, particularly those renting out vehicles (the proprietary name *Rentacar* was registered in the US in 1924; see **rent-a- (1921)**)

> 1961 *Daily Telegraph*: Dictators!!! When you liberate a territory or mop up a colonialist enclave, are you disappointed and upset to receive only a tepid welcome from the people? Let *rentacrowd* help you! We can supply cheering crowds for all occasions.

> 1970 *Guardian*: The strategy was based upon a tactic which Oxford students called Rentamob…a hard core of rioters who could turn a demonstration into a confrontation.

> 1976 *Times*: Squatters in London are reported to be using children in a 'rent-a-kid' system, as a means of being rehoused.

rent boy *n* (1969) a young male homosexual prostitute. Slang

> 1969 *Jeremy*: At the upper-end of the scene is the kept-boy who has little or nothing in common with the humbler 'rent-boy'.

reprography *n* (1961) the branch of technology concerned with the copying and reproduction of documentary and graphic material. From German *Reprographie*, formed from *Reproduktion* 'reproduction' + *Photographie* 'photography'. The adjective *reprographic* is also first recorded in 1961. See also **Xerox (1952)**

> 1967 *Financial Times*: The almost unpronounceable word 'reprography' is in. It covers a field with ill-defined boundaries, edging at its simplest into pencil-making and at its most sophisticated into desk-top photosetting.

roadie *n* (1969) an assistant employed by a touring pop group, etc. whose duties include the erection and maintenance of equipment. Formed from *road*, as in *road manager*

> 1969 Fabian & Byrne: Bill, the roadie, buys me a drink.

rocker *n* (1963) someone who performs, dances to, or enjoys rock music; often applied specifically to a teenager or young adult of a type characterized by liking rock and roll, typically wearing long hair and a leather jacket, and riding a motor-cycle. Outbreaks of violence between the rockers and their rivals the mods (see **mod (1960)**) made the headlines in Britain in the early 1960s

> 1964 *Spectator*: Brighton cancelled its proposed 'beat festival' next month on hearing that the Mods and Rockers were coming in force.

> 1973 John Wainwright: He was…a nineteen-year-old who had once identified himself as a greaser and, before that, as a Rocker, but who now led a provincial chapter of Hell's Angels.

Roy *n* (1960) a smart, fashionable, or 'smooth' man. Australian colloquial. From the male personal name

> 1960 *Encounter*: A Roy…would patronise *Art Nouveau* every pay-day…for arty knick-knacks for his lovely Wahroongah home.

run-up *n* (1966) a period of time or series of occurrences leading up to some important (often political) event

> 1968 *Listener*: The run-up to the election of Oxford's new Poetry Professor has aroused a good deal of mirthful interest.

safari park *n* (1969) an area of parkland where wild animals are kept in the open and through which visitors can drive in motor vehicles. A development welcomed both by (some) anti-zoo campaigners and by owners of stately homes, for whom such parks could bring in valuable additional revenue

> 1969 *Times*: Opened early this summer Windsor Safari Park covering an area of 140 acres on the north edge of Windsor Great Park has proved very successful.

sailboard *n* (1962) a craft consisting of a moulded board like a surfboard with a swivelling mast that has a single sail. Not in wide use until the later 1970s, when it was also converted into a verb. See also **windsurf (1969)**

> 1962 D. Klein: Another boat that may tempt you because it can give you a great deal of fun at rather low cost is what is called a *sailboard*—that is, a sort of surfboard equipped with centerboard, rudder, and sailing rig.

> 1978 B. Webb: You can ski in any mountainous region where there is snow, just as you can sailboard on any water, whether it be an ocean or a reservoir.

SALT *n* (1968) negotiations, involving especially the USA and the Soviet Union, aimed at the limitation or reduction of nuclear armaments. An acronym formed from the initials of *Strategic Arms Limitation Talks*. Often (redundantly) in the phrase *SALT talks*

> 1969 *New Scientist*: The progress of SALT is likely also to be slow.

> 1973 E. Osers: The first ceilings set by the Salt Talks may prove to be an important landmark in limiting the arms race.

samizdat *n* (1967) the clandestine or illegal copying and distribution of literature (originally and mainly in the USSR); an 'underground press'; a text or texts produced by this. From Russian, an abbreviation of *samoizdátel'stvo* 'self-publishing house', from *samo-* self + *izdátel'stvo* 'publishing house'

> 1967 *Times*: A vast and newly educated [Soviet] population…do not pass around the precious *samizdat* (unpublished) manuscripts.

satellite television *n* (1966) Originally, the use of an earth-orbiting satellite to relay a television signal from one country to another (e.g. across the Atlantic), from where it could then be broadcast in the conventional way. When the prospect of individual subscribers receiving television signals directly from a satellite was discussed, the term *satellite-to-home* was often used ('What about direct satellite-to-home broadcasting?… Perhaps the only way in which the federal government could expect to keep abreast of the developments in communications technologies would be to set up a Department of Communication', *Economist* (1967)). But when theory became commercial reality, in the mid 1980s, although the official term was *direct broadcasting by satellite*, or *DBS* for short (first recorded in 1981), *satellite television* (or *satellite broadcasting*, or just plain *satellite*) was what most people called it. Compare **cable television (1965)**

> 1966 *BBC Handbook*: The BBC's first satellite television transmissions were shown in 1962.

> 1989 *Which?*: There are also several monthly magazines with a mix of technical information and features about the films and other programmes on satellite and cable.

scag, skag *n* (1967) heroin. US slang. Compare the earlier sense, 'a cigarette', first recorded in 1915. Ultimate origin unknown

> 1973 E. Bullins: Most of the guys that we usta swing with are gone, man. In jail, on wine or scag.

scam *n* (1963) a swindle, a racket. Slang, originally US. Origin unknown

> 1966 *Wall Street Journal*: They're known as 'scam' operators, promoters who set up ostensibly legitimate businesses, order large amounts of merchandise on credit, sell it fast and strictly for cash— and then go 'bankrupt', leaving their creditors unpaid.

scenario *n* (1962) a predicted sequence of events. From the earlier sense 'outline of the plot of a film, play, etc.' A metaphor that by the 1970s was in danger of becoming a cliché (Robert Burchfield, editor of the *Supplement to the Oxford English Dictionary*, noted 'The over-use of this word in various loose senses has attracted frequent hostile comment')

1962 Herman Kahn: The scenario begins by assuming a crisis; everybody is on edge. A Soviet missile is accidentally fired.

1971 *Observer*: Several of the computer 'scenarios' include a catastrophic and sudden collapse of population.

1980 *Journal of the Royal Society of Arts*: The best scenario…that we can envisage is one in which all those who want to do formal work will have an opportunity of doing two or three days a week.

schlocky *adj* (1968) shoddy, trashy. Slang, originally and mainly US. Formed from *schlock* 'trash', which is first recorded in 1915

1968 *New York Times*: Playing the 'special guest star' in a series of schlocky European films.

score *v* (1960) Of a man: to achieve intercourse (*with* a woman). Slang, originally US; part of the lexicon of male boasting, with misogynistic undertones

1960 R. G. Reisner: I scored with that chick.

1976 David Craig: They talk about 'taking' a woman… Or, 'Did you score last night?'—like some great goal, scheming and forcing.

scrape *n* (1968) a dilatation of the cervix and curettage of the womb, especially as a means of inducing an abortion. Slang

1968 J. Hudson: The word got around…that she got a bad scrape.

scuzzy *adj* (1969) dirty, grimy. North American slang. Perhaps a blend of *scummy* and *fuzzy*

1976 *Daily Colonist* (Victoria, British Columbia): Perhaps Mr. Vander Kalm has good intentions about evicting scuzzy malingerers from the dole.

seg, seggie *n* (1965) A colloquial abbreviation of *segregationist* 'an advocate of racial segregation', which is first recorded in 1954. US

1970 *New Yorker*: Fulbright for the first time openly appealed for black votes, because he believed that he couldn't win without them and that the 'seggies'…would vote against him no matter what he did.

1971 *Harper's Magazine*: When people wore the American flag then it was to show that they were not segs, because the segs of course wore the Confederate flag.

self-assembly *adj* (1966) Denoting items (e.g. furniture) sold in a kit for later assembly

1966 in G. N. Leech: Peerless brings within your reach…the luxury of a Built-in Bedroom at a price you can really afford With Dovetail Self-assembly Units.

self-destruct *adj* (1966) Denoting a mechanism enabling a missile or other device to destroy itself under certain conditions. The verb *self-destruct* is first recorded in 1969. See also **destruct (1958)**

1966 R. W. Taylor: There's a double safeguard in a self-destruct system that would operate automatically in case of navigational error.

1969 *Daily Colonist* (Victoria, British Columbia): This message will self-destruct in 10 seconds but the printed message is the one that lives on.

self-starter *n* (1960) someone who acts on their own initiative at work—a favourite of writers of job advertisements. The term was originally applied to a starting device for a motor vehicle in the 1890s

1960 *Times*: The Man: Must be a self-starter yet able to work within references given to him.

serial *adj* (1961) Of a person, action, etc.: habitual, inveterate, persistent, or sequential. Originally US. The initial application was to a murderer, and it continues to be used mainly with reference to criminals who repeatedly commit the same offence (e.g. *serial rapist*). The commonest collocation is probably **serial killer (1981)**. In the 1990s the usage branched off in a new, facetious direction

a1961 S. Kracauer: [He] denies that he is the pursued serial murderer.

1986 *Sunday Times*: It is in the United States…that serial killings have become a crime epidemic.

> 1992 *Economist*: The shah, the diary proves, was a serial adulterer.

> 1993 *Independent on Sunday*: Behind the barbed-wire in Southern California, 'active retirees' become serial golfers, swimmers, gymnasts.

services *n* (1967) the provision of petrol, refreshments, etc., for motorists in buildings constructed near to or beside a motorway or other major road; the group of buildings themselves

> 1975 Catherine Storr: She was passing the Heston Services, she'd be at the Henley exit in another quarter of an hour.

sexcapade *n* (1965) a sexual escapade

> 1965 Frederick Raphael: We are not complicating our holiday with disgusting sexcapades.

sex change *n* (1960) a change of sex brought about artificially by surgical means, treatment with hormones, etc. The term had been used before by biologists to denote a natural gender-reversal ('These results…, while providing virtual proof of sex-change from male to female in a section of the male population, point also to the probable occurrence of two types of males in P[atella] vulgata', *Nature* (1946)), but once journalists and their headline-writers had got their hands on it, it was virtually lost to them. The papers also pioneered an adjectival use, denoting someone who has undergone such a change

> 1960 *Twentieth Century*: Sex-change may well seem, as The Times said, 'unprepossessing' as a subject for comedy.

> 1984 *Daily Telegraph*: A sex-change Kiss-a-Gram girl stepped into the Marlborough Street dock yesterday clad in a see-through bra, black knickers, and fishnet stockings with suspender belt.

sexist *n* (1965) somene who advocates the idea that one sex is superior to the other (usually, that men are superior to women) or discriminates against members of the supposed inferior sex. The adjective *sexist* is first recorded in 1968, as is the noun *sexism*, denoting the idea or the discrimination. A coinage based on **racist (1932)** which before long had inspired a range of other -*ists* and -*isms* denoting various sorts of discrimination (see **-ism (1965)**)

> 1965 P. M. Leet: When you argue…that since fewer women write good poetry this justifies their total exclusion, you are taking a position analogous to that of the racist—I might call you in this case a 'sexist'—who says that since so few Negroes have held positions of importance…their exclusion from history books is a matter of good judgment rather than discrimination.

> 1968 C. Bird: There is recognition abroad that we are in many ways a sexist country… Sexism is judging people by their sex where sex doesn't matter.

> 1971 *Publishers' Weekly*: The Women's National Book Association panel during NBA Week on 'sexism' in children's books.

sheltered *adj* (1961) Denoting a place for living or working (or suitable work) provided for the mentally or physically infirm, where special assistance and facilities are available

> 1961 *Oxford Mail*: The three-storey house [for patients of a mental hospital in the final stages of readjustment to community life]…was opened last month and is known officially as a 'sheltered hostel'.

> 1977 *New Society*: Patients leaving Herrison [Mental Hospital] have been 'graded' according to the kind of home they can cope with outside. Those least able to run their own lives are in sheltered accommodation.

shiatsu *n* (1967) a kind of therapy, of Japanese origin, in which pressure is applied with the thumbs and palms to certain points on the body. From Japanese, literally 'finger-pressure'

> 1967 *Telegraph* (Brisbane): A Japanese physiotherapist…believes that his shiatsu finger massage is good for treating high blood pressure, insomnia and hernia.

shoat *n* (1969) the offspring of a sheep and a goat. Originally Australian; a further example of the 20th century's partiality for naming animal hybrids with lexical hybrids (see **swoose (1920)**). See also *geep* **(1971)**

> 1969 D. F. Elder: Although it has not appeared in print, the radio and television news have also been using the word 'shoats'.

shrink *n* (1966) a psychiatrist. Slang, originally US. From *head-shrinker* 'a psychiatrist', a joky coinage first recorded in 1950

> 1966 Thomas Pynchon: It was Dr Hilarius, her shrink or psychotherapist.

shuttle, space shuttle *n* (1969) a manned space vehicle with wings enabling it to land like an aircraft and be used repeatedly. The usage was actually coined by John Wyndham in a fictional context in 1960 ('The acceleration in that shuttle would spread you all over the floor'), but not applied to a real vehicle until the end of the decade. It came into its own in the 1980s, when a series of such vehicles was launched by the US to carry out a range of space operations. The first flight, of a shuttle named 'Columbia', took place in 1981

> 1969 *New Scientist*: Another shuttle plying on a regular basis between Cape Kennedy and this large space laboratory.

> 1981 *Daily Telegraph*: The American space shuttle landed on a dry lake bed in California's Mojave Desert yesterday to complete the maiden flight of the first re-usable rocketship.

Sigint, SIGINT *n* (1969) An abbreviation of *signal(s) intelligence* 'intelligence derived from the monitoring, interception, and interpretation of radio signals and similar transmissions'. See also **Elint (1961)**

> 1972 *New Scientist*: Generally speaking the larger part of the staff of all Sigint headquarters consists of scientists and engineers.

single *adj* (1969) Designating a person who is bringing up a child or children without a marital partner. Mainly in the terms *single parent* and *single-parent family*, standard politically correct vocabulary until, towards the end of the century, it was realized that *single* might seem to discriminate against the unmarried (*unmarried mother*—first recorded in 1834—was the term *single parent* had been invented to replace), so *lone parent* was pressed into service instead. See also **one-parent family (1969)**

> 1969 J. Sprey: Stigmatization of the single-parent family, and especially of single parents, does occur.

> 1976 *Women's Report*: This, coupled with the fact that more women are voluntarily becoming single mothers by refusing to have their babies adopted has caused the government to set up a Cabinet Committee on Family Affairs.

singles bar *n* (1969) a bar which caters for young unmarried people in search of social companions. Mainly US

> 1969 S. M. Coy: Singles bars…are generally frequented by those under thirty… The good singles bars are crowded, which provides protective covering for the girl who is timid.

singularity *n* (1965) a region in space-time at which matter is infinitely dense (as within a black hole). From the earlier mathematical sense, 'a point at which a function takes an infinite value'

> 1965 *Physical Review Letters*: An exterior observer will always see matter outside $r = 2m$, the collapse through $r = 2m$ to the singularity at $r = 0$ being invisible to him.

sitcom *n* (1964) A contraction of *situation comedy* 'a television or radio comedy programme in which the humour is derived from the reactions of a regular set of characters to a range of situations' (first recorded in 1953). Originally US

> 1964 *Life*: Even Bing Crosby has succumbed to series TV and will appear in a sitcom as an electrical engineer who happens to break into song once a week.

sitter *n* (1961) a participant in a sit-in or sit-down

> 1961 *Guardian*: There are still people who think that marchers and sitters can be dismissed because some are oddly dressed.

ska *n* (1964) a kind of pop music of Jamaican origin, characterized by a fast tempo and emphasis of the off-beat. It is similar to reggae, but lighter and with a more fluid rhythm. Origin unknown

> 1971 *Guardian*: West Indian ska or blue beat music, latterly taken up by skinheads.

skateboard *n* (1964) a narrow platform mounted on roller-skate wheels, on which the rider coasts along, usually in a standing position. Formed from *skate*, on the model of *surfboard*. *Skateboarding* (also first recorded in 1964) began in California, and by the mid 1970s had become a worldwide youth cult

1964 *Life*: Skateboards appeared last fall in southern California.

1964 *Surfer*: Some of the skateboarders have set up slalom courses, timing each other from standstill starts.

1978 *Morecambe Guardian*: Coun. Mrs Taylor said that if any children still felt strongly about having no skateboarding park they should contact her so that a united effort could be made.

skinhead *n* (1969) a white youth (typically one of a gang), characterized by wearing workman-like clothing and heavy boots, and by a tendency to aggressive behaviour. The term originated in US slang of the early 1950s, applied to someone with a crewcut, and when this new youth cult arose in Britain in the late 1960s, the members' very short haircuts made the transference a natural one. The shortened *skin* is first recorded in 1970

1969 *Daily Mirror*: A group of teenagers…wear tight and rather short jeans, collarless T-shirts, exposed braces, big steel-capped boots and hair erased almost to their scalps. The lack of hair is what gives them their generic names…crop-heads, skin-heads or peanuts. The boots are good for kicking.

1971 *Daily Telegraph*: Gangs of Hell's Angels and skinheads marred Easter Monday seaside outings.

1978 R. Westall: Those Midland sods must be crazy… I shouted the rudest things you can shout at skins.

skinny-dip *v* (1966) to swim naked. Slang, originally US

1966 *Punch*: Nearly a year has passed since three members of the San Francisco Sexual Freedom League went skinny-dipping in the San Francisco bay.

skyjack *v* (1961) to hijack (an aeroplane); a favourite ploy of terrorists from the 1960s onwards. From *sky* + **hijack**. The derivative *skyjacker* is also first recorded in 1961

1961 *New York Mirror*: Pan Am Jet skyjacked to Havana.

1970 *Time*: Aboard the plane was Leila Khaled, 24, the Palestinian guerrilla who attempted to skyjack an El Al airliner over Britain last month.

1982 *Daily Telegraph*: The skyjackers…were said to have threatened crew members.

slash *n* (1961) a thin sloping line (/). Originally US; it has largely supplanted the earlier *solidus* in general usage. See also **backslash (1982)**

1976 Ted Allbeury: Reference SC49 slash two.

sleaze *n* (1967) sordidness, sleaziness. A back-formation from *sleazy* 'sordid', which is first recorded in 1941. The application to 'financial or other corruption' evolved in the early 1980s (see **sleaze (1983)**)

1967 *Listener*: For all its brazen sleaze, Soho is a pretty fair working model of what a city neighbourhood should be.

smudger *n* (1961) a photographer, especially a street or press photographer. Slang. From dated slang *smudge* 'photograph taken by such a person' (first recorded in 1931), perhaps from the blurring of a hastily taken snapshot, although first applied in prison slang to a picture of a fingerprint

1988 *National Trust Magazine*: Ian is…a 'smudger'. His assignments, or shoots, take him all over the world.

sniffer dog, sniffer *n* (1964) a dog trained to detect specific odours, especially those of drugs or explosives

1975 Antony Beevor: We are using…sniffer dogs at ports and airports so as to increase our chances of catching the explosive coming in.

sod off *v* (1960) to go away. Slang

1960 Julian Symons: Now sod off and get your identification parade done.

software *n* (1960) the programs and procedures required to enable a computer to perform a specific task, as opposed to the physical components of the system. Modelled on **hardware (1947)**

1960 *Communications Association Computing Machinery*: Nearly every manufacturer is claiming compatibility with all other equipment via such software as Cobol.

soul music *n* (1961) a type of music popularized by black singers which incorporates elements of rhythm and blues and gospel music. Often shortened to *soul* (also first recorded in 1961). See **soul (1946)**

> 1961 *Sunday Times*: The contemporary jazz cult of 'blues roots'—otherwise described as 'soul' or 'funk'.

> 1974 *Black World*: Soul music belched from windows where Black women wearing tired faces gazed impassively down at the hopeless street.

spacearium *n* (1962) a large room arranged so that scenes representing space may be projected on to its interior. A blend of *space* and **planetarium (1929)**

> 1962 *Times*: Five separate exhibits…will include such things as the 'Spacearium'.

spaced (out), spacy, spacey *adj* (1968) in a heightened state of consciousness, (as if) from taking drugs; disoriented from reality. Slang, mainly US

> 1971 J. Mandelkau: I remember being really spaced out and someone handing me a ladybird—telling me how nice they tasted.

> 1975 *Globe & Mail* (Toronto): 'You get pretty spacey after doing a lot of interviews,' she said. 'One time someone asked me if Dylan had changed a lot and I was so spacey I said, "Well, he doesn't bum drinks any more." '

spacewalk *n* (1965) an act or spell of physical activity undertaken in space outside a spacecraft. *Spacewalker* and *spacewalking* are also first recorded in 1965. See also **extravehicular activity (1965)**

> 1965 *Newsweek*: Thirteen new layers had been added [to his spacesuit]…to protect his torso and legs against micro-meteorites and the extreme temperatures on his spacewalk… Spacewalker White had trouble sleeping, due to the excitement… He was firmly convinced that spacewalking is an easily mastered art.

spacewoman *n* (1962) a female traveller in space; also, a woman who comes from another planet

> 1963 *Daily Telegraph*: Russia's first space woman, Valentina Tereshkova, 26, waving at Prestwick yesterday when her plane made a two-hour refuelling stop.

spaghetti *n* (1963) complex roadways forming a multi-level junction, especially on a motorway. Colloquial. The term **spaghetti junction**, originally applied to the Gravelly Hill interchange near Birmingham (see the quote below) and subsequently used generically, is not recorded before 1971

> 1966 *Guardian*: Details of one of the biggest pieces of motorway spaghetti so far designed in Britain were published… It is the Gravelly Hill interchange on the M6.

speed *n* (1967) an amphetamine drug, especially methamphetamine. Slang. From its stimulant effect

> 1969 Fabian & Byrne: Now he was on speed the paranoid fantasies were really beginning.

splashdown *n* (1961) the alighting of a spacecraft on the sea. The related verb *splash down* is first recorded in 1962

> 1961 *Washington Post*: They [i.e. several warships] are strung out about 60 miles apart, and their mission is to retrieve Shepard after 'splashdown'.

> 1962 *Daily Telegraph*: Cdr. Walter Schirra…'splashed down' safely in the Pacific at 10.28 (BST) last night.

sponsored *adj* (1967) Denoting a fund-raising activity (originally a walk), usually organized on behalf of a charity, in which each participant obtains pledges from sponsors to donate a certain sum for each unit completed

> 1967 *Oxfam News*: Teenage support for Oxfam increased… The 'sponsored walk' caught on.

> 1970 *Times*: People taking part in a sponsored walk along the Grand Union Canal…to raise funds for the British Council for Rehabilitation of the Disabled.

> 1977 *Cornish Times*: The sponsored 'slim in' was won by Mrs V. Humphries.

stagflation *n* (1965) a state of the economy in which stagnant demand is accompanied by severe inflation. A blend of *stagnation* and *inflation*. Compare **slumpflation (1974)**

> 1965 Iain Macleod: We now have the worst of both worlds—not just inflation on the one side or stagnation on the other, but both of them together. We have a sort of 'stagflation' situation.

> 1971 Rhodes Boyson: The result of all this extra state interference…has been…what might be called rampant stagflation, that is to say stagnation in production and raging inflation which…destroys belief in the future.

stand-by *n* (1961) (a passenger with or wishing to buy an air ticket under) a system of seat allocation whereby passengers do not book in advance, but may board at a cheaper rate the next flight with spare unbooked capacity

> 1961 E. Lathen: Four stand-bys who were convinced that by keeping in motion their chances of getting on a plane were improved.

starter *n* (1966) a dish eaten as the first course of a meal, before the main course. A native English term which has largely taken the place of the more exotic *hors d'oeuvre*

> 1966 *Vogue*: Starters include fish soup, cock-a-leekie, duck-liver pâté.

steaming *adj* (1962) complete, utter; used for reinforcing terms of abuse. A British slang usage which enjoyed a brief vogue

> 1962 *Listener*: A cautionary tale concerning a real steaming nit of a British civilian.

> 1965 A. Garner: Roland! You great steaming chudd! Come back!

stereo *n* (1964) a stereophonic record player, CD player, etc. By the 1970s, when stereophony had become the norm and cassettes had taken their place beside records, *stereo* was the standard term, replacing the earlier **record player**. See also **stereo (1954)**

> 1964 *House & Garden*: The wall unit houses the stereo.

stop-and-go *adj* (1961), **stop-go** *adj* (1962) designating a policy of alternately restricting demand, in order to contain inflation, and expanding credit, in order to reduce unemployment. *Stop-go* quickly supplanted *stop-and-go*. *Stop-go* originated in the 1910s, *stop-and-go* in the 1920s, both applied to traffic signs. Also occasionally used as a noun, denoting a 'stop-go policy'

> 1961 *Times*: The short-term 'stop-and-go' remedies of recent years…deal with the symptoms rather than the disease.

> 1962 *Daily Telegraph*: It is precisely these 'stop-go' policies of successive Chancellors which have been a major cause of our export troubles.

> 1964 Samuel Brittan: This was the event which turned the business community violently against 'stop-go' and made it look with a less jaundiced eye on national planning.

straight *n* (1967) someone who conforms to the conventions of society; someone who does not take drugs; a heterosexual. Slang, originally US. From the adjective *straight* 'conventional, heterosexual'

> 1967 W. & J. Breedlove: The easy atmosphere…the abundant evidence of abundant wealth attract not only 'straights', but a variety of sexual thrill-seekers.

street-wise *adj* (1965) familiar with the outlook of ordinary people in an urban environment; cunning in the ways of modern urban life. Originally US. See also **street-smarts (1976)**

> 1965 *New Yorker*: A [social] worker therefore had to be wary as well as trustful, be security minded as well as loving, and be 'street-wise' as well as compassionate.

> 1981 *Daily Telegraph*: Their [i.e. young blacks'] values place a premium on being 'street-wise',…that is, being able to survive in the rough and tough world of the streets.

Strine *n, adj* (1964) (an) Australian; Australian English. A representation of the alleged Australian pronunciation of *Australian*, coined by Alistair Morrison in 1964 under the pseudonym 'Afferbeck Lauder' (Strine pronunciation of 'alphabetical order')

> 1980 *Daily Telegraph*: He settled into his cramped, double-glazed Australian train cabin ('Roomette' in Strine).

supercontinent *n* (1963) one of the large land masses that are thought to have existed in the geological past and from which two or more of the present continents are thought to be derived. A later coinage than the synonymous *protocontinent* (first recorded in 1958), but now in wider use

> 1963 *Scientific American*: According to Wegener all the continents had been joined in a single supercontinent about 200 million years ago.

supremo *n* (1963) someone who has overall charge of some department of government or sphere of activity. Colloquial. From the earlier sense, 'a supreme (military) leader' (see **supremo (1944)**)

> 1976 Harold Wilson: The successful attack by other ministers to prevent [Herbert Morrison] from becoming an economic supremo.

> 1983 *Private Eye*: A short list of possible replacements…included…the ruthless supremo of the Royal Philharmonic Orchestra.

surgical *adj* (1965) Designating swift and precise military attack, especially from the air. Originally US; a notorious piece of military double-speak, conferring the illusion of dispassionate accuracy on murderous mayhem

> 1965 T. C. Sorensen: The idea of…a so-called 'surgical' strike…had appeal to almost everyone first considering the matter, including President Kennedy.

> 1971 *Harper's Magazine*: Even the language of the bureaucracy—the diminutive 'nukes' for instruments that kill and mutilate millions of human beings, the 'surgical strike' for chasing and mowing down peasants from the air by spraying them with 8,000 bullets a minute—takes the mystery, awe, and pain out of violence.

survivable *adj* (1961) capable of being survived; not fatal. *Survivable* has been used in the sense 'capable of surviving' since the late 19th century, but this rather more obvious meaning is not recorded before 1961

> 1967 *Times Review of Industry*: The attitude to safety in survivable accidents, while officially condoned, is indefensible.

sus out, suss out *v* (1966) to work or figure out; to investigate, to discover the truth about (a person or thing). Slang. From *sus* 'to suspect or surmise', which is first recorded in 1953. Compare **sus (1936)**

> 1966 *Queen*: Youth susses things out on its own.

> 1969 Fabian & Byrne: When chicks came round I enjoyed sussing them out, and trying to guess which one would last and which one would be dropped.

> 1971 *It*: Everybody seems to have at least two nicknames plus their birth-signs so every little chickie can think they've got it sussed.

sustainable *adj* (1965) capable of being maintained at a certain rate or level. A specialization of the much earlier general meaning 'capable of being upheld or defended'

> 1965 *McGraw-Hill Dictionary of Modern Economics*: A condition of sustainable economic growth means that economic stagnation will not set in.

sweeper *n* (1964) In soccer, someone who plays as the last line of defence except the goalkeeper, across the width of the field

> 1964 *Times*: Moore…played a giant part in his role as 'sweeper' of the rear.

> 1976 *Denbighshire Free Press*: Even with Bernie Welsh operating as sweeper behind a defensive line of four, Courtaulds were far from impressive at the back when the ball was in the air.

swinger *n* (1964) a person who is sexually promiscuous, specifically one who advocates or engages in group sex or the swapping of sexual partners. Slang. The related verbal noun *swinging* is also first recorded in 1964

> 1966 Thomas Pynchon: I had a date last night with an eight-year-old, And she's a swinger just like me.

> 1970 E. M. Brecher: What happened during the 1960's was that group sex in public—swinging—emerged from the brothels and became an established though minor feature of American urban and suburban life.

swinger *n* (1965) a lively person who keeps up with what is considered fashionable; someone who is 'with it'. Colloquial. See also **swinging (1958)**

> 1966 *Economist*: No attempt has been made to attract the wilder London 'swingers' of *Time*-fame.

swingometer *n* (1965) a device consisting of a dial with a movable pointer, used to demonstrate, especially on television, how a likely or observable 'swing' should influence the outcome of an election. Made famous in the 1960s by Professor Robert McKenzie, but later commentators (e.g. Peter Snow) used similar devices on television election broadcasts

> 1965 *BBC Handbook*: Robert McKenzie demonstrating the Swingometer.

> 1974 *Daily Telegraph*: After five or six results, Robert McKenzie's famous swingometer accurately showed what was to be in the event a majority of 40 or so for Labour over Conservative.

switched on *adj* (1964) aware of all that is considered fashionable and up to date. Slang

> 1964 *House and Garden*: I…want…to open a department store which caters for switched-on people.

> 1970 D. Devine: Her mother wasn't switched on, she knew nothing of modern fashion.

tab *n* (1961) a tablet or pill, specifically one containing LSD or another illicit drug. Slang, originally US

> 1971 *Daily Telegraph*: Whenever anybody had any money it nearly always went on drugs, with LSD at £1 a 'tab' (tablet).

tab *n* (1963) a device, usually comprising a ring and short tongue of metal, by means of which a tin can be opened. Originally US. The fuller form **pull-tab** is first recorded in 1965

> 1963 *Wall Street Journal*: The beer drinker opens the can by pulling off the tab.

take-away *adj, n* (1964) Designating cooked food sold to be eaten away from the premises of sale. First recorded as a noun, denoting a shop selling such food, in 1970, and denoting a take-away meal in 1982

> 1964 *Punch*: Posh Nosh…was serving take-away venisonburgers.

> 1981 M. Hardwick: Proprietor of…a small string of burger eateries and takeaways.

> 1990 Ruth Rendell: He hadn't made a fortune in order to sit in his house eating takeaways and watching videos.

take-out *adj, n* (1968) (a shop selling food) prepared on the premises to be eaten elsewhere. Mainly North American. Compare **take-away (1964)**

> 1972 *Evening Telegram* (St. John's, Newfoundland): Commercial site. Formerly used as a Pizza Take-Out.

talk show *n* (1965) a **chat show (1969)**

> 1965 *Times Literary Supplement*: There are now literally thousands of talk-shows.

Tamla Motown *n, adj* (1964) The name of two US record labels, *Tamla* and *Motown*, launched in 1960 by Berry Gordy Jr., used to designate a style of music characterized by a heavy beat and influenced by gospel music, which was made popular by the black artists he employed

> 1968 P. Oliver: Rhythm and blues, rock 'n roll, the Tamla-Motown sound and the techniques of the gospel singer.

tank top *n* (1968) a sleeveless upper garment with round neck and deep armholes, often of knitted material and similar to the top of a one-piece bathing-suit, worn by men or women and fashionable in the late 1960s and 70s. The name comes from *tank suit*, a US term for a one-piece bathing costume of the 1920s worn in a tank or swimming pool

> 1968 *New Yorker*: Miss Farrell—a tall, pretty ballerina dressed in a purple tank top and baggy rubber warm-up pants.

> 1977 Miller & Swift: Even the latter have given up whalebone corsets and starched winged collars without assuming they have to switch to miniskirts or tank tops.

target *v* (1961) to aim (a nuclear weapon) at a target. Originally US. The derived adjective *targetable* is first recorded in 1968

> 1964 *Financial Times*: The Soviet presence…comprises…a force of about 100 MRBMs targeted on Japan.

> 1968 *New York Times*: The United States will in the next few years add to its arsenal missiles capable of putting into space a number of individually targetable warheads.

target *v* (1966) to mark out or identify (a place, person, etc.) as a target. Originally US. The derived adjective *targetable* is first recorded in 1972

> 1966 *Guardian*: US policy is to target North Vietnamese military targets only.

> 1972 *Scientific American*: Land-based intercontinental ballistic missiles…can readily be located with the aid of surveillance satellites, so that they must be regarded as 'targetable' in the event of an enemy first strike.

teach-in *n* (1965) an informal debate (often of some length) on a matter of public, usually political, interest, originally between the staff and students of a university. Hence, a conference attended by members of a profession on topics of common concern. Originally US. Modelled on **sit-in (1937)** and the like (see **-in (1960)**)

> 1965 *Times*: This free-for-all debate…was called by the ugly new jargon name of 'teach-in'—a concept recently invented at Harvard, which has crossed the Atlantic.

> 1965 *Economist*: Universities all over the country [i.e. USA] have conducted informal 'teach-ins' on Vietnam, running from eight in the evening to eight the following morning.

teeny-bopper *n* (1966) a girl in her teens or younger, especially one who is a fan of pop music and follows the latest fashions. Colloquial

> 1966 *Telegraph* (Australia): The teenybopper is aptly named because her two distinguishing features are her teeny size and her cool boppy with-it attitude to life.

telecom *n* (1963) An abbreviation of *telecommunication* (first recorded in 1932). In present-day usage (on the model of *telecommunications*) mainly plural, the singular form having been monopolized by the name of *British Telecom*, a British telecommunications company separated from the Post Office in 1981

> 1964 Douglas Macarthur: By 'telecom' I was directed to use the Navy and the Air Force to assist South Korean defenses by whatever use I could make of these two arms.

tequila sunrise *n* (1965) a cocktail containing tequila and grenadine. It enjoyed a vogue in the 1970s, but its lurid appearance handicapped any aspirations to a sophisticated image

> 1976 *Daily Telegraph*: A Tequila Sunrise has become the 'in' drink at many ski resorts and single bars. It is tequila and orange juice, with half an ounce of grenadine poured on top to filter dramatically down through the drink.

termination *n* (1961) the ending of a person's employment; dismissal. Euphemistic, mainly North American

> 1961 *Wall Street Journal*: They qualify for termination payments and most are eligible for deferred pensions.

> 1982 *Chicago Sun-Times*: He and fellow workers were informed of the terminations at 10:30 a.m. Wednesday and told to 'pack up and leave immediately'.

termination *n* (1969) an induced abortion. Euphemistic

> 1969 *Times*: Women denied a legal abortion commonly seek termination elsewhere.

> 1973 *Times*: The pregnant women walking about the hospital ward were all in for abortions. Or terminations, as they called them—a much nicer word.

thankfully *adv* (1966) one is thankful that. Originally US. A usage development similar to that of **hopefully (1932)**, albeit not quite so universally condemned

> 1966 W. Follett: The 'suicide needle' which—thankfully—he didn't see fit to use.

> 1982 *Daily Telegraph*: Thankfully, however, the old style has not entirely disappeared.

theme park *n* (1960) an amusement park organized round a unifying idea or group of ideas. Originally US; the concept and the term were exported to Europe in the late 1960s, but did not catch on in a big way until the 1980s (when *theme* began to take on a new life of its own as an adjective—see **theme (1983)**)

> 1960 *American Peoples Encyclopedia Year Book*: While most established parks and kiddielands were profitable, the theme parks, seeking to duplicate Disneyland's success, were often in trouble.

> 1989 *Holiday Which?*: Local conservationists are even more horrified by a new proposal—including a Disney-style theme park—covering 1,000 acres.

Third World *n* (1963) the countries of the world, especially those of Africa and Asia, which during the Cold War were aligned with neither the Communist nor the non-Communist bloc; hence, the underdeveloped or poorer countries of the world, usually those of Africa, Asia, and Latin America. A translation of French *tiers monde*, a term formulated by A. Sauvy in the mid 1950s. (The corresponding *First World* and *Second World*, though never widely used, denote respectively the West and the Communist bloc)

> 1963 *Economist*: Relations between Europe and the third world nowadays.

> 1964 *Economist*: The ingredients common to most 'third world' countries (poverty, ignorance, love-hate of the former colonial powers).

thong *n* (1967) a simple shoe held on the foot by a strap between the toes; a **flip-flop (1970)**. Australian and US. The full form *thong sandle* is first recorded in 1965

> 1967 *Coast to Coast 1965–6*: Her feet, in scuffed leather thongs, were none too clean.

threatened *adj* (1960) Of a wild animal or plant: in danger of becoming rare or extinct

> 1960 *Oryx*: Australia's threatened mammals.

> 1966 *Red Data Book*: The object of these lists and sheets of threatened species is not only to draw universal attention to the dangers facing some unique creatures,…but also to provide the factual information necessary for action.

tiger *n a tiger in one's tank* (1965) energy, vigour. An instance of an advertising slogan which became at least a semi-permanent part of the language—in this case, the Esso Petroleum Company's 'Put a tiger in your tank'

> 1965 *Guardian*: Esso's tiger has pounced on to the national consciousness within two months. The phrase 'Put a tiger in your tank' has become part of everyday conversation.

> 1981 *New Zealand Tablet*: Young girls must be made to realise that boys of the same age have a 'tiger in their tank' as far as sexual desire goes.

tights *n* (1965) a woman's or girl's one-piece stretchable garment covering the legs and body up to the waist, worn in place of stockings, which were impractically revealing beneath the fashionable miniskirt (the demise of stockings and suspenders was greeted with relief by women, with regret by men). The term was used at the end of the 19th century for an undergarment taking the place of knickers and stockings, but the 1960s usage almost certainly comes from the tights worn by dancers, actors, etc.

> 1965 Peter O'Donnell: Modesty wore…a full black skirt, with black stretch tights.

> 1968 S. E. Ellacott: For some years previously [to 1966], during cold weather, women had worn 'tights' (pantee stockings), and these were now developed in sheer nylon for everyday wear with mini-skirts.

Tipp-Ex *n* (1965) A proprietary name (registered in Germany—where it was coined from German *tippen* 'to type' and Latin *ex* 'out'—in 1962 and in Britain in 1972) for a sort of typewriter correction fluid. A boon to careless secretaries the world over. The name came to be used generically, the alternative **white-out** (first recorded in 1977) never really catching on. By the 1980s it was being used as a verb

> 1977 *Private Eye*: Freelance PS/Sec jobs 1 hour upwards undertaken… Have Tipp-Ex will travel.

> 1983 Harold Evans: So many staff lists had names erased that anyone sacked was later said to have been 'Tipp-Exed'.

together *adj* (1968) fashionable, up-to-date; hence used as a general term of commendation. Slang

> 1968 *Daily Mirror*: No finer honour can be bestowed on a man down the King's Road than to be called a together cat.

together *adj* (1969) composed, self-assured; free of emotional difficulties or inhibitions. Colloquial

> 1969 Fabian & Byrne: I reckoned it was no good putting on a together image if you were all screwed up inside.

> 1971 *New Yorker*: A young lady of twenty-two who's been through what Twiggy has been through has got to be a very together person to survive.

toke *n* (1968) an inhalation of smoke from a cigarette or pipe containing marijuana or other narcotic substance. US slang. From the verb *toke* 'to smoke a marijuana cigarette', first recorded in 1952, whose origins are unknown

> 1968 *Harper's Magazine*: If he still took a toke of marijuana from time to time...still! Mailer was not in approval of any drug.

tokenism *n* (1962) the practice or policy of making merely a token effort or granting only minimal concessions, especially to minority or suppressed groups. Originally US

> 1980 *Jewish Chronicle*: Philip Rosenthal...waffled on about 'tokenism' in his factory, where two workers sit on the board, as if real democracy had been achieved.

ton-up *adj, n* (1961) (Denoting) a speed of 100 m.p.h., or a motor-cyclist who achieves this. From the earlier use of **ton** in the same sense (1954)

> 1961 *Daily Telegraph*: The term 'Ton Up' is used by young motor-cyclists to indicate doing 100 m.p.h.

> 1961 *Harper's Bazaar*: Gangs, rebels without a cause and ton-up kids.

topless *adj, adv* (1964) Of a garment: not covering the breasts; hence, of a woman: naked or almost naked above the waist; bare-breasted. The application to places where bare-breasted women work (e.g. as waitresses) is first recorded in 1967. There is an isolated instance of the word on record from the 1930s referring to men's swimwear ('With another bathing-suit season at hand, local law-makers are aiming their ordinances at males on the score of topless suits rather than at underclad females', *Time* (1937)), but the application to women is a child of the 1960s

> 1964 *San Francisco Chronicle*: Saigis introduced San Francisco's first topless bathing suit for women.

> 1966 *Observer*: The appearance of topless waitresses.

tower block *n* (1966) a multi-storey block of flats (or sometimes offices). The 1950s' and 60s' solution to the problem of high-density housing, later so reviled that *tower block* became a dirty word. Sometimes shortened to just *tower*

> 1967 A. J. Marshall: The newest and nicest tower block is Centre Point.

> 1970 *Times*: The towers, cheerless in their four tones of dun-colour.

track record *n* (1965) known facts about past achievements or behaviour taken as a guide to future performance. Originally US; a metaphor drawn from the athletics track, where the term denotes literally 'the performances achieved by a particular athlete in the past'

> 1965 *Life*: Wilder has had a series of extremely successful pictures... We were betting on his track record that this one would be too.

trade-off *n* (1961) a balance achieved between two desirable but incompatible features; a sacrifice made in one area to obtain benefits in another; a bargain, a compromise

> 1961 *Hovering Craft & Hydrofoil*: Propulsion system integration allowing trade-offs between the requirements of lift and forward thrust can be achieved in a variety of ways.

trank *n* (1967) A slang abbreviation of **tranquillizer**

> 1980 A. Skinner: We'll have to go back to slipping tranks into his coffee.

tranny, trannie *n* (1969) A colloquial abbreviation of **transistor (radio)**

> 1969 *Nova*: 'How do you feel about the Love Generation now?'... 'Sick to my stomach,' he replied, tuning into *The Archers* on his tranny to get back in touch with decent values.

transcendental meditation *n* (1966) a method of relaxation and meditation based on the theory and practice of yoga popularized in the West by the Maharishi Mahesh Yogi. In vogue in the late 1960s and early 70s, on the back of a general enthusiasm amongst the youth of the West for Eastern mysticism

> 1966 C. F. Lutes: The system on which Maharishi's teaching is based—a simple method of transcendental meditation...—is indeed systematic and produces measurable and predictable results and is therefore scientific.

tratt, trat *n* (1969) A colloquial abbreviation of *trattoria*. The in place to eat in cosmopolitan swinging London at the end of the 1960s

> 1969 *Queen*: Luigi…who served you dinner in last week's trendy tratt.

traumatic *adj* (1962) distressing, emotionally disturbing. A generalized use of the psychiatric term, denoting severe emotional damage, which dates from the late 19th century

> 1962 Aldous Huxley: Memories of traumatic events in childhood.

> 1977 Edward Heath: Whatever the outcome, the impact on the United States of the decade of war in Vietnam was traumatic.

trendy *adj, n* (1962) fashionable, up to date, following the latest trend. First recorded as a noun, 'a trendy person', in 1968. From the beginning, a two-edged term: it can be used admiringly, but there is often also a suggestion of slavish and uncritical pursuit of the latest vogue

> 1962 *Punch*: I saw the headline 'The Trendiest Twin Set'.

> 1968 Joan Fleming: She was well in with what is now called the Chelsea set…, there are trendies and *personae non gratae* amongst them.

> 1972 *Lancet*: Pathobiology (a trendy name for general pathology) seems to be a fashionable subject in the United States.

trial separation *n* (1968) a temporary separation of a married couple, with a view to making a decision on whether to divorce. Modelled with 1960s irony on **trial marriage** (first recorded in 1906)

> 1968 *Listener*: We are telling our friends that he's not around because we've agreed to a trial separation.

Trimphone *n* (1965) The proprietary name of a type of lightweight telephone with a high-pitched quavering (or 'warbling') ringing tone

> 1965 *Times*: The new instrument is called a Trimphone and, in the words of the Post Office, it does not ring, it warbles.

trippy *adj* (1969) of or like a hallucinatory experience induced by a drug. Colloquial, mainly US

> 1976 Logan & Woffinden: In 1966 [The Grateful Dead] chose their name; in keeping with the band's image, it was a decision made under the influence of various drugs… The band thought it seemed vaguely appropriate, and certainly it had trippy connotations.

Trot *n* (1962) An abbreviation of *Trotskyist* or **Trotskyite**. Usually a term of abuse, often for someone even vaguely left-wing

> 1962 Doris Lessing: I was a hundred per cent party member, and there was Harry, a dirty Trot, so there were high words and we parted for ever.

tube *n* (1969) a bottle or can of beer. Australian, colloquial

> 1969 *Listener*: This…extrovert chunders…his way through the kangaroo valley of Earl's Court…buoyed up by innumerable tubes (bottles) of Foster's Beer.

turn off *v* (1965) to put off, repel. Slang. The related noun, *turn-off* 'something or someone that repels you', is first recorded in 1975

> 1965 *Harper's Bazaar*: Humperdinck turns me off.

> 1975 *New York Times*: Patrons dined on cervelle Grenobloise. 'Sounds better in French,' said the chef… 'Brains is a turn-off.'

turn on *v* (1965) to arouse interest, enthusiasm, or sexual response. Slang. The related noun, *turn-on* 'something or someone arousing or exciting', is first recorded in 1969

> 1965 *Harper's Bazaar*: Bach really turns me on.

> 1967 J. Hayes: The excitement in her eyes deepened. 'You turn me on, man.'

> 1969 *Telegraph* (Brisbane): I think I'm more of a turn-on now than I ever was when I was trying to conform to that curvy image.

TVP *n* (1968) An abbreviation (registered as a proprietary name in the US in 1969) of *textured vegetable protein*, a protein food derived from vegetables but given a texture held to resemble meat. Modern science's answer to food shortages and the cruelty of factory farming, or the degradation of our culinary heritage, depending on your point of view. See also **Quorn (1987)**

> 1968 *Guardian*: What TVP has been created from is mercifully not revealed.

twink *n* (1963) a male homosexual, or a young person regarded as an object of homosexual desire. US slang. Origin uncertain; perhaps related to *twink* 'twinkling (of an eye)'

> 1978 Armistead Maupin: Where are the twinks, anyway?… Who needs to waste a night staring at these old Gucci queens.

twist *n the twist* (1961) a dance to pop music in which the hips are gyrated. Earlier dances were named 'the twist' in the 1890s ('They're ready an' willin', An' fair at Kadrillin', But my little Flo does the twist', *Sunday Times* (1894)) and the 1920s (' "The Twist", created by M. Camille de Rhynal…is designed to cultivate gliding and swaying movements', *Daily Telegraph* (1928)), but the term did not catch on then as in the 1960s. Also first recorded as a verb in 1961

> 1961 *Guardian*: I have read recently that a new dance has been introduced in America called 'The Twist'… It is a week with only one new film, a small loud monstrosity called 'Hey, Let's Twist'.

> 1965 Muriel Spark: My mother makes a party for the girls to do the Twist.

two-way mirror *n* (1967) a mirror which lets through enough light for an observer at the back to see through it, without being seen from the front

> 1967 John Gardner: They directed total concentration through the sighting side of a two-way mirror.

UDI *n* (1965) An abbreviation of *unilateral declaration of independence*. Originally applied to the illegal declaration of independence from Britain made by the Ian Smith-led white government of Southern Rhodesia in 1965, but subsequently applied, both seriously and facetiously, to other such actions

> 1965 *Economist*: They shrug off…the threat of Britain imposing sanctions if Mr Ian Smith's government made a unilateral declaration of independence ('UDI').

> 1980 *Times*: Both he and his wife Avis are from Yorkshire—not quite the kind that think Yorkshire should declare UDI.

unaligned *adj* (1961) pursuing a policy of having no affiliations with any of the world's main power blocs. Synonymous with the earlier (and longer-lived) **non-aligned (1960)**

> 1961 *Guardian*: India and the 'unaligned nations'.

unban *v* (1968) to remove a ban or prohibition from (a publication, person, group, etc.). Often used in South African political contexts

> 1968 *Guardian*: Book censorship has eased since the Dail passed a law which un-bans a book after 12 years in purdah.

> 1979 Winnie Mandela: The first thing I'll do when I'm unbanned (if I ever am) is to go to church and thank God for letting your letter reach me.

unisex *adj* (1968) characterized by a style (of dress, appearance, etc.) that is designed or suitable for either sex. Unisex clothing was pioneered by the French designer André Courrèges

> 1968 *Life*: With-it young couples…are finding that looking alike is good fashion as well as good fun. The unisex trend was launched by…the teen-agers.

> 1969 *New Yorker*: Unisex metallic trouser suits.

unleaded *adj* (1965) Of petrol, etc.: without added lead. The benefits of such fuel in preventing air pollution were taken on board in the last third of the century, and by the 1980s *unleaded* was in common enough parlance to be used as a noun, meaning 'lead-free petrol'

> 1965 *Oil & Gas Journal*: The industry association will make a study next year of the cost of producing unleaded gasoline.

> 1981 J. D. MacDonald: He pulled up to the pump… He took six and four-tenths gallons of unleaded, which came to eight sixty-four.

unreal *adj* (1965) remarkable, amazing, wonderful. Slang, mainly North American and Australian
> 1986 *Truckin' Life*: I reckon your magazine is unreal. I've never missed an issue for the last four years.

upper *n* (1968) a drug, especially an amphetamine, often in the form of a pill, which has a stimulant or euphoric effect. Slang, originally US. From the idea of 'raising' one's mood
> 1969 Fabian & Byrne: I wasn't used to so many uppers all at once.

uptight *adj* (1969) characteristically formal in manner or style; correct, strait-laced. Compare the earlier meaning, 'tense', which dates from the 1930s
> 1969 *Manchester Guardian Weekly*: Who would have thought that an uptight institution like the august Oxford University Press would have done a thing like this? Here is a…spirited and spiritous piece of autobiography…served up as a book.

upwardly mobile *adj* (1964) See **upward mobility (1949)**

urban guerrilla *n* (1967) a guerrilla operating in cities or towns and involved in kidnapping, bombing, etc.
> 1967 George Jackson: I have made inroads into political economy…and when I can get hold of them some of the works on urban guerrilla warfare.

Valium *n* (1961) A proprietary name (registered in the US in 1961 and in Britain in 1962) for the drug diazepam, used especially as an anti-anxiety agent, hypnotic, and muscle relaxant. Origin unknown. Along with **Librium (1960)**, notorious as the dependency sedative of the 1960s
> 1972 *Guardian*: She had taken an overdose of Valium after getting drunk the night before.

VAT *n* (1966) An abbreviation of **value-added tax (1935)**, usually pronounced as three separate letters, but occasionally as a single word. The tax was first imposed in the UK in 1973 (see **VATable (1973)**)
> 1966 *Economist*: This may be true of the conventional VAT.

VDU *n* (1968) An abbreviation of *visual-display unit*, a device for displaying on its screen data stored in a computer, and usually incorporating a keyboard for manipulating the data. Within a dozen years the television-like screens had become an unremarked part of the office environment. *Visual-display unit* itself is first recorded in 1968 too, but the term *visual display*, denoting the display of computer information via the screen of a cathode-ray tube, dates back to the early 1950s
> 1968 *British Medical Bulletin*: The data-terminal…may consist of a 'video display unit' (VDU), in effect the combination of a television-like display tube with a keyboard.

Velcro *n* (1960) A proprietary name (registered in Britain in 1960) for a fabric made in narrow strips for use as a fastener, one strip having tiny loops and the other hooks so that they can be fastened or unfastened simply by pressing together or pulling apart. From French *velours croché* 'hooked velvet'
> 1961 *Practitioner*: We have been experimenting for some time with the new Bri-nylon fastener, 'velcro', using it particularly for patients who have difficulty in doing up buttons, trousers and belts.

vibes *n* (1967) instinctive feelings, atmosphere. Slang. Short for *vibrations* in the same sense, a usage which can be traced back to the late 19th century
> 1970 John Lennon: 'You give off bad vibes.' That's what George said to [Yoko Ono] and we both sat through it, and I didn't hit him, I don't know why.

video *n* (1968) a video recording
> 1968 *Observer*: The days of the disc, in the pop world at least, are numbered. For soon will come the video. We will have the top 20 videos which you plug into your home video-machine.

videodisc *n* (1967) a disc on which (moving or static) visual images have been recorded in non-representational form for subsequent reproduction on a television screen or the like. Videodiscs eventually came seriously onto the market in the early 1980s, but lost out commercially to video-tapes
> 1967 *New Scientist*: We shall soon have on the market the video-disc, about the size of a gramophone record and costing about 22 shillings.
> 1982 *New Scientist*: Video discs are the video equivalent of the long-playing record.

videotape *v* (1964) to record on videotape

> 1964 *Times*: Even an expert cannot tell the difference between live and video-taped programmes.

villain *n* (1960) a professional criminal. British police slang, made familiar to the general public largely via television crime dramas

> 1975 *Sunday Telegraph*: A flying squad officer said: 'As far as we know these are no ordinary villains. We believe they are Irish IRA.'

vox pop *n* (1964) popular opinion as represented by informal comments from members of the general public, especially when used for broadcasting; statements or interviews of this kind. From Latin *vox populi* 'voice of the people'

> 1964 Hall & Whannel: In television…we could include…the use of the brief survey of popular opinion on any topic by means of the posed question (the so-called 'vox pop').

wall-to-wall *adj* (1967) extending from one end or extreme to the other; allowing no unfilled space; ubiquitous. Originally US. Usually used disparagingly. From the earlier literal application to carpets (see **wall-to-wall (1953)**)

> 1973 *Listener*: A respite from wall-to-wall Mozart on Radios 3 and 4.

wally *n* (1969) an unfashionable person; one who is foolish, inept, or ineffectual. Slang. Origin uncertain; perhaps a use of the male forename *Wally* (compare *Charlie* 'a fool'), but compare also Scottish *wallydrag, wallydraigle* 'a feeble or worthless person'. Not in widespread use until the mid 1970s

> 1983 *Evening Star* (Ipswich): He shrugged off Ms. Ford's throw as temperamental but I bet he felt a right wally.

washerette *n* (1968) a launderette. Mainly US

> 1976 *Honolulu Star-Bulletin*: Washerette in prime location. 10 washers & 5 dryers. Good lease.

Wasp *n* (1962) a member of the American white Protestant middle or upper class descended from early European settlers in the US. Often derogatory. For the etymology, see the first quote below

> 1962 E. B. Palmore: For the sake of brevity we will use the nickname 'Wasp' for this group, from the initial letters of 'White Anglo-Saxon Protestants'.

> 1963 *Times*: There is such a thing as a 'Human Engineering Laboratory'; whether a man is a Wasp (white Anglo-Saxon Protestant) can decide his career.

water cannon *n* (1964) a device for shooting a jet of water at high pressure. A new riot-control device popular with civil authorities who in the mid and late 1960s had widespread student unrest to deal with

> 1982 *Listener*: People had begun to take to the streets, defying martial law, tear-gas, water-cannon and bullets.

Watusi, Watutsi *n* (1964) a type of dance to pop music. From the name of a people inhabiting Rwanda and Burundi. Also used as a verb

> 1964 *Time*: A pretty eyeful slaps on new records and dances it all by herself. That way, it's called the Watutsi.

> 1966 *Punch*: They…fed on lotus and daiquiri, they frugged and watutsied.

way in *adj* (1960) conventional; fashionable, sophisticated. Modelled on **way out** 'unconventional' (1959)

> 1967 *Punch*: There's a real way-in guy looking like how a guy on *The Times Saturday Review* ought to look like.

Weight Watchers *n* (1961) A proprietary name used especially for (members of) an organization, Weight Watchers International Inc., formed to promote dieting as a means of slimming, or any of its associated clubs

> 1964 *New York Herald Tribune*: Weight Watchers is an Alcoholics Anonymous for compulsive eaters.

welcome *adj you're welcome* (1960) A polite formula used in response to an expression of thanks. Prevalent particularly in US English, and sometimes criticized as a rote response, particularly when used by service-industry employees. See also **have a nice day (1971)**

1960 *Times*: The coloured lift attendant in South Carolina who had that attractive way of saying, almost singing, 'You're welcome' whenever we thanked her.

welly, wellie *n* (1961) A colloquial British abbreviation of *wellington (boot)*. A low-profile word which expanded its horizons later in the century, both as a metaphor for 'acceleration' (see **welly (1977)**) and, in *green welly*, as a symbol of the English rural *haute bourgeoisie*

1961 *Guardian*: The ground floor we converted back into a hall, for coats and wellies, etc.

wet look *n, adj* (1968) a glossy appearance, as if wet. Applied especially to a chemical finish given to fabrics to make them appear shiny and wet, fashionable in the late 1960s and early 70s

1970 D. Uhnak: Her lips, shining with a wet-look lipstick, quivered.

1971 *Daily Telegraph*: The chair and stool covered in white wet-look fabric.

wheel and deal *v* (1960) to engage in scheming or shrewd bargaining, especially of a political or commercial nature. Colloquial, originally US. The noun *wheeler-dealer* is also first recorded in 1960

1963 *Economist*: Two Dallas oil millionaires,...described as 'a pair of old-line Texas wheeler-dealers'.

1967 *Listener*: Frost is wheeling and dealing off camera.

wheelie *n* (1966) the stunt of raising the front wheel off the ground while riding a bicycle or motor-cycle. Slang, originally US

1966 *New York Times*: A popular sport for young bicycle riders is 'doing a wheelie'. This means lifting the front wheel off the ground and balancing on the rear wheel alone.

wholefood *n* (1960) unrefined food containing no artificial additives. The original connotation was to some extent food for crankies, but the term gradually joined the mainstream

1960 *Mother Earth*: We should like to hear from further growers who may have available supplies of wholefood, especially winter salads, parsnips [etc.].

1978 *Peace News*: If you are interested in wholefoods, running a shop collectively and a political awareness of food please contact us.

wide-bodied, wide-body *adj* (1968) Of a large jet aircraft: having a wide fuselage, allowing for the accommodation of many more passengers than a standard fuselage. *Wide-bodied*, the commoner form, is not recorded until 1970

1968 *Flight International*: BAC foresees a demand for standards matching the high-capacity wide-body aircraft of the long-haul routes on short/medium-haul routes.

1970 *Times*: About £200m. is being requested to get the proposed BAC 3–11 wide-bodied, 250-seater subsonic airliner off the ground.

wimpy *adj* (1967) feeble and ineffectual; like a **wimp (1920)**

1984 *Melody Maker*: Dennis had a brilliant artist last summer, really strong drawings, but now it's gone back to being a bit wimpy.

window *n* (1965) a period outside which the planned launch of a spacecraft cannot take place if the journey is to be completed, owing to the changing positions of the planets. The usage broadened out in the 1970s to 'a (limited) period of opportunity'

1967 *New York Times*: The Soviet and American vehicles flew to Venus close together because both were fired during one of the periodic 'windows' for such shots.

1980 *New York Times*: To intimidate the Americans with a Soviet 'window of opportunity' to knock out Minuteman missiles.

windsurf *v* (1969) to go board-sailing. Originally US. A back-formation from *windsurfer* 'a sailboard', which is first recorded in the same year and in the US is a proprietary name

1969 *Christian Science Monitor*: Depending on the wind and water conditions, older as well as young people can windsurf.

winklepicker *n* (1960) a shoe with a long pointed toe, fashionable amongst teenagers in the late 1950s and early 60s. The reference is to the pin needed to extract winkles from their shells to eat

1960 *Spectator*: The incredibly pointed custom-built shoes in which teenagers keep other teenagers at arm's length… The shoes, called winklepickers, look like something out of Grimm's fairy tales.

Womble *n* (1968) an imaginary animal depicted as inhabiting Wimbledon Common, invented by the writer Elizabeth Beresford. A shortening of *Wombledon*, a fanciful alteration of *Wimbledon*. The Wombles achieved a brief minor cult status in Britain in the mid 1970s

1975 *Sunday Express*: In addition to the Wombles pop group and the TV series, there are Womble jigsaws, Womble dolls, Womble T-shirts, Womble pillow cases… Now…there are Womble-approved crisps.

women's liberation *n* (1966) the liberation of women from subservient social status and all forms of sexism; also (usually with capital initials) a militant movement with these aims. The shortened form *women's lib* is first recorded in 1969 (see **lib (1969)**). The abbreviation, in particular, became a target for trivializers, and within a decade or so supporters had largely abandoned it in favour of *feminism* (a late-19th-century coinage). See also **women's movement (1902)**

1966 *New Left Review*: Fourier was the most ardent and voluminous advocate of women's liberation and of sexual freedom among the early socialists.

workaholic *n* (1968) someone who is addicted to work, or who voluntarily works excessively hard and unusually long hours. Originally US. Coined from *work*, on the model of *alcoholic*, it went on to inspire a range of other more or less facetious *-aholic* formations (see **-aholic (1965)**)

1973 *Bulletin* (Sydney): The workaholic, as an addict is called, neglects his family, withdraws from social life, and loses interest in sex.

worker-director *n* (1968) a worker who is also on the board of directors of a firm—an idea that was nurtured but failed to flourish in the industrial-democracy climate of the 1960s and 70s

1968 *Economist*: The proposal—that worker-directors should be put on the boards of a number of nationalised industries…—is a waste of time.

workfare *n* (1968) a policy of requiring recipients of welfare money to do some work in exchange for this benefit. Originally US. Coined from *work*, on the model of **welfare**

1968 *Harper's*: One of Evers' programs is what he calls workfare; he has said that everybody ought to work for what he gets.

1969 Richard Nixon: What America needs now is not more welfare but more 'workfare'.

working *adj* (1964) Denoting a meal at which those present discuss business. Originally (and mainly) in *working lunch*

1964 *Guardian*: After these meetings there was a 'working' lunch at the British Embassy.

1970 *Daily Telegraph*: Union chiefs and chairmen of five nationalised industries had a 'working dinner'…last night.

worst-case *adj* (1964) that is or pertains to the worst of a number of possibilities. Originally a technical term in statistical analysis, its use by contingency planners, especially in the now clichéd *worst-case scenario*, brought it into the public domain

1964 R. F. Ficchi: It is first assumed, using a worst-case analysis technique, that the mean beam of the receiver and transmitter antenna are in direct line of sight.

1980 *Times*: Analysts believe that the Kremlin drew up a 'worst-case' scenario which took into account both an embargo on American grain and a threat to the Moscow Olympics.

xerox *v* (1965) to reproduce by **xerography (1948)**; to photocopy. See also **Xerox (1952)**

1966 E. V. Cunningham: Anything you want copies of, why we'll Xerox it out.

yippie, yippy *n* (1968) a member of a group of politically active hippies, originally in the US. Coined from the initials of *Youth International Party*, on the model of **hippie (1953)**

1968 *Listener*: One student outlines his own theories to me. 'This whole scene began with Dylan, the Beatles, and of course pot.' Another complains that the militants need a sense of humour and hopes the Yippies move in with their 'politics of ecstasy'.

yonks *n* (1968) a very long time. British slang. Mainly in the phrase *for yonks*. Origin unknown

1968 *Daily Mirror*: I rang singer Julie Driscoll… She said: 'I haven't heard from you for yonks.'

zap *n* (1968) liveliness, energy, power, drive; also, a strong emotional effect. Slang, originally US. From the interjection **zap (1929)**

> 1968 *New York Times*: When the heat's too much and the gin's lost its zap…, tranquilize your jangled nerves with the Swinging Wonder.

Zapata moustache *n* (1968) a type of moustache in which the two ends extend downwards to the chin, fashionable in the late 1960s and early 70s. Named after the Mexican revolutionary Emilio Zapata (1879–1919), who was portrayed with a moustache of this kind by Marlon Brando in the film *Viva Zapata!* in 1952

> 1998 *Observer*: My Cambridge dons in 1977 were all retired hippies with safari suits, Zapata moustaches and bogus Maoist opinions.

zappy *adj* (1969) lively, amusing, energetic; striking. Slang

> 1969 *Guardian*: The Minister wore in his lapel…a zappy coloured badge of the 'Cocoa makes you sterile' type.

> 1984 *Listener*: The company felt the need for a zappier profile.

zazzy *adj* (1961) flashy, colourful, vivid. Slang, mainly US. Perhaps a blend of *zippy* and *jazzy*, but compare also *pizzazz, sassy,* and *snazzy*

> 1961 *Encounter*: Death seemed to follow me through the zazzy carnival of Miami.

zip code *n* (1963) a series of digits representing a particular area in a US city, etc., used in addressing mail. *Zip* is an acronym formed from *Zoning Improvement Plan*, and was initially usually spelt *Z.I.P.* or *ZIP*

> 1963 *New York Times*: Z.I.P. codes, for the present at least, are for big business, and more particularly big users of the mails such as publishers, banks, insurance companies and mail-order houses.

zit *n* (1966) a pimple. Slang, originally US. Origin unknown

> 1975 *Maclean's Magazine*: When did you last have a zit on your face?

There are party decades and hangover decades. After the exuberance of the 1920s came the gloom of the 30s. And now, in the 70s, the reaction to the Swinging Sixties set in. At the end of the century the decade tended to be looked back on without affection by those who lived through it, memorable mainly for not being the 60s. The Western world received a check to its long postwar run of prosperity, largely precipitated by the rapid rise in oil prices in the early years of the decade, and inflation and unemployment walked abroad. The leader of the world's most powerful nation was forced to resign in disgrace: an episode summed up in the single word *Watergate*. And Abba bestrode the popular entertainment scene.

Our collective confidence took a series of knocks. We were destroying our environment; new diseases were appearing to which we had no answer (*Lassa fever, legionnaires' disease*); and even though we had reached the moon, we did not seem quite to know where to go from there. Against this background, terrorism inexorably extended its tentacles.

The growing realization of what we were doing to our planet found its response in *environmentalism*. The 70s were the first *green* decade. *Ecofreaks* appeared, scattering their *smiley faces* about them. The *counter-culture* of the *New Age* preached the virtues of *alternative technology*. The *energy crisis* forced us all to take the *gas guzzlers* seriously, and search for *renewable* sources of energy. *Doomwatch* was in fashion, and *CFCs* made their ominous début, with their threat of *global warming*. We learnt that we must recycle, and the first *bottle banks* sprouted in the streets. Even sounds could be pollutants: *noise pollution*. We condemned *speciesism*, embraced *bioethics*, and discovered the existence of a whole new geopolitical region: the *South*. When it all got too heavy, we could just *bliss out*.

What sort of society were the *baby boomers* helping to create? One in which the *poverty trap* lurked, and the *bag lady* started to appear in city centres, but one also with the urge to *gentrify*, to preserve its *heritage*, and to sleep on *futons*. One in which long-anonymous *carers* found a name, and many of their charges acquired new ones: *crumblie, wrinklie*. One in which we learnt to live with *full-frontal* nudity, and had to find time for *quality time* with our children.

But if there was one phenomenon above all that marked out the 70s it was the gender issue. The 60s feminist campaign against sexism began to bear fruit; women were becoming *liberated*. *Sexual politics* could not be ignored, and *women's studies* were well up the agenda at universities and colleges. The *libbers* pursued their guerrilla war with the *male chauvinists*. The *gender gap* was closing, and expectant fathers were demanding *paternity leave*.

Not the least of the effects of the feminist revolution was on the English language. The revolutionaries found sexist assumptions ingrained in the very fabric of the lexicon, particularly in the ambisexual use of *man* and the various masculine personal pronouns. Why should a woman who chaired a meeting be referred to as a *chairman*? How could anyone justify alluding to human history as the history of *man*, or of *mankind*? Was it not discriminatory to say 'If anyone wants to leave, *he* should do so now'? We were asked to kindly adjust our vocabulary.

The chairman could become the *chairperson*, and likewise the spokesman could become the *spokesperson*. The neutral element -*person* spawned scores of new formations, many of them patronizingly facetious. It remains in limited use at the end of the century, although other more euphonious solutions have often been found preferable (*chair* for *chairman*, *fire-fighter* for *fireman*). Polemical coinages such as *herstory* (for *history*) have for the most part remained marginal. The answer to the subtler problem of the masculine pronouns remains in the balance. Orthographic tricks such as *s/he* are of no relevance to the spoken language. Formulations like *he or she*, or *she or he*, become tiresome if often repeated. The most promising candidate as a non-sex-specific pronoun remains *they*, which has actually been used in this role, particularly in the environment of indefinite pronouns such as *somebody* and *anyone*, since at least the 16th century ('If…a psalm escape any person, or a lesson, or else if they omit one verse or twain', *Pilgrimage of Perfection* (1526)), and can be quoted from eminent writers from then to the present day ('Nobody else…has so little to plague them', Charlotte Yonge (1853); 'Nobody does anything well that they cannot help doing', John Ruskin (1866)), but which continues to irk the self-appointed language police. See also *themself* (1992)

Insistence on or conformity to such non-sexist usage was a major force behind the growth of *politically correct* vocabulary, which had its full efflorescence in the 1980s.

Also in anticipation of the 80s, the 70s were a decade greatly exercised by money, and the language of capitalism, the terminology of the *bean counters*, made considerable strides. Corporate manoeuvrings produced *buy-outs*, *unbundling*, *asset-stripping*, and *golden handshakes*. No doubt there was some *creative accounting* going on, and perhaps even some *laundering* of funds. We could pick up our cash from an *automated teller* or a *cashpoint*, or simply use *plastic money*—a *debit card*, perhaps—or even pay by *direct debit*. In the UK, buyers and sellers had to cope with the vocabulary of a new currency: was it to be *pee* or *pence*? Meanwhile, economists and financiers bemused us with talk of *PSBR*, *supply side*, *petrodollars*, and *index-linked granny bonds*.

Those in work could perhaps take advantage of *flexitime*, or experiment with *job sharing*. But the 70s were not the happiest of times in the workplace: it was the decade of *industrial action* and *flying pickets*, culminating in the UK in the 'Winter of Discontent'. Many lost their jobs, and found out all about the *job centre* and the *giro cheque*. The market in new euphemisms for 'firing an employee' was brisk: *dehire*, *deselect*, *outplace*, *release*. Sacking half the workforce was *downsizing*.

The major change in the UK's political and economic circumstances was its joining of the European Economic Community in 1973. This ushered in a period in which English was increasingly beset by European jargon. We grew familiar with the *green pound*, *E-numbers*, wine *lakes*, and the mysterious *snake*. In future there would be the prospect of *EMU* and the *single currency*, the *ECU* and the *euro* (already under active discussion), not to mention a continuing flow of often hostile or mocking *Euro-* (1962) compounds.

Closer to home in Britain, the troubles in Northern Ireland were taking a grip, and we had to add *plastic bullet* and *rubber bullet, car bomb* and the verb *kneecap, no-go area* and *Provo* and *Bloody Sunday* to our vocabulary. The prospect of *proximity talks* was well in the future. On the wider political scene it was a polarized time, with the *hard left* (or *loony left*) in the ascendancy, *Militant Tendency* active in the Labour party, and *Thatcherism* on the horizon. In the US the concept of *spin* was invented, which would permeate politics round the world in the final quarter of the century.

The computer continued its march towards the centre of our lives, bringing with it copious amounts of new terminology, at first arcane, now commonplace: *floppy disk* and *hard disk, microprocessor* and *window* and the dreaded *virus.* We acquired *personal computers* or *word processors,* and to print the result of our labours, the *dot matrix,* the *daisy wheel,* and later the *laser printer.* We could sit at our *workstation* in our *paperless* office, communicate via the *Ethernet,* and hope the whole system did not *crash*; or perhaps, with the help of the computer, we could simply *telecommute* from home. *User-friendly touch screens* facilitated our transactions, and we had barely heard of *hacking* and the need for *data protection.* And to cater to our recreational needs, there was *Space Invaders.*

Towards the end of the decade the mass-market video arrived, and *couch potatoes* could use their *Betamax* to record their favourite *miniseries* or *docutainment* programme, or to watch *action replays* of the latest sporting *megastars* in action. *Teletext* services such as *Ceefax* were coming on stream, *electronic mail* was arriving, and music buffs had the prospect of being able to play *compact discs* on their *music centres.* And what sort of music would they be listening or dancing to? If they were young, it would very likely be *heavy metal, punk rock* (inspiration of the characteristic youth look of the decade—spiky coloured hair and leather clothes with chains, safety pins, etc.), *New Wave, rap,* or possibly *salsa.*

It was the era of *hot pants* and *leg-warmers, Doctor Martens* and *flip-flops, bomber jackets* and *bustiers, loon pants, skinny* sweaters, and *Afghan coats. Trainers* graduated from the jogging track to the high street, and the *trouser suit* (1939) made a big comeback.

The upwardly mobile could plump for *nouvelle cuisine,* cook their chicken in a *chicken brick,* join the race for *Beaujolais nouveau,* go green with a *Vegeburger,* or yellow with a *piña colada.* The downmarket choice was *pub grub, junk food,* a *ready meal,* or a *Big Mac.*

And the craze of the decade? *Streaking.*

action replay *n* (1973) a playback (at normal speed or in slow motion) of a recorded incident in a sports match, etc., especially immediately after the action occurs. A far-reaching development of the video age, allowing television spectators (and in due course spectators at the ground, via a large screen) to cheat real time and enabling incidents (and officials' decisions about them) to be micro-scopically examined. The terms *instant replay* and simply *replay* are also used (the noun *replay* had been used in the audio field since the early 1950s)

> 1974 *Cleveland* (Ohio) *Plain Dealer*: The scoreboards will be placed on each side and the instant replay screens at each end.

> 1977 Jim Laker: The action replay can be of great help…in showing the reason for a batsman's dismissal.

Afghan coat *n* (1973) a kind of sheepskin coat or jacket worn with the skin side outside, sometimes embroidered and usually having a shaggy border. All the rage in the early 1970s, when Eastern folk art was cool

> 1973 *New Musical Express*: Afghan sheepskin coat.

> 1980 *New York Times*: Special on Afghan coats, cheap.

Agent Orange *n* (1970) a mixture of 2,4-D and 2,4,5-T which was used as a defoliant in the Vietnam war. So named from the colour-coded stripe on the drums in which it was shipped

> 1972 *New Scientist*: It was reported by the Washington Post that more than a million gallons of Agent Orange (the most powerful defoliant used in Vietnam and banned since April, 1970) was being shipped back to the United States.

airhead *n* (1972) someone who is foolish, simple-minded, or stupid. Slang, originally and mainly North American

> 1980 *Maclean's Magazine*: One of the many airheads who move torpidly through the $40-million mistake known as *Raise the Titanic* says in a throat-clutching voice: 'A ship that big down that deep!?!?'

alderperson *n* (1973) Used as a non-sex-specific substitute for *alderman* or *alderwoman* (see **person (1971)**). Originally and mainly US

> 1973 *Wisconsin State Journal*: 'They're very willing to work with us,' he said, 'but they've been yelled at by past alderpeople.'

alternative *adj* (1970) Applied to a lifestyle, culture, etc. regarded by its adherents as preferable to that of contemporary society because it is less conventional, materialistic, or institutionalized, and often more in harmony with nature. A usage modelled on **alternative society (1969)**

> 1970 Anthony Sampson: Cyclops has died. Strange Days has died. Grass Eye and Zig Zag ail. The alternative Press is in trouble all round.

> 1982 *New Zealand Listener*: There is another non-rigid non-school with what in today's language we could call an alternative life-style.

> 1983 *British Medical Journal*: One of the few growth industries in contemporary Britain is alternative medicine.

alternative technology *n* (1972) (a) technology designed to conserve natural resources and avoid harm to the environment, especially by harnessing renewable energy sources such as wind- or solar power

> 1991 *Whole Earth Review*: Computers are not alternative technologies. They are energy consumptive and lock a person into the system of Earth destruction.

animatronics *n* (1971) a technique of constructing robot models in accurate likenesses of humans, animals, etc., which are programmed to perform intricate, lifelike bodily movements in synchro-nization with a pre-recorded soundtrack. Originally US; a shortening of the earlier term *audio-animatronics* (a proprietary name in Britain), which was coined from *animation* and **electronic**

> 1992 Armistead Maupin: To me, the kids looked like animatronics figures, robots from a ride at Disneyland.

Apex, APEX *n* (1971) An acronym formed from the initial letters of *Advance Purchase Excursion*, a system whereby airline tickets for scheduled flights can be bought at a reduced rate on certain conditions (usually including payment in advance and a specified interval between outward and return flights)

> 1971 *Time*: The West Germans argued that…APEX would only add confusion to…fares.

> 1980 *Times*: Travel notes… Low season Super-Apex £282.

asset *n* (1977) a resource available to an armed force; a piece of military hardware. Originally US. The chilling bureaucracy of war: a lethal weapon becomes an item on a balance sheet

> 1977 *Aviation Week & Space Technology*: U.S. Air Forces Europe…plans to increase its air assets greatly in this central region of the North Atlantic.

> 1996 *Jane's Defence Weekly*: Information from battle-management assets like AWACS can be piped via datalink into the cockpit of modern fighter aircraft and combined with the aircraft's own sensor picture.

asset-stripping *n* (1972) the practice of selling off the assets of a company (especially one recently taken over) in order to make a profit, without regard for the company's future. A favourite wheeler-dealer's ploy of the 1970s and 80s; see also **unbundle (1977)**. *Asset-stripper* is also first recorded in 1972

> 1972 *Observer*: The asset stripper's aim is to find a company rich in assets but down on its luck… Asset stripping has become the short cut to great wealth for young men with a burning ambition to make as much money as possible, with as little effort as possible.

> 1977 *Guardian Weekly*: Inquires in detail into Slater Walker's forays into industry but finds little evidence of industrial efficiency but plenty of asset stripping.

automatic teller *n* (1971), **automated teller** *n* (1974) a computerized machine that automatically provides cash or performs other functions of a bank cashier when a special card is inserted. Usually in *automatic teller machine* (the abbreviation *ATM* is first recorded in 1976). A successor to the slightly more specific **cash dispenser (1967)**. See also **cashpoint (1973)**, **hole-in-the-wall (1985)**

> 1971 *American Banker*: Depositors seal their deposits in envelopes which are provided and insert them in the 'automatic teller', which flashes a Thank You sign and issues a receipt.

> 1974 *Computers & People*: Installations of cash-dispensing and automated teller machines in proliferation by both thrifts and commercial banks.

ayatollah *n* (1979) See **ayatollah (1950)**

baby-boomer *n* (1974) a product of the post-World War II **baby boom (1941)**. Originally US; later abbreviated to *boomer*. A term that began to feel necessary when the postwar generation grew up, and advertisers, businesses, and politicians realized that they should be paid attention

> 1974 *Time*: 'We'—the baby boomers—had the schools, the attention of the media, [etc.].

> 1989 *New Yorker*: The script is ambitiously constructed, tracing the relationships of several boomer-age parents with their kids, their siblings, and their own parents.

back to basics (1975) A catch-phrase applied to a movement or enthusiasm for a return to fundamental principles (e.g. in education) or to policies reflecting this. Originally US. It did not impinge much on British consciousness until 1993, when it was adopted as a slogan by the Conservative Party ('It is time to get back to basics: to self-discipline and respect for the law, to consideration for others, to accepting responsibility for yourself and your family, and not shuffling it off on the state', John Major, Conservative Party Conference (1993)). Numerous fallings from grace amongst government ranks soon enabled opponents to turn the phrase back on those who had sponsored its use

> 1975 *New York Times*: The style and tone of the churches have undergone a major adustment…, gradually turning toward a 'back-to-basics' approach.

> 1994 *Vanity Fair*: 'Back to Basics' has so far involved three resignations, nine girlfriends, one close male friend, two violent deaths and two…'love children'.

bag lady *n* (1972) a homeless woman, often elderly, who carries her possessions in shopping bags. Originally US, but as the homeless began to appear in greater numbers on the streets of British cities in the 1980s the term became familiar on the eastern side of the Atlantic

1972 S. R. Curtin: Letty the Bag Lady…would pack all her valuables in two large shopping bags and carry them with her.

1984 Martin Amis: They even had a couple of black-clad bagladies sitting silently on straight chairs by the door.

barbie *n* (1976) a barbecue (see **barbecue (1931)**). Colloquial, originally and mainly Australian; along with several other Australianisms it made some inroads into British English in the 1980s and 90s, largely via watchers of popular Australian television soap operas such as *Neighbours*

1976 *Australian* (Sydney): He propounded the natural and national virtues of the Aussie beach barbie with beer and prawns, and the big chunder.

1993 *Mother & Baby*: We grown-ups were free to get the barbie sizzling or relax on the doorstep with a well-deserved drink.

barefoot doctor *n* (1971) a paramedical worker with basic medical training, especially one working in rural China. A literal translation of Chinese *chijiaoyisheng*

1971 *China Quarterly*: Dr. Horn…gives by far the most detailed account I have seen in English of the training, role, and supervision of the peasant-doctors (or 'barefoot doctors'), and their relationship to the mobile medical teams.

bean-counter *n* (1975) an accountant, especially one who compiles statistical records or accounts. Hence widely used as a term of contempt for financial planners or statisticians, viewed as being more interested in figures than in the creative aspects of the businesses they serve, or for anyone excessively concerned with accounts or figures

1986 *Independent*: The highly respected beancounters at Price Waterhouse have failed to recognise that times are changing in the City.

Beaujolais Nouveau *n* (1972) A commercial name for young Beaujolais wine (in French literally 'new Beaujolais'), sold during the first year of a vintage. From the mid 1970s to the late 1980s the practice developed (strenuously promoted by the growers and merchants) of rushing the latest vintage of Beaujolais across the Channel as soon as it had been released (around the middle of November), often accompanied by various headline-catching stunts. Disenchantment following too many years of thin and barely fermented grape juice eventually cooked Beaujolais Nouveau's goose

1979 *Daily Telegraph*: Prices for Beaujolais Nouveau…should be around £2 to £2.25 per bottle.

Betamax *n* (1975) A proprietary name for a videocassette format developed by the Japanese firm Sony. It was formed from Japanese *beta-beta* 'all over' and *max*, an abbreviation of English *maximum*, in allusion to the condensed format in which the signal is recorded. The format was widely used in the television industry, but in the domestic market it largely lost out to the rival **VHS (1982)**

1975 *Popular Photography*: But Sony…won't give up: its new Betamax ½in. cassette system uses tape very sparingly.

big hair *n* (1978) a bouffant hairstyle, especially one which is teased, permed, or sprayed to create volume. Originally US. Often taken as characteristic or symbolic of rich, powerful, or aggressive women

1991 *Guardian*: I expressed my concern that I didn't want a power hairdo, that bouffant meringue known affectionately as Big Hair.

Big Mac *n* (1970) A proprietary name (registered in the US in 1973, with claim of use since 1957) for the largest in a range of hamburgers sold by McDonald's fast-food outlets

1970 *Forbes* (New York): [McDonald's] tested big burgers—today's big seller—for years before adopting the Big Mac.

binge *v* (1976) to eat heavily, often furtively and as part of a compulsive cycle of eating and fasting

1976 Susie Orbach: The goal is for the compulsive eater to give up tortuous starving and bingeing.

bioethics *n* (1971) the discipline dealing with ethical questions that arise as a result of advances in medicine and biology

1978 *Observer*: The first successful completion of a pregnancy begun in the laboratory does raise some interesting issues. They fall into that area of debate which the Americans call…'bio-ethics'.

biofeedback *n* (1970) a technique in which electronic equipment is used to enable a person to monitor bodily processes and parameters that are normally involuntary or unperceived, so that he or she can learn to modify them

> 1970 *Journal of Transpersonal Psychology*: Gardner Murphy must be given due credit for stimulating and promoting bio-feedback research…and for his effort…to establish the Bio-Feedback Research Society, which met for the first time in 1969.

bionic *adj* (1976) outstandingly gifted or competent. Colloquial; a popular 1970ism thanks to the US television series *The Six Billion Dollar Man*, which featured a 'bionic' man (i.e. one containing electronic components) who performed superhuman feats (see **bionics (1960)**)

> 1976 *Guardian*: Among the splendid women in the cast, Prunella Gee stands out…as a bionic Julie Christie who proves to be the unprincipled Eternal Female Principle.

> 1977 *Private Eye*: Am I not right in thinking that the Faraday catchment area includes the delightful Ealing home of Margaret Jay, lovely daughter of Stoker Jim Callaghan and wife of the bionic Peter?

biotechnology *n* (1972) the branch of technology concerned with modern forms of industrial production utilizing living organisms, especially micro-organisms, and their biological processes. A reapplication of a term which had originally (see **biotechnology (1947)**) been applied to what would now more usually be called 'ergonomics'

> 1972 (title of periodical): Biotechnology and bioengineering symposium.

> 1982 *Times*: Biotechnology appeared to have staked out half a dozen major industries, each of which would be transformed by new manufacturing processes based on cell culture, genetic engineering, or the catalysing powers of enzymes.

birth *adj* (1977) Denoting a natural (as opposed to an adoptive) parent (or sometimes, in the case of the female parent, the one who physically gave birth as opposed to the genetic mother). Usually in *birth mother* and *birth parent*

> 1977 *New York Times*: A small but apparently growing number of adults…have started searching for their biological parents, or their 'birth parents', as some prefer it.

> 1995 *Coloradoan* (Fort Collins): Under an open adoption, the birth mother plays an active role in her baby's future by choosing who will raise the child.

blanket *n* (1977) Used in such expressions as *blanket protest* and *on the blanket* with reference to supporters of the Irish Republican cause held in the Maze prison (near Belfast) and elsewhere, who wore blankets instead of prison clothes, as a form of protest against being treated as criminals rather than as political prisoners

> 1978 *Economist*: The boys on the blanket have never won the same support beyond their immediate circle of friends and families that those who were interned could rely on.

blaxploitation *n* (1972) the exploitation of blacks, especially as actors in films of historical or other interest to blacks. A blend of *black* and *exploitation*, on the model of **sexploitation (1942)**

> 1972 *New York*: This blaxploitation picture's about a pre-Civil War slave.

bliss out *v* (1973) to reach a state of ecstasy. US slang; usually in the past participial adjective *blissed out*, denoting a state achieved particularly by young Western devotees of mystical Eastern religious cults. Probably modelled on **freak out (1965)**

> 1973 *National Observer* (US): A 'soul rush' of blissed-out young pilgrims is heading for the Western mecca of The Most Important Movement in the History of Mankind.

> 1973 *Newsweek*: Initiates learn to see a dazzling white light, hear celestial music, feel ecstatic vibrations… The process is called 'blissing out'.

Bloody Sunday *n* (1972) A name given to Sunday, 30 January 1972, when 13 civilians were shot and killed by British troops trying to disperse anti-internment protesters in the Bogside, Londonderry, Northern Ireland. It was borrowed from an earlier 'Bloody Sunday', 13 November 1887, when many people were injured in the dispersal of a socialist demonstration in Trafalgar Square, London

> 1972 *Listener*: The First Battalion of the Parachute Regiment pulls out of Northern Ireland at the end of the month… Incidents like Bloody Sunday…have earned the Paras a reputation for toughness.

blush *adj, n* (1979) Denoting a pale rosé wine. A marketing term invented in the US to help sell large amounts of rosé wine produced from a glut of red Zinfandel grapes. The wine proved unsuited to sophisticated tastes, so the term has fallen into disfavour

> 1996 *Houston Chronicle*: A blush wine called white zinfandel, panned by critics but loved by the soda-pop pinheads.

BMX *n* (1978) organized bicycle-racing on a dirt-track, especially for youngsters. Also applied to a bicycle used for this or similar activities, especially one which is robust and highly-manœuvrable. Originally US; an abbreviation of *bicycle moto-cross*, with the *X* standing for *cross*

> 1978 *Washington Post*: When police began chasing the teens off their makeshift race courses, a parents' group known as the Rockville BMX Association was organized to help teenagers find a site for a permanent race course.

> 1979 *Telegraph* (Brisbane): That infernal BMX—you know, that dragster-cross bicycle with the technicolor wheels.

boat people *n* (1977) refugees who leave their country by boat. The term was originally applied to refugees from Vietnam and other South-East Asian countries who fled by putting to sea in small boats, rafts, etc.

> 1977 *Chicago Tribune*: Repressive rule in the south has created a new classification of refugees, 'the boat people'. These are the thousands of families of Vietnamese...who push off in leaky boats and rafts into the South China Sea.

bomber jacket *n* (1973) a fashionable style of usually leather jacket, front-zippered and tightly gathered at waist and cuffs. It was modelled on the flight jackets worn by U.S.A.F. aircrew— hence the name

> 1985 *Listener*: There was the Intourist taxi driver in his Western trainers and Western bomber jacket.

bonk *v, n* (1975) to have sexual intercourse (with). A British colloquialism which did not really take off until the mid 1980s, when it was discovered and gleefully exploited by tabloid headline-writers ('Bonking Boris', in reference to the German tennis player Boris Becker's sex life, created a big alliterative impression in 1987). Probably a metaphorical extension of *bonk* 'to hit' (first recorded in 1931), on the model of *bang*. The noun *bonk* 'an act of sexual intercourse' is first recorded in 1984

> 1975 *Foul*: Rita is currently being bonked by the entire Aston Villains defence!

> 1984 McConville & Shearlaw: 'They're not even bonking any more.'... Entirely cross-sexual, with women being just as likely to say they bonk as are men... 'Did you have a good bonk last night?'

> 1986 *Daily Telegraph*: Fiona...has become so frustrated that she has been bonking the chairman of the neighbouring constituency's Conservative association.

> 1987 *Sun*: Fans who were at the concert...were still convinced that Carol had 'bonked' the virgin— and one of the band... It certainly looked like she and the boy were bonking.

born-again *adj* (1977) characterized by the extreme (or fanatical) enthusiasm of the newly con-verted or re-converted. Originally US; a metaphorical extension (often fairly disparaging) of **born-again (1961)**

> 1982 *Observer*: Nott has never been a true, born-again monetarist.

> 1985 Jonathan Raban: They're a bit born-again about smoking now.

> 1998 *Observer*: I have always been sceptical that Rupert Murdoch can be converted into a born-again European.

bottle bank *n* (1977) a collection point (typically a large metal box with a hole in the top or side) to which members of the public can take empty bottles for recycling

> 1977 *Grocer*: Bottle banks start.

> 1984 *Which?*: Why not take your old non-returnable glass bottles to your local bottle bank instead of throwing them away?

bottle out *v* (1979) to lose one's nerve; to back out of an action due to a last-minute draining away of courage. British slang, derived from **bottle** 'courage' (1958)

> 1985 *Times*: Why did Ken Livingstone 'bottle out' and vote to set a legal GLC rate?

brain-dead *adj* (1976) having suffered irreversible loss of function in the cerebrum and brain-stem of such a degree that respiration and circulation continue only if artificially maintained. An adjective based on **brain death**, a term first recorded in 1964 but largely restricted to medical and medico-legal texts until the 1970s, when discussion of the precise definition of psysiological death (prompted by advances in artificial life-support) entered the public domain. By the early 1980s it had been hijacked (originally in the US) as a contemptuous term for someone considered feeble-minded, stupid, or moribund

> 1976 *Time*: Because Karen was not 'brain dead', few lawyers were surprised when Judge Robert Muir ruled against any 'pulling of the plug'.

> 1990 *Daily Mirror*: I squealed as…Randy Ron…dropped his G-string to have his way with brain-dead yomping freak Billy.

brilliant *adj* (1971) wonderful, fantastic. Youth slang; in the 1980s it metamorphosed briefly into **brill (1981)**

> 1983 James Kelman: Man man who would've thought of me getting paid back money like that. Brilliant.

> 1984 Sue Townsend: I allowed Pandora to visit me in my darkened bedroom. We had a brilliant kissing session.

bucket shop *n* (1973) a retailer of cut-price airline tickets, aiming to undercut the market by working outside the official system. Mainly British; a re-application of an originally 19th-century term for an establishment where small-time gambling on the commodity markets took place, to the accompaniment of alcoholic drink sold from a bucket

> 1976 *Holiday Which?*: Bucket shops (as well as other travel firms) usually advertise in the small ads of *The Times, Time Out*, [etc.].

bulimia *n* (1976) an emotional disorder, occurring chiefly in young women, in which binges of extreme overeating alternate with depression and self-induced vomiting, purging, or fasting, and there is a persistent over-concern with body shape and weight. Ultimately from Greek *boulimia* 'great hunger', which was formed from the intensive prefix *bou-* (originally from *bous* 'ox') and *limos* 'hunger'. English had used it as a medical term (usually in the form *bulimy*) since at least the late 14th century, denoting extreme or pathological hunger, especially in the insane, but this usage (in full *bulimia nervosa*) recognizes a newly diagnosed psychological illness, in many ways the reverse of *anorexia nervosa* (a term which dates from the 1870s). The derived *bulimic* is first recorded as an adjective in 1977 and as a noun in 1980. See also **anorexic (1907)**

> 1976 *Scientific American*: After about two years a second phase [of anorexia], called bulimia, usually develops, in which the victim alternately fasts and gorges herself.

> 1977 *Behavior Therapy*: None of the patients in the studies cited were bulimic anorexics.

> 1980 *Washington Post*: Bulimics may not exhibit the outward signs of starvation that are the hallmark of the anorexic.

> 1985 *Woman's Own*: She developed another slimmer's disease—bulimia nervosa. 'For four months I stuffed myself with food then purged myself.'

bungee jumper *n* (1979) someone who jumps from a great height (e.g. from a bridge or precipice) while secured by an elasticated rope attached to the ankles or to a safety harness. The practice spread during the 1980s and 90s, both among those with a subterranean boredom threshold and as a means of raising money for charity (see also **extreme (1974)**). It has its origins in the South Pacific island of Pentecost, where men jump from a wooden tower attached only by a vine, with the purpose of encouraging the yam harvest. The word *bungee* itself, denoting an elasticated rope, is first recorded in 1930. It is presumably the same word as the somewhat earlier British slang *bungee* or *bungy* denoting an indiarubber eraser, but the origins of this are uncertain—probably it partly suggests the 'bouncy sponginess' of rubber

> 1979 *New York Times*: Five Britons who call themselves the 'Bungee Jumpers' leaped from the Golden Gate Bridge today, their falls broken by thick rubber bands that stopped them short of the water.

bustier *n* (1979) a short, close-fitting, often strapless bodice or top worn by women as a fashion garment. A borrowing from French, where it was derived from *buste* 'bust'

> 1989 *Times*: Young ladies were sunbathing topless or even naked in Hyde Park or wearing bustiers in Oxford Street.

buy-out *n* (1976) the purchase of a controlling share in a company. Often in *management buy-out* (first recorded in 1977), a buy-out in which senior management gain control of a company

> 1979 *Time*: At the end of 1978, Time Inc. completed a buyout of A.T.C. for a total price of $175.6 million.

> 1980 *Financial Review* (Australia): The British generally call it the 'management buy-out' but the meaning is the same—a company, very often the subsidiary of a large group, is bought 'out' by its senior directors.

cable *v* (1979) to equip with cable for the reception of cable television (see **cable television (1965)**)

> 1979 *Washington Post*: So far, only the east central part of the county is cabled.

> 1982 *Nature*: If most British dwellings can be 'cabled up'—linked to some broadband distribution system capable of handling more like forty than four distinct video signals, as at present.

car bomb *n* (1972) a bomb concealed by terrorists in a car, especially in one that is parked

> 1972 *Times*: The explosion of a car bomb without warning in a loyalist street.

carer *n* (1978) a person whose occupation is the care of the sick, aged, disabled, etc. Also applied to someone who looks after a disabled or elderly relative at home, often at the expense of her or his own career. A modern specialization of *carer* 'one who cares', which dates back at least to the 17th century. The related adjective *caring* (as in *caring professions*) is first recorded in 1976 (see **caring (1966)**)

> 1978 *Age & Ageing*: A much lower proportion of patients with chief carers in social classes one and two were admitted than those in three, four and five.

> 1982 *Times*: More money should be spent on the carers—those people, mainly women and mainly unpaid, who look after old and handicapped relations.

cashpoint *n* (1973) An alternative name for a **cash dispenser (1967)**

> 1973 *Times*: A cash dispenser which can issue variable amounts of money has been introduced by Lloyds Bank… Known as Cashpoint, the service is at present available at several branches in Essex.

> 1984 *Financial Times*: Charges for cashpoint withdrawals and direct debits will remain at 20p.

CAT *n* (1975) See **CT (1974)**

CD *n* (1979) See **compact disc (1979)**

Ceefax *n* (1972) The proprietary name for a teletext system operated by the BBC (see **teletext (1974)**). Coined by respelling the first elements of *seeing* and *facsimile*

> 1983 *Listener*: Telesoftware is carried by teletext—in other words, it is part of the BBC's Ceefax service.

cellular *adj* (1977) Designating a mobile radio-telephone system in which the area served is divided into sections or 'cells' a few miles across, each with its own short-range transmitter/receiver linked to an automatic switching centre, so that the same frequency can be used in different parts of the area simultaneously and the capacity is thereby increased. With the technology in place, the world awaited the tidal wave of mobile phones (see **mobile phone (1965)**). See also **cellphone (1984)**

> 1977 *Wireless World*: Cellular mobile radio going ahead.

> 1984 *Sunday Times*: So much has been written about developments in cellular car telephones…that the prospective buyer is almost bound to be confused.

CFC *n* (1976) An abbreviation of *chlorofluorocarbon* (first recorded in 1947), any of a class of stable compounds of carbon, fluorine, and chlorine whose presence in the atmosphere is thought to cause damage to the ozone layer. They have been widely but quietly used as refrigerants and aerosol propellants and in the plastics industry for several decades, and it was not until doubts surfaced about their safety that their name became at all well known (usually in the abbreviated form)

> 1976 *New Scientist*: The official view on CFCs and the ozone layer.

chairperson *n* (1971) a chairman or chairwoman: usually intended as an alternative that avoids specifying the sex of the office-holder. For some reason, this was the main coinage around which the controversy about non-sex-specific *person* raged in the 1970s (see **person (1971)**). Opponents attacked it on political and aesthetic grounds. Subtler arguers claimed that in practice it was only applied to women, and that men were still called *chairmen* (although in practice this was not always so—see the second example below). Seekers of the middle way advocated the use of the genderless *chair* (' Martha Layne Collins...is to serve as chair of the Convention', *New Yorker* (1984)), a usage which dates back to the 17th century

> 1971 *Science News*: A group of women psychologists thanked the board for using the word 'chair-person' rather than 'chairman'.

> 1984 Sue Townsend: Dear Chairperson, Arthur, it is with the deepest regret that I offer my resigna-tion as vice-chairperson of the Elm Ward Labour Party.

chaos *n* (1974) (a state characterized by) behaviour which is governed by deterministic laws but which is so unpredictable as to appear random, owing to its extreme sensitivity to changes in para-meters or its dependence on a large number of independent variables. The study of such states is termed *chaos theory* or *chaology* (both first recorded in 1987)

> 1974 *Science*: Li and Yorke's general theorem for cycles of period 3 may be extended...to show that equations of the generic form of 1 and 2 will enter a regime of chaos, with an uncountable number of cycles of integral period along with an uncountable number of aperiodic solutions

> 1987 *Nature*: A survey of how determinism fares in various branches of physics, including classical mechanics, relativity theory..., probabilistic theories, modern chaos theory and the quan-tum theory.

charm offensive *n* (1979) the adoption of a plausible manner or cooperative approach as an ex-pedient strategy for achieving a goal. Usually used with reference to politicians, and with the implication of ingratiation and insincerity

> 1996 *Financial Times*: Nato's new secretary general...pledged himself yesterday to launch a 'charm offensive' aimed at winning the confidence of Russia.

cheers *interj* (1976) thank you. British colloquial; apparently the drinking toast put to a new use
> 1978 *U & Non-U Revisited*: Do any small favour for a young Englishman these days and he will thank you by saying 'cheers'.

cherry-pick *v* (1972) to select or pick out only that which is most outstanding, advantageous, profitable, etc. Usually used with negative connotations, by someone who disapproves

> 1975 *Business Week*: Many customers are trading down to cheaper brands. Others are doing more 'cross-shopping' from store to store, cherry-picking the specials.

> 1991 *Kiplinger's Personal Finance*: Small groups don't have enough people to spread the risk, so insurers cherry-pick.

chicken brick *n* (1970) a two-part earthenware container inside which a chicken can be cooked. An ethnic utensil (it is of Tuscan origin) which no self-respecting Habitat-furnished British kitchen would have been without in the late 1970s and early 80s

> 1982 *Habitat Catalogue 1982/83*: Terracotta chicken brick that cooks any meat to golden, tender succulence in its own juices.

child benefit *n* (1975) a regular government payment made in Britain (and also New Zealand) to the parents of children up to a certain age. In Britain it replaced family allowance in 1975
> 1977 *Belfast Telegraph*: If you want Child Benefit, we want your Family Allowances book.

chocoholic, chocaholic *n* (1976) a compulsive eater of chocolate. See **-aholic (1965)**
> 1976 *Business Week*: Sheron says he used to be a 'chocoholic', but lost 50lb in nine months last year.

CJD *n* (1975) An abbreviation of *Creutzfeldt-Jakob disease*, a communicable degenerative disease of the human brain. The disease was identified in the 1930s and named (in German) *Creutzfeldt-Jakobsche Krankheit*, after the German neurologists Hans G. Creutzfeldt (1885–1964) and Alfons M. Jakob (1882–1927). It did not achieve a high public profile until the 1990s, when fears grew that it might be caused by eating meat infected with the cattle disease BSE (see **BSE (1987)**); then, not surprisingly, the abbreviation was frequently preferred to the full form. See also **human BSE (1992)**

> 1996 *Private Eye*: The trigger of the current scare was the 10 new cases of CJD in persons under the age of 42, said to resemble the pattern of disease presented by BSE cows.

cling film *n* (1975) plastic film so thin that it attaches readily to an object round which it is wrapped, sold commercially to cover and preserve food

> 1975 *Food Manufacture*: British Cellophane Ltd. announce the introduction of a polyethylene cling film for fresh food wrapping—BCL Cling Film 301.

clocking *n* (1974) the practice of winding back the milometer (colloquially *clock*) of a vehicle so that it registers a falsely low mileage, and the vehicle can be passed off to potential purchasers as less heavily used than it is. British slang

> 1994 *BBC Top Gear Magazine*: In the US they have legislation which has all but prevented clocking—The Truth of Mileage Act—and carries heavy penalties.

club class *n* (1978) a class of fare between first class and tourist class on a passenger aircraft, etc., and designed especially for the business traveller. Part of the on-going late-20th-century proliferation of names for various fare categories in the travel industry which seek, often simultaneously, to maximize the prestige of the category and to euphemize its non-first-class status. In this particular case, the subliminal message is the exclusivity of the club

> 1978 *Times*: Club class would be available to full economy-fare passengers and would be intended mainly for businessmen.

cod war *n* (1973) A journalistic name given to a long-running intermittent quarrel between Iceland and Britain over the former's extension of its fishing limits. This had its beginnings as far back as 1953, but the term *cod war* was coined in response to a new outbreak of hostilities when Iceland extended its limit to 80.5 km (50 miles) in 1973. The model was later exploited in **beef war (1996)**

> 1973 *Guardian*: Sir Alec Douglas-Home…was launching into…the need to avoid actions which would 'hot up this cod war'.

cold calling *v, n* (1972) making unsolicited calls on prospective customers, either by telephone or in person, in order to sell them goods or services

> 1972 *Times*: She and Ken used to set off for the City, 'cold calling' on travel agencies…that might have jobbing work.

> 1978 *New York Times*: Bonified appointments with customers who are waiting for you. No cold calling.

collateral damage *n* (1975) destruction or injury beyond the intent or expectation of an aggressor, usually occurring in a civilian area surrounding a military target. Commonly used as a euphemism for 'accidentally killing civilians'. US military jargon which reached a wider audience during the Gulf War

> 1975 *Aviation Week*: Low-and-moderate yields also would be developed to replace Pershing 1-A nuclear warheads for greater military effectiveness and less collateral damage.

> 1991 *Washington Post*: Weapons of such precision that military targets can be detected, isolated and killed almost without collateral civilian damage.

community service *n* (1972) unpaid socially beneficial work done under supervision as an alternative sentence to imprisonment. Imposed in Britain under the terms of a 'community service order'

> 1972 *Criminal Justice Act*: Where a person who has attained the age of seventeen is convicted of an offence punishable with imprisonment, the court by or before which he is convicted may…make an order (in this Act referred to as 'a community service order') requiring him to perform unpaid work in accordance with the subsequent provisions of this Act.

compact disc *n* (1979) a disc on which sound or data is recorded digitally as a spiral pattern of pits and bumps underneath a smooth transparent protective layer and reproduced by detecting the reflections of a laser beam focused on the spiral. By the end of the 1980s such discs had largely replaced LPs and tapes as the main medium of audio recording. The widely used abbreviation **CD** is also first recorded in 1979. See also **CD ROM (1983)**

> 1979 *Materials Engineer*: As the laser moves toward the outer edge, the Compact Disc slows down from 500 to 215 rpm.

> 1979 *New Scientist*: Although the Compact Disc (CD) system indubitably works as claimed and could offer an attractive alternative to today's grooved records…CD is sure to receive far hotter competition from Japan than the compact cassette.

> 1984 *What Video?*: My musical examples came from what is still one of the best examples of CD recording around.

confrontational *adj* (1975) aggressive, deliberately seeking conflict

> 1982 *Observer*: Why is the United States pursuing these confrontational tactics?

contraflow *n* (1975) road-traffic flow or movement alongside and in a direction contrary to an established or usual flow, as during road-works. British; an exciting new use for a word which had hitherto largely languished as a technical term in the paper-making industry

> 1975 *Daily Mail*: There are…contra-flow bus lanes (in which buses go against the flow of other traffic).

> 1983 *Daily Telegraph*: A contraflow will apply between junctions 14 and 15…until August.

cot death *n* (1970) the unexplained death of a baby in its sleep. See also **SIDS (1970)**

> 1970 *Guardian*: 'Cot death' relates to children not known to be ill…who die unexpectedly.

couch potato *n* (1979) someone who spends leisure time passively or idly sitting around, especially watching television or videotapes. Slang, originally US. Reputedly coined by Tom Iacino as a pun on US slang *boob-tuber* 'television addict', from *boob tube* 'television' (the potato being a type of tuber), but maybe it simply arose by association with *vegetable* 'inert person'. Either way, its neat encapsulation of vacuous indolence ensured its success in the censorious 1980s. Registered as a proprietary term in the US in 1984, with claim of first use in 1976. See also **mouse potato (1994)**

> 1979 *Los Angeles Times*: The Humboldt State Marching Lumberjacks…and the Couch Potatoes who will be lying on couches watching television as they are towed toward the parade route.

counter-culture *n* (1970) a radical culture, especially amongst the young, that rejects established social values and practices. Originally US; applied specifically to the 'hippie' culture of the late 1960s and early 70s. Compare **alternative society (1969)**

> 1970 *Atlantic Monthly*: Some 400 newspapers and magazines now serve the counter culture… More than one underground 'wire service' exists, along with radical film and video-tape studios and street theater troupes and poster artists. The preferred name for this considerable activity is 'alternative media'.

cowboy *n* (1972) a person without qualifications who competes against established traders or operators, providing shoddy goods or services usually at low (or inflated) prices; someone who is recklessly unscrupulous in business. British colloquial

> 1977 *Listener*: In the next decade, as the rich seams of double glazing, wall coating and so on get worked out, it is likely that the cowboys will move into quite new areas.

crash *n, v* (1972) (to undergo) a sudden failure which puts a computer system out of action, often with the loss of data

> 1972 *Computer Journal*: If there is a crash, we have an armoury of little programs to aid the system programmers in sorting out the system.

> 1973 *Scientific American*: A computer can 'crash', or fail, for any number of reasons. Usually the cause can be traced either to the failure of an electronic component or to a flaw in the program.

creative accounting *n* (1973) the modification of financial accounts to achieve a desired end; falsification of accounts that is misleading but not illegal

> 1973 *Harper's Magazine*: The extent to which Equity Funding's earnings before 1970 were the result of 'creative accounting' is still unclear.

crumblie, crumbly *n* (1976) an elderly or senile person, especially one older than a wrinkly (see **wrinkly (1971)**). Slang

> 1976 *Times*: The girl's great-grandmother, who died recently at 102, was called 'the crumblie'.

> 1984 Sue Townsend: At the end of the party Rick Lemon put 'White Christmas' by some old crumblie on the record deck and all the couples danced romantically together.

CT *n* (1974), **CAT** *n* (1975) An abbreviation (in the case of *CAT* pronounced as an acronym) of *computerized* (*axial*) *tomography*, a method of X-raying a plane section of a body in which a computer controls the motion of the X-ray source and detectors, processes the data, and produces the image. Usually used in combination with *scan, scanner*, etc.

> 1974 *Radiology*: CT scans were clearly positive.

> 1975 *Journal of the American Medical Association*: The brain, an immobile structure of relatively homogeneous density is ideal for CT.

> 1979 L. Shainberg: He had an X-ray of his cerebral tissue called a CAT-scan.

daisy wheel *n* (1977) a kind of removable printing unit for typewriters and printers, in which the printing elements are on the sides of arms radiating from a central hub and forming a flat wheel which is automatically rotated to bring a selected character in front of the hammer

> 1979 *New Scientist*: 'Daisy wheel' printers are now ousting 'golfballs' in word processing systems.

data protection *n* (1975) the legal regulation of access to data held in computer storage

> 1985 *Library Association Record*: Data Protection: A Guide for Library and Information Management…provides a comprehensive study of the data protection issue… The Data Protection Act is examined in detail.

date rape *n* (1975) rape of a woman by a man she is dating or with whom she is on a date. Originally and mainly US

> 1991 *New York Times*: Most date rape cases come down in the end to Her versus Him.

de-accession *v* (1972) to remove an entry for (an exhibit or book) from the accessions register of a museum, library, etc., usually in order to sell the item concerned. Used as a camouflage word (the practice does not encourage new benefactors), but by the end of the century its cover had been well and truly blown

> 1972 *New York Times*: The Museum of Art recently de-accessioned (the polite term for 'sold') one of its only four Redons.

debit card *n* (1975) a plastic card issued by an organization, giving the holder access to an account, via an appropriate computer terminal, especially in order to authorize the transfer of funds to the account of another party when making a purchase, etc., without incurring revolving finance charges for credit. Originally US. Compare **credit card (1952)**

> 1977 *McGraw-Hill Yearbook of Science & Technology*: Unlike bank credit cards…, debit cards… are presently used mainly in a local or regional environment.

deconstruct *v* (1973) to subject to deconstruction, a strategy of critical analysis associated with the French philosopher Jacques Derrida (b. 1930), directed towards exposing unquestioned metaphysical assumptions and internal contradictions in philosophical and literary language, and emphasizing the meaning of words in relation to each other rather than to referents in the real world; to analyse and reinterpret in accordance with this strategy, which has been both influential and controversial (i.e. reviled) in the last quarter of the century. Both *deconstruct* and *deconstruction* are first recorded in an English translation of Derrida's work

> 1973 D. B. Allison: The prerogative of being cannot withstand the deconstruction of the word… One cannot attempt to deconstruct this transcendence.

> 1976 G. C. Spivak: Ricoeur delivers hermeneutic interpretations of several texts that Derrida deconstructs.

> 1979 *London Review of Books*: We are not in favour of the current fashion for the 'deconstruction' of literary texts, for the elimination of the author from his work.

def *adj* (1979) excellent, great, cool. Slang, originally and mainly US Black English. Often used in the expression *def jam* 'excellent music'. Its origins are disputed: it probably represents a Jamaican variant of *death*, used as a general intensifier (for which there is some evidence from the first decade of the 20th century), but it is often explained as a shortened form of *definite* or *definitive*

    1979 S. Robinson et al.: I'm 'a get a fly girl Gonna get some spank 'n' Drive off in a def OJ.

    1986 *Village Voice* (New York): 'It's Yours'—TLA Rock and Jazzy Jay (Partytime, 1984). Here's the first def jam that made the others possible.

dehire *v* (1970) to dismiss (someone, especially an executive) from employment. Originally US; one of a range of late-20th-century euphemisms designed to take the sting out of the sack (see also **downsize (1979)**, **outplace (1970)**)

    1970 *Guardian Weekly*: The pinched corporation…fires the chairman of the board. Fires is a rude word, but the bouncing of the boss is happening now on such a scale that Wall Street is mushrooming with firms bearing the weird names of 'Dehiring Consultants, Inc.' and 'Executive Adjustment Advisers'… In a depression, the boss is sacked and jumps from a window. In the 'recedence', he is 'dehired'.

deselect *v* (1979) Of a local constituency party: to reject (a sitting Member of Parliament) as constituency candidate at a forthcoming election, especially under the Labour Party's reselection procedure. A re-application of a verb which had occasionally been used, equally euphemistically, in the US since the late 1960s to denote dismissing an employee or rejecting a candidate (see **deselect (1968)**). The related noun *deselection* is also first recorded in 1979

    1979 *Times*: By the example of expulsion or the threat of de-selection the Labour right is to be cowed and cajoled into submission.

    1983 *Daily Telegraph*: Two 'deselected' Labour M.P.s are standing as independents.

detox *n, v* (1972) (to subject to) a process of removing the toxic effects of alcohol or other drugs. Originally US

    1978 *New York Times Magazine*: I went to detox again…and it's been five years since I came out and I haven't had a drink or pill since… They did get me detoxed and clean. They told me I was an alcoholic.

direct debit *n* (1976) an order requiring a bank to pay bills, etc. by regularly transferring the requisite amount from a customer's account to that of the creditor. A further step towards the cashless economy

    1994 *Guardian*: Some Natfhe members at the college have their union subscription deducted by 'check-off', but others pay by direct debit.

do, doo *n* (1972) excrement, especially canine. A euphemism which exploits the blank vagueness of the verb *do*. Not recorded in print until the 1970s, but reliably remembered in use around 1920, and recorded ambiguously in the sense either 'excrement' or 'act of defecating' in 1930. It leapt to fame in reduplicated form when US president-elect George Bush used it metaphorically in a speech in 1989 in the expression *in deep doo-doo*, meaning 'in serious trouble'

    1974 P. Gzowski: About as naughty as I got on the air was to talk about 'doggy do'.

    1994 N. McCall: I got myself into deeper doo-doo while trying to clean up my act.

Doctor Martens *n* (1977) A proprietary name (registered in Britain in 1977, with claim of use since 1965) for a type of heavy laced walking boot or shoe with a cushioned sole, often associated with aggressive young men. Commonly abbreviated to *Doc Martens*. The boot's name comes from its German inventor, Dr Klaus Maertens

    1983 *New York Times*: The new look is…everything in gray and black, with stiletto heels on girls and Doctor Marten's ankle boots on guys.

    1984 Sue Townsend: Today I drew some money out of my Building Society account, and bought my first pair of Doc Marten's. They are bully-boy brown and have got ten rows of lace holes.

docutainment *n* (1978) a genre of film, etc. which includes documentary material and seeks to both inform and entertain. Originally and mainly North American; a blend of *documentary* and *entertainment*

    1983 *Washington Post*: 'I call it "variety docutainment",' says the production's executive producer, Cindy Walker… 'We'll be using documentary inserts combined on stage with drama, song and dance.'

doomwatch *n* (1970) observation intended to avert danger or destruction, especially of the environment by pollution or nuclear war. The term was suggested by the name of a BBC television series first broadcast in 1970 ('BBC-TV's new scientific soap-opera, *Doomwatch*, has been fortunate in its first selection of topics to warn us about', *New Scientist* (1970)). The derived *doomwatcher* is first recorded in 1971

> 1970 *Guardian*: The Government Chemist…tested 50 tins of tuna bought throughout the country… Mr Prior said:…'We shall be getting on with this—this Doomwatch, if you like to call it that.'

> 1978 *Nature*: As WMO sees it, hard evidence does little to support many of the disaster hypotheses of the doom-watchers… There is one major exception: the problem of increasing CO2 in the atmosphere.

dot matrix *n* (1975) a letter-sized rectangular or square array of positions that are selectively filled to create an alphanumeric character on paper or a VDU screen. Usually in *dot-matrix printer*— standard technology for producing computer print-out before the advent of laser printers

> 1975 *Electronic Design*: A dot-matrix printer, the Model 9316, offers speeds to 173 char/s.

down-market *adj, adv* (1970) at, towards, or being the cheaper end of the market; cheap, popular

> 1970 *Times*: It really is…cheering that Courtaulds, who have always seemed so determinedly down-market in their approach…should wake up to the fact that good design is…essential.

> 1973 *Listener*: Readers who have asked about the matter can be told that there is no reason to believe the paper will move 'down-market' in search of popularity.

downsize *v* (1979) to reduce the size of. Originally and mainly US; widely used as a euphemistic cover for reducing the size of an organization by dismissing employees (compare the later and even more weaselly **rightsize (1987)**). It was not an entirely new usage, but a generalization of the slightly earlier *downsize* 'to design or build a car of smaller size', which came out of the energy crisis of the early 1970s

> 1982 *Fortune*: Right now he's 'downsizing' the company, and hopes to achieve 1982 cost savings of about $600 million.

dream team *n* (1972) a team (in sports, etc.) that is perfect or ideally matched. Originally US

> 1972 J. McGinniss: Do you know what Federated Press is starting?… A collection of the smartest, prettiest girl reporters. They're bringing them all to New York and calling them the dream team.

drive-time *adj, n* (1975) (Designating a radio programme broadcast at) one of two periods in the day, corresponding to the morning and evening rush hours, in which large numbers of commuters listen to the radio in their cars. Originally US

> 1975 *New York Times*: Recent studies showed 51% increase in FM morning drive time listening from '73 to '75 and 42% increase in afternoon drive time.

> 1993 *Coloradoan* (Fort Collins): 'Shock jocks'…are beginning to dominate morning drive-time FM radio.

dub *n* (1974) a re-mixed version of a piece of recorded music, often with the melody line removed and including various special effects, which was developed in Jamaica and is popular especially in reggae and other black music. From *dub* 'to mix in new elements in a soundtrack'. See also **dub (1982)**

> 1974 C. Gillett: Dub wise skank: talk over.

> 1983 *Listener*: As we pull up outside a reggae shop in the Lower Clapton Road, loud and bass-heavy 'dub' music with a patois talkover 'toast' booms into the bus.

earner *n* (1970) an activity that brings in money for the person engaged in it. British slang; often in the phrase *a nice little earner* 'a means of making easy or illicit profit', which was popularized by the Thames TV series *Minder* (1979–93)

> 1987 *Sunday Telegraph*: The family letting rooms on the quiet, or the person who has a 'nice little earner' on the side.

easy peasy *adj* (1976) childishly or ridiculously simple. British colloquial; an arbitrary reduplication of *easy*, in imitation of children's language

> 1976 *Evening Standard*: I'm short of money this week… How do I get to work?… Easy peasy… I run to the station, leap the barrier, clobber the train driver, dress up in his clothes [etc.].

Ebonics *n* (1975) African-American vernacular English, especially as considered to be a language in its own right, rather than a non-standard dialect of English. Originally US; a blend of *ebony* and *phonics*, first recorded as the title of a book by R. L. Williams

> 1996 *Daily Progress* (Charlottesville, Virginia): The Oakland school board voted to recognize Black English, or 'Ebonics', as a second language.

EC *n* (1973) An abbreviation of *European Community*, a title that superseded *European Economic Community* (see **EEC (1958)**). The change in designation was intended to de-emphasize the purely economic role of the Community (particularly following the link-up in 1967 with the European Coal and Steel Community and the European Atomic Energy Community), and prepare the ground for closer political union. The full form is recorded in informal use since the late 1950s ('The Six are the European Community, fore-runner of the continental political union…that is to be when General de Gaulle is gone', *Economist* (1958)), and the abbreviation since 1973 (sometimes in early use standing for *European Communities*), but they did not become official until the 1980s. See also **European Union (1991)**

> 1973 *Business Week*: Europe: The EC feud over nuclear fuel.

> 1980 *Daily Telegraph*: The abbreviation EEC is now taboo…'The European Community' is the Council [of Ministers]'s approved designation, with the abbreviation EC.

ecofreak *n* (1970) a fanatical conservationist or environmentalist

> 1980 *Guardian Weekly*: Alexandre Hebert,…a staunch anarchist trade unionist, has nothing but disdain for 'those eco-freaks who want to turn back the wheels of history'.

ECU, ecu *n* (1970) An abbreviation of *European Currency Unit*, denoting originally a notional unit used for pricing goods within the European Economic Community, and towards the end of the century applied to the actual monetary units used for the common currency within the European Union. Modelled on *écu*, the name of various French gold or silver coins of former times, and sometimes written thus. Compare **euro (1971)**, and see also **Exchange Rate Mechanism (1978)**

> 1970 *Guardian*: M. Rey, president of the EEC Commission in Brussels, yesterday forecast the écu (crown) as the name of the future European currency… [It] would…stand for 'European Currency Unit'.

> 1972 *Times*: The European currency unit, the Ecu, failed to make an impact.

electronic mail *n* (1977) the sending of non-spoken information between individuals over a telecommunication network to a selected location or locations where it is stored for subsequent retrieval, typically via a personal computer. The term is also applied to the information sent. More commonly referred to at the end of the century by its abbreviation **e-mail (1982)**

> 1977 *Science*: An electronic mail system is becoming practical today, because of the wide availability…of electronic communication channels.

EMU *n* (1972) An abbreviation of *economic and monetary union*, a programme for full economic unity within the European Union, based on the phased introduction of the ECU as a common currency (see **ECU (1970)**, **single currency (1975)**). Initially proposed as a way of solving currency difficulties in France and Germany (at this stage it was often taken to stand for *European Monetary Union*), it was relaunched in 1989 following the publication of the Delors report, a three-stage plan for introducing a common currency and aligning the economies of the member states. Often pronounced /'iːmjuː/, like the bird

> 1972 *Times*: The initiative for EMU is a result of the currency crises of 1969 involving France and Germany.

> 1990 *International Management*: The EC's main debate a few months ago centred on 'EMU', or how to achieve economic and monetary union after 1992.

end *n* **at the end of the day** (1974) eventually; when all's said and done. An expression that was apparently born a cliché

> 1976 *South Notts. Echo*: 'At the end of the day,' he stated, 'this verifies what I have been saying against the cuts in public expenditure.'

> 1982 Bill Beaumont: But, at the end of the day, it is an amateur sport and everyone is free to put as much or as little into the game as he chooses.

energy crisis *n* (1970) a serious shortage of energy-producing fuels. A term called into being mainly by the large price increases imposed by oil-exporting countries in the early 1970s, which caused severe disruption in Western economies

> 1971 *Washington Post*: Although some progress has been made in dealing with the U.S. 'energy crisis', the likelihood of…blackouts in the coming year is not being ruled out.

> 1974 *B.B.C. Handbook 1975*: One…fairly brief consequence of the energy crisis was the decision to close down all television networks at 10.30 pm.

enterprise zone *n* (1978) a designated zone within an area of high unemployment and low investment, usually in an inner city, where the government encourages new enterprise by granting financial concessions such as tax and rate relief to businesses

> 1978 *Times*: A suggestion that 'enterprise zones' should be created in Britain's derelict inner cities…was made last night by Sir Geoffrey Howe…in a speech to the Bow Group.

E-number *n* (1977) a code number preceded by the letter *E*, assigned to an additive that accords with EU Food Additive directives, and listed as an ingredient on the packaging of food or drink. The *E*, short for *Euro* or *European*, was in due course re-interpreted as standing for 'additive', and came to be used in such combinations as *E-free* ('Who could have imagined mammoth supermarket chains majoring their promotion campaigns on E-free food as they do now?', *She* (1988)) and on its own ('Thr arn't any E's in Panda's licoric', advertising slogan (1988))

> 1977 *Grocer*: Other labelling disagreement stems from EEC Commission recommendations that all additives be declared by their name or by their 'E' number (an 'E' number means the additive has been approved).

> 1986 *Financial Times*: A merry dance of dietary fibre, polyunsaturates and E-numbers.

environmentalism *n* (1972) concern with the preservation of the environment, especially from the effects of pollution; the politics or policies associated with this

> 1972 *Science News*: The arguments in the United States over environmental problems have not yet reached these basic levels, even though environmentalism got its first major impetus there.

epidural *n* (1970) an injection of anæsthetic into the space outside the membrane covering the spinal cord, used especially to control pain during childbirth by producing a loss of sensation below the waist without affecting consciousness. A noun use of the adjective *epidural*, first recorded in 1882

> 1970 *Guardian*: If I was in a lot of pain I would be offered an 'epidural'.

Ethernet *n* (1976) a type of local area network of computers in which all stations can receive all messages

> 1995 *Macworld*: The 9500 has a 10BaseT Ethernet connector (in addition to an AAUI connector) so you can more easily attach to Ethernet networks.

euro *n* (1971) A name proposed for the monetary unit of the European **single currency (1975)**, based on the prefix **Euro-**, and officially accepted by the European Commission in December 1995. The euro came into force in most countries of the European Union (see **Euroland (1999)**) on 1 January 1999, although notes and coins will not be available until 2002. Compare **ECU (1970)**

> 1971 *Guardian*: How would you feel about paying your bills in Euros…? 'Euro' is the name…thought the ideal one for a European currency.

> 1995 *Economist*: As the Euro is likely to replace only the currencies of EU members with the strongest currencies at first, it will be a significantly 'harder' currency than the basket ecu.

> 1999 *Observer*: 'Do euros mean I have to make different arrangements when I go on holiday?' 'No. Everything you've been doing before, you can still do—at least for the next three years.'

Exchange Rate Mechanism *n* (1978) a method of stabilizing exchange rates within the European Monetary System, by which the currencies of some EC countries are linked to the ECU (see **ECU (1970)**) to limit excessive exchange-rate fluctuations. Often known by the abbreviation *ERM*. Britain joined in 1990, but had to withdraw in somewhat embarrassing circumstances in 1992 (see **Black Wednesday (1992)**)

> 1978 *Financial Times*: The ECU will be used…as the denominator…for the exchange rate mechanism.

> 1991 *Economist*: Sterling's membership of the exchange-rate mechanism was acceptable at the current wide 6% band because 'it is in a way like anchoring something to the gold standard'.

Exocet *n* (1970) A proprietary name for a kind of rocket-propelled short-range guided missile of French manufacture, used especially in tactical sea warfare. French *exocet* means literally 'flying fish'. The term did not become familiar to lay audiences until the Falklands War of 1982, when the Argentinians used Exocets against British forces

> 1983 *Annual Register 1982*: On 4 May HMS Sheffield, a type 42 destroyer, was sunk by a French-made Exocet air-to-sea missile.

expert system *n* (1977) a computer program or group of programs designed to store and apply the knowledge of experts in a given field, so that others can use it for deciding, evaluating, or inferring in that field

> 1983 *International Management*: ICOT is concentrating for now on the development of two 'expert systems'—intelligent computer programs that can solve problems or reach conclusions usually requiring the knowledge of human experts.

explicit *adj* (1971) Of a magazine, film, etc.: describing or portraying nudity or sexual activity graphically or in detail. Euphemistic

> 1971 *Hansard Lords*: There are, my expert friend said, still some prohibitions…in the cinema—including what he calls 'explicit penetration'.

> 1972 R. Michael: His films are not explicit—no genitals for instance—and they are often intentionally droll and whimsical.

extreme *adj* (1974) Designating (a participant in) a sport performed in a hazardous environment or involving a high physical risk. Originally apparently a mountaineering term, it spread in the 1980s to skiing and thence to a range of increasingly white-knuckle activities, as people sought ever more hair-raising sources of an adrenaline buzz (see also **bungee jumper (1979)**, **canyoning (1992)**)

> 1974 R. Messner: As technique improved, difficulties were overcome and every Alpine face was conquered; the extreme climbers…became non-competitive.

> 1996 *Chicago Tribune*: The 'extreme sports' of bungee jumping, street luge and mountain biking.

face *n in your face* (1976) Initially an exclamation of derision or contempt, originating among US basketball players, but soon developing into an adjective, meaning 'aggressive, provocative, brash'. In this latter usage, it began to spread into British English in the 1990s

> 1976 C. Rosen: 'Stuffed!' shouted the taller boy. 'Doobie got himself stuffed!…In yo' face, Doobie!'

> 1996 *Independent*: A broad canvas of British artists, the provocative, in-your-face double act Gilbert and George and Turner Prize winner Damien Hurst infamous among them.

factoid *n* (1973) something that becomes accepted as a fact, although it is not (or may not be) true. Applied specifically to an assumption or speculation reported and repeated so often that it is popularly considered true—a concept elaborated by the US writer Norman Mailer (b. 1923)

> 1973 Norman Mailer: Factoids…that is, facts which have no existence before appearing in a magazine or newspaper, creations which are not so much lies as a product to manipulate emotion in the Silent Majority.

first-time buyer *n* (1973) a buyer of property who has not previously owned a home, and therefore has no house to sell

> 1973 *Times*: The Building Societies Association was taken unawares by the Government's specific proposals to help first-time buyers.

fixed link *n* (1974) (a tunnel, bridge, etc. built to accommodate) a (projected) permanent means of transit between Britain and France, especially by road or rail. A term favoured by insiders in the 1970s, when advance planning for the link was getting under way but the tunnel/bridge decision had not yet been taken. See also **Chunnel (1928)**

> 1974 *Economist*: As so much of the traffic will be road vehicles and their passengers, it is worth asking whether a rail tunnel is the best form of a fixed link with France, rather than a road bridge or bridge/tunnel.

flagship *adj* (1977) being the leading product, model, etc., in a range (and therefore promoted as representing the range and establishing its public image)

> 1977 *Listener*: Flagship programmes on BBC TV were offered as remedies.

> 1978 *Daily Telegraph*: Opel's new flagship model, the three-litre Monza coupé.

> 1981 *Times*: THF's flagship hotel, Grosvenor House.

flasher *n* (1974) See **flash (1968)**

flexitime, flextime *n* (1972) an arrangement whereby employees, while working a contracted number of hours, are free to vary (within prescribed limits) their starting and finishing times. The variant *flextime* was registered as a proprietary name in Britain in 1972 and in the US in 1974, but it seems never to have been quite as popular as *flexitime*. Both may be modelled ultimately on German *Gleitzeit*, literally 'sliding time'. Workers absent under such an arrangement were at first often said to be *flexing off*

> 1972 *Business Week*: 'Everybody told us flexi-time was pie in the sky,' says Gösta Rehn.

> 1972 *Times*: New working hours are based on the 'flextime' principle, with a 'core time' of three hours during the day when everyone must be at work.

flip-flop *n* (1970) a plastic or rubber sandal consisting of a flat sole and straps. In US and Australian English usually termed a **thong (1967)**. The word imitates the sound the wearer makes when walking along

> 1970 *Observer*: Milligan has a beard and wears flip-flops with jeans.

floppy disk *n* (1972) a small flexible plastic disc with a magnetic coating used as an inexpensive light-weight moderate-capacity storage device for computer information. After some initial uncertainty, *disk* became the standard spelling in British as well as American English. Compare **hard disk (1978)**

> 1972 *Computer Design*: Century Data Systems has introduced the CDS–100 'floppy disc' drive, a portable storage device that utilizes a single, removable, disc cartridge as the recording medium.

flying picket *n* (1974) (a member of) a group of striking workers who picket premises or organizations other than those at which they are employed, especially one which travels from another area to a striking site or sites in order to reinforce local pickets. British

> 1984 *Times*: 138 pits are on strike or are 'picketed out' by flying pickets from…militant coalfields.

food processor *n* (1974) an electrical kitchen appliance for mixing, chopping, shredding, and otherwise preparing foods for cooking or for the table

> 1974 *House Beautiful*: The food machine that does nearly everything is the innovative Food Processor made by Cuisinarts.

fractal *n* (1975) a mathematically conceived curve such that any small part of it, enlarged, has the same statistical character as the original. A term borrowed from French, where it was coined (from Latin *fractus* 'broken') by the mathematician Benoît Mandelbrot and introduced by him in *Les Objets Fractals* (1975)

> 1977 B. B. Mandelbrot: Many important spatial patterns of Nature are either irregular or fragmented to such an extreme degree that…classical geometry…is hardly of any help in describing their form… I hope to show that it is possible in many cases to remedy this absence of geometric representation by using a family of shapes I propose to call fractals—or fractal sets.

frag *v* (1970) to kill or wound (a disliked superior officer, especially one overzealous for combat), especially by means of a fragmentation grenade. US military slang—a product of the Vietnam War. The noun *frag*, an abbreviation of *fragmentation grenade*, is first recorded in 1966

> 1971 *New York Times Magazine*: Goddammit, if no one was watching, I'd frag the sonuvabitch.

freak out, freak *v* (1970) to become angry; to lose self-control. Slang, originally US; a development of **freak out** 'to undergo a drug-induced experience' (1965)

1979 *Honey*: They both totally freaked out. They were both standing over me saying 'You must have an abortion'.

1984 *Australian*: I…was confronted by a car with a video camera pointed at me. I just freaked. If I'd have caught him.

full frontal *adj* (1970) Usually in the expression *full frontal nudity*, denoting the totally naked body seen from the front, revealing the sexual organs. Mainly used in the context of stage performance: the catalyst was the musical *Hair* (1968) which, to the consternation of guardians of public morals, included naked performers letting it all hang out

1970 *Private Eye*: Despite outraged reaction from…the Scottish establishment…full frontal nudity in the theatre will soon strike north of the border for the first time.

futon *n* (1972) a low-slung Japanese-style bed or mattress. The Japanese word *futon* denotes a sort of bed-quilt or thin cotton mattress which is laid on a mat on the floor at night and can be rolled up and put away during the day, and as such it has been used in English in descriptions of Japanese culture since the late 19th century. The new usage reflected sudden middle-class fashionability of the adapted mattress or bed in the West in the 1970s and 80s

1974 Kate Millett: His mother came upstairs to help me measure for a new *futong*.

1986 *Artseen*: They fall onto the stripped-pine futon.

F-word *n* (1973) A euphemistic formulation for referring to the word *fuck* in circumstances where it would be taboo. Originally US. As other once embargoed items (e.g. *shit*) have emerged from the closet, it has gradually replaced the previous circumlocution **four-letter word (1934)**. In the late 1980s the pattern produced a flurry of look-alikes, both serious (*C-word* for *cunt*) and polemical (*L-word* for *liberal*, used by those for whom *liberal* is a dirty word: 'Hillary is a liberal (the bad L-word)', *Independent* (1993)), and also facetious (see the third quote below)

1973 *New York Times Book Review*: I ain't got time to be outraged about these books. I dismiss them. The kids use the expression 'f-word', the 'f-word', when they want to talk about it without saying it. Well, I say, 'f-word' them books, and 'f-word' the pretentious writers who write them.

1988 *Gazette* (Montreal): The appearance of the f-word in a City page A-3 news story in *The Gazette* May 3 offended Wallace Norman of Dollard des Ormeaux.

1995 *Daily Telegraph*: Others describing such an incident might have used an f-word—'feckless' or, in extremes, 'a foozler'. Benaud opted for: 'What a shemozzle!'

garbology *n* (1976) Dr. William Rathje's term for the scientific study of the refuse of a modern society; the investigation of material discarded by a society, considered as an aspect of social science. Originally US; the alternative *garbageology* is sometimes encountered. Not to be confused with **garbologist (1965)**, an upmarket word for a dustman

1976 *Telegraph* (Brisbane): Garbology…is, [Dr. Rathje] believes, a social science.

gas-guzzler *n* (1973) a motor vehicle, especially a large car, that uses fuel extravagantly. US slang (from *gas* = 'gasoline'); a sign that the necessity for energy conservation was beginning to sink in (see **energy crisis (1970)**). The term was possibly inspired by a reference in the late 1960s to 'gas-guzzling dinosaurs' [i.e. outmoded vehicles] by the US politician George Romney

1973 *Washington Post*: Most of the gas-guzzlers have big engines of 400 cubic inches or better.

-gate *suffix* (1973) An ending denoting an actual or alleged scandal (and usually an attempted cover-up), in some way comparable with the Watergate scandal of 1972 onwards (see **Watergate (1972)**). Added (on the model of *Watergate*) to the name of the place where the scandal occurred, or somewhere linked with it (e.g. *Dallasgate, Irangate*); to the name of a person or organization implicated in it (e.g. *Muldergate*); or to something connected with it (e.g. *Winegate*). See also **Irangate (1986)**

1973 *Saturday Review World* (US): Inevitably, the brouhaha of Bordeaux became known as Winegate.

1975 *Modern People*: Shocking Dallasgate revealed.

1978 *Observer*: The South African Government easily defeated…an attempt…to force its resignation over 'Muldergate'—the Information Department scandal.

1987 *Daily Telegraph*: [Oliver] North will be asked about his accepting the gift of a security gate at his home, a sub-plot that has become known as Gategate.

geep *n* (1971) the offspring of a goat and a sheep. Note the plural form in the first quote below, following the model of *sheep*. The early preferred term for this blended animal was **shoat (1969)** (the cause of *geep* was perhaps not helped by the fact that it is also US slang for an obnoxious person). *Geep* came to the fore in the 1980s, applied to a cross produced by genetic engineering

1971 *New Scientist*: Hundreds of people have claimed success in breeding shoats or geep.

1987 *Listener*: Others team have fused goat embryos with sheep embryos, to produce a new life-form they call a geep.

gender gap *n* (1977) the difference in (especially political) attitudes between men and women. Modelled on **generation gap (1967)**

1977 Desmond Morris: They argue that the gender gap belongs to man's ancient past and is no longer relevant in the modern world.

1982 *Newsweek*: The White House is opening the loophole to help close the 'gender gap'—data that show women are disproportionately dubious about administration policies.

gentrify *v* (1972) to renovate or convert (housing, especially in an inner-city area) so that it conforms to middle-class taste; also, to make (an area) middle-class. Usually used disparagingly, with the implication of swamping genuine working-class culture with effete bourgeoiserie. *Gentrification* soon followed

1972 J. I. M. Stewart: The humbler dwellings…were well-groomed rather than neat, and their little gardens had been gentrified as effectively as had their low parlours.

1973 *Times*: The switch to owner-occupation has shifted overcrowding to the north of the borough which already suffered acutely before the 'gentrification' process began.

1977 *New York Times*: Newcomers are 'gentrifying' working-class Islington and should be resisted, not welcomed.

geriatric *n* (1974) a patient in a geriatric ward or institution. By the end of the decade, used as a more or less contemptuous term for an old or senile person

1974 *New Statesman*: Ban all hospital treatment for miners, and send geriatrics and mental defectives back to their pit villages.

1982 *Spectator*: Hua Kuo-feng was replaced by Teng Hsiao-ping but a number of geriatrics remained.

giro cheque *n* (1972) a cheque issued through the giro system, a system of transferring money within a country's financial institutions. In Britain, such cheques are used for social security payments, so *giro cheque*, and especially its abbreviation *giro*, are particularly associated with them

1976 *Southern Evening Echo* (Southampton): A 31-year-old woman told the Department of Health and Social Security she had not received her giro cheque.

1981 *Sunday Times*: If it's a Wednesday I check straight away that I've got my Giro.—A. Benson, unemployed.

glitz *n* (1977) an extravagant but superficial display; showiness, ostentation, especially show-business glamour or sparkle. Originally US; a back-formation from **glitzy (1966)**

1977 *New Republic*: Stoppard's plays have been marked by undergraduate cleverness and glitz and ultimate sterility.

1985 *Toronto Life*: There was too much Third-World esoterica and not enough Hollywood glitz.

global warming *n* (1977) a long-term gradual increase in the earth's temperature, thought to be caused by various side-effects of modern energy consumption such as the augmented greenhouse effect

1977 *Economist*: Even a doubling of carbon dioxide could be serious: a global warming of nearly three degrees centigrade, and possibly over eleven degrees in parts of the Arctic.

1989 *Nature*: A Senate resolution calling on the United States to take the lead in setting up an international convention to slow global warming.

go *v go for it* (1975) to attempt to obtain something. Colloquial, originally US; usually used in the imperative as an expression of encouragement

> 1987 *Poetry Review*: 'Keep writing, keep submitting, keep a positive attitude.' In a word, Go for it!

> 1990 *New Woman*: In the 'go for it' decade there was a neglect of the inner side of our relationships.

golden handcuffs *n* (1976) benefits (e.g. a private health scheme or a company car) provided to employees in order to induce them to remain in their jobs and not move to another company. Originally US; inspired by **golden handshake (1960)**.

> 1982 *Wall Street Journal*: Getty Oil is trying to lock 'golden handcuffs' on explorationists by offering them four-year loans 'up front' equal to 80% of an employee's salary.

gonzo *adj* (1971) wild, eccentric, far-fetched. Slang, mainly US. Originally used by Hunter Thompson in an article in *Rolling Stone* to characterize his own type of committed, subjective journalism characterized by factual distortion and exaggerated rhetorical style (see the first two quotes below). The ultimate source is probably Italian *gonzo* 'simpleton'

> 1971 Hunter Thompson: But what was the story? Nobody had bothered to say. So we would have to drum it up on our own. Free Enterprise. The American Dream. Horatio Alger gone mad on drugs in Las Vegas. Do it *now*: pure Gonzo journalism.

> 1972 R. Pollack: I ask Hunter to explain… Just what is Gonzo Journalism?… 'Gonzo all started with Bill Cardosa,…after I wrote the Kentucky Derby piece for *Scanlan's*…the first time I realized you could write *different*. And…I got this note from Cardosa saying, "That was pure Gonzo journalism!"… Some Boston word for weird, bizarre.'

> 1985 *New Yorker*: He has a small, weird triumph with his gonzo psycho docudrama.

good buddy *n* (1976) A term of address among users of a Citizen's Band or similar radio system. Slang, mainly US

> 1976 *New York Times Magazine*: 'Hey, there, eastbounders. You've got a Smokey in the grass at the 93-mile marker…he's takin' pictures.' 'Aaay, we definitely thank you for that info, good buddy. We'll back 'em down a hair.'

-gram *suffix* (1979) Used in various often (allegedly) humorous combinations based on *telegram*, denoting a message delivered by a representative of a commercial greetings company, especially one outrageously dressed to amuse or embarrass the recipient, in the manner indicated by the first element (e.g. *Gorillagram* (a proprietary name in the US), *Rambogram*, *strippergram*, etc.). See also **kissogram (1982)**

> 1979 *Maclean's Magazine*: For singing-telegram junkies bored by the same old song and dance, Cookie climbs into a furry suit to deliver Gorillagrams.

> 1982 *Private Eye*: Singing telegrams, Gorillagrams,…Strip-a-Grams…for…anniversaries etc.

> 1985 *Time*: Youngsters will soon be able to pop Rambo vitamins, and New Yorkers can send a Rambogram, in which a Stallone look-alike will deliver a birthday message or carry out a tough assignment.

grand unified theory *n* (1978) a theory in physics in which the strong, the weak, and the electromagnetic interactions are treated mathematically as different manifestations of a single force. A term developed from the earlier *unified (field) theory* (first recorded in 1935), denoting a field theory that describes two or more of the four interactions (originally gravitation and electromagnetism) previously described by separate theories

> 1978 *Nuclear Physics*: We have mainly studied three aspects of grand unified theories of the strong, weak, and electromagnetic interactions.

granny bond *n* (1977) A colloquial name for an index-linked British National Savings certificate available originally only to a person of pensionable age

> 1977 *Sunday Times*: The 1,200,000 pension-age people (men over 65, women over 60) who have money tucked away in National Savings Retirement certificates—now endearingly known as granny bonds.

green *adj* (1972) relating to or supporting environmentalism, especially as a political issue; belonging to or supporting an ecological party. Also used more loosely to mean 'environmentalist, ecological'. The association of the colour green with the environmentalist lobby, especially in Europe, dates from the early 1970s in West Germany, notably with the *Grüne Aktion Zukunft* 'Green Campaign for the Future', and the *grüne Listen* 'green lists (of ecological election candidates)', both of which emerged mainly from campaigns against nuclear power stations. Its initial manifestation in English was as part of the name of *Greenpeace*, an international organization which campaigns in support of conservation and the protection of the environment. See also **greens (1978)**

> 1972 R. Keziere: A bringing-together of the peace and environmental movements…Greenpeace seemed like a concept that might create such an alliance.

> 1978 *Economist*: European politics are turning green; or so the ecologists would have us believe.

> 1979 *Now!*: The rebuff to 'green', environmentalist ideals is displayed by the drop in the Centre Party's vote from 24 to 18 per cent.

> 1985 *Sunday Times*: The 5,000-strong Ecology Party swapped its 'too middle class' name for the Green Party at its annual conference in Dover yesterday.

green pound *n* (1974) the unit of account in which prices of agricultural commodities fixed by the Common Agricultural Policy of the European Union are converted into sterling (the exchange value of the green pound is established annually)

> 1974 *Financial Times*: Britain and Ireland have what is labelled a Green Pound because sterling is floating in relation to the currencies of other EEC members.

> 1987 *Times*: Mr Jopling has dismissed as 'not enough' a devaluation of nearly 4 per cent in Britain's 'green pound', the special money used in agricultural trade.

greens *n* (1978) the members or supporters of an ecological party, often specifically the one in (West) Germany (*die Grünen*); also applied more broadly to people committed to environmentalism or ecology, especially as a political issue. A noun use of the adjective **green (1971)**

> 1978 *Economist*: The Greens are more likely to take votes from the Social Democrats and the Liberals than from the Christian Democrats.

> 1986 *New Socialist*: If the government's greens…get their way, then the pollution from Drax B may yet be cleaned up.

grey market *n* (1979) trading in a security before its official quotation on the Stock Exchange. A specialized use of the earlier sense, 'unofficial or unorthodox trading (in a "grey" area legally or morally)', which is first recorded in 1946

> 1984 *Daily Telegraph*: In the Commons, Mr Hattersley, Shadow Chancellor, attacked the Government over the development of the 'grey market' in the shares.

hacking *n* (1976) the use or programming of a computer as an end in itself, for the satisfaction it gives. Someone who does this is called a *hacker* (also first recorded in 1976). Colloquial, originally US; reputedly first used at the Massachusetts Institute of Technology. The back-formed verb is first recorded in 1983. In the early 1980s the word developed the more sinister connotation of breaking electronically into others' computer systems (see **hacker (1983)**)

> 1976 J. Weizenbaum: The compulsive programmer spends all the time he can working on one of his big projects. 'Working' is not the word he uses; he calls what he does 'hacking'… The compulsive programmer, or hacker as he calls himself, is usually a superb technician.

> 1983 G. L. Steele: At MIT, I would sometimes work nights for a month at a time. Now that I am married, I find that I can hack only in spurts.

hang *v* **let it all hang out** (1970) to be uninhibited or relaxed. Slang, originally US

> 1978 R. Westall: When my parents quarrel, they…fight in hoarse whispers. But like a lot of upper-middles…Derek and Susan let it all hang out.

happening *adj* (1977) exciting, lively, trendy, up-to-the-minute, hip; that is 'where the action is'. Slang, originally US; from the notion of 'what is happening now'. See also **happening (1959)**

> 1977 Cyra McFadden: Who could live anywhere else? Marin's this whole high-energy trip with all these happening people.

> 1990 *Radio Times*: My kind of day is a Saturday when we've had a totally happenin' week on Children's BBC.

harassment *n* (1975) the subjecting of a person to aggressive pressure or intimidation through unwanted sexual advances. When originally conceptualized by feminists, the offence was termed *sexual harassment*, to distinguish it from other forms of harassment, but so preponderant is the usage that by the 1990s plain *harassment* (almost always stressed, *à la* US English, on the second syllable) was widely understood to mean 'sexual harassment'

> 1975 *New York Times*: Sexual harassment of women in their place of employment is extremely widespread.

> 1993 *New York Times Book Review*: The increasing emphasis on woman's essential weakness and man's essential bestiality that underlies many of the current debates about rape, harassment and pornography.

hard *adj* (1975) Designating a strict or hard-line faction at the wing of a political party or of the political spectrum. Mainly in *hard left* and *hard right*. Compare **soft (1977)**

> 1975 *New Left Review*: For the foreseeable future, then, the hard right has the initiative in Turkey.

> 1976 *National Observer* (US): It is a fact that the hard-left liberals don't like him.

hardball *n* (1973) tough uncompromising dealings or activity in politics, business, etc. Slang, mainly US; often in the phrase *play hardball*. *Hardball* as a term for 'baseball' (contrasted with *softball*, played, not surprisingly, with a softer ball) dates from the 1880s

> 1973 P. J. Buchanan: There are things that are certainly utterly outrageous… Then, there is dirty tricks, then there is political hardball, then there is pranks.

> 1983 *Fortune*: If anyone wants to play hardball, Cub can operate in the 5% to 6% range and still be profitable, because its costs are so lean.

hard disk *n* (1978) a computer disk that is rigid and has a large storage capacity, as distinct from the smaller-capacity **floppy disk (1972)**

> 1982 *Times*: Hard disks are made to a far higher degree of precision, using an aluminium platter that is extremely finely ground and polished before the magnetic oxide coating is applied.

Harvey Wallbanger *n* (1970) a cocktail made from vodka or gin and orange juice. The second half of its name apparently reflects its effect on the drinker

> 1981 Tim Heald: The Mounties…ordered a brace of Harvey Wallbangers.

have a nice day (1971) Used as a conventional formula on parting. Originally and mainly US. Considered (and in some quarters reviled) as the archetypal American parting shot. See also **welcome (1960)**

> 1971 Dorothy Halliday: The admonitions of the freeway from the airport are wholly American: *Keep off the Median… Have a Nice Day*.

Hazchem *n* (1976) A conflation of *hazardous chemical*, designating a system of codes and symbols for labelling dangerous chemicals in order that they can be easily identified and safely handled, especially when being transported or in the event of an accident. Mainly British and Australian

> 1979 N. Wallington: The Hazchem Code obviously saves valuable time.

> 1997 *Guardian*: In industry, you often see doors with orange signs that say 'HAZCHEM'; remember, this isn't Hebrew for 'prayer room'.

heavy metal *n* (1973) a type of loud, vigorous rock music characterized by the use of electronically amplified instruments (typically guitar, bass, and drums), a heavy, usually fast beat, intense or spectacular performance, and often a clashing, harsh musical style

> 1973 *Crawdaddy*: They find no comfort in glitter or Heavy Metal—Black Sabbath, Black Oak Arkansas and their ilk.

> 1980 *Daily Mirror*: The names of Heavy Metal groups like Deep Purple and Motorhead are inscribed on the back of his leather jacket.

her indoors *pron* (1979) one's wife or girlfriend; also applied more generally to any woman occupying a postion of authority who is regarded as domineering. British colloquial; often spelt *'er indoors* to reflect the original 'Cockney' flavour. The phrase was popularized by the Thames Television series *Minder* (1979–93), in which the leading character Arthur Daley habitually referred to his wife (who never appeared on screen) as 'her indoors'. The series' original writer, Leon Griffiths, apparently first heard it used by 'a taxi-driver drinking companion of his'

> 1979 Leon Griffiths: That's what her indoors doesn't understand Terry. A young bird keeps you feeling young.

> 1984 *Guardian*: These days, her indoors (and Mr Walker too) are said to be seldom off the phone with words of wisdom for Mr MacGregor.

heritage *n* (1970) Used quasi-adjectivally in the context of preserving or exploiting local and national features of historical, cultural, or scenic interest, especially as tourist attractions. By the 1980s the usage had proliferated to such an extent that it seemed to jaundiced observers that its idea of a packaged, touristic past had all but supplanted *history*. Its status was further enhanced in the 1990s when Britain appointed its first Secretary of State for the National Heritage, responsible for such areas as the arts, museums, and sport

> 1970 *Nature*: The idea of the 'heritage highway', a route which links places in the life of national figures…seems to me to be a sort of motorized nature trail.

> 1986 *Financial Times*: Cadw has struck a blow for the entire heritage industry.

> 1988 *Breakfast Time* (BBC): If you're interested in history, or heritage, as we're supposed to call it today, you can have a good day out today, as all the National Trust properties are open for free.

herstory *n* (1970) history emphasizing the role of women or told from a woman's point of view. A feminists' polemical punning alteration of *history*, fancifully reinterpreted as *his story*, implying that history has in the past been viewed predominantly from the male perspective. Always in fairly limited usage, but it seems likely to survive the century

> 1988 *Sunday Times*: In a series of hot back-flashes we get the 'herstory' so far. As luck would have it, the dead woman was a writer and reader of modern herstory.

heterosexism *n* (1979) prejudice and antagonism shown by heterosexual persons towards homosexuals; discrimination against homosexuals. The adjective and noun *heterosexist* is also first recorded in 1979. Compare **homophobia (1969)**

> 1979 J. Penelope: Heterosexism designates, in particular, those central social structures which prescribe heterosexuality as the only 'natural' sexual interest.

> 1979 *Ms*: At least one heterosexist assumption expressed in Signe Hammer's article should not pass unquestioned. There are some of us who as daughters competed with Daddy to possess Mommy.

high-tech *adj, n* (1972) Short for *high-technology*, denoting the production or utilization of highly advanced and specialized technology (first recorded in 1964). Also applied specifically to a style of architecture and interior design that imitates the functionalism of industrial technology

> 1978 Kron & Slesin: Some people call this phenomenon 'the industrial style', but we call it 'high-tech'. High-tech…is a term currently used in architectural circles to describe buildings incorporating prefabricated…building components.

> 1980 *New Age* (US): A pocket calculator, a very high-tech gadget.

Hispanic *adj, n* (1972) (someone) Spanish-speaking. Applied especially to someone of Latin-American descent living in the United States

> 1972 *New York Times Magazine*: The fictional melting pot has become a pousse-café in which every layer is jealous of, or hostile to, every other layer; in a fever of ethnicity, Italians, Jews, Orientals, Blacks, Hispanics and others have withdrawn into themselves.

> 1980 *Times*: Hispanic children in Los Angeles are taught entirely in Spanish.

hit list *n* (1976) Originally, a list of people to be assassinated, but soon transferred metaphorically to 'a list or group of people, etc., against which some concerted action is intended'

> 1976 *Time*: One intelligence official…bitterly labeled **Counterspy**'s roster of CIA agents as nothing more or less than 'a hit list'.

> 1985 *Times Educational Supplement*: By the time talks resume…the Government's 'hit list' of rate-capped authorities in 1986 to 1987 would be published.

home video *n* (1977) the production or use of video recordings, especially of feature films, intended to be watched at home

> 1977 *Economist*: Home video looks like being the next major consumer electronics market.

> 1983 *New York Times*: Only six years ago, the business that Hollywood calls 'home video'...did not exist.

hot pants *n* (1970) brief shorts worn briefly by girls and young women as a fashion garment. Inspired no doubt by the earlier metaphorical *hot pants* 'inflamed sexual desire', which dates from the 1920s

> 1970 *Women's Wear Daily*: As for hotpants, we haven't seen anything in the market... They're going to have to be styled very imaginatively. Otherwise, they're going to look like old-fashioned short shorts.

> 1971 *New Scientist*: Where we once had ladies in gowns and earrings to elocute the score at us, we now have hot-panted dolly-birds who can't add up.

> 1971 *Daily Telegraph* (November): Hotpants have rather quickly died a fashion death.

HRT *n* (1973) An abbreviation of *hormone-replacement therapy*, a term first recorded in 1967 and denoting the replacement of oestrogenic hormones as a means of alleviating the unpleasant symptoms experienced by some menopausal women

> 1973 *Good Housekeeping*: For women on HRT there is no menopause, no hot flushes, backaches nor depression.

human shield *n* (1977) a person or group of people placed in the line of fire so as to fend off any kind of attack. The term was widely used in the late 1980s in connection with the situation in Lebanon, but its real moment of fame came in 1990, when President Saddam Hussein of Iraq held a group of Westerners captive in order to dissuade the US and its allies from attacking following the Iraqi invasion of Kuwait. Several of the hostages were placed at military and industrial installations

> 1989 *Financial Times*: Thirty-nine right-wing French MPs arrived yesterday from Paris to join the 'human shield' around Gen Aoun, who also received the unexpected 11th-hour support of 6,000 'Lebanese forces', or Phallange militiamen.

> 1990 *Washington Post*: Americans...reportedly were taken from the Mansour-Melia Hotel in Baghdad on the night of Oct. 29 and are now presumed to be 'human shields' at an undisclosed strategic site in Iraq.

hypermarket *n* (1970) a very large self-service store, usually situated outside a town, having an extensive car park and selling a wide range of goods. An Anglicization of French *hypermarché* (the concept was imported from France—see the quote below)

> 1971 *Times*: The catalyst has been the imminent arrival in the United Kingdom of Carrefour hypermarkets.

immunocompromised *adj* (1974) Of a patient: having an impaired immune system, especially as a result of illness. A term which came into its own in the 1980s, the Aids decade

> 1989 D. Leavitt: You take a woman in her sixties, immunocompromised, and...I wouldn't have put money on her getting this far.

index-linked *adj* (1970) Designating bonds, pensions, etc., of which the value is adjusted according to the level of the cost-of-living index or some other economic indicator. *Index-linking* and the back-formed verb *index-link* are first recorded in 1974

> 1970 *Guardian Weekly*: The scope for cutting any kind of tax is therefore limited unless some incentive to save can be invented. An index-linked bond might provide such an incentive.

> 1974 *Daily Telegraph*: If it becomes necessary...to index-link a large proportion of their deposits some form of index linking of mortgages would have to be considered.

industrial action *n* (1971) action such as a strike, a go-slow, working to rule, etc., taken by industrial or other workers. Useful as a cover-term, but there was almost certainly also a euphemistic impulse behind its coinage, avoiding the rebarbative *strike*. It was an obvious target for jokes about the inappropriateness of the word 'action'

> 1971 *Times*: The Times regrets that, in common with other national newspapers, it will probably be unable to publish tomorrow because of industrial action.

in your face *interj, adj* (1976) See **face (1976)**

item *n* (1970) a pair of lovers; a couple. Colloquial, originally US; usually used in the expression *be an item*, denoting that two people are involved in an established romantic or sexual relationship, especially a socially acknowledged one. Rare in British English before the 1990s

> 1970 T. Coe: 'What was Maundy's relationship with Dearborn?' Remington said, 'They were an item once, long ago… Before Ronnie.'

> 1996 *Just Seventeen*: My mate had a fling with one of his and they hung out together, even though they weren't officially an item.

jetfoil *n* (1972) a type of passenger-carrying hydrofoil with a stabilization and control system based on that of an aircraft. A proprietary name in the US

> 1974 *Times*: Macao is about an hour away by hydrofoil and when the jetfoils are introduced later this year the time will be cut to 45 minutes.

job centre *n* (1972) a government office that lists and advertises current job vacancies in an area. As well as a sprucing up (see the first quote below), Britain's labour exchanges got a new name (*labour exchange* dates from the 1860s): *job centre* is down-to-earth but snappy

> 1972 *Times*: Forget about the Government employment exchanges…think about the bright, new offices with a new image and a sign outside saying job centre.

> 1973 *Guardian*: Britain's first Job Centre will be opened this afternoon. Job Centres are the modern version of what have…been called employment exchanges or…labour exchanges.

job-seeking *n* (1972) looking for a job. Originally US. An attempt to promote a positive attitude to unemployment, or an attempt to cover it up in persiflage, depending on your point of view, but either way somewhat weaselly. The concept became familiar in Britain in 1993 with the introduction of the 'jobseeker's allowance' (see **jobseeker (1993)**)

> 1972 *Saturday Review* (US): Job-seeking itself can be costly.

job-sharing *n* (1972) a working arrangement in which two or more people are employed on a part-time basis to perform a job which would otherwise have been available only to a person able to work full-time, and share the renumeration and other benefits

> 1972 *Guardian*: The report will ask for a massive injection of Government money into the docks industry…There [were]…also proposals for job-sharing schemes.

jobsworth *n* (1970) an official or other employee who insists on petty rules and bureaucracy, especially in refusing or vetoing a particular course of action. Colloquial; from the expression 'It's more than my job's worth (to let you …)'

> 1987 *Punch*: Now we all know park-keepers—'jobsworths' to the man. (It's more than my job's worth to let you in here/play ball/walk on the grass/film my ducks.')

junk food *n* (1973) food that appeals to popular (especially juvenile) taste but has little nutritional value. Originally US

> 1973 *Washington Post*: How many children are going to fill up on junk foods and be too full to eat a nutritious lunch now?

kalashnikov *n* (1970) a type of rifle or sub-machine gun made in the Soviet Union. The name, particularly as applied to the rifle (also known as the 'AK 47') became associated in the last quarter of the century with left-wing guerrilla groups supplied with arms, directly or indirectly, by the Soviet Union

> 1970 *New York Times*: A ragtag group of fedayeen bearing kalashnikovs, hand grenades and often Pepsi-Cola bottles, swarms around the headquarters area.

karaoke *n* (1979) a form of entertainment, originating in Japan, in which a person sings the vocal line of a popular song to the accompaniment of a pre-recorded backing tape, and the voice is electronically amplified through a loudspeaker system for the audience. It was introduced in the US and Britain in the late 1980s, with considerable success (in the early 1990s, every other English pub seemed to have a karaoke machine to beguile its customers, who seemed on the whole not to be driven out by the vocalists' efforts). The Japanese word is a compound of *kara* 'empty' and *oke* 'orchestra', which is a shortened form of *okesutora*, a Japanization of English *orchestra*

> 1990 *Independent*: The brewers are now introducing *Karaoke* into selected pubs on a trial basis.

> 1992 *Premiere*: This new combi player plays hundreds of karaoke video music titles, hits from the '50s through the '80s, all with on-screen lyrics.

kiddie porn *n* (1977) child pornography. A term with a particulary high profile in the last decade of the century, with such material widely available on the Internet

> 1995 *Wired*: The kiddie porn debate pitted morality cops and grandstanding politicians on one side against artists, writers, and intellectuals on the other.

kiss and tell (1970) Denoting the public revelation of one's sexual exploits (usually implying the embarrassment of former sexual partners). Originally US; often used metaphorically in the political arena to suggest the revealing of confidential information gained through any close or privileged relationship

> 1970 *Harper's*: It is kiss-and-tell time for Lyndon Johnson's White House inner circle. But those who relish bloody and Byzantine tales will be unsatisfied by this discreet chronicle.

> 1992 *Independent*: Turning from erotic fiction to carnal fact, Thomas also produced a 1988 autobiography, *Memories and Hallucinations*, an unusual combination of literary monograph and tabloid kiss-and-tell.

kneecap *v* (1975) to shoot (someone) in the knee (or leg) as a form of punishment. A practice associated with Northern Ireland, where it is used against those who have incurred the wrath of a terrorist organization

> 1975 *Daily Telegraph*: Man 'kneecapped' in Carrickfergus.

> 1975 *Observer*: Ulster's gunmen have found they can get hold of Government cash by giving victims a 'knee-capping'—their grim colloquialism for a bullet in the legs…Kneecapping…has replaced tarring and feathering as the province's most common form of terrorist punishment… 'This so-called kneecapping is really a misnomer, because the kneecap itself is rarely touched.'

lake *n* (1974) a surplus of a particular liquid commodity, especially as a result of overproduction under the terms of the Common Agricultural Policy within the European Union. In practice mainly used with reference to wine. A coinage inspired by the parallel **mountain (1969)** for foodstuffs

> 1974 *Daily Telegraph*: The Common Market has a 'wine lake' estimated at 8 million litres…—and yesterday a Labour MP called for some of it to be brought to Britain.

laser printer *n* (1979) a non-impact printer in which a laser is used to form a pattern of dots on a photosensitive drum corresponding to the pattern of print required on a page. Technology which, when it replaced the **daisy wheel (1977)** and the **dot matrix (1975)**, transported commercial and personal correspondence from the age of the typewriter to an era in which a letter looks like a page out of a book

> 1985 *Personal Computer World*: Laser Jet is a quiet, eight page-per-minute tabletop laser printer.

Lassa fever *n* (1970) an acute febrile virus disease that occurs in tropical Africa with a high mortality rate. It got its name from Lassa, a village near Mubi in northeast Nigeria, where it was first reported in 1969

> 1970 *Times*: Lassa fever infection can involve almost all the body's organs; symptoms may vary. The virus produces a fever as high as 107°F, mouth ulcers, a skin rash with small haemorrhages, pneumonia, infection of the heart leading to cardiac failure, kidney damage, and severe muscle aches.

launder *v* (1973) to transfer (funds of dubious or illegal origin), usually to a foreign country, and then later to recover them from what seem to be 'clean' (i.e. legitimate) sources. The usage arose from the Watergate inquiry in the US in 1973–4 (see **Watergate (1972)**)

> 1973 *Guardian*: Suitcases stuffed with 200,000 dollars of Republican campaign funds; money being 'laundered' in Mexico.

> 1973 J. M. White: Phoenix is a city where the Mafia is well entrenched; its booming real-estate, building and service industries are ready-made havens for 'laundering' the extortion and gambling money from Nevada and California.

lava lamp *n* (1970) a transparent electric lamp containing a viscous liquid in which a brightly coloured waxy substance is suspended, rising and falling in constantly changing shapes when the lamp is switched on. Regarded with hindsight as symbolic of the bad taste of the late 1960s and early 70s, although at the end of the century they enjoyed something of a retro-chic comeback. The alternative term *lava light* (registered in 1968 as the proprietary name *Lava Lite*) is first recorded in US English in 1967

> 1970 *Toronto Daily Star*: We bought a Lava lamp…and, three days after delivery, it exploded, spewing the hot liquid contained in the fixture over our drapes, hi-fi, and rug.

LCD *n* (1973) An abbreviation of *liquid crystal display*, a visual display, especially of segmented numbers or letters, in which liquid crystals are made visible by temporarily modifying electrically the way they reflect and scatter ambient light. By the end of the decade they were ubiquitous in clocks and watches, public information displays, etc.

> 1973 *Electronics*: What is claimed to be the first watch using a field-effect LCD, the Teletime, has been introduced by Gruen Industries.

leading edge *n* (1977) the forefront of progress or development, especially in technology. Widely used as an adjective. A slightly later synonym is **cutting edge (1985)**

> 1977 *Scientific American*: We are a young, publicly held, leading-edge technology company.

> 1983 *Fortune*: Professors, commonly assumed to be on the leading edge of thought.

learning difficulties *n* (1975) difficulties experienced by a schoolchild in learning one or more subjects to the level of proficiency expected of his or her contemporaries, especially because of social problems or mental or physical handicap. A piece of educationists' jargon intended to replace earlier synonyms (e.g. *backward, educationally subnormal*) which had become taboo (although in due course their schoolmates reportedly taunted such children in the playground with 'LD! LD!')

> 1975 *Language for Life*: Specialists in reading, learning difficulties, drama and 'immigrant' language teaching.

> 1995 *Times Educational Supplement*: Kenel Lane School is a campus school catering for pupils from 2–19 years with a multiplicity of special educational needs including…profound and multiple learning difficulties and autism.

legionnaires' disease *n* (1976) a severe form of bacterial pneumonia, often accompanied by mental confusion, which is caused by *Legionella pneumophila* and is associated especially with infected water systems. So called from the outbreak in July 1976 that affected people attending a Legionnaires' Convention in Philadelphia

> 1977 *Lancet*: It is already important for clinicians to think of legionnaires' disease when severe pneumonia proves resistant to standard therapy.

leg-warmer *n* (1974) either of a pair of tubular, typically knitted garments covering the leg from ankle to thigh, originally worn by ballet dancers at rehearsal, and subsequently by (young) women, often as a fashion accessory

> 1974 *Dance Magazine*: At last a fashion-wise…line of garments that can be worn for dance, sports…or street wear… Leg Warmers…Midriff Top…Swing Skirt.

> 1984 Sue Townsend: No Selina this morning, so I had to make do with going into town with Pandora, who wanted to buy a pair of neon pink legwarmers.

libber *n* (1971) a campaigner for a particular political freedom. A derivative of **lib (1969)**. In practice, when used on its own it is taken to mean 'women's liberationist'

> 1971 *Telegraph* (Brisbane): Women's libbers are preparing to do battle with the police in Baltimore.

> 1973 *Times*: *The Female Woman* sorts out…the contemporary confusion of ideas about the sexes which the Libbers have…worse confounded.

liberate *v* (1970) to free from social conventions, especially male domination. Mainly used in the form of the past participial adjective. See also **women's liberation (1966), lib (1969)**

> 1970 *New Yorker*: It is not only men liberated. It is *women* liberated.

> 1973 David Jordan: He resents me because I'm a liberated woman who can support herself.

liberation theology *n* (1972) a theory, originating amongst Roman Catholic theologians in Latin America, which interprets liberation from social, political, and economic oppression as a vital part of the Christian message. A translation of Spanish *teología de la liberación*, a term coined by G. Gutiérrez in 1968. It was originally rendered in English as *theology of liberation*; the formulation *liberation theology*, which caught on, was introduced by R. R. Ruether in 1972 as the title of a book. The derived *liberation theologian* is first recorded in 1976

> 1973 P. E. Berryman: Latin American liberation theology arises out of an experience: the discovery of institutionalized violence and the dimensions of oppression.

> 1976 *Christian Socialist*: The radical Catholics of South America (who include Archbishop Helder Camara of Brazil and the 'liberation theologians').

lig *v* (1976) to obtain entertainment or refreshment at another's expense; to freeload. British slang: the *ligger*, the sponger, hanger-on, and gate-crasher of parties, became a boringly familiar figure on the fashionable social scene in the 1980s, especially in the entertainment and pop music world, where free hospitality is all around. The verb *lig* had its origins as a dialectal variant of *lie* 'to recline', and first appeared in the late 1950s, with the meaning 'to lounge about'

> 1976 *Zigzag*: The Feelgoods, now ligging and gigging around America.

> 1982 *Soundmaker*: The usual droves of music biz liggers.

> 1985 *Radio Times*: [I] suddenly twigged what ligging was all about when I got my first job as a researcher on Aquarius. I found…I could get free tickets for everything, everywhere.

line dancing *n* (1975) a form of folk-dancing, especially to country music, in which participants stand face to face in two long lines. Originally US

> 1975 *New Yorker*: It's an album of pictures: line dancing, marathon dancing, the Lindy.

line in the sand *n* (1978) a limit or boundary; a level of tolerance or a point beyond which one will not go. Originally US; a favourite metaphor of politicians and diplomats wanting to sound tough in the last quarter of the century. Often in the expression *draw a line in the sand*

> 1978 *Washington Post*: Notwithstanding the supposed public revulsion toward more federal spending, waste and bureaucracy-building, Congress seems to have gone out of its way to draw a wide line in the sand in front of Carter.

> 1996 *Scotsman*: Whenever John Major draws a line in the sand, you can be sure some Eurosceptic bully will come along and kick it in his face.

listings *n* (1971) lists providing details of forthcoming concert, film, or theatre performances, television schedules, etc., often printed as part of a newspaper or magazine. Commonly in the expression *listings magazine*, denoting a widespread cultural vade-mecum of the late 20th century

> 1971 *Time Out*: *Time Out* is published every Thursday. Listings run from Friday to Thursday each week.

> 1991 *History Workshop*: London listings magazines have a regular section for the tours on offer, with daily summer choice of up to seven.

lone *adj* (1976) Designating a parent who does not live with a partner and thus has most or all of the responsibility for bringing up a child or children. Preferred latterly to **single**, as it avoids suggesting 'unmarried' (and hence excluding the divorced, widowed, etc.)

> 1976 *Economist*: In 1956, only 56,000 lone mothers were living on supplementary benefit…; in 1974, the figure was 245,000.

> 1997 *Glasgow Herald*: The proportion of children living in lone-parent families has almost tripled since 1972 and there were 12 lone mothers to every lone father.

lookism *n* (1978) prejudice or discrimination on the grounds of appearance (i.e., uglies are done down and the beautiful people get all the breaks). One of the longer-lasting PC '-isms' of the last quarter of the century (see **-ism (1965)**). The derived *lookist* is not recorded before 1990

> 1978 *Washington Post Magazine*: [Fat people] are rallying to help each other find sympathetic doctors, happy employers and future mates. They are coining new words ('lookism'— discrimination based on looks, 'FA'—Fat Admirer).

> 1990 *Toronto Star*: He still looks great—oops, that makes me a lookist.

> 1997 *Plain Dealer*: Now, it's blatant lookism to say so, but deer are cuter than cows.

loon pants, loons *n* (1971) a style of close-fitting casual trousers widely flared from the knees to the ankles. Apparently from **loon** 'to pass the time in leisurely pursuits' (1966)

> 1971 *Melody Maker*: New velvet and cord loon pants with 28" flare… New cotton drill loons and military trousers.

> 1974 D. Winsor: I wriggled into a pair of brown velvet loons, dropped a cream lace tunic over them.

loony left *n* (1977) the extreme left wing of a political party, especially the Labour Party, viewed as being extremist or fanatical. A favourite bugaboo term of the political right in the late 1970s and 80s, intended to make the voters' flesh creep. The left sometimes responded with *loony right* (' "Red Dawn", described widely as of the loony-right and paranoid, was not a very good movie', *New York Times Magazine* (1985)), but it lacked the alliteration that made *loony left* a success

> 1977 *Economist*: The views of the loony left are well known in the democratic world.

> 1987 *City Limits*: The press has branded Deirdre Wood a 'loony lefty'.

male chauvinism *n* (1970) an attitude attributed to men of excessive loyalty to members of the male sex and of prejudice against women. Originally US. The adjective and noun *male chauvinist* are also first recorded in 1970, as are the first traces of *male chauvinist pig*, a term of contempt and abuse for a male chauvinist. Plain *chauvinism*, with the implication 'male chauvinism', is first recorded in 1968: 'The chauvinism…they met came from individuals and was not built into the institution itself', *Voice of the Women's Liberation Movement*

> 1970 *Time*: European women have accepted their lot much more readily than their American counterparts. Recently, however, growing numbers…have launched their attack on male chauvinism.

> 1970 *New Yorker*: Hello, you male-chauvinist racist pig… Repent Male Chauvinists.

> 1972 *Punch*: I know, I know; me male chauvinist pig, you Jane. But the exercise has finally woken me up to ask—why should there be separate magazines for men and women at all?

mandy *n* (1970) A colloquial abbreviation of **Mandrax (1963)**

> 1971 *Frendz*: Avoid dealing while tripping on Acid, Speed or Mandies—you'll goof on the action.

marginalize *v* (1978) to render or treat as marginal; to remove from the centre or mainstream; to force or confine (an individual, social group, activity, etc.) to the periphery of any sphere of influence or operation. Originally a sociologists' term (perhaps adapted from French *marginaliser*, which occurs in this sense slightly earlier), it was taken up enthusiastically by various interest groups and liberation movements, and became one of the main social buzzwords of the 1980s

> 1978 *Dædalus*: That Rousseau was self-taught…seemed to discredit and marginalize him all the more.

> 1987 Caryl Phillips: Society, taking its lead from the media and its politicians, begins to reject a whole class and marginalizes them in the job market.

mean machine *n* (1976) a sports team of extremely high ability. Slang, originally North American; applied in the mid 1980s specifically to the Australian men's 4 × 100m freestyle relay swimming team

> 1986 *Telegraph* (Brisbane): Swimmer Neil Brooks, one of the stars of Australia's 'mean machine', had more than fans waiting for him after his guest appearance at the Sydney Rugby league grand final yesterday.

> 1991 *Rugby World & Post*: The All Black mean machine, battle-hardened if a little bruised from its Bledisloe Cup exertions.

megastar *n* (1978) an exceptionally famous, well publicized, or successful superstar, especially in the world of entertainment

> 1978 *Business Week*: With the number of movie roles declining, and such megastars as John Wayne succumbing to big advertising dollars, the stigma of making commercials has faded.

> 1990 *She*: Sometimes, when I'm doing my shows, I [i.e. Edna Everage] see people in the audience slipping from their seats into a kneeling position and I say, 'Get up! Off your knees! Back into your seat!' After all, I'm just a megastar, no more than that.

me generation *n* (1978) Applied to the people of the 1970s to characterize their supposedly obsessive preoccupation with personal fulfilment and self-gratification during that decade. Later re-
applied to the people of the 1980s to characterize their supposed selfishness and materialism

> 1978 *Journal of Technical Writing & Communication*: The 'me generation' is obsessed with self.

> 1985 *Sunday Telegraph*: At more than 60 American campuses, apartheid has suddenly inflamed
> the 'me generation' that was thought to be too materialistic to care.

MEP *n* (1976) An abbreviation of *Member of the European Parliament*. The parliament is the principal representative and consultative body of the European Union, originally set up (as the
European Parliamentary Assembly) under Article 138 of the Treaty of Rome, and since 1979 elected
by direct universal suffrage throughout the EU

> 1976 *Times*: There is no doubt that the British Government can devise a means of electing MEPs.

metal detector *n* (1971) a device which gives a signal when it encounters a metal object buried in
the ground. Widely used by treasure-hunters and amateur archaeologists

> 1971 B. St. J. Wilkes: Metal detectors are sold quite extensively in the US and Canada to amateur
> 'prospectors' to aid their hunt for gold.

microprocessor *n* (1970) a processor small enough to be accommodated on a single chip, or just a
few chips, and capable of serving as the central processing unit of a computer of comparable size

> 1970 *Institute of Electrical & Electronics Engineers Transactions on Computers*: LX-1 is an
> integrated circuit prototype of a microprocessor which is being used as a design vehicle to study the
> problems associated with the design and implementation of a similar computer constructed with
> large-scale integrated circuits.

microwave *n, v* (1974) See **microwave oven (1965)**

Militant Tendency *n* (1979) a Trotskyist political organization, originally comprising the supporters of the weekly newspaper *Militant*, which was set up in 1964. It was at no time an official
subdivision of the British Labour Party; however, in the mid 1980s, it was alleged to be involved in
infiltration of the Labour Party, and a number of its members were expelled from Labour Party
membership. The seeds of the name were sown in the mid 1960s ('Grant and Co's insistence not
only that Militant should be a "tendency" paper but that it must also be a "youth and labour"
paper', R. Protz, quoting from ?1964 in *Observer* (1975)), but it did not become institutionalized
until the late 1970s. The shortened formulation *Militant* is first recorded in 1980

> 1979 *Economist*: The Militant Tendency is just another faction in the Labour Party.

> 1980 *Economist*: The major advance which Militant has made inside the Labour party is to capture
> the official youth organisation.

minibar *n* (1976) a small lockable refrigerator in a hotel room, stocked with drinks and often snacks
which guests can consume and have charged to their bills. By the end of the century they had
become part of the background scenery in all but the most modest hotels (saving on room-service
labour costs)

> 1991 *Business Traveller*: Each guest room is equipped with hairdryer, trouser press, minibar and
> satellite TV.

miniseries *n* (1972) a television series, usually of short duration, that treats a single complete theme
or plot in a predetermined number of episodes. A popular television genre of the 1970s and 80s

> 1985 *Woman's Own*: Another TV mini-series, this time about the life and loves of George
> Washington.

mission statement *n* (1976) a formal summary of the aims and values of a company, organization, or individual. Originally US; a piece of business jargon often ridiculed as portentous and
pious

> 1976 *Aviation Week & Space Technology*: The formal mission statement of the 8th Air Force is a
> model of simplicity.

> 1992 *IndustryWeek*: The departmental management developed a mission statement that talked of
> meeting the company's information needs in a timely and cost-effective fashion.

mole *n* (1974) a secret intelligence agent who gradually achieves a position deep within the security defences of a country or organization. Also used more broadly to denote anyone within an organization or in a position of trust who betrays confidential information. The metaphor has been traced back as far as the 17th century (the underlying idea of someone burrowing away in the dark is a fairly obvious one), and certainly *mole* was used in an espionage context earlier in the 20th century ('I also have certain moles at my command...When the Cirque Doré mobilizes itself it has many eyes and ears', John Buchan (1925)), but its modern currency is due to its use by the British author of spy fiction John le Carré (see the second quote below for his account of its origins). Compare **sleeper (1955)**

> 1974 John le Carré: Ivlov's task was to service a mole. A mole is a deep penetration agent so called because he burrows deep into the fabric of Western imperialism.

> 1976 John le Carré: A 'mole' is, I think, a genuine KGB term for somebody who burrows into the fabric of a bourgeois society and undermines it from within.

> 1984 *Times*: Clearly therefore, we suggest, this points to a 'mole' within British Telecom Prestel headquarters.

moment *n at this moment in time* (1972) now. A notorious circumlocution of the 1970s and 80s

> 1972 Gordon Bromley: What can we actually do to help at this moment in time?

> 1973 *Guardian*: The usual stuff about meaningful confrontations taking place...at this moment in time.

mondo *adv, adj* (1979) very much, extremely; considerable, huge. Slang, originally and mainly US. A word with a bizarre etymology. Italian *mondo* means 'world'. In 1961 an Italian film appeared called *Mondo cane*, literally 'world for a dog', which received the English title *A Dog's Life*. It depicted eccentric forms of human behaviour, and *mondo* came to be used in (often mock-Italian) pastiches on the film's name, denoting bizarre worlds (e.g. *mondo weirdo*). In these expressions, *mondo* came to be reinterpreted as an adverb meaning 'very' (probably helped by a vague resemblance to Spanish *mucho*), and its new career was born

> 1986 *Stereo Review*: He's so mondo cool, even though he's not British and doesn't have spiked hair!

moon buggy *n* (1971) a vehicle designed for use on the moon. Earlier termed *moon bug* (1963) and *moon car* (1965)

> 1971 *Guardian*: The astronauts will have a powered moon buggy called Rover.

Moonie *n* (1974) A dismissive nickname for a member of the Unification Church, a religious sect founded in 1954 by the Korean industrialist Sun Myung Moon (b. 1920). By the 1970s the cult's strategies for recruiting and retaining its members had brought it a certain notoriety

> 1976 *Fiji Times*: Last year, two of their children left home to cast their lot in with 'the Moonies'.

Moral Majority *n* (1979) Originally, the name of a political movement of evangelical Christians, founded in the US in 1979 by the Reverend Jerry Falwell, advocating an ultra-conservative political and social agenda, especially on issues such as abortion and religious education. It was probably modelled at least partly on **silent majority (1955)**. In 1986 the movement was renamed the 'Liberty Federation', but by then the term had taken on a generic application to any group claiming to hold majority views (typically highly conservative) on moral matters

> 1986 *Times*: Appropriating a term hitherto used by the political right (especially in the United States)...Mr Kinnock declared himself...to be speaking for the real 'moral majority' of Britain, broad-minded and compassionate.

mouthfeel *n* (1973) the sensation of flavour, consistency, etc. produced in the mouth by an item of food or drink. Originally US; a piece of food-industry jargon

> 1995 *Fine Cooking*: Fat...moistens sandwiches..., gives a tender richness to meats..., and it adds richness, texture, and great 'mouth-feel' to desserts.

mover and shaker *n* (1972) a person who influences events, especially events of importance in the world. The expression has its origin in a line from 'Ode' (1874) by the English poet Arthur O'Shaughnessy (1844–81): 'Yet we are the movers and shakers Of the world for ever, it seems.' (The poem was set to music by Elgar as *The Music Makers* (1912). Its prevailing mood of wistful regret contrasts strangely with the thrustfulness of the expression for which it is now mainly remembered.) It is sometimes reversed to *shaker and mover*, and as it came into commoner use in the 1980s it was often shortened to simply *shaker*. Usually used in the plural

> 1972 F. Knebel: The rich movers and shakers…always manage to manipulate the Congress for their own benefit and screw the rest of us.

> 1988 *Sunday Times*: Puttnam, 1963 edition, a 22-year-old proletarian meteor photographed by…David Bailey as one of a portfolio of Sixties shakers like Paul McCartney and Michael Caine.

Muppet *n* (1970) A proprietary name (registered in the US in 1972, with claim of first use in 1954) for any of a number of glove and rod puppets and marionettes (chiefly representing animals) first popularized in the children's television programme *Sesame Street*, and for playthings depicting them. Coined by their creator, Jim Henson (1936–90), probably based on *puppet*, and possibly influenced by *marionette*, although Henson himself denied this (see the quote below)

> 1978 *Time*: Henson…says that 'muppet' was simply a word that sounded good to him. The sound combination of puppet and marionette is merely an explanation that happens to sound logical.

music centre *n* (1974) a stereophonic system combining record-player, radio, and cassette tape recorder in a single unit, typically with separate loudspeakers. The latest in 1970s mass-market hi-fi, and in many ways the direct evolutionary descendant of the **radiogram (1932)**

> 1974 *Hi Fi for Pleasure*: Model G 2601 KL…is a music centre with everything.

nanotechnology *n* (1974) the branch of technology that deals with dimensions and tolerances of 0.1 to 100 nanometres, or, more broadly, with the manipulation of individual atoms and molecules. Coined from Greek *nanos* 'dwarf'

> 1974 N. Taniguchi: From the emergent needs based on these industrial requirements, the system of ultra fine finishing or 'Nano-technology' has been introduced.

network *v* (1976) to make use of one's membership of a 'network' of colleagues, friends, acquaintances, etc., usually on an informal basis, and especially for the exchange of information, etc., or for professional or other advantage. Originally US

> 1979 *Working Woman*: The way networking works in real life for both men and women goes something like this: when you need help, someone you have known over a period of time, for whom you have done services and favors of friendship, takes your need as the opportunity to return them.

> 1980 M. S. Welch: This book will show you how to network.

New Age *n* (1971) a cultural movement covering a broad range of beliefs and activities and characterized by a rejection of modern Western-style values and culture and the promotion of a more integrated or holistic approach in areas such as religion, medicine, philosophy, astrology, and the environment. The term, with its messianic overtones, was first used as long ago as the 1840s, and crops up from time to time in 19th- and early-20th-century theosophical and mystical writings, but it was the 1970s that saw its institutionalization. It is often used adjectivally. See also **Age of Aquarius (1967)**, **New Age traveller (1986)**

> 1971 D. Spangler: Findhorn strengthens this movement, sometimes called the 'New Age movement', and becomes a cornerstone of the universal foundation of new, inspired confidence.

> 1987 *Sunday Express Magazine*: Most of them listen to New Age music—waves lapping, whales calling, amplified heartbeats and so on. None of them listen to the Beach Boys.

New Wave *n* (1976) a style of rock music, popular in the late 1970s, that was originally associated with punk rock (see **punk rock (1971)**), but later developed its own, more restrained character

> 1976 *Listener*: The Pistols are…the best known of the 'new-wave', or 'punk-rock' groups.

> 1980 *Washington Post*: The first bands I heard referred to as New Wave were Englishmen—Elvis Costello and Joe Jackson and the Police.

nice one *n* (1972) something performed well. Colloquial. Popularized in Britain in the phrase 'Nice one, Cyril', originally used in a televison advertisement for 'Wonderloaf', and subsequently taken up by football fans as a chant aimed at the Tottenham Hotspur player Cyril Knowles. A song was written based on this (see the first quote below). Hence used as an exclamation of commendation (but often with its message ironically inverted)

> 1973 Spiro & Clarke: Nice one, Cyril, Nice one, son. Nice one, Cyril, Let's have another one.

> 1990 Maureen Lipman: 'They're on the top table with Her Royal Highness. We're on Table No 5 with no one we know.' 'Nice one,' I said darkly.

no-go area *n* (1971) an area to which entry is impossible or forbidden for specified people, groups, etc.

> 1971 *Guardian*: For journalists and others, the Bogside and Creggan estates are 'no-go' areas, with the IRA in total effective control.

> 1972 *Guardian*: The Duke of Norfolk has decreed the Royal Enclosure at Ascot a 'no-go' area for the miniskirted or hotpanted lass.

noise pollution *n* (1970) an excessive or annoying degree of noise in a particular area (e.g. from traffic, aircraft engines, or audio devices)

> 1970 *Science Journal*: The greatly improved noise pollution characteristics of VTOL compared not only with conventional aircraft (CTOL) but with short take off and landing craft (STOL).

non-dairy *adj* (1972) Designating foodstuffs resembling dairy products but containing no animal fats. A term rich in resonances of the technologized food of the last third of the 20th century, conjuring up particularly the little individual pots of 'non-dairy creamer' offered with coffee at fast-food outlets

> 1972 *Which?*: The non-dairy ice creams we found with the highest amount of non-fat milk solids were *Ross Tudor…and Marine Ices.*

> 1994 *Successful Retirement*: I found…three varieties of 'nondairy' creamer.

nouvelle cuisine *n* (1975) a style of originally French cooking that avoids traditional rich sauces and emphasizes the freshness of the ingredients and attractive presentation. A borrowing from French, literally 'new cooking'. The term was introduced in 1974 by the two French food critics Henri Gault and Christian Millau. Nouvelle cuisine was pioneered by the French chefs Paul Bocuse, Jean and Pierre Troisgros, and Michel Guérard (who introduced his own variation called *cuisine minceur*). Intensely fashionable in the late 1970s, it was subsequently reviled for merely painting pictures on a plate and leaving eaters in need of a square meal

> 1978 Conran & Hobhouse: These three-star chefs have between them changed French cooking radically. The new style…which they have developed together over the years is called Nouvelle Cuisine, and its principles are that food should have a 'lyrical lightness'.

> 1982 Jane Grigson: Even manuals of nouvelle cuisine, in which fruit is put to new savoury uses, neglect the gooseberry.

nubile *adj* (1973) Of a woman: sexually attractive. *Nubile* began the century meaning, as it had for nearly 300 years, 'marriageable', but somewhere around the middle of the century this new sense began to emerge, and the old one has been virtually lost. It mainly arose from (not uncommon) contexts in which either interpretation was possible, but with the benefit of hindsight its form and sound seem to fit its new meaning like a glove

> 1973 *Times*: Some of the slimmest and most nubile girls in London, animadverted on by the Chancellor in his Budget statement, were on parade in London yesterday beneath the chandelier and haze of perfume of Christian Dior's thrice-repeated display of spring fashion.

> 1975 Tim Heald: Waiting by the lift doors was a nubile blonde.

ocker *n* (1971) a rough, uncultivated, or aggressively boorish Australian male (the female of the species is sometimes referred to as an *ockerina*). Originally an Australian nickname (first recorded in 1916) for someone called 'Oscar'. It was used as the name of a character devised and played by Ron Frazer (1924–83) in the Australian television series *The Mavis Bramston Show* (1965–68), and was hence applied generically

> 1971 G. Johnston: The big man would be a good player, a vigorous clubman, a hearty participant in the companionship of the club bar. He was a type Julian had sometimes talked to him about, what the boy called an 'Ocker'.

> 1975 *TV Times* (Australia): The cult of the ocker is sweeping Australia.

optical fibre *n* (1970) a very thin transparent fibre used in **fibre optics (1957)** to transmit light

> 1970 *Science Journal*: Nobody has yet produced glass which meets all the challenging require-
> ments of optical fibres.

outplace *v* (1970) to help (a redundant employee, especially an executive) in finding new employment. Originally US. Often used as a euphemism for 'to make redundant' or 'to sack'. See also
dehire (1970)

> 1970 *Time*: Instead of simply bouncing a subordinate, the boss can send him to a firm that special-
> izes in helping unwanted executives to find new jobs. The practitioners have even coined a
> euphemistic description for the process: 'outplacing' executives who have been 'dehired'.

> 1981 William Safire: If your boss threatens to fire you, put him down with 'You can't outplace me—I
> quit!'

outro *n* (1971) a concluding section, especially one which closes a broadcast programme or musical
work. A colloquial variation on *intro* (which is first recorded in the 1920s)

> 1985 *Music Week*: Dave Goodman...has added a straight orchestral intro and outro.

outsource *v* (1979) to obtain (goods, especially component parts) by contract from a source outside an organization or area; also, to contract (work) out

> 1979 *Journal of the Royal Society of Arts*: We are so short of professional engineers in the motor
> industry that we are having to outsource design work to Germany.

overstayer *n* (1977) an immigrant who stays beyond the time permitted by a work permit.
Originally a New Zealand usage, applied to Polynesian immigrants

> 1977 *New Zealand Woman's Weekly*: We have heard so much lately about the overstayers and
> while agreeing wholeheartedly that the law must be held in regard and obeyed, I have been wonder-
> ing if we realize just how much we depend on some of these Island people.

page three girl *n* (1975) a scantily-clad or nude female model whose picture appears as a pin-up
in the popular press. Originally applied specifically to such a girl regularly featured on page three
of the British tabloid *Sun* (and the term *Page Three* was registered as a proprietary name by the
Sun's owners). The break-through display of nipples in a mass-market newspaper brought the
Sun great commercial success in the 1970s and 80s, but towards the end of the 1990s its proprietors
judged that the readers were jaded and craved greater seriousness, so the nipples disappeared

> 1975 *Sun*: Lovely Jackie Brocklehurst makes her bow today as a super Sun Page Three girl.

> 1986 *Times*: Prostitution and 'page three' girls were the subjects chosen by a senior circuit judge.

palimony *n* (1979) compensation claimed especially by the deserted party after the separation of an
unmarried couple living together. Colloquial, originally US; a blend of *pal* and *alimony*.

> 1981 *Times*: Miss Barnett...has alleged in a separate civil action seeking 'palimony' (financial sup-
> port) that she and Mrs King became lesbian lovers in 1972.

paperless *adj* (1971) in which paper is not used as a medium for the storage, transmission, etc., of
information; computerized. Often in the expression *paperless office*

> 1975 *Business Week*: Some believe that the paperless office is not that far off. Vincent E. Giuliano of
> Arthur D. Little, Inc., figures that the use of paper in business for records and correspondence
> should be declining by 1980, 'and by 1990, most record-handling will be electronic'.

paramedic *n* (1970) an auxiliary medical worker (e.g. a laboratory assistant). In general usage, most
commonly applied to someone (e.g. an ambulance driver) who, although not a doctor, is trained
to give basic medical treatment

> 1974 *Telegraph* (Brisbane): Paramedics tried artificial respiration, but to no avail.

passive smoking *n* (1971) the inhalation of smoke involuntarily from the tobacco being smoked
by others, considered as a health risk. Possibly a translation of German *Passivrauchen*. The related
passive smoker is first recorded in 1976

> 1971 G. Richardson: Some studies give attention to the fact that non-smokers cannot avoid inhal-
> ing smoke when breathing smoky air, the so-called 'passive smoking'.

> 1976 *Medical Journal of Australia*: This type of smoker is known as a passive or second-hand
> smoker.

paternity leave *n* (1973) temporary absence from work granted to a man in the period up to and following the birth of his child

> 1975 *Times*: The Greater London Council…agreed tonight that fathers on their staff should normally be allowed up to five days paternity leave.

patrial *n* (1971) someone who has the legal right of abode in the United Kingdom. A term introduced in the 1971 Immigration Act; it was adapted from the existing but little-used adjective *patrial* 'of one's native country'

> 1971 *Sunday Times*: The draft Bill…lays down that a patrial basically is: 1. A person born in the UK or one of whose parents or grandparents were; 2. A naturalised citizen; 3. A former citizen of the Commonwealth already resident in Britain.

pay-and-display *adj* (1976) Designating a system of car-parking in which the driver buys a ticket for a specified period of time and displays it in the car while it is parked

> 1976 *Lancaster & Morecambe Guardian*: The existing charge of 12p for two hours will be cut to 10p for up to an hour to solve problems at pay-and-display machines.

pay-per-view *n* (1978) a system of television broadcasting in which viewers pay a fee to watch certain specified programmes (usually feature films or sporting events). Originally US, where the abbreviation *PPV* is not uncommon. See **pay television (1956)**

> 1995 *Economist*: These extra channels will allow pay-TV companies to offer…'pay-per-view', where customers are charged for individual programmes such as boxing or football matches.

peace process *n* (1975) negotiations towards the peaceful settlement of an established conflict. A term originally associated with US Secretary of State Henry Kissinger's shuttle diplomacy of the 1970s. In the 80s it was much used in the context of Middle East peace negotiations, and in the 90s it was inherited by the attempts to bring peace to Northern Ireland

> 1975 *Economist*: They claim that he has no idea where Mr Kissinger's piecemeal peace process is leading, beyond the short-sighted hope that acquiescence in it will at least buy time.

> 1994 *Financial Times*: Mr Major has won plaudits for his handling of the peace process.

pee *n* (1971) A representation of the pronunciation of *p*, an abbreviation of *penny*, the name of a unit of decimal currency introduced in Britain on 15 February 1971. The 'old' penny had gone under the abbreviation *d* (for Latin *denarius*), which no one ever attempted to pronounce. However, the abbreviation for the 'new' penny (see **new penny (1966)**) swiftly passed into the spoken language, and was briefly deemed to deserve a more impressive orthographic form than mere *p* (no doubt with a facetious side-glance at *pee* 'urine'). The usage did not long survive the end of the 1970s. See also **pence (1971)**

> 1971 *Observer*: Everyone at the Decimal Currency Board has taken to calling new pence 'pee'.

> 1974 Ruth Rendell: May I trouble you for forty-two pee?

pence *n* (1971) Used colloquially as an alternative singular form to *penny* when decimal currency was introduced in Britain in 1971 (see **new penny (1966)**). Speakers seemed somehow reluctant to use *penny* for the new coin, perhaps because it was still too strongly associated with the 'old' penny, and turned the previous plural into a singular—sometimes even going so far as to invent a new plural *pences*

> 1971 *Record* (Oxford University Press): The computer was found to be rounding up to the nearest pence the Bank Code Numbers on the Wages Slips.

> 1973 *Daily Telegraph*: In our village shop a customer asked for some small change but the shopkeeper was unable to oblige as she was very short of 'two pences and one pences'.

> 1979 *Daily Telegraph*: A taxi passenger who refused to pay an extra charge of one pence on his fare…was killed by the driver, police said in Manila.

people mover *n* (1971) A term applied to any of a range of means of conveying people from one place to another. Originally US

> 1971 J. P. Romualdi: A 'people mover', a vehicle smaller than a streetcar…will provide continuous service between the old campus in town and the new campus in the suburbs.

> 1974 *Times*: Magnetic levitation, vacuum tubes, vertical take-off aircraft, and small-scale automatic and semi-automatic 'people-movers' of all kinds for urban situations.

performance art *n* (1971) a form of visual art in which the activity of the artist forms a central feature, combining static elements with dramatic performance

> 1971 *Rolling Stone*: A...work of performance art was staged by...cars whose drivers all sounded their horns according to a pre-arranged score, and the noise was broadcast by a local radio station.

persistent vegetative state *n* (1972) a condition of indefinite duration, resulting from brain damage, in which a patient recovering from a coma retains brainstem functions such as reflex responses and may appear wakeful, but has no cognitive functions or other evidence of cerebral cortical activity. A term called into being largely by late-20th-century medicine's skill in keeping such patients alive. (The colloquial use of *vegetable* to denote such people ('I hope and pray she will die with dignity and not be reduced by a stroke into a vegetable', Barbara Castle (1980)) appears to have had its beginnings in the 1930s.) The abbreviation *PVS* is first recorded in 1985. See also **brain-dead (1976)**

> 1972 *Lancet*: Patients with severe brain damage due to trauma...may now survive indefinitely... Such patients are best described as in a persistent vegetative state.

> 1996 *Independent*: Now many patients who, 20 years ago, would have died quick and painless deaths, linger on in PVS.

person *n* (1971) Used in place of *man* in a range of compound forms in order to avoid an invidious exclusion of women. Mainly found in the titles of jobs and offices that can be held by either sex, but also used more widely in various fanciful and often allegedly amusing combinations (e.g. *henchperson*). Initially the earnest political correctness of some advocates of the usage made it the butt of heavy-handed humour, resulting in such nonce coinages as *Personchester* and *personhole cover*, but by the end of the century it had been more or less comfortably absorbed into the language. Its plural is almost invariably *persons* rather than *people*. See also **alderperson (1973)**, **chairperson (1971)**, **personkind (1972)**, **spokesperson (1972)**, **waitperson (1980)**

> 1971 *Scientific American*: If there is any doubt at the counter, let him show the salesperson this ad.

> 1972 *Listener*: Two young black women will almost certainly join Representative Shirley Chisholm in Congress...putting up the number of black 'Congresspersons' to at least 14.

> 1973 *Listener*: Chairperson Mitchell and her henchpersons looked at the way education brainwashes girls.

> 1976 *Oxford Times*: Builders' merchants require yardperson.

> 1976 *Journal of the Royal Society of Arts*: The exercise known amongst marketing men, or should I say marketing persons, as market segmentation.

> 1977 *Evening News* (Worcester): Person required for general cleaning duties in car showroom.

> 1978 *Amateur Photographer*: We saw nothing in cine to rival the spectacular application of high-technology design to still cameras for everyman (sorry, everyperson).

personal computer *n* (1976) a computer designed for use by an individual, especially in an office or business environment. Commonly abbreviated to *PC*, which is first recorded in 1978

> 1976 *Byte*: You can do such modelling...using the personal computer as a central element.

> 1982 *Computerworld*: Then the next year the PC (Personal Computer) came out and you saw that for $3,000 you could do the same thing you had paid all that money for.

personkind *n* (1972) the human race. Originally US; an early stab at a non-sexist substitute for *mankind*, but in the long run alternatives such as *humankind* and *human race* seem to have been found more acceptable

> 1972 *Time*: Readers and writers of both sexes must resist onefully [i.e. not 'manfully'] any meaningless neologisms. To do less is to encourage another manifestation of prejudice—against reason, meaning and eventually personkind itself.

> 1984 *Australian Personal Computer*: The personal computer is, perhaps, the worst thing that ever happened to personkind.

petrodollar *n* (1974) a notional unit of currency available in a petroleum-exporting country. Often used in the context of the surplus of petroleum exports over imports of all other goods

1974 *Globe & Mail* (Toronto): What emerged in Washington…was a growing concern over the swiftly accelerating petrodollar holdings of the Arabs.

PG *n* (1972) An abbreviation of *parental guidance*. Used as a classification symbol for a film certified for viewing by anyone but which contains scenes which may be unsuitable for children. Originally North American

1976 *New Yorker*: Why would anybody want a PG-rated Peckinpah film?

photofit *n* (1970) a method of building up a picture of someone suspected of a crime by assembling a number of photographs of individual facial features. Also applied to a picture so formed. See also **identikit (1961), E-fit (1994)**

1974 John Gardner: They showed…a straight and recent picture of Peppe, together with some photofits put together to show the [Mafia] don in a permutation of disguises.

pig out *v* (1978) to make a pig of oneself by over-eating; to have an eating binge. Slang, originally and mainly North American; often followed by *on*

1981 Jane Fonda: Troy and Vanessa…pig out for days on leftover Halloween candy.

piña colada *n* (1975) a long drink made with pineapple juice, rum, and coconut. A borrowing from Spanish, where it means literally 'strained pineapple'. The drink enjoyed a vogue in the second half of the 1970s, but never really acquired a sophisticated image

1978 *Chicago*: There was gin and piña coladas and talk about Estée Lauder…and money…and clothes.

piss artist *n* (1975) Originally applied to someone who drinks heavily and therefore gets 'pissed' (i.e. drunk); a more general application stemmed from the drunkard's characteristic blend of boastfulness and incompetence. British slang

1977 *Custom Car*: I refer to the auto/driver self-destruct mechanism know as 'booze'. A piss artist behind the wheel of a 1935 Austin Seven was a killer.

1977 *Private Eye*: Malcolm Derek Winn. Photographer, traveller, piss-artist. Whereabouts known? Box 1215.

plastic bullet *n* (1972) a type of projectile made of PVC, which is fired from a riot-gun and is used especially by security forces in riot-control. See also **rubber bullet (1971)**

1972 *News Letter* (Belfast): New devices for riot control, including a plastic bullet, have been issued to the Army in Northern Ireland.

plastic money *n* (1974) credit cards, debit cards, etc. as a method of payment. Colloquial, originally US. Later shortened to simply **plastic (1980)**

1974 *Time*: About 503 million credit cards are in use in the U.S. today—proof enough that 'plastic money' is replacing the folding kind.

plc *n* (1973) An abbreviation of *public limited company*, which replaced *limited* as the official designation of a British limited-liability company under the terms of the 1980 Companies Act

1973 *Daily Telegraph*: Although the proposed new form of incorporation for small companies is temporarily shelved, a new designation for listed companies is introduced. Out goes 'Ltd' and in comes 'PLC' or 'Public Limited Company'.

1980 *Daily Mail*: Following the implementation of…the 1980 Companies Act…we will be faced with names which resemble the lyrics of a Goodies song: ICI plc; RHM plc; [etc.].

pointy-head *n* (1972) a supposed expert or intellectual. US colloquial, used derogatorily

1972 *Times*: Mr Wallace…dismissed it quickly at the end of his address as 'the most callous, asinine, stupid thing that was ever conceived by some pointy-head in Washington DC'.

politically correct *adj* (1970) conforming to a body of liberal or radical opinion, especially on social matters, characterized by the advocacy of approved causes or views, and often by the rejection of language, behaviour, etc., considered discriminatory or offensive. Originally US; often used as a term of derision by those who do not espouse such views. The expression is recorded as long ago as the late 18th century in the neutral sense 'correct from a political point of view' (' "The United States", instead of the "People of the United States", is the toast given. This is not *politically correct*', J. Wilson (1793)), but as a term in its own right it had to await the liberalization of the 1960s and its backlash. The now frequent abbreviation **PC** is first recorded in 1986, the noun *political correctness* in 1979

> 1970 T. Cade: A man cannot be politically correct and a chauvinist too.

> 1975 P. Gerber: If a literary thesis were unmistakable and politically correct, a favorable reception for the work was assured.

> 1986 *Los Angeles Times*: The key to this was found not in her message songs—like many of her ilk, she tends toward smug political correctness.

> 1991 *Village Voice* (New York): I've been chided by a reader for using the word *gringos* and informed that European American is politically correct.

pooper-scooper *n* (1976), **poop-scoop** *n* (1978) an implement used for clearing up faeces, especially dog faeces fouling public places. Originally North American

> 1978 *Daily Telegraph*: It may soon be common to see people holding a dog lead in one hand and a 'poop scoop' in the other.

> 1978 *Daily Telegraph*: The 'pooper-scooper' law in New York requires dog-owners to pick up anything their dogs drop.

Popemobile *n* (1979) A popular name for a specially-designed vehicle with a raised viewing platform surrounded by bullet-proof glass, used by the Pope when on an official visit to a foreign country. This type of vehicle was introduced by Pope John Paul II

> 1979 *Irish Times*: The Pope drove through the crowds in the specially constructed 'Popemobile'.

> 1982 Gerald Priestland: The usual 'Popemobile' has been harshly renamed the SPT or 'Special Papal Transport'.

pop festival *n* (1970) an event at which several pop groups perform to a mass audience, typically over several days and in the open air. The legendary exemplar is Woodstock, a pop festival held in fields outside Bethel, New York in 1969

> 1970 *Guardian*: Pop festivals…are big business.

> 1971 *Daily Telegraph*: The Isle of Wight County Council last night rejected all three farm sites proposed by Richard Roscoe, a promoter, for staging a pop festival.

POSSLQ *n* (1979) a long-term sexual partner, especially a live-in one. This entrant in the 'word-for-a-nonmarried-sexual-partner' stakes was apparently coined in 1978 as an acronym from the initial letters of *partner* (or *person*) *of opposite sex sharing living quarters* by Arthur J. Norton, a member of the US Census Bureau. It was never adopted by the Bureau, and its bizarre form means that it has never been regarded as much more than a joke word. Compare **significant other (1977)**

> 1979 *National Review* (US): The Feds, as usual, screwed it up by creating POSSLQ, or Persons of Opposite Sex Sharing Living Quarters, which could refer to married couples as well as unmarried or newborn twins, or just about anybody.

> 1993 *Independent on Sunday*: It's not *terrifically* poetic, as in 'Come live with me and be my POSSLQ'.

Post-it *n* (1975) The proprietary name for a piece of often yellow note-paper with an adhesive strip on one side, designed to be stuck prominently to an object or surface and easily removed when necessary, and used for appending temporary notes. Often called more fully *Post-it note* or, colloquially, *yellow sticky* (first recorded in 1986). By the end of the century it was a common sight to see documents, books, etc. sprouting these little bits of yellow paper

> 1992 *College & Research Libraries News*: Don't put that handy little 'yellow sticky' a.k.a. Post-it™ note on library materials or you could cause staining and permanent damage.

poverty trap *n* (1972) a situation in which an earned increase to a low income is offset by the consequent loss of means-tested state benefits

> 1972 *Daily Telegraph*: The idea was to prevent families falling into the 'poverty trap'—the situation in which a pay rise can mean the poor are worse off because they lose a disproportionate number of State benefits.

power *n* (1970) Used with a preceding adjective or noun to designate a movement to enhance the status of the specified group or the beliefs and activities of such a group. Modelled on **black power (1966)** and **flower power (1967)**

> 1970 Jennie Melville: I'm working to establish Parent Power right now.

> 1972 *Pride of Lions* (Columbia University): What is important is that you come out, have gay pride and leave the dance with a sense of Gay power.

> 1972 *Guardian*: Pupil power flexes its muscles in London today. The organisers have called on all London secondary school-children to join them in a one-day general strike.

power-sharing *n* (1972) a sharing of political power. Often applied specifically to an arrangement in Northern Ireland in the early 1970s by which minority parties exercised some measure of political power in cooperation with the majority. This was effectively brought to an end by a general strike in 1974

> 1978 Patrick Cosgrave: It was widely believed that if there had not been a general election in February 1974 his Northern Ireland 'power-sharing' executive would have worked.

prequel *n* (1973) a book, film, etc. in which the events portrayed precede those of an existing completed work. A combination of *pre-* and *sequel* to which more than one writer has laid claim (see the first two quotes below)

> 1977 *National Observer* (US): Cammer…has just written a book, *Freedom from Compulsion*… He calls it a 'prequel' to his earlier book, *Up from Depression*. ' "Prequel" is a word I coined', he explains. 'It's a sequel except it's on a subject that comes before.'

> 1977 *Globe & Mail* (Toronto): The Silmarillion, for which Tolkien coined the term Prequel, describes not only the creation of Middle Earth, but of the universe.

> 1979 *Films & Filming*: In this 'prequel' Tom Berenger stars as Butch Cassidy and William Katt as Sundance.

prioritize *v* (1973) Initially, to designate as worthy of prior attention, to give priority to; latterly also, to determine the order in which (items) are to be dealt with, to establish priorities for (a set of items). Originally US

> 1973 T. H. White: The storefront operators in the counties that Malek had 'prioritized' had identified independents, wavering Democrats and 'don't knows'.

> 1981 *Times*: In the Nato headquarters…we are well used to prioritizing our targets.

privatize *v* (1970) See **privatization (1959)**

proactive *adj* (1971) Of a person, policy, etc.: that creates or controls a situation by taking the initiative or by anticipating events (as opposed to responding to them). Also used latterly to mean 'innovative, tending to make things happen'. Mainly management or business jargon. Coined from *pro-* and *reactive*, perhaps with a subliminal memory of the earlier psychology term *proactive*, denoting a mental process that affects a subsequent process

> 1971 A. J. R. Reiss: Citizens usually bring matters to police attention… The police department deals with such requests as a *reactive* organization… The police also acquire information by intervening in the lives of citizens on their own initiative. In this capacity, they serve as a *proactive* organization.

> 1985 *Globe & Mail* (Toronto): If you are the proactive and innovative individual we are looking for…we invite you to submit a resume in confidence.

pro-choice *adj* (1975) in favour of upholding a woman's legal right to choose whether to have an abortion. Originally and mainly US; first recorded as a noun, denoting a 'pro-choice' policy. Essentially a euphemism for 'pro-abortion'; compare **pro-life (1976)**

> 1975 *Ms*: The legal battles…have virtually all been decided in favour of pro-choice.

> 1986 *Parliamentary Affairs*: 'Pro-life' senators opposing those allied with the 'pro-choice' movement.

prog *n* (1975) A colloquial British shortening of *programme*; a usage particularly associated with the singer and disc-jockey Jimmy Young, presenter of a prog on BBC radio

> 1975 *Listener*: Nice to have you with us on the prog, we say, don't we, fans?

pro-life *adj* (1976) opposed to inducing abortions. Originally US; first recorded in the derivative *pro-lifer*, denoting an anti-abortionist. One of the more obnoxious weasel-words thrown up by late-20th-century polemical word-coiners, implying as it does that those who wish women to be able to have abortions are against life. Out of the same stable, but less successful, was *pro-family* ('Some "pro-family" activists…noisily pressed their antiabortion and "morality" platform', B. Frishman (1984)). Those opposed to this stance counter-coined with *anti-choice*, first recorded in 1978 ('What hypocrisy to call such anti-humanitarian people "pro-life". Call them what they are—antichoice', *Ms* (1978)). Compare **pro-choice (1975)**

> 1976 *National Observer* (US): Carter…had misled proabortionists and prolifers.

> 1979 *Time*: As the oldest of eleven children (all married), I'd like to point out our combined family numbers more than 100 who vote only for pro-life candidates.

property developer *n* (1970) someone who buys land, buildings, etc. and increases their value, especially by new building. A hate figure of the 1970s, seen as making excessive profits while transforming inner-city landscapes into bleak wildernesses. (*Developer* in this general sense is first recorded in 1938)

> 1970 *Harper's Bazaar*: Property developers…wreaked vandalism upon the cities and countryside of England.

Provo *n* (1971) a member of the Provisional I.R.A., a faction favouring terrorist action which split from the official I.R.A. towards the end of 1969. The name was probably at least partially modelled on *Provo* 'a member of a group of young Dutch political activists of the 1960s', from an abbreviation of French *provocateur*

> 1971 *Guardian*: In their bombing campaign the Provos seem to have hit on a policy…described as being the best way to bring down Stormont.

proximity talks *n* (1975) diplomatic discussions or negotiations in which opposing parties do not meet but are in close proximity to each other and talk through intermediaries. A device to enable communication to take place between two sides who are not on speaking terms

> 1975 *Economist*: 'Proximity' talks, which means that the intermediary would have to shuttle a shorter distance, between Israeli and Egyptian teams sitting in next-door rooms.

PSBR *n* (1976) An abbreviation of *public-sector borrowing requirement*, the amount a government has to borrow to make up the difference between its income from tax and other sources and its expenditure. A term which first came forcefully to public notice in Britain during the economic crisis of 1976 ('The borrowing requirement (a euphemism for government overspending)', *Times* (1976)), which required a large baling-out loan from the International Monetary Fund, conditional on a £1 billion cut in public spending

> 1976 *Economist*: The £11½ billion public sector borrowing requirement (PSBR).

> 1986 *Daily Telegraph*: This year's PSBR looks like turning out at a little under £7 billion.

psycho-babble *n* (1976) jargon that is much influenced by the concepts and terminology of psychology and is used especially by lay people in referring to their own personality or relationships. Colloquial and derogatory; originally US. Popularized as the title of a 1977 book by R. D. Rosen

> 1980 *Times Literary Supplement*: The book is written in colloquial American spliced with psychobabble, a language in which the highest commendation is to say of someone 'She was a person.'

pub grub *n* (1978) food served in a pub. British. A signal not only of the transformation of the traditional British pub from beer station to civilized place of refreshment by the latter part of the century, but also of the increasing tendency to use colloquial language (here *grub*) in situations where at the beginning of the century it would have been out of the question

> 1978 *Country Life*: There are 'lounge bars' and 'singing bars' and many places advertising 'pub grub'.

pump *v pump iron* (1972) to exercise with weights as a form of fitness training or body-building technique. Colloquial, originally US

> 1976 *New York Times*: Arnold Schwarzenegger…, believed by many to have the world's most perfect male body, was pumping iron the other day at the Mid-City Gym.

punk *n* (1976) a punk rocker; an adherent of the punk youth cult

> 1976 *Sunday Times*: Johnny Rotten and the Sex Pistols are punks. They sing 'Anarchy in the UK.'

> 1977 *Evening News*: London's growing army of punks have developed a powerful animosity for teds… For the uninitiated, punks…are the ones who match short, ragged hair with short ragged leather jackets.

punk rock *n* (1971), **punk** *n* (1974) a loud, fast-moving style of rock music characterized by aggressive and deliberately outrageous lyrics and performance. Its most high-profile exponents were the band 'The Sex Pistols'. In the later 1970s punk developed in Britain into a youth cult whose adherents, *punk rockers* (1976), rejected middle-class values and standard pop culture and dressed in a provocative style (e.g. with spiky day-glo hairstyles and leather clothing with chains, safety pins, etc.). The original *punk* in *punk rock* came from the mainly US adjective *punk* 'worthless, rotten'. See also **New Wave (1976)**

> 1971 *Creem*: [Rudi Martinez is] doing the knee-drop, and the splits and every other James Brown move. He's the only one in punk-rock who's still got 'em and he's makin' a comeback.

> 1974 *New Yorker*: I was getting a naïve kick out of watching a woman play rock-and-roll punk.

> 1976 *Sunday Times*: Punk-rockers hate Mick Jagger (also, Led Zeppelin, Yes and Genesis) as much as they hate critics… Punk will fade. Its apologists are ludicrous.

pyramid selling *n* (1972) a system of marketing in which each buyer secures the participation of further buyers: a stock of goods is sold on and on to an ever larger set of buyers, at a higher price every time, until at last the final buyers are left with a stock that is unsaleable except at a loss. It is illegal in many countries

> 1972 *Daily Telegraph*: A company whose cosmetic business is said to involve 'pyramid selling'—a system whereby a franchiser sells to others the right to market goods—was banned in the High Court yesterday from operating its bank account.

Pythonesque *adj* (1975) (characteristic) of *Monty Python's Flying Circus*, a popular BBC television comedy series of the 1970s, noted especially for its absurdist or surrealistic humour

> 1975 *Guardian*: A range of comic methods that stretches from Pythonesque funny walks…to comedy of manners.

> 1977 *Time Out*: It veered from the Pythonesque, mostly due to the presence of the Cleese-like Julian Hough, to the twee.

quality time *n* (1977) time spent in giving someone one's undivided attention in order to strengthen a relationship, especially between a parent and child. A symptom of the manically busy last quarter of the century in Western culture, when both parents usually went out to work and a special phrase had to be coined to denote time spent relaxing with their children

> 1977 *Business Week*: The time they spend with their children is 'quality time, not quantity time,' say the mothers, echoing the claim of many executive fathers, and the children's home life is frequently more stimulating.

> 1995 *Evening Argus* (Brighton): Leo… Your feelings of love return today and you'd be wise to spend quality time with a partner, re-establishing the bonds between you.

quango *n* (1973) a semi-public administrative body outside the civil service but financed by the exchequer and having members appointed by the government. An acronym, but its elements are disputed: it is commonly explained as standing for *quasi-autonomous national government organization*, but this is not independently recorded before 1976, and it is considerably predated by *quasi-nongovernmental organization* ('In recent years there has appeared on the American scene a new genus of organization which represents a noteworthy experiment in the art of government… We may call it the quasi nongovernmental organization', *Annual Report of the Carnegie Corporation* (1967)). Either way, its connotations are usually negative, suggesting placemanship and the exercise of undemocratic authority

> 1973 C. Hood: It was the Americans who first drew attention to the importance of what they have labelled the 'grants economy', the 'contract state' and the 'quasi-non-government organisation' (Quango).

> 1976 *Observer*: A new species of animal is multiplying in the undergrowth of Britain—the QUANGO, or Quasi Autonomous National Governmental Organisation.

> 1978 *Economist*: A quango covers just about everything from the Price Commission to the Police Complaints Board and the British Waterways Board.

> 1979 *Daily Telegraph*: Anthony Barker of Essex University, describes the gathering as his act of atonement for having, he claims, invented the word quango…10 years ago.

quantum leap *n* (1970) a sudden large increase or advance. The metaphor comes from the world of quantum physics, where the term denotes 'an abrupt transition between one stationary state of a quantized system and another, with the absorption or emission of a quantum'

> 1977 *New Yorker*: The imperial Presidency did not begin with Richard Nixon although under him abuses of the office took a quantum leap.

radical chic *n* (1970) the fashionable affectation of radical left-wing views or of dress, style of life, etc., associated with such views. A concept introduced by the American writer Tom Wolfe in a 1970 article in *New York*

> 1970 Tom Wolfe: Radical Chic invariably favors radicals who seem primitive, exotic, and romantic, such as the grape workers…the Panthers…and the Red Indians… Radical Chic…is only radical in style; in its heart it is part of Society and its traditions. Politics, like Rock, Pop, and Camp, has its uses; but [etc.].

> 1977 *Rolling Stone*: Right now bisexuality is the big radical chic on campuses.

railcard *n* (1977) a pass entitling the holder to reduced fares on the railway. British

> 1977 *Times*: The senior citizens' Railcards will become available from April 1 for a full year regardless of the date of purchase.

rap *n* (1979) a style of popular music developed by New York blacks in the 1970s in which words, usually improvised, are spoken rhythmically and often in rhyming sentences over an instrumental backing. *Rapper* and the related verb *rap* are also first recorded in 1979. A development from **rap** 'improvised repartee' (1965)

> 1979 *Billboard*: The Philadelphia-based rapper, Kurtis Blow, will soon record a 'Christmas Rapping' 12-inch record 'with holiday appeal'.

> 1982 *Face*: There is even a Rap single of 'Mama' available.

ready meal *n* (1979) a complete dish (or sometimes two or more dishes packaged together) which needs only brief heating in a microwave or conventional oven to prepare it for eating

> 1995 *Daily Telegraph*: The brand leads the field in vegetarian ready-meals. The beefless burgers were introduced in June.

recreational *adj* (1972) Designating the taking of a drug on an occasional basis for pleasure, especially when socializing (as opposed to addictive consumption). Originally US, with more than a tinge of euphemism, or at least special pleading

> 1972 *New York Times*: [The] percentage includes both drug abusers and recreational users, but does not include students who have merely experimented with drugs.

> 1994 *Independent on Sunday*: With youngsters now beginning to overdose on 'recreational' dance drugs like Ecstasy, they say, hardcore venues such as the Hangar should close.

reflexology *n* (1976) a form of therapeutic procedure practised in alternative medicine which involves massaging the soles of the feet. It is based on the belief that various parts and organs of the body have reflexes in the feet

> 1976 M. Segal: Like acupuncture, reflexology has been used by the Chinese for 5,000 years… We, as reflexologists, do the same by trying to relax the patient and relieve nerve tension.

refusenik *n* (1975) a Jew in the Soviet Union who has been refused permission to emigrate to Israel. A partial translation of Russian *otkaznik*, which was formed from the stem of *otkaznat'* 'to refuse'

> 1975 *Nature*: If, as is often the case with scientists, the initial application is rejected, one may spend months or years as a 'refusnik', with neither the opportunity nor the necessary time to keep up one's reading or think about one's own research.

> 1980 *Radio Times*: Tonight Avital talks about her life since she left Russia, a life of waiting and campaigning to free her husband and other Jewish refusniks from jail in the USSR.

regretfully *adv* (1976) it is to be regretted (that). A curious substitution for the expected *regrettably* which presumably owes a lot to **hopefully (1932)**, and which, when spotted by the eagle-eyed purist, arouses equal ire with that usage

> 1976 *New Statesman*: Regretfully, that is no ground for leniency towards him.

> 1977 *Times Literary Supplement*: The investigators, who must regretfully remain anonymous, have produced…a richness of archaeological potential which it will take years to absorb and assess.

relaunch *n* (1970) a reintroduction of an established product, institution, programme, etc. to the public by means of a publicity campaign. A piece of commercial persiflage camouflaging the pretence that something that had previously flopped is suddenly new and interesting. The related verb usage is first recorded in 1971

> 1970 *Daily Telegraph*: The re-launch had the desired effect and Vim's share of the market increased from 33 p.c. to 38 p.c.

> 1971 *Daily Telegraph*: The company was relaunched nearly two years ago… It was originally part of Henry Bowen-Davies' £8m Davies' Investment group which collapsed in 1967.

release *v* (1976) to dismiss (an employee). US euphemistic

> 1976 *National Observer* (US): The two most difficult things I ever had to do were, one: tell 23 teachers we were going to release them [etc.].

renewable *adj, n* (1971) (a source of energy) that is not depleted by its utilization

> 1978 *Nature*: Renewable sources of energy—wind, wave, sun, geothermal heat and the like— are…taken seriously at the United Kingdom Atomic Energy Authority.

> 1980 *Times*: The CEGB decision to take the first commercial steps for wind-powered electricity makes it easier…to take renewables seriously.

rent strike *n* (1970) a refusal to pay rent, usually by a number of people (originally often students) as a form of protest

> 1973 *Freedom*: Let the Trade Union movement now show its regard for the value of education by giving…support to student rent-strikes.

replay *n* (1973) See **action replay (1973)**

resource *v* (1975) to supply with resources. A transformation of the noun *resource* into a verb: an example of the sort of word-class conversion that has been a common feature of English word formation for hundreds of years, but which at the end of the 20th century continues to raise hackles (particularly when, as is often the case, it features in the language of bureaucrats)

> 1975 *Listener*: I would have gone in for smaller [school] units…resourced from some central agency.

> 1979 *Observer*: Social workers have been inadequately trained and inadequately resourced to meet the expectations upon them.

retro *n, adj* (1974) (characterized by) a style or fashion (of dress, music, etc.) that harks back to the past, especially in a nostalgically retrospective way. An adaptation of French *rétro*, an abbreviation of *rétrograde* first recorded in 1973

> 1974 *Guardian Weekly*: The icy charms of the Group TSE's productions, beginning as far back as 1969's 'Eva Peron', have been in the vanguard of the French vogue for 'retro'.

> 1986 *Times*: Black patent Grace Kelly handbags, long black gloves and high-heeled slingbacks are retro accessories to the elegant look.

right-on *adj* (1970) in accordance with received radical opinion of the time; also, more broadly, modern, trendy. Colloquial, originally US; a development of the exclamation *right on!*, denoting full agreement or approval (' "Only in a capitalist society could art be turned to profit." "Right on", ' *Melody Maker* (1970)), which is first recorded in 1925

> 1970 *Time*: In Boston, Homans is known as a 'right-on lawyer'—he defends blacks, war protesters and poor people.

> 1976 *Spare Rib*: I had just read *Sappho was a Right-On Woman* by Sidney Abbott and Barbara Love.

ring-pull *adj, n* (1970) Denoting a seal on a drink can or similar container which is broken by pulling a ring attached to it. As a noun, applied to the ring itself. A slightly more specific term than the earlier **tab (1963)**, **pull-tab (1965)**

> 1970 *Times*: Easy opening devices are undergoing considerable development—and ring-pull and zip-top cans are already available.

roller disco *n* (1978) a discothèque at which the dancers wear roller-skates; disco-dancing on roller-skates

> 1978 S. Boorstin: Skaters pursuing their passion…under the strobe lights of a roller disco.

rubber bullet *n* (1971) a type of projectile made of rubber, which is fired from a riot-gun and is used especially by security forces in riot-control. See also **plastic bullet (1972)**

> 1971 *Guardian*: The soldiers, wearing gas masks and riot helmets, fired nine rounds of rubber bullets.

> 1980 *Journal of the Royal Society of Arts*: Fire hoses as favoured on the Continent or rubber bullets favoured by the Army in Ireland.

rule(s), OK (1975) Used originally in wall graffiti to affirm the superiority of a gang, football team, etc., but the formula was widely taken up and reapplied in the late 1970s and early 80s. British, and traced back by some to the Glasgow razor-gangs of the 1930s

> 1975 *New Society*: Chelsea rule—okay.

> 1976 *Sunday Express*: He kept going on and on: '…there are certain standards to be maintained in first-class compartments.'… And when he left the train…he gave…a look which said: 'First Class Rules—O.K.?'

Sagbag *n* (1974) The proprietary name (registered in Britain in 1974) of an informal chair consisting of a large bag filled with polystyrene granules which accommodates itself to the form of the sitter

> 1978 *Evening Standard*: June Mendoza's picture of La Rippon, shoeless in a denim jump-suit and reclining fetchingly in a purplish sag-bag.

salsa *n* (1975) (a dance performed to) a kind of dance music of Latin American origin which incorporates elements of jazz and rock music. *Salsa* is Spanish for 'sauce', but this particular application comes from American Spanish, where a *salsa* is specifically a relish containing a variety of chopped-up ingredients—hence, music that is a blend of different styles

> 1981 *Weekly Guardian*: Salsa music drifts out of the bar as a group of grease-spattered youths tinker with the engine of a new Toyota.

screwdriver *adj* (1972) Designating, usually disparagingly, a factory for the assembly of components manufactured elsewhere. The subtext is 'rich country builds such a facility in a poor country, in order to exploit its cheap labour, and pockets the profits from the finished article'. Usually in the expression *screwdriver plant*

> 1972 *Times* (Jamaica Supplement): Mr Manley has also spoken in disparaging terms of 'screwdriver' industries.

> 1991 *Sunday Times*: Although many Japanese factories begin life as 'screwdriver plants', assembling imported components, the domestic component steadily increases.

self-catering *n* (1970) catering for oneself, especially providing one's own domestic services (e.g. meals and cleaning) in rented holiday accommodation. Often used adjectivally of holidays and vacation accommodation

> 1970 *Country Life*: There has also been a discernible movement towards self-catering holidays, in farmhouses, chalets, caravans and cottages.

selfish *adj* (1976) Of a gene or genetic material: tending to be perpetuated or to spread although of no effect on the phenotype. A usage popularized by the British evolutionist Richard Dawkins in his 1976 book *The Selfish Gene*. The underlying idea is that the gene's fundamental ambition is to perpetuate itself (via the organism it inhabits)

> 1976 Richard Dawkins: Let us understand what our own selfish genes are up to, because we may then at least have the chance to upset their designs.

sell-by date *n* (1973) a date marked on food packaging to indicate the latest recommended date of sale, especially for perishable goods. Widely used metaphorically in such phrases as *past its sell-by date*, denoting obsolescence

> 1973 *Which?*: Most of the date stamps will be 'Sell by…' dates.

> 1987 *Daily Telegraph*: Socialism: the package that's passed its sell-by date.

Selsdon man *n* (1970) Used originally and mainly by political opponents to denote an imagined person or people believed to be pursuing the proto-Thatcherist policies outlined at a conference of British Conservative Party leaders held at the Selsdon Park Hotel near Croydon, Surrey, 30 January–1 February 1970. They included support for a market economy (as opposed to state intervention), rejection of compulsory wage control, and a refusal to rescue industrial 'lame ducks'. The coinage was inspired by *Piltdown man* (see **Piltdown (1912)**) and similar anthropological appellations

> 1970 Harold Wilson: Selsdon Man is designing a system of society for the ruthless and the pushing.

> 1974 *Times*: Selsdon man went wrong because it appeared to make the Conservative Party into a set of decimalized economic liberals.

Sensurround *n* (1974) The proprietary name (registered in the US in 1976, with claim of use since 1974) of a special-effect technique whereby a cinema audience is apparently surrounded by low-frequency sound and air vibrations generated from the soundtrack of a film

> 1977 *Time*: *Rollercoaster* is the latest—and so far least—excuse to trot out Sensurround, that technology that is still in search of a character and, for that matter, a plot worthy of its woofers.

sex aid *n* (1977) something (e.g. a dildo, a novelty condom, or a pornographic magazine) intended to stimulate (flagging) sexual desire or enhance sexual pleasure

> 1977 *Gay News*: I should like to dismiss this neat little toy as a sex-aid for sadomasochists.

sexual politics *n* (1970) the principles determining the relationship of the sexes. A term coined by the feminist campaigner Kate Millett, and used by her as the title of a 1970 book

> 1970 Kate Millett: The prospect of radical change in sexual politics… So we proceed to the counter-revolutionary sexual politicians themselves—Lawrence, Miller and Mailer.

shaft *v* (1970) to copulate with. Slang

> 1970 G. Lord: There was this young girl among them, not even sixteen yet…like as not being shafted by every dirty long-haired crud in town.

s/he *pron* (1977) A written representation of *she or he*, used to save space or as an attempt to create a more gender-equal form

> 1977 *Gay News*: The questionnaire asks congregations whether they would call a minister to their pulpit if s/he were gay.

> 1978 *American Educator*: A child's sexual orientation is determined before s/he enters school.

shuttle diplomacy *n* (1974) diplomatic activity involving a series of journeys to and fro, especially by a mediator travelling between disputing parties. The term was initially associated particularly with the methods of Henry Kissinger, US Secretary of State 1973–76

> 1974 *Between Lines* (Newtown, Pennsylvania): So beware of an over-celebration of Kissinger's shuttle diplomacy, heroic as it's been.

> 1979 Henry Kissinger: The October 1973 Middle East war and the 'shuttle diplomacy' that followed.

sicko *n* (1977) someone who is mentally ill or sexually perverted. Slang, originally US

> 1977 Joseph Wambaugh: But, Clarence, listen! She's a sicko. Some kinda fruitcake or somethin.

> 1982 *Chicago Sun-Times*: Is it asking too much for these sickos to stop bothering decent women?

SIDS *n* (1970) An acronym formed from the initial letters of *sudden infant death syndrome* 'the sudden unexpected death of an apparently healthy infant for whom a routine autopsy fails to identify the cause of death'. See also **cot death (1970)**

> 1970 J. B. Beckwith: I personally feel the term 'Sudden Death Syndrome' should at least be amplified to include the word 'infant'… I should like, therefore, to cast my vote for the term 'Sudden Infant Death Syndrome' (SIDS).

significant other *n* (1977) a sexual partner or spouse. Originally North American; one of a string of candidates tried out for the vacancy when changing social conventions created the need for a non-sex-specific term for a (long-term cohabiting) sexual partner (see also **POSSLQ (1979)**). This one was an adaptation of an already existing piece of social psychologists' jargon denoting 'someone with great influence on the self-opinion, behaviour, etc. of another, especially a child' (first recorded in 1940)

> 1994 *Internet World*: If you're perennially late with flowers and other gifts for your significant other, you'll be delighted to know there's now a florist on the Internet.

Silicon Valley *n* (1974) an area in which industries associated with information technology are concentrated. Applied originally and specifically to the Santa Clara valley, southeast of San Francisco, where many leading US microelectronic firms are located. From the use of silicon in making computer chips. A parallel area of Scotland, roughly between Glasgow and Edinburgh and containing IT towns such as Livingston, Cumbernauld, and Glenrothes, was nicknamed 'Silicon Glen'

> 1974 *Fortune*: They have turned part of Santa Clara County into 'Silicon Valley', the world capital of semiconductor technology.

single currency *n* (1975) a currency proposed for use by the member states of the European Union (in full the *single European currency*), specifically one based on the **euro (1971)** and implemented in 1999

> 1975 *Economist*: Hopes for a single European currency by 1980 now look absurdly optimistic.

> 1995 *Independent*: So, the top political heads of Europe have concluded that the new single currency should be named after a prefix.

single-issue *adj* (1977) concentrating single-mindedly on one particular political issue rather than (as mainstream politicians usually do) covering the entire range. Originally US

> 1977 *Time*: The right-to-lifers are single-issue individuals… They vote on what he or she says about abortion.

sink *adj* (1972) Applied to a socially deprived area, or to a school, estate, etc. in such an area

> 1972 *Daily Mail*: The downward spiral of decline in the 'sink' areas could be broken if the school led the way.

> 1972 *Guardian*: It is a pity…that there is not a 'sink' schools conference, like the Headmasters' Conference of the public schools, to act as a general champion of the rights of urban schools.

skinny *adj* (1970) Of clothing: tight-fitting

> 1970 Dorothy Halliday: Janey's friends…in skinny sweaters and bell-bottomed corduroy trousers.

sledging *n* (1977) verbal intimidation of a batsman by the fielders in an attempt to break his concentration. Originally Australian

> 1983 *Guardian*: Geoff Howarth says he intends to complain about the amount of swearing, sledging and unchecked short-pitched bowling New Zealand have faced.

Sloane Ranger *n* (1975) an upper-class and fashionable but conventional young person, especially a female one who lives in London. The term was formed by replacing the *Lone* of *Lone Ranger* (a well-known hero of western stories and films) with *Sloane* (part of the name of *Sloane Square*, on the border of Belgravia and Chelsea, London, in or near which many such people live). Coined by Martina Margetts, a sub-editor on *Harpers & Queen*, it was introduced by the style writer Peter York in an article in the magazine in October 1975, and further defined by him and Ann Barr in the *Official Sloane Ranger Handbook* in 1982 (where the colloquial *Sloanie* is first recorded). Often also shortened to simply *Sloane*. See also **Hooray Henry (1959)**

> 1975 Peter York: The Sloane Rangers…are the nicest British Girl… The Sloane Rangers always add tone. They never put on prole accents, like self-conscious Oxford boys in the sixties… Once a Sloane marries and moves to Kennington and starts learning sociology through the Open University, she is off the rails… Sloane Ranger pet hates…incense, Norman Mailer.

> 1980 S. Allan: She wore a cashmere sweater…a Sloane ranger type.

> 1982 Barr & York: Sloane Rangers hesitate to use the term 'breeding' now (of people, not animals) but that's what background means… 'A Sloanie has a pony' is…ingrained in the Sloane mind.

> 1986 *Listener*: She has to be literally beaten by her mother into marrying Cary Elwes-Guildford—who resembles a low-grade Sloanie with a taste for whores and bad liquor.

slumpflation *n* (1974) a state of economic depression in which decreasing output and employment in industry are accompanied by increasing inflation. A blend of *slump* and *inflation*, inspired by the rather wittier **stagflation (1965)**

> 1974 William Rees-Mogg: So-called stagflation and slumpflation are the inevitable reflection of the progressive divergence between a rising nominal and a falling real supply of money.

> 1976 *Economic Journal*: Chronic slumpflation has given rise to much agonising reappraisal of doctrines that were hardening into orthodoxies.

smart *adj* (1972) Of a weapon or other device: capable of some independent and seemingly intelligent action. Used especially in *smart bomb*, a powered missile which is guided to its target by an optical system

> 1972 *Guardian*: Three out of four [missions] have been using 'smart' bombs.

> 1977 *Scientific American*: When smart traffic signals become ubiquitous and are linked to a control center, the traffic cop at the intersection will become obsolete.

smiley face *n* (1972) a round cartoon-style representation of a smiling face, usually black on yellow, often used as an international symbol of hope, peace, solidarity, etc. in youth culture. In the late 1980s it came to be associated with acid house

> 1972 *Times*: China—new from France with the Smiley face in black on yellow. In packs of four: cups and saucers, £2.55; tea plates £2.45.

Smokey Bear, Smokey *n* (1974) a state policeman. US Citizen's Band users' slang. The name comes from the hats worn by US state troopers, reminiscent of that worn by Smokey Bear, an animal character used in US fire-prevention advertising

> 1978 *Weekend*: Long distance lorry drivers in America try to avoid smokey bears and tend to drink road tar. Or, in English, avoid state police and drink coffee.

snake *n* (1972) a narrow range of fluctuation in rates of exchange, agreed to in 1972 by certain member countries of the EEC. A metaphor based on the idea of a snake wriggling up and down: it was elaborated still further in *snake in the tunnel*, denoting this range in relation to a wider range of fluctuation agreed in the foreign exchange markets

> 1972 *Economist*: Europe's currencies will try to be held inside the celebrated 'snake' wriggling within the overall 4.5 per cent dollar 'tunnel'.

> 1972 *Accountant*: It would take over the day-to-day running of the so-called 'snake in the tunnel' system of exchange rate margins which Britain opted out of when the £ was floated on June 23rd.

snuff *adj* (1975) Denoting a pornographic photograph or film involving the actual killing of a person. From slang *snuff* (*out*) 'to kill'

> 1976 *New Musical Express*: The 'snuff movie', a kind of ultimate pornography that has at its climax the supposedly unfaked murder of a young woman.

soaraway *adj* (1977) making rapid or impressive progress. A epithet probably best known for its alliterative application to the British tabloid *Sun* (by the *Sun*'s own publicists)

> 1977 *Zigzag*: All the great American pop styles rolled into one but fueled with the energy of the super soaraway seventies.

> 1982 *Observer*: He'll soon be writing for Britain's best and liveliest soaraway Sunday newspaper.

social market *n* (1975) an economic system based on a free market operated in conjunction with state provision for those (such as the elderly or sick) unable to sell their labour. Short for *social market economy* (first recorded in 1956), which itself is a translation of German *soziale Marktwirtschaft*, coined by A. Müller-Armack in 1948. See also **third way (1990)**

> 1975 *Times*: Such a policy ought to be modelled on the one successful postwar anti-inflationary policy, Dr. Erhard's social market policy, a label which has been given to Sir Keith Joseph's policies.

soft *adj* (1974) Designating a kind of technology that uses renewable resources such as wind or solar power and human or animal exertion and is not harmful to the natural environment.

1974 *Harper's Magazine*: The term 'soft technology' was coined amid the British counter-culture in 1970. Technology which is soft is gentle on its surroundings, responds to it, incorporates it, feeds it. A nuclear power-generating station doesn't qualify. A wooden windmill with cloth sails grinding local grain does.

soft *adj* (1977) Designating a comparatively moderate or centrist section of a political party, or the section of the political spectrum which lies between the 'hard' or extreme faction and the centre. Mainly in *soft left*. Compare **hard (1975)**

1977 *Economist*: Unless the party's election rules were changed it would still be unlikely that Labour MPs would turn to Mr Tony Benn as their leader, but the chances of their choosing a 'soft left' candidate would be strong.

solvent abuse *n* (1977) the use of certain solvents (e.g. toluene) for their stimulant effect. A broader (and somewhat more pompous) term than **glue-sniffing (1963)**

1977 *Lancet*: Investigation of the 42 patients…showed that 'sniffing' was a group activity involving mainly adolescents aged 12–19 years, all of whom had a previous history of solvent abuse.

sorry *interj* (1972) Used interrogatively to request repetition of words that the speaker failed to catch or to understand. A shift into new territory for the apologetic **sorry (1914)** (based on the idea of apologizing for one's ineptness in not hearing or understanding), perhaps prompted by a pervading uneasiness among British speakers about the 'politeness' of such available alternatives as *pardon* and *what*

1972 Tom Stoppard: Miss Moore, is there anything you wish to say at this stage? *Dotty* (*in the sense of 'Pardon?'*): Sorry? *Bones*: My dear, we are all *sorry*—.

South *n* (1975) A collective name for the industrially and economically less advanced countries of the world, typically situated to the south of the industrialized nations. Usually used in a specific contrast with *North*

1979 *Newsweek*: The turbulent years of the 1970s have witnessed an uneasy confrontation between the North and the South, and a largely unresolved debate on a whole series of specific economic problems.

spa *n* (1974) a supposedly therapeutic bath containing hot aerated water. Originally and mainly US; often used in combinations (*spa bath* and *spa pool*). See also **Jacuzzi (1966)**

1977 *Times*: The latest craze [in Los Angeles] is bathing with your friends…in a jacuzzi or spa-bath.

space *n* (1976) that portion of the universe occupied by a particular individual, regarded as being an element of their individuality. Originally US

1976 *New Times*: Werner Erhard…has created the 'space' for them to 'be' and given them the 'opportunity' to 'take responsibility' for their lives.

1980 G. B. Trudeau: Seriously, I think I know where you're coming from, and I'd like to share that space.

Space Invaders *n* (1979) The name of an animated computer game in which players attempt to defend themselves against a fleet of enemy spaceships

1980 *Washington Post*: A world-class Space Invaders player can keep the machine going for an hour.

spaghetti junction *n* (1971) a complex junction of roads at different levels. Often applied specifically to the Gravelly Hill interchange on the M6 near Birmingham (see the quote at **spaghetti (1963)**)

1971 *Evening News* (Worcester): Worcester will have its own 'spaghetti junction' if the big multi-level interchange is ever constructed in the Arboretum.

1980 S. Brett: He got held up…under the spaghetti junction between the M23 and M25 because of road works.

speciesism *n* (1975) discrimination against or exploitation of certain animal species by human beings, based on an assumption of humankind's superiority. Of all the many antidiscrimination -*isms* modelled on **racism** and **sexism** (see **-ism (1965)**), this has stood the test of time better than most. The associated *speciesist* is also first recorded in 1975

> 1982 *Times*: Animals have rights… There are forms of 'speciesism' as corrupting as 'racism' or 'sexism'.

speed bump *n* (1975) a ramp in the road intended to jolt a moving motor vehicle, thereby encouraging motorists to reduce their speed (see **traffic calming (1987)**). An earlier synonym was *sleeping policeman* (first recorded in 1973), which flourishes particularly in Caribbean English, but this was perhaps too quirky to find official favour. In its wake has come a clutch of alternatives, variations on the *speed bump* theme (*traffic bump, road hump*, etc.), but *speed bump* itself has generally led the field

> 1975 *Public Works*: Speed bumps had been installed in many apartment complexes and shopping center parking lots.

spin *n* (1978) a bias or slant on information, intended to create a favourable impression when it is presented to the public. Originally US; often in such phrases as *put a positive spin on*. The metaphor appears to come from baseball (or possibly pool), where spin is imparted to the ball to make it travel in the desired direction. A key term in late-20th-century news management, in which **spin doctors (1984)** are always keen to put the most favourable gloss on a story and journalists equally intent on removing it

> 1978 *Guardian Weekly*: The CIA can be an excellent source [of information], though, like every other, its offerings must be weighed for factuality and spin.

> 1979 *Washington Post*: American spokesman Jody Powell gave a press briefing and put a negative spin on the talks.

> 1998 *Observer*: It has introduced a culture based on lies and spin and false bonhomie.

spokesperson *n* (1972) someone authorized to speak on behalf of another person, group, or organization. Created as a non-sex-specific alternative to *spokesman* and *spokeswoman*, and one of the more successful and long-lived of such coinages (see also **person (1971)**)

> 1972 *Guardian*: The spokesperson (non-sexist term) for UCWR complained that she had been 'physically assaulted by a university administrator'.

> 1981 *Economist*: As a feminist fillip Miss Joan Lestor…has been made spokesperson for women's rights and welfare.

squat *n* (1975) a house, flat, or building occupied by squatters; the place where a squatter lives. From the verb *squat* 'to occupy an uninhabited building without permission', which dates from the late 19th century

> 1975 *Guardian*: He's at 14 Algernon Road. It's a squat.

> 1977 Margaret Drabble: They'd been hosed out of their last squat.

squeaky clean *adj* (1975) Probably originally denoting hair that has been washed and rinsed so clean that it squeaks. Hence used more broadly of anything that is completely clean and, very often, figuratively, of something or someone that is above criticism or beyond reproach

> 1975 *Country Life*: No one…is in a position to criticise… No one is, in the current idiom, that squeaky-clean.

> 1976 Newton Thornburg: Still towelling his hair, Bone returned to the living room… 'Behold, the squeaky clean Richard Bone.'

stairlift *n* (1977) a device that can be built into a domestic staircase for the conveyance of disabled or infirm people up and down stairs

> 1980 *BSI News*: Stairlifts and homelifts are now extensively used in domestic situations, where they can be an invaluable aid to the disabled or infirm person.

stakeholder *n* (1976) Used prenominally to designate types of organization in which all who participate have a stake in the success of the organization's activities. A high-profile term only in the 1990s, particularly in the expression *stakeholder economy* 'a national economy which gives all members of society a stake in its success', which was adopted as a campaign slogan by the British Labour party in January 1996

> 1976 R. E. Thomas: Three approaches are considered here, the shareholder approach advocated by free enterprise theorists…, the stakeholder approach, as portrayed by Dahrendorf, and the Marxist approach.

> 1996 *Times*: What, finally, about the broader idea of creating a 'stakeholder economy' on the German model? Although certain changes in corporate governance are likely…Mr Blair has become much cooler about the 'stakeholder' concept since he delivered his famous speech in Singapore.

stealth *adj* (1979) denoting a branch of technology concerned with rendering aircraft hard to detect by radar, or an aircraft designed in accordance with this. Originally US; first recorded in 1979, but prefigured in 1975: 'Advanced Research Projects Agency has funded studies on high-stealth aircraft through USAF Aeronautical Systems Div.', *Aviation Week & Space Technology*. The futuristic and menacing shape and all-black coloration of the B2 stealth bomber (developed in great secrecy and used in the Gulf War) caught the public imagination

> 1979 *Aviation Week & Space Technology*: Key technologies that have been identified are the following: Stealth technology. Engines and fuels. Avionics.

> 1981 *New Scientist*: In the air the US will go ahead with the B1 bomber and will develop the 'Stealth' bomber, an aircraft that will employ as yet unperfected technology to make itself invisible to enemy radar.

Stockholm syndrome *n* (1978) the observed tendency of hostages to try to cooperate with or even help their captors. The Stockholm bank robbery referred to in the quote below, which gave the syndrome its name, took place in 1973

> 1978 *Practitioner*: Mr Vaders had a mild case of 'Stockholm syndrome'… Named after the dramatic and unexpected realignment of affections in the Sveriges Kreditbank robbery, this syndrome consists of a positive bond between hostage and captor, and feelings of distrust or hostility on the part of the victim towards the authorities.

streaking *n* (1973) the action of running naked in a public place. A craze of the early 1970s which began on US college campuses and has left its legacy in the occasional unclothed invader of sports grounds. *Streaker* is also first recorded in 1973, and the verb *streak* (a back formation) in 1974

> 1973 *Time*: Another statistic in a growing Los Angeles-area fad: streaking… Streakers generally race nude between two unpredictable points.

> 1974 *Runner's World Magazine*: During the winter of 1958–9 a group of us 'streaked' all over Berkeley.

> 1977 Desmond Morris: The phenomenon of 'streaking'…is a strange example of an act that only has value as a deliberate Overexposed Signal.

street credibility *n* (1979) status or reputation amongst one's peers in the world of urban street youth culture. The shortened form *street cred* soon appeared (see **cred (1981)**). The adjective *street-credible* is first recorded in 1984

> 1979 *Sounds*: Levine has real street credibility (not like some wimp who wears Mary Quant's latest range, went to public school and then tells the world he's as street level as the Cockney Rejects).

> 1986 *Sunday Express Magazine*: Talking Heads are sufficiently street-credible in three-quarters of the known universe.

street fighter *n* (1970) someone who is combative (especially in the tough environment of the urban streets)

> 1970 Kim Platt: I promised my mother I would only marry a street fighter.

street-smarts *n* (1976) the ability to live by one's wits in an urban environment; the quality of being **street-wise (1965)**. US slang

> 1976 *New York Times*: To be free, however, requires street-smarts, the cunning of the survivor.

Strimmer *n* (1978) A proprietary name (registered in Britain in 1978) for an electrically powered grass trimmer that has a nylon wire rotating at high speed on a central spindle instead of a cutting blade. A blend of *string* and *trimmer*

> 1984 *Times*: Black and Decker is to…warn customers about defective strimmers.

string, string bikini *n* (1974) a bikini with a minimal amount of cloth

> 1974 *Times*: The String, a sort of cache-sexe sized bathing suit from Brazil which is now sweeping America.

strip *n* (1974) the clothing worn by and distinguishing a football team. It is unclear whether etymologically it is clothing with 'strips' of different colours on it, or clothing to which a player 'strips' down

> 1977 *Shoot*: The national strip of Zambia is green jerseys, orange shorts, and black stockings.

substance abuse *n* (1975) the use of a substance for its narcotic or stimulant effect, whether it was produced for that purpose (e.g. alcoholic drink) or not (e.g. glue). Originally US; useful as both a cover term and a euphemism

> 1984 Joan Didion: A clinic on East 61st Street that specialized in the treatment of what the therapist called adolescent substance abuse.

suck *v* (1971) to be contemptible or disgusting. Slang, originally US; the underlying metaphor is probably the subservience and hence contemptibleness implied by fellatio, anilingus, etc.

> 1971 *It*: Polaroid sucks! For some time the Polaroid Corporation has been supplying the South African government with large photo systems…to use for photographing blacks for the passbooks…every black must carry.

> 1978 M. Gordon: All the hotels have the same pictures. The last one, the food sucked.

suit *n* (1979) A derisive term for a business executive, seen as being boring, conventional, an 'organization man', always male, and of course always wearing a suit to work (and perhaps in bed too). The original contrast was with lower-ranking employees, who may wear overalls, a uniform, etc. Originally US

> 1979 T. Sullivan: McBride was an exception to the usual 'suits' at the Bureau.

supercool *adj, n* (1970) (someone) extremely relaxed, laid-back, sophisticated, etc. Slang, originally US

> 1970 Tom Wolfe: The pimp style was a supercool style that was much admired or envied.

> 1975 *Radio Times*: James Coburn was the nicest of all those Bond-type supercools.

superfly *n* (1973) someone who sells illegal drugs, a drug pusher. US slang. The term comes from the 1972 film *Super Fly*, about a cocaine dealer in Harlem, which in turn got its name from *superfly*, a term of approval applied to high-quality drugs (first recorded in 1971)

> 1973 *Black Panther*: The high level dope pushers, the 'Super Flys', were the target.

supergrass *n* (1978) a criminal who gives a substantial amount of information to the police about other criminals, especially ones involved in terrorism or other major crimes. British

> 1983 *Listener*: Following information from a supergrass, dozens of people alleged to be members of it had been arrested.

supermodel *n* (1977) a highly successful and internationally famous fashion model

> 1977 *Time*: Supermodel Margaux Hemingway dreamed up the idea of posing in high fashion in Jimmy's home town to make people think of plain old Plains as a fashion capital.

> 1992 *Sun*: Supermodel Claudia Schiffer has ditched her boyfriend to wed Prince Albert of Monaco, it was claimed last night.

> 1998 John Carey: What would [George Orwell] feel, confronted with new Labour, the Diana cult, fat cats, supermodels, and millions of zombies propped in front of World Cup telescreens?

supply-side *adj* (1976) of that part of the economy concerned with supply (as opposed to demand). Used to designate a policy designed to increase the incentives to produce and invest, by means of tax cuts—as embraced by right-wing governments in the 1980s. The derived *supply-sider* 'an advocate of supply-side policies' is first recorded in 1980. (The related but less frequent *demand-side* is first recorded in 1975)

> 1976 *Wall Street Journal*: Supply-side fiscalism… Supply-side fiscalists…agree that tax changes do not affect total demand, but they emphasize the effects on supply.

> 1981 *Christian Science Monitor*: The supply-siders who persuaded President Reagan to seek a balanced budget by cutting taxes.

surrogate *adj, n* (1978) a woman whose pregnancy arises from the implantation in her womb of a fertilized egg or embryo from another woman. Used adjectivally mainly in *surrogate mother*, but also sometimes applied to relatives of the woman who stand in an analogous position towards the child. The related noun *surrogacy*, hitherto rarely used in the general sense 'the position of a surrogate', is first recorded in 1982

> 1978 *Times*: The demand for surrogates remained strong… Despite potential legal problems, some have already opted for surrogate mothers.

> 1979 *Scientific American*: Will this research lead…to the use of 'surrogate parents', where, for example, rich women might pay poor women to carry their children?

> 1982 Walters & Singar: The objections to surrogacy based on fears of financial exploitation…are very real.

talk radio *n* (1972) a radio format in which the presenter chats about issues of the day, usually with listeners who call in by telephone to air their opinions. Originally US; the implied contrast is with the rest of commercial radio, where music dominates programming and talk is at a minimum

> 1995 *Independent*: He obviously doesn't think there's any socially redeemable value to Talk Radio. As he said in Thursday's *Independent*, 'It's just mindless wittering and gratuitous insults.'

tax haven *n* (1973) a country that attracts companies or individuals by its low taxes

> 1973 *Times*: The Briton wanting to minimize his taxes through getting paid in a tax haven.

telecommute *v* (1974) to work from home (especially at what is traditionally an office job), communicating with one's place of employment, colleagues, etc., by telephone line or data link. *Telecommuter* soon followed

> 1974 *Economist*: As there is no logical reason why the cost of telecommunication should vary with distance, quite a lot of people by the late 1980s will telecommute daily to their London offices while living on a Pacific island if they want to.

> 1975 *Economist*: Telecommuting is coming. When production is properly automated even in service industries, probably 60% of American breadwinners will be brainworkers… Telecommuter terminals will stop social interaction at the workplace.

teletext *n* (1974) a system in which a user's television set is adapted so as to be able to show alphanumeric information (e.g. news, sports results) selected from displays transmitted using the spare capacity of existing television channels. See also **Ceefax (1972)**

> 1975 *Electronics & Power*: In March 1974, the British Radio Equipment Manufacturers' Association, BBC and IBA reached agreement on a unified standard system, known as teletext, based largely on the ceefax system.

televangelist *n* (1973) an evangelical preacher who uses the mass media, and particularly television, to promote especially fundamentalist doctrine. Originally and mainly US; a blend of **television** and *evangelist*. The term (and its derivative *televangelism*, first recorded in 1980) did not come into widespread use until the 1980s, when a range of sexual and financial scandals hit the headlines involving leading US televangelists such as Jim Bakker and Jimmy Swaggart

> 1973 *Time*: Televangelist Rex Humbard with map showing TV broadcast centers.

> 1980 *Pantagraph* (Bloomington, Illinois): Televangelism has been around for years, but just now it's making more of an impact than it ever has.

> 1987 *Independent*: With mutual hatreds now so vividly exposed, the 'televangelists' may find it difficult in future to retain the support of their flocks.

temazepam *n* (1970) a drug used to treat insomnia, and as a sedative before operations. It is also often abused by drug addicts. Probably modelled on the earlier tranquillizer-name *oxazepam*, but the origin of the element *tem-* is not known

> 1984 *Daily Telegraph*: [He] chose temazepam, a hypnotic drug marketed…for transient insomnia under the trade name of Normison.

temp *v* (1973) to work as a temp. The noun *temp* had been used for a 'temporary employee' since the 1930s (see **temp (1932)**), but the specific application to a 'temporary secretary', which is what this verb usage is based on, only started to emerge in the late 1960s

> 1973 *Times*: Bored with temping? We specialise in short term assignments…in the artistic and creative fields.

> 1974 *Harpers & Queen*: You meet such civilized people when temping for Bernardette.

textile *n* (1979) A nudists' term for a non-nudist, especially one who wears a swimming costume on the beach

1983 *Times*: The topless generally inhabit the more remote ends of the beach well away from the 'textiles'.

Thatcherism *n* (1979) the political and economic policies advocated by Margaret Thatcher (see next), especially as contrasted with those of earlier Conservative leaders. Its main tenets are generally held to be monetarism, privatization, and self-help

1979 *Times*: The party was fighting off the shrill divisiveness of Thatcherism, with its simple monetarist policies.

1982 *Daily Telegraph*: At heart, Thatcherism is a liberal economic reaction to the collectivism and corporatism of the past 40 years.

Thatcherite *adj, n* (1976) (someone) supporting the views or policies of Margaret Thatcher (b.1925), British politician, leader of the Conservative Party from 1975 and Prime Minister 1979–90

1976 *Economist*: Tory constituency rooms were by 1974 fuller of anti-Butler Thatcherites than Mr Heath dreamed.

1977 *Times*: The Thatcherite philosophy can be summed-up in two words, 'non-interference'.

1982 *Daily Telegraph*: With the exception of that large part of the Labour party which is now authentically Bennite, we are all, to a greater or lesser extent, Thatcherites now.

theatre *adj* (1977) Designating nuclear weapons for use within a particular 'theatre of operations' (in the context of the Cold War thought of as Europe) as opposed to intercontinental or strategic weapons, or their targets

1980 *Daily Telegraph*: Theatre nuclear missiles…have a longer range than battlefield weapons but cannot be fired as far as inter-continental missiles.

third age *n* (1972) the period in life of active retirement; old age. A euphemism translated from French *troisième âge*

1972 *Times*: We have devised a package deal for elderly people from the Continent… We are attempting to attract some Belgian old age pensioners. In Belgium it is called the third age.

1980 *Washington Post*: The seven senior citizens—or 'Dancers of the Third Age'—continually delight audiences, wherever they perform.

throw *v throw away the key* (1976) to send someone to prison for life; hence, more broadly, to punish someone with utmost severity for a crime. Based on the idea of a cell door that cannot be unlocked once locked. An expression characteristic of the late-20th-century backlash against the liberalism of the 1960s

1997 *Independent*: At a major one-day conference…leading thinkers opposing today's 'lock 'em up and throw away the key' approach will point a different way.

time-sharing *n* (1976) the ownership or right to use of a property, especially as a holiday home, for a fixed limited time each year. Originally US; an adaptation of a term originally used in computing, denoting simultaneous access to a central processor by more than one user

1976 *Time*: In exchange for guaranteed occupancy over an extended period time-sharing resorts offer low prices, [etc.].

1980 R. Rejnis: A time-share can be very inexpensive…compared to hotel costs.

tinny *n* (1974) a can of beer. Australian colloquial

1974 *Telegraph* (Brisbane): In olden days audiences took the equivalent of a cut lunch and a few tinnies to the theatre and expected to be entertained for hour after hour.

toll-free *adj, adv* (1970) Denoting a telephone service in which the calls (typically in response to an advertisement) are paid for by the receiver. Mainly North American. See also **Freefone (1959)**

1970 *Globe & Mail* (Toronto): For reservations, call toll-free 368–7474.

touch screen *n* (1974) a VDU screen that is also a computer input device operated by touching it

1974 *Management Informatics*: As a first step, a prototype touch screen was designed and constructed in our Laboratory by Mr. Stephen Salter.

touchy-feely, touchie-feelie *adj* (1972) A usually dismissive epithet applied to people given to the tactile expression of feelings (e.g. by touching and hugging), motivated by emotion rather than intellect. Originally US; the term arose out of the encounter groups of the 1960s, whose members often sought psychological benefit through close physical contact with each other

> 1972 *Tuscaloosa* (Alabama) *News*: A considerable amount of time is spent in encounter groups, gestalt training, psychodrama or 'T groups'… On almost every campus where this approach has been tried it has caused an uproar. Faculty critics deride it as 'touchy-feely' education, with strong undercurrents of anti-intellectualism.

> 1995 *Daily Telegraph*: We Greens are quite touchy-feely types. But because you go to a Green Party Conference it doesn't mean you want to be hugged all the time.

trainer *n* (1978) a soft running shoe without spikes; a training shoe (the term *training shoe* itself is first recorded in 1973). They started off as athletes' equipment but by the 1980s they were fashion items, particularly among teenagers

> 1978 *Guardian*: The Poynton Jemmers, a women's morris dance side…are in mufti tonight… But no trainers or pumps: it's clogs or nothing.

> 1982 *New Society*: Skinny teenage boys in the ubiquitous parkas, jeans and trainers.

transputer *n* (1978) a computer chip that incorporates all the functions of a microprocessor, including memory. A blend of **transistor** and **computer**

> 1978 I. M. Barron: The word 'transputer' has been coined to describe the computer on a chip. The word is derived from…'computer' and 'transistor'.

trash *v* (1970) to vandalize (property or goods). US colloquial; originally applied especially to students destroying property as a means of protest

> 1970 *New York Times*: The new breed of campus revolutionaries…are now turning to what they call 'trashing'—the setting of fires, hurling of rocks, smashing of windows.

> 1971 *Time*: Backstage at *Comes a Day* he got drunk and trashed his dressing room.

tree-hugger *n* (1977) someone who cares for trees or for the environment in general. Originally and mainly US; used as a term of patronizing contempt for environmentalists. The underlying idea is of someone who adopts a position embracing a tree to prevent it from being chopped down; it apparently had its genesis in 1973 when villagers in Uttar Pradesh, India staged a campaign of this sort

> 1995 *Mother Earth News*: Perhaps, in time, history will give us a proper title like Enlightenment or Romantics. About all I hear these days is Tree-Hugger and Environmentalist Wacko.

Trekkie *n* (1976) a fan of the US science-fiction television programme *Star Trek* (1966–68), which achieved cult status in the last quarter of the century

> 1976 *New Yorker*: Of course, I didn't know George was a Trekkie when I married him.

trouser-suited *adj* (1973) See **trouser suit (1939)**

tug of love *n* (1973) a conflict of affections. Usually applied specifically (mainly by journalists) to a contest for custody of a minor. The term may have been suggested by the title of a comedy 'The Tug of Love' by Israel Zangwill (1907)

> 1973 *Times*: The Houghton committee was set up after some highly-publicized 'tug of love' cases, and recommended making it easier for long-term foster-parents…to adopt.

> 1977 *Daily Mirror*: Back home in the arms of her mother, a tiny tug-of-love girl sleeps peacefully. The girl…had been taken to California after being snatched by her father.

turf war *n* (1979) a dispute over territory, especially between criminal gangs. Often applied metaphorically to areas of legitimate involvement. Colloquial, originally US

> 1979 *Washington Post*: 35 killings occurred in one recent six-month period in turf wars between local gangs.

> 1995 *Coloradoan* (Fort Collins): In New Jersey…, a turf war between attorneys and brokers has simmered for more than 20 years.

turn-off *n* (1975) See **turn off (1965)**

unbundle *v* (1977) to split (a company or business conglomerate) into its constituent businesses or assets, often with the intention of selling off some parts. There was a particular boom in this form of asset-stripping in the mid 1980s, when the financier Sir James Goldsmith earned his nickname 'the Great Unbundler'

> 1989 *Independent*: The decision of BAT to unbundle its US retail holdings comes at a…bad time.

> 1989 *Observer*: 'He was not well-publicised when he worked for Goldsmith,' says James Wood, a former associate of the great unbundler.

underperform *v* (1975) to perform in a manner which falls below expectation. Usually used of a business company or other institution, and first recorded as a transitive verb, denoting the achievement of a lower share price than the general market

> 1975 *Dun's Review*: A company that fits the criteria…might underperform the market for several years before somebody wants to acquire it.

> 1976 Business Week: Institutions…underperform over the all-important long term.

> 1977 *Daily Mail*: What's wrong with comprehensive schools…is…not that they fail to teach children properly… They just 'underperform'.

unsocial hours *n* (1973) socially inconvenient working hours (e.g. at night or at weekends). A concept invoked mainly in claiming extra payment

> 1973 *Times*: A proposed unsocial hours payment in recognition of the odd times of the day and night that a [train] driver has to report for duty.

> 1982 *Economist*: If the government is to avoid the annual pay squabble with the nurses the new review body should first establish realistic pay scales…taking into account the unsocial hours.

upfront *adj, adv* (1970) open(ly), frank(ly). Colloquial, originally US

> 1970 John Lennon: That game of 'Well, I'm going to be up-front because…a few people said she'd got a lousy name in New York.'

> 1978 Mario Puzo: He would…make them understand in a nice way that he would trade space for a piece of ass. He was that upfront about it.

upfront *adj, adv* (1972) (paid) in advance. Colloquial, originally US

> 1972 *Britannica Book of the Year* (US): Actors demanding $1 million up front.

> 1975 *New Yorker*: I'd like to suggest that we get most of the people involved below the line, so we won't need much of that scarce up-front bread.

up-market *adj, adv* (1972) at, towards, or being the more expensive or sophisticated end of the market; quality

> 1974 *Daily Telegraph*: An 'up-market' £1,950 version of the Austin Allegro, hand-finished by the Vanden Plas coachbuilders.

> 1975 *Daily Telegraph*: Lyons-Tetley go up-market a bit with their Red Label and Orange Label [tea].

user-friendly *adj* (1977) easy to use; designed with the needs of users in mind. Originally used with reference to computers, but its range of application soon broadened out. Its underlying morphological pattern, too, quickly found imitators (see **-friendly (1982)**)

> 1977 Birss & Yeh: STDS-I does not provide the user with a sufficiently 'user-friendly' interface to allow noncomputer scientists to easily work with a data base.

> 1979 *Interfaces*: User friendliness is a term coined by Harlan Crowder to represent the inherent ease (or lack of ease) which is encountered when running a computer system.

> 1984 *Listener*: No TV show (not even the news) could close without reference to this user-friendly family of dolls.

valet *v* (1972) to clean (a motor vehicle)

> 1972 *Drive*: It's not difficult to imagine an owner confining his chauffeur to valeting the car, while he hogs the driving.

VATable, vatable *adj* (1973) liable to value-added tax. Colloquial. VAT (see **VAT (1966)**) was first imposed in the UK in 1973

1973 *Times*: A glance at how Alice is faring will show how plays themselves are affected. At present she and her like are VAT-able and non VAT-able according to circumstances.

1976 *Daily Telegraph*: The last [i.e. higher indirect taxes] would put up the cost of living but, to a large extent, the extra cost of vatable items…is voluntary.

Vegeburger *n* (1972) A proprietary name (registered in the US in 1976) for a flat savoury cake similar in shape to a hamburger but containing vegetables or vegetable protein rather than meat (see **burger (1939)**)

1986 *Listener*: Free festivals are market-places for everything hippies most like to sell, from hashish to vegeburgers.

verbal *n* (1973) abuse; also, an insult. British slang

1973 *Time Out*: We faced them, and gave them a load of verbal across the street.

1982 *Observer*: Each 'ball' consisted of a distinctly lethargic head-high bouncer…, followed by a rousing collection of verbals (money will be paid to lip-reading viewers for translation).

video *v* (1971) to make a video recording of.

1984 *What Video?*: My work…is videoing anything to do with the emergency services (road accidents, fires etc.).

video game *n* (1973) a game played by electronically manipulating images displayed on a television screen. In the mid 1970s people in bars, amusement arcades, etc. all seemed to be playing electronic table tennis, batting a point of light back and forth across a screen

1973 *Business Week*: The astonishing ability of the video game to lure quarters from the public and the electronic techniques used in its design are forcing major changes on the coin-operated game business.

virus *n* (1972) a computer program or section of programming code which is designed to sabotage a computer system by causing itself to be copied into other parts of the system, often destroying data in the process. Originally a science-fiction term; the real thing did not appear until the early 1980s, when the word *virus* was adopted for it. See also **vaccine (1986)**

1972 David Gerrold: You know what a virus is, don't you?…The VIRUS program does the same thing.

1984 F. Cohen: We define a computer 'virus' as a program that can 'infect' other programs by modifying them to include a possibly evolved copy of itself.

walkabout *n* (1970) an informal stroll through the crowd by a member of the Royal Family or other public figure. A usage adapted from the earlier 'Aboriginal migration into the bush', which is of Pidgin English origin. The practice was one of the earliest ploys in the British Royal Family's campaign to demystify itself

1970 *Daily Telegraph*: The Queen realised she was on to a winner with her New Zealand 'walkabouts'.

wanker *n* (1972) a contemptible or incompetent (male) person. British slang; an adaptation of the earlier *wanker* 'masturbator'. *Wank* 'to masturbate' emerged (in print) in the 1940s, but its origins are unclear. Probably it comes from a dialectal verb meaning 'to hit, slap'

1972 Alfred Draper: 'Get out, you fucker,' screamed a youth… Another said, 'You wanker,' and indulged in a masturbatory gesture.

1981 Peter Niesewand: They're such a bunch of wankers… You can't trust them to do anything properly.

water bed *n* (1970) a plastic mattress filled with water, designed as an alternative to a conventional bed. A term which, at least to begin with, gave rise to giggles and knowing winks about the mattress's supposed aphrodisiac qualities. Not a neologism: in the 19th century it was applied to a water-filled mattress used for invalids ('Our kind Bishop had him removed to his House the day he was taken ill and planned a water bed to place him on', A. N. Brown (1844))

1970 *Time*: His efforts to improve it led him [i.e. C. P. Hall] to a much splashier creation… It is the water bed.

Watergate *n* (1972) The name of a building in Washington D.C. containing the national head-quarters of the US Democratic Party, which was burgled on 17 June 1972 by people connected with the Republican administration, trying to find material that would help in the re-election of President Richard Nixon. Widely used in allusion to the circumstances leading to the resignation of President Nixon in 1974, and subsequently applied metaphorically to any large-scale political or commercial scandal. See also **-gate (1973)**

> 1972 *New Republic*: The very name, 'the Watergate caper', tells how funny it is.

> 1972 *Time*: By coming down hard on Mitchell, the Democrats hope they can make Watergate a devasting—and durable—campaign issue.

welly, wellie *n* (1977) a kick (as if with a wellington boot). Also applied to something thought of as accomplished with a sudden forceful kick, such as acceleration in a motor vehicle. British slang; based on colloquial **welly** 'wellington boot' (1961)

> 1977 *Daily Mirror*: The girl they call 'Daredevil Divi' gave the car a bit more wellie. In racing language, this meant she was stepping on the accelerator.

> 1979 *Guardian*: The tactic most likely to succeed in the conditions was the long welly upfield.

wetware *n* (1975) chemical materials organized so as to perform arithmetic or logical operations. A coinage modelled on **hardware** and **software**, and frequently applied, often humorously, to the brain, as having this ability

> 1975 *Nature*: An electronic computer is made up of hardware and software; a chemical automaton needs an additional component, a chemical reaction system which might be called 'wetware'.

> 1977 *New York Times*: Computer scientists have lately begun talking about 'wetware', which is the human brain.

whistle-blower *n* (1970) someone who reveals (discreditable) secrets about an organization, especially one to which he or she belongs. Originally US; from the expression *blow the whistle* 'to expose wrongdoing', first recorded in 1934. The companion noun *whistle-blowing* is first recorded in 1971

> 1970 *New York Times*: When they reflect more fully on how well the majority leader handled a whistle-blower and protected their interests.

> 1971 *New Scientist*: The Code [of Good Conduct of The British Computer Society] contains secrecy clauses that effectively prohibit Nader style whistle-blowing.

white-out *n* (1977) a white liquid that can be brushed on to paper to obliterate marks and provide a white surface on which to type or write afresh. More usually known by the proprietary name **Tipp-Ex (1965)**

> 1977 Lilian O'Donnell: You changed the date… Did you cover the original entries with a strip of paper, or did you use white-out?

wide-bodied *adj* (1970) See **wide-bodied (1968)**

windfall tax *n* (1973) a tax levied on an unforeseen or unexpectedly large profit, especially one that is considered to be excessive or unfairly obtained. Originally US; familiarized in Britain in the mid 1990s when such a tax was proposed by the Labour party on the profits of privatized utilities

> 1995 *Independent on Sunday*: The Labour Party is threatening to apply a 'windfall tax' to excess profits made by monopolies.

window *n* (1974) a defined part of a VDU display, such as may be allocated to a particular category of information. See also **Windows (1983)**

> 1974 *AFIPS Conference Proceedings*: The display screen is divisible into rectangular, possibly overlapping 'windows'.

wind up *v* (1979) to provoke (someone) deliberately, especially by telling untruths. British colloquial; the derived noun *wind-up*, meaning 'an imposture', is first recorded in 1984

> 1979 *Time Out*: The kids are proud of the successful thieving they have done, and though they'll 'wind you up' (take the piss) as much as they can, the conversation becomes deadly serious on certain topics.

> 1984 *Times*: My recollection of this is quite clear. I thought it was a wind-up to be honest with you.

wobbly *n* (1977) a sudden fit of temperament or uncontrollable anger. Slang; mainly in the phrase *throw a wobbly*. Probably a variation on the earlier synonym *wobbler*, first recorded in 1942—the underlying idea being the uncontrollable shaking of someone having a fit

> 1978 Denis Norden: Not only did she throw a wobbly at the slightest murmur of tango rhythms, even the sight of a piano-accordion brought her out in hives.

wolly *n* (1970) a uniformed police officer, especially a constable. British slang; origin uncertain, but perhaps connected with *walloper*, 1950s British slang for 'police officer'

> 1970 G. F. Newman: The wollies were out in their cars, patrolling for drunks and discontents.

women's studies *n* (1972) academic studies concerning women, their role in society, etc. Originally US

> 1972 *Newsweek*: In the classroom, many women think less of competing with men than of learning about themselves. 'Women's studies' was nearly unknown before 1970; now 78 institutions have complete women's studies programs.

woofter, wooftah *n* (1977) a homosexual man. Contemptuous slang; an arbitrary alteration of **poofter (1910)**, which is itself an extension of *poof*

> 1977 *Private Eye*: The headshrinker had been reduced to a nervous wreck, and was prepared to dismiss the rabidly heterosexual Tynan as a wooftah.

word processor *n* (1970) a keyboard device incorporating a computer programmed to store, amend, and format text that is keyed in, a printer to print it automatically, and usually also a screen to display it. Also first recorded in 1970 is *word processing*, denoting the storing and organizing of texts by electronic means, especially using a word processor

> 1970 *Administrative Management*: In 1970…ITEL…introduced its 'Word Processor'… 'Word processing', a concept that combines the dictating and typing functions into a centralized system.

> 1984 David Lodge: A roomful of secretaries…would wait patiently beside their word-processors, ready to type…his latest reflections.

workstation *n* (1977) a desk with a computer terminal and keyboard; also applied to the terminal itself

> 1983 *What's New in Computing*: Featured above in teak: printer stand, linking quadrant and 3' by 2' workstation with monitor shelf.

wrinkly, wrinklie *n* (1971) an old or middle-aged person. Slang, often used self-mockingly. See also **crumblie (1976)**

> 1983 *Church Times*: I am a wrinkly whose monthly cheque from the Church Commissioners is labelled 'Diocesan Dignitary'.

Youth Opportunities Programme *n* (1977) a government-sponsored scheme introduced in Britain in 1978 to provide temporary work experience for unemployed young people and replaced in 1983 by the Youth Training Scheme (see **Youth Training Scheme (1981)**). Better known under its abbreviation *YOP*, first recorded in 1978 and also applied to someone on the scheme

> 1977 *Department of Employment Press Notice*: Up to 230,000 unemployed youngsters each year will have a chance of work experience or training under a new £160 million Youth Opportunities Programme announced today by Mr. Albert Booth, Secretary of State for Employment.

> 1978 *Times Higher Education Supplement*: Young people…eligible for the YOP in Cardiff…will be asked for their views.

> 1983 *Financial Times*: All I had to do was take on a YOP as a personal assistant.

zipless *adj* (1973) Denoting a brief but passionate sexual encounter. Slang; mainly in *zipless fuck*, a term introduced by Erica Jong in her novel *Fear of Flying*

> 1973 Erica Jong: My response…was…to evolve my fantasy of the Zipless Fuck… Zipless because when you came together zippers fell away like petals.

> 1978 Gore Vidal: Girls who feared flying tended to race blindly through zipless fucks.

The 1980s The 1980s
The 1980s The 1980s
The 1980s The 1980s
1980s 1980s The 1980s
1980s The 1980s The
1980s The 1980s The 1980s

The 1980s

The 1980s are chiefly remembered for money. Not only was there a lot of it about in the Western economies: those who had it relished it, boasted about it, consumed conspicuously with it, even worshipped it. To be *seriously* rich was no trivial matter. It was the decade of *dosh* (1953). The financial sector contributed generous amounts of new vocabulary to the English language, as did the changes in society brought about by the considerable rearrangements of wealth.

Politically, deregulation was in the air. Patience with post-war state controls was wearing thin, and people were ready to pass the levers of power into the hands of a right-wing government that would allow (or promise) more scope for individual initiative (in Britain, the Conservative Thatcher government had come into office in 1979, and by the end of 1980 the American electorate had voted the Republican Ronald Reagan into the presidency). In the world of high finance, this meant a clearing away of restrictions on how the money men were permitted to operate, and on the sort of fiscal schemes and manoeuvrings they could indulge in. As far as the British stock market was concerned, the climactic moment was the *Big Bang* of October 1986, which removed a whole range of previous restrictive practices. All the novel phenomena required names, and the fertile brains of financiers (at home with a menagerie of bulls, bears, and stags) obliged with an array of outlandish metaphors that have come to symbolize the decade: *dawn raid* and *white knight, golden hello* and *golden parachute, greenmail* and *grey market* and *swaption*. Readers of the financial and business columns of the newspapers would puzzle over *arbs* and *derivatives*, new acronyms like *EFTPOS* and *EPOS, PEP* and *PIN*, new concepts such as *ethical* investment and *internal markets*. In the Far East the *tiger* (or *dragon*) economies were cranking themselves up, and from Japan came the notion of *zaitech*. Payment increasingly meant *plastic*, with the prospect of being able to *swipe* your *smart card*. Britain now had *pound coins*, but hard cash was further threatened by *telebanking*. The bubble of economic euphoria was burst on *Black Monday* (19 October 1987), when share prices around the world hit the floor. Was it just a *blip*, or was a long recession on the way? Only the 1990s would tell.

People who had a lot of money in their pocket were intent on spending it—and not discreetly. If you had it, you flaunted it; it was the era of *conspicuous consumption* (1899), of *loadsa* money. The quintessential figure of the decade was the *yuppie*, the high-earning 25–30-year-old business executive, lawyer, stockbroker, etc. with the smart car, the *mobile phone* (1965) (or *cellphone*), and the *Filofax* (1931) (or *personal organizer*). The *raison d'être* of the coinage was a *life-style* (1961), and it was to be the first of a rash of such life-style coinages. The lexical fashion fad of the 1980s left a legacy of *buppies, dinkies,* and *woopies,* not to mention non-acronyms such as *empty-nester. Stressed-out thirty-somethings* relaxed in *wine bars, shopaholics* shopped till they dropped, the *chattering classes* chattered, *foodies* held olive-oil tastings, and *power-dressing* was the fashion statement that mattered. The tabloids entertained their readers with tales of *bimboes* (1920) and *himboes, bimbettes* and *toy boys.*

But if the rich got richer in the 1980s, the poor also got poorer. The supposed benefits of *trickle-down* (1944) were slow to show themselves. The *underclass* (1918) was growing; *cardboard cities* were appearing. While politicians were berating the *dependency culture,* growing unemployment swelled the numbers on *income support* and attending *job clubs.* No employee seemed safe from the dreaded *UB40.* This was the world not of the sharp suit but of the *shell suit.* The happy partying of the early part of the decade had given way to the sound of *lager louts* breaking glass.

The political mantras of the decade were *privatize* (1970) and *monetarist* (1963). In Britain, Margaret Thatcher proclaimed the *enterprise culture* and the joy of *marketization.* Her government (bone-*dry* by the middle of the decade, having been purged of *wets*) pursued the *feel-good factor,* but managed to upset *Middle England* with the *poll tax* (officially named the *community charge*). The *leaderene* gained a reputation for *handbagging* all who tried to thwart her. Meanwhile, self-destructive tendencies within the Labour party led the *Gang of Four* to break away and form the *SDP* (later combined with the Liberals to become the *Liberal Democrats*); its main contribution to the English language during its brief career was '*fudge* and mudge'. Television arrived in the British parliament, and with it the strange practice of *doughnutting. Emily's List* set out to increase the number of women MPs. Ominously, the terms *sleaze* and *spin doctor* appeared for the first time in the political lexicon.

On the international scene, the 80s got into their stride with the Falklands War (1982), the winning of which (despite the obfuscation of *Haigspeak*) did wonders for Margaret Thatcher's electoral prospects (the so-called *Falklands factor*). The conflict's lexical legacy (*Argie,* an insult word for Argentinians; an unpleasant new use of *gotcha;* and the verb *yomp*) was for the most part mercifully short-lived.

The nuclear stakes were being raised by *SDI* (popularly known as *Star Wars*), a futuristic scheme for defence against Soviet missiles on which the US saw fit to spend the profits of *Reaganomics.* The deployment of cruise missiles in Britain led to the establishment of *peace camps,* and there were chilling forecasts of *nuclear winter,* but disarmament diplomacy continued, adding *build-down, START,* and *zero option* to its bizarre lexicon. The Soviet monolith was breaking up, a process which propelled the terms *glasnost* and *perestroika* temporarily into the English language. The satellite states of eastern Europe grasped their independence (Czechoslovakia in a *velvet revolution*), and by the end of the decade it was clear that the forty-year Cold War was over—and that the West had won it.

In the 1980s, *cyberspace* infiltrated the interstices of the everyday world. Computer technology leaped ahead, enriching the English language with *dongle* and *toggle.* Only an ageing minority were not, it seemed, *computerate,* and able to cope with *booting, downloading,* and *dragging,* recognize an *icon* or a *spreadsheet,* or use a *laptop,* a *palmtop,* or a *touchpad.* While the grown-ups were *teleworking,* the kids could play *Pac-man* or *Game Boy. Hackers* were becoming a problem, but there were now *vaccines* to counter the threat of viruses.

Increasingly, though, the computer's most pervasive influence on the modern world lay in the area of communication. It was the decade which saw the beginnings of the *Internet* and the *information superhighway*, of *e-mail* and the *telecottage*, of *domains* and *newsgroups*. The days of *snail mail* were numbered. The era of the *virtual* was coming.

The media was transforming itself on all fronts. *DBS* (satellite television) arrived, and *dishes* (or in a few cases *Squarials*) sprouted all over the country. *Infotainment* was on offer, and *rolling news* (complete with *sound bites*). Alternatively, if you had a *camcorder*, you could make your own *video nasty* (but preferably not a *splatter* movie). Sounds were portable in the shape of *ghetto-blasters* and *Walkmans*, and the enticing *jewel boxes* of CDs filled the record-shop shelves. *Chat lines* and *help-lines* reflected a revitalized telephone industry. In the increasingly competitive world of print journalism, reporters *doorstepped* their victims and indulged in *feeding frenzies*. It was not a decade for the shy and retiring: the representative media figure was perhaps the *shock jock*.

Environmental concerns grew ever more powerful, as the extent of human depredations became increasingly evident. We embraced the concept of *biodiversity*, eagerly bought *eco-friendly* and *cruelty-free* products, nodded over the necessity for a *carbon tax*, and supported the construction of *wind farms*. From its fringes (*eco-terrorists* and *New Age travellers*) to its solid middle-class centre, the environmental movement was a force to be reckoned with.

One of the key facts of the decade was *Aids*. Unknown at its beginning, by 1989 the terminology of the disease was familiar wherever English was spoken: *buddy, HIV, PWA, AZT* (some areas of the world had a different name for it: *slim* in Africa, for instance). The official answer was *safe sex*: not an easy concept to popularize at a time when the media were obsessed by *bonking*. Nevertheless, *Femidoms* and *dental dams* were added to the prophylactic armoury. (For purely contraceptive purposes there was the *abortion pill* or, if it was too late for that, the reviled *abortuary*.) Other diseases lined up to attack us: *ME* (or *yuppie flu*), *repetitive strain injury, sick-building syndrome*. Then there was all that *techno-stress* to deal with. Nor did our animals escape: cattle succumbed in droves to the dreaded *BSE* (colloquially *mad cow disease*), and suddenly beef was off the menu.

A prolific and vibrant youth culture produced a myriad new dances and styles of music (many of them of *hip-hop* origin). There was *moshing, body-popping*, and *moonwalking, break dancing, dirty dancing*, and *slam dancing* (there was also *lap dancing*, but that was not the same sort of thing at all). It was the decade of *Acid House, raves*, and *warehouse parties*, of *goths* and *greboes* and *thrash metal*, of the *lambada* and the *bhangra* beat. *Garage* took on a whole new meaning. It was a culture that got its highs from *ecstasy* (or *Es*, or *Adam*). *Designer drugs* were the fashion of the decade, *Prozac* the favourite happy pill, and *crack* the new market leader.

Youth slang shuffled its approval words with enough dexterity to keep adults guessing. One moment it was *crucial*, the next *wicked*. *Brill, fabby, gnarly, massive, mega, radical*, and *tubular* all had their turn at one time or another.

Meanwhile, *PC* language made further strides. Pets became *animal companions*, prostitutes *sex workers*, and to avoid charges of *ableism*, any deviation from the norm had to be described in terms of being *challenged*. *Fattist* or *sizeist* comments were to be severely discouraged. Even in a *post-feminist* age, *person* was still alive and well and producing offspring: *waitperson*. The *New Man* proudly made his debut (although alas within a decade he would have transformed himself into a *New Lad*).

abled *adj* (1981) able-bodied; not disabled. A polemical coinage, formed in contradistinction to *disabled*, and often used euphemistically as the second element in compounds (particularly *differently abled*) seeking to avoid the negative associations of *disabled*

> 1981 *Washington Post*: The disabled vary like the abled. Some are terminally ill, some are teenagers paralyzed by car accidents.

> 1990 *Amateur Stage*: All the young members of this group suffer from cerebral palsy but insisted 'We are not disabled, we are differently abled'.

ableism *n* (1981) discrimination in favour of able-bodied people; prejudice against or disregard of the needs of the disabled. A term originally used by US feminists. The alternatives *able-bodism* and *able-bodiedism* were briefly tried in British English later in the 1980s, but (hardly surprisingly) they never caught on. See **-ism (1965)**

> 1981 *Off our Backs*: One must imagine trying to show a woman with lower body paralysis that she is 'accepted' by saying, 'We're all less strong than we'd like to be,' to realize how *ableist* it is to say 'We're all crazy'… 'Ableism'—that is, the systemic oppression of a group of people because of what they can or can not do with their bodies or minds—is the result of… ignorance.

abortion pill *n* (1985) an anti-hormone drug, usually a progesterone-blocker (e.g. mifepristone, also known as RU-486), which is used to induce early abortions and usually acts by preventing implantation of the embryo

> 1991 *New Scientist*: Why no explicit reference to the increasing ethical dilemmas raised by modern science, from animal rights to the abortion pill RU486?

abortuary *n* (1985) a clinic where abortions are performed. Originally and mainly US; a blend of *abortion* and *mortuary*. A polemical usage favoured by opponents of induced abortions

> 1985 *Chicago Tribune*: They are killing our children in these abortuaries, pulling their little arms and legs off.

Acid House *n* (1988) a type of house music with a very fast beat, a spare, mesmeric, synthesized sound, and usually a distinctive gurgling bass noise. Also applied to the youth cult associated with this music, characterized by a vogue for warehouse parties, a revival of psychedelia, and the taking of hallucinogenic drugs. *Acid* may well be the slang term for LSD (see **acid (1966)**), although many cultists claim that it comes from the record *Acid Trax* by Phuture (in the slang of Chicago, where this music originated in 1986, *acid burning* means 'stealing', and the music relies heavily on 'sampling', a polite word for stealing musical extracts)

> 1988 *Observer*: Drugs fear as the 'acid house' cult revives a Sixties spectre… 'Acid house' started in four London clubs… In the past month it has 'taken off', spreading to other clubs throughout the country.

Adam *n* (1985) the hallucinogenic drug 3,4-methylenedioxymethamphetamine. Slang, originally US. The name was probably coined by reversing *MDMA*, the drug's abbreviated chemical name, dropping the first *m*, and pronouncing the resulting word—no doubt also with a side-glance at the drug's allegedly paradisal effects. It never caught on to the same extent as its synonym **ecstasy (1985)**

> 1985 *Los Angeles Times*: On the street, its name is 'ecstasy' or 'Adam', which should tell how people on the street feel about it.

Aid *n* (1984) Used as the second element in the names of events, etc., organized to raise money for particular charitable causes. The original one was *Band Aid*, based on the name of the rock music group formed by Bob Geldof in October 1984 to raise money for famine-relief in Ethiopia. It was followed by *Live Aid* and many others

> 1984 *Times*: Do They Know It's Christmas, [a record] on which Boy George, Sting, George Michael, members of Duran Duran, Status Quo, and U2 appear under the joint name of Band Aid.

> 1985 *Times*: The failure of Live Aid to penetrate the poorer countries is unlikely to affect adversely the amount of money it makes.

> 1985 *Times*: The fashion world is smouldering with gossip about Fashion Aid, which takes off like a rocket at the Albert Hall tonight.

AIDS, Aids *n* (1982) An acronym formed from the initial letters of *acquired immune deficiency syndrome* (also first recorded in 1982), denoting an illness (often if not always fatal) in which opportunistic infections or malignant tumours develop as a result of a severe loss of cellular immunity, which is itself caused by earlier infection with a retrovirus, HIV, transmitted in sexual fluids and blood. See also **slim (1985)**

> 1982 *Morbidity & Mortality Weekly Report* (US Centers for Disease Control): CDC defines a case of AIDS as a disease, at least moderately predictive of a defect in cell-mediated immunity, occurring in a person with no known cause for diminished resistance to that disease… The infant had no known contact with an AIDS patient.

> 1985 *Daily Telegraph*: A cancer clinic in the Bahamas has been ordered to close…after two patients…were given serum infected with HTLV-III, the deadly virus which causes Aids.

air-kiss *v* (1985) to pretend to kiss (someone) without making lip-contact. Elaborate greeting ceremonies based on this practice (which received a big boost from Aids panic) spread to the hitherto reserved Anglo-Saxon culture in the 1980s, often causing embarrassment if one of the parties was operating different conventions from the other (e.g. two swoops or three?). The characteristic accompanying vocalization is often represented as **mwah (1994)**. Also used as a noun

> 1985 *People*: At a recent party, people were air-kissing. They were joking about it, but they weren't kissing.

> 1992 R. Brown: She gave me the necessary hug, the cheek-to-cheek air kiss.

Air Miles *n* (1982) A proprietary name for a consumer incentive scheme under which credits redeemable for free air travel are issued to frequent flyers or with qualifying transactions, or given as a bonus by some employers

> 1995 *Guardian*: The accumulation of air miles has become one of the ruling obsessions of modern American life.

A list *n* (1984) a (notional) roster of the most celebrated or sought-after individuals (often in the context of their desirability as guests and the prestige they confer on the events they attend); hence, a social or professional elite. Originally US; often used adjectivally to denote pre-eminence and prestigiousness. The possibilities of a hypothetical hierarchy are also occasionally explored further down—e.g. *B list* and (the dregs) *Z list*

> 1990 *Sunday Times*: Even so, in the trade's terms, it was an A-list event, graced by such luminaries as Derek Cooper, Paul Levy and Lady Arabella Boxer.

alternative comedy *n* (1980) comedy that is not based on stereotypes (especially sexual or racial ones), or on conventional views of humour, but often includes an element of black humour or sur-realism and an aggressive style of performance. *Alternative comedian* is first recorded in 1981, the (not very right-on) *alternative comedienne* in 1986

> 1980 *Time Out*: Alternative comedy has come of age and you have nothing to use but your chains.

> 1981 *Sunday Times*: Throughout, Alexei Sayle, the alternative comedian, had sat in the aisle spurn-ing the bourgeois comfort of a seat.

> 1986 *Melody Maker*: Alternative comedian Ade Edmondson and alternative comedienne Jennifer Saunders introduce their alternative sprog.

animal companion *n* (1980) a pet. Coined mainly to avoid the connotations of ownership or speciesism perceived to be present in the word *pet*

> 1980 *Business Week*: If you know someone who has lost a beloved animal companion, it may help to know that vets and psychiatrists are paying much attention to the problem of how to deal with the resultant grief.

annus horribilis *n* (1985) a disastrous or particularly unpleasant year. A modern Latin invention, literally 'dreadful year', modelled on *annus mirabilis* 'wonderful year'. It was given a high profile when Queen Elizabeth II used it to describe the year 1992, in the wake of the fire in Windsor Castle and the breakdown of the marriages of Prince Charles and Prince Andrew

> 1988 *Sunday Times*: In the past *annus horribilis*, BT's black and yellow cubicles have sprouted in every town and village in the land.

> 1992 Queen Elizabeth II: 1992 is not a year I shall look back on with undiluted pleasure. In the words of one of my more sympathetic correspondents, it has turned out to be an 'annus horribilis'.

anorak *n* (1984) a boring, studious, or socially inept young person (caricatured as typically wearing an anorak); especially, one who pursues an unfashionable and solitary interest with obsessive dedication. British colloquial

> 1995 Jayne Miller: The Beatles have become almost an obsession. I try to get out-takes and rare records, I'm almost anorak level about it—getting really excited if I can hear John Lennon cough.

arb *n* (1983) A colloquial abbreviation of *arbitrageur* 'someone who buys and sells the same stock on different markets in the hope of making a profit'. A ubiquitous stock-market figure in the wheeling-and-dealing early 1980s

> 1983 *Securities Week*: As with most tender offers, large amounts of the target stock accumulated in the hands of arbitrageurs. Paine Webber only solicited stock from arbs.

Argie *n, adj* (1982) (an) Argentinian. A term of contempt, used initially in the context of the Anglo-Argentinian conflict over sovereignty of the Falkland Islands (1982) and occasionally revived subsequently by British tabloid headline-writers (e.g. for Anglo-Argentinian soccer matches)

> 1982 *Daily Telegraph*: We yelled at the Argies.

> 1982 *Private Eye*: It is my proud privilege to loan the ship to the British Government for use in our heroic crusade against the Argie hordes.

> 1998 *Sun*: Sun prayer mats can't foil Argies.

awesome *adj* (1980) marvellous, wonderful, stunning. Slang, originally and mainly US. A meaning that has dribbled down from the original 'awe-inspiring' via 'remarkable' (see **awesome (1961)**), part of the perennial search for new ways to enthuse, and further ammunition for the 'English-going-to-the-dogs' faction

> 1982 *Guardian*: It's so awesome, I mean, fer shurr, toadly, toe-dully!

> 1986 *Making Music*: I just know it'd be an awesome band.

AZT *n* (1985) An abbreviation of *azidothymidine* (first recorded in 1974), a substituted derivative of thymidine that has been used to inhibit the replication of HIV, the Aids virus

> 1987 *Scientific American*: The prospect of long-term use has…heightened concerns about AZT's considerable toxicity to bone-marrow cells, the precursors of blood cells.

backslash *n* (1982) a symbol in the form of a backward-sloping diagonal line (\) used in programming notation. A new punctuation mark introduced to the world courtesy of the computer. See also **slash (1961)**

> 1982 *Byte*: Arguments enclosed in backslashes refer to disk-file operations… In some cases, [commands] are bordered by special characters, such as back slashes.

Baker day *n* (1988) any of several days in the British state-school year set aside for in-service training of teachers. Named informally (and not altogether affectionately) after Kenneth Baker, who was British Education Secretary at the time they were introduced

> 1991 *Times Educational Supplement*: The Baker days…concentrate on key stage 1.

ballistic *adj* (1981) wildly angry, furious. Slang, originally US; often in the phrase *go ballistic*. The underlying reference is probably to the rapid ascent of a ballistic missile, but a more literal use of *go ballistic* is on record, meaning (of a ballistic missile) 'to go into freefall when its guidance system cuts out'

> 1988 George Bush: I get furious. I go ballistic. I really do and I bawl people out.

balti *n* (1984) a type of cooking from northern Pakistan, characterized by highly spiced dishes typically served in wide metal pans (*balti* means literally 'bucket' in Urdu) accompanied by nan bread. Restaurants serving this cuisine (known as *balti houses*) began to appear in Birmingham in the mid 1980s, and had spread nationwide in Britain by 1990

> 1984 *Curry Magazine*: Can anyone tell me what Balti is?… Some unusual dishes on the menu are Curried Quail, Balti chicken or meat.

> 1987 *Good Food Guide 1988*: Highlights are the superb balti dishes, cooked and served in blackened iron pans.

been there, done that (1983) A slogan of someone fully experienced in or familiar with something, especially to the point of boredom or complacency. Colloquial. It comes with a range of elaborations, notably *been there, done that, got the T-shirt*

> 1991 *Ski Survey*: Rosemary Burns has been there, done that and got the T-shirt. She gives fellow sufferers her sympathy and sound advice.

bell *n* (1982) a telephone call. British colloquial; usually in the phrase *give someone a bell*. A reminder of the days when telephones made a sound like a bell, rather than a bird-like twitter

> 1985 *Music Week*: Give them a Bell on 402 3105.

bender *n* (1985) a shelter made by covering a framework of bent branches with canvas or tarpaulin. British slang, used particularly by environmental protesters. See also **twigloo (1995)**

> 1995 *Daily Telegraph*: Mr Gummer has overruled the appeal and given the settlers six months to move their wood and canvas homes known as…'benders'.

bhangra *n* (1987) a type of pop music originating in the Asian community in Britain and incorporating elements of both Punjabi folk and Western music. It borrowed its name from Punjabi *bhangra*, the name of a traditional Punjabi male folk-dance

> 1988 *Sunday Telegraph*: It is getting big: so big that soon bhangra, like reggae before it, will break through the ethnic barrier.

Big Bang *n* (1986) A colloquial name for the deregulation of the London Stock Exchange on 27 October 1986, when a number of complex changes in trading practices were put into effect simultaneously. People had been working their way towards the metaphor (which is of course based on the name of the theory of instantaneous creation of the universe—see **big bang (1950)**) for some years (for instance, 'It is argued that a "big bang" approach, with all changes in Stock Exchange rules taking place on a single day…, would allow firms to make rational plans', *Financial Times* (1983); and again, 'The removal of the minimum commissions guaranteed to the 250-member firms of the [Stock] Exchange is now likely to happen in one go—by what is known as the "big bang" approach', *Times* (1984))

> 1986 *Sunday Express*: After the Big Bang tomorrow, the City will never be the same again… From tomorrow,…the distinction between brokers and jobbers disappears.

big girl's blouse *n* (1983) an effeminate or ineffectual male; one regarded as weak, cowardly, emotionally oversensitive, or lacking in common sense. British slang; probably in northern dialectal use before the 1980s, but only then did it achieve national exposure. Also in the form *great girl's blouse*

> 1983 K. Bryson et al.: *Naff ballet roles*… The big girl's blouse in 'Les Sylphides'.

big mo *n* (1980) the impetus for a successful election campaign, derived from prevailing public opinion, a politician's popularity, etc. Originally and mainly US; *mo* is short for *momentum*. A favourite term of President George Bush, who did much to popularize it. It no doubt owes much to the earlier US naval slang term *Big Mo* for the battleship USS *Missouri*

> 1988 *Times*: Big mo—decisive momentum—was even used unadorned on the cover headline in *Time* magazine this week now that Mr Bush has finally captured the elusive elixir. You get big mo after exploiting the bounce of early victories.

bimbette *n* (1982) an adolescent **bimbo (1920)**

> 1988 *Arena*: A gathering of playboys just wasn't a party unless there was at least one… scantily clad bimbette swimming around in a bathtub of shampoo.

biodiversity *n* (1987) diversity of animal and plant life, as represented by the number of extant species. A term reportedly proposed by Walter G. Rosen in 1986. Diversity of life forms is seen as essential to keeping the machinery of the Earth going—as many farmers who embraced monoculture in the 1960s later came to realize

> 1987 *Nature*: Here biodiversity increases with the introduction of understory vegetation.

bioethics *n* (1986) the ethical aspects of various techniques of human intervention in biological processes, such as genetic engineering and birth control

> 1986 *Dædalus*: From faint whisperings…that gathered strength in the sixties and emerged in force in the seventies, bioethics has become an established presence in medicine.

Birtism *n* (1988) the policies introduced into the BBC by John Birt, Deputy Director-General 1987–92 and Director-General from 1992, characterized by an emphasis on the explanatory function of current-affairs broadcasting and a market-based approach to the elements of programme-making. Often a negative term, signalling disapproval of the policies, as is the derived *Birtist*, also first recorded in 1988

> 1988 *Sunday Times*: For many at the meeting, the idea that the flamboyant, original and free-thinking Janet Street-Porter had notions of journalism not dissimilar to those of the allegedly dull and dreary Birtists came as something of a shock.

> 1993 *Guardian*: Now an iron structure has been set in place in news and current affairs to make sure that producers do not have freedom, that they conform to what has become known as Birtism.

Black Monday *n* (1987) The name given to Monday 19 October 1987, the day on which the world's stock markets crashed (beginning in New York). Not exactly the most original of epithets: *black* has been used since the Middle Ages to name a *dies horribilis*, and indeed the day of the Wall Street crash in 1929 was called by some *Black Thursday* (see also **Black Wednesday (1992)**). People with a more lurid imagination named it *Meltdown Monday*

> 1988 *Life*: The Dow Jones, once up 712 points for the year, drops 508 points on Black Monday. Paper losses total $500 billion.

blip *n, v* (1983) a temporary movement in statistics, usually in an unexpected or unwelcome direction; hence any kind of temporary problem or hold-up. As a verb, used to denote figures suddenly rising on a graph. The underlying idea is of a blip or sudden peak on a radar trace. The usage emerged from financial jargon into the public domain in Britain in 1988, when the Chancellor of the Exchequer, Nigel Lawson, reportedly announced that a large increase in the Retail Price Index was just a 'temporary blip'

> 1989 *Listener*: Nigel Lawson's dilemma is the Conservative Party's also. Is the first tremor on its happy political landscape merely a 'blip', as the Chancellor has called the storm that has gradually engulfed him.

> 1989 *New York Times*: Prices moved higher during overnight trading, and blipped a shade higher still following the release of the G.N.P. figures.

board-sailing *n* (1980) An official name for windsurfing (see **windsurf (1969)**), introduced because of difficulties with the proprietary status of *Windsurfer*. The derived *board-sailor* (or *sailer*) is also first recorded in 1980. See also **sailboard (1962)**

> 1980 *Washington Post*: Other events added for Los Angeles were board sailing (also known as 'wind-surfing'), [etc.]… Winner tried twice before to set new board-sailing distance records.

> 1980 *New York Times*: For the advanced board sailor, there is now a sailboard…designed for use only in winds of more than 15 knots.

body-popping *n* (1984) a style of (street-)dancing popular among teenagers, especially in urban areas, and characterized by robotic, jerking movements. Originally US: the dance style developed on the streets of Los Angeles in the late 1970s, and by the mid 80s it had spread throughout the English-speaking world. It eventually merged with **break dancing (1982)** in general hip-hop culture

> 1984 *New York Times*: The girls wanted to go back to Covent Garden to watch the punks and body-poppers.

> 1985 *Times*: The mechanical movements of body popping can be traced to mime and to robotic disco dancing.

bog-standard *adj* (1983) basic or unmodified; unexceptional or uninspired. Slang, mainly British. Its origins are obscure. It appears first to have been applied to motorcycles, and it has been suggested that it is an alteration of *box-standard*—the underlying idea being of a new motorcycle straight out of its packing-case, not modified by its owner. Alternatively, there may be some link with obsolete Cambridge slang *bog-wheel* 'bicycle'

> 1983 *Australian Personal Computer*: Decryption of a 30-byte cipher block takes about five minutes, using a bog-standard Z80 running at under 2 Mhz clock rate.

> 1995 *Empire*: A bog-standard biography with a cheap Psycho sales gimmick, you can't help thinking Perkins deserved better.

bondage trousers *n* (1980) trousers, often of black leather, of a style favoured by punk rockers, hung with chains, safety-pins, zips, etc.

> 1980 *Daily Mirror*: They think if you put on a pair of bondage trousers you're a Punk.

bonkbuster *n* (1988) a type of popular novel characterized by frequent explicit sexual encounters between the typically glamorous and wealthy characters. Etymologically, *bonking* (see **bonk (1975)**) meets the *blockbuster* 'a best-selling book'

> 1994 *Guardian*: As the extra-curricular activities of discomfited Tories continue to entertain the nation, Mrs Currie's 564-page political 'bonkbuster' beds down nicely with the assorted scandals *du jour*.

boot *v* (1980) to prepare (a computer) for operation by causing an operating system to be loaded into its memory from a disc or tape, especially by a bootstrap routine; also, to cause (an operating system or a program) to be loaded in this way. Often used with *up*. An abbreviation of **bootstrap (1953)**

> 1986 *Courier-Mail* (Brisbane): If you boot up your system without the keyboard being plugged in, you will see an error message.

> 1986 *What Micro?*: Once you boot up and run the new Mac one difference is immediately apparent.

Bork *v* (1987) to defame or vilify (someone) systematically, especially with the aim of obstructing or preventing them from holding public office. US. The term commemorates Robert Bork (born 1927), a judge whose nomination to the US Supreme Court in 1987 was rejected following a large amount of unfavourable publicity for his allegedly illiberal and extreme views

> 1991 *New Republic*: 'We're going to Bork him', the National Organization for Women has promised. But if they succeed, liberals may discover that they have Borked themselves.

bouncy castle *n* (1986) a large inflatable in the form of a stylized castle, in which children can play. From the late 1980s onwards, it seemed that no fete in Britain was complete without one of these bulbous constructions lolloping in the background

> 1986 *Guardian*: Supervised children's holiday activities…tuition in many sports…; fun sessions including rollerskating, swimming, and bouncy castle.

boxercise *n* (1985) A proprietary name for a fitness routine or type of aerobics which incorporates moves and exercises from boxing, sometimes with the use of gloves, punchbags, etc. The latest in a line of *exercise* blends which goes back to **dancercise (1967)**

> 1992 *Future Fitness UK*: Boxercise…includes shadow boxing, jumping rope, punching drills, friendly sparring and killer sets of abdominal crutches.

brat pack *n* (1985) a group of young Hollywood film stars of the mid 1980s (e.g. Emilio Estevez, Matt Dillon, Patrick Swayze, and Tom Cruise) popularly regarded as enjoying a rowdy fun-loving lifestyle; hence applied more broadly to any precocious and aggressive clique. The term was coined by David Blum in a 1985 article about the film *St Elmo's Fire*; it is a punning reference to the *rat pack*, the group of rowdy young stars led by Frank Sinatra in the 1950s

> 1986 *City Limits*: Andie…is torn between desire for rich kid Blane…and contempt for his brat pack lifestyle.

break dancing *n* (1982) a style of dancing popularized by US blacks, often individual or competitive, and characterized by a loud insistent beat to which dancers perform energetic and acrobatic movements, sometimes spinning around on their backs on the pavement or floor. Pioneered during the late 1970s by teams of black teenage dancers in the south Bronx, New York City. The original literal meaning was dancing to fill the 'break' in a piece of rap music

> 1982 *Village Voice* (New York): The Smurf is a fusion dance…a dance incorporating smoothed out elements of break dancing.

brill *adj* (1981) wonderful, marvellous. British slang; a shortening of **brilliant (1971)**. Originally youth-speak, and, like most such enthusiasm-words, fairly short-lived; by the middle of the decade it was curling up at the edges

> 1982 *Pony Club Annual*: What a brill idea.

> 1983 *Guardian*: It may have been an awful night…but the meat and potato pies were brill.

> 1986 *Sunday Express Magazine*: Here's a clue. Fab brill Hellmann's Mayonnaise.

Brilliant Pebbles *n* (1988) a defence strategy conceived as part of the US Strategic Defence Initiative in which incoming enemy missiles are intercepted and destroyed by numerous small heat-seeking missiles. *Brilliant* refers to the missiles' inbuilt computer guidance

> 1992 *Syracuse Herald*: Clinton…intends to scrap the massive space-based defense system known as Brilliant Pebbles.

BSE *n* (1987) An abbreviation of *bovine spongiform encephalopathy* (also first recorded in 1987), a fatal neurological disease of cattle characterized by behavioural disorders including unsteady gait and nervousness. It was first identified in Britain in 1986, and is thought to have been caused by feeding infected animal products to cattle. Its jaw-cracking name was usually either abbreviated to *BSE* or colloquialized to **mad-cow disease (1989)**. See also **human BSE (1992)**

> 1987 *Economist*: Bovine spongiform encephalopathy (BSE) twists the tongues of vets and wrecks the brains of cows.

buckminsterfullerene *n* (1985) a stable form of carbon, whose nearly spherical, hollow molecule consists of 60 carbon atoms arranged in a shape with 12 pentagonal faces and 20 hexagonal ones. Named after Richard Buckminster Fuller (1895–1983), the US architect who conceived the similarly shaped geodesic dome. Often referred to more manageably as a *buckyball*

> 1991 *New Scientist*: A soccer-ball-shaped molecule made of 60 carbon atoms, buckminsterfullerine, can become a superconductor if it is 'doped' with a small quantity of potassium atoms.

buddy *n* (1984) someone who befriends and provides support for someone suffering from an incapacitating disease, especially Aids. Originally US

> 1987 *Observer*: Buddies start off as strangers yet often end up as the people closest to their PWAs.

build-down *n* (1983) a systematic reduction of nuclear armaments, by destroying two or more for each new one deployed. US military/political jargon, coined as a deliberate contrast to *build-up*, and presumably partly modelled also on *run-down* and *wind-down*

> 1983 *New York Times*: The reaction to the build-down concept has been gratifying… This plan, referred to as a 'build down', was offered originally by Senators William S. Cohen…and Sam Nunn… Under their proposal, every time a new land-based warhead was deployed, two older ones would have to be destroyed.

bunny *n* (1989) a person. Used colloquially in the expression (*not*) *a happy bunny* to indicate (slightly condescendingly and often with a degree of understatement) that someone is (not) pleased with their lot

> 1991 *Toronto Star*: On the very morning they met, they learned that they had to cut 'only' $2 million. And they had one month to find that money… They were not happy bunnies.

buppie *n* (1984) a member of a socio-economic group comprising young black professional people working in cities. Originally US; one of the earliest of the **yuppie (1982)** clones, and also, despite its often offensive tinge, one of the longest-lasting

> 1984 *People Weekly* (US): Bryant Gumbel and Vanessa Williams are both Buppies. Of course, it wouldn't be Yuppie to be Miss America unless you are the first black one.

camcorder *n* (1982) a portable video camera incorporating a built-in video recorder. A blend of *camera* and *recorder*. The earlier term *videocamera* (first recorded in 1978) does not imply a recording facility

> 1982 *Economist*: Manufacturers of video tape recorders…have agreed that these 'camcorders' will all use the same standard 8mm. video tape.

canteen culture *n* (1987) an established set of attitudes within the lower ranks of the British police, characterized by resistance to the introduction of modern managerial standards and practices, and at its most extreme associated with male chauvinist and racist views. From the idea of such views being exchanged off-duty in police-station canteens

> 1995 *Guardian*: Officially Britain's police are committed to eradicating racism in their ranks… But are their efforts being undermined by the 'canteen culture' of rank and file officers?

cap *v* (1983) See **rate-capping (1983)**

carbon tax *n* (1986) a tax levied on fossil fuels with the aim of discouraging the production of harmful carbon dioxide by their being burnt. Originally US

> 1993 *New Scientist*: Britain is the only member of the European Community blocking a carbon tax.

car-boot sale *n* (1985) an outdoor sale at which people gather to sell unwanted possessions, produce, etc., from the boots of their cars. British; later widely curtailed to **boot sale (1992)**. Compare **garage sale (1966)**

> 1985 *Company*: We cram our own homes solid with junk and then cruise the local car-boot sales in the hope of acquiring someone else's.

car bra *n* (1986) Originally, a protective cover that fits over the front end of a car, guarding it against wear and tear. Subsequently applied also to a similarly placed carbon-based cover that absorbs the microwaves used in radar equipment, minimizing the chance of getting caught by a radar speed trap

> 1989 *Car & Driver*: I keep reading ads for car bras that are supposed to suck up police radar signals and permit one to sail through traps.

cardboard city *n* (1982) an area of a large town where homeless people congregate at night under makeshift shelters made from discarded cardboard packing cases, etc. Originally US. A sight increasingly familiar in the West in the 1980s as unemployment and various stringent social policies deprived more and more people of a home

> 1990 *Independent*: Beggars on our streets, cardboard cities…are the results of…political indifference.

cashback *n* (1988) a facility offered by retailers (especially supermarkets) by which a customer can withdraw a limited amount of cash when making a credit or debit card purchase, the amount of which is added to the bill. An adaptation of the earlier usage, 'an incentive to buyers by which in return for purchasing something they receive a cash refund' (first recorded in 1973)

> 1993 *Daily Mail*: Nearly one in ten now gets cash elsewhere, often from a supermarket. For example, Sainsbury's has a cash-back scheme, which allows you to add extra to your bill if you pay by debit card.

casual *n* (1980) a (male) youth belonging to a peer group favouring a casual style of dress and conventional appearance, often characterized as aggressively nationalistic and associated with football-related violence. In many respects the Casuals' cult was the successor to the Mods (see **mod (1960)**)

> 1980 *Daily Mirror*: A Casual, 17-year-old printer, Jeff McNamara, lives in a skinhead stronghold in East London. Yet he dresses defiantly in smart slacks.

> 1992 D. McLean: Football's a game, fighting's more than that. Football's something you just do, or just watch, but a casual, that's something you *are*.

CD ROM *n* (1983) a compact disc (see **compact disc (1979)**) on which text or data is stored and which is used as a read-only memory. It revolutionized the publishing business, making it possible to offer large reference works and commercial databases from which a maze of information is available at the touch of a computer key

> 1983 *Electronics*: The CD ROM, which is expected to hit the market next year, can hold 525 megabytes of formatted data.

cellphone *n* (1984) a hand-held or mobile radio-telephone providing access to a cellular radio network (see **cellular (1977)**)

> 1989 *Satellite Times*: There were only about half a dozen others…taking trans-Atlantic phone calls on a cellphone.

challenged *adj* (1985) disabled, handicapped. Originally North American. One of the highest-profile politically correct euphemisms of the 1980s, inspired by replacing the negative connotations of 'handicap' with a more positive notion of rising to a challenge. It was, however, easily mocked: alongside serious usages like *physically challenged* and *mentally challenged* came facetious coinages such as *vertically challenged* 'short', *follicularly challenged* 'bald', and *hymenally challenged* 'non-virginal'

> 1985 *New York Times*: The disabled skiers, whom Mr. Kennedy prefers to call 'physically challenged', achieve speeds on difficult runs that would be daunting to most competitors.

1995 *Freedom: Canada's Guide for the Disabled*: Sources suggest that there may be well over four million people in Canada considered as challenged due to a wide variety of disabilities.

1996 *Good Food*: Celebrity chefs…take centre stage and teach the culinarily-challenged to cook.

champagne socialist *n* (1987) A derisive term for someone who espouses socialist ideals but enjoys a wealthy and luxurious lifestyle. Originally and mainly British

1995 *New Yorker*: He was often to be found in the company of London's so-called 'champagne socialists'—anti-Thatcherites like Margaret Drabble and anti-Americans like Harold Pinter.

chaology *n* (1987) the scientific study of **chaos (1974)**

1987 *Nature*: The concepts and methods of chaology have penetrated into virtually all branches of science.

charge-capping *n* (1987) See **rate-capping (1983)**

chat line *n* (1984) a telephone or electronic mail service which enables subscribers to exchange casual conversation, either individually or by means of a conference line, with other subscribers or with employees of the service. In the late 1980s chat lines came under a cloud for allowing children to run up huge phone bills without their parents' knowledge

1991 *Independent on Sunday*: Yesterday there were 20 [advertisements] promoting pornographic 'chat lines' in which one is, for instance, invited to 'talk dirty'.

chattering classes *n* (1985) a social group consisting of articulate members of the educated middle class, typically seen as holding liberal opinions (notably opposition to the Thatcher government of the 1980s) and given to debating social, political, or cultural issues amongst themselves. British colloquial, and usually used with dismissive contempt (generally by someone who might him- or herself be regarded as belonging to the group). Reportedly coined by the journalist Frank Johnson in the early 1980s, and popularized by Alan Watkins in the *Observer*

1987 *Daily Telegraph*: Does anybody really care who is elected Chancellor of the University of Oxford? Only the chattering classes are exercised.

Chiantishire *n* (1986) A humorous name applied to Tuscany, or more specifically to the area around Chianti, in allusion to the popularity of the area as a holiday destination for British tourists, and the large number of British expatriates living there. A usage popularized by the British novelist John Mortimer

1986 *Independent*: 'Chiantishire'—the English-dominated countryside around Florence—has about it an 'atmosphere of weekend Surrey'.

Childline *n* (1986) (the charitable organization that runs) a telephone help-line service established in Britain in 1986 which offers help and advice to children experiencing problems, especially physical or sexual abuse; also applied subsequently to similar services elsewhere. See also **help-line (1980)**

1986 *Times*: Esther Rantzen, the television presenter, is to head ChildLine, a charity which was launched yesterday to help children in danger.

chill *v* (1985) to pass time idly; to hang around, especially with other members of a group. Slang, originally and mainly US; usually followed by *out*. A development of the earlier slang *chill* (*out*) 'to relax, calm down, take it easy', which is first recorded in 1979

1985 J. Simmons et al.: Now the Adidas I possess for one man is rare Myself, homeboy, got fifty pair Got blue and black 'cause I like to chill And yellow and green when it's time to get ill.

1988 *New Musical Express*: The perfect Xmas prezo would be to spend it at home 'chilling out'…with the Schoolly family.

ciabatta *n* (1985) a type of open-textured Italian bread made with olive oil. Modern Italian, and Cal-Ital, food was the fashion of the 1980s, and the ciabatta was among its most widely successful manifestations. The word in Italian dialect means literally 'old, down-at-heel shoe, slipper', which the loaf may be said to resemble (in shape)

1993 *Independent on Sunday*: The British high street ciabatta, oozing with oil, soft of crumb and supple of crust, is actually a modern invention.

clamp *v* (1983) to fit (an illegally parked vehicle) with a wheel clamp in order to immobilize it. A shortening of the verb *wheel-clamp*, which is also first recorded in 1983 (see **wheel clamp (1980)**)

> 1990 *Holiday Which?*: We've been clamped!! One just can't avoid *every* potential hazard!!

cold fusion *n* (1982) nuclear fusion taking place at a temperature lower than ordinarily required, especially at or near room temperature. A holy grail of physics, because it would provide low-cost energy for the rest of time. Several announcements in the 1980s and 90s that it had been achieved proved premature

> 1992 *Wilson Quarterly*: Many supposed 'breakthroughs' are only beginnings, and some have little more substance than cold fusion.

commit *v* (1982) to make a serious (personal, business, etc.) commitment. Originally and mainly US; an adaptation of the reflexive usage *commit oneself* into an intransitive usage. Often used in the context of committing oneself to a serious sexual relationship

> 1982 *Business Week*: Investors are simply unwilling to commit at fixed rates far into the future.

> 1991 *Premiere*: Warshawski fits into the tradition of lonely-guy operatives, emotionally guarded (if not wounded) and largely unable to commit.

community charge *n* (1985) a tax or charge for local services levied on adult residents of a community, introduced as a flat-rate charge in Scotland in 1989 and elsewhere in Britain in 1990, replacing household rates. *Community charge* was the official name for it, but in the country at large it was generally known as the **poll tax (1985)**. Widely reviled for its perceived unfairness, it was replaced in 1993 by a **council tax (1991)**

> 1989 *Which?*: Do you have any questions about how the poll tax (or 'community charge') works?

compassion fatigue *n* (1983) an indifferent or unsympathetic attitude towards others' suffering as a result of overexposure to charitable appeals. Originally US; the term became familiar in Britain in the wake of the large-scale fund-raising events of the mid-eighties, the initial trigger of which was the Ethiopian famines of 1984–85. Its ultimate models were probably *combat fatigue* and *battle fatigue*, dating from the World War II period. It started off a mini-rash of *fatigue* formations, many of them facetious ('There were signs yesterday of princess fatigue', *Guardian* (1996)); see also **information fatigue syndrome (1994)**

> 1985 *New York Times*: Geldof, the Irish rock musician who conceived the event and spearheaded its hasty implementation, said that he 'wanted to get this done before compassion fatigue set in', following such projects as the African fund-raising records 'Do They Know It's Christmas?' and 'We Are the World'.

computerate *adj* (1981) familiar with the theory and practice of computing. A coinage modelled on *literate* and **numerate**, and indeed perhaps formed by concertinaing *computer-literate*, which is first recorded in 1976. The related noun **computeracy (1969)** did not come into general use before the early 1980s

> 1984 *New Scientist*: Chapman and Hall are looking for a numerate and computerate person with publishing experience.

contra *n* (1981) a Nicaraguan counter-revolutionary, especially a member of the forces opposing the Sandinista government between 1979 and 1990 and supported by right-wing governments in the West. A borrowing from Spanish, where it is an abbreviation of *contrarrevolucionario* 'counter-revolutionary'

> 1984 *New Yorker*: When Nicaragua…announced a series of reforms this fall, Reagan and his men announced themselves…encouraged but not nearly pleased enough to cease encouraging the contras.

cook-chill *adj* (1982) Denoting food sold in a pre-cooked and refrigerated form, for consumption within a specified time, usually after thorough reheating. Originally a technical term in the food industry, it leapt to fame in the late 1980s after numerous cases of listeriosis were linked with such food inadequately reheated

1990 *Which?*: The Department of Health has already advised people in at-risk groups not to eat cook-chill foods cold, and—if you buy one to eat hot—to make sure that it's reheated until it's 'piping hot'.

crack *n* (1985) a potent highly addictive crystalline form of cocaine made by heating a mixture of it with baking powder and water until it is hard, and breaking it into small pieces which are inhaled or smoked for their stimulating effect. Slang, originally US; since the late 1980s widely used in the fuller form *crack cocaine*, especially in official parlance. The term refers both to the fact that the hard-baked substance has to be 'cracked' into small pieces for use, and to the 'cracking' sound the pieces make when smoked

1986 *US News & World Report*: Crack…has rocketed from near obscurity to national villainy in the past six months.

crackhead *n* (1986) someone who habitually takes or is addicted to crack cocaine. Slang, originally US. The use of *-head* for 'drug-taker' originated in *hophead* 'opium addict', first recorded in 1911

1986 *Time*: A recent survey…indicates that…more than half the nation's so-called crackheads are black.

cred *n* (1981) credibility, reputation, status amongst one's peers. Originally in the phrase *street cred*, a shortening of **street credibility (1979)**, but gradually the emphasis shifted from the sharp world of urban street culture to mere fashionability or 'hipness', and the *street* was quietly dropped. Later still *cred* came to be used adjectivally, meaning 'fashionable, trendy'

1981 *Guardian Weekly*: A couple of expressions have only come my way in the last month or so. One is 'street wise' and the other 'street cred'.

1985 *International Musician*: I know that walking down main street with an oboe in hand does nothing for the street cred.

1986 Bob Geldof: 'Cred' was achieved by your rhetorical stance and no one had more credibility than the Clash.

1991 *Hot Air*: Annie Nightingale's got the most cred show in the air… Tune in and groove.

cringe-making *adj* (1983) causing one to cringe, especially with embarrassment or dismay; unspeakably inadequate. British colloquial; a new formation based on earlier models such as **shy-making (1930)**

1998 *Private Eye*: Jeff Ennis, Labour MP for Barnsley East and Mexborough,…has been awarded a special OBBN [i.e. Order of the Backbench Brown Nose] for his recent cringe-making performance during prime minister's questions.

crop circle *n* (1988) a circular area in a field of standing crops, usually wheat or other cereal, in which the stalks have been flattened, typically in concentric rings. Hailed by some as evidence of visits by extraterrestrials, pooh-poohed by the more sceptical as man-made hoaxes. Also known as *corn circles* (first recorded in 1989)

1992 *Science News*: The study of these mysterious crop circles has itself grown into a thriving cottage industry.

crucial *adj* (1987) very good or important; great, fantastic. A British teen and (largely) pre-teen slang approval adjective of the late 1980s, popularized by children's television presenters and other media personalities, notably the comedian Lenny Henry

1990 *New Statesman*: Martha (aged seven): 'Lenny Henry, he wrote the "guide to cruciality", so we don't say crucial no more.'

cruelty-free *adj* (1986) involving minimal cruelty to animals; usually applied specifically to consumer goods produced without involving any cruelty to animals in the development or manufacturing process—in other words, a good marketing slogan to bring disgruntled animal lovers back into the consumer fold

1992 *Looks*: The natural girl is a barefaced beauty and she's determined to stick to her principles—it's only the cruelty-free beauty products for her.

crystal meth *n* (1984) the drug methamphetamine in a powdered crystalline form, used illegally by injection, inhalation, oral absorption, etc. as a stimulant

> 1990 *Rolling Stone*: I used to shoot up crystal meth on a regular basis in high school.

cutting edge *n* (1985) the forefront of progress or development, especially in technology. Widely used as an adjective. A slightly earlier synonym was **leading edge (1977)**

> 1985 *Times*: If…the cutting edge of blue skies research becomes somewhat blunted, [etc.].

> 1990 *Premiere*: The company also puts out *Gorgon*, on horror movies, and *Impact*, on cutting-edge pop culture.

cyberpunk *n* (1983) a subgenre of science fiction characterized by a bleak, high-tech setting in which a lawless subculture exists within an oppressive society dominated by computer technology. Coined, possibly by Gardner Dozois, to describe the work of a number of writers in the mid 1980s, notably William Gibson (whose 1984 book *Neuromancer* is seminal) and Bruce Sterling. A combination of **cybernetics**, the science of control systems, and **punk**, probably in allusion to the harshness and shockingness of punk rock

> 1989 *Listener*: It's the Rhetoric of the New. Pitched somewhere between the SF genre of cyberpunk and the mainstream brat novel.

cyberspace *n* (1982) the notional environment within which electronic communication takes place, especially when represented as the inside of a computer system; space perceived as such by an observer but generated by a computer system and having no real existence; the space of virtual reality. A term coined by the science-fiction writer William Gibson, and first used by him in a short story in 1982. He based it on **cybernetics (1948)**. It became the progenitor of a wide range of *cyber-* compounds in the 1980s and 90s, relating to computer-mediated electronic communications, the use of the Internet, and virtual reality—for example, **cybernaut**, *cyberart*, *cyberhippy*, *cyberlawyer*, *cyberworld*. See also **cyberpunk (1983)** and **cybercafé (1994)**

> 1984 William Gibson: Molly was gone when he took the trodes off, and the loft was dark. He checked the time. He'd been in cyberspace for five hours.

> 1993 *Guardian*: The search for a kidnapped girl from a small town in California has leapt into cyberspace as her picture criss-crosses the world's computer networks, databases and electronic mail systems.

DAT *n* (1985) See **digital audio tape (1981)**

dawn raid *n* (1980) a swift operation effected early in stock-market trading whereby a stockbroker obtains for his or her client a markedly increased shareholding in a company (often preparatory to a take-over) by clandestine buying from other substantial shareholders

> 1981 *Bookseller*: Following his 'dawn raid' last July, which gained him 29.4 per cent of BPC, Robert Maxwell…clearly plans to secure and consolidate his control of the group.

DBS *n* (1981) An abbreviation of *direct broadcasting by satellite*, television broadcasting in which viewers have special aerials to pick up the signal direct from the satellite used to receive and retransmit it. The specialist's term for what is more generally known as **satellite television (1966)**

> 1986 *Stage & Television Today*: ITN has put together a schedule for DBS operators.

deacon *v* (1980) to ordain as a deacon. A usage called into being by the Church of England's admittance of women to deacon's orders

> 1980 *Church Times*: Everyone agreed that the cathedral protest had been dignified. But many were puzzled that it should occur now, as ten women had already been deaconed… This is the first public deaconing of a woman in the Diocese of Llandaff.

Deely-bobbers *n* (1982) A proprietary name (registered in the US in 1982, with claim of use since 1981) for a variety of children's novelty headgear consisting of a pair of ornaments (e.g. balls) attached antenna-like by springs or wires to a head-band. It was actually a recycling of a US trade-name previously applied (in the early 1970s) to a make of construction toy comprising a number of inter-linking building blocks

> 1982 *New Statesman*: Deely-bobbers—the glittering, bouncing baubles on wire which are the latest craze in headgear—caused a row in a hospital's X-ray department when all the staff there decided to wear them at once.

demerge *v* (1980) to separate one or more firms or trading companies from a large group. A back-formation from the noun *demerger*, which had been in use since the 1940s, but never with such frequency as in the 1980s, when antagonism to large corporations and the profitability of asset-stripping combined to encourage the break-up of multiple concerns. See also **unbundle (1977)**

> 1980 *Economist*: The government hit on encouraging large firms to 'demerge'.

> 1983 *Times*: House of Fraser directors were last night believed to be ready to recommend share-holders to vote against a proposal by Lonrho that it demerge Harrods from the rest of the…group.

dental dam *n* (1986) a thin sheet of latex used as a protection against infection during oral sex, especially cunnilingus. An innovation prompted largely by the fear of Aids. Originally US

> 1996 Pauline Adams (*Somerville for Women*): A generation alerted to the dangers of Aids kept itself informed not only about condoms but also about dental dams.

dependency culture *n* (1988) a social or political climate in which people rely on money or services provided by the State. Applied particularly, and disapprovingly, by right-wing theorists to reliance on State benefits by the unemployed or poor, viewed as robbed by this largesse of the motivation to provide for themselves or to improve their situation

> 1992 *Economist*: During the boom years of the mid-1980s…conservative works chronicling the growth of a black dependency culture in America's ghettos multiplied.

derivative *n* (1985) a financial arrangement or instrument (such as a future, option, or warrant) whose value derives from and is dependent on the value of an underlying variable asset, such as a commodity, currency, or security. Usually used in the plural. The term moved from financiers' jargon into the public domain in the 1990s with the news of large losses being made by speculators in derivatives, notable examples being the collapse of the British bank Barings in 1995, precipitated by the illegal activities of derivatives trader Nick Leeson, and huge losses by a Japanese bank speculating in copper in 1996

> 1996 *Economist*: Put simply, derivatives have flourished because a series of recent developments have transformed them into a cheap and efficient way of moving risk about within the economic system.

designer drug *n* (1983) a drug synthesized to mimic a legally restricted or prohibited drug without itself being subject to such restriction. Also used more broadly to denote any recreational drug with an altered structure. The term imports the 'fashionability' implications of **designer (1966)**

> 1983 *Sacramento Union*: Thirty-four people have died in the last four years after using 'designer drugs', heroin look-alikes concocted in underground laboratories and hitting the streets one step ahead of government regulations.

designer stubble *n* (1987) a short bristly growth of stubble on a man's unshaven face, worn for a carefully groomed yet rugged and masculine appearance. Fashionable in the late 1980s and early 90s. It works best if the stubble is dark. See **designer (1966)**

> 1989 *Guardian*: Designer stubble of the George Michael ilk has also run its bristly course.

desktop publishing *n* (1984) the production of printed matter similar in quality to that of typeset books by means of a printer (such as a laser printer) linked to a desk-top computer. The abbreviation *DTP* is first recorded in 1986

> 1984 *Financial Times*: When Xerox looked for a new way to market its revolutionary but commercially unsuccessful 'Star' workstation…, it settled on what it called a 'document creation system'—in other words, a desk-top publishing unit.

des res *n* (1986) An abbreviation of *desirable residence*, estate-agent-speak for 'a house or or other dwelling-place that is a highly desirable purchase'. British. Estate agents' reputation for probity and plain-speaking being what it is, *des res* is usually used ironically

> 1987 *Punch*: So the charmed grove was exchanged for a des res in Summertown, Oxford.

digital audio tape *n* (1981) magnetic tape on which sound is recorded digitally, analogous to digital recording on compact discs. More familiar in the long run via its abbreviation **DAT**, first recorded in 1985, which is occasionally treated as an acronym and pronounced /dæt/.

> 1981 *Business Week*: No less than five totally incompatible prototypes of digital-audio tape decks have been unveiled this fall by as many Japanese companies.

> 1985 *New Scientist*: DAT makes existing audio cassette recorders obsolete.

dinky *n* (1986) An acronym coined (on the model of **yuppie (1982)**) from the initial letters of *double* (or *dual*) *income, no kids*, denoting either partner of a usually professional working couple who have no children (*yet*, as the final -*y* is sometimes interpreted) and are characterized, especially by advertisers and marketers, as affluent consumers with few domestic demands on their time and money—in other words, the perfect target. Originally North American. The abbreviated *dink* is first recorded in 1987 (the surprise registered in the final quote below is no doubt due to the fact that *dink* is also US slang for 'penis', 'twerp', and 'Communist Vietnamese soldier'). Similar but less successful coinages in the lifestyle-acronym-mad mid 1980s include *oink* 'one income, no kids' and *tinkie* 'two incomes, nanny, and kids'

> 1987 *Observer*: People who will live in Docklands are empty nesters, dinkies, two incomes, two cars.

> 1987 *New York*: When a friend referred to two young professionals as 'a couple of dinks', it was a bit surprising... Double Income, No Kids.

dinomania *n* (1987) obsessive enthusiasm for dinosaurs, especially as a group phenomenon. Originally US. A coinage which did not take off until the release in 1993 of the phenomenally popular Steven Spielberg film *Jurassic Park*, about the cloning of dinosaurs

> 1996 *Guardian*: He has fun with the only book of Edgar Allan Poe that was a hit in his lifetime (it was about shells) and with the dinomania launched by Jurassic Park, and asks whether God really does have an inordinate fondness for beetles (25 per cent of all named species, so far).

dirty dancing *n* (1987) a type of fast, erotic dance in which couples dance very close together with a pronounced movement of the hips—a style which led naturally into the **lambada (1988)**. The term was popularized by a film of the same name which came out in 1987

> 1988 *Gold Coast Bulletin* (Australia): Dirty Dancing, the new dance craze, is really good clean fun.

> 1991 Julian Barnes: When he walked in I thought, You can take me dirty dancing any day of the week. Really tasty, long black hair, brilliant.

dis, diss *v* (1980) to put (someone) down; to show disrespect for (a person) by insulting language or dismissive behaviour. Slang, originally US Black English, and popularized by the spread of hip hop. An abbreviation of *disrespect*

> 1987 *New York Times*: The victim, according to detectives, made the mistake of irritating Nuke at a party. 'He dissed him', Sergeant Croissant said.

disappear *v* (1983) to abduct (someone) for political reasons and typically detain or kill them, without making their fate known. A transitive usage associated particularly with South American military dictatorships

> 1983 *New York Times*: In Latin America we whisper that somebody has made someone else disappear—that 'they' have 'disappeared' him or her.

> 1987 Elmore Leonard: Our two Nicaraguan doctors were disappeared, one right after the other.

dish *n* (1980) a concave antenna used as a receiving aerial for the domestic reception of satellite television. A usage based on the radar *dishes* and the *dishes* of radio telescopes that had become familiar since the 1940s

> 1980 *New Scientist*: Even a dish of just under a metre in diameter...has such a tight beam that the dish must be aimed at the satellite to an accuracy of within half a degree.

dog's bollocks *n* (1989) the very best; the height of excellence. British slang, initially associated particularly with the humorous magazine *Viz*. Perhaps from the notion of the prominence of the testicles in certain breeds of dog (' "It sticks out like a dog's bollocks", said of something that the speaker considers is patently obvious', Paul Beale, *Partridge's Dictionary of Slang* (1984)), but it probably also continues the tradition of earlier formations such as *the cat's nuts* (see **cat's whiskers (1923)**)

> 1989 C. Donald et al. (title): Viz: the dog's bollocks: the best of issues 26 to 31.

> 1995 *Times*: Before Tony Blair's speech, a chap near me growled: "'E thinks 'e's the dog's bollocks.' Well he's entitled to. It was a commanding speech: a real dog's bollocks of an oration.

domain *n* (1983) a region of a computer network, especially the Internet, corresponding to a particular country, organization, etc., which is used in the network address of individual computers

> 1995 *Economic Development Review*: In 1991, the Internet boasted about 9,000 commercial 'domains', the electronic equivalent of a storefront address. Today, more than 21,700 different commercial domains are registered.

dongle *n* (1982) a software protection device which must be plugged into a computer to enable the protected software to be used on it. An invented word (perhaps subliminally suggested by **toggle (1982)**)

> 1982 *MicroComputer Printout*: The word 'dongle' has been appearing in many articles with reference to security systems for computer software [refers to alleged coinage in 1980].

doorstep *v* (1981) Of a press or media reporter, photographer, etc.: to call on (someone) or wait on their doorstep, in order to obtain an interview, photograph, etc. British; originally journalists' slang, but as the usage has spread, the usual implication has been of intrusiveness

> 1985 *Guardian*: Sara's views about the 'frightful men' from that newspaper who doorstepped her.

doughnutting *n* (1989) the clustering of members round a speaker in a parliamentary debate, especially in order to give the impression to television viewers that the speaker is well supported or to conceal low attendance. The practice is said to have originated in Canada, but the term *doughnutting* (based on the idea of the ring-shaped North American doughnut) appears not to have been used there. It enjoyed a brief vogue in Britain when the broadcasting of proceedings in the House of Commons began

> 1989 *Daily Telegraph*: Viewers of Commons television coverage which starts in November have been warned to watch out for the practice of 'doughnutting'—whereby MPs cluster artificially around colleagues speaking in debates.

download *v* (1980) to transfer (especially software) from the storage of a larger computer system to that of a smaller one.

> 1982 *Which Computer?*: The existing software…will be down-loaded onto the new machine.

drag *v* (1983) to move (text, graphics, etc.) across a computer screen using a mouse or similar device

> 1983 *Byte*: Finally, I pick up the title with the cursor, 'drag' it to a new location and leave it there.

dragon *n* (1985) any of the more successful smaller economies of East and South-East Asia, especially those of Hong Kong, Singapore, Taiwan, and South Korea, and, in the early 1990s, Malaysia, Thailand, and the Philippines. Commonly used in the form *little dragon*. It eventually lost out to the longer-established synonym **tiger (1981)**

> 1993 *Time*: One of Asia's four rapidly developing 'Little Dragons'—along with South Korea, Taiwan and Hong Kong— Singapore is the smallest and in some ways most successful.

drop-dead *adv* (1985) very, stunningly (attractive). Slang, originally US; mainly in the phrase *drop-dead gorgeous*. A development of the earlier adjectival usage of *drop-dead* (first recorded in 1970), meaning 'stunning, exceptional' or 'breath-taking' (as if striking you dead)

> 1990 *Los Angeles*: Priscilla Presley arrives straight from a television interview, looking drop-dead gorgeous.

drug czar *n* (1989) a person responsible for co-ordinating and implementing measures for controlling and reducing the problem of illegal drug use in a given area. Originally US, based on the well established American use of *czar* for 'someone with supreme authority'. It crossed the Atlantic in the late 90s, when the newly elected Labour government in Britain decided to appoint such an official

> 1989 *New York Times*: The opposition of these intellectuals, the Bush Administration's blustery drug czar wrote in The Washington Times, was 'partly rooted in general hostility to law enforcement and criminal justice'.

> 1997 *Daily Telegraph*: Tony Blair posed with a 'Dennis the Menace' ecstasy tablet yesterday as he announced that Labour would appoint a 'drug tsar' to oversee the fight against 'one of the great evils of our time'.

dry *n* (1983) a politician, especially a member of the British Conservative party, who advocates economic stringency and individual responsibility, and uncompromisingly opposes high government spending. Used mainly in specific contrast with **wet (1980)**

> 1984 *Times*: It is hard to see economic dries such as Mr. Ridley buying the channel tunnel arguments now.

dub *n* (1982) a type of Black performance poetry, originally performed extempore and accompanied by dub or other recorded music (see **dub (1974)**), but subsequently also written down

> 1982 D. Sutcliffe: Johnson has…brought his poetry to young Black people on record, where it becomes a kind of 'dub'.

> 1982 *New Musical Express*: I consider Louise Bennett to be the mother of the young dub poets.

du jour *adj* (1989) of the day; of the present time. Used with a variety of connotations, ranging from impermanence through repetitiveness to fashionability. The ultimate source is French *plat du jour* 'dish of the day', which has been used in English since at least the first years of the 20th century. It came to be employed in other gastronomic contexts ('The vegetable du jour is always lima beans', J. C. S. Smith (1984)), and broadened out metaphorically from there

> 1989 *Christianity Today*: Religiously oriented swindles have become the 'fraud du jour' of the investment world.

> 1997 *Daily Telegraph*: Adult Attention Deficit Disorder…is…according to the latest surveys, taking over from chronic depression as the disease *du jour*.

E *n* (1988) (a tablet of) the drug ecstasy (see **ecstasy (1985)**)

> 1990 *New Musical Express*: 'People will dance to anything now,' muses Mal. 'I blame the E meself!'

eco-friendly *adj* (1989) not harmful to the environment; also applied to products manufactured with explicit regard to the environment

> 1989 *Daily Telegraph*: The only way that eco-friendly products are going to take off is for them to be presented by manufacturers and retailers as high tech and modern.

eco-terrorist *n* (1988) someone who participates in *eco-terrorism*. This term, first recorded in 1990, has been used with two deeply antagonistic meanings: 'violence carried out to further environmentalist ends', and 'politically motivated damage to the natural environment'

> 1988 *Arena*: He came up with the idea for *Tourist Season*, the story of eco-terrorists taking on the grossness of the tourist trade.

> 1990 Alvin Toffler: A second wing [of an environmental pressure group]…might well step up from eco-vandalism to full-scale eco-terrorism to enforce its demands.

> 1991 *Time*: Saddam's eco-terrorism raised the amount of carbon dioxide that humans are pumping into the atmosphere by up to 2%.

ecstasy *n* (1985) the hallucinogenic drug 3,4-methylenedioxymethamphetamine. Slang, originally US; so named from its effect on the user. Widely used on the rave scene in the later 1980s and the 90s as a provider of energy for all-night dancing, despite the occasional fatality linked with it. Often abbreviated to **E (1988)**. See also **Adam (1985)**

> 1987 *Times*: Police impounded £10,000-worth of a drug known as 'ecstasy' yesterday…the first time it has been found in Britain.

edgy *adj* (1986) controversial, unconventional; not ordinary or run of the mill. The underlying idea is of being 'near the edge' of danger. Slang

> 1992 *Vibe*: More singles and videos followed: all radio-friendly yet edgy, accessible yet fantasy-tinged.

Eftpos, EFTPOS *n* (1982) An acronym formed from the initial letters of *electronic funds transfer at point of sale*, a system of cashless payment in which money is electronically transferred directly from the customer's account to the retailer's, using the customer's charge or debit card

> 1990 *Accountancy*: An increasing number of credit card transactions are now captured electronically using an Eftpos…terminal.

electronic mailbox *n* (1981) an individual facility for receiving and storing electronic mail (see **electronic mail (1977)**) for retrieval by a recipient

> 1981 *Computerworld*: ETC/EM features electronic mailboxes, automatic message routing and broadcasting, correspondence archiving, [etc.].

e-mail, email *n*, *v* (1982) An abbreviation of **electronic mail (1977)** which by the middle of the 1980s had established itself as the standard term. First recorded as a verb in 1987

> 1982 *Computerworld*: ADR/Email is reportedly easy to use and features simple, English verbs and prompt screens.

> 1986 *Times*: Electronic mail—now known universally as e-mail. The partnership of word processor and e-mail almost eliminate [*sic*] the need for paper.

> 1994 *Loaded*: For Sonic Youth we would first e-mail them at SERV@CORNELL.EDU.

Emily's List *n* (1985) Originally, a US organization which campaigns and raises funds for women wishing to become Democratic candidates, particularly those who are pro-abortion. In the 1990s the name was taken up for a similar organization in the UK (founded by Barabara Follett) to increase the representation of women in the (Parliamentary) Labour party. *Emily* is an acronym (on the model of the female forename), formed from *early money is like yeast*

> 1985 *New York Times*: A group of prominent Democrats has formed a new fund-raising network to concentrate exclusively on soliciting early campaign contributions for Democratic Senate candidates who are women… The Washington-based group has chosen the name Emily's List, with 'Emily' standing for 'Early Money Is Like Yeast'.

> 1996 *Daily Telegraph*: Emily's List, the organization which gives financial help to aspiring Labour women MPs who support pro-choice policies on abortion.

empower *v* (1986) to make (a person or group) stronger and more confident, especially in controlling their life and claiming their rights. A pre-echo of what might be called this 'pregnant' sense can be found in the writings of William Penn in 1690 ('Who empowered them as their work witnesseth'), but as a widespread usage it is definitely a child of the 1980s

> 1986 C. Lasch: Communitarianism…rejects the kind of liberalism that seeks to 'empower' exploited groups by conquering the state.

> 1991 *Utne Reader*: While Afrocentrism helps empower blacks, it labels homosexuality a 'deviation' that weakens black culture.

empty-nester *n* (1987) a parent whose children have grown up and left home; also, one of a (married) couple with no children. One of the life-style encapsulations of which the 1980s were so fond

> 1993 *Albuquerque* (New Mexico) *Journal*: A motherly voice describes herself and her husband as 'empty nesters' who got involved in the environmental movement and ended up as 'enviro-nuts'.

enterprise culture *n* (1980) a model of capitalist society which specifically emphasizes and encourages entrepreneurial activity and speculation, financial self-reliance, etc.

> 1980 *Economist*: Sir Keith [Joseph] himself would agree that industrial policy now begins and ends with the treasury: an economic policy designed to foster the 'enterprise culture'.

EPOS *n*, *adj* (1980) An abbreviation of *electronic point of sale*, a computerized system of stock control in shops, in which bar-codes on goods for sale are scanned electronically at the till, which is in turn linked to a central stock-control computer

> 1990 *Which?*: All of the supermarkets…now have some branches with the EPOS system.

Estuary English *n* (1984) A term applied (with reference to the estuary of the River Thames) to a variety of British accent identified as spreading outwards from London, mainly into the southeast of England, and containing features of both received pronunciation and such regional accents as Cockney. The concept was not widely publicized until the 1990s (and then in a somewhat alarmist way, as yet more evidence of linguistic degradation)

> 1984 David Rosewarne: What I have chosen to term *Estuary English* may now and for the foreseeable future be the strongest native influence upon RP.

> 1993 *Sunday Times*: It is the classless dialect sweeping southern Britain. Estuary English, the 'high cockney' diction typified by Ken Livingstone, Nigel Kennedy and Lord Tebbit, has taken…a hold on the way millions speak.

ethical *adj* (1980) relating to or being investment in enterprises whose activities do not offend against the moral principles of the investor. In the 1990s the scope of the adjective moved on still further, to cover, for example, a country's foreign policy

> 1980 *National Journal* (US): Pension Funds and Ethical Investment, commissioned by California's Consumer Services Agency, looks at the basis for such investing

Euro-sceptic *n, adj* (1986) someone, especially a politician, who is sceptical about the benefits to Britain of increasing cooperation with fellow members of the European Union, especially one who strongly opposes greater political or economic integration. By the 1990s the term had become virtually a euphemism for those on the right wing of the Conservative Party who distrusted all things EU-ish and would rather Britain withdrew altogether—of whom the measured doubt and self-questioning implied in *sceptic* was not a notable feature

> 1986 *Times*: Mrs Thatcher is seen in most of the EEC as a Euro-sceptic at best.

> 1990 *Daily Telegraph*: It would be very regrettable if anyone sought to divert the party down a Euro-sceptic path.

Eurotrash *n* (1983) A contemptuous term for rich European socialites, especially ones living or working in the US. Originally US; based on *trash* 'worthless people' (as in *white trash*)

> 1983 *People*: 'We are Eurotrash,' [Couturier] says of some of his acquaintances. 'We are obnoxious. We are spoiled. We are brats… But…we can also work a lot.'

exit poll *n* (1980) an unofficial poll in which people leaving a polling station are asked how they have voted, used in predicting the result of an election. Originally US

> 1987 *Oxford Diocesan Magazine*: The polls remained…stable (except for that curiously errant 'exit poll' put out by the BBC which accepted the possibility of a hung parliament).

eye-candy *n* (1984) superficially attractive images which provide visual entertainment but fail to engage the intellect. Colloquial, originally and mainly US. A parallel contemporary coinage was *ear-candy*, denoting light undemanding pop music. The ultimate model for both is probably *nose candy*, a slang term for cocaine taken by inhalation which dates from the 1930s

> 1984 D. Seyler & C. Boltz: This ad also features an elegantly dressed woman with conspicuous cleavage, which advertising executives reportedly refer to as 'eye candy'.

> 1997 *Daily Telegraph*: But *Baywatch*, we are told, is not just mildly salacious eye-candy.

fabbo *adj* (1984), **fabby** *adj* (1989), **faberoonie** *adj* (1990) wonderful, marvellous. *Fab*, the youth slang approval word of the early to mid 1960s (see **fab (1957)**), enjoyed a brief revival in the 1980s, and underwent some further embellishments

> 1984 Sue Townsend: A brilliant day today. School broke up for eight fabbo weeks.

> 1989 *Victor*: I think 'Victor' is the best, fabbiest, greatest, most entertaining, best value boys' comic in the whole world.

> 1990 *Fast Forward*: You remember that faberoonie day out Sean had with the excellent *Skee=Beaz jet-ski team*?

Falklands factor *n* (1982) the effect of the Falklands conflict of 1982 on the popularity of British political parties, specifically the electoral boost it was perceived as giving to Margaret Thatcher and the ruling Conservative Party, which had previously been going through a period of unpopularity. Also termed the *Falklands effect*

> 1982 *Washington Post*: One of the Social Democrats' four co-leaders, William Rodgers, said, 'The Falklands factor is a major one' in the disappointing showing of his party.

> 1986 *Observer*: With the Libyan Legacy taking over from the Falklands Factor, the only question about Thursday's local elections is the extent of Labour's gains.

fantasy football *n* (1984) a competition in which participants select imaginary teams from among the real players in an actual football league and score points according to the actual performance of their players. Originally US, and applied to American football, but when the craze spread to British newspapers in the 1990s, it was diverted to soccer. Its success prompted the extension of the concept to other sports, such as *fantasy cricket* and *fantasy basketball*. (A parallel US phenomenon which has not crossed the Atlantic is the *rotisserie league* (first recorded in 1980), in which participants 'buy' actual players (originally baseball players) and score points according to their performances. The term comes from *La Rotisserie*, the name of a restaurant in Manhattan, New York City, where the league was devised)

> 1984 *New York Times*: 'Fantasy Football' is not so much a new idea as the formalization of an old parlor game.

> 1994 *Guardian*: In the past year the Telegraph introduced fantasy football and other games with cash prizes.

fashion victim *n* (1984) a slavish follower of trends, especially in clothing fashion

> 1992 Roger Graef: When the precious jeans were finally on board, he sheepishly conceded there was nothing he could point to which distinguished them from any others—except the label… I felt there was some value in hinting to them that they might be fashion victims rather than connoisseurs.

fattist *adj, n* (1987) (an advocate or practitioner) of unfair discrimination against fat people. One of the more successful of the minor -*ist* creations of the 1980s, modelled on **racist**, **sexist**, and the like. The related *fattism* is first recorded in 1988

> 1988 *Time*: What [Rita Freedman] calls fattism, an inclination to associate thinness with prettiness and goodness, and obesity with lassitude and lack of discipline.

> 1989 *Daily Telegraph*: Mr Lawson has been the subject of grossly fattist caricatures in the popular prints, especially this week.

fatwa, fatwah *n* (1989) an edict or statement issued (as if) by a religious authority, especially one pronouncing a death sentence or calling for some other form of extreme punishment. The Arabic word was borrowed into English in its original sense, 'an edict issued by a Muslim juridical authority', as long ago as the 17th century, but it failed to make much impression until in 1989 the Ayatollah Khomeini, religious leader of Iran, issued such a ruling sentencing the British novelist Salman Rushdie to death for publishing *The Satanic Verses* (1988), a book which many Muslims considered blasphemous and highly offensive. As a result it quickly extended itself metaphorically in various directions. (The Rushdie fatwa was lifted in 1998)

> 1989 *Guardian*: When the Catholic archbishop came out against Noriega, and fatwahs against him were read out in church, the church services in the middle class suburbs turned into political demonstrations against the regime.

> 1995 *Saturday Night*: In 1974, when the splendid Hank Aaron hit his 715th dinger, overtaking the Babe's career record of 714 homers, he suffered something like a fatwa, requiring police protection against the many death threats he received.

feeding frenzy *n* (1989) a voracious competition between would-be purchasers or consumers, especially an instance of insatiable public or media appetite for a news story or its protagonists. The expression had its origins in American English in the 1950s as a term for an aggressive group attack by sharks or other carnivorous fish, and by the 1970s it was being widely used metaphorically ('Which he says has prompted some journalists to act like "sharks in a feeding frenzy"', *San Diego Union* (1977))

> 1989 *Premiere*: I read how the book's author, Kim Wozencraft, had helped manipulate the industry into what Lehman calls a 'feeding frenzy' for the film rights to the book.

> 1994 *Guardian*: There had been a 'feeding frenzy' of speculation and gossip at the House of Commons following news of the MP's death.

feel-good factor *n* (1984) a feeling of satisfaction and well-being derived from a particular object, circumstance, etc. Originally US, but used particularly in British political jargon in the late 1980s and the 90s to denote a feeling of well-being and (financial) security prevailing in a nation, believed to lead to increased consumer spending and satisfaction with the government in power. The ultimate model for the usage is *Doctor Feelgood*, a hypothetical doctor who readily prescribes mood-enhancing drugs, such as amphetamines, for recreational use; he was made famous in a US hit song of 1967

> 1984 *Industry Week*: The 'feel good' factors are the same in Japan as in the United States because human nature is inherently the same East and West.

> 1987 *Business Week*: Thatcher is benefiting from the 'feel good' factor among voters.

Femidom *n* (1989) A proprietary name for a contraceptive sheath worn inside the vagina. A blend of *feminine* and *condom*. The generic alternative *female condom* is first recorded in 1988

1990 *Independent*: They were anything but a joke: Femidom, which was invented by a Danish nurse and tested by volunteers, is still undergoing worldwide trials and should be available in Britain next year.

flame *v, n* (1983) (to post) an electronic message which is destructively critical, abusive, or intended to provoke dissent or controversy. Originally part of the in-slang of the electronic community, it became more widely known in the 1990s as the Internet's influence spread

1993 *C Users Journal*: It always disappoints me to read some flame from a reader who is mostly demonstrating his lack of tact or inability to express an opinion without insulting anyone.

flatline *v* (1980) to die. Originally medical slang, referring to the sudden flatness of the line on a heart or brain monitor when a patient dies. It was taken up and popularized by the science-fiction writer William Gibson in his novel *Neuromancer* (1984), but it did not come into widespread use until the 1990s, following the release of the film *Flatliners*, about medical students who experiment with death. Its subsequent use has been mainly metaphorical, relating especially to finance

1984 William Gibson: He flatlined on his EEG… 'Boy, I was *daid*'.

1992 *Spy*: Not that it was a bad magazine, but it was a fiscal flatliner—with one of Brown's early issues…carrying just 14 pages of ads.

focus group *n* (1984) a group of people chosen to be representative of the population as a whole or of a specific subset of the population, and brought together to take part in guided discussions about consumer products, political policies, etc., so that their attitudes and opinions can be studied. In the 1990s, a leading target of those who see marketing techniques driving principles out of politics

1997 *Times*: The party chairman…insisted on testing the poster with focus groups of floating voters.

foodie *n* (1982) someone who is (obsessively) interested in food; a gourmet. The product of the postwar revolution which made it possible in Anglo-Saxon countries to regard food as an object of enthusiasm and study rather than as a necessary evil. The term was popularized by the publication of Ann Barr and Paul Levy's *The Official Foodie Handbook* in 1984

1982 *Harpers & Queen*: Foodies are foodist. They dislike and despise all non-foodies… The [colour] supplements encouraged the foodie movement.

F Plan Diet *n* (1982) The proprietary name (registered in the US in 1984) of a type of high-fibre diet devised by Audrey Eyton. The *F* stands for 'fibre'—i.e. food material such as bran and cellulose that is not broken down by the process of digestion: what used to be known as **roughage (1927)**

1983 *Financial Times*: The newly promoted F plan diet, which underlined the nutritional value of beans, fortuitously coincided with the Heinz campaign message.

freebase *n* (1980) cocaine purified by heating with ether, and taken by inhaling the fumes or smoking the residue. Slang, originally US; reported in use since 1978, but first widely known in 1980, after the US comedian Richard Pryor was badly burned while preparing the drug. The 'base', or most important ingredient in cocaine, is 'freed' by the process of heating. The verb *freebase*, denoting either preparation or use, is also first recorded in 1980

1980 *New York Times*: A police lieutenant said Mr. Pryor had told a doctor the accident happened while he was trying to make 'free base', a cocaine derivative produced with the help of ether.

1985 *Times*: Cocaine…has traditionally been taken by sniffing but there are reports of 'freebasing', which involves heating the drug to remove impurities and then inhaling the fumes.

-friendly *suffix* (1982) suitable or well adapted to the stated thing; also, not harmful to the stated thing. A usage largely modelled on the successful and popular **user-friendly (1977)**, with perhaps a little help from the parallel German *-freundlich*

1982 *Economist*: I have relished the thought that Fortresses America and Albion may prove unable or unwilling to keep out such 'abominations' as 'environment-friendly packaging' or 'citizen-friendly legislation'.

1985 *Times Educational Supplement*: This subject is considered one of the least 'girl-friendly', because it is more geared towards traditionally masculine interests.

fuck-me *adj* (1981) inviting or perceived as inviting sexual interest; alluring, seductive. Slang; originally (and usually) in the expression *fuck-me shoes*

1981 L. Lochhead: Moira McVitie…shouts out 'Hiya there Verena is that you trying on some fuck-me shoes for yer man gettin back?'

1992 Julian Barnes: Have you ever looked at old men, the sort of old men who seduce young women? The roguish high-bummed stride, the fuck-me tan, the effulgent cuff-links, the reek of dry-cleaning.

fudge *n* (1980) an unsatisfactory or makeshift solution, especially one reached for the sake of expediency; also, sophistry, or prevaricatory or imprecise language or reasoning intended to obfuscate. A noun based on the verbal use of *fudge* to mean 'to prevaricate or temporize' which goes back to at least the late 19th century but which was popularized in 1980 in the phrase *fudge and mudge* (*mudge* in this context is just an arbitrary rhyme on *fudge*). Former Labour foreign secretary David Owen is the first on record as using it ('We are fed up with fudging and mudging, with mush and slush. We need courage, conviction, and hard work', *Guardian* (1980)), and it became for a while a rallying call among those right-wing members of the British Labour Party who eventually split off to form the SDP

1980 *Observer*: The right wing of the party believes that, in concocting his fudge, Mr Callaghan has sold the pass.

1986 *Sunday Express*: On secret ballots there is still a hint of fudge in the Brighton air.

full monty, full monte *n* (1986) everything which is necessary or appropriate; the works. British colloquial. An expression which backed into the spotlight thanks to the success of a 1997 British film called *The Full Monty*, about a group of unemployed men who take to stripping to earn some money. It has been reported in use well before the 1980s, but no written record of it has been discovered before 1986. Its origins (and hence the basis for preferring one or other of its spellings) remain obscure: it has been linked with Field Marshall Montgomery, the British World War II military commander whose nickname was 'Monty', and with the card game monte, but perhaps the most plausible explanation is that it is an abbreviation of the first name of *Montague Burton*, a British firm of mass-market men's tailors—the expression is often used in the context of a complete suit of clothing (or lack of one, following its film debut)

1995 *Guardian*: When conducting a funeral he wears the full monty; frock coat, top hat and a Victorian cane with metal tip.

fund-holding *adj* (1989) Denoting a general practice whose budget is controlled by its own doctor(s). A term which arose out of the NHS reforms introduced in Britain at the end of the 1980s by the Conservative government. The related *fund-holder* is first recorded in 1991

1989 *Independent*: As with self-governing hospitals, which the Bill firmly describes as 'NHS Trusts', ministers have changed the name from 'practice budgets' to 'fund-holding practices' to remove the word budget from the title.

1992 *Economist*: GP fundholders and opted-out hospitals are determined to defend their new-found privileges.

fussed *adj* (1989) interested, concerned, bothered, emotionally engaged in a topic. British colloquial; mainly used in negative contexts, indicating indifference

1989 *What Diet & Lifestyle*: I had thought of joining a slimming club, but Paul said he wasn't fussed.

Game Boy *n* (1989) A proprietary name for a hand-held electronic device, incorporating a small screen, which is used to play computer games loaded in the form of cartridges

1989 *USA Today*: Last weekend…Nintendo unveiled Game Boy, a hand-held portable version of its popular video game.

Gang of Four *n* (1981) the four founder-members of the Social Democratic Party (see **SDP (1981)**): Roy Jenkins, David Owen, William Rodgers, and Shirley Williams. The original of the 'Gang of' formula, applied to a group of people who are outspoken in their advocacy of a particular policy or who take a minority view on an issue, was the 'Gang of Four', a radical faction within the Chinese Communist Party which emerged in 1969 in response to the Cultural Revolution and was suppressed following the death of Mao Tse-tung in 1976; the name was a translation of Chinese *sìrénbāng*, literally 'four-person gang'. Adapted to 'Gang of Three', it was applied to three leading disaffected right-wing members of the British Labour Party who, following Labour's lurch to the left after its 1979 election defeat, were considering leaving the party ('Mr. William

Rodgers...brushed aside Mr. David Steel's appeal for Labour's so-called "Gang of Three" to give up their fight against the Left of their party', *Daily Telegraph* (1980)). When they were joined by Roy Jenkins, they became the 'Gang of Four'

> 1985 *Guardian*: He did not reserve his characteristic gentleness for Mr Bill Rodgers, one of Mrs Williams's co-defectors in the Gang of Four.

garage *n* (1987) a New York variety of house music, influenced by soul, and with powerful vocals and a strong emphasis on the lyrics. Named after Paradise Garage, a dance club in Manhattan, New York City

> 1987 *Blues & Soul*: From New York comes this 'garage' instrumental, basically more useful for dee-jays in a 'House' mix rather than a great record on its own merit.

gazunder *v* (1988) Of a house-buyer: to reduce the price offered to (a seller) for a property, especially shortly before exchange of contracts, threatening to withdraw if the new offer is not accepted. British colloquial; a facetious combination of **gazump (1928)** and *under*, perhaps partly inspired by a memory of the earlier euphemism *gazunder* 'chamber-pot'. The coinage was called into being by the house-price slump of the late 1980s

> 1988 *Gloucestershire Echo*: If one of them is nearing exchange of contracts there may be no alternative but to accept, to prevent the collapse of the chain. The vendor will have been gazundered.

gender bender *n* (1980), **gender blender** *n* (1983) someone, especially a pop singer or follower of a pop cult, who deliberately affects an androgynous appearance by wearing sexually ambiguous clothing, make-up, etc. The derived *gender-b(l)ending* is first recorded in 1984. The US tends to favour the *blender* variant, which perhaps has too many culinary associations for British speakers

> 1980 *Economist*: The cult hallows ambiguous sexuality: Mr David Bowie, the rock star 'gender bender', is a key hero.

> 1983 *Washington Post*: Boy George, with his urban beachcomber look and gender-blender confusions, manages to fit in and stand out.

> 1984 *Observer*: This 'gender-bending', as it has been dubbed, is not news in the world of popular music.

ghetto-blaster *n* (1981) a large portable stereo radio (and cassette player), especially one on which pop music is played loudly. Originally US. There was a vogue amongst inner-city youths, and especially blacks, in the US around 1978–82 for carrying around such radios with the volume turned up to danger level—whence the name. An even less politically correct alternative was *third-world briefcase*

> 1983 *Daily Mirror*: A beat throbbing from a ghetto-blaster—a giant, portable stereo system.

girl power *n* (1986) power exercised by girls. Often applied specifically to a self-reliant attitude among girls and young women manifested in ambition, assertiveness, and individualism. Linked in the 1990s with the briefly prominent 'riot girl' ethos (see **riot girl (1992)**), in which connection it is often spelt *grrl power*. Latterly associated mainly with the Spice Girls, a British all-female pop group

> 1986 *Los Angeles Times*: 'Girl Power: Health Power' motivates girls to assume long-term responsibility for their health and fitness.

> 1994 *Rolling Stone*: It has four all-girl bands... All amazing. Part of the grrrl-power underground that's so exciting.

> 1997 *J-17*: If something you've bought isn't up to standard, remember you're entitled to complain. Use your girl power and don't let the shop assistant fob you off!

glasnost *n* (1986) a declared Soviet policy from 1985 of greater openness and frankness in public statements, including the publication of news reflecting adversely on the government and political system; greater freedom of speech and information arising from this policy. The Russian word *glasnost* (literally 'the fact of being public') is recorded in dictionaries from the 18th century, but in the more general sense of 'publicity'. It was used in the context of freedom of information in the Soviet State by Lenin, and called for in an open letter to the Soviet Writers' Union by Aleksandr Solzhenitsyn in 1969, but did not become a subject of serious public debate in the Soviet Union until an *Izvestiya* editorial requested letters on the subject on 19 January 1985. Its use by Mikhail

Gorbachev on 11 March 1985 in a speech accepting the post of General Secretary of the CPSU subsequently led to its being associated particularly with his policies. With the benefit of hindsight, one of the first significant cracks in the wall of Communism, which was to collapse in Eastern Europe before the end of the decade. See also **perestroika (1986)**

> 1986 *New York Times*: Exposes of corruption, shortages and economic problems appear virtually daily in the [Soviet] press. It is a change that became evident after Mikhail Gorbachev came to office last March and called for more 'glasnost', or openness, in covering domestic affairs.

glass ceiling *n* (1984) an unofficial or unacknowledged barrier to personal advancement, especially of a woman or a member of an ethnic minority in employment. Originally US

> 1984 *Adweek*: Women have reached a certain point—I call it the glass ceiling. They're in the top of middle management and they're stopping and getting stuck.

gnarly *adj* (1982) excellent, wonderful, cool. US slang. A piece of Valspeak which apparently originated in 1970s surfers' slang, where it meant 'difficult, dangerous' (perhaps from the appearance of rough sea). It went on to be used more generally in the sense 'unpleasant, unattractive', and then seems to have done a flip-flop in the early 1980s into an approval adjective

> 1982 S. Black: Stylish belt. It looks totally gnarly.

> 1991 *Tulsa World*: This to me is gnarly. Cool. Radical. Intense. It makes a statement.

goalposts *n move* (*shift*, etc.) *the goalposts* (1984) to alter the terms of a procedure, agreement, argument, etc., usually without telling those affected; to change the rules. Colloquial

> 1989 *Dimensions*: Many companies have, in recent years, moved the corporate goalposts so that those who used to qualify no longer do so.

gobsmacked *adj* (1985) flabbergasted, astounded; speechless or incoherent with amazement. British slang, probably based on *gob* 'mouth'—the underlying idea being 'struck dumb as if by a smack in the face'. In spoken use for several decades, especially in Northern dialects, but not recorded in print until the 1980s, when its quirky earthiness suddenly endeared it to newspaper writers. The synonymous *gob-struck* is first recorded in 1988

> 1988 *Gay Times*: I was that gob-struck at the barefaced cheek of the man that I couldn't say anything coherent.

> 1989 *Daily Telegraph*: When told the price, between 10 and five times over estimate, he was 'gobsmacked'.

go-faster stripes *n* (1985) ornamental stripes adorning the side of a car or other vehicle. Regarded in some quarters as betraying a lack of style

> 1985 *Times*: The sales of a vehicle are affected more by go-faster stripes on the side than a better lock.

golden hello *n* (1983) a substantial sum offered to a senior executive, etc., as an inducement to change employers, and paid in advance when the new post is accepted. Yet another humorous variation on **golden handshake (1960)** coined in the feverish years of 1980s corporate rivalry

> 1983 *Observer*: Following the 'golden handshake', the 'golden hello' is taking root in British industry. Being paid a handsome lump sum before you even start a new job may sound too good to be true. But, last year alone, 50 top directors got such 'golden hellos'.

golden parachute *n* (1981) a long-term contractual agreement guaranteeing financial security to senior executives dismissed as a result of their company being taken over or merged with another. Originally US; a facetious coinage based on **golden handshake (1960)**

> 1990 *New York Times Book Review*: It wasn't long before most of RJR Nabisco's top executives 'pulled the rip cords on their golden parachutes'... Mr Johnson's alone was worth $53 million.

gothic *adj* (1983) Denoting a style of rock music, and the youth culture associated with it, deriving originally from punk, and characterized by the dramatically stark appearance of its performers and followers (white-faced with heavy black make-up and mainly black clothing with bulky metallic jewellery) and by mystical or apocalyptic lyrics. The style itself is called *goth* and its fans *goths* (both first recorded in 1986). The general air of sepulchral gloom linked them with Gothic fantasy of the early 19th-century variety, from which they took their name

> 1983 *New Musical Express*: Why is this gothic glam so popular?

1986 *City Limits*: Hamish and Dave Birkman battled against traditional dancefloor ideas with a complete mish mash of funk, rock, goth.

grant-maintained *adj* (1987) Designating a secondary school funded directly by central government rather than by a local authority. A concept introduced in the late 1980s by the Conservative government in Britain. The decision to become grant-maintained was, in theory at least, one left to each individual school; see also **opt out (1987)**

1993 *Times Educational Supplement*: Piqued that an avalanche of grant-maintained schools has not yet occurred, the Government is using fiscal measures to tip the balance and drive more schools to opt out.

grebo *n* (1987) (a member of) an urban youth cult in Britain characterized by musical tastes bridging heavy metal and punk rock, an aggressive or anti-social manner, and long hair and clothes reminiscent of the earlier biker or greaser generation. Possibly coined from *greaser* plus the ending *-bo*, as in *dumbo, jumbo*

1987 *Sounds*: This is Pop Will Eat Itself's triumphant, Grolsch soaked finale to a pimply pop pepped 12 song 'designer grebo' set.

greenmail *n* (1983) the practice of buying enough shares in a firm or trading company to threaten a take-over, thereby forcing the owners to buy them back at a premium in order to retain control of the business. Stock market jargon, originally US; a punning substitution of US slang *greens* 'money, dollars' for the *black* of *blackmail*. Also used as a verb

1983 *National Law Journal* (US): Corporations are scurrying to combat a perceived threat from those professional investors who practice 'greenmail'—putting pressure on a company to get a buy-out for cash.

1984 *Financial Times*: It is not every year that CJR will have the chance to greenmail St Regis.

gridlock *n* (1981) a situation in which no progress can be made; an impasse or deadlock. Originally US; a metaphorical use of the earlier *gridlock* 'a traffic jam affecting a whole network (or *grid*) of streets', which is first recorded in 1980

1985 *British Medical Journal*: The National Health Service is trapped in gridlock and lacks the incentives to break out.

hacker *n* (1983) someone who uses their skill with computers to try to gain unauthorized access to computer files or networks. Colloquial; a term which evolved from **hacking** 'the use of computers as a hobby' (1976). By the middle of the decade the back-formed verb *hack* was being used in this sense, usually accompanied by *into*

1983 *Daily Telegraph*: A hacker…yesterday penetrated a confidential British Telecom message system being demonstrated live on BBC-TV.

1985 *Times*: The equipment needed can be used quite legitimately…But it can also be used to hack into other people's computers.

Haigspeak *n* (1981) convoluted or obfuscatory language of a type supposedly characteristic of Alexander Haig, especially in his dealings with the press while US Secretary of State 1981–82

1983 Gerald Priestland: 'A flexible pluralistic dialogue',…'a comprehensive pressurized capability'…it all sounds like good, convincing Haig-speak.

handbag *v* (1982) to subject to a forthright verbal assault or to strident criticism, as if battering with a handbag. Used originally and mainly with reference to Margaret Thatcher, British Prime Minister 1979–90

1982 *Economist*: One of her less reverent backbenchers said of Mrs Thatcher recently that 'she can't look at a British institution without hitting it with her handbag'. Treasury figures published last week show how good she has proved at handbagging the civil service.

1988 *Guardian*: Don't we all…simply adore the idea of foreign politicians (male) and recalcitrant members of her own party (mostly male) being handbagged?

happy bunny *n* (1989) See **bunny (1989)**

hell *n from hell* (1987) exceptionally bad or unpleasant. Originally US; often used facetiously

1992 *Foreign Student & Au Pair Magazine*: The Au Pair from Hell…waits to be served dinner with the rest of the family unless asked to help dish up.

1994 *Sugar*: Next day, she returned from trawling the junk shops with the Curtains from Hell—dark purple and green tie-dyed horrors that soaked up more daylight.

help-line *n* (1980) a telephone service which specializes in providing information, advice, and help with problems. Originally US. See also **Childline (1986)**

1980 *New York Times*: Agencies to Coordinate Homebound Services…hired a social worker, set up a homebound helpline…and created public awareness and advocacy campaigns on behalf of shut-ins.

high-five *n* (1980) a gesture of celebration or greeting in which two people slap each other's palms, usually with their arms extended over their heads. Originally US basketball slang; *five* is from the fingers. First recorded as a verb in 1981

1980 *Maclean's Magazine*: They used to slap palms ('Gimme five, man'), but what they do now is reach high and bang hands up there ('The high five, man').

1981 *Washington Post*: The first Phil out of the dugout after the Maddox mash was Rose, jumping and high-fiving it, hair flapping, a 40-year-old acting 14.

himbo *n* (1988) an attractive but unintelligent young man; the male equivalent of a **bimbo (1920)**. Originally US; a journalistic coinage of around the time when bimbos were making all the front pages, intended to give equal billing to the mono-brain-celled beaux of female film stars and the like

1988 *Washington Post*: From a Melanie Griffith look-alike stuffed into her gown like salami in spandex to the macho himbo who strutted the Croisette wearing a 16-foot python like a stole around his shoulders and neck.

hip-hop *n* (1982) a youth subculture, originating amongst the black and Hispanic population of New York City, which comprises elements such as rap music, graffiti art, and break dancing, as well as distinctive codes of dress and speech; also, the music associated with this subculture, characterized by often politically inspired or motivated raps, delivered above spare electronic backing, and harsh rhythm tracks. Formed alliteratively from **hip** 'fashionable, cool' and *hop* 'dance'

1984 *Washington Post*: Like breakdancing, rap and hip hop in general flourished at street level despite overexposure in too many 'breaksploitation' films and a virtual end to exposure in the media.

HIV *n* (1986) An abbreviation of *human immunodeficiency virus*, either of two retroviruses (HIV–1, HIV-2) which cause Aids. The fact that the *V* stands for *virus* is often overlooked, resulting in the tautological *HIV virus*

1986 *Capital Gay*: An international committee on viral names has been looking into the problem, and was rumoured to have agreed on 'human immune deficiency virus' (HIDV or HIV).

1987 *Daily Telegraph*: One of the two blood donors had been found not to be carrying the HIV virus, but the other could not be traced.

hole-in-the-wall *n* (1985) an automatic cash dispenser installed in the (outside) wall of a bank or other building. Colloquial, mainly British

1987 *Today*: Three [banks], along with Bank of Scotland…are set to unveil their joint hole-in-the-wall cash machine network.

hoolivan *n* (1985) a type of police van carrying photographic and video equipment for observing crowd behaviour and identifying trouble-makers at football matches and other events. British; a blend of *hooligan* and *van*

1985 *Daily Telegraph*: The 'hoolivan' designed to detect trouble-makers in football crowds, was unveiled at the Chelsea-Luton match at Stamford Bridge last night.

hospital trust *n* (1989) a self-governing administrative body within the British National Health Service, comprising a hospital, or a group of neighbouring hospitals, which has withdrawn from local health authority control. Also known as an *NHS trust*. An element in the Conservative government's NHS reforms (see also **fund-holding (1989)**)

1991 *Pulse*: Mr Waldegrave…implicitly admitted at a press conference that hospital trusts and GP fund-holders would create a two-tier NHS service.

hothousing *n* (1985) the policy or practice of artificially accelerating the intellectual development of a child by intensive teaching from an early age. *Hothouse* had been used as a verb by education-ists since at least the early 1960s, denoting intensive education (the underlying idea is, of course, of forcing a plant in a hothouse or greenhouse). The theory that gave rise to this specialized applica-tion became fashionable in the US in the late 1970s

> 1988 *Observer*: Their father…wanted to test the hot-housing theory; that if you subject a normally intelligent child to intensive, specialised training in a particular discipline at a very early age, you will produce excellence.

house *n* (1986) a type of pop music, originally created by disc jockeys in dance-clubs, which typic-ally features the use of drum machines, sequencers, sampled sound effects, and prominent syn-thesized bass lines, in combination with sparse, repetitive vocals and a fast beat. Originally US; it probably took its name from the Warehouse, a night-club in Chicago where this music was first popularized around 1985. See also **Acid house (1988)**

> 1986 *Q*: Washington has Go-Go, The Bronx gave the world hip-hop and Chicago, that toddlin' town, steps forward with House Music.

> 1988 *New Statesman*: The pirates hype…the neo-disco known as house.

icon *n* (1982) a small symbolic picture of a physical object on a VDU screen, especially one that rep-resents a particular option (e.g. a small picture of a pen representing the word-processing option) and can be selected to exercise that option. Towards the end of the decade the *icon* was punningly joined by the *earcon*, denoting a symbolic sound representing an option (based on a reinterpreta-tion of *icon* as *eyecon*)

> 1982 *Computerworld*: Star's screen displays black characters on a white background. These are known as icons on the Star and are equivalent to the familiar physical object in an office.

income support *n* (1985) a means-tested welfare benefit introduced in Britain in 1988 to replace supplementary benefit

> 1985 *Daily Telegraph*: Income support is the name of the new benefit which will replace Supplementary Benefit, criticised by the Green Paper as too difficult for claimants to understand.

infomercial, informercial *n* (1981) an advertising film, usually shown on television, which pro-motes a product, service, etc. in an informative and purportedly objective style. Originally US, and associated particularly with the US businessman and politician Ross Perot. *Informercial* is a straight blend of *information* and *commercial*; *infomercial*, which has been more successful in the long run, is constructed using the prefix *info-*. This spawned a wide range of terms in the information-technology era of the 1980s and 90s, including *infomania, infopreneur, infosphere, infosystem,* and *infotech*. See also **infotainment (1980)**. The newspaper equivalent is **advertorial (1961)**

> 1981 *Christian Science Monitor*: Educational commercials, or so-called 'informercials'…are attract-ing much interest. J. Walter Thompson has been producing several at its own expense.

> 1991 *Time*: The Federal Trade Commission has cracked down on a handful of infomercials for unsubstantiated claims.

information superhighway *n* (1985) any of a number of projected national high-speed, high-capacity telecommunications networks linking homes and offices and permitting the trans-mission of a variety of electronic media, including video, audio, multimedia, and text. Based on the idea of a multi-lane road for high-speed traffic (see **superhighway (1925)**). Often abbrevi-ated in US English to *I-way*

> 1993 *New York Times*: One of the technologies Vice President Al Gore is pushing is the information superhighway, which will link everyone at home or office to everything else—movies and television shows, shopping services, electronic mail and huge collections of data.

infotainment *n* (1980) a form of television entertainment which seeks to present factual material in a lively and entertaining way

> 1988 *Courier-Mail* (Brisbane): Both shows are halfway between hard news and current affairs, being more in the lifestyle/'infotainment' mould. Will this 'infotainment' train ever run out of steam?

instant *n* (1985) a lottery ticket which can be scratched, opened, etc. to reveal immediately whether a prize has been won. Originally US, but familiarized in Britain following the introduction of the National Lottery in 1994. See also **scratch card (1982)**

> 1985 *Los Angeles Times*: Give me a six-play Megabucks and two instants.

> 1995 *Daily Telegraph*: Instants are on sale to the over 16s and we feel at that age and over, people are responsible enough to decide how much they spend.

internal market *n* (1989) a system of decentralized funding within an organization by which each department is responsible for its own budget and charges other departments at a market rate for services it provides

> 1991 *Pulse*: Only days before he was expected to compete in the NHS's new so-called internal market, north-east Thames region accepted…Dr David Keene's claim for a budget of £50 per patient to cover hospital referrals.

Internet *n* (1986) Originally applied to a set of linked computer networks operated by the US Defense Department, and hence to the global computer network which evolved out of this, providing a variety of information and communication services to its users, and consisting of a loose confederation of interconnected networks which use standardized protocols. Both these usages represent a specific application of *internet* 'a set of linked networks' (first recorded in 1974), which in turn is a shortening of the synonymous *internetwork*

> 1986 *Network World*: The electronic mail net runs over Internet, an international network of networks operated by the Department of Defense.

> 1997 *Times*: Where most tourist services on the Internet can only provide text and picture data on places of interest, InferNet is going one step better and including an accurate scale map of locations as well.

intifada *n* (1985) an Arab uprising or revolt, specifically the Palestinian insurrection in the Israeli-occupied West Bank and Gaza Strip, which began in late 1987. The word in Arabic means literally 'a jumping up (in reaction to some external stimulus)'. It is derived from the verb *intafada* 'to be shaken, shake oneself'

> 1988 *Daily Telegraph*: The *intifada* is unequivocally a demonstration of support for the PLO and an independent Palestine, not for any half-way arrangement in which Jordan plays a prominent part.

Irangate *n* (1986) a scandal involving allegations that profits from US arms sales to Iran had been diverted to aid anti-government guerrillas in Nicaragua. One of the more high-profile offspring of **Watergate (1972)**

> 1986 *Independent*: It is all too easy for Mr Reagan…to see 'Irangate' purely in domestic American terms.

IT *n* (1982) An abbreviation of **information technology (1958)**

> 1982 *Times*: Teletext and personal computers are IT, but Hollywood movies on a video machine are probably not.

jewel box *n* (1984) a flat square plastic case in which an audio CD is packaged and stored. A metaphor based on the size of such boxes, the extent to which their contents are prized, and the colourful designs with which many are embellished

> 1984 *New York Times*: What seem to have been ignored are the shortcomings of the original hard plastic 'jewel box' housing the Compact Disk.

job club *n* (1985) an organization set up in the UK either by a local community or by a Job Centre which aims to help the long-term unemployed find work, by offering encouragement and material support such as free postage and use of a telephone. One of a range of such government initiatives to counter the high unemployment of the early and mid 1980s

> 1985 *Financial Times*: A chain of 200 'jobclubs' is to be established by the end of next year to help the long-term unemployed.

keyhole surgery *n* (1988) surgery in which an instrument such as an optical-fibre endoscope, laparoscope, or arthroscope is used, via a very small incision, to view the operation area, and usually involving remotely controlled surgical instruments. A colloquial term; the official name is *minimally invasive surgery*

> 1994 *Guardian*: Keyhole surgery is used extensively in knee operations, with minimal scarring and faster recovery, and is being tried in hernia repair, although this is still controversial.

kicking *adj* (1989) exciting, lively; great, excellent. Slang; probably an extension of earlier 1980s slang 'having a fast, lively, musical beat'

> 1989 *Just Seventeen*: Her latest song is really kickin' and we think she's probably the best female newcomer.

> 1991 *Sun*: The joint was kicking.

killing field *n* (1983) a place of warfare or unrest involving heavy loss of life, especially as a result of massacre or genocide. Usually used in the plural. Popularized as the name of the film *The Killing Fields* (1984), about the massacre of three million Cambodians under Pol Pot's Communist Khmer Rouge regime in the mid 1970s

> 1983 *New York Times*: Foreign tourists could be flown in to see both the monument and a sample of Mr. Pol Pot's killing fields.

> 1995 *Focus*: The tens of thousands of ritualised revenge-killings that have in recent times transformed Haiti into a killing field.

kissogram, kissagram *n* (1982) a novelty telegram or greetings message sent through a commercial agency, which is delivered (usually by a provocatively dressed young woman) with a kiss, especially to amuse or embarrass the recipient. Probably the most successful of the facetious *-gram* coinages of the late 1970s and early 1980s (see **-gram (1979)**). However, it was not entirely a neologism: a 'Kissogram Post Card' (Valentine Series) was available in the 1900s. The sender could leave the imprint of a kiss on the face of the card, above a sentimental verse ('…But it's you that I'd rather be "kissing"').

> 1982 *Standard*: Kissagrams. 286 9531.

> 1984 *Times*: A kissogram employer who parked his car illegally rather than allow his scantily-clad girls to walk too far was fined £10 on each of nine charges.

lager lout *n* (1987) a young man who behaves in an aggressive, boorish manner, typically in a group, as a result of drinking too much alcohol, especially lager. British colloquial. Lager louts came into the spotlight in 1988 following a bout of press reports of post-pub violence in country towns previously thought of as quiet and peaceful

> 1987 C. Thompson: When the lager lout says that beer is an old man's drink, the reply is to ask if they have ever thought of growing up.

lambada *n* (1988) a fast rhythmical erotic dance of Brazilian origin, in which couples dance with their stomachs touching each other. The word in Brazilian Portuguese means literally 'a beating, a lashing'. The dance became suddenly fashionable at the end of the 1980s, perhaps as a result of the craze for **dirty dancing (1987)**

> 1989 *Los Angeles Times*: *Lambada* brings couple dancing back with a vengeance.

LAN *n* (1981) An acronym formed from the initial letters of *local area network* (first recorded in 1977), a network by means of which computers can communicate with each other, the quality of communication being higher than that achieved in wide area networks because of the relative proximity of the computers, which are typically in the same building or on the same site

> 1984 *Times*: 90 percent of office data systems do not require LANs as such.

lap dancing *n* (1988) erotic dancing or striptease performed close to, or sitting on the lap of, a paying customer. Originally US

> 1995 *Guardian*: Lap dancing has taken America's clubs by storm—and now the personalised strip show has arrived here.

lap-top *adj*, *n* (1984) (a computer) small and light enough to be used on one's lap. A coinage modelled on **desktop (1968)**. See also **palm-top (1987)**

> 1984 *Fortune*: Led by Tandy's four-pound Radio Shack Model 100…the lap-tops are selling briskly.

> 1984 *Byte*: Laptop portables such as Gavilan were stealing the show.

leaderene *n* (1980) Originally, a facetious or ironic nickname for Margaret Thatcher as British Leader of the Opposition and then Prime Minister; later applied during the 1980s to any (formidable) female leader. Coined (by Conservative MP Norman St John Stevas) from *leader*, perhaps by analogy with French *speakerine* 'female television presenter'; the spelling of the suffix probably comes from names like *Irene* and *Marlene*

> 1980 *Private Eye*: The Leaderene is devastatingly impressed by her new recruit, we were told.

level playing field *n* (1981) a state or condition of parity or impartiality; fair play. Colloquial, originally US. By the 1990s the expression had become a cliché, especially in the world of politics

> 1995 *Accountancy*: They are still not providing a level playing field in terms of opportunities for women.

Liberal Democrat *n, adj* (1989) (a member) of a British political party which was formed by merging the Liberal and Social Democratic parties (formed in 1988 under the name 'Social and Liberal Democrats' and renamed in 1989). Often used in the abbreviated form *Lib-Dem*, which is also first recorded in 1989

> 1989 *Times*: Mr Paddy Ashdown…is expected to announce this morning that the third force in British politics will be known as the Liberal Democrats.

> 1992 *Financial Times*: The uncertainty caused by a hung parliament with the Liberal Democrats holding the balance of power would have been worse… A second line of argument, propounded in this space immediately after the 1987 election, is that Labour should make its peace with the Lib-Dems.

life *n get a life* (1985) to adopt a more worthwhile and meaningful lifestyle (e.g. by making new acquaintances or developing new interests, and by abandoning one's usual pointless or solitary pursuits). Originally US college slang. Usually used in the imperative as a criticism aimed at sad or pathetic individuals

> 1993 *SFRA Review*: Shatner exhorts *Star Trek* fans to 'get a life!'

liposuction *n* (1983) a technique of cosmetic surgery in which particles of excess fat (Greek *lipos* 'fat') are loosened and then removed by being sucked through an incision using a vacuum pump. Hailed as the fatties' magic bullet: weight loss without the stress of dieting

> 1986 *Choice*: With liposuction bruising and rippling in the skin can occur where skin is very lax or excessive fat is removed.

loadsa (1987) Representing a casual pronunciation of *loads of*. British; popularized originally in the expression *loadsamoney*, a catchphrase of the comedian Harry Enfield, with which he satirized the yobbish plutocrats of the 1980s. It was subsequently taken up by journalists and headline-writers and put to other uses. Compare **lotta (1906)**, **lotsa (1927)**

> 1988 *Daily Telegraph*: Any claim that the Conservatives want to see the newly tax-cut flaunting their wealth in a vulgar, 'loadsamoney' fashion would horrify [Margaret Thatcher].

> 1988 *The Sport*: [A parliamentary bill to ban some types of pornography] stands no chance and would deprive loadsa people— men and women—of a lot of pleasure.

Lymeswold *n* (1981) The proprietary name of an English blue cheese, soft in texture and mild-tasting, introduced in 1982. It was invented to suggest bucolicism—there never was a real place called *Lymeswold* (although it may have been suggested by *Wymeswold*, the name of a town in Leicestershire). Despite the fanfare that accompanied its launch, the cheese never really caught on, and it was withdrawn from sale in 1992

> 1988 *Guardian Weekly*: While never personally threatening (the man is as mild as Lymeswold) his confrontations with authority and plain folk going about their business are…entirely unpredictable and demand reaction.

mad cow disease *n* (1989) A colloquial name for **BSE (1987)**, reflecting with black humour its effect on the behaviour of cattle suffering from it. Mainly British; the coinage produced a brief flutter of more or less frivolous look-alikes, such as *mad chicken disease*, and was widely borrowed in translation in countries which banned British beef (e.g. *vache folle* in French). See also **beef war (1996)**

> 1996 *Private Eye*: In the West Country it is common knowledge that 'mad cow disease' was present at epidemic levels long before it was 'discovered' by Maffia [i.e. Ministry of Agriculture, Fisheries, and Food] vets in Kent in 1985.

MailMerge *n* (1981) A proprietary name for a program that draws on a file of names and addresses and a text file to produce multiple copies of a letter each addressed to a different recipient. Later also used as a verb

> 1986 *British Journal of Aesthetics*: *Nota Bene* has…mailmerge, and automatic generation of tables and contents.

> 1991 *Which?*: To send a letter to lots of people, you can 'mailmerge' it.

make *v make my day* (1983) gratify me by acting in a way which justifies my being violent towards you. Colloquial, mainly US; popularized as a remark made by the character Dirty Harry (played by Clint Eastwood) in the film *Sudden Impact*

> 1984 *Washington Post*: He was going to tell voters Mondale was promising everything to the elderly, minorities, labor, teachers, women, small farmers and those with liberal defense and foreign policy views. And Mondale said: 'Go ahead. Make my day.'

> 1991 *Vanity Fair*: He's from the…Clint Eastwood 'Make My Day' school and we don't need that in 1991 in the chief of police.

marketization *n* (1980) the exposure of an industry or service to market forces; also, the conversion of a national economy from a planned to a market economy. A favourite term of the market-obsessed 80s

> 1980 Alvin Toffler: The evidence points to the end of the process of marketization, if not in our time, then soon after.

> 1993 *New Republic*: Does it advance or slow the marketization of the Russian economy?

massive *adj* (1984) Of pop groups, etc.: especially successful or influential. Slang

> 1984 *Sounds*: Personally, I'm convinced that the Immaculate Fools are going to be massive and that singer Kevin Weatherill has what could become a Voice of the 80s.

mattress money *n* (1980) the savings of private individuals, especially as a source of commercial revenue. US business slang, referring to the supposed custom of hiding savings inside or under the mattress

> 1990 *New York Times*: A main aim of the legitimized dollar exchange is to tap into the 'mattress money', the huge stash of dollars held by Poles…that has had little legitimate place in the economy.

max *n to the max* (1980) to the limit; totally. US slang, originally among teenage girls in California (see **Valspeak (1982)**). *Max* as an abbreviation of *maximum* has been around since at least the middle of the 19th century

> 1989 *The Face*: On stage and in interview, Sandra Bernhard works her sharp tongue to the max.

ME *n* (1982) An abbreviation of *myalgic encephalomyelitis* (first recorded in 1956), a disease of unknown cause but usually occurring after a viral infection, and characterized by headaches, fever, localized muscular pains, extreme fatigue, and weakness. It, or its diagnosis, became prevalent during the 1980s, and, partly because of the mystery surrounding it, it went under a number of alternative names, including *post-viral (fatigue) syndrome, chronic fatigue syndrome, Iceland disease* (from an outbreak in 1948–49 in Akureyri, northern Iceland), and **yuppie flu (1988)**

> 1990 *Health Now*: It is widely taken throughout Brazil as an antidote to stress and is potentially a very valuable supplement for increasing energy levels of ME sufferers.

medallion man *n* (1985) an often middle-aged man favouring tasteless and flashy clothes, especially an open-necked shirt displaying a medallion, frequently nestling in luxuriant chest-hair

> 1993 *Wine*: Mont Marçal…is regularly consumed by Julio Iglesias, king of the aging medallion men.

meeter and greeter *n* (1987) someone employed to greet and deal with customers, clients, or other members of the public. The professionalization of bonhomie

> 1987 *Nation's Restaurant News*: Anthony…still prefers the back-of-the-house to the front. Vince, on the other hand, is a born meeter-and-greeter.

meets *v* (1983) The third-person present singular of *meet*, used quasi-conjunctionally to mean 'combined with'. Originally US; a usage based on the title-formula 'X meets Y', used in books and especially films to suggest a momentous confrontation (e.g. 'Godzilla Meets King Kong')

1990 *Guardian*: Bob Dylan meets Half Man Half Biscuit meets Frank Zappa. Even more eclectic than that, Dutch band Trespassers W. do Brecht on acid.

mega *adj* (1982) huge, enormous. Colloquial, originally US; a transformation of the prefix *mega-* 'very large' into an adjective in its own right. By the middle of the decade it was being widely used as an approval word, meaning 'excellent, great', and also as an intensifying adverb

1982 *Guardian*: Valspeak is…the funnest, most totally radical language, I guess, like in the whole mega gnarly city of Los Angeles.

1987 *New Musical Express*: It's a crap record but I had to have it. Look at it. Isn't it mega? What a great sleeve!

megastore *n* (1982) a very large retail store, often one specializing in a particular type of product

1985 *Investors Chronicle*: Virgin and HMV have set up megastores.

Mexican wave *n* (1986) See **wave (1984)**

microlight *adj, n* (1981) (of or being) a small, low-speed, inexpensive, usually one-seater aircraft that has a small engine but can also soar and whose fuselage is an open framework without an enclosed cockpit. The term usually used in British English for what is known in the US as an *ultra-light* (1974)

1981 *Times*: Microlight flying will appeal to the Biggles factor in most adults… The microlight association defines the aircraft as one weighing no more than 150 kilogrammes with a minimum wing area of 10 square metres.

Middle England *n* (1983) the majority of middle-class people in England (sometimes specifically outside London), variously regarded as representative of traditional social values, provincial mores, or conservative political views. Modelled on *Middle America* (first recorded in this sense in 1968), and slightly predated by the parallel but rather less frequent *Middle Britain* ('Middle Britain thinks…one puff on the joint leads to the needle', *Listener* (1973))

1983 *Guardian Weekly*: Some of [Margaret Thatcher's] opponents snobbishly underestimated her popular appeal and her empathy with middle-class, Middle England into whose ranks were moving the upwardly mobile working class.

1995 *Sunday Times*: I trust officialdom will not be foolish enough to take the nurses on in a needless dispute. Middle England is watching.

minder *n* (1980) someone employed to accompany or assist another person, either to provide protection or advice, or to monitor that person's movements. The word has been used in British criminals' slang since the 1920s to denote a criminal's bodyguard. This semantic extension was no doubt set in train by the popularity of the Thames TV series *Minder* (1979–93), about the activities of small-time London crooks. Later in the 80s it was broadened out still further to cover a political adviser, especially a senior politician who protects a less experienced one from embarrassment or mistakes, particularly in an election campaign

1988 *Times*: The minder, Mr Simon Burns, Conservative MP for Chelmsford, directed all enquiries about the plans of Mr Nigel Lawson to the press office.

1989 *Times*: Her London lawyer and minder…had struck a deal with a British newspaper to reveal the secrets she has so far coyly refused to disclose.

minimart *n* (1981) a small shop or supermarket, especially one that stays open late and sells household essentials

1994 *Daily Telegraph*: Her Royal Highness would also be advised to stroll from any earmarked residence to the following facilities, and measure the distance: launderette, pub, minimart, bus stop, newsagent.

Mockney *n* (1989) (someone who adopts) a form of speech perceived as an inauthentic and affected imitation of Cockney in accent and vocabulary, usually adopted to conceal the speaker's privileged background. British; a blend of *mock* and *Cockney*

1994 *Guardian*: In interview, Mick Jagger may be the world's most famous Mockney (compare his current roadie's slur to the polite vicar's son enunciating in blurred sixties' clips).

moonwalking *n* (1980) an exaggeratedly slow action, dance, or method of proceeding which resembles the characteristic weightless movement of walking on the moon. Applied specifically in the late 1980s to a style of dancing popularized by US entertainer Michael Jackson, involving appearing to move forwards while in fact sliding backwards

> 1980 *Christian Science Monitor*: One hang balloon thrill is 'moon walking': heating the balloon until you are almost weightless and then hopping across the landscape as if gravity were a figment of Sir Isaac Newton's imagination.

> 1988 *Los Angeles Times*: Kids think they were the first ones to come up with moonwalking and poplocking.

mosh *v* (1987) to dance in a violent manner involving jumping up and down and deliberately hitting other dancers, especially at a rock concert. Originally and mainly US. The origins of the word are not clear; it may be a variant of *mash* 'to crush to a pulp'

> 1987 *US News & World Report*: On the floor beside the stage, the boys begin to 'mosh', slamming shoulder to shoulder with abandon.

motion discomfort bag *n* (1984) A euphemism for *sick-bag*. US; based on the almost equally euphemistic *motion discomfort* for *travel sickness*, which is first recorded in 1978

> 1984 *Saturday Evening Post*: The motion-discomfort bag is basically dishonest... Motion discomfort is when your leg falls asleep... I don't think the airlines would go for 'throwing-up bag'.

mountain bike *n* (1980) a bicycle with a sturdy lightweight frame, fat deep-treaded tyres, and multiple gears, originally designed for riding on mountainous terrain. A fashion for the bikes started in the US and Canada in the early 1980s, and by 1990 they were cult items

> 1988 *The Face*: 80 per cent of all bikes sold in London are now mountain bikes.

mousse *n* (1982) a substance for setting or colouring the hair, sold as a foam or froth in a pressurized container. First recorded as a verb in 1984

> 1982 *Financial Times*: Anybody with soft, limp hair...might like to know about a new mousse created by Michaeljohn.

> 1984 *New York*: If all of America is soon to be moussed, what will the hair-care industry think of next?

muesli belt *n* (1981) an area regarded as being populated by prosperous middle-class health-food faddists. British; a humorous coinage based on the popularity of muesli among bourgeois healthy-eaters in the 1970s

> 1981 *Not The Church Times*: Team vicar required. An attractive post in S.W. London 'Muesli belt'.

multi-media *adj, n* (1981) Designating a computer system that combines text with audio, video, and still images to create an interactive application. A more specific use of the much earlier **multi-media** 'using more than one medium of expression' (1962)

> 1994 *New York Times*: For consumers, the effects of the new chips are most evident in software for presenting movie-style video and combinations of video, sound and text, known as multimedia programs.

multiplex *adj, n* (1982) (an entertainment complex) incorporating two or more cinemas, theatres, etc. on the same site. Originally US; the single, individual cinema was becoming an increasing rarity at the end of the century

> 1986 *Daily Telegraph*: The out-of-town multiplex is beginning to multiply fast even as the high street cinemas...are 'rationalised' out of existence.

necklace *n, v* (1985) (to kill with) a tyre soaked or filled with petrol, placed round the victim's neck and shoulders, and set alight, as a form of lynching or unofficial execution. Often used adjectivally, in such expressions as *necklace murder*. A gruesome metaphor employed in the context of attacks by South African black activists on fellow blacks suspected of betraying the black rights movement

> 1985 *Washington Post*: A group of young blacks caught him and pulled him to the ground. As he lay there they smashed rocks into his skull and body. Then came the 'necklace' burning.

> 1986 *Sunday Telegraph*: Last year, [Bishop Desmond Tutu] did shoulder his way through a crowd to save the life of a man who was about to be 'necklaced'.

New Age traveller *n* (1986) someone, especially an adherent of New Age philosophies (see **New Age (1971)**), who has deliberately rejected conventional ways of life and adopted a travelling existence. In many ways the fin-de-siècle equivalent of the hippie, and attracting much of the same opprobrium (dole-scrounging, loose morals, etc.). Their anti-urbanism embraces environmental concerns, and they are often to the fore in, for instance, protests against new roads

> 1994 *Arena*: The collision with the rag-tag army of fossilized hippies, white dreads and old punks who were bobbing along on the free festival circuit created a mutant subculture—labelled New Age Travellers by the Tory press—whose lineage can plausibly be traced back to the Levellers, Diggers and other antinomian religious cults of the 1640s.

New Man *n* (1982) a man who rejects sexist attitudes and aims to be caring, sensitive, and non-aggressive and to take a substantial role in his household's domestic routine. A product of 1970s feminism who for a historical moment in the 1980s was widely taken as a role model, but who as the decade moved on came more and more to be regarded as a wimp

> 1985 *Chicago Tribune*: Does the New Woman Really Want the New Man?… The answer, as you might guess, is a frustrated no.

New Romantic *n* (1980) a follower of a British youth cult and fashion of the early 1980s which combined elements of punk and glam-rock to form a style in which both sexes dressed in flamboyant clothes and often wore make-up

> 1981 *Melody Maker*: Any similarity between Brum's Duran Duran and London's so-called New Romantic movement is merely…sartorial.

newsgroup *n* (1983) On the Internet or other computer network: a forum for the discussion of, and exchange of information about, a particular subject

> 1994 *Guardian*: You want to know everything there is to know about…baroque music. You pick two dozen Usenet newsgroups out of the 3,000 or more available to you, and send a message to each: 'Can anyone tell me where I can get information about baroque music?'

NICAM, Nicam *n* (1986) An acronym formed from the initial letters of *near instantaneously companded audio multiplex*, denoting a digital system used in British television to provide video signals with high-quality stereophonic sound. It did not become widely available until the mid 1990s. To *compand* a signal, incidentally, is to compress its audio range on transmission and expand it again on reception; the word is a back-formation from *compander*, a blend of *compressor* and *expander*

> 1995 *Camcorder User*: Sporting Nicam digital sound, the VHS deck also has NTSC playback, dual Scart connectors and push-jog remotes.

Nicorette *n* (1980) The proprietary name (registered in the US in 1981) of a type of nicotine-flavoured chewing-gum used to reduce dependency on tobacco

> 1984 *Daily Telegraph*: Nicorette became available in 1980 and I have been challenging the authorities ever since to try to get it available on the National Health.

NIMBY, nimby *n* (1980) An acronym formed from the initial letters of 'not in my backyard', a slogan expressing objection to the siting of something unpleasant, such as nuclear waste, in one's own locality (although by implication not minding if it is dumped on someone else in consequence). Originally US; reputedly coined by Walter Rodger of the American Nuclear Society. The derivative *nimbyism* is first recorded in 1986

> 1980 *Christian Science Monitor*: A secure landfill anywhere near them is anathema to most Americans today. It's an attitude referred to in the trade as NIMBY—'not in my backyard'.

> 1988 *Economist*: Over 90 Tory backbenchers, including some keen Thatcherites, have joined a parliamentary group dedicated to Sane Planning: doublespeak for 'not-in-my-back-yard', or nimbyism.

no-fly zone *n* (1988) an area in which military (and sometimes civil) aircraft are forbidden to fly, especially during a conflict. A military term made familiar to the general public through its frequent use in reports on the Gulf War and the conflict in former Yugoslavia

> 1993 *Coloradoan* (Fort Collins): The White House said Saturday that Iraq has moved its missiles out of threatening positions in the 'no-fly zone' of southern Iraq, ending the prospect of imminent U.S. military action.

nuclear winter *n* (1983) a period of extreme cold and devastation that has been conjectured to follow a nuclear war, caused by an atmospheric layer of smoke and dust particles shutting out the sun's rays

> 1983 Carl Sagan: We considered a war in which a mere 100 megatons were exploded, less than one per-cent of the world arsenals, and only in low-yield airbursts over cities. This scenario, we found, would ignite thousands of fires, and the smoke from these fires alone would be enough to generate an epoch of cold and dark almost as severe as in the 5000-megaton case. The threshold for what Richard Turco has called The Nuclear Winter is very low.

offender profiling *n* (1988) a system of itemizing and recording the probable psychological characteristics, *modus operandi*, etc. of the perpetrators of particular crimes so that these can be matched with the known habits and personalities of individual suspects

> 1993 *Guardian*: The police are building up a new comprehensive system of 'offender profiling' to assist in the hunt for murderers and rapists.

one-stop *adj* (1988) Denoting a shop or other premises in which a wide range of goods or services are available under one roof, so that the customer does not have to visit a large number of shops. Originally US

> 1988 *Architects' Journal*: Our freephone is your access to the biggest one-stop shop in town.

> 1994 *Accountancy*: The islands are trying to attract sophisticated, high net worth individuals and offer them one-stop banking, stockbroking and investment advice.

opt out *v* (1987) Of a school or hospital: to choose to withdraw from the control of a local authority. British: the term arose out of the Conservative government's policy in the late 1980s of encouraging schools and hospitals to become 'self-governing', with funding from central government rather than local councils. Such schools and hospitals were often described as *opted-out*. See also **grant-maintained (1987)**

> 1991 *Times Educational Supplement*: The principle of opting out encourages a selfish élitism and it calls in question the relationship between one school and others in its neighbourhood.

OTT *adj* (1982) extreme, exaggerated, outrageous. British slang; an abbreviation of *over the top*

> 1990 *Folk Roots*: Fans will be happy enough to get half a dozen previously unreleased tracks, including a typically OTT Watkins offering.

out of order *adj* (1984) Of a person or behaviour: unacceptable, objectionable, beyond the pale. British slang; from the earlier sense, 'against established rules of conduct or procedure'

> 1989 Martin Amis: I was out of order. Got taught a lesson.

> 1995 *Sugar*: Forcing your friend down and trying to take her top off is totally out of order *and* illegal.

PACE *n* (1987) An acronym formed from the initial letters of *Police and Criminal Evidence* Act, a UK Act of Parliament passed in 1984 which makes provision in relation to the powers and duties of the police and to the treatment of people in police detention, chiefly by standardizing the code of practice regarding the length of time for which police may detain a suspect without charge, and by providing the detainee with various rights, including the right to legal advice. The acronym became widely known at the end of the 1980s, as it filtered through TV crime dramas

> 1992 V. McDermid: One more stroke like this, Ms Brannigan, and you're going to be in a cell. And if you remember your law, under PACE I can keep you there for thirty-six hours before I have to get round to charging you with obstructing my investigation.

Pac-Man *n* (1981) The proprietary name of a computer game in which a player attempts to guide a voracious blob-shaped character through a maze while eluding attacks from opposing images which it may in turn devour. The origin of the name (which is also applied to the creature itself) is uncertain: it may refer to the fact that the creature's whole object in life is to 'pack' away (i.e. eat) everything that gets in its way

> 1982 *Observer*: Last year, $1 billion in 25 cent pieces was retrieved from machines in America playing one electronic game alone—Pac-Man.

palm-top *adj, n* (1987) (a computer) small enough to be held and used in the palm of the hand. Modelled on **lap-top (1984)**

> 1993 *Computing*: Whereas in the old days a portable was simply a PC you could carry…, now you can take your pick from portables, notebooks, sub-notebooks, palmtops and organisers.

PC, pc *adj, n* (1986) An abbreviation of **politically correct (1970)** and of *political correctness* (1979)

> 1986 *New York Times*: There's too much emphasis on being P.C.— politically correct.

> 1992 *Economist*: Subjects like science and engineering where the ravages of PC are unknown (or, at least, rare)

peace camp *n* (1981) a camp set up by peace campaigners, usually outside a military establishment, as a long-term protest against the build-up of (nuclear) weapons. The term is particularly associated in Britain with the camp set up outside the US airbase at Greenham Common in Berkshire in 1981

> 1986 *Economist*: Soviet newspapers are full of praise for the anti-nuclear activities of the women's peace camps at Greenham Common in Britain and elsewhere.

pear-shaped *adj go pear-shaped* (1983) to go wrong, go amiss. British colloquial; originally R.A.F. slang, and probably in restricted currency for some time before 1983, when it began to appear in public much more often. The underlying metaphor is not entirely clear, but probably it is nothing more mysterious than the notion of a pear as a sphere gone wrong

> 1983 J. Ethell & A. Price: There were two bangs very close together. The whole aircraft shook and things went 'pear-shaped' very quickly after that. The controls ceased to work, the nose started to go down.

> 1995 *FourFourTwo*: The day itself was one of those prize-winningly crappy days when everything went pear shaped.

PEP *n* (1986) An acronym formed from the intial letters of *personal equity plan*, an investment scheme intended to extend share-ownership in the UK, whereby investors could acquire shares (up to a given value) in UK companies without paying tax on dividends or capital gains. PEPs were phased out in 1998

> 1986 *Daily Telegraph*: PEPs are more flexible than pension arrangements.

perestroika *n* (1986) the reform of the Soviet economic and political system, first proposed at the 26th Communist Party Congress in 1979 and actively promoted under the leadership of Mikhail Gorbachev from 1985. The word means literally 'restructuring' in Russian. See also **glasnost (1986)**

> 1986 *Sunday Telegraph*: I can see Mr Gorbachev on television going on about something he calls Perestroika, roughly translated as 'the restructuring'.

personal organizer *n* (1985) a portable folder or wallet containing loose-leaf sections for storing personal information (such as appointments and addresses). The 1980s yuppie was lost without one. In Britain, usually known by the proprietary name **Filofax (1931)**. In due course computer technology caught up with pen and paper, and the term came to be re-applied to a pocket-sized microcomputer or software for a personal computer, providing similar functions to the loose-leaf folder

> 1985 *Los Angeles Times*: These busy people all rely on personal organizers—compact, three-ring binders designed to keep track of various aspects of one's life.

phwoar *interj* (1980) An enthusiastic expression of (usually lecherous sexual) desire. Mainly British; a spelt form representing an apparently naturally-arising vocalization of (male) lust (although *phew* and *cor* may lurk in its ancestry). Spellings vary enormously (*foooar, fwooah, phwooargh, phwooor*, etc.), but *phwoar* has become the canonical form. Popularized by the humorous magazine *Viz*

> 1980 *Viz*: Foooar! What juicy big pink tumblers!!

> 1994 *Phase*: All my male friends were saying 'Phwoar, lesbians. How much are we going to see? Yum.'

PIN *n* (1981) An abbreviation of *personal identification number*, a number allocated by a bank, etc., to a customer for use with a cash card. Mainly used in the phrase *PIN number*; the full form was never widely enough used for the tautology to be apparent

> 1981 *Sunday Times*: Cards with PIN numbers written on them have been stolen… It would be pointless to try a Lloyds' card without its PIN.

pindown *n* (1985) a system formerly operated in certain children's homes in Britain whereby children considered difficult to deal with were placed in solitary confinement for long periods. Variously explained as being from the notion of 'pinning' the child down, or of 'pinning' the problem down

> 1993 *Observer*: I was in solitary confinement for two months, without any day clothes or footwear or anything to do except stare out of the window… From day one I was put…on pindown.

plastic *n* (1980) credit cards, debit cards, etc. A shortening of the earlier **plastic money (1974)**, which referred to the material of which such cards are made, but also alluded to *plastic*'s connotations of artificiality and meretriciousness

> 1980 *Time*: Visa and MasterCard users will now have to pay more for using plastic.

policy wonk *n* (1985) See **wonk (1954)**

poll tax *n* (1985) The term in general use in Britain for the local tax officially known as the **community charge (1985)**. It is an ancient term, meaning literally 'per-capita tax' (*poll* is an old word for 'head'). It, or its earlier variant *poll-money*, had been in use since the 16th century, and it carries with it connotations of public unrest and anti-tax riots which the Conservative government introducing this latest version was anxious to avoid—hence the bland authorized name *community charge*. In the event, it got the riots anyway

> 1985 *Times*: It is the dreaded poll tax that I am referring to.

> 1988 *Annual Register 1987*: Particular emphasis was placed on the poll tax as a way of forcing local councils to become fully 'accountable' to all their electors.

post-feminist *adj, n* (1981) (a supporter) of the principles and attitudes regarded as formed in the wake of the feminist ideas of the 1960s and later (the word *feminism*, probably an adaptation from French, is first recorded in 1895). A term of fragmented application, signifying for some a negative idea of women enjoying the fruits of earlier feminists' struggles while rejecting their ideals, for others a positive era in which a reformed consciousness of women's rights has become a societal norm. *Post-feminism* is first recorded in 1983

> 1995 *Daily Telegraph*: It would be too simplistic to blame work…and I really believe in what *She* is about—a post-feminist magazine for grown-up women.

Pot Noodle *n* (1988) A proprietary name for a fast-food dish consisting of a plastic tub filled with flavoured noodles, which can be prepared for eating by pouring on hot water. It achieved a certain symbolic status *vis-à-vis* junk food in the late 1980s

> 1989 A. Davies: Why couldn't the little rat stay home with his videos and his pot noodles?

pound coin *n* (1980) a coin worth one pound sterling, introduced in the UK on 21 April 1983 and subsequently superseding the pound note

> 1980 *Times*: Anyone who travels regularly on the London Underground…will realize that a British pound coin cannot be long delayed.

> 1983 *Daily Telegraph*: The arrival of the new pound coin has triggered off something of a new 'Green Piece' movement in St. Austell, Cornwall, this week.

power dressing *n* (1980) a style of dressing for work and business intended to convey an impression of efficiency and confidence. Applied particularly to clothing adopted by some women to fit in with the ruthless business ethic of the 1980s, characterized by the use of shoulder-pads to create a more masculine-looking outline

> 1989 *Dimensions*: Power dressing for executive women is dead. No-one wants a square-cut, double-breasted jacket with aggressive shoulders now.

pray-TV *n* (1981) religious broadcasting, especially television evangelism that dominates a time-slot or network. Colloquial North American—a pun on **pay-TV (1956)**

> 1983 *Maclean's Magazine*: The commission…voted to approve 'pray TV', a national satellite-distributed religious broadcasting service.

presenteeism *n* (1989) the practice of being present at one's place of work, especially for more hours than required by one's terms of employment. A word sporadically recorded since the 1930s as a conscious antonym of **absenteeism (1922)** ('Certainly he is an absentee…—if he adopted the habit of dropping in at the works and making well-meant suggestions …, is it likely that his presenteeism would be helpful?', H. Withers (1931)), but the connotations of a pathological work-place attendance are a product of the job insecurity of the 1980s and 90s

> 1989 *Eurobusiness*: Executives might be suffering from levels of stress that impair their performance…through what she calls 'presenteeism'—being at work but not fully available psychologically.

> 1995 *Independent on Sunday*: According to Cary Cooper, professor of organisational psychology at the University of Manchester Institute of Science and Technology, downsizing…has led to a pheno-menon he has termed 'presenteeism'.

> 1995 *Daily Telgraph*: The old problem of absenteeism has been replaced by 'presenteeism', with staff continuing to arrive at the office each morning even when sick, because they feared their jobs would disappear while they were gone.

prion *n* (1982) a hypothetical infectious particle consisting only of protein, and thought to be the cause of some diseases (e.g. BSE). Formed by rearrangement of the initial letters of *proteinaceous infectious particle*

> 1987 C. A. Clarke: Scrapie…is caused by an organism containing neither DNA nor RNA and called a prion.

Prozac *n* (1985) A proprietary name for the antidepressant drug fluoxetine hydrochloride, de-veloped in the early 1970s by US drug company Lilly Industries. The wonder-drug happy pill of the late 1980s; more soberly regarded in the 1990s following reports of side-effects such as excessive assertiveness and aggression

> 1993 *Spy*: Prozac can make a hormone-addled young adult less sensitive, more confident, less homesick, and able to have a good time at parties.

PWA *n* (1986) An abbreviation of *person with Aids*

> 1986 *Guardian Weekly*: He found a place to live thanks to the Shanti Project, a charity subsidised by the municipality to help PWAs. It makes houses available to Aids victims

quality circle *n* (1980) a group of employees, originally in Japanese industry, who meet to consider ways of resolving problems and improving production in their organization. Fashionable in the 1980s among Western managers desperate for the secret of Japanese business success

> 1984 *Listener*: The current vogue for 'quality circles' *à la japonaise* is no more than recognition of the need…for harnessing the creativity, commitment and energy of ordinary managers and workers.

Quorn *n* (1987) A proprietary name for a type of textured vegetable protein (see **TVP (1968)**) made from an edible fungus and used as a meat substitute in cooking. It comes from the name of the manufacturer, Quorn Specialities Ltd. of Leicester, which itself is named after the village of Quorn (now Quorndon) (the local Quorn Hunt gets its name from the same source, which would no doubt upset vegetarian consumers of Quorn)

> 1991 *Which?*: Tasters said the Quorn worked well and that the flaked almonds in the curry gave it a good texture.

radical *adj* (1983) wonderful, marvellous. Originally and mainly US; a youth slang approval adjec-tive which evolved from 1970s surfers' slang: 'at the limits of control or safety'

> 1985 E. Lochhead: The Young Mothers' Meeting we had there was Really Radical.

rainbow coalition *n* (1982) a political grouping of minority peoples and other disadvantaged elements, especially for the purpose of electing a candidate. Originally US; from the notion of all the diverse colours of the rainbow. A concept embraced in particular by the US Democratic Party's Jesse Jackson when running for a presidential nomination in the early 1980s

> 1982 *Austin* (Texas) *American Statesman*: Hightower boasts he will beat the incumbent with the help of 'The Rainbow Coalition: the blacks, the browns, the white liberals and the Yellow Dog Democrats'.

ram-raid *n* (1987) a form of smash-and-grab raid in which premises are broken into by ramming a vehicle through a window or wall. Originally and mainly British; the method was pioneered in the Northeast of England. Verbal uses and derivatives such as *ram-raider* soon developed

> 1987 *Evening Chronicle* (Newcastle): Thieves drove through the shutters of a Tyneside warehouse and loaded up with television sets and video recorders. The ram-raid took place last night.

> 1991 *Independent*: Ram-raiding—using cars as battering rams to break into shops—is the latest threat to stores in the North-east.

rate-capping *n* (1983) the imposition of upper limits on the amount of money which a local authority can spend and also levy through rates, especially as practised in Britain by the Conservative government in the early 1980s, which thought that councils were spending too much on local services. The back-formed verb *rate-cap* soon followed. Later in the 1980s, when other forms of local taxation were introduced in Britain (see **community charge (1985)** and **poll tax (1985)**), the element *cap* was adapted to fit them

> 1983 *Daily Telegraph*: The Government's rate-capping plan was 'yet another giant stride along the path of tight Whitehall control over life in Britain'.

> 1984 *Guardian*: Opposition cries of derision, as when the name of Portsmouth appeared among the rate-capped.

> 1989 *Independent*: The major cost would come in lost interest on cash flow because most people would delay paying until the lower, charge-capped, demand arrived.

> 1990 *Guardian*: The Court of Appeal yesterday dismissed the second stage of the legal campaign by 19 Labour local authorities against the Government's decision to cap their poll tax levels and order cuts in their budgets.

rave *n* (1989) a large, originally often illegal party or event, with dancing to fast electronic pop music, and sometimes associated with the recreational use of drugs such as LSD and Ecstasy. Also applied to electronic dance music of the type played at such events. Raves were usually held in rural locations such as fields and large barns, their location kept secret until the last moment to avoid the attentions of the police. An extension of **rave** 'lively party' (1960). The related *raver* 'someone who attends a rave party' is first recorded in 1991

> 1991 *New Musical Express*: When you're at a rave there's 10,000 ravers going mental—you can't beat the energy.

> 1991 *Sun*: If you want to dress for success on the rave scene you'll need a proper selection of pukka gear… Heat can't escape through the material and the raver comes out of the club feeling like a roast chicken.

Reaganomics *n* (1980) the economic policies of Ronald Reagan, US President 1980–88, especially those of promoting free-market forces in commerce and reducing the taxation of earnings from investment. Unfortunately the tax-cutting was accompanied by unprecedented levels of government expenditure (e.g. on **Star Wars (1983)**), and the result was a record deficit. The idea behind the coinage was not new—*Nixonomics* was applied in 1969 to the economic policies of Richard Nixon—but *Reaganomics* set the ball rolling. It was followed by, among others, *Thatchernomics* and **Clintonomics (1992)**. See also **Reaganism (1966)**

> 1986 *Observer*: Kemp is the darling of the conservatives, a man who represents Reaganomics in its purest form.

real *adj* **get real** (1987) to be realistic; to abandon a naive or dishonest opinion. Usually used in the imperative. Recorded in US college slang in the late 1960s in the sense 'to tell the truth', which is probably the forerunner of the late-20th-century usage

> 1987 Kathy Lette: 'Shit, Jo. I didn't know he meant anything to you.' 'Get real. He doesn't.'

> 1993 *Caves & Caving*: For those who feel that politics have no place in caving or other sporting activities—get real!

reinvent oneself *v* (1989) to assume a new and often radically different character or guise, often so as to cope with changed circumstances or to revive a flagging public image. Originally US

> 1998 *Radio Times*: Lesser men might have despaired but Bryan Forbes simply reinvented himself once more. He became a novelist.

repetitive strain injury *n* (1983) (a medical condition characterized by) pain or impairment of function in tendons or muscles, typically in the lower arms and hands, due to prolonged performance of repetitive actions. A health risk threatening all those who sit at computer keyboards in the last quarter of the 20th century. Commonly known by the abbreviation *RSI*

> 1996 *Daily Telegraph*: An American computer manufacturer has become the first to be found guilty of being responsible for repetitive strain injuries in a $4 million compensation verdict that is sending shock waves through the multi-billion dollar industry.

reverse-engineer *v* (1980) to examine (a product) in order to find out details of construction and operation, especially with a view to manufacturing a similar product; also, to make (something) by this method. A neat euphemism, widely resorted to in the field of computers

> 1990 *Scientific American*: The flourishing international trade in pirated and reverse-engineered software threatens the health of U.S. software producers.

rightsize *v* (1987) to convert to an appropriate or optimum size. Originally and mainly US; usually used as a euphemism to denote reducing the size of an enterprise by sacking some of its workforce, and therefore much in vogue as the economically priapic 1980s deflated. Compare **downsize (1979)**

> 1990 *Business Week*: He adds that 'we're right-sizing our organisation' by reexamining how work is done. Layoffs could result.

road rage *n* (1988) violent anger caused by the stress and frustration of driving a motor vehicle. Used particularly in connection with acts of violence committed by one motorist against another which are provoked by the supposedly objectionable driving of the victim. The foremost example of a rash of *rage* coinages in the late 1980s and 90s, reflecting the frustration and barely suppressed aggression of late-20th-century urban life: others include *trolley rage* (affecting supermarket customers), *phone rage,* and *golf rage*

> 1995 *Guardian*: A driver was jailed for 18 months yesterday for a 'road rage' attack after which a pensioner died.

> 1995 *Independent*: Courts should be given power to order 'rage counselling' for aggressive motorists.

Rollerblade *n* (1985) The proprietary name (registered in the US in 1985) of a type of roller-skate with wheels set in one straight line beneath the boot, giving an appearance and action similar to that of an ice-skate. Originally invented as a way of training for ice-hockey on dry land, they became part of street culture in the late 1980s. First recorded as a verb in 1988

> 1991 *Boston*: One cruises on a bike, one coasts on roller blades, three ride skateboards.

> 1992 *Men's Health*: I go mountain biking and Rollerblading and I ski-race.

rolling news *n* (1982) a service in which a broadcasting channel or station is dedicated entirely to news reports, which are broadcast 24 hours a day

> 1993 *Guardian*: We're not allowed to call it rolling news (a vulgar, commercial concept). No, this will be 24-hour news, not just segments uniformly repeated.

roll-over *n* (1981) the accumulative carry-over of lottery prize money to the following draw (as when no participant has selected the winning combination), typically added to the value of the jackpot. Originally US; the term became familiar in Britain in the 1990s, following the introduction of the National Lottery

> 1981 *Milwaukee Journal*: Lottery jackpot rollover close to $4 million… The Lotto 47 jackpot went unclaimed…and will offer at least $4 million in the next drawing.

> 1995 *Daily Mail*: Saturday's National Lottery draw will be a rollover after no one matched the six winning numbers in last night's draw.

Rubik's cube, Rubik cube *n* (1980) a puzzle consisting of a cube seemingly formed by 27 smaller cubes, uniform in size but of various colours, each layer of nine or eight smaller cubes being capable of rotation in its own plane; the task is to restore each face of the cube to a single colour after the uniformity has been destroyed by rotation of the various layers. Named after the Hungarian teacher Ernö Rubik, who patented the puzzle in Hungary in 1975. There was a brief but intense craze for it in the early 1980s

1980 D. Singmaster: This edition has been retitled since the Magic Cube is now being sold as Rubik's Cube… [The Ideal Toy Corp.] has renamed the cube as 'Rubik's Cube' on the grounds that 'magic' tends to be associated with magic.

runner *n do a runner* (1981) to escape by running away. British slang; applied especially to someone evading capture by the police. Also used more broadly to denote a hasty and unceremonious departure

1986 *Times*: He had been put into police cells and given a kicking after he 'tried to do a runner'.

safe pair of hands *n* (1983) capableness, reliability, or trustworthiness, especially in the management of a situation. Sometimes used with the implication of stolid dependability, without imagination or flair. A metaphorical use of the original cricketing sense 'reliability in catching the ball', which dates from the mid 19th century

1988 *Observer*: John Wakeham believes him to possess 'a safe pair of hands', which, coming from a former Chief Whip, is high praise indeed.

safe sex *n* (1983) sexual activity in which precautions are taken (e.g. wearing a condom) to ensure that the risk of spreading sexually transmitted diseases, especially Aids, is minimized. Also termed, less ambitiously, *safer sex*

1990 *Mediamatic*: Part-parody, part safe-sex education, her presentation uses a combination of home movies, slides, vignettes.

1995 *Daily Telegraph*: John Bowis, the impressively girthed health minister, was in a Soho café for the launch of 'Cruise Cards', promoting 'safer sex'.

sanpro *n* (1985) A contraction of *sanitary protection*, a collective euphemism (first recorded in 1939) for the products (e.g. tampons and sanitary towels) used by women during menstruation. Largely an advertising industry term, which emerged around the time when television authorities were considering allowing such products to be advertised on TV

1989 *Marketing*: Delaney feels that reticence about advertising sanpro and condoms is often the result of 'hypocrisy and squeamishness'.

satanic abuse *n* (1987) sexual abuse or killing, especially of children, alleged to be committed as part of a satanic worship ritual. Originally US; lurid reports of such goings-on spiced up the tabloids in the late 1980s and early 90s

1990 *Social Work Today*: Despite increasing evidence at child care conferences that satanic abuse existed, there was a lack of overall co-ordination.

1994 *Post* (Denver): Akiki…had the misfortune to be misidentified as a practitioner of Satanic Ritual Abuse (SRA).

scratch card *n* (1982) a card used in a competition, with a section coated in a waxy substance which can be scratched away to reveal whether a prize has been won. In Britain associated particularly with the *Instants* game run in conjunction with the National Lottery (see **instant (1985)**)

1993 *Independent*: He is proposing a form of telebingo involving scratch cards with winning numbers shown on screen during selected ad breaks.

SDI *n* (1984) An abbreviation of *Strategic Defense Initiative*, a US project to develop and deploy satellite-mounted devices (e.g. lasers) to destroy enemy missiles in flight. A 'brain'-child of President Ronald Reagan, it was much touted to begin with (gaining the nickname **Star Wars (1983)**), but gradually its impracticability sank in, and most of it was quietly shelved

1984 *New York Times*: The [Defense and Administration] officials…are now referring to the President's plan as 'S.D.I.', for 'strategic defense initiative'.

1985 *Daily Telegraph*: Gen Chervov, a Soviet arms control spokesman, had suggested that if Russia decided to counter SDI, it would not attempt to match it but would seek a lower cost solution.

SDP *n* (1981) An abbreviation of **Social Democratic Party**, a British political party founded in 1981 by disaffected right-wing members of the Labour Party (see also **Gang of Four (1981)**). Following early successes in by-elections the party's popularity faded, and at the end of the decade it merged with the Liberal Party (see **Liberal Democrat (1989)**)

1981 *Times* (headline): SDP launched with aim of 'reconciling the nation'… (advert) If you share our aims you can join the SDP by filling in the application and returning it with a subscription.

section *v* (1984) to cause (a person) to be compulsorily detained in a mental hospital in accordance with the provisions of the relevant section of the Mental Health Act of 1983 or (formerly) that of 1959. British; a euphemism in the *certify* and *commit* tradition

> 1987 *Openmind*: The author uses the case of Mrs Z as an example. Sectioned by her husband, she was then confined in a secure unit.

Semtex *n* (1985) a malleable, more or less odourless plastic explosive, manufactured in several grades and known largely through its use by terrorists. Its name was given to it by its manufacturers, probably based on *Semtín*, the village in Eastern Bohemia, Czech Republic, where it is made, plus the initial syllable of *explosive* or *export*

> 1988 *Daily Telegraph*: The Czechs were replying to a Foreign Office request for help in fighting terrorism and in tracing the growing consignments of Semtex reaching the IRA from Col Gaddafi of Libya.

serial killer *n* (1981) someone who murders repeatedly, often with no apparent motive and usually following a characteristic predictable pattern of behaviour. The application of *serial* to murderers dates from at least the early 1960s (see **serial (1961)**), but the term *serial killer* came into prominence in the US in the mid 1980s in the wake of a number of notorious cases, notably the crimes eventually traced to Theodore Bundy and John Wayne Gacy

> 1990 *ArtForum*: Part of the calculated dementedness of the antisitcom *Married with Children* is the star family's surname, the same as that of notorious serial killer Ted Bundy.

seriously *adv* (1981) very, substantially. Originally US. As with **serious (1929)**, this usage started life in the financial sector (*seriously rich*), but branched out further in the late 1980s

> 1981 *Washington Post*: He became seriously rich, but in 1977 experienced a mid-wealth crisis.

> 1990 *Daily Telegraph*: The new deputy Governor of the Bank of England, Eddie George…is a Russian speaker ('seriously fluent', I am told).

sex worker *n* (1982) someone, typically female, who works in the sex industry (e.g. as a stripper, a nude model, or especially a prostitute). Usually intended as an alternative term that avoids stereotyping and negative connotations and that legitimizes prostitutes, etc. as service workers like any others

> 1991 *Utne Reader*: The telephone companies rake in millions every year, the tele-sex services ring up millions every week, and the phone sex workers can make a pretty penny as well.

shareware *n* (1983) computer software, often distributed informally, which is available free of charge for evaluation, after which a fee is usually requested for continued use. Originally US. One of the earliest (and longest-lasting) of a tidal wave of new coinages based on the *-ware* of **software** that began to appear in the early 1980s (others included *bannerware, charityware*, and *shovelware*). See also **vapourware (1984)**

> 1983 *InfoWorld*: It certainly was a different bag of mail I received in response to the last shareware installment. Usually…the ratio of downloaders requesting programs to the uploaders donating them is about 20 to 1.

shell suit *n* (1989) a type of tracksuit which has a showerproof, often brightly coloured nylon outer shell with a thin inner lining. British; popular as casual leisure wear in the early 1990s, but often taken as a touchstone of naff unstylishness

> 1989 *Burlington Home Shopping Catalogue 1989/1990*: Shell suit by Adidas. Strong nylon outer. Hardwearing suit features two side pockets, attractive contrast piping.

> 1993 R. Rankin: I never had a lot of time for good taste. I'm a take-me-as-you-find-me sort of guy, know what I mean? Give me a shellsuit, a pit-bull terrier and a wife to smack around after I've had a few, and I'm happy.

shock jock *n* (1986) a talk-radio disc-jockey who is deliberately offensive or provocative and frequently abusive to callers, often in an effort to entertain or in addressing some controversial issue. A phenomenon that developed in America in the second half of the 1980s, and made an unsuccessful foray into Britain in the mid 90s

> 1990 *Village Voice* (New York): The airwaves bristle with the sexual dis of shock-jocks, stand-up sociopaths, metal marauders, and rough rappers.

shopaholic *n* (1984) a compulsive shopper. Originally US. A phenomenon that arose out of the credit boom of the early 1980s. The suffix *-aholic/-oholic* 'compulsive consumer or buyer' enjoyed something of a boom then too: other roughly contemporary but mainly shortlived coinages include *clothesaholic, creamaholic*, and *nutaholic* (see also **chocoholic (1976)** and **workaholic (1968)**, and see **-aholic (1965)**)

> 1984 *Washington Post*: [The rumour] that Diana is a 'shopaholic'…was described as 'absolute rubbish'.

… short of a … *adj* (1983) Used to express the notion of lack of intelligence or common sense in terms of a specified deficiency in a desirable or standard quantity of something (e.g. *a brick short of a load, a few sandwiches short of a picnic, sixpence short of a shilling*). Expressions of the underlying idea of deficiency can be found as far back as the mid 19th century, especially in Australian English ('Let no man having, in colonial phrase, "a shingle short" try this country. He will pass his days in Tarban Creek Asylum', G. C. Mundy (1852)), but 'x short of a y' seems to be a late-20th-century formulation

> 1983 R. Thomas: Velveeta's sort of pretty and halfway smart, even if she is six bricks short of a load.

> 1992 *Making Music*: If someone's obviously several bananas short of a milkshake, how you deal with it depends on whether they're the star of the show.

> 1993 Lowe & Shaw: I thought either I had something very wrong with me physically, or I was two sandwiches short of a picnic.

short-termism *n* (1986) concentration on short-term investments, projects, etc. for immediate profit, at the expense of long-term security or development. British—and indeed the phenomenon, characteristic of companies with dividend-hungry shareholders to please, is often diagnosed as one of the causes of Britain's 20th-century economic underperformance

> 1986 *Independent*: The growing friction between industry and the City over the alleged 'short termism' of financial institutions' investment attitudes.

sick building syndrome *n* (1983) the set of adverse environmental conditions found in buildings that are inadequately ventilated, air-conditioned, etc.; also, the symptoms (e.g. headaches, dizziness, breathing problems) experienced by the people who live or work there

> 1990 *Garbage*: Airtight and chemical-laden, office environments may cause 'sick building syndrome', a condition characterized by fatigue, nausea, and respiratory illness.

sizeist, sizist *adj, n* (1981) (someone) discriminating against others on the grounds of size (i.e. how tall or short—or sometimes fat or thin—they are). Originally US. The associated noun *sizeism* is of the same vintage. See **-ism (1965)**

> 1981 *New York Times*: Your reference to '5-foot 1-inch bricklayer Joseph Zangara,' who shot at (Franklin) Roosevelt, can only feed this sizist prejudice.

> 1989 *Economist*: [He] often mimicked Sir Michael's gait in what can only be described as a sizist way.

slam dancing *n* (1981), **slamming** *n* (1983) a form of dancing to rock music (originally at punk rock concerts) in which participants deliberately collide violently with each other. Originally US

> 1992 *Option*: Now that Nirvana has brought slam-dancing to MTV, the mosh pit is getting a lot of attention.

sleaze *n* (1983) corruption involving politicians or government officials. A back-formation from *sleazy* 'sordid, disreputable', or a semantic extension of the earlier **sleaze** 'sordidness, sleaziness' (1967), first recorded in 'The sleaze factor', a chapter heading in the book *Gambling with History* by the US journalist Laurence Barrett. It remained current during the Reagan administration of the 80s, usually in that phrase *sleaze factor*, and moved to the UK towards the end of the decade, when a number of scandals began to engulf the Conservative government. Many involved financial corruption (e.g. the so-called **cash for questions (1994)** affair, in which several MPs accepted payment for asking particular questions in the House of Commons), but the term was also applied to sexual scandals involving MPs, something of a return home for *sleazy*, which originally often connoted sexual squalor

> 1988 *Courier-Mail* (Brisbane): Mr Meese…had become the outstanding symbol of the so-called 'sleaze factor' which has bedevilled the Reagan administration.

> 1995 *Daily Telegraph*: Although Tory disunity and uncertainty about Britain's economic prospects are undoubtedly the main reasons underlying voter discontent with the Government, the 'sleaze factor' is almost certainly making an independent contribution.

slim *n* (1985) The name given to **Aids (1982)** in Central Africa, after the severe weight loss associated with the disease

> 1986 *Listener*: Museveni's government has now been forced at least to recognise the AIDS problem (called 'Slim' in East Africa).

smart card *n* (1980) a plastic bank card or similar device with an embedded microprocessor, used in conjunction with an electronic card-reader to authorize or provide particular services, especially the automatic transfer of funds between bank accounts. Originally US

> 1988 *Times*: The beauty of the algorithm…is that it can be built into hardware that will fit even on 'smart cards', and enables the identity of end-users to be checked in less than a second.

snail mail *n* (1983) ordinary (as opposed to electronic) mail. E-mail user's slang, poking rhyming fun at the slowness of the conventional post. Originally US

> 1991 *Whole Earth Review*: The cost of e-mail is an advantage that increases in importance as the cost of snail-mail and the more expensive delivery services…increase.

social *n the social* (1981) social security. British slang

> 1981 *Times*: I'm getting two wages, one from prison, and one from the social.

> 1983 John Wainwright: They were both 'on the social'.

Social Democratic Party *n* (1981) a British political party founded in 1981 (see **SDP (1981)**). Its members were known as *social democrats*

> 1981 *Guardian*: The Social Democratic Party will be launched today.

> 1981 *Times*: We have gained the sympathy of a quarter of Britain's voters, and between a third and two-fifths if Social Democrats fight together with Liberals.

sound bite *n* (1980) a brief extract from a recorded interview, speech, etc., usually edited into a news report on account of its aphoristic or provocative quality. Also applied to a phrase or sentence intended by its speaker to be quoted in this way. Originally US. The term came to prominence in the 1988 US presidential election campaign, and has come to be shorthand for the superficiality of late-20th-century political discourse

> 1980 *Washington Post*: Remember that any editor watching needs a concise, 30-second sound bite. Anything more than that and you're losing them.

spelling checker *n* (1980), **spell checker** *n* (1983) a computer program which checks the spelling of words in files of text, usually by comparing them with a stored list of acceptable spellings. Originally US

> 1983 *Graphic Arts Monthly*: The composition and editing package includes…a spell checker.

spin doctor *n* (1984) a political press agent or publicist employed to promote a favourable interpretation of events to journalists. Originally US. *Doctor* comes from the various figurative uses of the verb *doctor* (ranging from 'to patch up, mend' to 'to falsify'); on *spin*, see **spin (1978)**. Sometimes also called (in the US) a *spin meister*

> 1984 *New York Times*: They won't be just press agents trying to impart a favourable spin to a routine release. They'll be the Spin Doctors, senior advisers to the candidates.

> 1995 *Guardian*: The party's spin doctors were alarmed to hear the BBC was covering the speech and delighted to hear that it had not 'made' the news bulletin.

> 1998 *Sunday Times*: Head-hunters have spent two months trying to find an ideal candidate for the new strategic post as the Queen's 'spin doctor'.

splatter *adj* (1980) Denoting a cinema genre in which many characters die violently or gruesomely, their bodies apparently 'splattered' across the screen. Compare **snuff (1975)**

> 1993 *Guardian*: The producer of a 'splatter movie' (described as one in which 'blood and body parts are distributed in substantial quantities') set part of the film in a graveyard.

spod *n* (1989) someone (especially a computer enthusiast) who lacks social skills or is boringly studious; a nerd. British slang. Its origins are unclear, although it is first reported as Eton College slang. The adjective *spoddy* soon followed, suggesting at least a *post hoc* association with teenage spottiness

 1991 *Esquire*: They just struck me as spotty spods.

 1997 *T3*: Rubik's Cube...no-one apart from a few spoddy kids in the '80s ever managed to solve it anyway.

spreadsheet *n* (1982) a computer program that allows any part of a rectangular array of positions or cells to be displayed on a VDU screen, with the contents of any cell able to be specified either independently or in terms of the contents of other cells

 1983 *Daily Telegraph*: A good spreadsheet will let you put in all your figures, then just press one specified key and do all the calculations at once producing your completed accounts.

Squarial *n* (1988) The proprietary name of a type of diamond-shaped dish aerial for receiving satellite-television broadcasts. A blend of *square* and *aerial*, sometimes, in early use, also spelled *squaerial*. The company that produced the aerials, British Satellite Broadcasting, merged with Sky Television in 1990, and production of the aerial ceased

 1989 *Times*: More than a million British homes will have dishes or 'squarials' by the end of 1989.

squeegee *n* (1985) a (young) person with a squeegee or other sponge who cleans the windscreen of a car stopped in traffic, especially at traffic lights, and solicits payment from the driver. Often in fuller phrases such as *squeegee bandit, kid, thug*, etc.

 1985 *Washington Post*: When rush-hour traffic backs up along the downtown streets here, the 'squeegee kids' are in business.

 1991 *Evening Standard*: 'Squeegees', the growing urban tribe who molest waiting motorists at busy road junctions.

START *n* (1981) An acronym formed from the initial letters of *Strategic Arms Reduction Talks*, discussions (superseding **SALT** in 1981) held between the US and the Soviet Union; also applied to the *Strategic Arms Reduction Treaty* signed by the US and the Soviet Union in December 1987

 1981 *Washington Post*: Rostow suggested that the well-known acronym SALT, which stands for Strategic Arms Limitation Talks, now become START, for Strategic Arms Reduction Talks.

Star Wars *n* (1983) A nickname for the **SDI (1984)**, based on the title of a popular science-fiction film released in 1977

 1985 *Radio Times*: President Reagan believes his 'Star Wars' defence initiative may end the threat from nuclear weapons.

steaming *n* (1987) a form of robbery in which a gang passes rapidly through a public place, train, etc. robbing bystanders or passengers by force of numbers. *Steamer* for such a robber is first recorded in 1987 too, and *steam* can also be used as a verb. British slang, possibly inspired by *steam in* 'to become involved in a fight or brawl'

 1987 *Hackney Gazette*: 'Steaming' gangs will return—police. Hackney's steaming mobs laid low at the weekend—but a senior policeman has warned that the giant gangs of muggers will return.

 1988 *Sunday Times*: Last November, steamers...hit crowds outside a rock concert at Hammersmith Odeon.

street cred *n* (1981) See **cred (1981)**

stressed out *adj* (1983) debilitated or exhausted as a result of stress. Colloquial, originally US

 1983 *MacNeil/Lehrer Report*: The place where people can bring their children when they were feeling very, very stressed out.

stripagram *n* (1981) a novelty telegram or greetings message intended to entertain or embarrass the recipient, which is sent through a commercial agency and delivered by someone who does a striptease on delivery. One of the more tenacious of the facetious *-gram* coinages of the late 1970s and early 1980s (see **-gram (1979)**)

 1990 *Sunday Express*: I wondered if she'd enjoyed being a kissagram girl. She groaned. 'I was particularly upset when they said I was a stripagram. I was a singing telegram.'

subsidiarity *n* (1982) the principle that a central authority should have a subsidiary function, performing only those tasks which cannot be performed effectively at a more immediate or local level. Originally adapted into English in 1938 from German *Subsidiarität*, and applied specifically to a principle in Roman Catholic social doctrine (originally enunciated by Pope Pius XI (1857–1939)) that social problems should be dealt with at the most immediate (or local) level consistent with their solution. It was often used with overtones of hostility to state intervention, but this new overtly political usage is a product of the Eurocrats of the European Community

> 1982 *Times*: The 'principle of subsidiarity'—a meaningless or even misleading phrase in English—is being discussed in the European Parliament in connection with eventual revision of the Treaty of Rome. It is defined to mean that the European Community's activities should be limited to those which are better performed in common than by member states individually.

sug *v* (1980) to attempt to sell something to someone while pretending to conduct market research. An acronymic verb, coined from the initial letters of *selling under guise*

> 1983 *Which?*: Have you been sugged?… An MRS survey found that one in five people believe they have been the victims of 'sugging'.

sunrise industry *n* (1980) a new and expanding industry (e.g. computer technology). Often contrasted in early use with *sunset industry*, denoting an old, dying industry such as ship-building, but that term has not stayed the course so well

> 1980 L. C. Thurow: We do need the national equivalent of a corporate investment committee to redirect investment flows from our 'sunset' industries to our 'sunrise' industries.

surtitles *n* (1983) captions projected on to a screen or otherwise displayed above the stage during the performance of an opera, especially to translate the libretto or explain the action. Originally North American, and registered as a proprietary name in Canada. A move in the late-20th-century campaign to make opera less elitist

> 1986 *Stage & Television Today*: I'm all against surtitles, because the vertical ping-pong you have to play…means that you can never relax.

survivalist *n* (1982) someone who practises outdoor survival skills, or who trains in the use of combat equipment for survival. Often a camouflage term for a militaristic gun-enthusiast who enjoys playing soldiers. The derived *survivalism* is first recorded in 1985

> 1985 *Survival Weaponry*: If you feel strongly about some aspect of Survivalism…write us a letter.

> 1986 *Daily Telegraph*: Under present laws, no licence is required to sell or buy the weapons favoured by survivalists, apart from firearms and air guns over a certain strength.

swaption *n* (1987) the right to enter into a swap contract (involving exchanging the payments of the interest or principal of debts in such a way that each party has the debts in a more convenient form) at preset rates by an agreed future date

> 1995 *Time*: The London headquarters of Barings was struggling with the division that championed derivatives—financial instruments that use the public's massive bet on securities to create a parallel universe of side bets, some straightforward (like futures) and some arcane (like swaptions).

swipe *n* (1983) an electronic device for reading information magnetically encoded on a credit card, identity card, etc., usually incorporating a slot through which the card is passed. Originally US. Often in *swipe card*, denoting a card for use in such a device. First recorded as a verb, denoting the passing of a card through such a device, in 1986 (*wipe* is used synonymously)

> 1983 *American Banker*: A direct debit system that links a 'swipe' card reader and PIN…pad to an electronic cash register.

> 1986 *Chain Store Age*: When a cashier accepts payments by a VISA credit card, for example, he presses the VISA button on the CAT and swipes the card through the automatic card reader.

tag *n, v* (1980) (to decorate with) a nickname or other identifying mark written or sprayed as the signature of a graffiti artist, often in elaborately decorative style (e.g. on the wall of a building or the side of a train). Originally US

> 1980 *New York Times Magazine*: It is close to a decade since the advent in New York of graffiti tags, often simply newly minted nicknames or random combinations of letters… SE 3, a 19-year-old graffiti graduate, remembers tagging around his family's brownstone on the Upper West Side.

tamper-evident *adj* (1982) Of packaging: designed to make obvious any improper interference with a product, especially a foodstuff or medicine, before sale. A usage resulting from a growing trend in the 1980s for people of malicious intent to introduce substances (e.g. poison or sharp objects) into products on shop shelves, often with a view to extorting money from the store. Originally US

> 1989 *Group Profile, Hillsdown Holdings plc*: Recent product developments have included… 'tamper-evident' packaging on Chivers, Hartley's and Rose's preserves.

technobabble *n* (1981) outlandish or pretentious (pseudo-)scientific jargon. Colloquial, originally US; modelled on **psychobabble (1976)**

> 1981 *People Weekly* (US): To help separate technology from technobabble, *People* turned to Tracy Kidder, 36, whose book *The Soul of a New Machine* describes the building of a new computer.

technostress *n* (1983) (psychosomatic illness caused by) stress arising from working in an environment dominated by computer technology. Originally US

> 1983 *Washington Post*: A new exercise guide featuring an array of do-at-your-desk stretches designed to combat techno-stress.

Teflon *n, adj* (1983) The name of the non-stick coating (see **Teflon (1945)**), applied bemusedly to politicians whose reputation remains undamaged by scandal or misjudgement, or who manage to deflect criticism on to others, so that nothing 'sticks' to them. Originally US, and referring specifically to Ronald Reagan, US President 1981–89, whose ability to sail unscathed through all difficulties earned him the epithet *Teflon (coated) President*

> 1983 P. Schroeder, *Congress Record*: After carefully watching Ronald Reagan he is attempting a great break-through in political technology—he has been perfecting the Teflon coated Presidency. He sees to it that nothing sticks to him.

> 1985 *Times*: His skill in ducking out of tricky situations…has led to his being dubbed the Teflon Prime Minister, because nothing sticks.

telebanking *n* (1981) a method of carrying out banking transactions at a distance by electronic means. Originally US

> 1982 *Times*: British Linen Bank…is assessing the feasibility of cabling parts of central Scotland for multi-channel TV and 'telebanking'.

telecottage *n* (1989) a room or building, especially in a rural area, containing computers and telecommunications equipment for use by members of the local community. A translation of Swedish *telestuga*, which is based on *stuga* 'cottage'. Working by means of such a place is known as *telecottaging*

> 1989 *Times*: The first British telecottage, to be officially opened today week, has been set up in a school at Warslow, Staffordshire.

telemarketing *n* (1980) the marketing of goods, services, etc., by means of (often unsolicited) telephone calls to prospective customers. Originally US; the back-formed *telemarket* is first recorded in 1983

> 1983 *Inc.*: Al Felly…had a great way to telemarket his flowers.

> 1986 *East Anglian Daily Times*: Part-time tele-marketing vacancy working from home.

telemessage *n* (1981) a form of telegram introduced in Britain in October 1981 to replace the inland telegram, and abolished one year later

> 1981 *Times*: A new, cheaper form of telegram called the telemessage is to be introduced by British Telecom as an inland service next Monday.

teleworking *n* (1981) working at home rather than in the office, with the aid of various communications tools (e.g. e-mail). Originally US

> 1988 *Times*: How will teleworking cope with the lack of office fellowship, and living on top of the job?

theme *adj* (1983), **themed** *adj* (1986) Denoting a catering outlet in which all aspects of design and atmosphere are related to a particular unifying theme (e.g. pirates, Merrie England). A concept, and usage, evolved from the **theme park (1960)**. Later broadened out in application to other areas of retailing

> 1983 *Times*: A growth segment of the pub trade is emerging…theme pubs. Their hall mark is a design concept to create a particularly individual atmosphere (the theme) with varying combinations of restaurant, cocktail bar and normal bar service. Various theme restaurants have emerged in the past five years.

> 1986 *Evening Standard*: Cashier/receptionist reqd. for fashionable themed restaurant in the City.

> 1998 *Christie's leaflet*: Following the highly successful jewellery theme sales held in London in 1997—*Bijoux Français* and *Indian Jewellery*—we are holding a special sale devoted to *Bijoux Signés*.

thirty-something *n* (1981) an unspecified age between thirty and forty. Applied especially to members of the 'baby boom' generation entering their thirties in the mid 1980s. Colloquial, originally US; popularized as a catch-phrase by the US television programme *thirtysomething*, first broadcast in 1987, which dealt with the ups and downs in the lives of a group of such people. In the late 1980s the word formed a template for further age categorizations, especially *twenty-something* and *forty-something*

> 1989 *Publishers Weekly*: This comic strip collection chronicles the demands of a 'thirtysomething' career woman.

thrash *n* (1982) **thrash metal** *n* (1985) a style of fast, loud, harsh-sounding rock music combining elements of both punk rock and heavy metal. The term is a development of *thrash* 'short energetic (and usually fast and loud) passage of music', which originated as jazz musicians' slang in the 1960s

> 1984 *Sounds*: Hard-core thrash merchants Black Flag are to release a new LP.

> 1985 *Venue*: The band played an excellent set of high-speed thrash metal and were very well received.

tiger *n* (1981) any of the more successful smaller economies of East and South-East Asia, especially those of Hong Kong, Singapore, Taiwan, and South Korea, and, in the early 1990s, Malaysia, Thailand, and the Philippines. The synonym **dragon (1985)** was once also popular. The congratulatory name was quietly shelved later in the 1990s, when many of them struck the economic rocks, but the model, once established, could be reapplied elsewhere (e.g. the resurgent Irish economy has been referred to as the *Celtic tiger*)

> 1981 *American Banker*: A global shift in development…is taking place amid the booming trade activities of Japan and the 'Four Tigers', Hong Kong, Singapore, Taiwan and South Korea.

> 1990 *Times*: Sir Hugh found his hosts keen to develop a regional economic force resembling the 'tiger' economies of the Pacific Rim.

tired and emotional *adj* (1981) A British euphemism for 'drunk'. Not recorded in print until 1981, but in circulation well before that, and foreshadowed in 'Mr Brown had been tired and overwrought on many occasions', *Private Eye* (1967)

> 1981 Lynn & Jay: Another paper's headline was *Hacker tired and emotional after embassy reception*.

toggle *n* (1982) a computer key or command that is always operated the same way but has the opposite effect on successive occasions

> 1982 *Personal Computer World*: I find that the 'Install' program is unable to make the best of configuring for my printer as Wordstar expects toggles where the Epson has separate control codes for turning on and off certain modes.

touch pad *n* (1980) a computer input device in the form of a small panel containing different areas that need only to be touched to operate the computer

> 1983 *Your Computer*: Once out of its package the Wizzard takes on the appearance of a quite simple, compact unit, complete with two joysticks, touch pads and firing buttons.

tough love *n* (1981) care and concern expressed by encouraging a person to give up certain behaviours and take responsibility for themselves, stressing the importance of self-help rather than the indulgence of others. Originally US; the concept was eagerly embraced by politicians seeking to restrict state benefits

> 1981 *Washington Post*: Grappling with teen-age drug abuse… In many cases this means practising 'tough love'…by establishing curfews, enforcing house rules, chaperoning parties and forbidding drugs in the house.

toy-boy *n* (1981) an attractive young man who is 'kept' as a lover by an older person (typically a woman, but the word is also applied to homosexual catamites). British slang. A favourite of the tabloids in the 1980s, who exploited its essentially mocking message to the full

> 1983 *Financial Times*: At the start he is observed as Caesar's toy boy, stripped for the religious ceremony.

> 1987 *News of the World*: At 48 she is like a teenage girl again—raving it up with four different lovers including a toyboy of 27!

traffic calming *n* (1987) the deliberate slowing or restriction of road traffic, especially through residential areas, by means such as narrowing or obstructing roads, or limiting use of some thoroughfares or lanes to certain vehicles (such as bicycles or public transport). A literal translation of German *Verkehrsberuhigung.* See also **speed bump (1975)**

> 1991 *Courier-Mail* (Brisbane): Traffic calming works, residents of Red Hill said yesterday.

train-spotter *n* (1989) someone who enthusiastically studies the minutiae of a subject; a collector of trivial information. British; a metaphor based on the perceived earnest pointlessness of the hobby of train-spotting. Compare **anorak (1984)**

> 1992 *Face*: Containing over 3,000 entries…, and spanning 600 pages, this should settle a good few of those arguments about who starred in what and when. Not just for film train-spotters.

transgenic *adj* (1981) Of an organism: containing genetic material into which DNA has been artificially introduced from another organism

> 1981 Gordon & Ruddle: The feasibility of producing such genetically transformed mice, which we call 'transgenic' mice, depends upon several factors.

trial *v* (1981) to submit (something, especially a new product) to a test or trial

> 1982 *ICL News*: The 2946 [computer] was successfully trialled on the weekend of February 19.

triff *adj* (1984) See **terrific (1930)**

Trivial Pursuit *n* (1982) A proprietary name for a board game, first marketed in Canada in 1982, in which players advance by correctly answering general-knowledge questions from one of six subject areas, the subject being determined by the colour of the space on which a player lands

> 1988 *Oxford Diocesan Magazine*: Even the weaker pupils found some of the short Trivial-Pursuit-type questions insulting.

tubular *adj* (1982) wonderful, marvellous. A Valspeak approval adjective taken from US surfers' slang, where it denoted a hollow and curved wave, suitable for riding on

> 1982 *Time*: The Zappa's Valley girl becomes, like, a totally tubular national craze—for sure.

> 1990 Herbeck & Ross: They turned to Donatello, who struggled to come up with the perfect word to describe their exploits. But Donatello was at a loss. His brothers continued to top each other: 'Tubular!' 'Radical!' 'Dynamite!'

UB40 *n* (1983) (the index number of) a card issued to a claimant for unemployment benefit in the UK. The term (*UB* is short for *unemployment benefit*) dates from the early 1970s, when it was changed from *UI40* (short for *unemployment insurance*), but did not become widely known until the early 1980s, when severe unemployment set in. It was then also applied to an unemployed person

> 1983 *Time Out*: Half price tickets to UB40s and OAPs on Wednesdays.

> 1986 *Capital Gay*: Eight introductions will cost £95, although there is a reduction for students and holders of UB40s.

vaccine *n* (1986) a program designed to detect computer viruses (see **virus (1972)**), and prevent them from operating

> 1989 *New York Times*: Other vaccines screen the commands that programs send to the computer's operating system.

Valley Girl *n* (1982) a teenage girl from San Fernando Valley in southern California, especially one whose characteristic mode of speech is **Valspeak (1982)**

> 1982 *Guardian*: The Valley Girl, well-heeled with time on her hands, suburban and middle-class, is, first and foremost, a consumer.

Valspeak *n* (1982) a type of US slang which originated among **Valley Girls (1982)** and was later taken up more widely by youngsters in the US. Its main features are a small group of approval and disapproval words (e.g. **awesome**, **mega**, **tubular**, **grody**, **gross**, **gnarly**), frequent use of certain 'filler' words, especially **like** and *totally*, and a girlish, giggly style of delivery. Frank Zappa's daughter Moon Unit played a large part in popularizing it

> 1982 *People Magazine*: On the record, in pure, uncut Valspeak, Moon laments in bubbly staccato that, 'Like my mother like makes me do the dishes. It's like so *gross*.'

vapourware *n* (1984) a piece of software or other product for use in computing which, despite being publicized or marketed, either does not exist or has not (yet) been developed commercially. Originally US. See **shareware (1983)**

> 1984 *PC*: Esther Dyson…appropriately coined the term 'vapor ware' to refer to all the integrated windowing software that doesn't exist—apparently.

veal crate *n* (1988) a narrow wooden box or stall, designed to restrict movement, in which calves are confined while being reared in a method of veal farming which is now illegal in a number of countries. Originally US; familiarized in Britain in the 1990s by high-profile campaigns against such farming methods

> 1990 *Times*: We have been involved in a big campaign to get the EC to ban veal crates, and they have already been banned in England.

veejay *n* (1982), **VJ** *n* (1983) An abbreviation of *video jockey*, a term (modelled on **disc jockey (1941)**) denoting someone who presents a programme of pop videos, especially on television. Originally US

> 1983 *American Way*: VJs, or video jockeys, at MTV's studio cue up as many as 13 videos an hour.

vegelate, vegolate *n* (1985) A term (a blend of *vegetable* and *chocolate*) proposed (but not eventually adopted) within the European Community to designate chocolate that contains a certain proportion of vegetable fat other than cocoa butter. Since this would have affected the British chocolate industry in particular, it was seen as yet more evidence of anti-British sentiment in Brussels, or Paris, or both

> 1986 *Daily Telegraph*: Chocolate will keep its name…despite a French attempt to have it renamed 'vegolate'.

veg out *v* (1980) to pass the time in mindless or vacuous inactivity, especially by watching television. Slang, originally US; *veg* is short for *vegetate*

> 1988 *Independent*: Cold rubbery pizzas for paralytic lager louts vegging out in front of the late-night movie.

velvet revolution *n* (1989) a non-violent political revolution, especially one in which a totalitarian regime is replaced. A translation of Czech *sametová revoluce*, introduced into English by the series of events in Czechoslovakia which led to the ending of Communist rule in late 1989

> 1989 *New York Times*: This was a special way of declaring their faith in what has come to be called the velvet revolution, for its gentle, non-violent quality.

> 1990 *Independent*: Now that 'velvet' revolutions are all the rage, *Citizens* never shirks from examining the bloodlust of 1789.

VHS *n* (1982) An abbreviation of *Video Home System*, a videotape format which by the end of the 1980s had become the industry norm for home video. Compare **Betamax (1975)**

> 1984 *What Video?*: SKC…is also launching a range of high grade cassettes in standard lengths in VHS and Beta formats.

video nasty *n* (1982) a video film depicting scenes of violence, cruelty, or killing. A term which rode in on the back of the video rental boom in Britain in the early to mid 1980s, which brought such films into people's homes for the first time

> 1984 *Listener*: Unless one has seen a video nasty…it is difficult to imagine the depths of degradation to which certain producers are willing to sink.

videotext *n* (1980) an information system in which a television is used to display alphanumeric information selected by the user

> 1980 *New Scientist*: The British pioneered viewdata (now known as videotext according to international standards) with Prestel, but the Gallic Teletel is running hard to catch up.

viff *v* (1981) Of an aircraft: to change direction abruptly as a result of a change in the direction of thrust of its engine(s). A verb based on the acronym *VIFF*, from 'vectoring in forward flight', first recorded in 1972. The reference is specifically to the Harrier, an aircraft whose vertical-takeoff capability is achieved by a system known as 'vectored thrust': an arrangement of slats can be turned through 90 degrees to direct the power of the jet engine downwards. The high profile of the Harrier in the Falklands War helped to bring the word to public attention

> 1981 B. Gunston: No matter how inferior the starting position, the viffing Harrier invariably won the engagement.

virtual *adj* (1987) Denoting an electronic equivalent of something in the real world, generated by computer software. A development of a computing use of *virtual* which dates from the late 1950s, designating techniques for simulating memory space, disk storage, and operating environments. By the late 1980s computers could simulate real space which people could move about in and react with (e.g. using a helmet containing a screen). This was named *virtual reality*, and the new usage spread out from there. Latterly *virtual* has come to be used still more broadly to denote something imagined rather than physically present

> 1989 *Whole Earth Review*: Virtual Reality is not a computer. We are speaking about a technology that uses computerized clothing to synthesize shared reality.

> 1992 *Independent*: This spring the Open University is to start a course taught almost entirely on computer networks to explore the possibilities of 'virtual classrooms'.

> 1998 *Radcliffe Quarterly*: For Ella Fitzgerald, too, cookbooks could offer virtual meals.

VJ *n* (1983) See **veejay (1982)**

voice mail *n* (1980) a system for electronically storing, processing, and reproducing verbal messages left through the conventional telephone network. Originally US

> 1991 *Times*: 'I won't be around tomorrow but my voice mail will be active.' The voice on the answering machine belongs to Cheryl Costa.

waitperson *n* (1980), **waitron** *n* (1980) a waiter or waitress. US. *Waitperson* was coined as a non-sex-specific alternative to *waiter* and *waitress* (see **person (1971)**). That is how *waitron* has ended up too, but its originators apparently intended it (with its scientific sounding suffix -*tron*) to convey the mindless, robotic nature of waiting at tables. The contrast with *patron*, someone who is waited on, has also been pointed out. Neither word has successfully crossed the Atlantic

> 1980 *New York Times*: The young waiters and waitresses (referred to as 'waitpersons' on the menu)...wear a preppy uniform.

> 1985 *New York Times*: 'Are you our waitress?' he inquired politely. 'No,' the young woman answered, 'but I'm your waitron.'

walker *n* (1981) a male escort paid to accompany usually wealthy women in public or at social engagements. Originally US. The implication of the term is that no intimacy later takes place: he is there merely for show

> 1993 *Vanity Fair*: A dependable date for charity events—to which he insists on buying his own tickets, 'going Dutch', as he puts it—Woolley has fallen into the category of 'walker'. He often shows up in paparazzi shots with such ladies-about-town as Eleanor Lambert..., Dorothy Hirshon, and Iris Love.

Walkman *n* (1981) A proprietary name (registered in 1981) for small battery-operated cassette players and headphones capable of being worn by a person who is on foot (hence *walk*...). Widely used, especially in the 1980s, as a generic term, although strictly speaking the name is the property of Sony, the manufacturers (who a couple of years later registered the name *Discman* for a portable CD player). In the 1990s it has largely been replaced by the non-product-specific **personal stereo (1992)**

> 1981 *Japan Times*: Sony Walkmans, easy-driving Honda scooters and aluminum household Buddhist altars sold like hotcakes during 1981.

1984 Sue Townsend: They wear red satin side vent running shorts, sleeveless satin vests, white knee socks, Sony Walkman earphones and one gold earring.

wannabe, wannabee *n*, *adj* (1981) (an admirer or fan) seeking to emulate a particular celebrity or type, especially in appearance or dress. Slang, originally US surfers'; representing a casual pronunciation of *want to be*. Popularized in the mid 1980s through its application to the female fans of the US rock star Madonna, many of whom adopted her style of dress and make-up

1986 *Washington Post*: A morbid Madonna-wannabe fascinated with tabloid tales of bizarre deaths.

1990 *Sunday Times*: Word travels fast among the young literati and their wannabe friends.

warehouse party *n* (1988) a party held, usually illegally, in a warehouse or other spacious building, in which the main entertainment is dancing to pop music, especially house. Venues tended to be kept secret until the last moment, for fear of raids by police suspicious that these events were being used for drug-pushing

1988 *New Statesman*: Jazzie's part of this new environment started to shape itself early in 1986, via the magnet of illicit warehouse parties.

wave *n* (1984) a wave-like effect produced in a grandstand or stadium by successive sections of the crowd of spectators standing up, raising their arms, and sitting down again. Originally US, but publicized around the world through its popularity among spectators at the World Cup football competition held in Mexico City in 1986—whence the name *Mexican wave*, which it has subsequently gone by

1984 *New York Times*: This undulating human wave…apparently became popular at University of Washington football games a few years ago.

1986 *Today*: 100,000 fans had turned up at the Aztec stadium and performed the wave for two hours…on a day when there was no match.

1986 *Guardian*: An occasion and result that satisfied the partisan bulk of the 88,000 crowd. We even saw a passable Mexican Wave.

wet *n* (1980) a politician with liberal or middle-of-the-road views on controversial issues; applied specifically to a member of the Conservative Party opposed to the monetarist policies of Margaret Thatcher. Also used adjectivally. See also **dry (1983)**

1980 *Sunday Telegraph*: At least Sir Ian Gilmour and other political wets do not have their hair pulled.

1981 *Observer*: The term 'Wet' was originally used by Mrs Thatcher, who meant it in the old sense of 'soppy', as in 'What do you mean the unions won't like it, Jim? Don't be so wet.' It meant feeble, liable to take the easy option, lacking intellectual and political hardness. Like so many insults, it was gleefully adopted by its victims, and so came by its present meaning of liberal, leftish, anti-ideological.

1982 *Listener*: In considering the promotion of wet (or wettish) Ministers, she will tell herself that Pope was right.

wheel clamp *n* (1980) a clamp designed to be locked to one of the wheels of an illegally parked motor vehicle to immobilize it. First recorded as a verb in 1983. Compare **Denver boot (1967)**, and see also **clamp (1983)**

1981 *Times*: Illegal parking in London has become so widespread that the Government may bow to police demands to be allowed to use wheel clamps to immobilize offending vehicles.

1983 *Daily Telegraph*: Cars belonging to diplomats will no longer be wheel-clamped.

wheelie bin *n* (1984) a large refuse bin on wheels. Originally Australian, but later widely used in British English as this type of bin was introduced to cut rubbish-collecting costs

1984 *Courier-Mail* (Brisbane): Perhaps, when Mr Baines' wheelie bin arrives, I am sure he will have a change of mind when he sees for himself the improvement for all concerned.

white knight *n* (1981) a company that comes to the aid of one facing an unwelcome take-over bid. A notable example of the exuberant and often outlandish Stock Exchange slang of the 1980s, when imaginative new financial manoeuvrings needed imaginative new names. This one comes from the conventional image of the morally upright knight who saves the damsel from a fate worse than death

> 1990 *Business*: Adia…launched a hostile bid for Hestair… When Hestair found a white knight, BET, Adia refused to enter a bidding war.

wicked *adj* (1984) wonderful, marvellous, outstanding. US Black English and streetgang slang, adopted by British youth culture in the late 1980s. *Wicked* has been used ironically in US English since early in the 20th century to mean 'remarkably fine or admirable' ('Phoebe and I are going to shake a wicked calf', F. Scott Fitzgerald (1920)), but this 1980s usage is more likely inspired by the parallel use of *bad* as an approval adjective. That is first recorded in the 1890s in US Black English; it proliferated in 1920s jazz slang ('Ellington's jazzique is just too bad', Charters & Kunstadt (1927)), widened into general use in the 70s, and was picked up by the youth culture of the 80s ('We ran into some of the baddest chicks, man, we partied, we had a nice time', Gene Lees (1988))

> 1989 *Time Out*: I've been to loads of Acid House parties. We have a wicked time but never, not never, do we take any drugs.

> 1990 *Daily Telegraph*: The boy looked in wonder at the polyurethane and leather marvel and offered it the coolest of street compliments. 'Well wicked', he breathed.

wilding *n* (1989) a protracted and violent rampage in a street, park, or other public place by a gang of youths, who attack or mug people at random along the way. US slang; probably just based on the adjective *wild*, but it has also been suggested that it was originally a contraction of *Wild Thing*, a popular rap song of the time

> 1989 *Austin* (Texas) *American-Statesman*: Seven teen-agers are now charged as members of the gang who brutalized the woman during a night of 'wilding'.

wimmin *n* (1983) A semi-phonetic spelling of *women*, adopted by some feminists as one not containing the ending -*men*. Not a new form—it had been used in the past for suggesting a particular sort (or class) of accent (' "Wimmin's a toss up," said Uncle Penstemon', H. G. Wells (1910))—but the polemical purpose marks out a new usage

> 1983 *Sunday Times*: Return to Greenham Common, view the wool webs, the papier mâché masks, the eccentric re-spelling of words like 'wimmin', the improbable cosiness of the little tents in a landscape of wire fencing and policemen.

> 1983 *Listener*: Meanwhile, what of the Peace Women ('wimmin' in feminist placards) camped outside Greenham Common?

wind farm *n* (1980) a group of energy-producing windmills or wind turbines. One of many late-20th-century schemes for producing pollution-free energy

> 1980 *Sunday Times*: The plan is to set up one (windmill) of medium size as soon as possible to gain experience, and then to establish a 'wind farm', of about ten windmills, each capable of generating a megawatt of electricity.

Windows *n* (1983) The proprietary name of a window-based graphical computer user interface (see **window (1974)**)

> 1983 *Wall Street Journal*: Microsoft Corp. introduces its Microsoft Windows package, which is designed to make it easier to juggle several computer jobs simultaneously.

wine bar *n* (1981) an establishment that specializes in serving wine and usually food. The term had existed at a low level since at least the late 1930s, denoting broadly 'a bar at which wine is served', but the specific application to this sort of drinking and eating establishment (with connotations of sophistication/trendiness, underwritten—as with the cocktail bar of previous decades—by the absence of draught beer) is a 1980s development

> 1983 *Which?*: For an accurate description of over 200 wine bars across the country, this section of the book is unbeatable, with critical comments on the range of wines, and an assessment of the food and perceptive summing-up of the atmosphere.

wired *adj* (1982) in a state of nervous excitement; tense, anxious, edgy. Slang, originally and mainly US; often followed by *up*

> 1982 Armistead Maupin: 'Want some coffee?' 'I think I'll wait', said Mary Ann. 'I'm wired enough as it is'.

> 1983 Erin Pizzey: He's really wired up. It's fun to see him do the jumping for a change.

woodentop *n* (1981) a uniformed police officer. British slang. An epithet inspired ultimately by the *Woodentops*, a BBC television children's puppet programme first broadcast in 1955. The specific implication seems to be that uniformed officers have 'wooden tops' (i.e. are slow-witted), in contrast with the mental acuteness of detectives

1981 John Wainwright: I'm a copper. An ordinary flatfoot… A real old woodentop. That's me.

woopie *n* (1986) An acronym based on the initial letters of *well-off older person*, on the model of **yuppie (1982)**); a jocular term, used especially by advertisers and marketers, for a member of a socio-economic group comprising affluent retired people who pursue an active lifestyle. Originally North American

1989 *Property Weekly*: Woopies will stimulate demand into the 1990s says Connell.

wuss *n* (1984) a weak, ineffectual, or indecisive person, especially an effeminate man. Colloquial, originally and mainly US. Probably a back-formation from the synonymous and slightly earlier *wussy* ('Kong's a wussy. The truth is, Kong's acrophobic. That wasn't him climbing the Empire State Building; that was a stunt ape', *Washington Post* (1981)). This in turn may have come from *pussy* 'mild-mannered person', perhaps via the unrecorded reduplication *pussy-wussy*

1984 *Washington Post*: 'There are disadvantages,' says Hanks, shaking his head, as if sad. 'Everybody thinks I'm a wuss. And I don't impress any of the stunt women at all.'

1995 *Guardian*: Kirk and Picard are the only two decent Enterprise skippers available to stop him, as the wuss that commanded the Enterprise-B couldn't captain a canoe.

wysiwyg *n* (1982) An acronym (pronounced as if it were spelt *whizziwig*) formed from the initial letters of *what you see is what you get*, a slogan used in the computer industry denoting that what appears on the VDU screen exactly represents the eventual output

1984 *Scientific American*: The resulting interface between the computer and the user would then fall into the class of interfaces known as wysiwyg, which stands for 'What you see is what you get'.

yardie *n* (1986) a member of any of a number of West Indian, especially Jamaican, gangs engaged in usually drug-related organized crime. The word is derived from West Indian *yard* 'dwelling', probably in the sense 'home, Jamaica' used by Jamaican expatriates: *yardie* itself is applied in Jamaica not to a member of a local gang, but to a Jamaican who has been a gang-member abroad and returned home

1988 *Financial Times*: Errol Codling—reggae singer Rankin' Dread—the so-called Godfather of Britain's Yardie gangs, was deported to Jamaica, for questioning about murders.

yomp *v* (1982) to march with heavy equipment over difficult terrain. The word came into prominence when used by the Royal Marines during the Falklands conflict of 1982. Its origins have never been certainly identified. It has been compared by those familiar with the terminology of rally-driving with *yump* (of a rally car or its driver) 'to leave the ground while taking a crest at speed', which apparently comes from a Scandinavian pronunciation of *jump*, but whether there is any connection has not been confirmed. Its colourful sound and appearance made it popular with journalists and headline-writers in Britain, and it enjoyed some metaphorical usage (see the second quote below), but after a few years it faded from the scene. (The equivalent word in the Parachute Regiment was *tab*, of equally obscure origin)

1982 *Daily Telegraph*: And always in the cold light of the Falklands dawn, the…Marines…have been ready to 'yomp on' for the next stage of the journey.

1983 *Listener*: Mrs. Thatcher may begin yomping…around the hustings considerably sooner.

young fogey *n* (1980) a young person of noticeably conservative tastes or outlook. Recorded in occasional use since the first decade of the 20th century in implicit or explicit contrast with *old fogey* ('Fashions, outlook, the spirit and manners of the age—I found the lot beyond me… I was a young fogey', Dornford Yates (1929)), the expression did not become common until the 1980s. Its institutionalization in British usage is said to have arisen from a specific application to the novelist A. N. Wilson

1983 *Listener*: He implies that this is a consequence of the decline in educational standards of the past decades. Mr. Wilson, though he has many admirable qualities, is a bit of a professional young fogey.

1985 S. Lowry: The present resurgence of the Young Fogey ties up neatly with the reinvention of the class system that has been going on at least in the South of England ever since Tina Brown revamped *Tatler*.

Youth Training Scheme *n* (1981) a Government-sponsored scheme introduced in Britain in 1983 to replace the **Youth Opportunities Programme (1977)** and offering job experience and training for unemployed school leavers. Better known under its abbreviation *YTS*, first recorded in 1984

> 1981 *Hansard Commons*: We are able to ask the Manpower Services Commission to ensure that this new youth training scheme is in full operation by the autumn of 1983.

> 1984 *Times*: The YTS is not available for many 17-year-olds.

yuppie *n* (1982) a member of a socio-economic group comprising young professional people working in cities, of a type thought of as typifying the ethos of the 1980s: ambitious, go-getting, newly affluent, young, class-free, owing no debt to the past. Originally US; a hybrid word coined probably by grafting an acronym based on *Young Urban Professional* (or *Young Upwardly mobile Professional*) on to a basic model suggested by **hippie**. At first it had rivals in *yumpie* ('The yumpies climbing the ladder of success with great agility can be described as upscaling', *New York Times Magazine* (1984)), based on *Young Upwardly Mobile Professional*, and *yap* ('Phillips' Yaps believe in vigorous self-advancement, jogging and BMWs', *Sunday Times* (1984)), based on *Young Aspiring Professional*, but *yuppie* proved the fittest for survival, and went on to become perhaps the main buzzword of the 80s. Numerous derivatives were formed from it, including *yuppyish, yuppiedom, yuppieism*, and *yuppette* (see also **yuppify (1984)**), and it provided the role-model for a rash of look-alike words (e.g. **buppie** 'black yuppie', *guppie* 'gay yuppie', also 'green [i.e. environmentally concerned] yuppie', *Juppie* 'Japanese yuppie'). It was probably also the main inspiration behind the general fashion for acronymic lifestyle terms in the mid 80s (e.g. **dinky (1986), woopie (1986)**)

> 1982 Joseph Epstein: People who are undecided about growing up: they are college-educated, getting on and even getting up in the world, but with a bit of the hippie-dippie counterculture clinging to them still—yuppies, they have been called, the YUP standing for young urban professionals.

> 1984 *Times*: A new term has been introduced into the American political lexicon… It is 'Yuppie', which stands for Young, urban professional people.

> 1984 *Guardian*: The yuppies themselves, in the 25–34 age group, supported Senator Gary Hart in the primaries.

> 1984 *Washington Post*: Yuppiedom does not conduce to a realistic view of the human condition or of American society.

> 1984 *New York Times*: Yuppiness depends on the prestige of gaining; happiness on the satisfaction of giving.

> 1986 *Financial Times*: There is nothing yuppyish about the Folkes Group.

yuppie flu *n* (1988) An alternative name for **ME (1982)**, based on the notion that the disease attacks high achievers of the yuppie type

> 1990 *Daily Telegraph*: Graham…told Mr Patrick Cuff, the coroner, that his mother had suffered for several years from ME—myalgic encephalomyelitis, known as Yuppie Flu.

yuppify *v* (1984) to make (an area, building, clothing, etc.) characteristic of or suitable for yuppies. The connotations of the coinage (which was probably inspired by **gentrify (1972)**) are usually negative: traditional (working-class) area gets taken over by bourgeois trendy young upstarts who swamp its culture (and send house-prices through the roof). The derived *yuppification* is also first recorded in 1984

> 1984 *Listener*: They get into a district before anyone else and really yuppify it.

> 1987 *Observer*: Their 'bashers' (shacks) will be forcibly removed by police to make way for developers who want to 'yuppify' the Charing Cross area.

> 1987 *Independent*: What Dickens is describing, I suddenly realised, is yuppification. The trendies were moving in.

zaitech *n* (1986) investment in financial markets by a company as a means of supplementing the earnings which it receives from its principal operations. A partial Anglicization of Japanese *zaiteku*, which was formed from *zai* 'wealth' and *teku*, itself a Japanization of *tech*, short for *technology*

> 1986 *Washington Post*: Everyone seems to be trying his hand at deftly juggling securities using 'zaitech', or financial engineering.

zero option *n* (1981) a disarmament proposal that if the Soviet Union would withdraw its SS-20 missiles from Europe, the US would abandon its plan to deploy Pershing and cruise missiles there. The implication in the name is that both sides would end up with zero nuclear missiles in the given category. The proposal failed, but the nomenclature was revived in *zero-zero* or *double-zero*, a suggestion sprung on the surprised Americans by Mikhail Gorbachev at the Reykjavik summit in 1986, encompassing the withdrawal of shorter-range missiles as well; this was put into practice in the 1987 INF treaty. A further refinement was *triple-zero*, proposing the inclusion of battlefield nuclear weapons

> 1981 *Washington Post*: By reviving controversy about a moratorium and the 'zero option', Brandt's trip appears to have realized some of the fears of those in the West German government and opposition party.

> 1987 *New Scientist*: If Pershing II and Cruise are…to be negotiated away under the zero-zero option, and if Polaris is truly obsolescent…then the Labour Party 'unilateral' policy seems to differ very little in substance from that of the Alliance.

> 1987 *MacNeil/Lehrer NewsHour*: If we said yes to zero option, we said yes, yes to double zero option, and who knows, there may be a triple zero option involved in tactical nuclear weapons.

zero tolerance *n* (1982) non-acceptance of antisocial and especially criminal behaviour, typically by strict and uncompromising application of the law. Originally US; a political slogan of the law-and-order lobby which spread to Britain in the 1990s

> 1982 *Christian Science Monitor*: Beyond its 'zero tolerance' for drug abuse, the Navy also wants to root out another problem, alcohol abuse.

> 1997 *Daily Telegraph*: The Labour leader pledged his support for 'zero tolerance' schemes pioneered in New York…in which the police target even the most minor criminal behaviour.

The 1990s

As the millennium approached, the world seemed a fragmented place. The certainties of 1900 had been blasted by two world wars. At the end of the 1980s the Cold War ice had melted, opening up new possibilities and uncertainties. The stratified, deferential society inherited from the 19th century had given place to the '*people's*' democracy. A confident, optimistic belief in progress had faded; late-20th-century humanity was cynical about the efficacy of science and technology, and aware of the damage it had done to the world and its other inhabitants. Sensing the ultimate victory of capitalism, Professor Francis Fukuyama had even proclaimed 'the end of history'. And as if all that were not enough, the stoical, stiff-upper-lip British had become a sentimental, touchy-feely nation (if the public reaction to the death of Diana, Princess of Wales was anything to go by).

As Communism's grip on Eastern Europe loosened, nowhere was the outcome more bitter than in Yugoslavia. Civil war broke out in 1991 with the secession of Croatia and Slovenia. It smouldered on to the end of the decade, and introduced the sour euphemism *ethnic cleansing* into the English language. The other major hot conflict of the 90s was the Gulf War (1991), a punitive action by the United Nations to expel the Iraqi invaders from Kuwait. A number of US military euphemisms were brought to wider public notice as a result (notably *collateral damage* (1975) and *friendly* fire (1925)), and duly ridiculed. Several years after the war was over, sufferers from *Gulf War syndrome* were still trying to establish that it was caused by conditions they had encountered in Kuwait and Iraq. The military strategists drew the lesson that what was needed to police an increasingly volatile world was a *rapid-reaction force*.

To counterbalance this geopolitical fissiparousness (the number of independent states in Europe went up from 25 in the 1980s to approaching 40 in the late 90s), the European Community was enlarging itself. Under the terms of the 1992 Maastricht treaty, it transformed itself into the *European Union*. Such developments were not to the liking of *Eurosceptic* (1986) elements within the ruling Conservative party in Britain. They were encouraged in their doom-laden predictions by *Black Wednesday*, in which Britain was forced ignominiously to abandon its membership of the European Exchange Rate Mechanism. Britain's relations with its European partners reached rock bottom with the *beef war*.

The humbling of the pound spelled the beginning of the end for the British Conservative government, which had been in power since 1979. Shorn of its reputation for economic competence, and plagued by its own Euro-sceptics, who could exploit its tiny parliamentary majority to try to press their case, it stumbled along on a wave of unprecedented public unpopularity. Beset by accusations of *sleaze* (1983) and scandals such as *cash for questions*, it tried to identify the *green shoots* of economic recovery and establish *clear blue water* between itself and its political opponents. The electorate, however, was not convinced. In the general election of 1997, the government suffered a crushing defeat. Even MPs who had taken the precaution of the *chicken run* could not escape the landslide.

Taking the Tories' place, *New Labour*: a transformed Labour party which had abandoned its more extreme socialist policies in favour of the *third way*. Under *Blairism, tax and spend* was out, *welfare to work* and *tough love* (1981) were in. Having taken the lesson of more than a decade of internecine strife, the new government made sure its supporters stuck close to the party line: to be *off-message* was the greatest crime; any deviation would be spun back into line by the *spin doctors* (1984). Labour had learnt well from the *Clintonites* in the US how to gain and hold on to power.

The get-rich-quick-and-flaunt-it society of the 80s had evaporated in the recession of the early 90s. *Essex man* was no more (his place taken by *Islington person*), and *Essex girl* was keeping a lower profile. It was forecast as the 'caring decade', although *Generation X, job-seekers*, and sufferers from *negative equity* probably did not find it so. Nor, perhaps, did children, for it was a decade in which the realities of paedophilia, child pornography, etc. were laid bare (or supposedly—*false memory syndrome* cast doubt on the reliability of *recovered memory*), and the high-profile Louise Woodward case publicized *shaken baby syndrome*. The *V-chip* promised to control children's access to sex and violence on television.

Confidence returned with the end of the recession, and Britain reinvented itself as *Cool Britannia*, proprietor of *Britpop*. For entertainment, people had *docusoaps* on TV, *Aga sagas* in the bookshops, and *red top* tabloids on the news-stands: possible evidence of *dumbing down* for those in search of it. At work, there was a good chance you would be *hot-desking*, and the new institution of *dress-down* Friday reached Britain from the US.

The New Man had become the *New Lad*, with his *laddish* behaviour. The female backlash went over the top with *bobbitting*, a *girl power* (1986) solution not even *Viagra* could remedy. The gay community, meanwhile, had to face the new threat of *outing*.

Cybernauts and *Netties* surfed the *World Wide Web* (or the *Web* for short). To be in the swim you had to have your own *web site* or *home page*. You would hope to avoid the *spam* and the *mail bombs*, but the main fear in the *cybercafé* was the dreaded *millennium bug*, which threatened to make the world's computer systems crash when the clocks chimed midnight on 31 December 1999. At least *tamagotchis* (or *cyberpets*) would not be affected; they only succumbed if you neglected them.

So the century which began with such simple new pleasures as the jigsaw puzzle ended with human beings looking after a piece of electronic equipment as if it were a living pet. As people filed into the *Millennium Dome*, perhaps some pondered on what strange neologisms would be necessary to cope with humanity's bizarre inventiveness in the coming hundred years.

Aga saga *n* (1992) a type of popular novel set typically in a semi-rural location and describing the domestic and emotional lives of articulate middle-class characters. The gently mocking term, which seems to have been inspired mainly by the novels of British author Joanna Trollope (b. 1943), exploits the nostalgic association of Aga stoves with lost rural idylls

> 1994 *Independent on Sunday*: The success of Joanna Trollope's rural novels led to a whole wave of Aga Sagas from publishers hoping to cash in.

> 1995 *Daily Telegraph*: When contemporary women writers publish novels about other women of a certain class the critics call them 'Aga Sagas' and throw them on the fire.

alcopop *n* (1995) a carbonated, often fruit-flavoured drink containing alcohol. A controversial marketing development (which actually had its beginnings in the US in the 1970s), involving the alcoholizing of drinks typically consumed by children

> 1995 *Daily Telegraph*: 'Alcopop' sales fizz as young Britain gets the taste.

> 1996 *Independent*: The launch of two new alcoholic fruit drinks looks set to brew up another storm over criticism that the 'alcopops' encourage under-age drinking.

> 1997 *Guardian*: Alcopops contain about 5% alcohol.

angel dust *n* (1990) the drug clenbuterol, especially as used illegally to promote growth in cattle. Mainly British and Irish English; a revival of a term applied in the 1960s to the hallucinogen phencyclidine (see **angel dust (1969)**)

> 1990 *Daily Telegraph*: The Provisional IRA is profiteering from the sale of 'angel dust', an illegal substance used to promote growth in cattle.

applet *n* (1990) a small computer application program, especially one that executes a single task within a larger application. Formed by adding the diminutive suffix -*let* to *application*

> 1995 *Economist*: Sun's vision for Java is that its compact applets, many taking up less than 100,000 bytes, will do a single job well.

as if *interj* (1995) Used ironically to express incredulity or disbelief. Slang; a curtailed version of 'As if it were true!' or some such expression. There is actually a previous record of the usage in 1905, but there is no evidence of any continuity of use between this and *as if*'s sudden burst of fashionability in the 1990s. Compare **in your dreams** at **dream (1994)**

> 1995 *Just Seventeen*: You know how pools winners always say it won't change their lives? Yeah, right, as if.

> 1997 *FourFourTwo*: When Adams' contract was up a couple of summers ago, Spurs and Man Utd fans were all excited at the prospect of signing him. As if!

babelicious *adj* (1991) Of a person, especially a young woman: extremely sexy. Slang, originally and mainly US; a blend of **babe** 'sexually attractive young woman' (1915) and *delicious*. Introduced in the sketch 'Wayne's World' on the US television show *Saturday Night Live*, and popularized by the 1992 film *Wayne's World*

> 1991 M. Myers & R. Ruzan: The babelicious movie star.

> 1993 *Picture* (Sydney): Babelicious Debbie..won the utmost honour of becoming THE PICTURE Wet T-shirt/Luscious Body champion 1993.

bad hair day *n* (1991) a day on which one's hair is particularly unmanageable; hence, a day on which everything seems to go wrong. Colloquial, originally US

> 1994 *Post* (Denver): Soon you will notice how much less complaining you do, even on bad hair days.

bail bandit *n* (1991) someone who commits a crime while on bail awaiting trial. Colloquial

> 1993 *Independent on Sunday*: After a police campaign against 'bail bandits'…ministers are considering forcing a suspect to prove he would not be dangerous if allowed to wait at home instead of in jail.

ball-tampering *n* (1990) an infringement of the rules in cricket consisting of artificially altering the condition of the ball (e.g. by raising its seam with the fingernail or a metal object, or using an artificial substance to shine it). The practice is almost as old as the game itself, but the term arose out of a number of high-profile (alleged) incidents in the 1990s, notably when the England cricket captain Mike Atherton was accused of rubbing earth on the ball during a test match against South Africa in 1994. The formation itself is linguistically interesting in that it treats the normally intransitive *tamper* (which as a verb needs a following *with*) as if it could take a direct object

> 1994 *Guardian*: In the past 18 months we have had cricket's ball-tampering fiasco, football's brown envelopes, and now the suggestion that the alleged actions of the most powerful man in athletics might have been a contributory factor in the suicide of a journalist.

barmy army *n* (1991) A self-designation of a group of supporters of a particular sports team. British; originally used by soccer supporters, but in the mid 1990s applied specifically to a group of young vociferous fans following the England cricket team abroad

> 1991 *Independent*: 'Atkinson's Barmy Army' and their madcap rituals reflect the transformation he has effected at a deeply conservative club.

> 1996 *Sunday Telegraph*: The 'Barmy Army', English cricket's noisiest and most outrageous supporters, arrived in South Africa, raring to go, for the Test series this winter.

beef war *n* (1996) A journalistic name for the attempt of the British government to overturn the ban on the export of British beef and beef by-products imposed by the European Commission in March 1996, following the outbreak of BSE among British cattle herds. A coinage modelled on the **cod war (1973)** of the early 1970s, when Britain quarrelled with Iceland over fishing rights

> 1996 *Scotsman*: The plan had been to enlist President Chirac's help in the beef war against Germany, and get France to squash Bonn's veto on our semen and tallow exports.

benefit tourism *n* (1993) travelling to or within Britain in order to live off social security payments while untruthfully claiming to be seeking work. A polemical usage introduced in a speech made to the British Conservative Party conference in 1993 by Peter Lilley, Secretary of State for Social Security. *Benefit tourist* is also first recorded in 1993

> 1994 *Independent on Sunday*: Mr Lilley's clampdown on 'benefit tourism' has been attacked by the Government's own social security advisory committee.

> 1995 *Economist*: As for EU citizens using their right of entry to become 'benefit tourists', on March 20th the High Court upheld Britain's right to deny income support to unemployed EU citizens if they were not seeking work.

Big Beat *n* (1997) a form of dance music characterized by the use of rock-style guitars

> 1997 *Independent on Sunday*: The recent media frenzy around big beat and speed garage has been virtually ignored in Manchester.

Black Wednesday *n* (1992) 16 September 1992, the day on which the UK was forced by adverse economic circumstances to withdraw sterling from the European Exchange Rate Mechanism. So called because generally regarded as a disaster (and certainly it was an embarrassing piece of mismanagement which permanently wrecked the Conservative government's reputation for economic competence), but Eurosceptics hailed it with other epithets (such as 'White Wednesday')

> 1992 *Earth Matters*: The national coffers [are] much depleted after 'Black Wednesday'.

> 1992 *Economist*: The Bundesbank is thought to have lent the Bank around DM33 billion (£13 billion) through the ERM's 'very-short-term financing facility' on Black Wednesday.

Blairism *n* (1993) the political and economic policies of Tony Blair, leader of the British Labour Party since 1994 and Prime Minister 1997–, characterized by a willingness to combine a concern for social issues with an acceptance of many aspects of market-based economics. Supporters of Blair or his policies have been dubbed *Blairites* or sometimes **Blairistas (1995)**

> 1994 *Guardian*: A little more exposure to Blairism and evidence that it is not just a leadership phenomenon but running deep in the veins of the party itself, would make the balance of forces much tighter.

> 1995 *Guardian*: It is well worth re-reading that compromise text, for it meets virtually all the arguments for modernisation advanced by the Blairites, yet remains true to the spirit of Clause 4.

Blairista *n* (1995) A lampooning term for a fanatical supporter or apparatchik of Tony Blair (see **Blairism (1993)**), based on *Sandinista* 'a member of the revolutionary socialist party ruling in Nicaragua in the 1980s'

> 1995 *Independent*: Barrie Clement…makes the same mistake as Tony Blair and the Blairistas by assuming that those who voted for Mr Blair as leader of the Labour Party will now follow blindly wherever he chooses to lead them.

bless *interj* (1998) A shortened version, fashionable in the late 1990s, of such cosily indulgent exclamations as *bless you* and *bless his heart*, meted out to winsome children and small furry things

> 1999 *Observer*: What if I didn't get out much, and was simply grossly overdressed for lunch? If I were a receptionist—and I have been—I'd think, 'Oh, bless' and reward the party dress at lunch with a (big big) smile.

bobbitt *v* (1993) to amputate the penis of (especially a husband or lover) in an unpremeditated or vindictive manner, typically as an act of revenge for perceived sexual grievances. Originally US. The term comes from a 1993 incident (exhaustively reported in the world's media) in which Lorena Bobbitt cut off her husband John Wayne Bobbitt's penis with a kitchen knife in revenge for alleged acts of rape and abuse. It may have been influenced by a punning similarity to *bob it* (i.e. 'cut it short')

> 1993 *Pittsburgh Post-Gazette*: I have heard several people say that 'that no-good so-and-so should be bobbitted' or that 'bobbitting would serve that creep right'.

> 1996 *Independent*: One woman scorned bobbitted her boyfriend with a Stanley knife.

bone *n on the bone* (1992) Of meat: sold or cooked with the bones in place, not removed by filleting. A technical term of the butchery and catering trades which did not gain wide currency in British English until 1997, when the sale of beef on the bone was banned because of fears that it might cause Creutzfeldt-Jakob disease

> 1992 *Gourmet*: Fired up, the *tandoor* handles skewered veal tenderloins and lamb longs on the bone.

> 1997 *Daily Telegraph*: It is ironic to think that I know a great many sources where I could, if I so wished, buy heroin or crack cocaine illegally, but I will be unable to buy beef on the bone. Last week, I took possession of more than £200 worth of wing ribs of beef.

boot sale *n* (1992) A shortened form of **car-boot sale (1985)**. British

> 1992 *Daily Mirror*: I decided to supplement our low funds by knitting and selling items at a boot sale. Other booters are also down on their luck and trying to make ends meet.

Boxgrove man *n* (1994) an early human, fragmentary remains of which were found in a gravel pit at Boxgrove, Sussex in 1993

> 1994 *Guardian*: Boxgrove man—Europe's oldest human—dined off horsemeat, rhinoceros, giant and red deer, and cave bear.

Bridget Jones *n* (1998) an independent single woman in her thirties. Despite the prediction in the quote below, a usage which shows little sign of permanence. It comes from *Bridget Jones's Diary* (1996) by Helen Fielding, a humorous fictional diary recounting the highs and (more usually) lows in the life of a thirty-something female in 1990s Britain

> 1998 *Independent*: This year's list [of additions to the English language] might indeed have found some words and phrases to endure. Single, unattached women in their 30s risk being called Bridget Jones for years to come.

Britpop *n* (1995) the music of a loose affiliation of independent British groups performing in the mid 1990s (e.g. Blur, Oasis, Pulp, Radiohead), showing influences from a variety of British musical traditions (e.g. mod and punk). The term was originally coined in the mid 1980s as a generic term for British pop music ('Potent Brit Pop from the heart and soul of punk's long-gone Buzzcocks', *Chicago Tribune* (1986)), but in the 90s it came to be applied specifically to a new wave of British music produced as a self-conscious reaction against the prevalence of American musical styles

> 1995 *Arena*: A call to *Select* magazine's editor suggesting Suede and their peers were all part of a British reaction to the American grunge movement, and Britpop was born.

> 1996 *Independent*: Ex-punky indie-melodicists making it work for themselves in the post-Britpop world.

canyoning *n* (1992) (a sport involving) jumping into a fast-flowing mountain stream and careering down a mountainside at high speed. Originally US; one of a range of 'extreme' sports which became popular in the 1980s and 90s (see **extreme (1974)**)

1992 *Los Angeles Times*: One new French sports craze Catherine loves is 'canyoning'—riding down a waterfall without a rope.

1995 *Daily Mail Holiday Action*: Canyoning is another thrilling sport where you are carried along by the power of a waterfall.

cash for questions *n* (1994) Designating a series of incidents in the mid 1990s in which several Conservative MPs were alleged to have accepted money from private individuals in return for tabling specific questions in the House of Commons. The formula was revived in 1998 to accuse the Labour government of 'cash for access' (i.e. accepting payment for access to government ministers). See also **sleaze (1983)**

1994 *Daily Telegraph*: His comments reflect his concern over the damage to the Tory Party image from the recent 'cash for questions' controversy.

1996 *Observer*: Cash for questions seems tame stuff compared with the way the eighteenth-century Commons lubricated its business.

chicken run *n* (1995) the abandonment by a sitting MP of a marginal seat for a safer one. Applied specifically to the flight of Conservative MPs to safer seats in anticipation of rough times in the forthcoming general election (although such was the landslide in 1997 that many an anticipated safe haven proved illusory). An adaptation of the earlier *chicken run* designating the emigration of whites from Rhodesia in the period surrounding the introduction of black majority rule and the subsequent granting of independence as Zimbabwe in 1980. This in turn was a punning blend of *chicken run* 'an enclosure for domestic fowls', *chicken* 'a coward', and *run* 'to run away'

1995 *Observer*: Then there are the MPs who have taken the 'chicken run', abandoning seats likely to fall to Labour to move into the Tory heartlands.

Chill Can *n* (1994) A proprietary name (registered in the US in 1996) for a drinks can containing a device that when activated releases gas that cools the contents of the can

1997 *Daily Telegraph*: Britain is to urge the rest of Europe to halt the introduction of 'chill cans' at a meeting of environment ministers in Luxembourg today.

chill-out room *n* (1990) an area in a nightclub, usually with air-conditioning and seating, where quiet or ambient music is played. Used for recovering from the heat and frenetic activity of the dancefloor

1991 *Time Out*: A jazz/flamenco guitarist in the chill-out room and happy hour prices at the bar before midnight.

chuffing *adj, adv* (1995) A thinly disguised euphemistic alteration of *fucking*, used as an intensifying adjective and adverb. British slang; apparently originally a northern dialectal form, which infiltrated the general language in the 1990s

1995 *Loaded*: Whoever invented breasts, hot weather and skimpy clothing, and then put them all together was a chuffing genius.

clear blue water *n* (1994) a substantial and noticeable difference in ideology and policy between the British Conservative party and its political opponents, especially the Labour party. The metaphor was based on the idea of one boat being clearly ahead of another in a race, with a not very subtle reference to the traditional colour of the Conservatives. It was first used by the Conservative minister Michael Portillo and quickly became a political cliché

1994 *Observer*: Both Ministers believe that the Conservatives should put 'clear blue water' between themselves and Labour by moving further to the radical Right.

1995 *Independent*: I'm absolutely brassed off with all this talk of green shoots and clear blue water.

Clintonite *n, adj* (1992) (a supporter) of Bill Clinton, President of the US 1993–. One of a range of eponyms (others include *Clintonize, Clintonian, Clintonism*, and **Clintonomics**) which, to the extent that they have a political rather than a personal reference, began by implying a new philosophy that would break with the conservatism of the Reagan years, and went on to connote a Republican-in-Democrat's-clothing social marketism which strongly influenced **New Labour (1993)**

1992 *Seattle Times*: The sole Clinton supporter in Precinct 37-001 was warned that..her vote would not count. 'Well, that's our political system for you,' the die-hard Clintonite responded good-naturedly.

1992 *Sunday Telegraph*: 'Regardless of what happens to Bill, the nation will be exposed to Hillary Clinton,' intoned a close female friend in the Clintonite magazine, Vanity Fair.

1993 *Times*: The Clintonites of the new Labour party will be no better at winning elections than the prophets of Clause Four.

1993 *Observer*: A Clintonised wing of the Labour Party wants to import his language of political renewal on the cheap.

1995 *Economist*: It was a classically Clintonian exercise, so everyone assumed it would end in a classically Clintonian way: with a doughy-thick waffle.

Clintonomics *n* (1992) the economic policies of US President Bill Clinton (see **Clintonite (1992)**). Lexically, a follow-up to **Reaganomics (1980)**

1993 *Newsweek*: A favorite of business for tax breaks he backed in the Senate, this consummate insider will try to sell Clintonomics to Congress from his new post at the Treasury.

cone off *v* (1996) to mark off or close (a section of road) by means of traffic cones (see **cone (1953)**). British; encapsulating the perennial condition of British motorways

1996 *Market Trader & Shopkeeper*: Before very long I can see the pavements being coned off for the different grades of pedestrians.

consensualist *adj* (1997) marked by consensus; seeking agreement via the middle way, rather than adopting a confrontational approach. A usage associated particularly with the new Labour government elected in Britain in 1997

1997 *Guardian*: Under the listening regime of Mr Mandelson, in a consensualist age, there's no good reason why that shouldn't happen.

cool Britannia *n* (1993) A slogan encapsulating a supposed renaissance of pop culture in Britain in the mid 1990s, featuring bands, clothes designers, restaurateurs, etc. fashionable throughout the known world. It is a pun on *Rule Britannia*, and had actually been used in 1967 as the title of a song by the Bonzo Dog Doo Dah Band. By 1998 its appeal was wearing thin, amid accusations that politicians, particularly the new Labour government, were trying to cash in on the coolness

1993 *Sunday Times*: The children of cool Britannia may not know much about trigonometry, but they do know every art term in the book. On the other hand, your average American rock fan probably thinks dada is somebody you can borrow the car from.

1996 *Independent*: Cool Britannia discovers its style again; tourists are flocking to join in a cultural renaissance.

1996 *International Herald Tribune*: 'Cool Britannia' is inspiring the Yanks.

council tax *n* (1991) In the UK, a tax levied by local authorities, calculated according to whichever of several bands the estimated capital value of a property falls into, and introduced in 1993 to replace the unpopular **community charge (1985)**

1991 *Daily Telegraph*: Mr Major secured full Cabinet backing yesterday for a new local tax—expected to be called the Council Tax—which will be based on a two-person household, with a discount for a single person living alone.

1992 *Daily Mail*: The new council tax, designed to replace the community charge, is expected to be based on the 1990 value of properties.

crusty, crustie *n* (1990) one of a group of homeless or vagrant young people, generally living by begging in cities, and characterized by rough clothes, matted, often dreadlocked hair, and an unkempt appearance. An uncertain line divides them from **New Age travellers (1986)**. British; the name probably comes from *crusty* 'hard, crustlike', perhaps with reference to unwashed skin and clothes

1991 *Twenty Twenty*: A familiar sight on every city's streets— look for the matted hair, donkey jacket and the dog on a string lead—Crusties are the cult that got away.

cybercafé *n* (1994) a café where customers while eating and drinking can sit at computer terminals and log on to the Internet

1995 *.net*: Cyberia, the UK's first cybercafe…offers a pretty affordable way for anyone to play with the big daddy of Internet connections—if only for half an hour or so.

cybernaut *n* (1990) someone who uses various sensory devices in order to experience virtual reality. Later, and more widely, applied to someone who uses the Internet. In either case, the underlying idea is of a traveller in **cyberspace (1982)**

> 1994 *Computer Weekly*: If anyone could qualify for being a closet cybernaut, Mike Lunch, director of the PC division at Toshiba, has got his diploma.

cyberpet *n* (1996) A vernacular name for the **tamagotchi (1996)**

> 1998 *Mail on Sunday*: The Bishop of Southwell has condemned the craze for cyberpets, claiming the gadgets are creating a generation of children who relate more closely to machines than to people.

dadrock *n* (1997) A disparaging term for rock music played by middle-aged rock stars

> 1997 *Select*: The bits that sound like *Northern Exposure* incidental music are very pretty, mind, and when, as an opener 'Float My Boat', the traditionalist songwriting meets with the soft but distorted singing and fuzzy background guitar, Arnold show their big potential. They'll have to watch out they don't inaugurate the new genre: dadrock shoegazing.

dangerous dog *n* (1991) a dog of a breed notable for its strength and ferocity, legally defined as dangerous to the public in the Dangerous Dogs Act 1991, which set out restrictions on the import, breeding, and keeping of a range of named breeds (e.g. bandogs and pit-bull terriers—see **pit-bull terrier (1945)**) in the UK, following a series of widely reported attacks on children by such dogs. See also **wolf-dog (1996)**

> 1996 *Daily Telegraph*: [Bull mastiffs] are not on the dangerous dogs list.

decluttering *n* (1997) the art of discarding unnecessary items. A term associated with feng shui, the Chinese philosophy relating to the optimal siting and arrangement of a building, room, etc., which became fashionable in the West in the 1990s. The art might well be learned to advantage by hoarders everywhere, even non-feng shui devotees

> 1997 *Independent on Sunday*: Feng Shui expert Sarah Surety runs decluttering classes, teaching inadequates how to throw things away.

Dianamania, Dimania *n* (1996) a mass-hysterical reaction to the presence or idea of Diana, Princess of Wales (often colloquially known as 'Di'). Latterly applied specifically to the wave of public emotion caused in Britain and elsewhere by her death in a car crash in Paris on 31 August 1997

> 1996 *Guardian*: Though most reporters were still proclaiming the city gripped by Dimania, there were signs yesterday of princess fatigue.

> 1997 *Guardian*: The Christmas holiday period will be the first of two tests of whether the Dianamania was a late-summer madness or a lasting national rite of pasage... She may think such stuff is for politicians but, as she is likely to discover when Dimania revives this Christmas, the Queen is running for office.

> 1998 *Sunday Times*: Time for a foreign holiday if you are fed up with Dimania—this is only the start of a fortnight of mourning on television.

docusoap *n* (1998) a television genre consisting of (actual or semi-staged) unscripted footage of people going about their ordinary lives and work. It combines the actuality of the fly-on-the-wall documentary with the developing story-line of the soap opera. A usage anticipated in the US in the late 1970s by *docu-soap opera*, which denoted a dramatized scripted film of actual events. See also **docudrama (1961)**

> 1998 *Daily Telegraph*: Chris Terrill's 12-part docu-soap...charted the journey of the Galaxy, a 2000-passenger cruise ship bound for the Caribbean.

> 1998 *Independent*: Docusoaps are now beginning to get really serious ratings.

> 1998 *Daily Telegraph*: The speaker, Betty Boothroyd, is set to end the tradition of secrecy by approving the filming of a Channel 4 'docusoap' which will show politicians at work and play throughout the House of Commons.

don't ask, don't tell *adj, n* (1993) Designating a policy on homosexuality adopted by the US military in 1994, under which personnel are not asked about their sexual orientation and gays and lesbians are allowed to serve provided they do not openly reveal their sexuality. A usage which soon spread out metaphorically to other areas

> 1997 *San Diego Union-Tribune*: Soldiers accused of homosexuality often become the focus of investigations and may be discharged from the military if they are found to have violated the military's 'don't ask, don't tell, don't pursue' policy on gays.

> 1998 *News & Observer* (Raleigh, North Carolina): A particularly scrupulous veterinarian may explain it, but others observe a don't ask/don't tell policy. Unless you inquire, they won't tell you dead pets are simply dumped in the landfill.

dream *n in your dreams* (1994) Used to suggest that someone is being unrealistically optimistic. Compare **as if (1995)**

> 1994 Charles Grant: In your dreams, G-man. In your dreams.

> 1995 *English Today*: And Sarah goes to me I think he's quite flattered and I went, in your dreams!

dress-down *adj* (1990) Designating a day (usually Friday) on which office workers are encouraged to wear casual clothes. Originally US

> 1990 *Orlando Sentinel Tribune*: In the summer, our office has 'dress-down Fridays'. On these days we don't have to dress up quite as smartly as usual.

> 1997 *Times Union* (Albany, New York): If you're an executive, get with the program on dress-down day. It defeats the purpose if the big bosses are showing up in full dress for success while the workers are dressed casually.

dumb down *v* (1991) to become less intellectually challenging or sophisticated, especially in order to appeal to a mass audience. Originally US. The transitive form of the verb has been in use since the 1930s, but with a low profile (see **dumb down (1933)**); this intransitive usage accompanied a growing feeling towards the end of the century that US culture was becoming trivialized

> 1991 C. S. Stepp: I've never heard so many editors talking about readers, thinking about readers... It doesn't mean dumbing down. It means a stronger push for clarity.

> 1994 *Washington Post Book World*: America is dumbing down, one hears. Cultural illiteracy is said to be spreading like kudzu.

DVD *n* (1994) An abbreviation of *digital video disc*, a type of digital recording medium similar in appearance to a CD but with much-increased storage capacity. According to its manufacturers, the true expansion is *digital versatile disc*, but the *v* is now generally taken to mean *video*, probably because the principal reason for developing the disc was to allow a full-length feature film to be stored on one disc

> 1994 *Variety*: In May of this year, Sony and Philips announced the joint development of a quad density digital video disk—or DVD.

> 1997 *San Francisco Chronicle*: The first DVD players will be hitting the stores this month, priced from $599 to $1000.

DWEM *n* (1990) An acronym formed from the initial letters of *dead white European male*, a contemptuous term applied to famous male historical figures, especially writers, artists, and thinkers, whose work has dominated the curricula of Western schools and universities, and is now challenged by some as discriminatory and unrepresentative, especially sexist, and Eurocentric or insufficiently multicultural. Originally and mainly US

> 1990 *Forbes*: 'PC,' she smiled, using the new campus jargon for opinions that are 'politically correct'. That and 'DWEM' (dead white European male) are, I gather, two of the most common acronyms on campus.

> 1992 *New Republic*: I have usually taken comfort in the obvious response that DWEMs have given us habeas corpus and digitalis, cantatas and penicillin.

ecological footprint *n* (1992) (a measure of) the amount of land required to sustain a particular society, or the human race in general

> 1992 W. E. Rees: The total area of land required to sustain an urban region (its 'ecological footprint') is typically at least an order of magnitude greater than that contained within municipal boundaries or the associated built-up area.

1996 *Austin American-Statesman*: Humanity must learn to leave a smaller ecological footprint,…or the 21st century will be filled with unpleasant environmental surprises.

E-fit *n* (1994) an electronically produced photofit picture. A blend of *e* for 'electronic' and **photofit (1970)**

1995 *Daily Telegraph*: The suspects were identified to police from computer-enhanced photofits, or E-Fits, of the two men.

Essex girl *n* (1991) A humorously derogatory British term applied to a type of young woman, supposedly to be found in and around Essex, and variously characterized as vulgar, unintelligent, promiscuous, and materialistic. A coinage based on **Essex man**, but in this case the focus is social rather than political. The archetypal Essex girl garb includes unsubtle gold jewellery, white high-heeled shoes, short tight skirts, and probably, if the rash of politically incorrect Essex girl jokes going around in Britain in the early 1990s are to be believed (see the first quote below), knickers with no elastic

1991 *Independent*: How does an Essex girl turn the light on afterwards? She kicks open the car door… Essex Girl jokes are told on the radio; they are faxed around between offices.

1993 *Independent*: You can parade in shiny and pricey skin-tight leggings. You can be jazzed up with Essex-girl gold jewellery for weekends.

Essex man *n* (1990) A derogatory British term used to denote a supposed new type of Conservative voter, to be found especially in London and the south-east of England in the late 1980s, typically characterized as a brash, self-made young businessman who benefited from entrepreneurial wealth created by Thatcherite policies. A touchstone of Tory electoral success in the 1980s was held to be the regular return of Conservative members to Parliament by newly enriched working-class voters in a number of Essex seats (e.g. Basildon and Harlow) which had hitherto been solidly Labour

1990 *Sunday Times*: The mass of the tribe has changed: the life and soul of the new Conservative Party, and the bedrock of its support, is Essex man.

1994 *Guardian*: Essex Man has returned to his two-up two-down in Billericay and loadsamoney has been silenced under loadsadebts.

ethnic cleansing *n* (1991) the purging, by mass expulsion or killing, of one ethnic or religious group by another. A chilling euphemism introduced into English by courtesy of the inter-ethnic conflict within the area formerly known as Yugoslavia, which started in 1991, and particularly associated with the bitter fighting between the Bosnian Serbs and the Bosnian Muslims. A translation of Serbo-Croat *etničko čišćenje*

1994 *Imprimis*: The world still seems helpless to stop ethnic cleansing in Bosnia.

1995 *Times*: The area has a large number of towns and villages, many emptied of Muslims and Croats in three years of ethnic cleansing.

Euroland *n* (1999) A name for an (as yet) hypothetical political unit consisting of those countries within the European Union (Austria, Belgium, Finland, France, Germany, Ireland, Italy, Luxembourg, the Netherlands, Portugal, and Spain) which adopted the euro (see **euro (1971)**) as an official currency in 1999

1999 *Observer*: The launch of the euro makes it much cheaper to convert between the national currencies in Euroland. The exchange rate is legally fixed to six decimal figures, and it is illegal to offer different buy and sell rates.

1999 *Sunday Times*: Given the alternative of becoming the 51st state of the United States or joining euroland, which would we prefer?

European Union *n* (1991) a federation of (originally western) European states, established by the Maastricht Treaty in 1992, which is co-extensive with the European Community (see **EC (1973)**), and whose members send representatives to the European Parliament. The abbreviation *EU* is first recorded in 1993

1991 *World Press Review*: But only diehard Euro-skeptics believe that the European Union part of this scenario will never see the light of day.

1995 *Daily Mirror*: Despite what the anti-European politicians say, are we willing to accept being part of Europe, how much do we know about the EU and should we get closer to the European dream?

e-verdict *n* (1997) a judicial verdict communicated via the Internet. A term familiarized, if not introduced, by the proposed announcement of a verdict in this way by the US judge in the trial of British au pair Louise Woodward for murdering a baby in her charge. Modelled on **e-mail**

> 1997 *Forum on Computer Risks*: Judge Zobel was planning on delivering his decision on the Louise Woodward 'Au Pair' case via the World Wide Web…trouble is, his Internet Service Provider lost power at the exact time that he was trying to deliver his much-anticipated 'E-verdict'.

extropy *n* (1992) the concept that life is not limited by extropy, but will continue to expand in an orderly and progressive manner throughout the universe

> 1994 K. Kelly: 'Extropians', as promoters of extropy call themselves, issued a seven-point lifestyle manifesto based on the vitalism of life's extropy.

false memory syndrome *n* (1992) the apparent recollection during psychotherapy of child-hood sexual abuse, especially by a relation, which had not in fact taken place. See also **recovered memory (1993)**

> 1992 *Toronto Star*: The Browns have joined the FMS foundation, formed in February in the United States. FMS stands for false memory syndrome… [The Browns] now want to spread the word to other parents…who may be suffering in solitude.

> 1993 *New York Review of Books*: By virtue of his prodding…to get his patients to 'recall' nonexistent sexual events, Freud is the true historical sponsor of 'false memory syndrome'.

FAQ *n* (1991) An acronym formed from the initial letters of *frequently asked questions*, denoting a computer text file containing a list of questions and answers relating to a particular subject, espe-cially one giving basic information on a topic to users of an Internet newsgroup

> 1994 *Independent*: 'Respect other people's time and bandwidth' means, among other things, checking the 'FAQ' (Frequently Asked Questions) document before posting a query.

> 1997 *Linux Journal*: Are there FAQs about setting up Netscape 2.02 with Linux? After you unzip Netscape where do you put the files?

feminazi *n* (1990) A contemptuous term for a radical feminist. Slang, originally and mainly North American. A blend of *feminist* and **Nazi**

> 1990 Atlanta Journal & Constitution: Let commie-liberals, femi-nazis and other bleeding hearts quibble over that.

> 1992 R. H. Limbaugh: Here then is the definition and real agenda of the feminazi: radical feminists whose objective is to see that there are as many abortions as possible.

> 1994 *Ms*: I fight my way to my destination, finally arriving in bad mood, militant black woman, cranky feminazi.

flying bishop *n* (1993) a bishop in the Anglican Church appointed to minister, within another's diocese, to those who do not accept the ordination of women. Colloquial; a phenomenon result-ing from the decision in 1993 of the General Synod of the Church of England to authorize the appointment of female clergy

> 1994 *Guardian*: Since his appointment as a 'flying bishop' was announced last week, Bishop Gaisford—a fierce opponent of women's ordination—has been deluged with letters.

FOB *n* (1992) a supporter of US President Bill Clinton. A colloquial acronym formed from the initial letters of *Friend of Bill*. The usual underlying implication is 'a crony from Clinton's days as Governor of Arkansas'

> 1995 *Newsweek*: [A] lobbyist and FOB whose Hamptons political salon is in session when Congress isn't.

Fortean *adj* (1990) relating to or being paranormal phenomena. A coinage which commemorates Charles Hoy Fort (1874–1932), a US journalist and student of such phenomena. It has been used since 1973 in the title of the *Fortean Times*, a periodical devoted to the paranormal, but it did not come into widespread general use until the 1990s

> 1996 *ikon*: Fortean phenomena like spontaneous combustion and freaks of nature.

fund-holder *n* (1991) See **fund-holding (1989)**

gabber *n* (1992) (a follower of) a harsh, aggressive type of house music originating in Rotterdam, characterized by its extremely fast dance beat. A borrowing from Dutch, where it was originally a slang term for 'mate, fellow, lad'

> 1995 *Mixmag*: 21 year old gabber freak looking for m/f penfriends.

> 1997 *Observer*: 'It's the fastest dancing you've ever seen,' said DJ Curley, a veteran of the Dutch scene. 'Gabbers really bounce, kicking alternate legs forward while sticking out their bums.'

garagiste *n* (1992) the proprietor of a garage or filling station. A borrowing from French, used chiefly to poke snobbish fun at the infiltration of the ranks of Conservative MPs, hitherto the preserve of the aristocracy, knights of the shires, and the professional classes, by people in trade—a development attributed to Margaret Thatcher's period of leadership

> 1992 *Economist*: The squirearchy that used to reap its votes from a stable, deferential rural society is disappearing from Westminster. It is being replaced, in the words of Steve Norris, an anti-hunting Tory [MP], by *garagistes* like himself.

Generation X *n* (1991) a generation of young people perceived to be disaffected, directionless, and having no part to play in society; a 'lost generation'. The term can be traced back to a science-fiction novel by Charles Hamblett and Jane Deverson called *Generation X*, published in 1964, but did not gain wide currency until the appearance in 1991 of Douglas Coupland's *Generation X: tales for an accelerated culture*. A member of the generation is known as a *Generation Xer*, or simply as an *Xer*. See also **slacker (1994)**

> 1992 *Playboy*: Xers like their infotainment. The average Xer logs 23,000 hours in front of the TV before reaching the age of 20. They learned all they need to know about politics from Oliver Stone's *JFK*.

> 1994 *Rolling Stone*: Maybe it's the pandemic shrug of Generation X, the futility felt by the young when analyzed to death by self-styled experts, carpet-bombed by music videos and wired to 157 channels with nothing on.

genetically modified *adj* (1995) Of foodstuffs: containing or consisting of genetically altered plant or animal material. First recorded as a technical term in the biological sciences in 1970, but its application by producers and marketers to foods and consequent wider lay usage are a 1990s phenomenon. See also **GM (1996)**

> 1995 *Independent*: The new tomatoes are the first genetically modified fruit to be approved for human consumption in both the UK and the US. They will be processed into tomato purée.

GM *adj, n* (1996) Abbreviation of **genetically modified (1995)** or, occasionally, of *gentic modification*. By the end of the decade a bogey term, evoking thoughts of Frankenstein

> 1999 *Sunday Times*: Dr Stanley Ewan of Aberdeen University...measured their internal organs and found the stomach walls of the rats fed GM potatoes were grossly distended.

golden goal *n* (1994) the first goal scored during extra time in a soccer match, which ends the match and gives victory to the scoring side. A concept introduced to try and forestall the 'penalty shoot-out' as a way of deciding unresolved matches in a knock-out competition

> 1994 *Daily Mirror*: FIFA general secretary Sepp Blatter said yesterday that a system of sudden-death would be introduced in extra-time, with a goal—the 'golden goal'—ending the match.

goodfella *n* (1990) a member of the Mafia; a mobster. US colloquial. A usage inspired by *Goodfellas*, a 1990 film by Martin Scorsese about the world of the American Mafia; a reliable member of the Mafia is seen as a 'good fellow' by his companions

> 1990 *Village Voice* (New York): Like the goodfellas who become gangsters so they don't have to stand in line to buy bread, Scorsese can get his hands on any film he has a passion for.

granny dumping *n* (1991) the deliberate abandonment at an unfamiliar location of an elderly person by those responsible for him or her. A phenomenon first noted in the US in the early 1990s

> 1992 *Independent*: Government policy on community care of the elderly could see the arrival of 'granny dumping', which has occurred in the US, the conference was told.

green shoots *n* (1991) signs of economic recovery. A usage (based on the clichéd metaphor of new growth on a plant) brought to public notice in Britain when the Chancellor of the Exchequer, Norman Lamont, attempting to raise the spirits of the faithful at the 1991 Conservative Party

Conference in the depths of the recession, said 'The green shoots of economic spring are appearing once again'

> 1992 *New Republic*: Every week in the last four months of 1991 was marked by predictions from one minister or another that the recession was about to end. The 'green shoots' of recovery were now showing.

> 1993 *Computer Contractor*: Tax increases may be necessary but they carry the risk of jeopardising those fragile green shoots.

> 1995 *Independent*: I'm absolutely brassed off with all this talk of green shoots and clear blue water.

grey pound *n* (1996) the purchasing power of older people. A phenomenon of increasing interest to sellers at the end of the century, with the average age of the population rising decade by decade. The coinage follows a recently established pattern for identifying particular economic sectors by colouring the currency (e.g. *pink pound* for the purchasing power of gays, *blue pound* for the money spent on pornography)

> 1996 *Independent*: Saga, the company whose success is built squarely on the 'grey pound', has fixed its sights on a lucrative new market—radio for the over-55s.

grunge *n, adj* (1991) (in) a style of appearance or dress characterized by loose-fitting, layered, often second-hand clothes, ripped jeans, and heavy boots, favoured by fans of grunge music and also briefly appropriated by the retail fashion industry. The use of **grunge (1965)** with reference to informal music has been claimed since the late 1960s, and there is recorded evidence of it from the early 70s, but it seems not to have become a specific term until the beginning of the 90s, when it was applied to a style of rock music characterized by a raucous guitar sound which was developed by a number of mainly Seattle-based US groups. The term soon spread from there to the appearance of its fans

> 1993 *Chicago Tribune*: Still, designer grunge is a concept that doesn't play well in Seattle where the real grunge community wears a 'uniform' of layered, worn clothing.

> 1994 *Rolling Stone*: The group is discussing what it's like to be seen as grunge kids in the reality of post-Nirvana Aberdeen.

Gulf War syndrome *n* (1992) a disorder of the nervous system alleged to have been contracted by soldiers serving in the Gulf War of 1991. The causes (and indeed the existence) of the disorder are still disputed: suggested agents include the anti-nerve-gas medication given to troops destined for the Gulf, and harmful chemicals encountered on active service there. The condition has also been referred to as *desert fever, Desert Storm syndrome* (from the code name of the Allies' land campaign in the Gulf War), and *Persian War syndrome*

> 1992 *USA Today*: Hundreds of gulf war veterans…are reporting various illnesses they say are the result of service in the Persian Gulf. Dubbed 'gulf war syndrome', symptoms range from hair loss, fatigue and muscle aches to dizzy spells and shortness of breath.

> 1996 *Week*: Nicholas Soames, the Armed Forces Minister, has announced a full inquiry into Gulf War Syndrome and apologised for unknowingly misleading Parliament over the extent to which troops had been exposed to harmful pesticides during the Gulf War.

handbag *n* (1991) a form of electronic dance music, derived from house, characterized by its highly commercial appeal, catchy melodies, and an upbeat or euphoric mood. Originally a patronizing term based on the stereotypical image of women in nightclubs dancing with their handbags at their feet, supposedly suggestive of the music's unsophisticated, celebratory, crowd-pleasing quality

> 1991 *New Musical Express*: New Yawk drawling rap over Kraftwerk's 'The Model' just does not work, no way, no how. Handbag DJs will love it.

> 1992 *Face*: As it is, it's already taken over handbag clubs from Jason and Kylie.

happy-clappy *n, adj* (1990) (a member) of a Christian charismatic group. A mildly contemptuous term, based on the enthusiastic hand-clapping and other outward signs of emotion which often mark evangelical services

> 1992 *Sunday Times*: He's one of the happy-clappy lot. They're always speaking in tongues, casting out demons and frightening the old ladies.

1994 *Guardian*: Now Asian families have to live not only in fear of BNP attacks but with the threat of muddled happy-clappies patronising them every week.

heroin chic *n* (1994) a glamorization of the culture and appearance of heroin users, characterized especially by the use of very thin, wan fashion models

1994 *Washington Post*: Another musician-martyr with a mighty habit who may or may not enhance heroin chic among the fans.

1996 *Economist*: The worry is over 'heroin chic', marked by new trends in fashion and films such as 'Trainspotting'.

1998 *Guardian*: I find the heroin-chic thing disturbing... I never used people being high as a way of selling clothes.

home alone *adj* (1990) Designating a child left at home unsupervised while its parents are out or away. Also applied to the parents of such a child. A largely journalistic expression inspired by the 1990 Hollywood film *Home Alone*, which tells the story of a small boy accidentally left behind when his parents went on holiday

1993 *Coloradoan* (Fort Collins): 'Home alone' couple face abuse charges.

home page *n* (1993) a document created in a hypertext system (especially on the World Wide Web) which serves either as a point of introduction to a person, institution, or company, or as a focus of information on a particular topic, and which usually contains hypertext links to other (related) documents. Compare **Web site (1994)**

1993 *R & D*: At startup, Mosaic provides the user with a home page that contains a number of information links with which the user can begin his exploration.

1995 *Guardian*: Edward Kennedy was the first senator to establish a 'home page' on the Internet giving two way access to the public.

hot-desking *n* (1991) the practice of sharing desks, workstations, etc., between office workers on an ad hoc basis or rota system, rather than allocating individual desks, as a means of saving space and resources

1991 *Sunday Times*: The new trend, 'hot desking', is that desks are shared between several people who use them at different times. This has been made possible because more people are now working from home or with the customer.

1995 *Independent*: As businesses move towards teleworking and hot-desking, such portability could become crucial.

hotting *n* (1991) joyriding in stolen high-performance cars, especially dangerously and for display (e.g. with show-off stunts such as handbrake turns). British slang; probably based, with deliberate double entendre, on *hot* 'fast and powerful' and **hot** 'stolen', with perhaps a side-glance too at *hot-wire* 'to start the engine of (a car) by bypassing the ignition system'. The term *hotter*, for 'someone who engages in hotting', is also first recorded in 1991

1991 *Observer*: What started as a campaign against 'hotting'— displays of high-speed handbrake turns in stolen cars—has turned into a dispute over territory.

1991 *Guardian*: Police moved into the estate…to crack down on 'hotters', the youngsters who steal high performance cars and speed in front of crowds of more than 100.

HTML *n* (1992) An abbreviation of *Hypertext Markup Language*, a specification for generating World Wide Web pages which enables the viewing software to display text, images, and other resources and to execute links to other such pages; it also allows the user to create and print out documents

1994 *Computer Weekly*: HTML has 'tags' to tell your browser how to lay out the text it is receiving— 'text' that can include images, sounds and even live, digital video.

human BSE *n* (1992) a notional neurological disease resembling BSE that affects human beings. A usage that sprang from the long-running BSE epidemic in cattle and the fears that humans who ate BSE-infected beef might catch the disease themselves

1992 *Dogs Today*: And the professor thinks all this meddling in what animals eat could already have given BSE to human beings: 'I think Creutzfeldt Jakob's disease—which turns the brain into a sponge—could be human BSE. We're seeing about 50 cases a year. But as it takes 30 years to surface, we won't know if there's an epidemic on the way until it's too late.'

Iceman *n* (1991) the body of a man from the prehistoric period (probably about 3,300 BC), found preserved in ice in the mountains of the Tyrol on the Italo-Austrian border

> 1995 *Post* (Denver): If the Alps could have its Iceman, as the find is popularly called, then the Andes now has its Icewoman.

information fatigue sydrome *n* (1994) a condition of psychological stress induced by the attempt to assimilate or manipulate excessive amounts of information (*information overload*, a term first recorded in 1977). The quintessential late-20th-century managerial malaise. The term *information fatigue* (probably inspired by the earlier **compassion fatigue (1985)**) is first recorded in 1991

> 1994 *Straits Times* (Singapore): With so much bombardment of information, we sometimes tend to suffer from information fatigue-syndrome.

> 1997 *Business Times*: IFS... Short for Information Fatigue Syndrome, it's a new disease that managers are particularly prone to.

intermercial *n* (1997) an advertisement published via the Internet

> 1997 *Guardian*: Unfortunately, it's too early to celebrate the death of advertising online. What they're cooking up now is even worse: 'intermercials'.

internaut *n* (1992) an (expert or habitual) user of the Internet. Colloquial, originally US; a blend of **Internet** and **astronaut**, probably with the idea of 'cyberspace' in mind

> 1996 *New York Times*: Currently, internauts visiting the site can follow Tracy Bowden and other divers in their exploration of the treasure-laden Spanish galleon Concepcion.

internot *n* (1992) A facetious coinage (inspired by **internaut (1992)**) implying a range of negative relationships with the Internet, from 'someone who does not use the Internet' to 'someone opposed to the Internet'. Originally US

> 1992 *Computers in Libraries*: In the world of wide-area computer networking, the 'haves' and the 'have nots' could be called the 'Internauts' and the 'Internots'.

> 1996 *Internet World*: Is the Internet putting a strain on your relationship? Some Internauts are being confronted by InterNOTs!—significant others who want to know why they're spending so much time online and so little time with them.

Irishization *n* (1997) the process of making something Irish. A term applied specifically to a phenomenon of late-1990s Britain in which pubs hitherto of a traditional English character were turned into 'Irish' pubs, with vintage advertisements for Irish products, folksy Irish artefacts, and wall-to-wall Guinness

> 1997 *Independent on Sunday*: In Holloway Road, north London, the Nag's Head has become O'Neill's—a victim of the fake 'Irishisation' of pubs across the country.

Islington person *n* (1994) A usually derogatory British term for a middle-class, socially aware person (if male, *Islington man*) with left-wing views (characteristics supposedly typical of residents of Islington, a borough of North London)

> 1994 Cal McCrystal: Just as Essex Man, the distinctive lager-swilling Tory entrepreneur, represented the 1980s, Islington Man—more properly Islington Person—may turn out to be the most potent composite of the late 1990s.

> 1995 *Independent*: At the time of his election the Labour leader [Tony Blair] was portrayed as the ultimate Islington man.

Java *n* (1990) The proprietary name of a computer programming language used to create networking applications, especially interactive elements within World Wide Web pages. It alludes to Java coffee, a favourite drink of many US computer programmers, and was intended to reflect the richness and strength of the language

> 1996 *Economist*: Whereas Web pages are static documents, Java applets are real programs that you can control like any other software.

jelly *n* (1992) a capsule of the tranquillizer Temazepam reformulated as a gelatinous compound in an effort to prevent users injecting. British colloquial

> 1992 *Herald* (Glasgow): James Deas told the High Court in Glasgow he was going for chips with George Mitchell, 19, when they were stopped by youths and one asked 'Do you want to buy jellies? (the drug temazepam)'.

jobseeker *n* (1993) In Britain, an unemployed person required to demonstrate efforts to find work in order to qualify for government benefits. The semi-euphemistic *jobseeker* for 'unemployed person' is first recorded as long ago as 1942 (see also **job-seeking (1972)**), but this specific application stems from the introduction of the so-called *Jobseeker's Allowance* in 1993 (see the first quote below)

> 1993 *Guardian*: Similarly, the unemployed are now 'jobseekers', entitled to Jobseeker's Allowance provided they first sign a Jobseeker's Agreement.

> 1995 *Independent*: Pilot projects of workfare…could be launched after the Jobseeker's Bill becomes law.

juice box *n* (1991) a small carton with attached plastic straw containing a single portion of fruit juice. Evidence of their popularity litters 1990s urban environments

> 1991 *New Age Journal*: Environmentally unfriendly juice boxes have been snubbed in favor of old-fashioned whole milk in a reusable thermos.

jungle *n* (1992) a style of dance music, originating in Britain in the early 1990s, which incorporates elements of ragga, hip-hop, and techno, and is characterized by bare instrumentation consisting almost exclusively of very fast electronic drum tracks and slower booming synthesized bass lines. The origins of the name are disputed: it may be a reference to the music's rhythmic drumming and repetitive chanting, supposedly reminiscent of jungle-dwellers, or to the emphatically urban concerns of its lyrics (as in *concrete jungle*), but some have linked it with 'The Jungle', a name given to the Tivoli Gardens district of Kingston, Jamaica. Performers or fans are known as *junglists*

> 1994 *Rolling Stone*: If I say what jungle music's like, it makes it so banal. It's an attitude, very happy and organic, while hard-core techno is banging your head against a wall.

> 1994 *Echoes*: The junglists are in for a treat, too, with three firing drum 'n' bass versions of this track.

kit *n* (1994) clothing. British slang; used mainly in the phrase *get one's kit off*, denoting removal of one's clothes, usually for the benefit of a lecherous would-be observer. From the previous sense, 'a set of clothes for a particular activity' (e.g. *football kit*)

> 1994 *Observer*: I've written a highbrow piece of highly political literary fiction, but all anyone can say is 'get your kit off'.

> 1995 *Guardian*: Most of the males in the audience roar appreciatively, including one behind me who shouts: 'Get yer kit off!'

laddish *adj* (1991) indulging in behaviour and attitudes characteristic of a **New Lad (1991)**; uncouthly macho. Compare **blokeish (1957)**

> 1991 *Face*: We're all cackling in laddish glee. Things are looking up.

life *n get a life* (1991) start living a fuller or more interesting existence. Slang; used as a scornful admonition to someone whose way of life is viewed as unacceptably empty, dull, or 'sad' (e.g. nerds, wonks, anoraks, or train-spotters)

> 1995 *Internet World*: 'Get a Life' messages periodically appear—usually in impolite terms—advising *Star Trek* enthusiasts that they could be spending their time better elsewhere.

loved-up *adj* (1992) affected by the drug ecstasy. Slang, mainly British; from the popular idea that ecstasy is an aphrodisiac

> 1992 *Face*: The first people I met were…all set for a night's raving and loved-up to the eyeballs.

> 1995 *DJ*: The majority of 'loved-up' ravers will pass through the night happy and unscathed.

lovely jubbly *n* (1990) money, wealth. British slang. Originally, in the 1950s, the advertising slogan of an orange drink called 'Jubbly'. It was popularized by the character Del Boy in the BBC television sitcom *Only Fools and Horses*, and took on a new career as a generalized exclamation or adjective of pleased approval (as if *jubbly* were just a rhyming alteration of *lovely*)

> 1993 *Non-League Football Today*: The FA might get a bit upset as well without all that lovely jubbly clinking in at the till.

> 1997 *Inside Soap*: Enjoy three lovely jubbly episodes of the classic comedy featuring Del Boy, Rodney and Uncle Albert.

> 1997 *News of the World*: Presented in chronological order this collection is only available from Britannia and is not sold in any shops. Lovely Jubbly!

loyalty card *n* (1993) an identity card issued by a retailer to its customers so that each individual transaction can be recorded as part of a consumer incentive scheme under which credits are amassed for future discounts each time a purchase is made

> 1993 *Bookseller*: Publishers' restrictions do not, for example, allow us to issue a Dillons customer loyalty card.

> 1995 *Which?*: Loyalty cards may be popular, but rather than having to join special clubs to get savings, we think it's better if all customers can see cuts on shelf prices.

lunchbox *n* (1992) the male genitalia, especially as visible through tight clothing. British humorous slang. The immediate inspiration is a facetious comparison with the contents of a lunchbox (e.g. a banana and two apples, or conceivably a gherkin and two olives), but the underlying metaphor is no doubt the same as in the past was responsible for *packet*, *basket*, and indeed *box* itself being applied to the male genitals. A usage popularized by the *Sun* newspaper, which used it frequently in stories relating to the British sprinter Linford Christie

> 1998 *Guardian*: 'What is Linford Christie's lunchbox?' Mr Justice Popplewell…asked the Olympic gold medallist in bemusement. 'They are making a reference to my genitals, your honour,' replied the agitated athlete. 'I think it's disgusting.'

luvvy, luvvie *n* (1990) A British term of mockery for actors and actresses, especially ones considered particularly effusive or affected, of the sort who go around calling each other 'luvvy', 'darling', etc. (*luvvy* as a spelling of the term of address *lovey* dates from the 1960s)

> 1990 *Guardian*: The 43rd Cannes International Festival of Cinema… It's a rough deal for the poor luvvies being paid to watch movies and party.

> 1992 *Daily Telegraph*: Actors are always saying that the stage is the loneliest place in the world and I'd always thought it was hyperbolic luvvy talk.

mad *adj* (1991) Used as a generalized approval adjective among participants in the dance-music and rave culture of the 1990s. Apparently a development of US Black English *mad* 'remarkable, exciting', which is first recorded in 1970

> 1993 G. Donaldson: The superlative of the hour was not 'awesome' or even 'cool' but 'mad', as in 'mad house party'.

> 1995 *Represent*: There was a mad B-Boyin' jam with the French Crew Actual Force representing with mad flavas.

mail bomb *n* (1993) an abnormally large e-mail message, or an abnormally large number of e-mail messages, sent maliciously in the expectation that the receiving computer will be unable to cope. Probably a pun on the earlier *mail bomb* 'a bomb sent through the post' (first recorded in 1972). Such action is usually taken in retribution for some perceived violation of Internet etiquette

> 1994 *Guardian*: He was inundated with abuse, including a 'mail bomb'—eight million characters of gibberish designed to clog up his system.

millennium bug *n* (1995) the inability of certain computer software to deal correctly with dates later than 31 December 1999, threatening to bring computer systems worldwide crashing to a halt at the arrival of the millennium. Also sometimes referred to as the *millennium bomb*

> 1995 *Chicago Tribune*: To fix software that carries the millennium bug, the code must be run through a decompiling program that converts the computer code into languages like Cobol.

> 1996 *Times*: The Internal Revenue Service envisages taking 300 man-years to defeat the 'new millennium bug'.

Millennium Dome *n* (1997) a very large structure in the shape of a flattened dome constructed on the Greenwich Peninsula, SE London, to house a national exhibition celebrating the millennium in 2000. Often shortened contextually to simply *the Dome*. A project attacked widely during the course of its building on such varied grounds as its expense, the banality of its proposed contents, and the self-aggrandizing tendencies of its political master Peter Mandelson

1997 *Earthmatters*: Part of [the Millennium Experience] is going to be showing what our environment will be like, how we can sustain it, and how new technologies will shape our housing, our energy, transport and so on. We need the Millennium Dome and the rest of the Experience to present those things with the originality and the panache they deserve.

1998 *Observer*: An earlier scene had shown Draper walking Dainton around the Dome. 'Isn't it marvellous,' gushes Draper. 'Waste of money,' counters Dainton.

Millennium Product *n* (1997) a product designated under the Millennium Products Initiative as representing innovative and progressive British design

1997 *Daily Telegraph*: A plastic bucket may not sound high-tech, but it is saving lives in Rwanda, Burundi and Zaire. Oxfam's 14-litre water container, selected as one of the first Millennium Products, proves that good design need not be complicated.

Mini Disc *n* (1991) The proprietary name of a small recordable version of a magneto-optical compact disc

1992 *Playboy*: Sony's system, called the mini-disc, is actually a two-inch diameter compact disk. Like DCC tapes, minidiscs will incorporate track-finding codes and song-name display.

1994 *Rolling Stone*: If you want digital audio *and* recording capability, consider the MiniDisc.

misper *n* (1994) a person reported missing. British police slang; a conflation of *missing person* which was probably around before the 1990s but first came to public notice with the revelations about the murderous Gloucester builder Frederick West, who turned out to have been responsible for the deaths of many young female mispers. Further reinforced by its frequent use in the police soap opera *The Bill*

1995 *Guardian*: He…leaves the sister of a 'misper' in peace rather than ask 'And how did you feel?'

mobile *n* (1990) See mobile phone (1965)

monster *adj* (1991) remarkably successful or capable; outstanding. Slang

1991 *Sports Illustrated*: Sierra enjoyed a monster 1989…, but slipped to .280, 16 and 96 last year.

1992 *Option*: Perry had started working with Bob Marley, gathering a monster band.

1994 *M.E.A.T.*: Ur—the debut full-length from Vancouver act Salvador Dream—is just fuckin' monster!

morphing *n* (1991) a computing technique used to produce the special effect of smoothly transforming one film image into another by encoding both images into digital form and gradually manipulating parts of the first image to correspond with comparable parts of the second. Based ultimately on Greek *morphē* 'shape' (as in *metamorphosis*)

1993 Shay & Jody: ILM had employed computer generated imagery and advanced morphing techniques to transform actor Robert Patrick into a variety of wholly digital and puppet creations in his role as the shape-shifting liquid metal terminator in James Cameron's blockbuster film [i.e. *Terminator 2*].

mouse potato *n* (1994) someone who spends an excessive amount of time in front of a computer, especially one who uses it online. A facetious variation on the earlier **couch potato** 'someone who watches television or videos all the time' (1979), using **mouse** in the computer sense 'a pointing device'

1994 *Guardian*: Freddie is a mouse potato, an Internet addict.

1996 *Digital Dispatch*: Confirmed mouse potato Raphael Needleman can't wait for the convergence of TV and the Net.

MSP *n* (1995) An abbreviation of *Member of the Scottish Parliament*. Following a referendum in 1997, a Scottish Parliament with widely devolved powers is projected to begin its deliberations in 2000

1995 *Scotsman*: Each elector will be entitled to cast two votes, the first under the first-past-the-post system for one of 73 constituency MSPs elected from the existing Westminster constituencies.

multiculti *adj, n* (1991) A colloquial US shortening of *multicultural* or of *multiculturalism*. Its use creates an informal tone, which converts multiculturalism from a serious political issue to something more familiar and accessible

1993 Robert Hughes: Up come the conservatives, wringing their hands in the manner of the late Allan Bloom over rap, rock-'n'-roll, and the unearned Dionysiac ecstasies of mass multi-culti.

1995 *Entertainment Weekly*: Jane Smiley's satire of a Midwestern University is like a big college party to which everybody's invited. They're all here—the whole multi-culti, crazy-quilt gang that makes up modern academic life in America.

mwah *interj* (1994) A representation of the sound of an air kiss (see **air-kiss (1985)**)

1994 *Daily Telegraph*: The foyer beforehand was wall-to-wall *mwah!s* and Sheridan-how-lovely-to-see-you's.

1998 *Independent*: He is half-Czech, half-Spanish, beautifully groomed, deliciously perfumed, around 60, and a great air-kisser, mwah, mwah!

name and shame *v* (1991) to disclose publicly a person's or institution's (perceived) wrongdoing or failure. Originally US. A popular move in the morally self-righteous 1990s

1993 *Vancouver Star*: Juveniles should be named and shamed, not protected, so that they and their parents may be held responsible.

1998 *Mirror*: Jack Straw…is a strong advocate of tough punishments for juvenile drug offenders—including naming and shaming them, and fining their parents.

negative equity *n* (1992) the indebtedness that occurs when the market value of a property falls below the outstanding amount of a mortgage secured on it, representing a reversal of the favourable (and expected) situation in which a property is a valuable asset. A term in use since the 1950s in US financial jargon in broad application to assets generally. This specific British use arose out of a situation in which house prices, inflated by the boom of the 1980s, suddenly tumbled with the recession of the early 90s, catching out many people who had bought at the top of the market

1993 *Guardian*: The proportion of house owners with negative equity rose by a fifth over the past year as prices in some regions continued to fall.

netizen *n* (1993) a (habitual or keen) user of the Internet. A blend of *net* and *citizen*

1996 *Daily Telegraph*: Several Web sites have set up Valentine's Day pages to put love-lorn netizens in touch.

Nettie *n* (1994) a regular user of Usenet, a system of online discussion groups. Colloquial, often with a tinge of mockery

1994 *Daily Telegraph*: The temptations of surfing are irresistible to new netties but reality takes over.

New Britain *n* (1997) Britain viewed as being reinvigorated or reborn following the election victory of New Labour in 1997, and consequently vibrant, fashionable, etc.

1997 *Guardian*: The phrase has slowly entered the language, with New Britain replacing New Labour as chattering-class slang for fashionable or in.

New Labour *n* (1992) the British Labour party as it is after the internal reforms initiated by Neil Kinnock (party leader 1983–92), and carried through by John Smith (party leader 1992–94) and Tony Blair (party leader 1994–, prime minister 1997–). The changes affect both its constitution and internal workings (e.g. the introduction of 'one man one vote' for decision-making within the party) and its policies (characterized by a move towards the political centre; see **third way (1990)**). The use of *new* to suggest a radical political departure or change of direction is far from new (compare **New Deal (1932)**), and the term *New Labour* itself first came to prominence in 1989 to denote a breakaway wing of the New Zealand Labour party. See also **Blairism (1993)**

1995 *Independent*: The Labour front bench's prevarication over rail renationalisation has only added to the mistrust felt by rank and file trade unionists towards Mr Blair and 'New Labour'.

1997 *Mail on Sunday*: Rebel MP Tam Dalyell—thorn in the side on New Labour's pro-devolution campaign—said he would refuse to bow to threats to oust him before the next General Election.

New Lad *n* (1991) a (young) man who embraces sexist attitudes and the traditional male role as a reaction against the perceived effeminacy of the **New Man (1982)**, especially one who does so (or claims to do so) knowingly and with a sense of ironic detachment. British; brought to a wide audience in the 1990s BBC television sitcom *Men Behaving Badly*. See also **laddish (1991)**

1991 *Arena*: I was quite mystified by the New Lad, or rather his motives for trying to be anything more than the neanderthal he always will be.

THE 1990S —————————————————————————————————— | 594

> 1994 *Independent*: David Baddiel, for one, is convinced his New Laddishness appeals to women. 'I've got lots of women friends. They find my honesty refreshing,' he insists.

nigga *n* (1990) a black person. Originally and mainly US; a deliberate, politically motivated reclamation (albeit in altered form) by blacks of the word *nigger*, which had become taboo through its use as a term of contempt by whites. The plural is often spelt *niggaz*

> 1990 *Los Angeles Times*: After South Central Los Angeles was plastered with posters promoting N.W.A.'s new '100 Miles and Runnin' album with the tag line 'Tha Niggaz R Back', some of the most immediate response came not from fans but from alleged white supremacists who were unable to decipher the posters' origins.

nul points *n* (1994) a score of zero in a contest; a verdict of abysmal quality. A facetious British usage inspired by the Norwegian entry in the 1978 Eurovision Song Contest, *Mil Etter Mil* 'Mile after Mile' (sung by Jahn Teigen), which failed to elicit a single point from the international juries. The cod French, 'no points' (real French would be *nul point*), is probably a tribute to the long-time commère of the British presentation of the contest, Katie Boyle, who was famous for her immaculate French

> 1995 *Sporting Life*: 'All the shrewdies are on at long odds. Good luck to Pat Ryan and the team. Here's to Seanie!' Curryhills Fancy? Nul points from The Greyhound Life jury, I'm afraid.

> 1998 *Sunday Mirror*: England? Nul points. Sadly, NONE of the world's top footballers we asked said England (or Scotland) would win [the World Cup]. But then, what do they know?

offliner *n* (1997) someone who does not use the Internet. A sad and despised species in the online 90s

> 1997 *Computing*: Although it sounds bizarre to offliners, all those involved describe it as completely addictive.

off-message *adj, adv* (1993) departing from a planned or intended message. Applied specifically to a politician who departs from the official party line. Originally US, but taken up enthusiastically in Britain, especially by the media managers of New Labour, for whom loyal adherence to the script (being 'on message') is an acid test of political soundness and promotability

> 1993 *Washington Post*: The president essentially went 'off-message'. He moved from topic to topic…and promoted his economic plan only in passing.

> 1997 *Daily Telegraph*: A colleague said there had been a serious conflict among ministers because the commitment was '100 per cent off-message'.

> 1998 *Private Eye*: The Lib Dems' off-message response to planned benefit cuts.

OMOV *n* (1992) An acronym formed from the initial letters of *one member, one vote*, a principle of democratic election within an organization. It became a motto of advocates of voting reform within the British trade unions and Labour party in the 1990s, who saw the block voting arrangements then in place as damaging to Labour's image and electoral prospects

> 1994 *Guardian*: It states that without the dreaded OMOV, one member one vote, Labour will simply be written off as incapable of addressing the massive discontents in the political system.

out *v* (1990) to expose the undeclared homosexuality of (especially a prominent or public figure), originally mainly as a tactical move by gay-rights activists. Originally US. A verbal use of the adjective *out*, which is first recorded in the sense 'acknowledged openly as a homosexual' (i.e. 'out of the closet') in 1979

> 1995 *Maclean's*: 'I consider outing a supreme act of moral cowardice,' he said. 'In no case I am aware of have the outers offered counselling or support to the person they are outing.'

> 1996 *Face*: It's typical of Garber's style that *Vice Versa* is packed with juicy anecdotes about the sex lives of celebrities. She 'outs' dozens as bi—instead of exclusively straight or gay.

paleo-conservative *n* (1993) someone advocating old or traditional forms of conservatism; an extreme right-wing conservative. US; an insult word (reflecting the rise of the extreme right in US politics in the 90s) formed with the prefix *paleo-* 'of ancient, especially prehistoric, times'. Sometimes abbreviated to *paleo-con*

> 1993 Robert Hughes: Instead of common ground, we got demagogues urging that there is only one path to virtuous American-ness: palaeo-conservatives like Jesse Helms and Pat Robertson who think this country has one single ethic.

> 1995 *New York Review of Books*: Robertson…unlike Kirk and many 'paleocons', has consistently supported the Israeli right wing over the years.

Palookaville *n* (1990) an imaginary town characterized by stupidity, mediocrity, and ineptitude. US slang, based on *palooka* 'a stupid or mediocre person', which dates from the 1920s

> 1994 *Rolling Stone*: Critical buzz, MTV airplay and an endorsement from none other than late night monarch David Letterman combined to shoot this intriguing West Coast band from Palookaville to Platinumland.

people's *n* (1997) Designating something thought of as relating to, belonging to, or including all the ordinary members of the population, as opposed to an establishment élite. A concept that took off in Britain in the wake of the death of Diana, Princess of Wales, when the unexpectedly effusive public expressions of grief supposedly demonstrated, among other things, that it was the rank and file of Britain, not their rulers or the great and the good, who would determine the nature and extent of the nation's response. The term has its roots in the 19th century (an educational institution called the 'People's Palace' was opened in London in 1887), but since the 1930s it has been associated mainly with Communist regimes; this new usage is more mystical than political

> 1997 *Daily Telegraph*: The continuing myth that Tony Blair coined the phrase 'The people's Princess'… [It] was actually the title of the chapter about Diana in Anthony Holden's 1993 book about the House of Windsor, *The Tarnished Crown*.

> 1997 *Independent on Sunday*: If the Palace is to be converted into a 'living gallery' or 'people's palace', it would be closed to the public for state occasions.

> 1997 *Guardian*: They were joined by 'ordinary' people chosen as a cross-section of the nation, at the 'People's Banquet'.

> 1999 *Evening Standard*: The Government's proposals for an interim Chamber appear something of a dog's breakfast, including…the appointment of up to 20 'people's peers'.

personal stereo *n* (1992) a small battery-operated cassette player and headphones capable of being worn by a person who is on foot. A generic term that has largely come to replace the earlier tradename **Walkman (1981)**. First recorded in 1992, but probably in use well before then (the synonymous *personal hi-fi* is first recorded in 1985)

> 1992 *Which?*: If you want your children to keep their music to themselves during the holidays, a personal stereo is the ideal gift.

pharm *n* (1990) a place where genetically modified plants or animals are grown or reared in order to produce pharmaceutical products. Formed from the first syllable of *pharmaceutical*, with a punning play on *farm*. Also used in the derivative *pharming*

> 1991 *Longevity*: Others foresee the marriage of cloning with genetic engineering, yielding herds of 'pharm' animals.

> 1996 *Sacramento Bee*: Take the banana. As a pharming product, this tropical fruit is being transformed.

phat *adj* (1992) excellent, great. Originally denoting sexiness in a woman, this extended approval usage entered the general language via the vocabulary of hip-hop. Its ultimate origins are obscure: suggestions that it may have been formed from the initial letters of *pussy, hips, arse* (or *ass*), and *tits*, or of *pretty hole at all times*, have never been proved

> 1995 *Guardian*: The Criminal Justice Act put the rave under House arrest. But it's out and it's phat in Oxfordshire.

> 1995 *Echoes*: Here he turns in a rough-arsed stomping groove with off-beat disco bass and a phat kick that provide the base for clonky piano, stabby organ and sparse vocal drops.

poptastic *adj* (1992) Denoting fantastically good pop music, or an atmosphere or background associated with this. British humorous slang; a blend of **pop** and **fantastic**. Popularized by the BBC television comedy programme *The Harry Enfield Show*, in which the term was used as a catchphrase of 'Smashie and Nicey', spoof radio disc jockeys

> 1992 *New Musical Express*: December 1, 1991 was World AIDS Day… On that day, various poptastic things happened all over the world.

> 1994 *Daily Telegraph*: Some BBC2 art guru likes them so much that he has nicked their poptastic CD for himself.

Power Ranger *n* (1993) The proprietary name of a plastic toy figure resembling a character from the US children's television series *Mighty Morphin Power Rangers*. These American teenagers are regularly summoned to change into masked kung-fu heroes to do battle with the evil *Space Aliens* and other villains

> 1994 *Guardian*: The key to the toys' success is television. The characters are all tied in to a series about a group of teenagers able to 'morph' into crime-fighting Power Rangers.

> 1995 *Sugar*: Snap up one of these fab Power Ranger key-rings.

prebuttal *n* (1997) anticipatory rebuttal. A case of getting one's retaliation in first. Originally US, and usually used in political contexts: political parties' sophisticated computerized files on their opponents enable them to counter an accusation before it has been made

> 1997 *Guardian*: The rebuttal units of Millbank would become as insignificant as the prebuttal teams at Smith Square.

Premiership *n* (1993) the top division of the English Football League. A name intended to lend added class to the earlier *Premier League*, itself an aggrandizing term introduced in 1992 to make the First Division sound more impressive (what had been the Second Division as a result became the 'First' Division)

> 1993 *Radio Times*: The clash at Old Trafford is the real business of winning crucial premiership points and perhaps striking a psychological blow.

prenup *n* (1990) A colloquial US abbreviation of **prenuptial agreement (1916)**, reflecting the wide usage of that term from the 1980s onwards

> 1990 *Mirabella*: The De Loreans ($2000-a-month child support in spite of the prenup).

> 1991 *New York Times*: The couple's prenup linked alimony payments to whether the parties remained clean and sober.

puffa (jacket) *n* (1991) a type of thick, heavily padded warm jacket. Presumably so named on account of its puffed-up shape

> 1998 *BBC Match of the Day Magazine*: This season things have got worse with the proliferation of people with mobile phones and Puffa jackets who think they are John Motson.

pukka *adj* (1991) excellent, of the highest quality; fashionable. A fashionable British approval word of the 1990s, based on the earlier *pukka* 'genuine'. Also sometimes used as an adverbial intensifier

> 1991 *Independent*: I'm going to France soon.., so I'll look well pukka trendy.

> 1996 *Observer*: Girls mug girls for jewellery or pukka clothes.

radical centre *n* (1996) a political position that is neither extreme left-wing or extreme right-wing in traditional terms, but which espouses 'radical' policies. A response to the adversarial politics of previous decades which caught the mood of the 1990s. The derived *radical centrism* is first recorded in 1997. See also **third way (1990)**

> 1997 *PA News*: Mr Blair, opening Labour's first major press conference of the campaign, declared that his party had changed and become 'the new force for the radical centre in British politics'.

> 1997 *Guardian*: Yet the framework of the kind of 'radical centrism' which Labour advocates in other areas is already in place.

ragga *n* (1990) a style of pop music derived from reggae and incorporating elements from faster, electronically based styles, such as hip-hop and techno. An abbreviated form of *ragamuffin* (a somewhat earlier name for the music), probably influenced by Jamaican *raga raga* 'old ragged clothes'

> 1994 *Face*: When jungle first emerged from the hardcore underground, the world wouldn't listen. But with ragga taking it into new musical territory, it's now being hailed as the sound of modern urban Britain.

rapid-reaction force *n* (1990) a military unit capable of being dispatched at short notice to any part of the world and going into action there immediately. A favourite concept among military strategists at the end of the century, made possible by high-capacity long-range air transport

> 1990 Antony Beevor: The new NATO system of multi-national corps and a rapid reaction force begins to take shape.

1991 *US News & World Report*: A multinational airmobile division took part, a precursor of the alliance's new rapid-reaction force.

1993 Andy McNab: Soon afterwards, Stan joined the army and became part of the rapid reaction force. When independence was declared, Stan left the country in despair.

rebrand *v* (1994) to give (an old product, service, etc.) a new name so as to modernize its public image and (it is hoped) revive flagging sales

1994 *Buses*: The company has launched a two-pronged attack on neighbouring Greater Manchester, by the establishment of MTL Manchester to develop a network in Manchester and also by the rebranding of its St Helens operation as Lancashire Travel.

recovered memory *n* (1993) a repressed memory, especially of childhood sexual assault, claimed to be restored during psychoanalysis. A term arising as part of the late 20th century's anxiety over sexual abuse of children. The validity of the procedure is hotly contested, and *recovered memory syndrome* is often characterized as **false memory syndrome (1992)**

1993 *Sunday Times*: 'Recovered memory syndrome', in which children and adults 'discover' under therapy that they were abused as children, is one of the most painful issues dividing American society.

red route *n* (1991) a road (typically an important arterial route leading into the centre of a city) to which stringent parking regulations apply, keeping it clear for through traffic. British. The first experimental red route (marked at the roadside with a double red line) was introduced between Highgate and Limehouse in 1991

1995 *Evening Standard*: Despite calls from environmentalists for a more radical approach to traffic control through active discouragement of car use and the development of public transport, the Government is pressing on with the kerbside management of 315 miles of Red Route.

red top *adj, n* (1997) Designating a tabloid newspaper at the 'lower' end of the market, aimed at a C2 and D readership (e.g. the *Mirror, Star*, and *Sun*). British; from the red masthead characteristic of such papers

1997 *Daily Telegraph*: The reason is that all the downmarket tabloids—'red tops'—are losing circulation, and have been doing so for a long time. The process may have accelerated since the death of Diana, Princess of Wales. The Press Complaints Commission's new code of conduct…will not make life easier for the red tops or their editors.

respect *n* (1990) Used, originally in Black English, to denote regard or esteem, without deference on the part of the speaker, but often an indication that he or she accepts or approves of the person or thing spoken of. Often used interjectionally

1990 *Face*: At one huge rave last summer, the DJ announced, 'Respect is due to the visuals', and everyone broke out in a massive round of applause.

1992 *Face*: For services to British fashion, this season's FACE award winner: Lionel Blair. Respect!

riot girl, riot grrl *n* (1992) a member of a movement of young feminists expressing their resistance to the sexual harassment and exploitation of women especially through aggressive punk-style rock music. See also **girl power (1986)**

1992 *Gazette* (Montreal): The main way riot girls express themselves is through dozens of girl fanzines. The small, Xeroxed-and-folded booklets are filled with grrl talk, art and articles.

1995 *Guardian*: When the Riot Grrl movement began in America in 1991, its intention was to redress the balance of power via the punk rock underground using slogans (words like 'rape' and 'slut' written in black marker pens on exposed stomachs or bare arms), fanzines, meetings and women-only shows.

road-kill *n* (1992) a person or thing that is useless or moribund. North American colloquial; a blackly metaphorical diversion of the earlier meaning 'an animal killed by a vehicle on a road' (first recorded in 1972)

1993 *Esquire*: We all know any number of men who can cook a virtuoso…dish or two, but outside of this they are strictly roadkills in the kitchen.

road pricing *n* (1991) a system of traffic control by which drivers must make a payment for using a particular stretch of road

> 1991 *Canberra Times*: Road pricing needs to be developed and introduced whereby car users pay a charge according to the degree of restraint which is thought to be desirable in relation to the levels of congestion likely to be caused.

> 1991 *New Scientist*: Richmond hopes that it will be able to persuade other boroughs in the capital to join forces and set up a London-wide scheme of road pricing.

saddo *n* (1992) someone who is seen as socially inadequate, unfashionable, or otherwise contemptible; a nerd. Colloquial; a derivative of **sad (1938)**

> 1992 *New Musical Express*: It is now widely acknowledged (except by saddoes) that *Dr Who* stopped being good after Jon Pertwee in 1974.

> 1994 *Sugar*: Take to faxing your boyfriend instead of phoning him. Only saddos use phones.

> 1994 *.net*: He actually met his wife through CompuServe, but is not a saddo in spite of this.

safe haven *n* (1991) a protected zone in a country designated for members of a religious or ethnic minority. This specific application of the term came to public notice after the Gulf War, when such zones were established for Kurds who were being persecuted by Saddam Hussein's troops. It was subsequently widely used in relation to the former Yugoslavia

> 1994 *Star-Ledger* (Newark): NATO warplanes yesterday buzzed Bihac, and only darkness and failure to find their targets prevented air strikes intended to silence Serb shelling of the 'safe haven'.

screenager *n* (1996) a teenager highly skilled at and experienced in the use of computers

> 1996 *Time Out New York*: Occasionally, though, that becomes a drive to make up new words and catchphrases ('screenagers', 'the paranoid reciprocal').

screen saver *n* (1990) a computer program, originally designed to prevent screen damage, which automatically blanks the screen or displays an animated sequence when there has been no input for some time. An increasingly familiar part of the office landscape in the 1990s

> 1994 *Guardian*: The screen-savers include Hopping Elephants, Man With Baby Carriage and Queen Victoria.

shaken-baby syndrome *n* (1992) the set of often fatal symptoms (e.g. brain damage) caused by shaking a baby violently. Originally US; widely publicized in 1997 by the case of the British 'au pair' Louise Woodward, who was charged with murdering a US baby, Matthew Eappen, by shaking him

> 1995 *Coloradoan* (Fort Collins): An autopsy confirmed that the boy died of shaken-baby syndrome.

> 1997 *New Scientist*: To the local doctors who treated and examined Eappen, it looked like a clear case of child abuse by violent shaking or 'shaken baby syndrome'—a view they propounded in court.

sig *n* (1991) text at the end of an e-mail message or similar online communication identifying or giving information about the writer, often in an individualistic way. A shortening of *signature*. Because the file containing a person's sig message on Unix systems is called *.sig* (said as 'dot sig'), this form of the term is often used

> 1996 Online posting: Load up one of the .vew files, type in your .sig in the message area and then save the .vew file to your custom views directory.

slacker *n* (1994) someone, particularly a member of the current generation of young adults, perceived to lack a sense of direction in life. A usage inspired by the 1991 film *Slackers*, featuring a former student unable to move beyond the student lifestyle and lacking any ambition. Compare **Generation X (1991)**

> 1995 *Wired*: The tone is set by graphic artists and wannabe musicians and common-or-garden slackers off to drink cheap beer on Dad's money.

> 1995 *Guardian*: 'It's certainly a reaction to the slacker thing, which was so "anti-style",' says Paul Tunkin, promoter of the London club Blow Up.

slaphead *n* (1990) a bald or shaven-headed person. Slang, perhaps based on the idea that a hairless head can be slapped directly on the scalp. Usually derisive, especially when the hair-loss is natural rather than a fashion choice

> 1991 *Gazette* (Montreal): The current rage in London, Paris, Berlin and New York is the Slaphead look... A Slaphead is someone (and there are no gender-based limitations here) who is bald either by nature or by choice—yes, by choice!

> 1995 *FourFourTwo*: Attention British hair loss sufferers! This amazing new technique developed in North Shields will end your slaphead nightmare forever.

slapper *n* (1990) a promiscuous or tarty woman, especially one who is no longer young. British slang; perhaps from an earlier dialect sense 'big, strapping woman', or conceivably an alteration of *schlepper* 'worthless person' (of Yiddish origin)

> 1995 *Observer*: Frostrup's face clouds over. 'And when Germaine Greer wears short skirts! She was on Clive Anderson wearing a very short skirt. If I'd have done that, everyone would have said, "Oh, look at that old slapper!" '

sleazebuster *n* (1994) someone employed to combat sleaze. Originally recorded in the context of sexual sleaziness, but latterly also applied to political corruption

> 1994 *Guardian*: According to yesterday's Today, 1.1 million 'tartcards' were collected by 'council sleazebusters' out to clean up the streets.

> 1997 *Scotsman*: Sir Gordon Downey, Westminster's sleazebuster, has spent the past six months conducting a painstaking inquiry into the cash-for-questions affair.

> 1997 *Mirror*: Parliamentary sleazebuster Sir Patrick Neill has advised Labour to hand back Ecclestone's cash gift.

Snowblades *n* (1997) A trademark for half-length skis used for their high manoeuvrability in turning and jumping

> 1999 *Observer*: When a daredevil 14-year-old performed a modest ski jump last week in front of a small group of onlookers, he caused an avalanche of sales of Snowblades throughout the UK and much of Europe. It helped that the teenager was Prince Harry.

social chapter *n* (1991) a document dealing with social policy, especially workers' rights and welfare, forming part of the Maastricht Treaty signed by members of the European Community in 1991

> 1993 *Times*: Mr Major...promised that he would protect British industry from excessive labour market regulation with his famous opt-out from the social chapter.

SoHo *n* (1991) An acronym formed from the initial letters of *small office, home office*, denoting the small-business sector of the economy, especially that part of it which is home-based. Originally US, and used especially in the context of information-technology marketing. The capitalization reflects the earlier *SoHo*, the nickname of an area in Manhattan, *south of Houston* Street

> 1994 *Computing*: It has been unable to completely fulfil orders from any of its chosen sectors, from SoHo to corporates, over the past nine months.

sorted *adj* (1991) well organized or controlled; fully prepared or equipped. British slang; a curtailed version of *sorted out*. Often used with the specific implication 'supplied with illegal drugs'. Latterly also used, often interjectionally, as a generalized adjective of approval

> 1991 *Independent*: A dealer wanders around. He pulls out a plastic bag from his pocket... 'Are you sorted? It's good stuff, it'll keep you going all night,' he says.

> 1993 *Super Bike*: Late 900s are reliable and well-sorted and most earlier models should have had major modifications carried out.

> 1995 *Independent*: If he's a waster then get yourself out of there and get a life. If he's sorted then take a leaf out of his book and 'chill out'.

> 1995 *Daily Telegraph*: Peterlee is sorted, it's mad because you can do what you want.

spam *n, v* (1994) to flood the Internet with tedious or inane postings, especially sending the same message or advertisement to large numbers of newsgroups. Such a message is termed a *spam*. Originally US; from the tinned meat brand-name (see **Spam (1937)**), but the reason for the application is unclear: some have linked it with the *Monty Python* sketch in which Spam appears with every item on a restaurant menu, others with the notion of Spam hitting the fan and filling the surrounding environment

> 1995 *Everybody's Internet Update*: The alt.current-events.net-abuse Usenet newsgroup is the place to discuss spamming and other obnoxious advertising.

spamdex *n, v* (1997) to scatter keywords abundantly throughout a computer text so that it will be retrieved by World Wide Web search engines. Such misleading keywords are termed *spamdexes*. A coinage based on **spam (1994)**

> 1997 *Computer Weekly*: In the usual online cat-and-mouse fashion, Web search engines are now developing strategies to filter out spamdexes.

speed camera *n* (1992) a camera, often hidden, that is equipped with a motion sensor that detects motorists exceeding the speed limit and photographs them

> 1994 *Daily Telegraph*: About 6,000 motorists a week are incurring fines and licence endorsements after being caught speeding on film by 'Gatso' speed cameras.

splurgundy *n* (1998) sparkling red wine from Australia. Australians, who have a taste for the beverage not widely shared in the rest of the world, used to call it *sparkling burgundy*, but following the 1993 EU trade agreement, the use of European regional names for Australian wines was phased out, so this unofficial blend was coined to take its place

> 1998 *Sunday Times*: Splurgundy may be a wine of merit, but there's no denying that it is also an acquired taste.

spread betting *n* (1992) a form of betting in which the better wins or loses money according to the margin by which the value of a particular outcome varies from the spread of expected values quoted by the bookmaker

> 1992 *Daily Telegraph*: Sporting Index is a new and well-connected firm of bookmakers, set up to concentrate on what is called spread-betting. If you want to bet on the number of fences which a horse…will clear at Aintree, you can buy or sell his chances as if he were a share. Buyers start to make money once he has jumped 23 fences, sellers hope he will jump fewer than 21.

> 1995 *Guardian*: Spread betting, the latest craze in bookmaking, has introduced the volatility of the stock market into high-rolling wagers on football matches.

stalk *v* (1990) to harass or persecute (a person, especially a celebrity) with unwanted and obsessive attention. A phenomenon recognized since the 1980s, and increasingly high-profile in the 90s. The persecutor is known as a **stalker**

> 1990 *Daily Mail*: A fan...stalked...star Stephanie Zimbalist for 18 months, writing 200 letters threatening: 'I'll get you'.

> 1993 *Independent on Sunday*: This week the media have been using the word 'stalker' to describe the sort of obsessed fan who follows tennis stars around.

> 1994 *Coloradoan* (Fort Collins): The attacks on Kerrigan and Seles, and the stalking of other women, are alarmingly looking more like a trend than isolated incidents.

> 1995 *Guardian*: For five years, she was stalked by a man who would taunt and threaten her, hiding in the shadows in restaurants and shops, never showing his face.

storming *adj* (1991) wonderful, fantastic. A slang approval adjective that evolved from the earlier use of *storming* to mean 'wildly successful, booming'. Often spelled *stormin'* for that genuine demotic touch

> 1991 *New Musical Express*: A fine and storming time was had by all.

> 1995 *Time Out*: Eleven hours of full-on fun as the stormin' daytime club takes over these double-arched dancefloors.

> 1996 *Daily Telegraph*: Mum, Dad and Claire wish Christopher Yat a storming day tomorrow as he celebrates the big 7.

superpub *n* (1995) a very large licensed premises serving alcoholic drinks and usually also food, and typically also a variety of other attractions, such as video games and a DJ

> 1996 *Independent on Sunday*: The business is making its mark with the superpub. These vast, hangar-like spaces, up to 6,000 square feet of floorspace, are enormous compared to the normal local.

> 1997 *Publican*: Booming town centre superpubs have drawn fire from trade leaders, who accuse them of boosting crime.

> 1997 *Face*: What do you get when three Superpubs set up in a small Hertfordshire town? '*Blood Alley*', according to the media. Some people blame the size of the new bars for the trouble.

surf *v* (1993) to move from site to site on (the Internet), sampling the contents. Probably an extension of the earlier metaphorical application of *surf* to hopping from channel to channel on the television

> 1994 *Guardian*: It costs 20 times as much to 'surf' the world-wide Internet in Germany as it does in the US.

sword opera *n* (1997) a television drama series set in ancient times, featuring frequent bouts of swordplay and other stylized violent action (e.g. *Xena: Warrior Princess*). A coinage modelled on **soap opera (1939)**

> 1997 *Economist*: Television series about doctors, policemen and lawyers suffer from 'high demographic specificity', he says, but 'sword operas' such as Hercules, with their dramatic stories and simple distinctions between right and wrong, have, on this argument, a universal interest.

tamagotchi *n* (1996) a hand-held electronic toy in which an animated pet displayed on a small screen must be kept 'alive' by pushing buttons at regular intervals to simulate feeding, exercise, etc. An acquisition from Japanese, where it means literally 'lovable egg'. The craze for the toys reached Britain in 1997. They are also called in the vernacular **cyberpets (1996)**)

> 1997 *Church Times*: 'Can I have a Tamagotchi?' was a school-holiday litany daily intoned by our youngest daughter.

> 1998 *Belfast News Letter*: A French motorist killed a cyclist and injured another when she took her eye off the road trying to save her Tamagotchi virtual pet. The 27-year-old woman became distracted when the electronic pet, which was attached to her car key ring, started to send out distress signals.

tank *v* (1992) to fail, usually spectacularly; to 'bomb'. US slang

> 1992 *Spy*: There's trouble all over the Disney empire: EuroDisney is tanking.

> 1993 *Spy*: Hollywood wants to show it cares, that despite...the recent Ices T and Cube vehicle *Trespass*, it yearns to film more than gratuitous slaughter. (Besides, *Trespass* tanked badly.)

tax-and-spend *adj* (1991) Designating (with disapproval) a politician or policy committed to high taxation in order to maintain high public expenditure. A demonizing word of the 1990s political lexicon, with which right-wingers beat liberals about the head (the expenditure criticized is always on things like welfare and public services, never on, e.g., defence)

> 1991 *Economist*: With the federal budget in massive deficit, not even a tax-and-spend Democrat president, were one elected in 1992, would find it easy to be more generous.

technoplegia *n* (1997) paralysis brought on by fear of using technological equipment. A humorous coinage based on the suffix *-plegia* (from Greek *plege* 'blow, stroke'), which is used in the names of various sorts of paralysis (e.g. *hemiplegia, paraplegia*)

> 1997 *Guardian*: The word that best describes the self-styled technophobics is this: technoplegia, paralysis brought on by something technical.

TESSA *n* (1990) An acronym formed from the initial letters of *tax-exempt special savings account*, a type of savings account allowing savers to invest a certain amount in a bank or building society with no tax to pay on the interest, provided that the capital remains in the account for five years. It was introduced in 1990 by John Major when he was Chancellor of the Exchequer

> 1990 *Guardian*: The first Tessa...to be launched since the Chancellor introduced them in the Budget, it offers 13 per cent tax-free for 5.5 years.

themself *pron* (1992) himself or herself. The use of *they* and its derivatives (including *themselves*) as a non-sex-specific alternative to *he* or *she* dates back at least to the early 16th century, but it has come into particular prominence in the final third of the 20th century (see p. 456). One of its interesting spin-offs is this modified form of the third-person plural reflexive pronoun, with *-self* substituted for *-selves* to fit in with a singular referent

> 1992 *English Today*: Walking through Pilsen, the casual observer might easily think themself back in 1945.

third way *n* (1990) an alternative mode approximately midway between two prevailing and antagonistic systems. Originally applied to the Swedish policy of neutrality between East and West, in the 1990s it became a buzzword in the US and Britain for those advocating a new radical centrist approach, breaking the mould of conflict between political parties of the left and right. See also **radical centre (1996)**, **social market (1975)**, **stakeholder (1976)**

> 1990 *Independent*: Our capitalists and communists have always, out of hand, condemned the Third Way, or socialist alternative to Stalinism.

> 1998 *Observer*: The third way Brazilian style might not just offer a way forward for Brazil but some lessons for us in Britain.

trailer trash *n* (1993) people who live permanently in caravans or mobile homes and are regarded as being common, antisocial, unsightly, feckless, or otherwise beyond the pale of civilization. Mainly US; based on the American *trailer* 'mobile home'

> 1993 Lowe & Shaw: Getting the permission's the hard bit, getting past all the narrowminded people who don't want trailer trash down the road.

Trustafarian *n* (1992) a young person from a wealthy background who affects the lifestyle and attitudes of the inner-city ghetto. British; a contemptuously humorous blend of *trust fund* (frequently such people's means of support) and **rastafarian**

> 1994 *Guardian*: Here, for instance, is the home of 'Trustafarians'—rich white kids who subscribe to the notion of West London bohemia—and here, for the older generation, is a politically correct mix of creeds, colours and ideologies.

twigloo *n* (1995) a tree-house made of branches, especially one built and occupied by environmental protesters. British; a blend of *twig* and *igloo*

> 1995 *Daily Telegraph*: She lives in a tree house, known as a 'twigloo', at Slyward Camp.

> 1996 *Times*: Inside the rucksack is also a citizens' band radio base station and handset, and a mobile telephone. All ensure constant contact with the 15 CB stations linking the 'twigloo' camps along the nine-mile route.

twoc, twock *v, n* (1990) (to commit) the offence of stealing a car. British, originally police slang; an acronym formed from the initial letters of *taking without owner's consent*

> 1990 *Oxford Times*: Twoc…is police shorthand for the offence of taking and driving away a vehicle without its owner's consent… From the victim's point of view, 'only a twoc' has a very hollow ring to it.

> 1993 *Guardian*: [He] reckons most joyriders steal cars for fun, not profit, although he recently took a twocked car to a breakers in Manchester which was run by a gang of professional car thieves.

unfeasibly *adv* (1990) unbelievably, remarkably. A colloquial intensifier suddenly created out of the adjective *unfeasible* 'impossible', which had been inoffensively around since the early 16th century but never attracted much attention

> 1990 *Mountain*: Hadaway…takes the dirty central wall, *Buster Gonad* (with an unfeasibly hard move at E5 6b) takes a hanging flake on the right, just left of the innocuous groove of *Roger Mellie*.

> 1995 *Nature*: More than 200,000 miles away, men in short-sleeved nylon shirts and unfeasibly thick spectacles gather round a console.

V-chip *n* (1993) a device which, when installed in a television set, can be programmed by the user to block or scramble any television programme that contains an unacceptable level of violence, sex, or offensive language (as indicated by a code inserted into the signal by the broadcaster). The main purpose of the chip is to block the reception of unsuitable programmes when children are watching television unsupervised. The *V* stands for *viewer*, although it has come to be widely interpreted as *violence*

> 1993 *Vancouver Sun*: The 'V-chip' technology, being developed in Vancouver, would encode the soundtracks of every movie and television show with a violence-rating signal.

> 1996 *Daily Telegraph*: Last year's communications bill ordered all computer and television manufacturers to implant a 'v-chip' gadget in future circuits.

Viagra *n* (1998) The proprietary name of a drug used for treating male impotence by stimulating penile blood flow. Manufactured by the Pfizer company, its active ingredient is sildenafil citrate. Its apparent success led, unsurprisingly, to a stampede of hopeful purchasers

> 1998 *Daily Telegraph*: The drug works by stimulating blood flow and is reportedly effective on women as well as men. Many people who are not impotent are thought to be trying Viagra to see if it improves their sex lives. Viagra has few notable side-effects except mild headaches in some people.

> 1998 *Sunday Times*: Frank Dobson, the health secretary, insists that the NHS will prescribe Viagra only to men who have 'sound clinical reasons' for taking the drug.

waif *n* (1991) a fashionable young woman, with clothes and hair suggesting a ragged style, characterized by extreme thinness and apparent fragility. A look popularized in the 1990s by such supermodels as Kate Moss

> 1991 *Premiere*: She has so many layered waif outfits.

> 1994 *New York*: One of Stasi's main claims to fame is starting the controversy over the low body weight of superwaif Kate Moss.

Web *n* (1994) A shortened version of **World Wide Web (1990)**

> 1994 *American Scientist*: The first components of the system were working by 1991, but the Web did not begin to spread outside the high-energy physics community until 1993.

> 1995 *New York Times*: Some people believe the Web is the most important advance in publishing since the printing press.

Web site *n* (1994) a document or set of linked documents, usually associated with a particular person, organization, or topic, that is held on a computer system and can be accessed as part of the World Wide Web. Compare **home page (1993)**

> 1994 *.net*: Pore over fascinating trivia on The Death of Rock 'n' Roll, a…Web site that provides detailed information on rigamortis rockers who are prematurely pushing up the daisies.

> 1996 *Interzone*: They experience difficulty in separating their website lives from their real lives, and find the freedom of the former infinitely preferable to the limitations of the latter.

welfare-to-work *adj* (1996) Designating a policy or measure encouraging unemployed people to find a paid job rather than relying on unemployment benefit

> 1996 *Independent*: Alongside the penal system we need to look at a much wider agenda, including welfare-to-work strategies; special programmes for troubled young people…; and the planning, ownership and social ecology of housing estates.

wet bike *n* (1997) An alternative name for a *jet-ski* (first recorded in 1991), a vehicle powered by a petrol engine which travels over the water on skis. Increasingly common off beaches in the 1990s but controversial because of noise levels and possible danger to other sea-users

> 1997 *Sunday Times*: Ban wet bikes from all forthcoming EU Special Areas of Conservation…and from all beaches monitored under the EU's 1976 bathing water directive.

wingback *n* (1997) In soccer, a fullback who may advance attackingly down the wing. The term (modelled on the much earlier *centreback*) first became widely familiar thanks to media coverage of the 1998 World Cup

> 1997 *Daily Mail*: Liverpool's Stig Bjornebye, the 27-year-old Norway wingback who has played in every game for the Anfield club this season, has signed a five-year contract.

wired *adj* (1990) making use of computers and information technology to transfer or receive information. Often with the specific implication 'connected to the Internet'

> 1995 *Wired*: My host Martin Klima…has an Internet address and a 486. He's got WordPerfect and Paradox and Corel Draw. By Prague standards, Martin is one wired dude.

> 1995 *Just Seventeen*: Get wired! Learn about the Internet and suss out the information super-highway.

wolf-dog *n* (1996) a dog which is a hybrid between a wolf and a dog. A concept not covered when the Dangerous Dogs Act was passed in Britain (see **dangerous dog (1991)**). The common option of naming such a hybrid with a blend of its component animals' names was not taken in this case, presumably on the one hand because of a certain unpronounceability and on the other because of political incorrectness

> 1996 *Daily Telegraph*: The RSPCA has warned the public to steer clear of hyrid 'wolf-dogs' being sold for £400 as Britain's latest family pet and said to be replacing the pit-bull as the favourite with macho dog lovers.

World Wide Web *n* (1990) a visually based system for accessing information (text, graphics, sound, video) by means of the Internet, which consists of a large number of 'documents' tagged with cross-referencing links by which the user can move between sources. Originally intended as a tool by which particle physicists might exchange information, by 1993 it had been taken up far more widely, and by the end of the century, computer addresses prefixed by the abbreviation *WWW* have become an everyday sight. See also **Web (1994)**

> 1990 T. Berners-Lee & R. Calliau (title): WorldWideWeb: Proposal for a HyperText Project.

> 1994 *Guardian*: The World Wide Web…is poised to create an egalitarian new cybersociety for all, regardless of creed, colour or class.

> 1995 *Internet World*: As a WWW site administrator, or Webmaster, becomes comfortable with the site's basic functionality, more advanced features can be added.

> 1998 *Radio Times*: You'll find more to interest you at the fascinating Windrush website (*www.bbc.co.uk/education/windrush*).

zero-emission(s) vehicle *n* (1990) a motor vehicle which does not emit pollutant gases. Originally US; sometimes abbreviated to *ZEV*. In practice the term is generally applied to electric cars. The search for a commercially viable one continues at the end of the millennium

> 1991 *Popular Science*: Under present regulations, a Zero Emissions Vehicle (ZEV) is defined…as one producing no tailpipe pollutants, without regard to emissions produced in the manufacture of the vehicle.

zorbing *n* (1996) an extreme sport involving hurtling down slopes or into rapids in a large perspex ball. A variant in which the inside of the ball is lubricated is known as *hydro-zorbing*

> 1996 *Guardian*: Bungee jumping and the latest tourist craze, zorbing—climbing into a large ball and rolling down a hill— have prompted the hasty introduction of a safety code for adventure-tour operators in New Zealand.

> 1996 *Guardian*: He told me I had gone down the first time in the classic novice manner, doing what is known in Zorbing nomenclature as a 'washing machine'.

Index

EP 338
epidural 472
EPOS 536
equalize 137
equal opportunity 137
ergonomics 338
Ernie 339
-eroo 205
escalate 339
escalation 205
escalator 20
escapist 206
Eskimo pie 138
espresso 273
Essex girl 584
Essex man 584
establishment 138
estrogen 138
Estuary English 536
Ethernet 472
ethical 536
ethnic 273
ethnic cleansing 584
ethnicity 339
ethnic minority 273
ethnocentric 20
Eton crop 138
eurhythmics 83
euro 472
Euro- 405
Eurocrat 405
Euroland 584
Europe 339
European Union 584
Euro-sceptic 537
Eurotrash 537
Eurovision 339
evacuate 206
evacuee 206
eventide home 83
e-verdict 585
Exchange Rate
  Mechanism 472
exclusive 20
executive 20
existential 206
existentialism 273
exit poll 537
Exocet 473
expansionism 20
expert system 473
explicit 473
expressionism 20
extermination camp
  274
extra-marital 138
extra-sensory perception

206
extraterrestrial 406
extravehicular activity
  406
extreme 473
extropy 585
extrovert 83
eye-candy 537
eye shadow 206

F

fab 339
fabbo 537
fabby 537
faberoonie 537
fabulous 339
face 473
face-lift 206
face-lifting 138
facial 83
facilitator 406
faction 406
factoid 473
factory farming 406
fag 138
faggot 83
fail-safe 274
Falklands factor 537
fall-out 339
false memory syndrome
  585
falsies 274
family allowance 138
family planning 206
family values 406
fan dancer 206
fan mail 139
Fanny Adams 83
fantasize 139
fantastic 207
fantasy football 537
Fany 83
fanzine 274
FAQ 585
farmerette 83
far-out 340
fascism 139
fascistization 139
fashion victim 538
fast food 340
fast-forward 274
fast one 139
fast worker 139
fat cat 139
Father's Day 274

fattist 538
fatwa, fatwah 538
Fauvist 83
fave 207
fax 274
feature film 84
fed up 21
feed 207
feeding frenzy 538
feel-good factor 538
feel up 207
fellow-traveller 207
felt-tip pen 340
Femidom 538
feminazi 585
ferro-concrete 21
fibre 21
fibreglass 207
fibre optics 340
fibrositis 21
fifth column 207
fighter 84
filing cabinet 21
filling station 139
film 21
film star 84
Filofax 207
filter-tip 208
final solution 274
fine-tune 406
fire-power 84
fire-watching 274
firing squad 21
first-time buyer 473
First World War 275
fish finger 340
fish stick 340
fission 208
fission bomb 275
five-star 84
fixate 139
fixation 84
fixed link 473
fixit 84
flagship 474
flak 208
flake 21
flakey 340
flaky 340
flame 539
flame-thrower 84
flapper 139
flares 406
flash 406
flasher 474
flatlet 140
flatline 539

flaunt 140
flavour-of-the-month
  275
Fletcherize 21
flex 22
flexible response 407
flexitime, flextime 474
flick 140
flick knife 340
flight attendant 275
flip-flop 474
flipping 84
flip side 275
float 407
floating voter 22
floodlight 140
floor polish 22
floosie 22
flopperoo 208
floppy disk 474
flow chart 140
flower children 407
flower people 407
flower power 407
fluoridate 275
fly-by-wire 407
flying bedstead 341
flying bishop 585
flying bomb 275
flying doctor 140
flying-ground 22
flying picket 474
flying saucer 275
fly-over 22
FOB 585
focus group 539
foil 276
foodie 539
food parcel 84
food processor 474
fool-proof 22
footage 85
football pool 140
foreplay 140
for it 22
fork-lift truck 276
format 407
Formica 276
formula 141
Fortean 585
FORTRAN 341
foundation garment
  141
four-letter word 208
four-minute mile 341
fox-trot 85
F Plan Diet 539

fractal 474
frag 474
fraternization 276
freak 407, 474
freak out 407, 474
freaky 407
freebase 539
freedom-fighter 276
freedom ride 407
free expression 276
Freefone 341
free world 341
freeze-drying 276
French roll 277
Freudian 85
Freudian slip 341
fridge 141
friendly 141
-friendly 539
Frigidaire 141
Frisbee 341
Fritz 85
front 141
front line 85
frug 408
fruit gum 208
fruit machine 208
fry 141
fuck-me 539
fuck off 141
fudge 540
fuehrer 209
fuel rod 277
fuel-tank 22
führer 209
full frontal 475
full monty, full monte 540
fundamentalism 142
fund-holder 585
fund-holding 540
funk-hole 22
funky 341
furphy 85
fuselage 22
fusion 277
fussed 540
futon 475
futurism 23
futurology 277
fuzz 142
F-word 475

G

G 142
gabber 586

gaff 209
galleria 408
Gallup poll 277
Game Boy 540
game show 408
gamesmanship 277
gamma ray 23
gangbang 277
gangland 85
Gang of Four 540
gang shag 142
garage 23, 541
garage sale 408
garagiste 586
garbiologist 408
garbologist 408
garbology 475
garden centre 408
garden gnome 277
garden suburb 23
garden town 85
garlic bread 341
gas 23, 342
gas attack 85
gas chamber 277
gas gangrene 85
gas-guzzler 475
gas helmet 85
gas mask 85
gasper 86
gasser 278
gas station 209
-gate 475
gate-crasher 142
gay 209, 342
gazump 142
gazunder 541
gear 408
geep 476
gee-string 211
Geiger counter 142
gen 278
gender 408
gender bender 541
gender blender 541
gender gap 476
gene 86
generation gap 408
Generation X 586
genetically modified 586
genetic engineering 409
genetic fingerprint 409
genetics 23
genocide 278
Gentleman's Relish 23
gentrify 476

geopolitical 23
geostationary 409
geriatric 142, 476
geriatrics 23
germ warfare 209
Gestapo 209
ghetto-blaster 541
ghost 143
ghost-write 143
G.I. 209
G.I. bride 278
Gibson 210
Gibson girl 24
gift-wrap 210
gig 143
GIGO 409
gimlet 143
gin-and-it 210
ginormous 278
gin-rummy 278
gippy tummy 278
girdle 143
Girl Guide 24
girl power 541
Girl Scout 24
giro cheque 476
gismo 279
git 278
gite 409
gizmo 279
glad rags 24
glamour boy 210
glasnost 541
glass ceiling 542
glitch 409
glitterati 342
glitz 476
glitzy 409
global village 409
global warming 476
glue-sniffing 410
G-man 210
GM 586
gnarly 542
gnome 210, 342
go 477
goalposts 542
gobbledygook 279
gobsmacked 542
gob-stopper 143
go-faster stripes 542
gofer 410
go-getter 86
go-getting 143
goggle-box 342
go-go 410
go-kart 342

gold-digger 143
golden-ager 410
golden goal 586
golden handcuffs 477
golden handshake 410
golden hello 542
golden parachute 542
golfer 86
gong 143
gongoozler 24
Gonk 410
gonzo 477
good buddy 477
goodfella 586
good-time girl 143
goofus 143
googly 24
googol 279
goo-goo eyes 24
goon 143, 210, 279, 342
goose-stepper 144
go-slow 210
gotcha 211
gotcher 211
gothic 542
gracing 144
grafter 24
-gram 477
grand 86
grand unified theory 477
granny bond 477
granny dumping 586
granny glasses 410
grant-maintained 543
grass 211
grass roots 86
Great War 86
grebo 543
green 477
green belt 211
greenhouse effect 144
greenmail 543
green pound 478
greens 478
green shoots 586
gremlin 279
grey market 478
grey pound 587
gridlock 543
groceteria 86
grody 410
groove 211
groovy 211
gross 343
grotty 410

radiogenic 166
radiogram 232
radioize 166
radiolocation 299
radiology 46
radio receiver 46
radio telescope 299
radiotherapy 46
radiothon 433
radish 166
radon 102
ragga 596
railbus 233
railcard 499
railodoc 167
railodok 167
railophone 102
rainbow coalition 556
rain forest 46
rally 233
RAM 361
ramjet 299
ram-raid 557
rand 433
rap 46, 433, 499
rapid-reaction force 596
raspberry 167
Rasta 361
Rastafarian 361
rate-capping 557
ratings 300
rationalize 167
ration book 102
rationing 102
rat-race 233
ratty 46
raunchy 434
rave 167, 434, 557
rave-in 434
rave-up 434
raygun 233
rayon 167
readership 167
read-only 434
ready meal 499
Reaganism 434
Reaganomics 557
real 557
Realpolitik 102
real time 362
rebrand 597
recce 300
recession 167
record 233
recordist 233
record player 233
recovered memory 597

recreational 499
recycle 167
red 102
redbrick 300
redcoat 362
redevelop 233
red-eye 434
Red Guard 434
red menace 168
red route 597
red shift 168
red top 597
redundant 168
re-enter 434
re-entry 300
reffo 300
reflation 234
reflexology 499
refugee 103
refusenik 499
refute 434
reggae 435
regression 103
regretfully 500
reinforced concrete 46
reinvent oneself 557
reject 234
relaunch 500
release 500
relegate 103
Remembrance Day 168
Remembrance Sunday
  300
remote control 46
renewable 500
rent-a- 168
renta- 435
rent boy 435
rent party 168
rent strike 500
reparations 168
repetitive strain injury
  558
replay 500
repossess 234
repress 46
reprography 435
request 168
reserved occupation 103
resistance 234, 300
resource 500
respect 597
rest home 168
retro 500
rev 46, 169
reverse-engineer 558
revisionism 47

revusical 234
rhesus 300
rhubarb 301
ribbon development
  169
Rice Krispies 234
right-on 500
rightsize 558
ring-pull 501
ring road 169
riot 47
riot girl, riot grrl 597
ripple 234
Ritz 169
roadability 169
roadie 435
road-kill 597
road pricing 597
road rage 558
road safety 169
road sense 169
road sign 47
robomb 301
robot 169, 234, 247
robot bomb 301
robotics 301
rock 47, 301, 362
rock and roll 362
Rockefeller 234
rocker 435
rocket 103
rocket aeroplane 169
rocket airplane 169
rocket plane 169
rocket-ship 170
rock 'n' roll 362
rock salmon 235
rodent officer 302
rodent operative 302
rodent operator 302
rodeo 103
role 103
role model 362
role-playing 302
Rollerblade 558
roller disco 501
rolling news 558
roll-on 302
roll-over 558
Rolls-Royce 47
röntgenoscopy 47
roquette 47
Rorschach test 170
Rosebud 104
Rosie Lee 170
Rosy Lee 170
rotisserie 363

Rottweiler 47
roughage 170
roundabout 170
Roxy 302
Roy 435
royal 170
RSJ 302
rubber bullet 501
Rubik's cube, Rubik cube
  558
ruddy 104
rule(s), OK 501
rumba 170
rumpus room 302
runner 559
running dog 235
run-up 435
runway 170
Ryvita 171

S

s 184, 501
S.A. 171
sabotage 104
sack dress 363
sacred cow 104
sad 235
saddo 598
Sadie Hawkins day 235
sado-masochism 235
safari 47
safari park 436
safe haven 598
safe pair of hands 559
safe sex 559
safety island 235, 247
Sagbag 501
sailboard 436
salariat 104
saleing 48
salesperson 171
sales resistance 171
Salk vaccine 363
salmonella 104
saloon 48
saloon car 48
salsa 501
SALT 436
salvage 104
samey 171
samizdat 436
sanctions 104
sandwich 104
sandwich counter 105
sandwich course 363

undercarriage 115
underclass 115
underdeveloped 313
undergraduette 115
underground 377
underpants 248
underpass 57
underperform 512
underprivileged 248
underwhelm 377
undies 57
unfeasibly 602
unflappable 377
unidentified flying object 377
unilateral disarmament 182
unilateralism 377
unisex 449
unit 249
United Nations 313
unit trust 249
unleaded 449
unputdownable 313
unquote 249
unreal 450
unsocial hours 512
unwind 249
up 115
up-do 249
upfront 512
uplift 182
up-market 512
upper 450
up-tight 249
uptight 450
upwardly mobile 450
upward mobility 313
urban guerrilla 450
urban renewal 377
use 377
user-friendly 512
usherette 183
utility 313

V

V 314
V-1 314
V-2 314
vaccine 567
vacky 314
vacuum cleaner 58
vacuum-pack 378
vakky 314
valet 512

Valium 450
Valley Girl 567
Valspeak 568
value added tax 249
valve set 183
vamp 115
vampish 183
vanishing cream 116
vapour trail 314
vapourware 568
VAT 450
VATable, vatable 512
V-bomber 378
V-chip 602
V.D. 183
VDU 450
veal crate 568
VE Day 314
veejay 568
vegan 314
Vegeburger 513
vegelate, vegolate 568
Vegemite 183
veg out 568
Velcro 450
veleta 58
velodrome 58
velvet revolution 568
venture capital 315
verbal 513
Veronal 58
Vespa 378
vet 58
VHS 568
Viagra 602
vibes 450
victory roll 315
video 249, 378, 450, 513
videodisc 450
video game 513
video nasty 568
videophone 378
videotape 378, 451
videotext 568
Viet Cong 378
view 250
viewer 250
viff 569
villain 451
-ville 378
vinyl 250
V.I.P. 250
virgin 183
virtual 569
virus 513
vision 116

visual aid 116
vital statistics 379
vitamin 116
Vitaphone 183
VJ 568, 569
VJ Day 315
vo-do-deo-do 183
voguey 183
voguish 183
voice mail 569
voice-over 315
Volstead 184
vorticism 116
vote-getter 58
vox pop 451
voyeur 58
voyeurism 184
V sign 315
VTOL 379

W

wah-wah 184
waif 603
waitperson 569
waitron 569
wakey, wakey 315
waldo 315
Waldorf salad 116
walkabout 513
walkathon 250
walker 569
walkie-talkie 250
walking wounded 116
Walkman 569
Wall Street crash 184
wall-to-wall 379, 451
wally 451
walrus moustache 116
Walter Mitty 379
wanker 513
wannabe, wannabee 570
war bride 117
war cabinet 117
war crime 58
war effort 117
warehouse party 570
warfarin 379
war of nerves 315
Warsaw Pact 379
war to end war 184
war trial 315
washerette 451
washing-up machine 250
Wasp 451

watch in 184
water bed 513
water cannon 451
Watergate 514
water-plane 117
water ski 251
water waving 184
water wings 58
Watusi 451
wave 570
wavicle 184
way in 451
way out 379
weave 316
Web 603
Web site 603
weegie 380
week-end 58
weepie 184
Weight Watchers 451
weirdo 380
welcome 451
welfare 59
welfare state 316
welfare-to-work 603
well- 184
wellie 452, 514
wellington 59
welly 452, 514
West 316
western 117
Western Front 117
wet 570
wet bike 603
wet look 452
wetware 514
wham-bam 380
wham-bang 380
whammy 316
wha-wha 184
wheel and deal 452
wheel clamp 570
wheelie 452
wheelie bin 570
whirlybird 380
whistle-blower 514
whistle-stop 316
white collar 117
white dwarf 185
white hope 117
white knight 570
white line 185
white-out 514
white supremacy 59
white-wall tyre 380
whizz-bang 117
whizz-boy 251